# T'es branché? 1A

## Annotated Teacher's Edition

### Authors

Colleen C. Josephson

Terry L. Meyers

Emily Wentworth

### Contributing Writer

Patricia Teefy

EMC Publishing

ST. PAUL

**Editorial Director:** Alejandro Vargas

**Developmental Editor:** Diana I. Moen

**Associate Editors:** Nathalie Gaillot, Patricia Teefy

**Assistant Editor:** Kristina Merrick

**Production Editor:** Bob Dreas

**Cover Designer:** Leslie Anderson

**Text Designer:** Leslie Anderson

**Production Specialist:** Julie Johnston

Care has been taken to verify the accuracy of information presented in this book. However, the authors, editors, and publisher cannot accept responsibility for Web, e-mail, newsgroup, or chat room subject matter or content, or for consequences from application of the information in this book, and make no warranty, expressed or implied, with respect to its content.

**Trademarks:** Some of the product names and company names included in this book have been used for identification purposes only and may be trademarks or registered trade names of their respective manufacturers and sellers. The authors, editors, and publisher disclaim any affiliation, association, or connection with, or sponsorship or endorsement by, such owners.

We have made every effort to trace the ownership of all copyrighted material and to secure permission from copyright holders. In the event of any question arising as to the use of any material, we will be pleased to make the necessary corrections in future printings. Thanks are due to the aforementioned authors, publishers, and agents for permission to use the materials indicated.

ISBN 978-0-82196-672-3

© 2014 by EMC Publishing, LLC

875 Montreal Way

St. Paul, MN 55102

Email: educate@emcp.com

Website: www.emcschool.com

Printed in the United States of America

22 21 20 19 18 17 16 15 14 13     1 2 3 4 5 6 7 8 9 10

# Meet the Textbook Authors

**Toni Theisen**, the 2009 ACTFL Teacher of the Year and ACTFL President in 2013, is a National Board Certified Teacher of French at Loveland High School in Loveland, Colorado and the Thompson School District World Language Curriculum Representative. She holds an M.A. in Foreign Language Teaching and an M. A. in Education of Diverse Learners. She is also a Google Certified teacher.

A passionate and active world language advocate, Theisen has presented numerous workshops, keynotes, and webinars for national, regional, and state conferences and institutes. Also an author, she has written several middle and high school French language series and many articles on Multiple Intelligences, Differentiated Instruction, and Technology for the 21st-century learner. Theisen presented "Activating Communication" as part of the first ACTFL Webinar series and also presented at the 2011 LARC (National Language Acquisition Resource Center) STARTALK Institute at San Diego State University.

Theisen led the effort in 2009 to revise the Colorado World Languages Academic Standards and co-chaired the revision committee of the National Board for Professional Teacher Standards for WLOE (World Languages Other than English) in 2009. Most recently she chaired the ACTFL 21st Century Skills Map committee in collaboration with the Partnership for 21st Century Learning.

Theisen's many additional honors include the ACTFL Nelson Brooks Award for the Teaching of Culture, the Colorado Governor's Award for Excellence in Teaching, the SWCOLT Excellence in Teaching Award, and the Genevieve Overman Memorial Service Award from the Colorado Congress of Foreign Language Teachers.

**Jacques Pécheur** is the Chief Editor of the French review *Le français dans le monde*. He has worked as Director of the Cultural Center of Palermo and Sicily, and as Cultural Ambassador to the French Embassy in Switzerland. As head of the Mission to the General Delegation for the Languages of France (DGLF), Pécheur has conducted numerous missions to promote multilingualism, the French language, and la Francophonie in the world. He also worked for the French Ministry of Foreign Affairs, the European Council, the European Union, and the Intergovernmental Agency of la Francophonie (AIF). As such he was entrusted with conducting and managing conferences and training workshops in more than 50 countries.

Pécheur's numerous involvements in political, cultural, and language-related occupations have led him to gain expertise in language policies and the language marketplace. As someone who has developed many strategies to promote the learning of French, Pécheur has been a spokesman in numerous conferences related to language learning, and has published many articles. His 20 years of experience in *Le francais dans le monde*, as well as his many publications on French civilization, cinema, and contemporary literature, have shaped his proactive approach to the editorial world.

Honorary member of the AATF, Pécheur is recognized in the United States by the Cultural Services of the French Consulate in the United States (SCAC), the Alliance Française, and many American universities.

# Table of Contents

# Scope and Sequences

## *T'es branché?* Level 1

| Vocabulaire | Fonctions | Culture | Structure | Stratégies |
|---|---|---|---|---|
| **Unité 1**    **Bonjour, tout le monde!** | | | | |
| *Essential question: In what ways is learning another language beneficial?* | | | | |
| • Greetings<br>• Nationalities (in **Vocabulaire actif**) | • Introduce oneself<br>• Introduce someone else<br>• Respond to an introduction<br>• Ask someone's name (in **Pour la conversation**) | • Greetings<br>• Popular first names<br>• **La Francophonie:** Francophones in France and North America (in **Points de départ**) | | |
| • Respond to **Ça va?**<br>• Say good-bye | • Ask how someone is<br>• Say how I am doing | • Back to school<br>• Ways to say good-bye<br>• **La Francophonie:** Europe and North Africa | | **Communication:** Register in speaking and writing (in **Stratégies communicatives**) |
| • Locations<br>• Parents | • Extend an invitation<br>• Accept an invitation<br>• Refuse an invitation | • French teens<br>• **La Francophonie:** Sub-Saharan Africa, Caribbean, and South America<br><br>**Produits:**<br>**La Négritude** | | **Culture:** Assess comfort level with Francophone cultures (in **La culture sur place**)<br><br>**Fine art:** Impressionistic techniques (Jean Béraud) (in **Le monde visuel**)<br><br>**Reading:** Answer the five "W" questions and decipher words (in **Lecture thématique**) |
| **Unité 2**    **Les passe-temps** | | | | |
| *Essential question: What do activities and pastimes reveal about a culture?* | | | | |
| • Pastimes<br>• Olympic sports<br>• Weather<br>• Food | • Ask what someone likes to do<br>• Say what I like to do<br>• Say what I don't like to do | • **Pari Roller**<br>• Olympics<br>• Paris<br><br>**La Francophonie (Sports):**<br>• **Tour de France**<br>• Hockey in Canada<br><br>**Produits:**<br>Cubism in Paris | • Subject pronouns<br>• **tu** vs. **vous**<br>• Present tense of regular **-er** verbs | |
| • More pastimes<br>• Adverbs | • Ask how much someone likes to do something<br>• Say how much I enjoy doing things | • Lyon<br><br>**La Francophonie (Les passe-temps):**<br>• Mancala in Africa<br><br>**Produits:**<br>Guignol | • Position of adverbs | **Communication:** Cognates |

| Vocabulaire | Fonctions | Culture | Structure | Stratégies |
|---|---|---|---|---|
| • Nouns:<br>  Sports<br>  Music<br>  Pastimes<br>• Numbers 0–20 | • State my preferences<br>• Ask what someone prefers<br>• Agree and disagree | • Count on fingers<br>• Rachid Taha and World music<br>• Singer Corneille<br>• **Fête de la musique**<br><br>**La Francophonie (Instruments):**<br>• Kora in Africa | • Gender of nouns and definite articles<br>• The verb **préférer**<br>• Negation with **ne... pas** | **Culture:**<br>Sports viewing habits<br><br>**Fine art:**<br>Coloration (Béatrice Boisségur)<br><br>**Reading:**<br>Paraphrasing and finding meaning in repetition |

## Bilan cumulatif: Unités 1 – 2

## Unité 3  À l'école

*Essential question: How does education shape individuals and societies?*

| | | | | |
|---|---|---|---|---|
| • Classroom objects<br>• Numbers 20–100 | • Say what I need<br>• Ask what someone else needs<br>• Ask what something costs<br>• State what something costs | • Carrefour<br>• School supplies<br>• The euro and the Eurozone<br>• Online instruction | • Indefinite articles<br>• Plurals of articles and nouns<br>• Present tense of the irregular verb **avoir**<br>• **Avoir besoin de** | |
| • Classroom subjects<br>• Adjectives<br>• Time expressions | • Describe a class<br>• Ask for a description of someone<br>• Describe someone | • 24-hour clock<br>• Wednesday afternoon<br>• Classes and exams<br>• The **lycée** and the **bac**<br>• Naming schools<br><br>**La Francophonie:**<br>• French Polynesia<br><br>**Produits:**<br>**Le paréo** in French Polynesia | • Telling time<br>• Present tense of the irregular verb **être**<br>• Agreement and position of regular adjectives | **Communication:**<br>Combine sentences |
| • Places in school<br>• Places in the city | • Ask where someone is going<br>• Ask when someone is going somewhere<br>• Ask why someone cannot do something<br>• Establish a place and time to meet | • **La cantine** and school meals<br>• **Lycées hôteliers**<br>• **Fête de la musique**<br>• English words of French origin<br><br>**La Francophonie (Éducation):**<br>• Education in Mali | • Present tense of the irregular verb **aller**<br>• **À** + definite articles<br>• Forming questions with **est-ce que** | **Culture:**<br>Reflect on learning about French schools and compare them to schools in the United States<br><br>**Fine art:**<br>Focal point (Robert Doisneau)<br><br>**Reading:**<br>Point of view and Context clues |

| Vocabulaire | Fonctions | Culture | Structure | Stratégies |
|---|---|---|---|---|
| **Unité 4    Le weekend ensemble** | | | | |
| *Essential question: What activities do friends in other countries do together?* | | | | |
| • Soccer<br>• Soccer clothes<br>• The **métro** | • Give a reason<br>• Set a time and place to meet<br>• Suggest a different time | • Soccer in France<br>• Soccer clubs<br>• Famous soccer players<br><br>**Produits:**<br>The media and soccer in France | • **Aller** + infinitive<br>• Forming questions | |
| • Food and drink<br>• Numbers 100–1.000 | • Understand what the server will ask<br>• Order food<br>• Ask for the bill | • Cafés and **bistrots**<br>• Paris cafés and famous writers<br>• Fast food chains in France<br><br>**Produits:**<br>**Le croissant** | • Present tense of the irregular verb **prendre**<br>• Avoir expressions: **avoir faim/soif** | **Communication:**<br>Use adjectives and adverbs |
| • Movie genres<br>• Early, on time, and late | • Make a prediction<br>• Respond to a prediction | • French cinema<br>• French comedies<br>• *Bienvenue chez les Ch'tis*, French comedy<br><br>**Produits:**<br>French film starring Johnny Depp | • The interrogative adjective **quel**<br>• Present tense of the irregular verb **voir** | **Culture:**<br>Remakes of French films<br><br>**Fine art:**<br>Poster art<br><br>**Reading:**<br>Identify the conflict in a story and recognize false cognates |
| **Bilan cumulatif: Unités 3 – 4** | | | | |
| **Unité 5    Les gens que je connais** | | | | |
| *Essential question: What is the nature of relationships in other cultures?* | | | | |
| • Family members<br>• Physical descriptions<br>• Numbers 1.000–1.000.000 | • Ask for a description<br>• Point out resemblances | • The metric system<br><br>**La Francophonie:**<br>• Martinique<br><br>**Produits:**<br>Zouk music | • Possessive adjectives<br>• Indefinite articles in negative sentences | |
| • Months of the year<br>• Birthdays<br>• Descriptions of character | • Ask someone's age<br>• Tell my age<br>• Tell what gift I am giving<br>• Plan a party with others | • Birthdays and saints' days<br>• **La FNAC**<br><br>**La Francophonie (Fêtes d'anniversaire):**<br>• Birthday celebrations in Guadeloupe, North Africa, and Sub-saharan Africa | • Present tense of regular verbs ending in **-ir**<br>• Dates<br>• Expressions with **avoir: J'ai... ans**<br>• Present tense of the irregular verb **offrir** | **Communication:**<br>Ask questions to extend a conversation |
| • French-speaking African countries and nationalities<br>• Professions | • Find out someone's profession<br>• Ask where someone comes from<br>• Tell where I come from | • Singers Amadou and Mariam<br><br>**La Francophonie:**<br>Sub-saharan Francophone Africa<br><br>**Produits:**<br>African masks | • **C'est** vs. **il/elle est**<br>• Present tense of the irregular verb **venir**<br>• **De** + definite articles | **Culture:**<br>Collect anecdotal evidence about a Francophone family<br><br>**Fine art:**<br>Composition (Alfred Wolf)<br><br>**Reading:**<br>Theme and Monitoring comprehension |

| Vocabulaire | Fonctions | Culture | Structure | Stratégies |
|---|---|---|---|---|

## Unité 6    La rue commerçante

*Essential question: How is shopping different in other countries?*

| Vocabulaire | Fonctions | Culture | Structure | Stratégies |
|---|---|---|---|---|
| • Articles of clothing<br>• Colors | • What to ask the salesperson<br>• What the salesperson says | • Shopping online<br>• French flea markets<br>• High fashion houses in Paris<br><br>**La Francophonie (Vêtements):**<br>Clothing in West Africa | • Present tense of the verb **acheter**<br>• Present tense of the irregular verb **vouloir**<br>• Demonstrative adjectives | |
| • Stores and grocery items<br>• Quantities | • Sequence my activities | • Superstores vs. small shops<br>• French cheeses<br>• Metric measurements<br><br>**Produits:**<br>**Le pâté** | • Present tense of regular verbs ending in **-re**<br>• Expressions of quantity | **Communication:**<br>Tell a story through pictures |
| • Fruits and vegetables | • Make a purchase at the market<br>• Respond to questions from the vendor | • Outdoor markets<br>• Slow food movement<br><br>**La francophonie (Le marché):**<br>**Les souks** in North Africa<br><br>**Produits:**<br>North African arts and crafts | • The partitive article<br>• The partitive in negative sentences | **Culture:**<br>Go shopping online<br><br>**Fine art:**<br>Black and white photography **d'après-guerre** (Sabine Weiss)<br><br>**Reading:**<br>Setting and Word families |

## Bilan cumulatif: Unités 5 – 6

## Unité 7    À la maison

*Essential question: What makes a house a "home"?*

| Vocabulaire | Fonctions | Culture | Structure | Stratégies |
|---|---|---|---|---|
| • Stories in a building<br>• Rooms in a house<br>• Furniture in the kitchen and living room | • Give a tour of a house or an apartment<br>• Ask where someone lives<br>• Agree and disagree | • Housing in France<br>• Bathrooms in France<br><br>**La Francophonie (Habitations):**<br>North African dwellings, focus on Algeria<br><br>**Produits:**<br>**Le raï** | • Ordinal numbers | |
| • Meals<br>• Table setting | • Give directions in the kitchen | • Marseille<br>• Provence<br>• Regional culinary specialties<br><br>**Produits:**<br>*The Starry Night* by Van Gogh And "**La Marseillaise**" | • Comparative of adjectives<br>• Present tense of the irregular verb **devoir**<br>• Present tense of the irregular verb **mettre** | **Communication:**<br>Write descriptions |

| Vocabulaire | Fonctions | Culture | Structure | Stratégies |
|---|---|---|---|---|
| • The bedroom and bathroom<br>• Computer and other technology | • Say that I don't understand<br>• Talk about computers | • Technology and French youth<br>**La Francophonie:**<br>• New Brunswick<br>• The **Grand Dérangement** of the Acadians<br>• Singer Natasha St-Pier<br>**Produits:**<br>Zydeco music | • Present tense of the irregular verb **pouvoir** | **Culture:**<br>Evaluate whether student's home is like or unlike Francophone homes<br>**Fine art:**<br>Impressionism and Cubism (Paul Cézanne)<br>**Reading:**<br>Rhyme Scheme and Deciphering new grammatical structures |

## Unité 8 À Paris

*Essential question: How do major world cities tell their stories?*

| Vocabulaire | Fonctions | Culture | Structure | Stratégies |
|---|---|---|---|---|
| • Weather<br>• Seasons<br>• Pets | • Extend an invitation<br>• Accept or refuse an invitation | • Paris<br>• Parisian pastries<br>**La Francophonie (Une autre capitale):**<br>Port-au-Prince<br>**Produits:**<br>**La galette des rois** | • Present tense of the irregular verb **faire**<br>• Expressions with **avoir: avoir froid, avoir chaud, avoir envie de** | |
| • Places in the city<br>• Monuments in Paris | • Excuse oneself<br>• Describe actions that took place in the past<br>• Sequence past events | • **Notre-Dame**<br>• **L'arc de triomphe**<br>• **La tour Eiffel** | • **Passé composé** with **avoir**<br>• Irregular past participles<br>• Position of irregular adjectives | **Communication:**<br>Personal narrative |
| • Time expressions | • Express actions that took place in the past<br>• Sequence past events | • **Le jardin des Tuileries**<br>• **Le métro** | • **Passé composé** with **être**<br>• Position of adverbs in the **passé composé** | **Culture:**<br>Identify customs and React to French culture<br>**Fine art:**<br>Pointillism (Paul Signac)<br>**Reading:**<br>Personification and Making inferences |

## Bilan cumulatif: Unités 7 – 8

## Unité 9 En forme

*Essential question: How do people stay healthy and maintain a healthy environment?*

| Vocabulaire | Fonctions | Culture | Structure | Stratégies |
|---|---|---|---|---|
| • Parts of the body<br>• Parts of the face | • Say it is necessary to do, or not do, something | • **La sécu** in France<br>• **"Manger-bouger"** ad campaign<br>• **Le thermalisme**<br>**Produits:**<br>Homeopathic medications | • Present tense of the irregular verb **falloir** | |

| Vocabulaire | Fonctions | Culture | Structure | Stratégies |
|---|---|---|---|---|
| • Illnesses and other health expressions | • Ask for advice<br>• Give advice | **La Francophonie:**<br>Rwanda<br>• Fighting AIDS in Rwanda<br>• Home health care workers in Rwanda<br><br>**Produits:**<br>Languages and language education in Rwanda | • The imperative | **Communication:**<br>"How-to" writing |
| • Environmental problems<br>• Environmental solutions<br>• Endangered species | • Persuade someone<br>• Respond to persuasion | • **Les Verts** in France<br>• **Vélib' Paris**<br><br>**Produits:**<br>*La souris verte*, online magazine for young people | • Verbs + infinitives<br>• **De** + plural adjectives | **Culture:**<br>Hunting for diabetes education aids in Francophone countries<br><br>**Fine art:**<br>Cubism (Roger de La Fresnaye)<br><br>**Reading:**<br>Characterization, Text organization, and Making a prediction |

## Unité 10    Les grandes vacances

*Essential question: How do travel experiences shape our worldview?*

| Vocabulaire | Fonctions | Culture | Structure | Stratégies |
|---|---|---|---|---|
| • Places in North America<br>• Quebec essentials<br>• Compass directions | • Tell someone where a place is located | **La Francophonie:**<br>• Quebec<br>• Montreal<br>• **FrancoFolies** festival in Montreal<br><br>**Produits:**<br>Maple syrup | • Prepositions before cities, countries, and continents | |
| • At the train station<br>• Features of the countryside | • Remind someone to do something<br>• Wish someone a good trip | • Departments and regions of France<br>• Loire castles<br>• Tours | • Other negative expressions | **Communication:**<br>Writing a postcard |
| • European countries<br>• European nationalities<br>• Expressions for giving directions | • Ask for directions<br>• Give directions | **La Francophonie:**<br>• Switzerland<br>• Geneva<br>• International museum of the **Croix-Rouge**<br><br>**Produits:**<br>Swiss watches | • Superlative of adjectives | **Culture:**<br>Interviewing a traveler who has visited a Francophone location<br><br>**Fine art:**<br>Perspective (Achille Varin)<br><br>**Reading:**<br>Imagery and the Progression of stanzas |

**Bilan cumulatif: Unités 9 – 10**

# T'es branché? Level 2

| Vocabulaire | Fonctions | Culture | Structure | Stratégies |
|---|---|---|---|---|
| **Unité 1  Comment je passe l'été** | | | | |
| *Essential question: What do young people do in the summer in other cultures?* | | | | |
| • Holidays in France, Quebec, and the United States | • Ask someone if they celebrate a particular holiday<br>• Ask when something takes place and respond | • Quebec City<br>• 400th anniversary of the founding of Québec<br>**La Francophonie (Les fêtes):**<br>• Celebrations in Quebec and France<br>• Native Singer Samian<br>**Produits:**<br>**Le cirque du soleil** | • Present tense of regular verbs ending in **-er**, **-ir**, and **-re**<br>• Negation<br>• Possessive adjectives<br>• Forming questions<br>• Dates | |
| • Television programs<br>• Television professions | • Ask for an opinion<br>• Give an opinion<br>• Find out what someone is thinking<br>• Agree or disagree | **La Francophonie:**<br>• Luxemburg<br>• French and Luxemburg TV channels<br>• Reality shows in France<br>**Produits:**<br>• Canal +<br>• "La Nouvelle Star" | • Present tense of the irregular verbs **avoir** and **être**<br>• Indefinite articles in negative sentences<br>• Demonstrative adjectives<br>• Agreement and position of adjectives<br>• Comparative of adjectives | **Communication:**<br>Create a TV commercial |
| • Rides and attractions at amusement parks | • Inquire about future plans<br>• Respond | • French fair **la Fête des Loges**<br>• Amusement parks and other attractions in France<br>**La Francophonie (Parcs d'attractions):**<br>**La Ronde**<br>**Produits:**<br>**Le Parc d'Astérix** | • Present tense of the irregular verbs **aller** and **faire**<br>• **De** and **à** + definite articles<br>• The irregular verb **venir** and **venir de** + infinitive<br>• Telling time | **Culture:**<br>Investigate bilinguism in Canada<br>**Fine art:**<br>Realism (Jean-Louis Ernest Meissonier)<br>**Reading:**<br>Paraphrasing and Learning from the title |
| **Unité 2  Dans la capitale** | | | | |
| *Essential question: What stories does Paris tell about art and architecture?* | | | | |
| • Art terms<br>• Types of paintings | • Describe a painting | • The **Louvre**<br>• The **musée d'Orsay**<br>• The **Centre Pompidou**<br>**Produits:**<br>La *Joconde* | • Present tense of the irregular verb **suivre**<br>• **Passé composé** with **avoir**<br>• Present tense of the irregular verbs **mettre**, **prendre**, and **voir** | |
| • Places in the neighborhood | • Say I'm lost<br>• Tell someone not to worry<br>• Ask for directions<br>• Give directions | • Paris **arrondissements**<br>• **Le Quartier latin**<br>• **Saint-Germain des Prés**<br>**Produits:**<br>**La Sainte-Chapelle** | • Present tense of the irregular verbs **vouloir**, **pouvoir**, **devoir**, and **falloir**<br>• Irregular past participles<br>• Imperative | **Communication:**<br>Describe art |

| Vocabulaire | Fonctions | Culture | Structure | Stratégies |
|---|---|---|---|---|
| • Modes of transportation<br>• Versailles | • Ask about transportation<br>• Respond | • Tourist offices<br>• The R.E.R.<br>• **Versailles** | • Present tense of the irregular verbs **partir** and **sortir**<br>• **Passé composé** with **être**<br>• Superlative of adjectives | **Culture:**<br>Explore **le musée d'Orsay**<br><br>**Fine art:**<br>Modern Art (Marc Laberge)<br><br>**Reading:**<br>Drama basics and Finding evidence in the text |

**Bilan cumulatif: Unités 1 – 2**

**Unité 3**  La vie quotidienne

*Essential question: How do the routines of people in other cultures differ from mine?*

| | | | | |
|---|---|---|---|---|
| • Toiletries<br>• Daily routine | • Complain<br>• Respond to a complaint<br>• Express frustration<br>• Respond | **La Francophonie:**<br>• Cameroon<br>• Goals of the community of **la Francophonie**<br><br>**Produits:**<br>**Le Ngondo** | • Present tense of reflexive verbs<br>• Irregular plural forms of nouns and adjectives | |
| • Household items<br>• Household chores | • Make comparisons<br>• Respond to comparisons<br>• Express injustice | **La Francophonie:**<br>• Ivory Coast<br>• Artists from the Ivory Coast<br>• Africa today<br>• African immigrants in France today<br><br>**Produits:**<br>**Zouglou** music | • Present tense of the irregular verb **s'asseoir**<br>• The imperative of reflexive verbs | **Communication:**<br>Tell a story through pictures |
| • More reflexive verbs | • Find out if someone remembers something<br>• Recount past events | **La Francophonie:**<br>• Senegal<br>• Senegalese artists<br>• **Griots**<br>• Singer Youssou N'Dour<br><br>**Produits:**<br>**L'hymne national sénégalais** | • **Passé composé** of reflexive verbs | **Culture:**<br>Examine the controversy of Halal meat in fast-food restaurants<br><br>**Fine art:**<br>Batik (Anonyme)<br><br>**Reading:**<br>Sensory details and Making inferences |

**Unité 4**  Autrefois

*Essential question: How does the past shape us?*

| | | | | |
|---|---|---|---|---|
| • Farm<br>• Farm animals | • Reminisce<br>• Describe past events | • Agriculture in France<br>• World ranking of France's agricultural products<br>• French rural life today<br><br>**Produits:**<br>**Emmental** | • Imperfect tense<br>• Present tense of the irregular verb **croire** | |

| Vocabulaire | Fonctions | Culture | Structure | Stratégies |
|---|---|---|---|---|
| • Professions of the past | • Describe past events | • Montmartre<br>• Toulouse-Lautrec<br>**Produits:**<br>Poster art | • **Il y a** + time<br>• Imperfect and **passé composé** | **Communication:**<br>Write an oral history |
| • University life | • Make a suggestion | • Demonstrations<br>• May 1968<br>• University of Vincennes vs. Sorbonne | **Si on** + imperfect | **Culture:**<br>Discover the reasons why people demonstrate<br>**Fine art:**<br>Impressionism's use of light (Camille Pissarro)<br>**Reading:**<br>Text organization and Fact vs. opinion |

**Bilan cumulatif: Unités 3 – 4**

## Unité 5    Bon voyage et bonne route!

*Essential question: What do you need to know to travel successfully?*

| Vocabulaire | Fonctions | Culture | Structure | Stratégies |
|---|---|---|---|---|
| • At the airport | • Describe a health problem<br>• Give instructions | • **Air France**<br>• Airports in Paris<br>• Bordeaux<br>**Produits:**<br>**Les Nubians**, hip-hop group from Bordeaux | • Direct object pronouns: **me**, **te**, **nous**, **vous** | |
| • Types of cars<br>• Exterior of cars<br>• Interior of cars | • Express that I'm looking forward to something | • **Peugeot-Citroën** and **Renault** car companies<br>• Learning to drive in France<br>**Produits:**<br>**Renault** and General Motors | • Direct object pronouns: **le**, **la**, **l'**, **les**<br>• Direct object pronouns in the **passé composé**<br>• Present tense of the irregular verb **conduire** | **Communication:**<br>Write a dialogue |
| • Hotel room<br>• French breakfast<br>• North American breakfast | • Ask for a hotel room<br>• Ask if something's included in the price<br>• Understand what the receptionist asks | • Hotels, inns, and bed & breakfasts in France<br>• Luxury hotels and the movies<br>**Produits:**<br>Sofitel, hotel chain | • Indirect object pronouns: **lui**, **leur**<br>• Indirect object pronouns: **me**, **te**, **nous**, **vous**<br>• Present tense of the irregular verb **boire**<br>• The adjective **tout** | **Culture:**<br>Find a hotel that meets your needs<br>**Fine art:**<br>Pop art (François Le Diascorn)<br>**Reading:**<br>Motif and Cause and effect |

## Unité 6    Les arts maghrébins

*Essential question: How do other cultures enrich our lives?*

| Vocabulaire | Fonctions | Culture | Structure | Stratégies |
|---|---|---|---|---|
| • Things we read<br>• Things we write | • Say what a book is about<br>• Introduce an author or a novel<br>• Borrow something | **La Francophonie:**<br>• Morocco<br>• French language comic books<br>**Produits:**<br>• Henna decoration in North Africa<br>• *Le racisme expliqué à ma fille* by Tahar Ben Jelloun | • Present tense of the irregular verb **lire**<br>• Present tense of the irregular verb **écrire** | |

| Vocabulaire | Fonctions | Culture | Structure | Stratégies |
|---|---|---|---|---|
| • Music genres<br>• Musical instruments | • Ask if someone plays a particular instrument<br>• Say what instrument I play | **La Francophonie:**<br>• Algeria<br>• **Raï** music<br>• Singer Faudel<br>• North African music instruments<br><br>**Produits:**<br>*Indigènes*, French film about North African soldiers | • Present tense of the irregular verb **savoir**<br>• Present tense of the irregular verb **connaître** | **Communication:**<br>Write a character sketch |
| • Accessories and fabrics<br>• Jewelry | • Begin and end a letter<br>• Thank someone formally | **La Francophonie:**<br>• Tunisia<br>• **Souks**<br><br>• How to write a formal letter<br><br>**Produits:**<br>Carthage | • Present tense of the irregular verb **recevoir**<br>• Present tense of the irregular verb **ouvrir** | **Culture:**<br>Reflect on negotiating a price in North African souks and in North America<br><br>**Fine art:**<br>Perspective in modern photography (Peet Simard)<br><br>**Reading:**<br>Images and Refrain |

## Bilan cumulatif: Unités 5 – 6

## Unité 7    En province

*Essential question: How do smaller communities enrich a country's culture?*

| Vocabulaire | Fonctions | Culture | Structure | Stratégies |
|---|---|---|---|---|
| • Foods and courses | • Compliment the host or hostess<br>• Politely refuse more food<br>• Offer help | • Alsace<br>• Strasbourg<br><br>**La Francophonie (Une autre province):**<br>**Kabylie** in Algeria<br><br>**Produits:**<br>**La choucroute garnie** | • The relative pronouns **qui** and **que**<br>• The partitive<br>• The pronoun **en** | |
| • French regions and their adjectives | • Ask a friend what's new<br>• Find out someone's associations with a place<br>• Say I like a suggestion | • Normandy<br>• Rouen<br><br>**Produits:**<br>• French influence on the English language<br>• Bayeux tapestry<br>• Cider<br>• Claude Monet museum in Giverny | • Interrogative pronouns | **Communication:**<br>Combine sentences |
| • Things to eat and drink in a **crêperie**<br>• Youth hostels | • Understand what the server asks<br>• Order food | • Brittany<br>• Saint-Malo<br>• Youth hostels<br><br>**Produits:**<br>Food specialties of Brittany | • Stress pronouns | **Culture:**<br>Explore regional identity<br><br>**Fine art:**<br>Still lifes (Paul Cézanne)<br><br>**Reading:**<br>Refrain and tone, and Anticipating vocabulary |

| Vocabulaire | Fonctions | Culture | Structure | Stratégies |
|---|---|---|---|---|

## Unité 8   Les Antilles

*Essential question: What are the benefits of encountering other cultures?*

| Vocabulaire | Fonctions | Culture | Structure | Stratégies |
|---|---|---|---|---|
| • Flora in Guadeloupe<br>• Fauna in Guadeloupe | • Ask what someone prefers<br>• State ambivalence | **La Francophonie:**<br>• Guadeloupe<br>• **Parc national de la Guadeloupe**<br>• Green tourism<br><br>**Produits:**<br>"Prière d'un Petit enfant nègre" by Guy Tirolien | • Present tense of the irregular verb **vivre**<br>• Pronoun **y** | |
| • Carnival in Martinique<br>• Weddings | • Make an observation | **La Francophonie:**<br>• Martinique<br>• Carnival in Martinique<br><br>**Produits:**<br>*La Rue Cases-Nègres* | • Double object pronouns | **Communication:**<br>Circumlocution |
| • Water management<br>• Seafood | • Say what I'm in charge of<br>• Express appreciation | **La Francophonie:**<br>• Haiti<br>• Toussaint Louverture<br>• Haitian cuisine<br><br>**Produits:**<br>Haitian music | • **Depuis** + present tense | **Culture:**<br>Find a good humanitarian organization<br><br>**Fine art:**<br>Seascapes (Claude Salez)<br><br>**Reading:**<br>Theme and Citing others' works |

## Bilan cumulatif: Unités 7 – 8

## Unité 9   La vie contemporaine

*Essential question: What influences and changes contemporary society?*

| Vocabulaire | Fonctions | Culture | Structure | Stratégies |
|---|---|---|---|---|
| • Features of smartphones<br>• Steps for taking a digital photo | • Ask someone to lend me something<br>• Say that I know or do not know how to use something<br>• Express what someone was happy about | • French transportation technologies: aviation, space program, rail<br><br>**Produits:**<br>Rubber from Indochina and Michelin | • Conditional tense | |
| • Problems in contemporary society<br>• Possible solutions | • Hypothesize<br>• Propose solutions | • Nuclear energy<br>• Objectives and problems in French education<br>• Unemployed young people<br><br>**Produits:**<br>French **Grandes Écoles** | • Conditional tense in sentences with **si** | **Communication:**<br>Write a proposal |

| Vocabulaire | Fonctions | Culture | Structure | Stratégies |
|---|---|---|---|---|
| • Job sectors<br>• Today's professions | • Express my future goals<br>• Give a reason | **La Francophonie:**<br>• Belgium<br>• Famous Belgians<br>• Brussels<br>• European Union<br><br>**Produits:**<br>Flemish/French song by Jacques Brel | • Future tense | **Culture:**<br>Investigate what new words in **Le Petit Larousse** reveal about contemporary French culture<br><br>**Fine art:**<br>Textures of acrylic paints (Daniel Cacouault)<br><br>**Reading:**<br>Dystopias in fiction and Social commentary |

## Unité 10    En vacances

*Essential question: What opportunities does travel afford us?*

| Vocabulaire | Fonctions | Culture | Structure | Stratégies |
|---|---|---|---|---|
| • At the beach | • Say I've been wanting to do something for a long time | • French Riviera<br>• Nice<br>• Chagall museum<br>• Matisse museum<br><br>**Produits:**<br>The **promenade des Anglais** in Nice | • Adverbs<br>• Verbs + infinitives | |
| • Camping | • Say I need something<br>• Ask someone to return something as soon as possible | • Alps<br>• Grenoble<br>• Camping in France<br><br>**Produits:**<br>**Téléphérique** in Grenoble | • Present tense of the irregular verb **dormir**<br>• Comparative of adverbs | **Communication:**<br>Travel writing |
| • Continents and bodies of water<br>• Adventure tourism | • Ask what to bring | **La Francophonie:**<br>• French Guiana<br>• Kourou<br>• Prisons<br><br>**La Francophonie (Tourisme d'aventure):**<br>Adventure tourism in France and French Guiana<br><br>**Produits:**<br>• Poems of Léon Gontran-Damas<br>• *Papillon* | • Superlative of adverbs | **Culture:**<br>Compare French and American vacation destinations<br><br>**Fine art:**<br>Point of view (Delphine D. Garcia)<br><br>**Reading:**<br>Point of view and Characterization |

## Bilan cumulatif: Unités 9 – 10

# T'es branché? Level 3

| Vocabulaire | Fonctions | Culture | Structure | Stratégies |
|---|---|---|---|---|
| **Unité 1   Les moments de la vie** | | | | |
| **Essential question:** *Comment les objectifs et les intérêts des Francophones évoluent-ils avec le temps?* | | | | |
| • Human emotions<br>• Teen destinations | • Say where I met someone<br>• Advise someone<br>• Tell someone not to worry<br>• Describe how someone seems | • Teen socialization<br>• **Maisons des Jeunes et de la Culture (MJC)**<br>**Produits:**<br>French blogs | • Present tense of regular -**er**,-**ir**, and -**re** verbs<br>• Present tense of irregular verbs<br>• **Depuis** + present tense | |
| • Different types of families<br>• Childhood games and activities | • Explain how something happened<br>• Say what I discovered<br>• Ask for a suggestion | • Different types of families in France<br>**La Francophonie (Les familles):**<br>• Families and family values in Africa<br>• **Provence-Alpes-Côte d'Azur**<br>**Produits:**<br>Perfumes and Grasse | • The irregular verb **courir**<br>• **Passé composé** with **avoir**<br>• **Passé composé** with **être**<br>• Imperfect tense<br>• Imperfect and **passé composé** | **Communication:**<br>Write a personal narrative |
| • Weddings<br>• Workplaces | • Say I don't care<br>• Say where I'd like to work | • Preparatory and Ivy league schools<br>• Civil and religious marriage ceremonies<br>**La Francophonie (Le mariage):**<br>• Marriage ceremony in Maghreb<br>**Produits:**<br>French wedding cake | • Conditional tense<br>• Conditional tense with **si**<br>• Future tense | **Culture:** Describing adolescent cultures<br>**Fine art:**<br>Line drawing (Édouard Albert)<br>**Reading:**<br>Setting and Using context clues (***Les petits enfants du siècle***, Christiane Rochefort) |
| **Unité 2   Les rapports personnels** | | | | |
| **Essential question:** *Qu'y a-t-il d'universel dans les rapports entre les gens?* | | | | |
| • Christmas eve dinner | • Talk on the phone<br>• Invite someone<br>• Respond affirmatively to an invitation<br>• Say that a proposal works for me | • Christmas Eve holiday<br>**Produits: Bûche de Noël**<br>**La Francophonie (Les fêtes):**<br>• Ramadan<br>• **Aïd-el-Fitre** | • Interrogative pronouns<br>• Direct object pronouns | |
| • Descriptions: shapes, sizes, material, and usage<br>• Kitchen utensils | • Ask for help<br>• Respond to a request for help | • Classic French cooking<br>• **La nouvelle cuisine**<br>**Produits:**<br>Le Cordon Bleu | • Indirect object pronouns<br>• **C'est** vs. **il/elle est** | **Communication:**<br>Using circumlocution |

| Vocabulaire | Fonctions | Culture | Structure | Stratégies |
|---|---|---|---|---|
| • Dinner table topics of conversation | • Express that I can't stop myself<br>• Say someone is right<br>• Ask about dinner table topics | • Traditional meal for Christmas Eve<br>• Rules of table etiquette<br>**Produits:** French wine | • Relative pronouns **qui, que**<br>• Relative pronouns **ce qui, ce que** | **Culture:** Identify food preferences<br>**Fine art:** Landscapes behind portraits (Jules Ernest Renoux)<br>**Reading:** Dialogue and Conflict (*Deux couverts*, Sacha Guitry) |

**Bilan cumulatif: Unités 1 – 2**

**Unité 3    La Francophonie**

*Essential question: Comment les Francophones restent-ils fidèles à leurs traditions?*

| Vocabulaire | Fonctions | Culture | Structure | Stratégies |
|---|---|---|---|---|
| • Extended family members<br>• States in the United States | • Say where my ancestors came from<br>• Say where my ancestors settled | • **Alliance Française** and its outreach programs<br>• French immigration to Quebec and **île d'Orléans**<br>• French-Canadian immigration to New England | • Pronouns **y, en**<br>• Double object pronouns | |
| • Types of stories<br>• Words from a North African children's story | • Start a fairy-tale | **La Francophonie:**<br>• Tunisia<br>• Immigration of **Maghrébins** in France<br>**La Francophonie (Les contes):**<br>• Overview of **contes maghrébins**<br>**Produits:** North African cuisine | • Reflexive verbs | **Communication:** Describe in detail |
| • Types of housing<br>• Home repair terms | • Respond to an introduction<br>• Say where I grew up<br>• Give a compliment | • HLMs and **allocations familiales**<br>**La Francophonie:**<br>• Senegal **(Logement):**<br>• African housing<br>**Produits:** Oral tradition in Africa | • Comparative of adverbs<br>• Superlative of adverbs | **Culture:** Needs of new immigrants<br>**Fine art:** Primitive Art (Cécile Delorme)<br>**Reading:** Make cultural inferences, Gender criticism (*Une si longue lettre*, Mariama Bâ) |

| Vocabulaire | Fonctions | Culture | Structure | Stratégies |
|---|---|---|---|---|

## Unité 4   Préparatifs de départ

*Essential question: Qu'est-ce qu'on doit connaître de sa destination pour réussir son voyage?*

| Vocabulaire | Fonctions | Culture | Structure | Stratégies |
|---|---|---|---|---|
| • Sports and activities to do on vacation | • Ask someone's opinion<br>• React positively to someone's opinion<br>• React negatively to someone's opinion | **La Francophonie:<br>La Réunion**<br>• Chamonix and other **stations de ski** in France<br><br>**La Francophonie<br>(Stations de ski):**<br>• Switzerland<br><br>**Produits:**<br>Training Saint Bernard dogs | • Present participle<br>• Negation<br>• Other negative expressions | |
| • At the ski resort<br>• Ski clothing and equipment | • Say what I must do<br>• Tell someone they'll have an opportunity<br>• Say I was expecting something | • Haute Savoie traditions and specialties<br>• **Classes de neige**<br><br>**Produits:<br>La raclette savoyarde**<br><br>**La Francophonie<br>(La récréation):**<br>Aquatic or "bleu" activities in Saint-Martin | • **Savoir** vs. **connaître**<br>• Subjunctive of regular verbs after **il faut que**<br>• Subjunctive of irregular verbs | **Communication:**<br>Write a "how-to" piece using subjunctive |
| • Other winter sports<br>• Travel planning expressions | • Say I'm doing something different<br>• Tell someone to not hurt himself or herself | • Volunteer travel experiences in Francophone countries<br><br>**Produits:**<br>Sports in the Winter Olympics | • Subjunctive after impersonal expressions | **Culture:** Volunteer travel experiences<br><br>**Fine art:** Classicism (Sébastien Bourdon)<br><br>**Reading:**<br>Structure and Meaning, Allusions ("**Heureux qui, comme Ulysse, a fait un beau voyage,**" Joachim du Bellay) |

## Bilan cumulatif: Unités 3 – 4

## Unité 5   Comment se renseigner en voyage

*Essential question: De quelles compétences ai-je besoin pour réussir un séjour?*

| Vocabulaire | Fonctions | Culture | Structure | Stratégies |
|---|---|---|---|---|
| • At the hotel<br>• Hotel amenities | • Ask for information | **La Francophonie:**<br>• Monaco<br>• Monte Carlo<br>• Rainier family<br><br>**Produits:<br>Le Bal de la Rose** | • Subjunctive after expressions of wish, will, desire | |
| • Food in Bourgogne: meats, dishes, sauces | • Ask about restaurant specialties<br>• Ask what a dish is served with | • Dijon and its region<br>• Food specialties in Bourgogne<br><br>**Produits:** Dijon museum and mustard<br><br>**La Francophonie<br>(La cuisine):**<br>• North African dishes | • Subjunctive after expressions of emotion<br>• Subjunctive after expressions of doubt or uncertainty | **Communication:**<br>Write a movie review |

| Vocabulaire | Fonctions | Culture | Structure | Stratégies |
|---|---|---|---|---|
| • Movie expressions | • Say what I'm not in the mood for<br>• Report a review of a film<br>• Ask someone's reaction (to a piece of art)<br>• Express disagreement | • **Le septième art**<br>• **Les Césars**<br><br>**Produits:** Lumière brothers and birth of cinematography | • Interrogative adjective **quel**<br>• Interrogative pronoun **lequel** (**duquel, auquel**) | **Culture:** Planning a trip online<br><br>**Fine art:** Cartoons (Christian Cailleaux)<br><br>**Reading:** Comedy Sketch, Straight Man ("**Les croissants**," Fernand Reynaud) |

## Unité 6     On se débrouille en France.

### Essential question: Comment s'intégrer à une autre culture?

| Vocabulaire | Fonctions | Culture | Structure | Stratégies |
|---|---|---|---|---|
| • Banking terms<br>• University departments | • Open a bank account<br>• Get a credit card<br>• Make a promise | • French banks<br>• French universities and free education<br><br>**Produits:**<br>**La Carte bleue** | • Future tense in sentences with **si**<br>• Future tense after **quand** | |
| • Things to read | • Ask what a book is about<br>• Say I can't decide | • French reading habits<br>• Le Clézio<br><br>**Produits:**<br>French TV shows about books<br><br>**La Francophonie (Les écrivains):**<br>Maryse Condé | • Verbs + **de** + nouns<br>• Relative pronoun **dont** | **Communication:** Persuade someone to read a book or see a movie |
| • At the post office | • Say what I need<br>• Specify items | • French post office and its services<br><br>**Produits:**<br>Films that feature mail carriers | • Demonstrative adjectives<br>• Demonstrative pronouns | **Culture:** Problem solving **sur place**<br><br>**Fine art:** Cartoon art (Marjane Satrapi)<br><br>**Reading:** Narrator and Narration, Direct and Indirect Reporting (**Petropolis**, Marjane Satrapi) |

## Bilan cumulatif: Unités 5 – 6

## Unité 7     Les Arts

### Essential question: Comment l'art est-il un reflet de la culture?

| Vocabulaire | Fonctions | Culture | Structure | Stratégies |
|---|---|---|---|---|
| • Art descriptions<br>• Art movements | • Say when a painting was painted<br>• Describe an artist's approach<br>• Describe colors in a painting | • **Académie, salons**<br>• **Atelier** vs. **en plein air**<br>• **Salon des refusés**<br><br>**Produits:**<br>Monet painting that gave name to Impressionnists, *Sunday in the Park with George* | • Agreement and position of adjectives<br>• Comparative of adjectives<br>• Superlative of adjectives | |

| Vocabulaire | Fonctions | Culture | Structure | Stratégies |
|---|---|---|---|---|
| • Music | • Describe an artist's development<br>• Say that an artist was successful<br>• Describe an artist's ability to connect with his or her audience | • The modern French song and its themes<br>**Produits:**<br>"La vie en rose"<br>**La Francophonie (Les chansons):**<br>Quebec group<br>**Produits:** "Mon pays," Gilles Vigneault | • The irregular verb **plaire** | **Communication:**<br>Compare and Contrast |
| • Poetry | • Describe how an artist raises themes<br>• Describe how a work of art takes a position<br>• Describe what an artist worked on<br>• Attribute new inventions<br>• Describe how an artist fits into a culture | • French poets<br>**Produits:**<br>Apollinaire's **calligrammes** | • **Pour** + infinitive<br>• Subjunctive after **pour que** | **Culture:**<br>Compare French and American music<br>**Fine art:**<br>Multiple exposure (Walter Limot)<br>**Reading:** Free Verse and Oxymorons ("**Familiale**," Jacques Prévert) |

## Unité 8 La France hier et aujourd'hui

*Essential question: Comment le passé influence-t-il le présent?*

| Vocabulaire | Fonctions | Culture | Structure | Stratégies |
|---|---|---|---|---|
| • French Revolution | • Express what someone was obligated to do<br>• Find that someone is forced to do something | • Louis XVI and Marie-Antoinette<br>• **Les États généraux**<br>• La *Déclaration des Droits de l'homme et du citoyen*<br>**Produits:**<br>La Conciergerie, guillotine, **La *Déclaration des Droits de la femme et de la citoyenne***<br>**La Francophonie (La révolution):**<br>Arab Spring in Tunisia | • Expressions with **faire**<br>• **Faire** + infinitive | |
| • Applying and interviewing for a job | • Indicate quantity<br>• Say I did something in vain | • European Union Institutions<br>**Produits:**<br>Flag of E.U. | • Expressions with **avoir**<br>• Past infinitive | **Communication:**<br>Write a CV |
| • Health care terms<br>• Debate terms | • Express that someone has a right<br>• Express that someone can afford something<br>• Say I want to discuss something more later | • Rights of the French citizen under **la sécu:** unemployment, health care, family, disabled protection, retirement<br>**Produits:**<br>La crèche | • Expressions with **être**<br>• Pluperfect tense | **Culture:**<br>Rights issues and challenges the press faces abroad<br>**Fine art:**<br>Theatrical photography (Joseph Nicéphore Niépce)<br>**Reading:**<br>Word families and setting (*Le bourgeois gentilhomme*, Molière) |

| Vocabulaire | Fonctions | Culture | Structure | Stratégies |
|---|---|---|---|---|

## Unité 9    Récits de la vie contemporaine

*Essential question: Quels sont les défis de la vie contemporaire?*

| Vocabulaire | Fonctions | Culture | Structure | Stratégies |
|---|---|---|---|---|
| • Emotions | • Express how someone looked | • Recent changes to French school system<br>• **Le bac** and student stress<br><br>**Produits: Les annales du bac** | • Past conditional tense<br>• Past conditional tense with **si** | |
| • Physical description: hair, age, ethnicity, clothing | • Say I realized something | • Different types of French police<br>• Crime in France<br><br>**Produits: Une déclaration de vol**<br>**Le château d'If** | • Possessive adjectives<br>• Possessive pronouns | **Communication:**<br>Tell a story through pictures |
| • Reactions | • Say I did not expect something | • Internet resources for teens<br><br>**Produits: Loisirs ados** | • Indefinite adjectives<br>• Indefinite pronouns | **Culture:**<br>Interview a French speaker about challenges of life today<br><br>**Fine art:**<br>Book illustrations (Anonymous)<br><br>**Reading:**<br>Characterization and **Le passé simple** (Les Misérables, Victor Hugo) |

## Unité 10    La culture des affaires

*Essential question: Qu'est-ce qu'on apprend de la culture d'un pays en étudiant son économie?*

| Vocabulaire | Fonctions | Culture | Structure | Stratégies |
|---|---|---|---|---|
| • Export products | • Say where an item was made | • French attitude toward globalization<br>• **Luxury products** and LVMH<br><br>**Produits:** Louis Vuitton brand | | |
| • Types of companies<br>• French and U.S. trade | • Ask if someone's been here a long time<br>• Say I wanted to get away | • France's position in world trade<br>• Multinational companies<br>• French business etiquette and taboos<br><br>**Produits:** Ariane rockets | | **Communication:**<br>Make a storyboard to sell a North American product in France |
| • Professional qualifications<br>• Job positions within a company | • Describe adaptability<br>• Say what I'm interested in | • Evolution of French marketing strategies<br><br>**Produits:**<br>Advertisements for **La vache qui rit** | | **Culture:**<br>How globalization affects our lives<br><br>**Fine art:**<br>Advertising photography<br><br>**Reading:**<br>(*14.99 €*, Frédéric Beigbeder) |

## Bilan cumulatif: Unités 9 – 10

# Introduction

*T'es branché?* was designed to give French teachers a program that focuses on the three modes of communication—interpersonal, presentational, and interpretive—while ensuring their students become proficient in the five skill areas. Based on detailed surveys involving hundreds of experienced French educators, the textbook program responds to teachers' expressed interests and priorities. The filmed dialogues in the *Rencontres culturelles* section were written in France by native speakers, so that students learn idiomatic and natural expression. Grammar exercises are designed to build proficency. Students develop reading skills with comprehensible input paragraphs in the vocabulary practice section. They also learn to appreciate literary writing in *Lecture thématique*. Activities move from mechanical exercises to more creative and open-ended projects. An essential question molds all the learning in any given unit.

Because paired, small group, and cooperative group activities are at the heart of today's student-centered classroom, *T'es branché?* offers many opportunities for students to work with their classmates on activities and projects that have clear guidelines and expectations. Students assume a more active role in their learning as they focus on how to learn as well as how to communicate in French. Opportunities for critical thinking can be found throughout the program, for example, in comparing francophone cultures to American culture and French grammar to English grammar.

Finally, the *T'es branché?* program was written to incorporate the National Standards. Let's look at how the textbook covers 2.1 and 2.2 from the standards below, for example. Students read culture notes about practices in the francophone world, as well as the content in *Produits* boxes that describe products from these locations. *Perspectives* are presented that may be in the form of a poem or song or quote from a French-speaker about their beliefs, experience, or observations. A new approach to teaching culture is presented in *La culture sur place*, allowing students to engage with francophone culture as they investigate topics of interest to teens and reflect on their "experience." Whatever element you are teaching, *T'es branché?* provides the tools you need to address standards in the following areas:

## Communication

### Communicate in Languages Other Than English

**Standard 1.1:** Students engage in conversations, provide and obtain information, express feelings and emotions, and exchange opinions.

**Standard 1.2:** Students understand and interpret written and spoken language on a variety of topics.

**Standard 1.3:** Students present information, concepts, and ideas to an audience of listeners or readers on a variety of topics.

## Cultures

### Gain Knowledge and Understanding of Other Cultures

**Standard 2.1:** Students demonstrate an understanding of the relationship between the practices and perspectives of the culture studied.

**Standard 2.2:** Students demonstrate an understanding of the relationship between the products and perspectives of the culture studied.

## Connections

### Connect with Other Disciplines and Acquire Information

**Standard 3.1:** Students reinforce and further their knowledge of other disciplines through the foreign language.

**Standard 3.2:** Students acquire information and recognize the distinctive viewpoints that are only available through the foreign language and its cultures.

# Comparisons

## Develop Insight into the Nature of Language and Culture

**Standard 4.1:** Students demonstrate understanding of the nature of language through comparisons of the language studied and their own.

**Standard 4.2:** Students demonstrate understanding of the concept of culture through comparisons of the cultures studied and their own.

# Communities

## Participate in Multilingual Communities at Home & Around the World

**Standard 5.1:** Students use the language both within and beyond the school setting.

**Standard 5.2:** Students show evidence of becoming life-long learners by using the language for personal enjoyment and enrichment.

Since a modern challenge in world language instruction is reaching all students—those with varying abilities, backgrounds, interests, and learning styles—the *T'es branché?* program has many opportunities beyond the textbook to help meet those needs. The Annotated Teacher's Edition provides suggested activities for different types of learners, from those with special needs to those who would benefit from enrichment. The Workbook contains Basic and Advanced activities so that students can make progress from where they begin and at their own pace. The online Drill and Practice games provide immediate feedback, allowing students to find out what they need more practice on well in advance of the test. Online Pre-tests also have immediate feedback, so that students can find out what they need to study more before their assessment experiences. Tailor-made products such as these ensure that each student makes progress and meets their potential as they embrace the French language and francophone culture.

# Common Core State Standards

The Common Core State Standards (CCSS) initiative seeks to raise academic standards for students and provide articulation of academic standards between states. The CCSS is designed for courses in English Language Arts, History/Social Studies, Science, and Technical Subjects, each containing four strands: Reading, Writing, Speaking and Listening, and Language. Having CCSS drive curricula will result in new assessment benchmarks for students.

*T'es branché?* was designed with the CCSS in mind. It emphasizes the purpose behind the communication by labeling activities that provide interpersonal (speaking-listening or writing-reading), interpretive (reading, listening, viewing), and presentational (writing, speaking, representing visually) communication. The goal of the textbooks is to move students from novice, to intermediate, to advanced proficiency levels by the time they complete the *T'es branché?* four-level program. Connections activities in *T'es branché?* that are specific to history and science allow students to learn about francophone history and scientific contributions made by Francophones. Technology skills are developed, as in the readings of *Points de départ*, where students research online using search words provided, and the *Projets finaux*, which allows for individual, pair, and group work using technology such as the Internet, video, smartphone, and online programs. *T'es branché?* uses the CCSS to make sure all students are ready for post-secondary learning, working, and becoming global citizens. A correlation of *T'es branché?* to the CCSS is at the end of the Annotated Teacher's Edition front pages.

Welcome to *T'es branché?*!

# Key Features: Student Textbook

## Students are excited to speak... targeted communic...

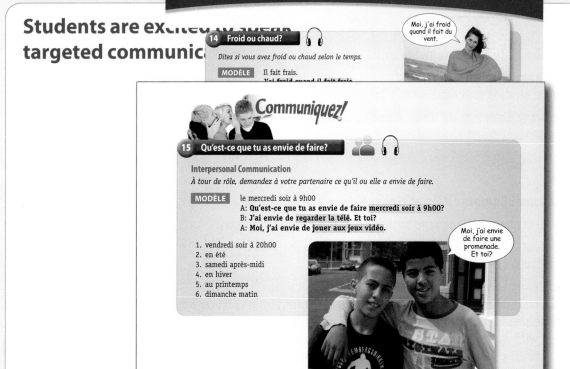

**14  Froid ou chaud?** 🎧

*Dites si vous avez froid ou chaud selon le temps.*

**MODÈLE**  Il fait frais.
J'ai froid quand il fait frais.

*Moi, j'ai froid quand il fait du vent.*

### Communiquez!

**15  Qu'est-ce que tu as envie de faire?** 👥🎧

**Interpersonal Communication**

*À tour de rôle, demandez à votre partenaire ce qu'il ou elle a envie de faire.*

**MODÈLE**  le mercredi soir à 9h00
A: **Qu'est-ce que tu as envie de faire mercredi soir à 9h00?**
B: **J'ai envie de regarder la télé. Et toi?**
A: **Moi, j'ai envie de jouer aux jeux vidéo.**

1. vendredi soir à 20h00
2. en été
3. samedi après-midi
4. en hiver
5. au printemps
6. dimanche matin

*Moi, j'ai envie de faire une promenade. Et toi?*

Leçon A | quatre cent sept **4 0 7**

## and opportunities for creative self-expression.

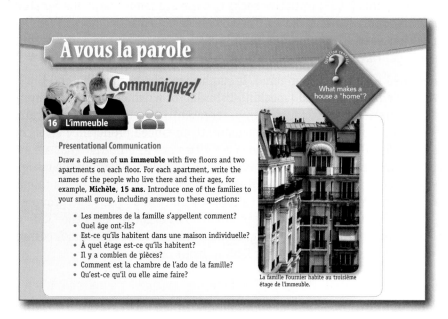

### À vous la parole

### Communiquez!

**16  L'immeuble** 👥

**?** What makes a house a "home"?

**Presentational Communication**

Draw a diagram of **un immeuble** with five floors and two apartments on each floor. For each apartment, write the names of the people who live there and their ages, for example, **Michèle, 15 ans.** Introduce one of the families to your small group, including answers to these questions:

- Les membres de la famille s'appellent comment?
- Quel âge ont-ils?
- Est-ce qu'ils habitent dans une maison individuelle?
- À quel étage est-ce qu'ils habitent?
- Il y a combien de pièces?
- Comment est la chambre de l'ado de la famille?
- Qu'est-ce qu'il ou elle aime faire?

La famille Fournier habite au troisième étage de l'immeuble.

## Unit content is centered on an essential question to anchor learning:

**Unit 3**  How does education shape individuals and societies?

**Unit 5**  What is the nature of relationships in other cultures?

**Unit 7**  What makes a house a "home"?

**Unit 9**  How do people stay healthy and maintain a healthy environment?

## Students analyze the essential question in the *Projets finaux* section.

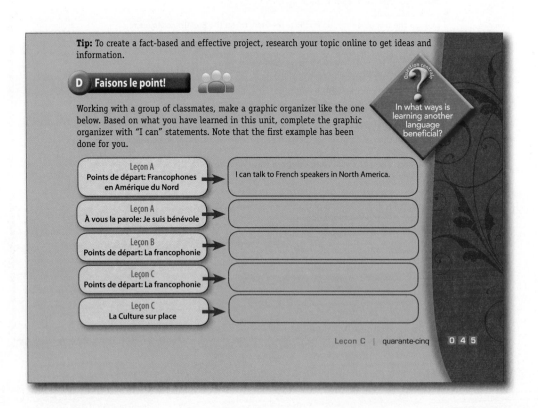

**Tip:** To create a fact-based and effective project, research your topic online to get ideas and information.

**D   Faisons le point!**

Working with a group of classmates, make a graphic organizer like the one below. Based on what you have learned in this unit, complete the graphic organizer with "I can" statements. Note that the first example has been done for you.

In what ways is learning another language beneficial?

| Leçon A Points de départ: Francophones en Amérique du Nord | → | I can talk to French speakers in North America. |
| Leçon A À vous la parole: Je suis bénévole | → | |
| Leçon B Points de départ: La francophonie | → | |
| Leçon C Points de départ: La francophonie | → | |
| Leçon C La Culture sur place | → | |

Leçon C  |  quarante-cinq  **0 4 5**

## La culture sur place

### Les remakes de films français

#### Introduction

One place to find modern versions of a culture's collected stories is in movies. In this section, you and your classmates will use the Internet to learn about French movies that have been "remade" in the United States.

#### Investigation

Moviemakers in the United States often borrow ideas and themes of movies from other cultures. You and your classmates will use the suggestions below to identify American movies based on French films.

---

**10  Un remake d'un film français**

First, use one or more of the following techniques to find a list of American remakes of French films:

- enter the phrase "remakes américains de films français" in an online search engine. Click on a site that comes up and see if it includes a list of remakes.
- search for "remake of French films" on the Internet Movie Database site (www.imdb.com).
- look up the box office results for "Remake-French" on the Box Office Mojo site (www.boxofficemojo.com/genres.com).

Second, select a movie that you are familiar with or that interests you.

Third, look for information that will help you answer the following questions.

1. Compare the French title with the American title. Do they have the same meaning? Or, has the title completely changed?
2. In what ways are the plots similar?
3. In what ways is the American remake different from the French original version? For example, are the main characters the same? Did the setting change? Are elements of the plot different?
4. How popular were the French and American versions in each country? (You may want to include information about box office earnings, film critiques, fan pages, etc.)

---

**11  Un film français et américain**

Share your research with your small group.

---

# The francophone world is seen through its

## • Practices

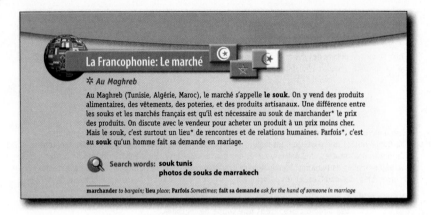

## • Products

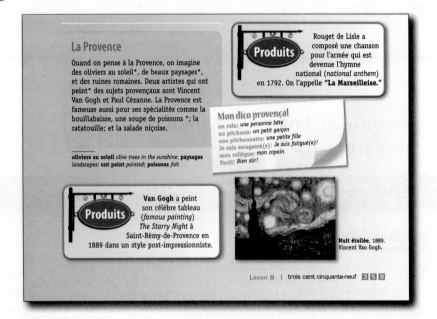

## • and Perspectives.

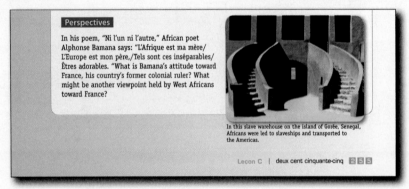

# Students master core vocabulary by reading comprehensible-input texts…

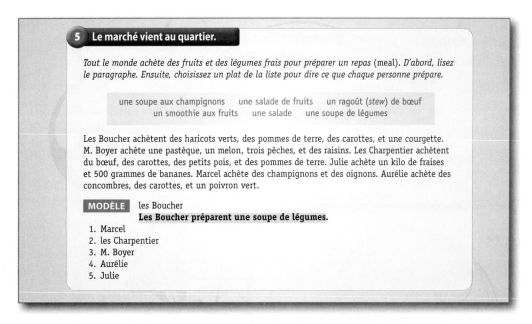

**5  Le marché vient au quartier.**

*Tout le monde achète des fruits et des légumes frais pour préparer un repas (meal). D'abord, lisez le paragraphe. Ensuite, choisissez un plat de la liste pour dire ce que chaque personne prépare.*

> une soupe aux champignons    une salade de fruits    un ragoût (*stew*) de bœuf
> un smoothie aux fruits    une salade    une soupe de légumes

Les Boucher achètent des haricots verts, des pommes de terre, des carottes, et une courgette. M. Boyer achète une pastèque, un melon, trois pêches, et des raisins. Les Charpentier achètent du bœuf, des carottes, des petits pois, et des pommes de terre. Julie achète un kilo de fraises et 500 grammes de bananes. Marcel achète des champignons et des oignons. Aurélie achète des concombres, des carottes, et un poivron vert.

**MODÈLE**  les Boucher
**Les Boucher préparent une soupe de légumes.**

1. Marcel
2. les Charpentier
3. M. Boyer
4. Aurélie
5. Julie

# and doing meaningful activities with high frequency vocabulary.

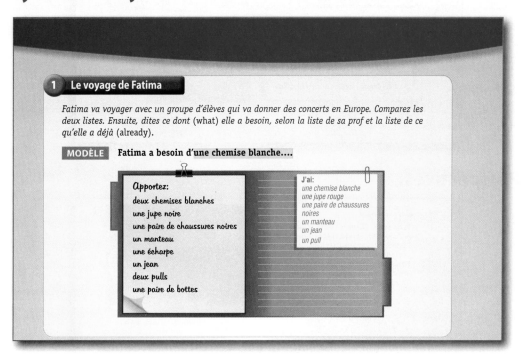

**1  Le voyage de Fatima**

*Fatima va voyager avec un groupe d'élèves qui va donner des concerts en Europe. Comparez les deux listes. Ensuite, dites ce dont (what) elle a besoin, selon la liste de sa prof et la liste de ce qu'elle a déjà (already).*

**MODÈLE**  **Fatima a besoin d'une chemise blanche….**

Apportez:
deux chemises blanches
une jupe noire
une paire de chaussures noires
un manteau
une écharpe
un jean
deux pulls
une paire de bottes

J'ai:
une chemise blanche
une jupe rouge
une paire de chaussures noires
un manteau
un jean
un pull

# Students connect to each structure topic...

- ## visually

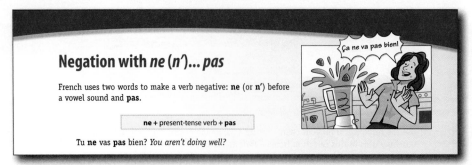

- ## contextually

- ## meaningfully

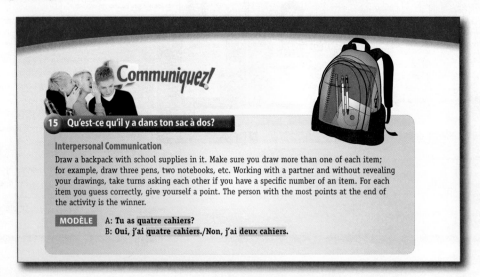

# Students make meaningful reading/writing connections.

## Le Petit Nicolas

### 22 Activités d'expansion

1. Use the responses from your chart to write a paragraph describing the point of view Goscinny uses in this selection from *Le Petit Nicolas*.
2. Rewrite the classroom scene above from the teacher's or George's point of view, using the third-person or first-person point of view.
3. Write a scene for a play based on the selection. Include parts for a narrator, the teacher, Georges, Maixent, and Joachim. Perform your scene for the class.

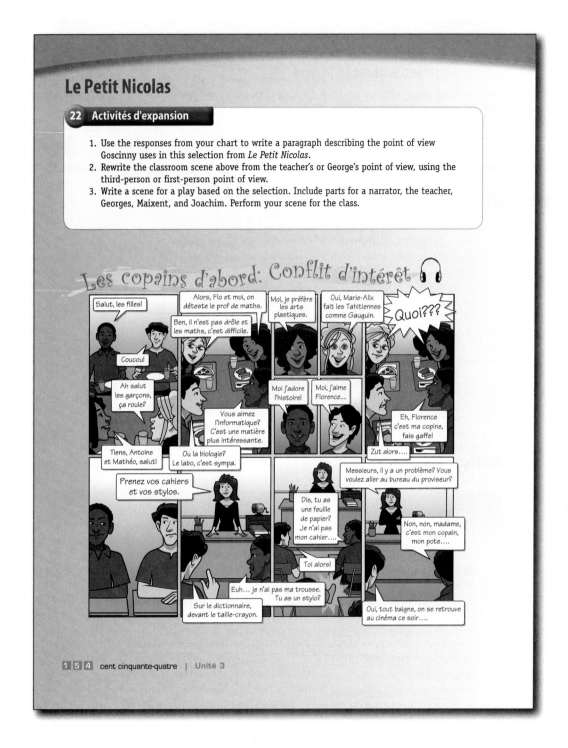

# *T'es branché?* provides two opportunities for reviewing:

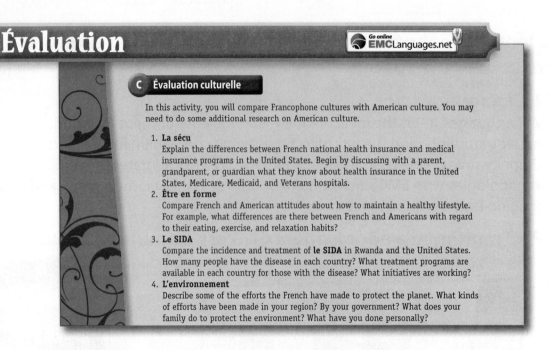

## Évaluation

**Go online EMCLanguages.net**

**C   Évaluation culturelle**

In this activity, you will compare Francophone cultures with American culture. You may need to do some additional research on American culture.

1. **La sécu**
   Explain the differences between French national health insurance and medical insurance programs in the United States. Begin by discussing with a parent, grandparent, or guardian what they know about health insurance in the United States, Medicare, Medicaid, and Veterans hospitals.

2. **Être en forme**
   Compare French and American attitudes about how to maintain a healthy lifestyle. For example, what differences are there between French and Americans with regard to their eating, exercise, and relaxation habits?

3. **Le SIDA**
   Compare the incidence and treatment of **le SIDA** in Rwanda and the United States. How many people have the disease in each country? What treatment programs are available in each country for those with the disease? What initiatives are working?

4. **L'environnement**
   Describe some of the efforts the French have made to protect the planet. What kinds of efforts have been made in your region? By your government? What does your family do to protect the environment? What have you done personally?

## Unité 8 Bilan cumulatif

**Go online EMCLanguages.net**

### Speaking

VII. Tell the four stories suggested by the images.

A. Bruno et Caro    B. Antoine et ses copains    C. Malika    D. tu

1. Give the date, identify the season in each illustration, and describe the weather.
2. Describe what the people are doing in each illustration.
3. Then describe two to three activities that you like to do during each season.

# Key Features: Technology for Students

**Students have the technological tools they need to excel and learn at their own pace:**

- **EMCLanguages.net**
  **EMCLanguages.net** is the ideal blended-learning environment for world language students, and the ultimate, time-saving companion for teachers. This innovative online Learning Management System integrates proven methodologies with EMC's rich content to deliver authentic, interactive, and engaging learning experiences.

- **EPUB multimedia eBook offers delivery on multiple devices.**

- **Electronic flash cards help students master core vocabulary.**

une chemise

- **e-visuals allow for motivating vocabulary practice.**

| prêt-à-porter | chaussures | accessoires | mon panier |

**Faites votre shopping en ligne!**

lamodeados.fr

*Toute la mode du printemps!*

**La mode des filles**

Pantalon Fantaisie
Couleur: fushia
25,99 €

Jupe bicolore
Couleur: pas de variation
12,99 €

Pull-tunique
Couleur: vert, beige, blanc
21,99 €

**Pour les garçons**

Short Cargo KAPORAL
Couleur: disponible en beige,
gris ou noir
15,99 €

T-shirt manches longues
Couleur: orange, bleu ou vert
27,99 €

Tenue Élégance
Couleur: pas de variation
67,99 €

- **Online Pre-tests offer immediate feedback.**

### Unité 1

### Leçon B

Complete the mini-dialogues by filling in the blanks.

1. -Salut, Nasser!
   -Salut, Aurélie! [          ]?
   -Oui. Top!

2. -Bonjour Professeur Novak. [          ]?
   -Très bien merci, Marcus.

3. -Ça va Mélanie?
   - Non, pas [          ].

4. -Au [          ]!
   -Ciao!

5. -Salut!
   -À [          ]!

6. -Moi, ça va. Et toi?
   -Comme [          ].

- **New continuous storyline DVD series, filmed on location in Nice, excites students.**

- **QR codes provide access to videos.**

Weihrauch, Michael/Tellus Vision Production AB, Lund Sweden

# Key Features: Teacher's Edition

Online, print, and electronic resources for the page in question are listed here.

The Reference Desk offers additional background information, linguistic and pronunciation notes, and other relevant information about items on the page.

The Communication box includes Interpersonal, Presentational, and Interpretive activities for additional practice.

Additional information about cultural Practices, Products, or Perspectives is offered here, or additional culture activities.

## RESOURCES

 e-visuals 28–29

 Workbook 1–6

 Flash Cards

🎧 Listening Activity

## Reference Desk

The basic formula for determining temperature conversions is as follows ($T_f$ = Temperature in Fahrenheit; $T_c$ = temperature in Celsius):

$$(T_f - 32) \times 5/9 = T_c$$
$$T_c \times 9/5 - 32 = T_f$$

## Communication

**Interpersonal: Paired Practice**
Have students research the weather online for about 20 international cities. In groups, students will take turns saying what the weather is in a city according to their findings.

**Interpersonal: Cooperative Groups**

To practice weather expressions, have students sit in small groups. One student starts a round by saying a weather word, such as **beau**. The next student must use the word in a complete sentence about, as in **Il fait beau**. The next student must say that phrase in the negative. The activity continues until all have had a turn.

## Culture

**Practices: Information**
Consider showing the i-Culture video entitled **"L'équitation"** (2010-2011) to provide your students with a culturally authentic perspective related to the theme of this **Leçon**.

**3 9 6**

---

## Leçon A

### Vocabulaire actif

**Quel temps fait-il?** 🎧

**En été...**
il fait beau.
il fait du soleil.
il fait chaud.

**En automne...**
il fait frais.
il fait du vent.

**En hiver...**
il fait froid.
il neige.
il fait mauvais.

**Au printemps...**
il pleut.

La température est de 20 degrés./Il fait 20 degrés. (Celsius).

Chloé a chaud.    Pierre a froid.

**3 9 6** trois cent quatre-vingt-seize | **Unité 8**

---

**Essential Instruction**

1. Write the seasons on the board with the prepositions **en/au** and the articles **l'/le**. Have students practice saying and spelling them. Point out the silent "m" in **automne**.
2. Ask students, **"Quel temps fait-il aujourd'hui?"** Project images of the weather expressions, act them out, or draw them on the board. Have students repeat as a class, then practice in pairs.
3. Explain the difference between **il fait froid/chaud** and **il a froid/chaud**.
4. Review and practice the Fahrenheit to Celsius conversion and vice versa.
5. Make the animal sounds in **Les animaux domestiques** and have students identify the animal. Demonstrate a few extra ones, such as **cocorico** (**le coq**/rooster), **meuh** (**une vâche**/cow), **hihan** (**un âne**/donkey), **coin coin** (**un canard**/duck).
6. Play the audio of **Pour la conversation** and have students repeat the sentences.
7. Present the vocabulary in **Et si je voulais dire...?**, explaining the difference between **il pleut** and **la pluie**, **il neige** and **la neige**.

Here you can find the essential parts of the day's lesson; these tips will help teachers organize the lesson and suggest a logical order of approach.

## Les animaux domestiques

un chat — Miaou!
un oiseau — Cui cui!
un cheval — Hî-hî-hî!
un chien — Ouaf ouaf!
un poisson rouge — Glou glou!

## Pour la conversation

**H**ow do I extend an invitation?

> **Tu as envie de** faire une promenade avec moi?
> *Do you want to take a walk with me?*

**H**ow do I accept an invitation?

> **Bonne idée! Je suis disponible.**
> *Good idea! I'm free.*

**H**ow do I refuse an invitation?

> **Désolé(e). Je suis occupé(e).**
> *Sorry. I'm busy.*

### Et si je voulais dire...?

| | |
|---|---|
| bruiner | *to drizzle* |
| **Il fait du brouillard.** | *It's foggy.* |
| **Il y a des éclairs.** | *It's lightning.* |
| **la grêle** | *hail* |
| **la neige** | *snow* |
| **la pluie** | *rain* |
| **la météo** | *weather report* |

**Leçon A** | trois cent quatre-vingt-dix-sept **3 9 7**

---

### RESOURCES

Workbook 7–8

### Communication

**Presentational: Cooperative Groups**

Have students write a description about a pet that belongs to their family, a friend, or a celebrity, including the pet's name and what the pet likes to do in certain weather. Ask them to accompany the paragraph with a photo or drawing. Students will make a gallery of pet portraits for the wall and present them to the class. Consider having a contest to vote for the most handsome, funniest, oddest, etc.

### Game

**Des animaux domestiques**
Have students use gestures and actions to "describe" their pets as the rest of the class shouts out French phrases such as **Il est grand! Il dit Miaou!**, etc. to match the actor's movements. Students should continue until they guess the pet.

### Connections

Teach students that the metric system is used in most of the world, including Europe. Give them a set of temperatures in Celsius and ask them to convert them to Fahrenheit temperatures.

### Critical Thinking

Ask students to come up with a rule for describing many weather conditions after looking at those on the page. Then ask them to come up with a rule for saying "I'm hot" or "I'm cold." (Many weather expressions use the third-person-singular form of **faire**, while people's body temperatures are described with **avoir**.)

**3 9 7**

---

**Differentiated Learning**
**Expand**
Have students respond **vrai** or **faux** in response to statements you make about the weather in various places and seasons. Ask students to describe the weather in favorite locations. Demonstrate a weather expression and have students say what it is. Switch roles.

**Special Needs Students**
**Linguistically Challenged**
1. To help organize the vocabulary for students, have them complete a chart according to headings such as seasons, weather expressions, verbs, etc. You could also organize weather expressions by adjectives (**beau/chaud/frais**, etc.), nouns (**du vent, du brouillard,** and **du soleil**), and verbs (**il pleut, il neige**).
2. Go over the use of **il y a + du/de la/des + nom,** using the **Et si je voulais dire...?** vocabulary.

---

Games may practice vocabulary, grammar, or culture knowledge.

Connections provides additional cross-curricular activities.

Critical Thinking activities ask students to apply, choose, interpret, solve, categorize, compare, contrast, criticize, distinguish, compose, construct, create, propose, etc.

Differentiated Learning tips help the teacher make sure advanced and slower-paced students have successful learning experiences.

Here teachers find tips for how to reach students with different learning styles, including multiple intelligences, or special needs.

# Components

*T'es branché?* is a comprehensive four-level French language program written to meet the needs of French students of all abilities in the twenty-first century. The first-level program includes the following components:

- Student Textbook
- Annotated Teacher's Edition
- Workbook
- Workbook Teacher's Edition
- At-Standard Assessment Manual
- Communicative Activities

- Listening Activities
- Audio Program
- DVD Manual
- TPR Storytelling Manual
- EMCLanguages.net

## Student Textbook

*T'es branché?* contains ten units. Each unit is composed of three lessons, labeled A, B, and C. All the units are designed similarly so that both teachers and students will know what to expect. Each lesson gives students the vocabulary, functions, structures, and cultural information necessary to communicate in authentic French about a variety of everyday situations designed to appeal to teenagers. Vocabulary and structures are recycled in the first-level textbook and subsequent textbooks so that students can attain mastery of the concepts that are introduced by the time they complete the program. The headphones icon 🎧 indicates activities that are recorded in the audio program.

*Unit Opener* – The unit begins with a photo spread, quotation (**Citation**) by a Francophone person of note, and fact (**À savoir**) that connect to the unit theme. The **Question centrale** is an essential question that frames the unit's contents, and that reappears throughout the unit. There is also a culture question accompanied by a photo for which students will find the answer somewhere in the culture readings of the unit. The electronic device pictured in the Unit Opener contains an image from the DVD program that accompanies the textbook; a question is asked to get students excited about seeing the episode that is aligned with the unit in question.

*Vocabulaire actif* – Each lesson begins with colorful photos or illustrations that introduce coherent vocabulary groupings in a meaningful context. Students need to know that they are expected to learn these words and expressions. Also in this section are one or more functions under the *Pour la conversation* heading, and more advanced vocabulary for the students who want to move at a faster pace (*Et si je voulais dire…?*) and assimilate even more vocabulary in order to express themselves. Vocabulary practice activities follow the presentation, culminating in questions that are designed to elicit responses from students about their lives (*Questions personnelles*). One of the vocabulary practice options includes a listening activity. Another is a paragraph or other text that puts comprehensible input into practice, allowing students to "read" and understand the vocabulary words before using them.

*Rencontres culturelles* – Next comes a short dialogue that dramatizes a situation typical of everyday life in Francophone regions. Written in France, these dialogues use authentic French speech and current expressions. Speakers may include one or more of the four main characters, their friends, parents, other relatives, or teachers. These teens all live in Paris.

> **Yasmine** is an Algerian girl who is dating Maxim. She likes to shop with Camille and finds biology difficult. She is good friends with the other teens below.
>
> **Maxime** is Yasmine's boyfriend. In Unit 8, Maxime and Yasmine have a romantic rendez-vous at the Tuileries. Maxime has a dog, and he has introduced Yasmine to his mother.
>
> **Camille** likes to go inline skating at Pari Roller on Friday nights. In Unit 6 she goes clothes shopping with Yasmine.
>
> **Julien** is an athletic boy who is good friends with Maxim. In Unit 10 he goes to Geneva with his parents.

These dialogues include the functions from the *Pour la conversation* box in the vocabulary spread. Also in the dialogue you will find an example of each structure topic that models for students how it can be used. All words in the dialogue are active vocabulary, though not all of them appear in the vocabulary presentation that precedes it. All dialogues were filmed in France, and the accompanying photo is a still shot from the film. A comprehension activity follows the dialogue to make sure students understand what transpired.

**Extension** – This is another dialogue but of a more advanced nature that requires students to read in context and perhaps even look up some words in their French-English dictionary. A critical thinking question follows each of these dialogues. The vocabulary in this dialogue will not be tested.

**Points de départ** – Directly after the dialogues, information about the francophone world is presented, in English through Unit 5, then in French beginning with Unit 6. These notes reflect the themes introduced in the first dialogue in the *Rencontres culturelles* section. Accompanying photos open a window on cultural practices, perspectives, and products. Certain products are defined and described in the *Produits* boxes, such as African masks, **pâté**, and Coco Chanel's little black dress. In this section, students are also asked to draw comparisons between Francophone cultures and their own (see *Comparaisons* graphic). After answering the *Questions culturelles*, students engage with culture further by participating in a discussion (*À discuter*) or reading a *Perspectives* note and answering a critical thinking question.

**Du côté des medias** – In this section, students read or skim or scan francophone realia and answer questions or complete an activity based on it. The realia ties into one of the notes in the *Points de départ*. Students might see a grocery store advertisement, a restaurant menu, or film ratings.

**La culture sur place** – In Lesson C, this section follows the culture notes and gets students to investigate and engage in an aspect of French culture. For example, students might be asked to examine American remakes of French movies, interview a traveler who has been to a francophone location, or shop online at French stores. The philosophy behind this section is explained in the Philosophy and Approach section of the Annotated Teacher's Edition front pages.

**Structure de la langue** – One or more grammar topics is presented and practiced in this section. You can find all the grammar topics covered in *T'es branché?* in the Scope and Sequence at the beginning of this Annotated Teacher's Edition. The contextualized practice activities that follow move from more mechanical activities to those that are more creative and open-ended. The activities allow for oral and written practice of the language structures, and students may be asked to work with a partner or group. Practice for one of the grammar topics includes a listening activity. (Unit 1 contains no grammar.) Where there is a model, the model sentence is highlighted so students know which parts of the sentence to replace.

**À vous la parole** – A series of proficiency-based activities follows the grammar section. Students have an opportunity to practice interpersonal, presentational, and interpretive communication here as well as in the vocabulary and grammar sections. In this section, the vocabulary, structures, and culture all come together and are integrated into activities that may be cooperative, task-based, oral, or written. For example, students may be asked to conduct a survey, engage in a dialogue at a store or restaurant, develop a book of recipes, perform metric conversations, organize a fashion show, or plan a trip to do humanitarian work.

**Prononciation** – This section is presented at the end of Lesson A in each unit. Written by a pronunciation expert in France who works with English speakers, it centers on pronunciation problems English speakers have with French sounds and pronunciation patterns.

**Stratégie communicative** – This section is presented at the end of Lesson B in each unit. Students learn various strategies for successful function-based oral and written communication activities. For example, students learn how to decode cognates, combine sentences to make longer sentences, write a postcard, practice descriptive writing or the art of communication, and tell a story through pictures.

***Lecture thématique*** – This section is presented at the end of Lesson C in each unit. Authentic texts in French are studied with scaffolding that allows students to learn about literature, Francophone authors, and francophone art. First, students read a paragraph about the author, which concludes with a question designed to get students to focus on one of the main ideas of the text. Next, students learn a strategy with which to approach the text, always accompanied by a graphic organizer. A secondary tool for understanding another aspect of the text is highlighted with the *Outil de lecture*. With the pre-reading question, students connect to the theme of the text by comparing it to their own experience or observations. During reading questions, alongside the text, check to make sure students comprehend what is happening in the text. A post-reading question asks students to draw a main conclusion about the text. A painting or other art form accompanies the text. Students learn to appreciate art and art periods and techniques in *Le monde visuel*, which is designed to promote literacy in the visual arts. In the *Activités d'expansion*, students use the information from their graphic organizer to write about the meaning of the text in the first activity. Then, other, more creative activities connect students to the text. Further reading is provided in the *Les copains d'abord* cartoon; here students have the opportunity to learn some idioms and slang expressions in French. The *Lecture thématique* section provides students opportunities to improve their reading skills and helps to prepare them for the AP language exam.

***Projets finaux*** – This section was designed for teachers who prefer performance-based assessment to traditional testing, or who like unit work to culminate in a meaningful project. The first activity, *Connexions par Internet*, provides a cross-curricular project that may be connected to art, architecture, math, science, or any number of academic disciplines. The focus of *Communautés en ligne* is to have students build online communities in the French-speaking world in projects that relate to the unit's theme. *Passez à l'action!* provides an engaging activity for students to work with their classmates to complete a project. Finally, *Faisons le point!* asks students to pull together all their learning from the unit and analyze it; one format occurs in odd-numbered units, another in even-numbered units.

***Évaluation*** – There are six opportunities for reviewing unit content in this section: (A) listening comprehension; (B) oral communication; (C) culture comparisons; (D) written expression; (E) oral or written response to a visual; and (F) telling a story that uses unit content.

***Vocabulaire*** – All words and expressions introduced as active vocabulary in *T'es branché?* appear in the end-of-unit vocabulary list.

***Bilan cumulatif*** – Based on the AP exam, this section appears after every even-numbered unit and provides an assessment of listening, reading, writing, and speaking skills.

## Annotated Teacher's Edition

This Annotated Teacher's Edition contains a front section and an annotated version of the student textbook.

Front Section:

- Scope and Sequence charts for Levels 1 – 3
- Introduction
- Key program features
- Description of all the components in the program
- Author biographies
- Philosophy and approach
- Transcript of Textbook Listening Activities
- Correlation to Common Core State Standards

Annotated Version of the Student Textbook:

- Correlations of ancillary materials to the textbook (*Resources*)
- Answers to both oral and written activities
- Informational notes for teachers in the *Reference Desk*
- Culture notes or activities about products, practices, or perspectives (*Culture*)
- Interpersonal, presentational, or interpretive communicative activities (*Communication*)

- Total Physical Response (TPR) activities
- Activities that use critical thinking skills (*Critical Thinking*)
- Additional cross-curricular activities (*Connections*)
- Games
- Additional activities or adaptations of textbook activities (*Expansion*)

The annotated version of the expanded student textbook contains icons in the Resource boxes at the top of the wraparound pages. These icons are:

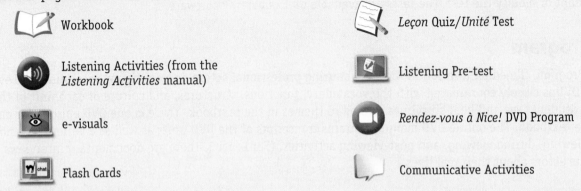

Workbook

Listening Activities (from the *Listening Activities* manual)

e-visuals

Flash Cards

*Leçon* Quiz/*Unité* Test

Listening Pre-test

*Rendez-vous à Nice!* DVD Program

Communicative Activities

## Workbook

The workbook reviews and expands on the material covered in the textbook with additional written exercises that reinforce students' language skills and cultural awareness. To make sure the workbook provides for differentiated instruction, there are basic activities marked with an "A" and more advanced activities marked with a "B," for example "1A" and "6B."

## Workbook Teacher's Edition

This is the student workbook, but with answers in bold.

## Communicative Activities

Since effective communicative activities are integral to the success of a proficiency-oriented French-language program, this online manual provides additional oral and written communicative practice for students. Information gap activities and situation cards allow for interpersonal communication and student-to-student interaction. Also in this manual are conversation grids, activities based on an illustration, and surveys; an e-mail writing activity; and a writing activity based on the conversation grids, activities based on an illustration, or surveys.

## Listening Activities

This online manual provides seven additional listening comprehension activities for each unit, two for each lesson and a cumulative dialogue that synthesizes the vocabulary and grammar from the whole unit. Students are provided with an answer sheet they fill in while they listen. These activities help prepare students for the listening comprehension sections of the Unit Tests in the Assessment Program. An answer key is provided at the end of the manual that also includes complete scripts.

## Textbook Audio Program

The online audio program contains language-production activities, and all the listening comprehension activities in the textbook: one vocabulary and grammar activity for every lesson, the listening activity in the *Évaluation* section, and the first activity of the *Bilan cumulatif*. The *Vocabulaire actif*, dialogues, *Points de départ*, and reading selection have also been recorded.

## Assessment Manual

The *T'es branché? Assessment Manual* is a print version of the At-Standard test that is also found as a prescribed test on the *Teacher Resources DVD* (see Multimedia Technology and Teacher Resources DVD). It contains Lesson Quizzes, Unit Tests, and Proficiency Tests. Each quiz tests student achievement in vocabulary, culture, structure, and speaking. There are three quizzes for each unit, or one per lesson. The Unit Tests contain these sections: vocabulary, structure, proficiency writing, speaking, listening comprehension, reading, and culture. Teachers are encouraged to test their students in the areas that have been practiced in class during the unit. For teachers who want to adapt or modify the test, the tests are available on ExamView® software.

## DVD Program

The DVD Program, filmed on location in Nice and starring professional actors, is a continuous storyline for Levels 1-2. Each DVD is closely coordinated with the vocabulary, functions, structures, and culture of each unit of the textbook. Students see and hear storylines related to themes in the textbook. There is one DVD episode for each unit in the textbook. The online DVD manual contains transcripts of the DVD units as well as a variety of innovative pre-viewing, during viewing, and post-viewing activities. (For Level 3, there are documentary interviews with some of the actors about their real lives.)

## TPR Storytelling Manual

Each unit of this manual contains three mini-stories, one for each lesson, and a comprehensive unit story that are correlated to the content of *T'es branché?* Teachers can present each mini-story and unit story as a class reading, a homework reading, or a reading comprehension assessment. In the beginning of the manual, the TPR Storytelling philosophy is explained, and there is an introductory story that uses high-frequency vocabulary so teachers can see if they like the TPR storytelling approach and decide if they would like to incorporate the stories for the units into their instruction. Each story is accompanied by a series of illustrations.

## Lectures thématiques

Additional readings, including some realia pieces, are available in this manual. The format is similar to the *Lecture thématique* section of the student book.

## Activities for Mastery

The activities presented here offer ideas for instruction from an experienced French teacher who has taught all the levels of high school French. Whether teachers have a few minutes at the end of the class, or need to introduce or reinforce a concept, *Activities for Mastery* is there to help teachers plan their instruction with activities that are fun, educational, and innovative.

## Copy Masters

To save time in the class, there is a manual with blackline masters for all the graphs, charts, maps and other graphics that are in the student edition.

# Multimedia Technology

## EMCLanguages.net

EMCLanguages.net is EMC Publishing's online resource center for many of the *T'es branché?* ancillary materials. Online delivery of classroom materials allows students to access them in an electronic, interactive format and connect to the classroom in new ways using blended instruction. Visit EMCLanguages.net to see all that is available for your students.

- **Lesson Planner**

  Each day's lesson plan, whether for a traditional class or block scheduling, presents the core materials from the textbook and key ancillaries to include in instruction. Teachers can access the ancillary manuals within the lesson planner.

- **e-visuals**

  These digital "transparencies" reinforce the vocabulary presented in the textbook. Some of them are interactive.

- **Electronic Flash Cards**

  These flash cards are an essential component of the differentiated-learning classroom because students can practice over and over again until they master the vocabulary. Each vocabulary word is illustrated and the vocabulary word or expression is also visible spelled out.

- **Drill and Practice Games**

  Students master the vocabulary and structures in *T'es branché?* with activities that provide immediate feedback, telling students if their answer is right or wrong.

- **WebQuests**

  A WebQuest is an inquiry-oriented activity for which students use online resources. There is a WebQuest for each lesson of *T'es branché?*

- **Pre-AP Listening**

  Students hear a short listening segment and answer multiple-choice questions as on the AP test. If they get any of the questions wrong, they can then see and hear the video in order to have a more successful listening experience.

- **Pre-tests**

  There is a pre-test for each lesson of *T'es branché?* Students receive immediate feedback by completing sentences about vocabulary, grammar, culture, and listening so that they know what they need to review before they take each Lesson Quiz or Unit Test.

- **ExamView® Assessment Program**

  Teachers choose between a prescribed test for At-Standard, Slower-Paced, or Advanced students, or they can make their own test that responds to the needs of their students. There is a quiz for every lesson. Each quiz consists of vocabulary, culture, structure, and speaking. Each prescribed Unit Test covers vocabulary, structure, proficiency writing, speaking prep, speaking, listening comprehension, reading, and culture.

## Teacher Resources DVD

The Teacher Resources DVD is a one-stop resource where teachers can find all the resources for the program:

- Annotated Teacher's Edition
- Textbook Audio Program
- Lesson Plans
- Workbook
- Drill and Practice Games
- e-visuals
- Textbook Dialogue Videos
- DVD Program
- Listening Activities
- Activities for Mastery
- Communicative Activities
- Copy Masters
- Lectures thématiques Manual
- TPR Storytelling
- Pre-AP Listening
- Electronic Flash Cards
- Assessment (ExamView® and Print)

# Philosophy and Approach

## World Language Learning in the 21st Century

### By Toni Theisen

Our world is an ever increasingly diverse, globalized, and complex, media-saturated society. Our 21st-century learners need a multi-sensory and multi-layered learning environment that is designed to inspire creativity, synthesis, and collaboration, as well as provide opportunities to analyze, reflect, and evaluate. So what are the critical skills and multiple literacies that our students will need in order to successfully participate in the global community of today's world? How do we engage them in meaningful contexts that are relevant and challenging? How do we provide project-based learning opportunities that help students reach higher levels of proficiency? How do we help students set personal learning goals and become self-directed learners? How do we personalize learning?

Quite often 21st-century skills are equated with technology. True, technology is a part of the skills learners will need to master, but this concept is much broader. In 2010 ACTFL, in collaboration with the Partnership for 21st Century Skills organization, created the ACTFL World Languages 21st Century Skills Map for Pre-K-16. The Partnership for 21st Century Skills P21 is a national organization that advocates for 21st-century readiness for every student framed within 12 skill areas and four interdisciplinary themes.

**Here are the twelve skills statements from the ACTFL World Languages 21st Century Skills Map and their topics:**

1. **Communication**
   Students as effective communicators use languages to engage in meaningful conversation; to understand and interpret spoken language and written text; and to present information, concepts, and ideas.

2. **Collaboration**
   Students as collaborators use their native and acquired languages to learn from and work cooperatively across cultures with global team members, sharing responsibility and making necessary compromises while working toward a common goal.

3. **Critical Thinking and Problem Solving**
   Students as inquirers frame, analyze, and synthesize information as well as negotiate meaning across language and culture in order to explore problems and issues from their own and different perspectives.

4. **Creativity and Innovation**
   Students as creators and innovators respond to new and diverse perspectives as they use language in imaginative and original ways to make useful contributions.

5. **Information Literacy**
   Students as informed global citizens access, manage, and effectively use culturally authentic sources in ethical and legal ways.

6. **Media Literacy**
   Students as active global citizens evaluate authentic sources to understand how media reflect and influence language and culture.

7. **Technology Literacy**
   Students as productive global citizens use appropriate technologies when interpreting messages; interacting with others; and producing written, oral, and visual messages.

8. **Flexibility and Adaptability**
   Students as flexible and adaptable language learners are open-minded, willing to take risks, and accept the ambiguity of language while balancing diverse global perspectives.

9. **Initiative and Self-Direction**
   Students as life-long learners are motivated to set their own goals and reflect on their progress as they grow and improve their linguistic and cultural competence.

10. **Social and Cross-Cultural Skills**

Students as adept language learners understand diverse cultural perspectives and use appropriate socio-linguistic skills in order to function in diverse cultural and linguistic contexts.

11. **Productivity and Accountability**

Students as productive and accountable learners take responsibility for their own learning by actively working to increase their language proficiency and cultural knowledge.

12. **Leadership and Responsibility**

Students as responsible leaders leverage their linguistic and cross-cultural skills to inspire others to be fair, accepting, open, and understanding within and beyond the local community.

## Interdisciplinary Themes

### Global Awareness

Language education and cultural understanding are at the heart of developing global awareness for students. In order to understand and address global issues, it is important to understand the perspectives on the world that speakers of other languages bring to the table. By learning other languages, students develop respect and openness to those whose culture, religion, and views on the world may be different. Language students are able to interact with students from the target language in order to discuss and reach solutions regarding global issues.

### Financial, Economic, Business, and Entrepreneurial Literacy

Students in language classes learn about the financial and economic issues from the target language culture and are able to compare and contrast with those of the U.S. According to the Committee for Economic Development (CED), "...cultural competence and foreign language skills can prove invaluable when working on global business teams or negotiating with overseas clients." Those who are able to communicate with others in their native language will naturally feel more empowered to negotiate with those around the world as they engage in entrepreneurial activities.

### Civic Literacy

Language learners become aware of the judicial, legislative, and government functions of the target language country/countries and are able to compare and contrast those with the civil liberties and responsibilities in the U.S. Because they can communicate in the target language, they are able to engage in discussions with other students to participate in activities in which they discuss civic life in their respective countries.

### Health Literacy

Language learners are engaged in a value-added activity as they can address global health and environmental issues in the target language and understand materials that were written for native speakers of that language. They have access to information because they can understand the language and can thus engage in global discussions on health, environmental, and public safety issues as they prepare for careers in these fields.

So by focusing on these essential skills, the interdisciplinary themes and the integration of technology in a meaningful, relevant standards-based curriculum, teachers can empower students to actively participate in the global community.

Sources:

ACTFL World Languages 21st Century Skills Map

Partnership for 21st Century Skills

# Oral Proficiency in the 21st Century

### By Toni Theisen

"I want to learn how to speak the language" is the most common goal of most world language learners. But what is oral proficiency and how do learners demonstrate their progress toward this goal?

At the center of the national standards are the three modes of communication. The interpersonal and the presentational modes are focused on both oral and written communication. In the interpersonal mode learners engage in conversation, provide and obtain information, express feeling and emotion, and exchange opinions. This mode occurs in two-way, spontaneous exchanges that involve negotiation of meaning and is unrehearsed. Activities and strategies include debates, discussions, phone calls, Skyping, asking for and giving directions, and conversations with friends about making plans.

In the presentational mode, learners present information, concepts and ideas to an audience of listeners or readers on a variety of topics. It is one-way, planned and can be rehearsed. There is no feedback from another person. Some activities and strategies include creating videos, telling a story, delivering a speech, creating a public service announcement or other podcasts, or presenting a skit or play.

Teachers can assess language performance in terms of ability to use the language effectively and appropriately in real-life situations using a rubric that can measure proficiency. Students need to demonstrate what they "can do." The Linguafolio is an excellent source for "can do" statements at different proficiency levels. The "can do" statements are a perfect resource to use to create learner targets for each thematic unit, help students set personal goals and provide a clearer explanation to parents about what their children are learning in their language classes.

Open-ended performance assessments are the best ways to determine growth in oral proficiency. Rubrics and feedback should be put in kid-friendly terms, so students know what they can do to improve. Each assessment needs to be designed to show what a student is able to do with the language in order to elicit meaningful feedback.

With *T'es branché?*, students gain practice in the three modes of communication in vocabulary and structure activities, as well as the *À vous la parole* and *Projets finaux* sections. Rubrics for spoken and written communication can be found at emclanguages.net. A student contract on the Unit Opener page makes it clear to students what material they will be responsible for learning and helps them take ownership of this content from the beginning. Students reflect on what they can do and what they can learn to do better in *Faisons le point!* at the end of each unit. The final projects are designed to showcase student learning and make students feel successful, engaged, and purpose-driven in their French language learning experiences with *T'es branché?*

# A New Emphasis in Teaching Culture: Explore and Investigate *sur place*

### By Pamela M. Wesely

Foreign language teachers have examined and debated the issue of teaching culture in the foreign language classroom for many years. One of the ways that *T'es branché?* attempts to respond to this debate is through the presentation of *La culture sur place* sections in every unit. They are designed to engage students differently with francophone culture(s) by promoting a spirit of inquiry and treating the students as social actors, not as passive recipients of culture. The idea of developing intercultural competence in the language classroom rather than relying solely on teaching *about* the target culture(s) is not a new one, but it is one that has rarely been incorporated into a textbook.

The format of these sections varies throughout the text, but generally one of six different styles of activity is used for each one.

- **Submersion:** Students are encouraged to feel that they are "on location" in a francophone culture observing, asking questions, finding answers, drawing conclusions, and finding different perspectives and viewpoints. They report on their findings to the class.
- **Poll:** Students conduct a survey of their fellow students that parallels a survey of French or Francophone people. The students can then draw conclusions from a comparison of the results, focusing on current characteristics and realities in francophone cultures, as well as the diversity of their own lives.
- **Advocacy:** Students write a plan for taking action, getting their voices heard, and/or advocating for a specific population in the face of human rights abuses, current events issues, or other potential areas for discussion.

- **Reaction:** Via self-assessment, students examine potential areas of discomfort with French or Francophone cultures, and perhaps identify what they might need to do to gain more comfort in or become more habituated to the practices of these cultures.
- **Comparison:** Students take two explicitly different but related phenomena (encompassing products, practices, and perspectives) in their own culture and the target culture(s) and examine why those two phenomena might be different.
- **Contact:** Students investigate the reality of one individual from a French-speaking culture through an interview conducted in written form or face-to-face.

  "Culture" in *La culture sur place* is thus not intended to be something to be learned, but rather something to be explored, questioned, and examined. Students will be able to use their 21st-century skills in applying themselves to get through the steps of these activities that are meaningful, structured, and that allow for student self-expression.

- **Note:** Some of the activities in *La Culture sur place* might take some preparation several weeks before the actual activity takes place. One notable example of this is the *Unité 5* activity involving identifying individuals from French-speaking countries for the students to interview.

## Teaching Grammar to Enhance Communication

"I took French for three years and I can't say anything." Perhaps you know someone with such an experience with language instruction. The drill-and-practice instruction of yesteryear relied on mechanical, repetitive exercises that were not linked to meaningful expression. Today's teachers still want their students to learn grammatical concepts incrementally so that their language production doesn't fossilize. They also want their students' oral and written expression to be comprehensible to native speakers, acceptable in different social contexts, and accurate. To reach these goals, today's teachers often provide activities that allow for structured input (learning the grammar rules and examining models), structured output (practicing the grammar point in communicative exercises), and communicative output (doing a communicative task that uses the grammar point).

### Structured Input

In *T'es branché?*, grammar points are presented concisely with the use of charts and examples. Students can use these pages as reference when they want to try to expand on their expression; they don't have to learn everything at once. For example, they may learn quickly how to use the **passé composé** in declarative sentences, but can refer back to the grammar presentation later in order to see how to form a question using inversion in the **passé composé** for an interview or survey. Many of the examples used in the grammar presentation come from the first *Rencontres culturelles* dialogue that students can hear and see as many times as they'd like on their mobile devices.

### Structured Output

*T'es branché?* begins with more mechanical activities, then builds to activities that are more creative, meaningful, and open-ended. A mechanical activity might ask students to insert the right preposition before the names of cities, countries, and continents they learned about in the culture readings. A creative activity might have them use the adverbs **bien**, **un peu**, **beaucoup** with the verb **aimer** to report on critics' reviews of new French films. A meaningful and more open-ended activity might include interviewing their partner about their lifestyle habits for the week and then writing sentences using **toujours**, **souvent**, or **ne (n')... pas souvent** or **ne (n')... jamais** to describe those weekly activities. For example: **Zach ne mange jamais de légumes frais.**

### Communicative Output

In the *À vous la parole* section, students put their knowledge of grammar to use in interpretive, presentational, and interpersonal communication activities. For example, they might use **il faut** in a conversation at the doctor's office, describe a photo of their family using possessive adjectives, or use a French TV guide to tell what programs they choose (**choisir**, regular **-ir** verb).

## Communicative Competence

Students build communicative competence by using *T'es branché?* in part because they learn grammar from a logical grammatical syllabus that builds on and recycles grammar points. Some teachers like to provide an immersion experience, having their students build structural knowledge naturally. For these teachers we have the TPR Storytelling manual, which is correlated to the textbook. Students will pick up on the grammar topics in the original story and soon be able to tell their own variation, using accurate and comprehensible grammar.

# Meeting the Needs of the 21st-Century Reader

**"Qui que vous soyez qui voulez cultiver, vivifier, edifier, attendrir, apaiser, mettez des livres partout."**

—Victor Hugo

*Whoever wishes to cultivate, enliven, edify, soften, pacify, put books everywhere.*

Reading research shows that successful readers read extensively, integrate information in the text with pre-existing knowledge, have a reading style that adapts to the text, are motivated, read for a purpose, and rely on different skills to comprehend a text. The readings in *T'es branché?* were designed to provide contextual reading activities that hone all of these skills and guide the reader to greater comprehension. These readings are always accompanied with supports to make every French student a successful reader.

## Successful Readers Read Extensively

In *T'es branché?* students read the dialogues (the second one in *Rencontres culturelles* is for students who want to go farther and faster), which incorporate the vocabulary, functions, structure, and culture of the lesson. In each lesson there is a comprehensible-input paragraph so that students can build understanding of the new vocabulary before using it. A piece of realia, such as a transportation schedule, calendar, movie schedule, map, or tourism website, appears in the section *Du côté des médias*. Beginning in Unit 6 of Level 1, students read the culture readings in French also. Their unit learning culminates in a literary selection, linked to the theme of the unit; pre-reading questions, strategies, guided reading questions, and post-reading questions help students feel that they can tackle literary selections with ideas and themes.

## Successful Readers Integrate Information in the Text With Pre-Existing Knowledge and Adapt to the Text

In the culture section, students are asked to connect to what they know about culture in the United States and Canada with *Comparaisons* questions, which become their starting point for comparisons with francophone cultures. The *Perspectives* questions ask students to consider a certain point of view of a French speaker in excerpts from songs, poems, blogs, etc. In the literary selection, students are asked a pre-reading question to connect the theme of the selection to their own experience. The repeated supports in these sections help students to adapt to the text, whether it is experiential (*Rencontres culturelles*), factual (*Points de départ*), opinion (*Perspectives*), informational (*Du côté des médias*), or literary (*Lecture thématique*).

## Successful Readers Are Motivated and Read for a Purpose

For whatever reason students are learning French (a love of languages, to test out of college French, to travel to French-speaking countries, to have an interesting career, etc.), the texts in *T'es branché?* underline their reasons for study, thus motivating them toward their goal. Students also read with a purpose: for enjoyment (the serial cartoon *Les copains d'abord*), for information (the culture section), to confirm prior knowledge (dialogues and the culture section), or to evaluate ideas (the literary selections), and to grapple with other points of view (*Perspectives*). Students who want to learn more about a certain culture topic will benefit from the "Search words" underneath each culture paragraph that connect them to texts online.

## Successful Students Rely on Different Skills to Comprehend a Text

Although woven throughout the various reading activities of each unit, specific strategies that can help students read more quickly and effectively receive greater focus in *Lecture thématique* and the manual with the same name, and include previewing, predicting, skimming and scanning, monitoring their comprehension, using text organization, tacking difficult vocabulary, visualizing, writing things down (with the help of graphic organizers), guessing from context, and paraphrasing.

Since research has shown that reading is the skill that endures the longest, French students who study with *T'es branché?* will be on their way to becoming life-long readers of French: successfully reading literary selections; reading nonfiction; and reading Internet, reference, and visual materials.

# Immersion Lessons in the Non-immersion Classroom

## Connecting to Literature and Art

"The subject matter class is a language class if it is made comprehensible to the language student."

—Krashen

Research has shown that immersion experiences provide the best experience for language acquisition outside of interaction with a native community. Beginning with Unit 6, the sections of *T'es branché?* that easily lend themselves to immersion experiences are the *Lecture thématique* and *Le monde visuel*, both in Lesson C. Students can build a literary and artistic vocabulary, which will result in an appreciation and understanding of literature and art.

## La littérature

Begin the reading lesson by asking students to read the **Rencontre avec l'auteur**. Identify the time period of the writer by making a timeline on the wall and placing the names of the authors, as you encounter them, where they belong, along with a flag identifying their nationality. Have students identify the question at the end of the paragraph that they should be able to answer after having read the selection; you may want them to write it in their notebook and jot down ideas as they come to them when they read. Have students share responses to the **Pré-lecture** question as a class, unless you consider the question personal and want students to write a response in their notebook. Although the strategy is presented in English, you can give directions on how to complete it in French. Since interaction is the key to a good immersion experience, have students compare their graphic organizers in pairs or small groups. Put useful expressions on the board to help students share information, such as, **J'ai mis....**, **Pourquoi n'as-tu pas considéré...?**, **J'ai une autre idée**, etc.

You may want to begin the selection by playing the audio recording. Point out that there will be words students won't know, but these words are glossed below the selection. Wherever possible, a French synonym is given. Ask students to answer the **Pendant la lecture** questions after listening to the recording, or pause the recording where there is a question in order to monitor their comprehension. Then have students share their responses to the **Post-lecture** question in pairs or small groups, and ask for volunteers to share once you reassemble as a class. Finally, students do the **Activités d'expansion**. Encourage students to publish their writings on the Internet and put some in their portfolio so they can see how they improve at analyzing literature over time.

## L'art

To familiarize your students with keys to understanding art as presented in **Le monde visuel**, you may want to have students keep a notebook in which they define the art terms they encounter with each new painting. Provide them with some words and expressions to answer the question(s) at the end of each paragraph. Have students work in pairs to answer the question(s).

In Level 2, you might begin with an overview of the basic art movements, since not all the art movements are covered in *T'es branché?*, so that students understand the basic characteristics of each movement. The chart that follows provides simple phrases you can use to distinguish these movements. Bring in art books and pass around paintings by the artists mentioned so students understand which artists are associated with each movement and the evolution of French art. Students should learn these types of paintings: **la nature morte**, **le portrait**, **l'auto-portrait**, **le paysage**, **la scène**. Post some examples in class and do a station activity in which they identify the type of painting and the movement.

## Overview of Art Movements

| Mouvement | Dates approximatives | Charactéristiques | Peintres |
|---|---|---|---|
| Renaissance | 1492 – 1600 | Inspirée par la Renaissance italienne<br><br>Conception nouvelle du portait<br><br>Débuts du paysage, par exemple, dans la *joconde* | Léonard de Vinci<br>Fouquet<br>Clouet<br>Dubreuil<br>(Ambroise) Dubois |
| Classicisme | 1575 – 1700 | Sujets nobles de l'antiquité, de la mythologie, de la Bible<br><br>La symétrie dans la composition | Poussin<br>Charles Le Brun |
| Baroque | 1625 – 1700 | Histoires viennent des légendes, de la mythologie, de la Bible<br><br>Couleurs chaudes et vives<br><br>Sentiments visibles sur les visages<br><br>L'asymétrie dans la composition<br><br>Impression du mouvement | Chardin<br>Fragonard<br>Lebrun<br>Lorrain<br>Poussin |
| Rococo | 1730 – 1789 | Compositions frivoles et légères<br><br>Scènes pastorales et aristocrates | Boucher<br>Watteau |
| Néo-classicisme | 1760 – 1830 | Inspiré par Rome antique<br><br>Style plus simple que rococo<br><br>Allégories, mythologie comme sujets | David<br>Gérard<br>Gros |
| Romantisme | 1775 – 1850 | Rejet du classicisme (trop rigide)<br><br>Désir de montrer l'idéal, les sentiments, l'exotique, les fantaisies du peintre | Delacroix<br>Gros<br>Géricault |
| Réalisme | 1830 – 1890 | Sujets les scènes de la vie courante<br><br>Observation<br><br>Stylisation<br><br>Coloration sombre | Corot<br>Courbet<br>Daumier<br>Millet<br>Fantin-Latour |
| Impressionnisme | 1850 – 1900 | Rejet de l'art académique<br><br>Note les impressions fugitives avec une touche rapide<br><br>Taches de couleurs juxtaposées se recomposent à une distance | Monet<br>Renoir<br>Pissarro<br>Sisley<br>Morisot<br>Bazille<br>Manet |
| Cubisme | 1907 – 1914 | Sujets décomposés<br><br>Formes géométriques | Picasso, Gris<br>Braque |

# Differentiated Instruction and *T'es branché?*

Differentiated instruction occurs when teachers design learning to meet individual student needs. It differentiates between **content** (the materials the student needs to learn); **process** (practice that allows the student to learn the material; **products** (projects that get the student to rehearse, apply, and extend his or her learning); and, according to Carol Ann Tomlinson, fosters a positive **learning environment** (the way the classroom functions and feels).

Tailoring activities to different ability levels in your classroom can be time-consuming, so having a program like *T'es branché?* that is designed to meet differing ability levels and learning styles means you won't have to develop many materials on your own. Below are a few examples from *T'es branché?* for each aspect of differentiated instruction.

## Content

1. **Use reading materials for different ability levels.**

   *T'es branché?* has a basic dialogue and a more advanced dialogue in each lesson; the advanced dialogue is called *Extension*. If a literary selection in *Lecture thématique* is too easy or hard for a student, pick an alternative for him or her in the *Lectures thématiques* manual. Ideas for differentiated learning appear in the Annotated Teacher's Edition wraparound notes.

2. **Present materials visually and auditorily.**

   For the visual learner, *T'es branché?* includes many activities based on a visual illustration, piece of realia, or graphic. Take advantage of the e-visuals and electronic flash cards for learning vocabulary, for example. Students are encouraged to fill out graphic organizers throughout *T'es branché?* to help them conceptualize and form ideas. *T'es branché?* has seven listening activities in every odd-numbered unit, eight for even-numbered units; also, the first dialogue in the *Rencontres culturelles* section is available as a video and an audio mp3 file; these listening activities will help students who learn best aurally.

3. **Use materials that result in analysis and evaluation.**

   While some students may find their comfort area in knowledge, comprehension, and application, *T'es branché?* allows for analysis and evaluation as students progress and move forward to reach their potential.

## Process

1. **Provide opportunities for students to work in pairs and groups.**

   Students learning with *T'es branché?* receive many opportunities to work cooperatively in pairs and groups.

2. **Adapt instruction to meet Multiple Intelligences and other learning styles.**

   Different learning styles are built into the activities of *T'es branché?*; suggestions for implementation appear in the Annotated Teacher's Edition wraparound notes.

3. **Provide differentiated testing.**

   With *T'es branché?*, students can be tested with a slower-paced test, an at-standard test, or an advanced test.

## Products

1. **Provide opportunities for communication.**

   With the *T'es branché?* program, students learn to enact dialogues (interpersonal communication); write memos, e-mails, postcards, etc. (presentational communication); and make presentations based on online research (interpretive/presentational communication).

2. **Provide challenging and engaging tasks.**

   The activities in *T'es branché?* move from those that are more mechanical to those that are meaningful, open-ended, and creative. Students practice recalling, check their comprehension, apply what they have learned, analyze, synthesize, and evaluate using *T'es branché?*

3. **Provide a variety of final projects based on learning styles.**

   Students have the opportunity to develop three types of final projects in *T'es branché?*: *Connexions par Internet*, *Communautés en ligne*, and *Passez à l'action!* In the first students do cross-disciplinary research in

French using presentational communication. In the second they reach out to or learn about a francophone community online that results in interpersonal or presentational communication. The third activity may have them designing the house of the future, researching French links to the Olympics, or donating books to Africa, often as a group activity.

### Learning Environment

People passing by your classroom will see a lot of activity when you teach with *T'es branché?*, but it is a good idea to have days for working quietly without distraction too to keep all your students comfortable. Qualitative assignments in *T'es branché?* mean that students dig deeper and go beyond comprehension questions; learning revolves around an essential question that ties each unit together and that allows for reflection on learning in *Faisons le point!* The technology that accompanies *T'es branché?* means that your students can be engaged every day with video, audio, interactive e-visuals, electronic flash cards—using a variety of electronic devices—having fun while they learn at their own pace because you have planned and organized instruction that accommodates their learning styles.

## Blended Learning in the Second Language Environment

### A Blended Learning Success Story

The overwhelming success of the Khan Academy, which provides free lessons on the Internet, is a wake-up call for teachers who are not using much online instruction in the classroom. Khan Academy currently has 3.5 million users per month, and its free lessons have been viewed more than 82 million times. The increased success rate of students using this free tool is a testament to the potential of blended learning.

### What Is Blended Learning?

Blended learning occurs when teachers combine face-to-face learning with online learning. With self-paced e-learning, students experience differentiated learning. In a blended learning environment activities that may have previously taken place during classroom time are moved online. In one model, student might meet in the traditional classroom only a couple times per week and do the rest of their learning online.

### What Kind of Blended Learning Experience Can I Create for My Students with *T'es branché?*

Today's students are digitally literate, interactive, experiential, social, and possess strong visual-spatial skills. They look for fast response times and are adept at multi-tasking. *T'es branché?* is motivated by the belief that to be successful teachers need to communicate in the language and style of today's students. To achieve this goal, we have created materials that coordinate with a blended learning approach that allows for three types of learning:

| Face-to-Face Learning | Self-Paced Learning | Online Collaborative Learning |
|---|---|---|

### Face-to-Face Learning

Classroom learning with *T'es branché?* centers on the three modes of communication: interpersonal, presentational, and interpretive, or a combination of these. Activities move from mechanical to meaningful to more creative and open-ended as students progress with concepts and information. Assessment is geared to the level of the student with three possibilities for testing: tests for the advanced learner, tests for the at-standard learner, and tests for the slower-paced learner.

## Self-Paced Learning

In today's student-centered classroom, students need to be able to learn at their own pace. To learn vocabulary, *T'es branché?* allows for students to learn words and expressions at their own pace with electronic flash cards and e-visuals, some of which are interactive. In the culture section, called *Points de départ*, students can find out more online about any covered topic by using Search words that are provided under each informational (cultural practices) paragraph. Students can learn each unit's content at their own pace with the interactive textbook; for example, they can listen to and watch the dialogues as many times as they need to. Students can see if they have learned the vocabulary and structure content by playing the *Drill and Practice Games*, which allow for immediate feedback. Immediate feedback is also provided in the online *Pre-tests* so that students can see what they need to go back and review before the Unit Tests. These are a few of the features of *T'es branché?* available on EMC's platform for online learning, emclanguages.net.

## Online Collaborative Learning

Students work collaboratively using *T'es branché?* in the *À vous la parole*, *La culture sur place*, and *Projets finaux* sections. Fun and worthwhile activities that they can participate in online include interviewing or surveying francophone teens, communicating with francophone communities, exchanging videos with other French or francophone classes, participating in a service project with other French speakers, posting and commenting on movie reviews, sharing and describing personal photos, and planning a class trip to a French-speaking location.

The blended learning approach of *T'es branché?* provides a technology-rich learning environment that responds to the needs and expectations of students and teachers of the 21st century and extends the second-language environment beyond the classroom. *T'es branché?* in conjunction with emclanguages.net speak the multi-media language of students today. *On est branché!*

# Pre-AP French Language and Culture

The new AP French Language and Culture exam is centered around themes, incorporates overarching essential questions, and focuses on the three modes of communication (interpersonal, presentational, interpretive). It also relies on authentic print, audio, and video materials, and requires students to comprehend cultural perspectives and make comparisons among cultures. These are some ways in which *T'es branché?* prepares students for the eventual AP French language exam:

- Units are organized thematically, for example, *La rue commerçante*, *Les gens que je connais*, and *Le weekend ensemble*.
- All units have an overarching question, a *Question centrale*, or essential question around which students frame their learning, for example: In what ways is learning another language beneficial? How is shopping different in other cultures? What makes a house a "home"?
- The culture readings (*Points de départ*) take students to French-speaking locations. The *Produits* boxes introduce key cultural products in French-speaking countries. The *Perspectives* questions get students to read excerpts from songs, poems, blogs, etc. and think about cultural perspectives in **la Francophonie**. Students also make comparisons to the cultures they know in this culture section. In *La culture sur place*, students experience French culture by investigating it and reflecting on it.
- Filmed dialogues (*Rencontres culturelles*) and a soap opera DVD program filmed in France allow for student engagement with authentic listening experiences. There are also seven listening opportunities in each unit, eight in the even units.
- *The Stratégies communicatives* provide clear and effective strategies to help students use the three modes of communication in activities that are meaningful, creative, and use criticial thinking skills.
- The *Lectures thématiques* present authentic texts from the French-speaking world (novels, poetry, dialogues, blogs, etc.) that students engage with using critical thinking skills. There are also readings in French in the culture section (beginning with Unit 6) and authentic texts in *Du côté des médias*.
- The *Projets finaux* allow students to build communities (*Communautés en ligne*), make connections (*Connexions par Internet*), and communicate in French to complete a French-based project (*Passez à l'action!*).

- Finally, the *Bilan cumulatif*, at the end of every other unit, provides a practice test experience in listening, reading, writing, composition, and speaking.
- The online resource Pre-AP Listening allows students to listen to audio that is followed by multiple-choice questions as on the AP French exam. However, since this is Pre-AP, students who can't answer the questions with audio alone are prompted to "watch" the video to help them understand before trying the questions again.

Students who use *T'es branché?* will learn to use French in real-life settings (Communities), demonstrate an understanding of francophone cultures (Culture), incorporate interdisciplinary learning (Connections), make comparisons between their cultures and languages and French-speaking cultures and French language (Comparisons), all the while communicating in French (Communication).

## *T'es branché?* and the International Baccalaureat

The International Baccalaureat (IB) program is recognized in many schools in 141 countries, with more than 1,300 schools participating in the United States. It seeks to develop global citizens with a strong sense of cultural awareness who recognize and develop universal human values. The program stimulates curiosity and inquiry as students learn and acquire knowledge across different disciplines in a quest toward lifelong learning.

With *T'es branché?*, students are exposed to **la Francophonie** in culture readings, activities, projects, and literature selections, so they move towards becoming global citizens who can embrace the big "C" and small "c" of places where French is spoken. They interact with Francophone students in *À vous la parole* and *Projets finaux* activities and projects. The section *La culture sur place* asks students to interact directly with Francophone culture as participants. Students see universal human values at work in the *Lecture thématique* selections and *Points de départ* sections, and build relationships working collaboratively with others in pair and group work. Pushing the boundaries of their knowledge in cross-disciplinary activities, they connect to math, literature, meteorology, art, science, technology, and many other subject areas.

Each unit of *T'es branché?* is organized around a *question centrale*, in a sense an umbrella under which all the content of the unit falls. At the end of the unit, students are asked to recapture and reflect on what they have learned and self-assess in the *Faisons le point!* section.

As students learn with *T'es branché?*, they begin to acquire important IB characteristics, becoming....

- **knowledgeable** about French language and culture
- **inquiring** about many subject areas
- **reflective** about human values, social issues, and their own learning process
- **open-minded** about other cultures, their values, and points of view
- **caring** about their classmates and Francophone students with whom they collaborate
- **communicative** as they interact orally and write memos, web pages, formal and informal letters, journal articles, reports on surveys they have taken, brochures, and critiques of books and films

With *T'es branché?* as a tool, IB students become great communicators who practice interpersonal, presentational, and interpretive language skills in activities and projects that are engaging, challenging, penetrating, and open-ended.

# Transcript of Textbook Listening Activities

The following is the transcript of the listening comprehension activities included in the *T'es branché?* These activities are recorded in the Audio Program. The following section contains a transcript of these recorded activities for teachers who prefer to read the activities aloud instead of using the recorded version. There is one vocabulary, one structure listening activity in each lesson, plus one in the *Évaluation* section; in every even unit there is also one for the *Bilan cumulatif*. (Unit 1 has fewer listening activities as it has no grammar.)

## Unité 1

### Leçon A

**Vocabulaire**

**1 Les présentations**

Listen to the following short introductions and decide if the person who is being introduced is male or female. Write **M** for male or **F** for female.

1. Raoul:       Bonjour, Myriam! Je te présente ma copine, Catherine.
   Myriam:    Salut, Catherine!

2. Raoul:       Salut, Jean! Je te présente mon copain, Ahmed. Il est algérien.
   Jean:       Salut, Ahmed!

3. Raoul:       Bonjour, Madame Duteil! Je vous présente Monsieur Pradier.
   Mme Duteil:  Enchantée, Monsieur Pradier!

4. Raoul:       Salut, Nathalie! C'est Thomas, mon camarade de classe.
   Nathalie:    Salut, Thomas!

5. Raoul:       Bonjour, tout le monde! Je vous présente Mademoiselle Gentille.
   Tout le monde:  Bonjour, Mademoiselle!

6. Raoul:       Salut, Hugo! C'est ma copine, Leïla. Elle est française.
   Hugo:       Salut, Leïla! Enchanté.

### Leçon B

**Vocabulaire**

**1 Bonjour ou au revoir**

Imagine you are on the streets of Paris listening to greetings and good-byes. Write **H** if the speaker says hello or **G** if the speaker says good-bye.

1. -Bonjour, Monsieur Sorette!
   -Bonjour, Madame Picard! Comment allez-vous?
2. -Salut, Hervé!
   -Salut, Gabrielle! À demain!
3. -Au revoir, Sophie!
   -Au revoir, Ahmed!
4. -À demain, Lilou!
   -À demain, Antoine!
5. -Salut, Christophe. Ça va?
   -Bonjour, Sabrina. Ça va très bien.
6. -À bientôt, Camille!
   -À bientôt, Jérémy!

## Leçon C

### Vocabulaire

### 1 On accepte, oui ou non?

You will hear a series of short conversations. Write **oui** if the second speaker accepts the invitation or **non** if he or she declines.

1. -On va au café?
   -Pas possible. J'aide ma mère.
2. -Tu voudrais aller à la teuf de Sandrine avec moi et ma copine Armelle?
   -Non, je ne peux pas.
3. -On va au centre commercial?
   -D'accord.
4. -Salut, Henri! Tu voudrais aller au centre commercial avec moi?
   -Je ne peux pas. Je dois faire mes devoirs.
5. -Salut, Ahmed! Je te présente mon copain, Xavier. On va au cinéma. Et toi?
   -Oui. Je veux bien.
6. -On va à la maison?
   -Eh bien, oui!
7. -Tu voudrais aller au café demain?
   -Non, je dois aider mon père.

### Évaluation

### A Évaluation de compréhension auditive

Listen to the dialogue, then read the statements below. Write **V** if the statement is **vrai** (*true*) and **F** if it is **faux** (*false*).

| | |
|---|---|
| Aïcha: | Bonjour, Maude. |
| Maude: | Bonjour, Aïcha. Comment ça va? |
| Aïcha: | Ça va bien, et toi? |
| Maude: | Pas mal. |
| Aïcha: | Je te présente mon cousin, Ahmed. Ahmed est algérien. |
| Maude: | Enchantée, Ahmed. |
| Ahmed: | Salut, Maude. On va au café. Et toi? |
| Maude: | Pas possible. Je dois faire mes devoirs. |
| Aïcha: | Bon alors, à demain. |
| Maude: | Oui, à demain. |

## Unité 2
## Leçon A

### Vocabulaire

### 1 Les projets de la semaine

Some students are talking about their week. In English write the day of the week each activity will take place.

1. Tu fais du vélo dimanche.
2. Mardi, je peux aller au cinéma.
3. Lundi, je fais du roller avec mes copains.
4. Jeudi, on va au café manger des hamburgers.
5. Vendredi soir, je fais du shopping après les cours.
6. Samedi, on va au centre commercial.
7. Mercredi, je peux sortir avec mes amis.

## Grammaire

### 10 Identifiez le sujet!

Write the letter of the French subject pronoun that could replace each name or set of names.

1. Élodie
2. Marcel et Joël
3. Marie et Bruno
4. Jeanne et Anne
5. Amadou
6. Leïla

## Leçon B

### Vocabulaire

### 1 C'est quelle activité?

Clément is asking his classmates about activities they enjoy. Choose the image that matches the activity you hear.

1. Clément: Salut, Fatima! Qu'est-ce que tu aimes faire?
   Fatima: J'aime beaucoup écouter de la musique.
2. Clément: Bonjour, Lucas! Qu'est-ce que tu aimes bien faire?
   Lucas: J'aime bien envoyer des textos.
3. Clément: Jean-Marc et Yasmine, qu'est-ce que vous aimez faire?
   Jean-Marc & Yasmine: Nous aimons lire.
4. Clément: Et vous, Maude et Mégane?
   Maude & Mégane: Nous aimons jouer aux jeux vidéo.
5. Clément: Cédric, tu aimes surfer sur Internet?
   Cédric: Oui, j'adore surfer sur Internet. C'est génial!
6. Clément: Et Coralie? Elle aime étudier?
   Cédric: Ah! Oui. Elle aime étudier.
7. Clément: Et Éric et Anaïs, ils aiment cuisiner?
   Cédric: Oui, ils aiment beaucoup cuisiner.

## Grammaire

### 8 On aime un peu, bien, ou beaucoup?

Fill out a chart like the one below. Listen to each sentence twice. Then write the activity each teenager likes to do under the heading that indicates the degree to which they like doing that activity. Listen first to the model.

**Modèle: Fatima aime beaucoup téléphoner.**

1. Lucas aime beaucoup écouter de la musique.
2. Coralie aime un peu lire.
3. Lucas aime un peu cuisiner.
4. Lucas aime bien surfer sur Internet.
5. Coralie aime beaucoup faire du sport.
6. Lucas aime bien étudier.
7. Coralie aime bien envoyer des textos.
8. Lucas aime un peu regarder la télé.
9. Coralie aime beaucoup jouer aux jeux vidéo.

## Leçon C

### Vocabulaire

### 1 Les numéros de téléphone

Florence wants to invite her classmates to a party. She asks Thomas for their phone numbers. Write each phone number you hear.

1. Florence:   Quel est le numéro de téléphone de Jasmine?
   Thomas:     C'est le 01.19.02.12.03.
2. Florence:   Quel est le numéro de Bertrand?
   Thomas:     C'est le 01.13.13.18.07.
3. Florence:   Et le numéro de Paul?
   Thomas:     C'est le 01.05.09.17.11.
4. Florence:   Quel est le numéro de Nasser?
   Thomas:     C'est le 01.06.08.10.13.
5. Florence:   Quel est le numéro de Moussa?
   Thomas:     C'est le 01.15.15.03.04.
6. Florence:   Et le numéro de Romane?
   Thomas:     C'est le 01.14.20.11.04.
7. Florence:   Quel est le numéro de Juliette?
   Thomas:     C'est le 01.05.07.18.16.

### Grammaire

### 13 Un e-mail de France

French teenagers have written an e-mail to your class. Listen to each sentence twice. If you hear a masculine noun, write **M**. If you hear a feminine noun, write **F**.

1. Nous aimons bien le sport.
2. Nous aimons beaucoup le football.
3. Nous aimons la télé.
4. Nous préférons le cinéma américain.
5. Nous aimons la musique alternative.
6. Nous préférons le hip-hop américain et français.
7. Nous aimons bien la pizza.
8. Nous aimons bien le roller.
9. Nous aimons un peu le basket.

### Évaluation

### A Évaluation de compréhension auditive

Listen to the phone conversation and decide if the statements you hear are **vrai (V)** or **faux (F)**.

Nayah:   Allô, Koffi?
Koffi:   Salut, Nayah. Tu vas bien?
Nayah:   Pas mal. Qu'est-ce que tu fais?
Koffi:   Je surfe sur Internet et j'écoute de la musique.
Nayah:   Qu'est-ce que tu écoutes?
Koffi:   J'écoute Rachid Taha. C'est génial!
Nayah:   Moi, je préfère le hip-hop.
Koffi:   Tu voudrais aller au concert mercredi?
Nayah:   Oui, je peux. J'invite Alexandre?
Koffi:   Ah, non. Il préfère la musique alternative!
Nayah:   Coralie? Elle aime bien le R'n'B et le hip-hop.
Koffi:   D'accord. Quel est le numéro de téléphone de Coralie?
Naya:    C'est le 05.03.13.20.19. À bientôt!
Koffi:   Salut!

Recorded statements:

1. Koffi surfe sur Internet.
2. Nayah écoute la musique.
3. Koffi écoute Rachid Taha.
4. Nayah préfère la musique alternative.
5. Le concert, c'est vendredi.
6. Koffi invite Alexandre au concert.
7. Coralie adore le R'n'B et le hip-hop.
8. Le numéro de Coralie est le 01.02.12.20.17.

## Bilan cumulatif

### Listening

**I.**

You will hear a short conversation. Select the reply that would come next. You will hear the conversation twice.

| | |
|---|---|
| Marie: | Salut, Djamel! |
| Djamel: | Salut, Marie! Tu vas bien? |
| Marie: | Oui, super! Mon weekend est génial! |
| Djamel: | Qu'est-ce que tu fais ce weekend, mon amie? |
| Marie: | Mon père et moi, on regarde un film pendant qu'il fait mauvais. Et toi, tu joues aux jeux vidéo? |
| Djamel: | Non, je ne joue pas aux jeux vidéo ce weekend. |
| Marie: | Eh bien, qu'est-ce que tu fais? |

**II.**

Listen to the conversation. Select the best completion to each statement that follows.

| | |
|---|---|
| Alexis: | Natasha! On va fait du roller? Il fait beau! |
| Natasha: | Alexis, moi je préfère surfer sur Internet quand il fait beau. |
| Alexis: | Ah bon! Je déteste ça l'Internet, les blogues, les textos, et la télé! Et bien moi, je préfère faire du sport! |
| Natasha: | Ah oui!? Tu aimes jouer au basket? |
| Alexis: | Oui j'aime bien le basket et le foot, et je préfère faire du roller quand il fait soleil. C'est mon passe-temps préféré en été! Et toi? |
| Natasha: | Moi, je n'aime pas faire du roller. Je regarde beaucoup les Jeux Olympiques à la télé: le patinage artistique et le hockey sur glace. Et toi? |
| Alexis: | Regarder les Jeux Olympiques avec mon père et ma mère, c'est mon passe-temps préféré le weekend! C'est génial! |
| Natasha: | Tu voudrais bien regarder la télé? |
| Alexis: | D'accord! On regarde le hockey sur glace, le patinage artistique, et le ski alpin! |

## Unité 3
### Leçon A

### Vocabulaire
#### 2 Les prix

Some students are buying school supplies and items for their bedroom at the store. Number your paper from 1-8. Then match the correct price to the picture of each item you hear.

A. 79,89€    B. 2,30€    C. 5,75€    D. 4,49€    E. 1,29€    F. 56,30€
G. 30,50€    H. 3, 99€

1. - Bonjour, madame. J'ai besoin d'une trousse. Elle coûte combien, s'il vous plait?
   - Elle coûte cinq euros soixante-quinze.
2. - Lilou, tu as besoin d'un dictionnaire?
   - Oui, d'un dictionnaire français-anglais. C'est combien?
   - Trente euros cinquante.

3. - Combien coûtent les cahiers?
   - Ils coûtent deux euros trente.
4. - Léa a besoin d'un crayon.
   - Ce n'est pas cher! Un euro vingt-neuf.
5. - Et le taille-crayon, il coûte combien?
   - Il coûte trois euros quatre-vingt-dix-neuf.
6. - Pardon, monsieur. Il coûte combien l'ordinateur portable HP?
   - Il coûte soixante-dix-neuf euros quatre-vingt-neuf.
7. - Maman, j'ai besoin d'un cédérom français-espagnol.
   - Cinquante-six euros trente. D'accord!
8. - Mathis, ils coûtent combien les cinq stylos?
   - Ils coûtent quatre euros quarante-neuf.

## Grammaire

### 13 Qu'est-ce qu'on a?

Select the correct answer for each question you hear.

1. Tu as un livre de maths?
2. Marielle a une feuille de papier?
3. Vous avez un taille-crayon?
4. J'ai mon cahier d'histoire?
5. Sébastien et Rose ont un cédérom?

## Leçon B

### Vocabulaire

### 2 Les emplois du temps

Listen to Rosalie and Mathis talk about their schedules. Write in French each class or activity in the order it is mentioned.

Mathis:    Salut, Rosalie!
Rosalie:   Salut Mathis! On a quels cours ce matin?
Mathis:    On a biologie à neuf heures. Puis, on a deux heures de maths avec Monsieur Lahalle.
Rosalie:   Vraiment? Après les maths, on a quoi?
Mathis:    On a anglais et après on mange à la cantine.
Rosalie:   Et cet après-midi? On a informatique, espagnol, et EPS, n'est-ce pas?
Mathis:    Oui, c'est ça!

## Grammaire

### 7 L'heure

Listen to each statement. Write **oui** if the time you hear matches the clock. Write **non** if it does not match.

1. Je vais à la maison à cinq heures et demie, le lundi.
2. Léa a cours de maths à dix heures et quart du matin.
3. Il est minuit vingt.
4. Kemajou et Jean-Luc jouent au foot à trois heures quarante-cinq le mercredi après-midi.
5. Tu as histoire-géo à neuf heures?
6. Le film sur Gauguin est à huit heures moins le quart du soir.
7. Le matin, Alexandre a cours à huit heures moins vingt-cinq.
8. On rencontre Thomas à quatre heures et demie, mercredi après-midi.
9. On va au centre commercial à trois heures moins le quart?
10. Sandrine mange le déjeuner à midi vingt-cinq.

## Leçon C

### Vocabulaire

### 2 Mercredi après-midi

Number your paper 1-6. Listen to Maxime interview his classmates about their activities on Wednesday afternoon. Identify each location.

1. Maxime: Omar, tu fais quoi le mercredi après-midi?
   Omar: J'étudie à la médiathèque.
2. Maxime: Et toi, Coralie?
   Coralie: Moi, je nage à la piscine.
3. Maxime: Salut Sabine, tu fais quoi mercredi après-midi?
   Sabine: Salut, Maxime! Je vais au café.
4. Maxime: Tu vas où, Sarah?
   Sarah: Je vais à la salle d'informatique pour mon projet d'histoire.
5. Maxime: Bonjour, Noémie! Tu fais du sport?
   Noémie: Non, moi, je fais mes devoirs à la maison.
6. Maxime: Et toi, Justin?
   Justin: Moi, je vais en ville au magasin de sports.

### Grammaire

### 16 Répondez aux questions!

A group of Tahitian teenagers is answering their friends' questions. Select the correct response to each question.

1. Est-ce que tu aimes ta prof de français?
2. Quand est-ce que vous avez chimie?
3. Combien coûte le taille-crayon?
4. Où est-ce que tu veux étudier samedi?
5. Avec qui est qu'ils vont au labo?
6. Tu as besoin de quoi pour le cours d'anglais?
7. Pourquoi est-ce que tu ne vas pas à la piscine avec nous?

### Évaluation

### A Evaluation de compréhension auditive

Listen to the conversation between Félix and his mother. Choose the appropriate answer to the questions.

| | |
|---|---|
| Félix: | Maman, j'ai besoin d'aller à Carrefour. |
| Maman: | Bien sûr. Tu veux y aller à quelle heure? |
| Félix: | À 5h30, après les cours. |
| Maman: | D'accord. Tu as besoin de quoi? |
| Félix: | J'ai besoin de crayons, de stylos, d'un cahier pour le cours de maths, de feuilles de papiers, et d'un cédérom français-anglais pour l'anglais bien-sûr. |
| Maman: | Pourquoi tu as besoin d'un cédérom? Tu as un livre d'anglais, n'est-ce pas? |
| Félix: | Oui, mais le prof veut aussi le cédérom. |
| Maman: | Il coûte combien? |
| Félix: | Il coûte 69 euros. |
| Maman: | Oh là là, c'est cher. Je téléphone au proviseur pour lui demander pourquoi tu dois acheter un cédérom avec ton livre d'anglais. |
| Félix: | Oh, non! Maman!!! |

## Unité 4
### Leçon A

#### Vocabulaire

#### 3  Mélanie fait du shopping.

Mélanie is shopping at a sporting goods store. Write the name of the person she is shopping for and what she is buying in English.

1. J'achète un ballon de foot pour Pierre.
2. Sandrine va avoir le maillot de l'équipe de Marseille.
3. Pour Koffi, les chaussettes de mon équipe.
4. Je vais acheter un blouson pour Samia.
5. J'achète un blason pour le blouson de Thierry.
6. Pour Norbert, une casquette.
7. Je donne une écharpe à mon copain Loïc.
8. Marie-Hélène… pour elle des chaussures de foot!

#### Grammaire

#### 10  C'est le weekend!

*C'est le weekend! Choisissez la lettre de l'image qui correspond à chaque activité que vous et vos amis allez faire.*

1. Ce weekend, Vincent va aider sa mère.
2. Timéo va regarder le film avec moi.
3. Parce qu'il fait beau, nous allons nager.
4. Elles vont acheter des maillots de notre équipe de foot.
5. Je vais prendre un sandwich.
6. Rahina et Myriam, vous allez jouer aux jeux vidéo.

### Leçon B

#### Vocabulaire

#### 2  Une fête chez Jérémy

*Écrivez **A** si la personne à la fête de Jérémy a soif ou **B** si elle a faim.*

1. -Tu voudrais quoi, Coralie?
   -Un jus d'orange.
2. -Et toi, Laurent, tu vas prendre un coca?
   -Non, je vais prendre une limonade.
3. -Koffi?
   -Pour moi, une pizza.
4. -Emma, qu'est-ce que tu voudrais?
   -Une quiche.
5. -Héloïse, tu prends quoi?
   -Je prends un café.
6. -Et toi, Salim?
   -J'aime les sandwichs. Je prends un sandwich au jambon.
7. -Et toi, Florence?
   -Pour moi, un coca!
8. -Noah, tu veux une crêpe à la confiture?
   -Oui, d'accord.
9. -Evenye, tu veux quoi?
   -Une eau minérale.
10. -Nicole, tu prends une glace?
    -Non, pour moi, un jus d'orange.

**Grammaire**

## 12 Qu'est-ce qu'on va prendre?

*Tout le monde prend quelque chose à manger ou à boire. Écrivez 1 si on parle d'une personne ou 2 si on parle de deux ou plusieurs personnes.* (Everyone is having something to eat or drink. Write **1** if what you hear refers to one person or **2** if it refers to two people or more.)

1. Je prends une limonade et un croque-monsieur.
2. Marcel prend un steak-frites.
3. Mon père et ma mère prennent des hamburgers.
4. Nous ne prenons pas une salade, nous prenons une quiche.
5. Tu prends une glace à la vanille et une eau minérale.

## Leçon C

**Vocabulaire**

## 2 Nous allons être à l'heure, n'est-ce pas?

*Regardez l'horaire des films et pour chaque phrase que vous entendez, décidez si les personnes vont être....*

A. en avance     B. à l'heure     C. en retard

1. Lois est devant le cinéma pour voir *Shrek* à 15h00.
2. Amir va au cinéma à 20h10 pour voir *Prince of Persia*.
3. Moi, je retrouve Cédric à 13h45 pour voir *Fatal*.
4. Alexandre va voir *Tournée* au ciné à 20h15.
5. Frédéric et Sandrine se retrouvent à 19h55 pour voir *Tournée*.
6. Kémajou achète un billet pour *Millenium 2*, à 21h00.
7. Saniyya et Amir se retrouvent devant le cinéma à 16h05 pour voir *Shrek 4*
8. Julie va voir *Prince of Persia* à 20h15.
9. On va voir *Fatal* à 13h55.
10. Nous achetons le billet pour *Millenium 2* à 21h30.

**Grammaire**

## 14 Qui voit quoi?

*Tout le monde* (Everyone) *voit un film ce weekend. Écrivez la lettre qui correspond à la forme du verbe voir que vous entendez dans chaque phrase.*

A. vois     B. voit     C. voyons     D. voyez     E. voient

1. Alain voit *Avatar* à 17h00.
2. Aline et moi voyons *Saw* au cinéma.
3. Martine et Françoise voient *Star-Trek*.
4. Je vois *Bienvenue chez les Ch'tis* pour rire!
5. Vous voyez *Harry Potter* ce weekend?
6. Nous voyons *Batman*.
7. Mohamed voit *New Moon* sur internet.
8. On voit Iron Man ensemble?

**Évaluation**

## A Évaluation de compréhension auditive

Listen as Marine and Khaled talk about their plans for Wednesday afternoon. For each statement you hear, write **V** if it is true (**vrai**) or **F** if it is false (**faux**).

| | |
|---|---|
| Khaled: | Salut, Marine. Tu voudrais aller au cinéma mercredi après-midi? |
| Marine: | Oui, j'aime beaucoup le cinéma. On va voir un film d'horreur ou une comédie? |
| Khaled: | Je préfère voir une comédie ou un film policier. |
| Marine: | On peut voir *Shrek 4* ou *Millenium 2*. |
| Khaled: | Oui, j'aime bien *Shrek 4*. À quelle heure? |
| Marine: | À 13h50 ou 16h30. |

| | |
|---|---|
| Khaled: | On va manger au café après les cours et on va à la séance de 16h30? |
| Marine: | Oui, d'accord. Nous nous retrouvons devant le Café des Artistes à midi. |
| Khaled: | On invite Sylvain et Rahina? |
| Marine: | Ils vont voir le match du PSG au Parc des Princes cet après-midi. |
| Khaled: | Bon, alors rendez-vous à midi. |
| Marine: | Oui, à bientôt. |

Recorded statements:

1. Khaled veut voir le match de foot du PSG au Parc des Princes.
2. Marine va voir le match du PSG avec Sylvain et Rahina.
3. Marine adore le cinéma.
4. Khaled veut voir un film de science-fiction.
5. Marine préfère une comédie ou un film policier.
6. Khaled et Marine décident de voir *Shrek 4*.
7. Khaled et Marine vont à la séance de 13h50.
8. Khaled et Marine décident de manger au Café des Artistes.
9. Khaled et Marine se rencontrent à midi et demie devant le Café des Artistes.
10. Khaled et Marine vont au cinéma avec Sylvain et Rahina.

## Bilan cumulatif

### Listening

**I.**

You will hear a short conversation. Select the reply that would come next. You will hear the conversation twice.

| | |
|---|---|
| Stéphane: | Dis, Virginie, qu'est-ce que tu voudrais faire après le cours d'espagnol? |
| Virginie: | Je voudrais aller au cinéma! |
| Stéphane: | Ah, le cinéma, j'adore! On y va à midi? |
| Virginie: | Non, je ne peux pas! J'ai besoin de manger un croque-monsieur et une glace! |
| Stéphane: | Très bien, mais on se retrouve quand? |

**II.**

Listen to the conversation. Select the best completion to each statement that follows.

| | |
|---|---|
| Alexis: | Allô, Séverine, c'est Alexis, ton camarade de classe! |
| Séverine: | Ah, salut Alexis! |
| Alexis: | Ça va? |
| Séverine: | Oui très bien, merci! Et toi? |
| Alexis: | Bien, merci! On va au match de foot dimanche. Dis, tu aimes le foot? |
| Séverine: | Oui, j'adore! J'aime aller au stade et regarder les matchs! |
| Alexis: | Moi aussi! Tu voudrais sortir dimanche avec moi et mes copains? |
| Séverine: | Oui, je veux bien! |
| Alexis: | Et bien, rendez-vous dimanche devant le stade! |
| Séverine: | On se retrouve après le déjeuner? |
| Alexis: | Oui, à 2h00! |

## Unité 5
### Leçon A

#### Vocabulaire

#### 5 Ma famille

*Simone décrit* (is describing) *sa famille. Regardez l'arbre généalogique* (family tree) *et dites si chaque phrase est* **vraie (V)** *ou* **fausse (F)**.

1. Je ressemble à mon père.
2. Ma sœur est Romane.

3. Mon oncle et ma tante ont deux enfants.
4. Raoul est mon oncle.
5. Anaïs est ma tante.
6. Ma cousine est Philippe.
7. Françoise est ma grand-mère.

## Grammaire

### 10 Comparons nos familles!

*Juliette compare sa famille à la famille de Xavier. Écrivez **J** si elle parle de sa famille, **X** si elle parle de la famille de Xavier, ou **J** et **X** si elle parle des deux familles.*

1. Sa cousine est très bête.
2. Mes frères sont sympa et intéressants.
3. J'adore ma famille. Elle est super!
4. Ses oncles sont un peu paresseux!
5. Je ressemble à ma grand-mère Thérèse.
6. J'aime beaucoup son père. Il est très généreux.
7. Son demi-frère a les cheveux roux.
8. Nos grands-pères sont aussi de très bons copains.

## Leçon B

## Vocabulaire

### 3 Les jumeaux

*Les jumeaux souvent se ressemblent. Écoutez chaque description et écrivez l'adjectif qui décrit le jumeau de cette personne.* (Twins often look and act alike. Listen to each description and write the adjective that describes that person's twin.)

**Modèle:** Vous entendez: Christian est méchant. Comment est sa sœur Delphine?
Vous écrivez: **méchante**

1. Madeleine est sympa. Comment est son frère Alain?
2. Kemajou est timide. Comment est sa sœur Rahina?
3. Saniyya est égoïste. Comment est son frère Nasser?
4. Noah est bavard. Comment est sa sœur Noémie?
5. Claire est paresseuse. Comment est son frère Sébastien?
6. Salim est diligent. Comment est sa sœur Leïla?
7. Émile est généreux. Comment est sa sœur Émilie?

## Grammaire

### 16 Les dates

*Catherine et sa sœur parlent des dates importantes. Écoutez leur conversation et écrivez les dates que vous entendez à la française: le jour/le mois. Par exemple, la date de Noël* (Christmas) *s'écrit* (is written) *25/12.*

**Modèle:** Vous entendez: L'anniversaire de Richard est le 12 mai.
Vous écrivez: **12/5**

1. L'anniversaire de mon père est le 31 juin.
2. Karim va avoir 13 ans le 8 janvier.
3. On va à la fête de Marie le 15 août.
4. C'est le 25 novembre. C'est l'anniversaire de ma sœur.
5. Nous n'allons pas à l'école le 1er mai en France.
6. Laura et Laurent vont voyager à Tahiti le 13 mars.
7. J'invite nos amis le 15 octobre pour l'anniversaire de Jean.
8. Nous offrons un CD à Valentin pour sa fête. C'est le 14 février.
9. En France, on ne va pas à l'école le 11 novembre.
10. Maxime, qu'est-ce que tu fais le 17 avril?

## Leçon C

### Vocabulaire

### 3 Les professions

*Choisissez l'image qui correspond à la phrase que vous entendez.*

**Modèle:** Vous entendez: M. Diouf? C'est un dentiste congolais.
Vous écrivez: **E**

1. Mlle Chérie est blonde et diligente. C'est une prof.
2. J'adore ce metteur en scène. Elle fait des films intéressants.
3. Mon père adore manger et c'est un bon cuisinier.
4. Il est français; il a les yeux bleus et les cheveux blonds. Il est chanteur.
5. Elle est intelligente. C'est une femme d'affaires.
6. Il gagne beaucoup de matchs. C'est un bon athlète et un footballeur.
7. Elle est diligente. Elle a les cheveux bruns et les yeux marron. C'est une actrice.
8. Elle aime écrire et lire des romans. Elle désire être écrivain.
9. Il est drôle et intelligent. C'est un testeur de jeux vidéo.

### Grammaire

### 16 Les pays d'origine

*Écrivez en anglais le nom du pays* (country) *d'où viennent ces personnes.*

**Modèle:** Vous entendez: Koffi vient du Togo.
Vous écrivez: Togo

1. Nous venons des États-Unis.
2. Tu viens du Canada.
3. Rahina vient du Cameroun.
4. Amidou vient de Côte-d'Ivoire.
5. Abdoulaye et Awa viennent du Gabon.
6. Marc et toi, vous venez de France.

### Évaluation

### A Évaluation de comprehension auditive

Listen to the conversation between Rahina and Mathéo. Afterward, you will hear some statements. Write **oui** if the statement is correct. Write **non** if the statement is incorrect.

Mathéo: Salut, Rahina. Tu vas à l'anniversaire d'Antoine vendredi soir?
Rahina: Oui, j'y vais. Quel âge a-t-il?
Mathéo: Il va avoir 18 ans le 23 juin. Il prépare une super teuf! Son oncle, le metteur en scène, offre à Antoine de voyager en Martinique.
Rahina: Quelle chance! Il vient de Martinique, n'est-ce pas?
Mathéo: Oui, sa famille vient de Fort-de-France. Sa mère va préparer des accras de morue et des crêpes. Ça va être délicieux!
Rahina: Quelle est la profession de son père?
Mathéo: Son père est dentiste.
Rahina: Et sa mère, elle est comment?
Mathéo: Elle est gentille. Et, c'est une super cuisinière.
Rahina: Tu offres quoi à Antoine?
Mathéo: J'offre un CD de Corneille. À vendredi alors?
Rahina: Oui, c'est ça. Salut!

Recorded statements:

1. C'est l'anniversaire de Rahina.
2. Mathéo ne va pas à l'anniversaire d'Antoine.

3. Antoine va avoir 18 ans.
4. La famille d'Antoine vient de Martinique.
5. La mère d'Antoine va acheter des accras de morue.
6. Le père d'Antoine est metteur en scène.
7. La mère d'Antoine est une bonne cuisinière.
8. Mathéo va offrir un CD de Corneille.

## Unité 6
### Leçon A

**Vocabulaire**

**3 Qu'est-ce qu'on porte?**

*Choisissez l'illustration qui correspond à chaque description que vous entendez.*

1. Justine porte une jupe rouge et des bottes noires. Elle est chic.
2. Amir porte un jean rose. C'est pas mal!
3. Nayah porte un jean, un tee-shirt jaune, et des baskets orange. C'est très sympa.
4. Moussa porte un jean et une veste blanche. Il est sympa!
5. Malika porte un beau manteau vert. C'est pas mal!
6. Anh porte une robe blanche et un chapeau bleu. Elle est très chic!
7. Théo porte un jean et une chemise noire. C'est pas mal!
8. Rahina porte un ensemble marron et des bottes beiges. Elle est chic!

**Grammaire**

**12 Faisons du shopping!**

*Choisissez le rayon (department) du magasin où M. et Mme Chambon et leurs enfants, Gabrielle (5 ans) et Julien (10 ans), trouvent les vêtements.*

A. rayon (*department*) garçons    B. rayon filles    C. rayon hommes    D. rayon femmes

1. Mme Chambon veut acheter un ensemble pour le travail. Elle choisit une jupe noire et un pull rose.
2. Gabrielle va bientôt avoir six ans. Ses parents veulent acheter une robe rose pour sa fête d'anniversaire samedi.
3. M. Chambon veut acheter un pantalon bleu et une chemise bleue pour le travail.
4. Julien et Gabrielle veulent acheter un ensemble pour faire du sport. Ils choisissent des shorts verts, des tee-shirts blancs, et des baskets.
5. Mme Chambon veut acheter un vêtement pour l'hiver. Elle choisit un anorak rouge.

### Leçon B

**Vocabulaire**

**6 La chronologie**

*Indiquez le magasin où François achète les choses que vous entendez.*

A. la boulangerie    B. la crémerie    C. la boucherie    D. le supermarché    E. la pâtisserie
F. la charcuterie

1. François prend du ketchup, de la mayonnaise, et de la moutarde.
2. Il achète aussi un kilo de bœuf.
3. Il choisit quatre tranches de jambon et un saucisson.
4. Il prend une tarte aux pommes pour samedi.
5. Je n'ai pas de lait ou de beurre; prends un camembert aussi.
6. Tu achètes une baguette et des croissants pour demain matin.

## Grammaire

### 19 Au supermarché

*Choisissez l'expression de quantité qui correspond à l'aliment (food) que Nicole achète.*

A. une boite    B. une bouteille    C. un kilo    D. un litre    E. un morceau
F. des tranches    G. un paquet    H. un pot

1. J'ai besoin de pommes.
2. J'achète du jambon.
3. J'ai besoin de lait.
4. J'achète aussi du fromage.
5. Je prends du café.
6. J'achète de l'eau minérale.
7. Je prends des pâtes.
8. J'ai besoin de moutarde.

## Leçon C

### Vocabulaire

### 3 À l'épicerie

*Choisissez l'illustration qui correspond à ce que les clients achètent au marché.*

1. Bonjour, madame. Je voudrais cinq bananes, s'il vous plaît.
2. Bonjour, monsieur. Je fais une ratatouille. J'ai besoin d'une aubergine, de tomates, d'olives, et de courgettes.
3. Madame, donnez-moi un kilo de pommes de terre.
4. Vos poires sont bien mûres? Je prends 500 grammes de poires, s'il vous plaît.
5. Je vais faire une tarte pour le déjeuner. J'achète 200 grammes de fraises, s'il vous plaît.
6. J'ai besoin de poivrons pour ma salade. Donnez-moi deux poivrons rouges, Monsieur.
7. Pour ma salade de fruits, je prends des raisins, des cerises, des pommes, et des oranges, s'il vous plaît, madame.
8. Monsieur, je prends deux kilos de champignons, s'il vous plaît.
9. Je prépare une salade niçoise. J'achète des haricots verts, des tomates, un concombre, un poivron rouge, des olives, et un orange pour le dessert. Merci, mademoiselle.
10. Donnez-moi deux grosses pastèques, s'il vous plaît, mademoiselle.

## Grammaire

### 16 Le marché

*Choisissez l'image qui correspond à la quantité de l'aliment qu'on décrit (describes).*

**Modèle**    You hear:    M. Martin prend du pain.
    You select:    **A**

1. J'achète un poulet.
2. Mme Mercier prend du jambon.
3. M. Laurent mange de la salade.
4. Justine désire une glace.
5. Claude prend de l'eau.
6. Mlle Michel mange de la tarte aux fraises.
7. Théo achète un saucisson.

## Évaluation

### A Evaluation de compréhension auditive

Jean-Luc and Christian are going to a market in a village while on vacation. Make a list in English of what they buy.

Jean-Luc:    Qu'est-ce qu'on prend pour le déjeuner et le dîner?
Christian:    Achetons des tomates, elles sont bien mûres, et des courgettes. Tout est frais!

| Jean-Luc: | Je n'aime pas les courgettes. Je préfère prendre des concombres et petits pois. Ils sont très bons et bon marché. |
| Christian: | D'accord. Nous avons besoin d'un kilo de champignons aussi. C'est délicieux! |
| Jean-Luc: | Bonjour, madame. Je voudrais un kilo de tomates bien mûres, deux kilos de courgettes, deux concombres, et 500 grammes de petits pois. C'est combien le kilo de champignons? |
| Vendeuse: | C'est cinq euros. |
| Jean-Luc: | C'est beaucoup trop! |
| Vendeuse: | Je vous fais un prix, quatre euros le kilo. |
| Jean-Luc: | D'accord, 500 grammes alors. Ça fait combien? |
| Vendeuse: | Onze euros, s'il vous plait. |

## Bilan cumulatif

### Listening

**I.**

You will hear a short conversation. Select the reply that would come next. You will hear the conversation twice.

| Vendeuse: | Vous désirez, Mademoiselle? |
| Demoiselle: | Je cherche des pêches. |
| Vendeuse: | Des pêches jaunes ou blanches? |
| Demoiselle: | Des pêches blanches. C'est combien le kilo, s'il vous plaît? |

**II.**

Listen to the conversation. Select the best completion to each statement that follows.

| Marion: | Céline, dis, tu veux bien aller faire du shopping avec moi? |
| Céline: | Oui, je veux bien! Quand ça, Marion? |
| Marion: | Après les cours? |
| Céline: | Génial! Qu'est-ce que tu veux acheter? |
| Marion: | J'ai besoin d'une robe pour la fête, samedi! |
| Céline: | Ah oui! Tu veux une robe de quelle couleur? |
| Marion: | Je voudrais une robe noire. J'aime les robes noires et rouges. |
| Céline: | Pas moi, je préfère les vêtements blancs et roses. Tu as trop de noir, Marion! |
| Marion: | Oui, mais moi, c'est ma couleur, le noir! |
| Céline: | On se retrouve devant la salle de classe de Mademoiselle Lecourt? |
| Marion: | Non, Je préfère devant la médiathèque à 17h00. |
| Céline: | Bon, à 17h00 devant la médiathèque, d'accord? |
| Marion: | D'accord! |
| Céline: | Je vais à la pâtisserie prendre deux tartes aux pommes d'abord: une pour toi et une pour moi, et après, c'est le shopping! |
| Marion: | J'adore faire du shopping avec toi, Céline! |

## Unité 7
### Leçon A

### Vocabulaire
#### 6 Chez moi!

*Écrivez **L** si la description de la maison est **logique** ou **I** si la description est **illogique**.*

1. Dans la chambre, il y a un évier.
2. Dans la salle à manger, il y a une table.
3. Dans le salon, il y a un tapis et une lampe.
4. Dans la salle de bain, il y a un frigo.
5. Dans la cuisine, il y a des placards.
6. Dans les toilettes, il y a une micro-onde.
7. Dans le couloir, il y a un fauteuil.

**Grammaire**

**15  La maison de Coralie**

*Coralie parle de sa maison à Julie. Écrivez **0** si la pièce que Coralie décrit (describes) est au rez-de-chausséeet **1** si c'est au premier étage.*

1. Mes parents et moi, on habite une maison charmante. Au rez-de-chaussée, il y a un grand couloir avec un tapis berbère et une table pour le téléphone.
2. À droite, il y a la cuisine et à gauche du couloir, il y a le salon et la salle de séjour.
3. Il y a aussi des W.C. avec un lavabo au fond du couloir.
4. La chambre de ma sœur Myriam est au premier étage à droite de ma chambre.
5. A côté de ma chambre, il y a aussi une salle de bains.
6. Au fond du couloir, il y a la chambre de mon frère Sébastien et le bureau de mon père. J'adore notre maison. Elle est fantastique!

## Leçon B

**Vocabulaire**

**2  À table!**

*La mère de Maxime explique comment mettre le couvert. Faites un dessin selon ses explications.*

1. Tu vas mettre la nappe sur la table.
2. Tu vas mettre quatre assiettes sur la table.
3. Tu vas mettre un couteau à droite de chaque assiette.
4. Tu vas mettre une fourchette à gauche de chaque assiette.
5. Tu vas mettre une cuiller au-dessus de chaque assiette.
6. Tu vas mettre un verre au-dessus et à droite de chaque cuiller.
7. Tu vas mettre une serviette sur chaque assiette.
8. Tu vas mettre le sel et le poivre sur la table.

**Grammaire**

**16  La recette de grand-mère**

*Écrivez les numéros 1-7 sur votre papier. Écoutez la grand-mère de Romane donner une recette d'une ratatouille. Choisissez l'illustration qui correspond à chaque phrase.*

1. D'abord, je mets de l'huile dans la poêle.
2. Tu mets un peu d'ail.
3. Puis, on met des oignons.
4. Ensuite, je mets des aubergines coupées en carrés.
5. Ensuite, tu mets les courgettes coupées en rondelles fines.
6. Beaucoup de cuisiniers mettent les tomates après les autres légumes.
7. Et ensuite, vous mettez du sel et du poivre. Voilà, c'est tout.

## Leçon C

**Vocabulaire**

**3  La chambre de Julien**

*Écrivez les lettres des illustrations qui représentent les meubles et les accessoires que Julien a dans sa chambre.*

Dans ma chambre, il y mon bureau rouge avec une chaise sous la fenêtre. Sur le bureau, il y a mon nouvel ordinateur. Il y a le clavier et la souris devant l'écran. J'ai une imprimante à droite du bureau à coté de mon armoire. Sur les murs, j'ai aussi une affiche de mon film préféré. Et toi, comment est ta chambre?

**Grammaire**

**15  La technologie: on peut...?**

*Écrivez les numéros 1-6 sur un papier. Écrivez **oui** si on peut faire les choses mentionnées ou **non**, si on ne peut pas les faire.*

1. Tu peux taper avec le mp3.
2. Mme Mercier peut télécharger un document avec son imprimante.
3. M. Laurent peut surfer sur Internet.
4. Vous pouvez cliquer avec la souris.
5. Ils peuvent démarrer l'ordinateur avec leur mp3.
6. Mlle Michel peut voir le site web sur l'écran.

## Évaluation

## A Évaluation de compréhension auditive

M. and Mme Petit are looking for an apartment. They have two children. Listen to their conversation with the real estate agent and read the sentences. Write **V** if the statement is **vrai** (true) or **F** if it is **faux** (false).

| | |
|---|---|
| L'agent immobilier: | Est-ce que vous préférez un appartement au rez-de chaussée ou au premier étage? |
| M. Petit: | Nous désirons un appartement au quatrième ou cinquième étage près d'une rue commerçante et d'une bouche de métro. |
| L'agent immobilier: | De combien de chambres avez-vous besoin? |
| Mme Petit: | Nous devons avoir trois chambres, quatre c'est mieux. |
| L'agent immobilier: | Et combien de salle de bains désirez-vous? |
| M. Petit: | Nous voulons deux salles de bains et deux W.C. Une avec baignoire et une douche pour nous, et une avec une douche pour les enfants. |
| L'agent immobilier: | Je pense avoir exactement ce que vous désirez. C'est un appartement avec quatre chambres, deux salles de bain, une cuisine moderne, et une salle à manger, un salon important, et un bureau. Il est au quatrième et dernier étage. Mais il n'y a pas de terrasse et seulement un W.C. séparé. Le marché est à côté le mercredi et le samedi, et vous pouvez être au métro dans cinq minutes. |
| M. et Mme Petit: | Pas de problème pour les toilettes. Ça a l'air super. Quand pouvons-nous le visiter? |
| L'agent immobilier: | Vous pouvez le voir mardi à 17h00? |
| M. et Mme Petit: | Oui, c'est parfait. À mardi alors. |

# Unité 8
## Leçon A

### Vocabulaire

### 4 Quel temps fait-il?

*Écrivez les numéros 1–6 sur votre papier. Écoutez la météo (weather forecast) des villes différentes. Ensuite, choisissez la lettre de l'illustration qui correspond à chaque description.*

1. Aujourd'hui, dimanche 20 mars, il pleut et il fait frais.
2. En ce beau jour de printemps, il fait frais et du soleil. La température est de 16 degrés.
3. Il fait mauvais et il fait du vent.
4. Sortez votre manteau! Il neige et il fait froid.
5. C'est l'été! Il fait beau et très chaud. Pourquoi pas nager?
6. Il ne fait pas froid mais il ne fait pas beau.

### Grammaire

### 13 Qu'est-ce que Malika fait?

*Écrivez les numéros 1–5 sur un papier. Écoutez et choisissez l'image qui correspond à chaque activité que Malika fait.*

1. Elle fait du shopping.
2. Elle fait une salade.
3. Elle fait ses devoirs.
4. Elle fait du vélo.
5. Elle fait une promenade avec une copine.

## Leçon B

### Vocabulaire

### 4 C'est où?

*Écrivez les numéros 1–7 sur un papier. Écoutez chaque description et écrivez la lettre de l'endroit (location) correspondant.*

1. Les touristes arrivent à l'aéroport Charles de Gaulle.
2. Ils choisissent un hôtel sur la rive gauche.
3. Ils prennent une photo du monument.
4. Ils font une promenade sur la grande avenue.
5. Ils vont au musée d'art.
6. Ils dînent à un restaurant algérien.
7. Ils vont à la gare pour aller à Lyon.

### Grammaire

### 13 Paris ou non?

*Si Brad parle de ses vacances de l'été dernier à Paris, écrivez P. S'il parle de sa vie à Boston maintenant, écrivez B.*

1. J'ai visité le monument à la place de la Concorde.
2. Nous faisons une promenade à Fort Point le dimanche.
3. On aime bien manger au restaurant Union Oyster.
4. Ma grand-mère n'a pas aimé le bateau-mouche.
5. Ma copine va acheter un manteau au centre commercial Roslindale.
6. On a fini notre visite au quartier Latin.
7. Le soir, nous avons attendu le bus devant l'arc de triomphe.
8. J'ai choisi de visiter La tour Eiffel notre dernier jour.

### Grammaire

### 19 Le weekend de Juliette

*Écrivez les numéros 1–8 sur votre papier. Écoutez la description de Juliette qui a passé le samedi dernier à Paris avec sa grand-mère. Ensuite, indiquez si chaque (each) phrase que vous entendez (hear) est **vraie** (true) ou **fausse** (false).*

Samedi, j'ai attendu ma grand-mère à la gare. Nous avons fait une promenade, puis nous avons mangé dans un restaurant italien. L'après-midi nous avons fait du shopping. Ma grand-mère m'a offert une belle robe bleue et un chapeau. Le soir, nous avons fait une promenade dans l'avenue des Champs-Élysées, la plus grande avenue de Paris. Là, on a pris une glace au café et on a discuté. Dimanche nous avons pris le petit déjeuner à l'hôtel.

1. Juliette a attendu sa grand-mère à l'aéroport.
2. Juliette et sa grand-mère ont nagé dans la Seine.
3. Elles ont mangé de la cuisine italienne.
4. Juliette a acheté une robe et un chapeau.
5. Elles ont fait une promenade sur les Champs-Élysées.
6. Le soir, elles ont vu un film.
7. Juliette a pris un dessert au café.
8. Dimanche elles ont pris des croissants à la pâtisserie.

## Leçon C

### Vocabulaire

### 4 Ça s'est passé quand?

*Écrivez les numéros 1–8 sur votre papier. Aujourd'hui, c'est samedi 17 mars. Écoutez les phrases et indiquez la date (en français) qui correspond à chaque description.*

1. Samedi dernier, j'ai visité le musée d'Orsay. J'ai adoré!

2. Hier soir, Alain et moi sommes allés à la cathédrale Notre-Dame.
3. Janine a passé une mauvaise journée mercredi dernier.
4. Nous sommes allés au cinéma hier après-midi.
5. Ils sont allés au jardin de Luxembourg dimanche dernier.
6. Je suis arrivée à la gare hier matin à 9h00.
7. Le weekend dernier, M. et Mme Gérard sont sortis au restaurant.
8. Je suis restée à l'hôtel lundi de la semaine dernière.

## Grammaire

## 15 Le passé ou le présent?

*Écrivez les numéros 1–8 sur votre papier. Écoutez les phrases et indiquez si chaque phrase est au passé composé (**PC**) ou au présent (**PRÉS**).*

1. Michelle est allée au Louvre avec son école la semaine dernière.
2. Jean est sorti avec des amis samedi soir.
3. Ils restent à l'hôtel.
4. Nathalie et Jasmine sont descendues du bus.
5. Je monte dans le métro.
6. Thibaut et moi, on est arrivé à la teuf à 21h00 heures.
7. Je rentre à deux heures du matin.
8. Nora et moi sommes revenu(e)s de Paris hier soir.

## Évaluation

## A Évaluation de compréhension auditive

Amélie went to Paris for Christmas vacation. Listen to her conversation with Pierre. Then, indicate if each sentence about her trip is **vrai** or **faux**.

| | |
|---|---|
| Pierre: | Alors, tes vacances à Paris? |
| Amélie: | C'était génial! J'ai adoré! Je suis allée avec mes parents et mon frère. Il a fait du soleil, mais il a aussi fait froid. |
| Pierre: | Ah bon. Quel âge a ton frère? |
| Amélie: | Il a 19 ans. Il a commencé ses études à l'université à Paris l'année dernière. |
| Pierre: | Alors, qu'est-ce que vous avez fait? |
| Amélie: | Oh, beaucoup. D'abord, nous avons visité trois grands musées. Nous sommes allés au Louvre, au Centre Pompidou, et au musée Grévin. |
| Pierre: | Tu as vu la *Joconde* de Léonard da Vinci? Elle est comment? |
| Amélie: | Bien sûr! Elle est très belle, mais très petite. Et tu ne peux pas prendre de photos. Moi, j'ai préféré le Centre Pompidou. |
| Pierre: | Où est le Louvre? |
| Amélie: | Le Louvre est près de la Seine. |
| Pierre: | Tu as pris le métro? |
| Amélie: | Oui, tous les jours. Quelle vue magnifique de Paris de la tour Eiffel! On a voulu aller manger au restaurant de la tour, mais c'est trop cher. |
| Pierre: | Tu as mangé des spécialités? |
| Amélie: | Pas vraiment, mais j'ai mangé beaucoup de pâtisseries. Les religieuses, c'est bon! |
| Pierre: | Vous avez fait une promenade aux Champs-Élysées? |
| Amélie: | Oui. Nous avons visité la place de la Concorde, l'arc de triomphe, et bien sûr, nous avons fait du shopping pour des souvenirs. |

Recorded statements:

1. Amélie a visité le Louvre, le Centre Pompidou, et le musée Grévin.
2. Elle a vu la *Joconde*.
3. Elle a préféré le Louvre comme musée d'art.
4. Amélie a pris le métro avec ses parents et son frère.
5. Amélie et sa famille ont mangé au restaurant de la tour Eiffel.

6. Elle a fait une promenade aux Champs-Élysées.
7. Amélie n'a pas acheté de souvenirs.
8. Amélie a passé de bonnes vacances.

## Bilan cumulatif

### Listening

**I.**

You will hear a short conversation. Select the reply that would come next. You will hear the conversation twice.

- Ah maman, hier Pascal et moi, nous avons....
- Oui, nous avons regardé....
- Dis, Pascal, laisse-moi finir!

**II.**

Listen to the conversation between a tourist and a French man. Select the best completion to each statement that follows.

Touriste:  S'il vous plaît, monsieur!
Français:  Oui, mademoiselle?
Touriste:  Pardon, excusez-moi, où est la bouche du métro le plus près d'ici?
Français:  Où désirez-vous aller, mademoiselle?
Touriste:  Je voudrais aller à la cathédrale de Notre-Dame.
Français:  Ah Paris et sa cathédrale! Et bien, le métro pour Notre-Dame est derrière vous.
Touriste:  Merci bien, monsieur!
Français:  Vous êtes touriste, mademoiselle?
Touriste:  Oui, c'est ma première fois dans la capitale.
Français:  Vous êtes anglaise? Américaine?
Touriste:  Non, je suis canadienne. Je suis de Montréal!
Français:  Ah, j'adore Montréal et les bateaux sur le fleuve Saint-Laurent.
Touriste:  Moi aussi, j'aime beaucoup Montréal, mais je préfère Paris—ses petits cafés, ses beaux monuments, ses musées, et ses cathédrales! Merci beaucoup, monsieur. Au revoir.

# Unité 9
## Leçon A

### Vocabulaire

### 3  Qu'est-ce que Jacques dit?

*Écrivez les numéros 1–10 sur votre papier. Écoutez Jacques et écrivez la lettre qui correspond à la partie du corps mentionné.*

1. Jacques  dit: "Touchez le nez."
2. Jacques  dit: "Touchez le cou."
3. Jacques  dit: "Touchez la main."
4. Jacques  dit: "Touchez la jambe."
5. Jacques  dit: "Touchez les yeux."
6. Jacques  dit: "Touchez le dos."
7. Jacques  dit: "Touchez le pied."
8. Jacques  dit: "Touchez l'estomac."
9. Jacques  dit: "Touchez la bouche."
10. Jacques  dit: "Touchez les doigts."

**Grammaire**

**11 Qu'est-ce qu'il faut faire pour être en forme?**

*Écrivez les numéros 1–10 sur votre papier. Écoutez chaque suggestion et écrivez **L** si elle est **logique** ou **I** si elle est **illogique**.*

1. Il faut faire du sport tous les jours.
2. Il ne faut pas manger de fruits et de légumes.
3. Il ne faut pas regarder la télévision six heures par jour.
4. Il faut manger beaucoup de chocolat pour maigrir.
5. Il faut jouer au basket au fitness.
6. Il faut faire une cure thermale pour se décontracter.
7. Il faut aller au supermarché quand on veut faire du sport.
8. Il ne faut pas prendre de l'eau.
9. Il ne faut pas porter des chaussures de sport pour faire du footing.
10. Il faut manger-bouger pour être en bonne santé.

## Leçon B

**Vocabulaire**

**5 On est malade!**

*Écrivez les numéros 1–9 sur votre papier. Écoutez chaque description et écrivez la lettre de l'image correspondante.*

1. Il a mal au dos.
2. Elle a mal aux oreilles.
3. Elle a mal à la gorge.
4. Il a mal à la tête.
5. Elle a un rhume.
6. Il a mal à la jambe.
7. Il a mal au bras.
8. Elle a mal au pied.
9. Elle a mal au ventre.

**Grammaire**

**12 Les bons conseils!**

*Écrivez les numéros 1–10 sur un papier. Écoutez chaque phrase et indiquez l'image qui correspond à la forme de l'impératif utilisée.*

1. Va chez le médecin quand tu as mal partout!
2. Faites de l'aérobic pour rester en bonne forme!
3. Mange des fruits et des légumes tous les jours!
4. Prenons le thème des accompagnateurs pour le devoir sur l'Afrique!
5. Allez au fitness pour faire un cours de yoga!
6. Regardons l'émission à la télé sur le Rwanda!
7. Allez voir le médecin si vous avez de la fièvre.
8. Finissons le cours de step et allons faire une cure thermale!
9. Quelle mauvaise mine! Demande des conseils à ta mère!
10. Dors bien!

## Leçon C

**Vocabulaire**

**6 Sauvons la planète!**

*Faites correspondre l'image avec la description pour indiquer ce que les Morin font pour sauvegarder l'environnement.*

1. La famille Morin habite dans une belle maison. Pour conserver l'énergie, ils ont installé des panneaux solaires sur le toit.

2. Monsieur Morin donne de l'argent pour aider les animaux en danger.
3. Marion recycle les papiers, les boîtes, et les bouteilles à la maison.
4. Christophe ne prend pas le bus pour aller à l'école. Il y va à pied.
5. La famille prend toujours leur voiture hybride quand ils font de longs voyages.
6. Pour aider à éliminer le dioxyde de carbone, Madame Morin circule à vélo.

**Grammaire**

**14 Engagé(e) ou non?**

*Écoutez les phrases suivantes et écrivez **E** si la personne est engagée et **NE** si la personne n'est pas engagée pour sauvegarder la planète.*

|  |  |
|---|---|
| **Modèle:** | -Tu veux recycler? |
|  | -Non, je ne veux pas recycler. |
| You write: | **NE** (pas engagé) |

1. -Pourquoi Marc ne veut-il pas acheter de canettes de coca?
   -Il n'aime pas recycler les boîtes d'aluminium.
2. -Qu'est-ce qu'on peut faire pour protéger les animaux des marées noires?
   -On ne peut rien faire.
3. -La ville de Lyon va-t-elle construire des éoliennes pour lutter contre la pollution?
   -Non, mais elle va construire des panneaux solaires sur le toit des usines.
4. -Ton père préfère acheter de l'engrais biologique ou de l'engrais chimique?
   -Il préfère acheter de l'engrais chimique parce que c'est moins cher.
5. -Est-ce que tu détestes circuler en voiture?
   -Non, mais j'aime mieux circuler en voiture hybride.
6. -Pourquoi est-ce qu'il faut aller à la conférence des Verts?
   -On désire s'engager à protéger les espaces verts dans les villes.

**Évaluation**

**A Évaluation de compréhension auditive**

Number from 1–12 on your paper. Then listen to the conversation between Anissa and Michel. Finally, indicate if each statement you hear is **vrai (V)** or **faux (F)**.

| | |
|---|---|
| Anissa: | Salut, Michel. Ça n'a pas l'air d'aller! Qu'est-ce que tu as? |
| Michel: | Oh, là là! Je ne sais pas. J'ai mal partout! |
| Anissa: | Tu as fait de l'exercice? |
| Michel: | Non, pas du tout. Je déteste faire de l'exercice. Je préfère regarder la télé ou surfer sur Internet. |
| Anissa: | À quelle heure est-ce que tu te couches? |
| Michel: | Normalement, vers 23h00. |
| Anissa: | Il faut dormir plus et, à mon avis, tu dois faire de l'exercice pour être en forme. Il faut faire du sport au moins trois ou quatre fois par semaine, bien manger, et boire beaucoup d'eau. |
| Michel: | Je déteste l'eau. Je préfère prendre du coca et j'aime trop manger des frites. |
| Anissa: | Voilà pourquoi tu as mauvaise mine. En plus, les boîtes de coca, c'est mauvais pour l'environnement. |
| Michel: | Mais je recycle. Ma famille s'engage à protéger l'environnement. On fait partie des Verts. On a même installé des panneaux solaires sur les toits de la maison. |
| Anissa: | Alors, mangez des produits bios! |
| Michel: | Mes parents et ma sœur préfèrent manger bio mais pas moi. Je n'aime pas les légumes. Aïe! J'ai mal au ventre et à la tête! J'ai des frissons aussi. |
| Anissa: | Et tu as de la fièvre. Peut-être que tu as la grippe. Je te conseille d'aller chez le médecin! |
| Michel: | Bonne idée! Je vais téléphoner maintenant. |

Recorded statements:

1. Michel est malade.
2. Michel a trop fait d'exercice.

3. Michel adore regarder la télé.
4. Anissa conseille à Michel de faire du sport.
5. Anissa pense que Michel va beaucoup dormir.
6. Anissa pense que Michel pollue avec les boîtes de coca.
7. Anissa pense que Michel a mauvaise mine.
8. Michel aime faire du sport et boire de l'eau.
9. La famille de Michel recycle.
10. Michel mange des produits bios.
11. Michel a très mal au dos.
12. Michel ne veut pas aller chez le médecin.

## Unité 10
### Leçon A

**Vocabulaire**

### 3 Ils viennent d'où au Québec?

*Écrivez les numéros 1–6 sur votre papier. Ensuite, écoutez les descriptions et choisissez la lettre de la ville qui correspond à chaque description.*

1. Cette ville, qui est située au sud-ouest de Rimouski, est la capitale du Québec.
2. Cette ville est située au sud de la ville de Québec et à l'est de Montréal.
3. C'est au nord de Québec sur le fleuve Saint-Laurent.
4. Cette ville est située entre Québec et Laval.
5. C'est entre Montréal et Trois-Rivières.
6. Cette grande ville est à l'ouest de Sherbrooke au bord du fleuve Saint-Laurent.

**Grammaire**

### 13 Quel pays habites-tu?

*Écrivez les numéros 1–8 sur votre papier. Ces personnes parlent du pays où elles habitent. Écoutez et écrivez la lettre qui correspond au continent où le pays ou la province est situé.*

1. Salut! Je m'appelle Koffi et j'habite à Abidjan en Côte-d'Ivoire.
2. Bonjour. Je suis Madame Abdou. J'habite à Bruxelles en Belgique.
3. Moi, c'est Rashid et j'habite à Alger en Algérie.
4. Je m'appelle Christine et j'habite à Los Angeles en Californie.
5. Je m'appelle Brian. J'habite à New York aux États-Unis.
6. Bonjour, je m'appelle Juliette et j'habite à Marseille en France.
7. Je suis Félix et j'habite à Montréal, au Canada.
8. Moi, c'est Demba. J'habite à Bamako au Mali.

### Leçon B

**Vocabulaire**

### 3 Les vacances à Québec!

*Annie parle de son voyage en train de Vancouver à Québec. Faites correspondre la phrase avec l'illustration.*

1. Pour aller chez ma cousine Armelle à Québec, je dois acheter un billet de train. C'est facile, je peux aussi l'acheter à la gare.
2. Heureusement, j'ai un siège confortable.
3. La voyageuse à côté de moi est très sympa.
4. À la gare, je regarde le tableau des arrivées et des départs.
5. Attention! Il faut composter mon billet!
6. Je vais prendre le déjeuner dans le wagon-restaurant du train.

## Grammaire

### 10 Le voyage de Julien!

*Écrivez les numéros 1–8 sur votre papier. Ensuite, écoutez l'histoire de Julien et indiquez si les phrases sont **vraies** (V) ou **fausses** (F).*

À la gare, Julien a composté son billet et ensuite est allé directement au wagon-restaurant. Il n'a rien trouvé, alors il a pris sa place. Normalement, Julien prend la voiture parce que c'est plus rapide. Il aime bien la voiture, mais en ville, il préfère faire du vélo! C'est sympa et moins polluer! Il fait du vélo tous les jours! Dans le train, Julien a regardé le paysage de la campagne. Les collines, les étangs, et les rivières sont très beaux! De la gare de Chenonceau, il est allé jusqu'au château à pied. Le château est très joli! C'est la première fois qu'il a visité un château de la Loire. Dans le train du retour, il a vu sa copine Aurélie. Ça alors, quelle coïncidence! Ils ont pris un café et ont parlé de leur visite du château.

Recorded statements:

1. Julien n'a jamais pris le train.
2. Il prend souvent sa voiture.
3. Il n'a rien mangé dans le train.
4. Il ne fait plus de vélo.
5. Il n'a rien vu par la fenêtre.
6. Il ne marche pas jusqu'à Chenonceau.
7. Il n'a jamais visité de châteaux avant sa visite à Chenonceau.
8. Il n'a vu personne pendant son voyage.

## Leçon C

### Vocabulaire

### 3 En vacances où?

*Écrivez les numéros 1–6 sur votre papier. Écoutez chaque description de vacances et choisissez la lettre du pays correspondant.*

A. l'Espagne    B. la France    C. la Suisse    D. la Belgique    E. l'Angleterre

1. -Salut, Eric. Tu as passé de bonnes vacances de printemps?
   -Salut, Marie. Super! Je suis allé dans les Alpes. J'ai fait du ski alpin et j'ai marché. Le paysage est magnifique! J'ai vu des cascades, et bien sûr de beaux lacs!
2. -Et toi, Cécile? Tu es allée où?
   -Je suis restée à la maison. Mais, j'ai fait beaucoup de choses. J'ai visité le musée du Louvre. J'ai traversé tout Paris à pied. Je suis allée à l'Opéra et j'ai fait des courses aux grands magasins avec une copine.
3. -Rahina, qu'est-ce que tu as fait pendant les vacances?
   -Je suis allée à Madrid pour voir ma famille. Je suis allée à la plage tous les jours. J'ai mangé de la paëlla, bien sûr!
4. -Salut, Johann, qu'est-ce que tu as fait pendant les vacances?
   -Moi? J'ai aidé mes grands-parents belges qui habitent à la campagne. Ils ont beaucoup d'animaux.
5. -Et toi, Karim? Qu'est-ce que tu as fait?
   -Je suis allé voir mes cousins anglais. Nous sommes restés dans un hôtel super au bord de la mer! Ensuite, on a traversé le pays en voiture.
6. -Et Gabrielle. Tu as aimé Genève? Qu'est-ce que tu y as fait?
   -Génial et super intéressant! J'ai visité la vieille ville et le musée de la Croix-Rouge. J'ai aussi fait du bateau sur le Lac Léman.

## 14 Qui est l'élève le plus...?

*Écoutez chaque description des personnes suivantes au superlatif et écrivez la lettre qui correspond à l'image la plus logique.*

1. Qui est l'élève la plus chic?
2. Qui est la plus petite élève?
3. Quel élève est le meilleur footballeur?
4. Qui est le plus grand élève?
5. Qui est l'élève le plus intelligent?
6. Qui est l'élève le plus bavard?

## Évaluation

### A Évaluation de compréhension auditive

*Écoutez Sandrine et Lucas décrire leur journée aux châteaux de la Loire. Choisissez la réponse appropriée.*

| | |
|---|---|
| Sandrine: | OK, il est 8h00. Nous avons le temps de visiter deux ou trois châteaux de la Loire aujourd'hui. |
| Lucas: | Ca dépend. On prend la voiture ou le bus? |
| Sandrine: | Pourquoi on ne fait pas de vélo? On peut faire de l'exercice et admirer la campagne. En plus, on peut s'arrêter quand on veut et peut-être faire un pique-nique au bord de la rivière! |
| Lucas: | D'accord, quel château on visite d'abord? |
| Sandrine: | Le plus grand des châteaux de la Loire, Chambord! |
| Lucas: | Tu as un plan pour y aller? |
| Sandrine: | Oui, regarde! C'est facile. Sur la route d'Orléans, on va tout droit. Le château est sur la droite. À gauche, il y a le village. |
| Lucas: | Oh! Regarde, il y a un bureau de poste et des cafés. En plus, on peut aller à Cheverny facilement après. |
| Sandrine: | Oui, c'est simple, on entre dans le village et on tourne à gauche et c'est tout droit. Tu es d'accord? |
| Lucas: | Oui, on peut faire Chambord et Cheverny et prendre le train pour retourner à la maison. |
| Sandrine: | Bonne idée, allons-y! |

## Bilan cumulatif

### Listening

**I.**

You will hear a short conversation. Select the reply that would come next. You will hear the conversation twice.

-Dis, Anne-Sophie! Tu as mauvaise mine!
-Oui, j'ai froid et j'ai très mal à la tête.
-Qu'est-ce que tu me conseilles, maman?

**II.**

Listen to the conversation. Select the best completion to each statement that follows.

| | |
|---|---|
| Mme Sanchez: | Bonjour, Monsieur Duris! |
| M. Duris: | Bonjour, Madame Sanchez! Comment allez-vous aujourd'hui? |
| Mme Sanchez: | Ah, pas très bien! Je suis très fatiguée, j'ai mal à la tête, à la gorge, et j'ai chaud! |
| M. Duris | Ah, madame, à mon avis vous êtes malade; il fait très froid aujourd'hui. Et puis, vous êtes très pâle ce matin. |
| Mme Sanchez: | Oh non, il ne faut pas rester comme ça! Bon, je dois aller chez le médecin. |
| M. Duris: | Bonne idée, Madame Sanchez! Et ne circulez pas à pied; le dioxyde de carbone, ce n'est pas bon pour vous! |
| Mme Sanchez: | Vous avez raison, Monsieur Duris! Je dois me protéger! Je vais prendre le train pour aller en ville! |

# Correlation of Common Core State Standards

| Common Core State Standards—ELA | Standards for Learning Languages | *T'es branché?* Level 1 |
|---|---|---|
| **Key Ideas and Details** | | |
| **Reading 1–3** | **Interpretive (Reading, Listening, Viewing)** | **Page Number** |
| 1. Read closely to determine what the text says explicitly and to make logical inferences from it; cite specific textual evidence when writing or speaking to support conclusions drawn from the text<br>2. Determine central ideas or themes of a text and analyze their development; summarize key supporting details and ideas<br>3. Analyze how and why individuals, events, or ideas develop and interact over the course of a text | Interpretive Communication (Standard 1.2) | 4, 5, 8, 13, 16, 19, 22, 23, 28, 36, 37, 41, 42, 43, 46, 52, 53, 56, 60, 72, 77, 81, 94, 96, 103, 111, 114, 119, 120, 126, 135, 138, 140, 143, 145, 153, 171, 182, 197, 198, 199, 207, 214, 215, 224, 235, 236, 253, 256, 263, 264, 265, 266, 280, 295, 299, 308, 313, 314, 317, 335, 342, 349, 356, 358, 361, 373, 376, 398, 401, 412, 415, 429, 431, 433, 437, 447, 454, 463, 475, 478, 488, 491, 503, 504, 505, 520, 531, 534, 547, 549, 559, 567 |
| | Cultures: Practices and Products (Standard 2.1 and 2.2) | 4, 5, 16, 22, 23, 24, 29, 31, 32, 35, 36, 37, 41, 42, 46, 55, 60, 72, 77, 81, 126, 128, 140, 143, 152, 153, 171, 182, 197, 198, 199, 208, 215, 224, 236, 253, 263, 264, 265, 266, 280, 295, 299, 313, 314, 317, 328, 335, 342, 349, 356, 358, 361, 376, 386, 398, 401, 412, 415, 429, 432, 433, 437, 446, 447, 451, 454, 463, 475, 478, 488, 491, 503, 504, 505, 520, 531, 534, 547, 549, 559, 567 |
| | Connections: Acquiring New Information (Standard 3.2) | 44, 106, 208, 266, 376, 433, 447, 464, 465, 475, 476, 478, 488, 549 |
| **Craft and Structure** | | |
| **Reading 4–6** | **Interpretive (Reading, Listening, Viewing)** | **Page Number** |
| 4. Interpret words and phrases as they are used in a text, including determining technical, connotative, and figurative meanings, and analyze how specific word choices shape meaning or tone<br>5. Analyze the structure of texts, including how specific sentences, paragraphs, and larger portions of the text relate to each other and the whole<br>6. Assess how point of view or purpose shapes the content and style of a text | Interpretive Communication (Standard 1.2) | 6, 7, 15, 57, 61, 65, 68, 69, 75, 86, 87, 89, 94, 102, 103, 108, 109, 110, 114, 115, 132, 133, 134, 136, 137, 139, 144, 147, 149, 152, 160, 164, 165, 172, 174, 178, 179, 180, 188, 190, 191, 194, 195, 203, 204, 207, 212, 220, 221, 227, 229, 231, 232, 233, 239, 241, 243, 244, 248, 249, 250, 258, 260, 261, 272, 276, 277, 284, 285, 287, 290, 291, 292, 293, 304, 305, 310, 311, 320, 323, 340-341, 350, 354, 355-356, 361, 364, 367, 371-372, 381, 392, 396-397, 404, 406, 409, 410, 411, 419-420, 423, 425, 430-431, 438-439, 443, 453, 460, 461, 467, 470, 471, 472, 479, 485, 486, 489, 496, 499, 510, 512, 516-517, 525, 529, 530, 531, 538, 544-545, 546, 554, 558, 566 |
| | Cultures: Practices and Products (Standards 2.1 and 2.2) | 6, 7, 12, 19, 26, 27, 54, 60, 69, 70, 71, 75, 86, 89, 110, 111, 112, 113, 122, 123, 124, 132, 134,146, 147, 148, 149, 166, 172, 173, 176, 181, 182, 189, 191, 193, 196, 203, 204, 205, 222, 223, 228, 234, 235, 240, 245, 247, 251, 252, 259, 260, 261, 262, 270, 278, 279, 284, 286, 294, 296, 297, 302, 303, 305, 306, 311, 312, 313, 320, 321, 322, 323, 324, 327, 332, 334, 336, 341, 342, 343, 344, 349, 350, 351, 357, 360, 361, 362, 363, 364, 373, 374, 375, 376, 382, 383, 385, 390, 398, 399, 405, 406, 407, 420, 421, 422, 423, 424, 426, 427, 431, 432, 440, 441, 443, 444, 461, 462, 466, 467, 468, 472, 473, 480, 481, 487, 499, 500, 501, 525, 526, 532, 533, 539, 540, 543, 546, 556, 568 |

| Common Core State Standards—ELA | Standards for Learning Languages | *T'es branché?* Level 1 |
|---|---|---|
| | Connections: Reinforce Other Disciplines (Standard 3.1) | 136, 462, 466, 472, 473, 558 |
| | Comparisons: Language (Standard 4.1) | 2, 9, 10, 19, 38, 46, 65, 115, 117, 128, 132, 133, 142, 149, 152, 153, 172, 175, 185, 188, 190, 203, 204, 226, 227, 239, 243, 258, 260, 284, 302, 304, 327, 347, 350, 359, 362, 365, 381, 404, 406, 439, 443, 467, 479, 496, 522, 539, 543, 551, 554 |
| | Comparisons: Cultures (Standard 4.2) | 9, 10, 38, 46, 82, 112, 113, 208, 350, 458, 468 |

## Integration of Knowledge and Ideas

| Reading 7–9 | Interpretive (Reading, Listening, Viewing) | Page Number |
|---|---|---|
| 7. Integrate and evaluate content presented in diverse formats and media, including visually and quantitatively, as well as in words<br>8. Delineate and evaluate the argument and specific claims in a text, including the validity of the reasoning as well as the relevance and sufficiency of the evidence<br>9. Analyze how two or more texts address similar themes or topics in order to build knowledge or to compare the approaches the authors take<br>10. Read and comprehend complex literary and informational texts independently and proficiently | Interpretive Communication (Standard 1.2) | 6, 7, 8, 14, 18, 25, 40, 52, 53, 82, 83, 127, 128, 129, 130, 141, 142, 152, 162, 168, 169, 170, 185, 186, 187, 200, 202, 206, 225, 226, 237, 254, 255, 265, 281, 282, 289, 299, 300, 315, 316, 318, 327, 346, 347, 348, 353, 359, 360, 377, 378, 379, 385, 387, 401, 402, 416, 434, 445, 446, 449, 454, 464, 465, 476, 477, 492, 493, 503, 518, 521, 522, 523, 528, 535, 541, 542, 550, 551, 552, 557, 558, 560 |
| | Cultures: Practices and Products (Standards 2.1 and 2.2) | 6, 7, 21, 47, 55, 58, 59, 60, 74, 78, 127, 128, 129, 141, 153, 168, 170, 186, 187, 201, 226, 237, 254, 255, 283, 301, 315, 316, 327, 346, 347, 348, 358, 359, 378, 379, 390, 401, 402, 416, 434, 435, 445, 446, 449, 454, 465, 477, 491, 492, 493, 502, 518, 541, 542, 551, 552 |
| | Connections: Reinforce Other Disciplines (Standard 3.1) | 21, 95, 185, 200, 237, 254, 255, 281, 282, 299, 300, 377, 387, 390, 413, 434, 445, 446, 449, 476, 491, 492, 493, 518, 522, 542, 550, 551, 552, 557, 559 |
| | Comparisons: Cultures (Standard 4.2) | 9, 20, 21, 33, 34, 39, 51, 57, 58, 59, 73, 74, 82, 83, 127, 128, 129, 141, 142, 153, 159, 169, 185, 186, 200, 208, 237, 254, 274, 281, 282, 300, 301, 316, 346, 347, 358, 359, 377, 387, 390, 394, 401, 402, 416, 417, 434, 464, 477, 492, 493, 522 |
| | Communities: Beyond the School Setting (Standard 5.1) | 237, 254, 255, 281, 299, 300, 307, 315, 346, 347, 359, 377, 464, 465, 476, 477, 492, 493, 502, 535, 542, 550, 551 |

## Range of Reading and Level of Text Complexity

| Reading 10 | Interpretive (Reading, Listening, Viewing) | Page Number |
|---|---|---|
| 10. Read and comprehend complex literary and informational texts independently and proficiently | Interpretive Communication (Standard 1.2) | 154, 197, 215, 226, 256, 263, 264, 267, 315, 316, 328, 329, 335, 345, 349, 387, 448, 454, 473, 494, 505, 536, 540, 559 |
| | Comparisons: Cultures (Standard 4.2) | 315, 328, 448, 538 |
| | Communities: Beyond the School Setting (Standard 5.1) | 494, 536, 559 |

| Common Core State Standards—ELA | Standards for Learning Languages | *T'es branché?* Level 1 |
|---|---|---|

## Text Types and Purposes

| Writing 1–3 | Presentational (Writing, Speaking, Visually Representing) | Page Number |
|---|---|---|
| 1. Write arguments to support claims in an analysis of substantive topics or texts using valid reasoning and relevant and sufficient evidence<br>2. Write informative/ explanatory texts to examine and convey complex ideas and information clearly and accurately through the effective selection, organization, and analysis of content<br>3. Write narratives to develop real or imagined experiences or events using effective technique, well-chosen details, and well-structured event sequences | **Presentational Communication (Standard 1.3)**<br>Present information, concepts, and ideas to an audience of listeners or readers on a variety of topics.<br>• Produce a variety of creative oral and written presentations (e.g. original story, personal narrative, script).<br>• Retell or summarize information in narrative form, demonstrating a consideration of audience.<br>• Create and give persuasive speeches and write persuasive essays.<br>• Produce expository writing. | 27, 42, 67, 75, 96, 97,101, 152, 154, 159, 192, 193, 201, 209, 213, 271, 287, 289, 308, 309, 332, 336, 384, 391, 429, 445, 450, 452, 473, 478, 480, 507, 543, 560, 568 |
| | **Comparisons: Language (Standard 4.1)**<br>Demonstrate understanding of the nature of language through comparisons of the language studied and one's own. | 86, 89, 289, 309, 473, 480, 507, 543 |

## Production and Distribution of Writing

| Writing 4–6 | Presentational (Writing, Speaking, Visually Representing) | Page Number |
|---|---|---|
| 4. Produce clear and coherent writing in which the development, organization, and style are appropriate to task, purpose, and audience<br>5. Develop and strengthen writing as needed by planning, revising, editing, rewriting, or trying a new approach<br>6. Use technology, including the Internet, to produce and publish writing and to interact and collaborate with others | **Presentational Communication (Standard 1.3)**<br>Present information, concepts, and ideas to an audience of listeners or readers on a variety of topics, knowing how, when, and why to say what to whom.<br>• Retell or summarize information in narrative form, demonstrating a consideration of audience.<br>• Self-edit written work for content, organization, and grammar. | 84, 94, 101, 159, 210, 211, 213, 216, 307, 319, 329, 387, 413, 445, 488, 495, 508, 557 |
| | **Cultures: Practices and Perspectives (Standard 2.1):**<br>Demonstrate an understanding of the relationship between the practices and perspectives of the cultures studied. | 11, 12, 17, 32, 35, 40, 47, 54, 62, 131, 136, 210, 211, 216, 257, 264, 261, 319, 326, 333, 417, 425, 445, 450, 484, 508, 510, 557 |
| | **Cultures: Products and Perspectives (Standard 2.2)**<br>Demonstrate an understanding of the relationship between the products and perspectives of the cultures studied. | 11, 25, 40, 211, 216, 261, 299, 307,319,326, 333, 445, 450 |
| | **Comparisons: Language (Standard 4.1)**<br>Demonstrate understanding of the nature of language through comparisons of the language studied and one's own. | 211, 329, 329, 558 |

| Common Core State Standards—ELA | Standards for Learning Languages | *T'es branché?* Level 1 |
|---|---|---|
| | **Communities: Beyond the School Setting (Standard 5.1)** Use the language both within and beyond the school setting. | 44, 98, 257, 271, 388, 488, 510, 550 |

## Research to Build and Present Knowledge

| Writing 7–9 | Presentational (Writing, Speaking, Visually Representing) | Page Number |
|---|---|---|
| 7. Conduct short as well as more sustained research projects based on focused questions, demonstrating understanding of the subject under investigation<br>8. Gather relevant information from multiple print and digital sources, assess the credibility and accuracy of each source, and integrate the information while avoiding plagiarism<br>9. Draw evidence from literary or informational texts to support analysis, reflection, and research | **Presentational Communication (Standard 1.3)** Present information, concepts, and ideas to an audience of listeners or readers on a variety of topics.<br>• Expound on familiar topics and those requiring research.<br>• Produce expository writing including researched reports.<br>• Use reference tools, acknowledge sources and cite them appropriately.<br>• Demonstrate an understanding of features of target culture communities (e.g. geographic, historical, artistic, social and/or political).<br>• Demonstrate knowledge and understanding of content across disciplines. | 14, 25, 42, 45, 60, 67, 73, 74, 80, 84, 85, 89, 93, 95, 98, 99, 125, 126, 142, 151, 157, 159, 202, 210, 211, 212, 225, 268, 269, 283, 307, 330, 332, 352, 387, 391, 408, 449, 493, 495, 498, 502, 510, 523, 524, 527, 528, 537, 541, 542, 552, 557, 561, 562 |
| | **Interpretive Communication (Standard 1.2)** Understand and interpret written and spoken language on a variety of topics. | 13, 30, 47, 90, 92, 97, 114, 115, 116, 125, 128, 202, 230, 268, 330, 380, 449, 495, 523, 524, 535, 537, 541, 542, 550, 553, 555, 561, 562, 563 |
| | **Cultures: Practices and Perspectives (Standard 2.1)** Demonstrate an understanding of the relationship between the practices and perspectives of cultures studied. | 13, 30, 42, 43, 45, 47, 56, 97, 98, 125, 128, 142, 144, 202, 225, 230, 269, 281, 282, 327, 332, 380, 385, 389, 418, 435, 449, 451, 464, 465, 466, 469, 474, 492, 493, 506, 522, 523, 524, 535, 536, 541, 542, 550, 552, 553, 562, 564 |
| | **Cultures: Products and Perspectives (Standard 2.2)** Demonstrate an understanding of the relationship between the products and perspectives of cultures studied. | 25, 47, 202, 269, 283, 332, 356, 389, 435, 449, 451, 469, 484, 527, 528, 541, 561, 562, 564 |
| | **Connections: Reinforce Other Disciplines (Standard 3.1)** Reinforce and further knowledge of other disciplines through the target language. | 225, 271, 330, 332, 387, 435, 449, 451, 493, 506, 509, 510, 523, 527, 528, 541, 561 |
| | **Connections: Acquiring New Information (Standard 3.2)** Acquire information and recognize the distinctive viewpoints that are only available through the target language and its cultures. | 225, 271, 283, 330, 332, 387, 449, 451, 493, 495, 506, 509, 510, 523, 542, 550, 561, 562 |
| | **Comparisons: Culture (Standard 4.2)** Demonstrate understanding | 100, 144, 151, 157, 202, 212, 225, 230, 269, 271, 330, 332, 382, 451, 493, 495, 509, 510, 523, 527 |

| Common Core State Standards—ELA | Standards for Learning Languages | *T'es branché?* Level 1 |
|---|---|---|

| Writing 10 | Presentational (Writing, Speaking, Visually Representing) | Page Number |
|---|---|---|
| 10. Write routinely over extended time frames (time for research, reflection, and revision) and shorter time frames (a single sitting or a day or two) for a range of tasks, purposes, and audiences | **Presentational Communication (Standard 1.3)** Present information, concepts, and ideas to an audience of listeners or readers on a variety of topics. <br>• Self-monitor and adjust language production. <br>• Self-edit written work for content, organization, and grammar. | 76, 80, 82, 83, 92, 93, 98, 101, 104, 138, 155, 157, 169, 170, 177, 181, 200, 206, 223, 228, 230, 271, 333, 368, 391, 443, 448, 450, 456, 503, 506, 511, 518, 560, 564, 565 |
| | **Cultures: Practices and Perspectives (Standard 2.1)** Demonstrate an understanding of the relationship between practices and perspectives of the cultures studied. | 60, 64, 79, 104, 135, 144, 155, 157, 158, 181, 183, 216, 226, 241, 242, 243, 244, 246, 262, 263, 286, 331, 344, 345, 370, 385, 391, 398, 441, 448, 450, 455, 506, 511, 518, 526 |
| | **Cultures: Products and Perspectives (Standard 2.2)** Demonstrate an understanding of the relationship between the products and perspectives of the cultures studied. | 60, 155, 166, 183, 331, 391, 448, 511 |

| Speaking and Listening 1–3 | Interpersonal (Speaking & Listening; Reading & Writing) | Page Number |
|---|---|---|
| 1. Prepare for and participate effectively in a range of conversations and collaborations with diverse partners, building on others' ideas and expressing their own clearly and persuasively <br> 2. Integrate and evaluate information presented in diverse media and formats, including visually, quantitatively, and orally <br> 3. Evaluate a speaker's point of view, reasoning, and use of evidence and rhetoric | **Interpersonal Communication (Standard 1.1)** Engage in conversations, provide and obtain information, express feelings and emotions, and exchange opinions. <br>• Engage in the oral exchange of ideas in formal and informal situations. <br>• Elicit information and clarify meaning by using a variety of strategies. <br>• State and support opinions in oral interactions. <br>• Self-monitor and adjust language production. <br>• Converse in ways that reflect knowledge of target culture communities (e.g., geographic, historical, artistic, social and/or political. | 4, 5, 6, 7, 8, 14, 18, 19, 21, 26, 27, 31, 36, 43, 46, 52, 53, 54, 59, 60, 63, 64, 65, 66, 67, 69, 70, 71, 72, 74, 75, 79, 80, 82, 83, 84, 86, 87, 88, 91, 92, 96, 98, 100, 103, 104, 114, 121, 131, 135, 139, 150, 152, 153, 157, 158, 159, 167, 173, 177, 183, 187, 190, 192, 196, 197, 198, 202, 206, 211, 226, 229, 230, 240, 242, 245, 246, 247, 257, 264, 278, 279, 285, 286, 287, 288, 295, 296, 297, 303, 305, 306, 307, 313, 319, 324, 325, 330, 331, 332, 336, 343, 344, 352, 357, 363, 367, 368, 369, 375, 378, 380, 383, 384, 388, 389, 390, 391, 399, 407, 417, 421, 424, 427, 428, 435, 437, 442, 450, 451, 456, 462, 469, 474, 482, 483, 489, 497, 508, 509, 510, 511, 519, 527, 528, 533, 536, 540, 541, 542, 548, 553, 555, 563, 564, 568 |
| | **Cultures: Practices and Perspectives (Standard 2.1)** Use appropriate verbal and non-verbal behavior in interpersonal communication. | 4, 5, 6, 7, 9, 10, 16, 17, 26, 29, 30, 38, 47, 56, 62, 66, 82, 136, 139, 142, 144, 150, 167, 174, 181, 182, 188, 196, 229, 257, 270, 279, 332, 352, 384, 414, 432, 442, 451, 482, 489, 497, 508, 511, 519, 527, 548, 564 |
| | **Cultures: Products and Perspectives (Standard 2.2)** Compare and contrast artifacts, themes, ideas, and perspectives across cultures. | 21, 23, 25, 32, 33, 34, 45, 51, 58, 59, 85, 114, 202, 212, 289, 296, 301, 316, 368, 389, 509, 564 |

| Common Core State Standards—ELA | Standards for Learning Languages | *T'es branché?* Level 1 |
|---|---|---|
| | **Connections: Acquiring New Information (Standard 3.2)** Use age-appropriate authentic sources to prepare for discussions. | 22, 44, 316, 529, 564 |
| | **Comparisons: Language (Standard 4.1)** Demonstrate an awareness of formal and informal language expressions in other languages and one's own. | 5, 9, 10, 16, 17,20, 26, 27, 46, 47, 63, 119, 257, 278, 527, 528, 553 |
| | **Communities: Lifelong Learning (Standard 5.2)** Establish and/or maintain interpersonal relations with speakers of the target language. | 257 |

## Presentation of Knowledge and Ideas

| Speaking and Listening 4–6 | Interpersonal (Speaking & Listening; Reading & Writing) | Page Number |
|---|---|---|
| 4. Present information, findings, and supporting evidence such that listeners can follow the line of reasoning and the organization, development, and style are appropriate to task, purpose, and audience 5. Make strategic use of digital media and visual displays of data to express information and enhance understanding of presentations 6. Adapt speech to a variety of contexts and communicative tasks, demonstrating command of formal English when indicated or appropriate | **Presentational Communication: (Standard 1.3)** Present information, concepts, and ideas to an audience of listeners or readers on a variety of topics. • Produce a variety of creative oral presentations (e.g. original story, personal narrative, speech, performance). • Retell or summarize information in narrative form, demonstrating a consideration of audience. • Create and give persuasive speeches. • Expound on familiar topics and those requiring research. • Self-monitor and adjust language production. • Use information about features of target culture communities (e.g. geographic, historical, artistic, social and/or political) in presentations. • Incorporate content across disciplines in presentations. | 19, 21, 40, 76, 91, 92, 93, 115-119, 120, 121, 151, 156, 159, 167, 206, 207, 212, 216, 246, 257, 331, 353, 368, 380, 389, 450, 456, 469, 508, 509, 528, 536, 542, 553 |
| | **Connections: Acquiring information (Standard 3.2)** Use age-appropriate authentic sources to prepare for discussions. | 331 |

# T'es branché? 1A

## Author

Toni Theisen

**With the collaboration of**
**Jacques Pécheur**

## Contributing Writers

**Caroline Busse**
Pasadena, CA

**Annie-Claude Motron**
Paris, France

**Nathalie E. Gaillot**
Lyon, France

**Virginie Pied**
Salt Lake City, UT

**Lynne I. Lipkind**
West Hartford, CT

**Ann Trinkaus**
Middletown, CT

**Todd Losié**
Detroit, MI

**Pamela M. Wesely**
Iowa City, IA

**Diana I. Moen**
St. Paul, MN

**EMC Publishing**

ST. PAUL

**Editorial Director:** Alejandro Vargas

**Developmental Editor:** Diana I. Moen

**Associate Editors:** Nathalie Gaillot, Patricia Teefy, Scott Homler

**Assistant Editor:** Kristina Merrick

**Director of Production:** Deanna Quinn

**Cover Designer:** Leslie Anderson

**Text Designers:** Diane Beasley Design, Leslie Anderson

**Illustrators:** Marty Harris; Patti Isaacs, Parrot Graphics; Katherine Knutson

**Production Specialists:** Leslie Anderson (lead), Jaana Bykonich, Ryan Hamner, Julie Johnston, Valerie King, Timothy W. Larson, Jack Ross, Sara Schmidt Boldon

**Copy Editor:** Mayanne Wright

**Proofreader:** Jamie Gleich Bryant

**Reviewers:** Sébastien De Clerck, Ojai, CA; Nicole Fandel, Acton, MA; Linda Mercier, Elizabethtown, PA; Gretchen Petrie, Medina, OH; Anne Marie Plante, Minneapolis, MN; Celeste Renza-Guren, Dallas, TX

Care has been taken to verify the accuracy of information presented in this book. However, the authors, editors, and publisher cannot accept responsibility for Web, e-mail, newsgroup, or chat room subject matter or content, or for consequences from application of the information in this book, and make no warranty, expressed or implied, with respect to its content.

**Trademarks:** Some of the product names and company names included in this book have been used for identification purposes only and may be trademarks or registered trade names of their respective manufacturers and sellers. The authors, editors, and publisher disclaim any affiliation, association, or connection with, or sponsorship or endorsement by, such owners.

**Credits:** Bridge Photo Credits, Photo Credits, Reading Credits, Art Credits, and Realia Credits follow the Index.

We have made every effort to trace the ownership of all copyrighted material and to secure permission from copyright holders. In the event of any question arising as to the use of any material, we will be pleased to make the necessary corrections in future printings. Thanks are due to the aforementioned authors, publishers, and agents for permission to use the materials indicated.

ISBN 978-0-82196-666-2
© 2014 by EMC Publishing, LLC
875 Montreal Way
St. Paul, MN 55102
Email: educate@emcp.com
Website: www.emcschool.com

Printed in the United States of America

22 21 20 19 18 17 16 15 14 13     1 2 3 4 5 6 7 8 9 10

# To the Student

**Bienvenue au monde de *T'es branché?*** Welcome to the world of ***T'es branché?*** As you learn French with this exciting and innovative series, you will enjoy many opportunities to explore contemporary life in the Francophone world through your textbook and supplemental materials, online research, and on-location videos filmed in France.

You are on a voyage of discovery. You will meet people from many French-speaking countries and find out what it is like to live there. You will gain knowledge of diverse cultures, traditions, history, and language that will make you travel-ready and multicultural.

From the first day of your apprenticeship at becoming a citizen of the world, you will communicate in French with your classmates, teachers, and other French-speaking teens around the world. You will become skilled at working with a partner, in a group, and at making presentations. You will realize that learning another language expands your horizons, develops your intellect, and prepares you to experience the rich and engaging world in which we live.

Why is it important to learn French? Did you know that...?

1. there are over 200 million people in the world in more than 50 countries on five continents who speak French
2. there are over 20 million French speakers nearby—win Canada, the Caribbean, South America, and even closer to home, in Louisiana, and New England
3. French is, either directly or indirectly, the means of communication of over a quarter of a billion people in Africa where it is the official language of 18 countries
4. French opens doors in Canada, the top trading partner of the United States
5. French is the Romance language most similar to English; about 30% of all English words can be traced to French, so learning French will improve your English-language skills
6. French is among the official languages of the United Nations, UNESCO, the International Monetary Fund, the International Labor Organization, the International Olympic Committee, the 31-member Council of Europe, the European Community, the International Red Cross, postal services around the world, the organization for African Unity, and the International Council of Sport Science and Physical Education (to name a few of the organizations)
7. a second language is often a college requirement and, through its connections to English, can boost your success at your studies
8. French gives you access to discoveries and prominent persons in the world of art, government, food, literature, architecture, science, medicine, technology, music, diplomacy, fashion, and cinema
9. French connects you to the history of the United States and the thousands of places whose names are derived from French

Whatever your personal reasons for learning French, have a good journey as you discover French language and culture!

**Bonne chance!** (*Good luck!*)

# Table of Contents

frites

# Les gens que je connais  217

# Administrative Map of France

# Map of Paris

CLICHY

LEVALLOIS-PERRET

Bd. Bessières

Av. de Clichy

Av. de St-Ouen

Boulevard Berthier

Bd Malesherbes

**Arche de la Défense**

Avenue Charles de Gaulle

NEUILLY-SUR-SEINE

Bd. G. St Or

17e

Bd des Batignolles

Gare Saint-Lazare

Av. de la Grande Armée

Bd Malesherbes

Bd

Haussmann

**Arc de Triomphe**

**Pl. Charles de Gaulle**

8e

Av. Foch

Bd Lannes

Av. Victor Hugo

Av. Kléber

**Avenue des Champs-Élysées**

**Place de la Concorde**

R. Royale

la Se

**Bois de Boulogne**

16e

Av. Bosquet

**Tour Eiffel**

Bd St-

**Champ de Mars**

**Invalides**

7e

Bd Suchet

**Statue de la liberté**

la Seine

Bd de Grenelle

Av. Émile Zola

Bd. Garibaldi

Bd Keplr

Rue de la Convention

15e

Bd Pasteur

Bd du Mont

Bd Exelmans

Avenue de Versailles

Rue de Vaugirard

**Gare Montparnasse**

Av. du Maine

Bvd

Victor

R. de Vouillé

BOULOGNE-BILLANCOURT

Bd Lefèbvre

Rue

ISSY-LES-MOULINEAUX

VANVES

Boulevard

Brune

MALAKOFF

MONTROUGE

0           1 Mile

0           1 Kilometer

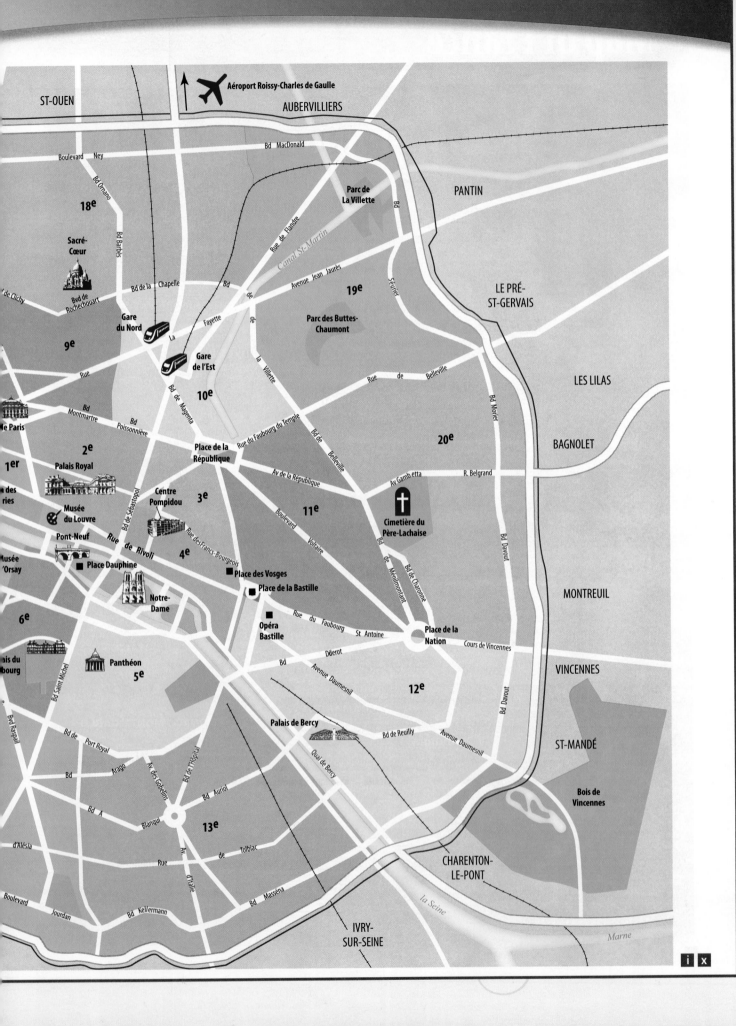

ST-OUEN

Aéroport Roissy-Charles de Gaulle

AUBERVILLIERS

Bd MacDonald

Boulevard Ney

Bd Ornano

18e

Sacré-
Cœur

Bd Barbès

PANTIN

Parc de
La Villette

Bd

LE PRÉ-
ST-GERVAIS

d de Clichy

Bvd de
Rochechouart

Bd de la Chapelle

Gare
du Nord

9e

Rue

Fayette

La

Avenue Jean Jaurès

Canal St-Martin

Rue de Flandre

de

19e

Parc des Buttes-
Chaumont

Séurier

LES LILAS

Gare
de l'Est

Bd de Magenta

10e

de

de la Villette

Rue

de

Belleville

Bd Morier

e Paris

Bd
Montmartre

Bd
Poissonnière

Bd

Rue du Faubourg du Temple

Place de la
République

20e

Bd de Belleville

Av Gambetta

R. Belgrand

BAGNOLET

2e

Palais Royal

Av de la République

11e

Cimetière du
Père-Lachaise

Bd Davout

1er

des
ries

Centre
Pompidou

Bd de Sébastopol

3e

Boulevard

Voltaire

Musée
du Louvre

Rue des Francs-Bourgeois

Pont-Neuf

Rue de Rivoli

4e

Place des Vosges

Bd de Ménilmontant

Bd de Charonne

MONTREUIL

Musée
'Orsay

Place Dauphine

Notre-
Dame

Place de la Bastille

Rue du Faubourg

St Antoine

Place de la
Nation

Cours de Vincennes

6e

Opéra
Bastille

Diderot

VINCENNES

ais du
bourg

Panthéon

Bd

Avenue Daumesnil

12e

5e

Bd Saint Michel

ST-MANDÉ

Bvd Raspail

Bd de

Port Royal

Palais de Bercy

Bd de Reuilly

Avenue Daumesnil

Bois de
Vincennes

Bd

Arago

Av des Gobelins

Bd de l'Hôpital

Bd Auriol

Quai de Bercy

d'Alésia

Bd A

Blanqui

13e

Av.

Rue

de

Tolbiac

d'Italie

CHARENTON-
LE-PONT

Boulevard

Jourdan

Bd Kellermann

Bd Masséna

la Seine

Marne

IVRY-
SUR-SEINE

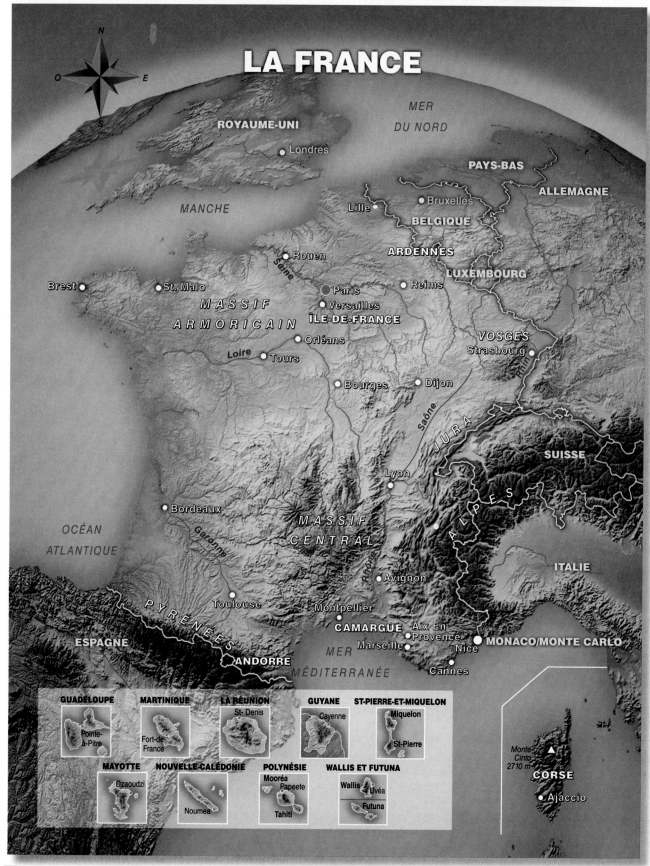

# 1 Bonjour, tout le monde !

*Rendez-vous à Nice !*

**Épisode 1:**
*La rentrée*

Go online
**EMC**Languages.net

un 0 0 1

## Essential Instruction

Ask your students to look at the video photos and try to determine what the first DVD episode will be about and the type of characters who will be in it.

1. Each unit opener spread will have a **Citation**, or quote, designed to connect students to the theme of the unit. The unit title **Bonjour, tout le monde!** was chosen because students will be introduced to people from throughout the francophone world in this unit and this textbook.
2. The francophone map shows two categories of French-speaking countries around the world: countries where French is the first language (purple) and countries where French is important (orange).
3. **À savoir** will present an interesting fact related to the content of the unit.

## Culture

**Perspectives: Information**

Open up a discussion about the notion of **francophonie** by asking where French is spoken in the Americas, the Caribbean, Africa, the Pacific, and the Far East. Pose some questions concerning the geographic location and distribution of francophone countries. Ask why French plays a greater role in the northwest of the African continent rather than in the east or south. Many francophone countries border the Atlantic. Is this significant? Have your students visited any of these French-speaking areas or know people from them?

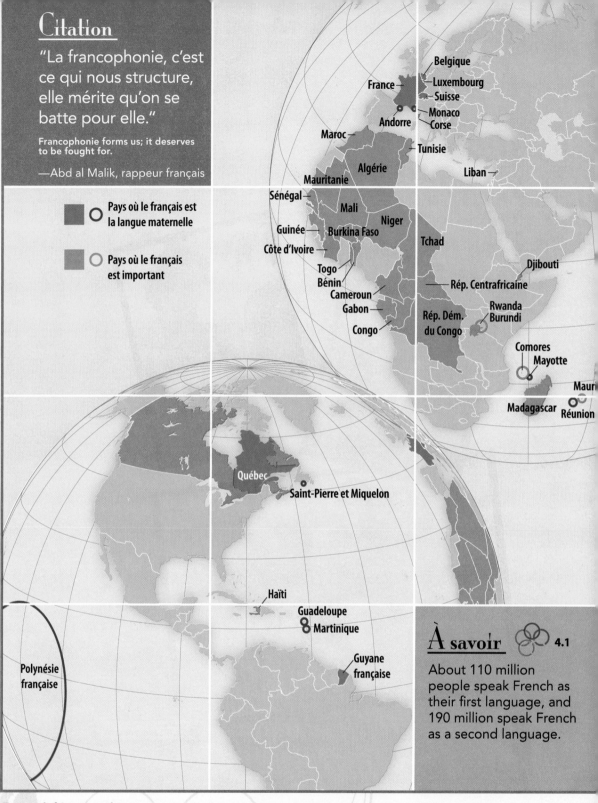

## Citation

"La francophonie, c'est ce qui nous structure, elle mérite qu'on se batte pour elle."

Francophonie forms us; it deserves to be fought for.

—Abd al Malik, rappeur français

Pays où le français est la langue maternelle

Pays où le français est important

## À savoir 4.1

About 110 million people speak French as their first language, and 190 million speak French as a second language.

**Essential Instruction**

1. Begin by asking students where French is spoken. Then point out those countries on the map. Draw attention to any countries they could not identify.
2. Help students discern that the purple countries are where French is the mother language and the orange countries are where French is important.
3. Ask if they know anyone who speaks French, and ask who in class has francophone origins.
4. Point out the student contract on p. 3. Ask students to read about what they will learn in this unit.
5. Ask students what language the rapper sings in (French). Tell them to look for the answer to the **Question centrale** as they move through the unit.
6. Show the relevant video clip from *Rendez-vous à Nice!*, Episode 1, and discuss the related question as a class.

# Unité 1

# Bonjour, tout le monde!

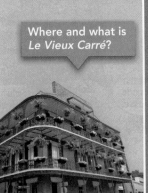

Where and what is *Le Vieux Carré*?

Question centrale

?

In what ways is learning another language beneficial?

Go online
EMCLanguages.net

**Who is the girl to the left of Jean-Charles?**

A. his girlfriend
B. his ex-girlfriend
C. a friend of his and Charlotte's

## Contrat de l'élève

**Leçon A** **I will be able to:**

>> introduce myself and others, respond to an introduction, tell my name.

>> use French greetings, recognize common first names from French-speaking countries, discuss locations where French is spoken in North America and who makes up the French-speaking population.

**Leçon B** **I will be able to:**

>> ask how things are going and tell how I am.

>> use expressions for saying good-bye, discuss **la rentrée** in France, and places in Europe and North Africa where French is spoken.

**Leçon C** **I will be able to:**

>> invite someone and accept or refuse an invitation.

>> discuss teens in France and where French is spoken in sub-Saharan Africa and the Caribbean.

trois 003

## Answers _____

The answer to the video question is C.

## Reference Desk

1. **The Question centrale** is designed to help frame students' learning around an essential question for the entire unit. Students will wrap up their ideas about the question in the section **Faisons le point!** in **Leçon C.**
2. The **Contrat de l'élève** shows students the core content of the unit that they must master: the functions, cultural topics, and elements of structure.
3. In each unit opener there will be a question, like this unit's question about **Le Vieux Carré**, that will be answered in one of the lesson's culture readings. Encourage your students to keep an eye out for the answer.
4. The image in the video viewer comes from this unit's DVD episode. Students can get an idea of what the episode will be about by reading the question. Students can review the video using their smartphones if they have software to scan the QR code.

## Differentiated Learning
### Decelerate
Review the names of the seven continents and tell students on which continents there are French speakers. Then proceed to name some specific locations.

### Accelerate
After students have looked at the map, ask them to infer why French is spoken in those regions (exploration, war, colonization).

## Learning Styles
### Kinesthetic Learners
Have kinesthetic learners come up and touch on a wall map the French-speaking countries that you name. Or, print blackline maps and have students color in the countries according to a key (where French is official language, etc.) and label with the country names in French.

## Reference Desk

1. In the **Vocabulaire actif** section, words and expressions that can be illustrated are introduced visually.
2. In Quebec, people use **bonjour** (*good day*) to say good-bye.
3. Students learn the abbreviations for **Monsieur** (**M.**), **Madame** (**Mme**), and **Mademoiselle** (**Mlle**) in the **Points de départ** (culture readings) of this lesson.
4. Use **Allô** only when answering the phone. **Un portable** is a cell phone, while **un téléphone fixe** is a landline.
5. Ask for student volunteers to model the use of **tu** vs. **vous** in introductions. Tell students to use **tu** with one person their age, younger, or with whom they are familiar, but **vous** when speaking to an adult or to two or more people.
6. **Et si je voulais dire…?** vocabulary is intended for students who want to proceed at a faster pace. This vocabulary is not included in the test or quiz banks, or in the end-of-unit or end-of-book vocabulary.

## Essential Instruction

1. On the first day of class, greet students with **Bonjour, tout le monde!** Write the expression on the board with its definition.
2. Explain to students that much of the vocabulary is presented visually at the beginning of the lesson so they should pay close attention to the pictures. They should know that the first unit is unique and that subsequent units will contain sections that this one does not.
3. Introduce yourself to the class in French, and model the sentences in **Pour la conversation**.
4. Then, ask students to greet and introduce themselves to at least two classmates and to ask them their names.
5. Read the list of names for pronunciation, and ask students to join in. Explain that some French boys' and girls' names are basically the same but that the addition of "e" changes the name to the feminine form, for example, **Michel→Michèle**, **René→Renée**.

## Pour la conversation

**H**ow do I introduce myself?

> **Je m'appelle** Sophie.
>
> *My name is Sophie.*

> **Je suis** Bruno.
>
> *I am Bruno.*

**H**ow do I respond to an introduction?

> **Bonjour!/Salut!**
>
> *Hello!/Hi!*

> **Enchanté(e).**
>
> *Delighted. (formal)*

**H**ow do I introduce someone else?

> **Je te/vous présente** Jean-Luc.
>
> *I'd like to introduce you to Jean-Luc.*

> **C'est** mon camarade de classe.
>
> *This is my classmate.*

**H**ow do I ask someone's name?

> **Tu t'appelles comment?**
>
> *What's your name?*

Je m'appelle Sandrine.

Je suis Saniyya.

Moi, c'est Evenye.

Je m'appelle Alexandre.

Je suis Khaled.

Moi, c'est Moussa.

### Les prénoms de filles

| | | |
|---|---|---|
| Aïcha* | Gabrielle | Nathalie |
| Alima** | Hamza* | Nayah** |
| Ambre | Héloïse | Nicole |
| Amélie | Inès | Noémie |
| Anaïs | Isabelle | Océane |
| Awa** | Juliette | Rahina** |
| Catherine | Justine | Romane |
| Charlotte | Laurence | Rosalie |
| Chloé | Lilou | Rose |
| Clara | Malika* | Sabrina |
| Coralie | Marianne | Sandrine |
| Élodie | Marie-Alix | Saniyya* |
| Émilie | Maude | Sarah |
| Emma | Mégane | Sophie |
| Evenye** | Méline | Stéphanie |
| Fatima* | Michèle | Valérie |
| Florence | Myriam* | Virginie |

### Les prénoms de garçons

| | | |
|---|---|---|
| Abdoulaye** | Jérémy | Nicolas |
| Alexandre | Justin | Noah |
| Alexis | Karim* | Olivier |
| Amidou** | Kemajou** | Paul |
| Amir* | Khaled* | Philippe |
| Antoine | Koffi** | Raoul |
| Augustin | Lamine** | Raphaël |
| Cédric | Louis | René |
| Clément | Lucas | Romain |
| David | Marc-Antoine | Salim* |
| Émile | Mathéo | Samuel |
| Étienne | Mathieu | Sébastien |
| Félix | Mathis | Simon |
| Gabriel | Mehdi* | Thomas |
| Guillaume | Michel | Timéo |
| Hugo | Moussa** | Vincent |
| Jean-Luc | Nasser* | Xavier |

\*prénoms d'origine arabe
\*\*prénoms d'origine africaine

**1  Les présentations**   1.2, 2.1

Listen to the following short introductions and decide if the person who is being introduced is male or female. Write **M** for male or **F** for female.

**2  Bonjour ou salut?**  1.2, 2.2

Say hello to the people pictured here. If they have a title, be sure to include it in your greeting.

1. Monsieur Rousset     2. Mademoiselle Serre

3. Martine     4. Bruno     5. Madame Tortevoie     6. Mademoiselle Vellard

*Communiquez!*

**3  Je te présente....**  1.1, 2.1, 2.2

**Interpersonal Communication**

Introduce each of the following people to your mother. Your partner will play the role of your mother. Follow the model. Throughout the text, the highlighted words are to let you know the part of the sentence you are replacing.

1. Monsieur Duharnais     2. Marie-France

**MODÈLE**  A: **Je te présente Mademoiselle Gaillot.**
B: **Enchantée!**

3. Madame Stein     4. Mademoiselle Sang     5. Jacques     6. Angèle

# Communiquez!

## 4 Un nouveau copain

### Interpersonal Communication

**1.1, 1.2**

Jean-Paul is introducing his new neighbor, Théo, to his friend Françoise. With two classmates, play the roles of the teens.

## 5 Les salutations

**2.1, 2.2**

Tell what you would say in each situation.

1. Miss Hadad, your neighbor, says hello.
2. Your classmate, Sylvie, wants to meet your mother.
3. You answer the phone.
4. Your parents want to know if your best friend, Karim, is Algerian.
5. You have just been introduced to a new male student, Amadou.
6. Someone asks your name.
7. Your neighbors, M. and Mme Meunier, greet you.
8. Your teacher, Mme Dubois, wants to meet your girlfriend.

---

# Communiquez!

## 6 À l'auberge de jeunesse

### Interpersonal Communication

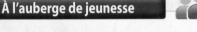

Two teens are checking in at the reception desk of a youth hostel in Quebec. With a partner, take turns playing the roles of the receptionist and each teen. Follow the model.

**1.1, 2.1, 2.2**

> **MODÈLE**
> A: **Tu t'appelles comment?**
> B: **Je m'appelle Salim,**
>    **Salim Belkassim.**
> A: **Français?**
> B: **Algérien.**

1. Sarah O'Connor    2. Bruno Dupont

Américaine?

Non, canadienne.

Leçon A | sept **007**

## Answers

**4** *Possible dialogue:*
  –Salut, Théo. Je te présente ma copine Françoise.
  –Bonjour, Françoise.
  –Bonjour, Théo.

**5**

1. Bonjour, Mademoiselle!
2. Sylvie, je te présente ma mère.
3. Allô, oui?
4. Oui, il est algérien.
5. Bonjour, Amadou!
6. Je m'appelle....
7. Bonjour, Monsieur et Madame Meunier!
8. Je vous présente ma copine, Sophie.

**6** *Answers will vary.*

### Expansion

Find out your students' backgrounds, and add these adjectives to **Activité 6**, for example, **mexicain(e)**, **chinois(e)**, and **japonais(e)**. Then, have students repeat the **Activité** using their own names.

### Communication

**Interpersonal: Paired Practice**
To familiarize students with greetings, do this **Activité** before listening to the recorded dialogues. Have students choose an identity—such as a cousin, teacher, store clerk, child—and write it on a piece of paper. Then divide the class in half and ask students to form two lines on either side of the classroom. All students hold up their signs. The first student in the line on one side greets the corresponding person in the opposite line (**Bonjour**, **Salut**, etc.). Next, these two students go to the back of the line. After everyone has had a turn and the line has re-formed, ask the students on the right to greet the students on the left. For variety, you could reverse or mix the order of the greeters' line.

## Multiple Intelligences
### Interpersonal
There are many different ways to organize your classroom to maximize productive interaction among students. Some **activités** work best in pairs, others in groups of three or four. Depending on the size and the maturity level of the class, you can experiment with different groupings. If you organize your classroom in semi-permanent "pods" of four students, you have pre-made groups for oral work without moving desks for every partner- or group-based **activité**.

## Answers

**7**

1. Camille greets Maxime by saying **Salut, Maxime!** Yasmine greets Mme Brochant by saying **Bonjour, Madame!** Camille is greeting a friend and can be informal, and Yasmine is greeting an adult, with whom she is more formal.
2. Camille introduces her friend Maxime to Julien.
3. Maxime's girlfriend is Yasmine. She is Algerian.
4. He would say **mon copain** instead of **ma copine**.
5. Yasmine is talking on the phone with Mme Brochant, Maxime's mother.
6. Yes, they know each other. Yasmine doesn't give her last name but is still recognized by Mme Brochant.
7. You can tell Maxime is at home because his mother calls out for him.

### Extension

The **animateur** is better with names than nationalities. He only gets one nationality right.

### Reference Desk

1. Usually there is one video dialogue, followed by a more advanced dialogue called **Extension** that is audio recorded only. Vocabulary from the video dialogue is included in the end-of-unit vocabulary and in assessments, whereas the new vocabulary in the **Extension** dialogue is not.
2. Camille, Maxime, Julien, and Yasmine are the four main characters who will be featured in the video dialogues. They live in Paris. Students will learn about their relationships, families, friends, interests, attitudes, and pastimes as the book progresses.

# Rencontres culturelles

## Salut!    1.2

Some teens in France are talking at the end of summer.

| | |
|---|---|
| Camille: | Salut, Maxime! |
| Maxime: | Ah! Salut, Camille. |
| Camille: | Je te présente Julien. |
| Maxime: | Salut, Julien. Et moi, je te présente Yasmine. |
| Camille: | Bonjour! |
| Julien: | C'est ta copine? |
| Maxime: | Oui, c'est ma copine. |
| Julien: | Elle est française? |
| Maxime: | Non, elle est algérienne. |

Maxime's mother is talking on the phone in their apartment.

| | |
|---|---|
| Mme Brochant: | Allô, oui? |
| Yasmine: | Bonjour, Madame! C'est Yasmine. |
| Mme Brochant: | Ah! Bonjour, Yasmine! |
| Yasmine: | Maxime est là? |
| Mme Brochant: | Oui, oui. Maxime! C'est ta copine! |

**7 Salut!**  1.1, 2.1, 2.2

*Répondez aux questions.*
(Answer the questions.)

1. How does Camille greet Maxime? How does Yasmine greet Mme Brochant? Why are these greetings different?
2. To whom does Camille introduce her friend?
3. Who is Maxime's girlfriend? What is her nationality?
4. What word would Maxime use for a friend if he were introducing a boy?
5. Who is talking on the phone?
6. Do they know each other? How can you tell?
7. Is Maxime at home? How do you know?

**0 0 8  huit** | Unité 1

### Extension  Bienvenue en France

A TV host, or **animateur**, is introducing the teen panel for an episode of the show **"Bienvenue en France."**

| | |
|---|---|
| Animateur: | Je vous présente mes invités: Tom, il est américain. |
| Tom: | Non, je suis canadien. |
| Animateur: | Et voici Luc. Luc, tu es.... |
| Luc: | Moi, je suis belge. |
| Animateur: | Yasmine, elle, elle est française. |
| Yasmine: | Ah! Non! Je suis algérienne! |
| Animateur: | Et toi Carlos? Tu es espagnol? |
| Carlos: | Oui, je suis espagnol. |
| Animateur: | Et voici Maria, l'Italienne. |
| Maria: | Ah! Non! Je suis portugaise! |

### Extension  Is the **animateur** better at remembering names or nationalities?

## Essential Instruction

1. Before listening to the recording of the video dialogue, review the difference between **Bonjour**, **Salut**, and **Allô**. All are greetings, but **Allô** is used only when answering the phone.
2. To ensure comprehension of the dialogues, first discuss the questions in **Activité 7** as a class, exploring different ways of addressing people.
3. Have the class listen to the dialogues, and then ask volunteers to read the roles.
4. Put students in small groups and ask them to read the cultural information on p. 9. Then ask them to summarize the information and share it with the whole class.

*Question centrale*

**?** In what ways is learning another language beneficial?

**RESOURCES**

📖 **Workbook 10–11**

### Saluts 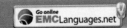 2.1, 4.1

People in France generally shake hands when they greet a person they don't know or a colleague at work. Their handshake consists of one up-and-down movement. They will also use the title (**M.**), (**Mme**), or (**Mlle**). When greeting a family member or friend, people usually kiss each other on the cheek. Depending on the region, they will give two, three, or even four kisses! These kisses are called **la bise**.

### Les prénoms les plus populaires  4.2

Many popular girls' names in France today end in the sound "ah" or "ee"—Clara, Emma, Léa, Amélie, and Lucie. Some common names, like Inès, come from other European cultures. Traditional names, such as Manon and Agnès, have also recently come back into fashion.

Popular boys' names today often end in the letter **o**—Léo, Théo, Hugo. Many also come from other European cultures. Two such names are Enzo (Italian) and Killian (Irish). Thomas, Mathias, and Lucas round out the list of today's top names. Although names of European origin remain the most popular, many French children have names from North or West Africa or Asia, such as Khaled, Youssopha, and Thi Loan.

What Francophone name would you choose?

🔍 **Search words: prénoms populaires**

### La Francophonie  4.2

❋ *Francophones d'ailleurs en France*

Five million foreign visitors and immigrants live in France out of a total of 66 million inhabitants. Many of them come from countries in North and sub-Saharan Africa that were once French colonies. When these people from places like Algeria, Morocco, Tunisia, Senegal, the Ivory Coast, Cameroon, Mali, and Madagascar arrived in France, they brought their cultural traditions with them. All over France, you can find restaurants serving ethnic cuisines, such as couscous from North Africa, and clothes made from the brightly colored fabrics of West Africa. The population of modern France can be called a mosaic of cultural diversity.

🔍 **Search words: immigration in france**

### COMPARAISONS  4.1

From the 18th century until 1993, there were strict regulations for naming a baby in France, limiting parents to traditional names. Today, however, the influence of other cultures can be seen in the names chosen for children. What are some popular names for boys and girls in the United States that come from other cultures?

*Couscous, a dish from North Africa, is served in many restaurants in France.*

Leçon A | neuf 0 0 9

**Reference Desk**

1. **Points de départ** is the section in which students read about francophone culture.
2. Culture readings are in English through **Unité 5**; they will be all in French beginning with **Unité 6**.
3. Most of the time two **bises** are given, especially in southern and eastern France, while in central France the number is normally three. However, in western France, four **bises** are common.
4. The **Comparaisons** box asks students to compare francophone culture with American culture. There will also be a **Comparaisons** box in the structure section.

---

**Differentiated Learning**

**Accelerate**

1. After students have listened to and/or watched the first part of the video dialogue, write out the lines on strips of paper. Place the first, fourth, seventh, and last sentences on the board. Ask students to come up and place the remaining lines in order. Ask two students to use their cell phones to act out the second part of the video dialogue.
2. For the **Extension** dialogue, ask for volunteers to play Tom, Luc, Yasmine, and Carlos while you play the **animateur** (*TV host*).

**Learning Styles**

**Visual Learners**

If your students are unfamiliar with couscous, you might bring in some raw couscous and explain that it is a hard-wheat semolina that is rolled into tiny balls of pasta and used in many African dishes, both savory and sweet. You might identify the equivalent starches used in Italian and Mexican cuisine.

Suggest that students might like to make some simple couscous dishes for their family or class. Online search words: couscous recipes

**8**

1. They kiss each other on the cheek (**la bise**).
2. There is only one up-and-down movement for the French handshake.
3. Léo and Enzo are names for boys; Léa and Manon are names for girls.
4. Five million foreign visitors and immigrants live in France.
5. Couscous is a popular dish of North-African origin.
6. About 80 percent of the population in Quebec speaks French.
7. The American states of Louisiana, Maine, New Hampshire, Vermont, Florida, and New York have French-speaking communities.

## Reference Desk

1. Find online and play a music video of **Beausoleil** (search words: **vidéo beausoleil**).
2. **Mon dico** is designed to teach some words about featured francophone culture.
3. The culture readings are followed by comprehension questions in **Unités 1 – 6** and **Activité**-based questions in **Unités 7 – 10**. **Perspectives** asks students to share their experiences and viewpoints; the **Perspectives** question is designed for students to examine different viewpoints in francophone cultures.

## Connections

**History**
Point out **Acadie** on a map of Canada. Have a student show where Louisiana is located. To review, ask students what brought the people from **Acadie** to Louisiana. For extra credit, ask students to research the full history of this displacement, how Henry Wadsworth Longfellow is connected to **Acadie** (his poem "Evangeline" is about two lovers who get separated during **le Grand Dérangement**), or why Mardi Gras is on Tuesday.

 **2.1, 4.1, 4.2**

✳ *Francophones en Amérique du Nord*

Did you know that French is widely spoken in parts of Canada and the United States? In fact, French is one of Canada's official languages, along with English. The province of Quebec has the largest Francophone community in Canada with around 80% of its population speaking French. The state of Louisiana also has French speakers, many of whom are descendents of the Acadians, who were forced to leave Canada in the 18th century. Many of them eventually settled in Louisiana where they became known as Cajuns. Their culture has greatly influenced Louisiana's language, food, and music. Other French-speaking groups in the United States include immigrants from Haiti who live largely in Miami and New York City and the descendants of Quebeckers who left home to work in the textile mills of Maine, New Hampshire, and Massachusetts.

🔍 **Search words: cajun louisiana**

### Mon dico Cajun

**Jambalaya:** *a spicy rice dish with meat or seafood*
**Zydeco:** *Cajun music with African-American influences*
**Mardi Gras:** *a public celebration on the last day before Lent*
**Le Vieux Carré:** *the French Quarter in New Orleans (literally, the "old" quarter)*
**Fais do do:** *a dancing party whose name comes from an expression meaning "Go to sleep"*

Beausoleil, a musical group specializing in Cajun music, is based in Lafayette, Louisiana.

**8 Questions culturelles**  **4.1, 4.2**

*Répondez aux questions.*

1. How do the French greet a family member or friend?
2. How does the French handshake differ from the American handshake?
3. Are Léa, Léo, Enzo, and Manon names for boys or for girls?
4. How many foreign visitors and immigrants live in France?
5. What is the name of a North African dish often served in France?
6. What percentage of the population living in Quebec speaks French?
7. Which American states have French-speaking communities?

### Perspectives

Do online research to find out information about immigration issues in France. Print an article or blog entry and bring it to class. Discuss how French attitudes about immigration compare to those in the United States.

Founded in 1608, after St. Augustine, Florida, and before New York, Quebec city is among North America's oldest cities.

## Essential Instruction

1. Looking at the pictures, ask students if they have traveled to Quebec, Louisiana, or other francophone regions. Ask for volunteers to locate these places on a wall map.
2. Put students in pairs to answer the **Questions culturelles**.
3. Look at the French ID card and ask the students how their school ID differs from this one. What are the advantages and disadvantages of a national ID vs. a school ID?
4. See **Copy Masters** ancillary for a blank copy of the **carte d'identité** in **Activité 9**.

## Du côté des médias

Most French citizens have a French national identity card, or **carte d'identité française**, although it is not mandatory to carry it. Not only do they use it to identify themselves, they can also use it instead of a passport for travel in some countries, such as those belonging to the European Union.

### 9 Carte d'identité française

 2.1, 2.2

Make a grid like the one that follows on a separate sheet of paper. Fill in the column in the middle with information from the **carte d'identité française**. Fill in the column on the right with your personal information, as if you were making your own **carte d'identité**.

| | | |
|---|---|---|
| Nom de famille/*Last name:* | | |
| Prénoms/*First names:* | | |
| Sexe/*Gender:* | | |
| Date de naissance/*Birthdate:* | | |
| Ville/*City:* | | |
| Département/*Department:* | | |

C'est ma carte d'identité.

**Answers** _____

**9**

**Nom de famille:** Agerone
**Prénoms:** Alexandre Michael Maxime
**Sexe:** M
**Date de naissance:** October 6, 1999
**Ville:** Villeneuve-Saint-Georges
**Département:** 94

### Reference Desk

1. Each culture reading section will be followed by at least one piece of realia from print sources or electronic media.
2. Ask your students what their parents and older brothers and sisters use when asked for identification.

### Expansion

This is a cross-curricular **activité** that uses math knowledge if students make the conversions using a formula. Suggest that students find and use an online metric converter to calculate Alexandre's height. Ask students to find their own height in meters.

**Learning Styles**
**Auditory Learners**
Play a short clip of Zydeco music from the Internet before students read the culture paragraph. Sound out how the word "Acadian" morphed into "Cajun."

Answers _____

**10**

1. The female names Camille, Anne-Marie, Chloé, and Christiane are similar to names in English.
2. The male names Michel, Vincent, and Alain are similar to names in English.
3. Fabien is the masculine name related to Fabienne.
4. T. Dubois' first name could be Thomas or Timéo.
5. S. Cassarin's first name could be Sabrina, Sandrine, Sarah, Sophie, or Stéphanie.
6. Michel Clémente is a man.
7. Jean-Paul has a compound first name.
8. Anne-Marie has a compound first name.
9. The last names Dubois, Ducôte, Dumont, and Duval indicate that their ancestors could have come from a wooded area, a coastal area, a mountainous area, or a valley.
10. The last names Charpentier, Chevalier, and Couturier indicate that their ancestors could have been carpenters, knights, or tailors.

### Expansion

Once students have learned the numbers 1 – 20 in **Unité 2**, **Leçon B**, you may want to come back to this page and have students give the phone numbers of people in the phone directory, for example: **–Quel est le numéro de téléphone de Michel Clémente? –C'est le 01.42.31.17.65.**

---

*Regardez l'annuaire (phonebook).*

**CASSARIN,** S.
  58 r Poissoniers 18ᵉ..............................01.46.06.72.02

**CHARPENTIER,** Camille
  56 quai Jemmapes 10ᵉ.........................01.42.06.57.14

**CHEVALIER,** Jean-Paul
  9 bd St. Denis 3ᵉ ................................01.42.72.65.11

**CHEYRE,** Hervé
  184 r Entrepreneurs 15ᵉ .....................01.45.78.21.29

**CLEMENTE,** Michel
  11 r Belleville 19ᵉ ..............................01.42.31.17.65

**COUTURIER,** Anne-Marie
  22 r Champ de Mars 7ᵉ.......................01.45.51.42.34

**DAULAUS,** Chloé
  15 r Moines 17ᵉ .................................01.42.28.22.83

**DE GIRY,** Fabienne
  45 r Linné 5ᵉ.....................................01.46.34.57.12

**DUBOIS,** T.
  1 r Charles Delescluze 11ᵉ...................01.48.05.20.43

**DUCOTE,** Vincent
  165 r Tobiac 13ᵉ ................................01.45.80.16.87

**DUMONT,** Alain
  35 bd Davout 20ᵉ...............................01.43.48.60.37

**DUVAL,** Christiane
  10 av Parmentier 11ᵉ .........................01.43.67.36.47

---

**10**   L'annuaire de Paris       **2.1, 2.2**

*Répondez aux questions. Pour les questions 9 et 10, consultez un dictionnaire français-anglais.* (Answer the questions. For questions 9 and 10, consult a French-English dictionary.)

1. Which female names are similar to names in English?
2. Which male names are similar to names in English?
3. What do you think is the masculine name related to "Fabienne"?
4. What could be the first name of T. Dubois if it's a man?
5. What could be the first name of S. Cassarin if it's a woman?
6. Is Michel Clémente a man or a woman?
7. Which man has a compound first name?
8. Which woman has a compound first name?
9. Which last names indicate an area the person's ancestors came from?
10. Which last names indicate a profession an ancestor had?

**Essential Instruction**

1. Discuss the questions in **Activité 10** as a whole class.
2. Model the pronunciation of several names, and then ask for volunteers to pronounce others.

# À vous la parole

## Communiquez!

**11** **Bulletin d'adhésion** ✿ 1.2, 2.1

### Interpretive Communication

The **Association Québec-France** is an organization dedicated to developing relationships between the people of Quebec and the people of France. Read the brochure. What two programs are being advertised?

Your teacher will give you a form for joining this organization. Fill it out and return it to him or her.

Un réseau unique de citoyens engagés dans la promotion de la relation franco-québécoise

**VENDANGES**
**jeunes de 18 à 35 ans**

Partez de 6 à 15 jours dans les vignobles et vivez cette expérience particulière de récolte du raisin et de découverte des régions de France!

*(septembre et octobre)*

**VOYAGE DÉCOUVERTE**
**adultes 35 ans et plus**

Ce programme est destiné aux adultes et permet aux participants de découvrir la France par l'accueil et la coopération des régionales de l'Association France-Québec.

*(à tous les deux ans)*

*Les conditions de participation aux programmes sont détaillées sur

**www.quebecfrance.qc.ca**

ASSOCIATION
Québec-France

Leçon A | treize **0 1 3**

## Differentiated Learning

### Adapt

1. Ask students to look at the photos to anticipate the content of the brochures.
2. Make a list of cognates to help students with comprehension.
3. Explain the concept of **faux amis** (*false cognates*) with the word **raisin** in the section **Vendanges**, and give the students **raisins secs**, the French word for raisins.
4. Ask how many students would like to participate in the **activité** described in **Vendanges**.

### RESOURCES

📖 **Communicative Activities**

**Answers** _____

**11** The form for students to fill out can be found in the **Copy Masters** ancillary. Some students may not feel comfortable providing the personal information that the form requests; offer the choice to complete the form with real or fictitious information.

### Reference Desk

1. In **À vous la parole**, students will engage in interpersonal, presentational, or interpretive communication, or a combination of these communication types.
2. Introduce students to the correct use of a French-English dictionary by reviewing with them the parts of speech and how they are identified in the dictionary (for example, v for verb, nm for a masculine noun and nf for a feminine noun). Then list on the board the words that are important to the brochure, such as **vendanges** and **raisin**. Challenge students to find the meanings of these words.

**Blended Instruction**
Consider using blended instruction, a combination of in-class learning and computer-mediated instruction or learning opportunities. Ask students to complete activities on the computer, using their cell or smartphone, or other emerging electronic technology. This will allow students to hone their tech skills and become more independent learners. Schedule routine Internet and e-book learning in class and in the lab.

## Communiquez!

**12** Je suis bénévole!

 1.1, 1.2

### Interpersonal Communication

You have volunteered to work on an international service project. Today you will meet two other team members from francophone locations around the world via live streaming on the Internet. Roleplay the following dialogue with two classmates. Switch roles to play all three parts.

- Greet team member A and introduce yourself. Then ask team member A's name.
- Team member A greets you and states his or her name. Then team member A introduces team member B.
- Greet team member B and respond to the introduction.
- Team member B responds.

Je m'appelle Jérémy.

## Communiquez!

**13** Les prénoms

1.3

### Presentational Communication

Choose a francophone name from the list of names in this lesson, from somewhere else in the textbook, or from the Internet. Research the meaning of the name online, using the key words below. Then create a large nametag with your name and a symbol of its meaning. Finally, introduce yourself to others in your group and explain the meaning of your name.

 **Search words: signification des prénoms**

Yasmine

### Essential Instruction

1. Present the French alphabet. Give each student an index card with a letter of the alphabet (including accent marks) written on it. Say a word for the class to spell collectively. The student holding the first letter says it aloud, the student holding the second letter says it aloud, and so on, until the word is spelled. Have students compete. Divide the class into two groups and give each a complete alphabet. Ask Team #1 to spell a word.

Give Team #2 a different word to spell. Award one point for each word spelled correctly. If a team fails to spell its word correctly, the other team gets a chance to spell the same word as well as its own word, thus earning two points.

2. Create a message and spell it out, for example, **J'adore mes élèves.** The first student to decode the letters earns a point.

3. Have students listen to **Activités B** and **C**.

# Prononciation  1.2

### A — L'alphabet français

*Repeat the phrases that come after the pronunciation of the letters. Think about rules of pronunciation as you say these easily recognizable words that are pronounced differently in French.*

| | | | |
|---|---|---|---|
| a = a | "a" comme Adam | n = enne | "n" comme novembre |
| b = bé | "b" comme Barbara | o = o | "o" comme orange |
| c = cé | "c" comme cinq | p = pé | "p" comme passeport |
| d = dé | "d" comme dollar | q = ku | "q" comme quatre |
| e = e | "e" comme Eugène | r = erre | "r" comme restaurant |
| f = effe | "f" comme famille | s = esse | "s" comme sport |
| g = gé | "g" comme girafe | t = té | "t" comme télévision |
| h = hache | "h" comme hamburger | u = u | "u" comme ultra |
| i = I | "i" comme immense | v = vé | "v" comme violet |
| j = ji | "j" comme jean | w = double vé | "w" comme Washington |
| k = ka | "k" comme ketchup | x = iks | "x" comme Xavier |
| l = elle | "l" comme latin | y = i grec | "y" comme Yasmine |
| m = emme | "m" comme moderne | z = zède | "z" comme zéro |

### B — Les accents

*Repeat each accented letter and word.*

| | |
|---|---|
| é = e accent aigu | bébé |
| è = e accent grave | première |
| ë = e tréma | Raphaël |
| ô = o accent circonflexe | hôtel |
| ç = c cédille | Ça va? |

### C — Les prénoms de filles

*Repeat the girls' names you hear that end in an unpronounced "e."*

Amélie
Mégane
Nathalie
Stéphanie
Marianne
Virginie

### D — Les sons nasaux

*Repeat the words with nasal vowels, then the words with non-nasal vowels.*

Nasal vowels: Justin / copain / américain / canadien
Non-nasal vowels: Justine / copine / américaine / canadienne

### E — Oui ou non?

*Write **oui** if the end of the name you hear is nasal or **non** if the end of the name is not nasal.*

**Differentiated Learning**
**Accelerate**
You may want to get your advanced students interested in etymology: the study of the meaning of words based on their Greek and Latin roots. Explain that the French word **bénévole** on p. 14 and the English word "benevolent" are both based on the Latin root meaning "good." Ask students to watch for more related words.

---

## Answers

**E**
1. non
2. non
3. oui
4. non
5. oui

## Reference Desk

1. Students learn how to pronounce the alphabet in French, which facilitates spelling. Have students practice the French pronunciation of the words on the list; point out English cognates.
2. **Activité B:** Learning the accents introduces students to some common French sounds or phonemes.
3. **Activité D:** Point out that the vowel is nasal and the end consonant is silent if there is no final "e." If there is a final "e," the consonant is pronounced and the vowel is not nasal.

## Expansion

**Activité A**
1. Have students design bingo cards with a French name in each square. Ask a student to spell out the names only. The winner spells back the names on the card.
2. Have each student choose and spell the name of a person or street from the **annuaire** on p. 12. Another student responds with the corresponding street or name of the person associated with the address.

**Activité B**
Introduce accents by spelling any French names with accents.

**Activité C**
Ask a student to spell any name from the list on p. 5, while others guess the name.

### Reference Desk

**Students** learned **Salut!**, meaning "hello," in **Leçon A**.

### TPR

1. Play **Jacques a dit** (Simon says) to practice gestures associated with **Leçon B** vocabulary. Say, **"Jacques a dit"** with an expression such as **Pas mal**. Students must respond with the correct gesture or they are eliminated.
2. Have students cut out four circles large enough to cover their face and draw facial features on each one to illustrate these expressions: **Très bien**, **Pas mal**, **Comme ci, comme ça**, and **Mal**.

### Game

**Telephone**
To practice answering the question **Ça va?**, divide students into two or three teams. Whisper one possible answer to the question to the first person on each team who in turn whispers it to the next person, and so on until the end of the line.

### Critical Thinking

**Application**
Challenge students to use their French with other French speakers in the community (older students, teachers, neighbors, etc.). Students can assess the experience and their comfort level in a Culture Journal, a notebook where they log French expressions and reflect on culture topics.

 **Leçon B**

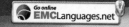

# Vocabulaire actif

## Ça va?

1.2, 2.1, 2.2, 4.1

**Et si je voulais dire...?**

| | |
|---|---|
| **Ça roule?** | *What's up? How are you?* |
| **Oui, j'ai la pêche.** | *Yes, I'm full of energy.* |
| **Ça va fort.** | *I'm doing great.* |
| **Plus ou moins.** | *More or less.* |
| **Bonne journée!** | *Have a good day!* |

016 seize | Unité 1

### Essential Instruction

1. Before students view the photos and/or hear the vocabulary, act it out using the French gestures illustrated. Ask the students what **Ça va?** and the responses probably mean. Then play the audio. Have students repeat each response numerous times, explaining that repetition is crucial to learning how to pronounce and remember new words.

2. Have the class ask you how you are. Tell students to show the gesture as you respond to **Ça va?** Then reverse the process by showing the gesture and having the class provide the French response.

3. Have students read and listen to **Pour la conversation**. Explain formal versus informal conversation illustrated by **et toi/vous**.

# Pour la conversation

**H**ow do I ask how someone is?

> **Ça va?**
>
> *How's it going? [informal]*

> **Comment allez-vous?**
>
> *How are you? [formal]*

**H**ow do I express how I am doing?

> **Très bien, et toi/vous?**
>
> *Very well, and you?*

---

**1** **Bonjour ou au revoir**  1.2

Imagine you are on the streets of Paris listening to greetings and good-byes. Write **H** if the speaker says hello or **G** if the speaker says good-bye.

---

**2** **Formel ou informel?**  2.1, 4.1

On a separate sheet of paper, draw a graphic organizer like the one below. Write each word or expression in the appropriate part of the diagram to indicate whether it is usually formal, informal, or neutral (neither formal nor informal).

À bientôt!
Il est français?
Comme ci, comme ça.
Et toi?
Salut!
Madame
Je te présente….
Comment allez-vous?

Monsieur
Au revoir!
Je vous présente….
Très bien.
Mademoiselle
Et vous?
Je m'appelle….
Ça va mal.

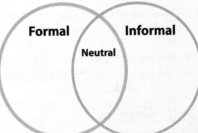

**Formal**   **Informal**

**Neutral**

---

**3** **Phrases brouillées**  2.1

Unscramble the words and punctuation marks below to write logical sentences.

1. va? / Bonjour, / Ça / Céline!
2. toi? / Pas / et / très / bien,
3. bien? / Yasmine! / Ça / Salut, / va
4. ci / ça. / Comme / Au / comme / revoir!

Ça va pas mal?

Leçon B | dix-sept **0 1 7**

---

**Reference Desk**

In this lesson, students practice how to formally and informally ask how someone is, and how to respond to the question.

**Communication**

**Interpersonal: Paired Practice**
To help students distinguish between when to use **Ça va?** and **Comment allez-vous?**, have pairs choose an identity, such as a cousin, mail carrier, teacher, convenience store clerk, or child. Students ask each other how they're doing, for example:

A: (teen) **Bonjour, Monsieur. Comment allez-vous?**

B: (elderly neighbor) **Très bien, et toi?**

A: **Comme ci, comme ça.**

---

**Differentiated Learning**
**Accelerate**
Ask students to create a dialogue based on the vocabulary in **Leçon B** on p. 16 and the functions in **Pour la conversation** on p. 17.

**Special Needs Students**
**Dyslexia**
Spelling in French can be challenging for some students, so instruct them to carefully copy the **Vocabulaire actif** onto index cards. Have them check spelling in small groups and rewrite any mis-spelled vocabulary twice on the other side of the card. Have all students pronounce each card within their group. Point out that both pronunciation and spelling require much practice and that they will have many opportunities to improve both skills.

# Communiquez!

**4** **Ça va?**  1.1, 1.2

## Interpersonal Communication

Ask how things are going for your partner, who will respond based on the expression. Then repeat the activity. One of you plays the role of a student and the other the role of your teacher.

1.

2.

3.

**5** **Ça va très bien? Non!**  1.1, 1.2

Respond to each situation using **Pas mal**; **Comme ci, comme ça**; **Pas très bien**; or **Ça va mal**.

1. Someone you really like has "defriended" you on your social network.
2. You got an A- on your math quiz.
3. It's the last day of vacation, and tomorrow you have to go back to school.
4. You are having an ordinary day with no good surprises and no bad disappointments.
5. You are a devoted basketball player, but your team lost the game, and you are not going to state.
6. It's Saturday morning and before you can meet your friends, you have to spend an hour cleaning up the garage.
7. You have a coupon for a free sandwich at a fast-food restaurant.
8. At the amusement park, you have to stand in line for an hour for the rollercoaster, but the wait was almost worth it.
9. You are developing a sore throat.

Ça va mal!

## Essential Instruction

1. After students read silently the **Ça va?** dialogue on p. 19, explain the meaning of any words they don't understand.
2. Play the dialogue twice, then have the students role-play it several times, changing roles each time.
3. Split the class into two groups (**Maxime** and **Tom**) to read aloud the dialogue as a chorus. Have a volunteer read the teacher's role. Then, have the groups switch roles.
4. Ask for volunteer groups to role-play the dialogue for the class.
5. Now that students are familiar with the dialogue, they may want to see and hear the dialogue video one more time.

# Rencontres culturelles

## Ça va?     1.2

On a day in September, two boys meet in the courtyard at school.

Maxime: Salut, Tom!
Tom: Salut, Maxime!
Maxime: Ça va?
Tom: Très bien, et toi?
Maxime: Pas mal.
Tom: Et avec ta copine Yasmine, ça va?
Maxime: Très bien... top!

(*A teacher, or* professeur, *approaches.*)

Prof: Ça va, Maxime?
Maxime: Bien, bien! Et vous, Monsieur, comment allez-vous?
Prof: Pas trop mal, pas trop mal.

(*The teacher leaves.*)

Tom: Eh bien, à bientôt.
Maxime: C'est ça... on s'appelle.

### 6 Ça va?  2.1, 2.2

*Répondez aux questions.*

1. How does Maxime ask Tom how things are going? How does Maxime ask his teacher how things are going?
2. Maxime says the English word "top." How does he feel things are going with his girlfriend?
3. Are things going best for Maxime, Tom, or the teacher?
4. What do you think Maxime means when he says **on s'appelle**? In what other expression have you heard the French word **appelle**?

### Extension    Devant l'ascenseur

Two women run into each other in front of the elevator of their apartment building.

Mme Perrin: Bonjour, vous allez bien?
Mme Rivoire: Oui, très bien, et vous?
Mme Perrin: Ça va comme ci, comme ça.
Mme Rivoire: Votre mari va bien?
Mme Perrin: Pas mal....
Mme Rivoire: Bon eh bien, bonne journée.
Mme Perrin: Bonne journée, au revoir.
Mme Rivoire: Oui. Merci. Sans doute à demain.

### Extension    How can you tell the women aren't close friends?

Leçon B | dix-neuf **0 1 9**

## RESOURCES

 **Dialogue Video**

### Answers _____

**6**

1. Maxime asks Tom "**Ça va?**" He asks his teacher the same thing more formally: "**Comment allez-vous?**"
2. Things couldn't be better.
3. Things are going best for Tom, who says "**Très bien.**"
4. **On s'appelle** means Maxime and Tom will call each other, probably on their **portable**. The root of this expression is also in **Tu t'appelles comment?**, which is used when asking what someone is called or named.

### Extension

The female neighbors aren't close friends because they use **vous** and **votre**.

### Reference Desk

1. Ask students what a synonym for **Très bien** is (**Top**).
2. Ask students where else they have seen the root word **appelle** (**Comment tu t'appelles?**) to help them see the relationship between "What are you called?" and "to call" on the phone.

## Differentiated Learning

### Expand
Ask students to create original exchanges based on the **Ça va?** dialogue.

### Decelerate
Play the video without sound to provide the context for the dialogue **Ça va?** Ask students to answer these questions: Where are the teens? Which person joins them? Which person leaves?

## Multiple Intelligences

### Logical-Mathematical
Read aloud the **Extension** dialogue and review the meaning and pronunciation of new words. Ask students to carefully copy the dialogue but to leave out a word in each line, replacing it with a blank. Students exchange the text with a partner who tries to complete the dialogue with the missing words. Students could also copy the dialogue but change several lines so they contain different words. Then have partners read aloud the re-worked dialogue.

**0 1 9**

**RESOURCES**

Workbook 17–18

**Reference Desk**

Students will have the opportunity to learn in depth about francophone countries throughout the ***T'es branché?*** series, for example in **Points de départ**.

# Points de départ

Go online EMCLanguages.net

Question centrale: In what ways is learning another language beneficial?

## C'est la rentrée! 4.2

At the beginning of September, French students go back to school. In the weeks leading up to **la rentrée**, students go shopping for a new book bag or backpack, new clothes, and school supplies. On the first day back, they find out who is in their class and who their teachers will be. In France, students usually stay with the same group of classmates for most of their courses. Between classes and before and after school, students often gather in the courtyard (**la cour**) to see old friends and make new ones.

Many French teens love to play soccer.

## Comment dit-on *au revoir?* 4.1

Teens often use **Salut** to mean **Au revoir**. Other options are **Bye** and **Ciao**, from Italian. Do you know which European languages use **Adiós**, **Arrivederci**, and **Auf Wiedersehen** to say good-bye?

**COMPARAISONS**

In what ways are schools in France different from those in the United States? Would you like to see these changes made to American schools?

## La Francophonie 4.2

### *En Europe*

In Europe, there are 75 million French speakers. They live in France, Switzerland, Belgium, and Luxembourg, as well as the principalities of Monaco and Andorra. France has just one official language, French. Switzerland has four official languages: French, German, Italian, and Romansch. Belgium and Luxembourg each have three. Belgians speak Flemish, French, and German. The people of Luxembourg speak French, German, or Luxembourgish. Only French is spoken in Monaco while both French and Spanish are spoken in Andorra.

Belgium's capital, **Bruxelles** (*Brussels*), is the seat of the European Parliament.



## Essential Instruction

1. When discussing **C'est la rentrée**, add any extra information you may know about French public education, such as the grading scale (0 – 20 instead of letter grades), the grade levels (11 – 0 instead of 1 – 12), the long lunch break, **le bac**, and the fact that French students have a different schedule each day of the week.
2. Then have students do the **Comparaisons** activity as a class or in small groups.
3. For the francophone countries mentioned on these pages, have each group of three or four create a three-column chart with categories such as: famous people, food, sports, movies. Ask groups to brainstorm items in each category, for example, "Belgian food: chocolate, waffles." Then have them share results with other groups or with the class. You could make this **activité** a contest, declaring the group that comes up with the most items the winner.

✳ *En Afrique du Nord*  **4.2**

In Algeria, Morocco, and Tunisia, all former colonies of France, French remains the preferred language in many political, intellectual, commercial, and artistic circles. While Arabic is the official language in these countries, some consider French the **langue d'ouverture**, a language that can lead to opportunities for multiculturalism (promotion of multiple cultures) and success. A new generation of creative writers, musicians, and filmmakers from these countries enrich cultural relations by bringing together French and ethnic traditions in their art.

Marrakech is a destination favored by many French tourists.

**7 | Questions culturelles**  **1.1, 2.1, 2.2, 3.1**

*Répondez aux questions.*

1. When do French teens go back to school?
2. What do French students use to carry their schoolwork and books?
3. What are three ways to say good-bye other than **Au revoir**?
4. Approximately how many people speak French in Europe?
5. In which European countries do people speak French?
6. Which Francophone countries in Europe have more than one official language?
7. Monaco and Andorra are not countries. What are they?
8. Which groups of people tend to speak French in North Africa?
9. In which areas of artistic expression have French-speaking North Africans made an important contribution?

**À discuter**

In what ways can a **langue d'ouverture** lead to "multiculturalism and success"? What do multiculturalism and success mean to you?

Today, Monaco is most famous for its sporting and cultural events, its beautiful resorts, and its lavish lifestyle.

**7**
1. French students go back to school in early September.
2. French students carry their school materials in either book bags or backpacks.
3. **Salut**, **Bye**, or **Ciao** are all ways to say good-bye.
4. There are 75 million speakers of French in Europe.
5. In Europe, you can use French in France, Switzerland, Belgium, Luxembourg, Monaco, and Andorra. In North Africa, you can use French in Tunisia, Algeria, and Morocco.
6. Switzerland, Belgium, and Luxembourg all have more than one official language.
7. Monaco and Andorra are principalities.
8. People in politics, academia, business, and the arts speak French in North Africa.
9. Writers, musicians, and filmmakers are giving a new voice to the French language.

**À discuter**
*Answers will vary.*

**Reference Desk**

Students will learn about **L'Algérie** later in this level, whereas a more thorough presentation of the other countries of **Le Maghreb** will be presented in subsequent levels.

**Differentiated Learning**
**Adapt**
Put students in small groups to discuss the **À discuter** question. Then ask a spokesperson for each group to summarize the discussion.

**Learning Styles**
**Visual Learners**
For enrichment, and to help students remember the countries, ask them to find photos online of the capital cities, scenic landscapes, and main tourist sites of one of the francophone countries mentioned. Students could then present these photos to the class in a slideshow presentation, poster board collage, or in a format of their choice.

## Answers

1. Three brands are listed: DDP, armanoah, and baifao.
2. *Printouts will vary.*

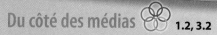 **Du côté des médias** 1.2, 3.2

### Culture

**Products: Information**
Students may be interested in looking at how school supplies for **la rentrée** in France differ from those in the United States. You might have them look for graph paper and fountain pens on a site that sells school supplies.

You learned that many French students buy book bags, or **cartables**, to put their school belongings in. Look at a couple that are on the market.

Accueil > Mode et beauté > Cartables, Sacs, Sacs à dos

**Cartable - DDP**

Marque : DDP
Type : Cartable

Voir le descriptif complet du produit

Voir le descriptif complet du produit

**Meilleur Prix**
15€
18 annonces:
15 neufs & 3 occasions
Voir les annonces
> Définir mes envies

**Vendeur: armanoah**

15€
Ajouter au panier

Etat : Occasion (Bon)

Envoi : point relais simple, point relais garanti, normal, suivi recommandé

Sac à dos 45x38x19cm, 1 petite poche devant contenant 1 porte-clés, une petite poche et des rangements à stylo + 2 grandes poches dont une avec porte-étiquette et une petitie poche plastifiée. Cartable utilisé l'année dernière avec quelques petits...

**Vendeur: baifao**

19€
Ajouter au panier

Etat : Occasion (Bon)

Envoi : point relais garanti, Suivi recommandé

Couleur(s) : rose Vends ce grand cartable (environ 45cmsx40cms) utilisé une année mais avec grand soin. Malgré le dessous rembourré, il y a 2 traces d'usure. Il y a 2 grandes poches intérieures, une petite pochette zippée en tissu à l'intéri...

Done

---

**8** **Les cartables**  2.1, 2.2

Answer the questions about **cartables**.

1. What is a brand name of **cartables** advertised above?
2. What kind of a **cartable** do you like? Enter **fournitures scolaires** into the search field of your favorite French search engine. Then choose your favorite **cartable** and print a copy of it to give your teacher.

 **022** vingt-deux | Unité 1

**Essential Instruction**

1. Your students can do **Activité 8** online during class or on their own time in a school computer lab or at home. You may want to ask them to complete an individual confidential form about Internet access at home before assigning computer **activités** to be done outside of class. Give extra time to students who do not have Internet access at home.

2. You may want to write all of the French grade levels on the board, showing the American equivalents, before doing **Activité 9** together as a class.

## Vocabulaire utile 1.2

**élèves:** *students*
**primaire:** *elementary school*
**collège:** *middle school*
**lycée:** *high school*

**6ème:** *sixth grade*
**5ème:** *seventh grade*
**4ème:** *eighth grade*

*Regardez le calendrier.*

### Expansion

Ask students to make a September calendar for events at your school, such as the date of **la rentrée des profs**, the date of **la rentrée des élèves**, **la réunion des parents et les profs**, and **les matchs sportifs**.

 **9 Un calendrier scolaire** 2.1, 2.2

*Répondez aux questions.*

1. What is the date of **la rentrée** for high school students?
2. What is the date of **la rentrée** for elementary and middle school students?
3. What is the date of the first day of classes for middle school students?
4. When is the teacher-parent meeting for eighth graders?
5. When is the teacher-parent meeting for seventh graders?
6. When is the teacher-parent meeting for sixth graders?

**❿**

1. French, German, and English words for "recommended" come after "Reservation."
2. The table of Swiss train trip fares is in Swiss francs.
3. A 2nd class one-way ticket from Luzern to Sarnen costs 8.20 Swiss francs or 13.60 for 1st class.
4. A round-trip fare from Interlaken Ost to Montreux costs 96.00 (2nd class) or 160.00 (1st class) Swiss francs.
5. The cheapest one-way trip is the 7.60 Swiss francs for travel from Interlaken Ost to Brenz.
6. The most expensive one-way trip is 114.00 Swiss francs.
7. The cheapest round-trip fare is 10.00 Swiss francs.
8. The most expensive round-trip fare is 228.00 Swiss francs.
9. A Eurail pass pays for unlimited travel in participating European countries.

## Critical Thinking

**Analysis**

Have students discuss or answer questions in their Culture Journal about train travel: Is train travel cheaper than flying? What are the advantages and disadvantages of travel by rail? Would they ever choose to travel by train? Why or why not?

*Regardez les prix des billets pour les trains suisses.*

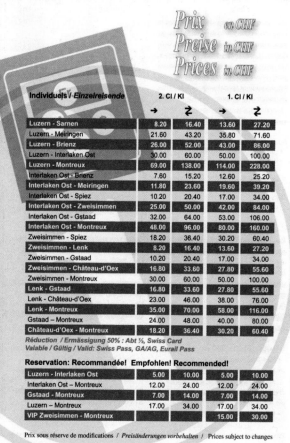

**In what ways is learning another language beneficial?**

**10 Le train en Suisse**  **2.1, 2.2**

*Répondez aux questions.*

1. Look at the heading for the bottom table. What languages come after "Reservation"?
2. Is the table of Swiss train trip fares in euros or Swiss francs?
3. How much is a one-way trip from Luzern to Sarnen?
4. How much is a round-trip fare from Interlaken Ost to Montreux?
5. What is the cheapest one-way trip?
6. What is the most expensive one-way trip?
7. What is the cheapest round-trip fare?
8. What is the most expensive round-trip fare?
9. What is a Eurail Pass (in red)? Do online research.

**Essential Instruction**

1. Before students do **Activité 10**, talk about train travel in general in Europe, asking them to consider why train travel is popular there. They might be interested in hearing about the bullet train, **le train à grande vitesse (TGV)**, that started service in France in 1981 and has expanded to include several European countries. Ask them to discuss whether or not bullet trains would be a good idea in the U.S. and for what reasons.

2. **Activité 11** can be done with partners if you do not have access to live streaming.

3. **Activité 12** could be assigned for enrichment to be done at home.

# À vous la parole

## Communiquez!

**11** Une autre visite

**1.1**

### Interpersonal Communication

Today you will connect again via live streaming with one of your partners on the international service project you began in **Leçon A**. With a partner, role-play the following conversation:

> Say hello.

> Say hello and ask how things are going.

> Respond. Add "And you?"

> Tell how you are.

> Say you'll see your partner soon.

> Say good-bye.

## Communiquez!

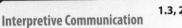

**12** La rentrée

**1.3, 2.2**

### Interpretive Communication

Search online for images and text related to **la rentrée** in France. Use the material you find to create an interesting collage. You might include photos, drawings, and text related to:

- School websites
- Lunch menus in a school's **cantine**
- School supplies
- Back-to-school clothing sales
- Tips for doing well in school
- Tips for staying healthy during the school year

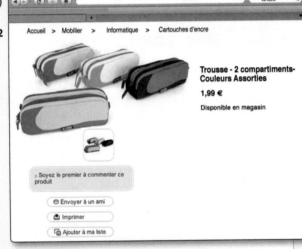

Create a bibliography citing the source for each image or text used. Describe your collage and what you learned about **la rentrée** to a small group of classmates.

**Answers** _____

**11** *Possible dialogue:*
—Bonjour, Claudette!
—Bonjour, Samantha! Ça va?
—Très bien, et toi?
—Pas mal.
—À bientôt!
—Au revoir!

**12** *Projects will vary.*

## Reference Desk

### Blended Instruction

Consider using blended instruction, a combination of in-class learning and computer-mediated instruction or learning opportunities. Ask students to complete activities on the computer, using their cell or smartphone, or other emerging electronic technology. This will allow students to hone their tech skills and become more independent learners. Schedule routine Internet and e-book learning in class and in the lab.

## Differentiated Learning
### Decelerate

The euro currency may be an abstract concept to students. To make it real for them, have them use an online currency converter to find out the monetary values of the train fares.

## Special Needs Students
### AD(H)D

Pair students to do **Activité 12**. Together they can decide what to include in their collage, who will find which items, and who will put the collage together.

# Stratégie communicative

## Register in Speaking and Writing

Should I speak or write formally or informally? This is the question you should ask yourself before addressing a French-speaking person. Register, or the degree of formality of the language you use, is an important aspect of communication. Use formal language with teachers and other adults you don't know well. Formal words and expressions you might use are **Bonjour**, **Comment allez-vous?**, **Et vous?** and **Je vous présente....** Informal words and expressions you might use include **Salut**, **Ça va?**, **Et toi?** and **Je te présente....**

**13  Bonjour ou Salut?**     2.1, 2.2, 4.1

Greet the following people, using **Bonjour!** or **Salut!** In formal conversations, be sure to include one of these titles: **Monsieur**, **Madame**, or **Mademoiselle**.

1. the mail carrier, M. Duval
2. your dog Max
3. your grandfather
4. your teacher, Mme Thorigny
5. the dentist, Mlle Gaillot
6. your cousin
7. the librarian, Mme Reverchon

Salut, Max!

**14  Dialogues**   1.1, 2.1, 2.2

### Interpersonal Communication

With a partner, play the roles below. Use **Ça va?** or **Comment allez-vous?** and **Et toi?** or **Et vous?** Follow the models. Responses to questions may vary.

> **MODÈLES**  a teen speaks to his neighbor, a man in his 40s
> A: **Comment allez-vous, Monsieur?**
> B: **Pas trop mal. Et toi?**
> A: **Très bien.**
>
> a sister speaks to her brother who just got home from college
> A: **Ça va, Noah?**
> B: **Comme ci, comme ça. Et toi?**
> A: **Bien.**

1. a student speaks to his or her teacher, Mme Ozier
2. an office employee speaks to her boss, M. Picard
3. a girl speaks to her cousin
4. a storekeeper speaks to a customer, Mlle Vallois
5. a classmate speaks to a classmate
6. a man at the bus stop speaks to the bus driver, M. Tripier
7. a teen speaks to another teen at a party

### Essential Instruction

1. Jigsaw **Activité 14**. Assign each pair of students a different conversation to share orally, first with another pair and then with the class. Suggest writing out what they are going to say, to help them feel more confident.

2. Before students begin **Activité 15**, have them repeat the pronunciation of **Je te/vous présente**, as well as the names in **Activité 15**. Ask for volunteers to role-play the scenarios for the class. Another option is to choose two rows of students to do the introductions chorally. Choose two new rows for each number.

# Communiquez!

## 15 Je te/vous présente....
**1.1, 2.1, 2.2, 4.1**

### Interpersonal Communication

Take turns introducing the following people. The first name is the person being introduced. The second name is the person he or she is being introduced to.

**MODÈLES** Michèle/Corinne
> A: **Je te présente Michèle.**
> B: **Salut, Michèle!**
> C: **Salut, Corinne!**

> M. Muller/Mlle Bonnet
> A: **Je vous présente M. Muller.**
> B: **Bonjour, M. Muller!**
> C: **Bonjour, Mlle Bonnet!**

1. Martine/Théo
2. Mme Martinez/M. Mathieu
3. Maxime/Claude
4. Mlle Petit/Mme Gauthier
5. Abdoulaye/Karim
6. M. Chevalier/Mlle Nicolas
7. Henri/Simone

Très bien, et toi?

Ça va?

## 16 Écrivez!
**1.3, 4.1**

Write a dialogue that includes the lines that follow. Remember to use the appropriate register for each character.

- Two people greet each other.
- Person A asks Person B how things are going.
- Person B responds and asks, "And you?"
- Person A responds, then introduces Person C to Person B.
- Person B greets Person C.

**Answers**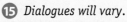

**15** *Dialogues will vary.*

**16** *Possible dialogue:*
—Bonjour, Monsieur!
—Bonjour, Madame!
—Comment allez-vous?
—Très bien, et vous?
—Pas trop mal. Je vous présente Madame Pécheux.
—Bonjour, Madame!

---

## Differentiated Learning
### Adapt
You may want to videotape the dialogues in **Activité 16**. Then show them to the class, and ask students to identify if the formal or informal register is being used.

### Multiple Intelligences
#### Bodily-Kinesthetic
To give students more practice in deciding which style of address is appropriate, create a classroom set of large flash cards with cues such as doctor, mail carrier, baby, teacher, cousin.

Then instruct students to hold up the cards and ask their classmates to answer the question **Ça va?** adding **Et toi?** or **Et vous?** according to the flash card cue. Students can ask each other the question as they circulate around the room. Remind them to include a handshake or **la bise**, depending on whom they are addressing and if they feel comfortable.

## Reference Desk

1. **Une teuf** is **verlan** for **une fête**. **Verlan** is a spoken language in which syllables are inverted. This slang developed in outlying areas of Paris in the 1970s and 80s. The singer Renaud celebrated **verlan** in his 1978 album *Laisse béton* (**laisse tomber**). Later, hip-hop artists appropriated **verlan**, and this slang saw a resurgence among youth. Other examples of this slang include **cainri** (**Américain**), **genhar** (**argent**), **teillebou** (**bouteille**), **teucha** (**chat**), **géman** (**manger**), **mifa** (**famille**), **meuf** (**femme**), and **zonmai** (**maison**).
2. Teens often refer to a movie theater as **le ciné** or **le cinoche**.
3. Students often remember the expression **Bonne idée** if you associate it with Easter ("bunny day").
4. **A+** is an abbreviation for **À plus tard**. It is often used as a closing in an e-mail, text message, letter, or postcard.

## Culture

**Products: Activity**
Consider showing the i-Culture video entitled **"Fille au Pair"** (2010 – 2011) to provide a culturally authentic lesson related to the theme of this **Leçon**.

## Leçon C

## Vocabulaire actif

*Go online* **EMC**Languages.net

**On va...?** 🎧 ✿ 1.2

C'est ma mère. C'est mon père.

à la teuf (fête)

CAFÉ DU NORD

au café

au centre commercial

au cinéma

à la maison

**Et si je voulais dire...?** 🎧

| Tu viens? | Are you coming? |
| Bonne idée! | Good idea! |
| Pourquoi pas? | Why not? |
| Ça ne me dit rien. | I'm not interested. |
| À plus tard. | See you later. |

028 vingt-huit | Unité 1

**Essential Instruction**

1. Model the pronunciation of the new words and expressions on p. 28, then check comprehension by asking, **Comment dit-on** in English using all of the expressions in French in a quick drill.

2. To practice the functions in **Pour la conversation** on p. 29, model a dialogue with a student in which you extend an invitation. Ask the class to tell you if the student accepted or declined the invitation.

3. Do **Activités 1** and **2** as a class to ensure comprehension.

# Pour la conversation

## How do I extend an invitation?

> **On va** au café?
>
> *How about going to the café?*

> **Tu voudrais aller...?**
>
> *Would you like to go...?*

## How do I accept an invitation?

> **D'accord.**
>
> *OK.*

> **Oui, je veux bien.**
>
> *Yes, I'd like that.*

## How do I refuse an invitation?

> **Pas possible. Je dois** faire mes devoirs.
>
> *It's not possible. I must do my homework.*

> **Je ne peux pas. J'aide** ma mère.
>
> *I can't. I'm helping my mother.*

---

**1  On accepte, oui ou non?**   **2.1, 2.2**

You will hear a series of short conversations. Write **oui** if the second speaker accepts the invitation or **non** if he or she declines.

**2  Les gens que je connais**   **2.1, 2.2**

Imagine you are Stéphanie and identify the people you know. Follow the model.

> **MODÈLE**  C'est **mon professeur.**

1.

2.

3.

4.

5.

6.

Leçon C | vingt-neuf **029**

---

**Answers** _____

**1** Script can be found in the front pages of the Annotated Teacher's Edition.

1. oui
2. non
3. oui
4. non
5. oui
6. oui
7. non

**2**

1. C'est ma camarade de classe.
2. C'est ma mère.
3. C'est mon copain.
4. C'est mon camarade de classe.
5. C'est mon père.
6. C'est ma copine.

### Reference Desk

1. The functions in this lesson practice extending an invitation and accepting or refusing an invitation.
2. Encourage students to incorporate the **Leçon A** vocabulary when refusing an invitation, for example, **Je ne peux pas. J'aide ma prof/mon copain/ma camarade de classe.**

---

**Differentiated Learning**
**Decelerate**
Ask students to identify the pictures of places in **Vocabulaire actif** in English. Then pronounce them in French and ask students to point to the right photo.

**Multiple Intelligences**
**Logical-Mathematical**
Sequential learners like information presented linearly, so be sure to practice the functions in **Pour la conversation** before these students listen to **Activité 1.**

**Answers** _____

**3**

1. 2
2. 5
3. 4
4. 1
5. 3

## Reference Desk

Ask students to use what they already know about a social network home page to help them guess what these tabs are for: **Accueil** (*Home Page*), **Profil** (*Profile*), **Compte** (*Account*), **Mur** (*Wall*), **Infos** (*Information*), **Photos**, **Partager** (*Share*).

**3** **Connectez-vous!**  **1.2, 2.1**

Luc signed on to his social networking site and discovered that the messages between Anne and him were scrambled. Help Luc make sense of the messages by rewriting them in the correct order.

## Mon réseau social          Accueil    Profil    Compte

### Luc Bolduc

| Mur | Infos | Photos |
|-----|-------|--------|
| Exprimez-vous... | | |

 **Luc Bolduc** Aujourd'hui j'aide ma mère      **Partager**
Ça va pas très bien!

samedi le 10 septembre           J'aime

Nouvelle
Messages
Événements
Amis

 1. **Tu voudrais aller au café algérien bientôt?**
samedi le 10 septembre

 2. **Ça va Luc?**
samedi le 10 septembre

3. **Oui, je veux bien. À bientôt.**
samedi le 10 septembre

 4. **Demain? Je ne peux pas. Je dois aider mon père!**
samedi le 10 septembre

 5. **Pas très bien! J'aide ma mère. On va à la teuf de Christine demain?**
samedi le 10 septembre

**Essential Instruction**

1. Ask students to complete **Activité 3** with a partner. Circulate in the room to answer any questions students may have. Ask students the date, which they should be able to guess since **septembre** is a cognate. Ask them to guess what day of the week **samedi** is.

2. For **Activité 4**, ask different pairs to present each of the dialogues. Tell the class to listen to whether or not the second speaker is accepting or declining the invitation.

# Communiquez!

**4  Je t'invite!**  1.1, 2.1, 2.2

**Interpersonal Communication**

With a partner, take turns inviting each other to the places in the photos below. When your partner invites you to do something, accept or decline the invitation.

**MODÈLE**  A: **On va au centre commercial?**
B: **Pas possible. Je dois aider mon père.**

1.

2.

3.

4.

On va au café?

D'accord!

Leçon C | trente et un **031**

**Expansion**

Have students create additional invitation dialogues. Ask for pairs of volunteers to model extending and responding to an invitation. Ask the class to write down if the second speaker accepts or refuses the invitation.

---

**Differentiated Instruction**
**Decelerate**
For **Activité 4**, write the possible responses on the board for students to choose from: **D'accord; Oui, je veux bien; Pas possible; Je dois aider mon père; Je ne peux pas; Je dois faire mes devoirs**, etc.

**Accelerate**
For **Activité 4**, ask more advanced learners to create a longer dialogue that includes greetings and asking how things are going, as well as an expression from **Et si je voulais dire…?**

**Special Needs Students**
**Social Anxiety/Behavioral Disorders**
Some students might prefer to prepare oral work at home, record it, and bring it in to class. If these students don't have a partner to work with at home, record the first line of the dialogue for them and ask them to record several different responses.

**Answers**

**5**

1. Julien
2. cinéma
3. contrôle
4. mère
5. Yasmine

**Extension**

The UGC movie theater is near a mall, which would allow the teen to do his or her shopping at the same time.

### Reference Desk

A possible translation of **Avec ton père ce n'est pas mieux** is *"Your dad isn't any better."*

# Rencontres culturelles

## Une invitation

2.1, 2.2

Yasmine calls Julien on her cell phone. Julien is at home in his bedroom.

Julien: Salut! C'est Yasmine?
Yasmine: Oui. Tu vas bien? Dis, Julien, on va au ciné avec Maxime. Tu voudrais venir?
Julien: Ah non, pas possible... on a un contrôle de maths.
Yasmine: Oui, je vois... ta mère est stricte....
Julien: Oh! Avec ton père ce n'est pas mieux.
Yasmine: Bon. Salut. À demain.

 **5 Une invitation**  2.1

*Complétez les phrases.* (Complete the sentences.)

1. Yasmine téléphone à....
2. Yasmine va avec Maxime au....
3. Julien a un... de maths.
4. La... de Julien est stricte.
5. Le père de... est strict.

**Extension** **On va au ciné?** 🎧

A couple of young people are sitting outside on the terrace of a café.

Paule: Ciné?
Étienne: D'accord!
Paule: Oui, je veux bien.
Étienne: Ah non, pas possible, je dois faire des courses.
Paule: Eh bien alors, on va à l'UGC Cité Ciné des Halles et tu fais tes courses au centre commercial.
Étienne: Bon, alors tu viens?
Paule: Je viens!

**Extension** What is the advantage of going to the movies at the UGC theater?

Paule et Étienne sont au café.

**Essential Instruction**

1. Ask students to look at the photos and anticipate the kind of exchanges that will take place.
2. Check for comprehension by asking the students to find the expressions that you give them in English.
3. Ask for a pair of volunteers to read the dialogue aloud after they have listened to the recording.

4. After students have read **Les ados,** have them compare French teens to American teens.
5. Explain that cognates (like **indispensable** in the graph on p. 33) are words with almost identical spellings and meanings in two languages and that French and English share many cognates because of their common Latin roots. Recognizing cognates will help students both with their reading and listening comprehension.

# Points de départ

 **Go online EMCLanguages.net**

*Question centrale*

**?**

In what ways is learning another language beneficial?

## Les ados  2.2, 4.2

Young people in France tend to be very individualistic, and they also have a certain degree of financial independence; 71% of teens between ages 15 and 17 receive roughly 29 euros in allowance each month. Teens spend a lot of time on the Internet writing and receiving e-mails and surfing the Web. Many teens also write their own blogs. Other favorite activities include listening to music, going to the movies, and talking to friends. Eight out of ten teens from ages 15 to 19 have their own cell phone, **un portable**.

 **Search words: convertisseur de devises** to find out the value of 29 euros

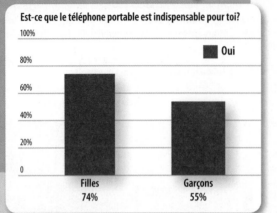

**Est-ce que le téléphone portable est indispensable pour toi?**

| | Oui |
| --- | --- |
| Filles | 74% |
| Garçons | 55% |

## La Francophonie  4.2

❊ *L'Afrique subsaharienne*

The people of sub-Saharan Africa speak many different languages. Some languages are limited to a small area in one country, while others are spoken by people in several different countries. Wolof, Peul, Bambara, and Malinke are just four of the languages spoken in the region. During the colonial period in Africa, the French language helped unify people of different languages and cultures living within the same country. French became the language of law, government, and education. Today French continues to be spoken in Senegal, the Ivory Coast, Cameroon, Burkina Faso, Gabon, Mali, Niger, Togo, and the Democratic Republic of the Congo. Many sub-Saharan artists have also blended their local traditions with the French language, producing films, works of art, and music for an international audience, for example, the songs of musician Youssou N'Dour from Senegal.

 **Search words: vidéo youssou n'dour**

Youssou N'Dour often performs in his native Africa.

---

## Differentiated Learning

### Decelerate
Help students find the countries mentioned in **La francophonie** on a map. Ask them to brainstorm a list of languages they know and then add those from the readings.

## Learning Styles

### Kinesthetic Learners
Prepare envelopes containing the dialogue sentences that you have cut into strips. Have pairs put them in logical order.

## Multiple Intelligences

### Logical-Mathematical
Challenge students with strong math skills to explain to the class how to convert sums from dollars to euros and vice versa without using a currency converter.

### Musical-Rhythmic
Play a Youssou N'Dour song in class and ask musically inclined students to categorize his music.

---

## RESOURCES

 **Workbook 24–25**

## Reference Desk

1. Francophone sub-Saharan African countries will be treated in more detail later in this level.
2. See **Copy Masters** ancillary for a blank survey to use with the paragraph entitled **Les ados**.

## Expansion

Students may be interested to see how American teens would respond to the survey about cell phone use. Have each student ask the question at the top of the graph to 10 boys and 10 girls, and record yes or no answers. Have them report on their findings. For example, if 7 of 10 boys said their cell phone is indispensable, they would say: "Seventy percent of American boys find using a cell phone indispensable." If any differences occur between the French and American survey results, ask students to hypothesize what might explain the differences.

## Culture

### Products: Information
Youssou N'Dour was born in 1959 in Senegal. His father was a laborer and his mother a **griot**, or traditional storyteller. A successful singer at age 13, he went on to join the group **L'Étoile de Dakar** in 1979. In 1981 his music hit the charts with the genre **m'balax**. Just like his mother and other **griots**, he sings about daily life, friendship, and holidays in Senegal, and is an ambassador for his country. His collaborators have included the likes of Peter Gabriel and Sting and others who express many different music genres. For the people of Senegal he is a national hero.

## ✳ Les Antilles et la Guyane française  4.2

**La Martinique** and **la Guadeloupe** are French overseas departments in the Caribbean. Although French is the official language, many people also speak Creole. Renowned writers from these islands whose works are in both languages include Aimé Césaire, Jean Métellus, and Léon Gontran-Damas. The islands are also known for their beautiful beaches which attract thousands of tourists each year. Nearby in South America is the overseas department of **la Guyane française** which attracts tourists as well, particularly those who enjoy ecotourism—responsible travel to pristine, protected areas that strive to maintain an environment relatively untouched by human intervention. However, French Guiana may be best known as home to Europe's satellite launching site.

 **Search words: martinique tourisme**
**guadeloupe tourisme**
**écotourisme en guyane**

Martinique is a Caribbean island and a department of France.

### Produits

Poet Aimé Césaire (1913–2008) from Martinique co-founded a movement called **la Négritude**. This philosophy rejected French cultural assimilation and sought to promote Africa and its culture, which was not valued by French colonial regimes. **4.2**

### COMPARAISONS

Where do you and your family and friends go on vacation? How do these places compare with Martinique, Guadeloupe, and French Guiana? **2.2, 4.2**

## Essential Learning

1. Using a world map, point out where **la Martinique**, **la Guadeloupe**, and **la Guyane française** are located. Tell students that these places, plus the island of **la Réunion**, located off the southeastern coast of Africa, are French overseas departments. Explain that France is divided into 96 departments including the Mediterranean island of Corsica, plus four overseas departments. France's overseas departments, or **les départements d'outre-mer**, can be compared to our states of Hawaii and Alaska, which are not in the continental United States. You may want to review the location of the other francophone countries mentioned previously in this unit.
2. Discuss answers to the questions in **Comparaisons**.
3. **Activité 7**: If possible, have students send a French text message to a classmate.

## 6 Questions culturelles  2.1, 2.2

*Répondez aux questions.*

1. What do French teens like to do most on the Internet?
2. What is the French word for a cell phone?
3. What are the names of four African languages?
4. In what arenas is French used in French-speaking African countries?
5. Who is Youssou N'Dour?
6. What are three of France's overseas departments in the Americas?
7. What body of water surrounds Martinique and Guadeloupe?
8. What languages do people speak in Martinique and Guadeloupe?
9. What is ecotourism?
10. Which overseas department is known for its ecotourism?
11. What is **la Guyane française** perhaps best known for?

The Ariane rocket is launched from the French National Space Center, or CNES, in Guiana.

### À discuter

Where could you use your French language skills in the western hemisphere? What would be your first choice for a vacation or study destination?

---

## Du côté des médias

## 7 Un texto/SMS  2.1

Rewrite the following sentences in the order of Méline's text message.

| | |
|---|---|
| T'es où? | *Where are you?* |
| Salut. | *Hi.* |
| Bisous | *Kisses* |
| Tu fais quoi? | *What are you doing?* |

SMS 10:10am
Slt. T ou? Tu fé koa? Biz Méline

**Answers** _____

**6**

1. French teens enjoy sending and reading e-mails on the Internet.
2. A cell phone is called **un portable.**
3. Four native African languages are Wolof, Peul, Bambara, and Malinke.
4. French is used in law, governmental administration, and education.
5. Youssou N'Dour is a musician from Senegal.
6. Martinique, Guadeloupe, and Haïti make up the French West Indies.
7. The Caribbean Sea surrounds Martinique, Guadeloupe, and Haiti.
8. Creole is the native language of the French West Indies, and French is also spoken.
9. Ecotourism is responsible travel to pristine, protected areas, as in French Guiana.
10. French Guiana is the French overseas department most known for its ecotourism.
11. French Guiana is most known as being the home to Europe's satellite launching site.

**À discuter**
*Answers will vary.*

**7**

1. Salut.
2. T'es où?
3. Tu fais quoi?
4. Bisous, Méline

**Differentiated Learning**
**Decelerate**
Before students read the culture paragraph on p. 34, ask them to skim for unfamiliar words; help them figure out from context what these words must mean. Write the answers to the questions in **Activité 6** on the board, and ask students to match the questions to the answers.

## Answers

**8**

1. French citizens can show a **carte d'identité nationale** if they don't have a passport.
2. If you're from Haiti or Turkey, you need to bring a visa in addition to a passport.
3. French and Creole are spoken in Martinique.
4. The euro is used in Martinique.
5. No, you are not required to get vaccines before coming to Martinique.

*Lisez les informations pour les voyageurs.*  **1.2**

martinique

**Infos voyageurs**
**FORMALITES D ENTREE**

**Pour les citoyens français**
La carte d'identité nationale ou le passeport.

**Pour les citoyens de la C.E.E.**
Passeport sans visa servant de carte d'identité officielle ou carte de séjour française en cours de validité.

**Pour les ressortissants des pays étrangers n'appartenant pas à la C.E.E.**
Passeport en cours de validité.

**Pour les ressortissants des USA, du Canada, et du Japon**
Pour un séjour de moins de 3 mois, une pièce d'identité muni d'une photo.
Un visa de régularisation gratuit leur sera délivré à l'arrivée.
Ce visa n'est valable que pour la durée du séjour et pour le seul département d'Outre Mer considéré

**Passeport et Visa**
Afrique du Sud - Bolivie - Dominique - Sainte Luce - Barbade - Jamaïque - Trinidad - Haïti - Honduras - San Salvador - République Dominicaine - Turquie
**LANGUES**
Français : langue usuelle
Créole : langue régionale
**MONNAIE**
L'Euro. Le dollar américain est accepté ainsi que les chèques de voyage et les cartes de crédit. Refus des chèques hors place dans certains établissements.
**EAU ET ELECTRICITE**
L'eau du robinet est potable partout. Des eaux minérales sont aussi proposées aux consommateurs. Le courant électrique est de 20 volts.
**POSTES TELECOMMUNICATIONS**
Téléphone : nombreuses cabines téléphoniques, réseau portables.
Télécopie.
Réseau Internet.
**LES VACCINS**
Pas de vaccin obligatoire pour se rendre en Guadeloupe, Martinique. En Guyane : vaccin contre la fièvre jaune obligatoire. Pour savoir où vous faire vacciner, vous pouvez consulter la liste des centres de vaccinations contre la fièvre jaune sur le site
www.chu-rouen.fr/cap/svhome.html
Toutefois pour les personnes arrivant d'Amérique du Sud et de certaines îles de la Caraïbe, un certificat international contre la variole et la fièvre jaune peut être demandé.

**VEGETAUX**
Quand vous prenez l'avion, il est strictement interdit de transporter des végétaux. Ces dispositions sont prises pour protéger certaines espèces particulièrement sensibles. Par exemple la banane aux Antilles ne résisterait pas à certaines formes de cercosporiose. Evitez donc d'emmener avec vous votre potager. Il ne passerait pas la Douane.

**ANIMAUX**
L'entrée des animaux domestiques dans le DOM, requiert quelques conditions : l'animal doit être tatoué, disposer d'un carnet de certificat avec ses vaccinations à jour et d'un certificat anti-rabique établi au moins 30 jours avant le voyage mais pas plus d'un an tôt. L'interdiction d'importer des animaux ne subit d'exception que si le dit animal a résidé dans un pays agréé (Australie....) pendant un mois après avoir vécu en France métropolitaine 6 mois sans discontinuer.

.../...

Espace visiteurs
Devenir membre
Appel d'offre
Email
Mot de passe
Mot de passe perdu
Espace annonceur
Ajouter une annonce
Gérer votre annonce
Faq
Parrainage
Affiliation
Création site Web
Photos & Vidéos
Cartes virtuelles
Photos Martinique
Photo panoramique
Fonds écran à télécharger
Services
Forum Antilles
Petites annonces Martinique
Annuaire
Météo
Climat
Météo Martinique
Alerte cyclonique
Information site
Faq visiteur
Charte d'utilisation
Conditions légales

Done

**8 Un voyage à la Martinique**  **1.1, 2.1, 2.2**

*Répondez aux questions.*

1. If French citizens don't have a passport, what proof of identity can they use instead?
2. If you're from Haiti or Turkey, what do you need to bring besides a passport?
3. What two languages are spoken in Martinique?
4. What currency is used in Martinique?
5. Are you required to get vaccines before coming to Martinique?

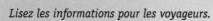

## Essential Learning

**1.** Ask students to skim and scan for answers to **Activité 8** questions. The new vocabulary on these pages offers a good opportunity to talk about cognates and how to decode for meaning. Ask your students if it is really necessary to understand <u>every</u> word that they read or hear in order to understand the main idea and to communicate.

**2. Activité 9:** Your class might find it interesting to complete the survey to elicit an American comparison to the French survey results.

## Les ados, les jeunes, et le téléphone portable

**1.2**

**As-tu déjà fait voler ton téléphone portable? (903 Votes)**

| | | |
|---|---|---|
| oui (189) | ▬▬▬ | 20.9% |
| non (679) | ▬▬▬▬▬▬ | 75.2% |
| plusieurs fois (35) | ▬ | 3.9% |

**Si tu pouvais, regarderais-tu la télé sur ton téléphone portable? (896 Votes)**

| | | |
|---|---|---|
| oui | ▬▬▬▬ | 68.7% |
| non (280) | ▬▬▬ | 31.3% |

**Combien de sms envoies-tu par jour? (849 Votes)**

| | | |
|---|---|---|
| de 0 à 3 (267) | ▬▬▬ | 31.4% |
| de 4 à 6 (264) | ▬▬▬ | 31.1% |
| de 7 à 10 (144) | ▬▬ | 17.0% |
| plus de 10 (174) | ▬▬ | 20.5% |

**Sondage réalisé par ADOSURF auprès de 12 à 25 ans**

---

**9** **Une enquête sur les portables**  **2.1, 2.2**

Identify each statement as essentially **vrai** (*true*) or **faux** (*false*).

1. This survey is about French young people and their laptops.
2. For each question, a different amount of teens responded.
3. The young people who participated in the survey were between 12 and 18 years old.
4. According to the survey, most teens have not had their phone stolen.
5. About 4% of teens have had their phone stolen more than once.
6. Most teens would not like to watch TV on their phones.
7. About 30% of teens send four to six text messages per day.
8. Seventeen percent of teens send more than ten text messages per day.

**Answers**

**9**

1. faux
2. vrai
3. faux
4. vrai
5. vrai
6. faux
7. vrai
8. faux

### Expansion

Have students interview ten friends or family members of different ages, using the same questions in the French survey. Then have them report on their findings, for example, "Sixty percent of respondents would watch TV on their cell phone." Is there a difference between older and younger respondents?

## Multiple Intelligences

### Interpersonal

Have students circulate and ask classmates three questions from the survey. Record the results and post on the board.

### Verbal-Linguistic/Intrapersonal

After doing **Activité 8**, have students create a postcard of their favorite francophone country (other than France) from this unit. One side of the postcard should have a photo or collage of photos they found or drew. On the other side, students write things they've learned about the location from doing online research, as if they're informing the postcard recipient. They can address the postcard to a real or imaginary person.

038

In **La culture sur place** students move beyond knowledge-based culture to simulated experiential culture. In this section they will solve problems and navigate through francophone cultures. For this lesson, there is no right or wrong answer. The objective of the **Activité** is to get students to decide how comfortable they are experiencing francophone culture and how comfortable they want to be by the end of the course.

**Critical Thinking**

**Evaluation**
Ask students to write about a real or imaginary experience of being "foreign" in a location. If they have never traveled outside the United States, ask them to imagine what the first week in this country would be like for a teen.

# La culture sur place

## Encounters with French Culture

### Introduction  1.2

When you learn about other cultures and languages, you also often learn that people may see things differently from the way you view them or do things differently from what you expect. You don't have to change who you are and become **français(e)** or **algérien(ne)** or **canadien(ne)** to communicate with Francophone people. However, you might find it interesting, enlightening, and even inspiring to learn how to engage and interact with people from another culture. In this section, you're invited to go "on location" and navigate through French-speaking cultures.

**10 Comment agir?**  2.1, 4.1, 4.2

Imagine you are experiencing each situation that follows and describe how you would react. Be sure to select a course of action with which you are comfortable. If you have trouble thinking of a reaction, look at the suggestions in the boxes. Other responses may be possible.

1. You are on a train ride in France. You'd like to ask the older woman sitting next to you if she minds if you open the window, but you're not sure what to say to get her attention. What do you do? Why?

   *You might tap her on the shoulder, wave at her, or say* **"Madame? Je peux...?"** *and gesture toward the window.*

2. You meet a French woman for the first time. You see her kiss your American friend twice on the cheek before she turns to greet you. What do you do? Why?

   *You might offer your hand, you might kiss her on both cheeks, or you might stop and ask what to do.*

3. You're saying good-bye to a new friend on your first day in France. He says **"Salut!"** as he waves and turns away. What do you do? Why?

   *You might say* **"Salut!"** *also,* **"Au revoir!"**, **"Bye!"** *or* **"Ciao!"**, *or you might just laugh.*

4. You receive a text message from a French-speaking friend: **"slt. T ou?"** How do you respond? Why?

   *You might respond using French abbreviations, or you might reply:* **"Je suis à la teuf/au ciné/au centre commercial/à la maison."**

**Essential Instruction**

1. Before beginning this section, ask your class to brainstorm what they already know about French culture by listing certain practices, for example, eating crêpes.

2. You may want to have students do **Activité 10** in pairs or groups to get a greater variety of reactions and responses. List the variety of responses on the board to show that multiple reactions are possible, and to reinforce that there is no right or wrong answer.

3. See **Copy Masters** ancillary for a blank "Taking Inventory" chart. Project the continuum on the board, and take a class survey. Consider having students re-take the survey two or three times during the year. Compare the results, and discuss why they have or have not changed.

## Taking Inventory  4.2

As you can see in the preceding situations, there may be more than one way to handle a situation in another culture. Look at the continuum below. Where do you fall in terms of your comfort level with the differences between your own culture(s) and francophone cultures? If you feel that you must always follow the customs of your own culture(s), you would fall to the left. If you feel that you might adopt many of the customs from the francophone world, you would fall to the right. Next, decide where on the continuum you would like to be when you finish this course. Discuss your ratings with a group of your classmates.

1   2   3   4   5   6   7   8   9   10

I am very comfortable in some U.S. cultures.

I would be somewhat comfortable in francophone cultures.

I would be very comfortable in francophone cultures.

# À vous la parole

*Question centrale*
In what ways is learning another language beneficial?

## 11 Les textos ou sms

2.1, 2.2

**Interpretive/Presentational Communication**

Now that you know some text messaging abbreviations in French, look for more of them online by using the key words below. Create a message for a classmate by changing some of the standard French words you know to SMS text. You may choose to send your message via phone or e-mail. If you don't have access to these technologies, just write your message on an index card and deliver it by hand. If your classmate has trouble deciphering your message, help him or her by saying your message aloud.

 **Search words:** **textos français**
**dico sms**
**langage sms**

## 12 Word Clouds

1.3, 2.1, 2.2

**Presentational Communication**

In this lesson you learned the names of some places and people, how to invite someone, how to accept or reject an invitation, some French-speaking destinations, and some SMS abbreviations. Choose some of your favorite new French and English words from this and previous lessons and make a word cloud. If you don't have access to word cloud applications online, write or design your words on a piece of paper with colored markers. Share your word cloud with your classmates. Tell them your five favorite words and why they are your favorites.

Ça roule?
D'accord!
langue d'ouverture
la teuf
algérien
Mardi Gras
texto
Kemajou

 **Search words:** **wordle, wordsift, abc ya word cloud**
to find Word Cloud applications

**Essential Instruction**

1. **Activités 11** and **12** are fun to do in the computer lab during class. Students can compare what they found online. If you assign them for homework, compare results in small groups the next day.
2. You may want to use whole group instruction with p. 41. Point out to students that two of the answers are provided because they are not included in the reading. The pre-reading question is designed to connect them to the reading, the strategy chart is to be completed as they read, and the **Outils de lecture** is designed to give them an attack strategy for the reading.
3. After students have read, discussed, and understood the reading, play the audio.

# Lecture thématique

## Belle du Seigneur

### Rencontre avec l'auteur  1.2

**Albert Cohen** (1895–1981) was a novelist and diplomat. Born in Greece, he settled in Switzerland where he studied law. Jewish himself, Cohen worked to create a safe haven for Jews during and after World War II. He is best known for his novel, *Belle du Seigneur*, which tells the story of the destructive romantic relationship between a woman named Ariane and a man named Solal. *Belle du Seigneur* won important literary prizes and is considered a masterpiece. As you read, try to answer the following question: What are the characters feeling?

## Pré-lecture

Think of a time you questioned a friend over and over again. Write a brief description of the situation and identify the emotions you felt.

## Stratégie de lecture  2.1, 2.2

### Answering the five "W" questions

The five "W" questions are Who, What, Where, When, and Why. If you can answer these questions about a reading, then you are on your way to finding the deeper meaning of the selection. Fill in a chart like the one below as you read the excerpt from *Belle du Seigneur*.

| Question words and questions | Answers |
|---|---|
| 1. **Who** are the two characters in this scene? | |
| 2. **What** does Solal want to know? | |
| 3. **Where** are the characters? | Agay, French Riviera |
| 4. **When** does the story take place? | 1930s |
| 5. **Why** does Solal want to know this third person's name? | |

## Outils de lecture

### Deciphering Words

When you see a word you do not know in a reading, ask yourself if there is a similar word, or cognate from English, or look at the words around it to help you decipher the meaning. If neither one of these strategies works, then look under the reading at the glossed words. Definitions here will be given in English, and in later units, some of them will be in French.

---

### Reference Desk

1. Students make a connection to literature in this section. Each reading section contains a strategy, a pre-reading question, during-reading questions, and a post-reading question.
2. In the **Rencontre avec l'auteur**, students find a brief biography of the writer.
3. In the **Stratégie de lecture**, students learn a literary term that they will apply to the selection. See **Copy Masters** ancillary for a graphic organizer that accompanies the **Stratégie de lecture**.
4. In the **Outils de lecture**, students learn how to apply a concept to help them read the selection more easily.

**Pendant la lecture**
1. The first speaker is a man.
2. Solal wants to know the last name, nationality, and first name of the other man.

 **13**

1. _Possible answer:_ In the chapter **Aveu**, Solal and Ariane are in Agay on the Riviera in the 1930s. Solal wants to know the last name, nationality, and first name of the other man in Ariane's life. He is jealous and demands a rapid response.
2. Ariane is a figure from Greek mythology and daughter of Minos, who was the king of Crete; she helped Theseus get out of the labyrinth by providing him with a spool. Solal is a Hebrew name meaning "guide."
3. Social Studies and nonfiction articles lend themselves to review using the five "W" questions (Who, What, Where, When, Why).
4. 1. Dis son nom, vite! Charbonneau. Quelle nationalité? Canadien. ...Son prénom? Robert
   2. .... Reed. ...? Américain. ...? Justin.
   3. .... Benjadid. ...? Algérien. ...? Karim.
   4. .... Lucas. ...? Français. ...? Thierry.

---

### Reference Desk

In the first line of the selection, **nom** is not glossed because students learned **prénom** on p. 5. **Nationalité** is not glossed because it is a cognate. **Allemand** is not glossed because of its proximity to **Allemagne** on the map of France at the beginning of the book.

---

 **2.1, 2.2**

| | |
|---|---|
| Solal: | Dis* son nom, son nom, vite*! |
| Ariane: | Dietsch. |
| Solal: | Quelle* nationalité? |
| Ariane: | Allemand. |
| Solal: | ...Son prénom? |
| Ariane: | Serge. |

_____
**Dis** _Say;_ **vite** _fast;_ **quelle** _what_

> **Pendant la lecture**
> 1. Is the first speaker a man or a woman?

> **Pendant la lecture**
> 2. What details does Solal want to know?

## Post-lecture

What does Solal feel that makes him question Ariane? With a group of classmates, brainstorm a list of other works of fiction (books, TV shows, plays, movies) that center on this emotion.

## Le monde visuel

French artist Jean Béraud (1849–1935) was influenced by Impressionist artists, who wanted to create an impression of a moment using techniques from broad brush strokes and swaths of color to mute, understated tones. Béraud liked to paint life in the Parisian salons, or drawing rooms, of the late 19th century. What is the setting of this painting, and in what ways is it impressionistic? How does the painting help you to interpret the reading selection?

_The Private Conversation_, 1904. Jean Béraud. J. Kugel Collection, Paris, France.

 **13 Activités d'expansion** **1.1, 1.3, 2.1, 4.2**

_Faites les activités suivantes._ (Do the following activities.)
1. Imagine that _Belle du Seigneur_ is being translated into English for the first time. Your job is to write the study guide for the chapter titled _Aveu_ ("Confession"). Use the information in your chart to write a paragraph in English about the background of this selection.
2. The names of the characters have meaning. Do online research to find out their meaning.

 **Search words: signification des prénoms**

3. The five "W" questions are useful when reading other types of publications besides literature. Work with a partner to make a list of them.

### Essential Instruction
1. Tell students the art was selected to help them understand the reading selection. What two people are having a conversation? What type of a conversation is it?
2. Describe the Paris metro, the scene of the cartoon on p. 43, before having students work on understanding the conversations that take place there. You may want to have them translate the conversations in groups of three and then read them aloud within their group.
3. Help students decode new words and phrases as a class before they break into groups.

4. With a partner, play the roles of Solal and Ariane, but imagine that the nationality and first names of the person being discussed change.

| MODÈLE | | |
|---|---|---|
| | Solal: | **Dis son nom, son nom, vite!** |
| | Ariane: | **Harndani.** |
| | Solal: | **Quelle nationalité?** |
| | Ariane: | **Algérien.** |
| | Solal: | **…Son prénom?** |
| | Ariane: | **Salim.** |

1. Robert Charbonneau/Canada
2. Justin Reed/USA
3. Karim Bendjadid/Algérie
4. Thierry Lucas/France

## Les copains d'abord: Dans le métro   1.2

## RESOURCES

**Pre-test**

*Leçon* **Quiz**

## Les copains d'abord

Here is the translation for **Les copains d'abord**:

A = Antoine
F = Florence
MA = Marie-Alix

A: Hello, Miss, my name is Antoine. What is your name? F: Oh, hello, I am Florence. Say *tu*, not *vous*. You're Canadian? A: Yes, that's right. (…and you, you are cool, super, neat. Do you want to go to the movies with me? No.Do you want to go to the coffee shop? Yes, to the coffee shop!) Say, do you…? F: Yes? Oh, hi honey. Yes I'm doing very well. I'm on my way to the mall.  See you tonight at the concert! MA: Good morning. F: Hi!  A: Delighted, miss. My name is Antoine. This is Florence. I am Canadian, she is French. Are you French? MA: Yes, from French Guyana. My name is Marie-Alix. Say *tu*, not *vous*. F: Oh, tonight, it's  Cheb Mami's concert at Bercy. My boyfriend and I are going. Do you want to come along? A: No, I cannot. MA: That's not possible, I am helping my mom, she is not feeling well.

List of slang and idiomatic expressions:
**cool**: *cool*; **chouette**: *cool*; **mon chéri**: *my darling*

**Differentiated Learning**
**Decelerate**
Have students work on **Activités d'expansion** with a partner and offer the option of selecting one **Activité**.

**Accelerate**
Assign #2, 3, and 4 of the **Activités d'expansion** and ask volunteers to share the results of the exercises.

**Multiple Intelligences**
**Interpersonal**
Ask interested students to create a skit in English that highlights jealousy, the theme of the reading selection, to help the class understand the feelings of Solal.

## Reference Desk

1. In **Connexions par internet**, students connect with another discipline such as technology, art, math, music, and social studies.
2. In **Communautés en ligne**, students will find out about francophone communities or interact with francophone communities or speakers.

## Expansion

1. See what students know about embassies and diplomacy, and from there discuss the French Embassy in Washington.
2. You might mention that France has been an ally of the United States since the Revolutionary War. Some students may have heard about LaFayette's contributions to America in History or Social Studies classes.
3. This is a good opportunity to introduce some French words about diplomacy that are used in English, such as **détente**, **rapprochement**, **laissez-faire**, **force majeure**, and **laissez-passer**.

## T'es branché?

# Projets finaux

**A** **Connexions par internet: La technologie** 3.2

**How accurate are online translators?**

Follow the steps below to experiment with an online French translator. Locate one by using your favorite French search engine, such as www.google.fr, and the key words below.

1. Type a short paragraph in English about where you went and what you did last weekend. Insert some details and slang into your text.
2. Find an online translator and paste your paragraph in the field titled **de l'anglais au français**.
3. Next, take the translated text (in French) and put it in the translator again. This time put the text in the field titled **du français à l'anglais**.

Now answer the following questions to evaluate your experiment. How accurate were the results? Give a percentage. How do you think your teacher could tell if you were to use an online translator? Discuss with a partner why your teacher might ask you not to use online translators and what you discovered about learning a second language from doing this activity.

 **Search words:  traducteur**

**B** **Communautés en ligne**
5.1

### La France aux États-Unis

Many countries have an embassy in Washington, D.C. Let's visit the French Embassy there to learn about France's presence in the United States and about the relationship between the two countries. Use the key words below to access the embassy's website. Then follow the directions below to explore the site.

The French Embassy in Washington, D.C., facilitates exchanges and communication between France and the United States.

1. Explore the site in English to see what kind of information is provided.
2. Make a chart with two columns. Label the left side "France's Embassy in Washington." Label the right side **Ambassade de France à Washington**.
3. In the left column, write ten things you learned about French-American relations.
4. In the right column, write ten facts you learned, for example, the name of the ambassador, the locations of the French consulates in the United States, services provided to French citizens, events, etc.

 **Search words:  ambassade de france à washington**

**Essential Learning**

1. Have all students do **Activité A** so they can see for themselves how online translators can distort language. This would be an appropriate time to emphasize that they will be using translators only when you instruct them to do so. There are some online dictionaries that you may choose to teach them to use later in the year.

2. Depending on time, you could choose (or have students choose) to do **Activité B** or **C**.
3. Ask students to complete **Activité D** individually to reflect on what they have learned in this unit, in particular regarding the **Question centrale**. Distribute copies of the graphic organizer, located in the **Copy Masters** supplement.

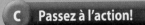 **C** **Passez à l'action!**  **1.3**

### Pourquoi j'apprends le français

You would like to encourage more people to learn French, so you are going to create a marketing tool to promote the French language and francophone culture. Look at some of the reasons to learn French below and study some possible products. Choose one from the list or come up with your own.

**Fashion:** Make a movie of a French fashion show.

**Cuisine:** Make a cookbook with French, French-Canadian, Swiss, Belgian, Caribbean, Cajun, or African recipes.

**Vocabulary development:** Create a blog about words with French origins.

**Sports:** Make a collage of sports played in the francophone world.

**Study abroad:** Make a brochure about colleges with study abroad programs in French-speaking locations, listing contact information.

**Business:** Make a graphic with the logos of famous French companies.

**Geography:** Create a map showing every country where French is spoken. Include a legend with each country's capital.

**Travel:** Make a poster with images of the top ten francophone locations you want to visit.

Possible formats you might use include: posters, flyers, brochures, PowerPoint™ presentations, movies, blogs, or word clouds.

**Tip:** To create a fact-based and effective project, research your topic online to get ideas and information.

**D** **Faisons le point!**   **2.1, 2.2**

Working with a group of classmates, make a graphic organizer like the one below. Based on what you have learned in this unit, complete the graphic organizer with "I can" statements. Note that the first example has been done for you.

> **Question centrale**
> ?
> In what ways is learning another language beneficial?

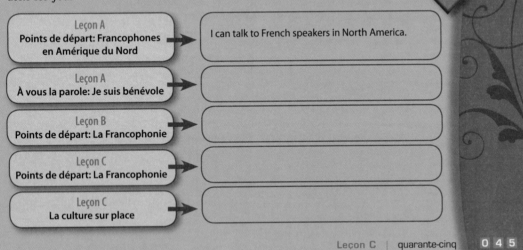

Leçon A
Points de départ: Francophones en Amérique du Nord → I can talk to French speakers in North America.

Leçon A
À vous la parole: Je suis bénévole →

Leçon B
Points de départ: La Francophonie →

Leçon C
Points de départ: La Francophonie →

Leçon C
La culture sur place →

Leçon C | quarante-cinq **0 4 5**

---

### Differentiated Learning
**Accelerate**
Challenge these students to use as much French as possible in their project for **Activité C**.

### Multiple Intelligences
**Intrapersonal vs. Interpersonal**
You might give students a choice, once they have completed the graphic organizer in **Activité D**, either to write a paragraph summarizing what they have learned or to hold a group discussion.

---

Answers _____

**C** *Activities will vary.*

**D** *Possible answers:*

**Leçon A:** I can talk to French speakers in North America.

**Leçon A:** I can work with other French speakers on international service projects.

**Leçon B:** I can travel to six places in Europe and speak French there. I can read books, listen to music, and see films by North Africans who create in French.

**Leçon C:** I can enjoy products from many countries in Africa. I can be a tourist in the Caribbean.

**Leçon C:** I can interact appropriately when greeting and taking leave of French speakers and demonstrate sensitivity when in francophone cultures.

### Reference Desk

1. Many **Projets finaux activités** are designed for students with verbal-linguistic and visual-spacial aptitudes.

2. Devise a general rubric for these projects that includes the following categories: engagement, creativity, language use, teamwork, etc. Let students know what they will be graded on ahead of time.

3. In **Faisons le point!**, students assess what they have learned using one of two types of graphic organizers. In the odd units, students are asked to write "I can...." statements and refer to specific **Activités** to demonstrate how the learning applies specifically to the **Question centrale**. In the even-numbered units, students reflect upon, analyze, and write about what they understand now that they didn't before; the connections they have made; what they did well or not so well to learn and use the content of the unit; and how they can improve upon their learning process. The graphic organizers for **Activité D** can be found in the **Copy Masters** supplement.

# Évaluation

 Go online EMCLanguages.net

## A  Évaluation de compréhension auditive   1.2

Listen to the dialogue, then read the statements below. Write **V** if the statement is **vrai** (*true*) and **F** if it is **faux** (*false*).

1. Maude introduces her cousin Robert to Aïcha.
2. Robert is from Canada.
3. Things aren't going well for Aïcha.
4. Maude invites Aïcha to a party.
5. Maude has homework to do.
6. The speakers will see each other the next day.

## B  Évaluation orale   1.1, 2.1, 2.2

With a partner, roleplay a conversation between two classmates talking to each other on the phone after school.

| | |
|---|---|
| Answer the phone. | Identify yourself. |
| Say hello and ask your classmate how things are going. | Answer and ask how your classmate is. |
| Say how things are going. Invite your classmate to go somewhere. | Say you can't go and give a reason. |
| Say that you'll call each other soon. | Say good-bye. |
| Say good-bye. | |

## C  Évaluation culturelle  4.1, 4.2

You will be asked to make some comparisons between francophone cultures and American culture. You may need to complete some additional research about American culture.

1. **Les immigrés**
   Compare the immigrant and foreign populations in France with those in the United States. Many immigrants in France come from former French colonies. What countries do they come from? Where do recent immigrants from the United States come from?

2. **Les adieux**
   Compare the expressions French teens use to say good-bye to expressions preferred by American teens. Do American teens use expressions from other languages like French teens do?

## Essential Learning

1. You may not have time to do all of these **Activités**, so choose the ones that you would like to do. Choose **Activités** based on: what you emphasized the most in Unit 1, which skills you think your students need to practice more, their unit assessment, or student interest.

2. It is a good idea for all students to do the **Évaluation orale**.

3. If you decide to do **Activité C**, divide the class in groups and assign each group a number.

4. If you want more written practice for your students, **Activité E** can be done as a written assignment.

3. **L'Europe et l'Amérique du Nord francophones**
   Compare the presence of French in Europe with the presence of French in North America. In which places is French an official language on each continent?

4. **Les langues dominantes**
   Compare the language of law, government, and education in sub-Saharan Africa to the language of international business. What advantages are there to having a dominant language in these areas?

5. **Les ados**
   Ask ten classmates what their favorite three activities are. How do your classmates' interests compare with those of French teens?

French teens attend a concert by Cheb Bilal, an Algerian singer whose songs are in French and Arabic.

**D** Évaluation écrite  2.1

You would like to practice French after school today and invite a classmate to join you. E-mail your classmate or pass an index card back and forth to ask how your classmate is and extend the invitation. Your classmate should respond appropriately. To make sure the messages are clear, do not use any SMS abbreviations.

**E** Évaluation visuelle  1.2, 2.1, 2.2, 4.1

Salle 24

Mlle Sang   Leïla   Léo   M. Savet

**Part 1:** Working in groups of four, each person selects an identity and makes a name tag based on the characters in the illustration. Introduce yourselves to each other, ask how things are going, and say good-bye. Be sure to address each other appropriately, using informal or formal language. Exchange name tags and repeat the activity until everyone has played each of the roles.

**Part 2:** Working in groups of four, each person assumes one of the identities. One person in the group knows everyone and introduces the others. Switch roles and repeat the scene until everyone has had a chance to make the introductions.

**F** Évaluation compréhensive  1.2, 2.1, 2.2

Create a storyboard with four frames. Write labels for each frame, showing how a student greets a fellow student and asks him or her to go somewhere. Finally, work with a partner to share your dialogue with a small group of classmates.

**Answers** _____

**D** *Possible answer:*
–Bonjour, c'est Paul.
–Salut, Paul.
–On va au ciné demain?
–Oui, je veux bien.
–Bon. À demain. On s'appelle.

**E** *Answers will vary.*

**F**

*Storyboards will vary.* Devise a rubric for grading students' storyboards. Keep in mind that they will be different in each unit, so it might be best to keep the criteria general: creativity or self-expression, language use, and following directions. See **Copy Masters** ancillary for a blank storyboard to use for **Activité F**.

**Differentiated Learning**

**Accelerate**
Ask students to complete all of the **Évaluation Activités** on this page spread.

**Special Needs Students**
**Linguistically Challenged Students**
You may want to allow these students to take an open-book test after completing the **Évaluation Activités** that you deem will help them be successful with the test.

All learners, especially challenged students, will benefit from using the electronic flash cards available for each unit. Encourage students to review vocabulary frequently with other students or family members.

**Flash Cards**

 *Rendez-vous à Nice!* **Episode 1**

 **Listening Pre-test D**

 *Unité* **Test**

## Reference Desk

1. The vocabulary list shows in which lesson a word or expression was introduced; look for the letters in red at the end of the entry.
2. At the end of every even-numbered unit, following the vocabulary list, there will be a **Bilan cumulatif** in which students review content through that unit. For example, in **Unité 4**, students will complete **activités** that use the vocabulary and structure of **Unités 1, 2, 3**, and **4**.

# Vocabulaire de l'Unité 1  1.2

**à** to *C*
**a: on a** we have *C*
**ah** Oh! *A*
**aider** to help *C*; **j'aide** I'm helping *C*
**algérien(ne)** Algerian *A*
**aller** to go *C*; **On va…?** Shall we go…? *C*; **Tu vas bien?** Are things going well? *C*
**allô** hello *[on telephone]* *A*
**américain(e)** American *A*
**au** to (the) *C*; **Au revoir!** Good-bye! *B*
**avec** with *B*
**bien** well *B*
**bientôt: À bientôt!** See you soon! *B*
**bon(ne)** good *C*
**bonjour** hello *A*
**c'est** this is, that is *A*; **C'est ça.** That's right. *B*
**ça: Ça va?** How's it going? *B*; **Ça va mal.** Things are going badly. *B*
un(e) **camarade: camarade de classe** classmate *A*
**canadien(ne)** Canadian *A*
**ce** it *C*
**comme: comme ci, comme ça** so-so *B*
**comment** how, what *A*; **Comment allez-vous?** *[form.]* How are you? *B*
un **contrôle** test *C*
un **copain, une copine** (boy/girl) friend *A*
**d'accord** OK *C*
**de** of, from *A*
**demain** tomorrow *B*; **À demain!** See you tomorrow! *B*
les **devoirs (m.)** homework *C*
**dis** Say… *C*
**dois: Je dois…** I must… *C*
**eh**: **eh bien** well *B*
**elle** she *A*
**enchanté(e)** delighted *A*
**est: elle est** she is *A*; **il est** he is *A*
**et** and *A*
**faire** to do, to make *C*; **faire mes devoirs** to do my homework *C*
la **fête** party *C*
une **fille** girl *A*
**français(e)** French *A*
un **garçon** boy *A*
**il** he *A*
**j'** I *C*
**je** I *A*
**là** there *A*
**la** the *C*
**le** the *A*
**m'appelle: je m'appelle** my name is *A*

**ma** my *A*
**madame (Mme)** ma'am (Mrs., Ms.) *A*
**mademoiselle (Mlle)** miss (Ms.) *A*
**mal** badly *B*
les **maths (f.)** math *C*
la **mère** mother *C*
**mes** my *C*
**mieux** better *C*
**moi** me *A*
**mon** my *A*
le **monde** everyone, world *A*
**monsieur (M.)** sir (Mr.) *A*
**ne (n')… pas** not *C*
**non** no *A*
**oh** Oh! *C*
**on** they, we, one *B*
**oui** yes *A*
**pas** not *B*; **pas mal** not bad *B*; **pas très bien** not very well *B*
le **père** father *C*
**peux: Je ne peux pas.** I can't. *C*
**possible** possible *C*
un **prénom** first name *A*
**présente: je te/vous présente….** I'd like to introduce you to…. *A*
le/la **prof** teacher *B*
**s'appelle: On s'appelle.** We'll call each other. *B*
**salut** hi *A*; bye *B*
**strict(e)** strict *C*
**suis: je suis** I am *A*
**t'appelles: Tu t'appelles comment?** What's your name? *A*
**ta** your *A*
**te** you, to you *A*
**toi** you *B*
**ton** your *C*
**top** awesome *B*
**tout** all *A*
**très** very *B*; **Très bien et toi/vous?** Very well, and you? *B*
**trop** too *B*
**tu** you *A*
**un** a, an *C*
**va: on va** they go, we go, one goes *C*
**vas: tu vas** you go *C*
**venir** to come *C*
**veux: Je veux bien.** I'd like that. *C*
**vois: je vois** I see *C*
**voudrais: tu voudrais** you would like *C*
**vous** you *A*

Places… see p. 28

# Unité 2

# Les passe-temps

*Rendez-vous à Nice!*

**Épisode 2:**

*Football ou études?*

Go online
EMCLanguages.net

1. Ask students why they think the African proverb was chosen for a unit on pastimes. (It takes practice to improve in sports and other leisure activities. Similarly, mastery of French is like acquiring sets of skills that require regular practice; the student will progress in "leaps" and "bounds"!) Ask students what English aphorism this quote brings to mind. (Practice makes perfect.)
2. Vocabulary terms and cultural information about soccer will be provided in **Unité 4, Leçon A**.
3. To put the **À savoir** into context, ask students to guess how many football and baseball organizations there are in the United States.

## Citation

"C'est en essayant encore et encore que le singe apprend à bondir."

It's in trying again and again that the monkey learns to leap.

—Proverbe africain

## À savoir

There are over 2,000 athletic organizations dedicated to soccer in France, a country about the size of Texas.

4.2

**Essential Instruction**

1. Set the stage for **Unité 2** by polling your students about their pastimes. Ask them to raise their hand if they participate in various hobbies, sports, and other leisure activities that you name.
2. Have students discuss in groups, then share with the class, their understanding of the **Question centrale**: What do the activities and pastimes the groups like to do reveal about American culture?
3. Review the **Contrat de l'élève** with students. Explain what they will learn, and expand on points they don't understand. Ask them what they are most excited about learning.
4. Show the relevant video clip from *Rendez-vous à Nice!*, Episode 2, and discuss the related question as a class.

# Unité 2

# Les passe-temps

Answers _____

The answer to the video question is A.

## Question centrale

?

What do activities and pastimes reveal about a culture?

**Go online**
**EMCLanguages.net**

**What is Patrick's mom about to tell him?**
A. He needs to improve his grades in English.
B. His grandfather passed away.
C. They are moving away.

Where is mancala played?

## Contrat de l'élève

**Leçon A** I will be able to:

>> ask what someone likes to do and say what I like to do.

>> talk about **Pari Roller**, the birth of the modern Olympics, Paris, the Tour de France, and ice hockey in Canada.

>> use subject pronouns, tell when to use **tu** or **vous**, form sentences using regular **–er** verbs, and recognize infinitives.

**Leçon B** I will be able to:

>> say how much I like to do something.

>> talk about Lyon and the game mancala.

>> use adverbs and know where to place them in a sentence.

**Leçon C** I will be able to:

>> ask about and state preferences, and agree and disagree.

>> talk about Rachid Taha and World Music, Corneille, and **la Fête de la musique**.

>> Identify masculine and feminine nouns, use definite articles, the verb **préférer**, and **ne (n')… pas** to make sentences negative.

cinquante et un **0 5 1**

## Reference Desk

1. Ask students to read the **Question centrale** and hypothesize about what vocabulary and themes this unit will contain.
2. Ask students if they have ever heard of **mancala** and see if they can tell it is a game. **Mancala** is the subject of a culture reading in this unit, **Leçon B**.
3. Have students anticipate what will happen in the video clip by reading the video-related question and possible answers. Remind students that they can review the video using their smartphones if they have software to scan the QR code.
4. Tell students the contract shows them what functions, culture, and structure they'll be learning in this unit.

## Culture

**Practices: Information**
Consider showing the i-Culture video entitled **"Au cinéma"** (2009 – 2010) to provide your students with a culturally authentic perspective related to the theme of this **Leçon**.

## Reference Desk

1. The vocabulary in **Leçon A** focuses on outdoor activities. The vocabulary in **Leçon B** focuses on indoor activities.
2. Explain the meaning of **Qu'est-ce que tu aimes faire?** and point out the responses.
3. Additional weather expressions will be introduced in **Unité 8, Leçon A. Faire** will be introduced as grammar in **Unité 8, Leçon A.**
4. Movie genres will be introduced as vocabulary in **Unité 4, Leçon C**; there will also be culture readings about **le septième art.**

## TPR

1. Develop a gesture for each verbal expression and introduce them to the class. Then say one of the expressions and have students give you the gesture to demonstrate their comprehension.
2. Have students draw one heart, two hearts, and three hearts on different sheets of paper. Ask the class how much they like different activities, for example, **Tu aimes jouer au foot?** Students hold up the appropriate heart to show if they like the **activité** a lot (3 hearts), so-so (two hearts), or a little (1 heart).

# Leçon A

## Vocabulaire actif

### Qu'est-ce que tu aimes faire? 1.2

**J'aime....**

**Je n'aime pas....**

faire du roller

faire du shopping

jouer au foot

faire du footing

aller au cinéma

sortir avec mes amis

faire du vélo

jouer au basket

Il fait beau.

Il fait mauvais.

## Essential Instruction

1. Model the pronunciation of the vocabulary expressions. Ask students to respond with thumbs up or down to indicate their preference.
2. Have students share with a partner if they like or don't like doing each **activité**.
3. Write the days of the week across the board. Explain that they are <u>not</u> capitalized in French. Explain the Latin origin of **di** and ask them to guess the meaning. Ask students to identify the planets that correspond to the days of the week.

4. Have students pronounce each day as you point to it. Erase one day at a time, but not in order. Leave the first letter. Students "read" the days, even the missing ones, until all are erased.

**Les Jeux Olympiques d'été:**

nager

plonger

faire de la gym

**Les Jeux Olympiques d'hiver:**

jouer au hockey sur glace

faire du patinage (artistique)

faire du ski (alpin)

**Tu manges...?**

des frites (f.)

des pâtes (f.)

de la pizza

une salade

**Les jours de la semaine**

lundi
mardi
mercredi
jeudi
vendredi
samedi
dimanche

**◄ Calendrier ►**

**OCTOBRE**

| lundi | mardi | mercredi | jeudi | vendredi | samedi | dimanche |
|-------|-------|----------|-------|----------|--------|----------|
|       |       |          |       |          | 1      | 2        |
| 3     | 4     | 5        | 6     | 7        | 8      | 9        |
| 10    | 11    | 12       | 13    | 14       | 15     | 16       |
| 17    | 18    | 19       | 20    | 21       | 22     | 23       |
| 24    | 25    | 26       | 27    | 28       | 29     | 30       |

**Et si je voulais dire...?** 🎧 1.2

| | |
|---|---|
| **Quel jour sommes-nous?** | *What day is it?* |
| **Nous sommes....** | *It is... (+ day of the week).* |
| **Quel temps fait-il?** | *What's the weather like?* |
| **faire de la musculation** | *to lift weights* |
| **faire du parcours** | *to do a fitness circuit or parcourse* |
| **faire du snowboard** | *to go snowboarding* |
| **danser** | *to dance* |
| **kiffer** | *to love [slang]* |
| **travailler** | *to work* |

Leçon A | cinquante-trois **053**

---

### Reference Desk

The negative expression **ne (n')… pas**, introduced as a lexical item in **Unité 1**, is a grammar topic in this lesson. Ask students which sentence in **Pour la conversation** makes a negative statement.

### Expansion

Have students re-do **Activité 4**, saying what day comes before.

## Pour la conversation

**H**ow do I ask what someone likes to do?

> **Qu'est-ce que tu aimes/vous aimez faire?**
> *What do you like to do?*

> **Tu aimes** manger des hamburgers?
> *Do you like eating hamburgers?*

**H**ow do I say what I like to do?

> **J'aime** sortir.
> *I like to go out.*

**H**ow do I say I don't like to do something?

> **Je n'aime pas** faire du ski.
> *I don't like to ski.*

**1** Les projets de la semaine  2.1

Some students are talking about their week. In English write the day of the week each activity will take place.

## Communiquez!

**2** Les agendas de Karim et Suzanne   2.1, 2.2

### Interpersonal Communication

Karim invites Suzanne to do different activities this week, but she can only do outdoor activities when it's nice out and indoor activities when the weather's bad. With a partner, play the roles of Karim and Suzanne using the information below. Follow the model.

**MODÈLE**

Karim: **Tu voudrais faire du shopping lundi?**
Suzanne: **Je ne peux pas. Il fait beau lundi. Tu voudrais faire du vélo?**
Karim: **D'accord.**

### Essential Instruction

1. Write questions and answers from **Pour la conversation** on the board. Review the meanings and pronunciation before listening to the audio.

2. After students do **Activité 1** (listening) and check answers, have them practice spelling the days of the week by dictating them to a partner. Have partners exchange and correct each other's paper.

3. Explain and model the pronunciation of **Tu voudrais faire…**, **Je ne peux pas**, and **D'accord** before completing **Activité 2**.

4. For **Activité 3**, give students a few minutes to write as many missing words as they can. Then have students work in groups to complete the e-mail. Review the answers as a class, and read the e-mail to the students to model the pronunciation. Have students read it aloud to practice pronunciation. Read the e-mail again, asking questions to ensure general comprehension this time.

## 3 Un e-mail d'une copine  2.1, 2.2

*Complétez le e-mail à Jessica de Québec.*

À: Jessica@yahoo.ca
Cc:
Sujet: Je me présente

Salut, Jessica!

Je m' __1__ Michèle. Je __2__ canadienne. Ça __3__ ? Moi, ça va très
bien! Qu'est-ce que tu __4__ faire? Moi, j'aime __5__ du shopping
avec ma mère. J' __6__ aller au cinéma avec mes copains. J'aime __7__
du vélo et j'aime __8__ au foot. Qu'est-ce que tu aimes __9__ ? J'aime
les pâtes! Et __10__ ?

À bientôt,

Michèle

---

## 4 Le calendrier

*Dites quel jour vient après.*
(Say what day comes after.)

**MODÈLE**  mercredi
**C'est jeudi.**

1. vendredi
2. lundi
3. mercredi
4. dimanche
5. mardi
6. jeudi
7. samedi   2.1, 2.2

---

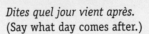

## 5 Tu aimes....  2.1, 2.2

**Interpersonal Communication**

With a partner, take turns asking and telling what
you like to do. If you have similar interests, invite
your partner to do something.

**MODÈLES**  faire du roller/manger des pâtes
A: **Tu aimes faire du roller?**
B: **Non, je n'aime pas faire du roller. Tu aimes manger des pâtes?**
A: **Oui, j'aime manger des pâtes.**
(B: **Tu veux aller au café jeudi?**
A: **Oui, je veux bien.**)

1. jouer au basket/faire du shopping
2. aller au ciné/manger des hamburgers et des frites
3. nager/sortir
4. faire du vélo/faire du ski alpin
5. aller au centre commercial/jouer au hockey sur glace
6. faire du roller/manger des pâtes

---

## 6 Questions personnelles

**Interpersonal Communication**

*Répondez aux questions.*

1. Qu'est-ce que tu aimes faire?
2. Tu aimes faire du roller?
3. Tu aimes aller au cinéma?
4. Tu aimes jouer au basket?
5. Tu aimes manger des salades?
6. Tu aimes manger de la pizza?

2.1, 2.2

tu ve allé o 6né 2m1?

---

Leçon A | cinquante-cinq **055**

---

### Answers

**3**
1. m'appelle
2. suis
3. va
4. aimes
5. faire
6. aime
7. faire
8. jouer
9. manger
10. toi

**4**
1. samedi
2. mardi
3. jeudi
4. lundi
5. mercredi
6. vendredi
7. dimanche

**5** *Dialogues will vary.*

**6** *Answers will vary.*

### Reference Desk

1. The text message says **Tu veux aller au ciné demain?**
2. Answers to **Questions Personnelles** will vary.

### Communication

**Interpretive/Interpersonal: Paired Practice**

Assign online research of other French text message abbreviations (keywords: **textos abbreviations, sms abbreviations**). Share findings. Have students write a text message to a classmate who responds.

**Interpersonal/Presentational: Paired Practice**

Have students interview each other about activities. Then, each student makes a Venn diagram and writes what he or she likes to do in the left circle, what the classmate likes to do in the right circle, and shared activities where the circles intersect.

### Expansion

Ask advanced students to do the part in parentheses. Provide them with additional destinations.

---

## Differentiated Learning
### Accelerate

1. Assign **Activité 2**, then play a game. Assign each student a day of the week. Say an **activité** from the exercise, e.g., **jouer au basket**. Students compare their day with the **activité** grid and call out the **activité** if it happens on their day.
2. Divide students into groups called **Karim** and **Suzanne**. Ask, "**Qu'est-ce que Suzanne (Karim) voudrait faire lundi (mardi, etc.)?**" Students who have that square from the table answer in unison: "**Suzanne voudrait faire du vélo lundi.**"

## Multiple Intelligences
### Logical-Mathematical/Interpersonal

Students do **Activités 5** and **6** with a partner. To practice writing, suggest that students pair up and text each other the questions and answers outside of school, as homework or an extra credit assignment. To verify the assignment, have students show you the text exchange for randomly selected numbers. Offer the option of writing the activities for students who do not want or are unable to text.

**Julien:** faire du sport; jouer au foot; jouer au basket; faire du vélo
**Camille:** faire du shopping; sortir; faire du roller
**Descriptions:** Julien aime faire du sport, jouer au foot, jouer au basket, et faire du vélo. Camille aime faire du shopping, sortir, et faire du roller.

### Extension

The vacation location: hot weather in summer, cold weather in winter.

### Reference Desk

1. **Un micro-trottoir** (*sidewalk microphone*) is an interview conducted on the street.
2. **Fais** and **fait** appear here as lexical items; the irregular verb **faire** appears as a grammar topic in **Unité 8, Leçon A**.
3. **Ne (n')... pas** is a grammar topic in this lesson.
4. Inform them that **si** is a French word with multiple meanings, one being "on the contrary" after a negative question.
5. Contrast **un soir** (*evening*) and **le soir** (*in the evening*).
6. **Pari Roller** is an organization that promotes inline skating as entertainment and sport.
7. The negative expression **ne (n')... rien** will be introduced in **Unité 10, Leçon B**, along with **ne (n')... personne**, **ne (n')... jamais**, and **ne (n')... plus**.

### Expansion

Ask students these comprehension questions based on the dialogue.
1. Qu'est-ce que Julien aime faire après les cours?
2. Camille aime faire du shopping?
3. Qu'est-ce que Camille aime faire quand il fait beau?
4. Pari Roller, c'est mercredi soir?

---

# Rencontres culturelles

## Qu'est-ce que vous aimez faire?     1.2

A journalist intern interviews Camille and Julien about young people's pastimes.

**Journaliste:** Qu'est-ce que vous aimez faire après les cours?
**Julien:** Moi, j'aime faire du sport. Je joue au foot et au basket, je fais du vélo.
**Camille:** Moi, j'aime faire du shopping, sortir avec mes amis....
**Journaliste:** Tu n'aimes pas faire de sport?
**Camille:** Si, j'aime faire du roller le vendredi soir quand il fait beau.
**Journaliste:** Tu fais Pari Roller?
**Camille:** Oui, c'est génial!

**7** **Qu'est-ce que vous aimez faire?**  2.1

Draw a grid with two columns. In one, write **Julien** and in the other write **Camille**. Write the activities each teen likes to do in the appropriate column. For example, you would write **faire du roller** in the diagram for Camille. Finally, describe to a partner what Julien or Camille likes to do.

**Extension** **Sports d'été et sports d'hiver**  1.2
Two teens discuss a low-cost vacation site they found online.

**Amadou:** Sports d'été ou sports d'hiver?
**Coralie:** Sports d'hiver!
**Amadou:** Alors là, on peut faire du hockey, du ski, du patinage....
**Coralie:** Ah bon... et les sports d'été, on fait quoi?
**Amadou:** Ben, il faut aimer nager, plonger, faire de la gym....
**Coralie:** Ah bon....
**Amadou:** Alors?
**Coralie:** Alors, rien!

**Extension** What type of climate do you think the vacation location has?

---

### Essential Instruction

1. Show the filmed dialogue, asking students to make a list of the activities they hear.
2. Point out the use of **si** as the substitute for **oui** to reply yes to a negative question.
3. Have students read aloud the dialogues in triads. Circulate to check pronunciation and answer questions.
4. Show the video again. Ask for volunteers to role-play the dialogue for the class before doing **Activité 7**.
5. If possible, show the class a video of **Pari Roller** from an online video sharing site.

# Points de départ

 *Go online* **EMCLanguages.net**

**Question centrale**
**?**
What do activities and pastimes reveal about a culture?

## Pari Roller  1.2

It's Friday, 9:30 P.M. Fifteen thousand skaters take off from the foot of the Montparnasse tower to complete an unofficial marathon—30 kilometers in all—through Paris streets. This event, organized by Pari Roller, has been taking place since 1994. How many miles is 30 km?

 **Search words:** **la tour montparnasse**
**pari roller**
**convertisseur kilomètres**

### COMPARAISONS

What large group sporting events take place in the United States? Do they occur as frequently as Pari Roller? 4.2

## Les Jeux Olympiques  1.2

Pierre de Coubertin founded the first modern Olympic Games in 1892. They took place in Athens, Greece, where 241 athletes, representing 14 nations, participated. In today's games, approximately 10,500 athletes participate, representing 200 delegations. Coubertin also designed the Olympic flag with its five rings and created the motto of the Games: **plus vite, plus haut, plus fort** (faster, higher, stronger). The original flag made its debut in 1920. The flame, symbol of the link between the modern and ancient Games, was added in 1928. In addition to the official flag and motto, the Olympics have three official languages: French, English, and the language of the host country.

 **Search words:** **jeux olympiques**

---

**Differentiated Learning**
**Expand**
1. Have students research online **Pari Roller**, **la Tour Montparnasse**, and **les Jeux Olympiques**, then share what they learned in small groups. Ask students to write three specific, interesting facts they learned about each topic.
2. Ask students to reflect upon and write about the **Question centrale**, perhaps in their Culture Journal, before sharing in their group.

**Special Needs Students**
**Linguistically Challenged**
Some students may have trouble understanding the dialogues without seeing a direct translation. To avoid frustration and help students who may miss some common, short words, show the video with subtitles.

---

## RESOURCES

 **Workbook 7–8**

## Reference Desk

1. Some students may be interested in learning the formula for converting kilometers to miles. One kilometer equals .62 miles, so to find out the equivalent in miles for 30 kilometers, multiply thirty by .62; the result is 18.6 miles. Here is the information for making other metric conversions:
   1 centimeter = .393 inches
   2.54 centimeters = 1 inch
   1 meter = 3.28 feet
   .3048 meters = 1 foot
   1.609 kilometers = 1 mile
   1 kilometer = .62 miles
2. Ask students to find out online when and where the next Summer and Winter Games will be held.

## Critical Thinking

**Application**
You may want to ask students to respond to the **Comparaisons** question in their Culture Journal.

## Connections

**Math**
To practice other metric conversions using distance, put the list of equivalencies on the board, and ask students to compute the following:
1. the size of a cafeteria lunch tray in centimeters
2. the length of their locker in centimeters
3. the height of the Statue of Liberty in New York
4. the height of the Statue of Liberty in Paris
5. the number of kilometers from your home town to Paris
6. the number of kilometers from Paris to London

# Paris  4.2, 2.1, 2.2

Yasmine, Maxime, Camille, and Julien all live in Paris, the capital of France. Called **la Ville lumière**, or "City of Light," Paris has 2.3 million inhabitants and 20 **arrondissements**. The Seine River divides the city in two parts: the Right Bank to the north and the Left Bank to the south. Paris is the world's top travel destination, thanks to architectural treasures (**la tour Eiffel**, **le Centre Pompidou**, and **la Grande Arche de la Défense**), world-class museums (**le musée du Louvre** and **le musée d'Orsay**), and monuments (**Notre-Dame** and **l'arc de triomphe**). Paris also has many famous wide avenues (**les Champs-Élysées**), charming squares (**la Place des Vosges**), and beautiful gardens (**les Tuileries** and **les jardins du Luxembourg**). Tourists also come to Paris for its fashion, luxury products, café life, excellent restaurants, and intellectual scene. Many famous writers and artists from all over the world have made their home in Paris over the years.

The **Centre Pompidou** exposes functional, color-coded pipes: blue for air, green for water, red for elevators, yellow for electricity, gray for corridors, and white for the building itself.

Search words: **pages de paris**
**tour eiffel site officiel**

**Produits** Paris is the birthplace of several artistic movements, including cubism in the early 20th century. Cubist art, attributed to Pablo Picasso and Georges Braques, is characterized by the use of geometric forms and the fragmentation of features arranged in an abstract manner.

Search words: **pablo picasso**
**georges braques**
**1.2, 2.1, 2.2, 4.2**

J'adore l'art cubiste!

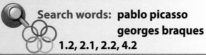

## Essential Instruction

1. Paris is an extremely high-interest topic for students, many of whom hope to go there someday. Create a slide show presentation or show a travel video to give students an overview of Paris. Alternatively, you can have your students jigsaw a list of Paris places to research online. Then they can present photos and a few interesting facts about the places.
2. Create a questionnaire to guide and enhance your students' visit to **la Tour Eiffel** website.
3. Have students research additional general information about **le Tour de France** and then share it in class.
4. Show an online video of the end of the **1989 Tour de France** (France's bicentennial year), which was the closest finish in the race's history. First, provide some background information about the two main competitors, Laurent Fignon (France) and Greg LeMond (U.S.A.).
5. Ask students to share their personal experiences and opinions about hockey, skating, and teams and individual competitors they like.

# La Francophonie: Sports

2.1, 2.2, 4.2

## ❋ Le Tour de France

Created in 1903, **le Tour de France** takes place each year in July. Stretching over three weeks and more than 1,800 miles, the course travels through France and its neighboring countries. Past winners of **le Tour** include Belgian rider Eddy Merckx, French champion Bernard Hinault, and Spanish cyclist Miguel Indurain. All these athletes have worn **le maillot jaune**, the champion's yellow jersey, several times. There is also a Tour de France for women athletes.

 **Search words: tour de france site officiel**
**tour de france féminin**

## ❋ Le hockey sur glace au Canada

2.1, 2.2, 4.2

Ice hockey is one of Canada's national pastimes. The country has six professional teams, the **Montréal Canadiens** being the oldest and biggest winner in the National Hockey League (NHL). Many Canadian players begin the sport as children, then play in the Junior Hockey leagues between the ages of 16 and 20 before moving on to the pros. It's not surprising that after ice hockey became an Olympic sport in 1920, the Canadians took home six of the seven first gold medals.

 **Search words: canadiens de montréal**

The Canadian National Hockey team scores a point against the Americans at the Vancouver Olympics.

**8**

1. an unofficial roller blade marathon
2. In 1982, the first modern Olympics games were created; in 1920, the original flag made its debut; and in 1928, the flame was added.
3. There are three: French, English, and the language of the host country.
4. the Seine River; into two parts, the Right bank to the north and the Left bank to the south
5. its architectural treasures (**la tour Eiffel**, **le Centre Pompidou**, **la Grande Arche de la Défense**), its museums (**le musée du Louvre** and **le musée d'Orsay**), and its monuments (**la cathédrale de Notre-Dame** and **l'arc de triomphe**).
6. a biking event through France and its neighboring countries that takes place yearly in July
7. the **Montréal Canadiens**

### Perspectives

*Answers will vary.* Students can find blogs and media articles about the topic online.

**9**

1. **faux**, the Winter Olympics were created in 1924
2. **faux**, they took place in Chamonix
3. **vrai**
4. **vrai**
5. **vrai**
6. **faux**, it is Rio de Janeiro

### Connections

**History**
Ask your students to study the chronology of the Olympics on this page and identify the locations in France where the modern Olympic Games have been held. (Answer: Paris, 1900 and 1924; Chamonix,1924; Grenoble, 1968; Albertville, 1992) Mark these cities on your wall map of France with colored pushpins.

---

## 8 Questions culturelles  1.3, 2.1, 2.2

*Répondez aux questions.*

1. What kind of event does Pari Roller sponsor?
2. What Olympic milestones occurred in 1892, 1920, and 1928?
3. What are the official languages of the **Jeux Olympiques**?
4. What is the name of the river that runs through Paris? How does it divide the city?
5. What attracts so many tourists to Paris?
6. What is **le Tour de France**?
7. What is the name of the professional hockey team from Montreal?

The main pyramid in the courtyard of the Louvre, Paris' largest and oldest art museum, serves as the primary entrance for tourists and artists.

### Perspectives

You have probably heard stories about athletes taking prohibited drugs to enhance their performance. Do online research about **le doping** and **le Tour de France**. In what ways is the French reaction to **le doping** in **le Tour de France** similar to or different from the American one?

---

## Du côté des médias

### L'histoire des Jeux Olympiques

| Date | Événement |
|------|-----------|
| 1896 | Athènes, premiers jeux modernes; rénovation des Jeux par Pierre de Coubertin |
| 1900 | Paris à l'occasion de l'Exposition universelle |
| 1904 | Saint-Louis, Missouri, premiers jeux aux USA |
| 1924 | Création des Jeux d'hiver à Chamonix |
| 1936 | Jeux de Berlin et l'injure faite à Jesse Owens |
| 1956 | Melbourne: premiers jeux dans l'Hémisphère Sud |
| 1968 | Mexico et le geste sur le podium des athlètes afro-américains; c'est la deuxième fois que la France accueille les Jeux d'hiver (Grenoble) |
| 1972 | Munich et l'attentat contre l'équipe d'Israël |
| 1976 | Montréal |
| 1980, 1984: | Moscou et Los Angeles: les Jeux de la fin de la "Guerre froide" avec le boycott réciproque |
| 1992 | Les Jeux d'hiver ont lieu à Albertville, en France |
| 1996 | Atlanta: le réveil du "Vieux Sud" |
| 2000 | Sydney, le tournant du Siècle |
| 2004 | Athènes: le retour aux origines |
| 2008 | Beijing: la démonstration de la puissance chinoise |
| 2016 | Rio de Janeiro: premiers jeux en Amérique du Sud |

## 9 Vrai ou faux?

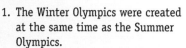

Read the Olympics timeline on the left. Decide if each statement is **vrai** (**V**) or **faux** (**F**). Correct any false statements.

1. The Winter Olympics were created at the same time as the Summer Olympics.
2. The first Winter Olympics took place in Montreal.
3. A terrorist attack occurred at the 1972 Olympics.
4. The United States went to Moscow to participate in the Olympics at the end of the Cold War.
5. The **Jeux d'hiver** were held in France three times.
6. Buenos Aires is the site of the first Olympics in South America.

1.2, 2.1, 2.2

### Essential Instruction

1. After students answer the questions in **Activité 8**, focus on **les Jeux Olympiques** in **Du côté des medias**. Have students write the numbers 1 – 16 on a piece of paper. Then say the English equivalent of the **événements** without saying the location. Tell students to look for cognate "clues" as they try to decode the French descriptions and identify the year in which the event took place.

2. Students may not know what a "subject pronoun" is, so first explain the concepts of 1st-, 2nd-, and 3rd- person subject pronouns in English. Give a subject pronoun in English and have students point to the appropriate person or number of people each pronoun signifies, for example, **toi** (student points to a classmate). Then, repeat the **activité** in French.

# Structure de la langue

  **1.2**

## Subject Pronouns

To talk to or about people, you can use subject pronouns to replace their names. Subject pronouns are either singular (referring to one person) or plural (referring to more than one person). Here are the subject pronouns in French.

| Singular | | Plural | |
|---|---|---|---|
| je | I | nous | we |
| tu | you (sing. informal) | vous | you (pl. or sing. formal) |
| il<br>elle<br>on | he<br>she<br>one/they/we | ils<br>elles } | they |

**Tu** aimes aller au cinéma?     *Do you like to go to the movies?*
Oui, **j'**aime aller au cinéma.     *Yes, I like to go to the movies.*

Note that **je** becomes **j'** when the next word begins with a vowel sound.

The pronoun **on** is singular even though it often refers to more than one person.

**On** va au centre commerical.     *We are going to the mall.*

**Il** replaces a masculine name; **elle** replaces a feminine name.

Julien? **Il** aime jouer au foot.     *Julien? He likes to play soccer.*
Et Camille? **Elle** aime jouer     *And Camille? She likes to play basketball.*
au basket.

**Elles** refers to two or more females. **Ils** refers to two or more males or to a combination of males and females.

Cédric et Sophie?     *Cédric and Sophie?*
**Ils** aiment faire du shopping!     *They love to go shopping!*

---

### Reference Desk

1. Ask students if they know what **Parlez-vous français?** means. Then ask them to look at the cartoon and tell you how many people **vous** refers to in this instance.
2. In English, "I" is a 1st-person pronoun, "you" is considered 2nd-person, and "he/she/it" are considered 3rd-person. In French grammar, pronouns are divided into singular and plural and the 1st-, 2nd-, and 3rd-person classification applies to both the singular and plural list. **Vous** is considered 2nd-person plural.
3. In French the subject pronoun used to refer to a thing or an idea depends on its antecedent, or the noun to which it refers.
4. Point out to students that when a sentence contains a masculine and a feminine subject, the pronoun **ils** is used. You might model this in class by having a boy and girl come to the front of the class. Say: **Caro et Léo? Ils aiment jouer au foot.** Or, you may want to ask students to deduce the rule. Also use same-sex pairings of students so students can anchor concepts of **ils** and **elles**.

### Communication

**Presentational: Cooperative Groups**

Ask groups of six students to make a one-frame cartoon in which they show their comprehension of another pronoun; if they want to use **vous**, the cartoon should show an example of the formal singular or informal plural usage. As a group, have them post their cartoons.

---

### Differentiated Learning
#### Accelerate
1. Ask students to research the original ancient Olympic Games in Greece.
2. Have students research and share with the class additional information about other events at the different Olympic Games listed on this page.

#### Multiple Intelligences
#### Bodily-Kinesthetic
1. To show the differences among the subject pronouns, divide the class into groups of six with a minimum of two students of each gender.

2. As you say a French subject pronoun, students take turns identifying the pronoun by standing in front of the person or people that represent the pronoun and pointing to them.
3. Demonstrate the game first. For example, say **nous** and form a group by standing next to another student or students. Next, say **vous** and stand in front of and point at a minimum of two students.

Script can be found in the front pages of the Annotated Teacher's Edition.

1. B/elle
2. C/ils
3. C/ils
4. D/elles
5. A/il
6. B/elle

**11**

1. tu
2. ils
3. je
4. elle
5. elles
6. nous
7. vous

**12**

1. elle
2. ils
3. il
4. elles
5. nous

## Critical Thinking

### Comparisons

Ask students to think of ways in which English speakers differentiate between the concept of **tu** and **vous**. (Possible answers: register levels, tone of voice, and forms of address, body language) Then discuss with students the benefits of being able to distinguish this in French because of the two different words for "you."

---

### 10 Identifiez le sujet!

Write the letter of the French subject pronoun that could replace each name or set of names.

A. il
B. elle
C. ils
D. elles

 **2.1, 2.2**

### 11 Aux Jeux Olympiques d'été  1.1

You are watching the opening ceremony at the Summer Olympics and listening to a group of French people who are talking about what they want to see at the Games. Identify the subject pronoun in the sentences you overhear.

1. Toi, tu veux voir la gymnastique.
2. Martine et Théo, ils désirent voir les nageurs.
3. Moi, je veux voir les plongeurs.
4. Élisabeth, elle désire voir la gymnastique.
5. Chloé et Marie-Ange, elles désirent voir les plongeurs.
6. Amadou et moi, nous désirons voir les nageurs.
7. Éric et toi, vous désirez voir la gymnastique.

### 12 Choisissez le sujet! **2.1, 2.2**

Choose the appropriate subject pronoun from the list to describe each person or group of people.

je   il   elle   nous   ils   elles

**MODÈLE**

**je**

1.

2.

3.

4.

5.

### Essential Instruction

1. Do **Activité 12** as a class, circling the subject pronouns on the board as students identify them. Model the pronunciation. Ask the class to identify the people to whom the pronouns refer. Circle them in a different color, and draw a line between the subject pronoun and the people to show the connection.

2. Review the concept of register on p. 26, **Unité 1** and the difference between **toi** and **vous**, and **tu** and **vous**. Discuss the **Comparaisons** question in the textbook. Ask if any students speak a language other then English. If so, ask them to share how the concept of register is expressed in that language.

## tu vs. vous  4.1

The subject pronouns **tu** and **vous** both mean "you," but are used in different ways. When you talk to one person,

Tu es branché?

use **tu** (the familiar form) with:
- a friend
- a person your own age
- a close relative
- a child
- a pet

use **vous** (the formal form) with:
- an acquaintance
- a person older than you
- a distant relative
- an adult you don't know
- a person of authority, such as a teacher or doctor

When talking to more than one person, always use **vous**.

Anne, Lucie, Amir, comment allez-vous?    *Anne, Lucie, Amir, how are you?*

Tu voudrais de la salade?

### COMPARAISONS  4.1

How is the plural form of "you" expressed in English?

Kirsten and Lance, are **you** ready for the quiz?
**You guys** get 15 minutes to study.
**You all** must take the test now.

### 13 Tu ou vous? 🎧 1.1, 4.1

Say if you would follow each exchange below with a sentence that uses **tu** or **vous**.

1. Salut, ça va?
2. Bonjour, les amis!
3. Au revoir, Madame!
4. À demain, Monsieur Duval!
5. Ah, Snoopy!
6. Anne et Michèle, on va à la maison?
7. Salim, on va à la fête?

COMPARAISONS: In English you can get the plural idea of "you" across by using names, "you guys," or by adding "all" to your sentence. In the southern United States, some people might say "y'all must take the test now."

### RESOURCES

📖 **Workbook 11**

Answers _____

⓭
1. tu
2. vous
3. vous
4. vous
5. tu
6. vous
7. tu

### Expansion

Ask students to write a list of the six closest (family, friends) and six most influential people (celebrities, athletes, teachers) in their lives. Then ask them to write down beside each name whether they would use **tu** or **vous** with each one.

### TPR

**Tu vs. vous**
Have each student write **tu** on one side of a piece of paper and **vous** on the other. Read off identities of people, for example, "your mail carrier" or "your cousin," and ask students to hold up the appropriate pronoun.

## Multiple Intelligences
### Bodily-Kinesthetic
1. Make five sets of index cards. Each set should have a girl's first name, boy's first name, **Monsieur X** (French surname), **Madame** X (surname), and **Mademoiselle** X (surname). Make another set with the **activité** vocabulary that students know.
2. Distribute a name tag and **activité** card to each student.
3. Have students circulate and greet each other formally or informally according to cues on their name tags.

4. Then students should ask about the **activité** on their card, using the appropriate pronoun depending with whom they are speaking. After the conversation, students switch cards and take leave.

### Logical-Mathematical
1. Have students create an eight-column grid that they label with the subject pronouns.
2. Write a name or names on the board that correspond to each subject pronoun. Students write them in the appropriate subject pronoun column.

**Workbook 12**

**Answers** _____

**14** Absorber; couper; passer

**15** *Answers will vary.*

### Reference Desk

In English grammar, infinitives are introduced with "to," for example, "to play." However, in French the infinitive form is usually shown by the final two or three letters, for example, **jouer**, **finir**, **attendre** (two letters); **recevoir** (three letters).

### Expansion

For **Activité 14**, ask students to make a list of 15 verbs they would like to know in French that they haven't learned yet. Have them use a French-English dictionary to find out what those verbs are and write them down in their infinitive form. Before students begin their research, you might tell them that many French verbs end in **-er**, **-ir**, or **-re**.

# Infinitives  1.2

A verb expresses action or a state of being. The basic form of a verb is called the infinitive. This form is found in the end vocabulary of this textbook and in French dictionaries. Many French infinitives end in **–er**, such as **présenter**, **aider**, **nager**, **aimer**, **manger**, **jouer**, and **plonger**.

*Paul aime jouer au foot.*

**14** **Je vois les infinitifs!**  2.1

Write a list of the **–er** infinitives that appear in this partial list of vocabulary for French speakers attending the **Jeux Olympiques d'hiver.**

**Alpine Skiing/Ski alpin**

| tactics | technique |
| --- | --- |
| absorb the bumps (to) | absorber les bosses |
| active lightening | allègement actif |
| aerodynamic | aérodynamique |
| airborne (to be) | être dans les airs |
| anticipation | anticipation |
| back grip | appui talon |
| breaking-stop | arrêt braquage |
| carving | conduite coupée |
| counter-turn | contre-virage |
| cross (to) | couper en traversée |
| cross the gate (to) | passer la porte |
| directional effect | effet directionnel |
| downhill ski | ski aval |

*Lexique anglais/français des sports olympiques* (INSEP 2001)

**15** **Qu'est-ce que tu aimes faire?**

Say that you do two outdoor activities when it is nice out, and two indoor activities when the weather's bad.

1. Quand il fait beau, j'aime....
2. Quand il fait mauvais, j'aime....
3. Quand il fait beau, j'aime....
4. Quand il fait mauvais, j'aime....

 1.1

*Quand il fait beau, j'aime faire du ski avec mon amie.*

**Essential Instruction**

1. Simplify the concept of an infinitive by explaining it as "the name of the verb." Add that in English an infinitive is expressed by "to" and the verb. Provide examples. Solicit infinitives in English to ensure comprehension. Next, explain that the infinitive of most verbs in French ends in **-er** (others end in **-ir** and **-re**).

2. Have students repeat aloud the lesson vocabulary, then do **Activité 15**.

3. Introduce the **-er** verb conjugation. Have students practice on an individual white board or sheet of paper. Give students a colored marker for pronouns and verb endings and a different color for verb stems. Ask students to write the subject pronouns in the order as listed for the verb **jouer**, p. 65. Solicit another infinitive from the lesson. Students should conjugate, holding up their board when finished. Have students correct, read the correct conjugation out loud, then move on to another infinitive.

# Present Tense of Regular Verbs Ending in –er  1.2

Regular verbs follow a predictable pattern. Regular **–er** verbs, such as **jouer**, have six forms in the present tense. To form the present tense of a regular **–er** verb, drop the **–er** ending from its infinitive to find the stem.

Now add the endings (**-e, -es, -e, -ons, -ez, -ent**) to the stem of the verb depending on the corresponding subject pronouns.

| Subject Pronouns | +Stem | +Ending |
|---|---|---|
| je | jou | e |
| tu | jou | es |
| il/elle/on | jou | e |
| nous | jou | ons |
| vous | jou | ez |
| ils/elles | jou | ent |

**On mange des pâtes?**

### Pronunciation Tip

Notice the shading in the conjugation of **jouer**. Despite the five different endings for the subject pronouns **je, tu, il/elle/on,** and **ils/elles**, all forms of the verb in dark yellow are pronounced identically. Only the **vous** and **nous** forms are pronounced differently.

Vous **jouez** au foot demain?  *Are you playing soccer tomorrow?*
Oui, je **joue** au foot.  *Yes, I'm playing soccer.*

Remember that **je** becomes **j'** when the next word begins with a vowel sound: **J'aime jouer au hockey**.

Each present tense verb form in French consists of only one word, but has more than one meaning.

André **nage**.  { *André swims.*
                  { *André is swimming.*

André **nage**?  *Does André swim?*

If an infinitive ends in **–ger**, the ending for the **nous** form is **–eons**.

Nous **nageons**.  *We are swimming.*
Nous **mangeons** une pizza.  *We are eating a pizza.*

### COMPARAISONS 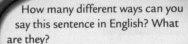 4.1

How many different ways can you say this sentence in English? What are they?

Luc joue au basket.

COMPARAISONS: Luc plays basketball. Luc is playing basketball. Luc does play basketball.

## RESOURCES

 e-visual 6

 Workbook 13–16

### Reference Desk

In French grammar the stem is called **la racine** and the ending **la terminaison**.

### Critical Thinking

**Application**
You may want to introduce **–er** verbs using the inductive method. Give each student a sheet of paper containing approximately 20 sentences that use different subject pronouns and an assortment of **–er** verbs that students have already seen. Put students in pairs, telling them to work together to try to sort out the sentences in order to recognize various patterns. Ask for a volunteer pair to explain the rules of using regular **–er** verbs. Then compare the typical **–er** verb chart to one using an English verb.

## Differentiated Learning
### Adapt
1. After students practice conjugating with singular pronouns, introduce the two-column conjugation chart, emphasizing how it is divided into singular and plural.
2. Students can also practice writing out this conjugation using white boards. Divide students into groups of four and write a list of infinitives on the board for students to conjugate. Have them help each other and peer-edit their work
3. Explain **j'**, and assign **j'aime** and **j'aide** for practice.

## Multiple Intelligences
### Verbal-Linguistic/Bodily-Kinesthetic
1. Bring a koosh ball (or something similar) to make oral drills more fun for your students.
2. Tell students that you will give them a cue, such as **jouer – tu** and then randomly throw the ball to a student who should respond with **tu joues**.
3. Tell students to listen carefully to the cue to know to whom you will throw the ball. Play the game until all have had a chance to participate.

## Answers

**16**

1. Non, il joue au foot.
2. Non, elles jouent au basket.
3. Non, il joue au foot.
4. Non, je joue au basket.
5. Non, ils jouent au foot.
6. Non, elle joue au basket.
7. Non, nous jouons au basket.

**17**

1. Elle mange des pâtes.
2. Tu nages.
3. Vous jouez au basket.
4. Marc et moi, nous plongeons.
5. Ils jouent au hockey.
6. Elle joue au foot.
7. Elles mangent de la pizza.

**18**

1. Florence et Alima nagent.
2. Je joue au basket.
3. Émile plonge.
4. David et Hugo jouent au basket.
5. Noémie nage.

---

**16 Au parc**   **1.1, 2.1, 2.2**

Anne calls to find out who is playing basketball and who is playing soccer at the park on Saturday. Answer her questions saying that the person asked about is playing the other sport.

**MODÈLE**   Vous jouez au foot?
**Non, nous jouons au basket.**

1. Julien joue au basket?
2. Marie-Alix et Delphine jouent au foot?
3. Marcel joue au basket?
4. Tu joues au foot?
5. Khaled et Amadou jouent au basket?
6. Madeleine joue au foot?
7. Vous jouez au foot?

Jean-Luc joue au basket.

---

**17 Le weekend**

*Dites ce que (what) tout le monde fait.*

**MODÈLE**    nous
**Nous mangeons une salade.**

1. Juliette

2. tu

3. vous

4. Marc et moi, nous

5. Félix et Alexis

6. Mlle Vellard

7. Rosalie et Saniyya
**2.1**

---

**18 Au club**   **1.1**

*Dites ce qu'on fait au club (fitness center).*

1. Florence et Alima
2. je
3. Émile
4. David et Hugo
5. Noémie

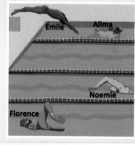

---

**Essential Instruction**

1. Some students may have difficulty with the transition from **tu** to **je** in a question-answer situation, so give some examples of questions and answers in English first. Ask them, "Do you like French?" ("Yes, I like French.")
2. Write on the board: "you → I" and its French translation: "**tu → je.**" Do the same for the other pronouns.
3. In **Activités 17** and **18**, translate the directions for the students. Suggest that they keep a list of French instructions and their meanings in their notes. Most students get frustrated when they can't understand the directions.
4. **Activité 19** can be done in a small group.
5. For **Activité 20**, students can create a photo album on the computer or print the photos they want to share with classmates.

# À vous la parole

## Communiquez!

**Question centrale**
? What do activities and pastimes reveal about a culture?

### 19 Les sports d'hiver ou d'été? 1.1, 1.3

**Interpersonal/Presentational Communication**

Poll ten to twelve of your classmates to find out if they like winter or summer sports. Record their responses in the chart like the one below that your teacher gives you.

**MODÈLE**

|       | les sports d'hiver | les sports d'été |
|-------|--------------------|------------------|
| Élodie |                   | ✓                |

Léo: **Tu aimes les sports d'hiver?**
Élodie: **Non, je n'aime pas les sports d'hiver.**
Léo: **Les sports d'été?**
Élodie: **Oui, j'aime les sports d'été.**

Tally the numbers in your chart. How many people like winter sports, summer sports, sports in both seasons, or don't like sports at all? Report your findings to your group.

**MODÈLE** **Simone, Marc, et Coralie aiment les sports d'hiver. Nathalie, Jean-Pierre, Martine, Élodie, et Thierry aiment les sports d'été. David aime les sports d'hiver et d'été. Bruno n'aime pas les sports.**

## Communiquez!

### 20 Pari Roller  1.3

**Presentational Communication**

Imagine you recently participated in the **Pari Roller** skating event in Paris. Create a photo album of eight famous Paris monuments you photographed during your skate. Make sure to label all the pictures with the names of and information about the monuments. Also include in your album five other photos you took, such as a Parisian café, store, or metro station.

The Eiffel Tower was built for the 1889 World's Fair by Gustave Eiffel.

---

**Answers** _____

**19** *Answers will vary.*

**20** *Photo albums will vary.*

### Reference Desk

If students poll ten students in **Activité 19**, the results are very easy to tabulate in percentages. For example, if six students prefer winter sports and four students prefer summer sports, they could report the percentages if they are not yet ready to write a summary as in the model. For example, they could write: **60% aiment les sports d'hiver; 40% aiment les sports d'été.**

**Blended Instruction**
Consider using blended instruction, a combination of in-class learning and computer-mediated instruction or learning opportunities. Ask students to complete activities on the computer, using their cell or smartphone, or other emerging electronic technology. This will allow students to hone their tech skills and become more independent learners. Schedule routine Internet and e-book learning in class and in the lab.

---

## Differentiated Learning
### Accelerate

1. Do **Activité 20** for enrichment. By the time students get to **Unité 8**, which is all about Paris, above-level students will be able write and present simple information about Paris monuments. These students could also conduct a poll about what their classmates like to do. Other students should respond with their top three choices. Ask the above-level students to make a list of the most popular activities, based on the poll results, and display it in the classroom.

## Special Needs Students
### Linguistically Challenged

1. For **Activité 16**, have students replace the names with subject pronouns.

2. Have students write **Activités 17** and **18** to practice spelling, the verb forms, and the illustrated vocabulary.

3. Ask these students to exchange papers in groups and correct their classmates' spelling. Tell students to re-write words they misspelled or sentences they didn't compose correctly.

**Answers** _____

 **B**

1. five
2. six
3. four
4. five
5. four

**D**

1. la
2. les
3. le
4. la
5. le

### Reference Desk

1. In **Activité A**, tap out the rhythm of the syllables to help students understand the equal emphasis on the syllables of each word.
2. In **Activité A**, the red **e** in **samedi** means you don't emphasize this vowel sound.
3. In **Activité B**, write out the sentences, located in the textbook Audio Program Manual, for visual learners.
4. In **Activité C**, students are asked to stress articles and syllables equally in a noun. The tendency for English speakers is to relax the **le** and **la** too much. By practicing the proper pronunciation early on, students can minimize pronunciation errors common to English speakers.
5. Help students who need more practice pronouncing definite articles. Read the following questions aloud, and ask students to answer affirmatively.
   1. Tu aimes le foot? (J'aime le foot.)
   2. Tu aimes le basket? (J'aime le basket.)
   3. Tu aimes le ski? (J'aime le ski.)
   4. Tu aimes le footing? (J'aime le footing.)

# Prononciation   1.2

## Rhythm

- In French, nearly equal emphasis is placed on each syllable.

 **A** Prononciation des syllabes

*Repeat these words, pronouncing each syllable with equal stress.*

1. (Two syllables)   lundi      jeudi      samedi      dimanche
2. (Three syllables)   mercredi   vendredi   le weekend   Il fait beau.

 **B** Comptons les syllabes!

*Number your paper from 1 to 5. The first time you listen, repeat the sentence. The second time, write the number of syllables you hear.*

| MODÈLE | **D'accord.** (2) |
| --- | --- |

## Pronouncing Definite Articles

- The articles for "the" in French—**le**, **la**, **les**—each have a different vowel sound, but all three should be stressed like any other word.

 **C** "Le," "la," et "les"

*Repeat each group of words. Pay close attention to how to pronounce the definite articles **le**, **la**, and **les**.*

1. le guide - la guide - les guides
2. le touriste - la touriste - les touristes
3. le photographe - la photographe - les photographes

 **D** La Prononciation de "le," "la," et "les"

*Number your paper from 1 to 5. Write **le**, **la**, or **les** to identify the definite article you hear in each sentence.*

| MODÈLE | You hear: | You write: |
| --- | --- | --- |
| | **Elle visite les États-Unis.** | **les** |

### Essential Instruction

1. Before doing the **Prononciation**, choose a short, rhyming poem to read to the class, such as **"Il pleure dans mon cœur"** by Paul Verlaine.
2. Tell them to listen to how the poem sounds, and then ask for their reaction.
3. Explain why French is often considered the most beautiful language in the world: because of the even rhythm and intonation and the equal balance of vowel and consonant sounds when spoken.
4. Ask students to look at the pictures on p. 69 and guess what the people are doing.
5. Review the concept of an "infinitive" (the non-conjugated verb form) and "conjugation" (putting the verb with its pronoun and into its usable form).
6. Clarify the meanings of the infinitives.
7. Model the pronunciation of the new vocabulary words and ask the students to find the only infinitive in the yellow box.

## Vocabulaire actif

 *Go online* **EMC**Languages.net

## Tu aimes un peu, bien, ou beaucoup? 🎧

Qu'est-ce que tu aimes faire à la maison?

🔵 1.1, 1.2, 2.1, 2.2

> J'aime un peu faire la cuisine.

> J'aime beaucoup écouter de la musique avec mon lecteur MP3.

> J'aime bien envoyer des textos.

> J'aime surfer sur Internet.

dormir

lire

étudier

regarder la télé

jouer aux jeux vidéo

téléphoner

### Et si je voulais dire...? 🎧

| | |
|---|---|
| **un magazine** | *magazine* |
| **un e-Zine** | *online magazine* |
| **un roman** | *novel* |
| **un SMS** | *text message* |
| **zapper** | *to flip through channels* |
| **un coup de fil** | *phone call* |

Leçon B | soixante-neuf **069**

## Reference Desk

1. Students learned **à la maison** in **Unité 1, Leçon C**.
2. A synonym for **un lecteur MP3** is **un iPod**; you can also abbreviate the expression and call it **un MP3**.
3. In English "cuisine" refers to a style of cooking, so students will have some familiarity with the word.
4. A synonym for **un texto** is **un SMS**.

## Critical Thinking

**Application**
Ask students what words in English come from **dormir** (dormant, dormancy, dormitory), what these English words have in common, and how they are related to the French word.

## Communication

**Presentational: Cooperative Groups**
Have students make a list of three activities from this unit that each of their family members likes to do, for example, Luke: **jouer aux jeux vidéos, écouter de la musique, faire du ski.** After each **activité**, students should write a + if the family member likes the **activité** a lot, = if he or she really likes it, and – if he or she likes it only a bit. Then, in groups, students tells how much their family members like each **activité**. (Since possessive adjectives and names of family members won't be introduced until **Unité 5, Leçon A**, you might tell students to use first names in all their sentences.)

## Multiple Intelligences
### Bodily-Kinesthetic
On the board, draw one heart next to **j'aime un peu**, two hearts for **j'aime bien**, and three hearts for **j'aime beaucoup**. Practice linking memory and body movement by asking students to gesture **un peu** by making a small circle with their hands, **bien** with a larger circle, and **beaucoup** with the largest circle when you ask them a question about how much they like an **activité**.

**069**

## Pour la conversation

**H**ow do I find out how much someone likes to do something?

> **Tu aimes beaucoup** lire?
> *Do you like to read a lot?*

**H**ow do I say how much I enjoy doing things?

> **J'aime un peu** lire.
> *I like to read a little.*
> **J'aime bien** envoyer des textos.
> *I really like to send text messages.*
> **J'aime beaucoup** faire du sport.
> *I like to play sports a lot.*

**1 C'est quelle activité?**   1.1, 2.1, 2.2

Clément is asking his classmates about activities they enjoy. Choose the image that matches the activity you hear.

A.    B.    C.    D.

E.    F.    G.

### Essential Instruction

1. Have students listen to the audio of the functions.
2. Do **Activité 1**; then, point to a few of these common classroom objects in the room to see if the students can recall the associated **activité**.
3. Ask students to do **Activités 2** and **3** with a partner and circulate in the room to help them.
4. Check for accuracy by asking individual students several of the questions in **Activité 3** out of order.
5. Ask the students to try to decipher the text message and ask the origin of the letters the French use for texting: SMS (Short Message Service). Have one student try to write the message in non-abbreviated French on the board. (**Bonjour, tu veux manger?**) You will need to provide them with the verb form **veux**.

## 2 Qu'est-ce qu'ils aiment faire?

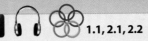 1.1, 2.1, 2.2

Match each image with the correct description. (♥ = un peu; ♥ ♥ = bien; ♥ ♥ ♥ = beaucoup)

A.

B.

C.

D.

E.

F.

G.

H.

1. Il aime beaucoup téléphoner.
2. Ils aiment un peu surfer sur Internet.
3. Elle aime beaucoup écouter de la musique.
4. Il aime bien faire la cuisine.
5. Elle aime bien regarder la télé.
6. Elle aime un peu jouer aux jeux vidéo.
7. Elles aiment bien envoyer des textos.
8. Ils aiment beaucoup faire du sport

## Communiquez!

## 3 Questions personnelles

1.1, 2.1, 2.2

**Interpersonal Communication**

With a partner, take turns asking and answering the questions.

1. Tu surfes sur Internet?
2. Tu aimes un peu écouter de la musique?
3. Tu aimes bien envoyer des textos?
4. Tu aimes beaucoup faire du sport?
5. Qu'est-ce que tu aimes lire?
6. Tu aimes regarder la télé?

J'aime bien faire de la gym.

**Differentiated Learning**

**Expand**

1. Write **J'aime un peu**, **J'aime bien**, and **J'aime beaucoup** on the board. Next to these phrases, write a list of the 11 infinitives the students know (**aimer, écouter de la musique, envoyer des textos, surfer, faire la cuisine, dormir, lire, étudier, regarder la télé, jouer, téléphoner**). Ask volunteers to express their opinions by matching the first part of the sentence with a verb of their choice.

2. After students have completed **Activité 3**, ask each student to present their partner's likes and dislikes, either in groups or in front of the class.

Answers _____

**2**
1. B
2. D
3. F
4. A
5. G
6. H
7. E
8. C

**3** *Answers will vary.*

**Dialogue Video**

**Answers** _____

**4**

1. Faux. Il aime beaucoup jouer aux jeux vidéo.
2. Vrai.
3. Faux. Elle aime beaucoup dormir.
4. Vrai.
5. Faux. Elle aime bien faire la cuisine.
6. Vrai.
7. Vrai.
8. Faux. Elle aime bien lire.

**Extension**

Samuel has scheduled more outdoor activities.

### Reference Desk

**Une enquête** is a survey; a **sondage d'opinion** is a formal opinion poll.

### Critical Thinking

**Analysis**

Explore the title word **enquête**. Explain that the circumflex accent replaces the letter "s" in an earlier version of the word derived from Latin, for example, "forest" from **forêt** and "hospital" from **hôpital**. Ask what English word comes from **enquête** and ask students what happens in an "inquest." Make the connection between a legal inquiry and a "survey."

### Expansion

For the **Extension** dialogue, you may choose to have students design and fill in their own weekly planner. You may want them to use their own phone or other electronic device, a page from a wall calendar, or a blank online weekly planner. Have them fill in their **activités** and a time for each. You might suggest they pick a recent week when they were quite busy.

# Rencontres culturelles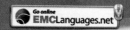

## Une enquête     1.2

Yasmine is reporting to her friends about **une enquête** she conducted for class in Lyon where her cousin lives.

Yasmine: C'est une enquête sur les activités préférées pendant le weekend. La question: Qu'est-ce que vous aimez faire?

Rose, "J'aime beaucoup dormir. C'est génial!"

Moussa, "Moi, j'aime beaucoup jouer aux jeux vidéo."

Xavier, "Moi, j'aime surfer sur Internet, écouter mon lecteur MP3, envoyer des textos à mes amis."

Isabelle, "Moi, j'aime bien lire, écouter de la musique, étudier."

Fatima, "J'aime bien faire la cuisine, regarder la télévision."

### 4 Une enquête  2.1, 2.2

Decide if each statement is **vrai (V)** or **faux (F)**. Correct any false statements.

1. Moussa aime un peu jouer aux jeux vidéo.
2. Xavier aime envoyer des textos.
3. Rose aime un peu dormir.
4. Isabelle aime bien écouter de la musique.
5. Fatima aime beaucoup faire la cuisine.
6. Xavier aime surfer sur Internet.
7. Fatima aime bien regarder la télévision.
8. Isabelle aime beaucoup lire.

**Extension** **Agenda électronique de Samuel** 1.1

lundi:
mardi: jeudi 19
mercredi: nager avec l'équipe
jeudi: jeux vidéo avec Timéo
vendredi: foot avec la classe
samedi: footing avec Koffi
dimanche: roller dans Paris
lire le roman *Belle du Seigneur*
basket au club

**Extension** Has Samuel scheduled more indoor or outdoor activities?

**072** soixante-douze | Unité 2

---

**Essential Instruction**

1. Have students watch the dialogue clip. Clarify vocabulary. Check comprehension with **Activité 4**.
2. Ask students to locate Lyon on a map, then read and summarize the paragraph on the city.
3. Show your class an example of Roman, Romanesque, Gothic, and Renaissance architecture so that they can understand the types of buildings in Lyon.
4. Invite students to use the online search words in **Points de départ** to learn more about Lyon and share what they discovered.
5. Mention that Lyon is a center of great gastronomic tradition, thus contributing to France's reputation for fine cuisine. Students will study foods in **Unité 4**.

# Points de départ

 Go online EMCLanguages.net

**Question centrale**

? What do activities and pastimes reveal about a culture?

## Lyon   4.2, 1.3

Lyon sits at the intersection where the **Rhône** and **Saône** rivers meet. With 1.6 million inhabitants, it is the third largest city in France. As an important crossroads for trade and a former capital in the Roman Empire, Lyon has had a rich past. You can still see traces of it in **Vieux Lyon** ("Old Lyon"), a neighborhood with Gothic and Renaissance houses, and the city's Roman theater. Today, Lyon is an important center for the chemical, mechanical, textile, and high tech industries. One high tech company, Infogrammes Entertainment, has produced several video games that have become international hits, including "Mission Impossible." Lyon also produces some of France's finest cuisine and has many well-known restaurants.

 **Search words: site officiel lyon**

The focal point of Lyon, **la Place Bellecour** is also France's biggest pedestrian square.

## Guignol  4.2, 1.3

 **Produits**

The puppet character Guignol was created at the beginning of the 19th century in Lyon. Guignol gave a voice to the city's workers. He expressed their concerns and spoke out against social injustice. Today an entire theatrical tradition takes its name from the Guignol character, and performances continue to comment on politics and society. Guignol doesn't perform alone; other characters include Gnafron, Guignol's friend; Madelon, his wife; and a policeman who often falls victim to Guignol's tricks.

 **Search words: théâtre du guignol à lyon**

### Connections

**Geography**
With a push pin mark Lyon on your wall map, and continue to add French cities in this way as they are introduced.

### Critical Thinking

**Analysis**
**Faire le guignol** means "to clown around." **C'est du guignol** means "It's a farce." Encourage students to speculate why these expressions developed. Or give the expressions to students and have them look them up in their French-English dictionary.

### Expansion

Ask students to find a restaurant and hotel in Lyon on the city's official website, as well as a tourist site or two. Then ask them to send you a virtual postcard that includes a description of what they like to see and do in Lyon. Virtual postcards are available on the official Lyon website.

**Differentiated Learning**
**Accelerate**
Teach the class the expression **faire le guignol en classe** (to act like a class clown). Ask them, **Tu aimes un peu/bien/beaucoup faire le guignol?** to encourage them to make connections with previously acquired vocabulary.

**Adapt**
Have students use paper lunch bags to make puppets and perform skits using vocabulary from **Unités 1** and **2**.

## Answers

**5**
1. It is the third largest city in France with 1.6 million inhabitants.
2. Gothic and Renaissance houses, the Roman theater
3. chemical, mechanical, textile and high tech industries
4. Its finest cuisine and restaurants
5. It is based on a puppet character, Guignol.
6. In Africa
7. Checkers and chess

**6**
1. December 8
2. It takes place in Lyon.
3. They light candles in their windows and walk through the streets carrying lights.
4. 04.72.10.30.30
5. www.lumieres.lyon.fr

**À discuter**
*Answers will vary.*

### Reference Desk

Explain to students that **mancala** is also referred to as **awalé** in many parts of Africa. Spectators of the game are often very vocal in their encouragement of the players.

### Culture

**Practices: Activity**
Organize a **mancala** tournament. Ask students to research online the game board and rules of the game. Then, have students create the game board. Ask them to collect and decorate enough egg cartons for each pair of students. Provide small playing pieces, such as beans or bingo chips. Play the game.

### Critical Thinking

**Evaluate**
The Latin root **lum**-: write the words "luminous" and "luminaries" on the board. Ask what the stem **lum**- refers to. Have students list words from the reading related to light.

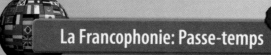

# La Francophonie: Passe-temps

1.3, 4.2

**※ Mancala en Afrique**

Mancala is a collection of traditional games that have been played in Africa for many hundreds of years. Players use strategies to "count and capture" stones, grains, or shells placed in small dishes or holes, or sometimes dug into the earth. Its closest equivalent in the West are the games of checkers and chess.

 Search word: **mancala**

**5 Questions culturelles**  1.1, 2.1, 2.2

*Répondez aux questions.*
1. How large is the city of Lyon?
2. What historical buildings might you visit in Lyon?
3. What kinds of businesses support Lyon's economy?
4. Apart from its history and industry, for what else is Lyon famous?
5. What is Guignol Theater?
6. Where do people play mancala?
7. Which Western games are similar to mancala?

The Guignol puppet show dates back to 1808 and is still performed in Lyon theaters today.

## Du côté des médias 1.3, 4.2

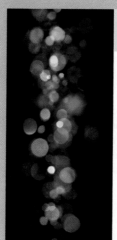

**Accueil**
**www.fetedeslumieres.lyon.fr**

Réservations: 04.72.77.69.69
Tous les ans, le 8 décembre, Lyon se transforme en une ville de lumière. Les bâtiments publics sont décorés de lumières, les gens placent des luminions sur les fenêtres, et les visiteurs et les habitants marchent dans les rues avec des lumières. **La Fête des Lumières** dure quatre jours et attire quatre millions de visiteurs. Beaucoup de personnes vont voir le spectacle extraordinaire des lumières créés par certains des meilleurs créateurs de lumière du monde.

 Search words: **fête des lumières lyon**

**6 La Fête des Lumières**

*Répondez aux questions.*
1. When is the festival?
2. Where does the festival take place?
3. What do people do during the festival?
4. What number can you call within France to reserve a hotel room?
5. Where can you find information online?

**À discuter** 1.1, 2.1, 2.2

How do the two games of chess and checkers compare to mancala?

**0 7 4** soixante-quatorze | Unité 2

**Essential Instruction**

1. Have students do **Activité 5** with a partner. Check comprehension by asking students to share their answers with the class.
2. Ask students to guess the meaning of **La Fête des Lumières** based on the photo and the comprehension questions in English.
3. Help students develop their "reading for meaning" skills. Emphasize the need to process the information in French rather than trying to translate it word for word into English. Read and discuss the passage for comprehension.
4. Ask students to re-read the passage. Explain that re-reading after discussing a text is a crucial step in developing reading comprehension.
5. Verify that students understand the grammatical term "adverb" on p. 75. Solicit some adverbs in English.
6. Model the pronunciation of the sentences in the yellow grid, noting the position of the bolded words.

**0 7 4**

# Structure de la langue

  *Go online* **EMC**Languages.net

## Position of Adverbs  1.2

Adverbs describe verbs, adjectives, and other adverbs. Adverbs tell how, how much, where, why, or when. Note that French adverbs usually come right after the verbs they describe.

*Caro aime beaucoup faire du sport.*

| beaucoup | J'aime **beaucoup** surfer sur Internet. | *I like surfing the Internet a lot.* |
| bien | J'aime **bien** envoyer des textos | *I really like sending text messages.* |
| un peu | J'aime **un peu** faire la cuisine. | *I like cooking a little.* |

### 7 La correspondante de Tanya  2.1, 2.2, 1.1

Read the e-mail Tanya's pen pal, Rahina, sent her. Tell how much Rahina likes each activity she mentions in her e-mail, based on the number of hearts.

À: TANYA
Cc:
Sujet: ce que j'aime

Chère Tanya,

J'aime ♥ lire. J'aime ♥♥♥ surfer sur Internet. J'aime ♥♥ étudier. J'aime ♥♥♥ envoyer des textos. J'aime ♥ faire la cuisine.

Bisous,
Rahina

### 8 On aime un peu, bien, ou beaucoup?

Fill out a chart like the one below. Listen to each sentence twice. Then write the activity each teenager likes to do under the heading that indicates the degree to which they like doing that activity. Listen first to the model.

|  | ♥ | ♥♥ | ♥♥♥ |
|---|---|---|---|
| **Modèle: Fatima** |  |  | **téléphoner** |
| 1. Lucas |  |  |  |
| 2. Coralie |  |  |  |

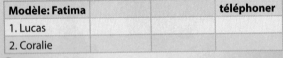 2.1, 2.2, 1.3

## COMPARAISONS

Where are adverbs usually placed in English?

I like doing homework a little.
I really like eating.
I like playing soccer a lot.

COMPARAISONS: In English adverbs can be placed at the end of the sentence or before the verb.

Leçon B | soixante-quinze **0 7 5**

### RESOURCES

 **Workbook 24–26**

**Answers** _____

**7**
J'aime un peu lire. J'aime beaucoup surfer sur Internet. J'aime bien étudier. J'aime beaucoup envoyer des textos. J'aime un peu faire la cuisine.

**8** Script can be found in the front pages of the Annotated Teacher's Edition.

Lucas: three hearts: écouter de la musique; two hearts: surfer sur internet, étudier; one heart: cuisiner, regarder la télé
Coralie: three hearts: faire du sport, play video games; two hearts: envoyer des textos, one heart: lire

### Reference Desk

Students may be interested to learn that the word "adverb" in English and French comes from the Latin for "an added word." In other words, the term "adverb" was invented to describe a word added to a verb to explain the verb or modify it further.

**Differentiated Learning**
**Adapt**
Have students pick the name of a classmate out of a bag and write him or her an e-mail, using adverbs in some of their sentences.

**Special Needs Students**
**AD(H)D**
Have students who find it difficult to stay on task alone at their desk complete the chart in **Activité 8** on the board. Getting up and moving around may refocus their attention on the task at hand.

## Communication

### Interpersonal: Paired Practice

Ask students to do the following oral **activité** with a partner. You and a friend are looking at your agendas to decide when to get together this week. In your conversation:
• Greet each other.
• Ask each other how things are going.
• Ask each other what you like to do.
• Say how much you like each **activité**.
• Decide on what day you can do an **activité** together.
• Say you'll see each other soon.

### Interpersonal: Cooperative Groups

Have groups write text messages to each other, asking how things are going. Students should find out if their classmates like to make phone calls, write text messages, study, watch TV, and play video games.

# À vous la parole

**9  Au téléphone**  1.3

### Interpersonal/Presentational Communication

Using the form your teacher gives you, write five activities you like to do the most from the list below, making sure your partner cannot see your list. With your backs turned, one of you phones the other. Ask your partner if he or she likes certain activities on the list. When you have discovered your partner's five favorite activities, tell your small group what your partner likes to do.

| | | |
|---|---|---|
| lire | manger de la pizza | faire la cuisine |
| jouer au hockey | jouer au basket | faire du roller |
| téléphoner | jouer aux jeux vidéo | aller au cinéma |
| faire du vélo | surfer sur Internet | envoyer des textos |
| faire du shopping | écouter un lecteur MP3 | |
| sortir avec des amis | dormir | |

**10  Un rendez-vous**  1.3

### Interpersonal Communication

You and a friend are looking at your agendas to decide when to get together this week. In your conversation:

• greet each other.
• ask each other how things are going.
• ask each other what you like to do.
• say how much you like each activity.
• decide on what day you can do an activity together.
• say you'll see each other soon.

On joue au basket demain?

## Essential Instruction

1. After having students do **Activité 9**, ask them to report to the class. Keep track of responses, and list the three favorite activities on the board.
2. For students curious about the negative construction, simply write, **Je n'aime pas + l'infinitif** on the board.
3. Read about cognates in **Stratégie Communicative**. Ask students to identify and tally on the board the patterns they see: **-ain** (-an), **-ie** (-y), **-é** (-y), **-ien** (-ian), **-que** (-ic).

4. Brainstorm other cognates previously encountered.
5. Have students find words in the sentences in **Activité 12** that follow the patterns identified above. Have students work with a partner to brainstorm a list of English words ending in -tion.
6. Ask students to locate Brazil on a map and identify its official language (Portuguese). Then, assign **Activité 12** as silent reading. Students answer questions with a partner.
7. Recycle adverbs by asking students about the reading: **Carlos aime un peu les sports?** Response: **Non, il aime beaucoup les sports.**

# Stratégie communicative

## Cognates  1.2

Words that have similar spellings and meanings in two languages are called cognates. For example, the words **activité** and "activity" are cognates. Look at the list of French and English cognates below. Do you see any patterns?

africain ⟷ African
économie ⟷ economy
possibilité ⟷ possibility

italien ⟷ Italian
université ⟷ university
politique ⟷ politics

### 11 Dans la presse  2.1, 2.2

Read the following headlines from the Internet and match them with the appropriate section of the magazine they came from.

A. Politique
B. Sports
C. Économie
D. Musique

1. **Concerts de jazz à Marseille en automne**
2. Élection présidentielle américaine en novembre
3. **Match de tennis à 10h00 à Wimbledon**
4. L'INFLATION DU DOLLAR CANADIEN

### 12 La vie de Carlos  1.2, 2.1, 2.2

Use your knowledge of cognates to read the following paragraph about Carlos. Then answer the questions.

Je m'appelle Carlos. Je suis brésilien. Au Brésil j'habite dans un appartement avec ma famille. Je suis étudiant à l'université de Nice. J'étudie la psychologie en France depuis septembre. J'adore le sport. Je suis un fan de football américain et de hockey. J'adore la cuisine japonaise et, oui, les sushis, c'est délicieux! J'adore la nature, les promenades en forêt et au bord de la côte. L'environnement, c'est important pour moi.

1. What is Carlos' nationality?
2. Where does he live and with whom?
3. What does he study and where?
4. What does he like to do?
5. What type of food does he like to eat?

**RESOURCES**

 **Pre-test**

 *Leçon* Quiz

Answers _____

 **11**

1. D
2. A
3. B
4. C

 **12**

1. He is from Brazil.
2. He lives in an apartment in Nice with his family.
3. He studies psychology at the university.
4. He likes to play sports, watch football and hockey, eat Japanese food, and take walks in the forest.
5. Japanese food

### Reference Desk

1. Over one-third of the new words and expressions in this unit are recognizable cognates.
2. Suggest that students start a glossary of French cognates they can add to as they go through the units in this book. Begin with a list of the cognates in this unit. With a partner, have them take turns checking each other's pronunciation of each word on their respective lists.

## Differentiated Learning
### Accelerate/Decelerate
Pair two above-level students together and ask them to model the "conversation" in **Activité 10** for the rest of the class. Have them use note cards if that allows them to feel more secure. Consider pairing students of different ability levels together so that the advanced student can help the struggling student. You may want to record an oral grade for this **activité** and place a videotaped or audio recording in students' portfolios for them to listen to at the end of the year and see how much progress they've made.

## Reference Desk

1. Students learned **jouer au basket/au foot, faire du footing/du roller** in **Leçon A**. Now the nouns for these sports are introduced, as well as some music genres.
2. Students learned **On va au cinéma?** in **Unité 1**, where **cinéma** meant "movie theater." Here it means "movies."
3. Students learned **faire du shopping** in **Leçon A** of this unit.
4. Another type of music, **le R'n'B**, is introduced in the dialogue. There is a culture reading about world music in this lesson.

# Leçon C

## Vocabulaire actif

### Qu'est-ce que tu préfères?   1.2

**les sports (m.)**

le basketball

le foot

le footing

le roller

**la musique**

le hip-hop

le rock

la musique alternative

la world

**les passe-temps (m.)**

le cinéma | le shopping

### Les nombres de 0 à 20

| | | | |
|---|---|---|---|
| 0 | zéro | 11 | onze |
| 1 | un | 12 | douze |
| 2 | deux | 13 | treize |
| 3 | trois | 14 | quatorze |
| 4 | quatre | 15 | quinze |
| 5 | cinq | 16 | seize |
| 6 | six | 17 | dix-sept |
| 7 | sept | 18 | dix-huit |
| 8 | huit | 19 | dix-neuf |
| 9 | neuf | 20 | vingt |
| 10 | dix | | |

### Et si je voulais dire...?

| | |
|---|---|
| **le football américain** | *American football* |
| **le baseball** | *baseball* |
| **le tennis** | *tennis* |
| **le volley (volleyball)** | *volleyball* |
| **faire les courses** | *to go grocery shopping* |
| **le reggae** | *reggae* |
| **la techno** | *techno* |
| **la zik** | *music [slang]* |
| **télécharger de la musique** | *to download music* |

## Essential Instruction

1. Write the title question **Qu'est-ce que tu préfères?** on the board.
2. Act out and have students guess the vocabulary as you poll them about which sport, music, and pastime they prefer.
3. After students have repeated the vocabulary several times, have them listen to the functions in **Pour la conversation.**
4. Explain the negative **ne (n')... pas**, and ask questions that elicit both affirmative and negative responses. Then do **Activité 2.**
5. Introduce the numbers 1–10, just as you presented the days of the week (p. 53), gradually erasing all the numbers. Ask for English cognates, for example, **deux:** duet, duo, double.
6. Then introduce the numbers 11–20, comparing them to 1–10, specifically 17–19, which are a combination of lower numbers.
7. Have students do **Activité 1**, a listening **activité** about phone numbers.

# Pour la conversation  1.3

> J'aime regarder le basket.

> Pas moi, je n'aime pas regarder le basket.

**H**ow do I state my preferences?

> **Moi, je préfère** lire les blogues.
> *Me, I like to read blogs.*

**H**ow can I find out what someone prefers?

> **Tu préfères** la world **ou** le hip-hop?
> *Do you prefer world music or hip-hop?*

**H**ow do I agree?

> **Moi aussi.**
> *Me too.*

**H**ow do I disagree?

> **Pas moi. Je n'aime pas....**
> *Not me. I don't like....*

**H**ow do I ask for a phone number?

> **Quel est le numéro de téléphone de** Yasmine?
> *What is Yasmine's phone number?*

## 1 Les numéros de téléphone   2.1

Florence wants to invite her classmates to a party. She asks Thomas for their phone numbers. Write each phone number you hear.

## Communiquez!

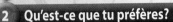

### 2 Qu'est-ce que tu préfères?

**Interpersonal Communication** 1.1

*Demandez (Ask) ce que votre partenaire préfère.*

**MODÈLE**   le roller/le foot
A: **Tu préfères le roller ou le foot?**
B: **Moi, je préfère le foot.**

1. la world/le hip-hop
2. les hamburgers/les frites
3. la pizza/les pâtes
4. le cinéma/le shopping
5. le footing/le basket
6. le foot/le roller

> Nous préférons le roller.

Leçon C | soixante-dix-neuf **079**

## RESOURCES

 **Workbook 29–30**

**Answers** _____

**1** Script can be found in the front pages of the Annotated Teacher's Edition.

1. 01-19-02-12-03
2. 01-13-13-18-07
3. 01-05-09-17-11
4. 01-06-08-10-13
5. 01-15-15-03-04
6. 01-14-20-11-04
7. 01-05-07-18-16

**2**

1. Tu préfères la world ou le hip-hop?
2. Tu préfères les hamburgers ou les frites?
3. Tu préfères la pizza ou les pâtes?
4. Tu préfères le cinéma ou le shopping?
5. Tu préfères le footing ou le basket?
6. Tu préfères le foot ou le roller?

*Responses to the questions above will vary.*

## Differentiated Learning
### Adapt

1. Have students create **Loto** (*Bingo*) cards. Call numbers for several rounds, then ask student volunteers to serve as callers. The winner must repeat back the numbers.
2. Play the game **Piqué** (*Stung*). Going quickly around the room, students count up to 20 and back down to zero. Add a twist like, "After every fifth number, the next student must say "**Bravo**" before the number." Students shout **"Piqué!"** if they hear an error in the pattern.

## Special Needs Students
### Social Anxiety

In the world language classroom, high profile activities such as Conjugation Koosh Ball or **Piqué** may cause anxiety for some students. Always preface such activities with clear guidelines and encouraging remarks. Remind students that making mistakes is part of the learning process. Speak privately with overly anxious students about accommodations that will encourage their participation. Consider letting the student observe or participate by keeping score or recording their responses at home.

**3**

1. C'est le zéro un, douze, dix-sept, quinze, dix-neuf.
2. C'est le zéro quatre, zéro sept, quatorze, dix-huit, treize.
3. C'est le zéro cinq, zéro trois, onze, seize, zéro six.
4. C'est le zéro deux, zéro neuf, vingt, dix, zéro deux.
5. C'est le zéro trois, zéro cinq, quatorze, dix-huit, douze.
6. C'est le zéro un, zéro huit, treize, onze, zéro quatre.
7. C'est le zéro quatre, quinze, zéro huit, seize, dix-neuf.
8. C'est le zéro trois, zéro deux, vingt, douze, zéro trois.
9. C'est le zéro deux, zéro six, dix-sept, treize, zéro sept.
10. C'est le zéro quatre, zéro neuf, dix, dix-huit, quatorze.
11. C'est le zéro un, zéro cinq, onze, zéro un, seize.

**4** *Activities will vary.*

**5** *Answers will vary.*

---

## Connections

### Math

Practice addition/subtraction in French. Teach students the words **plus, moins, égale** (plus, minus, equals). Make flash cards with the numbers 1–20. Divide the class into teams. Give students points for the correct phrase and answer.

---

## Expansion

Ask students to give the numbers in the **annuaire** page on p. 12. Explain that the first two numbers indicate the calling area. In this case, "01" indicates the Paris calling area.

---

### 3 Quel est son numéro de téléphone? **1.1**

**Interpersonal Communication**

With a partner, take turns asking for and giving the phone numbers below. Follow the model.

> **MODÈLE** Chloé: 01.20.18.09.16
> A: **Quel est le numéro de téléphone de Chloé?**
> B: **C'est le zéro un, vingt, dix-huit, zéro neuf, seize.**

1. Héloïse: 01.12.17.15.19
2. Augustin: 04.07.14.18.13
3. Kemajou: 05.03.11.16.06
4. Amélie: 02.09.20.10.02
5. Khaled: 03.05.14.18.12
6. Nayah: 01.08.13.11.04
7. Valérie: 04.15.08.16.19
8. Jean-Luc: 03.02.20.12.03
9. Mathéo: 02.06.17.13.07
10. Xavier: 04.09.10.18.14
11. Romane: 01.05.11.01.16

---

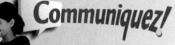

### 4 Tu préfères...?   **1.1, 1.3**

**Interpersonal/Presentational Communication**

Create four columns on a sheet of paper with these headings: **sports, activités, musique, lecture.** Write each item from the list on the right in the correct column. Then ask which items your partner prefers and circle his or her preferences. Report your partner's preferences to your group.

| | |
|---|---|
| le basket | le shopping |
| le cinéma | la world |
| le hip-hop | le foot |
| les blogues | le rock |
| la musique alternative | le footing |
| le ski | les textos |

> **MODÈLE** A: **Tu préfères le basket ou le foot?**
> B: **Je préfère le basket.**

(Student A circles **basket** and tells his or her group:)

**Myriam préfère le basket, le shopping, le hip-hop, et les textos.**

---

### 5 Questions personnelles    **1.3**

**Interpersonal Communication**

*Répondez aux questions.*

1. Tu aimes beaucoup le foot?
2. Tu préfères le footing ou le basket?
3. Tu aimes bien écouter de la musique?
4. Tu aimes beaucoup la musique alternative?
5. Tu préfères lire les blogues ou les textos?
6. Tu préfères le cinéma ou le shopping?

**0 8 0** quatre-vingts | Unité 2

---

**Essential Instruction**

1. Before doing **Activité 3**, assign online research on the French phone system and phone numbers. Then, ask students to share the results in class.
2. Have students become familiar with the dialogue (see teacher notes on p. 32) and complete **Activité 6**. Then, ask them to respond to **vrai/ faux** statements about the dialogue content. Vary this **activité** by having students create their own **vrai/faux** statements and sharing them in small groups.
3. Do a class role-play of the dialogue. Have the girls read **Maxime's** role in unison, and the guys read **Julien's**.

# Rencontres culturelles

## Un concert R'n'B

   1.2

Maxime phones Julien, who suggests they do something together the following evening.

**Maxime:** Tu vas bien?
**Julien:** Oui, ça va. Qu'est-ce que tu fais?
**Maxime:** J'écoute le nouveau CD de Rachid Taha. Je ne fais pas mes devoirs.
**Julien:** On va au concert?
**Maxime:** Quand?
**Julien:** Demain.
**Maxime:** Oui, je peux. Quel concert?
**Julien:** Tu préfères Taha ou Corneille?
**Maxime:** Corneille, un concert R'n'B.
**Julien:** Bon, d'accord. On invite les filles?
**Maxime:** Pourquoi pas?
**Julien:** Quel est le numéro de téléphone de Yasmine?
**Maxime:** C'est le 01.20.18.09....

### 6 Un concert R'n'B   2.1, 2.2

Say whether Julien or Maxime makes each of the following statements.

1. Je ne fais pas mes devoirs.
2. On va au concert?
3. Oui, je peux.
4. (Je préfère) Corneille, un concert R'n'B.
5. On invite les filles?
6. Quel est le numéro de téléphone de Yasmine?

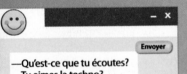

**Extension** Chat sur ordinateur  2.1, 2.2

—Qu'est-ce que tu écoutes?
—Tu aimes la techno?
—Non, je préfère le hip-hop.
—Moi, j'adore le reggae.
—Moi aussi.
—Et le cinéma?
—J'aime beaucoup le cinéma, surtout les films d'action américains. Et toi?
—Moi aussi.
—Et tu aimes lire les blogues?
—Plutôt des magazines en ligne....

**Extension** What do the two teens have in common?

## RESOURCES

 Dialogue Video

## Answers

**6**
1. Maxime
2. Julien
3. Maxime
4. Maxime
5. Julien
6. zero un, vingt, dix-huit, zero neuf, seize

## Reference Desk

1. **Tu vas bien?** is another way to ask **Ça va bien?**, which students learned in **Unité 1, Leçon B**.
2. The conjugated form **tu fais** is introduced here as a lexical item; students learn all the forms of the irregular verb **faire** in **Unité 8, Leçon A**.
3. **Quel** is also introduced as a lexical item; students learn the interrogative adjective **quel** in **Unité 4, Leçon C**.
4. Remind students that **le lundi** means "every Monday" or "on Mondays."
5. The phone number in this segment is not complete in the video or audio recording because this number may belong to someone and we do not want students to attempt to use this number.

## Differentiated Learning
### Accelerate
Divide students into groups of four. Have them play a game based on **Activité 4** and the days of the week. The first student says "**Je préfère le basket le lundi,**" and adds to the next person, "**Et toi?**" The second person must change both **activité** and day. No one can repeat an **activité**, but group members can help each other think of one. The first group to complete three rounds of play wins.

## Multiple Intelligences
### Bodily-Kinesthetic
Draw a large cell phone on the board. Ask student volunteers to "dial" phone numbers as you say them.

### Special Needs Students
### Auditory Impairment
Have students read the script while watching the dialogue video. Encourage them to look for visual clues to aid aural comprehension. Encourage them to listen again to the dialogue taking the time needed to process the sound, image, and script.

**081**

**Connections**

**Social Justice**
Expand on the **Comparaison** question under the R. Taha photo by having students work in groups to come up with a list of their favorite musicians that sing about social justice issues. Another way to expand on this topic is to ask students to research online benefit concerts in France or other francophone countries and the United States that focus on a particular social issue. Have each student create a poster about a singer or group's upcoming benefit concert to post in the classroom or hallway. Below the photo of the musician(s), students can write the location of the concert, the time, and the date the French way. Search words: **sos racisme**, **restaurants du coeur**.

# Points de départ

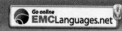

**Question centrale**
What do activities and pastimes reveal about a culture?

## Comment compter sur les doigts 2.1

zéro — un — deux — trois — quatre — cinq

six — sept — huit — neuf — dix

**COMPARAISONS**
How were you taught to count on your fingers? 4.1

## Rachid Taha et la World 1.1, 1.2, 1.3

World Music incorporates diverse styles of music from Africa, eastern Europe, Asia, Central and South America, and the Caribbean, as well as non-mainstream Western folk music. The genre took root in the 1980s and remains strong today, as seen in the popularity of Rachid Taha's recordings. Taha, who was born in Algeria but grew up in Lyon, is the king of rock in Arabic. He started out with a group he formed called **Carte de séjour** that gained national attention in France with its remake of the song "*Douce France.*" Today Rachid Taha performs alone, singing songs about tolerance, acceptance, and inclusion.

Search words: **vidéo rachid taha rock the casbah**

Rachid Taha performs at the Festival Nancy Jazz Pulsations in France.

**COMPARAISONS**
Can you think of a singer who performs songs in English about tolerance, acceptance, or inclusion? 4.2

## Corneille 1.1, 1.2, 1.3

Corneille Nyungura is an R&B singer-songwriter who has made albums in both French and English. Born in Germany, he spent most of his childhood in Rwanda, but now lives in Montreal, Canada. Audiences first discovered his unique sound, influenced by American artists Prince, Stevie Wonder, and Marvin Gaye, at the **Francofolies** festival in La Rochelle, France. The song he performed there, "*Parce qu'on vient de loin*" ("Because we come from far away"), became an instant hit. Today Corneille uses his fame to promote humanitarian causes, including participating in the Africa Live concert in 2005 to combat malaria and working with the Red Cross to help children victimized by war like him.

Search words: **vidéo parce qu'on vient de loin**

**Essential Instruction**

1. Ask your students to count on their fingers before demonstrating how it's done in French. Take a poll to find out if anyone already counts like the French do (with the thumb as number 1).
2. Depending on your time frame, you can expand the cultural points on these pages. If you have access to computers during class time, listen together to Rachid Taha and Corneille, watch the video **"Parce qu'on vient de loin,"** and ask students for their reactions.
3. Then have students put the keywords provided for these two artists, as well as **la Fête de la musique**, into their favorite search engine.
4. Ask students to share with a classmate or the class what they found.
5. For homework, have students write a paragraph, perhaps in their Culture Journal, about what they learned and found particularly interesting during their online research.

## Fête de la musique

 1.2, 4.2

Since 1982 it has been a tradition that on June 21 music invades the streets, squares, and cafés in all the cities and towns in France. Professionals and amateurs alike share their art for free. It's important to hear **Faites de la musique** ("Make music") as much as **Fête de la musique**. Each year there is a different theme such as women's music or music in French. Today **la Fête de la musique** is celebrated in 110 countries around the world and in over 340 cities. In France there are 18,000 concerts that assemble five million musicians who draw almost ten million spectators!

**Search words: fête de la musique**

## La Francophonie: Instruments

 4.2

✻ *La kora*

The kora is a stringed harp-lute instrument popular in West Africa. It is often played by griots, or hereditary storytellers. The player uses the thumb and index finger of both hands to pluck the strings. Today the kora has become a popular instrument in pop, world, and jazz music.

### 7 Questions culturelles

*Répondez aux questions.*  1.1

1. What is world music?
2. Where was Rachid Taha born?
3. What themes do Rachid Taha's songs address?
4. What kind of music does Corneille sing?
5. Which American singers influenced Corneille's music?
6. What kind of humanitarian work does Corneille do?
7. What happens on June 21 in France?
8. What is a kora?
9. Where do people play the kora?

**À discuter**

How do one's musical preferences reflect one's worldview?

## Du côté des médias

Read the chart below. Then answer questions in Activity 8.

| Le Hit Parade: meilleures ventes de singles en France |
| --- |
| ❶ Rain'B Fever Feat Magic System et Khaled — *Même pas fatigué* |
| ❷ Alizée — *Psychédélices* |
| ❸ Corneille — *Parce qu'on vient de loin* |
| ❹ Helmut Fritz — *Ça m'énerve* |
| ❺ Bisso Na Bisso — *Show ce soir* |
| ❻ King Kuduro — *Il faut danser!!!* |
| ❼ Bébé Lilly — *Les jeux vidéo* |
| ❽ Agnès — *Réalise moi/Release me* |
| ❾ Christophe Maé — *Mon p'tit gars* |
| ❿ Kidtonik — *Jusqu'au bout* |

### 8 Le Hit Parade francophone de l'année

Find video clips on the Internet of performers of this year's hit parade singing their songs. Tell your group which five videos you liked the best, what the music genre was, and why you liked each video.

**Search words: hit parade france nrj play list chante france radio**

1.1, 1.3

Leçon C | quatre-vingt-trois 0 8 3

## Multiple Intelligences
### Musical-Rhythmic

1. Ask your musically talented students to choose one of Rachid Taha's or Corneille's songs to learn, practice, and perform for the class. This can be done individually or in small groups and can be substituted for a homework assignment, awarded extra credit, or simply provide a way for your performers to be on stage.

2. Check local music organizations to try and find a willing **kora** player to demonstrate the instrument in class.
3. Check the radio station **NRJ** online and have students create a playlist of their favorite eight French songs this week.

**9** *Presentations will vary.*

**10** *Polls will vary.*

# La culture sur place

## Les sports que nous regardons

### Introduction

People's pastimes can reveal a lot about who they are. Many people spend their free time watching sports and are fans of local or regional sports teams. People's favorite sport, however, may vary from region to region or country to country. In this section, you will talk about your favorite spectator sports and learn about some of the sports commonly watched in France.

**9** **Les sports américains**  **1.3**

Write your personal sports profile and present it to your group. Tell what sports you like to watch, the team or players you admire, why you like (or do not like) watching sports, and what sports you do not like to watch.

**MODÈLE** **J'aime regarder le baseball. J'admire les Twins. Le baseball, c'est passionnant. Je n'aime pas regarder le hockey.**

| Vocabulaire utile | |
|---|---|
| **au stade** | – in the stadium |
| **à l'école** | – at school |
| **avec mes amis** | – with my friends |
| **avec ma famille** | – with my family |
| **ennuyeux** | – boring |
| **passionnant** | – exciting |
| **J'admire....** | – I admire.... |

**10** **Un sondage sportif**   **1.3**

Make a list of seven different sports Americans watch. Poll ten people you know to find out if they like each sport or not. Write a summary of your results. If seven out of ten students say yes, write: **70% des copains regardent le baseball.**

Look at the table below to find out which sports the people in France like to watch. Also look at the percentage of people who watch these sports.

**Est-ce que vous suivez\* l'actualité sportive\*?**

| Nom du sport | Pourcentages du public français |
|---|---|
| *Le foot* | 30% |
| *Le rugby* | 29% |
| *Le tennis* | 27% |
| *La Formule 1* | 25% |
| *Le patinage* | 21% |
| *Les sports de combat* | 20% |
| *L'athlétisme* | 20% |

\* **suivez** *follow;* **l'actualité sportive** *sports in the news*

### Essential Learning

1. Before students write their personal sports profile in **Activité 9**, have them repeat the **Vocabulaire utile** several times. Ask students to read their profile aloud to their group, then switch papers with a classmate and read aloud someone else's profile to learn from another perspective.

2. Ask each student to share something with the class (in French) about another student in his or her group.

3. In **Activité 10**, discuss the sports that the French prefer to watch. Provide a template for students to complete with what they think are the seven most popular sports among spectators in the United States. Have students combine polls and compare the results to the popular sports in France.

4. After doing **Activités 11** and **12** in class, as a "ticket out the door," have students write and hand in to you the written response to **Activité 9**.

La Formule 1

L'athlétisme

**11** *Discussions will vary.*

**12** *Diagrams will vary.*

**11 Les résultats**  1.1, 2.2

Discuss these questions with your group: How do viewing habits in France compare with those of the people you polled? Did any of the sports included on the list surprise you? Which sports did you expect to be included, but were not? Do you think people in other French-speaking countries share the same sports viewing habits?

**12 Comparaisons**  1.3

Your teacher will give you a copy of the following diagram. Write the sports watched in France in the circle labeled "French Culture." Write the sports from your poll in the circle labeled "My Culture(s)." The sports enjoyed by people in both countries should fall in the section where the circles intersect. Put a star by the sports that have the highest percentage of viewers. Discuss with your group what might explain the similarities and differences between sports viewing habits in the United States and France.

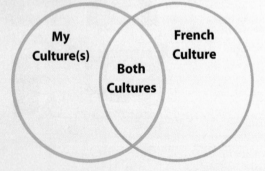

My Culture(s)    Both Cultures    French Culture

**Differentiated Learning**
**Accelerate**
Have students conduct the poll in **Activité 10** in French, by asking, "**Est-ce que tu regardes le...?**" Students need to answer with a complete sentence in French. Review the use of the negative: **Je ne regarde pas....** and **Je n'aime pas....**

**Multiple Intelligences**
**Visual-Spatial**
After completing **Activité 12**, have groups list all the sports they have learned so far in French, mak-ing sure that each student has a copy of the list from his or her group. Then, have students create a "word cloud" for France and one for the United States in class or at home, using an online search engine. Instruct them to write two or three times the sports that are the most popular in both cultures so that they will be highlighted in the word cloud. Ask students to share their word clouds with their classmates.

**Answers**

**13** Script can be found in the front pages of the Annotated Teacher's Edition.

1. M
2. M
3. F
4. M
5. F
6. M
7. F
8. M
9. M

**14**

1. Le CD est américain.
2. La fille est américaine.
3. Le centre commercial est français.
4. Le camarade est canadien. L'ami est canadien.
5. Le basket est américain.
6. Le cinéma est français.
7. La maison est française.
8. Le lecteur de MP3 est algérien.
9. La fille est américaine.

### Reference Desk

Introduce the notion of natural gender in French nouns, i.e. that girl, mother, grandmother, etc. are feminine nouns, and boy, father, grandfather, etc. are masculine nouns. Inform students that it is generally impossible to guess gender of common nouns in French. There are some clues, however, to help them, such as natural gender and some predictable word endings. For example, the ending **–tion** generally indicates a feminine noun, as in **information** (f.), **constitution** (f.), **libération** (f.). Sometimes patterns can be misleading. While -**euse** generally indicates a feminine noun (like **la serveuse**, the waitress), and -**eur** a masculine equivalent (like **le serveur**, *the waiter* or **l'auteur** (m.), *the author*), -**eur** is also a common ending for some feminine nouns (ex. **la grandeur**, *grandness* and **la hauteur**, *height*). In addition, while a final **e** at the end of a French *adjective* usually indicates a feminine adjective, many French *nouns* ending in **e** are masculine.

---

# Structure de la langue

Go online
EMCLanguages.net

## Gender of Nouns and Definite Articles

A noun is a person, place, or thing. Every French noun is masculine or feminine. When you learn a new noun, you need to remember if it is masculine or feminine. Here are the singular definite articles.

La télé ou le jeu vidéo?

| Definite articles | | |
|---|---|---|
| **masculine** | **feminine** | **English equivalent** |
| **le** weekend **l'**ami | **la** télé **l'**enquête | the |

 1.2

**13** **Un e-mail de France** 1.1

French teenagers have written an e-mail to your class. Listen to each sentence twice. If you hear a masculine noun, write **M**. If you hear a feminine noun, write **F**.

### COMPARAISONS

Are definite articles always needed in English?
I like pizza.
I eat spaghetti too. 2.1, 4.1

**14** **Le, la, ou l'?** 1.2, 2.2

*Donnez la nationalité de chaque chose ou personne.* (Give the nationality of each item.)

**MODÈLE** française
**La musique est française.**

 1.
 2.
 3.

 4.
 5.
 Amélie 6.

 7.
 8.
 9.

COMPARAISONS: No, definite articles are often omitted in English, but an article is almost always needed in a French sentence.

---

### Essential Instruction

1. Explore the notion of how gender is represented in various languages that students know about. Point out other languages that represent gender similarly to French (Romance languages, German, etc.).

2. Do **Activité 14** as a class. You may want to write all the adjectives on the board for students to choose from. They learned the adjectives in **Leçon A** of **Unité 1**, but may need help making the adjectives agree.

3. Ask students to write the words **le**, **la**, and **l'** on three index cards or small pieces of paper. Then say nouns they have already seen, such as **hip-hop**, **musique**, and **ami**. Tell them to hold up the appropriate article.

4. To help students remember the accent change in **préférer**, first show a visual mnemonic by drawing a line around the four conjugations of the verb that have the same accent pattern and tell students that this shape forms a boot. Then, point out that the forms with accents in the shape of a tent (**é è**) are pronounced the same.

## 15 Le MC Michel Druant  1.2

Read the paragraph about a young MC. Then determine how many definite articles are in the paragraph.

Michel aime le hip-hop. Il est MC à la discothèque, ou la boîte, de son oncle. Il aime beaucoup la musique américaine, surtout la chanson "Millie Fell off the Fire Escape" par Slug du groupe Atmosphere.

# Communiquez !

## 16 Tu aimes ou pas? 1.1

### Interpersonal Communication

Ask your partner six questions about what he or she likes. Record the answers. Then report to a third person the things your partner likes and does not like.

**MODÈLE** hip-hop
A: **Tu aimes le hip-hop?**
B: **Oui, j'aime le hip-hop./Non, je n'aime pas le hip-hop.**

| Tu aimes... | oui | non |
|---|---|---|
| le hip-hop? | ✔ | |
| le foot? | | |
| les pâtes? | | |

## The Verb *préférer*  1.2

**Préférer** is like a regular **–er** verb because it shares the same endings. But notice the pattern of its accent marks:

| préférer | |
|---|---|
| je préfère | nous préférons |
| tu préfères | vous préférez |
| il/elle/on préfère | ils/elles préfèrent |

> Nous préférons les sports d'hiver.

### Pronunciation Tip

The dark yellow shaded section shows you how the pattern changes from the infinitive; these forms all sound alike.

Like the verb **aimer**, the verb **préférer** can be followed by:

- a noun (with a definite article)
  Je préfère **la** musique alternative.     *I prefer alternative music.*

- an infinitive
  Mes amis préfèrent **écouter** le hip-hop.    *My friends prefer to listen to hip-hop.*

Answers

**15** Five

**16** *Conversations will vary.*

---

### Differentiated Learning
#### Decelerate
Place index cards with a definite article and a noun near objects in the classroom before you begin the lesson. Ask students to identify how many singular articles there are. Leave the cards in place for **Unité 3**.

#### Accelerate
Create and distribute a list of sentences where a definite article is used in French but not in English. Ask groups to brainstorm to see if they can figure out some rules governing the use of the definite article in English.

### Multiple Intelligences
#### Intrapersonal
Have students write a four-sentence e-mail in French about the music and groups they like and don't like. Have them read it to a partner or send it to a classmate. Some students may prefer to send the message to you.

⑰

1. Guillaume préfère écouter de la musique.
2. Joséphine et moi, nous préférons aller au café.
3. Gabrielle préfère téléphoner.
4. Charlotte et Abdoulaye préfèrent lire les blogues.
5. Vous préférez aller au concert.
6. Alexandre et Antoine préfèrent faire du roller.
7. Je préfère ... (*Answer will vary.*)

⑱

1. A: —Tu préfères le cinéma ou le shopping?
   B: —Je préfère ... .
2. A: —Tu préfères le basket ou le roller?
   B: —Je préfère ... .
3. A: —Tu préfères la world ou le hip-hop?
   B: —Je préfère ... .
4. A: —Tu préfères le foot ou le footing?
   B: —Je préfère ... .
5. A: —Tu préfères la pizza ou la salade?
   B: —Je préfère ... .
6. A: —Tu préfères l'hiver ou l'été?
   B: —Je préfère ... .
7. A: —Tu préfères la musique ou le sport?
   B: —Je préfère ... .
8. A: —Tu préfères la télé ou le cinéma?
   B: —Je préfère ... .

**17 Les grandes vacances**

*Dites ce qu'on préfère faire pendant les grandes vacances* (during summer vacation).

**MODÈLE** Élodie/nager  **1.1**
**Élodie préfère nager.**

1. Guillaume/écouter de la musique
2. Joséphine et moi, nous/aller au café
3. Gabrielle/téléphoner
4. Charlotte et Abdoulaye/lire les blogues
5. vous/aller au concert
6. Alexandre et Antoine/faire du roller
7. Et toi, qu'est-ce que tu préfères faire?

*Tu préfères sortir avec des amis?*

 Communiquez!

**18 Qu'est-ce que tu préfères?**    **1.1**

**Interpersonal Communication**

With a partner, take turns asking and telling each other which of the following things you prefer.

**MODÈLE** musique alternative/rock
**A: Tu préfères la musique alternative ou le rock?**
**B: Je préfère le rock.**

1. cinéma/shopping
2. basket/roller
3. world/hip-hop
4. foot/footing
5. pizza/salade
6. hiver/été
7. musique/sport
8. télé/cinéma

*Concert de rock*
*le 18 octobre*
*20h00*

**Essential Instruction**

1. Ask students to practice conjugating the verb **préférer** by doing **Activité 17** orally and then by writing it out.
2. Before students do **Activité 18**, review the pronunciation of the choices given, emphasizing words with silent letters or accents (**l'hiver**, **le hip-hop**, **l'été**, etc.).
3. Introduce negation, then have students create simple sentences (subject-verb-object) at the board. Next, have them insert **ne... pas** around the verb.
4. Point out that the **ne** is often eliminated in conversation; we recommend that students do not eliminate it yet. Compare this to the English negative, "do not" that becomes "don't."
5. At the board, have students conjugate at least two verbs that begin with consonants and two that begin with a vowel, such as **aimer** and **étudier**. Point out the elisions **j' → je n'**. Solicit examples and compare to English: Do not = don't, cannot = can't, etc.
6. Do **Activité 19** in pairs, after reviewing the model.

# Negation with *ne (n')... pas*  1.2

French uses two words to make a verb negative: **ne** (or **n'**) and **pas**.

> **ne** + present-tense verb + **pas**

Tu **ne** vas **pas** bien? *You aren't doing well?*

**Note: Ne** becomes **n'** before a vowel sound: On **n'**aime **pas** étudier! *We don't like studying!*

Ça ne va pas bien!

*Je n'aime pas jouer au foot.*

## COMPARAISONS  2.1, 4.1

How are sentences made negative in English?

> I'm not cooking tonight.
> I don't like to cook.

## 19 Qu'est-ce qu'on fait?  1.3

Anne guesses incorrectly what everyone is doing. Answer her questions based on the images.

**MODÈLE**

Olivier téléphone?
**Non, il ne téléphone pas.**
**Il joue aux jeux vidéo.**

1. Laurence et Nayah mangent?

2. Justine nage?

3. Clément et Paul jouent au basket?

4. David joue aux jeux vidéo?

5. Rose surfe sur Internet?

6. Marianne et Malika regardent la télé?

**COMPARAISONS:** To make a sentence negative in English, place "not" or "do not" (don't) before the verb.

## RESOURCES

👁 e-visual 7

📖 Workbook 37–39

### Answers

**19**

1. Non, elles ne mangent pas. Elles écoutent le lecteur de MP3.
2. Non, elle ne nage pas. Elle plonge.
3. Non, ils ne jouent pas au basket. Ils jouent au hockey.
4. Non, il ne joue pas aux jeux vidéo. Il joue au foot.
5. Non, elle ne surfe pas sur Internet. Elle regarde la télé.
6. Non, elles ne regardent pas la télé. Elles surfent sur Internet.

## Differentiated Learning
### Decelerate
For students who need more practice with the negative, project on the board 20 sentences that use a variety of subjects and **-er** verbs. Show only one sentence at a time and ask students to re-write it in the negative in their notes. Model the correct pronunciation of the negative sentence and have students repeat.

## Special Needs Students
### Dyslexia
To practice negative sentences, divide the class into groups of four and instruct students to collectively write a negative sentence. Circulate and correct the sentences. Students cut up and paper clip the words of the sentence together. Have students exchange sentences with other groups to reassemble them. When completed, have students read the sentences aloud to each other.

**20**

1. Le Cordon Bleu n'invite pas Justine.
2. Le Cordon Bleu n'invite pas Moussa.
3. Le Cordon Bleu n'invite pas Mathis.
4. Le Cordon Bleu invite Lamine.
5. Le Cordon Bleu n'invite pas Abdoulaye.
6. Le Cordon Bleu invite Saniyya.
7. Le Cordon Bleu n'invite pas Raphaël.

**21**

1. Vous aimez étudier.
2. Je n'aime pas étudier.
3. Monique n'aime pas étudier.
4. Fatima et Karim aiment étudier.
5. Tu aimes étudier.
6. Nasser n'aime pas étudier.

**20  Le Cordon Bleu**  1.2

Your French teacher has a friend at the local chapter of **Le Cordon Bleu**, a prestigious cooking school. The school wants to invite the students in her class who like cooking a lot. In order to determine who will attend the cooking class, your teacher took a survey to find out how students feel about cooking. Say who **Le Cordon Bleu** is inviting and not inviting, based on the results of the survey.

**MODÈLES**  Isabelle
**Le Cordon Bleu invite Isabelle.**

Cédric
**Le Cordon Bleu n'invite pas Cédric.**

1. Justine
2. Moussa
3. Mathis
4. Lamine
5. Abdoulaye
6. Saniyya
7. Raphaël

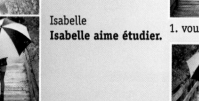

**Est-ce que tu aimes faire la cuisine?**

|  | un peu | bien | beaucoup |
|---|---|---|---|
| Abdoulaye | ✔ | | |
| Saniyya | | | ✔ |
| Justine | | ✔ | |
| Cédric | | ✔ | |
| Lamine | | | ✔ |
| Moussa | ✔ | | |
| Isabelle | | | ✔ |
| Raphaël | | ✔ | |
| Mathis | ✔ | | |

**21  Il fait beau?**  1.1

*Dites qu'on aime étudier quand il fait mauvais et qu'on n'aime pas étudier quand il fait beau.*

**MODÈLES**

Vincent et Noah
**Vincent et Noah n'aiment pas étudier.**

Isabelle
**Isabelle aime étudier.**

1. vous          2. je          3. Monique

4. Fatima et Leïla   5. tu          6. Nasser

**Essential Instruction**

1. Have a student conjugate the verb **inviter** on the board, then have the class repeat it. Ask another student to add the negative and have the class repeat it too, emphasizing the elision of the negative (**on n'invite pas**).
2. Review the pronunciation of the verb **aimer** in the negative before students do **Activité 21** orally with a partner.
3. Before students do **Activité 22**, have the class look at the model together. Then have two of your better students model #1 before you organize the class into pairs. It's a good idea to have struggling students work with an above-level student.

# Communiquez!

**22  Qu'est-ce que tu fais?**   1.1

### Interpersonal Communication

With a partner, take turns asking each other if you participate in these activities.

> **MODÈLE**  A: **Tu joues au foot?**
> B: **Non, je ne joue pas au foot.**
> **Tu joues au foot?**
> A: **Oui, je joue au foot.**

1. écouter la musique alternative
2. étudier la musique
3. inviter le prof au café
4. jouer aux jeux vidéo
5. jouer au hockey sur glace
6. plonger
7. surfer sur Internet
8. écouter la world

> Tu écoutes la musique alternative?

**Answers** _____

㉒

1. A: —Tu écoutes la musique alternative?
2. A: —Tu étudies la musique?
3. A: —Tu invites le prof au café?
4. A: —Tu joues aux jeux vidéo?
5. A: —Tu joues au hockey sur glace?
6. A: —Tu plonges?
7. A: —Tu surfes sur Internet?
8. A: —Tu écoutes la world?

*Answers will vary.*

## Differentiated Learning
### Accelerate
Have students write a paragraph in French about what they like to do and don't like to do when it's nice weather and when it's bad weather.

## Multiple Intelligences
### Visual-Spatial/Intrapersonal
Before doing **Activité 20**, you may want to present additional information about, or photos of, **Le Cordon Bleu**. Find out which students like cooking, who has been to a French restaurant, and what experience they have with French foods. Show them photos of some delicious-looking French foods, or ask students to bring in photos of French foods they find online.

## RESOURCES

**Communicative Activities**

## Answers

23 *Dialogues will vary.*

24 *Messages will vary.*

## Reference Desk

### Blended Instruction

Consider using blended instruction, a combination of in-class learning and computer-mediated instruction or learning opportunities. Ask students to complete activities on the computer, using their cell or smartphone, or other emerging electronic technology. This will allow students to hone their tech skills and become more independent learners. Schedule routine Internet and e-book learning in class and in the lab.

## Communication

### Interpretive: Cooperative Groups

You may want to do this **activité** with your class before asking them to do **Activité 24**. If you are comfortable providing a phone number to your students, prepare a voice-mail message for them and ask them to call you to retrieve the message. The next day in class, ask them to compare what they understood and correct if necessary.

## Game

Play Telephone. Have students form a line, and give one student a one-sentence message. The student must whisper it to the next student who, in turn, whispers it to another. The last student in the line must write the message on the board. Modify the game by playing it between groups with one member of a group delivering a message to the next group until it goes back to the originating group for correction.

What do activities and pastimes reveal about a culture?

### 23 Et toi? 1.1

**Interpersonal Communication**

For each category name an item that you like. Ask if your partner agrees. Follow the model.

> **MODÈLE** A: **J'aime le basket. Et toi?**
> B: **Moi aussi.**
> ou
> B: **Pas moi. Je préfère le foot.**

1. sport
2. passe-temps
3. genre de musique
4. musicien(ne)

J'aime Rachid Taha. Et toi?

Pas moi. Je préfère Corneille.

### 24 Message téléphonique  1.2, 1.3

**Presentational/Interpretive Communication**

Your teacher will give you a phone message form like the one on the right. Complete the form with a phone message for the classmate assigned you by your teacher. Then post your message on the bulletin board for your classmate to retrieve and read.

```
Message téléphonique

Jour: _____

Pour: _____

De: _____

Numéro de téléphone: _____

Message: _____

_____

_____

_____
```

092 quatre-vingt-douze | Unité 2

### Essential Instruction

1. Tally the results of **Activité 23** on the board. Recycle vocabulary by asking, "**Tu aimes... un peu, bien, beaucoup?**"

2. Distribute the phone message forms and ask students to complete a message to a secretly assigned classmate. Offer help as students work. Collect and post the forms. At the end of class, ask students to retrieve their message and make a phone call to the number on the pink slip.

3. Brainstorm a list of musical genres, then assign **Activité 25**.

# Communiquez!

## 25 Ma musique préférée

### Presentational Communication

Prepare a playlist of your favorite songs in one genre. Then tell your small group what genre of music you like a lot, show them your playlist on a sheet of paper, and say which song is your favorite. Sign your playlist in case your teacher wants to post them in the classroom.

> **MODÈLE** J'aime beaucoup la musique alternative. C'est mon playlist.... Je préfère la chanson "Can't Stop Feeling" de Franz Ferdinand.

 1.3

## Communiquez!

## 26 La musique francophone  1.3

### Presentational Communication

There are many different styles of francophone music. Research five of the artists from the following list. Find out what type of music they play and the names of some of their songs. If possible, also listen to recordings by the artists online. Then create a playlist of ten songs you recommend to your classmates.

Youssou N'Dour—Sénégal
Orchestra Baobab—Sénégal
MC Solaar—Sénégal
Baaba Maal—Sénégal
Zachary Richard—la Louisiane
Beausoleil—la Louisiane
Yannick Noah—France
Paris Combo—France
Emmanuel Moire—France
Souad Massi—Algérie
Faudel—France, d'origine algérienne
Amel Bent—France, d'origine algérienne
Kassav—les Caraïbes (*Caribbean*)
Angélique Kidjo—Bénin
Mes Aïeux—Québec
Garou—Québec
Cœur de pirate—Québec
Les Cowboys Fringants—Québec
Corneille—Québec, d'origine rwandaise
Amadou and Mariam—Mali

Yannick Noah

## Communiquez!

## 27 La Fête de la musique  1.3

### Presentational Communication

Your French club has decided to organize a **Fête de la musique**. As a member of the committee, you must choose a francophone singer or group and create a poster advertising the event. Your poster should include:

- who is hosting the event, for example: **La classe de Mme Briand présente....**
- a picture of the singer or the group
- a map showing the singer's or group's country of origin
- a list (or partial list) of the singer's or group's albums (**une discographie**)
- a phrase describing the singer's or group's style or genre
- the date, time, and location of the event

🔍 **Search words: chante france radio**

Answers _____
25 *Playlists will vary.*
26 *Playlists will vary*

## Multiple Intelligences
### Musical-Rhythmic

1. Select students who are particularly interested in music and ask them to do **Activité 26**. Post their lists for other students to see.
2. Do a cloze listening exercise with a song you select, such as Faudel's "**Mon Pays**." Find the lyrics online. Leave blanks for familiar words that you want students to listen for, making enough copies of the lyrics for each student. You might focus the listening exercise by selecting verbs, nouns, or adjectives and placing them at the top of the page. Distribute the lyrics and ask students to supply the missing words as you play the song several times. Review the lyrics and have students sing the song. Finally, ask students to express their opinion about the song, using **aimer** + adverb + name of song.

### Special Needs Students
### Visually Challenged

Team up any visually challenged student with a sighted student who likes to draw to collaborate on and create the poster in **Activité 27**.

# Lecture thématique

## Penser/Classer

### Rencontre avec l'auteur  1.2

**Georges Perec** (1936–1982) was the son of Polish immigrants who settled in Paris in the 1920s. A novelist, essayist, and poet, his work addresses the events of everyday life, memories, and human puzzles. In this excerpt from *Penser/Classer* (1985), published after the author's death, he examines how people categorize their lives. As you read, you will discover that one of the narrator's pastimes is travel. This leads him to wonder where he would actually like to live. But can he make up his mind?

## Pré-lecture  1.3

Make a list, for example, a shopping list, a list of the best songs, a list of your favorite TV programs, and share it with your partner.

## Stratégie de lecture  1.3

### Paraphrasing

When you paraphrase a text, you put its ideas in your own words. Paraphrasing will help you understand the author's main ideas. To help you understand the main ideas of this excerpt from *Penser/Classer*, fill in the chart your teacher gives you. As you read, write the names of the places mentioned in the selection, its location, and the line in which the narrator states how he feels about living there.

| Place | Location | Sometimes wants to live there | Sometimes doesn't want to live there | Doesn't want to live there a long time or forever |
|-------|----------|-------------------------------|--------------------------------------|---------------------------------------------------|
| 1. France | Europe | | line 1 | |

## Outils de lecture  1.2

### Repetition

Paying attention to what is repeated in a selection will help you understand the language of the reading and help you figure out its theme. The selection you are about to read repeats these phrases: *J'aime bien vivre*, and *Je n'aimerais pas vivre*. It is a good idea to understand what they mean before you begin a careful reading.

**1.2**

¹ J'aime bien vivre* en France et parfois* non

² J'aime bien vivre dans le Grand Nord
 mais pas très longtemps*

³ Je n'aimerais pas* vivre à Issoudun mais parfois si*

⁴ J'aurais bien aimé aller sur la lune* mais c'est un peu tard*

⁵ Je n'aimerais pas vivre au "Negresco"* mais parfois si

⁶ Je n'aimerais pas vivre en Orient mais parfois si

⁷ J'aime bien vivre à Paris mais parfois non

⁸ Je n'aimerais pas vivre au Québec mais parfois si

⁹ J'aimerais bien vivre à Xanadu* mais même,
 pas pour toujours.*

---

**Pendant la lecture**
1. What is the narrator doing? Is he perhaps thinking, dreaming, trying to make a decision?

**Pendant la lecture**
2. Is the narrator decisive? Justify your response.

**Pendant la lecture**
3. Has he traveled to countries outside of France?

---

**vivre** *to live;* **parfois** *sometimes;* **longtemps** *for a long time;* **Je n'aimerais pas** Je ne voudrais pas; **si** oui; **J'aurais bien aimé aller sur la lune** *I would have liked to have gone to the moon;* **tard** *late;* **le Negresco** un hôtel sur la Riviera; **Xanadu** *an imaginary exotic place;* **toujours** *always*

## Post-lecture  1.2

By the end of the selection, does the narrator make up his mind where he wants to live?

*Saint Germain-Des-Près*, c. 1998.
Béatrice Boisségur. Collection privée.

## Le monde visuel 3.1

Béatrice Boisségur (1956– ) is a contemporary painter whose vision includes this portrait of a Paris street in essentially dull, muted colors and limited coloration. How does she break with the monotone coloration and convey a whimsical, celebratory feeling in her painting?

---

---

Answers _____

 28 *Activites will vary.*

## Reference Desk

Poetry slams began in Chicago in 1984 when poet Mark Smith launched a poetry reading at a jazz club. Soon the idea spread to other cities, and the first national competition was held in 1990. Show a poet competing in a poetry slam before having students present their poems. Some students may be inspired to work collaboratively on a poem. Consider inviting guests to the event.

## Les copains d'abord

Here is the translation for **Les copains d'abord**:

A = Antoine; F = Florence; MA = Marie-Alix; M = Mathéo
A: Ouch! M: Oh, sorry, are you okay? A: Yeah, no harm. Say, your skateboard is cool! M: I can let you borrow it if you want. A: Oh, thanks, I love skateboarding! M: I prefer parkour. A: Me, I love jogging. M: I hate biking. A: Oh, I like girls. M: Got a girlfriend? A: Uh, no. I like a girl but she doesn't like me. M: Oh come on, go show off to her with my skateboard! F: Marie-Alix, I love to go shopping with you! MA: Me too! Shall we go to the café, now? F: Look, it's the guy in the subway. What's his name? MA: It is Antoine! Hi Antoine! A: Hi girls, how is it going? MA: Whoa, you skateboard really well! F: Yeah, not too bad. A: Thanks, Flo. You like my skateboard? F: It's *Florence*. MA: Antoine, come to the coffee shop with us. F: Oh no!

List of slang and idiomatic expressions:
**passer:** *give*; épater: *impress*;
**meuf:** *girl*; **Ça roule?** *How is it going?*

## 28 Activités d'expansion  1.1, 1.3

Complete the following activities.

1. Write a short paragraph that paraphrases the selection. Tell where the narrator wants to live sometimes, doesn't want to live sometimes, and where he doesn't want to live for a long time or at all.
2. Complete the phrases below with places you would like and not like to live.

Je voudrais vivre (*live*):
Parfois (*Sometimes*) oui:
Parfois non:
Pas très longtemps:
Pas pour toujours:

Finally, have a poetry slam in class and perform your work.

## Essential Instruction

1. Ask students to look at the cartoon and guess what pastime it will feature.
2. Explain interjections like "**Aïe**" (*ouch*). Brainstorm other interjections in English and provide the French equivalents (*whew*=**ouf**, *yuk*=**berk**, *shhh* = **chut**, etc.) Ask students to think of the English equivalent of **oui** and **ouais**.
3. Have students role-play the dialogues. Ask comprehension questions.
4. For **Activité A** of **Projets finaux**, search for and view online the animated short of "The Sweater." Ask students what contemporary sports teams are considered to be rivals and if they would wear the shirt of their favorite team's rival.

# T'es branché?

## Projets finaux

**A** | **Connexions par Internet: Littérature**    **1.2**

**"Le chandail de hockey"**

How can a hockey jersey be such a powerful symbol for national identity?

As you know, hockey is a very popular sport in Canada. "Le Chandail de Hockey" by Roch Carrier is a very famous children's story from Quebec about a hockey jersey and a little boy. Research the story and answer the following questions.

Question centrale

**?**

What do activities and pastimes reveal about a culture?

 **Search words: le chandail de hockey roch carrier**

**Part A**  **1.2, 2.1, 3.1**

1. Where does the story take place? (Locate the village on a map.)
2. Why is hockey popular in this small town?
3. The story begins with people listening to the hockey game on the radio. Imagine this scene. Who is there? What time of day is it? What is everyone doing? What emotions are expressed? What is the name of the famous hockey player and what is his jersey number?
4. What happened to the boy's jersey?
5. What did the mother do?
6. What did you learn about the English/French situation in Canada from the catalogue shopping incident?
7. How did the boy react to his new hockey jersey? Why?
8. What continued to happen?
9. How does the last scene show the boy's feelings towards his culture?
10. How is the hockey jersey a metaphor for cultural and linguistic identity?
11. Is there a team you identify with? How would you feel if your team jersey was ruined?

**Part B** **1.2, 1.3, 2.1**

Create a visual story with four to six frames and label them to show your understanding of the important events of the story. For example, one of your frames might show the Toronto jersey with the caption **Il n'aime pas le chandail de Toronto**. Tell the important events as you see them to your small group.

### Answers

**A**

1. It takes place in St Justine.
2. It is a deep part of Canadian culture.
3. *Answers will vary.*
4. It wore out.
5. She ordered the wrong one from a catalogue.
6. French is not spoken all over Canada.
7. He protests wearing it because it supports the opposite team.
8. He experiences more humiliation and frustration.
9. His culture is a major part of his identity.
10. The boy's older jersey represents the French team; the new one represents the English team.
11. *Answers will vary.*

### Reference Desk

1. In **"Le Chandail de Hockey,"** a boy's mother mistakenly orders a Toronto Maple Leafs hockey jersey for her son by mail, when he wants the number 9 jersey of the Canadiens' player "the Rocket."
2. The animated film version of Roch Carrier's **"Le Chandail de hockey"** is available at the National Film Board of Canada's website. Have students watch the film on their own time or show it in class.

---

**Differentiated Instruction**

**Accelerate**

Remove the verbal exchanges in the cartoon on p. 96 and ask students to work with a partner and fill in an alternate conversation.

**Decelerate**

Ask struggling students to study and use the pictures to interpret what is going on in the cartoon.

**Multiple Intelligences**

**Intrapersonal**

Ask an Intrapersonal student to explain to the class why Florence thinks **"Oh, non!"** (She knows Antoine likes her but is uncomfortable with that because she already has a boyfriend.)

**B** Communautés en ligne  1.3, 5.1

### L'importance du football en France

**Le football**, or soccer, is one of the most popular sports in the world. Many countries have several professional teams or clubs. Find out about France's passion for this sport by visiting the **Fédération Française de Football** (French Football Federation) and **Fédération Internationale de Football Association** (FIFA) Web sites. The second organization sponsors the World Cup. As you explore, answer these questions:

1. Who is on the national team of France that competes in the **Coupe du Monde** (*World Cup*)?
2. What are the French team's colors?
3. What is France's team logo?
4. What is the French mascot?
5. What is the team's nickname? Why do you think the team uses this name?
6. Who are the current popular players and where do they come from?
7. What are some of the most popular soccer clubs in France?
8. What is the closest soccer organization in your area?

 **Search words: fédération française de football, fédération internationale de football association**

**C** Passez à l'action!  1.1, 1.3, 2.1

### Why is French an official language of the Olympics?

In this unit, you learned about Pierre de Coubertin and the creation of the modern Olympic Games. Coubertin believed that an athletic competition among different nations would promote understanding across cultures and lessen the danger of war. In this same spirit, you would like to make your community more aware of the role francophone culture has played in the world. Create a presentation that illustrates Pierre de Courbertin's role in founding the modern Olympic games and explains why French is an official language of the Olympics. Then make your presentation available to your city or school library.

One of the most popular French soccer players, Thierry Henry plays for the French International team.

Possible formats you might use include: poster, Web page, PowerPoint™ slide show, video, or podcast.

**Tip:** Use French words, especially cognates, to spice up your presentation.

Canadian Governor General Michaëlle Jean gives a bilingual speech in English and French at the Vancouver Olympic games Opening Ceremony.

### Essential Instruction

1. Ask how many students play or watch soccer. Then, make sure students understand the directions for **Activité B** before they go online.
2. Before starting **Activité C**, ask how many students have watched the Olympics on TV. Ask them if they know why French is an official language of the Games.
3. Explain the meaning of **Faisons le point!** before asking students to individually fill in the graphic organizer. A copy of the graphic organizer can be found in the **Copy Masters** ancillary. Explain to students that reflecting on their learning is an important step in making progress in all of their subjects.

## D Faisons le point! 1.3

Your teacher will give you a chart like the one below. Fill it in to show what you've learned about the French language and francophone cultures in this unit.

*Question centrale*

**?**

What do activities and pastimes reveal about a culture?

| Je comprends | Je ne comprends pas encore | Mes connexions |
|---|---|---|
|  |  |  |

| What did I do well to learn and use the content of this unit? | What should I do in the next unit to better learn and use the content? |
|---|---|
| How can I effectively communicate to others what I have learned? | What was the most important concept I learned in this unit? |

Leçon C | quatre-vingt-dix-neuf **0 9 9**

**Differentiated Instruction**

**Decelerate**

Tell the class they will get a paired practice grade for completing **Activité B**. Then, pair each struggling student with an above-level student. This will perhaps help students who are struggling with French to get a better grade and feel successful. Help struggling students to understand what to do with the graphic organizer in **Activité D** by asking them questions individually, for example, for **Je comprends**: What was the title of the unit? What

pastimes did you learn how to say in French? Do you remember how to make a sentence negative? What are the genders of French words?

**Expand**

Ask students to work in groups to provide answers to the **Question centrale**: What do activities and pastimes reveal about a culture? Which parts of the unit illustrate the essential question?

# Évaluation

**A** **Évaluation de compréhension auditive**  1.1

Listen to the phone conversation and decide if the statements you hear are **vrai** (**V**) or **faux** (**F**).

**B** **Évaluation orale**  1.1

The radio show **La Zik** interviews young people about music and their other interests. With a partner, play the roles of Erica, an American guest on the show, and the interviewer. The interviewer asks Erica:

- her name.
- what she likes to do.
- if she likes music a little.
- if she prefers alternative music or hip-hop.

- if she prefers rock or world music.
- if she listens to Corneille and Taha.
- if she likes to go to concerts.

Erica responds to each question.

**C** **Évaluation culturelle**  4.2

You will be asked to make some comparisons between francophone cultures and American culture. You may need to complete some additional research about American culture.

**La Seine** separates the **rive droite** and **rive gauche** (Right and Left banks) of Paris.

### Pari Roller

1. Compare Pari Roller with sporting events that take place in your region. When do they occur? How many participants are there? What are the venues? How long have the sporting events been taking place?

### Deux capitales

2. Compare Paris with the U.S. capital. You may want to make a chart with one column of characteristics, for example, population, monuments, museums; one column for Paris; and one column for Washington, D.C.

### Les mouvements d'art

3. Compare the cubist movement in Paris to the modern art movement in New York. When did these movements occur? Who were the principal artists? Why did these art movements develop in these cities?

### La musique

4. France participates in **la Fête de la musique**. What music celebrations occur annually in your region? Compare the event in France with the events in your area. How are they similar? How are they different?

Answers _____

D *Answers will vary.*
E *Answers will vary.*
F *Answers will vary.*

## D Évaluation écrite  1.3

You will be arriving in Lyon in August to be an exchange student at a school there. Answer the questions below to help you write a letter to the principal so he can place you with the best possible host family. Make sure you begin your letter with **Bonjour Monsieur le Directeur** and end with **Merci**, followed by your signature.

1. Qu'est-ce que vous aimez manger?
2. Vous préférez le sport ou les jeux vidéos?
3. Vous aimez bien la musique?
4. Qu'est-ce que vous aimez faire le weekend?
5. Vous aimez surfer sur Internet et envoyer des textos?
7. Vous préférez lire ou regarder la télé?
8. Qu'est-ce que vous aimez faire quand il fait beau?
9. Qu'est-ce que vous aimez faire quand il fait mauvais?

## E Évaluation visuelle  1.3

Write a paragraph telling what each person in the picture likes to do in the park on Saturday.

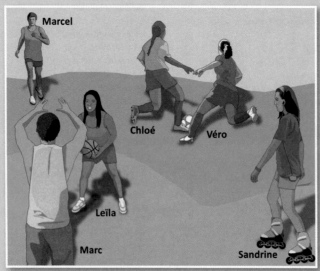

## F Évaluation compréhensive  1.3

Create a storyboard with four to six frames. Write labels for each frame, telling how some teens enjoy music. For example, they might listen to **Le Hit Parade** on their MP3 player, dance in a club, or go to a concert. Finally, "show and tell" your story to a small group of classmates.

**Differentiated Learning**

**Accelerate**
Challenge these students by asking them to complete all of the **Évaluation** activities.

**Decelerate**
Choose the most pertinent activities for your struggling students to complete. For example, if you are going to test only listening, speaking, and culture, have them do A, B, and C.

### Reference Desk

Students should use the electronic flash cards to review vocabulary.

### Games

1. Play Pictionary to review vocabulary. Create a set of vocabulary flash cards and put them in a large envelope or other container. Divide the class into two teams. One student picks a vocabulary word and draws it on the board while his or her teammates try to guess the word. Award a point for each word that students guess correctly during an allotted time.

2. Play vocabulary charades. Divide the class into two teams. One student picks a word and acts it out while teammates guess the word during an allotted time. Award a point for each word guessed correctly.

# Vocabulaire de l'Unité 2  1.2  

**à** at *B*

**une activité** activity *B*

**aimer** to like, to love *A*

**un(e) ami(e)** friend *A*

**après** after *A*

**aussi** also, too *C*

**beaucoup** a lot, very much *B*

**bien** really *B*

**un blogue** blog *C*

**un calendrier** calendar *A*

**un CD** CD *C*

**le cinéma** movies *A*

**un concert** concert *C*; **un concert R'n'B** R&B concert *C*

**un cours** course, class *C*

**de** of, any *A*; **de la** some *A*

**des** some *A*

**dormir** to sleep *B*

**écouter** to listen (to) *B*; **écouter de la musique** to listen to music *B*; **écouter mon lecteur MP3** to listen to my MP3 player *B*

**elles** they (f.) *A*

**une enquête** survey *B*

**envoyer** to send *B*; **envoyer des textos** to send text messages *B*

**l' été (m.)** summer *A*

**étudier** to study *B*

**faire: de la gymnastique** to do gymnastics *A*; **faire du footing** to go running *A*; **faire du patinage artistique** to (figure) skate *A*; **faire du roller** to inline skate *A*; **faire du shopping** to go shopping *A*; **faire du ski (alpin)** to (downhill) ski *A*; **faire du sport** to play sports *A*; **faire du vélo** to bike *A*; **faire la cuisine** to cook *B*

**fais: Je fais du vélo.** I bike. *A*; **Je ne fais pas…** I'm not doing… *C*; **tu fais** you do, make *A*;

**fait: Il fait beau.** It's beautiful out. *A*; **Il fait mauvais.** The weather's bad. *A*

**génial(e)** great, terrific, fantastic *A*

**un hamburger** hamburger *A*

**le hip-hop** hip-hop *C*

**l' hiver (m.)** winter *A*

**ils** they (m.) *A*

**l' Internet (m.)** Internet *B*

**inviter** to invite *C*

**les jeux-vidéo (m.)** video games *B*

**jouer** to play *A*; **jouer au basket(ball)** to play basketball *A*; **jouer au foot(ball)** to play soccer *A*; **jouer au hockey** to play hockey *A*; **jouer aux jeux vidéo** to play video games *A*

**le jour** day *A*

**l'** the *C*

**un lecteur MP3** MP3 player *B*

**les** the *A*

**lire** to read *B*

**manger** to eat *A*

**la musique** music *B*; **musique alternative** alternative music *C*

**nager** to swim *A*

**n'est-ce pas?** Isn't it so? *A*

**un nombre** number *C*

**nous** we *A*

**nouveau** new *C*

**un numéro** number *C*; **un numéro de téléphone** phone number *C*

**octobre** October *A*

**ou** or *C*

**un passe-temps** pastime *A*

**pendant** during *B*

**(un) peu** (a) little *B*

**plonger** to dive *A*

**pourquoi** why *C*

**préféré(e)** favorite *B*

**préférer** to prefer *C*

**qu'est-ce que** what *A*; **Qu'est-ce que tu aimes faire?** What do you like to do? *A*; **Qu'est-ce que tu fais?** What are you doing? *C*

**quand** when *A*

**quel, quelle** what, which *C*

**la question** question *B*

**regarder** to watch *B*

**le rock** rock (music) *C*

**une semaine** week *A*

**le shopping** shopping *C*

**si** yes [on the contrary] *A*

**un soir** evening *A*

**sortir** to go out *A*

**un sport** sport *A*

**sur** on *B*

**surfer: surfer sur Internet** to surf the Web *B*

**la télé (télévision)** TV, television *B*

**téléphoner** to phone (someone), to make a call *B*

**un texto** text message *B*

**vas: Tu vas bien?** Are things going well? *C*

**le weekend** weekend *B*

**la world** world music *C*

Days of the week… see p. 53
Food… see p. 53
Numbers 1–20… see p. 78

### Essential Instruction

1. Explore the steps involved in "learning the vocabulary." Students should be able to recall the word or expression from English to French and from French to English. They should be able to spell and pronounce the word correctly. Students should be able to identify and understand the word or expression when they hear it. If students have learned the vocabulary in a specific context, they should be able to recognize and understand it in a different context as they proceed in their study of French.

2. Explain the expression **Bilan cumulatif** ("taking stock" of their learning) in **Unité 2**.

3. Assign the **Listening** section at least once.

4. Have students read the passage silently for comprehension; then, have them work with a partner to find where the answer to each question is contained in the text.

# Unité 2 Bilan cumulatif

## Listening   1.1

I. You will hear a short conversation. Select the reply that would come next. You will hear the conversation twice.

1. A. Je n'aime pas jouer au basket.
   B. J'aime beaucoup mon père.
   C. Je dois étudier quand il fait mauvais.
   D. Je préfère lire.

II. Listen to the conversation. Select the best completion to each statement that follows.

2. Natasha et Alexis....
   A. aiment faire du roller
   B. préfèrent surfer sur Internet
   C. aiment lire les blogues
   D. aiment beaucoup le sport

3. On regarde....
   A. Pari Roller
   B. les Jeux Olympiques d'été
   C. les Jeux Olympiques d'hiver
   D. la gym

## Reading  1.2

III. Read the paragraph about pastimes in France. Then select the best completion to each statement.

Qu'est-ce que les Français aiment faire? C'est simple! Leurs passe-temps préférés sont similaires aux passe-temps des Américains. Certains aiment faire du shopping, regarder des comédies ou des films d'action avec leurs copains. Ils sont fans de la musique, surtout de la world et de la pop américaine. Ils adorent aussi être au téléphone de longs moments avec leurs copains et donner rendez-vous aux copains au café après un ciné ou un concert. D'autres préfèrent regarder le sport à la télé avec un bon copain ou aller au café. Écouter le hip-hop et danser à la musique latine et américaine est aussi très populaire chez les Français. Les ados français aident aussi leurs parents le weekend. Ils aiment faire la cuisine et organiser des dîners en famille le dimanche.

1. Les passe-temps des Français sont....
   A. différents des passe-temps des Américains
   B. similaires aux passe-temps des Américains
   C. le hockey sur glace et le basketball
   D. la musique classique et latine

2. Les ados français préfèrent....
   A. des films d'action ou des comédies
   B. regarder le sport à la télé
   C. faire du vélo et sortir avec des copains
   D. jouer au hockey et faire du ski alpin

3. Le dimanche on aime....
   A. aller au café
   B. écouter la pop américaine
   C. manger en famille
   D. danser

**Answers**

 Script can be found in the front pages of the Annotated Teacher's Edition.
1. C

2. D
3. C

**III**
1. B
2. A
3. C

---

**Differentiated Learning**
**Accelerate, Decelerate**
Ask students to create an original paragraph that incorporates vocabulary and structure from **Unités 1–2**. Check these paragraphs for errors. Then give them to struggling students to do at home for extra reading practice at their own pace.

**IV**

1. va
2. Qu'est que
3. aimes
4. footing
5. fait
6. faire
7. fait mauvais
8. pas
9. aime
10. musique
11. aimes
12. alternative
13. centre commercial/cinéma

**V**

14. étudie
15. surfent
16. téléphone
17. préfèrent
18. écoutons
19. jouez
20. aime beaucoup

**VII**

Possible answer:
On aime beaucoup de sports à notre lycée. Moi, j'aime beaucoup jouer au foot. Mon ami François aime bien faire du ski. Quand il fait beau, nous aimons faire footing. Quand il fait mauvais, nous aimons jouer au basket. Beaucoup d'élèves aiment jouer au hockey. Et toi, qu'est-ce que tu aimes faire?

---

### Reference Desk

1. The **Composition** section will prepare students for the Proficiency Writing section of the unit test.
2. In the **Speaking** section, consider requiring students to ask questions as well in order to recycle previous material such as introductions.

---

## Writing  1.3

**IV.** Complete the paragraph with appropriate words or expressions.

Salut! Ça __1__? __2__ tu aimes faire? Tu __3__ faire du __4__? Quand il __5__ beau, j'aime __6__ du vélo. Quand il __7__, je n'aime __8__ sortir! J' __9__ bien écouter de la __10__. Tu __11__ le hip-hop ou la musique __12__? On va au __13__ demain soir?

**V.** Complete the paragraph with the correct form of the verbs.

Qu'est-ce qu'on fait ce weekend? Élodie __14__ ce weekend! Rachid et Philippe __15__ sur Internet. Je __16__ à ma copine samedi pour aller au café. Les amis __17__ aller au cinéma. Laurence et moi, nous __18__ de la musique alternative dimanche. Et vous? Vous __19__ au football? J' __20__ le football!

14. (étudier)
15. (surfer)
16. (téléphoner)
17. (préférer)
18. (écouter)
19. (jouer)
20. (aimer beaucoup)

## Composition  1.3, 2.1

**VI.** Write a postcard to your future host family in Quebec. Begin your postcard with **Chère famille Bouchard**, then:

- introduce yourself.
- say what activities you like to do and to what degree.
- say what sports you like to play.
- ask what the Bouchards like to do.
- say what you like to eat.

At the end of your postcard, say you'll see the family soon and sign your name.

## Speaking  1.1

**VII.** Bruno is a new exchange student from Lyon. Based on the pictures, tell him in French which sports teens like to play at Lake City High, and to what degree. Then ask him a couple questions about which sports he prefers.

---

### Differentiated Learning
#### Decelerate

1. To support struggling students in becoming more successful at the cloze exercise in **Writing IV**, provide them the answers in a list on the board.
2. Review with these students how to conjugate regular **-er** verbs and put the forms on the board for them to look at before they tackle **Writing V.**
3. Provide a completed postcard for struggling students to use as a model.

4. Write out line-by-line directions of what struggling students should say. Give students a choice in deciding which role they want to play.

### Special Needs Students
#### Dyslexic Students

Accommodate dyslexic students by telling them that they can complete the **Writing** section with their books open.

# Unité

# 3 À l'école

*Rendez-vous à Nice!*

**Épisode 3:**

*À la cantine et au parc*

cent cinq **105**

## Citation

"Le but de l'éducation, c'est d'apprendre à rencontrer le monde."

**The goal of education is to learn how to encounter the world.**

—Albert Jacquard, philosophe et généticien

### À savoir 4.2

A student who is 13 or 14 years old is in middle school, or **collège**, in France.

### Essential Instruction

1. Begin with a discussion of the **Question centrale**. Ask students if they have considered what their school programs are trying to accomplish and why. Ask what they know about the French school system. Tell them that many French schools are named for a famous person, such as **Louis Pasteur, Henri IV**, or **Louis le Grand**.

2. Read aloud the **Citation** and ask students what they think "encounter the world" means. Have them brainstorm a list of ways that they have or would like to "encounter the world." Create and post the list.

3. Have students read and ask questions about the **Contrat de l'élève**. Explain **élève** vs. **étudiant**. (**Étudiant(e)**) usually refers to university students, but sometimes high school students prefer this term to refer to themselves.) Ask them if there is anything specific about French schools that they would like to learn in this unit.

4. Show the relevant video clip from *Rendez-vous à Nice!*, Episode 3, and discuss the related question as a class.

# Unité 3
# À l'école

Go online
EMCLanguages.net

**Question centrale**

?

How does education shape individuals and societies?

What is happening in English class?
A. Patrick is late.
B. Jean-Charles changed his looks.
C. Charlotte is sick.

What is the name of this French artist?

## Contrat de l'élève

**Leçon A** **I will be able to:**

>> say what I and others need, and give prices.

>> talk about Carrefour, French school supplies, the euro, and e-learning in France.

>> use indefinite articles, the plural forms of nouns and articles, the irregular verb **avoir**, and the expression **avoir besoin de (d')**.

**Leçon B** **I will be able to:**

>> describe my teachers and classes and ask for descriptions.

>> talk about French school schedules, courses, and exams; the naming of francophone schools; and French Polynesia.

>> tell time and use **être**.

**Leçon C** **I will be able to:**

>> ask "where," "when," "with whom," and "why" questions and set a time and place to meet someone.

>> talk about lunches in French school cafeterias and use borrowed words from French.

>> use the verb **aller**, the preposition **à** with definite articles, and form questions using **est-ce que**.

cent sept **1 0 7**

**RESOURCES**

*Rendez-vous à Nice!*
**Episode 3**

Answers _____

The answer to the video question is A. This photo is from *Rendez-vous à Nice!*, Episode 2. Use this question about school to review the previous episode before selecting the link, which will bring you to Episode 3.

**Reference Desk**

1. Questions to explore with your students: Which French artist created the painting on this page? What is the subject matter and how does it pertain to the notion of **Francophonie**? Where is **la Polynésie**? Is this an Impressionist painting? (Compare it with the Picasso painting on p. 58.) Are your students familiar with any work by this artist?
2. Remind students that they can review the video using their smartphones if they have software to scan the QR code.

**Multiple Intelligences**
**Intrapersonal**
Have pairs research online and report on the scientist **Albert Jacquard**. Expand the discussion of education to include topics that students are interested in or concerned about. Ask them to consider the evolution of education in the United States. What was it like 100 years ago? Who went to school in the past and until what age? What factors influenced the development of mandatory school for all children?

### Reference Desk

1. The French **clavier** (keyboard) of **un ordi** (computer) has AZERTY in place of the American QWERTY.
2. Explain **un stylo à bille** (ballpoint), **un stylo à plume** (cartridge pen), and **un stylo à encre** (fountain pen). Many French use fountain pens.
3. French notebooks have graph paper; the vertical lines help with penmanship.
4. Provide additional classroom vocabulary: **une agrafeuse** (stapler), **le scotch** (adhesive tape), **un poster** (poster).
5. **Un prof** and **une prof** are widely used informally. The more formal **un professeur** is always masculine, despite the person's gender. **Un proviseur** or **une directrice** is a principal. **Un professeur principal** is a homeroom teacher.
6. To introduce prepositions, ask students who sits **derrière** or **devant** of them. Play a true/false game by asking students where things are in the classroom.

### TPR

Teach the command **Montrez-moi....** Students find objects or respond with thumbs up or down as you name them. Introduce **Mets....** and give commands like **Mets le stylo sur la chaise.**

### Communication

**Interpersonal: Paired Practice**
Use vocabulary flash cards to play Go Fish!

# Leçon A

## Vocabulaire actif

**Go online EMCLanguages.net**

### La salle de classe 🎧 ⊗ 1.2

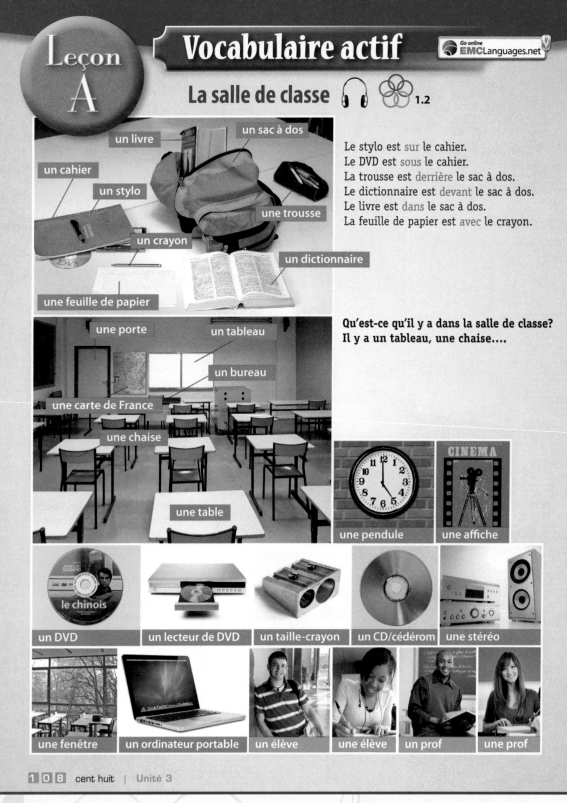

Le stylo est sur le cahier.
Le DVD est sous le cahier.
La trousse est derrière le sac à dos.
Le dictionnaire est devant le sac à dos.
Le livre est dans le sac à dos.
La feuille de papier est avec le crayon.

Qu'est-ce qu'il y a dans la salle de classe?
Il y a un tableau, une chaise....

### Essential Instruction

1. Have students listen to the audio of the nouns, then practice the vocabulary. Point to various objects and ask students to identify them. For example, point to the door and ask **C'est une porte?** Repeat with all vocabulary items. Next, use incorrect vocabulary and ask students to answer making corrections. For example, point to the classroom clock, and ask, **C'est une stéréo?** Students respond, **Non, c'est une pendule.**

2. Review numbers 1–20. Ask students to recite them in a round-robin pattern, then ask for **les numéros pairs et impairs**.

3. Explain how numbers 70–99 are formed by showing these math problems: 60 + 10 = 70, 60 + 11 = 71, 4 × 20 = 80, 4 × 20 + 1 = 81, etc. Teach students the symbols **plus** (+), **moins** (−), **fois** (×), **divisé par** (/) and have them do easy math problems.

4. Call out numbers and have students write them on the board.

| 20 | VINGT | 21 vingt et un | 22 vingt-deux… | 29 vingt-neuf |
|---|---|---|---|---|
| 30 | TRENTE | 31 trente et un | 32 trente-deux… | 39 trente-neuf |
| 40 | QUARANTE | 41 quarante et un | 42 quarante-deux… | 49 quarante-neuf |
| 50 | CINQUANTE | 51 cinquante et un | 52 cinquante-deux… | 59 cinquante-neuf |
| 60 | SOIXANTE | 61 soixante et un | 62 soixante-deux… | 69 soixante-neuf |
| 70 | SOIXANTE-DIX | 71 soixante et onze | 72 soixante-douze… | 79 soixante-dix-neuf |
| 80 | QUATRE-VINGTS | 81 quatre-vingt-un | 82 quatre-vingt-deux… | 89 quatre-vingt-neuf |
| 90 | QUATRE-VINGT-DIX | 91 quatre-vingt-onze | 92 quatre-vingt-douze… | 99 quatre-vingt-dix-neuf |
| 100 | CENT | | | |

# Pour la conversation  **1.2**

**H**ow do I say what I need?

> **J'ai besoin d'**une trousse.
>
> *I need a pencil case.*

**H**ow do I ask what someone else needs?

> **Tu as besoin d'**un cahier?
>
> *Do you need a notebook?*

**H**ow do I ask what something costs?

> La trousse, **elle coûte combien?**
>
> *The pencil case, how much does it cost?*
>
> Le cahier, **il coûte combien?**
>
> *The notebook, how much does it cost?*

**H**ow do I state what something costs?

> **Il coûte** 2,59 euros.
>
> *It costs 2,59 euros.*

**Et si je voulais dire…?**

| **le classeur** | *binder* |
|---|---|
| **la gomme** | *eraser* |
| **la règle** | *ruler* |
| **le stylo à bille** | *ballpoint pen* |
| **le feutre** | *marker* |

## 1 Qu'est-ce que c'est? **1.2**

*Identifiez!*

1.

2.

3.

4.

5.

6.

7.

8.

**RESOURCES**

 **Workbook 6–9**

**Answers**

**1**

1. une fenêtre
2. une porte
3. une pendule
4. une affiche
5. un taille-crayon
6. un bureau
7. un lecteur de DVD
8. un tableau

### Reference Desk

1. In Belgian, Swiss, and Acadian dialects, **septante (70)** is used instead of **soixante-dix**. In Swiss dialect, **huitante (80)**, or occasionally **octante**, is used instead of **quatre-vingts**. In Swiss, Acadian, Belgian, and central African dialects, people use **nonante (90)** instead of **quatre-vingt-dix**.
2. Review definite articles.
3. Add **x** to words ending in -**au** to make them plural (**un bureau/des bureaux**).
4. Review -**er** verbs before presenting **avoir**.
5. Highlight spelling: plural "s" in **quatre-vingts**, lack of **et** with **quatre-vingt-un** and **quatre-vingt-onze**, and use of hyphens.
6. Label classroom objects to reinforce vocabulary.

### Communication

**Interpersonal: Paired Practice**

Have partners play "Clap Math." One student says a number and claps: one = addition, two = subtraction, three = multiplication, four = division. Then he or she says the second number in the equation. The partner performs the calculation and gives the answer in French. Change roles.

**Presentational: Cooperative Groups**

Have groups pool together and display items from the **Vocabulaire actif**. Groups observe and list another group's collection. As groups share what they've displayed, partner groups compare it to what they wrote down.

## Differentiated Learning

### Accelerate

1. Teach the sequence of numbers 1-100. Make a master list of random numbers, and a corresponding set of those numbers on 3 × 5 cards. Distribute several cards to each student. Explain that you are going to call out numbers. When students hear a number on one of their cards, they should repeat it out loud, run to the board, and **write** it for the class.
2. Model the pronunciation of the **Et si je voulais dire…?** vocabulary, then have students listen to the audio.

## Special Needs Students

### Linguistically Challenged/AD(H)D

1. Instead of teaching all numbers from 20–100 at once, try the approach of teaching only the multiples of tens on the first day to make it more manageable for students. The next day, add multiples of five. Finally, complete the sequence on yet another day.
2. Teach the command, **Montrez-moi….** Students can point to the object to indicate understanding and answer using **Voilà….**

**109**

**2 Les prix**   1.2, 2.1, 2.2

Some students are buying school supplies and items for their bedroom at the store. Number your paper from 1–8. Then match the correct price to the picture of each item you hear.

A. 79,89 €   B. 2,30 €   C. 5,75 €   D. 4,49 €   E. 1,29 €
F. 56,30 €   G. 30,50 €   H. 3,99 €

  1.

  2.

  3.

  4.

  5.

  6.

  7.

  8.

**3 Dans la salle de classe**  1.1, 2.1, 2.2

*Dites où sont les fournitures scolaires de Fabien et Marianne.* (Say where Fabien's and Marianne's school supplies are.)

**MODÈLE**   le crayon de Fabien
**Le crayon de Fabien est sur le dictionnaire.**

1. le livre de maths de Marianne
2. le sac à dos de Fabien
3. la trousse de Marianne
4. le livre d'anglais de Fabien
5. la feuille de papier de Marianne
6. le livre de français de Fabien

Marianne   Fabien

# Rencontres culturelles

 Go online EMCLanguages.net

## On fait du shopping!

    1.2

Yasmine and Camille are at the Carrefour superstore in the school supplies section.

Yasmine: Bon… j'ai des stylos, un taille-crayon, et des cahiers pour écrire mes notes.
Camille: Tu as besoin d'un dictionnaire?
Yasmine: Oui! Il est où?
Camille: Là… devant toi, avec les cédéroms.
Yasmine: Il coûte combien?

*(Camille grabs it.)*

Camille: 28,50 euros.
Yasmine: Et en cédérom?
Camille: 44,90 euros!
Yasmine: C'est cher! Mais je prends le cédérom… pour mon ordinateur, c'est beaucoup mieux.
Camille: Et maintenant les trousses….
Yasmine: J'aime bien la bleue là. Total vintage! J'achète!

### 4 On fait du shopping!

.1, 2.2

*Répondez aux questions.*

1. Camille achète des stylos?
2. Yasmine achète des cahiers?
3. Yasmine a besoin d'un dictionnaire?
4. Le cédérom, il coûte combien?
5. Yasmine achète quelle trousse?

### Extension    À la caisse

A customer at Carrefour is checking out.

Caissière: Quarante-trois euros soixante… vous payez avec une carte de crédit?
Awa: Non, en espèces…. Voilà 50….
Caissière: Voilà six euros, 40 centimes. Votre ticket. Merci et au revoir.

### Extension    How much change does Awa get back?

## Differentiated Learning
### Accelerate
1. Challenge these students by asking questions about the picture in **Activité 3** and recycling the new vocabulary, for example, **Il y a quatre-vingt-deux élèves dans les chaises? Le prof a besoin d'élèves?**, etc.
2. Project an advertisement for school supplies from an online French catalogue and ask students to read the prices.
3. Model the **Extension** dialogue. Have students repeat and practice with a partner.

## Learning Styles
### Visual Learners
Have students draw and label the French classroom. Post their drawings around the room. Reassure students that their drawing will be reviewed for accuracy, not artistic merit, and ask students to circulate and critique the drawings, correcting any errors.

### Multiple Intelligences
#### Interpersonal
Have the students use **Activité 3** as a model to ask a partner where school items are in the classroom.

## Answers
**4**
1. Non.
2. Oui.
3. Oui.
4. 44,90€.
5. La bleue.

### Extension
Awa's purchase costs 43,60€. She gets 6,40€ in change.

### Reference Desk
Students will learn more about the euro on p. 113. However, they might enjoy discovering about it for themselves in the Culture Activity below.

### Culture

**Products: Activity**
Show students some real euros. Challenge them to discover what is pictured on the banknotes and coins. On the banknotes they should note that the architecture spans different styles across the ages but with generic designs common to Europe. On the coins, they should find one side has a common design and the other has an image issued by an individual member country. Look at different EU members' choices for their national design on the coins. Using real euros and a display of various school supplies "for sale," have the students copy the dialogue in a skit. As they get more confident handling the coins and banknotes, you can challenge them with even more items.

### Expansion

Ask further questions: Who is buying the articles? **Combien coûte le dictionnaire?** Visit the EU website to obtain posters and publications for your classroom.

111

# Points de départ

## Carrefour  1.2, 2.2

Carrefour is a French superstore, or **hypermarché**, that literally means "intersection." It sells everything from groceries and clothing to televisions and other electronics. You can find Carrefour stores throughout Europe, South America, and Asia.

**Search words: carrefour france**

How does education shape individuals and societies?

**Carrefour** (C
du positif chaque jour

**COMPARAISONS** 4.2

Do you have any superstores in your area like Carrefour? Is the store an international, national, or regional company?

## Les manuels et les fournitures scolaires  1.2, 2.2

Students in France buy most of their school supplies before classes begin in the fall. These include **une trousse**, a case to carry pens, pencils, and other small objects like erasers. Those students who can't afford to buy all their supplies receive government assistance to cover these expenses. Students attending **un collège**, or middle school, receive their textbooks free of charge. High school, or **lycée**, students also receive their textbooks for free or obtain vouchers to purchase the books themselves. The books students need are on a list provided by the school.

UNITED OFFICE
**2 cahiers et 1 bloc-notes**
• 2 cahiers A4 et A5 + 1 bloc-notes 12,5 x 20 cm.
• 75 feuilles.
*Le lot au choix*
**2.⁴⁹**

**Search words: fournitures scolaires**

PC Portable ASUS K50IN SX002C - 15.6" - 250 Go
<B><FONT COLOR="#FF0000">Prix exclusivement applicable sur le site int...

**499,99 €**

Quantité 1

| AJOUTER AU PANIER

Taille crayons Bulbo MAPED

**1,40 €**

Quantité 1

| AJOUTER AU PANIER

Sac à Dos Roulettes - OXBOW Broken

**43,92 €**
AU LIEU DE 49,99 €

Quantité 1

| AJOUTER AU PANIER

1 1 2   cent douze   |   Unité 3

1 1 2

## L'euro et l'eurozone  2.1, 2.2

The symbol for the euro is €. It is the currency used by those European Union countries joined together to create a single common market called the "eurozone." Created in 1999, the euro entered into circulation in France in 2002, replacing the French franc. Euro bills come in seven different denominations: €5, €10, €20, €50, €100, €200, and €500. They are identical, no matter which eurozone country prints them. The coins, however, have one side with a design unique to the country that minted them. The other side is the same in all countries. Coins come in values of 1 (**cent**, **centime**), 2, 5, 10, 20, and 50 cents as well as €1 and €2.

**Search words: euro**
**billets et pièces en euro**

The front of the euro bills features doors and windows, which symbolize the free alliance between member countries of the Eurozone.

### COMPARAISONS 4.2

Find prices for an MP3 player, laptop computer, and backpack in France. Then use a currency converter to find out how much they cost in dollars. Are these items more or less expensive in the United States?

## La formation en ligne  2.1, 2.2

Just as in the United States, many French universities and businesses offer online education and training. Twenty-four percent of all workers in France have now taken an online course or received online training. Schools offer distance learning, different types of e-learning, and other educational opportunities via today's modern technology. In fact, France recently dedicated an entire year to e-learning and online education in its schools.

### COMPARAISONS 4.2

What commitment has your school made to e-learning? What are the advantages of online learning? What are the disadvantages?

Some French schools offer e-learning classes as early as 1st grade.

**5**

1. A "hypermarket" that sells everything including food, clothing, appliances, and furniture. **Carrefour** means intersection and is among France's top retailers.
2. The government provides or distributes vouchers for required books.
3. A pencil case carried by most students in France.
4. The symbol € represents the euro currency.
5. The eurozone includes European Union member states that have adopted the euro currency; research online for the complete updated list of EU member states that use the euro. The United Kingdom, Switzerland, Norway, and Russia do not use or plan to use the euro.
6. 2002
7. Based on 100 cents, the euro notes are 500- , 200- , 100- , 50- , 20- , 10- and 5-euro notes. There are coins in the amounts of 2-€, 1-€, 50-cents, 20-cents, 10-cents, 5-cents, 2-cents, and 1-cent.
8. Online learning is increasingly popular in France.

**À discuter**
*Answers will vary.*

 **6**

1. Most expensive: **Trousse DDP Indie**; least expensive: **Trousse Ronde Fille**
2. euros
3. round
4. **fourre tout**
5. **Ajouter au panier**

## Reference Desk

An unofficial symbol of the French Republic, **Marianne** represents the values of liberty, equality, and fraternity. Research which French actresses have served as the model for **Marianne** since 1969.

---

 **5  Questions culturelles**   **1.1, 1.2**

*Répondez aux questions.*

1. What is Carrefour?
2. Who pays for student textbooks in France?
3. What is **une trousse**?
4. What is the symbol for the euro?
5. What is the eurozone?
6. In what year was the euro introduced in France?
7. What denominations does the euro bill come in?
8. How common is online learning in France?

**À discuter**  **1.1, 2.2**

Which way do you learn best, with a teacher in a traditional classroom or online? Provide advantages and disadvantages for both educational approaches.

The tail side of this 20-cent coin depicts Marianne, a symbol of the French Republic.

## Du côté des médias  **1.2**

*Lisez les publicités.*

 **6  Les trousses**  **1.1, 2.1**

*Répondez aux questions.*

1. Which brand of **trousse** is the most expensive? The least expensive?
2. What currency are the prices in?
3. What shapes do the **trousses** come in?
4. What is a synonym for **une trousse**?
5. How do you say "Add to my basket"?

**Essential Instruction**

1. Bring, or ask students to bring, euros to class for review. If no euros are available, search for pictures online or explore the European Commission's website on the euro.
2. Point out the photo of the euro coin in **Activité 5**. Then, show students various representations of **Marianne** that you find online, such as depicted by Delacroix in the painting *La Liberté guidant le peuple*. Do we have an equivalent common national personification of the United States government? How is Uncle Sam similar and different from the French figure **Marianne**?

# Structure de la langue

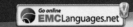 

**RESOURCES**

 **Workbook 13–15**

## Indefinite Articles  1.2

You learned that definite articles precede a noun and that **le** and **la** indicate whether the noun is masculine or feminine. **Un** and **une** ("a," "an," or "one") are indefinite articles. They also indicate the gender of a noun. **Un** is used for masculine nouns and **une** is used for feminine nouns.

Alors, *un coca* et *une pizza*?

Il y a **un** stylo et **une** trousse sur la table.
*There is a pen and there is a pencil case on the table.*

**7 Véro surfe sur Internet**   1.2, 1.3

Véro is looking online for inexpensive school supplies and items for her bedroom. Say how much each item costs.

**MODÈLE** pendule 24 €

**Une pendule coûte vingt-quatre euros.**

1. 8 €

2. 27 €

3. 15 €

4. 19 €

5. 88 €

6. 12 €

7. 22 €

### Answers

**7**
1. Une trousse coûte 8 €.
2. Un sac à dos coûte 27 €.
3. Une affiche coûte 15 €.
4. Un DVD coûte 19 €.
5. Une stéréo coûte 88 €.
6. Un CD coûte 12 €.
7. Un dictionnaire coûte 22 €.

**Comparaisons**
The indefinite article *a* becomes *an* before vowel sounds.

### Expansion

You may want to introduce some classroom commands in this lesson (for example: **écoutez**, **regardez**, **écrivez**, **lisez**, **complétez**, **fermez**, **ouvrez**). You may also wish to adapt **Activité 7, Véro surfe sur internet**, for paired communicative practice. Suggest that two students will share the room and will need to shop online together, or have one student play the role of Véro's parent who will discuss purchases with his or her daughter.

### COMPARAISONS  4.1

Do indefinite articles in English change according to the gender of the noun?
- We need a boy to play the lead in the school play.
- We need a girl on our team.

COMPARAISONS: Indefinite articles do not change according to the gender of the noun in English.

Leçon A | cent quinze **115**

---

## Special Needs Students
**Linguistically Challenged/Speech Impairment**
Have these students strengthen their non-verbal language skills by creating a map of the European Union and of the eurozone. Ask them to illustrate, using color coding, the overlap between those countries that are part of the EU and those that use the euro currency. Invite them to share their work with the other class members.

**8**

1. Il y a un DVD et une trousse.
2. Il y un livre et une feuille de papier.
3. Il y a un sac à dos et un stylo.
4. Il y a une carte et un ordinateur portable.
5. Il y a un taille-crayon et un crayon.

**9**

1. J'ai besoin d'un cahier.
2. J'ai besoin d'un crayon.
3. J'ai besoin d'un stylo.
4. J'ai besoin d'une trousse.
5. J'ai besoin d'une carte.

### TPR

Make **Activité 8** a physical activity by asking students to participate in a pretend fire drill. Then ask them what is left behind on their desks. Ask them what they would want most to take with them in case of emergency. (For example, **J'ai besoin de mon agenda**...)

### Connections

Discuss what your students' different teachers have requested that students bring for supplies at the start of the new academic year. Do different courses of study require different items?

**8 Exercice anti-incendie** 🎧 🍀 **1.2, 1.3**

Say what Mme Canvel's students left on their desks during a fire drill.

**MODÈLE** Il y a un cahier et une feuille de papier.

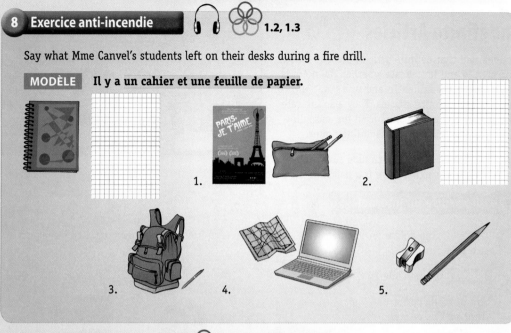

1.
2.
3.
4.
5.

**9 Ma liste de shopping** 🍀 **1.2**

The image shows school items you have left over from last year. The list contains items you need this year. Compare the two and say what you need.

5 cahiers
4 crayons
6 stylos
1 trousse
1 carte de France

**MODÈLE** (You already have four notebooks, but you require five, so you need to buy one.)
You say: **J'ai besoin d'un cahier.**

### Essential Instruction

1. Differentiate between a concrete noun (experienced with one of the five senses) and an abstract noun (not experienced with one of the five senses). Have students brainstorm French concrete and abstract nouns they know.
2. Review rules for determining gender of nouns in French. Explain that certain noun endings are always feminine (**-té**, **-ion**, **-ie**, etc.) or masculine (**-eau**, **-al**, etc.).
3. Review definite (specific) and indefinite (general/non-specific identification of items one can count) articles.
4. Practice identifying nouns and articles using pictures.

# Plurals of Articles and Nouns  1.2

Véro aime le stylo?

You add an **s** to make most nouns plural.

J'aime beaucoup les **concerts**.  *I like concerts a lot.*

The plural form of the definite articles **le**, **la**, and **l'** is **les** (*the*).

J'aime **les** sacs à dos vintage.  *I like vintage backpacks.*

The plural form of the indefinite articles **un** and **une** is **des** (*some*).

J'achète **des** crayons.  *I'm buying some pencils.*

## COMPARAISONS  4.1

Does the article change in English when the noun is plural?

• I'm watching the soccer game.
• I going to see the World Cup soccer games.

## Communiquez!

### 10  Mes préférences 🎧  1.3

**Interpersonal Communication**

With a partner, take turns asking and answering questions about what you prefer.

**MODÈLE**  concerts R'n'B/concerts rock

A: **Tu préfères les concerts R'n'B ou les concerts rock?**
B: **Moi, je préfère les concerts rock. Et toi, tu préfères...?**

1. CDs français/CDs américains
2. sports/passe-temps
3. salades/pâtes
4. hamburgers/frites
5. trousses françaises/trousses américaines
6. DVDs américains/DVDs canadiens
7. affiches de cinéma/affiches de rock

Tu préfères les hamburgers ou les frites?

Je préfère les hamburgers.

COMPARAISONS: There are no plural articles in English; speakers place "the" in front of both singular and plural nouns.

---

### Differentiated Learning
**Accelerate**
Have students guess the English cognate of the **Activité 8** title word **incendie**. Clarify that the English adjective incendiary means used or adapted to setting on fire. Invite students to define incendiary remark (remark intended to elicit a heated reaction).

### Multiple Intelligences
**Verbal-Linguistic**
Play a memory game. Begin by saying what you are buying in French. Each student repeats and adds to the list. Continue until all have participated.

---

## RESOURCES

📓  **Workbook 16–17**

**Answers** _____

**Comparaisons**
In English, articles do not change when they modify a plural noun. Discuss how we listen for the "s" sound in English to indicate a plural noun. What do we listen for in French? (**les** instead of **le**, **la**, or **l'**)

**10**  *Possible answers:*

1. A. Tu préfères les CDs français ou les CDs américains?
   B. Je préfère .... Et toi, tu préfères ....?
2. A. Tu préfères les sports ou les passe-temps?
   B. Je préfère .... Et toi, tu préfères ....?
3. A. Tu préfères les salades ou les pâtes?
   B. Je préfère .... Et toi, tu préfères ....?
4. A. Tu préfères les hamburgers ou les frites?
   B. Je préfère .... Et toi, tu préfères ....?
5. A. Tu préfères les trousses françaises ou les trousses américaines?
   B. Je préfère .... Et toi, tu préfères ....?
6. A. Tu préfères les DVDs américains ou les DVDs canadiens?
   B. Je préfère .... Et toi, tu préfères ....?
7. A. Tu préfères les affiches de cinéma ou les affiches de rock?
   B. Je préfère .... Et toi, tu préfères ....?

## Communication

**Interpretive: Cooperative Groups**
Write and display scrambled sentences with plural nouns. (Example: **coûtent/les/euros/bloc-notes/49€/deux.**) In small groups, have students unscramble sentences as you display the answers. Or, cut sentence strips into word pieces and distribute a set to each group. The first group to reassemble the sentence correctly wins.

**11**

1. J'achète des cahiers.
2. J'achète des affiches de rock.
3. J'achète des feuilles de papier.
4. J'achète des stylos.
5. J'achète des CDs.
6. J'achète des DVDs.

**12**

1. Il y a une porte.
2. Il y a des cartes.
3. Il y a un dictionnaire.
4. Il y a des livres.
5. Il y a des CDs.
6. Il y a un DVD.
7. Il y a une pendule.
8. Il y a un bureau.
9. Il y a des ordinateurs.

## Communication

### Interpersonal: Paired Practice

Have students make a list of 10 – 15 plural nouns with the indefinite article. Then, ask them to pair up with a partner for a quick drill of the singular of each noun and the article **un** or **une**. When students have finished the round, have one student rotate to another partner. Continue play until all students have worked with several partners.

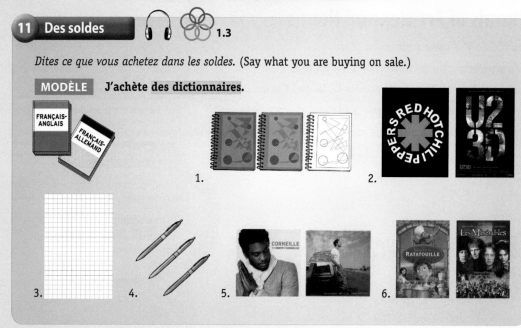

**11  Des soldes**  1.3

*Dites ce que vous achetez dans les soldes.* (Say what you are buying on sale.)

**MODÈLE**  **J'achète des dictionnaires.**

1.
2.
3.
4.
5.
6.

**12  Dans ma salle de classe**  1.3

*Dites ce qu'il y a dans votre salle de classe.* (Say what there is in your classroom.)

**MODÈLES**  carte de France
**Il y a une carte de France.**

fenêtres
**Il y a des fenêtres.**

1. porte
2. cartes
3. dictionnaire
4. livres
5. CD
6. DVD
7. pendule
8. bureau
9. ordinateurs

### Essential Instruction

1. Write on the board the singular and plural of several nouns from p. 118 (**ami, amie, amis, carte, cartes, ordinateur, ordinateurs**, etc.). Model the pronunciation. Reinforce that the final -**s** is not generally pronounced in French.
2. Add the definite articles to the nouns and emphasize the elision of **le/la** before a vowel (**l'ami, l'amie, les amis**, etc).
3. Add the indefinite articles (**un ami, des amis, une amie, des amies,** etc.) to the nouns too.

Point out that the -**n** of **un** is pronounced before a vowel.
4. Ask students to change nouns you provide from singular to plural and vice versa.
5. Write the irregular verb **avoir** on the board. Point out that the pronunciation of the **tu** and **il/elle/on** forms is identical, and the liaison of the **ils/elles** form.
6. Ask students to identify the endings that they know (**nous, vous**).
7. Explain that this high-frequency verb recurs in many French expressions.

# Present Tense of the Irregular Verb *avoir*

 1.2

The verb **avoir** (*to have*) is irregular, which means its forms don't follow a regular pattern based on the stem.

| avoir | | | |
|---|---|---|---|
| j' | **ai** | nous | **avons** |
| tu | **as** | vous | **avez** |
| il/elle/on | **a** | ils/elles | **ont** |

## 13 Qu'est-ce qu'on a?
 1.3

Select the correct answer for each question you hear.

A. Oui, et elle a un crayon.
B. Oui, ils ont un cédérom.
C. Non, j'ai un livre de français.
D. Oui, tu as trois cahiers dans ton sac à dos.
E. Non, nous avons des stylos.

### COMPARAISONS

Is the verb "to have" irregular in English too?

- I have a pencil case.
- You have a pen.
- Ben has a sheet of paper.
- Joy has a pencil.
- We have a math book.
- They have a dictionary.

## 14 Les fournitures scolaires
 1.3

*Dites ce que chaque* (*each*) *personne a.*

**MODÈLE** la prof
**La prof a un ordinateur portable et deux feuilles de papier.**

1. je

2. Marielle

3. tu        4. Abdoul        5. Yasmine

COMPARAISONS: The verb "to have" is irregular in English also.

**Differentiated Learning**
**Adapt**
Have students who need a tactile or visual prompt do **Activité 14** with the actual items listed in the **Activité** that you provide or they may have.

---

**RESOURCES**

📓 **Workbook 18–19**

**Answers** _____

🔟③ Script can be found in the front pages of the Annotated Teacher's Edition.

1. C
2. A
3. E
4. D
5. B

🔟④

1. J'ai un livre de maths et deux stylos.
2. Marielle a une feuille de papier et un crayon.
3. Tu as deux CDs et un taille-crayon.
4. Abdoul a un DVD sur Paris et un plan de Paris.
5. Yasmine a deux cahiers et une carte de France.

**Comparaisons**
**To have**
In English, the verb "to have" is irregular in the 3rd person singular.

### Communication

**Interpersonal: Cooperative Groups**
Have each student make a grid with five squares across and ten squares down. Across the top, have them write the names of five classmates; from top to bottom, have them write the words for ten school-related objects they know in French. Each student interviews the five classmates listed on his or her grid, asking if each person has each of the objects on his list. (For example, **Thomas, tu as une trousse?**) The interviewee responds accordingly. The student records the answers and summarizes the results with written sentences on the back of his or her sheet: **Il y a quatre classeurs. Il y a deux gommes. Il y a dix-sept feutres....**

## Critical Thinking

**Evaluate**
Ask students to translate literally and figuratively the **avoir** expression: **Nous avons besoin de stylos.**

## Culture

**Perspectives: Activity**
Have students research earthquake disaster aid to Haiti's school communities. Survey student participation in relief efforts in their area.

## Game

**Write It Right!**
Arrange six desks at the front of the room. Randomly place a card labeled with a different subject pronoun and various classroom items on each desk. Have teams go to the back of the class. Assign each a color and a set of matching colored cards. When you signal, a member from each team goes to desk #1 with a card and writes a sentence using the subject pronoun, verb **avoir**, articles, and displayed objects. A second signal indicates students should leave cards face down. Repeat round two with another set of students. Continue until teams have visited each desk. Collect and correct sentences.

**1 2 0**

---

### 15 Qu'est-ce qu'il y a dans ton sac à dos?  1.1

**Interpersonal Communication**

Draw a backpack with school supplies in it. Make sure you draw more than one of each item; for example, draw three pens, two notebooks, etc. Working with a partner and without revealing your drawings, take turns asking each other if you have a specific number of an item. For each item you guess correctly, give yourself a point. The person with the most points at the end of the activity is the winner.

**MODÈLE** A: **Tu as quatre cahiers?**
B: **Oui, j'ai quatre cahiers./Non, j'ai deux cahiers.**

## An *avoir* Expression  1.2

To say that you need something or that you need to do something, use the expression **avoir besoin de** (*to need*). Remember that **de** becomes **d'** before a word beginning with a vowel sound.

Tu **as besoin d'**étudier?    *Do you need to study?*
Oui, **j'ai besoin de** faire mes devoirs.    *Yes, I need to do my homework.*

*Didier a besoin de dormir.*

### 16 Des fournitures scolaires pour Haïti  1.3

Students in M. Tremblay's class signed up to send school supplies to Haiti after the earthquake. Say what everyone needs to buy, according to the list.

| Noms | Fournitures scolaires |
|---|---|
| **Modèle** Brigitte | 2 dictionnaires |
| 1. Bruno et Hugo | 6 taille-crayons |
| 2. je | 100 feuilles de papier |
| 3. Brigitte et Salim | 36 stylos |
| 4. Maxime | 24 crayons |
| 5. Saniyya et Martine | 2 dictionnaires |
| 6. Alexandre | 3 trousses |

**MODÈLE** **Brigitte a besoin d'acheter deux dictionnaires.**

**1 2 0** cent vingt | Unité 3

---

**Essential Instruction**

1. Contrast the **-er** verb conjugation with that of **avoir**. Ask students to note the differences. Explain that **avoir** has no real stem, although five of the forms share the beginning letter **a**.
2. Teach the structure of the expression **J'ai besoin d'étudier**. Mention that the expression can be followed by either a verb in the infinitive or by a noun.
3. After students practice the expression **avoir besoin de** plus an infinitive, practice the expression followed by a noun.
4. Pair students to do **Activité 15** and ask them to present the results of their conversations to the class.
5. Ask students to prepare **Activité 18** at home and then share that information with a partner in class.
6. Have students practice the expression **avoir besoin de** by conducting a survey of their classmates about what they need to do particular **activités**, such as **faire les devoirs**, **lire**, **écouter de la musique**, etc.

# À vous la parole

## Communiquez!

### 17 J'ai besoin de....  1.1

**Interpersonal Communication**

You and a friend run into each other while buying school supplies. In your conversation:

- greet each other.
- ask each other how things are going.
- tell each other three items you need.
- discuss how much each item costs.
- say good-bye.

**Question centrale**
How does education shape individuals and societies?

> Le livre de maths, il coûte combien?
>
> Il coûte 15 euros.

## Communiquez!

### 18 Je fais ma liste! 1.3

**Presentational Communication**

Make of list of ten items you need for school. Find a French online store like Top Office that sells school supplies, or **fournitures scolaires**. Write down prices for the items you find. You may want to add to or modify your list based on what you find online. Describe your online purchases to your partner, following the model. Next, convert the prices to dollars with an online currency converter. Compare the prices with those of an online store in the United States. Present your findings to your partner. (Be sure to list the online sites you used.)

**MODÈLE** J'ai besoin d'un cahier. À Top Office il coûte 2,60 euros.

 Search words: **fournitures scolaires en ligne, convertisseur monnaie**

**Answers** _____

**17** *Conversations will vary.*
- A. Bonjour.
- B. Salut!
- A. Comment vas-tu?
- B. Très bien et toi?
- A. Comme ci, comme ça.
- B. J'ai besoin de crayons, de stylos, et de feuilles de papier.
- A. Les crayons coûtent 3 €, les stylos coûtent 5€, et les feuilles de papier coûtent 6€.
- B. C'est cher! D'accord. Salut!
- A. Salut, Ciao

## Reference Desk

### Blended Instruction
Consider using blended instruction, a combination of in-class learning and computer-mediated instruction or learning opportunities. Ask students to complete activities on the computer, using their cell or smartphone, or other emerging electronic technology. This will allow students to hone their tech skills and become more independent learners. Schedule routine Internet and e-book learning in class and in the lab.

## Connections

### Media
After completing the tasks of the project, have students create an advertisement that shows American items and prices on one side and French items and prices on the other.

---

## Differentiated Learning
### Accelerate
Have students translate literally in English the expression **avoir besoin de**. Compare to the English equivalent "to need." Then, solicit other expressions describing states of being, such as thirsty, cold, hot, etc. Teach how to say these in French.

## Multiple Intelligences
### Intrapersonal
Have groups prepare a presentation on studying abroad at a high school in a francophone country of their choice. Ask them to include information about class schedules, activities available to students, and pictures.

### Interpersonal/Bodily-Kinesthetic
Ask partners to show, tell, and ask questions about items in their backpack, purse, or pencil case.

## Special Needs Students
### Behavioral Problems/At-risk Teens
Ask students to focus on the cartoon on p. 120 and complete the sentence **Didier a besoin de/d'....** Expand to include different situations, for example, **à l'école**, **à la maison**, etc.

**Answers**

 **E**

1. /u/
2. /y/
3. /y/ /u/
4. /y/
5. /u/

## Expansion

In the language lab, show twenty words in quick succession on a screen the students can see. Some words will have a pronounced final consonant and many will not. Use words from **Unité 3** such as **cahier, trombone, dessin, livre, ordinateur, papier,** etc. Have students record their pronunciation of each word they see. Alternately, you could read a list of words and ask students to mark one of two columns on their paper, for either "A. pronounced" or "B. not pronounced." In the appropriate column, they must write down the letter of the consonant that was or was not pronounced. Discuss their answers and review together.

# Prononciation  1.2

## Pronouncing Letters at the End of a Word

- In general, letters at the end of a word are not pronounced.

 **A** Consonnes non prononcées

*Repeat these examples of words in which the last consonant is not pronounced.*

1. le français – le concert – devant – le cours
2. Elle a un accent mexicain. – Elle a un accent canadien. – Elle a un accent coréen.

**B** Mots qui terminent en -r

The letter **r** is one of a small number of exceptions. It is pronounced at the end of a word, but not in the case of **-er** verbs. Repeat the following phrases that end in **r**.

1. Oui, du roller. 2. J'ai un ordinateur. 3. C'est cher.

## Liaison

- When a final consonant sound that is not normally pronounced is carried over to a word starting with a vowel, this is called **liaison**. One example is the letter **t**.

 **C** Pratiquons la liaison!

*Repeat the following examples of liaison.*

1. C'est_intéressant. 2. C'est_important. 3. Il est_énergique.

## Pronouncing Numbers

- When **un, deux, trois, huit, six, dix, vingt,** and **cent** are followed by a consonant, the last consonant of the number is not pronounced.

 **D** Les nombres

*Repeat the following phrases that incorporate numbers.*

1. Un dessin. 4. Dix cahiers.
2. Six romans. 5. Vingt papiers.
3. Huit chansons. 6. Cent livres.

## The Vowels /y/ and /u/

- The vowel **/y/** is the same sound as in **tu**. The vowel **/u/** is the same sound as in **vous.**

 **E** Écoutez!

*Write* **/y/** *if you hear a vowel as in* **tu** *and* **/u/** *if you hear a vowel as in* **vous.**

## Essential Instruction

1. Connect the concept of liaison in pronunciation to a liaison officer (a "middle person").
2. The /y/ in **tu** can be challenging for students since it doesn't exist in English. To help students, have them say "ee" as if smiling while holding a finger on either side of the mouth. Next, tell them to continue to pronounce "ee" as they purse their lips, extending them as far out as possible. They will naturally pronounce the /y/.
3. Ask students in French how many classes they have. Tell them that French **lycéens** often take up to ten different courses, but that most don't meet every day.
4. Teach the adjectives on p. 123, and have partners create sentences with them, for example, **L'art est intéressant.**

## Vocabulaire actif

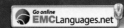

### Les matières   1.2

les sciences (f.): la biologie

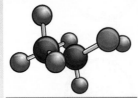
la physique

la chimie

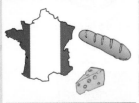
les langues (f.): le français

l'anglais (m.)

l'espagnol (m.)

l'allemand (m.)

les maths (f.)

les arts plastiques (m.)

la musique

l'éducation physique et sportive (l'EPS) (f.)

l'informatique (f.)

l'histoire (f.)

facile

difficile

drôle

énergique

intéressant(e)

intelligent(e)

## Communication

**Interpersonal: Paired Practice**

Pair students and have them figure out how many minutes they have a particular class each week. They can write it out or say it to each. **Modèle: la chimie – J'ai la chimie trois cents minutes par semaine.**

## Critical Thinking

**Comparisons**

Ask students to compare symbols and expressions to indicate different times of day in English (A.M., P.M., at night, etc.) and French (24-hour clock, **du matin, de l'après-midi, du soir**). Have students research and share what A.M. and P.M. mean. A.M. means *ante meridiem* (before noon) and P.M. means *post meridiem* (after noon). Point out that **di** in the days of the week in French also comes from the latin *diem* for day.

**Quelle heure est-il?**   **1.2**

Il est une heure.

Il est neuf heures.

Il est midi.

Il est minuit.

Il est trois heures et quart.

Il est six heures et demie.

Il est cinq heures moins le quart.

du matin | de l'après-midi | du soir

ouvert à 9h00 | ouvert à 14h00 | fermé à 19h30

## Pour la conversation   1.2

**H**ow do I describe my classes?
> **Mon cours de maths est difficile.**
> *My math class is difficult.*

**H**ow do I ask for a description of someone?
> **Elle est comment** ta prof d'informatique?
> *What is your computer teacher like?*

**H**ow do I describe my teacher?
> **Elle est** intéressante.
> *She is interesting.*

**Et si je voulais dire...?**

| | |
|---|---|
| **l'algèbre (f.)** | *algebra* |
| **la géométrie** | *geometry* |
| **la littérature** | *literature* |
| **la menuiserie** | *woodshop* |
| **la mécanique** | *autoshop* |
| **le chinois** | *Chinese* |
| **Je suis nul(le) en....** | *I'm not good at....* |
| **Je suis doué(e) en....** | *I'm good at....* |

**1 2 4** cent vingt-quatre | Unité 3

**Essential Instruction**

1. Use an analog clock with moveable hour and minute hands to introduce telling time in French.
2. Ask students to repeat the hours only. Point out the **liaison** in **deux heures, trois heures,** and **quatre heures.** Explain that an "s" or "x" between two vowels is pronounced as "z" and an "f" between two vowels is pronounced as "v." Next, add half hour, then quarter hours, emphasizing the use of **moins** to express quarter to the hour.
3. Listen to the audio of all **vocabulaire actif**.
4. In **Activité 1**, define **l'emploi du temps** and have students read aloud the paragraph in pairs to practice pronunciations.
5. As students look at their charts, ask questions about Hélène's schedule.
6. Do **Activité 2** with the audio and review the answers as a class.
7. Clarify the directions before assigning **Activité 3**.

## 1  L'emploi du temps d'Hélène  1.2, 1.3

Create a class schedule for Hélène based on the description below that tells when she has each class.

Hélène a maths lundi à huit heures, jeudi à onze heures, vendredi à deux heures, et samedi à huit heures. Elle a français lundi à neuf heures et à dix heures, mercredi à huit heures, jeudi à trois heures, et vendredi à onze heures. Elle a espagnol lundi à onze heures, jeudi à deux heures, et samedi à dix heures. Elle a anglais lundi à deux heures, mercredi à neuf heures, et jeudi à neuf heures. Elle a arts plastiques lundi à trois heures et quatre heures. Elle a histoire-géo mardi à huit heures et à neuf heures et jeudi à une heure. Elle a physique mardi à onze heures, à une heure, et à deux heures. Elle a EPS mardi à trois heures et à quatre heures, et vendredi à huit heures. Elle a informatique mercredi à dix heures, vendredi à quatre heures, et samedi à neuf heures. Elle a musique mercredi à onze heures. Elle a biologie vendredi à neuf heures et à trois heures. Hélène mange à quelle heure?

### L'emploi du temps d' Hélène

| heures | LUNDI | MARDI | MERCREDI | JEUDI | VENDREDI | SAMEDI |
|--------|-------|-------|----------|-------|----------|--------|
| 8h à 9h | | | | | | |
| 9h à 10h | | | | | | |
| 10h à 11h | | | | | | |
| 11h à 12h | | | | | | |
| 12h à 13h | | | | | | |
| 13h à 14h | | | | | | |
| 14h à 15h | | | | | | |
| 15h à 16h | | | | | | |
| 16h à 17h | | | | | | |

## 2  Les emplois du temps   1.2, 2.1

Listen to Rosalie and Mathis talk about their schedules. Write in French each class or activity in the order it is mentioned.

## 3  L'agenda de Djamal  1.2, 1.3

Dites ce que Djamal fait (*is doing*). Complétez chaque phrase avec l'heure correcte d'après son agenda (*according to his day planner*).

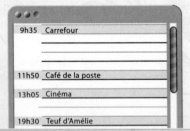

1. Djamal achète des cahiers....
2. Il mange un hamburger et des frites....
3. Il est au cinéma....
4. Il est à la teuf d'Amélie....

A. à sept heures et demie
B. à midi moins dix
C. à une heure cinq
D. à dix heures moins vingt-cinq

Leçon B | cent vingt-cinq  1 2 5

---

### TPR

Have students make individual clocks using a paper plate for the face and construction paper and a round fastener for the hands. Say a time and have students show you the time on their clocks. Or, play a **Jacques a dit** game with a leader calling out the time to the students standing up by their desks. Incorrect or slow answers eliminate a student. Students can also quiz each other in pairs taking turns to call out.

---

## Multiple Intelligences
### Visual-Spatial/Verbal-Linguistic

Assign students to find and bring in pictures that clearly illustrate each school subject. Then have them show their pictures in small groups, while the other students identify the subject represented in the picture and ask questions about when and how each class is. Tell students to help each other with pronunciation.

**Answers** _____

**4**

1. Sciences. C'est un cours de biologie.
2. Pour elle, le cours est difficile.
3. La prof est stricte mais énergique.
4. Le prof est tahitien.
5. Non, elle n'a pas cours mercredi.

**Extension**

Tahiti and other Polynesian islands are French overseas territories. Also, the computer science teacher is from Tahiti.

**Game**

**School Subject Relay Game**
As a review of **les matières**, put desks in rows. Each row is a team. Ask the first person in each row (team) to go to the board. Call out a subject matter and an adjective. The first student who has written a correct sentence on the board wins a point for his team. Continue by calling out different courses and adjectives.

---

# Rencontres culturelles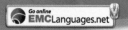

## Les cours et les profs   1.2, 2.1, 2.2

Maxime and Yasmine meet in the courtyard at their school, **le lycée Georges Brassens**.

Maxime: Qu'est-ce que tu fais à 10h00?
Yasmine: J'ai deux heures de biologie, un cours qui est difficile.
Maxime: Deux heures! Elle est comment la prof?
Yasmine: Stricte mais… énergique. Et toi, tu fais quoi?
Maxime: J'ai histoire avec M. Mataoa.
Yasmine: Oh! Le prof tahitien? Il est très drôle et très intéressant.
Maxime: On va au centre commercial après?
Yasmine: Non, je ne peux pas parce que j'ai mon cours d'anglais à 1h30.
Maxime: Mais on n'a pas cours le mercredi après-midi!

**4 Les cours et les profs**

2.1, 2.2

*Répondez aux questions.*

1. Yasmine a un cours de maths ou de sciences à 10h00?
2. Comment est le cours de Yasmine?
3. La prof de biologie est comment?
4. Le prof d'histoire est canadien ou tahitien?
5. Yasmine a besoin d'aller (*to go*) au cours d'anglais mercredi?

**Extension** **Dans la salle d'informatique**

1.2, 2.1

David and Amidou, two French students, are in the computer lab chatting with their American key pal, Kate, online.

David: Ici c'est la nouvelle salle informatique de notre collège. On a 20 ordinateurs, trois télés avec des lecteurs de DVD, un vidéoprojecteur pour le cinéclub, et on peut aussi écouter des CD.
Kate: Et derrière toi, c'est quoi le poster?
Amidou: C'est une affiche, de la publicité pour le tourisme tahitien. En fait, c'est un tableau de Gauguin.
Kate: Tahiti? Pourquoi Tahiti?
Amidou: Tahiti et d'autres îles de la Polynésie sont des îles françaises…. En plus, on a une prof tahitienne ici, Madame Temaru, la prof d'informatique.

**Extension** For what two reasons is there a poster of Tahiti in the computer lab?

---

**Essential Instruction**

1. Tell students about the singer-songwriter **Georges Brassens** (1921–1981).
2. Instruct students to use visual clues to help understand the video.
3. Act out the dialogue to foster comprehension. Model correct pronunciation.
4. Have students read the dialogue silently, discuss new vocabulary, and then watch the video again. Poll students about what they understand.
5. Have students practice each role of the dialogue with a partner, then do **Activité 4**.

6. Read **L'heure officielle**. Ask questions to elicit the 24-hour clock times listed on the arrival board on p. 127. Then, have students translate them into non 24-hour times, using **de l'après-midi** or **du soir**. Provide additional practice.
7. Discuss the pros and cons of the French school schedule after reading **Mercredi après-midi**. Explain that Saturday morning classes were officially dropped in 2008.
8. Ask if students had to take major tests before entering high school.
9. Explain that some French students choose a technical school, rather than traditional high school.

# Points de départ

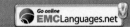 Go online
**EMCLanguages.net**

**Question centrale**
**?**
How does education shape individuals and societies?

## L'heure officielle  1.2, 4.2

The 24-hour time system (**l'heure officielle**) is used in French-speaking countries to give schedules for movies, transportation, classes, sporting events, and TV programs. One advantage to this system is not having to say A.M. or P.M. or "in the morning," "in the afternoon," or "in the evening" (**du matin**, **de l'après-midi**, **du soir**). To use **l'heure officielle**, continue counting to 24 for every hour after 12 noon. For example, 1:30 P.M. becomes 13h30. The expressions **et quart**, **et demie**, and **moins le quart** are not used in official time.

```
DEPART        DE

Trains au départ              De
Zeit   Nach
Time   Destination
Heure  Destination

11ʰ13   LONDON SAINT PANCRAS
11ʰ55   BRUXELLES-MIDI LIEGE AACHEN
12ʰ55   BRUXELLES LIEGE AACHEN KOLN
12ʰ55   BRUXELLES BERCHEM ROTTERDAM
12ʰ58   LILLE FLANDRES
13ʰ01   CALAIS FRETHUN LONDON SAINT
14ʰ22   ORRY-LA-VILLE CHANTILLY-GOUV
14ʰ55   BRUXELLES-MIDI
15ʰ13   ASHFORD LONDON SAINT PANCRAS
15ʰ55   BRUXELLES LIEGE AACHEN KOLN
15ʰ55   BRUXELLES BERCHEM ROTTERDAM
15ʰ58   LILLE FLANDRES
```
The train to Lille departs at 3:58 p.m.

## Mercredi après-midi 1.2, 4.2

French teenagers usually don't have school on Wednesday afternoon, but they sometimes attend classes on Saturday morning. School cafeterias usually offer lunch on Wednesday but not on Saturday.

## Les cours et les examens  1.2, 4.2

School attendance at **un collège** (middle school) or **un lycée** (high school) takes up 950 hours each year in an average French teen's life. In France, school attendance is mandatory until students earn a diploma at the end of middle school. Students in middle school mostly take the same general courses. When they move on to high school, they choose a specialization, such as literature, science, economics, or technical studies.

MINISTÈRE DE L'ÉDUCATION NATIONALE,
DE LA RECHERCHE ET DE LA TECHNOLOGIE

ACADÉMIE DE CRÉTEIL

**DIPLÔME**
**DU BACCALAURÉAT GÉNÉRAL**

Students who pass the bac exams receive their diploma in July.

Students spend three years at the **lycée**. In their second year, they begin preparing for **le bac**, an exit exam they must pass in order to receive a diploma. About 80% of students pass the exam the first time around. If students fail **le bac**, they will need to repeat their last year of high school and retake the exam. Only those students who pass will be allowed to attend a state university, which, like their previous schooling, is also free.

## RESOURCES

 **e-visuals 10–11**

 **Workbook 29–31**

## Reference Desk

Compare French and American grade levels, using the following table.

| | |
|---|---|
| **Preschool** | **École Maternelle** |
| Elementary school | **Cycle Élémentaire** |
| 1st grade | Cours Préparatoire (CP) or 11ème |
| 2nd grade | Cours Élémentaire I (CE I) or 10ème |
| 3rd grade | Cours Élémentaire II (CE II) or 9ème |
| 4th grade | Cours Moyen I (CM I) or 8ème |
| 5th grade | Cours Moyen II (CM II) or 7ème |
| **Junior High/ Middle School** | **First Cycle Collège** |
| 6th grade | 6ème |
| 7th grade | 5ème |
| 8th grade | 4ème |
| **High School** | **Lycée** |
| 9th grade | 3ème |
| 10th grade | Seconde |
| 11th grade | Première |
| 12th grade | Terminale |

For French students the **Baccalauréat** serves as admittance to universities.

## Critical Thinking

### Comparisons

Discuss how schools differ between the United States and francophone countries. What are the grade equivalents to French grade levels? How similar or different are our school calendars? Are notions about the length of the school year changing? Students may do research to find out about recent debates on these matters. Have students research the grade levels in francophone countries and make a poster to show the equivalencies.

---

**Differentiated Learning**
**Accelerate**
1. Ask students to read the **Extension**, first silently and then aloud in pairs.
2. Before reviewing the dialogue as a class, have pairs tell each other what they understand and discuss the answer to the **Extension** question.
3. Ask volunteers to role-play the dialogue for the class.

**Multiple Intelligences**
**Verbal-Linguistic**
After students have completed **activités** for the video, have them write a personalized dialogue with a partner, using the video dialogue as a template. Ask students to practice and present their dialogue to others in the class.

# La Francophonie

### Mon dico polynésien

**Gauguin:** A 19th-century French artist who painted Tahitian landscapes and people.
**Pirogues:** Dug-out canoes used for racing and traditional ceremonies.
**Tatouage:** Body decorations traditionally applied as a rite of passage in adolescence.
**Marae:** Large stone structures traditionally used to worship ancient Polynesian gods and celebrate war.
**Ahimaa:** Ancient earthen ovens still in use today.
**D'autres mots polynésiens:** *kai* (manger); *farani* (français); *va'a* (pirogue)

**4.1**

## ✳ *La Polynésie française*

**1.2**

French Polynesia is an overseas French territory made up of five groups of islands, numbering about 120 islands in all. Papeete, the largest city and located on the island of Tahiti, is the capital. French is the official language, but many inhabitants also speak native Polynesian languages. French Polynesia's economy is based largely on tourism and the exportation of pearls.

🔍 **Search words: visiter tahiti tahiti pratique**

The long shaped **toere** drums are traditional Tahitian instruments.

**4.2**

### Produits

**Le paréo** is a garment worn by men and women in French Polynesia. Lightweight and made of one large piece of brightly colored and decorated fabric, it is perfect for the tropical climate. Many people around the world have adopted the **paréo** as a beach cover-up.

### COMPARAISONS

What do you know about Hawaii? Make a list of five to six things you know, then do online research to find out if those things are true about Tahiti too since they are relatively close geographically.

**2.1, 2.2**
**4.2**

## Je vais au Lycée Gauguin  1.2, 2.1

Many French schools are named after people who have played an important role in French culture. Schools take their names from people in the arts like Claude Monet and Jacques Brel, in the sciences like Marie Curie and Louis Pasteur, or from literary greats, such as Victor Hugo and Émile Zola. Schools may also bear the name of historical figures like King Henri IV and former French president François Mitterrand. This tradition is practiced throughout the francophone world, where schools often receive the names of local heroes. **Le Lycée Gauguin** in Papeete, Tahiti and **le Lycée Schœlcher** in Fort-de-France, Martinique are two examples.

🔍 **Search words: lycée paul gauguin à papeete lycée henri iv paris**

For Paul Gauguin, the natural beauty of Tahitian women with their bright apparel contrasted with the artifice of Western Europe.

## 5 Questions culturelles

**4.2**

*Répondez aux questions.*

1. On which day do French students not have class in the afternoon?
2. School attendance is mandatory in France until when?
3. What is **le bac** and why is it important?
4. What is French Polynesia?
5. Who was Paul Gauguin?
6. What is a **pareo**?
7. Where do many French schools get their names?

French students who wish to attend the university like the Université de Nice must receive at least 10 out of 20 on their **bac** exam.

### Perspectives

France spends 6.8% of its Gross National Product (GDP), or 6.8% of all the money the country earns in a year, on education. This averages out to over 7,000 euros per student. What do these numbers tell you about French values toward education?

## 6 Air Tahiti Nui

**2.1, 2.2, 4.2**

*Répondez aux questions.*

1. What is the name of this airline company?
2. The airline flies to Tahiti from which cities?
3. In which countries are these cities located?
4. Which city is the closest to Tahiti? The farthest away?
5. How do you say "Welcome" in French Polynesia? In other French-speaking countries?
6. Tahiti is in between which two continents?

### COMPARAISONS

**2.1, 2.2**
**4.2**

Is your high school named after someone famous? What did this person do to become famous? In what ways do the names of schools in your area differ from the names chosen in the Francophone world?

### Du côté des médias

*Regardez l'image et trouvez Tahiti.* **2.1, 2.2**

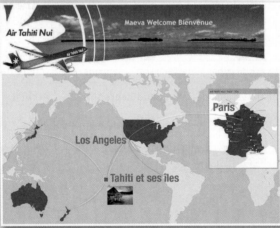

---

## Answers

**5**

1. Wednesday.
2. Until the end of middle school when students take the **brevet** exam.
3. **Le bac** is an exit exam and a requirement to receive a diploma and attend French university.
4. The South Pacific overseas territory of French Polynesia is comprised of five island groups. The capital is Papeete on the island of Tahiti.
5. Paul Gauguin was a post-impressionist artist, famous for paintings of people and landscapes of Tahiti.
6. The **pareo** is a loose, colorful garment traditionally worn by both men and women in Polynesia.
7. Many French schools are named after important cultural, historical, and political figures.

**Perspectives**
*Answers will vary.* Convert the French per student expenditure into U.S. dollars and compare to expenditures in their district. In France, the educational system helps to forge a national identity. Expenditures per pupil put France near the top of industrialized countries in terms of investment in education. The Organization for Economic Co-operation and Development maintains educational statistics and information on outcomes for a number of countries for purposes of assessment and international comparison.

**6**

1. Air Tahiti Nui
2. Paris, Los Angeles, Auckland, Tokyo.
3. France, the United States, New Zealand, and Japan.
4. Closest: Auckland, farthest: Paris.
5. Maeve. Bienvenue.
6. South America and Australia.

**Comparaisons**
*Answers will vary.*

---

### Differentiated Learning

**Accelerate**

Have these students research and report to the class on aspects of the French education system such as the various diplomas, types of schools, sections of **le baccalauréat**, extra-curricular **activités**, sports, higher education, tuition and fees, and the "campus" concept. (Does it exist in France?)

**Special Needs Students**

**Linguistically Challenged**

For students who find it difficult to do a lot of reading, have groups of four jigsaw the readings on the **Points de départ** pages and report to each other. (Two groups may have the same topic in a large class.)

You may want to write the six topics across the board and have students write two interesting or important facts under the topic. Each group can send one or two people to do the writing. Meanwhile, the remaining group members are reporting to another group.

# Structure de la langue

## Telling Time  1.2

To ask what time it is in French, say **Quelle heure est-il?** Always use the word **heure(s)** in your answer, for example **Il est deux heures**. The abbreviation for **heure(s)** is **h**: **2h00** = 2:00. To say that it's noon or midnight, use **Il est midi** or **Il est minuit**.

To say that it's quarter after the hour, add **et quart** or **quinze**.

| | |
|---|---|
| Il est cinq heures **et quart**.<br>Il est dix-sept heures **quinze** (17h15). | It's 5:15. |

To say that it's half past the hour, add **et demi(e)** or **trente**.

| | |
|---|---|
| Il est minuit **et demi**. | It's 12:30. |
| Il est six heures **et demie**.<br>Il est dix-huit heures **trente** (18h30). | It's 6:30. |

To say it's quarter to the hour, add **moins le quart** before the next hour or **quarante-cinq** after the hour using the official time.

| | |
|---|---|
| Il est **trois heures moins le quart**.<br>Il est **quatorze heures quarante-cinq** (14h45). | It's 2:45. |

To say how many minutes after the hour but before the half hour, add the number of minutes.

| | |
|---|---|
| Il est cinq heures **vingt**.<br>Il est dix-sept heures **vingt** (17h20). | It's 5:20. |

To say how many minutes before the next hour, say the next hour, and add **moins** and the number of minutes before the next hour, or use the official time and say the number of minutes after the hour.

| | |
|---|---|
| Il est **quatre heures moins dix**.<br>Il est **quinze heures cinquante** (15h50). | It's 3:50. |

To ask at what time something happens, use **à quelle heure**.

| | |
|---|---|
| On va au cinéma **à quelle heure**? | At what time are we going to the movies? |

To say at what time something happens, use **à** and the time.

| | |
|---|---|
| On va au cinéma **à 8h15** du soir. | We are going to the movies at 8:15 P.M. |

## Essential Instruction

1. Using an analog clock, add minutes, having students say the time as you move the clock hands. Point out that, similar to English, both numbers and expressions (**et demie**, etc.) are used in French.
2. The students won't have difficulty with digital times, such as 2:40 (**2h40**), when looking at a digital clock. However, when they see an analog clock, some will have difficulty making the transition from "2:40" to "20 to three" or from **2h40** to **trois heures moins vingt**. Point out the math connection and write the formula, **trois heures – 20** to help students as they practice the French.
3. Do listening **Activité 7**, then ask students to say the 24-hour clock and regular times listed on each clock.
4. Have students do **Activité 8** as a chorus or with a partner.
5. For **Activité 9**, draw a completed sample schedule on the board and then have students do the exercise with a partner.

## 7 L'heure   2.1

Listen to each statement. Write **oui** if the time you hear matches the clock. Write **non** if it does not match.

1.    2.    3.    4.    5.

6.    7.    8.    9.    10.

## 8 Quelle heure est-il? 2.1

*Répondez à la question.*

1.    2.    3.

4.    5.    6.    7.

## Communiquez!

### 9 On étudie ensemble?   1.1

**Interpersonal Communication**

You and your partner want to find a time to study together for the upcoming social studies test. Write down your class schedule and the time each class begins. Then ask each other questions until you find a time you can study together.

> **MODÈLE**
> A: **Tu as cours à 7h30?**
> B: **Oui, j'ai anglais à 7h30.**
> A: **Tu as cours à 2h50?**
> B: **Non, je n'ai pas cours. Je peux étudier.**

**Workbook 34**

**Answers**

⑩
1. Émilie et Richard sont de Paris.
2. Tu es de Lyon.
3. Hamza est de Marseille.
4. Abdoulaye et Amadou sont de Nice.
5. Vous êtes de Bordeaux.
6. Laurence et Rahina sont de Lille.

⑪
*Answers may vary.*
1. Tu es à la maison.
2. Ils ne sont pas à la maison.
3. Je suis à la maison.
4. Vous n'êtes pas à la maison.
5. Joëlle est à la maison.
6. Malika et moi, nous sommes à la maison.

**Comparaisons**
Yes, the verb "to be" is irregular in English, too, in both present and past tenses.

### Reference Desk

For **Activité 11**, you may want to review the formation of negative sentences.

---

# Present Tense of the Irregular Verb *être*  1.2

The verb **être** (*to be*) is irregular.

| être | | | |
|---|---|---|---|
| je | **suis** | nous | **sommes** |
| tu | **es** | vous | **êtes** |
| il/elle/on | **est** | ils/elles | **sont** |

Use **être**:
• with adjectives

| Vous **êtes** américains? | *Are you American?* |
| Non, nous **sommes** canadiens. | *No, we're Canadian.* |

• to say the city you are from

| Je **suis** de Chicago. | *I'm from Chicago.* |

Les fans sont français?

---

**10  Des Français**  2.1, 2.2

Say what French city people are from.

1. Émilie et Richard/Paris
2. tu/Lyon
3. Hamza/Marseille
4. Abdoulaye et Amadou/Nice
5. vous/Bordeaux
6. Laurence et Rahina/Lille

---

**11  À la maison ou pas?** 2.1, 2.2

*Dites si l'on est à la maison ou pas.*

| MODÈLES | Elle surfe sur Internet. |
| | **Elle est à la maison.** |
| | Tu fais du vélo. |
| | **Tu n'es pas à la maison.** |

1. Tu fais la cuisine.
2. Karim et Étienne jouent au foot.
3. Je regarde la télé.
4. Vous nagez.
5. Joëlle écoute de la musique sur l'ordinateur.
6. Malika et moi, nous regardons la télé.

---

**COMPARAISONS**  4.1

Is the verb "to be" irregular in English too?
• I am happy.
• You are sad.
• Julia is angry.
• We are content.
• Bill and Pete are energetic.

COMPARAISONS: The verb "to be" is irregular in English also.

---

**Essential Instruction**

1. Write the verb **être** on the board. Model the pronunciation. Have students orally conjugate the verb as a class and then individually by pointing to random students to say the next form as you cycle through the conjugation. Have students write simple sentences using all forms of the verb and exchange with a partner for correction.
2. Ask students where they are from originally: **Tu es d'où?** They answer: **Je suis de...** (+ city).
3. Have students do **Activités 10** and **11** in pairs or as a class.
4. Do **Comparaisons** together.
5. Provide a visual aid, such as a chart, to explain the forms of adjectives:

| | Masculine | Feminine |
|---|---|---|
| Singular | **intéressant** | **intéressante** |
| Plural | **intéressants** | **intéressantes** |

6. Have students brainstorm adjectives they know so far. Add cognates that follow similar patterns, such as **moderne, classique, intelligent, patient, italien,** and **parisien**. Drill students on the forms of each adjective, emphasizing spelling and pronunciation changes.

# Agreement and Position of Regular Adjectives  1.2

C'est un garçon génial!

Adjectives are words that describe nouns or pronouns. They agree with the noun or pronoun in gender (masculine or feminine) and in number (singular or plural).

1. To make most adjectives feminine, an **e** is added to the masculine form.

| masculine adjective + e = feminine adjective |
| --- |

Mon cours est intéressant.  La chimie est intéressant**e**.

Adjectives ending in a consonant often double the consonant and add an **e** for the feminine form.

Il est canadien.  Elle est canadie**nne**.

If the adjective already ends in **e**, there is no change in the feminine form.

M. Lucas est **drôle**.  Mlle Nero est **drôle**.

2. To make most adjectives plural, an **s** is added to the singular form.

| singular adjective + s = plural adjective |
| --- |

J'ai un devoir difficile.  J'ai des devoirs difficile**s**.

La fille est française.  Les filles sont française**s**.

If the adjective already ends in **s**, there is no change in the plural form.

Étienne est **français**.  Jacques et Louis-Do sont **français**.

3. Adjectives usually come after the nouns they describe.

La prof **américaine** est Mme Jones.
Tu aimes les sciences **physiques**?

 **COMPARAISONS** 4.1

Where are adjectives usually placed in English sentences?
- She wore a red dress.
- It was an expensive purchase.

Marine est intelligente.

COMPARAISONS: In English, adjectives are usually placed before the noun.

Leçon B | cent trente-trois 133

**Workbook 35–39**

**Answers**

**Comparaisons**
In English, adjectives are usually placed before the noun they modify.

## Game

**C'est qui?**
Put students in groups of five or six and distribute a small piece of paper to each student. Instruct students to describe themselves using two positive and respect-ful adjectives. Put all the pieces of paper in an envelope. Pass the envelope around the group and have each person pull out a piece of paper and try to guess which group member the two adjectives on the paper describe. For exam-ple, one might guess, **Caroline est diligente et sympa.** You may also have them add what courses the student they guess likes, **Et elle adore les arts plastiques.** Confirm if the guess is correct. Continue until all have the chance to guess.

**Differentiated Learning**
**Expand**
To practice memorizing the **être** forms, divide stu-dents into groups of four or five and have them conjugate the verb orally in a round robin until you signal for them to stop. When you signal again, they should continue where they left off. To practice writing the forms, have them do a round robin with one white board per group to pass around.

**Special Needs Students**
**Linguistically Challenged**
Distribute thirteen note cards to each student. Have them write the word **être**, each subject pronoun (combine **il**/**elle**) and verb form on a separate card. On the back of each card, have them write the English translation. Tell them to shuffle the cards and re-create the chart on p. 132 without looking in the book. Finally, test their knowledge by giving them verbal cues such as "you plural." They hold up the cards for **vous êtes** and say the words.

## 12 Facile, difficile, ou intéressant? 1.2, 2.1, 2.2

*Dites que les cours suivants sont faciles ou difficiles et intéressants. Notez que les adjectifs vont être masculins ou féminins.*

**MODÈLE** **La chimie est difficile et intéressante.**

1.

2.

3.

4.

5.

6.

Salut, je m'appelle....

Hallo, ich heiße....

¡Hola! me llamo....
7.

## 13 Il est midi. 1.2, 2.1, 2.2

*Décrivez (Describe) les objets des élèves dans cette salle de classe.*

**MODÈLE** stylos (4)/canadien
**Il y a quatre stylos canadiens.**

1. trousse (1)/algérien
2. dictionnaire (1)/français
3. affiches (2)/canadien
4. sacs à dos (5)/américain
5. feuilles de papier (4)/français
6. carte (1)/américain
7. CDs (3)/algérien

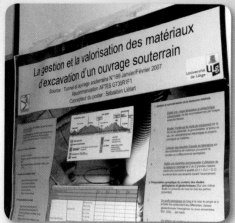

Il y a une affiche française dans la classe.

## Essential Instruction

1. Have students do **Activité 12** orally in pairs.
2. Have students write **Activité 13** on the board and go over the sentences together, repeating each answer.
3. Have pairs write out the dialogue in **Activité 14**, and then share their dialogue with another pair for correction. Once all four students have discussed the corrections and made adjustments to each of their dialogues, they can practice and present them to the class.
4. Before students do **Activité 15**, read aloud the profile to model pronunciation for the class. Ask them what they don't understand, and then read the questions to the entire class, having them answer **oui** or **non** chorally. Explain again areas they don't understand.

# À vous la parole

## Communiquez!

**Question centrale?**

How does education shape individuals and societies?

### 14 L'emploi du temps

1.1

#### Interpersonal Communication

Compare your class schedule with your partner's class schedule. In your conversation:

- greet each other.
- ask each other how things are going.
- tell each other the classes you are taking.
- compare the times and days of the week your classes meet.
- ask your partner what two of his or her teachers are like.
- say you'll see each other soon.

> Moi, je commence à 8h00.

> Je commence à 9h00 le vendredi, et toi?

## Communiquez!

### 15 Mon profil en ligne

1.2, 2.1

#### Interpretive Communication

Read Karine's profile on her social networking site. Answer the questions that follow in complete sentences.

**Mon réseau social**                                    Accueil    Profil

**Karine Duplessis**

| Mur | Infos | Photos |

Exprimez-vous...

Partager

#### Goûts et intérêts

**Âge**              J'ai seize ans (et demi).

**Personnalité**     Je suis intelligente, énergique, et drôle. J'aide ma mère et mon père avec leur magasin électronique.

**Musique**          J'aime bien le hip-hop et la musique alternative. Je n'aime pas le rock et la musique classique!

**Matières**         J'aime bien les sciences. J'étudie la biologie et la chimie parce que c'est intéressant!

1. Karine a 14 ans?
2. Elle est intelligente?
3. Elle est sérieuse (serious)?
4. Elle aime écouter de la musique?
5. Elle aime étudier les langues?

---

## Differentiated Learning

### Accelerate
Students can create their own sentences in the formats of **Activités 12** and **13**. This can be an oral or written round-robin activity, or it can be a contest between groups of three in which they write as many sentences as possible within a given time limit, using different nouns and adjectives in each sentence.

### Decelerate
Open-ended exercises like **Activité 14** may be challenging for some students. Write a dialogue with missing words and have students complete the sentences.

## Special Needs Students

### Auditory Impairment
For students who have difficulty hearing the difference between the masculine and feminine forms of adjectives, provide additional listening practice by saying pairs of examples such as, **Dominique est canadien. Dominique est canadienne.** Students raise one hand if they hear the masculine and two hands for the feminine form of the adjective. Give them some adjectives they haven't had such as **grand/grande** and **petit/petite**.

---

**Answers** _____

**14** *Conversations will vary.*

**15**

1. No. She is 16½.
2. Yes. She's intelligent, energetic, and funny.
3. Perhaps. She helps her family in their electronics store.
4. Yes. She enjoys hip-hop and alternative music.
5. No. She enjoys studying biology and chemistry.

## Reference Desk

### Blended Instruction
Consider using blended instruction, a combination of in-class learning and computer-mediated instruction or learning opportunities. Ask students to complete activities on the computer, using their cell or smartphone, or other emerging electronic technology. This will allow students to hone their tech skills and become more independent learners. Schedule routine Internet and e-book learning in class and in the lab.

## Expansion

Have students make up similar dialogues and perform them for the class. Assign students to write a blog about their schedules, specific classes, and opinions of their school. Set up a class website with a section devoted to student profiles in French. Ask students to research French audiences' reaction to the film *The Social Network* and discuss their findings. Assign further exploration of the **bac L**, **bac S**, and **bac ES**, including information about specific course of study for each **bac**, career options, level of difficulty, and popularity. Have students share their findings.

**Answers** _____

**Combining Sentences**
**Qui** means who.
**Quand** means when.
**Où** means where.

J'ai une amie. Elle est française.
Nous mangeons ensemble au café. Il fait mauvais.
C'est un café. Il est difficile de parler anglais.

 **16**

1. Le français est une langue qui est facile.
2. Paris est une ville qui est chère.
3. J'ai des cours qui sont intéressants.
4. Au cinéma, j'aime les films français quand ils sont intelligents.
5. On va à la médiathèque où les élèves étudient.
6. J'aime les magasins où les Français achètent des affiches et des T-shirts.
7. On va au parc quand il fait beau.

**17**

1. J'ai une copine qui est algérienne.
2. Elle est dans ma classe de biologie qui est intéressante.
3. Elle aime jouer au foot quand il fait beau.
4. On va à la cafétéria où on mange ensemble.

 **18** *Answers will vary.*

## Reference Desk

Explain how two simple sentences combine to form the model sentences with a dependent and independent clause. Define **qui** as a relative and interrogative pronoun. Tell students to use the relative pronoun **qui** if the next word is a verb.

# Stratégie communicative

## Combining Sentences  1.2, 3.1

Read the combined sentences below. What do you think each connecting word means? What two ideas are being combined?

> J'ai une amie **qui** est française.
> Nous mangeons ensemble au café **quand** il fait mauvais.
> C'est un café **où** il est difficile de parler anglais.

### 16 Mon voyage à Paris   2.1

Combine each set of Jenny's sentences about her trip to Paris, using **qui** (*who*), **quand** (*when*), or **où** (*where*).

1. Le français est une langue. C'est facile.
2. Paris est une ville. Elle est chère.
3. J'ai des cours. Ils sont intéressants.
4. Au cinéma, j'aime les films français. Ils sont intelligents.
5. On va à la médiathèque. Les élèves étudient à la médiathèque.
6. J'aime les magasins. Les Français achètent des affiches et des T-shirts dans les magasins.
7. On va au parc. Il fait beau.

*Paris est une ville qui est chère.*

### 17 Une très bonne amie  2.1

Complete the portrait below of a friend by finishing the sentences with a word or expression from the box.

| à la cantine | biologie | il fait beau |
| algérienne | est intéressante | |
| jouer au foot | on mange ensemble | |

1. J'ai une copine qui est….
2. Elle est dans ma classe de… qui….
3. Elle aime… quand….
4. On va… où….

### 18 Un portrait  2.1

Now write a description of yourself, someone you know, or an imaginary person that combines sentences using **qui**, **quand**, and **où**.

**Essential Instruction**

1. Go over the meanings of the three example sentences at the beginning of the **Stratégie Communicative** section on p. 136.
2. You may wish to introduce the term relative pronoun when referring to "connecting words."
3. In **Activité 16**, point out that the subject is eliminated when you use the relative pronoun **qui** to combine sentences. Have students write out the **Activité**, and then go over it together.
4. **Activité 17** can be done orally with a partner or in writing for more spelling practice.
5. **Activité 18** can be a homework assignment where students add a picture of the person they choose. Have them share their work in small groups, or with a partner.
6. Practice the relative pronouns. Prepare 10 to 15 sentences that answer **qui**, **quand**, and **où** questions. As you read a sentence, students call out the question that would elicit the response.
7. Explain the lesson title **Les Endroits**.

# Leçon C

## Vocabulaire actif

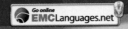

### Les endroits   1.2

**Je vais....**

à la cantine

au bureau du proviseur

au labo

à la médiathèque

à la salle d'informatique

à la piscine

au magasin

en ville

chez moi

### Et si je voulais dire...?

| | |
|---|---|
| **à la bibliothèque** | *at the library* |
| **au centre aquatique** | *at the aquatic park* |
| **au parc** | *at the parc* |
| **au stade** | *at the staduim* |
| **à la Maison des Jeunes** | *at the community center* |
| **à la discothèque** | *at the club* |
| **en boîte** | *at the nightclub* |

## RESOURCES

**Workbook 40–43**

**Listening Activities**

## Communication

**Interpretive: Cooperative Groups**

Have students take photos of classrooms and other areas where activities take place around school. Ask students to upload the pictures to a shared site or copy them to a flash drive. Display the pictures as a series on a screen for the class to view. Have one student at a time approach the screen and point to two locations while describing what course or activity he or she studies or does there.

## Differentiated Learning

### Accelerate

Teach the **Et je voulais dire...?** vocabulary and model the pronunciation. Ask students questions about if and when they go to, or are in, some of these places.

### Decelerate

Some students will have more difficulty with open-ended writing activities, such as **Activité 18**. You might choose one person and start the sentences you want the students to finish in French.

**Answers** _____

**1**

1. Angèle va au labo pour le cours de chimie.
2. Elle aime étudier à la média-thèque.
3. Elle surf sur internet à la salle d'informatique.
4. Elle mange des pâtes à la cantine.
5. Elle achète des cahiers au magasin.
6. Elle nage à la piscine.
7. Elle aime faire les devoirs à la maison.

**2** Script can be found in the front pages of the Annotated Teacher's Edition.

1. F,  Omar va à la médiathèque.
2. C,  Coralie va à la piscine.
3. A,  Sabine va au café.
4. E,  Sarah va à la salle d'informa-tique.
5. B,  Noémie va à la maison.
6. D,  Justin va au magasin de sports.

### Game

**Pass the Hat**
Cut three colored sheets of paper into small pieces. On one color, write names of subjects of study. On a second color, write differ-ent school locations where classes and activities are held. On the third color, write -**er** verb infini-tives. Put all pieces in a hat or other container. Arrange desks in a circle so that students can pass the hat around. Each person must randomly pick three different col-ored pieces of paper. Each student must then make and share a sen-tence using the stimulus words on the papers.

## Pour la conversation  1.2

How can I find out where someone is going next?

> **Où est-ce que tu vas après** le déjeuner?

*Where are you going after lunch?*

How can I find out when someone is going somewhere?

> **Quand est-ce qu'**on y va?

*When are we going there?*

How can I ask why someone can't do something?

> **Pourquoi est-ce que tu ne peux pas?**
*Why can't you (do it)?*

How can I establish a place and time to meet someone?

> **On se retrouve** à la piscine **à** 4h00.
*We'll meet at the pool at 4:00.*

**1** Angèle bouge!  1.2, 1.3

Angèle is always on the move. Complete each sentence with a location from the box to say where she does the following activities.

| à la piscine | à la salle d'informatique | à la maison |
| au magasin | au labo | à la cantine | à la médiathèque |

1. Angèle va... pour (*for*) le cours de chimie.
2. Elle aime étudier....
3. Elle surfe sur Internet....
4. Elle mange des pâtes....
5. Elle achète des cahiers....
6. Elle nage....
7. Elle aime faire les devoirs....

Angèle nage à la piscine.

**2** Mercredi après-midi

Number your paper 1–6. Listen to Maxime interview his classmates about their activities on Wednesday afternoon. Identify each location.

 1.2

 A.  B.  C.

 D.  E.  F.

**Essential Instruction**

1. Remind students of the online vocabulary flash cards.
2. Play the audio of **Pour la conversation**, then point out the key words **Où**, **Quand**, **Pourquoi**.
3. Do **Activité 2** as a class. Ask if students wish to hear the exercise again.
4. Have students share with a partner at what time they go to some of the places presented on p. 137. Ask them to report about their partner's schedule.
5. Before assigning **Activité 4**, review the days of the week. Expand on what students already know by teaching them that the days of the week in French derive from the Latin names for the planets: Monday→**lundi**→day of the moon, Tuesday→**mardi**→day of Mars, etc.
6. Do **Activité 5** as a class, then ask partners to repeat the exercise.

## 3  La journée scolaire de Christiane

 1.2, 2.1, 2.2

*Lisez* (Read) *le paragraphe, puis* (then) *répondez aux questions.*

Christiane va au labo à 9h15. Elle va à la médiathèque à 11h20. Elle va à la cantine à midi. Elle va à la salle d'informatique à 13h30. Elle va à la salle de musique à 14h35. Elle va à la piscine à 16h00. Elle va à la maison à 18h55.

1. Christiane mange à quelle heure?
2. Elle a besoin d'un ordinateur à quelle heure?
3. Elle a chimie à quelle heure?
4. Elle étudie à quelle heure?
5. Elle nage à quelle heure?
6. Elle regarde la télé à quelle heure?

## Communiquez!

### 4  On fixe un rendez-vous!

1.1, 2.1

**Interpersonal Communication**

With a partner, take turns finding a time to do four activities from the list below.

| jouer aux jeux vidéo   surfer sur Internet   étudier |
| manger de la pizza   jouer au basket |
| nager   jouer au foot   écouter de la musique |

**MODÈLE**

A: **Tu voudrais écouter de la musique?**
B: **Oui. Quand est-ce qu'on écoute de la musique?**
A: **Mercredi à 3h30.**
B: **D'accord.**

Quand est-ce qu'on va au cinéma?

### 5  Questions personnelles

*Répondez aux questions.* 1.1, 2.1

1. Tu manges à la cantine à quelle heure?
2. Où est-ce que tu vas après le déjeuner?
3. Tu étudies à la médiathèque?
4. Où est-ce que tes amis se retrouvent vendredi soir?
5. Tu es en ville samedi?

**RESOURCES**

 chat  **Flash Cards**

**Answers**

**3** *Answers may vary.*

1. Christiane mange à midi.
2. Elle a besoin d'un ordinateur à 13h30.
3. Elle a chimie à 9h15.
4. Elle étudie à 11h20.
5. Elle nage à 16h00.
6. Elle regarde la télé à 18h55.

**4** *Answers will vary.*

**5** *Answers will vary.*

**Game**

**Sentences**
Have the class form a circle. Start the game by saying a subject pronoun. The next student must provide the correct form of the verb for the subject. The following student must add a word to the sentence that makes sense. Continue the game. See how long of a sentence the students can make. When a sentence ends, the next student must start a new one. Challenge students by requiring that they only use the vocabulary from the unit.

**Learning Styles**
**Kinesthetic Learners**
Make **Activité 1** more interactive. Write the sentences and completion on strips of paper, put them in envelopes, and ask partners to match them to make complete sentences.

**Special Needs Students**
**Dyslexia**
Provide a visual support by drawing a map of Christine's destinations on the board. Have students complete the map with the times Christine does specific activities.

139

**Answers**

**❻**

1. Maxime désire aller à la piscine.
2. À 2h00 Yasmine va au labo voir la prof de biologie.
3. Camille désire aller à la piscine à 4h.
4. Camille a besoin d'aller au bureau du proviseur, puis chez elle.
5. On se retrouve à la piscine à 4h.

## Extension

Inès and Cédric are supposed to meet because they have to do a presentation on Polynesia.

## Communication

### Interpretive: Cooperative Groups

Have students research images of various school subjects and activities. Print these pictures or save them in a file to show on the screen for the class. Hold or show an image and call out a time such as "**deux heures de l'après-midi.**" Students must take turns to express at what time and where they do the activity or study the subject matter. For example, a student might answer: **À deux heures de l'après-midi, j'étudie la physique au laboratoire.** Use some of these statements later as material for a **dictée**.

# Rencontres culturelles

## Après le déjeuner      1.2

Julien, Maxime, Yasmine, and Camille are talking about what to do after having lunch together in **la cantine**.

Julien: Où est-ce qu'on va après ce "délicieux" déjeuner?
Maxime: On va à la piscine?
Yasmine: Oui, mais quand est-ce qu'on y va?
Maxime: Maintenant... à 2h00.
Yasmine: Alors, je ne peux pas!
Julien: Et pourquoi est-ce que tu ne peux pas?
Yasmine: J'ai besoin d'aller au labo... voir la prof de biologie.
Julien: Camille, tu vas à la piscine?
Camille: Est-ce qu'on peut y aller à 4h00? Moi, je dois aller au bureau du proviseur, puis chez moi....
Maxime: Et moi j'ai besoin de... je n'ai rien à faire!
Julien: Alors, nous, on va en ville et on se retrouve à la piscine à 4h00.

### 6  Après le déjeuner  2.1, 2.2

*Complétez les phrases.*

1. Maxime désire aller à....
2. À 2h00 Yasmine va au... voir la prof de....
3. Camille désire aller à la piscine à....
4. Camille a besoin d'aller au....
5. On se retrouve à la piscine à....

### Extension  On se retrouve dans la médiathèque  2.1, 2.2

Two students are talking in the **médiathèque**.

Gabrielle: Où est-ce qu'il est, Justin?
Cédric: En salle de dessin.... Mais pourquoi est-ce qu'Inès n'est pas là? On a rendez-vous ici à la médiathèque à 3h00....
Gabrielle: Pour travailler?
Cédric: Oui, on fait une recherche sur la Polynésie. On doit faire un exposé.

### Extension  Who is supposed to meet and what do they plan to do?

## Essential Instruction

1. Before listening to the dialogue on p. 140, present the context (four friends making plans). Then instruct students to listen first for a general sense of what the dialogue is about. The second time they listen, they should focus on adding details to their understanding. Explore why the word **délicieux** is in quotes.
2. Ask students to role-play the conversation on p. 140 in groups of four. Circulate among groups to help with pronunciation. Call on students to present.
3. Explain **médiathèque** in the **Extension** dialogue.
4. Assign each **Points de départ** cultural reading to a group. Ask students to read and report the essential information to the class, including one similarity and one difference between France and the United States.
5. Have small groups discuss the **Comparaisons** questions, and then share their views with the class.

# Points de départ

**Go online**
**EMCLanguages.net**

How does education shape individuals and societies?

## À la cantine  1.2, 4.2

Students in France often eat lunch in the school cafeteria, or **cantine**, but many also leave campus. Even students in **collège** can go off campus for lunch with their parents' permission. **Lycée** students don't need parental permission.

Meals served in the cantine consist of traditional French dishes, such as **pâté en croûte** (meat in pastry crust) or **quiche** (cheese and egg pie) for the first course, and **escalope de poulet à la strogonoff** (chicken Stroganoff) or **bœuf bourguignon** (beef stew) for the main dish. However, a movement now exists in France to teach students more about healthy eating with some schools making a commitment to serve only organic products.

Bread accompanies all meals in French school cafeterias.

## Les chefs à l'école 1.2, 4.2

In **les lycées hôteliers**, students train to work in the hotel-restaurant industry. Those who plan to become chefs learn to prepare gourmet dishes which are then served in the **cantine** to the student body. In addition to hands-on training, future chefs also have the opportunity to learn from master cooks with their own restaurants.

### COMPARAISONS

What kind of food choices do students make at your school? What choices are the healthiest? Is your school committed to teaching students healthy eating habits?

2.1, 2.2, 4.2

## La Francophonie   1.2, 4.2

❋ *L'éducation au Mali*

As in other parts of the francophone world, the Malian educational system inherited some principles from the French colonial system. Since its independence in 1960, Mali has initiated several educational reforms to educate its people. School is now compulsory from grades one through nine. However, for many, staying in school is a challenge due to economic circumstances. While 49% of the school-aged population attends primary school, only 13% go on to secondary school. There are several types of schools in Mali, ranging from public institutions; to schools that combine religious and secular instruction; to **écoles coraniques** where students learn to read, write, and recite passages from the Koran, the sacred book of millions of Muslims around the world.

---

### RESOURCES

**Workbook 48–49**

**Answers**

**Question centrale**
Education helps to teach values, knowledge, and cultural norms.

**Comparaisons**
*Answers will vary.*

### Culture

**Perspectives: Activity**
In **À la cantine** you may ask students to devise an American menu that could be served in a French school cafeteria.

### Critical Thinking

**Analysis**
Discuss the differences in French and American habits and practices concerning school meals. How long do French students have for a lunch break compared to your students? Ask them to research the school lunch practices in Quebec, Polynesia, and a few African francophone countries and compare their findings.

---

**Special Needs Students**
**Dyslexia**
You can use the reading selections in English to teach and review the fundamentals of phonology, which is likely something these students struggle with in English. They need to learn to decode (read words) and encode (apply the sounds to the written language). Being more aware of how the sounds and parts of language function will help them in their study of French. If need be, research online elements of both decoding and encoding to better assist these students.

**7**

1. Students eat lunch in the cantine. Lycée students, and middle-school students with parental permission, are allowed to leave school grounds for lunch.
2. Traditional French meals with a first course, main dish, salad, and dessert choices.
3. A **lycée hotelier** is a specialized school to prepare students for careers in the hotel and restaurant industries.
4. Student chefs actually prepare gourmet meals that are served to the student body.
5. A Koranic school is an institute of religious learning common wherever there are communities of Muslims. The focus is on recitation of Koranic verses and religious lessons.
6. The Norman conquest of England in 1066.
7. Government, law, art, literature, fashion, and cuisine, to name a few.
8. Familiar terms may include à la carte, collage, ballet, café, chauffeur, fiancé, and mousse.

## À discuter

*Possible answers:* Introduce healthy options and locally produced and organic foods to the school menu. Launch informational campaigns to promote a diet that will encourage overall health. Eliminate or reduce access to vending machines. Stock vending machines with healthier options.

### Communication

**Products: Cooperative Groups**

Divide students into groups of four. Have them brainstorm words used in the English language that they know or think are French that fall into the categories of government, law, art, literature, fashion, and cuisine.

## Les mots d'origine française  1.2, 4.1, 4.2

In the year 1066, a region in the northwestern part of France called Normandy conquered England. Consequently, about one third of all words in the English language have French origins. This means that students who want to learn French probably already know around 15,000 words! French terms are used to talk about government, law, art, literature, fashion, and cuisine. When you order a quiche, chicken fricassee, a croissant, or crepes, or cook with consommé or a bouquet garni, you are using words that have been borrowed from French. Do any of these other French words look familiar—a la carte, collage, ballet, café, chauffeur, fiancé, mousse? Can you think of more examples?

Géraldine mange un croissant.

**Search words: french words in english**
**borrowed words from french**

### 7 Questions culturelles  1.3, 2.1

*Répondez aux questions.*

1. Where do French students go to eat lunch?
2. What kind of food is served in French schools?
3. What is a **lycée hôtelier**?
4. How is the cafeteria food at a **lycée hôtelier** different from the food served in other French high schools?
5. What is **une école coranique**?
6. After what historic event did French words begin to appear in the English language?
7. What are three fields that use a lot of French terms?
8. What are four French words used in English?

Gratin dauphinois, a potato dish, is often served in French cantines.

**À discuter**

In what ways can schools help teach students healthy eating habits?

## Essential Instruction

1. Expand on the reading about words of French origin by showing students that there is a relationship between the letters "g" and "w" in French and English, for example, **Guillaume**/William, **guerre**/war, **garde-robe**/wardrobe.
2. Do **Activité 7** in small groups. Review the answers as a class.
3. Instruct the class to scan the questions in **Activité 8** before reading the menu. Note the date of the weekly menu and explain the importance of **le 11 novembre** in France. Armistice Day is a national holiday and commemorates the end (literally the "stopping/laying down of arms") of the fighting in WWI. Ask students if we celebrate this holiday. (Veteran's Day) Ask if we have an additional holiday to remember our soldiers. (Memorial Day)

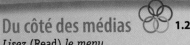

## Du côté des médias  1.2

*Lisez (Read) le menu.*

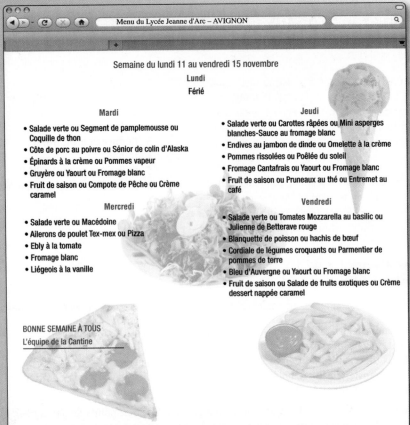

Menu du Lycée Jeanne d'Arc – AVIGNON

### Semaine du lundi 11 au vendredi 15 novembre

#### Lundi
Férié

#### Mardi
- Salade verte ou Segment de pamplemousse ou Coquille de thon
- Côte de porc au poivre ou Sénior de colin d'Alaska
- Épinards à la crème ou Pommes vapeur
- Gruyère ou Yaourt ou Fromage blanc
- Fruit de saison ou Compote de Pêche ou Crème caramel

#### Mercredi
- Salade verte ou Macédoine
- Ailerons de poulet Tex-mex ou Pizza
- Ebly à la tomate
- Fromage blanc
- Liégeois à la vanille

#### Jeudi
- Salade verte ou Carottes râpées ou Mini asperges blanches-Sauce au fromage blanc
- Endives au jambon de dinde ou Omelette à la crème
- Pommes rissolées ou Poêlée du soleil
- Fromage Cantafrais ou Yaourt ou Fromage blanc
- Fruit de saison ou Pruneaux au thé ou Entremet au café

#### Vendredi
- Salade verte ou Tomates Mozzarella au basilic ou Julienne de Betterave rouge
- Blanquette de poisson ou hachis de bœuf
- Cordiale de légumes croquants ou Parmentier de pommes de terre
- Bleu d'Auvergne ou Yaourt ou Fromage blanc
- Fruit de saison ou Salade de fruits exotiques ou Crème dessert nappée caramel

BONNE SEMAINE À TOUS
L'équipe de la Cantine

---

### 8 Le menu du Lycée Jeanne d'Arc  2.1, 2.2

*Répondez aux questions suivantes.*

1. Why do you think there is no menu on Monday?
2. On what days is salad served?
3. On what day are carrots or asparagus possible choices other than salad?
4. On what day can students have pork for their main course?
5. How many choices do students get for the main course?
6. On what days is yogurt served?
7. What American influences do you see on the menu?
8. Are there any other foods on the menu you recognize?
9. How do these menus from a French cafeteria compare to your school menus?

Leçon C | cent quarante-trois 143

---

Answers _____

**8**
1. Monday is a school holiday.
2. Salad is served Tuesday, Wednesday, Thursday, and Friday.
3. Thursday.
4. Thursday.
5. Two.
6. Tuesday, Thursday, and Friday.
7. Fish caught in Alaska, Tex-Mex chicken, and perhaps pizza are American influences on the menu.
8. *Answers will vary.*
9. *Answers will vary.*

### Critical Thinking

**Comparisons**
How does this French **lycée** menu compare to your students' school menu? What do the differences say about the ideas that are of importance to one culture or the other?

---

**Differentiated Instruction**

**Expand**
Since the students will not know the names of all the items on the French menu, name some items in English and ask them to find them in French (for example, chicken wings, steamed potatoes, ground beef, etc.). Give students some hints where to find the items, for example: **C'est sur le menu le dernier jour de la semaine,** etc.

143

# La culture sur place

## L'école en France et aux États–Unis  1.2

### Introduction

You have learned a number of interesting facts about what it's like to go to school in France. Did any of these facts surprise you? Or, are French schools like you expected them to be? How does the French school experience compare with your own experience in the United States?

Read the list on the right that refers to French school traditions. What do you remember about each one? Review the **Points de départ** readings in Units 1 and 3 if you need help recalling information.

> **L'école en France**
> 1. **la cour**
> 2. **la trousse**
> 3. **l'éducation en ligne**
> 4. **le bac**
> 5. **le mercredi après-midi**
> 6. **la cantine et la cuisine française**

**9**  **Que sais-je?** 2.1

Write what you remember about each tradition in the list above, then answer these questions:

- Do you have a tradition similar to this in your own school? If so, what is it? If not, have you ever heard of such a tradition before?
- How is this tradition different from your own school experiences?
- If you transferred to a school in France, would you easily adapt to this tradition or would it be difficult?

Share your thoughts about each tradition with a partner. On what points do you agree? On what points do you disagree? Can you persuade your partner to come around to your way of thinking, or do you simply have different values?

### Taking Inventory

As we saw in **Unité 1**, your comfort level may vary when coming into contact with different aspects of cultures other than your own. Something that may affect your comfort level is how deeply a cultural behavior or product impacts your life. Your reaction may be quite different in situations where you can remain an observer than where the culture directly affects your experience.

**10** **Ma liste**  1.1, 2.1

Take a look again at the traditions listed above. If you were to move to France, which one would have the greatest impact on your life? Which one would have the least impact? Rewrite the list, ordering each tradition according to the affect it would have on you. Begin with the tradition that would affect you the most. Discuss your list with some classmates. Do you share the same views?

## Essential Instruction

1. Model the pronunciation of **aller**.
2. Ask students to notice if any forms of **aller** are regular. Only the **nous** and **vous** stem resembles the infinitive and both have the same ending as regular -**er** verbs. Draw a line around the irregular forms of the verb (**je**, **tu**, **il/elle/on**, **ils/elles**) and point out that this outline is in the shape of a boot. Explain that while **aller** is considered irregular, it does follow a pattern. Suggest students note cuthat this is can be referred to as a "boot" verb (irregular within the boot).

3. Explain the literal meaning of **je vais** vs. the idiomatic expression **je vais bien**.
4. Do a rapid substitution drill as a whole class. Write a simple sentence on the board: **Je vais en France**. Then give students a new subject at random and have them repeat the new sentence with the subject and the correct conjugation.

# Structure de la langue

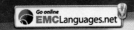 

## Present Tense of the Irregular Verb *aller*  1.2

*Les ados vont à la discothèque.*

The verb **aller** (*to go*) is an irregular verb. It's the only **–er** verb that is irregular.

| aller | | | |
|---|---|---|---|
| je | **vais** | nous | **allons** |
| tu | **vas** | vous | **allez** |
| il/elle/on | **va** | ils/elles | **vont** |

Comment **vas**-tu?        *How are you?*

The verb **aller** has more than one meaning. It can be used:

1. to talk about going somewhere

   On **va** à l'école.        *We're going to school.*

2. to talk about how things are going in general

   Ça **va**?                *How are things going?*

   Comment **allez**-vous?   *How are you?*

   Je **vais** très bien.    *I'm very well.*

*L'élève qui étudie la chimie va au labo.*

## Game

### Charades

Divide the class into two teams. Have a student volunteer go to the front of the room. The student audience calls out a time of day. The student volunteer must act out an (appropriate) activity listed in the unit vocabulary that he or she does at that particular time of day. The students on the opposite team must figure out what activity the actor is expressing. Award one point for stating the activity with a correct subject and verb and two points if the answer includes where the activity takes place.

---

### 11 Les notes  2.1, 2.2

French students are graded on a point system, with 20 points being the top score. A score of 18 is considered excellent, 12-13 good, and anything under 10 is not passing. Say how the following students would respond to the question **Ça va?** based on their grade in math class. Possible answers are **Ça va très bien**, **Ça va bien**, and **Ça va mal**.

1. Fatima/19
2. Amélie/9
3. Timéo/12
4. Mehdi/8
5. Awa/7
6. Mathieu/18

### 12 Samedi   2.1, 2.2

*Dites où tout le monde va samedi et à quelle heure.*

**MODÈLE** Nayah
**Samedi Nayah va en ville à trois heures moins vingt-cinq.**

1. Philippe

2. les filles

3. nous

4. tu

5. vous

6. je

---

### Essential Instruction

1. Discuss and have students compare the cultural information about grades in **Activité 11**, p. 146, to the practices in their school. Which system might they prefer? Why?
2. **Activité 13** provides the opportunity to explore several French cities. Ask students if they can associate any products with the cities in the exercise (**Limoges/porcelaine, Dijon/moutarde**).
3. Write on the board: **J'aime Paris. / Je vais à Paris.** (no article here!)
   **J'aime la ville de Paris. / Je vais à la ville de Paris.** (fem. article)
   **J'aime le cinéma. / Je vais au cinéma.** (masc. article)
   **J'aime l'école. / Je vais à l'école.** (article before vowel)
   **J'aime les magasins. / Je vais aux magasins.** (plural article)
   Point out which forms of the definite article are combined with the preposition **à**.

## 13 On voyage en France!

Say that everyone is going from one city in France to another, following the indicated route on the map.

**MODÈLE**   M. et Mme Carlson/Rennes
**M. et Mme Carlson vont de Rennes à Brest.**

1. Mlle Smith/Limoges
2. tu/Lyon
3. Shannon et Nicole/Dijon
4. je/Lille
5. Mark et toi, vous/Nice
6. Dan et Matt/Bordeaux
7. Ma mère et moi, nous/Paris

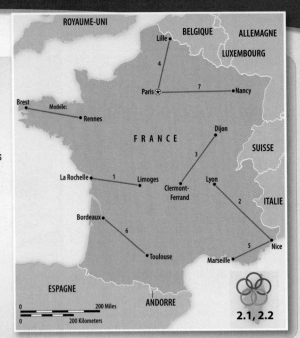

2.1, 2.2

# À + Definite Articles  1.2

Les touristes vont au magasin de luxe.

The preposition **à** (*to, at, in*) does not change before the definite articles **la** and **l'**.

Nous allons **à la** piscine.     *We're going to the pool.*
Tu étudies **à la** médiathèque?     *You're studying in the media center?*

Before the definite articles **le** and **les**, however, **à** changes form:

| à + le = au | to (the), at (the), in (the) |
|---|---|
| à + les = aux | to (the), at (the), in (the) |

Paul mange un hamburger **au** café.     *Paul is eating a hamburger at the cafe.*
Vous allez **aux** magasins?     *Are you going to the stores?*

Leçon C   |   cent quarante-sept   1 4 7

**Differentiated Learning**
**Expand/Accelerate**
Expand on **Activité 12** by asking the students where they go at different times. Then have them ask the same questions of you and each other.
Expand **Activité 13** by assigning groups online research of one of the cities mentioned. Ask students to find out three to five facts about their location and report to the rest of the class.

**13**
1. Mlle Smith va de Limoges à La Rochelle.
2. Tu vas de Lyon à Nice.
3. Shannon et Nicole vont de Dijon à Clermont-Ferrand.
4. Je vais de Lille à Paris.
5. Mark et toi, vous allez de Nice à Marseille.
6. Dan et Matt vont de Bordeaux à Toulouse.
7. Ma mère et moi, nous allons de Paris à Lille.

Use the geographical **préposition** **à** with cities. If a city name begins with **le**, then **à** becomes **au**. Refer to your French classroom map for city names in French.

### TPR

Have students plan a "dream" (**idéal**) itinerary for travel around the world. What cities will they visit? Have one student come up to the classroom map and state where they are going and call on another student to show these cities on the map. The class can vote on the itineraries they consider the most exotic or exciting. Use correct geographical prepositions.

## Answers

**14**

1. Tu es au labo.
2. Nous sommes à la médiathèque.
3. Vous êtes au café.
4. Elle est à l'école.
5. Je suis aux magasins.
6. Ils sont à la piscine.

**15**

1. Karim va au lycée.
2. Karim va au bureau du proviseur.
3. Karim va au cours de musique.
4. Karim va à la cantine.
5. Karim va au laboratoire.
6. Karim va à la salle d'informatique.
7. Karim va à la piscine.

**14 Ils sont où?**

**2.1, 2.2**

*Dites où tout le monde est.*

> piscine   café   école   labo
> magasins   médiathèque

1. J'étudie la chimie.
2. Vous étudiez.
3. Nous mangeons une pizza.
4. Ariane écoute la prof.
5. Tu fais du shopping.
6. Kemajou et Romain nagent.

Tu fais du shopping au magasin.

**15 La journée scolaire de Karim**    2.1, 2.2

*Dites où Karim va pendant sa journée scolaire.*

 1.     2.     3.

 4.     5.     6.     7.

### Essential Instruction

1. Ask students where they do the **activités** in **Activité 14**.
2. Say a series of declarative sentences and repeat the same sentence, but as yes/no questions using intonation only. Ask students to raise one hand if they hear a sentence and two if they hear a question.
3. Explain the use of **Est-ce que (qu')** at the beginning of the sentence to create a yes/no question. Provide the translation "Is it that…?"
4. Tell students that **Est-ce que (qu')** provides the listener a clue that the speaker is asking a question.
5. Write a yes/no question on the board and ask how one might change it to an information question. Add question words to the beginning of the yes/no question to show how to form this type of question.
6. Do **Activité 16**, advising your students to listen for the question word.
7. Discuss the **Comparaisons** as a class.

# Forming Questions with *est-ce que*  1.2

*Avec qui est-ce que Renée va au cinéma?*

To ask a question that can be answered by "yes" or "no":

1. Raise your voice at the end of a sentence.

   Camille a un cours de musique?      *Camille has a music class?*

2. Use the expression **est-ce que** before the subject of the sentence. **Est-ce que** has no meaning by itself; it serves only to change a statement into a question. Before a word beginning with a vowel sound, **est-ce que** becomes **est-ce qu'**.

   **Est-ce que** Khaled est français?      *Is Khaled French?*
   **Est-ce qu'**il aime jouer au foot?      *Does he like playing soccer?*

To form a question that asks for information, use a specific question word followed by **est-ce que**, a subject, and a verb.

**Où est-ce que** tu vas?      *Where are you going?*
**Pourquoi est-ce que** tu vas au magasin?      *Why are you going to the store?*
**Quand est-ce que** tu vas au magasin?      *When are you going to the store?*
**Avec qui est-ce que** tu vas?      *With whom are you going?*

### 16 Trouvez les questions!   2.1, 2.2

A group of Tahitian teenagers is answering their friends' questions. Select the correct response to each question.

- A. J'ai besoin d'une trousse.
- B. On se retrouve à la médiathèque.
- C. Nadine.
- D. Elle est intéressante.
- E. Je dois faire mes devoirs.
- F. Il coûte 2,53 €.
- G. Le mercredi à deux heures et demie.

### COMPARAISONS  4.1

Look at the English translations of the questions asking for information. What rule do you follow for forming this type of question in English?

COMPARAISONS: To form questions using question words in English, put the question word at the beginning of the sentence before the inverted subject pronoun and verb.

Leçon C | cent quarante-neuf **149**

---

**RESOURCES**

  **Workbook 58–61**

**Answers**

**Comparaisons**
Start with the question word. In the present progressive, the helping verb is next followed by the subject followed by the -ing form of the verb.

**16** Script can be found in the front pages of the Annotated Teacher's Edition.

1. D
2. G
3. F
4. B
5. C
6. A
7. E

## Reference Desk

Students will learn to make questions using inversion in **Unité 4**. When forming a question about oneself, one does not use inversion but rather makes the question using **est-ce que je**….

## Communication

**Interpersonal: Cooperative Groups**

Put students in groups of four. Have each student write three sentences on separate notecards, one sentence each about three other students in the group. For example, **Georges aime jouer aux jeux vidéo à la médiathèque.** Place all cards face down. Have each student choose a card at random and transform it into a question using **est-ce que** or with a question word such as **où, pourquoi, quand,** or **avec qui** and **est-ce que**. Another student in the group must answer the question out loud.

---

**Differentiated Learning**
**Expand**
To have your students practice question formation, write a sentence on the board, for example, **Tu vas à la piscine.** First, have them change it to a question by adding a question mark. Then, have students change it to a question using **Est-ce que (qu')**. Finally, have students change it to a "why" or "where," etc. question. Repeat the process with additional sentences, including ones that start with **il(s)**, **elle(s)**, and names that start with a vowel sound.

**Multiple Intelligences**
**Intrapersonal**
Have students write six questions they would like to ask anyone they choose. They need to use all the question words, **est-ce que(qu')**, and verbs and vocabulary they have already had. Then they share these orally in groups. You can also have them write answers to their own questions.

**149**

### Communication

**Interpersonal: Cooperative Groups**

On your classroom blog, make a question corner where you ask questions about your school or your activities. **Modèle: Où est le cours de danse lundi? Est-ce que j'ai besoin d'un dictionnaire pour mon cours d'histoire?**

---

 Communiquez!

**17** **Des questions!**   1.1

**Interpersonal Communication**

*Formez des questions avec **est-ce que** et posez-les (ask them) à votre partenaire.*

1. Le français est intéressant.
2. Elle est américaine.
3. C'est un cours difficile.
4. Tu as une trousse.
5. Tu as un sac à dos.
6. Ton CD est total vintage.
7. L'école est géniale.

Est-ce que ta prof d'anglais est intéressante?

Oui, elle est intéressante.

**18** **Mon portable**   2.1

What question did you ask for each of these responses on your cell phone? State each question.

1. On se retrouve au café à 5h30.
2. Non, les cours sont difficiles.
3. Non, nous avons besoin d'aller au labo à 14h45.
4. Je vais à la cantine à 12h00.
5. Oui, j'ai un dico français-anglais.
6. Je vais au centre commercial avec Valérie.
7. Je vais à la piscine dimanche.
8. Je vais au magasin parce que j'ai besoin d'un cahier.

---

### Essential Instruction

1. For **Activité 17**, tell students to write yes/no questions (not "where," "when," etc.), and remind them to change the subject-verb combination when they answer, for example, **Tu as→J'ai.**
2. The Internet research for **Activité 19** can be done in the lab or outside of class. If you have paper and markers in your room, have your students do the Venn diagram in class. Otherwise, give them large paper so they can do it at home. The next day, have them use the diagram to create sentences according to the model.
3. You may want to wait to do **Activité 20** until your students have learned food vocabulary or until National Foreign Language week at the beginning of March.
   If they do create menus, have them look for dishes in cookbooks as well as online.
4. Make **Activité 21** an online research competition between groups of three. The word cloud can be done in class or at home.

# À vous la parole

## Communiquez!

How does education shape individuals and societies?

### 19 Robert Doisneau et la salle de classe d'hier

 1.3

**Presentational Communication**

Use the key words **Robert Doisneau** and **école** to search the Internet for some of this famous photographer's images of children in French classrooms more than 50 years ago. Draw a Venn diagram and label the two circles **l'École d'aujourd'hui** and **l'École d'hier**. In the **l'École d'aujourd'hui** circle, list objects found in today's schools that you didn't see in Doisneau's photographs. In the **l'École d'hier** circle, list objects in the photographs that you wouldn't see in today's schools. List objects that would be found in both schools in the section where the circles intersect. Discuss your Venn diagram with that of your partner.

**MODÈLE**    Dans l'école d'hier il n'y a pas d'ordinateurs.

## Communiquez!

### 20 Le menu à la cantine
1.3, 4.2

**Presentational Communication**

It is International Week at your school. Research foods from French-speaking countries to create a francophone menu for your school cafeteria. You might look for information on school websites in French-speaking countries, consult French restaurant menus online, or find recipes from different francophone countries. When creating your menu, make sure it is healthy and contains a variety of foods. List dishes according to courses (first course, main course, and dessert) and include some photos to show your classmates what they will be eating.

**Bœuf bourguignon** is a beef dish from Bourgogne, in the north of France.

## Communiquez!

### 21 Mon vocabulaire est abondant!

 1.3

**Presentational Communication**

Do online research to find French words that are used regularly in English. List 30 of them, some that you already know and some that are new to you. Categorize each word according to the field in which it is used: politics, fashion, art, cuisine, etc. Then create a word cloud by hand or using an online program. Explain your word cloud to your partner or group.

 **Search words:** french words in english
borrowed words

---

**Answers** _____

19 *Answers will vary.*

20 *Answers will vary.*

21 *Answers will vary.*

**Question centrale**
Education helps to teach values, knowledge, and cultural norms.

## Reference Desk

**Blended Instruction**
Consider using blended instruction, a combination of in-class learning and computer-mediated instruction or learning opportunities. Ask students to complete activities on the computer, using their cell or smartphone, or other emerging electronic technology. This will allow students to hone their tech skills and become more independent learners. Schedule routine Internet and e-book learning in class and in the lab.

## Culture

**Products: Activity**
Are there any French restaurants in your neighborhood or area? What do they serve on the menu? What are some well-known French restaurants in the United States? Find some menus from these restaurants online and make a display for the classroom. Compare and discuss where you would like to go to eat French food.

## Differentiated Learning
**Decelerate**
You may want to have these students do **Activité 20** with a partner. Each pair chooses a different francophone country. Have them do the research in class and provide web sites where they can find menu items. Specify the number of dishes students need to find for each course. Tell them to find and include photos of the dishes.

## Multiple Intelligences
**Intrapersonal**
As a follow-up to their research of foods from different francophone countries, ask students to make a list of four dishes they discovered that they would like to try. You may wish to offer extra credit to students who make one of the dishes and report on it in class with photos and the recipe.

## Expansion

Have students use a medium that you designate, such as a moviemaker or drawing program, to design and present the ideal 21st century classroom. Be sure to have them label the room and items in it with classroom and other vocabulary that they know.

# Lecture thématique

## Le Petit Nicolas

### Rencontre avec l'auteur  1.2

**René Goscinny** (1926–1977) is a French author, best known for his work on the comic books _Astérix_ and _Lucky Luke_. In 1959, he published _Le Petit Nicolas_, a series of humorous children's stories about a little boy growing up in the 1950s. The stories interpret events from a child's viewpoint and poke fun at adult perceptions. The excerpt you are about to read takes place in an elementary school classroom. What is funny about the new student's name?

### Pré-lecture  2.1, 2.2

Tell a true or imaginary story about someone who joined a class as a new student.

### Stratégie de lecture 1.1

**Point of view**

Point of view is the vantage point from which a story is told. It reflects the perspective of the person telling the story. In the first-person point of view, one of the characters tells the story and uses the pronoun "I." The reader only knows what the character knows or observes. In the third-person point of view, the narrator tells the story from outside the action and knows everything and uses "he" or "she." As you read, think about how the point of view shapes the story and how the story would be different told from someone else's point of view. As you read, fill in a chart like the one below, answering each question.

| Questions | Réponses |
|---|---|
| 1. Is the narrator a character in the story? | |
| 2. Does the narrator comment on events in the story, or just tell what happens? | |
| 3. Does the narrator tell the story from a first-person point of view, using words like **je**, **me**, **moi**, **nous**? | |
| 4. Who is telling the story? | |

### Outils de lecture  1.2, 4.1

**Context clues**

To understand words in context, take into account the words around the word whose meaning you are trying to figure out. In this reading, the teacher says, **"Dis ton nom à tes petits camarades"** to the new student. What would be one of the first things a teacher would do with a new student? Take these context clues into account: **Dis** means "says" and you know the meaning of **camarade (de classe)**. What does the teacher want the new student to say to his new classmates?

**Essential Instruction**

1. If you have an _Astérix_ comic book, cartoons by René Goscinny, or a copy of _Le Petit Nicolas_, show them to your students.
2. Go over the pre-reading **activités** for _Le Petit Nicolas_ together as a class and discuss the **Stratégie de lecture**.
3. Role-play this passage from the story **"Djodjo"** using some kind of prop to indicate who you are at the moment. Students love seeing their teachers ham it up. Point out that MacIntosh is a Scottish surname, and that **JoJo** is a common French nickname for **Georges**. Compare the English and French "g" sounds, so they see where the nickname **Djodjo** comes from.
6. Then play the audio and do the questions together.
7. Refer back to **Activité 19**, p. 151, and the photos students found online by Robert Doisneau when you do **Le monde visuel** as a class.

**1.2, 2.1, 2.2, 4.1**

Nous avons un nouveau en classe. (...)

"Mes enfants," a dit* la maîtresse, "je vous présente un nouveau petit camarade. Il est étranger* et ses parents l'ont mis* dans cette école pour qu'il apprenne* à parler français." (...)

"Dis ton nom à tes petits camarades."

Le nouveau n'a pas compris*. (...) Comme le nouveau ne disait rien,* la maîtresse nous a dit qu'il s'appelait Georges MacIntosh.

"*Yes*," a dit le nouveau, Dgeorges.

"Pardon, mademoiselle," a demandé* Maixent, "il s'appelle Georges ou Dgeorges?"

La maîtresse nous a expliqué qu'il s'appelait Georges mais que dans sa langue, ça se prononçait Dgeorges.

"Bon," a dit Maixent, "on l'appellera Jojo."

"Non," a dit Joachim, "il faut prononcer Djodjo."

"Tais-toi* Djoachim," a dit Maixent et la maîtresse les a mis tous les deux au piquet.*

---

*a dit *said*; étranger *pas français*; l'ont mis *put him*; pour qu'il apprenne *so that he can learn*; n'a pas compris *didn't understand*; ne disait rien *said nothing*; a demandé *asked*; Tais-toi *Shut up*; les a mis tous les deux au piquet *put both of them in the corner facing the wall*

> **Pendant la lecture**
> 1. What happened in class?

> **Pendant la lecture**
> 2. Where is Georges from?

> **Pendant la lecture**
> 3. What is funny to the French students about the new student's name?

> **Pendant la lecture**
> 4. Why did the teacher punish Maixent and Joachim?

*Information scolaire*, 1956. Robert Doisneau.

## Post-lecture  **1.1, 2.1, 2.2**

Is the teacher's punishment of Maixent and Joachim fair? In what ways has classroom discipline changed since the 1950s?

## Le monde visuel **2.1, 2.2, 4.2**

French photographer Robert Doisneau (1912–1994) is known for his post-World War II black and white photos of Paris and its residents. A focal point in a work of art is the point the artist draws you to, for example, the lines of the walls draw your eyes to the bold cross in the window. Who is the main focal point in the photo? What is the boy's position in the photo? What is he concentrating on?

Leçon C | cent cinquante-trois **1 5 3**

**Answers** _____

 *Answers will vary.*

## Les copains d'abord

Here is the translation for **Les copains d'abord**:

A = Antoine
F = Florence
MA = Marie-Alix
M = Mathéo
P = Professor

M: Hi girls! A: Howdy! F: Hi boys, how is it going? MA: Hey, Antoine and Mathéo, hi! MA: So, Flo and me, we hate the math teacher. F: Well, he isn't funny and math is hard. M: Do you like computer science? It's a more interesting subject. A: Or biology? Labs are cool. MA: Personally, I prefer art. F: Yes, Marie-Alix draws Tahitians like Gauguin. M: Me, I love history! A: Me, I love Florence... F: and MA: What??? M: Eh, Florence is my girl, better watch out! A: Oh, my bad...P: Take out your notebooks and your pens. M: Eh... I don't have my pencil case. You got a pen? A: On top of the dictionary, in front of the pencil sharpener. M: Say, do you have a piece of paper? I don't have my notebook... A: Oh, you! P: Is there a problem, gentlemen? Would you like to go to the principal's office? M: No, no, ma'am, he's my friend, my bud... A: Yes, it's all good, we're going to a movie tonight...

List of slang and idiomatic expressions:
**Ben**: *well;* **fais gaffe:** *watch out;* **zut alors**: *darn;* **mon pote**: *my bud*

## Expansion

Have students make a cartoon reflecting school life or a funny event that happened in elementary school.

---

1. Use the responses from your chart to write a paragraph describing the point of view Goscinny uses in this selection from *Le Petit Nicolas*.
2. Rewrite the classroom scene above from the teacher's or George's point of view, using the third-person or first-person point of view.
3. Write a scene for a play based on the selection. Include parts for a narrator, the teacher, Georges, Maixent, and Joachim. Perform your scene for the class.

*Les copains d'abord: Conflit d'intérêt* 1.2

### Essential Instruction

1. Ask students to look at the cartoon while you read it for them so they can see the order of the conversations. Go over words they don't understand, having them repeat new words.
2. Then, have groups of five read and role-play the cartoon.
3. Choose topics from **Projets finaux** that reflect your students' interests, maturity level and age, and correspond to your time frame and preferences. Modify or shorten to suit your needs. For example, for **Activité A**, have students work in pairs to research three or four web sites on one of the six topics that they then present to the class. Make a list of all websites presented, check them out for appropriateness, and hand out a master list to everyone. On a lab day, give students a chance to explore all the sites.

# T'es branché?

## Projets finaux

### A  Connexions par Internet: Study Skills and Tools

1.3, 2.1, 2.2

**How Can I Improve My French by Using Resources on the Internet?**

To become more proficient in another language, you need to constantly practice and interact with people who speak the language. The Internet offers many opportunities to do just that. The following activity will help you design a personal action plan for practicing French. Here are some steps to follow to write a comprehensive plan:

1. Outline a personal goal for using Internet sites and activities to increase your language proficiency.
2. Practice listening to French. Listening to native speakers from different parts of the francophone world will help you increase your comprehension. Research five sites and/or activities that will help you practice listening to French. Write a brief description of each site.
3. Practice reading French. Reading different types of texts to get information and guessing the meaning of unknown words by using context clues are excellent language learning strategies. Research five sites where you can read different types of text in French. Write a brief description of each site.
4. Practice speaking French. There are many ways you can practice your speaking skills. You might make your own French podcast or join one of the many communities that connect students around the world. Research five sites and/or organizations where you can practice speaking and connecting with other French speakers. Write a brief description of each site.
5. Practice French grammar. Grammar provides the framework for a language, and it allows you to communicate accurately. French grammar will help you with basic survival and communicating in the language. Research five sites where you can practice and/or learn French grammar. Write a brief description of each site.
6. Learn French through the media and by exposing yourself to culture. French music, videos, e-zines, electronic books, movies, and many more types of media are available to you. Research five media or cultural sites and write a brief description of each one.

What has this activity taught you about learning French? Write a short paragraph about your experience.

**Differentiated Learning**
**Accelerate**
Have above-level students choose one of the three topics in **Activité 22** to write about outside of class. If time allows, ask them to share their written product with each other.

### Reference Desk

You may want to tell students that the first step in their work should be to assign specific roles to each group member.

### Expansion

Find a French-speaking school through an online exchange program and collaborate on the video project.

**B  Communautés en ligne**  1.3

#### Une vidéo de notre école

Your school has joined an international collaboration project called **Notre école**, or "Our School." Work with a group of four to five students to create a video showing what your school looks like and what it's like to study there. To produce your video, you will need to:

1. Film the outside of your school, the entrance, and several sites around the building(s). Show how students arrive at school and where they wait for classes to begin.
2. Film the inside of the school. Show some of the classrooms, the cafeteria, the gym, and the auditorium or theater.
3. Film the inside of a classroom. Show how the walls are decorated and what students have on their desks.
4. Write a script in French that describes everything you film and record it to accompany the images. You may want to rehearse filming so you can write the script ahead of time and record it as you film. Or, you may wish to do a voice-over.

**Note:** Be careful to film only students whose parents have provided permission for them to be in this movie. Also, never give out any personal information about a student. This includes the student's name, phone number, or e-mail address.

C'est où les autobus scolaires arrivent.

C'est la classe de maths.

#### Essential Instruction

1. For **Activité B**, have each group write a script. Give your students a list of specific vocabulary and grammar to include, such as school rooms, school subjects, use of **à** + definite article, and the verbs from **Unité 3**.
2. Have the class vote on which script they want to use for their class video. Enjoy the video together as a class. You may want to show them the videos from the other beginning-level French classes you teach.
3. For **Activité C**, you may want to have students do only the country profile and find pictures of Mali, if your time is limited.
4. Give students a chance to first discuss in groups how each of the sections of the unit relates to the **Question centrale**. Then review as a class.
5. For **Activité D**, distribute copies of the graphic organizer found in the **Copy Masters** supplement.

**C** **Passez à l'action!**  **1.1, 1.3**

### Dons pour les écoles d'Afrique

Schools in many poor areas of French-speaking Africa often lack the necessary funds to provide all children with a quality education. Your French class has decided to help one of these schools in Mali, West Africa, by sending school supplies. To complete this project:

Les élèves maliens sont dans la salle de classe.

1. Create a country profile of Mali. Include the size of the population, its literacy rate, birth rate, per capita income, life expectancy, and facts about the geography of the country.
2. Find images of Mali's cities, people, food, buildings, famous sites, geography, etc.
3. Find the name of a school in Mali.
4. Share your research with others to better understand the country's and particular school's needs.
5. Consult with your teacher to find out how to send packages to Africa.
6. Make a list of people and organizations you might contact to help you carry out your project.
7. Make a list of the school supplies you would like to collect and the quantities of each one.
8. Decide how many of each item you need.
9. Plan an event to raise money for the supplies or for individuals to donate them.
10. Make arrangements to mail the supplies to the school in Mali.

**D** **Faisons le point!**  **1.3, 2.1, 4.2**

Fill in a diagram like the one that follows to demonstrate your understanding of how education shapes individuals and societies. An example has been done for you.

> *Question centrale*
> ?
> How does education shape individuals and societies?

| | |
|---|---|
| **Leçon A** Points de départ: La formation en ligne → | Society gets a tech-savvy workforce. |
| **Leçon A** Points de départ: Les manuels.... → | |
| **Leçon B** Points de départ: Les cours et les examens → | |
| **Leçon B** À vous la parole: L'emploi du temps → | |
| **Leçon C** Points de départ: Les chefs à l'école → | |

---

### Differentiated Learning

**Accelerate**

If you don't have the opportunity for the entire class to write a video script, **Activité B** will offer a challenge to above-level students.

**Expand**

Have volunteers do the actual filming for the class. Keep in mind that some students don't drive, and they may have difficulty getting together outside of class. You might offer them an incentive for their extra work.

### Multiple Intelligences

**Musical-Rhythmic**

Have volunteers add audio to the video, such as music and sound effects.

---

**Answers** _____

**C** *Answers will vary.*

**D**

**Leçon A:** Society gets a tech-savvy workforce.

**Leçon A:** Nowadays more people are purchasing school supplies online in France.

**Leçon B:** French students must pass the **Baccalauréat** to go to college/university.

**Leçon B:** Social networking is an important part of students' lives now and an education tool.

**Leçon C:** The English languages uses French words in everday vocabulary.

**Leçon C:** There are some differences between the school system in France and in the United States.

**Leçon C:** Experiences have changed since Doisneau's days.

**Leçon C:** **Le monde visuel:** Classroom discipline has changed in the last century.

**Leçon C:** **Connexions par Internet:** I can improve my French by using resources on the Internet.

**Leçon C:** **Communautés en ligne:** Making a video serves as effective documentation.

**Leçon C:** **Passez à l'action:** Sending school supplies to poor countries is an effective way to help students who have fewer educational opportunities.

**Answers** _____

**A** Script can be found in the front pages of the Annotated Teacher's Edition.

1. C
2. B
3. B
4. B
5. C
6. A

**B** *Conversations will vary.*

A. Qu'est-ce que tu as à huit heures?
B. Moi, j'ai biologie à huit heures. Et toi, qu'est-ce que tu as à neuf heures moins cinq?
A. J'ai EPS. Après, j'ai anglais à dix heures et le déjeuner à midi. Et toi? Tu as le déjeuner à midi aussi?

---

# Évaluation

**A**  Évaluation de compréhension auditive   2.1

Listen to the conversation between Félix and his mother. Choose the appropriate answer to the questions.

1. Qu'est-ce que Félix demande à sa mère?
   A. D'aller à la piscine.
   B. De jouer au foot avec son ami Karim.
   C. D'aller à Carrefour.

2. À quelle heure est-ce qu'il veut aller au magasin?
   A. À 4h30.
   B. À 5h30.
   C. À 6h30.

3. De quoi est-ce que Félix a besoin?
   A. De crayons, de stylos, de cahiers, d'un dictionnaire, et d'un cédérom.
   B. De crayons, de stylos, d'un cahier, de feuilles de papiers, et d'un cédérom.
   C. De crayons, de stylos, d'un cahier, de feuilles de papiers, et d'un ordinateur.

4. Pourquoi est-ce que Félix a besoin d'un cédérom?
   A. Pour le cours d'allemand.
   B. Pour le cours d'anglais.
   C. Pour le cours de français.

5. Combien coûte le cédérom?
   A. 49 €
   B. 59 €
   C. 69 €

6. Qu'est-ce que la mère de Félix décide de faire?
   A. Téléphoner au proviseur.
   B. Acheter le cédérom.
   C. Téléphoner au prof d'anglais.

**B**  Évaluation orale      1.1

Students at your school just received class schedules for next fall. Work with a partner to compare your Monday schedules.

**MODÈLE**   A: **Qu'est-ce que tu as à huit heures?**
             B: **Moi, j'ai biologie à huit heures. Et toi, qu'est-ce que tu as à neuf heures moins cinq?**

---

**Essential Instruction**

1. Do **Activité A** and review as a class.
2. For **Activité B**, have students share and ask questions about their own daily schedule or an imaginary one that they write.
3. Have students discuss the topics in **Activité C** in small groups and then share with the class.
4. Ask students to write **Activité D** outside of class, and then have volunteers read their memo to the class the next day.

5. For **Activité E**, assign students to find or draw a picture of a classroom as homework. In class, have pairs describe the pictures. Then have them exchange pictures with another pair so they have a second picture to describe.
6. For **Activité F**, artistic students will enjoy creating storyboard frames. You might provide students a choice of templates on which they only fill in the captions.

## C Évaluation culturelle  4.2

You will be asked to make some comparisons between francophone cultures and American culture. You may need to complete some additional research about American culture.

1. **Les cours**
Compare the classes and schedules in French and American secondary schools. Do American and French students study the same subjects? Do their classes meet on the same days? Do their classes last the same amount of time?

2. **Les examens**
Compare standardized testing in your school with standardized testing in French schools. Which educational system is more rigorous?

3. **Les noms des écoles**
Compare the name of your school with the names of schools in France and other French-speaking countries. What field or discipline did the person your school is named after contribute to? What fields or disciplines are reflected in the names of francophone schools?

4. **Les dépenses**
Compare the amount spent per pupil in France with the amount spent per pupil in your state. Which better funds the education of its children?

5. **Les cantines**
Compare French and American cafeteria food. What conclusions can you draw about the type of food that is offered? Are there healthy choices on both American and French cafeteria menus?

6. **Les devises**
Compare the coins and bills of French and American currency.

## D Évaluation écrite  1.3

Your French teacher asks you to write a memo to new students to give them a better idea of what school will be like. Let them know what school supplies they need to buy, what classes the students have, how the teachers are, and where students go for lunch.

## E Évaluation visuelle  1.3

Describe the French classroom. Tell what items appear in the room and where they are located in relation to each other, and what the teacher needs on her desk.

## F Évaluation compréhensive  1.1, 1.3

Create a storyboard with six frames. Write captions for each frame, telling about your or an imaginary character's day at school. Finally, share your story with a small group of classmates.

**C**

1. *Answers will vary.* Typically, students in France study more subjects and their courses meet fewer times per week, but are often longer.
2. *Answers will vary.* In France, standardized tests (**brevet**, **bac**) are cornerstones of the national education system. Standardized tests are important, but perhaps less so than in the United States where they are not nationalized. Most people characterize the French educational system as more rigorous, particularly in the **lycée**.
3. *Answers will vary.*
4. *Answers will vary.*
5. *Answers will vary.* Students may conclude that French cafeterias offer more home-style cooking, more inventive cuisine, and more fresh fruits and vegetables.
6. Students might point out that the euro has fewer denominations in bills and coins than the U.S. dollar. They might also note that green is the primary color used for all denominations of dollar bills, whereas each denomination of euro bills is a different color. Euro coins bear specific characteristics of the country in which they were issued.

**D** *Answer will vary.*

**E** *Answer will vary.*

**F** *Answer will vary.*

### Reference Desk

**Activité E** may be structured as an end-of-unit graded oral task. Record the **Activité** for later assessment, or conduct the **Activité** face-to-face with students.

**Differentiated Learning**
**Decelerate Students**
Have students read through and translate, if you wish, the questions and answer choices in listening **Activité A** before doing the exercise.

Before assigning writing **Activité D**, brainstorm with students and write on the board vocabulary that falls into the categories to include for the memo: school supplies, school subjects, places around the school, and opinions.

## RESOURCES

 **Flash Cards**

 *Rendez-vous à Nice!*
**Episode 3**

 **Listening Pre-test D**

 *Unité* **Test**

# Vocabulaire de l'Unité 3  1.2

**acheter** to buy *A*
une **affiche** poster *A*
l' **allemand (m.)** German (language) *B*
**alors** so, then *C*
l' **anglais (m.)** English (language) *B*
l' **après-midi (m.)** afternoon *B*
les **arts plastiques (m.)** visual arts *B*
**aux** to (the) *C*
**avoir** to have *A*; **avoir besoin de** to need *A*
la **biologie** biology *B*
la **bleue** the blue one *C*
le **bureau** desk *A*; office *C*
un **cahier** notebook *A*
la **cantine** cafeteria *C*
**ce (m.)** this *C*
un **cédérom** CD *A*
**cher, chère** expensive *A*
**chez: chez moi** at home *C*
la **chimie** chemistry *B*
**combien** how much *A*; **Il coûte combien?**
  How much does it cost? *A*
**coûter** to cost *A*
**dans** in *A*
le **déjeuner** lunch *C*
**délicieux, délicieuse** delicious *C*
**demi(e)** half *B*; **et demi(e)** half past *B*; **Il est**
  **six heures et demie.** It is six thirty. *B*
**derrière** behind *A*
**devant** in front of *A*
**difficile** difficult *B*
**drôle** funny *B*
l' **école (f.)** school *A*
**écrire** to write *A*
l' **éducation physique et sportive (EPS) (f.)**
  gym class *B*
**en** in *A*; **en ville** downtown *C*
un **endroit** place *C*
**énergique** energetic *B*
l' **espagnol (m.)** Spanish (language) *B*
**est-ce que** (phrase introducing a question) *C*
**être** to be *B*
**euh** um *A*
un **euro** euro *A*
**facile** easy *B*
une **feuille de papier** sheet of paper *A*
le **français** French (language) *B*
la **France** France *A*

l' **heure (f.)** hour, time, o'clock *B*; **Quelle heure**
  **est-il?** What time is it? *B*
l' **histoire (f.)** history *B*
**il y a** there is/are *A*
l' **informatique (f.)** computer science *B*
**intelligent(e)** intelligent *B*
**intéressant(e)** interesting *B*
le **labo** lab *C*
la **langue** language *B*
le **magasin** store *C*
**maintenant** now *A*
**mais** but *A*
la **matière** class subject *B*
le **matin** morning *B*
**midi** noon *B*; **Il est midi.** It is noon. *B*
**minuit** midnight *B*; **Il est minuit.** It is midnight. *B*
les **notes (f.)** grades *A*
la **nuit** night *B*
**où** where *A*
**parce que** because *B*
**peut** can *C*
la **physique** physics *B*
la **piscine** swimming pool *C*
**pour** for *A*
**prends: je prends** (see **prendre**) I'll take *A*
un **proviseur** principal *C*
**puis** then *C*
un **quart** quarter *B*; **et quart** a quarter past *B*;
  **moins le quart** a quarter to *B*
**qui** who, that *B*
**quoi** what *B*
**retrouve: on se retrouve….** we'll meet…. *C*
**rien: ne (n')… rien** nothing *C*
un **sac à dos** backpack *A*
une **salle** room *A*; **une salle de classe** classroom *A*
les **sciences (f.)** science *B*
**sous** under *A*
**tahitien(ne)** Tahitian *B*
**total: Total vintage!** It has a totally vintage look! *A*
une **trousse** pencil case *A*
une **ville** city *C*; **en ville** downtown *C*
**voir** to see *C*
**y: On y va?** Are we going there? *C*

Classroom… see p. 108
Numbers 20–100… see p. 109
Places in school… see p. 137

# 4 Le weekend ensemble

*Rendez-vous à Nice!*

**Épisode 4:**

*Cours de salsa!*

Go online
**EMC**Languages.net

cent soixante et un **161**

1. Explore the theme introduced by the **Question centrale**. Students will discover they share common interests with their Francophone peers and learn interesting cultural aspects about pastimes in this unit.
2. Have students use the photo on p. 162 and the verb **aller** to help answer the **Question centrale**. Discuss café culture around the world and in local communities.
3. Soccer, or **le foot(ball)**, is perhaps the most popular sport in most countries worldwide. After students complete **Leçon A**, plan a soccer day when students can wear soccer jerseys for the international and local teams they support, and discuss teams and players.
4. Point out that **football américain** is used to distinguish American football from soccer.

## Culture

### Perspectives: Activity

Have students research Georges Brassens, iconic post-WW II French singer/songwriter/poet. Play a Brassens song in class. Tell students Brassens is known for his **jeux de mots** and point out one example. Discuss what his attitude is toward the topic he is singing about.

## Citation

"L'amitié n'exige rien en échange, que de l'entretien."

Friendship doesn't require anything in exchange, except for being nurtured.

Georges Brassens—auteur, compositeur, chanteur français

## À savoir 1.2

The city of Paris has approximately 10,000 cafés.

## Essential Instruction

1. Ask students the **Question centrale**. Then ask them what the word **ensemble** in the unit title might mean. To introduce the unit, have students discuss briefly what they like to do with friends.
2. Review the **Contrat de l'élève**. Ask students to guess what the French words might mean given the context. Answer questions students may have about the content of the **contrat**. Then, ask them to predict what the most popular activities for French youth probably are.
3. Poll the class to find out what they know about soccer, cafés, fast food, and movies.
4. Show the relevant video clip from *Rendez-vous à Nice!*, Episode 4, and discuss the related question as a class.
5. Finally, read the **Citation** to the class. Ask them what "nurtured" means, and if they agree with the quote. Briefly introduce Georges Brassens.

# Unité 4

# Le weekend ensemble

## RESOURCES

 *Rendez-vous à Nice!*
**Episode 4**

**Answers** _____

The answer to the video question is C.

## Question centrale

**?**

## What activities do friends in other countries do together?

Go online
**EMCLanguages.net**

**Why is Chadia's mom upset?**
A. Her daughter wants to move out.
B. Her daughter wants to quit school.
C. Her daughter wants to date someone.

Which famous writers frequented this Parisian café?

## Contrat de l'élève

### Leçon A I will be able to:

>> make plans, setting the time and place to do something.

>> talk about soccer in France and a famous French soccer player.

>> talk about the future using **aller** + infinitive and form questions using inversion and **n'est-ce pas**.

### Leçon B I will be able to:

>> order food and drinks in a café and ask for the bill.

>> talk about **le fast-food** and famous cafés in France.

>> use the verb **prendre** and the expressions **avoir faim/soif**.

### Leçon C I will be able to:

>> make and respond to predictions.

>> talk about the history of cinema in France and some popular comedies.

>> use all forms of **quel** and **voir**.

cent soixante-trois **163**

## Reference Desk

The photo shows one of Paris' historic literary **cafés**, **Les Deux Magots** in the **Place Saint-Germain-des-Prés**. Students can research the origins of this café's unusual name and also the famous café scene of the Left Bank. Challenge your students to find out the name of its nearby rival (the **Café de Flore**, pictured on p. 167). On your classroom wall map of Paris, mark the location of these and other cafés featured in **Unité 4**. You may wish to show clips of Paris from the film *Midnight in Paris* in which, while visiting contemporary Paris, the main character, a writer, travels back in time and discovers Paris and the literary and artistic café scene of the 1920s and 1930s.

## RESOURCES

 e-visual 12

 Workbook 1–5

 Flash Cards

 Listening Activity

### Reference Desk

Assign online research of the professional soccer teams mentioned in this unit. You may wish to ask students to make a wall display showing different international teams, the players, the team mascot, logo, and slogan. Have students talk about teams and players with whom they are familiar or follow, and post the team record during the soccer season. Discuss the popularity of soccer in your school district as well as statewide, nationally, and in the world. Has soccer (**le football**) been an Olympic sport?

### Culture

**Practices: Information**
Consider showing the i-Culture video entitled **"Le foot"** (2009-2010) to provide your students with a culturally authentic perspective related to the theme of this **Leçon**.

 **Leçon A**

## Vocabulaire actif

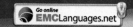 Go online EMCLanguages.net

### Le football   1.2

un stade

une équipe

un ballon de foot

un footballeur

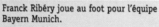

une bouche de métro

Franck Ribéry joue au foot pour l'équipe Bayern Munich.

Bayern Munich joue **contre** Lyon au stade.

Ribéry **marque un but!**

Est-ce que Bayern Munich va **gagner** ou **perdre**?

un ticket de métro

### Essential Instruction

1. Ask students who know soccer to explain the rules of the game. Research and share statistics about the popularity of soccer around the world. Find online and show a video of France's official soccer team, **Les Bleus**.
2. Have students listen to the audio and repeat the vocabulary for **Le football**.
3. Mention that the players and clubs featured here will be presented later in the unit. Explain that **Lyon** is one of France's largest cities.
4. Play the audio for **Pour la conversation** and have students practice the sentences several times, substituting another city for **Marseille** or changing the time or the place of the **rendez-vous**.

une écharpe

le blason de l'équipe

une casquette

un maillot

un short

des chaussettes

des chaussures

# Pour la conversation 🎧 ✿ 1.2

**H**ow do I give a reason?

> Je vais soutenir Marseille **parce qu'ils sont les meilleurs.**
>
> *I'm going to support Marseille because they're the best.*

**H**ow do I set a time and place to meet someone?

> **Rendez-vous à** 3h00 **devant** la bouche du métro.
>
> *Let's meet at 3:00 in front of the subway entrance.*

**H**ow do I suggest a different time?

> **Disons** 3h15.
>
> *Let's say 3:15.*

| Et si je voulais dire...? 🎧 | |
|---|---|
| **un abonnement** | *season tickets* |
| **un club** | *soccer association* |
| **des gants (m.)** | *gloves* |
| **un siège** | *seat* |
| **un supporter** | *fan* |
| **un survêtement** | *track suit* |
| **le vestiaire** | *locker room* |

Leçon A | cent soixante-cinq **165**

## Reference Desk

To provide an adequate model for the adjective **meilleur**, write **mon meilleur ami** on the board and then a chart with **meilleur, meilleure, meilleurs**, and **meilleures** to introduce masculine and feminine singular and plural forms.

## Culture

**Products: Activity**
What do students think is written on the football scarf? The answer (**Allez Paris**) will give you a chance to connect the slogan and the verb **aller**. What team is the young girl rooting for? Have your students research the **Paris Saint-Germain** team logo. What iconic Parisian monument and what royal symbol are featured on its design? (Answer: the Eiffel Tower and the white royal cradle of Louis XIV.)

What does a **métro** entrance have to do with soccer? (You can take **le métro** to **le Parc des Princes**, the stadium that is the home to the **Paris Saint-Germain** football club.)

## Differentiated Learning
### Expand
Reinforce the vocabulary and the French alphabet by having students practice spelling the vocabulary with a partner. Then ask the class to write vocabulary words as you say them. Students should correct their own work.

### Accelerate
Present the vocabulary in **Et si je voulais dire...?**

## Multiple Intelligences
### Visual/Intrapersonal
Ask students to find a photo of a player wearing a soccer, basketball, or tennis uniform and label it with the vocabulary on p. 165. This could be a photo they find online, in a magazine, or of themselves. Then have them write three sentences in French about the player, what team he or she plays for, and whether the team is going to win or lose. Ask students to show their photo and read their sentences in groups.

**❶**

1. Les tickets sont dans la casquette.
2. Les chaussettes sont avec les chaussures.
3. L'écharpe est sous le ballon.
4. Le blouson est sur la chaise.
5. Le maillot est sur l'écharpe.

**❷**

1. Amadou
2. Béatrice
3. Amadou
4. Amadou
5. Amadou et Béatrice

**❸** Script can be found in the front pages of the Annotated Teacher's Edition.

1. Pierre, a soccer ball
2. Sandrine, a jersey
3. Koffi, socks
4. Samia, a jacket
5. Thierry, a team logo
6. Norbert, a cap
7. Loïc, a scarf
8. Marie-Hélène, shoes

**1** | **Un fan se prépare pour le match.**  **2.1, 2.2**

Malick has all his clothing and equipment laid out in preparation for getting dressed for today's game. Tell where the first item is in relation to the second.

**MODÈLE** ballon de foot/écharpe
**Le ballon de foot est sur l'écharpe.**

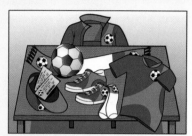

1. tickets/casquette
2. chaussettes/chaussures
3. écharpe/ballon
4. blouson/chaise
5. maillot/écharpe

**2** | **Un fan de foot**  **1.2, 2.1, 2.2**

_Lisez le paragraphe. Ensuite, identifiez la personne décrite_ (described).

Amadou est un supporter de l'équipe de Marseille. Il est au stade avec sa copine Béatrice. Il a le blason de l'équipe sur sa casquette et son maillot. Il aime beaucoup regarder les matchs de football. Pas Béatrice. Pour elle, le foot n'est pas intéressant. Mais Amadou est content! Pourquoi? Un footballeur marque un but, et l'équipe de Marseille gagne!

1. Cette personne aime beaucoup l'équipe de Marseille.
2. Cette personne n'aime pas le foot.
3. Cette personne est contente que l'équipe de Marseille gagne.
4. Cette personne a une casquette et un maillot avec le blason de l'équipe de Marseille.
5. Cette personne regarde le match au stade.

**3** | **Mélanie fait du shopping.**   **2.2**

Mélanie is shopping at a sporting goods store. Write the name of the person she is shopping for and what she is buying in English.

### Essential Instruction

1. Review prepositions before students do **Activité 1** in pairs.
2. After students read the paragraph in **Activité 2** silently, then aloud with a partner, go over any words they don't understand or can't pronounce. Assign the identifications as pair work.
3. Do **Activité 3** with the audio.
4. Reinforce pronunciation by having students repeat the vocabulary in **Activité 5** before doing the activity. For a change of pace, you may want to divide the class into two groups and do the activity chorally, with you as the conductor.

## 4 Des vêtements pour le match de football

*Alex et Philippe vont au match de football. Qu'est-ce qu'Alex va acheter pour s'habiller comme (to dress like) Philippe?*

1.3

| MODÈLE | **Alex va acheter** des chaussures **à la boutique du PSG.** |

---

# Communiquez!

1.1, 2.1

## 5 Où? Quoi? Pourquoi?

### Interpersonal Communication

*À tour de rôle, demandez où va votre partenaire et pourquoi. Utilisez les éléments donnés dans chaque colonne pour créer vos conversations.* (With a partner, take turns asking each other where you are going and why. Use information from each column in your conversations.)

| Où? | Pourquoi? |
|-----|-----------|
| au café | pour soutenir le club |
| en ville | j'aime nager |
| à la piscine | c'est un bon café |
| à Carrefour | mon cours est difficile |
| au stade | c'est génial |
| à la médiathèque | je dois faire mes devoirs |
| au bureau du proviseur | j'aime faire du shopping |

| MODÈLE | A: **Où est-ce que tu vas?**<br>B: **Je vais** au café.<br>A: **Pourquoi est-ce que tu vas** au café?<br>B: **Parce que** c'est un bon café! |

---

# Communiquez!

## 6 Questions personnelles

1.1

### Interpersonal Communication

*Répondez aux questions.*

1. Est-ce que tu aimes bien le football?
2. Est-ce que tu vas au stade pour regarder des matchs?
3. Qui achète les tickets?
4. Tu portes une écharpe quand tu regardes un match au stade?
5. Est-ce que tu as le maillot d'une équipe américaine?

---

### Reference Desk

Have students explore online and compare the **Café de Flore** pictured here, and **Les Deux Magots**. How much does it cost to have coffee inside, or outside (**terrasse**)? Ask questions using the verb **regarder**, a key verb to use with spectator sports (at a stadium, on TV, and at a Parisian café).

### Game

**Vocabulary Identification**
Have pairs draw a picture of each vocabulary item on pages 164–165, spread out over the paper and numbered, but not labeled. Play the "Fastest Finger in France." As you say a vocabulary word or expression, students try to point to it first.

---

## Differentiated Learning

### Accelerate
Ask students to use the vocabulary in **Activité 5** to write original sentences, for example, **Je vais à la piscine parce que j'aime nager.** Encourage students to include vocabulary they have learned from previous units.

### Decelerate
Have students write the answers to **Activité 6** (in class or at home) and share their answers with a partner.

## Special Needs Students

### Linguistically Challenged
In **Activité 5**, first have students match the places with the appropriate reasons. Some have more than one choice. Then, have students put together the two columns, writing sentences that start with **Je vais**. Tell them to use **parce que** to join the two parts. Write a model on the board, for example, **Je vais au café parce que c'est génial.** Explain the difference between using **pour soutenir le club** and **parce que** (followed by subject + verb).

**Answers** _____

**7**

1. Il désire acheter un maillot.
2. Ça coûte 38 euros.
3. Il achète un blason pour son blouson.
4. Ils vont au stade pour regarder le match.
5. Julien est un supporter de PSG ; Maxime est un supporter de Marseille.
6. Il va l'attendre devant la bouche du métro.
7. Maxime va porter son maillot de Marseille.

**Extension**

Ribéry has yet to prove his reputation for **l'équipe de France**.

**Communication**

**Presentational: Cooperative Groups**

Have students use the dialogue to create a skit. Suggest that they use their own soccer outfits for props.

# Rencontres culturelles

## On va au match de foot!     1.2

Maxime and Julien are shopping online.

Julien: Le maillot là, il coûte combien?
Maxime: Il est en solde... 38 euros.
Julien: C'est un peu cher, n'est-ce pas? Donc, j'achète un blason pour mon blouson.
Maxime: Allons-nous au stade voir le match de PSG contre Marseille?
Julien: Parce que tu veux voir perdre le PSG!
Maxime: Je vais soutenir l'équipe de Marseille parce qu'ils sont les meilleurs!
Julien: Bon, rendez-vous à 3h00? Je vais t'attendre devant la bouche du métro.
Maxime: Disons 2h45. Je vais porter mon maillot de Marseille!
Julien: Ça ne me surprend pas. Tu achètes les tickets sur Internet, et je te rembourse après?

**7** **On va au match de foot!**   **2.1, 2.2**

*Répondez aux questions.*

1. Qu'est-ce que Julien désire acheter?
2. Ça coûte combien?
3. Qu'est-ce qu'il achète?
4. Où est-ce qu'ils vont pour regarder le match de PSG?
5. Qui est un supporter du PSG? de Marseille?
6. Où est-ce que Julien va attendre Maxime?
7. Qu'est-ce que Maxime va porter au match?

**Extension** **Le petit Napoléon**   **1.2, 2.1, 2.2**

Dans le métro, Léa et Quentin parlent d'un match à la télé.

Léa: Et le match dimanche?
Quentin: Génial! Ribéry est un footballeur fantastique!
Léa: C'est vrai qu'on l'appelle "le petit Napoléon" au Bayern de Munich?
Quentin: Oui, les supporters l'adorent.
Léa: Et il a marqué?
Quentin: Comme d'habitude... un but et une passe décisive. Et le but, de la folie!
Léa: On va voir ce qu'il va faire avec l'équipe de France....

**Extension** What remains undecided about Ribéry?

**168** cent soixante-huit | Unité 4

**Essential Instruction**

1. Show the filmed dialogue and have small groups summarize what they understood. Ask a volunteer from each group to share with the class. Next, ask pairs to read aloud the dialog twice, changing roles. Review the meaning and pronunciation of new words. Encourage students to add new vocabulary to their personal dictionary if you're having them keep one. Finally, show the filmed dialogue again.

2. In **Activité 7**, ask volunteers to provide answers orally or have pairs write out complete answers and then read their sentences to another pair of students.

3. For the **Points de départ** on pp.169–170, after they have read about each cultural topic, have students do online research using the search words given.

# Points de départ

## Le foot en France  1.2, 1.3

Soccer has been a popular sport in France since 1880. Major cities, such as Marseille, Lyon, Bordeaux, Toulouse, Paris, and Lille, have their own professional soccer teams, or clubs. Amateur teams for both men and women, and for of all ages, exist in communities large and small. Schools in France do not organize competitions for soccer or any other sport. Young people can begin playing competitively at age 14. Soccer also has the largest television following of any sport in France. Some 21 million viewers tuned in to watch the last **Coupe du monde**, or World Cup, finals.

 **Search words:** **ca montrichard, club de football**

*Question centrale*

What activities do friends in other countries do together?

Océane enjoys playing soccer in France.

### Produits

All media outlets in France cover soccer. There are newspapers like *L'Équipe*, magazines like *Onze*, TV programs such as "Jour de foot," and radio shows like "Le grand direct" to give soccer die-hards all the details they could want. **4.2**

### COMPARAISONS

What is the most popular sport in the United States according to ticket sales and/or TV viewership? **4.2**

## Les clubs de foot  1.2, 1.3

Two soccer clubs have ruled the sport in France: the **Olympique Lyonnais**, from the city of Lyon, and the national French team, nicknamed **Les Bleus**. The **Olympique Lyonnais** have gained fame by dominating their national league (**Ligue 1**) in recent years while **Les Bleus** have performed well internationally, winning the World Cup in 1998 and coming in second place in 2006. **Les Bleus** also won the European Championship in 1984 and 2000. France is one of only seven countries to have won the World Cup in soccer since the tournament began in 1930.

**Les Bleus**, the famous 1998 **Coupe du Monde** winners, include Zinédine Zidane (10), Fabien Barthès (16), and Lilian Thuram (15).

 **Search words: olympique lyonnais site officiel, équipe de france, coupe du monde 1998**

---

### Reference Desk

Explain that French high schools do not have sports teams, cheerleading squads, marching bands, drum majors, or color guards. Discuss the roles these groups play in supporting high school sports.

Discuss the World Cup/**la Coupe du Monde**. What countries will host the next several FIFA (**Fédération Internationale de Football Association**) World Cup championships? (Brazil in 2014, Russia in 2018, and Qatar in 2022) Has the United States ever hosted a championship? (Yes, in 1994, when Brazil beat Italy.) What was special about the World Cup final in 1998? (France was host and won the championship over Brazil 3 - 0.) Who are the recent champions? (Spain beat the Dutch in 2010 in South Africa.) As you discuss these events, practice present tense verb conjugations for **regarder, gagner, jouer, adorer, aimer, marquer, porter, acheter**, etc.

---

**Differentiated Learning**
**Adapt**
1. If there is no opportunity to do online work during class, assign online research for homework.
2. For extra credit, ask students to find the answers to the **Comparaisons** question and report to the class the next day.

**Multiple Intelligences**
**Bodily-Kinesthetic**
Outside have students practice kicking a soccer ball with their feet and head or play a soccer game.

**Answers** _____

1. Soccer has been a popular sport since 1880.
2. There are professional and amateur soccer teams in France.
3. The team **Olympique Lyonnais** has recently dominated French professional soccer.
4. **Les Bleus**, the national French team, won the World Cup in 1998.
5. Franck Ribéry scored the fastest goal ever.

**À discuter**
_Answers will vary._

### Expansion

Use a discussion of famous French players to practice spelling in French. Have students pick a favorite French soccer player and write a short description about him or her. Ask volunteers to read their description without mentioning the name of the player to the class. When someone guesses the player, he or she must not say the name, but rather spell it out in French for the class to assess. Both the name and the spelling must be correct to win.

### Culture

**Products: Activity**
Ask "teams" of students to adopt a player per team and make biographies with photos to add to your pantheon of soccer stars on the classroom wall. What are the accomplishments of Michel Platini, Éric Cantona, or Thierry Ribéry, for example?

## Les meilleurs joueurs de foot  1.2, 1.3

Michel Platini, Éric Cantona, Zinédine Zidane, Thierry Henry, and Franck Ribéry are considered some of France's most outstanding players in recent years. Ribéry is considered the best French player today and attracts thousands of fans wherever he plays. An athlete known for his speed and technique, he scored the fastest goal ever, after only 13 seconds of play. In both league and international games, Ribéry often scores the deciding goal that takes his team to victory.

🔍 **Search words: franck ribéry photos, vidéo, biographie**

### 8 Questions culturelles  2.1, 2.2

_Répondez aux questions._

1. How long has soccer been a popular sport in France?
2. What types of soccer teams are there in France?
3. What is the name of the latest soccer team to dominate national French soccer?
4. In what year did the French national team win the World Cup?
5. What famous French soccer player scored the fastest goal ever?

**À discuter**

How do you balance competition and teamwork in your life?

Another name for **un club de foot** is **une association de football**.

**Essential Instruction**

1. In groups, have students read **Les meilleurs joueurs de foot**, do **Activité 8**, and discuss **Du côté des médias**. Ask which sports listed in the television program they would like to watch, and have them compare those to the ones they watch on American television.

2. Have students reflect in their Culture Journal on what they have especially enjoyed learning about the cultural topics they researched in the **Points de départ**.

3. Have students do **Activité 9** in pairs or do the Game on p. 171 as a class.

## Du côté des médias

*Lisez le programme.*

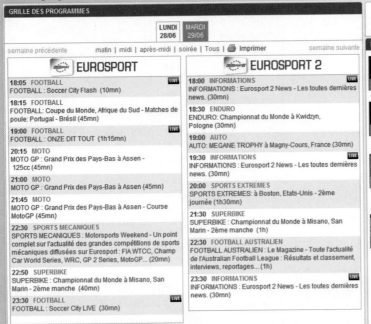

### Critical Thinking

**Comparisons**
What sports, familiar to your students, are not featured in the Eurosport programming? How does this French programming compare to American sports coverage on TV? Have students survey each other about the different types of sports they watch. Ask them to share what they learned about their classmates' preferences.

### Game

**What's on TV?**
Have selected students take turns calling out the time of an event, and ask students to respond telling the channel and the sport featured on the program for that time.

---

**9** Les sports à la télé  **1.2, 2.1, 2.2**

*Répondez aux questions.*

1. How many soccer programs are there on the Eurosport channels?
2. How many motorcycle shows are there on Eurosport?
3. How many cycling shows are there on Eurosport?
4. At what times can you listen to sports news on Eurosport 2?
5. Eurosport 2 features football from which country at 22h30?
6. What words would you enter to search for a program about the World Cup?

There are over 20 motorcycle races per year in France.

Leçon A | cent soixante et onze **171**

---

### Differentiated Learning
**Expand**
Incorporate a variety of ways to review telling time, using the TV schedule on p. 171. For example, say a time from the schedule and have students call it out in English. Or, have students call out the sport that is being broadcast at a particular time. Ask students to translate orally and in writing the time from the 24-hour clock, for example, **20:15→8:15 P.M.** You might also have students read aloud the times in a 12-hour format, such as **huit heures et quart du soir.**

### Learning Styles
**Auditory Learners**
You may want to play several brief radio reports from **Eurosport** or another radio show or French sports TV program, such as **TV5.** Ask students to identify what sport is being described and provide other details of what they hear.

**Answers**

**10** Script can be found in the front pages of the Annotated Teacher's Edition.

1. C
2. F
3. A
4. E
5. D
6. B

## Communication

**Interpersonal: Paired Practice**

Put several dozen slips of paper marked with infinitives related to sports and activities into a hat or container. Have students sit in a large circle with space to walk around the center. Select two students randomly and ask them to draw a paper from the hat. These students must then come to the center of the circle and converse, asking each other what they are going to do and answering with the verb **aller** and the infinitives marked on their paper slips. When the students have finished their conversation, continue to offer the hat to other students until all have participated. In another round, have a student choose a slip of paper and ask the question to another student at random, who must answer and elaborate as appropriate.

# Structure de la langue

 Go online EMCLanguages.net

## Aller + Infinitive  1.2

To say what you are going to do in the near future, use a present tense form of **aller** followed by an infinitive.

| aller + | infinitif |
|---------|-----------|
| going to + | Infinitive |

**Karim va gagner le match?**

Qu'est-ce que tu **vas faire**?    *What are you going to do?*
Je **vais aller** au match.    *I'm going to go to the game.*

To say what you are not going to do, put **ne (n')** before the form of **aller** and **pas** after it.

Xavier **ne** va **pas** porter le maillot.    *Xavier isn't going to wear the jersey.*

### 10 C'est le weekend!   2.1, 2.2

*C'est le weekend! Choisissez la lettre de l'image qui correspond à chaque activité que vous et vos amis allez faire.*

A.

B.

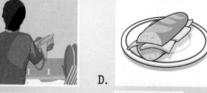
C.     D.

E.     F.

### COMPARAISONS 4.1

In French, the near future is expressed with aller + infinitive. How is the near future expressed in English?

Sarah va porter un blouson.
Sarah is going to wear a jacket.

COMPARAISONS: In English the near future is also expressed with a conjugated verb followed by an infinitive.

**Essential Instruction**

1. Before introducing the **futur proche**, review the conjugation of the verb **aller**. Write subject-verb combinations with **aller** on the board, such as, **je vais étudier** and **tu vas sortir**. Ask the class what they mean, and ask students to make each sentence negative. Then, have students ask a partner questions about future weekend activities using the infinitives listed on the board. Finally, have students report two activities their partner will do next weekend.

2. Review the directions in **Activités 11** and **12**. Then, have students do these in pairs.

3. You may wish to have students present one of the conversations from **Activité 12**.

**11**
1. Sabrina va porter un blouson.
2. Antoine et moi, nous allons porter des maillots.
3. Madame, vous allez porter une écharpe.
4. Justin et Karim, ils vont porter des chaussures.
5. Rosalie et Valérie, elles vont porter une casquette.
6. Moi, je vais porter un maillot.
7. Toi, tu vas porter des chaussettes.

**12** See **modèle** for questions. *All answers to the questions will vary.*

**11** Au stade   **2.1, 2.2**

*Indiquez les articles de la boutique du PSG que les personnes suivantes vont porter au match de football demain.* (Say what items from the PSG boutique the following people are going to wear to the soccer game tomorrow.)

**MODÈLE**   Hugo
**Hugo va porter des chaussettes.**

1. Sabrina

2. Antoine et moi, nous

3. Madame, vous

4. Justin et Karim

5. Rosalie et Valérie

6. Moi, je

7. Toi, tu

## Communiquez!

**12** Qu'est-ce qu'on va faire ce weekend?   **1.1**

**Interpersonal Communication**

*À tour de rôle, demandez à votre partenaire ce qu'il ou elle va faire et ne va pas faire ce weekend.*

**MODÈLE**   regarder un match au stade/écouter de la musique
**A: Est-ce que tu vas regarder un match au stade?**
**B: Non, je ne vais pas regarder un match au stade. Et toi, est-ce que tu vas écouter de la musique?**
**A: Oui, je vais écouter de la musique.**

1. regarder la télévision/sortir samedi soir
2. faire les devoirs/jouer aux jeux vidéo
3. aller au ciné/envoyer des textos
4. nager/plonger
5. aller à la médiathèque/faire du roller
6. jouer au basket/faire du footing

**Answers** _____

**13** *Answers will vary.*

**13** Pendant les vacances   2.1

*Dessinez un symbole pour six activités que vous allez faire pendant les vacances (while on vacation). Votre partenaire va deviner (guess) ces activités. Chaque fois que vous ou votre partenaire devine une activité, cette personne gagne un point. La personne qui gagne le plus de points gagne le jeu.*

**MODÈLE** A: **Tu vas aller au cinéma?**
B: **Oui, je vais aller au cinéma./Non, je ne vais pas aller au cinéma.**

## Forming Questions  1.2

• **n'est-ce pas**

One way to ask a question in spoken French is to add the expression **n'est-ce pas** to the end of a sentence. **N'est-ce pas** means "isn't that so" but may be interpreted in various ways, depending on context. It is usually a question answered by saying **oui** or **non**.

*Chloé va-t-elle plonger?*

| | |
|---|---|
| C'est toujours un peu cher, **n'est-ce pas?** | *It's still a bit expensive, isn't it?* |
| On aime beaucoup les soldes, **n'est-ce pas?** | *We like sales a lot, don't we?* |

### Essential Instruction

1. Review the instructions for **Activité 13**. Have students add important instruction words to their personal dictionary. Some additions might be **dessiner**, **diviner**, and **chaque fois**. Give students time to reflect and draw symbols of six activities that they can refer to when doing **Activité 13** in pairs or small groups.

2. Read as a class the explanation of **n'est-ce pas**. Ask students to create more examples orally in a round robin.

3. To introduce question formation with inversion, ask the students if they have ever heard the question **Parlez-vous français?** Then proceed with the explanation on p. 175.

4. Take students through the entire conjugation of **parler** pronouncing each question. Then show them how to invert each form and add the "**t**" (**parle-t-il, parle-t-elle**).

5. Discuss the question in **Comparaisons**, having the class come up with more examples of inversion.

## • inversion

A more formal way to ask a question in French, especially in written French, is to invert, or reverse the order of the verb and its subject pronoun. With simple inversion, the order is:

> verb - subject pronoun

**Fait-il** mauvais aujourd'hui?       *Is the weather bad today?*
[t]

**As-tu** besoin d'aller à la médiathèque?  *Do you need to go to the media center?*

Note that a hyphen connects the verb and its subject pronoun.

Inverting the subject pronoun **je** and its verb is not common. Instead, use **est-ce que** or raise your voice at the end of a sentence to form a question with **je**.

Est-ce que **j'**ai besoin d'un ticket?     *Do I need a ticket?*

When **il**, **elle**, or **on** are the subjects of a question and the verb form ends in a vowel, add a **t** between the verb and its subject pronoun. This **t** is pronounced.
                          [t]

Quand porte-**t**-il le blason?      *When does he wear the team logo?*

If the subject of the sentence is a noun, add the appropriate pronoun after the verb. This pronoun agrees with the subject noun in gender and in number.

Les footballeurs portent-**ils** le maillot   *Do the soccer players wear the blue jersey for*
bleu pour le match?   [t]          *the game?*

Sonia va-t-**elle** acheter un ballon de foot?  *Is Sonia going to buy a soccer ball?*
[t]

## COMPARAISONS   4.1

Does inversion ever occur when forming questions in English?

You are hungry.
Are you **thirsty** too?

COMPARAISONS: Inversion occurs in question formation in English also, with the subject pronoun and verb being switched from a normal declarative sentence: subject + verb + object.

Marcel va-t-il marquer un but?

---

## Differentiated Learning
### Expand
Create sentences that students will transform into yes/no and informational questions. Cut up each sentence into individual words and paperclip together. Have groups put the pieces of each question in order.

## Multiple Intelligences
### Bodily-Kinesthetic
Use a koosh ball to practice question formation. Have students stand in a circle. Say a sentence and a question word. Throw the ball to a student who must transform the sentence using the question word you provided and **est-ce que**. That student then says a sentence and a question word and throws the ball to another student. To prepare for this activity, have students write a list of sentences that they can use. Vary this game by asking students to create a question using inversion.

**Interpersonal: Paired Practice**
Have partners face each other. Using their quadrant illustrations from p. 174 for reference, instruct each pair to practice making and answering questions using inversion, **est-ce que**, and **n'est-ce pas**. Use a whistle or other signal to indicate when students should exchange papers with another pair and practice again.

**Answers** _____

**14**

1. Tu as les euros, n'est-ce pas?
2. Tu as les casquettes, n'est-ce pas?
3. Tu as les écharpes, n'est-ce pas?
4. Tu as le sac à dos, n'est-ce pas?
5. Tu as le blouson, n'est-ce pas?
6. Tu as les sacs à déjeuner, n'est-ce pas?

 **15**

1. Allez-vous au cinéma vendredi soir?
2. Jouons-nous aux jeux vidéo?
3. Étudie-t-elle la biologie dans le labo?
4. Vas-tu au match de basket?
5. Envoient-ils des textos dans la cantine?
6. Jouent-ils au foot samedi?
7. Écoutons-nous la prof d'histoire?
8. M. Michaud est-il intéressant?

**16**

1. A: Tu as un ballon de foot? As-tu un ballon de foot?
2. A: Les footballers portent des casquettes? Les footballers portent-ils des casquettes?
3. A: La prof d'anglais va aller au stade? La prof d'anglais va-t-elle aller au stade?
4. A: Tu voudrais voir l'équipe après? Voudrais-tu voir l'équipe après?
5. A: L'équipe va perdre? L'équipe, va-t-elle perdre?

---

**14** Nous allons au stade!  **2.1, 2.2**

Your friend is gathering things to bring to the French soccer game. Make sure he or she isn't forgetting anything essential!

 **Tu as le blason, n'est-ce pas?**

  1.  2.  3.

 4.  5.  6.

---

**15** Formons des questions!

*Utilisez l'inversion pour changer les phrases en questions.* (Use inversion to turn the statements into questions.)

1. Vous allez au cinéma vendredi soir.
2. Nous jouons aux jeux vidéo.
3. Elle étudie la biologie au labo.
4. Tu vas au match de basket.
5. Ils envoient des textos à la cantine.
6. Il joue au foot samedi.
7. Nous écoutons la prof d'histoire.
8. M. Michaud est intéressant.

 **2.1, 2.2**

L'équipe va-t-elle perdre? Non, elle ne va pas perdre.

---

**16** Pardon?  **2.1, 2.2**

*Votre partenaire n'entend rien au stade. Répétez chaque question en utilisant l'inversion. Ensuite, changez de rôles.* (Your partner can't hear well in the stadium. Repeat each question below using inversion. Then, switch roles.)

**MODÈLE** A: **Tu joues au football?**
B: **Pardon?**
A: **Joues-tu au football?**

1. Tu as un ballon de foot?
2. Les footballeurs portent des casquettes?
3. La prof d'anglais va aller au stade?
4. Tu voudrais aller voir l'équipe après?
5. L'équipe va perdre?

**1 7 6** cent soixante-seize | Unité 4

---

**Essential Instruction**

1. Have students do **Activité 14** with a partner.
2. After students write **Activité 15** individually, have them exchange papers with a partner and correct. Ask volunteers to write answers on the board and collectively correct.
3. You may want to have students do **Activité 16** as a chorus, with you re-stating the answer after they have given it, so that all students can hear if they used inversion correctly.
4. Do a quick brainstorm to see how students think the **Question centrale** is answered in **Leçon A**.
5. Have pairs present the dialogue in **Activité 17** to the rest of the class.

# À vous la parole

## Communiquez!

**Question centrale**
What activities do friends in other countries do together?

### 17 Combien d'euros pour soutenir mon équipe?

  1.1

**Interpersonal Communication**

You and a friend meet to go shopping at a French sporting goods store. In your conversation:

- greet each other.
- ask each other how things are going.
- find out what sports the other person likes.
- find out each other's favorite team.
- talk about what items you want to buy.
- say what you are going to buy and tell how much the items cost.
- tell each other good-bye.

## Communiquez!

### 18 Je suis un fan!  1.1, 1.3

**Presentational Communication**

Soccer is popular all around the world, and there are many professional teams in French-speaking countries. Start a collection of soccer trading cards by making two of your own.

1. Look online at examples of soccer trading cards.
2. Research a player on the French national team (**Les Bleus**).
3. Find a player from another francophone country, such as Senegal, Mali, or Algeria.
4. In French, write down each player's name, age, birthday, hometown, team name, position played, and other information you might find on a trading card.
5. Now make two cards. On one side, draw or glue a picture of the player. On the other side, write the information you found in French. Make copies of each card to post or trade with other students.

---

## RESOURCES

📖 **Communicative Activities**

### Answers

**17** *Answers will vary.*

**18** *Collections will vary.*

---

## Reference Desk

Check in with students about how they respond now to the **Question centrale**. How has what they've learned since the beginning of the **Unité** shaped their answer? Ask students to brainstorm key words or phrases from this lesson such as **rendez-vous au café**, **le foot**, **soutenir un club**, **acheter une écharpe**, etc. to inspire answers in French to the question.

### Blended Instruction

Consider using blended instruction, a combination of in-class learning and computer-mediated instruction or learning opportunities. Ask students to complete activities on the computer, using their cell or smartphone, or other emerging electronic technology. This will allow students to hone their tech skills and become more independent learners. Schedule routine Internet and e-book learning in class and in the lab.

---

## Differentiated Learning
### Decelerate

Show students a sample dialogue you create for **Activité 17** before asking them to create their own conversation. Or, have students list possible ways of expressing each item to use as a reference as they complete the dialogue.

## Multiple Intelligences
### Visual-Spatial

Assign students **Activité 18** to do at home. Have them create cards for soccer or another sport they choose and share their cards with classmates via a social media site.

Answers

**D**

1. F
2. M
3. M
4. F
5. F
6. M

# Prononciation  1.2

## Intonation

- In a sentence or clause, intonation rises or falls on the last syllable.

**A** **Les films**

*Repeat each pair of sentences. Pay close attention to the difference in intonation between the statement and the question in each pair.*

1. C'est un film policier.  Tu aimes les films policiers?
2. C'est une comédie.  Tu aimes les comédies?
3. C'est un film d'action.  Tu aimes les films d'action?
4. C'est un thriller.  Tu aimes les thrillers?

**B** **Au café**

*Repeat each pair of sentences, noting the slight rise in intonation in the middle of the second sentence.*

1. Je voudrais un sandwich.  Je voudrais un sandwich, s'il vous plaît.
2. Je voudrais un coca.  Je voudrais un coca, s'il vous plaît.
3. Je voudrais un café.  Je voudrais un café, s'il vous plaît.
4. Je voudrais une omelette.  Je voudrais une omelette, s'il vous plaît.

## The Nasal Sound /ɛ̃/, as in *le pain*

- The nasal sound /ɛ̃/ can be spelled **ain** or **in**. The **n** is not pronounced unless it occurs at the end of a word and the next word begins with a vowel.

**C** **Expressions nasales**

*Repeat the words and phrases that you hear.*

1. copain – matin – faim
2. Vers cinq heures. Vers quinze heures. Vers vingt heures.
3. alpin – demain

- With names, the **n** at the end is not pronounced, even if it is followed by a vowel, for example, **Justin est un copain.**

**D** **Les nationalités**

*Listen to the last vowel sound in these words and write **M** if it is nasal to indicate a masculine adjective of nationality. If the end vowel is not nasal, write **F** to indicate a feminine adjective.*

178

# Leçon B

## Vocabulaire actif

Go online EMCLanguages.net

### Au café   1.2

avoir faim/avoir soif

J'ai faim.                    J'ai soif.

un croque-monsieur

une eau minérale

une glace à la vanille

une limonade

un jus d'orange

un sandwich au fromage

---

### Reference Desk

1. Point out that in the United States, depending on the type of establishment, servers often bring the check while customers are still eating. In casual restaurants in the United States one commonly hears, "You can pay me when you're ready." In France, the check must be requested and generally doesn't come while people are still eating.

2. Most restaurants in France offer a two- or three-course meal, usually with appetizer, main course, and dessert (or coffee) at a fixed price that is generally more economical than ordering **à la carte**.

3. Students should address a waiter or waitress in France using formal language. In the United States, many restaurants strive to create an informal atmosphere in which wait staff will introduce themselves by their first name. In France waiters are friendly, but they usually maintain formal register in speaking with guests, especially if they are brand new customers. Along with **s'il vous plaît**, you may also wish to teach students **s'il te plaît**.

---

**Multiple Intelligences**
**Bodily-Kinesthetic**
To reinforce meaning, act out **j'ai faim** and **j'ai soif** and then ask the students, **Et toi?** They can answer affirmatively or practice the negative structure **Je n'ai pas faim/soif.**

un sandwich au jambon

une omelette

une quiche

un steak-frites

**les desserts (m.):**

une glace au chocolat

une crêpe

**les boissons(m.):**

un coca

un café

| 100 | cent |
| 101 | cent un |
| 102 | cent deux |
| 200 | deux cents |
| 201 | deux cent un |
| 202 | deux cent deux |
| 300 | trois cents |

| 400 | quatre cents | 800 | huit cents |
| 500 | cinq cents | 900 | neuf cents |
| 600 | six cents | 1.000 | mille |
| 700 | sept cents | | |

## Pour la conversation 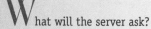 1.2

**W**hat will the server ask?

> **Vous désirez?**
> *What would you like?*

> **Et comme** boisson?
> *And to drink?*

**H**ow do I order in a café or restaurant?

> **Donnez-moi** la spécialité du jour.
> *Give me the daily special.*

> **Je vais prendre** le menu fixe.
> *I'll take the fixed-price menu.*

**H**ow do I ask for the bill?

> **L'addition, s'il vous plaît.**
> *The bill, please.*

### Et si je voulais dire...?

| | |
|---|---|
| **un café au lait** | *coffee with milk* |
| **un citron pressé** | *lemonade* |
| **un lait chocolat** | *chocolate milk* |
| **une menthe à l'eau** | *water with mint flavored syrup* |
| **un Orangina** | *orange soda* |
| **un thé** | *tea* |
| **un croque–madame** | *croque–monsieur with egg on top* |
| **un sandwich au pâté** | *pâté sandwich* |
| **Vous avez choisi?** | *Have you decided?* |

### Essential Instruction

1. Point out the use of the preposition **à** + the definite article in **un sandwich au fromage, une glace à la vanille,** etc., to designate the major ingredient or flavor of the food item. Explain the difference between **le menu fixe** and **à la carte**.

2. Model the pronunciation of the numbers. Connect the word **mille** to what students may already know about the metric system, or related English words, such as millennium (a 1000th anniversary or period of time). Teach the expression **merci mille fois**.

3. Have students create and present mini-dialogues using the vocabulary and expressions.

4. Ask for a student volunteer to be the server in **Activité 3** and tell the chef (you) what he or she needs.

## 1 Avez-vous faim? Avez-vous soif?  2.1, 2.2

*Ces personnes ont faim et/ou soif. Écrivez la lettre de l'image qui correspond à chaque phrase.*

A.　　　　B.

1. Martine a soif.
2. Claude a très soif.
3. J'ai faim.
4. Tu as faim et soif.
5. Bruno a très faim.

C.

D.　　　　E.

Chloé et Martin ont-ils faim ou soif?

## 2 Une fête chez Jérémy  2.1

*Écrivez **A** si la personne à la fête de Jérémy a soif ou **B** si elle a faim.*

A. La personne a soif.
B. La personne a faim.

## 3 Au Café du Sport  1.3

Imagine you are the server at the café. Write down a list of what everyone is ordering to take to the kitchen.

Martine et moi, nous allons prendre des sandwichs au jambon et des limonades. Karim va prendre une quiche et un coca. Saleh et Justine vont prendre des crêpes et des cocas. Tu vas prendre un croque-monsieur et un café. Marie-Alix va prendre un steak-frites et une eau minérale.

**Answers** _____

**1**
1. D
2. C
3. A
4. E
5. B

**2** Script can be found in the front pages of the Annotated Teacher's Edition.
1. A
2. A
3. B
4. B
5. A
6. B
7. A
8. B
9. A
10. A

**3** *Answers will vary.*

### Reference Desk

1. Introduce evocative idioms to your students, like **avoir une faim de loup** or **avoir soif d'apprendre**. Ask students to illustrate these sayings and display them in class. Discuss the difference between the literal translation and the actual, familiar meaning of these expressions. What idiomatic expressions using food vocabulary do we use in English?
2. The word **faim** is commonly mispronounced by English speakers and confused with something that resembles **femme**. Remind students about silent final consonants in French.

### Learning Styles
**Visual Learners**
Write the numbers 100, 101, 110, 200, 201, 220, etc., on the board and spell them out in an adjacent column. Highlight the letter "s" in a different color. Explain that the plural "s" is added only to numbers ending in 00.

### Multiple Intelligences
**Visual-Spatial**
To reinforce the expressions **avoir faim** and **avoir soif**, use flash cards, e-visuals, or bring in pictures of the food and beverage items presented in the vocabulary. Have students answer as a class with **Nous avons faim** or **Nous avons soif** according to the visual prompt. Then, ask students to answer individually with either **j'ai faim** or **j'ai soif**. Finally, have them ask you the question, **Vous avez faim/soif?**

### Expansion

Design three blank checks on a sheet of paper. Make copies for each student. Tell students about a meal, including prices in euros, they had at **Les Deux Magots**, **le Café de Flore**, and **la Brasserie Lipp**. Have students write down the prices, add them up, and make out a check to pay for each meal.

**4** La commande  2.1

*Dans votre groupe, donnez votre commande (order) au serveur.*

MODÈLE **Je vais prendre un hamburger et des frites.**

1.

2.

3.

4.

5.

6.

7.

**5** Problèmes de maths  2.1, 2.2

*Donnez les solutions à ces problèmes mathématiques.*

MODÈLE    $342 + 651 = 993$
**neuf cent quatre-vingt-treize**

1. $285 - 137 = ?$
2. $178 + 602 = ?$
3. $202 - 101 = ?$
4. $433 + 141 = ?$

5. $113 + 257 = ?$
6. $314 + 553 = ?$
7. $979 - 389 = ?$
8. $543 + 457 = ?$

9. $678 + 221 = ?$
10. $276 + 178 = ?$
11. $745 + 133 = ?$

### Essential Instruction

1. Teach **plus**, **moins**, and **égale**.
2. Before assigning **Activité 5** in pairs, review numbers 1–99. Have students stand and count off from 1–99. Each student who says a multiple of the number five (or another number you choose) must sit down. Vary this activity by directing students to count off by even or odd numbers (**pairs** or **impairs**).
3. Expedite the work in **Activité 6** by dividing the class into three groups. Assign one receipt to each group. When finished, students exchange their answers with another group for peer correction.
4. Ask students to read the **Questions personnelles** silently for comprehension, then to interview a partner. Write the results of popular preferences on the board.

## 6 De nouveaux cafés
2.1, 2.2

The owners of four new cafés need to buy **chaises**, **tables**, and **parasols** (*umbrellas*). Write out the total cost in euros of these items.

**MODÈLE**

73 chaises @ 12€
24 tables @ 20€
24 parasols @ 31€
Total 👉
9/11/13      16h26

**Les chaises coûtent huit cent soixante-seize euros, les tables coûtent quatre cent quatre-vingt euros, et les parasols coûtent sept cent quarante-quatre euros.**

**1. Café Bernard**

42 chaises @ 11€
11 tables @ 23€
11 parasols @33€
Tot
3/2/13      13h48
SERVICE IS NOT INCLUDED
THANK YOU

**2. Café Toulon**

110 chaises @ 7€
30 tables @ 21€
30 parasols @ 19€
Tot
15/11/13      9h50
SERVICE IS NOT INCLUDED
THANK YOU

**3. Café Grand Prix**

25 chaises @ 17€
5 tables @ 26€
5 parasols @ 35€
total 👉
21/11/13      18h50

## Communiquez!

## 7 Questions personnelles
1.1

### Interpersonal Communication

1. Tu aimes aller au café?
2. Qu'est-ce que tu manges au café?
3. Tu préfères un sandwich ou un hamburger?
4. Qu'est-ce que tu aimes comme boisson?
5. Est-ce que tu préfères un coca ou une limonade?
6. Qu'est-ce que tu aimes comme dessert?
7. Tu préfères une glace au chocolat ou une glace à la vanille?

*Je mange une glace au café.*

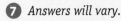

## Answers

**6**

1. Les chaises coûtent **quatre cent soixante-deux** euros, les tables coûtent **deux cent cinquante-trois** euros, et les parasols coûtent **trois cent soixante-trois** euros.
2. Les chaises coûtent **sept cent soixante-dix** euros, les tables coûtent **six cent trente** euros, et les parasols coûtent **cinq cent soixante-dix** euros.
3. Les chaises coûtent **quatre cent vingt-cinq** euros, les tables coûtent **cent trente** euros, et les parasols coûtent **cent soixante-quinze** euros.

**7** *Answers will vary.*

### Reference Desk

Both **cent** and **vingt** have a final "s" when multiplied by another number and not followed by another number. For example, **400** is written as **quatre cents**, but **405** is written as **quatre cent cinq**. Also: **vingt joueurs** and **quatre-vingt-trois tickets**, but **quatre-vingts spectateurs**. **Cent** is invariable when it relates to a percentage figure: **90 pour cent des élèves**. **Mille** (1000) is never changed (7000 = **sept mille personnes**).

Leçon B  |  cent quatre-vingt-trois **183**

### Learning Styles
### Auditory Learners

1. For listening practice of numbers, say several numbers between 0–1.000 and ask students to write the corresponding numerals on dry-erase boards or paper. Check their answers.
2. For **Activité 5**, ask for a volunteer to go to the board to compute the math problems. The first student to arrive at the answer gets to say that number out loud for the student at the board, who will then write it on the board. Continue with other volunteers.

**Answers**

1. Elles sont au café.
2. Non, Yasmine a un peu faim.
3. Elle va prendre un jus d'orange et un sandwich au fromage.
4. Camille va prendre un coca, un croque-monsieur, une salade, et des frites.
5. Camille va prendre une crêpe à la confiture et Yasmine une glace à la vanille.

**Extension**

Nicolas and Marie seem to be a couple because Marie says, "À la nôtre," whereby the collective implies they are "an item."

## Reference Desk

1. Point out the difference between **la carte** (the menu) and **le menu** (a fixed-price meal formula). In addition to fixed-price meals, many restaurants also offer the **plat du jour**, or daily special. This is usually available in a fixed-price meal format, but it can also be ordered separately. Point out too that **à la carte** means choosing items individually rather than as part of a fixed-price **menu**.
2. Remind students reading the **Extension** dialogue of the two pronunciations of "G" in French: as a soft consonant in the combination **ge** and **gi**, as in **Orangina, fromage**, and **génial**, and a hard "G" in the combination **ga, go,** and **gu**, as in **gants, Magots**, and **guignol**.

# Rencontres culturelles

## Bon appétit!     1.2

Camille and Yasmine are at the café.

Camille: Tu as faim?
Yasmine: Un peu, mais j'ai surtout soif.
Serveuse: Vous désirez?
Yasmine: Un jus d'orange, mais on va regarder la carte....
Camille: Et moi un coca. Ah, je sais, donnez-moi un croque-monsieur avec... une salade et des frites, s'il vous plaît.
Yasmine: Tout ça? Bon, alors moi, je vais prendre un sandwich au fromage.

Serveuse: Voilà, mesdemoiselles. Bon appétit!
Y et C: Merci.

Serveuse: Des desserts?
Camille: Oh! Oui... une crêpe à la confiture.
Yasmine: Euh non. Pour moi, rien merci... enfin si... je prends une glace à la vanille.
Serveuse: Très bien.

### 8 Bon appétit!   2.1, 2.2

*Répondez aux questions.*

1. Où sont Camille et Yasmine?
2. Est-ce que Yasmine a très faim?
3. Qu'est-ce qu'elle va prendre?
4. Qu'est-ce que Camille va prendre?
5. Les filles vont prendre quels desserts?

**Extension** Le restaurant du coin

Nicolas a invité (*has invited*) Marie à manger dans un restaurant du quartier.

Nicolas: Alors, poisson ou viande?
Marie: Poisson.
Nicolas: Menu ou plat du jour?
Marie: Plat du jour: la bouillabaisse!
Nicolas: Pour moi, le menu—la salade grecque, les côtes d'agneau. J'ai très, très faim!
Marie: Et comme boisson?
Nicolas: Comme toi.
Marie: Alors, de l'eau minérale. Je te sers.
Nicolas: À la tienne!
Marie: À la nôtre!

**Extension** Are Nicolas and Marie a couple? Justify your response.

**Essential Instruction**

1. Show the filmed dialogue. Then ask the class to read the dialogue. Explain any new vocabulary, model the correct pronunciation, and have students practice the dialogue three times in groups of three, playing a different role each time. Ask students to do **Activité 8** with their dialogue partners. Show the video a second time, and ask students how much more they understood.

2. Read **Les cafés et les bistros**. Ask the students to reflect on why so many cafes in France have disappeared. Survey the class about where they get together with friends and ask if anyone has seen the film **Amélie**.

3. Ask if students know any books written by the authors mentioned in **Les cafés et les écrivains**. Write some titles on the board.

# Points de départ

 **Go online** **EMC**Languages.net

**Question centrale**

**?**

What activities do friends in other countries do together?

**RESOURCES**

 **Workbook 25–26**

## Les cafés et les bistros  1.2, 3.1, 4.2

At the beginning of the 20th century, there were 500,000 cafés and bistros in France. Today about 35,000 remain. Nevertheless, the French still think of the corner café as a place where regulars gather to talk about what's going on in the neighborhood and where friends meet to catch up on each other's lives. The film *Le fabuleux destin d'Amélie Poulain* provides a glimpse into this tradition. Today, Internet cafés and small restaurants serving organic food have replaced some of the traditional cafés in order to meet the needs of their 21st century clientele.

There are some Internet cafés in Paris.

 **Search words: le fabuleux destin d'amélie poulain**

**Reference Desk**

You may choose to show selected scenes from the movie **Amélie**. French films often have strong content and should be carefully screened before use in classrooms.

 **Produits**

The **croissant** is served in many French cafés. Similar in shape to an American crescent roll, it is a buttery flaky bread or pastry. The word "croissant" first appeared in a dictionary in 1863, and the first recipe was published in 1891, but it is unclear when the croissant was invented.

 4.1, 4.2

## Les cafés et les écrivains  1.2, 3.1, 4.2

French author Albert Camus (1913–1960) also frequented Les Deux Magots.

Many Parisian cafés have become famous over the years because of the writers associated with them. In the 18th century, writer-philosophers like Voltaire met over coffee to discuss politics at the café Procope. In the 1920s, American writers Ernest Hemingway and F. Scott Fitzgerald used to frequent the cafés La Coupole, Le Dôme, and Le Select on **le boulevard Montparnasse.** In the 1940s and 1950s, Jean-Paul Sartre and Simone de Beauvoir, two writers associated with a literary and artistic movement called existentialism, used to write at two other Left Bank establishments, the Café de Flore and Deux Magots. Today this literary tradition continues at the Café Drouant where each year France's highest literary honor, the Prix Goncourt, is awarded.

 **Search words: pages de paris, cafés**

## Differentiated Learning
### Accelerate
Have students read the **Extension** dialogue silently. Then divide the class in half and have each half role-play a character. Switch roles.

### Decelerate
Ask students to bring in pictures of the people and places mentioned in the paragraph **Les cafés et les écrivains** and present one or two interesting facts about each.

## Special Needs Students
### Auditory Impairment
Encourage students to listen to the dialogue outside of class so they can pause and take more time to process it when needed, bringing sound, picture, and script together.

**9**

1. 465,000
2. They have become famous because they were frequented by famous writers.
3. It rewards literary texts.
4. Quick
5. Students choose two: Flunch, Paul, Délifrance, la Brioche Dorée, le Relais H, la Viennoisière, Pizza del Arte
6. burgers, pizzas, crêpes, waffles, gyros, sandwiches

**Perspectives**

French people tend to be conscious of the health problems caused by too much fast food.

---

## Culture

**Products: Activity**

Have students discuss the following topics in groups and share the results of their conversations.

**Le fast-food:** Are the French highly influenced by American fast-food? If so, in what ways?

**Les Prix littéraires:** Do we have literary prizes in America? Has the café intersected with literature and art in America?

**History of cafés:** European cafés have a long history of association with writers and artists. Students can research the history of European cafés and study the development from inns and public houses (or "pubs"), links to the discovery of the New World and the importation of tea and coffee, the rise of the French salon in the 18th c., coffee houses, taverns, and clubs, the influence of travelers and immigrants, changing eating habits and new freedoms, postwar creativity, and global travel.

---

## Les fast-foods  1.2, 3.1, 4.2

McDonald's, or **chez McDo**, is the number one fast-food chain in France. Quick is a French equivalent. Both of these restaurant chains, as well as KFC, Subway, Pizza Hut, and Planet Sushi, can be found in towns, cities, and shopping malls all over France. Other French fast-food restaurants include Flunch, Paul, Délifrance, la Brioche Dorée, le Relais H, la Viennoisière, and Pizza Del Arte. In addition to chain restaurants, there are snack shops everywhere. They sell crepes, waffles, gyros, and other types of sandwiches. Some people in France call fast food the **mal bouffe** because it has led to a growing problem of obesity and other medical problems.

 **Search words: quick hamburger restaurant, flunch, pizza del arte, délifrance**

---

**9** **Questions culturelles**  2.1, 2.2

*Répondez aux questions.*

1. How many cafés and bistros have disappeared since the beginning of the 20th century?
2. Why are the Procope, La Coupole, and the Café de Flore famous?
3. What does the **Prix Goncourt** reward?
4. What is the French equivalent of McDonald's?
5. What are the names of two French fast-food restaurants?
6. What types of fast food are available in France?

**Perspectives**

What attitudes toward American fast food do the French hold?

The Quick fast-food chain originated in Belgium.

---

**Essential Instruction**

1. Have the students complete **Activités 9** and **10** in pairs. Connect student learning of **à** + definite article in **un sandwich au fromage** to **une soupe aux légumes** (major ingredient).
2. Discuss possible reasons why the French fast food company **Quick** chose an American name for its chain. Compare to stores or restaurants in the United States with French names and what kind of image they project.
3. Remind students to use the formal **vous** with the **serveur**, but **tu** between the two customer friends when role-playing **Activité 11**. Switching from **tu** to **vous** will help cement proper pronoun usage in students.

## Du côté des médias

*Lisez la carte.*

**10  Au restaurant végétarien du Québec**  1.2, 2.1, 2.2

1. What is a **soupe aux légumes**?
2. What comes with a serving of quiche?
3. How much extra does a **salade César** cost?
4. Until what time are sandwiches served?

### Menu Végétarien
Vegetarian Menu

*Soupe aux légumes gratinée / Baked vegetable soup* ...6.95

#### Quiches

Les quiches sont servies avec salade du chef (pour César + $1.50)
Quiches are served with a chef's salad (for Caesar + $1.50)

*Quiche aux 5 fromages / 5 Cheese Quiche* ...9.95
Suisse, Brick, Mozzarella, Gruyère et Parmesan

*Quiche Provençale / Vegetable Quiche* ... 9.95
Avec tomates, courgettes, oignons, olives noires et fromage suisse, Brie et Mozzarella
With tomatoes, zucchini, onions, black olives and Swiss, Brie and Mozzarella cheese

#### Sandwiches

*Servis jusqu'à 17 h. / Served until 5 pm*
Les Sandwiches sont servis sur pain baguette avec salade du chef (César ou soupe + $1.50).
Sandwiches are served on a French baguette with a chef's salad (Ceasar or soup + $1.50)

*Avocat végétarien / Vegetarian avocado* ...8.95
Avec laitue, tomates, avocats et pesto
With lettuce, tomatoes, avocado and pesto

*Végétarien au fromage / Cheese Vegetarian* ...8.95
Avec fromage Brie, oignons caramélisés et tomates
With Brie cheese, caramelised onions and tomatoes

## Communiquez!

**11  Vous désirez?** 1.1

### Interpersonal Communication

With two classmates, act out the following scene between two customers and their server. In the conversation:

- the server and the two customers greet each other.
- the server asks what the customers would like from the menu above.
- each customer politely orders something from the menu.
- the server repeats the order and thanks the customers.

**RESOURCES**

 **e-visual 14**

 **Workbook 27**

**Answers** _____

**10**

1. a vegetable soup
2. a chef salad
3. $1.50
4. 5:00 p.m

**11** *Conversations will vary.*

---

**Differentiated Learning**
**Adapt**
Ask students to find online and print out a French menu to share with the class and use it in **Activité 11**.

**Learning Styles**
**Visual Learners**
For fun, ask students to research French idiomatic expressions with food, such as **manger sur le pouce** (to have a quick bite to eat) and illustrate them. Discuss and display the results around the classroom.

## Structure de la langue

**Answers**

Answers _____

12 Script can be found in the front pages of the Annotated Teacher's Edition.

1. 1
2. 1
3. 2
4. 2
5. 1

### Reference Desk

Point out to students the difference between using **manger** and **prendre** with respect to food. Write **Je mange une salade.** and **Je prends une salade.** on the board. What is the difference in meaning? The first sentence indicates that you are in the process of eating something. In the second sentence, you are going to have or choose that food item. Ask students to describe situations or scenarios when they would use one or the other of these similar statements. Mention the use of **prendre** when referring to eating a meal, such as in **Je prends le déjeuner à la cantine.**

## Present Tense of the Irregular Verb *prendre*  1.2

The verb **prendre** means "to take" and is irregular. **Prendre** can also mean "to have" when referring to something to eat or drink.

| prendre | | | |
|---|---|---|---|
| je | **prends** | nous | **prenons** |
| tu | **prends** | vous | **prenez** |
| il/elle/on | **prend** | ils/elles | **prennent** |

Est-ce que Justine prend une décision?

Qu'est-ce que tu **prends**? *What are you taking?*
**Je prends** mon cahier d'histoire. *I'm taking my history notebook.*

The **d** is pronounced [t] in the inverted forms of **il/elle/on: Prend-on une glace?**
　　　　　　　　　　　　　　　　　　　　　　　　　　[t]

Other verbs that follow the pattern of **prendre** include **apprendre** (*to learn*) and **comprendre** (*to understand*).

---

**12  Qu'est-ce qu'on va prendre?**
　　　　　　　　　　　　　　　　　　　　　　　　2.1

*Tout le monde prend quelque chose à manger ou à boire. Écrivez **1** si on parle d'une personne ou **2** si on parle de deux ou plusieurs personnes.* (Everyone is having something to eat or drink. Write **1** if what you hear refers to one person or **2** if it refers to two people or more.)

**COMPARAISONS**
　　　　　　　　　　　　　　　　4.1

Prendre is also used in a number of idiomatic expressions that can't be translated word for word into English. One such expression is prendre une décision (*to make a decision*). How many idiomatic expressions in English can you think of that use the verb "to take"?

COMPARAISONS: A few idiomatic expressions that use the verb "to take" include: to take a fancy (to something), to take away, to take off, to take (something) out on someone, to take to someone, to take someone up (on an offer), to take into account.

### Essential Instruction

1. Write the forms of the verb **prendre** on the board, model the pronunciation, and do a round-robin practice. Ask students **Qu'est ce que tu prends pour le déjeuner aujourd'hui?** Elicit several responses from the class.
2. Discuss **Comparaisons** together and the concept of idiomatic expressions. Provide some examples of idiomatic expressions in English and ask students to make a short list of some others.

Explain that in England the expression "to take a decision" is commonly used instead of "to make a decision," revealing the influence of French on English spoken in Britain.
3. Have the class do **Activité 13** in pairs.

## 13 On prend quoi?  2.1, 2.2

*Dites ce que tout le monde prend.*

> un lecteur mp3   des euros   un blason du PSG   des chaussures de foot
> un dictionnaire français-allemand   un stylo

1. Je vais jouer au foot.
2. Joëlle va avoir un cours d'allemand.
3. Tu vas aller à la teuf d'Éric.
4. Abdoul et moi, nous allons aller au match.
5. Hamza et Clara vont faire les devoirs.
6. Guillaume et toi, vous faites du shopping.

## 14 Les amis au café 2.1, 2.2

*Dites ce que tout le monde prend au café.*

1. les footballeurs

2. Michèle

3. moi, je

4. toi, tu

5. Nathalie et toi, vous

6. Karim et moi, nous

Answers _____

**13**

1. Je prends des chaussures de foot.
2. Elle prend un dictionnaire français-allemand.
3. Tu prends un lecteur mp3.
4. Nous prenons un blason du PSG.
5. Elles prennent un stylo.
6. Vous prenez des euros.

**14**

1. Les footballeurs prennent des crêpes.
2. Michèle prend un croque-monsieur.
3. Moi, je prends une glace au chocolat.
4. Toi, tu prends une quiche.
5. Nathalie et toi, vous prenez une limonade.
6. Karim et moi, nous prenons un steak-frites.

### Expansion

Have students make food and beverage picture cards or use vocabulary flash cards. Ask them to identify the item(s) on the cards using a sentence. For example, for a picture of ice cream, a student might say, **Je prends une glace!** Review and emphasize the use of the partitive with **prendre**. Have students sort out cards to make a complete meal and say what they are going to have.

Leçon B | cent quatre-vingt-neuf **189**

---

**Differentiated Learning**
**Expand**
Practice the verb **prendre** orally by asking students to respond to your cues. For example, you might ask, **Je prends une glace. Et vous?** to which the student responds, **Nous prenons une glace.** Use a different subject in each question as you continue this exercise.

**Special Needs Students**
**Auditory Impairment/Linguistically Challenged**
Prepare flash cards with subject pronouns and conjugated verb forms that the pairs can visually match.

**Answers** _____

**15** *Role plays will vary.*

### Reference Desk

Discuss the error in the phrase **Je suis faim** with your students. Ask if they understand why this is such a common error by English speakers who are learning to speak French. Ask students for the correct way to express this idea. Poll the class to find out if they have come across other French expressions that have caused problems for them so far.

 *Communiquez!*

**15 Au Café Splendide!** 1.1

**Interpersonal Communication**

*Avec deux partenaires, jouez les rôles du serveur et deux clients dans un café. Le serveur demande ce que (what) les clients prennent et les clients commandent quelque chose (order something) à manger et à boire (to drink). Utilisez la carte et suivez le modèle.*

Qu'est-ce que vous prenez?

**MODÈLE**

A: **Qu'est-ce que vous prenez?**
B: **Moi, je prends une salade et un coca. Et toi, qu'est-ce que tu prends?**
C: **Moi, je prends une pizza et une eau minérale.**
A: **D'accord... vous prenez une salade, une pizza, un coca et une eau minérale.**

 ***Avoir* Expressions: *avoir faim/soif***

1.2

You already know the expression **avoir besoin de** (*to need*). Two more **avoir** expressions are **avoir faim** (*to be hungry*) and **avoir soif** (*to be thirsty*).

Chloé a soif et Michel a faim.

 **COMPARAISONS** 4.1

J'ai soif.

Literally, the French sentences says "I have thirst." Which verb is used to express hunger and thirst in English?

I am hungry.
She is thirsty.

COMPARAISONS: To express hunger and thirst in English, speakers use the verb "to be."

**190** cent quatre-vingt-dix | Unité 4

**Essential Instruction**

1. Have groups prepare and present the dialogue for **Activité 15**. Review with students when to use the formal **vous** form, such as with wait staff in a restaurant. Discuss how to appropriately get the attention of a waiter or waitress in French (**S'il vous plait.**) and compare that to American practices ("Excuse me.", etc.) in the same situation.

2. Introduce the expressions **avoir faim/soif** by holding up pictures of food and drink items and say that you are hungry or thirsty. Randomly distribute pictures of food and beverage items. Ask if the students are hungry or thirsty. Have students ask a partner about what they eat and drink when they are hungry and thirsty.

16
1. Gabrielle prend un coca.
2. Alima et Cédric prennent une pizza.
3. Moi, je prends un sandwich au fromage.
4. Rose prend une omelette et une limonade.
5. Virginie et Sandrine prennent un steak-frites.
6. Augustin et toi, vous prenez une limonade.
7. Alexandre prend une quiche.
8. Toi, tu prends une glace au chocolat.

 **16  À Flunch**    2.1, 2.2

*Vous êtes à Flunch avec des amis. D'après (Based on) les images, dites si ces personnes ont faim, soif ou les deux. Ensuite, dites ce qu'elles prennent.*

**MODÈLE**  Hugo et Antoine
**Ils ont faim. Donc, ils prennent un sandwich au jambon.**

1. Gabrielle et Annie  2. Alima et Cédric  3. moi, je

4. Rose  5. Virginie et Sandrine  6. Augustin et toi, vous

7. Alexandre  8. toi, tu

Rose a-t-elle faim ou soif?

Leçon B  |  cent quatre-vingt-onze  **191**

**Game**

Divide students into two teams. Have them line up facing each other. One student begins by naming a food, beverage, or a noun related to items needed for sports. The corresponding partner from the other team responds with an expression appropriate for the item, using **avoir** (**faim/soif/besoin de**). For example, if the first student says, **une eau minérale**, the partner might say, **J'ai soif! Je prends une eau minérale!** When finished, pairs go to the end of the opposite line.

**Differentiated Learning**

**Expand**
Ask students to guess where the name **Flunch** came from. Could it be a combination of two words (fast and lunch)?

**Decelerate**
Have students translate sentences from French that contain the idiomatic expressions with **avoir**. To reinforce the difference between English and French, you might also have them translate sentences into French that require these expressions.

**Answers** _____

**17** *Conversations will vary.*

**18** *Answers will vary.*

## Reference Desk

For **Activité 18**, you may want to provide students with a list of websites for two or three each of a variety of cafés (vegetarian, famous cafés, organic, and sports) to help them get started. To reinforce their cultural understanding, students could point to the location of this café on your wall map of Paris as they speak.

### Blended Instruction

Consider using blended instruction, a combination of in-class learning and computer-mediated instruction or learning opportunities. Ask students to complete activities on the computer, using their cell or smartphone, or other emerging electronic technology. This will allow students to hone their tech skills and become more independent learners. Schedule routine Internet and e-book learning in class and in the lab.

# À vous la parole

**Communiquez!**

**Question centrale** — What activities do friends in other countries do together?

## 17 On va au café? 1.1

### Interpersonal Communication

You invite a new student to meet your friends at a café. One person in your group will play the role of the server. In your conversation:

- greet each other.
- introduce the new student.
- ask each other how things are going.
- the server greets the group and everyone orders something to eat and drink.
- the server repeats the order and leaves.
- discuss what you are going to do this weekend.
- the server returns with the food and wishes everyone a good meal.
- one person asks for the check.
- the server brings the check and everyone discusses the cost of each item.
- tell each other good-bye.

**Communiquez!**

## 18 Découvrez les cafés de Paris! 1.3

### Presentational Communication

Find a café, for example, a cybercafé, a sports café, a vegetarian café, an organic café, in Paris for each person below. Then write the name and address of the café and a sentence in French (see the model).

> **MODÈLE** **Brad va au Café du Stade.**

1. Clarissa is a vegetarian who eats eggs.
2. Justin likes to use the Internet while having lunch.
3. Mrs. Petersen believes in the slow food movement.
4. Brad likes to watch sporting events while eating a sandwich.
5. Ms. Blair will only eat food that has not been sprayed for insecticides.
6. Mr. Burton likes to frequent cafés where artists like Picasso used to spend time.

**192** cent quatre-vingt-douze | Unité 4

## Essential Instruction

1. For **Activité 17**, if possible, provide props such as a serving tray, menus, a waiter's apron, and a tablecloth.

2. For **Activité 19**, have students categorize the underlined elements in the second version of the story by parts of speech. You may wish to have them add these words to their personal dictionary, if they have one, according to part of speech. Learning about language in this way can increase students' understanding of their own language.

3. When assigning **Activité 20** remind students to keep meaning as well as structure in mind as they select words from the box.

# Stratégie communicative

## Writing Descriptions

To make a story more interesting, include adjectives, adverbs, and other details.

 **19 Comparez les paragraphes** 2.1, 2.2

The two stories below are essentially the same, but the second version has more detail. Make a list of the adjectives, adverbs, and other details that make the second version of the story more interesting.

C'est samedi. Il fait beau. J'ai soif. Je veux sortir avec mes amis au café. Je veux aller au café pour prendre une boisson et une glace. Après, je vais voir un film avec Corinne et son copain, Lucas! Il est comment Lucas? Ah, c'est une surprise!

C'est samedi. Il est 4h00. Il fait beau et j'ai très soif. Je veux sortir avec mes amis au café algérien devant le cinéma. Je voudrais aller au café pour prendre une eau minérale avec une glace à la vanille ou au chocolat. Après, je vais voir un film américain avec Corinne et son nouveau copain, Lucas! Il est comment Lucas? Ah, c'est une surprise!

 **20 Le portrait de Lucas** 2.1, 2.2

*Complétez chaque phrase avec un adjectif ou adverbe de la liste pour améliorer (improve) ce portrait de Lucas.*

| canadien | difficile | intéressant | intelligent | drôle | beaucoup de |
| génial | alternative | américaines | nouveau | bien | |

1. Le... copain de Corinne s'appelle Lucas.
2. C'est un garçon....
3. Il aime... films, surtout les comédies....
4. Il aime... écouter la musique....

 **21 Un portrait** 1.3

Imagine you see a girl with your friend's jacket with the PSG logo at a café and decide to call your friend. Write what you say to her: describe the girl, where you see her, what she is doing, and what she is wearing, plus any other important details.

**Answers**

**19** 4h00, très soif, algérien, une eau minérale, à la vanille, au chocolat, américain,

**20**
1. nouveau
2. intéressant/génial/intelligent/ drôle
3. beaucoup de; américaines
4. bien; alternative

**21** *Answers will vary.*

### Reference Desk

For **Activité 19**, have students work in pairs or do peer editing using a checklist before turning in their assignment.

### Expansion

Make a list of activities to do, such as **voir un film**, **regarder le match**, **prendre le métro**, **sortir au café**, etc. using as much vocabulary as possible from the **Unités** so far. As you read out the list, ask students to respond spontaneously with appropriate adjectives, such as **c'est génial**, **intéressant**, etc. Adjectives after **c'est** are in the masculine form.

**Differentiated Learning**

**Accelerate**
Have students create their own description of a person or scene, including as much detail as possible. Ask them to exchange with a partner who will then create a drawing to correspond to the description.

**Decelerate**
Make a template of the conversation for **Activité 17** in which you begin each sentence for the students to complete. To further simplify the activity, write out a sample conversation, and underline the parts that you want the students to change.

# Vocabulaire actif

 Go online **EMC**Languages.net

## Au cinéma   1.2

### Les genres (m.) de film

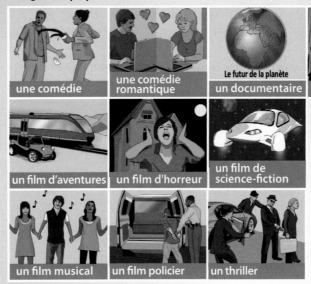

une comédie

une comédie romantique

un documentaire · Le futur de la planète

un drame

un film d'action

un film d'aventures

un film d'horreur

un film de science-fiction

un film musical

un film policier

un thriller

 Paris, je t'aime

Paris, je t'aime

19h30 · le guichet

en avance

Paris, je t'aime

19h30 · le guichet

à l'heure

Paris, je t'aime

19h30 · le guichet

en retard

### Essential Instruction

1. Introduce movie genres by asking your students, **Qui aime les comédies?** and providing an example of a recent film to reinforce understanding. Ask students to name a comedy they like and add to a list on the board. Do this with all the movie genres. You may wish to explain the use of **de/d'** between nouns, such as in **un film d'action** (a movie of action).

2. After listening to the audio and practicing pronunciation of the new vocabulary, poll the class about who is early, late, or on time to various classes or other places.

3. Present the expressions in **Pour la conversation**, and ask students to name a genre or specific movie that would elicit the response **Tu vas rire.** or **Tu vas pleurer.**

Clovis Cornillac

**un acteur**

Vanessa Paradis

**une actrice**

Clovis Cornillac **joue le rôle** d'un pingouin (*penguin*) dans le film *Happy Feet*.
George Miller est **le metteur en scène** de *Happy Feet*.

## Pour la conversation   1.2

**H**ow do I make a prediction?

> **Tu vas aimer ça.**
> *You're going to like it.*

> **Tu vas rire.**
> *You're going to laugh.*

> **Tu vas pleurer.**
> *You're going to cry.*

**H**ow do I respond to a prediction?

> **Peut-être.**
> *Maybe.*

> **On va voir.**
> *We'll see.*

**Et si je voulais dire...?**

| | |
|---|---|
| **l'écran (m.)** | *screen* |
| **un billet de cinéma** | *movie ticket* |
| **chialer** | *to cry (slang)* |
| **un navet** | *bad movie* |
| **le stand** | *concession stand* |

Leçon C | cent quatre-vingt-quinze **195**

**Differentiated Learning**
**Expand**
1. Have students brainstorm a list of recent, older, and classic films to serve as a reference when discussing movies. Display on the board or make enough copies for everyone. Have students identify the genre of each movie they recognize.
2. Have students spell the movie genres in French to a partner.

**Learning Styles**
**Visual Learners**
Ask students to create their own flash cards by finding pictures that represent each movie genre. Add genres such as **une tragédie**, **un mystère**, **un western**, and **un dessin animé**. Have students share their flash cards in groups and ask the others to say what type of film is being depicted.

**1** **On va au cinéma?**   2.1, 2.2

*Dites si les personnes suivantes sont en avance, à l'heure, ou en retard pour le film* Les Ch'tis *qui commence* (that begins) *à 19h20.*

**MODÈLE** toi, tu/19h30
**Tu es en retard.**

1. moi, je/19h05
2. Thomas et Philippe/20h00
3. elle/19h20
4. nous/19h25
5. Guillaume/19h00
6. vous/19h20
7. toi, tu/19h10

M. Lemaire est à l'heure.

**2** **Nous allons être à l'heure, n'est-ce pas?**

*Regardez l'horaire des films et pour chaque phrase que vous entendez, décidez si les personnes vont être....*

A. en avance    B. à l'heure    C. en retard

 2.1, 2.2

**CINÉMA**
**Les Enfants du Paradis**
**21/12/13**

**Shrek 4** - 16h15
**Millenium 2** - 21h15
**Fatal** - 13h35
**Tournée** - 19h55
**Prince of Persia** - 20h10

**3** **Mon film favori**  1.1, 2.1

In your group, ask the person on your right what their favorite movie is. They will tell you what genre of movie it is.

**MODÈLE** A: **Quel film est-ce que tu préfères?**
B: **Je préfère** *les Pirates des Caraïbes*. **C'est un film d'aventures et une comédie.**
(It is not necessary to give the film title in French, but if you're interested you can search online to see what the French call it.)

**Essential Instruction**

1. Review the pronunciation and meanings of **en avance**, **à l'heure**, and **en retard** before having students listen to **Activité 1**.
2. As students do **Activité 3** in groups, have them list their favorite movies. At home, ask them to check online to see if their movie has been shown in France and what its French title is.
3. For **Activité 4**, have students read silently and answer the questions in complete sentences.

Answers _____

4
1. C'est une célèbre actrice française.
2. Elle joue le rôle d'une serveuse dans un café parisien.
3. *Amélie* est une comédie.
4. Oui, ils l'adorent.
5. Elle joue avec Tom Hanks.
6. C'est un thriller.
7. Elle joue dans *Ensemble, c'est tout*.
8. Elle joue le rôle de Coco Chanel.

5 *Answers will vary.*

## 4 Une actrice française

1.2, 2.1, 2.2

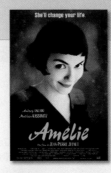

*Lisez le paragraphe et répondez aux questions.*

Audrey Tautou est une célèbre actrice française. Dans la comédie *Le fabuleux destin d'Amélie Poulain,* sorti en 2001, elle joue le rôle d'une serveuse dans un café de Paris. Les Français et les Américains l'adorent! Elle change de direction avec *Pas sur la bouche,* un film musical de 2003. En 2006, Mlle Tautou joue dans le film américain *Da Vinci Code,* un thriller, avec Tom Hanks. Aussi en 2006, elle joue dans *Hors de prix,* une comédie. En 2007, elle joue dans deux films importants: *Ensemble, c'est tout,* une comédie dramatique et *Coco avant Chanel,* un drame. Dans ce film, elle joue le rôle de Coco Chanel.

1. Qui est Audrey Tautou?
2. Quel rôle joue-t-elle dans *Le fabuleux destin d'Amélie Poulain*?
3. C'est quel genre de film?
4. Est-ce que les Américains aiment *Amélie*?
5. Avec quel acteur américain joue-t-elle dans *Da Vinci Code*?
6. C'est quel genre de film?
7. Elle joue dans quelle comédie dramatique?
8. Elle joue le rôle de qui dans le film *Coco avant Chanel*?

At the end of the movie, *Coco avant Chanel,* all the models come out to show Coco Chanel's most famous designs.

*Communiquez!*

## 5 Questions personnelles

 1.1

**Interpersonal Communication**

*Répondez aux questions.*

1. Est-ce que tu préfères les comédies, les films d'aventures, ou les films de science-fiction?
2. Tu préfères les thrillers, les documentaires, ou les films d'horreur?
3. Quel(s) drame(s) regardes-tu?
4. Quand tu voudrais voir un film est-ce que tu préfères regarder un DVD à la maison ou aller au cinéma?
5. Au cinéma, est-ce que tu arrives en avance, à l'heure, ou en retard?
6. Tu vas rire au nouveau film de Judd Apatow?

---

**6**

See model and #1 for A's answers in each dialogue.

1. A: Je voudrais voir une comédie.
   B: On va à *Le concert*? Tu vas aimer ça.
   A: D'accord. À quelle heure?
   B: à 20h30/22h00!
2. B: On va à *Les dents de la mer*? Disons à 18h40/21h50!
3. B: On va à *Le père de mes enfants*? Disons à 20h10/22h30!
4. B: On va à *Le fabuleux destin d'Amélie Poulain*? Disons à 17h00/19h30/10h15!
5. B: On va à *Space Cowboys*? Disons à 20h20/22h50!

## Communiquez!

**6 Quel film?** ✿ 1.1, 1.2, 2.1, 2.2

### Interpersonal Communication

With a partner, read the film guide and make plans to see a movie from each genre below. Be sure to make a prediction about how your partner will react to each film.

**MODÈLE**
A: **Je voudrais voir un documentaire.**
B: **On va à *Être et avoir*? Tu vas aimer ça.**
A: **D'accord. À quelle heure?**
B: **Disons à 19h25!**

1. une comédie
2. un film d'horreur
3. un drame
4. une comédie romantique
5. un film de science-fiction

Je voudrais voir une comédie.

On va à *Bienvenue chez les Ch'tis*?

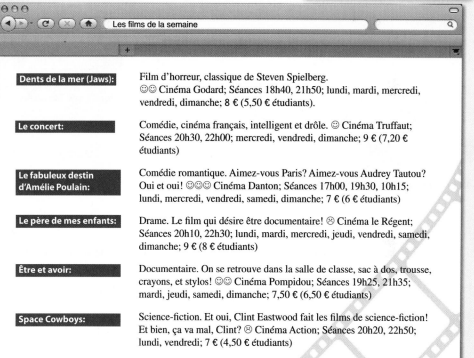

Les films de la semaine

| | |
|---|---|
| **Dents de la mer (Jaws):** | Film d'horreur, classique de Steven Spielberg. ☺☺ Cinéma Godard; Séances 18h40, 21h50; lundi, mardi, mercredi, vendredi, dimanche; 8 € (5,50 € étudiants). |
| **Le concert:** | Comédie, cinéma français, intelligent et drôle. ☺ Cinéma Truffaut; Séances 20h30, 22h00; mercredi, vendredi, dimanche; 9 € (7,20 € étudiants) |
| **Le fabuleux destin d'Amélie Poulain:** | Comédie romantique. Aimez-vous Paris? Aimez-vous Audrey Tautou? Oui et oui! ☺☺☺ Cinéma Danton; Séances 17h00, 19h30, 10h15; lundi, mercredi, vendredi, samedi, dimanche; 7 € (6 € étudiants) |
| **Le père de mes enfants:** | Drame. Le film qui désire être documentaire! ☹ Cinéma le Régent; Séances 20h10, 22h30; lundi, mardi, mercredi, jeudi, vendredi, samedi, dimanche; 9 € (8 € étudiants) |
| **Être et avoir:** | Documentaire. On se retrouve dans la salle de classe, sac à dos, trousse, crayons, et stylos! ☺☺ Cinéma Pompidou; Séances 19h25, 21h35; mardi, jeudi, samedi, dimanche; 7,50 € (6,50 € étudiants) |
| **Space Cowboys:** | Science-fiction. Et oui, Clint Eastwood fait les films de science-fiction! Et bien, ça va mal, Clint? ☹ Cinéma Action; Séances 20h20, 22h50; lundi, vendredi; 7 € (4,50 € étudiants) |

### Essential Instruction

1. Role-play the model conversation in **Activité 6**, then assign the activity in pairs. Ask each pair to present a dialogue to the class. Make a list of the movies used, and poll your students to find out their opinion of them using the guide. Ask, **Qui l'aime passionnément? Beaucoup? Un peu? Pas du tout?**

2. Show students an online video clip from ***Bienvenue chez les Ch'tis,*** then play the filmed dialogue. Have pairs read aloud the dialogue and do **Activité 7** together as a class.

# Rencontres culturelles

 Go online EMCLanguages.net

## On va au ciné!     1.2

Maxime and Yasmine are returning from a **kiosque à journaux** where they went to see what movies are playing.

Maxime: Bon alors, on va à la séance de 14h30 ou de 16h45?
Yasmine: De 16h45. Mais on voit quoi?
Maxime: Nous allons toujours voir un film d'aventures!
Yasmine: Ou un film policier. Ah! Je veux voir *Bienvenue chez les Ch'tis*.
Maxime: La comédie avec Dany Boon?
Yasmine: Ben oui, et Kad Merad.
Maxime: On va rire alors?
Yasmine: Peut-être. On va voir! Si tu veux pleurer, on peut aller voir *La Rafle*.
Maxime: Je veux bien voir *La Rafle* aussi, mais pas aujourd'hui.
Yasmine: On se retrouve où et à quelle heure?
Maxime: Devant le guichet. On arrive un peu en avance, disons 16h15.

### 7 On va au ciné!   2.1, 2.2

*Répondez aux questions.*

1. Maxime et Yasmine vont à quelle séance?
2. Qu'est-ce que Yasmine désire voir?
3. *Bienvenue chez les Ch'tis* est un film d'aventures ou une comédie?
4. C'est un film avec Johnny Depp?
5. Pourquoi est-ce qu'on va rire?
6. On se retrouve où et à quelle heure?
7. Maxime aime être à l'heure ou en retard?

### Extension  À chacun son goût    2.1, 2.2

Laura interviewe Théo et Lucie pour le journal du lycée, le *ClasseEcho*.

Laura: Quel genre de films est-ce que vous aimez voir?
Théo: Moi, surtout les films de science-fiction, les films d'horreur, les films d'action.
Lucie: Moi, j'aime surtout les comédies, les films d'aventures, les films dramatiques.
Laura: Lui, action, elle, évasion, vous n'allez pas souvent au cinéma ensemble....
Lucie: C'est vrai! Mais on aime discuter nos films après.

### Extension  Why don't Lucie and Théo go to the movies together very often?

---

### Answers

**7**

1. Ils vont à la séance de 16h45.
2. Elle désire voir le film *Bienvenue chez les Ch'tis*.
3. C'est une comédie.
4. Non, c'est un film avec Dany Boon et Kad Merad.
5. On va rire parce que c'est une comédie.
6. On se retrouve devant le guichet à 16h15.
7. Maxime aime être en avance.

### Extension

Because they don't like the same kinds of movies.

### Expansion

Label several large posters with headers for different **genres de film**. Have each student research French titles for an American film and a famous French film on French entertainment guides Internet sites. Students will then list their films on the most pertinent poster. For example, *Les 400 coups* (a French classic by director François Truffaut) would be placed on the poster for **drames**, and *La Guerre des étoiles* (*Star Wars*) on the poster for **films d'aventures**.

---

## Differentiated Learning

### Adapt
Assign **Activité 7** for homework. Have students answer in complete sentences for more practice in spelling, sentence construction, and using new vocabulary correctly.

### Accelerate
Ask students to organize their answers from **Activité 6** in a detailed paragraph about their movie preferences.

## Learning Styles

### Visual Learners
Have students use *Pariscope* or an online French search engine to plan an evening at the movies, including selecting a film they wish to see, a cinema where the film is showing, the cost of tickets, and what time they will see it.

### Reference Desk

The comedy ***Bienvenue chez les Ch'tis*** (*Welcome to the Sticks* or *Welcome to the Land of the Ch'tis*) affectionately pokes fun at the peculiarities of the local language of Picard and those living in the two northern regions, Nord-Pas-de-Calais and Picardy, who speak the language and who are considered not very **branché**!

### Expansion

Have students research online examples of Picard and other regional languages and compare them to simple French phrases that they know. Discuss the origins of Picard and the French regional and national government policies to support these regional languages. Extend the conversation to regional stereotypes and respect for those who speak differently or have different customs from one's own.

### Culture

**Perspectives: Activity**
Give each group the name of a French director and ask them to research the director's vision and share it with the class.

# Points de départ

What activities do friends in other countries do together?

## Le cinéma en France  1.2, 1.3

The French film industry began at the end of the 19th century. Today, studios such as Pathé and Gaumont produce about 220 films a year and distribute them to some 4,400 screens around France. Every year, theaters sell 200 million tickets, approximately 85 million of them for movies produced in France.

**Pathé** produces films, distributes them, and owns 92 movie theatres in France.

The French film industry has managed to thrive over the years thanks in part to the financing it receives from private investment and the French government. For example, money earned from taxes on private television channels and from movie ticket and DVD sales are given back to the film industry to help pay for new productions. Two events celebrate this success each year: **les Césars**, the French version of the Academy Awards held in February, and the Cannes Film Festival on the Riviera in May.

🔍 **Search words: cinéma français**

### COMPARAISONS

Which film genre is the most popular in the United States?

**4.2**

## Les comédies françaises  1.2, 1.3

Comedy is the most important genre in French cinema. Some French comedies have been adapted and remade in the United States, including *Three Men and a Baby* (***Trois hommes et un couffin***), *The Birdcage* (***La Cage aux folles***), and *True Lies* (***La Totale***). Police comedies, ensemble comedies, and parodies are all popular in France. A number of French comedies have become enduring and beloved classics, including ***Mon Oncle*** (*My Uncle*), ***La Cage aux folles*** and ***Le Dîner de cons***, which was remade in the United State as *Dinner for Schmucks*.

🔍 **Search words: allociné**

 **Produits**

Another French-American film connection is Johnny Depp, who had a small part speaking French in the film ***Ils se marièrent et eurent beaucoup d'enfants*** (...*And They Lived Happily Ever After*), which came out in 2004. The mother of his children is French actress-singer Vanessa Paradis. On the set of *Public Enemies* (2009), he and French actress Marion Cotillard spoke French when they didn't want others to understand what they were saying.

 **3.1**

### Essential Instruction

1. Assign online research using the search words in **Points de départ** and have students report three interesting facts on each topic.
2. Have students read silently the three cultural paragraphs, then do **Activité 8** and discuss the **Comparaisons** question and **Produits**.
3. Ask pairs to complete **Activité 9**, then review as a class.

## Bienvenue chez les Ch'tis

With more than 20 million tickets sold in France, **Bienvenue chez les Ch'tis** (*Welcome to the Land of Shtis*), starring Dany Boon, is the most popular French movie of all time. A tribute to earlier French comedies, it contains numerous references to French movies made in the 1950s and 1960s.

 **Search words: bienvenue chez les ch'tis site officiel**

### 8 Questions culturelles  2.1, 2.2

*Répondez aux questions.*

1. What are the names of two major French film studios?
2. About how many movies does France produce a year?
3. How are French films paid for?
4. Which movie genre do the French prefer?
5. What types of comedies are popular?
6. What is the title of a classic comedy?
7. *Bienvenue chez les Ch'tis* pays tribute to French comedies from what era?
8. Who stars in *Bienvenue chez les Ch'tis*?

Dany Boon and the rest of the cast from *Bienvenue chez les Ch'tis* attended the 61st **Festival de Cannes**.

### À discuter

How are teen movie viewing preferences different from those of adults?

## Du côté des médias

### 9 Le film est bon?  1.3

*Lisez le tableau (chart).*

This is a summary of what critics from the entertainment guide *Pariscope* think of certain films. Write sentences summarizing their findings, using **aimer... beaucoup**, **un peu**, or **n'aimer... pas**. Follow the model.

> **MODÈLE** *Le petit Nicolas*/V. Gaucher et A. Gaillard
> **Ils aiment beaucoup *Le petit Nicolas*.**

1. *L'imaginarium du docteur Parnassus*/Bernard Achour
2. *Une exécution ordinaire*/Éric Libiot
3. *Vincere*/Françoise Delbecq
4. *Un prophète*/Pierre Murat
5. *Le ruban blanc*/Fabrice Leclerc
6. *Les herbes folles*/V. Gaucher et A. Gaillard

*Les critiques aiment:*
*passionnément ★★★*
*beaucoup ★★*
*un peu ★*
*pas du tout*

### cotation des critiques

| | V. Gaucher et A. Gaillard | Bernard Achour | Éric Libiot | Françoise Delbecq | Pierre Murat | Fabrice Leclerc |
|---|---|---|---|---|---|---|
| Vincere | ★★★ | | ★★★ | ★★ | ★ | ★★★ |
| Le petit Nicolas | ★★★ | ★ | ★ | | ★ | ★★ |
| Les herbes folles | ★ | | | ★★★ | ★★ | ★★ |
| L'imaginarium du docteur Parnassus | ★★ | | ★ | ★★★ | | ★★ |
| Une exécution ordinaire | ★★★ | ★ | ★ | | ★★★ | |
| Un prophète | ★★★ | ★★★ | ★★★ | | ★★★ | ★★★ |
| Le ruban blanc | ★★★ | ★ | ★★★ | ★★★ | ★★★ | |

Leçon C | deux cent un **201**

# La culture sur place

## Les remakes de films français  1.2

**What activities do friends in other countries do together?**

### Introduction

One place to find modern versions of a culture's collected stories is in movies. In this section, you and your classmates will use the Internet to learn about French movies that have been "remade" in the United States.

### Investigation

Moviemakers in the United States often borrow ideas and themes of movies from other cultures. You and your classmates will use the suggestions below to identify American movies based on French films.

> **10 Un remake d'un film français**  **1.2, 1.3, 2.1, 2.2, 4.2**
>
> First, use one or more of the following techniques to find a list of American remakes of French films:
>
> - enter the phrase "remakes américains de films français" in an online search engine. Click on a site that comes up and see if it includes a list of remakes.
> - search for "remake of French films" on the Internet Movie Database site (www.imdb.com).
> - look up the box office results for "Remake-French" on the Box Office Mojo site (www.boxofficemojo.com/genres.com).
>
> Second, select a movie that you are familiar with or that interests you.
>
> Third, look for information that will help you answer the following questions.
>
> 1. Compare the French title with the American title. Do they have the same meaning? Or, has the title completely changed?
> 2. In what ways are the plots similar?
> 3. In what ways is the American remake different from the French original version? For example, are the main characters the same? Did the setting change? Are elements of the plot different?
> 4. How popular were the French and American versions in each country? (You may want to include information about box office earnings, film critiques, fan pages, etc.)

> **11 Un film français et américain**  **1.1, 2.2**
>
> Share your research with your small group.

# Structure de la langue

 *Go online* EMCLanguages.net

## The Interrogative Adjective *quel*

1.2

The adjective **quel** means "which" or "what" and is used to ask questions. **Quel** agrees in gender and number with the noun it precedes.

|  | **Masculine** | **Feminine** |
|---|---|---|
| **Singular** | quel | quelle |
| **Plural** | quels | quelles |

À **quelle** heure est le film?    *At what time is the film?*
Vous désirez **quel** dessert?    *Which dessert would you like?*

The forms of **quel** may also come directly before the verb **être**. In this case, **quel** agrees with the noun following **être**.

**Quel est** le genre du film?    *What is the film's genre?*

*Quel café est-ce qu'Amadou prend?*

**COMPARAISONS**

4.1

What question words replace quel in English?

What movie are you seeing?
At which movie theater?

### 12   Quand on veut préciser

2.1, 2.2

*Complétez avec **quel, quelle, quels,** ou **quelles**.*

1. Tu aimes… actrices?
2. Et… acteurs préfères-tu?
3. Johnny Depp joue dans… genres de film?
4. On voit son nouveau film à… cinéma?
5. On va à… séance?
6. Rendez-vous à… bouche de métro?

### 13   Qu'est-ce que tu dis?

2.1, 2.2

*Utilisez l'adjectif **quel** pour demander plus (more) d'information sur les projets de ton ami(e) pour ce weekend. Suivez le modèle.*

| MODÈLE | A: **Je fais du sport ce weekend!** |
|---|---|
|  | B: **Tu fais quel sport ce weekend?** |

1. <u>Les devoirs</u> vont être difficiles!
2. <u>Les amies</u> se retrouvent au café samedi!
3. Les élèves vont voir <u>un film</u> à 19h00.
4. Nous invitons <u>une prof</u> au stade pour regarder le match de football.
5. J'invite <u>les filles</u> à la teuf.

Quelles filles?

J'invite les filles à la teuf.

COMPARAISONS: The question words that replace **quel** in English include "what" and "which."

## Answers

**12**
1. quelles
2. quels
3. quels
4. quel
5. quelle
6. quelle

**13**
1. B: Quels devoirs vont être difficiles?
2. B: Quelles amies se retrouvent au café?
3. B: Les élèves vont voir quel film à 19h00?
4. B: Vous invitez quelle prof au stade pour regarder le match de football?
5. B: Tu invites quelles filles à la teuf?

### Communication

**Interpretive: Paired Practice**

To practice **quel**, distribute vocabulary picture cards. Have students ask each other which they prefer when shown two cards from the same category. For example, **Quel acteur préfères-tu?** or **Quelle équipe est-ce tu préfères?**

### Expansion

To practice the forms of **quel**, read ten sentences, such as, **Je préfère la glace au chocolat.** For each phrase, students will write down the question that best corresponds, for example: **Quelle glace préfères-tu?** (feminine singular). Do this as a multiple choice exercise by pre-printing student answer sheets.

### Learning Styles

**Kinesthetic/Visual Learners**
Give groups several minutes to write on the board a list of as many **quel** + noun combinations they can think of. The group with the most correct forms of **quel** wins the competition.

203

### Reference Desk

Point out that "to watch" is a voluntary action and "to see" is involuntary. Ask them which verbs pertaining to sound are voluntary and involuntary (i.e. *to listen* is voluntary, *to hear* is involuntary).

### Communication

**Interpersonal: Paired Practice**

Have pairs make two sets of note cards. On cards in the first set, students write a different subject pronoun. On each card in the second set, they write the name of a film title or genre, two teams in a soccer match, or a café in Paris. Students take turns selecting one card from each set and forming a question using **voir**. The other student responds. For example, **Pierre et toi /un documentaire – Est-ce que vous voyez un film documentaire? Oui, nous voyons un documentaire.** Encourage students to be as creative as they can in their answers.

# Present Tense of the Irregular Verb *voir*  1.2

The verb **voir** (*to see*) is irregular.

| voir | | | |
|---|---|---|---|
| je | **vois** | nous | **voyons** |
| tu | **vois** | vous | **voyez** |
| il/elle/on | **voit** | ils/elles | **voient** |

*Tu vois des animaux?*

**Pronunciation Tip**

The shaded area shows the verb forms that all sound the same.

**Spelling Tip**

In the **nous** and **vous** forms, the "i" from the infinitive changes to "y."

Quel film **voyez**-vous? — *What film are you seeing?*

Nous **voyons** une comédie romantique. — *We are seeing a romantic comedy.*

**14 Qui voit quoi?**  2.1, 2.2

*Tout le monde* (Everyone) *voit un film ce weekend. Écrivez la lettre qui correspond à la forme du verbe* **voir** *que vous entendez dans chaque phrase.*

A. vois
B. voit
C. voyons
D. voyez
E. voient

**COMPARAISONS**  4.1

The verbs "to see" and "to watch" are similar in both French and English, but their meanings are distinct. Can you complete these sentences?

I want to... the new sitcom on TV.
I want to... my grandmother this weekend.

COMPARAISONS: The sentences should be completed like this:
I want to **watch** the new sitcom on TV.
I want to **see** my grandmother this weekend.

**Essential Instruction**

1. Introduce the verb **voir** by asking what and whom students see in the class. Review the verb **regarder** and compare its use to **voir**.
2. Have students listen to the audio of **Activité 15** and respond.
3. Have the students do **Activité 16** with a partner.

## 15 Qu'est-ce qu'on voit? 🎧  2.1, 2.2

À tour de rôle, demandez à votre partenaire ce qu'on voit du Café de la Tour (Tower).

**MODÈLE** Michèle
A: Qu'est-ce que **Michèle voit?**
B: **Elle voit un magasin.**

1. on

2. les filles

3. tu

4. Amir

5. Marianne, Mégane, et Sandrine

6. vous

## 16 On fait le tour de l'école

You are giving your French host family a tour of your school. Describe to them what there is to see.

1. Dans la cantine, vous....
2. Ici, dans la médiathèque, nous....
3. Dans la salle de classe, on....
4. Le bureau du proviseur est devant nous. On....
5. C'est la piscine. Je....

2.1, 2.2

C'est la salle d'informatique. Tu vois la prof?

## Culture

**Products: Activity**
Divide the class into four research teams. One team each will research the **Césars**, the Cannes International Film Festival awards, the BAFTAS (British film awards), and the Oscars given for the last two years of cinema. Which categories of film were honored the most? Make a chart to combine your findings and present to the class.

## Reference Desk

**Blended Instruction**
Consider using blended instruction, a combination of in-class learning and computer-mediated instruction or learning opportunities. Ask students to complete activities on the computer, using their cell or smartphone, or other emerging electronic technology. This will allow students to hone their tech skills and become more independent learners. Schedule routine Internet and e-book learning in class and in the lab.

# À vous la parole

**Question centrale**

What activities do friends in other countries do together?

### 17 Le ciné-club  1.1

**Interpersonal Communication**

In order to help you choose a film for **le ciné-club**, ask your classmates what genre of movie they prefer. Insert their responses in a chart like the one below. Finally, write a summary (**Activité 18**).

*Je préfère les films d'horreur.*

| Quel genre de film est-ce que tu préfères? | | | | | | | | | | |
|---|---|---|---|---|---|---|---|---|---|---|
| | 1 | 2 | 3 | 4 | 5 | 6 | 7 | 8 | 9 | 10 |
| films d'action | | | | | | | | | | |
| drames | | | | | | | | | | |
| comédies | | | | | | | | | | |
| etc. | | | | | | | | | | |

## Communiquez!

### 18 Les résultats  1.3

**Presentational Communication**

Present the results of **Activité 17**. Say what types of movies your classmates prefer.

**MODÈLE**

**Cinq élèves préfèrent les comédies, deux préfèrent les drames, deux préfèrent les comédies romantiques et un préfère les films de science-fiction.**

### 19 Allociné  1.2, 1.3

**Interpretive**

**Go to** *www.allocine.fr* and click on "sorties de la semaine." Research a French movie so that you can provide a presentation to your group about:

- le nom du film en français
- le genre du film (comédie? drame?)
- le nom du metteur en scène
- le nom de l'acteur qui joue le rôle principal

Remember to cite your Internet sources.

**Essential Instruction**

1. For **Activité 17**, have students circulate to survey and record the answers of their classmates about their film preferences. To vary this activity draw the grid on the board and invite one student to the front of the class who will survey the entire class and tally the results. Have students individually write out **Activité 18**. Point out the cognate **résultats**. Ask the students if they have seen any French films. List them on the board.

2. Approach the reading strategy by asking the students if they can name a film in English that illustrates the three kinds of conflicts.

3. Teach the students that false cognates in French are called **faux amis**. Explore why this is an appropriate name. Provide some examples; ask students to research other examples online and share them with classmates. Search word: **faux amis**.

# Lecture thématique

## LOL

### Rencontre avec l'auteur

An anonymous blogger describes the movie *LOL* (2009) in the selection you are about to read. *LOL* tells the story of a 16-year-old French girl.

### Pré-lecture  1.3

Think of a movie or television program about a teen that made an impact on you. Tell a classmate about the movie, summarizing the story.

### Stratégie de lecture  1.2

#### Identifying the Conflict in a Story

The plot of a film or story often centers on a conflict of some sort. There are three types of external conflict in a story. The main character may struggle (1) against another character, (2) against forces of nature, or (3) against society or social norms. Create a chart like the one below. As you read, look for two examples of conflict in the story. Then describe each conflict in the appropriate column of your chart.

|    | Person vs. Person | Person vs. Nature | Person vs. Society |
|----|-------------------|-------------------|--------------------|
| 1. |                   |                   |                    |
| 2. |                   |                   |                    |

### Outils de lecture  1.2

#### False Cognates

In Unit 2 you learned that cognates are words that resemble and have the same meaning as English words, for example, **compliquer** and **essentiel** in this reading. But watch out for false cognates that look like English words but have a different meaning. In this reading you will come across the verb **ignore**, which looks like "ignore" in English but actually means "to not know."

Movie stills by ©2008_Pathe_Production_ Bethsabee Mucho_TF, Films Production_M6 Films. LOL official movie poster.

---

**Answers**

**Pendant la lecture**
1. LOL est un autre nom de Lola.
2. Le film *LOL* est une comédie.

**Post-lecture**
Possible answer: normal

**Le monde visuel**
The poster art for *LOL* is very realistic as it shows actual photographs.

**Connections**

**Art**
Each student chooses a favorite film and then draws and illustrates a poster to advertise the film. The film must be titled appropriately in French and artwork must be original. Display the finished posters and have peers from another French class at school vote for the best poster.

 **2.1, 2.2**

LOL? Ca veut dire "Laughing Out Loud"—mort de rire—en langage MSN.

C'est aussi comme ça que les amis de Lola l'appellent.*

Pourtant,* le jour de sa rentrée, Lola n'a pas le cœur* à rire.

Arthur, son copain, la provoque en lui disant* qu'il en aime une autre.*

Et sa bande de copains a le don* pour tout compliquer.*

Tout comme sa mère, Anne, avec qui le dialogue est devenu* impossible, et pas seulement parce qu'elle ignore* ce que LOL signifie....

Et pourquoi Anne traite-t-elle son ado comme une enfant en lui mentant* sur l'essentiel, par exemple sur le fait qu'elle revoit son ex-mari en cachette?*

De son côté, Anne se demande pourquoi sa douce* petite fille est si triste.*

De la fusion à la confusion, les relations mères-filles bouillonnent* d'amour et de LOL.

**Pendant la lecture**
1. Quel est un autre nom de Lola?

**Pendant la lecture**
2. *LOL* est un drame ou une comédie?

l'appellent *call her;* **Pourtant** *however;* **cœur** *heart;* **en lui disant** *by telling her;* **une autre** *another;* **le don** *gift;* **tout compliquer** *make it all worse;* **est devenu** *has become;* **ignore** *doesn't know;* **mentant** *lying;* **en cachette** *in secret;* **douce** *sweet;* **triste** *sad;* **bouillonnent** *boil*

 **Search words:** **lol film**
**blog lol le film officiel**

## Post-lecture  **2.1, 2.2**

How would you describe Lola's life—too good to be true, normal, or melodramatic?

## Le monde visuel  **3.2, 4.2**

Poster art became commercially viable with the introduction of commercial lithograghy in the 1870s. The most famous creator of poster art at that time was Henri de Toulouse-Lautrec, whose use of stylized images and large swaths of color still influence many cinematic posters of today. Look at some examples of Toulouse-Lautrec's poster art of Paris nightlife online. In what ways does the poster art for LOL differ essentially?

**Essential Instruction**

1. Have students scan the reading for cognates and list on the board. Point out the French abbreviation of **adolescent (ado)**. Ask students to identify the French equivalent for certain vocabulary and expressions, such as, "texting," "She (Mom) wonders," "the important things," "LOL," etc. After students listen to and read the text silently, check to see if comprehension increased.

2. Identify and classify the conflict according to the chart on p. 207.

3. Ask students to identify the characters in the cartoon. Emphasize the flow of the conversation. Write any new vocabulary words on the board.

4. Finally, have students role-play the cartoon in groups of five. Ask volunteers to present to the class.

## 20 Activités d'expansion    1.3

1. Refer to your chart and write a paragraph describing the conflicts in Lola's life. What type of conflicts are they? Are these conflicts common ones for teens? Do you think these conflicts will be resolved by the end of the movie?

2. Complete the following sentences to write a review for a movie you've seen about a teen's life.

   Je recommande.... / Je ne recommande pas le film....
   C'est un(e)... (*genre*)
   Le héros/l' heroïne s'appelle....
   Le problème de... (*nom du héros/de l' heroïne*) est....
   À la fin (*end*), il/elle....
   C'est un film.... (*adjectif*)

## Les copains d'abord: Vive le foot!   1.2

Leçon C | deux cent neuf   **209**

**RESOURCES**

**Pre-test**

*Leçon* Quiz

Answers _____

*Answers will vary.*

### Les copains d'abord

Here is the translation for **Les copains d'abord:**

A = Antoine
F = Florence
MA = Marie-Alix
M = Mathéo
S = le serveur

A: What are they doing? We're going to miss the World Cup! MA: It's on Canal + (TV channel), right? What time? A: At eight o'clock sharp. The French team is super well prepared. MA: I like Thierry Henri, he's really cute. S: What would you like? A: You want another coke? MA: Yes, and some dessert, too. A: Say, do you like horror movies? MA: Not too much, I prefer comedies. A: Well, there's a romantic comedy at the Pathé tomorrow. Shall we go? MA: Uh... with Flo and Mathéo? S: Here you go. MA: Thanks, Antoine. A: No, you and me. Shall we meet in front of the theatre at 7:00? M: Sorry, we're late... F: ...but we have everything: the caps, the team logos, and jerseys on sale. Shall we go watch the match? MA: OK, maybe.... A: It'll be great!

List of slang and idiomatic expressions:
**Qu'est-ce qu'ils font?**: *What are they doing?*; **louper**: *miss*; **vachement**: *very*; **canon**: *very cute*

**Differentiated Learning**
**Accelerate**
Ask students what Lola and her mother have in common. Ask them what advice they would give to Lola and her mother. Have students use vocabulary learned in this unit for critiquing a film to write a reaction to the reading.

*T'es branché?*

# Projets finaux

## A Connexions par Internet: Littérature

 1.3

### Les romans français

Many French movies have been based on novels, and sometimes the movies have the same title. Select a novel from the list below or find a French novel on your own that has been adapted to the screen and read a summary of it.

> *Bonjour tristesse*, Françoise Sagan
> *Le château de ma mère*, Marcel Pagnol
> *Le comte de Monte Cristo*, Alexandre Dumas
> *En plein cœur*, Georges Simenon
> *Les Misérables*, Victor Hugo
> *Le tour du monde en 80 jours*, Jules Verne

Next, present the novel to a group of your classmates. In your presentation, be sure to include....

- the title of the novel and name of the author
- when the novel was written
- a description of the main character
- what the main character wants or has a conflict with
- the names of people who directed and starred in the movie based on the novel (If more than one movie has been made, select the one that interests you most.)

## B Communautés en ligne

  1.3, 2.1

### Le football américain

Your partner class in France would like to learn more about American football. Work with four classmates to make a ten-minute video about the basics of football. Your video should explain the object of the game, how many players there are on a team, the names of some of the powerhouse professional teams in the United States, and some details about your school's football team. Give each member of your group a task: writing the narrative, filming, adding the soundtrack, editing. Finally, present your video to the class who will vote on which video to send to your partner school in France. Use as much French as you can in your video.

## Essential instruction

1. Ask groups to select **A** or **B** as their one final project. Reserve a day in the lab or in class for them to work on their project. Have each group present its work to the class or in groups.
2. You may want to put each group's cartoon from **Activité C** online.
3. For **Activité D**, distribute to students the graphic organizer found in the **Copy Masters** supplement. Explain that reflecting on their learning is an important step in the learning process that extends beyond the foreign language class. Review the **Question centrale** and how the unit addressed it.

## C  Passez à l'action!  1.3

### Une bande-annonce

Work with three other students to create an outline for **une bande-annonce** (*film trailer*) in French for a current film or remake of an older movie. The eventual film trailer will be between 30 and 60 seconds in length.

1. Research movies and **les bandes-annonces** on websites, such as **allocine.fr**. Choose a movie, and discuss with your group what information to include in a film trailer.
2. Include the following in your outline....

   - the movie title in French
   - the names of the actors starring in the film
   - the film genre
   - one thing that the film is about or that happens in the film
   - **la sortie du film**, or when the movie comes out
   - if you will feature video or photo stills from the movie
   - what the soundtrack will be
   - a list of the sources you used (credits)

## D  Faisons le point!  2.1, 2.2, 4.1

Your teacher will give you a chart like the one below. Fill it in to show what you've learned about the French language and francophone cultures in this unit.

Question centrale
What activities do friends in other countries do together?

| Je comprends | Je ne comprends pas encore | Mes connexions |
| --- | --- | --- |
|  |  |  |

| What did I do well to learn and use the content of this unit? | What should I do in the next unit to better learn and use the content? |
| --- | --- |
| How can I effectively communicate to others what I have learned? | What was the most important concept I learned in this unit? |

---

**Answers** _____

**C** *Presesntations will vary.*

**D** *Answers will vary.*

### Reference Desk

If they feel comfortable, ask students to share their chart from **Faisons le point!** Pair up students who need extra practice in one area with another who feels confident of the material. Peer tutoring can be a highly effective way to reach struggling students.

### Communication

**Presentational: Cooperative Groups**

Have students work in groups to design, act in, and record a film trailer to advertise a current movie. All dialogues must be in French.

### Learning Styles
### Visual/Auditory Learners

If time allows, show a French film, or 10 – 15 minutes of a film, to pique student interest. You may wish to offer extra credit to those who watch an entire film on their own time. Have them write up a simple synopsis and critique. Suggest that students organize a film party, perhaps during National French Week, and invite other classmates.

**Answers** _____

**A** Script can be found in the front pages of the Annotated Teacher's Edition.

1. F
2. F
3. V
4. F
5. F
6. V
7. F
8. F
9. F
10. F

**B** *Answers will vary.*

**C** *Answers will vary.*

### Reference Desk

For #5 of **Évaluation culturelle**, you may want to make some of your own DVDs available to students or encourage students who have access to online movie services to try watching one or two French films. Provide appropriate suggestions.

### Critical Thinking

**Comparisons**

Many people contend that French films focus much more on human relationships than do U.S. films. French movies generally have fewer special effects. Some would say that French cinema often ignores the convention of a clean and tidy resolution or ending at the conclusion of each film. Ask students what they believe are some typical conventions in American films.

---

# Évaluation

**A** **Évaluation de compréhension auditive**  **2.1, 2.2**

Listen as Marine and Khaled talk about their plans for Wednesday afternoon. For each statement you hear, write **V** if it is true (**vrai**) or **F** if it is false (**faux**).

**B** **Évaluation orale**  **1.1, 1.3**

You and a friend are making plans for the weekend. In your conversation:

- tell two activities you each plan to do this weekend.
- discuss a couple activities you'd like to do and pick one.
- make arrangements for when and where to meet.

After your conversation, report your plans to the class.

*Rendez-vous à 3h00 devant le cinéma?*

*Disons 3h15.*

**C** **Évaluation culturelle**  **1.3, 2.2, 4.2**

In this evaluation, you will be asked to compare francophone cultures with American culture. You may need to complete additional research about American culture.

1. **Les sports populaires**
   Which sports in the United States are as popular as soccer in France? Who are some of today's sports heroes in the United States? Can you name any well-known French or American soccer players? In your opinion, is soccer becoming a more popular sport? Does your school have a soccer team?

2. **Les cafés**
   Do you ever spend time in cafés? How are French cafés different from those in the United States? Are cafés in France increasing or declining? Are cafés becoming more or less common in your community?

3. **La cuisine**
   What do Americans think of French cuisine? What evidence is there that American cuisine has become more common in France?

4. **Le café et les arts**
   How do cafés in your area compare to the French literary café scene in the 1940s and 50s?

Crêpes have crossed the Atlantic to the United States.

5. **Le cinéma**
   Have you ever seen a French movie? If you have, how was it similar to the American movies you've seen? How was it different? Which film genre is the most popular in France? Which is the most popular in the United States? What are the ties between the French and American film industries?

**Essential Instruction**

1. For **Activité C**, divide the class into five groups and assign each group one topic. Have groups discuss and create a visual to accompany the report that they make to the class. Assign a student to take notes using an online note-taking program and post it to the class webpage.

2. You may wish to use **Activités D**, **E**, or **F** for assessment.

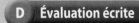 **D** **Évaluation écrite**  **1.3**

Write an e-mail inviting a friend to do four different activities with you this weekend.

**MODÈLE** **On va faire du roller?**

 **E** **Évaluation visuelle** **1.3**

Write a dialogue between two friends deciding on a movie to see. In your dialogue:

- discuss the movie genres you both prefer.
- decide on a movie to see.
- make a prediction about the movie or respond.
- choose a showing to attend.
- agree on where and when to meet.

 **F** **Évaluation compréhensive** **1.3**

Create a storyboard of six frames. Sketch what you like and don't like to do on the weekend and write a two-sentence caption for each frame. Share your storyboard with your classmates.

**Reference Desk**

It is recommended that teachers assign the first three evaluation activities. The written, visual, and comprehensive evaluation activities may be assigned according to students' multiple intelligences (written: verbal-linguistic; visual: visual-spatial; comprehension: interpersonal). Put students in small groups to work together.

**Differentiated Learning**
**Decelerate**
Have students work with a partner to complete
**Activité D**, **E**, or **F**.

Prepare a storyboard template that you ask students to fill with captions.

# Vocabulaire de l'Unité 4  1.2

**à** on, with *B*; **à l'heure** on time *C*; **à la vanille** vanilla *B*
un **acteur, une actrice** actor, actress *C*
l' **action (f.)** action *C*
l' **addition (f.)** bill *B*
**apprendre** to learn *B*
**arriver** to arrive *C*
**attendre** to wait (for) *A*
**aujourd'hui** today *C*
**avance: en avance** early *C*
une **aventure** adventure *C*
**avoir: avoir faim** to be hungry *B*; **avoir soif** to be thirsty *B*
un **ballon (de foot)** (soccer) ball *A*
**bienvenue** welcome *C*
un **blouson** jacket *A*
une **boisson** drink *B*
**bon: Bon appétit!** Enjoy your meal! *B*
une **bouche: bouche du métro** subway entrance *A*
un **but** goal *A*
**ça** that *A*
la **carte** menu *B*
le **chocolat** chocolat *B*
une **comédie** comedy *C*; **comédie romantique** romantic comedy *C*
**comme** for *B*
**comprendre** to understand *B*
**contre** versus, against *A*
**désirer** to want *B*
le **dessert** dessert *B*
**disons** let's say *A*
un **documentaire** documentary *C*
**donc** so, therefore *A*
**donner** to give *B*; **donnez-moi** give me *B*
un **drame** drama *C*
**du** of the *A*
l' **eau (f.)** water *B*; **eau minérale** mineral water *B*
**en** on *A*; **en avance** early *C*; **en retard** late *C*; **en solde** on sale *A*
**enfin** finally *B*
**ensemble** together *C*
une **équipe** team *A*
un **film** film *C*; **film d'action** action movie *C*; **film d'aventures** adventure movie *C*; **film d'horreur** horror movie *C*; **film de science-fiction** science fiction movie *C*; **film musical** musical *C*; **film policier** detective movie *C*
un **footballeur, une footballeuse** soccer player *A*
**gagner** to win *A*
le **genre** type *C*
le **guichet** ticket booth *C*

l' **heure (f.): à l'heure** on time *C*
le **jambon** ham *B*
**jouer un rôle** to play a role *C*
un **kiosque à journaux** newstand *C*
l' **it** (object pronoun) *C*
**marquer** to score *A*
un **match** game *A*
les **meilleurs (m.)** the best *A*
le **menu fixe** fixed-price menu *B*
**merci** thank you *B*
**mesdemoiselles (f.)** plural of **mademoiselle** *B*
le **métro** subway *A*
un **metteur en scène** director *C*
**mille** thousand *B*
**perdre** to lose *A*
**peut: on peut** we can *C*
**peut-être** maybe *C*
**pleurer** to cry *C*
**porter** to wear *A*
**prendre** to take, have (food or drink) *B*
**rembourser** to reimburse *A*
le **rendez-vous** meeting *A*
se **retrouver** to meet *C*
**rire** to laugh *C*
un **rôle** role *C*
**s'il vous plaît** please *B*
**sais: je sais** I know *B*
la **science-fiction** science fiction *C*
une **séance** film showing *C*
une **série** series *C*
un **serveur, une serveuse** server *B*
**si** if *C*
**solde: en solde** on sale *A*
**soutenir** to support *A*
la **spécialité du jour** daily special *B*
un **stade** stadium *A*
**surprend: ça ne me surprend pas** that doesn't surprise me *A*
**surtout** especially *B*
**te (t')** you *A*
un **thriller** thriller *C*
le **ticket** ticket *A*
**toujours** still *C*
**tout: Tout ça!** All that! *B*
**veux: tu veux** you want *A*
**voilà** here is/are *B*
**voir** to see *C*

Clothing… see p. 165
Food… see pp. 179–180

**Essential Instruction**

1. Do the Listening review together in class.
2. You may wish to assign the Reading section as homework.

# Unité 4 Bilan cumulatif

## Listening   2.1, 2.2

I. You will hear a short conversation. Select the reply that would come next. You will hear the conversation twice.

1. A. Il est midi.
   B. Disons devant le bureau du proviseur.
   C. À une heure.
   D. On se retrouve au cours d'espagnol.

II. Listen to the conversation. Select the best completion to each statement that follows.

1. Alexis....
   A. est dans la salle de classe
   B. téléphone à Séverine
   C. présente un nouveau camarade de classe
   D. désire faire du sport

2. Alexis et Séverine se retrouvent....
   A. au café pour prendre une pizza
   B. à la médiathèque pour faire les devoirs
   C. au stade pour voir un match de foot
   D. au magasin pour faire du shopping

## Reading  1.2, 2.1, 2.2

III. Read the letter from Rémi to Marianne. Then select the best completion to each statement.

Bonjour Marianne,

Comment ça va? Moi, ça va! C'est dimanche et je suis content! Et oui, c'est la finale de foot et on se retrouve avec les deux meilleures équipes de football en Europe. Oh, le match va être très intéressant. Tu vas rire, mais j'aime les deux équipes. Oui. Il est possible d'aimer la France et l'Espagne! Disons que j'aime beaucoup l'équipe espagnole. Elle est énergique et les footballeurs aiment jouer avec le ballon de foot. Ils envoient le ballon devant et derrière. C'est drôle et intéressant! J'aime soutenir l'équipe de France parce que c'est la France et je suis français! Le match France-Espagne, tu vas l'aimer, Marianne!

Bisous,

Rémi

1. Rémi aime....
   A. l'équipe française et l'équipe espagnole
   B. l'équipe espagnole
   C. l'équipe française
   D. l'équipe italienne

2. L'équipe espagnole est....
   A. géniale
   B. toujours en avance
   C. énergique
   D. drôle et intéressante

3. Rémi aime l'équipe française parce qu'....
   A. elle est intelligente
   B. il est français
   C. il est italien
   D. il n'aime pas le football espagnol

Answers _____

Script can be found in the front pages of the Annotated Teacher's Edition.

1. C

1. B
2. C

**III**
1. A
2. C
3. B

**Answers** _____

**IV**
1. B
2. A
3. B
4. B
5. A
6. C
7. B
8. A or C

**V**
9. allons
10. aiment
11. il aime
12. ai
13. avons
14. voyons
15. allons
16. prennent

**VI** _Answers will vary._

**VII** _Answers will vary._

# Writing  2.1

IV. Complete the paragraph by writing an appropriate word or expression.

Midi, c'est l'heure du __1__ .                           A. menu fixe  B. déjeuner  C. blouson
Les élèves sont au café, et ils regardent __2__ .        A. une carte  B. une heure  C. une séance
"Qu'est-ce que vous désirez?" dit __3__ .                A. le croque monsieur  B. la serveuse  C. le guichet
Philippe a très __4__ .                                  A. frites  B. faim  C. addition
Il prend un __5__ .                                      A. sandwich  B. guichet  C. coca
Il a soif, donc il prend aussi une __6__ .               A. séance  B. chaussette  C. boisson
Coralie dit " __7__ " un steak-frites.                   A. On peut  B. Donnez-moi  C. Surtout
Après, Coralie et Philippe disent " __8__ !"             A. merci  B. l'addition  C. bon appétit

V. Complete the paragraphs with the correct form of the verb in parenthese.

Nous __9__ voir deux équipes de football aujourd'hui.                9. (aller)
Les spectateurs français __10__ l'équipe de Paris.                   10. (aimer)
Mon ami Marc est espagnol; il __11__ beaucoup l'équipe espagnole.    11. (aimer)
Et moi, je préfère soutenir les Français. Je (J') __12__ le          12. (avoir)
blason de l'équipe française sur mon blouson!
Après un match, nous __13__ faim et soif.                            13. (avoir)
Nous __14__ la serveuse.                                             14. (voir)
"Nous __15__ prendre une pizza et des cocas."                        15. (aller)
Souvent, mes amis __16__ une glace aussi. Moi, non.                  16. (prendre)

# Composition  1.3, 2.1, 2.2

VI. Your friends have asked you to meet them at the Café des Sports at 18h00. Since you will arrive first, they've asked you to order for everyone. Write the conversation between you and the server.

# Speaking  1.3

VII. Tell a story suggested by the images.

**Essential Instruction**
Have students speak about the pictures in VII, or propose that they find another set of pictures that would illustrate the vocabulary and structures from the unit.

# 5 Les gens que je connais

*Rendez-vous à Nice!*

**Épisode 5:**

*S.O.S devoirs*

Go online
**EMC**Languages.net

1. Have students look at the photo on p. 218. Is this a particularly French scene? Who is pictured (young, old)? What do the people seem to be celebrating? What are they sharing (smiles, happiness, love, being together as a family)? This is a good time to introduce the **-er** verb **partager** from the quote by Arletty. Ask students to reflect on the relationships we share, how important family is in all cultures, and links that unite us as humans around the world.

2. Point out the key words of the quote: **l'amour**, **l'amitié**, **rire** and **s'aimer**. Your students are familiar with **aimer**, but the reflexive verb **s'aimer** introduces the concept of reciprocity. By extension for **rire**, you can introduce **sourire** as you study the image.

## Citation

"L'amour, l'amitié, c'est surtout rire avec l'autre, c'est partager le rire que de s'aimer."

Love and friendship, more than anything, mean to laugh with another person, because to laugh together is to share affection.
—Arletty, actrice française

## À savoir  2.2

Actress **Akissi Delta** produced a television drama in the Ivory Coast called **"Ma famille."** The show has been a favorite for over a decade across Africa.

**Essential Instruction**

1. Review the unit title, the **Question centrale**, and the **Contrat de l'élève**. Ask students what they will learn in this unit.
2. Explain the term "francophone countries."
3. Read aloud the **Citation** and ask students their opinion of this definition of friendship.
4. Show the relevant video clip from *Rendez-vous à Nice!*, Episode 5, and discuss the related question as a class.

# Unité 5

# Les gens que je connais

## Reference Desk

Ask students to be on the lookout for the answer to the culture question as they read the culture paragraphs in **Points de départ**. In 1902 St. Pierre, the former capital of Martinique, was devastated by a volcanic eruption that destroyed the entire town and its inhabitants. Fort-de-France is now the capital.

### Question centrale

## What is the nature of relationships in other cultures?

Go online
EMCLanguages.net

**Why are Patrick and Charlotte's mothers laughing?**

A. The are making fun of Patrick's English.
B. They think Patrick has a crush on Charlotte.
C. They are setting him up to study with Charlotte.

What is the name of the active volcano that destroyed St. Pierre, the former capital of Martinique?

## Contrat de l'élève

**Leçon A  I will be able to:**

>> propose something to eat and ask if I look like someone.

>> name measurements in the metric system and talk about Martinique.

>> use possessive adjectives.

**Leçon B  I will be able to:**

>> ask someone's age and tell my age, tell what gift I'm giving, and plan a party.

>> discuss holidays in Francophone countries.

>> use **–ir** verbs and **offrir** in the present tense, the expression **avoir… ans**, and give dates.

**Leçon C  I will be able to:**

>> ask what someone's profession is, ask where someone is from, and tell what country I'm from.

>> discuss French-speaking Africa and performers Amadou and Mariam.

>> use **c'est** and **il/elle est**, the verb **venir**, and **de** + definite articles.

deux cent dix-neuf  2 1 9

**Differentiated Learning**
**Decelerate**
Have students work in small groups to review the **Contrat de l'élève**, asking them to list functions and vocabulary in English that correspond to certain items in the **Unité** overview.

## Reference Desk

1. The French word **parents** is also used to refer to relatives in general.
2. Note that **grand** remains the same for (masculine) **grand-père** and (feminine) **grand-mère**.
3. The French often use **demi-frère** and **demi-sœur** for either *half-* or *step- brother/sister*. Use **beau-frère** and **belle-sœur** to say *brother-in-law* and *sister-in-law*. Other **membres de la famille** (m.) might include **le bébé** (*baby*), **le neveu** (*nephew*), **la nièce** (*niece*), **le petit-fils** (*grandson*), **la petite-fille** (*granddaughter*), **l'époux** (m.) or **l'épouse** (f.) (*spouse*), **l'ex-mari** or **l'ex-femme** (*ex-husband/wife*), **le beau-père** (*step father*, *father-in-law*), **la belle-mère** (*step mother*, *mother-in-law*), **les beaux-parents** (m.) (*stepparents, in-laws*), **les petits-enfants** (m.) (*grandchildren*), **le fils unique** (*only son*), **la fille unique** (*only daughter*), **l'enfant unique** (m./f.) (*only child*), **une gosse** (f.)/**les gosses** (slang for *kid(s)/children*), **un/les jumeau(x)** and **une/les jumelle(s)** (f.) (*twins*), and **divorcé(e)** (*divorced*).
4. Point out that one does not use an article with **fils/fille/enfant unique**.

## Critical Thinking

### Application
Have students label their relationships on a real or fictional family tree. Include the family terms mentioned in **Reference Desk** and challenge students to decipher the meanings.

# Leçon A

# Vocabulaire actif

## La famille de Théo   1.2

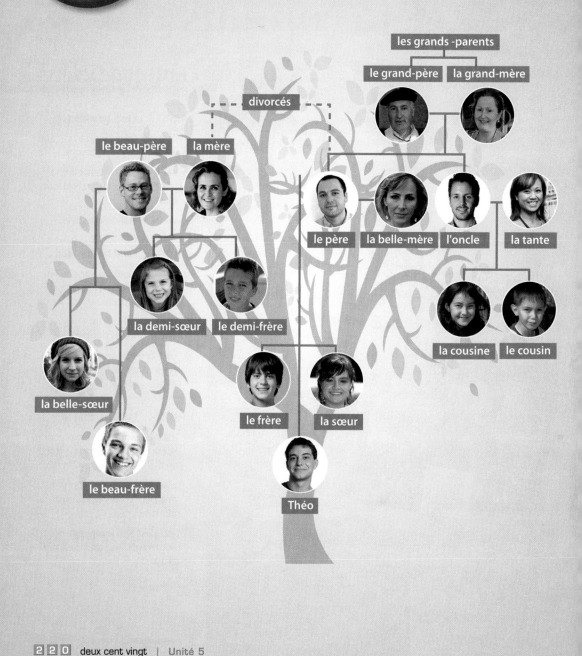

## Essential Instruction

1. Use photos of your own family or create a family tree to present the vocabulary. Television families like the "Simpsons" and "Modern Family" can be useful for this because students know the relationships of the characters.
2. Ask who's who on Theo's family tree. Be sure to teach the expression **une famille recomposée**. Have students guess the meaning of **beau-père** and **belle-mère**. You may also wish to teach **divorce** and **deuxième mariage**.
3. Note the exception to the adjective/noun agreement in **demi-sœur** and **grand-mère**. The rule in French states that if the first word explains the second, there is no agreement.
4. Point out that, depending on the context, **femme** means woman or wife.
5. Ask students to discern the meaning of **les cheveux roux**. Explain that **rouge** is never used to describe hair color.
6. Review the eye, hair, and size vocabulary by asking students to describe specific students.
7. Briefly review the numbers students learned previously, then point out that **mille** is always invariable.

**C'est la famille de M. Perrin.**

la femme · la fille · M. Perrin · le fils · les enfants

**C'est la famille de Mme Angelou.**

Mme Angelou · les parents · le mari

Alexandre a les cheveux blonds et les yeux bleus.

les cheveux roux

les yeux verts

les cheveux noirs

les yeux marron

les cheveux bruns

les yeux gris

grand(e)

de taille moyenne

petit(e)

| | |
|---|---|
| 1.000 | mille |
| 1.001 | mille un |
| 1.002 | mille deux |
| 2.000 | deux mille |
| 3.000 | trois mille |
| 1.000.000 | un million |
| 2.000.000 | deux millions |
| 3.000.000 | trois millions |

## Pour la conversation

**1.2**

How do I ask what someone is like?

> **Comment est** ma tante?
> *What is my aunt like?*

How do I point out resemblances?

> **Tu ressembles à** ton grand-père.
> *You look like your grandfather.*

### Et si je voulais dire...?

| | |
|---|---|
| **les cheveux blancs** | *white hair* |
| **les cheveux bouclés** | *curly hair* |
| **les cheveux ondulés** | *wavy hair* |
| **les cheveux frisés** | *tightly curled hair* |
| **les cheveux raides** | *straight hair* |
| **Je porte des lentilles/lunettes.** | *I wear contacts/ glasses.* |

Leçon A | deux cent vingt et un **221**

### Reference Desk

1. Teach the **-er** verb **ressembler à quelqu'un/quelque chose**.
2. Ask students to note that to qualify parts of the body in English one uses the possessive and the verb "to be," for example, "Her eyes are blue." In French, however, one uses definite articles (**le, la, l', les**) and the verb **avoir: Elle a les yeux bleus**.
3. The adjective **noir** is also used to refer to eye color. The invariable adjective **marron** is only used for eye color.

### TPR

Collect several dozen pictures (from magazines or online) of people of varying sizes with different hair and eye color. Divide students into two teams. Project three different pictures at a time and call out a description. The first student to go to the board and select the correct description wins a point for the team. Continue playing until all have had a turn.

---

**Differentiated Learning**
**Accelerate**
Ask students to prepare a detailed description of a family member that includes the vocabulary in **Et si je voulais dire...?**

**Multiple Intelligences**
**Visual-Spatial/Verbal-Linguistic**
Ask students to bring in a picture (a photo, a magazine picture, or a picture they find online) of someone and prepare three or four sentences using the new vocabulary. Have them share their photo and descriptions in small groups.

**1**
1. C
2. A
3. B

**2** *Answers will vary.*

**3** *Answers will vary.*
1. J'ai les cheveux….
2. J'ai les yeux….
3. Je ressemble à….
4. J'ai X frère(s) et X sœur(s). Non, je n'ai pas de frères ou de sœurs.
5. Mes cousins s'appellent X, Y, etc.… Je n'ai pas de cousins.

### Reference Desk

Emphasize that the nouns **les cheveux** and **les yeux** are masculine and plural, regardless of the gender of the person described. Consequently, the adjective will also be masculine plural. Contrast the sentence **Elle a les cheveux blonds et les yeux bleus.** to **Elle est blonde.** In the latter, the adjective is feminine because it modifies the subject **elle**.

---

**1** Des familles françaises   **1.2, 2.2**

*Choisissez la description qui correspond à chaque image.*

A. Mme Diouf a deux filles, Rahina et Naya. Elles ont les cheveux noirs et les yeux noirs comme leur mère.

B. M. Russac a les cheveux blonds et les yeux bleus. Il a deux fils, Alexis et Simon. Simon a les cheveux noirs. Alexis a les yeux bleus de son père.

C. M. et Mme Djellouli ont deux enfants—une fille, Leïla, et un fils Salim. Leïla ressemble à son père et Salim ressemble à sa mère.

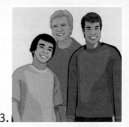

1.   2.   3.

**2** Des descriptions  **2.1, 2.2**

*Décrivez la taille (size), les cheveux, et les yeux des personnes suivantes.*

**MODÈLE**   un(e) camarade de classe

**Chloé est de taille moyenne. Elle a les cheveux blonds et les yeux bleus.**

1. ton frère ou sœur ou cousin(e)
2. un(e) prof
3. ton acteur préféré
4. ton actrice préférée
5. toi-même (*yourself*)

**3** Questions personnelles

*Répondez aux questions.* **2.1, 2.2**

1. Est-ce que tu as les cheveux bruns, noirs, blonds, ou roux?
2. Est-ce que tu as les yeux gris, marron, verts, noirs, ou bleus?
3. Tu ressembles à qui?
4. Est-ce que tu as des frères et des sœurs, ou tu es enfant unique (*only child*)?
5. Comment s'appellent tes cousins?

> J'ai les cheveux blonds.

### Essential Instruction

1. Model pronunciation again by reading the descriptions in **Activité 1** to the class.
2. Assign **Activité 2** and **Activité 3** as pairwork. Ask students to share several things in groups that they learned about their partner.
3. Have students write **Activité 4** and exchange with a classmate for peer correction. Then do a choral reading of the prices.
4. After listening to **Activité 5**, ask students questions about the various relationships in the family tree.

## 4 Des chefs-d'œuvres de la peinture française  1.3

*Écrivez le prix que les acheteurs (buyers) ont payé (paid) pour ces peintures.*

1. *Bal du moulin de la Galette* de Renoir
78.100.000 dollars

2. *Portrait de l'artiste sans barbe* de Van Gogh
94.500.000 dollars

3. *Le bassin aux nymphéas* de Monet
80.451.178 dollars

4. *Le vase paillé* de Cézanne
36.900.000 dollars

## 5 Ma famille   2.1

*Simone décrit (is describing) sa famille. Regardez l'arbre généalogique (family tree) et dites si chaque phrase est **vraie** (**V**) ou **fausse** (**F**).*

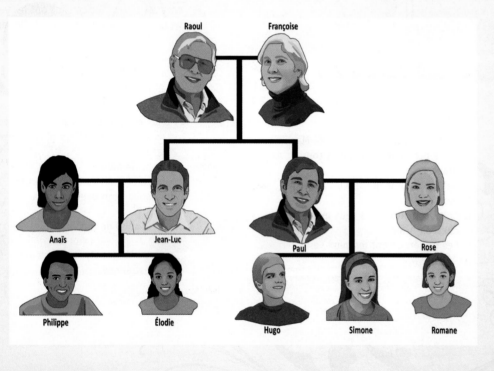

### Connections

**Art**
Students can research recent **ventes** (sales) of French paintings at **Hôtel Drouot** in Paris and international auction houses such as Sotheby's and Christie's and make a list of prices reached. Explore student opinions of the value of art.

**Differentiated Learning**
**Decelerate**
For **Activité 3**, ask students to write the beginning of each answer, for example, **j'ai les…**, **je ressemble à…**, etc. Next, have them compare (and make any necessary corrections to) what they wrote with the phrases you write on the board. Instruct students to refer to their guide as they discuss with a partner.

**Special Needs Students**
**Auditory Impairment**
Provide multi-sensory input by distributing the audio transcript for **Activité 5** so that students can refer to it as they listen.

**Answers** _____

**6**

1. L'oncle René arrive chez Julien.
2. Julien ressemble à son grand-père.
3. Tante Anne-Sophie prépare les accras.
4. Tante Anne-Sophie a les yeux marron et les cheveux bruns.
5. Les cousins de Julien ont les yeux verts.

**Extension**

Amélie's mother and Amélie's aunt (her mother's sister) are estranged.

# Rencontres culturelles

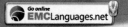

## Réunion de famille     1.2

Julien's Uncle René has just arrived from Martinique to visit his sister's family in Paris.

**La mère de Julien:** Julien, c'est ton oncle René. Il a voyagé 7.000 kilomètres pour nous voir à Paris!

**Julien:** Bonjour, mon oncle!

**René:** Tu ressembles beaucoup à ton grand-père!

**Julien:** Vraiment? C'est comment la Martinique?

**René:** La Martinique est petite, mais géniale! On mange très bien là-bas. Tu dois manger les accras de morue de ta tante Anne-Sophie. Délicieux!

**Julien:** Comment est ma tante? A-t-elle les yeux verts comme mes cousins?

**René:** Non. Elle a les yeux marron et les cheveux bruns. Tes cousins ont les yeux verts, comme les yeux de ma belle-mère!

---

**6 Réunion de famille**

2.1, 2.2

*Identifiez la personne ou les personnes du dialogue.*

1. Cette personne a voyagé de la Martinique.
2. Cette personne ressemble à son grand-père.
3. Cette personne prépare les accras de morue.
4. Cette personne a les yeux marron et les cheveux bruns.
5. Ces personnes ont les yeux verts.

**Extension** **Recherches généalogiques**

L'oncle d'Amélie parle de l'histoire de leur famille.

**L'oncle:** Ma belle-sœur, c'est-à-dire ta mère, et sa sœur ne se parlent plus depuis 20 ans!

**Amélie:** À cause de quoi?

**L'oncle:** À cause de moi! Ta tante a quitté Paris pour venir avec moi à la Martinique.

**Amélie:** Un vrai coup de foudre!

1.2, 2.1

**Extension** Which family members are estranged?

## Essential Instruction

1. Show the filmed dialogue. Then ask students to read through and sketch a family tree of the family members mentioned: **l'oncle René** from Martinique, his wife **Anne-Sophie** (originally from Paris), her sister **Amélie**, and her son **René** from Paris. Clarify why the sisters are estranged and explain the two meanings of **un coup de foudre**, literally "strikes of lightening" and figuratively "love at first sight."

2. Divide the class into pairs to read the dialogue aloud, having students change roles. Then, show the filmed dialogue again.

3. Ask students to use the search words in **Points de départ** to find out more about the cultural topics. Perhaps they could do this for extra credit.

# Points de départ

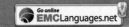 Go online **EMCLanguages.net**

## Le système métrique  1.2, 2.1, 3.1

In France, people use the metric system of measurements, developed by a commission of French scientists in 1789 just after the French Revolution began. The metric system uses centimeters, meters, and kilometers instead of inches, feet, and miles to measure distances. Weight is measured in grams and kilograms instead of ounces and pounds, while volume is measured in liters, not ounces, quarts, or gallons. Weight, volume, and size are tied to the same standards. This means one liter weighs one kilogram and fills a ten-centimeter square cube.

🔍 **Search words: conversion unités de mesure**

**FRANCE**

| 50 | 🏘️ |
| 90 | 🛣️ |
| 130 | 🛣️ |

**Question centrale**
**?**
What is the nature of relationships in other cultures?

The speed limit in France is 30 miles per hour in most cities, 43 miles per hour on main roads, and 80 miles per hour on national freeways.

### COMPARAISONS

Use formulas for metric conversion to find equivalents for:
- a kilometer
- 7,000 kilometers
- a meter
- a kilogram
- a liter

2.1, 4.2

🔍 **Search words: metric conversion formulas**

## La Francophonie

✴ *Antilles: La Martinique*

1.2, 3.2

Martinique, the "Island of Flowers," is an island located in the Caribbean Sea. Like nearby Guadeloupe, it is a French overseas **département**. This means that its citizens share the same rights and responsibilities as French citizens in mainland France. French people like to vacation in Martinique, and some residents of Martinique seek work in France. Martinique is a mountainous island with an active volcano. The last major eruption of Mont Pelé occurred on May 8, 1902. It destroyed the capital city of St. Pierre and killed some 30,000 people. After the disaster, the capital was moved to Fort-de-France, where it remains today.

Martinique has a unique cultural heritage due to the African, French, and other ancestors of its people. This blending of cultures can be especially seen in the island's traditional foods—cod fritters (**accras de morue**), creole sausage (**boudin créole**), and Caribbean pork stew (**Colombo de porc**)—and language. Creole is the term used to refer to this "blended" identity and to the language many native **Martiniquais** speak. The Creole language is a combination of several other languages, including French, Indian, and African languages

Since Mont Pelé erupted in 1902, the former capital, Saint-Pierre, is now a small city with only 5,000 inhabitants.

## RESOURCES

 **Workbook 7–8**

### Reference Desk

1. Despite the efforts of numerous kings prior to the French Revolution, France had no unified system of weights and measures, which made commerce and trade extremely laborious. In 1795, there were more than 700 different methods of measuring which varied from city to city and often depended on the object being measured. The body was the favorite point of reference for such measurements, for example, **le doigt** (*finger*), **la paume** (*palm*), **le pied** (*foot*), **le pas** (*a step*), or **la brasse** (*fathom*), to name a few.

2. On the speedometer of an American car, one can see the relationship of miles to kilometers. For example, 62 miles mph = 100km/hr and 62 miles = 100kms.

3. There are only three countries in the world that do not use the metric system as their official system of measurements: United States, Myanmar (formerly Burma), and Liberia. Within these countries the metric system is often used, especially in scientific and international contexts. The United Kingdom has laws allowing the use of other systems of measurement, such as the pound.

4. "Metropolitan France" refers to "mainland" France on the European continent in contrast to the Overseas Departments of Martinique, Guadeloupe, Réunion, and French Guiana.

---

## Differentiated Learning
### Expand

Show students a world map and have volunteers use push pins to mark the overseas French **départements**, including **la Martinique** and **la Guadeloupe**. Compare the relationship of France and these **départements d'outre-mer** to that of the United States and Puerto Rico, U.S. Virgin Islands, Guam, etc.

### Multiple Intelligences
**Visual-Spatial/Bodily-Kinesthetic**
Help students understand weight in grams in concrete terms (compared to ounces and pounds) by providing sand, sugar, or rice, plastic bags, and scales that measure grams. Have partners weigh different amounts and then convert to ounces. Label several amounts and display in class.

### Learning Styles
**Auditory Learners**
Find online and stream talk radio from Martinique for your students. Discuss any discernible accent and Creole expressions that they may hear.

Create an audio file of several Francophone speakers and post to your class page for students to access.

**7**

1. 1793 by a Napoleonic decree.
2. in kilometers
3. in the Caribbean Sea, south of Guadeloupe
4. Mont Pelée erupted on May 8, killing 30,000 inhabitants and destroying the city of Saint-Pierre.
5. Fort-de-France
6. African, French, and other ethnic backgrounds
7. a mix of mostly French, African, English, and Amerindian dialects typically spoken in informal and family contexts
8. Antilles dance music influenced by American R'n'B

**À discuter**
*Answers will vary.*

**8**

1. au beach-volley
2. le 25, 26, et 27 mars
3. à Anses d'Arlet en Martinique
4. une radio francophone de musique populaire
5. Air Caraïbes

## Reference Desk

1. In 1790, the National Academy of Sciences of Paris standardized the decimal system and defined the meter to be one 10-millionths of the distance from the equator to the Earth's Pole.
2. One of two known survivors of the 1902 Mont Pelée eruption was a prisoner name Cyparis.
3. The majority of the multi-racial, multi-ethnic population of Martinique is of African and African-white-Indian heritage. Other groups are East Indian, Chinese, and Indian Tamil.
4. The official language of Martinique is French, which is used by the government, schools, newspapers, and media.
5. **Zouk** means "party" or "festival" in Antillean Creole and refers to a musical genre made popular by mid-80s French Antilles groups such as Kassav'. Originally, **zouk** referred to a dance based on the 19th century Polish mazurka.

---

**Produits**

**Zouk** is a style of dance music, influenced by American R'n'B, that originated in the Antilles in the 1980s. The word zouk also refers to the type of dance performed to zouk music.

 **Search words: zouk vidéos**

**1.2**

**Mon dico Créole**  **4.1**

| | |
|---|---|
| Bonjou! | Bonjour! |
| Bonswa! | Bonsoir! |
| O revwa! | Au revoir! |
| Kombyen li ye? | C'est combien? |
| Ki sa wap etidye? | Qu'est-ce que vous étudiez? |
| Ou pale creole? | Vous parlez créole? |
| Fode mwen alé. | Je dois aller. |

**7** **Questions culturelles**  **1.1, 2.1, 2.2**

*Répondez aux questions.*

1. When was the metric system invented?
2. Instead of miles, how is distance measured in the metric system?
3. Where is Martinique located?
4. What happened in 1902?
5. What is the capital of Martinique today?
6. What is the ethnic heritage of Martinique's population?
7. What does the word creole refer to?
8. What is zouk?

**À discuter**

How would you describe Martinique's relationship with France? Can you think of a similar relationship the United States has with an island?

**Accras de morue**, a typical creole dish, has Portuguese origins.

## Du côté des médias

**8** **Un tournoi de beach-volley!** **1.2, 2.1**

*Répondez aux questions.*

1. On va jouer à quel sport?
2. Quelles sont les dates du tournoi (*tournament*)?
3. Où est la compétition?
4. Qu'est-ce que c'est que NRJ? (Faites des recherches en ligne.)
5. Quelle ligne aérienne (*airline*) soutient le "Défi des îles"?

**Tournoi de Beach-Volley les 25, 26 et 27 mars aux Anses d'Arlet**

---

## Essential Instruction

1. Have students study the vocabulary in **Mon dico créole**. What similarities do they see between Martinique Creole and French?
2. Have students write their answer to the question in **À discuter** in their Culture Journal. Then have them share in groups what they've written.
3. To introduce the concept of possessive adjectives, act out sentences like, **C'est mon livre.**

**C'est ton cahier. C'est notre salle de classe.** Then, to emphasize that the adjective agrees with the item(s) possessed and not the gender of the person who possesses the item(s), point to a male student's pen and say, **C'est son stylo.** Then repeat the sentence and point to a female student's pen. Contrast the French possessive adjectives with how possession is expressed in English.

# Structure de la langue

 *Go online* **EMCLanguages.net**

## Possessive Adjectives 🎴 1.2

Possessive adjectives show ownership or relationship, as in "my" computer, "his" flash drive. In French, possessive adjectives have different forms depending on the nouns they describe. They agree in gender (masculine or feminine) and in number (singular or plural) with what is possessed.

*Tu me présentes à tes parents?*

|  | Singular | | | Plural | |
|---|---|---|---|---|---|
|  | **Masculine** | **Feminine before a Consonant Sound** | | | |
| my | **mon** | **ma** | | **mes** | |
| your | **ton** | **ta** | | **tes** | |
| his, her, one's, its | **son** | **sa** | | **ses** | |
| our | **notre** | **notre** | | **nos** | |
| your | **votre** | **votre** | | **vos** | |
| their | **leur** | **leur** | | **leurs** | |

(**oncle** with masculine/feminine singular; **cousine** with feminine singular; **parents** with plural)

The possessive adjective agrees with what is possessed, not with the owner.

    **Leurs** cousins ont les cheveux roux.    *Their cousins have red hair.*

**Son**, **sa**, and **ses** may mean "his," "her," "one's," or "its," depending on the gender of the owner.

    Luc aime bien **sa** belle-mère.    *Luc really likes his stepmother.*
    Claire et **son** frère ont les yeux verts.    *Claire and her brother have green eyes.*

Before a feminine singular word beginning with a vowel sound, **ma**, **ta** and **sa** become **mon**, **ton**, and **son**, respectively.

    Luc? J'ai **son** affiche.    *Luc? I have his poster.*

*C'est ton dictionnaire d'espagnol?*

*Oui, c'est mon dictionnaire.*

### COMPARAISONS

What are the possessive adjectives in English?
    Emily is my sister.
    Is Leon your brother?
    He lives with his mother.
    He has her eyes.
    We like our cousins.
    We have their blond hair.

4.1

COMPARAISONS: The possessive adjectives in English are "my," "your," "his," "her," "our," and "their."

## Differentiated Learning
### Expand
Have students expand on the chart of possessive adjectives by asking them to add a noun to each possessive adjective, for example, **mon père**, **ma mère**, **mes cousins**. Remind them that **sa**, **son**, and **ses** can refer to his/her/its.

## Multiple Intelligences
### Visual-Spatial
Draw a simple cartoon of a boy, a girl, one dog, and two dogs. Point first to the boy and one dog and ask students to respond with the appropriate French possessive adjective. Do the same to elicit the responses in French for "her dog(s)" and "their dog(s)."

Expand on this activity by having students create their own visual representation of all of the possessive adjectives. Have them share their illustrations with others and use as a reference.

### Reference Desk

1. To explain more easily why **sa** becomes **son** before a word beginning with a vowel, explore with students the musicality or rhythm of the French language. Write C-V-C-V-C-V on the board to show how French uses the consonant-vowel alternance, which allows the language to flow.
2. Challenge students to tell you the meaning of **Notre-Dame**.

---

**9** **Au lycée**  **2.1, 2.2**

*Les étudiants du Lycée Victor Schoelcher à Fort-de-France ont besoin de leur livre d'histoire, d'une feuille de papier, et d'un stylo pour leur cours d'histoire. Regardez les bureaux de ces étudiants et dites ce dont (what) ils ont besoin.*

1. Maude     2. Romain

**MODÈLE**     mon frère
**Il a besoin de sa feuille de papier et de son livre d'histoire.**

3. Raphaël     4. ma cousine

5. Nicolas     6. Emma

---

**10** **Comparons nos familles!** 🎧  **2.1, 2.2**

*Juliette compare sa famille à la famille de Xavier. Écrivez **J** si elle parle de sa famille, **X** si elle parle de la famille de Xavier, ou **J** et **X** si elle parle des deux familles.*

---

## Communiquez!

**11** **Ma famille**  **1.3**

**Presentational Communication**
*Décrivez une photo de votre famille en répondant à ces questions.*

1. Qui est-ce?
2. Il ou elle ressemble à qui?
3. Il ou elle a les cheveux de quelle couleur?
4. Il ou elle a les yeux de quelle couleur?
5. Qu'est-ce qu'il ou elle aime faire?

---

**Essential Instruction**

1. Have students prepare **Activité 11** ahead of time, then share about their family members in groups.
2. To illustrate the concept of indefinite articles in negative sentences in French, write a sentence in English in both the affirmative and negative. Add the translation of the sentences in French underneath. Ask students to compare and comment on what differences they notice.

# Indefinite Articles in Negative Sentences  1.2

The indefinite articles **un**, **une**, and **des** become **de** or **d'** *(a, an, any)* in a negative sentence.

| | |
|---|---|
| Tu as **une** sœur? | Non, je n'ai pas **de** sœur. |
| Mme Blondel a **des** enfants? | Non, elle n'a pas **d'**enfants. |

However, **un**, **une**, and **des** do not change after a form of the verb **être** in a negative sentence.

Ce ne sont pas **des** maillots de l'équipe.
*They're not the team's jerseys.*

*Non, je n'ai pas de cousine, j'aime la cuisine!*

## 12 Est-ce que tu as…?  1.1

**Interpersonal Communication**

*Demandez si votre partenaire a les parents ou profs suivants. Ensuite, changez de rôles.*

> **MODÈLE** un prof tahitien
> A: **Est-ce que tu as un prof tahitien?**
> B: **Non, je n'ai pas de prof tahitien.**
> **Et toi, est-ce que tu as un prof tahitien?**
> A: **Oui, j'ai une prof tahitienne, Mlle Mataoa.**

*Est-ce que tu as une sœur?*

*Non, je n'ai pas de sœur.*

| | |
|---|---|
| 1. une prof française | 5. des cousins |
| 2. un prof algérien | 6. des tantes |
| 3. un frère | 7. un oncle |
| 4. une sœur | |

## 13 Les affaires de Juliette et Joëlle

*Juliette et Joëlle sont des sœurs qui partagent la même chambre. Dites ce qu'elles ont et n'ont pas, selon l'illustration.* (Juliette and Joëlle are sisters who share a room. Say what they have and don't have, according to the illustration.)  2.1

> **MODÈLE** Juliette a **un livre de maths**, mais Joëlle n'a **pas de livre de maths.**

**Juliette**          **Joëlle**

Leçon A | deux cent vingt-neuf **229**

## RESOURCES

Workbook 13–15

### Answers

**12** *Possible answers:*
1. Non, … pas de prof française.
2. Non, … pas de prof algérien.
3. Non, … pas de frère.
4. Non, … pas de sœur.
5. Non, … pas de cousins.
6. Non, … pas de tantes.
7. Non, … pas d'oncle.

**13**
1. Juliette a un livre de maths, mais Joëlle n'a pas de livre de maths.
2. Juliette a des CDs américains, mais Joëlle n'a pas de CDs américains. Elle a des CDs français.
3. Juliette a un ordinateur portable, mais Joëlle n'a pas d'ordinateur.
4. Juliette a un iPod, mais Joëlle n'a pas d'iPod.
5. Juliette a un dictionnaire anglais, mais elle n'a pas de dictionnaire français.
6. Joëlle a un dictionnaire anglais et un dictionnaire français.
7. Joëlle a une trousse mais Juliette n'a pas de trousse.
8. Joëlle a un sandwich au fromage, mais Juliette n'a pas de sandwich…
9. Joëlle a des feuilles de papier, mais Juliette n'a pas de feuilles de papier.
10. Joëlle a des CDs français, mais elle n'a pas de CDs américains

### Expansion

Have paired students gather and display on their desks items such as school and art supplies or images of sports that they play. Have pairs examine another pair's display and describe what each member has or doesn't have. Pairs then present orally on what their counterparts have displayed. Finally, ask students to describe the displays in writing.

---

**Differentiated Learning**
**Accelerate**
To encourage students to process information in French, have each one present his or her family member portrait for **Activité 10** to the class from memory. If students need a prompt, have them hold up a card with a key word to remind them of their thought.

**Special Needs Students**
**Auditory Impairment/Linguistically Challenged**
Some students might have difficulty distinguishing the difference between a short word like **un** or **de** in sentences such as **Il a un livre, elle n'a pas de livre.** Write several examples on the board, then read them aloud, exaggerating the pronunciation. Have them repeat example sentences like these many times to reinforce auditory memory.

# À vous la parole

 **Communiquez!**

 *Question centrale* — What is the nature of relationships in other cultures?

**14** **Je me présente.**   **1.1**

**Interpersonal Communication**

Imagine you are at a party where you don't know anyone. Introduce yourself to another student, giving your name. Then tell the student a little about yourself, including your favorite activities and something about the members of your family. After exchanging introductions with your partner, move on to the next student and introduce yourself again. Continue until you have spoken with four different students. Write a paragraph about one of the people you interviewed.

**Communiquez!**

**15** **Bienvenue!** **1.1, 1.3**

**Interpersonal/Presentational Communication**

Awa is an exchange student from **Sénégal**, and Christophe has just arrived at your school from Belgium. Choose one of them to interview for the school newspaper. Write questions to find out the student's age, favorite activities and foods, the town or city where he or she is from, who the members of the student's family are, as well as their names, favorite activities, and foods. Then, role-play the interview with a classmate and write the article for the school newspaper.

**Communiquez!**

**16** **Un faire-part de naissance** **1.2, 2.1, 4.2**

**Interpretive Communication**

**Un faire-part de naissance** is a birth announcement sent out to family, friends, and colleagues. Sending a **faire-part de naissance** to friends and relatives is a very important tradition in French culture. Go online to find an example. Take notes on what you understand. Then show the **faire-part** to your classmates and describe the facts about the baby.

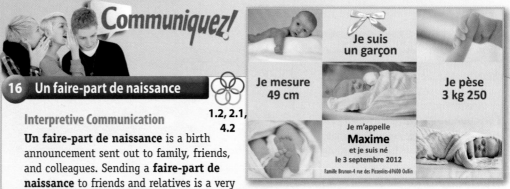

Je suis un garçon

Je mesure 49 cm

Je pèse 3 kg 250

Je m'appelle **Maxime** et je suis né le 3 septembre 2012

Famille Brunon-4 rue des Pissenlits-69600 Oullin

# Prononciation    1.2

## Linking Consonants

- In French you don't normally pronounce the last consonant in a word, such as the **s** in **gris** or the **t** in **est**. But when you do pronounce the last consonant, like the **r** in **père**, and the next word begins with a vowel, you link the two sounds together.

  Mon père est blond.

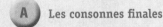 **A** Les consonnes finales

*Repeat each sentence. Pay attention to final consonants.*

1. Mon père est brun. Il est brun.
2. Ma mère est blonde. Elle est blonde.
3. Mon frère est roux. Il est roux.

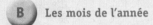 **B** Les mois de l'année

*Repeat each sentence. Pay attention to the pronunciation of the months.*

1. Septembre est frais (*cool*).
2. Octobre est pluvieux (*rainy*).
3. Novembre est humide.
4. Décembre est froid (*cold*).

## Pronunciation of the Letter "a"

- The vowel /a/ in **ma** or **famille** is different from the nasal vowel /ã/ in **grand**.

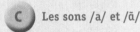 **C** Les sons /a/ et /ã/

*Repeat the sounds /a/ and /ã/ in the words and sentences that follow.*

1. mars, avril, janvier
2. Il va manger.
3. Il va changer.

**D** Les âges

*To practice the pronunciation of /a/ and the nasal vowel, repeat the questions and statements.*

1. Quel âge a Stéphane? Il a trente ans.
2. Quel âge a Romane? Elle a quarante ans.
3. Quel âge a Marianne? Elle a soixante ans.
4. Quel âge a Suzanne? Elle a cent ans.

**E** Distinguez!

*What do you hear in each sentence? Write **A** for the sound /a/ or **B** for the sound /ã/.*

### RESOURCES

☑ **Pre-test**

✎ *Leçon* Quiz

Answers _____

**E**

1. A. /a/
2. B. /ã/
3. A. /a/
4. B. /ã/
5. B. /ã/
6. A. /a/

### Reference Desk

Remind students that although there are general rules governing pronunciation in French, just as in English, there are always exceptions. Use the acronym CaReFuL (careful) as an **aide-mémoire** (mnemonic) to help students remember to pronounce the final consonant of words ending in C/R/F/L. Examples: **chic/blanc**, **bonjour/au revoir**, **actif/un chef**, **un animal**. Exceptions to the C/R/F/L rule: **une clef**, verbs ending in -**er**, such as **parler**, **manger**, etc., words ending in -**ier** such as **panier**. You may also wish to point out that while the final consonant (other than c/r/f/l) is not usually pronounced, there are words that end in other letters that are pronounced. Some examples are **un club**, **un anorak**, **le foot**, **top**, **Astérix**, **mars**. Point out that a word that ends in -**n** and not followed by a vowel is nasal, and often not pronounced. Examples: **brun**, **juin**, **mon**.

---

**Differentiated Instruction**
**Accelerate**
Use the **faire-part de naissance** in **Activité 16** as a reference to ask students questions to elicit answers with the negation of indefinite articles. For example, **Le bébé a des cheveux, des dents?** Response: **Non, il n'a pas de cheveux, pas de dents**. To challenge further, ask them what else the baby has or does not have.

**Multiple Intelligences**
**Visual-Spatial**
Have these students design an announcement for their own birth.

### Reference Desk

Reinforce daily dates and numbers. At the start of class, ask a different student each day to announce the full date to the class. On occasion, incorporate the date or the date of a student's birthday into a quick **dictée** with other relevant unit material. (For example, **Aujourd'hui, nous sommes le 20 octobre 2011.** Or, **Aujourd'hui c'est l'anniversaire de…. Il/Elle a X ans.**)

### Culture

**Practices: Information**
Consider showing the i-Culture video entitled **"La fête surprise"** (2010-2011) to provide your students with a culturally authentic perspective related to the theme of this **Leçon**.

### Expansion

Have students select an adjective (or several adjectives) from the vocabulary list that best describes them and create a visual. This can be done as an acronym, for example STP (**sympa, timide, premier**). Vary this activity by asking students to create a visual using their first name and adjectives for each letter. Brainstorm additional adjectives to expand the list.

**232**

---

# Leçon B

## Vocabulaire actif

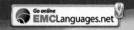 Go online EMCLanguages.net

### Bon anniversaire! 1.2

**les mois (m.) de l'année (f.)**

 janvier
février
mars
avril
mai
juin

 juillet
août
septembre
octobre
novembre
décembre

**Comment sont-ils?**

 Sarah est bête.
Didier est intelligent.

 Claude est égoïste.
Chloé est généreuse.

 Michèle est diligente.
Théo est paresseux.

 Angèle est bavarde.
Karim est timide.

 Martine est sympa.
Léo est méchant.

**l'anniversaire**

 une carte
 un gâteau
 un cadeau
 une carte cadeau

**232** deux cent trente-deux | Unité 5

**Essential Instruction**

1. Ask students to identify cognates as you introduce the vocabulary. Point out that **anniversaire** is a **faux ami** and that the months are not capitalized in French unless they are the first word in a sentence. Write on the board: **Tu as quel âge? J'ai 14 ans.** Ask them to compare to the English and identify what is different (use of **avoir** vs. the verb "to be"). Review the formation of adjectives and introduce **eux→euse**. Model pronunciation and have students repeat all vocabulary.

2. Introduce **Pour la conversation** with the audio.

| bavard | bavarde |
| bête | bête |
| diligent | diligente |
| égoïste | égoïste |
| généreux | généreuse |
| méchant | méchante |
| paresseux | paresseuse |
| sympa | sympa |
| timide | timide |

## Pour la conversation

1.2

**H**ow do I ask someone's age?

> **Tu as quel âge?**
>
> *How old are you?*

**H**ow do I tell my age?

> **J'ai... ans.**
>
> *I'm... years old.*

**H**ow do I tell what gift I'm giving?

> **J'offre** un CD à Alice.
>
> *I'm giving Alice a CD.*

**H**ow do I plan a party with others?

> **Tu peux apporter** les boissons?
>
> *Can you bring the drinks?*

### Et si je voulais dire...?

| de l'argent | *money* |
| une boîte de chocolats | *box of chocolates* |
| un bouquet de fleurs | *bouquet of flowers* |
| canon | *beautiful/handsome* |
| faible | *weak* |
| moche | *ugly* |
| pauvre | *poor* |
| riche | *rich* |

Leçon B | deux cent trente-trois 233

### Reference Desk

1. "I'm ... years old." Some students struggle with this construction in French that requires the verb **avoir** (*to have*) instead of **être** (*to be*). Explain that the student may not be understood unless the rules of the language are followed.
2. As students learn **bouquet**, it is a good opportunity to discuss the fact that many English words come from French. Brainstorm a list of French words that are used in English such as **croissant**, **à la carte**, **chic**, **critique**, **petite**, **détour**, **impasse**, **rendez-vous**, etc. Students will sometimes assume that the English pronunciation of a word spelled the same as in French is correct.

### Expansion

Depending on the size of your class, you may want to post the months of the year around the room and ask students to stand under the month of their birthday. Then, as you go around the room, each person says his or her birthday. Vary this activity by having a student ask another across the room **Quelle est la date de ton anniversaire?** The student replies and then asks the question to another student. Continue the activity until all have had the chance to ask and answer the question.

### Learning Styles
#### Visual Learners
Create a calendar template with the months of the year. Have students add their own illustrations that symbolize the months.

### Multiple Intelligences
#### Bodily-Kinesthetic
Poll your students about their birthday month by asking **Qui a un anniversaire en janvier?** etc. and have them form groups accordingly. Within each group, have students use the questions in **Pour la conversation** to ask each other how old they are on their birthday.

## Answers

**1**

1. mars
2. août
3. juin
4. novembre
5. janvier
6. juillet
7. décembre
8. février
9. septembre
10. avril
11. octobre
12. mai

**2** *Possible answers:*

1. Marie-Alix est paresseuse. Elle n'est pas diligente.
2. Salim est timide.
3. Julien est bête.
4. Abdoulaye est diligente.
5. Juliette est bavarde.
6. Alain est égoïste.
7. Bernard est généreux.
8. Anne est méchante.
9. Antoine est généreux.

### Game

**À vos dicos!**

Challenge your students to find more French adjectives (and expand their English vocabulary at the same time). First of all, ask students to list five adjectives to describe the latest movie or sports match they've seen. Compare their results. How many different adjectives did they use? Discuss how they could broaden or fine-tune their descriptions with new adjectives. Now divide the class into two teams. Distribute French-English dictionaries. Within a set time period, have students brainstorm and search for as many new and different adjectives as they can from English to French. Compare and combine their French lists afterwards. Have students take turns writing each new word in a different colored marker onto an oversized poster for everyone to see.

**2 3 4**

---

**1  Les mois**   **2.1, 2.2**

*Identifiez le mois qui correspond au chiffre (number), par exemple, janvier est 1.*

1. 3
2. 8
3. 6
4. 11
5. 1
6. 7
7. 12
8. 2
9. 9
10. 4
11. 10
12. 5

Noël est en décembre.

**2  Ils sont comment?** **2.1, 2.2**

*Décrivez chaque personne.*

**MODÈLE**  Nicole
**Nicole est généreuse.**

Lutte contre le cancer

1. Marie-Alix

2. Salim

3. Julien

Magali est bavarde.

4. Abdoulaye

blah, blah, blah
5. Juliette

Je suis la meilleure footballeuse de l'équipe
6. Julie

7. Bernard

8. Anne

9. Antoine

**2 3 4**  deux cent trente-quatre | Unité 5

---

**Essential Instruction**

1. Do **Activité 1** as a class with the audio.
2. Ask students to provide the feminine as you call out the masculine adjectives from the **Vocabulaire actif**. Give students the feminine adjective and have them provide the masculine form. Then, assign **Activité 2** as pair work.
3. Have volunteers write the answers to **Activité 3** on the board.
4. Read aloud and review the instructions and model in **Activité 4**.
5. Expand on **Activité 5** by having students write a similar description of several family members. Instruct them to exchange papers with a partner who will read, then say the ages of their partner's family.
6. Assign **Activité 6** as homework to prepare for pair work tomorrow.

**3** Script can be found in the front pages of the Annotated Teacher's Edition.

1. sympathique
2. timide
3. égoïste
4. bavarde
5. paresseux
6. diligente
7. généreuse

**3** Les jumeaux  **2.1, 2.2**

*Les jumeaux souvent se ressemblent. Écoutez chaque description et écrivez l'adjectif qui décrit le jumeau de cette personne.* (Twins often look and act alike. Listen to each description and write the adjective that describes that person's twin.)

**MODÈLE** Vous entendez: Christian est méchant. Comment est sa sœur Delphine?
Vous écrivez: **méchante**

**4** On offre un cadeau d'anniversaire.   **2.1, 2.2**

*Choisissez un cadeau qui correspond aux intérêts et besoins de chaque personne. Ensuite, expliquez (explain) pourquoi vous offrez ce cadeau.*

| |
|---|
| une carte cadeau pour le magasin Printemps |
| un ordinateur portable |
| une comédie sur DVD |
| un CD |
| des chaussures de sport |
| une écharpe avec le blason de PSG |

**MODÈLE** Je m'appelle Francine. J'aime sortir avec mes amis et nous aimons aller aux concerts.
**J'offre un CD à Francine parce qu'elle aime la musique.**

1. Je m'appelle Marc et j'aime bien le sport. J'aime faire du footing dans le parc, mais j'ai besoin de chaussures.
2. Je suis Céline et j'adore lire les blogues! J'aime jouer aux jeux vidéo. Je surfe beaucoup sur Internet.
3. Je suis Julien, un fan du football. J'aime regarder l'équipe de Paris au stade.
4. Je suis Mlle Dupont. J'aime faire du shopping au centre commercial.
5. Je m'appelle François. J'aime rire! Je vais au cinéma le samedi soir.

**4** *Possible answers:*

1. J'offre des chaussures de sport à Marc parce qu'il aime le sport.
2. J'offre un ordinateur portable à Céline parce qu'elle aime surfer sur l'Internet.
3. J'offre une écharpe à Julien avec le blason de PSG parce qu'elle/il aime le foot/le sport.
4. J'offre une carte cadeau pour le magasin Printemps à Mlle Dupont parce qu'elle aime faire du shopping.
5. J'offre une comédie sur DVD à François parce qu'il aime les films comiques.

**5** Quel âge ont-ils?  **1.2**

*Lisez le paragraphe suivant. Quel âge a chaque personne dans la famille de Florence? Écrivez le nom de chaque personne et leur âge en chiffres (numbers) comme ça:* **nom, 13 ans.**

Florence a quinze ans. Son frère Émile a seize ans. Leurs parents ont quarante-cinq ans. Leur grand-mère a soixante-six ans.

**6** Questions personnelles

Mon amie est généreuse et sympa.

*Répondez aux questions.*

1. Qu'est-ce que tu offres à ton ami(e) pour son anniversaire?
2. En quel mois est-ce que tu organises une fête pour l'anniversaire de ton ami(e)?
3. Qui apporte les boissons? la musique?
4. Qu'est-ce qu'on va manger?
5. Comment est ton ami(e)?
6. En quel mois est ton anniversaire? **2.1, 2.2**

**5**

1. Florence a 15 ans.
2. Son frère Émile a 16 ans.
3. Leurs parents ont 45 ans.
4. Leur grand-mère a 66 ans.

**6** *Answers will vary.*

1. J'offre… à mon ami(e) pour son anniversaire.
2. Son anniversaire est ….
3. J'apporte des boissons / X apporte la musique.
4. On va manger du gâteau.
5. Mon ami(e) est grand(e), etc.
6. Mon anniversaire est ….

**Differentiated Learning**

**Decelerate**
Point out that students can use their English to help recognize the months of the year. To help with spelling, ask students to note the differences (usually only one letter) with the months in English. Have the students practice in groups, first spelling the months orally with the French alphabet and then in writing. Have them exchange papers to check the spelling.

**Learning Styles**

**Visual Learners**
Use pictures that symbolize a particular holiday or celebration and ask questions such as, **En quel mois est (la fête de) Noël?**

**Multiple Intelligences**

**Interpersonal/Intrapersonal**
Have groups use the adjectives listed in the **Vocabulaire actif** in sentences to describe people whom they know.

**Culture**

**Practices: Activity**
Have students research **grands magasins** in Paris, such as **FNAC, Bon Marché,** and **Galeries Lafayette**, and design a **carte cadeau** in euros for one of these stores.

**Answers** _____

**7**

1. Julien va avoir son anniversaire.
2. Camille, Maxime, et Yasmine vont organiser une super teuf/une fête.
3. Maxime désire offrir une carte cadeau de la FNAC.
4. Yasmine pense que l'idée de Maxime n'est pas géniale et que Maxime est paresseux.
5. Camille parle de DVDs parce que Julien est passionné de cinéma.
6. Julien n'aime pas les films bêtes.
7. Maxime va choisir les DVDs.
8. On finit la discussion chez Maxime.

### Reference Desk

Point out the nuance between **offrir** and **donner** in French. The verb **offrir** means more to propose something with the hope that it will be accepted. **Donner** is simply "to give." Study these examples: **offrir un cadeau**, **offrir de l'aide**, **offrir de l'argent en échange d'un service**, **donner de l'amitié**, **donner un livre**, **donner un coup**.

### Communication

**Presentational: Cooperative Groups**

Ask students to choose a favorite gift they've received and draw a picture of it on a card. Each student will describe the gift and who gave it. Afterwards, students should discuss a present they have given someone.

### Game

**Les dates**

Divide students into two teams and ask one member from each team to come to the board. Give a date, for example, **le douze juillet**. The first student at the board to say and write out the date in French wins a point.

---

# Rencontres culturelles

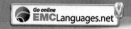

## Quel cadeau offrir?     1.2

Julien's friends are planning to celebrate his upcoming birthday.

Yasmine: Bon. Qu'est-ce qu'on offre à Julien?

Maxime: Ah! Son anniversaire, c'est le 23 février! Il va avoir 15 ans!

Yasmine: C'est un samedi. Alors, on va faire une super teuf!

Camille: Qu'est-ce qu'on va acheter comme cadeau?

Maxime: Je sais! Une carte cadeau de la FNAC!

Yasmine: Maxime, tu es paresseux! Tu ne veux pas faire un peu de shopping?

Maxime: C'est que... je suis généreux!

Camille: Ah! Julien est passionné de cinéma, non? Alors, nous lui offrons des DVD!

Maxime: Quels films choisissons-nous?

Camille: Des films sympa et intelligents. Julien n'aime pas les films bêtes.

Yasmine: Bon. Maxime, tu choisis les DVD, d'accord?

Maxime: C'est ça. Et on finit la discussion chez moi. Je peux vous offrir une pizza!

---

### 7 Quel cadeau offrir?
2.1, 2.2

*Répondez aux questions.*

1. C'est bientôt l'anniversaire de qui?
2. Qu'est-ce que Camille, Maxime, et Yasmine vont organiser?
3. Quel cadeau Maxime désire-t-il offrir?
4. Est-ce que Yasmine aime l'idée de Maxime? Pourquoi, ou pourquoi pas?
5. Pourquoi Camille parle de DVD?
6. Quels films est-ce que Julien n'aime pas?
7. Qui va choisir les cadeaux?
8. Où est-ce que les amis finissent la discussion?

---

**Extension** **Samuel, un nouveau copain**

Élodie a été malade hier. Emma lui parle d'un nouvel élève à l'école.

Emma: Samuel, c'est son nom.

Élodie: Il est comment?        1.2, 2.1,

Emma: Je le trouve un peu timide. Mais qui     2.2 sait? Il est peut-être juste un peu réservé?

Élodie: Comme toi l'année dernière! Tu te souviens... toi qui ne voulais parler à personne? Et ben, raconte-moi tout! Il est sympa?

Emma: Oui... enfin, je crois. Il est martiniquais. Il vient d'arriver des Antilles avec sa famille.

**Extension** What does Emma tell Élodie about Samuel, the new student?

---

**Essential Instruction**

1. Show the filmed dialogue **Quel cadeau offrir?** and have small groups review what they understood. Then have them read the dialogue aloud. Confirm that all students understand. Show the filmed dialogue again, and assign **Activité 7** orally in groups.

2. Have students read about **la FNAC** in the **Points de départ** and discuss similar stores that they know.

3. Ask partners to interview each other about family celebrations, and then share something they learned about their partner.

4. Have students read aloud and discuss the topics in **Points de départs**.

# Points de départ

 **Go online EMCLanguages.net**

 **What is the nature of relationships in other cultures?**

## Joyeux anniversaire! Bonne fête!  1.2, 5.1

In France, people often celebrate birthdays with a party, cake, and gifts just like in the United States. To wish someone a happy birthday in French, you say **Bon anniversaire!** or **Joyeux anniversaire!** Another day many people celebrate in France and other European countries is their saint's day. Each day of the year is associated with a Christian saint, so if an individual is named after a saint, such as Anne, Catherine, François, or Vincent, he or she may receive gifts or treats on that particular saint's day.

## La Francophonie  1.2, 3.1, 5.1

✽ *Fêtes*

In her autobiography, Antillean writer Maryse Condé writes about her mother's huge birthday parties attended by the entire family. She tells of how her many brothers and sisters would create skits and write poems in their mother's honor, and how the children where her mother taught would sing songs and present her with bouquets of flowers.

Many Muslim families in the Middle East and Africa don't always celebrate a child's birthday. They give parties and presents to their children, as well as gifts to less fortunate young people not related to them, during such festivals as **Aïd-el-Kébir** (also known as **Aïd-al-Adha** or **Tabaski**).

## La FNAC  1.2, 5.1

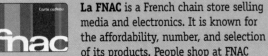

**La FNAC** is a French chain store selling media and electronics. It is known for the affordability, number, and selection of its products. People shop at FNAC stores or online to find a wide variety of products ranging from books and music to software and portable communications devices. Customers can also buy and reserve tickets for the theater, concerts, and other events at the FNAC. One of the most successful retailers in Europe, it also sponsors book fairs, literary prizes, and even campaigns that promote culture and the arts.

### COMPARAISONS  4.2

The United States is a very diverse country, made up of people from many places who brought their traditions, celebrations, and cultures with them. What special days does your family celebrate? What special foods do you eat on those days? What types of activities do you do? Do you give presents on those days?

Leçon B | deux cent trente-sept **2 3 7**

## RESOURCES

 **Workbook 21–22**

## Reference Desk

**Aïd-el-Kébir**, or "Festival of Sacrifice," is an important religious holiday for Muslims worldwide to commemorate the willingness of Abraham (Ibrahim) to obey God's command to sacrifice his son Ishmael before God intervened, providing a ram to sacrifice instead. **Eid** (or **Aïd**) is honored by spending time at the mosque with family and friends, offering a sacrifice, expressing gratitude for food and shelter, and helping the poor.

## Culture

### Practices: Information
The French enjoy 11 national holidays and, by law, are entitled to five weeks of paid vacation, which most citizens take during July and August. Many holidays, for example Christmas and Easter, celebrate France's Christian tradition. Others, such as Armistice Day (November 11, 1918) or Victory Day (May 8, 1945), commemorate France's involvement in the great world wars. France celebrates Labor Day on May 1, International Worker's Day.

**Le quartorze juillet**, or **Bastille Day**, is France's national holiday. It commemorates the storming of the Bastille prison on July 14, 1789, marking the beginning of the modern nation and the end of the French monarchy. **Bastille Day** has become somewhat of an international celebration. Find out from the local Alliance Française or other French cultural institution what local festivities are offered.

## Connections

### History
Have students research a holiday including its origins, history, and significance, in France or another francophone country, and then create a visual (poster, online dossier) to share in class.

## Differentiated Learning
### Decelerate
Pair challenged students with above-level students to collaborate on understanding the dialogues. Prepare a worksheet with questions in English for pairs to complete about the dialogues. Emphasize the importance of teaching or helping someone else as one effective way to learn and retain new material.

## Special Needs Students
### AD(H)D
Reading activities can confound some students because they don't know what to focus on first. Have students look at headings and illustrations and ask them what they expect to read.

### Multiple Intelligences
### Visual-Spatial
Have students explore the **FNAC** store website and identify a birthday gift for a friend or family member. Ask students to share what they found and give details, including the price.

**8**

1. People in France often celebrate birthdays with a party, cake, and gifts.
2. To wish someone a happy birthday in French, you say **Bon anniversaire!** or **Joyeux anniversaire!**
3. Many people in France and other European countries celebrate their saint's day. According to the Catholic calendar, each day of the year is associated with a Christian saint. If a person is named after a saint, he or she may receive gifts or treats on that particular saint's day.
4. The Antillean writer Maryse Condé writes about how big and lively her mother's birthday parties were.
5. **Aïd-el-Kébir** literally means **la grande fête** in Arabic. It is one of the most important Islamic celebrations and commemorates Abraham's willingness to sacrifice his son Ishmael as ordered by Allah. At the last moment, Allah sent the archangel Gabriel to replace Ishmael with a ram. To honor this complete submission to Allah's will, many Muslims ceremoniously sacrifice a sheep or ram.
6. One can buy electronics, books, CDs, DVDs, and software.
7. One can also purchase music, theater, and performance event tickets at **FNAC**.

**À discuter**
*Answers will vary.*

1. Véronique: le 4 février
2. Yvette: le 13 janvier
3. Hervé: le 17 juin
4. Pascal: le 17 mai
5. Catherine: le 24 mars
6. Jules: le 12 avril
7. Françoise: le 9 mars

---

**8** Questions culturelles  2.1, 2.2

*Répondez aux questions.*

1. How are birthday celebrations in France similar to those in the United States?
2. How do you wish someone a happy birthday in French?
3. What other special day do some people celebrate in France?
4. How does writer Maryse Condé describe her mother's birthday parties?
5. What is **Aïd-al-Kébir**?
6. What can you buy at **la FNAC**?
7. What other services does this retailer provide?

**La mosquée**, or mosque, is the place of prayer and religious gatherings for Muslims all over the world.

**À discuter**

What do personal, national, and religious celebrations all have in common?

## Du côté des médias

**9** Les fêtes  2.1, 2.2

*Choisissez la date pour la fête des ados avec les prénoms suivants.*

**MODÈLE** Sylvain
May 4

1. Véronique
2. Yvette
3. Hervé
4. Pascal
5. Catherine
6. Jules
7. Françoise

**Prénoms des saints**

| JANVIER | FEVRIER | MARS | AVRIL | MAI | JUIN |
|---|---|---|---|---|---|
| 1 V Jour de l'an | 1 L Ella | 1 L Aubin | 1 J Hugues | 1 S Fête du travail | 1 M Justin |
| 2 S Basile | 2 M Présentation | 2 M Charles le Bon | 2 V Sandrine | 2 D Boris | 2 M Blandine |
| 3 D Geneviève | 3 M Blaise | 3 M Guénolé | 3 S Richard | 3 L Philippe-Jacques | 3 J Kévin |
| 4 L Odilon | 4 J Véronique | 4 J Casimir | 4 D Isidore | 4 M Sylvain | 4 V Clotilde |
| 5 M Edouard | 5 V Agathe | 5 V Olive | 5 L Irène | 5 M Judith | 5 S Igor |
| 6 M Mélaine | 6 S Gaston | 6 S Colette | 6 M Marcellin | 6 J Prudence | 6 D Norbert |
| 7 J Raymond | 7 D Eugénie | 7 D Félicité | 7 M J-B. de la Salle | 7 V Gisèle | 7 L Gilbert |
| 8 V Lucien | 8 L Jacqueline | 8 L Jean de Dieu | 8 J Julie | 8 S Armistice 1945 | 8 M Médard |
| 9 S Alix | 9 M Apolline | 9 M Françoise | 9 V Gautier | 9 D Pacôme | 9 M Diane |
| 10 D Guillaume | 10 M Arnaud | 10 M Vivien | 10 S Fulbert | 10 L Solange | 10 J Landry |
| 11 L Pauline | 11 J ND de Lourdes | 11 J Rosine | 11 D Stanislas | 11 M Estelle | 11 V Barnabé |
| 12 M Tatiana | 12 V Félix | 12 V Justine | 12 L Jules | 12 M Achille | 12 S Guy |
| 13 M Yvette | 13 S Béatrice | 13 S Rodrigue | 13 M Ida | 13 J Rolande | 13 D Antoine de P. |
| 14 J Nina | 14 D Valentin | 14 D Mathilde | 14 M Maxime | 14 V Matthias | 14 L Elisée |
| 15 V Rémi | 15 L Claude | 15 L Louise | 15 J Paterne | 15 S Denise | 15 M Germaine |
| 16 S Marcel | 16 M Julienne | 16 M Bénédicte | 16 V Benoît-Joseph | 16 D Honoré | 16 M J. F. Régis |
| 17 D Roseline | 17 M Alexis | 17 M Patrice | 17 S Anicet | 17 L Pascal | 17 J Hervé |
| 18 L Prisca | 18 J Bernadette | 18 J Cyrille | 18 D Parfait | 18 M Eric | 18 V Léonce |
| 19 M Marius | 19 V Gabin | 19 V Joseph | 19 L Emma | 19 M Yves | 19 S Romuald |
| 20 M Sébastien | 20 S Aimée | 20 S Printemps | 20 M Odette | 20 J Bernardin | 20 D Silvère |
| 21 J Agnès | 21 D Damien | 21 D Clémence | 21 M Anselme | 21 V Constantin | 21 L Eté |
| 22 V Vincent | 22 L Isabelle | 22 L Léa | 22 J Alexandre | 22 S Emile | 22 M Alban |
| 23 S Banard | 23 M Lazare | 23 M Victorien | 23 V Georges | 23 D Didier | 23 M Audrey |
| 24 D Fr. de Sales | 24 M Modeste | 24 M Catherine1 | 24 S Fidèle | 24 L Donatien | 24 J Jean-Baptiste |
| 25 L Conv. de Paul | 25 J Roméo | 25 J Annonciation | 25 D Marc | 25 M Sophie | 25 V Prosper |
| 26 M Paule | 26 V Nestor | 26 V Larissa | 26 L Alida | 26 M Bérenger | 26 S Anthelme |
| 27 M Angèle | 27 S Honorine | 27 S Habib | 27 M Zita | 27 J Augustin1 | 27 D Fernand |
| 28 J Th. d'Aquin | 28 D Romain | 28 D Gontran | 28 M Valérie | 28 V Germain | 28 L Irénée |
| 29 V Gildas | | 29 L Gwladys | 29 J Cath. de Sienne | 29 S Aymar | 29 M Pierre-Paul |
| 30 S Martine | | 30 M Amédée | 30 V Robert | 30 D Ferdinand | 30 M Martial |
| 31 D Marcelle | | 31 M Beniamin | | 31 L Visitation | |

IMAGE DE CALENDRIER.COM

**Essential Instruction**

1. Have students do **Activité 8** and **Activité 9** in pairs.
2. As you present the verb **finir**, write the conjugation on the board with the endings in a different color. Review both the spelling and the pronunciation of the stem and endings.
3. To help students remember the verb meanings, make connections to what they already know.

For example, **réfléchir** is related to the English verb "to reflect," **maigrir** is related to the English adjective "meager." Explain that **rougir** really means "to turn red." Ask students what French color adjectives are contained in the verbs **blanchir**, **jaunir**, **noircir**, and **verdir** to help them discern the meaning.

# Structure de la langue

  Go online EMCLanguages.net

## RESOURCES

Workbook 23–25

## Present Tense of Regular Verbs Ending in *-ir* 1.2

Many French verb infinitives end in **-ir**. Most of these verbs are regular, such as **finir** (*to finish*) and **choisir** (*to choose*). Their forms follow a predictable pattern. To form the present tense of a regular **-ir** verb, drop the **-ir** ending from the infinitive to find the verb stem, then add the appropriate ending.

Je choisis le vert.

Now add the endings (**-is, -is, -it, -issons, -issez, -issent**) to the stem of the verb depending on the corresponding subject pronouns.

| finir | | | |
|---|---|---|---|
| je | fin**is** | nous | fin**issons** |
| tu | fin**is** | vous | fin**issez** |
| il/elle/on | fin**it** | ils/elles | fin**issent** |

Je **finis** le gâteau pour sa fête d'anniversaire.

*I am finishing the cake for her birthday party.*

En général, ma tante **choisit** les meilleurs cadeaux.

*My aunt generally chooses the best presents.*

**Note:** The verb **offrir** (*to give* or *offer*) is irregular. It will be presented later in this lesson.

| Some common **-ir** verbs: | |
|---|---|
| **grandir** | *to grow* |
| **grossir** | *to gain weight* |
| **maigrir** | *to lose weight* |
| **réfléchir (à)** | *to think over, consider* |
| **réussir (à)** | *to succeed, to pass (a test)* |
| **rougir** | *to blush* |

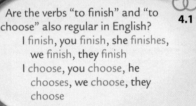

## COMPARAISONS 4.1

Are the verbs "to finish" and "to choose" also regular in English?
I finish, you finish, she finishes, we finish, they finish
I choose, you choose, he chooses, we choose, they choose

COMPARAISONS: The verbs "to finish" and "to choose" are also regular in English.

## Culture

Have students look up (by first name) the saint's **fête** (feast day) for their birthday. What feast day is celebrated then? Do any students have birthdays on their feast day? You can make a class calendar that is marked with all students' birthdays and feast days. When you practice saying the date, include the feast day. Also write out the full day with the feast day on the board and ask students to answer: **Quel jour sommes-nous?** Depending on your preference, explore traditions other than Christianity which honor certain individuals. Survey students about the origin of their names. Have them research and share about the significance of their first and last names.

## Differentiated Learning
### Adapt

1. To help students pronounce the forms of the regular -ir verbs, tell them to say the infinitive **finir**. Then, take off the -r and say **fini-**. Finally, model this stem with the endings: **-s, -s, -t, -ssons, -ssez,** and **-ssent**. Remind students that the final consonant of the singular is silent, as are the final syllables of the plural forms. Have students repeat this process with other -ir verbs.

2. Drill the conjugation chorally or toss a koosh ball to call on students individually to give the verb form when you say a pronoun or name.

## Multiple Intelligences
### Verbal-Linguistic

Students will benefit from knowing that there are three translations for the present tense of almost any French verb. **Je finis** means "I finish," "I am finishing (I'm finishing)," and "I do finish." Ask them to provide the three English meanings for each conjugated form.

**10**

1. Mehdi et Romain choisissent la carte Go Sport.
2. Inès et Coralie choisissent la carte Carrefour.
3. Je choisis la carte Quick.
4. Vous choisissez la carte FNAC.
5. Lilou et moi, nous choisissons la carte FNAC ou Carrefour.
6. Je choisis la carte Go Sport.
7. Tu choisis la carte FNAC ou Carrefour.
8. Laurence choisit la carte FNAC ou Carrefour.

**11** *Follow the model. Answers will vary.*

## Expansion

As a follow-up of the activity suggested on p. 235, have students discuss their preferences for gift cards. From which store(s) in France or the United States would they like to receive gift cards and why? What kind of gift cards do their family members prefer?

---

**10** **Quelle cartes cadeaux choisissent-ils?**  2.1, 2.2

*Dites quelle carte cadeau ces personnes choisissent pour offrir à leurs amis.*

**MODÈLE** Guillaume a besoin d'un nouveau sac à dos./Sébastien
**Sébastien choisit la carte cadeau Carrefour.**

1. Alima a besoin d'un ballon de foot./Mehdi et Romain
2. Mamadou a besoin de chaussures de foot./Inès et Coralie
3. Julie aime manger des hamburgers et des frites./je
4. Héloïse aime les concerts./Anaïs et toi, vous
5. Noémie a besoin d'un dictionnaire./Lilou et moi, nous
6. Marc-Antoine désire un maillot du PSG./je
7. David a besoin d'un cédérom./tu
8. Martin désire le nouveau CD de Franz Ferdinand./Laurence

## Communiquez!

**11** **Les emplois du temps** 1.1

### Interpersonal Communication

*Bruno et Serge désirent savoir quand l'autre finit ses cours pour trouver le temps de jouer au football.* (Bruno and Serge want to find out when the other finishes class so they can find a time to play soccer.) *Avec un partenaire, jouez les rôles de Bruno et Serge.*

**MODÈLE** Bruno: **Quand est-ce que tu finis les cours lundi?**
Serge: **Je finis à 14h45. Et toi, quand est-ce que tu finis?**
Bruno: **Je finis à 15h30.**

**Bruno**

| Jour | Ses cours finissent à.... |
|------|---------------------------|
| lundi | 15h30 |
| mardi | 14h45 |
| mercredi | 16h00 |
| jeudi | 16h30 |
| vendredi | 14h45 |
| samedi | 11h50 |

**Serge**

| Jour | Ses cours finissent à.... |
|------|---------------------------|
| lundi | 14h45 |
| mardi | 15h30 |
| mercredi | 15h15 |
| jeudi | 14h45 |
| vendredi | 16h30 |
| samedi | 11h50 |

Quand est-ce que tu finis les cours mercredi?

Je finis à 16h00.

---

### Essential Learning

1. Project, or have students go online to research, the website of the French stores and restaurants whose gift cards are pictured in **Activité 10**. What kinds of things can one purchase at these places? Then, do the activity chorally.
2. Briefly review telling time before assigning **Activité 11** in groups.
3. For **Activité 12**, remind students that the verb **donner** means "to give," but that "to give/offer a present" is expressed by **offrir un cadeau**.
4. Review the months of the year and show your students how to write dates in French. Contrast this to English. Explain that most of the world expresses dates by day/month/year. You may wish to discuss possible reasons for this difference.

**12 La fête d'anniversaire**  2.1

*Xavier est content. Hugo lui donne (is throwing him) une fête d'anniversaire. Complétez son e-mail avec les formes convenables des verbes* **choisir, finir, grossir,** *et* **rougir.**

| À: | Hugo |
|---|---|
| Cc: | |
| Sujet: | Mon anniversaire |

Salut, Hugo!

Une fête pour mon anniversaire, c'est sympa. Tu es généreux! (Je __1__ !) On va faire une super teuf! Qu'est-ce que tu vas __2__ comme gâteau? Je préfère les gâteaux au chocolat. Moi, je vais manger le gâteau, mais Andrée et Clara, ça, c'est différent. Elles ne veulent pas __3__ . On va avoir aussi des fruits et des boissons? Comme ça, les filles vont être contentes. Oui, c'est bien. Nous __4__ le dîner avec le gâteau ou des fruits.

À+! Xavier

## Dates  1.2

To express the date in French, follow this formula:

**le** + number + month

C'est **le 19 mars.**
Nous sommes **le 19 mars.** } It's March 19.

C'est le 14 février.

An exception to this rule is "the first" of any month. Use **le premier** before the name of a month.

C'est **le premier mai.**
C'est **le 1ᵉʳ mai.** } *It's May first.*

When a date is abbreviated, the day comes before the month: 12/7 is July 12.

---

**Differentiated Learning**
**Accelerate**
Ask students to create comprehension questions in French about **Activité 12** and lead a review of the exercise.

**Multiple Intelligences**
**Interpersonal**
Ask students to rewrite **Activité 12** as a dialogue, then perform it for the class.

---

**Answers** _____

**12**

1. rougis
2. choisir
3. grossir
4. finissons

## Communication

**Interpretive: Cooperative Groups**
Tear off the months of an old calendar and distribute one month to each cooperative group of several students. Have one student point to different days, one for each of the other students in the group to identify. For example, as the student points to August 28, another student says **C'est le vingt-huit août.** Each group member takes a turn in selecting dates for the others to identify. For further practice, students can also identify the day of the week and the name of the feast day.

### Culture

**Practices: Activity**
Have students make an academic year calendar with photos from your school or town, and student artwork. They can include dates of American holidays and school events for francophone e-pals. If your overseas partners send a calendar, then students can compare vacation times, number of school days, and other school-related information.

### Communication

Assign students to write a description of a family member or friend whom they admire, including age, date of birth, and qualities of the person. Ask students to present their description to the class.

---

## 13 Les jours fériés  2.1

*Écrivez les dates en français de ces jours fériés (holidays).*

**MODÈLE**   1/1
**le premier janvier**

9/4
**le neuf avril**

1. 9/4
2. 1/5
3. 8/5
4. 17/5
5. 28/5
6. 14/7
7. 15/8
8. 11/11
9. 25/12

## 14 Les dates spéciales  2.1

*Écrivez la date en français de chaque fête américaine ou événement.*

1. Valentine's Day
2. New Year's Day
3. Saint Patrick's Day
4. Independence Day (U.S.)
5. Halloween
6. April Fools' Day
7. Christmas
8. New Year's Eve
9. your birthday
10. the last day of school

In France, it is common to eat raw oysters squirted with lemon juice on New Year's Eve.

## Communiquez!

## 15 Les anniversaires de mes amis

**Interpersonal Communication**
*Écrivez les noms de cinq amis et échangez (exchange) votre liste avec la liste d'un partenaire. Votre partenaire va demander la date d'anniversaire de chacun de vos amis et la noter. Échangez encore (again) vos listes et corrigez les dates.*

**MODÈLE**   Rahina
A: **C'est quand, l'anniversaire de ton amie Rahina?**
B: **Son anniversaire est le 11 juin.**

C'est quand l'anniversaire de Patrick?

C'est le 12 février.

---

**Essential Instruction**

1. Have students do **Activité 13** and **Activité 14** at the board or write out the activity, then peer-correct.
2. You may want to briefly discuss some of the religious and cultural holidays recognized in the United States, such as Thanksgiving, Hanukah, Ramadan, or Kwanzaa and whether or not they exist or are widely celebrated in France.
3. Suggest that students add birthdays of family members when doing **Activité 15** in pairs.
4. Review the instructions for **Activité 16** before listening to the exercise.
5. Review the conjugation of the verb **avoir** and the **avoir** expressions students have already learned. Then add the expression **avoir... ans** and have students ask about and give the age of family members in pairs.

## 16 Les dates   2.1

*Catherine et sa sœur parlent de dates importantes. Écoutez leur conversation et écrivez les dates que vous entendez à la française: le jour/le mois. Par exemple, la date de Noël (Christmas) s'écrit (is written) 25/12.*

**MODÈLE**   Vous entendez:   L'anniversaire de Richard est le 12 mai.
             Vous écrivez:     **12/5**

# Expressions with *avoir*  1.2

You have already learned three expressions with the verb **avoir: avoir besoin de** (*to need*), **avoir faim** (*to be hungry*), and **avoir soif** (*to be thirsty*). Another expression is **avoir... an(s)** which is used to tell how old someone is. To ask someone's age, you can say: **Tu as quel âge?**

Tu as quel âge?          *How old are you?*
J'**ai** quatorze **ans**.   *I'm fourteen (years old).*

## 17 On a quel âge?   2.1

*Donnez l'âge de tout le monde selon leur date de naissance (birthdate).*

1. L'actrice et chanteuse Vanessa Paradis a quel âge?
   mille neuf cent soixante-douze
2. L'acteur Johnny Depp a quel âge?
   mille neuf cent soixante-trois
3. Le footballeur Franck Ribéry a quel âge?
   mille neuf cent quatre-vingt-trois
4. Le chanteur Corneille a quel âge?
   mille neuf cent soixante dix-sept
5. Le chanteur Rachid Taha a quel âge?
   mille neuf cent cinquante-huit

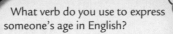

**COMPARAISONS**

What verb do you use to express someone's age in English?   **4.1**

Amber is 15 years old.
Tom and Jim are only 14.

COMPARAISONS: To express a person's age, English speakers use the verb "to be."

Leçon B   |   deux cent quarante-trois   **243**

**Answers**

**16** Script can be found in the front pages of the Annotated Teacher's Edition.

1. 31/6
2. 8/1
3. 15/8
4. 25/11
5. 1/5
6. 13/3
7. 15/10
8. 14/2
9. 11/11
10. 17/4

**17** *Calculate answers according to the present year.*

## Connections

**History**
Make up a list of 20 important dates in world history. Include a few with significance for franco-phone cultures, for example 1789 (French Revolution) and 6/6/44 (D-Day). Give out sheets of paper with these dates expressed only in numerical fashion. Then ask students to write out the complete dates in French with words. For 1789, they will answer: **mille sept cent quatre-vingt-neuf**. For 6/6/44, they will answer: **le six juin mille neuf cent quarante-quatre**. Students should pay attention to spelling and the French way of expressing dates. Ask students to note the significance of these dates. Discuss their findings.

As a follow-up, challenge students to make up a list of only dates that are significant for francophone culture. They might look up the date of the Battle of Waterloo (18 June 1815), the birth of Louis XIV (5 September 1638), the death of Joan of Arc (30 May 1431), the Battle of Quebec (13 September 1759), or the recent earthquake in Haiti (12 January 2010). They could design a poster or timeline for display in the classroom illustrating these events.

**Differentiated Learning**
**Accelerate**
For **Activité 17**, have students create additional questions similar to those in the exercise, using the birth dates of other famous people. Have them ask their questions to the class or a partner.

**Decelerate**
Before students answer the questions in **Activité 17**, help them write each year given in numerals. Go over the meaning of the instructions, having them add **tout le monde** and **selon** to their list of instructions.

**Special Needs Students**
**Auditory Impairment/Linguistically Challenged**
For students who have difficulty understanding dates when they hear them, provide extra practice using white boards. Give dates and have students write both the French and English version in two columns, for example, **le quinze septembre** would be written **le 15.09** and 9/15.

**243**

### Reference Desk

As your students become familiar with **offrir**, expand their knowledge base by introducing the verbs **ouvrir**, **couvrir**, **découvrir**, and **souffrir** that have a similar conjugation. Challenge your students to brainstorm what they think the conjugations would look like, then confirm the conjugation. Once you introduce this verb family, have students create sentences using all of the verbs. Provide further practice activities to anchor understanding.

---

**18** L'album de photos de grand-mère  **2.1**

*Vous regardez l'album de photos de votre grand-mère. Elle est née (was born) en 1950. Elle a quel âge dans chaque photo?*

**MODÈLE** 1960
**Ma grand-mère a dix ans en mille neuf cent soixante.**

1. 1965

2. 1969

3. 1977

4. 1983

5. 2000

# Present Tense of the Irregular Verb *offrir* 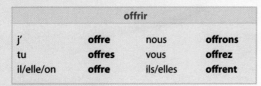 1.1

The verb **offrir** (*to offer, to give*) looks like an **–ir** verb, but it is irregular.

| offrir | | | |
|---|---|---|---|
| j' | **offre** | nous | **offrons** |
| tu | **offres** | vous | **offrez** |
| il/elle/on | **offre** | ils/elles | **offrent** |

**Spelling Tip**

Note that in the present tense of **offrir** has the endings of an **–er** verb.

Qu'est-ce qu'on **offre**?     *What are we giving?*

Qu'est-ce que Sophie offre à sa grand-mère?

**Essential Instruction**

1. Have students provide information to a partner about two additional family members after doing **Activité 18**.
2. Emphasize that **offrir** is conjugated like an **-er** verb.
3. When assigning **Activité 19**, you may wish to write on the board the formula **offrir** + **quelque chose** (direct object) + **à quelqu'un** (indirect object) to help students include all necessary components in their sentences.
4. Review the instructions for **Activité 20**, and then have students take turns asking each other questions with a partner.

## 19 Les cadeaux d'anniversaire

 2.1, 2.2

*Dites ce que tout le monde offre.*

**MODÈLE** Jean-Luc/son beau-père
**Il offre un cadeau à son beau-père.**

1. Emma/sa cousine
2. moi, je/mon oncle
3. Gabrielle et Paul/ leurs cousins

4. René/son cousin
5. Charlotte et moi, nous/notre belle-sœur
6. Océane et Annick/leur grand-mère
7. toi et Ambre, vous/votre cousin
8. toi, tu/ta prof de français

## Communiquez!

### 20 Les fêtes

1.1

**Interpersonal Communication**

*Posez des questions à votre partenaire sur ce qu'il ou elle offre à certaines personnes comme cadeau. Puis, changez de rôles.*

**MODÈLE** ta grand-mère/son anniversaire
A: **Qu'est-ce que tu offres à ta grand-mère pour son anniversaire?**
B: **J'offre une écharpe à ma grand-mère pour son anniversaire.**

> Qu'est-ce que tu offres à ton ami pour la Saint-Valentin?

> J'offre un CD à mon ami pour la Saint-Valentin.

1. ton père/la fête des Pères
2. ton ami(e)/la Saint-Valentin
3. ta mère/la fête des Mères
4. tes parents/leur anniversaire de mariage
5. ton frère ou ta sœur/son anniversaire
6. ton ami(e)/son anniversaire

### Answers

**19**
1. Elle offre une chemise à sa cousine.
2. Moi, j'offre un CD à mon oncle.
3. Gabrielle et Paul, ils offrent un DVD à leurs cousins.
4. René offre une trousse à son cousin.
5. Charlotte et moi, nous offrons un blouson à notre belle-sœur.
6. Océane et Annick offrent une écharpe à leur grand-mère.
7. Toi et Ambre, vous offrez un gâteau d'anniversaire à votre cousin.
8. Toi, tu offres un dessert à ta prof de français.

**20** *Answers to questions will vary. Questions follow model.*

### Communication

**Presentational: Cooperative Groups**
Give each student six cards and a plain envelope. Have students put the name of a family member or friend on one side of each card, noting the relationship and drawing a birthday gift they would give that person on the other side of the card. Students place their cards in the envelope and decorate it to look like a wrapped present. Next, each student pulls out three cards from the envelope and explains what the **cadeau** is and whom it is for. For the remaining three cards, students write a description to hand in.

### Learning Styles
**Visual Learners**
Have students draw or find images of eight objects they know how to say in French. Using the model from **Activité 19** have them write a sentence using a different subject pronoun and the correct form of the verb **offrir** under each image. Finally, have them share their work with a partner or post in the classroom.

# À vous la parole

**What is the nature of relationships in other cultures?**

  **1.1**

## 21 Quelle est la date de ton anniversaire?

### Interpersonal Communication

Form a circle with your classmates around the room to represent the calendar year. The door of the room marks the beginning of the year, or **janvier**. Ask the classmates closest to you when their birthday is, then arrange yourselves clockwise in the circle according to the month you were born. When everyone has found their place, each student will say when their birthday is. Listen carefully to make sure everyone is in the correct place!

## 22 Une carte d'anniversaire

**1.3, 2.1**

### Interpretive/Presentational Communication

Your teacher will come around the room with a bag. Pull out the name of a classmate and send him or her a virtual birthday card with a message. For example, you might wish your classmate a happy birthday and ask what he or she is going to do or ask how old he or she is now.

 **Search words: cartes de vœux virtuelles**

> Je veux inviter Awa, Anne, et Justin.

> Je peux téléphoner à nos amis.

## 23 Une surprise!

**1.1**

### Interpersonal Communication

You and a classmate are planning a surprise birthday party for a friend. In your conversation:

- greet each other.
- ask each other how things are going.
- confirm the date of your friend's birthday.
- decide on a gift to give him or her.
- decide whom is going to bring the sandwiches, cake, beverages, and music.
- say whom you want to invite and write a list of names.
- say who will send the invitations or phone your friends.
- exchange phone numbers so that you can do more planning later. Say good-bye.

### Vocabulaire utile

**envoyer les invitations** *send invitations*; **téléphoner à un copain** *phone a friend*; **continuer la discussion** *continue the discussion*

 **246** deux cent quarante-six | Unité 5

# Stratégie communicative

## L'Art de la conversation

There is an art to carrying on an interesting conversation. You may have mastered this art in English, but how do you improve your conversation skills in French? The answer is easy. Ask questions! Most people like to talk about themselves. Let's begin by reviewing how to ask someone for information. Here is a formula for asking information questions:

| question word + **est-ce que (qu')** + subject + verb | **Pourquoi est-ce que** tu vas au Café de Paris? *Why do you go to the Café de Paris?* |

Other question words and expressions you can use are:

| **où** *where* | **comment** *how* | **avec qui** *with whom* |
| **quand** *when* | **qui** *who* | **que** *what* |

### 24 Je continue la conversation.  2.1, 2.2

*Imaginez que vous parlez avec ces personnes. Choisissez la question qui suit logiquement (that logically follows) chaque phrase.*

1. Alexandre: Je vais au stade le weekend.
2. Michèle: J'aime faire du jogging.
3. Myriam: Je vais au centre commercial ce soir.
4. Marianne: J'étudie avec Hugo.
5. Mehdi: Je vais au parc après l'école.
6. Lamine: Je vais aller à Lyon.

A. Qui est Hugo?
B. Pourquoi est-ce que tu vas au stade le weekend?
C. Quand est-ce que tu vas aller à Lyon?
D. Où est-ce que tu aimes faire du jogging?
E. Qu'est-ce que tu vas faire au parc?
F. Comment est-ce que tu vas au centre commercial?

## Communiquez!

### 25 Je peux participer dans une conversation.   1.1

**Interpersonal Communication**

*Parlez avec un partenaire:*

1. du cinéma
2. d'un(e) camarade de classe
3. des dates d'anniversaire
4. des projets pour le weekend
5. de la famille

*Prolongez la conversation avec une question.*

---

**Differentiated Learning**
**Decelerate**
For **Activité 23**, create a template, omitting key words and expressions that the students must complete in French.

**Accelerate**
Have students write a dialogue for two of the topics in **Activité 25** and share them in a group.

**Special Needs Students**
**Linguistically Challenged**
For **Activité 25**, give students the choice of one or two topics. Provide them with specific facts and/or vocabulary to include. Provide the beginning of sample sentences to help them discuss each topic.

**RESOURCES**

 Pre-test

 *Leçon* Quiz

Answers _____

24
1. B
2. D
3. F
4. A
5. E
6. C

25 *Answers will vary.*

## Communication

### Presentational: Paired Practice

Draw up a list of topics, for example, sports, fashion, the arts, education, population, great leaders, health, nature/environment, etc. Have pairs select a topic that they will then research for several of the African francophone countries listed in the **Vocabulaire actif**. For example, students interested in fashion could research local outfits typical to each country. Those interested in numbers could perhaps research facts and figures related to population, health, education level, income, or other issues. A student interested in animals could research the status of the elephant or animal reserves from country to country. Have groups collaborate to share the results of their findings.

# Leçon C

# Vocabulaire actif

Go online
EMCLanguages.net

## L'Afrique francophone   1.2

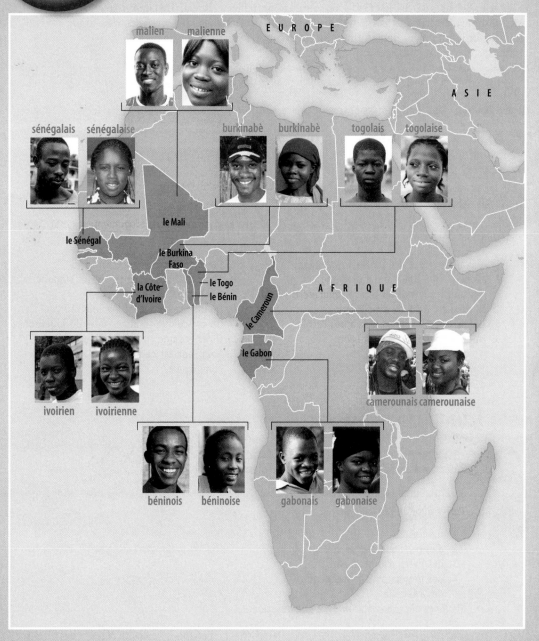

### Essential Instruction

1. Ask students to observe the map of Africa and reflect on why French is spoken in these countries and to share what they know about this area of the world. Explain that, in addition to French, people also speak many different African languages. Many Africans are **bilingue** or **trilingue**. Teach the word polyglots (poly = many + glot = tongues).

2. Explain that, generally speaking, **profession** has the connotation of being more intellectual or white-collar work, whereas **métier** implies a trade or manual labor.

3. Ask students if they can identify the jobs that are not cognates, based on the pictures. Clarify meanings, and then listen to the audio of the vocabulary.

# Des professions et des métiers   1.2

## RESOURCES

 e-visuals 18–19

 Workbook 31–32

un agent de police

une athlète

une avocate

un cuisinier

un homme d'affaires

un médecin

un ingénieur

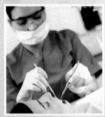

une dentiste

un écrivain

une chanteuse

un metteur en scène

un graphiste

un testeur de jeux vidéo

## Critical Thinking

### Application
Discuss with your class the advantages for today's job seekers of knowing a foreign language. What professions are open to those with foreign language skills? Have each student make a card giving the description and title of a job or profession that embraces foreign language skills, and display these as a job board on your wall. Expand this discussion by assigning research of job listings that list French, or another language, as a qualification. Ask students to create a list of local and regional companies that do business with France or other francophone countries. Post the list to your class webpage or in the classroom. If possible, contact one of the companies and explore inviting an employee who speaks French on the job to visit your class.

## Learning Styles
### Kinesthetic/Auditory Learners
Have students circulate and interview each other about languages other than English which are spoken at home. How many students are **bilingue** or **trilingue**?

### Visual Learners
Ask students to observe the map and find the country that looks like a rooster. When the people of Cameroun are asked where they live, they often respond, "in the head of the rooster," or "in the tail of the rooster," etc.

## Multiple Intelligences
### Musical-Rhythmic
Students who are well-versed in music may be familiar with the rich, contemporary music scene in Africa. Ask them to find music from one of the francophone countries mentioned in this lesson and share it with the class.

2 4 9

**Reference Desk**

Students must learn that, unlike in English, one does not use an indefinite article when using the verb **être** and mention of a profession. In French one says **Il est ingénieur** or **Ma tante est chanteuse** without **un** or **une**. When using **c'est + profession**, remind students to use an article: **C'est un mécanicien.** (see p. 258)

| | | | |
|---|---|---|---|
| un agent de police | un dentiste | un agent de police | une dentiste |
| un athlète | un écrivain | une athlète | un écrivain |
| un avocat | un chanteur | une avocate | une chanteuse |
| un cuisinier | un metteur en scène | une cuisinière | un metteur en scène |
| un homme d'affaires | un graphiste | une femme d'affaires | une graphiste |
| un médecin | un testeur de jeux vidéo | un médecin | un testeur de jeux vidéo |
| un ingénieur | | un ingénieur | |

## Pour la conversation  1.2

**H**ow do I find out what someone's profession is?

> **Quelle est votre profession?**
> *What is your profession?*

> **How do I state my profession?**

> **Je suis actrice.**
> *I'm an actrice.*

**H**ow do I ask where someone comes from?

> **Vous venez/Tu viens d'où?**
> *Where do you come from?*

**H**ow do I say where I come from?

> **Je viens** des États-Unis.
> *I come from the United States.*

> **Je viens** du Canada.
> *I come from Canada.*

> **Je viens** de France.
> *I come from France.*

**Et si je voulais dire...?**

| | |
|---|---|
| **un(e) secrétaire** | *secretary* |
| **un boulanger, une boulangère** | *baker* |
| **un boucher, une bouchère** | *butcher* |
| **un épicier, une épicière** | *grocery store owner* |
| **un pâtissier, une pâtissière** | *pastry chef* |
| **un caissier, une caissière** | *cashier* |
| **un pompier** | *fire fighter* |
| **un(e) vétérinaire** | *veterinarian* |
| **un chercheur, une chercheuse** | *researcher* |

**Essential Instruction**

1. Ask students to scan the vocabulary and identify cognates. As you model the pronunciation, have them note any jobs that are invariable (do not have a feminine form) and those whose pronunciation changes in the feminine of each profession. To practice further, call out the masculine and ask students to respond together with the feminine. Then do the reverse.

2. Define non-cognate words. Explain the helpful tip that French words that begin with **é-** sometimes correspond to English words that begin with an "s," hence the relationship between the word **écrivain** and the English word "scribe." Give other examples that students have already seen, such as **écharpe** (*scarf*), **école** (*school*), **États-Unis** (*United States*).

3. After listening to the functions in **Pour la conversation**, reinforce the question **D'où venez-vous?** by asking as many other students as possible during a set amount of time where they are from.

4. Do **Activités 1** and **2** as a class and reinforce correct pronunciation.

**1**
1. camerounaise
2. ivoirien
3. sénégalaise
4. malienne
5. togolais
6. gabonais

**2** *Possible answers:*
1. Mme Renette est médecin.
2. M Odinot est avocat.
3. Mme Touzain est femme d'affaires.
4. M Vivot est dentiste.
5. M Toussaint est chanteur.
6. Mlle Soyer est écrivain ou graphiste

**1 Des étudiants de l'Afrique**  🎧 ✿ 2.1, 2.2

*Des élèves de l'Afrique se présentent* (are introducing themselves). *Complétez chaque phrase avec l'adjectif de nationalité convenable.*

1. Je m'appelle Alima. Je viens du Cameroun. Je suis….
2. Je m'appelle Amidou. Je viens de la Côte-d'Ivoire. Je suis….
3. Je m'appelle Naya. Je viens du Sénégal. Je suis….
4. Je m'appelle Evenye. Je viens du Mali. Je suis….
5. Je m'appelle Kemajou. Je viens du Togo. Je suis….
6. Je m'appelle Koffi. Je viens du Gabon. Je suis….

Je vous présente Mlle Fanta. Elle est gabonaise.

**2 Quelle est sa profession?** ✿ 2.1, 2.2

*Dites la profession de ces personnes.*

MODÈLE  Mme Dumont
**Mme Dumont est cuisinière.**

1. Mme Renette    2. M. Odinot    3. Mlle Touzain

4. M. Vivot    5. M. Toussaint    6. Mlle Soyer

**Expansion**

Make a list of professions and distribute to small groups. Ask students to work together by contributing the name of a well-known person or film or literary character to match each profession. Have students share orally or post their lists.

**Differentiated Instruction**
**Expand**
Give students a 3 x 5 card each and have them write their name on one side and three professions in French that they are interested in pursuing in the future on the other. Allow students to use a dictionary or online resource to find the French translation of any profession that is not on the list. Collect the cards. Students guess which classmate wrote the list as you read off the professions.

**Learning Styles**
**Auditory/Visual Learners**
Brainstorm a list of famous names and ask the students to identify their professions with **Il est….** or **Elle est….** Alternatively, show the students pictures of famous people or of people doing various jobs to elicit the same responses.

**Kinesthetic Learners**
Call out a profession and have students act it out. Do this activity in reverse. Students act out a profession and others guess.

**3** Script can be found in the front pages of the Annotated Teacher's Edition.

1. B
2. C
3. H
4. D
5. G
6. J
7. I
8. A
9. F

**4** Answers will vary.

## Communication

**Interpersonal: Paired Practice**

Have partners fold a sheet of paper into three columns and add the labels "professions," "francophone countries," and "francophone first names." Refer students to the list of names in **Unité 1**. They then draw up a list of 10 items to place in each column. One student randomly chooses an item from two of the columns and creates sentences about a person. For example, a student selects a name and a country, but must provide the nationality (which he must ascertain from the country name). **Modèle: Il est haïtien et il s'appelle Fernand.** The partner repeats the information, but adds to the description by including information from the remaining column, in this case, professions. For example, **Il est haïtien, il s'appelle Fernand, et il est médecin**. Continue the exercise, alternating **rôles**.

---

**3 Les professions**   **2.1, 2.2**

*Choisissez l'image qui correspond à la phrase que vous entendez.*

> **MODÈLE** Vous entendez: M. Diouf? C'est un dentiste congolais.
> Vous écrivez: **E**

A.

B.

C.

D.

E.

F.

G.

H.

I.

J.

**4 Questions personnelles**  **2.1**

*Répondez aux questions.*

1. Tu viens d'où?
2. Tes parents, ils sont américains?
3. Quelle est la profession de tes grands-parents ou ton oncle et ta tante?
4. Quelle profession est-ce que tu vas choisir?
5. Quelle profession est-ce que tu préfères, graphiste ou testeur de jeux vidéo?

> Je voudrais être graphiste.

**Essential Instruction**

1. For **Activité 3**, explain to students that they will need to listen for both the profession and the adjective agreement.
2. Model correct responses in **Activité 4** by first having students ask you the **Questions personnelles** using **vous**. Then assign the activity in pairs.
3. Before you show the filmed dialogue, ask students if they have heard of Amadou and Mariam. What kind of music might they play and what instruments could they use? Have the students read the dialogue silently, identify cognates, and ask questions about new vocabulary. Model the pronunciation, asking them to repeat each sentence after you, then show the filmed dialogue a second time. Check for comprehension with **Activité 5**.

# Rencontres culturelles

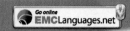 **Go online EMCLanguages.net**

## On prépare un projet culturel!

    **1.2**

To prepare for a culture project, Yasmine tells Maxime about Amadou and Mariam, her favorite African singers.

| | |
|---|---|
| Maxime: | D'où viennent-ils? |
| Yasmine: | Amadou et Mariam? Ils viennent du Mali. |
| Maxime: | Et quelle est leur profession? |
| Yasmine: | Ils sont chanteurs et compositeurs. |
| Maxime: | Je voudrais être chanteur un jour. |
| Yasmine: | C'est une bonne profession. Mais tu chantes bien, toi? Et bien, moi, je voudrais être écrivain ou peut-être médecin! |
| Maxime: | Mademoiselle n'est pas paresseuse! Tu travailles bien à l'école. |
| Yasmine: | Non. Mais toi, tu es un peu bavard! Je veux préparer mon projet culturel, pas parler de professions! |

**5** **On prépare un projet culturel!**   **2.1, 2.2**

*Complétez les phrases.*

1. Yasmine prépare un....
2. Elle aime bien..., des chanteurs et compositeurs africains.
3. Amadou et Mariam... du Mali.
4. La future profession de Maxime est....
5. Yasmine désire être... ou....

**Extension** **Comment choisir sa profession?**   **1.2, 2.1, 2.2**

Sébastien, un reporter pour le journal du lycée, interviewe des élèves pour trouver la profession qu'ils veulent exercer un jour.

| | |
|---|---|
| Sébastien: | Quelle profession aimerais-tu exercer et pourquoi? |
| Étudiante 1: | Cuisinière! Pour les saveurs et pour le plaisir que l'on donne aux autres. |
| Étudiant 2: | Journaliste... par passion de l'écriture et par intérêt pour le monde qui change. |
| Étudiant 3: | Avocat... parce que j'aime les causes perdues! |
| Étudiante 4: | Ingénieur... parce que c'est l'art de faire et de défaire et d'imaginer d'autres solutions. |

**Extension** Which reason for choosing a profession comes closest to one you would have? Explain.

---

---

## Culture

### Practices: Information
Before the 19th century, access to Africa by European expansionists was impeded to the north by the Sahara, and difficult conditions (insects, parasites, diseases) near the coastal areas. As Europeans made progress with the inventions of weapons and development of remedies (quinine), colonization accelerated and, by the end of the 19th century, the entire continent of Africa was under the rule of European colonial powers with deleterious effects. Research maps of Africa from the 18th to 20th centuries to show the evolution of this period.

## Critical Thinking

### Comparisons
Many local and regional museums, universities, and colleges have collections of African art. Research and contact such organizations to arrange a guided tour of the collection, or have students explore the collections online. Ask students to compare what they learn about African masks to any practices from their own family or ethnic groups.

# Points de départ

 Go online EMCLanguages.net

 **La Francophonie**

**1.2, 3.1, 5.1**

*Question centrale* **?** What is the nature of relationships in other cultures?

❋ *L'Afrique francophone*

Sub-Saharan Francophone Africa refers mainly to West Africa and Central Africa. It includes the nations of Senegal, the Ivory Coast, Cameroon, Benin, Togo, Gabon, Burkina Faso, and Mali....

European traders brought African slaves to the Americas from the 15th to the 19th century. Heavy colonization of Africa didn't begin until the 19th century in what is called the "Scramble for Africa." By the 1960s, most African colonies had gained their independence, bringing the colonial period to an end. After independence, several of the former colonies modeled their educational systems on the one in France and used French in business and governmental affairs.

Peanuts, food for men and animals, are an important export crop in West Africa.

Many Africans earn a living from farming and herding, even in the dry and hot regions of the Sahel, just south of the Sahara. Coffee, cacao, cotton, and peanuts are important export products. Africa also exports minerals and other raw materials, such as natural gas, petroleum, rare metals, and diamonds. Africa is home to many artists who have greatly influenced Francophone culture. African writers like Kourouma, Birago Diop, Tchicaya U Tam'si, Henri Lopès, Mariama Bâ, and Mongo Beti are popular in both Africa and Europe, and musicians and singers, such as Youssou N'Dour and Akon have become international stars.

 **Search words: carte afrique francophone de l'ouest akon video**

**Mon dico africain** **4.2**
une France au-revoir: *used car from France*
faire le show: *have fun*
coco taillé: *shaved head*
Ça fait deux jours. *It takes a long time.*
On dit quoi? Ça va?

 **Produits**

African masks are more than decorative objects. They play an important role in tribal ceremonies and are used to communicate with the spirits. Made of wood and carved by hand, they vary from region to region. Masks from Gabon are often white, representing dead ancestors. Many Malian and Cameroonian masks look like animal heads.

 **Search words: masques africains**

**2.1, 2.2, 4.2**

West African mask

## Essential Instruction

1. Before reading the text **L'Afrique francophone**, ask a volunteer to identify the Sahara Desert on the map of Africa. Brainstorm what students know about the theme of the reading and create a word cloud online with their contributions. Divide students into small groups and have them read and summarize each paragraph, and then share three important points of information for each paragraph. Ask if they have seen any films or read anything that explores what they read about.

2. After they read about **Amidou et Mariam** in class, have students research the singers online for homework. Ask students to share their research. Play one of **Amadou et Mariam's** songs from the Internet. Then do **Activité 6** as a class.

## Amadou et Mariam 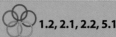 1.2, 2.1, 2.2, 5.1

Amadou Bagayoko and Mariam Doumbia are from Mali. They met at Mali's Institute for the Young Blind where they discovered a shared love for music. Eventually they married and had children. Their unique sound blends traditional Malian music with rock and roll, as well as Syrian and Cuban musical genres, as seen through the use of guitars, violins, and trumpets. Their music has often been described as "Afro blues." One of their albums, with Latin music star Manu Chao, was called *Dimanche à Bamako*. In 2010 they published their autobiography, *Away from the Light of Day*.

Amadou and Mariam have given concerts all over the world, including in the United States.

 Search words: **amadou et mariam en concert**
**amadou et mariam site officiel**

### COMPARAISONS

Can you name any American musicians who have been influenced by World music? 2.1, 2.2, 3.1, 5.1

## 6 Questions culturelles 2.1, 2.2

*Répondez aux questions.*

1. Can you name four countries that are considered part of sub-Saharan Francophone Africa?
2. What was the "Scramble for Africa," and when did it take place?
3. When did colonialism end in Francophone Africa?
4. What are some of Africa's export products?
5. Can you name two areas in which Africans are contributing to Francophone culture?
6. What purpose do masks serve in Africa?
7. Who are Amadou and Mariam? What kind of music are they known for?
8. What does the name of their album *Dimanche à Bamako* mean?

### Perspectives

In his poem, "Ni l'un ni l'autre," African poet Alphonse Bamana says: "L'Afrique est ma mère/ L'Europe est mon père,/Tels sont ces inséparables/ Êtres adorables. "What is Bamana's attitude toward France, his country's former colonial ruler? What might be another viewpoint held by West Africans toward France?

In this slave warehouse on the island of Gorée, Senegal, Africans were led to slaveships and transported to the Americas.

Leçon C | deux cent cinquante-cinq 255

**7**

1. Une série humoristique, comique, tragique, sentimentale
2. 300 épisodes
3. 7 ans
4. *Answers will vary.*
5. *Answers will vary.*

## Expansion

Have students research TV programs in other francophone countries and draw up program cards following the model of the one for **Ma Famille** pictured on p. 256.

## Du côté des médias

**7** **Ma famille**  **1.2, 2.1, 2.2**

*Lisez l'information sur ce programme qui passait (used to be on) à la télévision en Côte-d'Ivoire et répondez aux questions.*

1. What kind of TV show is *"Ma famille"*?
2. How many episodes were made?
3. For how many years was this program on TV?
4. Can you think of any TV programs in the United States like *"Ma famille"*? What are they?
5. Watch an episode posted on the Internet. What do you think the episode was about? How many of the words did you understand?

 **Search words: épisode ma famille**

| Ma Famille | |
|---|---|
| **Titre original** | *Ma Famille* |
| **Genre** | Série humoristique, comique, tragique, sentimentale |
| **Créateur(s)** | Akissi Delta |
| **Production** | LAD Production |
| **Pays d'origine** | Côte d'Ivoire |
| **Chaîne d'origine** | La Première |
| **Nombre de saisons** | 7 |
| **Nombre d'épisodes** | 300 |
| **Durée** | Environ 1h/1h+ |
| **Diffusion d'origine** | 2002–2009 |

## Essential Instruction

1. Clarify the vocabulary in the graphic **Ma Famille**. Create a template similar to that in **Activité 7** and have students complete it with information about a television show about family that they know and that has family as its central theme. Post in the classroom for others to see.
2. Use the question in the "Introduction" of **La culture sur place** to explore the theme of family. Establish boundaries of responsive and respectful interaction as students devise questions to learn about an e-pal's family. You may wish to have students write to another classmate if e-pals are not available to you.
3. Secure parental/guardian and school administration permission before exchanging student contact information with a Francophone pen pal or e-pal.

# La culture sur place

## Enquête culturelle: Nos familles

### Introduction

As you know, not all families are alike, even in one culture. How many different types of families do you know? In this activity, you will contact someone in a French-speaking country to learn about his or her family.

### Investigation

**8  Des questions pour un(e) Francophone**  2.1, 4.1, 5.2

> Moussa, tu viens d'une famille nucléaire?

Use the vocabulary that you have learned in this chapter and what you know about asking questions in French to create a list of at least ten interview questions to ask about someone's family. You may wish to consult your teacher about the types of questions to ask.

After you have written your list of questions, your teacher will give you contact information for someone from a French-speaking country. You will then communicate with him or her either through e-mail or some other form of electronic communication. Be sure to keep a record of your correspondence or communication since you will report what you learn to the class. For example, you might record your conversation or print your e-mails.

#### Vocabulaire utile

**une famille nucléaire** – *a nuclear family*
**une famille élargie** – *an extended family*
**une famille monoparentale** – *a single-parent family*
**une famille recomposée** – *a blended family (which includes step-parents and step-children)*

### Taking Inventory

**9  Présentation et discussion**     1.1, 1.3, 2.1

Prepare a report of what you learned to present to your group. Summarize your interviewee's responses to your questions in French. Once everyone in your group has given their presentation, compare and contrast your interviewees' families. Some questions to consider are:

1. What do the families have in common? How are they different?
2. How are these families similar to ones you know in the United States?
3. What general conclusions can you draw about families from French-speaking countries in comparison to families in the United States?

**Answers**

**8** *Answers will vary.*

**9** *Presentations and discussion will vary.*

### Communication

**Interpersonal: Paired Practice**
Refer your students to free online French pen pal sites like e-pals, europapages, or other similar sites. If you don't have access to these sites, ask students to write their letter to a partner that you assign to them. Have students exchange and reply to the e-mails. If you know someone in a French-speaking country, see if he or she can connect with you and your students via an online video call service.

**Who's Who Loto**
Prepare a list of at least 35 historical and contemporary personalities that students know, of different nationalities and professions. Use this list to practice **C'est** and **il/elle est** + nationalities and professions or **venir** + **de** + country. Next, create a 16-square **Loto** (French bingo) template (**Loto** spelled across the top, numbers 1-4 down the left side). Have each student complete a **Loto** card with nationalities randomly selected from the list. Provide **jetons** (game chips).

As you play **Loto**, call out a name, profession, and country of origin from the list of personalities. Students mark the corresponding nationality if it's on the card. For example, if you call out **William**, **prince**, **Angleterre**, students could mark **anglais**. The first student to get four in a row calls out **Loto**. Have the winning student create sentences with **c'est** and **il est** when reading back the answers. To make this activity more challenging, call out the person's name and profession, but not the country of origin. Students must guess the nationality. You can also make country or professions **Loto** cards.

# Structure de la langue

## C'est vs. il/elle est  1.2

Both **c'est** and **il/elle est** mean *he is* or *she is* as well as *it is*.

Use **c'est**:

- with an article/possessive adjective and a noun
  **C'est** un sac à dos.
  **C'est** mon affiche.
- with an article, a noun, and an adjective
  **C'est** un étudiant diligent.

**C'est** becomes **ce n'est pas** in a negative sentence.

> **C'est** un bon athlète, mais **ce n'est pas** un footballeur.  *He's a good athlete, but he's not a soccer player.*

Use **il/elle est**:

- with an adjective by itself
  **Elle** est malienne.    *She is Malian.*
  **Elle** est généreuse.    *She is generous.*
- with a profession
  **Elle** est femme d'affaires.    *She is a businesswoman.*

The plural for of **c'est** is **ce sont**. The plural form of **il/elle est** is **ils/elles sont**.

> **Ce sont** des testeurs de jeux vidéo.    *They are video testers.*
> **Ils sont** canadiens.    *They are Canadian.*

Adjectives of nationality are not capitalized like they are in English. However, a noun referring to a person's nationality is.

> Elle est ivoirienne. }    *She is Ivorian.*
> C'est une **Ivoirienne**. }    *She is an Ivorian.*

C'est un magicien.

Le lapin? Il est invisible.

**COMPARAISONS**

An antecedent is something that comes before, for example, to indicate gender. What type of antecedent would you need to see before translating these sentences? Why? **4.1**

C'est un agent de police.
C'est un médecin.

COMPARAISONS: Because both **agent de police** and **médecin** are masculine professions, there would need to be an antecedent indicating gender before these sentences to know if someone is describing a man or a woman. For example, you could use a title like **M.** or **Mme.**

**Essential Instruction**

1. Introduce the **Structure de la langue**. First show students pictures of people doing different jobs and ask **Quelle est sa/leur profession?** As students respond, write on the board the formula **il/elle est** and **ils/elles sont** + adjective or profession. Emphasize again that one does not use an article before a profession in French with the verb **être**. Next, as you point to various objects that students know, ask **Qu'est-ce que c'est?**

Write the formula **C'est un/une/possessive adjective...** + singular noun and **Ce sont des/possessive adjective** + plural noun as students answer.

2. For **Activité 10**, ask the class to "divine" the meaning of the verb **deviner**.

3. Do **Activité 11** as a class and then assign students to repeat the activity with a partner.

**10**
1. C'est Amadou et Mariam.
2. C'est Corneille.
3. C'est Ribéry (Zidane).
4. C'est Steve Carrell.
5. C'est J.K. Rowling.
6. C'est Vanessa Paradis.

**11**
1. C'est mon père. Il est avocat. Il est américain. Il est très sympa.
2. Ce sont mes amies Claire et Susan. Elles sont des élèves intelligentes. Elles sont françaises.
3. C'est ma prof d'histoire. C'est une Ivoirienne. Elle est énergique.
4. C'est mon amie. C'est une Française. Elle est intéressante.

## 10 Devinettes  2.1, 2.2

*Devinez l'identité des personnes.*

1. C'est un couple africain. Ce sont des chanteurs. Leur genre, c'est la world.
2. C'est un chanteur R'n'B. C'est un Canadien. Il est généreux.
3. Il n'est pas paresseux. C'est un footballeur énergique. C'est un Français.
4. C'est un Américain. Il a les cheveux noirs. C'est un acteur drôle de *The Office*.
5. C'est un écrivain avec les initiales J.K. Elle est anglaise. Ses livres? Ils sont très intéressants.
6. C'est une actrice et une chanteuse. C'est une Française. Elle est sympa. Le père de ses enfants est Johnny Depp.

Vanessa Paradis.

## 11 Les gens que je connais 2.1, 2.2

*Complétez ces titres (captions) de photo de l'album de Josyanne avec* **il est, elle est, elles sont, c'est,** *ou* **ce sont.**

**MODÈLE** … ma mère. … médecin. … diligente.
**C'est ma mère. Elle est médecin. Elle est diligente.**

1. … mon père. … avocat. … Américain. … très sympa.

2. … mes amies Claire et Susan. … des élèves intelligentes. … françaises.

3. … ma prof d'histoire. … une Ivoirienne. … énergique.

4. … mon amie. … une Française. … intéressante.

**Differentiated Learning**
**Expand/Decelerate**
The apparently simple concept of **il/elle est** vs. **c'est un/une** is deceptively complicated for students. Provide extra practice activities and revisit the concept from time to time throughout the year. Point out that there are two ways to say, "He is a teacher." (**C'est un prof/Il est prof.**) However, there is only one way to say, "He is a good teacher." (**C'est un bon prof.**)

**Special Needs Students**
**Linguistically Challenged**
Bring in a photo of someone and integrate the structure introduced on these pages to tell who the person is, what he or she does, does not do, etc. and what kind of person he or she is. Then ask students questions about the person to check comprehension and practice the structures.

## Answers

 ⑫

1. Anne et Luc Perrin viennent à l'exposition de Gauguin.
2. Moi, je viens à l'exposition de Gauguin.
3. Océane et Lucie Morel viennent à l'exposition de Gauguin.
4. Marie-Alix Richard vient à l'exposition de Gauguin.
5. Thomas Martin vient à l'exposition de Gauguin.

### Reference Desk

After students have studied **venir** and **revenir**, challenge them to find the connection with **devenir**, **souvenir**, and **prévenir**. How does the prefix change the meaning of each verb? Can students surmise each meaning according to the different Latin prefixes? Have them compare and connect the French prefixes to their English counterparts. Ask students to brainstorm a list of words in English with these prefixes and do research to find out if the words are the same or similar in French.

## Present Tense of the Irregular Verb *venir*  1.2

The verb **venir** (*to come*) is irregular. Other verbs that follow the same pattern are **devenir** (*to become*) and **revenir** (*to come back*).

| venir | |
|---|---|
| je **viens** | nous **venons** |
| tu **viens** | vous **venez** |
| il/elle/on **vient** | ils/elles **viennent** |

Quand est-ce que vous **venez**?  *When are you coming?*
Je **viens** le 16 juin.  *I'm coming June 16.*

*Avec qui est-ce que Nathalie vient au pique-nique?*

### Pronunciation Tip

The singular forms of **venir** all sound the same.

**COMPARAISONS**

In French venir means "to come' and revenir means "to come back." What English verbs contain the prefix re-? What does it mean? **4.1**

### 12 L'exposition de Gauguin 🌸 2.1, 2.2

*Dites qui vient avec la classe de français à l'exposition de Gauguin. Si vous voyez un "✔" sous "Permission," les parents ont dit (have said) que cette personne peut y aller.*

| Permission | Noms |
|---|---|
| ✔ | Anne et Luc Perrin |
| ✔ | moi |
| | Fatima et Nasser Aknouch |
| ✔ | Océane et Lucie Morel |
| | Jérôme Fontaine |
| ✔ | Marie-Alix Richard |
| | toi |
| ✔ | Thomas Martin |
| | Virginie Faure |

**Paysage à Arles**, 1888.

COMPARAISONS: Here are some verbs that begin with the prefix re-, which indicates that an action is occurring again: reacquaint, reactivate, reaffirm, reappear, reapply, rearrange, recheck, recopy, restart.

### Essential Instruction

1. Connect the verb **venir** to the English word "venue" (a place where people come together for an event), as in a concert venue. Model the verb **venir** by stating where you come from, then asking students the same question until you have used all subject pronouns. Add questions using **revenir** and **devenir** and toss the koosh ball to individuals to answer. Use choral conjugation to drill all the forms.
2. For the **Comparaisons** question, brainstorm some English verbs on the board that begin with the prefix **re-**. Ask students to discern the meaning ("to do something again"). Then provide several verbs in French that function this way (**réactiver, réapparaître, recopier, recommencer**, etc.).
3. Assign **Activités 12** and **13** with a partner. Review months and/or numbers first if necessary.
4. As they learn countries, states, provinces, and regions, revisit and practice the use of **de** + definite article + geographic place.

# Communiquez!

## 13 Les grandes vacances  2.1, 2.2

*Dites quand ces personnes reviennent de vacances.*

> **MODÈLE**  Karim/20.7
> **Karim revient le 20 juillet.**

1. Stéphanie/22.7
2. Philippe et toi, vous/18.8
3. je/29.7
4. Augustin et Sandrine/31.8
5. Sarah et moi, nous/25.8
6. Maude et Justine/27.7
7. tu/18.8
8. Éric/1.8

Ma tante revient le 25 juillet.

## *De* + **Definite Articles**  1.2

The preposition **de** (*of, from*) contracts with the definite articles **le** and **les** to form **du** and **des**.

| | |
|---|---|
| **de + le = du** | *from (the), of (the)* |
| **de + les = des** | *from (the), of (the)* |

**De** does not contract with the definite articles **la** and **l'**.

*C'est le steak-frites du cuisinier?*

| | |
|---|---|
| C'est l'anniversaire **de la** prof. | *It's the teacher's birthday.* |
| Le premier mois **de l'**année est janvier. | *The first month of the year is January.* |

To say where someone comes from, use a form of **venir** followed by:

- **de** or **d'** if the place is a city
  Amir **vient d'**Annecy.     Je **viens de** Paris.
- **de** or **d'** if the country is feminine
  Elle **vient d'**Algérie.     Il **vient de** France.
- **du** if the country is masculine     Je **viens du** Canada.
- **des** if the country is plural     Nous **venons des** États-Unis.

Leçon C | deux cent soixante et un **261**

## RESOURCES

 **Workbook 40–41**

**Answers** _____

**13**

1. Stéphanie revient le 22 juillet.
2. Philippe et toi, vous revenez le 18 août.
3. Je reviens le 29 juillet.
4. Augustin et Sandrine reviennent le 31 août.
5. Sarah et moi, nous revenons le 25 août.
6. Maude et Justine reviennent le 27 juillet.
7. Toi, tu reviens le dix-huit août.
8. Éric revient le premier août.

### Reference Desk

In general, cities in French have no gender, for example, **Nath vient de Lyon**. However, there are some exceptions, for example **Le Caire** (*Cairo*), **Le Havre**, **La Rochelle**, **Les Eyzies**, **La Nouvelle Orléans**.

### TPR

Randomly distribute a card with a sentence that contains a form of **de** + definite article, but omit this word from any card, for example, **Je / viens /** (blank card) **/ supermarché**. To other students, distribute cards on which you have written **de la, du, des, de l'**. Ask the student with the correct preposition card to join the others and line up in order to formulate a correct sentence.

---

**Differentiated Learning**
**Decelerate**
Group together students of varying abilities. Create a sentence completion exercise, for example, **Il vient** (*from*)... **Canada. C'est le blason** (*of*)... **Lyon. Je reviens** (*from*)... **Algérie. C'est l'anniversaire** (*of the*)... **prof de maths.**, etc.

**Learning Styles**
**Visual Learners**
Use a chart or some other visual mapping to present the preposition **de** + definite articles that students can refer to when doing the exercises.

14

1. C'est le football du footballeur.
2. C'est le dictionnaire de la prof.
3. C'est le sandwich du proviseur.
4. C'est le film d'Audrey Tautou.
5. C'est le prof des élèves.
6. C'est le stade des footballeurs.
7. C'est le dessert de la cuisinière.

15

1. ...vient/viennent du Gabon.
2. ...vient/viennent de France.
3. ...vient/viennent du Bénin.
4. ...vient/viennent du Canada.
5. ...vient/viennent de Côte d'Ivoire.
6. ...vient/viennent du Mali.
7. ...vient/viennent du Burkina Faso.
8. ...vient/viennent du Sénégal.

16 Script can be found in the front pages of the Annotated Teacher's Edition.

1. United States
2. Canada
3. Cameroon
4. Ivory Coast
5. Gabon
6. France

## Reference Desk

Perhaps the most common question asked of a traveler abroad is "Where do you come from?" Have students practice their answer to this question in French. Besides saying, for example, **Je viens des États-Unis.** to indicate their country of origin, they can use this expression to say where they have just travelled from.

## Connections

**Music**
Have students research the Pan-African hip-hop festival WAGA. Expand the research to include the history and influences that led to the emergence of the hip-hop genre in francophone countries. Learn about some of the musicians listed on the poster. Are they still performing? What is the focus of their music? If appropriate, have students listen to the music and share their opinions.

---

**14  C'est à qui?**  **2.1, 2.2**

*Dites à qui sont les choses suivantes.*

**MODÈLE**  l'élève
**C'est le livre de l'élève.**

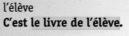

1. le footballeur   2. la prof   3. le proviseur

4. l'actrice
   Audrey Tautou

5. les élèves   6. les footballeurs   7. la cuisinière

## Du côté des médias

**15  Un festival international du hip-hop**

**Interpretive Communication**  **2.1, 2.2**
*Dites d'où vient chaque groupe ou chanteur au festival de hip-hop.*

**MODÈLE**  le Togo
**Ali Jezz vient du Togo.**

1. le Gabon
2. la France
3. le Bénin
4. le Canada
5. la Côte-d'Ivoire
6. le Mali
7. le Burkina Faso
8. le Sénégal

**16  Les pays d'origine**   **2.1**

*Écrivez en anglais le nom du pays (country) d'où viennent ces personnes.*

---

**Essential Learning**

1. Have students do **Activités 14** and **15** in pairs. Do a quick practice drill of **de** + definite article with the countries in **Activité 15**. Say the name of the country and ask students to respond in chorus with the correct preposition. For example, if you say **Le Gabon**, students reply **du Gabon**, etc.

2. For **Activité 17**, have groups of three or four select, summarize, and report on two of the **petites annonces**.

# À vous la parole

## Communiquez!

**Question centrale**

What is the nature of relationships in other cultures?

**17** Les petites annonces  1.2, 2.1

### Interpretive Communication

Read each classified ad below. Then write a sentence profiling the type of person who should apply for the job.

**MODÈLE**

**CHERCHE graphiste**

**Description:**

Tahiticlic recherche graphiste freelance installé en Polynésie Française pour divers projets: flyer, plaquette, design web.

**Lieu:** Papeete

**Contact:** Merci d'envoyer vos tarifs à Fabien: graphix@tahiticlic.com

*http://www.toutannoncer.com/emploi/cherche-graphiste-freelance*

Accueil > Petites annonces > Collaboration - Offres

**Someone interested in working as a graphic designer in Tahiti, who has experience with Web design, would be interested in this position.**

**1. CHERCHE ingénieur**

**Description:**

Ingénieur industriel ou civil en mécanique/électromécanique (idéalement précédé par un graduat en mécanique)

**Lieu:** Belgique

**Contact: AW Europe**, Avenue de l'Industrie, 19, 1420 - Braine-L'Alleud, Belgique

Présentation Recrutement@aweurope.be

tél : 02/3891204
fax : 02/3860804

*http://www.aweurope.be/*

**2. CHERCHE chanteuse**

**Description:**

Recherche, pour une production pop dance, une chanteuse à la couleur de voix Nubienne, Orientale, Nord africaine qui parle français, espagnol et eventuellement portugais.

**Lieu:** Ornans, France

**Contact:** *http:// www.vincentleclere.fr*

**3. CHERCHE acteur**

**Description:**

Nous recherchons un acteur homme de 25-30 ans pour le tournage d'une publicité à Toulouse, dans la semaine du 23 au 29 août. Merci d'envoyer des photos.

**Lieu:** Toulouse

**Contact:** Pour contacter Alix, écrire à *webmaster@lunox-production.com*

**4. CHERCHE testeur jeux vidéo**

**Description:**

Le studio de Paris recrute plusieurs testeurs pour une production sur console next gen. Votre mission: identifier les bugs d'un jeu vidéo, tester des outils nécessaires à la production, utiliser les logiciels Word et Excel et l'informatique.

**Lieu:** Paris

**Contact:** Audrey CHATELET; Ubisoft, 28, rue Armand Carrel, 93100 Montreuil-sous-Bois, France

*http://www.ubisoftgroup.com*

**Answers** _____

**17** *Answers will vary.*

### Expansion

Students may wish to research online **les offres d'emploi** listed in the **les petites annonces** column of francophone or European Union newspapers to further identify employment opportunities that require foreign language skills. Have students work together to create an online "Jobs offered/wanted" newspaper page.

### Reference Desk

**Blended Instruction**

Consider using blended instruction, a combination of in-class learning and computer-mediated instruction or learning opportunities. Ask students to complete activities on the computer, using their cell or smartphone, or other emerging electronic technology. This will allow students to hone their tech skills and become more independent learners. Schedule routine Internet and e-book learning in class and in the lab.

## Differentiated Learning
### Decelerate

Some students will benefit more from having a worksheet to complete with more exact information they find in the classified ads.

## Multiple Intelligences
### Verbal-Linguistic

After completing **Activité 17**, have students create their own **petite annonce** based on the language used in the activity. They can write these with a partner and then share them with another pair, or you can post them around the classroom and have students decide which job they would like to apply for.

## Answers

**18**

1. Laurence is looking for a summer job watching pets while people are on vacation.
2. The name of her school is called Lycée Drummondville.
3. She is a senior.
4. She loves dogs.
5. She will feed and play with the animals, and take them outside.

**19** *Answers will vary.*

### Reference Desk

You may want to review grade levels with students here.
**Collège** (*middle school*): 6th grade = **6ème** (**sixième**), 7th grade = **5ème**, 8th grade = **4ème**, 9th grade = **3ème**, **Lycée** (*high school*): 10th grade = **Seconde**, 11th grade = **Première** (*year of the Bac français exam*), 12th grade = **Terminale** (*year of the Bac exam*)

 **1.2, 2.1, 2.2**

## 18 Garde d'animaux

### Interpretive Communication

**Élève veut garder vos animaux**

Je suis en terminale au Lycée Drummondville et je cherche comme beaucoup d'élèves un petit job pour les mois de juin, juillet, et août. Si vous désirez partir en vacances et vous avez des animaux, je peux les garder. Je vais jouer avec vos animaux et, bien sûr, je vais nourrir vos animaux le matin et le soir. Je vais aussi sortir vos animaux si vous le désirez. J'aime énormément les chiens et les chats, mais j'aime tous les animaux. Je suis à votre disposition.

Laurence T.
01.04.21.78.15

A. Answer these questions in English to demonstrate your comprehension of the ad.

1. What kind of job is Laurence looking for?
2. What is the name of her school?
3. What grade is she in?
4. How does she feel about dogs?
5. What services does Laurence provide for pets?

B. Write a similar ad for the type of summer job you would like to have.

## 19 Tu connais la chanson?

  **1.1, 1.2, 2.1**

### Interpretive Communication

Find a song you like at Amadou and Mariam's official website. Click on "ALBUMS." See if there are some words you understand in one of the songs. Then search for the lyrics to the song. Type up a copy of the lyrics, leaving blanks for words you think your partner will know. Exchange song sheets and ask your partner to listen to the song and write in the missing words. To make it easier for him or her, you can write the words and expressions at the top of the song sheet. Finally, correct the song sheet once the blanks have been filled in.

 **Search words: amadou et mariam site officiel**
**paroles (+ *name of song*)**

### Essential Learning

1. Review new vocabulary in **Activité 18**. Point out that **partir** and **sortir** are irregular -**ir** verbs (presented in Level 2, **Unité 2**), but that **nourrir** is regular. Have partners read aloud the paragraph and complete **A**. Assign **B** as homework and have students peer-edit their work in class the next day.
2. Pre-select several songs for students to use in **Activité 19**. Have pairs prepare a cloze-listening of a song and lead the class in the activity.
3. Assign further research and report on Andrée Chedid. Find an interview with the author online and listen to it in class. Prepare for the reading by discussing the **Pré-lecture** question. Have students draw their family tree. Ask volunteers to post their family portraits in class.
4. Have students identify phrases in the four statements of the **Stratégie de lecture** that they already know. Define new vocabulary.
5. Discuss the **Outils de lecture** before reading and listening to the selection.

# Lecture thématique

## L'Enfant multiple

### Rencontre avec l'auteur  1.2

**Andrée Chédid** (1920–  ) was born in Cairo, Egypt, and then moved to Paris in the 1940s. Her books focus on the lives of everyday people, their tragedies and hopes. Omar-Jo, the Lebanese protagonist of *L'Enfant multiple* (1989), leaves for Paris to start a new life in a new country. In the excerpt you will read he meets up with a ride operator at a carnival with whom he would like to work. What does Omar-Jo want more than a job?

### Pré-lecture  1.3

Do you have friends that feel as close or closer than members of your own family? Draw a portrait of you and your "extended" family. Put yourself in the middle with your blood relatives, friends, and other people who feel like family around you.

### Stratégie de lecture  1.2, 2.1, 2.2

#### Theme

A theme is the main idea or message of a literary work. It is a statement or opinion about a topic that the author expresses or implies. A universal theme is a message about life that people of different cultures can understand. To help you find the theme in this reading, find the following lines in the text and write down what you think each one means or implies in a chart like the one below.

|  | Signification |
|---|---|
| 1. Je ne fais partie de rien. |  |
| 2. Un homme qui aime son manège, je n'ai pas besoin de savoir d'où il vient. Il est de ma famille. |  |
| 3. Pas la famille de sang, mais l'autre. Parfois ça compte beaucoup plus. On peut la choisir. |  |
| 4. Oui, maintenant, je te choisis! |  |

### Outils de lecture  1.2

#### Monitor your comprehension

This selection is a dialogue. A dialogue might occur in a literary work for a number of reasons, such as to show an exchange of information or how one character gets something from another. In this reading, Omar-Jo wants something from the carnival worker. As you read this selection, look for clues that will help you figure out what Omar-Jo wants. If you still don't know by the end of the selection, read the passage again, maybe with the help of a French-English dictionary. Or, discuss with a partner what you understand and share your insights.

**Differentiated Learning**
**Accelerate**
After confirming that students understand the meaning of the four statements in the **Stratégie de lecture**, have your students discuss what is revealed about the speaker.

Answers _____

Pré-lecture
*Portraits will vary.*

Stratégie de lecture
*Possible answers:*

1. Someone is individualistic.
2. There are relationships that are instinctual.
3. Family goes beyond blood ties.
4. One can choose one's family.

**Pendant la lecture**
1. Omar says that he is not a member of anything.
2. Omar chooses the carnival worker.

**Post-lecture**
*Answers will vary.*

**Le monde visuel**
*Possible answer:* The composition is based on balancing differently proportioned pieces (objects and people). Except for the ferris wheel, all other objects and the people are on a symmetrical plane. This composition gives balance to the ferris wheel which appears to be moving and perhaps falling.

---

**Expansion**

**At the Fair**
Students may wish to use the theme of **la fête foraine** to work with a partner or in a group to write a short story that takes place at a fair. Students who have photos showing a fairground with rides can share them as inspiration for illustrations for the story. Characters can have varying nationalities and professions, meet at the fair, and tell of their background. Each student should contribute at least two sentences to the communal story.

---

 **1.2, 2.1, 2.2**

| | |
|---|---|
| Le forain:* | Tu fais partie d'une bande*? |
| Omar-Jo: | Non, je ne fais partie de rien. |
| Le forain: | Si je t'emploie*, il faut quand même que je sache* d'où tu viens! |
| Omar-Jo: | Je ne te demande pas d'où tu viens. Un homme qui aime son manège*, je n'ai pas besoin de savoir d'où il vient. Il est de ma famille. |
| Le forain: | De ta famille? |
| Omar-Jo: | Pas la famille de sang*, mais l'autre. Parfois* ça compte* beaucoup plus. On peut la choisir. |
| Le forain: | Tu veux dire* que tu m'as choisi? |
| Omar-Jo: | Oui, maintenant je te choisis! |

> **Pendant la lecture**
> 1. What does Omar-Jo say when asked if he is a gang member?

> **Pendant la lecture**
> 2. Who chooses whom?

**forain** *carnival worker;* **fais partie d'une bande** *belong to a gang;* **t'emploie** *hire you;* **il faut quand meme que je sache** *I must know at least;* **manège** *merry-go-round;* **sang** *blood;* **Parfois** *Sometimes;* **compte** *counts;* **Tu veux dire...?** *Do you mean...?*

## Post-lecture  2.1, 2.2

Do you think the carnival worker will hire Omar-Jo? Why, or why not?

## Le monde visuel 3.2

When artists create a work of art, they think about its composition, or how all the elements in the piece fit together to create a unified whole. Many artists combine elements to create balance or symmetry. How does the photographer compose the elements in this photograph: the chair swing ride, the Ferris wheel, the snack stand, the building in the background, and the people in the foreground? Is there balance or symmetry? Explain.

*Fête foraine,* 2003. Alfred Wolf.

---

**20 Activités d'expansion**

1. What do you think the theme of the reading selection is? Is it a universal theme? Write a paragraph of at least five sentences presenting your ideas. Use the quotations from your chart to support your position. Then tell whether or not you agree with the theme.
2. Omar-Jo is from Lebanon. How do you think he learned French? Research the French connection with Lebanon. Use the search words **le liban et les français** ou **langues au liban**. Prepare a map or other document to share with a group of classmates.

**Essential Learning**

1. Have your students listen to the dialogue, then read it silently. Give them a chance to decode the meaning of the exchange between the characters before discussing it as a class. Listen to the dialogue once more and discuss the question in the **Post-lecture**. Have pairs role-play the dialogue.

2. Ask students to observe the cartoon **Tout est relatif** and guess the content (location, mood, relationships, etc.). Role-play the cartoon for the class while students follow along. Then ask students to role-play in groups of four. Answer any vocabulary questions and discuss slang expressions, such as **Quelle poisse!** and **Ça craint!** Caution students about mindful use of familiar language. Ask for volunteer groups to role-play the comic strip for the class.

# Les copains d'abord: Tout est relatif 🎧 ✳ 1.2

## Les copains d'abord

Here is the translation for **Les copains d'abord:**

A = Antoine
F = Florence
MA = Marie-Alix
M = Mathéo

F: So, how is it going with Antoine, is it love at first sight? MA: No, he's nice but a bit nerdy. MA: And his type is blond hair and green eyes... F: Not me, I like black hair and brown eyes... MA: Actually, he likes girls that look like his grandma! F: Oh, that stinks! MA: ...and he looks like a fish! F: Yes, he is kind, but unattractive. M: Antoine, what's wrong? A: I need to go to Québec for my sister's wedding. What a drag! M: You're lucky! I have an uncle in Mali and a half sister in Congo, but I have to stay in Paris! A: Well, I would like to stay here with Marie-Alix. M: So, it's love at first sight? A: Yes, she is charming, intelligent, gorgeous, sweet... ideal!

List of slang and idiomatic expressions:
**le coup de foudre:** *love at first sight;* **ça craint:** *it stinks;* **moche:** *ugly;* **une morue:** *lit.* a codfish, implying ugly; **Quelle poisse!:** *What a drag!;* **canon:** *really cute*

**A**

| 10/11 | 425 km | 212,50€ |
|---|---|---|
| 21/11 | 337.5 km | 168,75€ |
| 8/12 | 112.5 km | 56,75€ |
| 19/12 | 550 km | 275,00€ |
| 13/1 | 462.5 km | 231,25€ |
| 27/1 | 718.75 km | 359,00€ |

Total reimbursement depends on exchange rate.

**B** *Answers will vary.*

**C** *Possible answers:*

1. The manuscript was a liturgical book of hours with texts used at each hour of the liturgical day.
2. during the Middle Ages (11$^{th}$ – 16$^{th}$ centuries)
3. a hand-written manuscript supplemented with ornamentation, often gold or silver
4. the Limbourg brothers, originally from the area now known as the Netherlands
5. a rich noble or merchant who supported artists and artisans by commissioning paintings, sculptures, or manuscripts
6. writing material made from sheep, calf, or occasionally pig skin
7. *Answers will vary.*
8. *Answers will vary.*
9. *Answers will vary; various professions that were practiced at that time.*
10. *Answers will vary.*

### Expansion

Have partners find the distance in miles and kilometers of two francophone cities in different countries, such as Alger–Dakar, Hanoi-Québec, etc.

## Projets finaux

**A Connexions par Internet**  **2.1, 2.2**

### Le système métrique

Gerald Browne, who lives in Milwaukee, Wisconsin, works as a consultant for an international organization in France. He needs your help with his travel report. Recreate the chart below, writing the dates as they do in France and converting the miles to kilometers. Browne will be reimbursed for mileage at half a euro per kilometer, so also figure out the total of what he is owed and what his compensation will be in dollars.

 Search words: **convertisseur kilomètres**

| Dates | Ville | Distance en miles | Total en euros/dollars |
|---|---|---|---|
| 11/10 | Minneapolis, Minnesota | 680 | |
| 11/21 | Indianapolis, Indiana | 540 | |
| 12/8 | Chicago, Illinois | 180 | |
| 12/19 | Cleveland, Ohio | 880 | |
| 1/13 | Des Moines, Iowa | 740 | |
| 1/27 | Fargo, North Dakota | 1,150 | |

**B Communautés en ligne**  **1.3**

### Mon album de photos

**Presentational Communication**

Find or create four photos of different members of your family and write a description for each photo. Give the name, age, birthday, and a physical description of each family member. Then tell what that person likes to do or is doing in the photo. Create a website for your photo album, or share them in another way with French-speaking teens you know. If you do not want to describe your real family, you may use the definition of family from the reading selection.

**C Passez à l'action!**   **1.3**

### Les Très Riches Heures du Duc de Berry: Un calendrier historique et artistique

Art often reflects the history and daily life of a particular country. *Les Très Riches Heures du Duc de Berry* is a famous set of illuminated manuscripts from the Middle Ages. It contains illustrations for each month of the calendar year. Research this famous work online and answer the following questions.

1. Why were these manuscripts created?
2. When were they produced?
3. What is an "illuminated" manuscript?
4. Who were the artists?

### Essential Instruction

1. Have students work in pairs to complete **Activité A**. Once students convert both the dates to the French order and the miles to kilometers, have them complete the activity with another pair.
2. For **Activité B**, offer the option to use one's own family, a TV or movie family, or an imaginary family. Project photos as students share their albums.
3. For **Activité C**, once students complete and share about the research, provide blank calendar templates and instruct them to design their own calendars. Post the results for all to see.
4. To do **Activité D**, distribute copies of the graphic organizer located in the **Copy Masters** supplement. Then divide the class into seven groups, assigning each group a different topic. Next ask groups to present their topic to the rest of the students who can add missing details if necessary. Finish this review by revisiting the **Question centrale**.

5. Jean de Berry was the patron of these manuscripts. What is a "patron"?
6. What ingredients were used to create these paintings?
7. Study six of the paintings for different months closely, then describe each one.
8. What professions can you identify in the images?
9. From these manuscripts, what do you learn about life in the Middle Ages?
10. Based on the images, what do you think was important to people back then?

In small groups of six, create your own calendar showing the months, seasons, scenery, and events in your town or region. Each group member will be responsible for two calendar months. Once your calendar is completed, present it and explain it in French to the class.

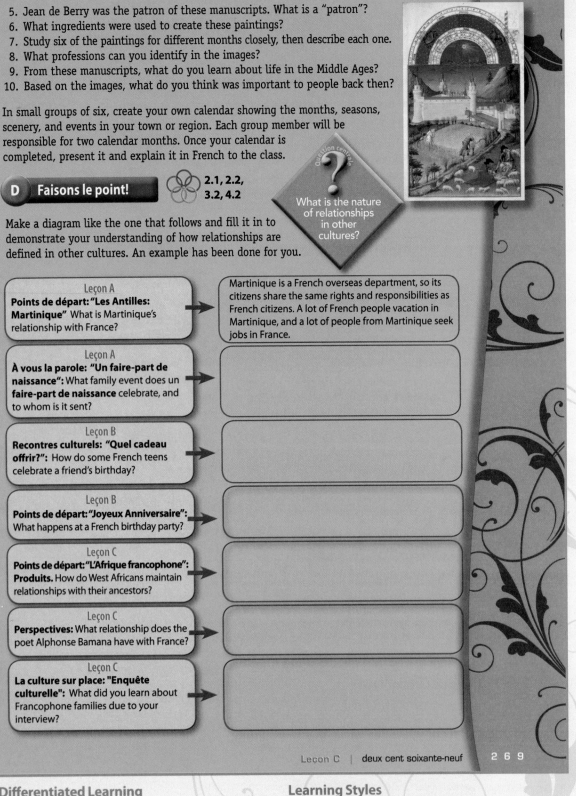

## D  Faisons le point!

2.1, 2.2, 3.2, 4.2

**Question centrale**

? What is the nature of relationships in other cultures?

Make a diagram like the one that follows and fill it in to demonstrate your understanding of how relationships are defined in other cultures. An example has been done for you.

**Leçon A**
**Points de départ: "Les Antilles: Martinique"** What is Martinique's relationship with France?

→ Martinique is a French overseas department, so its citizens share the same rights and responsibilities as French citizens. A lot of French people vacation in Martinique, and a lot of people from Martinique seek jobs in France.

**Leçon A**
**À vous la parole: "Un faire-part de naissance":** What family event does un **faire-part de naissance** celebrate, and to whom is it sent?

→

**Leçon B**
**Recontres culturels: "Quel cadeau offrir?":** How do some French teens celebrate a friend's birthday?

→

**Leçon B**
**Points de départ: "Joyeux Anniversaire":** What happens at a French birthday party?

→

**Leçon C**
**Points de départ: "L'Afrique francophone": Produits.** How do West Africans maintain relationships with their ancestors?

→

**Leçon C**
**Perspectives:** What relationship does the poet Alphonse Bamana have with France?

→

**Leçon C**
**La culture sur place: "Enquête culturelle":** What did you learn about Francophone families due to your interview?

→

Answers _____

**D**

**Leçon A:** **Un faire-part de naissance** celebrates a birth announcement and is sent to family, friends, and colleagues.

**Leçon B:** Some French teens organize birthday parties for their friends.

**Leçon B:** To celebrate birthdays, the French have parties and give presents and serve cake. In the Antilles, some families create skits, write poems, and sing songs.

**Leçon C:** Many West Africans use masks in ceremonies in which they commune with the spirits of their dead ancestors.

**Leçon C:** In his poem, Bamana speaks of seeing Europe or France as the father.

**Leçon C:** *Answers will vary.*

**Leçon C:** Writer Andrée Chédid says you can create your own family in addition to the one you are born with.

## Expansion

Students may wish to create a colorful calendar with each month illustrated by a photo from a different francophone country or region. Illustrations might show New Orleans at Mardi Gras, Quebec in December, Paris in July, various African countries in different seasons, etc.

## Differentiated Learning
### Adapt
Some students may prefer to adapt the graphic in **Activité D** and use the format found in even-numbered units.

## Learning Styles
### Visual/Kinesthetic Learners
For **Activité C**, have students research *Les Très Riches Heures du Duc de Berry* online, answer the questions from the **Activité**, then select two images to describe and critique. Offer those students who are interested the opportunity to create their own image using the style of the original manuscripts.

**A** **Évaluation de compréhension auditive**   **2.1, 2.2**

Listen to the conversation between Rahina and Mathéo. Afterward, you will read some statements. Write **oui** if the statement is correct. Write **non** if the statement is incorrect.

1. C'est l'anniversaire de Rahina.
2. Mathéo ne va pas à l'anniversaire d'Antoine.
3. Antoine va avoir 18 ans.
4. La famille d'Antoine vient de Martinique.
5. La mère d'Antoine va acheter des accras de morue.
6. Le père d'Antoine est metteur en scène.
7. La mère d'Antoine est une bonne cuisinière.
8. Mathéo va offrir un CD de Corneille.

**B** **Évaluation orale**  **2.1**

> Nous allons acheter une écharpe pour Coralie.

> Et une carte d'anniversaire!

You and a friend are planning a birthday party for Coralie and have come up with a guest list. There is room for two more guests at the table. Each of you suggests someone to invite, stating the person's name, age, physical description, and what they like to do. Next, plan the details of the party by saying:

- the date and time of the party.
- what you will each buy Coralie, based on her personality, likes, or pastimes.
- who will buy the cake.
- who will bring the sandwiches and beverages.
- who will choose the music.

**C** **Évaluation culturelle**  **1.3, 3.1, 3.2, 4.2, 5.1**

You will be asked to make some comparisons between Francophone cultures and American culture. You may need to complete some additional research about American culture.

1. **Le système métrique**
   Make a list of the measurements you use on a daily basis when buying bottled products, cooking, driving, stating the temperature, etc. Next to the American measurements, write the metric system equivalents. (You may use a metric converter online.)
2. **La Martinique**
   Write a note to someone from Martinique planning to visit your state. Describe how things are different or the same where you live to those same topics in Martinique. Some things you might talk about are the climate, food, language, and music.

**Essential Learning**

1. Review as a class the listening **Activité A**.
2. Have students choose a partner and write the dialogue for **Activité B**. Provide in-class time for peer-editing and practice before students present to the class. To lower students' anxiety level about speaking in French in front of the whole class, let them use note cards that contain a clue for each line of their dialogue.
3. Ask students to select one or two topics from **Activité C** which interest them. Have groups of six students present the topics.
4. Assign either **Activité D** or **E** to do at home, reminding students to use only vocabulary they have learned up to this point. Ask volunteers with the best writing to share with the whole class.
5. Consider using **Activité F** as the **Unité 5** assessment.

3. **Les fêtes**
   Compare a holiday or special occasion your family celebrates with one from the French-speaking world. Compare the reasons for the celebration, the food, activities, and gift-giving traditions.
4. **Le shopping en ligne**
   Compare France's FNAC, Quebec's Archambault, and the American online site from which you buy music, books, video games, etc. Compare the criteria on the chart your teacher will give you, then rate all three online stores accordingly.
5. **Les écrivains francophones en Afrique**
   In small groups, have each member select an author from the culture reading "L'Afrique francophone" in the **Points de départ** section of **Leçon C**. Do online research to fill in the chart your teacher will give you about your author.
6. **World Music**
   Compare the musical instruments and styles used by Amadou and Mariam with those of an American musician who has recorded a World Music album.

The legendary zouk band **Kassav** performed in Paris to raise money for Haitian earthquake victims.

**Answers** _____

**D** *Answers will vary.*

**E** *Letters will vary.*

**F** *Storyboards will vary.*

### Communication

**Presentational: Paired Practice**
Have students work with a partner to adapt the **Évaluation écrite** into a dialogue, including as much vocabulary and and as many structures from **Unité 5** as possible. Provide time in class for practice and peer-editing of dialogues. Finally, ask students to present their dialogues.

 **D** **Évaluation écrite**    1.3, 5.1

Imagine you are hosting a Francophone student who will live with you for the school year. Write him or her a letter introducing the members of your family. Give their names, ages, physical and character descriptions, professions, and birthdays. Begin your letter with **Cher** before the name of a boy or **Chère** before the name of a girl, and close your letter with **Amitiés** and sign your name.

 **E** **Évaluation visuelle**    1.3

Write a paragraph describing the family in the illustration. Identify everyone by name and relationship, give their ages, birthdays, and professions. Describe the color of their hair and eyes, and tell what kind of person they are.

  **F** **Évaluation compréhensive**     1.3

Create a storyboard with six frames. Write captions for each frame, telling about a friend's birthday party. Finally, share your story with a partner or a small group of classmates.

**Learning Styles**
**Visual Learners**
Give students the option of doing **Activité F** instead of **Activité D** or **Activité E**. Students who choose this **Activité** will be above level linguistically and/or often appreciate the visual, creative process.

**Special Needs Students**
**AD(H)D**
Many students need and prefer more structured, step-by-step activities in order to be successful. You may want to write additional, more guided instructions for some of the **Évaluation Activités** to support students who could benefit from them.

## RESOURCES

 **Flash Cards**

 *Rendez-vous à Nice!* **Episode 5**

 **Listening Pre-test D**

 *Unité* **Test**

# Vocabulaire de l'Unité 5  1.2

**à** in *A*

les **accras de morue (m.)** cod fritters *A*

l' **Afrique (f.)** Africa *C*

l' **âge (m.)** age *B*; **Tu as quel âge?** How old are you? *B*

l' **an (m.)** year *B*

l' **année (f.)** year *B*

un **anniversaire** birthday *B*

**apporter** to bring *B*

**avoir: avoir… an(s)** to be…years old *B*; **avoir quel âge** to be how old *B*

**bavard(e)** talkative *B*

le **Bénin** Benin *C*

**béninois(e)** Beninese *C*

**bête,** unintelligent *B*

le **Burkina Faso** Burkina Faso *C*

**burkinabè** from, of Burkina Faso *C*

un **cadeau** gift *B*

le **Cameroun** Cameroon *C*

**camerounais(e)** Cameroonian *C*

le **Canada** Canada *C*

une **carte** card *B*; **une carte cadeau** gift card *B*

**chanter** to sing *C*

**choisir** to choose *B*

**comme** like *A*

**comment: Comment est…?** What is… like? *A*

un **compositeur une compositrice** composer, songwriter *C*

**connais: je connais** I know *A*

la **Côte-d'Ivoire** Ivory Coast *C*

**culturel, culturelle** cultural *C*

**des** from (the), of (the) *C*

**devenir** to become *C*

**diligent(e)** diligent *B*

la **discussion** discussion *B*

**divorcé(e)(s)** divorced *A*

**dois: tu dois** you must *A*

**du** from (the) *C*

**égoïste** selfish *B*

les **États-Unis(m.)** United States *C*

**être: Nous sommes le (+ date).** It is the (+ date). *B*

une **famille** family *A*

**finir** to finish *B*

**francophone** French-speaking *C*

le **Gabon** Gabon *C*

**gabonais(e)** Gabonese *C*

un **gâteau** cake *B*

**généreux, généreuse** generous *B*

les **gens (m.)** people *A*

**grand(e)** tall, big, large *A*

**grandir** to grow *B*

**grossir** to gain weight *B*

**ivoirien(ne)** from, of the Ivory Coast *C*

un **kilomètre** kilometer *A*

**là-bas** over there *A*

**leur, leurs** their *A*

**lui** to him/her *B*

**maigrir** to lose weight *B*

le **Mali** Mali *C*

**malien(ne)** Malian *C*

la **Martinique** Martinique *A*

**méchant(e)** mean *B*

un **métier** job *C*

un **million** a million *A*

un **mois** month *B*

**notre, nos** our *A*

**nous** us *A*

**offrir** to offer, to give *B*

**paresseux, paresseuse** lazy *B*

**parler** to speak, to talk *C*

**passionné(e)(de)** passionate (about) *B*

**petit(e)** little, short, small *A*

**premier, première** first *B*

**préparer** to prepare *B*

la **profession** profession *C*; **Quelle est votre profession?** What is your profession? *C*

un **projet** project *C*

**que** that *B*

**réfléchir (à)** to think over, consider *B*

**ressembler (à)** to ressemble *A*

**réussir (à)** to succeed, pass (a test) *B*

**revenir** to come back *C*

**rougir** to blush *B*

le **Sénégal** Senegal *C*

**sénégalais(e)** Senegalese *C*

**son, sa, ses** his, her, one's, its *A*

**super** super *B*

**sympa** nice *B*

la **taille** size *A*; **de taille moyenne** of average height *A*

**timide** shy *B*

le **Togo** Togo *C*

**togolais(e)** Togolese *C*

**ton, ta, tes** your *A*

**travailler** to work *C*

**votre, vos** your *A*

**vous** to you *A*

**voyager** to travel *A*

**vraiment** really *A*

Family members… see pp. 220–21

Hair and eye color… see p. 221

Months of the year… see p. 232

Professions… see pp. 249–50

# Grammar Summary

The material in this section contains information presented in Textbook 1A and Textbook 1B.
The Grammar Summary is listed in alphabetical order.

## Adjectives

### Agreement of Regular Adjectives

| Masculine | Masculine Plural | Feminine | Feminine Plural |
|---|---|---|---|
| | + s | masculine adjective + e | masculine adjective + es |
| grand | grands | grande | grandes |

### Exceptions

| Masculine | Masculine Plural | Feminine | Feminine Plural |
|---|---|---|---|
| Adjectives ending in **e** <br> bête | + s <br> bêtes | no change <br> bête | + s <br> bêtes |
| Adjectives ending in **n, l** <br><br> bon <br> intellectuel | + s <br><br> bons <br> intellectuels | double consonant + e <br><br> bonne <br> intellectuelle | double consonant + es <br><br> bonnes <br> intellectuelles |
| Adjectives ending in **s** <br><br><br> gros | no change <br><br><br> gros | double consonant + e <br><br><br> grosse | double consonant + es <br><br><br> grosses |
| Adjectives ending in **eux** <br> généreux | no change <br> généreux | -euse <br> généreuse | -euses <br> généreuses |

### Irregular Adjectives

| Masculine | Masculine Before a Vowel | Masculine Plural | Feminine | Feminine Plural |
|---|---|---|---|---|
| beau | bel | beaux | belle | + s |
| nouveau | nouvel | nouveaux | nouvelle | |
| vieux | vieil | vieux | vieille | |
| frais | | | fraîche | |
| cher | | } + s | chère | |
| blanc | | | blanche | |
| long | | | longue | |

### Position of Adjectives

| Article + Noun | + Adjective |
|---|---|
| des stylos **bleus** | |

**Exceptions**

beau, joli, nouveau, vieux, bon, mauvais, grand, petit, gros *(BAGS: beauty, age, goodness, size)*

| Article + Adjective | + Noun |
|---|---|
| une **belle** voiture | |

## Comparative of Adjectives

| | | | | | |
|---|---|---|---|---|---|
| **plus** | *(more)* | **+ adj** | **+ que** | *(than)* |
| **moins** | *(less)* | **+ adj** | **+ que** | *(than)* |
| **aussi** | *(as)* | **+ adj** | **+ que** | *(as)* |

## Superlative of Adjectives

**For regular adjectives, placed after the noun**

**le/la/les** + noun + **le/la/les** + **plus** + adjective

**For adjectives placed before the noun**

**le/la/les** + **plus** + adjective + noun

**Exception**: bon = le/la/les **meilleur**(e)(s)

## Interrogative Adjective *quel*

| Masculine | Masculine Plural | Feminine | Feminine Plural |
|---|---|---|---|
| quel | quels | quelle | quelles |

## Possessive Adjectives

| Masculine | Feminine | Plural |
|---|---|---|
| mon | ma | mes |
| ton | ta | tes |
| son | sa | ses |
| notre | notre | nos |
| votre | votre | vos |
| leur | leur | leurs |

# Adverbs

| | |
|---|---|
| assez | mal |
| beaucoup | peu |
| bien | un peu |
| déjà | trop |
| enfin | vite |

## Expressions of Quantity

| | | |
|---|---|---|
| assez de | une boîte de | une bouteille de |
| beaucoup de | un paquet de | un pot de |
| peu de | un morceau de | une tranche de |
| un peu de | un gramme de | un kilo de |
| trop de | un litre de | |

# Articles

## Indefinite Articles

| Singular | | Plural |
|---|---|---|
| **Masculine** | **Feminine** | |
| un | une | des |

## Definite Articles

| Singular | | | Plural |
|---|---|---|---|
| **Before a Consonant Sound** | | **Before a Vowel Sound** | |
| **Masculine** | **Feminine** | | les |
| le | la | l' | |

## *À* + Definite Articles

| Singular | | | Plural |
|---|---|---|---|
| **Before a Consonant Sound** | | **Before a Vowel Sound** | |
| **Masculine** | **Feminine** | | aux |
| au | à la | à l' | |

## *De* + Definite Articles

| Singular | | | Plural |
|---|---|---|---|
| **Before a Consonant Sound** | | **Before a Vowel Sound** | |
| **Masculine** | **Feminine** | | des |
| du | de la | de l' | |

## Partitive Articles

| Before a Consonant Sound | | Before a Vowel Sound | In the Negative |
|---|---|---|---|
| **Masculine** | **Feminine** | | **pas de** coca |
| du | de la | de l' | **pas de** viande |
| | | | **pas d'**eau minérale |

# C'est vs. il/elle est

| c'est | vs. | ce n'est pas |
|---|---|---|
| C'est un ballon de foot. | | Ce n'est pas un gâteau. |
| **c'est** | **vs.** | **il/elle est** |
| C'est un garçon. C'est une fille. | | Il s'appelle Karim. Elle s'appelle Amélie. |
| **ce sont** | **vs.** | **ils/elles sont** |
| Ce sont des étudiants. Ce sont des étudiantes. | | Ils sont sportifs. Elles sont sympa. |

# Negation

| | |
|---|---|
| ne (n')… pas | Il **ne** joue **pas**.<br>Il **n'**a **pas** joué. |
| ne (n')… plus<br>ne (n')… jamais<br>ne (n')… personne<br>ne (n')… rien | Elle **n'**aime **plus** les frites.<br>Nous **ne** dansons **jamais**.<br>Vous **n'**invitez **personne**?<br>Ma grand-mère **ne** comprend **rien**. |

# Numbers

| Cardinal Numbers | Ordinal Numbers |
|---|---|
| un | premier, première |
| deux | deuxième |
| trois | troisième |
| quatre | quatrième |
| cinq | cinquième |
| six | sixième |
| sept | septième |
| huit | huitième |
| neuf | neuvième |
| dix, etc. | dixième, etc. |

# Prepositions

## Prepositions before Cities, Countries, Continents

| City<br>(no article) | Masculine<br>(le Japon) | Feminine<br>(la France) | Plural<br>(les États-Unis) |
|---|---|---|---|
| à | au | en | aux |

# Pronouns

## Subject Pronouns

| Singular | Plural |
|---|---|
| je | nous |
| tu | vous |
| il/elle/on | ils/elles |

# Questions

## Forming Questions

| | |
|---|---|
| using **n'est-ce-pas** | Il fait chaud, **n'est-ce pas**?<br>Ils regardent un DVD, **n'est-ce pas**? |
| using **est-ce que** | **Est-ce qu'**il fait chaud?<br>**Est-ce qu'**ils regardent un DVD? |
| using **inversion:** Verb-Subject | **Fait-il** chaud?<br>**Regardent-ils** un DVD? |

# Telling Time

| | | | |
|---|---|---|---|
| **Il est** une **heure** | …et quart. | …et demie. | …moins le quart. |
| Il est midi. | | | |
| Il est minuit. | | | |

# Verbs

## Regular Verbs—Present Tense

| -er<br>aimer | | | |
|---|---|---|---|
| j' | aim**e** | nous | aim**ons** |
| tu | aim**es** | vous | aim**ez** |
| il/elle/on | aim**e** | ils/elles | aim**ent** |

| -ir<br>finir | | | |
|---|---|---|---|
| je | fin**is** | nous | fin**issons** |
| tu | fin**is** | vous | fin**issez** |
| il/elle/on | fin**it** | ils/elles | fin**issent** |

| -re<br>vendre | | | |
|---|---|---|---|

| je | vend**s** | nous | vend**ons** |
|---|---|---|---|
| tu | vend**s** | vous | vend**ez** |
| il/elle/on | vend | ils/elles | vend**ent** |

## Irregular Verbs—Present Tense

| acheter | | | |
|---|---|---|---|
| j' | ach**è**te | nous | achetons |
| tu | ach**è**tes | vous | achetez |
| il/elle/on | ach**è**te | ils/elles | ach**è**tent |

| aller | | | |
|---|---|---|---|
| je | vais | nous | allons |
| tu | vas | vous | allez |
| il/elle/on | va | ils/elles | vont |

| avoir | | | |
|---|---|---|---|
| (avoir besoin de/avoir chaud/avoir faim/avoir froid/avoir soif) | | | |
| j' | ai | nous | avons |
| tu | as | vous | avez |
| il/elle/on | a | ils/elles | ont |

| devoir | | | |
|---|---|---|---|
| je | dois | nous | devons |
| tu | dois | vous | devez |
| il/elle/on | doit | ils/elles | doivent |

| être | | | |
|---|---|---|---|
| je | suis | nous | sommes |
| tu | es | vous | êtes |
| il/elle/on | est | ils/elles | sont |

| faire | | | |
|---|---|---|---|
| je | fais | nous | faisons |
| tu | fais | vous | faites |
| il/elle/on | fait | ils/elles | font |

| falloir |
|---|
| il faut |

| mettre | | | |
|---|---|---|---|
| je | mets | nous | mettons |
| tu | mets | vous | mettez |
| il/elle/on | met | ils/elles | mettent |

| offrir | | | |
|---|---|---|---|
| j' | offre | nous | offrons |
| tu | offres | vous | offrez |
| il/elle/on | offre | ils/elles | offrent |

| pouvoir | | | |
|---|---|---|---|
| je | peux | nous | pouvons |
| tu | peux | vous | pouvez |
| il/elle/on | peut | ils/elles | peuvent |

| préférer | | | |
|---|---|---|---|
| je | préf**è**re | nous | préférons |
| tu | préf**è**res | vous | préférez |
| il/elle/on | préf**è**re | ils/elles | préf**è**rent |

| prendre | | | |
|---|---|---|---|
| je | prends | nous | prenons |
| tu | prends | vous | prenez |
| il/elle/on | prend | ils/elles | prennent |

# Irregular Verbs—Present Tense *continued*

| venir | | | |
|---|---|---|---|
| je | viens | nous | venons |
| tu | viens | vous | venez |
| il/elle/on | vient | ils/elles | viennent |

| voir | | | |
|---|---|---|---|
| je | vois | nous | voyons |
| tu | vois | vous | voyez |
| il/elle/on | voit | ils/elles | voient |

| vouloir | | | |
|---|---|---|---|
| je | veux | nous | voulons |
| tu | veux | vous | voulez |
| il/elle/on | veut | ils/elles | veulent |

## Regular Imperatives

| -er chanter | -ir choisir | -re pendre |
|---|---|---|
| Chante! | Choisis! | Prends! |
| Chantons! | Choisissons! | Prenons! |
| Chantez! | Choisissez! | Prenez! |

## Expressing the Near Future

| aller + Infinitive |
|---|
| Nous allons dîner. |

## *Passé composé* with *avoir*

| avoir + past participle |
|---|

| -er verbs → é | -ir verbs → i | -re verbs → u |
|---|---|---|
| Nous avons gagné. | Tu as fini. | On a attendu. |

| Irregular Past Participles | | | | | |
|---|---|---|---|---|---|
| avoir | → **eu** | devoir | → **dû** | être | → **été** |
| faire | → **fait** | mettre | → **mis** | offrir | → **offert** |
| pouvoir | → **pu** | prendre | → **pris** | vendre | → **vendu** |
| venir | → **venu** | voir | → **vu** | vouloir | → **voulu** |

## *Passé composé* with *être*

| être + past participle (+ **agreement** in gender and number) | | | | | |
|---|---|---|---|---|---|
| je | suis | arrivé(e) | nous | sommes | arrivé(e)s |
| tu | es | arrivé(e) | vous | êtes | arrivé(e)s |
| il | est | arrivé | ils | sont | arrivés |
| elle | est | arrivée | elles | sont | arrivées |

Some of the verbs that use *être* as the helping verb in the **passé composé** are:

| Infinitive | Past Participle |
|---|---|
| aller | **allé** |
| arriver | **arrivé** |
| entrer | **entré** |
| monter | **monté** |
| rentrer | **rentré** |
| rester | **resté** |
| retourner | **retourné** |
| partir | **parti** |
| sortir | **sorti** |
| descendre | **descendu** |
| vendre | **vendu** |
| venir | **venu** |

## Verbs + Infinitives

| aimer | aller | désirer |
|---|---|---|
| devoir | falloir | pouvoir |
| préférer | venir | vouloir |

Nous préférons faire du ski.

# Vocabulaire

## Français–Anglais

This vocabulary list combines words from Textbook 1A (Units 1 to 5) and Textbook 1B (Units 6 to 10). The number at the end of each definition is the Unit in which the word is first presented.

## A

à to 1; at 2; on 4; in 5; by 9; À *bientôt.* See you soon. 1; à *bord* on board 7; à *côté (de)* beside, next to 7; À *demain.* See you tomorrow. 1; à droite on the right 7; à gauche on the left 7; à *l'heure* on time 4; à mon avis in my opinion 9; à pied on foot 9; à vélo by bike 9

un **accompagnateur, une accompagnatrice** home health worker 9

**accompagner** to accompany 10

les **accras de morue (m.)** cod fritters 5

un **achat** purchase 6
**acheter** to buy 3

un **acteur, une actrice** actor 4
l' **action (f.)** action 4
une **activité** activity 2
l' **addition (f.)** bill 4
l' **aérobic (m.)** aerobics 9
un **aéroport** airport 8
une **affiche** poster 3
l' **Afrique (f.)** Africa 5
l' **âge (m.)** age 5; *Tu as quel âge?* How old are you? 5

un **agent de police** police officer 5
l' **agriculture (f.)** agriculture 9
**ah** oh 1
**aider** to help 1
**aimer** to like, love 2
l' **air (m.)** air 6
**algérien(ne)** Algerian 1
l' **Allemagne (f.)** Germany 10
l' **allemand (m.)** German (language) 3
**allemand(e)** German 10
**aller** to go 1; *Tu trouves que... me va bien?* Does this... look good on me? 6; *Vas-y!* Go for it! 6
**allô** hello (on telephone) 1
**alors** so, then 3
l' **aluminium (m.)** aluminum 9; *en aluminium* made of aluminum 9
**américain(e)** American 1
un(e) **ami(e)** friend 2
un **an** year 5

un **ananas** pineapple 6
l' **anglais (m.)** English (language) 3
**anglais(e)** English 10
l' **Angleterre (f.)** England 10
un **animal** animal 8; *animaux en voie de disparition* endangered species 9
une **année** year 5
un **anniversaire** birthday 5
les **antirétroviraux (m.)** antiretroviral drugs 9
**août** August 5
un **appartement** apartment 7
s' **appeler: je m'appelle** my name is 1; *On s'appelle.* We'll call each other. 1; *tu t'appelles* your name is 1
**apporter** to bring 5
**apprendre** to learn 4
**après** after 2
l' **après-midi (m.)** afternoon 3
l' **argent (m.)** money 8
une **armoire** wardrobe 7
**arrêter** to stop 9
s' **arrêter** to stop 8
une **arrivée** arrival 10
**arriver** to arrive 4
les **arts plastiques (m.)** visual arts 3
**assez (de)** enough (of) 6
une **assiette** plate 7
un(e) **athlète** athlete 5
**attendre** to wait (for) 4
**Attention!** Watch out!, Be careful! 7
**au** to (the) 1; in (the), on (the) 8; *au bout (de)* at the end (of) 10; *au-dessus de* above 7; *au fond (de)* at the end (of) 7; *Au revoir.* Good-bye. 1
une **aubergine** eggplant 6

**aujourd'hui** today 4
**aussi** also, too 2; as 7
un **autobus** bus 10
l' **automne (m.)** autumn 8
**autre** other 7
**autrement** otherwise 6
**aux** at (the), in (the), to (the) 3
**avance: en avance** early 4
**avec** with 1
une **aventure** adventure 4
une **avenue** avenue 8
un **avion** airplane 8
un **avis** opinion 9; *à mon avis* in my opinion 9
un(e) **avocat(e)** lawyer 5
**avoir** to have 3; *avoir... an(s)* to be... year(s) old 5; *avoir besoin de* to need 3; *avoir bonne mine* to look healthy 9; *avoir chaud* to be hot 8; *avoir envie de* to want, to feel like 8; *avoir faim* to be hungry 4; *avoir froid* to be cold 8; *avoir mal (à...)* to be hurt, to have a/an... ache 9; *avoir mal au cœur* to feel nauseous 9; *avoir mauvaise mine* to look awful 9; *avoir quel âge* to be how old 5; *avoir soif* to be thirsty 4; *avoir un petit air du pays* to look like (something from) my country 7
**avril** April 5

## B

une **baguette** long thin loaf of bread 6
une **baignoire** bathtub 7
un **ballon (de foot)** (soccer) ball 4
**banal(e)** banal 8
une **banane** banana 6

un **banc** bench 7

une **banque** bank 8

le **bas** bottom 8

le **basket (basketball)** basketball 2

un **bateau** boat 8

**bavard(e)** talkative 5

**beau, bel, belle** beautiful, handsome 7

**beaucoup** a lot, very much 2; *beaucoup de* a lot of 6

un **beau-frère** stepbrother 5

un **beau-père** stepfather 5

**beige** beige 6

**belge** Belgian 10

la **Belgique** Belgium 10

une **belle-mère** stepmother 5

une **belle-sœur** stepsister 5

**ben** well 7

le **Bénin** Benin 5

**béninois(e)** Beninese 5

**berbère** Berber 7

**bête** unintelligent 5

le **beurre** butter 6

**bien** well 1; really 2

**bientôt** soon 1; *à bientôt* see you soon 1

**bienvenue** welcome 4

un **billet** bill (money) 6; ticket 10

la **biologie** biology 3

**biologique** organic 9

**blanc, blanche** white 6

un **blason** team logo 4

**bleu(e)** blue 5; *la bleue* the blue one 3

un **blogue** blog 2

**blond(e)** blond 5

un **blouson** jacket 4

le **bœuf** beef 6

une **boisson** drink 4

une **boîte (de)** can (of) 6

un **bol** bowl 7

**bon(ne)** good 1; *Bon Appétit!* Enjoy your meal! 4; *bon marché* cheap 6; *Bon voyage!* Have a good trip! 10

**bonjour** hello 1

les **bottes (f.)** boots 6

la **bouche** mouth 9; *bouche du métro* subway entrance 4

une **boucherie** butcher shop 6

**bouger** to move 9

une **boulangerie** bakery 6

le **bout** end 10; *au bout (de)* at the end (of) 10

une **bouteille (de)** bottle (of) 6

une **boutique** shop 6

le **bras** arm 9

**brun(e)** brown, dark (hair) 5

un **bureau** desk, office 3; *bureau du proviseur* principal's office 3

le **Burkina Faso** Burkina Faso 5

**burkinabè** from, of Burkina Faso 5

un **but** goal 4

# C

**c'est** this is, that is, it is 1; *C'est ça.* That's right. 1; *C'est le (+ date)* It's the (+ date) 5; *C'est le top!* That's awesome! 1

**ça** it, this 1; that 2; *Ça fait combien?* How much is it? 6; *Ça va?* How are things going? 1

une **cabine: cabine d'essayage** dressing room 6

un **cadeau** gift 5

un **café** café 1; coffee 4

un **cahier** notebook 3

un **calendrier** calendar 2

un(e) **camarade de classe** classmate 1

le **camembert** camembert cheese 6

le **Cameroun** Cameroon 5

**camerounais(e)** Cameroonian 5

la **campagne** country(side) 10

le **Canada** Canada 5

**canadien(ne)** Canadian 1

un **canapé** sofa 7

une **cantine** school cafeteria 3

une **capitale** capital 10

une **carotte** carrot 6

un **carré** square 7; *en carrés* in squares 7

une **carte** map 3; menu 4; map 5; *carte cadeau* gift card 5

une **cascade** waterfall 10

une **casquette** cap 4

une **cathédrale** cathedral 8

une **cause** cause 10

**causer** to cause 9

un **CD** CD 2

**ce** it 1; this 3; *ce, cet, cette,*

*ces* this, that, these, those 6; *ce que* what 9

un **cédérom** CD 3

**cent** (one) hundred 3

un **centre** center 1; *centre commercial* mall, shopping center 1

une **cerise** cherry 6

une **chaise** chair 3

une **chambre** bedroom 7

un **champignon** mushroom 6

une **chanson** song 7

**chanter** to sing 5

un **chanteur, une chanteuse** singer 5

un **chapeau** hat 6

une **charcuterie** delicatessen 6

**charmant(e)** charming 7

un **chat** cat 8

un **château** castle 10

**chaud(e)** hot 8; *avoir chaud* to be hot 8; *il fait chaud* it's hot 8; *j'ai chaud* I am hot 8

une **chaussette** sock 4

une **chaussure** shoe 4

un **chemin** way, path 10

une **chemise** shirt 6

**cher, chère** expensive 3

**chercher** to look for 6

un **cheval** horse 8

les **cheveux (m.)** hair 5

**chez** to, at the house (home) of 3; *chez moi* at/to my house 3

**chic** chic 6

un **chien** dog 8

la **chimie** chemistry 3

**chimique** chemical 9

le **chocolat** chocolate 4

**choisir** to choose 5

**chouette** great 8

un **ciné (cinéma)** movie theatre 1; *le cinéma* movies 2

**cinq** five 2

**cinquante** fifty 3

**cinquième** fifth 7

**circuler** to drive, to get around 9

une **classe** class 1

un **clavier** keyboard 7

une **clé USB** USB key 7

**cliquer** to click 7

**un** **coca** cola 4

**le** **cœur** heart 9; *avoir mal au cœur* to feel nauseous 9

**le** **coin** corner 8; *du coin* on the corner 8

**une** **colline** hill 10

**combattre** to fight 9

**combien** how much 3; *Ça fait combien?* How much is it? 6; *C'est combien le kilo?* How much per kilo? 6; *Il coûte combien?* How much does it cost? 3

**une** **comédie** comedy 4; *comédie romantique* romantic comedy 4

**comme** for 4; like 5; *comme ci, comme ça* so-so 1

**commencer** to begin 7

**comment** how, what 1; *Comment allez-vous? [form.]* How are you? 1; *Comment est...?* What is... like? 5

**commerçant(e)** shopping, business 6

**un** **compositeur, une compositrice** composer, songwriter 5

**composter** to validate (a ticket) 10

**un** **composteur** ticket-stamping machine 10

**comprendre** to understand 4

**un** **concert** concert 2; *concert R'n'B* R&B concert 2

**un** **concombre** cucumber 6

**la** **confiture** jam 4

**connais: je connais** I know 5

**conseiller** to advise 9

**consommer** to consume 8

**continuer** to continue 9

**contre** versus, against 4

**un** **contrôle** test 1

**un** **contrôleur, une contrôleuse** ticket collector 10

**un** **copain, une copine** (boy/girl) friend 1

**le** **corps** body 9

**côté: à côté (de)** beside, next to 7

**la** **Côte-d'Ivoire** Ivory Coast 5

**le** **cou** neck 9

**une** **couleur** color 6; *De quelle(s) couleur(s)?* In what color(s)? 6

**un** **couloir** hallway 7

**couper** to cut 7

**une** **courgette** zucchini 6

**un** **cours** course, class 2

**le** **couscous** couscous 6

**un(e)** **cousin(e)** cousin 5

**un** **coussin** pillow 7

**un** **couteau** knife 7

**coûter** to cost 3

**le** **couvert** table setting 7; *mettre le couvert* to set the table 7

**un** **crayon** pencil 3

**une** **crémerie** dairy store 6

**une** **crêpe** crêpe 4

**un** **croissant** croissant 6

**un** **croque-monsieur** grilled ham and cheese sandwich 4

**une** **cuiller** spoon 7

**la** **cuisine** cooking 2; kitchen 7

**un** **cuisinier, une cuisinière** cook, chef 5

**une** **cuisinière** stove 7

**culturel, culturelle** cultural 5

**une** **cure** spa treatment 9

# D

**d'abord** first of all 6

**d'accord** OK 1

**dans** in 3

**de/d'** of, from 1; some, any 2; *De quelle(s) couleur(s)?* In what color(s)? 6

**décembre** December 5

**décontracté(e)** relaxed 9

**un** **degré** degree 8

**déjà** already 8

**le** **déjeuner** lunch 3

**délicieux, délicieuse** delicious 3

**demain** tomorrow 1; *À demain.* See you tomorrow. 1

**demander** to ask (for) 7; *demander le chemin* to ask for directions 10

**démarrer** to start 7

**demi(e)** half 3; *et demie* half past 3

**un** **demi-frère** half-brother 5

**une** **demi-sœur** half-sister 5

**une** **dent** tooth 9

**un(e)** **dentiste** dentist 5

**un** **départ** departure 10

**un** **département** department 10

**dernier, dernière** last 8

**derrière** behind 3

**des** some 2; from (the), of (the) 5

**désagréable** unpleasant 8

**descendre** to go down, to get off 8

**désirer** to want 4

**désolé(e)** sorry 8

**un** **dessert** dessert 4

**dessus: au-dessus de** above 7

**une** **destination** destination 10

**deux** two 2

**deuxième** second 7

**devant** in front of 3

**devenir** to become 5

**une** **devise** motto 10

**devoir** to have to 7

**un** **devoir** assignment 9; *les devoirs (m.)* homework 1

**un** **dictionnaire** dictionary 3

**difficile** difficult 3

**diligent(e)** diligent 5

**dimanche** Sunday 2

**dîner** to have dinner 7

**le** **dîner** dinner 7

**le** **dioxyde de carbone** carbon dioxide 9

**une** **direction** direction 10

**dis** say 1; *disons* let's say 4

**une** **discussion** discussion 5

**disponible** free 8

**divorcé(e)(s)** divorced 5

**dix** ten 2

**dix-huit** eighteen 2

**dix-neuf** nineteen 2

**dix-sept** seventeen 2

**dixième** tenth 7

**un** **documentaire** documentary 4

**le** **doigt** finger 9; *doigt de pied* toe 9

**dois** (see **devoir**) 1

**donc** so, therefore 4

**donner** to give 4; *donnez-moi* give me 4

**dormir** to sleep 2

**le** **dos** back 9

**une** **douche** shower 7

**douze** twelve 2

**un** **drame** drama 4

**un** **drapeau** flag 10

**droite: à droite** to the right 7; *à droite de* to (on) the right of 7; *tout droit* straight ahead 10

**drôle** funny 3

**du** some 2; of (the) 4; from (the) 5; about (the) 8; *du coin* on the corner 8

**un** **DVD** DVD 3

# E

**l'** **eau (f.)** water; *eau minérale* mineral water 4

**une** **écharpe** scarf 4

**un** **éclair** eclair 8

**une** **école** school 3

**écouter** to listen (to) 2; *écouter de la musique* to listen to music 2; *écouter mon lecteur MP3* to listen to my MP3 player 3

**un** **écran** monitor, screen 7

**écrire** to write 3

**un** **écrivain** writer 5

**l'** **éducation physique et sportive (EPS) (f.)** gym class 3

**un** **effet** effect 9; *l'effet de serre* greenhouse effect 9

**égoïste** selfish 5

**eh: eh bien** well 1

**électrique** electric 9

**un(e)** **élève** student 3

**éliminer** to eliminate 9

**elle** she 1; it 3

**elles** they 2

**embrasser** to kiss 8

**une** **émission** television program 9

**en** in 3; on 4; of (pronoun) 8; by 9; *en aluminium, plastique* made of alumnum, plastic 9; *en avance* early 4; *en face de* across from 10; *en ligne* online 6; *en retard* late 4; *en solde* on sale 4; *en ville* downtown 3; *en voiture électrique* by electric car 9; *en voiture hydride* by hybrid car 9

**enchanté(e)** delighted 1

**un** **endroit** place 3

**l'** **énergie (f.)** energy; *énergie nucléaire* nuclear energy 9; *énergie solaire* solar energy 9

**énergique** energetic 3

**un** **enfant** child 5

**enfin** finally 4

**s'** **engager** to commit to, to be committed to 9

**l'** **engrais (m.)** fertilizer 9

**une** **enquête** survey 2

**ensemble** together 4

**un** **ensemble** outfit 6

**ensuite** next 6

**entre** between 10

**entrer** to enter, to come in 8

**l'** **environnement (m.)** environment 9

**envoyer** to send 2; *envoyer des textos* to send text messages 2

**une** **éolienne** wind turbine 9

**l'** **épaule (f.)** shoulder 9

**une** **épicerie** grocery store 6

**l'** **EPS (f.)** gym class 3

**une** **équipe** team 4

**un** **espace** area 9

**l'** **Espagne (f.)** Spain 10

**l'** **espagnol (m.)** Spanish (language) 3

**espagnol(e)** Spanish 10

**essayer** to try (on) 6

**est** (see **être**) 1

**l'** **est (m.)** east 10

**est-ce que** (phrase introducing a question) 3

**l'** **estomac (m.)** stomach 9

**et** and 1; *et demie* half past 3; *et quart* quarter past 3

**un** **étage** floor, story 7; *le premier étage* the second floor 7

**un** **étang** pond 10

**les** **États-Unis (m.)** United States 5

**l'** **été (m.)** summer 2

**être** to be 3; *être au courant* to know, to be informed 9; *être d'accord* to agree 7; *être libre* to be free 8; *être en (bonne, mauvaise) forme* to be in (good, bad) shape 9; *être en train de (+ infinitive)* to be (busy) doing something 7; *être occupé(e)* to be busy 8; *être situé(e)* to be located 10; *être vert* to be environmentally friendly 9; *Nous sommes le (+ date).* It's the (+ date). 5

**étudier** to study 2

**euh** um 3

**un** **euro** euro 3

**l'** **Europe (f.)** Europe 10

**un** **évier** sink 7

**exactement** exactly 8

# F

**face: en face de** across from 10

**facile** easy 3

**faim: avoir faim** to be hungry 4

**faire** to do, to make 1; *faire de la gym (gymnastique)* to do gymnastics 2; *faire du footing* to go running 2; *faire du patinage (artistique)* to (figure) skate 2; *faire du roller* to in-line skate 2; *faire du shopping* to go shopping 2; *faire du ski (alpin)* to (downhill) ski 2; *faire du sport* to play sports 2; *faire du vélo* to bike 2; *faire la connaissance (de)* to meet 10; *faire la cuisine* to cook 2; *faire les courses* to go grocery shopping 6; *faire marcher* to run, make (something) work 9; *faire mes devoirs* to do my homework 1; *faire une promenade* to go for a walk 8

**fais: je fais** (see **faire**) 2

**fait:** *Ça fait combien?* How much is it? 6; *il fait beau* it's beautiful out 2; *il fait chaud* it's hot 8; *il fait du soleil* it's sunny 8; *il fait du vent* it's windy 8; *il fait frais* it's cool 8; *il fait froid* it's cold 8; *il fait mauvais* the weather's bad 2; *Quel temps fait-il?* What's the weather like? 8

**falloir** to be necessary, to have to 9; *il faut* it is necessary, one has to/must, we/you have to/must 9

une **famille** family 5

**fatigué(e)** tired 8

**faut** (see **falloir**) 9

un **fauteuil** armchair 7

une **femme** wife 5; *femme d'affaires* businesswoman 5

une **fenêtre** window 3

**fermer** to close 7

une **fête** party 1

une **feuille de papier** sheet of paper 3

**février** February 5

la **fièvre** fever 9

la **figure** face 9

une **fille** girl 1; daughter 5

un **film** film 4; *film d'action* action movie 4; *film d'aventures* adventure movie 4; *film d'horreur* horror movie 4; *film de science-fiction* science fiction movie 4; *film musical* musical 4; *film policier* detective movie 4

un **fils** son 5

**fin(e)** fine 7

**finir** to finish 5

un **fitness** health club, gym 9

un **fleuve** river 8

**fond: au fond (de)** at the end (of) 7

le **foot** soccer 2

un **footballeur, une footballeuse** soccer player 4

le **footing** running 2

une **forêt** forest 10

**forme: être en (bonne, mauvaise) forme** to be in (good, bad) shape 9

**fort(e)** strong 7

un **foulard** scarf 6

un **four** oven 7

une **fourchette** fork 7

**frais, fraîche** fresh 6; cool 8; *il fait frais* it's cool 8

une **fraise** strawberry 6

le **français** French (language) 3

**français(e)** French 1

**francanadien(ne)** from, of French-speaking Canada 10

la **France** France 3

**francophone** French-speaking 5

un **frère** brother 5; *beau-frère* stepbrother 5; *demi-frère* half-brother 5

un **frigo** refrigerator 7

les **frissons (m.)** chills 9

les **frites (f.)** French fries 2

**froid(e)** cold 8; *avoir froid* to be cold 8; *il fait froid* it's cold 8; *j'ai froid* I am cold 8

le **fromage** cheese 4

un **fruit** fruit 6; *une tarte aux fruits* fruit tart 6

## G

le **Gabon** Gabon 5

**gabonais(e)** Gabonese 5

**gagner** to win 4

un **garçon** boy 1

une **gare** train station 8

un **gâteau** cake 5

**gauche: à gauche** on the left 7; *à gauche de* to (on) the left of 7

**géant(e)** giant 9

**généreux, généreuse** generous 5

**génial(e)** fantastic, great, terrific 2

le **genou** knee 9

un **genre** type 4

les **gens (m.)** people 5

une **glace** ice cream 4; *glace à la vanille* vanilla ice cream 4; *glace au chocolat* chocolate ice cream 4

la **gorge** throat 9

un **gorille** gorilla 9; *gorille des montagnes* mountain gorilla 9

**gourmand(e)** fond of food 8

le **goûter** snack 7

un **gramme (de)** gram (of) 6

**grand(e)** big, large, tall 5

une **grand-mère** grandmother 5

les **grands-parents (m.)** grandparents 5

un **grand-père** grandfather 5

**grandir** to grow 5

un(e) **graphiste** graphic designer 5

**grave** serious 8

la **grippe** flu 9

**gris** grey 5

**gros, grosse** big, fat, large 6

**grossir** to gain weight 5

un **guichet** ticket booth 4

un **guide** guidebook 10; *guide touristique* tourist guide 8

la **gym (gymnastique)** gymnastics 2; *faire de la gym (gymnastique)* to do gymnastics 2

## H

un(e) **habitant(e)** inhabitant, resident 10

**habiter** to live 7

un **hamburger** hamburger 2

les **haricots verts (m.)** green beans 6

le **haut** top 8

l' **heure (f.)** hour, o'clock, time 3; *à l'heure* on time 4; *Quelle heure est-il?* What time is it? 3

**hier** yesterday 8

le **hip-hop** hip-hop 2

l' **histoire (f.)** history 3

l' **hiver (m.)** winter 2

un **homme** man 5; *homme d'affaires* businessman 5

l' **horreur (f.)** horror 4

un **hôtel** hotel 8; *hôtel de ville* city hall 8

**huit** eight 2

**huitième** eighth 7

**humanitaire** humanitarian 10

**hybride** hybrid 9

## I

**ici** here 7

une **idée: Bonne idée!** Good idea! 8

**il** he 1; it 3

**il y a** there is/are 3

**ils** they 2

un **immeuble** apartment building 7

**impossible** impossible 7

une **imprimante** printer 7

**imprimer** to print 7

l' **informatique (f.)** computer science 3

un **ingénieur** engineer 5

**installer** to install 9

un **instant** moment 9; *pour l'instant* for the moment 9

**intelligent(e)** intelligent 3

**intéressant(e)** interesting 3

**international(e)** international 10

(l') **Internet (m.)** Internet 2

un(e) **invité(e)** guest 7

**inviter** to invite 2

l' **Italie (f.)** Italy 10

**italien(ne)** Italian 10

**ivoirien(ne)** from, of the Ivory Coast 5

# J

la **jambe** leg 9

le **jambon** ham 4

**janvier** January 5

un **jardin** garden, park 8

le **jasmin** jasmine 7

**jaune** yellow 6

**je (j')** I 1

un **jean** jeans 6

**jeudi** Thursday 2

les **Jeux Olympiques (m.)** Olympic Games 2

des **jeux vidéo (m.)** video games 2

**joli(e)** pretty 6

**jouer** to play 2; *jouer au basket (basketball)* to play basketball 2; *jouer au foot (football)* to play soccer 2; *jouer au hockey sur glace* to play ice hockey 2; *jouer aux jeux vidéo* to play video games 2; *jouer un rôle* to play a role 4

un **jour** day 2; one day, someday 5

une **journée** day 8

**juillet** July 5

**juin** June 5

une **jupe** skirt 6

un **jus** juice 4; *jus d'orange* orange juice 4

**jusqu'à** until 10

# K

le **ketchup** ketchup 6

un **kilo (de)** kilogram (of) 6

un **kilomètre** kilometer 5

un **kiosque à journaux** newsstand 4

# L

**là** there 1

**là-bas** over there 5

un **labo (laboratoire)** science lab 3

un **lac** lake 10

**laisser** to leave, to let 9; *Laisse-moi finir!* Let me finish! 8

le **lait** milk 6

une **lampe** lamp 7

une **langue** language 3

**le, la, l'** the 1; it (object pronoun) 4

un **lecteur de DVD** DVD player 3; *lecteur de MP3* MP3 player 3

un **légume** vegetable 6

**les** the 2

**leur, leurs** their 5

un **lien** link 7

la **ligne** figure 8; *en ligne* online 6

une **limonade** lemon-lime soda 4

**lire** to read 2

un **lit** bed 7

un **litre (de)** liter (of) 6

un **livre** book 3

une **livre** pound 6

un **logiciel** software 7

**loin (de)** far (from) 10

**long, longue** long 7

**louer** to rent 10

**lui** to him/her 5

**lundi** Monday 2

le **Luxembourg** Luxembourg 10

**luxembourgeois(e)** from, of Luxembourg 10

un **lycée** high school 9

# M

**m'appelle: je m'appelle** my name is 1

**madame (Mme)** Ma'am, Mrs., Ms. 1

**mademoiselle (Mlle)** Miss, Ms. 1

un **magasin** store 3

**mai** May 5

**maigrir** to lose weight 5

un **maillot** jersey 4; *maillot de bain* bathing suit 6

la **main** hand 8; *la main dans la main* hand in hand 8

**maintenant** now 3

**mais** but 3

une **maison** house, home 1

**mal** badly 1; *Ça va mal.* Things are going badly. 1; *avoir mal (à...)* to be hurt, to have a/an... ache 9

**malade** sick 9

un(e) **malade** sick person 9

une **maladie** illness 9

le **Mali** Mali 5

**malien(ne)** Malian 5

**manger** to eat 2

un **mannequin** model 6

un **manteau** coat 6

un(e) **marchand(e)** merchant 6

un **marché** outdoor market 6; *marché aux puces* flea market 6

**marcher** to walk 9; *faire marcher* to make (something) work 9

**mardi** Tuesday 2

une **marée** tide 9; *marée noire* oil slick 9

un **mari** husband 5

**marquer** to score 4

**marron** brown 5

**mars** March 5

la **Martinique** Martinique 5

un **match** game 4

les **maths (f.)** math 1

la **matière** class subject 3

le **matin** morning 3

**mauvais** bad 8; *il fait mauvais* the weather is bad 2

la **mayonnaise** mayo 6

**me (m')** me 4

**méchant(e)** mean 5

un **médecin** doctor 5

une **médiathèque** media center 3

les **meilleurs (m.)** the best 4

un **melon** melon 6

**même** same 6

un **menu fixe** fixed menu 4

**merci** thank you 4

**mercredi** Wednesday 2

une **mère** mother 1; *belle-mère* stepmother 5

**mesdemoiselles (f.)** plural of *mademoiselle* 4

un **métier** job 5

le **métro** subway 4

un **metteur en scène** director 4

**mettre** to put (on), to set 7; *mettre le couvert* to set the table 7

se **mettre: mets-toi devant l'écran** place yourself in front of the TV 9

un **meuble** piece of furniture 7

un **micro-onde** microwave 7

**midi** noon 3

**mieux** better 1

**mille** thousand 4

un **millefeuille** layered custard pastry 8

un **million** million 5

une **mine** appearance, expression 9

une **minute** minute 7

**minuit** midnight 3

**moche** ugly 6

**moi** me 1

**moins** less 7; *moins le quart* quarter to 3

un **mois** month 5

**mon, ma, mes** my 1

le **monde** everyone, world 1

un **moniteur** monitor 7

**monsieur (M.)** Mr., sir 1

une **montagne** mountain 9

**monter** to go up, to get in/on 8

**montrer** to show 8

un **monument** monument 8

un **morceau (de)** piece (of) 6

**mort(e)** dead 9

**morue: accras de morue (m.)** cod fritters 5

une **mosquée** mosque 7

la **moutarde** mustard 6

**moyen(ne)** medium 5

**mûr(e)** ripe 6

un **musée** museum 8

la **musique** music 2; *musique alternative* alternative music 2

# N

**n'est-ce pas?** isn't that so? 2

**nager** to swim 2

une **nappe** tablecloth 7

**naviguer** to browse 7

**ne (n')... jamais** never 10

**ne (n')... pas** not 1

**ne (n')... personne** no one, nobody, not anyone 10

**ne (n')... plus** no longer, not anymore 10

**ne (n')... rien** nothing 3

**neige: il neige** it's snowing 8

**neuf** nine 2

**neuvième** ninth 7

le **nez** nose 9

**niçoise: une salade niçoise** tuna salad 6

**noir(e)** black 5

un **nombre** number 2

**non** no 1

le **nord** north 10

une **note** grade 3

**notre, nos** our 5

**nous** we 2; us 5

**nouveau** new 2; *nouvel, nouvelle* new 8

le **Nouveau-Brunswick** New Brunswick 7

**novembre** November 5

**nucléaire** nuclear 9

la **nuit** night 3

un **numéro** number 2; *numéro de téléphone* phone number 2

# O

**obligatoire** mandatory 8

**occupé(e)** busy 8; *être occupé(e)* to be busy 8

un **océan** ocean 9

**octobre** October 2

l' **œil (m.)** eye 9

un **œuf** egg 6

**offrir** to offer, to give 5

**oh** oh 1

**oh là là** oh dear, oh no, wow 9

un **oignon** onion 6

un **oiseau** bird 8

une **olive** olive 6

une **omelette** omelette 4

**on** they, we, one 1; *On s'appelle.* We'll call each other. 1

un **oncle** uncle 5

**onze** eleven 2

**orange** orange 6

une **orange** orange 4

un **ordinateur** computer 3;

**ordinateur portable** laptop computer 3

l' **oreille (f.)** ear 9

**ou** or 2

**où** where 3; when 8

**oublier** to forget 8

l' **ouest (m.)** west 10

**oui** yes 1

**ouille** ouch 9

un **ours** bear 9; *ours polaire* polar bear 9

**ouvre: elle ouvre** she opens 7

# P

**paie** (see **payer**) 7

le **pain** bread 6

un **pamplemousse** grapefruit 6

un **panda** panda 9; *panda géant* giant panda 9

un **panneau** panel 9

un **pantalon** pants 6

le **papier** paper 3; *une feuille de papier* sheet of paper 3

un **paquet (de)** packet (of) 6

**par** with 7

un **parc** park 7

**parce que** because 3

**pardi (régional)** of course 7

**pardon** pardon me 8

les **parents (m.)** parents 5

**paresseux, paresseuse** lazy 5

**parler** to speak, to talk 5

se **parler** to talk to each other/ one another 8

les **paroles (f.)** lyrics 7

**partir** to leave 8

**partout** everywhere 9

**pas** not 1; *pas du tout* not at all 10; *pas mal* not bad 1; *pas très bien* not very well 1

**passer** to spend (time) 7

un **passe-temps** pastime 2

une **passion** passion 10

**passionné(e) (de)** passionate (about) 5

une **pastèque** watermelon **5**

le **pâté** pâté 6

les **pâtes (f.)** pasta 2

le **patinage (artistique)** (figure) skating 2

une **pâtisserie** bakery, pastry shop 6
**payer** to pay 9
un **payeur, une payeuse** someone who pays 9
un **pays** country 7
une **pêche** peach 6
**pendant** during 2; for 8
une **pendule** clock 3
**penser** to think 7
**perdre** to lose 4
**perdu(e)** lost 10
un **père** father 1; *beau-père* stepfather 5
une **personne** person 9; *ne (n')… personne* no one, nobody, not anyone 10
**persuadé(e)** persuaded 9
**petit(e)** little, short, small 5
le **petit déjeuner** breakfast 7
les **petits pois (m.)** peas 6
(un) **peu** (a) little 2; *un peu de* a little of 6
**peut** (see **pouvoir**) 3
**peut-être** maybe 4
**peux** (see **pouvoir**) 1; *Je peux vous aider?* May I help you? 6
une **photo** photo 7; *re-photo* another photo 8
la **physique** physics 3
une **pièce** room 7
le **pied** foot 9; *à pied* on foot 9
une **piscine** swimming pool 3
une **pizza** pizza 2
un **placard** closet 7
une **place** square 8
un **plaisir** pleasure 10
un **plan** city map 10
une **planète** planet 9
le **plastique** plastic 9; *en plastique* made of plastic 9
**pleurer** to cry 4
**pleuvoir** to rain 8; *il pleut* it's raining 8
**plonger** to dive 2
**plus** more 7; *le/la/les plus (+adjectif)* the most (+ adjective) 10
une **poire** pear 6
un **poisson (rouge)** (gold)fish 8
la **poitrine** chest 9

le **poivre** pepper 7
un **poivron** bell pepper 6
**polluant** polluting 9
**polluer** to pollute 9
un **pollueur, une pollueuse** polluter 9
la **pollution** pollution 9
une **pomme** apple 6; *une tarte aux pommes* apple pie 6
une **pomme de terre** potato 6
un **pont** bridge 8
le **porc** pork 6
un **portable** cell phone 7
une **porte** door 3
**porter** to wear 4
**possible** possible 1
une **poste** post office 8
un **pot (de)** jar (of) 6
le **poulet** chicken 6
**pour** for 3
**pourquoi** why 2
**pourrais: tu pourrais** you could 9
**pouvoir** can, to be able (to) 7
**préféré(e)** favorite 2
**préférer** to prefer 2
**premier, première** first 5
**prendre** to take, to have (food or drink) 4; *je prends* I'll take 3
un **prénom** first name 1
**préparer** to prepare 5
une **préposition** preposition 10
**près de** near 7
**présenter** to introduce 1; *Je te/vous présente…* I'd like to introduce you to… 1
**presque** nearly 9
**prêt(e)** ready 6
le **printemps** spring 8
un **problème** problem 7
un(e) **prof** teacher 1
une **profession** profession 5; *Quelle est votre profession?* What is your profession? 5
un **profil** profile 10
**profiter** to take advantage of 8; *profiter de* to benefit from 9; *tu profiterais de* you would benefit from 9
un **projet** project 5
une **promenade** walk 8

**protéger** to protect 9
**provençal(e)** from, of Provence 7
une **province** province 10
un **proviseur** principal 3
**puis** then 3
un **pull** sweater 6

## Q

**qu'est-ce que** what 2; *Qu'est-ce qu'elle a?* What's wrong with her? 9; *Qu'est-ce que tu aimes faire?* What do you like to do? 2; *Qu'est-ce que tu fais?* What are you doing? 2
un **quai** platform 10
**quand** when 2
**quarante** forty 3
un **quart** quarter 3; *et quart* quarter past 3; *moins le quart* a quarter to 3
**quatorze** fourteen 2
**quatre** four 2
**quatre-vingt-dix** ninety 3
**quatre-vingts** eighty 3
**quatrième** fourth 7
**que** that 5; than, as 7
le **Québec** Quebec 10
**québécois(e)** from, of Quebec 10
**quel, quelle** what, which 2
**quelqu'un** somebody, someone 10
**quelque chose** something 10
une **question** question 2
**qui** that, who 3
une **quiche** quiche 4
**quinze** fifteen 2
**quitter** to leave 9
**quoi** what 3

## R

la **radiation** radiation 9
un **raisin** grape 6
la **ratatouille** ratatouille 7
**réaliser** to realize 10
une **recette** recipe 7
**réchauffer** to heat up 9
**recycler** to recycle 9
**réfléchir (à)** to think over, consider 5
**regarder** to watch 2
une **religieuse** cream puff pastry 8

**rembourser** to reimburse 4

**remplacer** to replace 9

un **rendez-vous** meeting 4

**rentrer** to come back, to come home, to return 8

un **repas** meal 7

**re-photo** another photo 8

un **reportage** news report 9

une **résolution** resolution 9

**respiratoire** respiratory 9

**ressembler (à)** to resemble 5

un **restaurant** restaurant 8

**rester** to remain, to stay 8

**retourner** to return 8

se **retrouver** to meet 4; *on se retrouve....* we'll meet.... 3

**réussir (à)** to pass (a test), to succeed 5

**revenir** to come back 5; to return 8

le **rez-de-chaussée** the ground floor 7

un **rhume** cold 9

une **riad** riad 7

**rien: ne (n')... rien** nothing 3

**rigoler** to laugh 8

**rire** to laugh 4

une **rivière** river 10

une **robe** dress 6

le **rock** rock (music) 2

un **rôle** role 5

le **roller** in-line skating 2

une **rondelle** circular piece of food 7; *en rondelles* in circles 7

**rose** pink 6

**rouge** red 6

**rougir** to blush 5

une **route** highway, road, route 10

**roux, rousse** red (hair) 5

une **rue** street 6

le **Rwanda** Rwanda 9

# S

**s'appeler: On s'appelle.** We'll call each other. 1

**s'il vous plaît** please 4

un **sac à dos** backpack 3

**sais: je sais** I know 4; *tu sais* you know 9

une **salade** salad 2; lettuce 6; *salade niçoise* tuna salad 6

une **salle** room 3; *salle à manger* dining room 7; *salle de bains* bathroom 7; *salle de classe* classroom 3; *salle d'informatique* computer lab 3

un **salon** living room 7

**salut** hi, good-bye 1

**samedi** Saturday 2

un **sandwich** sandwich 4; *sandwich au fromage* cheese sandwich 4; *sandwich au jambon* ham sandwich 4

le **saucisson** salami 6

**sauvage** wild 9

**sauvegarder** to protect 9; to save 7

la **science-fiction** science fiction 4

les **sciences (f.)** science 3

une **séance** film showing 4

**seize** sixteen 2

un **séjour** living room 7

le **sel** salt 7

une **semaine** week 2

le **Sénégal** Senegal 5

**sénégalais(e)** Senegalese 5

**sentir** to smell 7; *Ça sent quoi?* What does it smell like? 7

**sept** seven 2

**septembre** September 5

**septième** seventh 7

une **série** series 4

un **serveur, une serveuse** server 4

une **serviette** napkin 7

le **shopping** shopping 2

un **short** shorts 4

**si** yes (on the contrary) 2; if 4

le **SIDA** AIDS 9

un **siège** seat 10

**simple** simple 10

un **site web** website 7

**situé(e)** located 10

**six** six 2

**sixième** sixth 7

le **ski (alpin)** (downhill) skiing 2

une **sœur** sister 5; *belle-sœur* stepsister 5; *demi-sœur* half-sister 5

**soif: avoir soif** to be thirsty 4

le **soir** evening 2

**soixante** sixty 3

**soixante-dix** seventy 3

**solaire** solar 9; *l'énergie (f.) solaire* solar energy 9

**solde: en solde** on sale 4

**soleil: il fait du soleil** it's sunny 8

**son, sa, ses** his, her, one's, its 5

**sortir** to go out 2; to come out 6

la **soupe** soup 6

une **souris** mouse 7

**sous** under 3

**soutenir** to support 4; *je soutiens* I support 4

un **souvenir** memory 8

**souvent** often 10

**souviens: je me souviens** I remember 10

une **spécialité: spécialité du jour** daily special 4

un **sport** sport 2

un **stade** stadium 4

une **statue** statue 8

un **steak-frites** steak with fries 4

le **step** step aerobics 9

une **stéréo** stereo 3

**strict(e)** strict 1

un **stylo** pen 3

le **sucre** sugar 7

le **sud** south 10

**suis** (see **être**) 1

**suisse** Swiss 10

la **Suisse** Switzerland 10

**super** awesome 5

un **supermarché** supermarket 6

**sur** on 2; of 8

**sûr(e)** sure 7

**surfer** to surf 2; *surfer sur Internet* to surf the Web 2

**surprend: ça ne me surprend pas** it doesn't surprise me 4

**surtout** especially 4

**survivre** to survive 9

**sympa** nice 5

**synchroniser** to synchronize 7

# T

**t'appelles: tu t'appelles** your name is 1; *Tu t'appelles comment?* What's your name? 1

une **table** table 3

un **tableau** chalkboard 3; painting 8; *tableau des arrivées et des départs* arrival and departure timetable 10

une **tablette** tablet 7

un **taf** work 7

**tahitien(ne)** Tahitian 3

une **taille** size 5; *de taille moyenne* of average height 5; *Quelle taille faites-vous?* What size are you? 6

un **taille-crayon** pencil sharpener 3

**tant pis** too bad 6

une **tante** aunt 5

un **tapis** rug 7

une **tarte** pie 6; *tarte aux fruits* fruit tart 6; *tarte aux pommes* apple pie 6

une **tasse** cup 7

**te (t')** you, to you 1

un **tee-shirt** T-shirt 6

une **télé (télévision)** TV, television 2

**télécharger** to download 7

**téléphoner** to phone (someone), to make a call 2

la **température** temperature 8

le **temps** weather 8; *Quel temps fait-il?* What's the weather like? How's the weather? 8

des **tennis (m.)** sneakers 6

une **terrasse** terrace 8

un **testeur de jeux vidéo** video game tester 5

la **tête** head 9

une **teuf** party 1

un **texto** text message 2

un **thème** topic 9

**thermal(e)** hydrotherapeutic 9

le **thon** tuna 6

un **thriller** thriller 4

un **ticket** ticket 4

**tiens** hey 6

un **tigre** tiger 9; *tigre de Sumatra* Sumatran tiger 9

**timide** shy 5

un **tissu** fabric 7

le **Togo** Togo 5

**togolais(e)** Togolese 5

**toi** you 1

les **toilettes (f.)** toilet 7

un **toit** roof 9

une **tomate** tomato 6

**ton, ta** your 1; *tes* your 5

**top** awesome 1; *C'est le top!* That's awesome! 1

**total(e): Total vintage!** It has a totally vintage look! 3

une **touche** key (on keyboard) 7

**toujours** always 10; still 4

un **tour** tour 8

**tourner** to turn 10

**tout(e), tous, toutes** all 1; *Tout ça!* All that! 4

un **train** train 10

une **tranche (de)** slice (of) 6

**travailler** to work 5

**traverser** to cross 10

**treize** thirteen 2

**trente** thirty 3

**très** very 1; *Très bien, et toi/vous?* Very well, and you? 1

**trois** three 2

**troisième** third 7

**trop** too 1; *trop de* too much of 6

une **trousse** pencil case 3

**trouver** to find 6

se **trouver** to be located 10

**tu** you 1

# U

**un** a, an 1; one 2

**une** a, an, one 3

une **usine** factory 9

# V

**va** (see **aller**) 1

les **vacances (f.)** vacation 10

une **valise** suitcase 10

une **vallée** valley 10

**vas** (see **aller**) 1; *Tu vas bien?* Are things going well? 2

un **vélo** bike 2; *à vélo* by bike 9

un **vendeur, une vendeuse** salesperson 6

**vendre** to sell 6

**vendredi** Friday 2

**venir** to come 1

**vent: il fait du vent** it's windy 8

le **ventre** stomach 9

un **verre** glass 7

**vers** towards 10

**vert(e)** green 5

une **veste** jacket 6

des **vêtements (m.)** clothes 4

**veux: je veux bien** I'd like that 1

**vieux, vieil, vieille** old 8

une **ville** city 3; *en ville* downtown 3

**vingt** twenty 2

**violet, violette** purple 6

une **visite** visit 10

**visiter** to visit 8

**vite** fast, quickly 8

une **voie** path 9; train track 10; *animaux en voie de disparition* endangered species 9

**voilà** here is/are 4

**voir** to see 3

se **voir** to see each other/one another 8

une **voiture** car 9; *voiture électrique* electric car 9; *voiture hybride* hybrid car 9

**votre, vos** your 5

**voudrais: je voudrais** I would like 5; *tu voudrais* you would like 1

**vouloir** to want 6

**vous** you 1, to you 5; *Vous voulez…?* Would you like…? 4

un **voyage** trip 8

**voyager** to travel 5

un **voyageur, une voyageuse** traveller 10

**vrai(e)** true 10

**vraiment** really 5

une **vue** view 7; *Quelle belle vue!* What a beautiful view! 7

# W

les **W.C. (m.)** toilet 7

un **wagon-restaurant** dining car 10

le **weekend** weekend 2

la **world** world music 2

# Y

**y: On y va?** Are we going (there)? 3

un **yaourt** yogurt 6

les **yeux (m.)** eyes 5

le **yoga** yoga 9

# Z

**zéro** zero 2

# Vocabulary

## English–French

This vocabulary list combines words from Textbook 1A (Units 1 to 5) and Textbook 1B (Units 6 to 10). The number at the end of each definition is the Unit in which the word is first presented.

## A

**a, an** un 1; une 3; *(a) little* (un) peu 2; *a little of* un peu de 6; *a lot* beaucoup 2; *a lot of* beaucoup de 6

**to be able (to)** pouvoir 7
**about (the)** du 8
**above** au-dessus de 7
**to accompany** accompagner 10
**ache: to have a/an... ache** avoir mal (à)... 9
**across from** en face de 10
**action** l'action (f.) 4
**activity** une activité 2
**actor** un acteur, une actrice 4
**adventure** une aventure 4
**to advise** conseiller 9
**aerobics** l'aérobic (m.) 9; *step aerobics* le step 9
**Africa** l'Afrique (f.) 5
**after** après 2
**afternoon** l'après-midi (m.) 3
**against** contre 4
**age** l'âge (m.) 5
**to agree** être d'accord 7
**agriculture** l'agriculture (f.) 9
**AIDS** le SIDA 9
**air** l'air (m.) 6
**airplane** un avion 8
**airport** un aéroport 8
**Algerian** algérien(ne) 1
**all** tout(e), toutes, tous 1; *All that!* Tout ça! 4
**already** déjà 8
**also** aussi 2
**aluminum** l'aluminium (m.) 9; *made of aluminum* en aluminium 9
**always** toujours 10
**American** américain(e) 1
**and** et 1
**animal** un animal 8
**another: another photo** re-photo 8
**antiretroviral drugs** les antirétroviraux (m.) 9
**any** d', de 2

**apartment** un appartement 7; *apartment building* un immeuble 7
**appearance** une mine 9
**apple** une pomme 6; *apple pie* une tarte aux pommes 6
**April** avril 5
**area** un espace 9
**arm** le bras 9
**armchair** un fauteuil 7
**arrival** une arrivée 10; *arrival and departure timetable* un tableau des arrivées et des départs 10
**to arrive** arriver 4
**as** aussi, que 7
**to ask (for)** demander 7; *to ask for directions* demander le chemin 10
**assignment** un devoir 9
**at** à 2; *at (the)* au, aux 3; *at my house* chez moi 3; *at the end (of)* au fond (de) 7; *au bout (de)* 10; *at the house (home) of* chez 3
**athlete** un(e) athlète 5
**August** août 5
**aunt** une tante 5
**autumn** l'automne (m.) 8
**avenue** une avenue 8
**awesome** top 1; super 8; *That's awesome!* C'est le top! 1

## B

**back** le dos 9
**backpack** un sac à dos 3
**bad** mal 1; mauvais 8; *the weather is bad* il fait mauvais 2
**badly** mal 1; *Things are going badly.* Ça va mal. 1
**bakery** une boulangerie, une pâtisserie 6
**banal** banal(e) 8

**banana** une banane 6
**bank** une banque 8
**basketball** le basket (basketball) 2
**bathing suit** un maillot de bain 6
**bathroom** une salle de bains 7
**bathtub** une baignoire 7
**to be** être 3; *to be able (to)* pouvoir 7; *to be busy* être occupé 8; *to be (busy) doing something* être en train de (+ infinitive) 7; *to be cold* avoir froid 8; *to be committed to* s'engager 9; *to be environmentally friendly* être vert 9; *to be free* être libre 8; *to be hot* avoir chaud 8; *to be how old* avoir quel âge 5; *to be hungry* avoir faim 4; *to be hurt* avoir mal (à...) 9; *to be informed* être au courant 9; *to be in (good, bad) shape* être en (bonne, mauvaise) forme 9; *to be located* être situé(e), se trouver 10; *to be necessary* falloir 8; *to be thirsty* avoir soif 4; *to be... year(s) old* avoir... an(s) 5
**bear** un ours 9; *polar bear* un ours polaire 9
**beautiful** beau, bel, belle 7; *It's beautiful out.* Il fait beau. 2
**because** parce que 3
**to become** devenir 5
**bed** un lit 7
**bedroom** une chambre 7
**beef** le bœuf 6
**to begin** commencer 7
**behind** derrière 3
**beige** beige 6
**Belgian** belge 10
**Belgium** la Belgique 10
**bench** un banc 7

to **benefit from** profiter de 9; *you would benefit from* tu profiterais de 9

**Benin** le Bénin 5

**Beninese** béninois(e) 5

**Berber** berbère 7

**beside** à côté de 7

**best: the best** les meilleurs (m.) 4

**better** mieux 1

**between** entre 10

**big** grand(e) 5; gros, grosse 6

**bike** un vélo 2

to **bike** faire du vélo 2; *by bike* à vélo 9

**bill** l'addition (f.) 4; *bill (money)* un billet 6

**biology** la biologie 3

**bird** un oiseau 8

**birthday** un anniversaire 5

**black** noir(e) 5

**blog** un blogue 2

**blond** blond(e) 5

**blue** bleu(e) 5; *the blue one* la bleue 3

to **blush** rougir 5

**boat** un bateau 8

**body** le corps 9

**book** un livre 3

**boots** les bottes (f.) 6

**bottle (of)** une bouteille (de) 6

**bottom** le bas 8

**bowl** un bol 7

**boy** un garçon 5

**bread** le pain 6; *long thin loaf of bread* une baguette 6

**breakfast** le petit déjeuner 7

**bridge** un pont 8

to **bring** apporter 5

**brother** un frère 5; *half-brother* un demi-frère 5; *stepbrother* un beau-frère 5

**brown** marron 6; *brown (hair)* brun(e) 5

to **browse** naviguer 7

**building: apartment building** un immeuble 7

**Burkina Faso** le Burkina Faso 5; *from, of Burkina Faso* burkinabè 5

**bus** un autobus 10

**business** commerçant(e) 6

**businessman** un homme d'affaires 5

**businesswoman** une femme d'affaires 5

**busy** occupé(e) 8

to be **busy** être occupé(e) 8; *to be (busy) doing something* être en train de (+ infinitive) 7

**but** mais 3

**butcher shop** une boucherie 6

**butter** le beurre 6

to **buy** acheter 3

**by** à 9; en 9; *by bike* à vélo 9; *by electric car* en voiture électrique 9; *by hybrid car* en voiture hybride 9

# C

**café** un café 1

**cafeteria: school cafeteria** une cantine 3

**cake** un gâteau 5

**camembert cheese** le camembert 6

**Cameroon** le Cameroun 5

**Cameroonian** camerounais(e) 5

**can (of)** une boîte (de) 6

**Canada** le Canada 5

**Canadian** canadien(ne) 1

**cap** une casquette 4

**capital** une capitale 8

**car** une voiture 9; *dining car* un wagon-restaurant 10; *electric car* une voiture électrique 9; *hybrid car* une voiture hybride 9

**carbon dioxyde** le dioxyde de carbone 9

**card** une carte 5

**careful: Be careful!** Attention! 7

**carrot** une carotte 6

**castle** un château 10

**cat** un chat 8

**cathedral** une cathédrale 8

**cause** une cause 10

to **cause** causer 9

**CD** un CD 2; un cédérom 3

**cell phone** un portable 7

**center** un centre 1; *shopping center* un centre commercial 1

**chair** une chaise 3

**chalkboard** un tableau 3

**charming** charmant(e) 7

**cheap** bon marché 6

**cheese** le fromage 4; *camembert cheese* le camembert 6; *cheese sandwich* un sandwich au fromage 4

**chef** un cuisinier, une cuisinière 5

**chemical** chimique 9

**chemistry** la chimie 3

**cherry** une cerise 6

**chest** la poitrine 9

**chic** chic 6

**chicken** le poulet 6

**child** un enfant 5

**chills** les frissons (m.) 9

**chocolate** le chocolat 4

to **choose** choisir 5

**circular: circular object or piece of food** une rondelle 7

**city** ville 3

**city hall** un hôtel de ville 8

**class** une classe 1; un cours 2; *class subject* la matière 3; *gym class* l'éducation physique et sportive (EPS) (f.) 3

**classmate** un(e) camarade de classe 1

**classroom** la salle de classe 3

to **click** cliquer 7

**clock** une pendule 3

to **close** fermer 7

**closet** un placard 7

**clothes** des vêtements (m.) 4

**coat** un manteau 6

**cod fritters** les accras de morue (m.) 5

**coffee** un café 4

**cola** un coca 4

**cold** froid 8; *I am cold* j'ai froid 8; *it's cold* il fait froid 8; *to be cold* avoir froid 8

**cold** un rhume 9

**color** une couleur 6; *In what color(s)?* De quelle(s) couleur(s) 7

to **come** venir 1; *to come back* revenir 5; rentrer 8; *to come home* rentrer 8; *to come in* entrer 8; *to come out* sortir 6

**comedy** une comédie 4; *romantic comedy* une comédie romantique 4

to **commit to** s'engager 9

**composer** un compositeur 5

**computer** un ordinateur 3; *computer lab* une salle d'informatique 3; *computer science* l'informatique (f.) 3; *laptop computer* un ordinateur portable 3

**concert** un concert 2

to **consider** réfléchir (à) 5

to **consume** consommer 8

to **continue** continuer 9

**cool** frais, fraîche 8; *it's cool* il fait frais 8

**cook** un cuisinier, une cuisinière 5

to **cook** faire la cuisine 2

**cooking** la cuisine 2

**corner** le coin 8; *on the corner* du coin 8

to **cost** coûter 3

**could: you could** tu pourrais 9

**country** un pays 7

**country(side)** la campagne 10

**course** un cours 2

**couscous** le couscous 6

**cousin** un(e) cousin(e) 5

**cream puff pastry** une religieuse 8

**crêpe** une crêpe 4

**croissant** un croissant 6

to **cross** traverser 10

to **cry** pleurer 4

**cucumber** un concombre 6

**cultural** culturel, culturelle 5

**cup** une tasse 7

to **cut** couper 7

## D

**daily special** une spécialité du jour 4

**dairy store** une crémerie 6

**dark (hair)** brun(e) 5

**daughter** une fille 5

**day** un jour 2; une journée 8; *one day, some day* un jour 5

**dead** mort(e) 9

**December** décembre 5

**degree** un degré 8

**delicatessen** une charcuterie 6

**delicious** délicieux, délicieuse 3

**delighted** enchanté(e) 1

**dentist** un(e) dentiste 5

**department** un département 10

**departure** un départ 10

**desk** un bureau 3

**dessert** un dessert 4

**destination** une destination 10

**dictionary** un dictionnaire 3

**difficult** difficile 3

**diligent** diligent(e) 5

**dining: dining car** un wagon-restaurant 10; *dining room* la salle à manger 7

**dinner** le dîner 7

to have **dinner** dîner 7

**direction** une direction 10

**director** un metteur en scène 5

**discussion** une discussion 5

to **dive** plonger 2

**divorced** divorcé(e)(s) 5

to **do** faire 1; *to do gymnastics* faire de la gym (gymnastique) 2; *to do my homework* faire mes devoirs 1

**doctor** un médecin 5

**documentary** un documentaire 4

**dog** un chien 8

**door** une porte 3

to **download** télécharger 7

**downtown** en ville 3

**drama** un drame 4

**dress** une robe 6

**dressing room** une cabine d'essayage 6

**drink** une boisson 4

to **drive** circuler 9

**during** pendant 2

**DVD** un DVD 3; *DVD player* un lecteur de DVD 3

## E

**ear** l'oreille (f.) 9

**early** en avance 4

**east** l'est (m.) 10

**easy** facile 3

to **eat** manger 2

**eclair** un éclair 8

**effect** un effet 9; *greenhouse effect* l'effet de serre 9

**egg** un œuf 6

**eggplant** une aubergine 6

**eight** huit 2

**eighteen** dix-huit 2

**eighth** huitième 7

**eighty** quatre-vingts 3

**electric** électrique 9

**eleven** onze 2

to **eliminate** éliminer 9

**end** le bout 10; *at the end (of)* au fond (de) 7; au bout (de) 10

**endangered species** les animaux en voie de disparition 9

**energetic** énergique 3

**energy** l'énergie (f.) 9; *nuclear energy* l'énergie nucléaire 9; *solar energy* l'énergie solaire 9

**engineer** un ingénieur 5

**England** l'Angleterre (f.) 10

**English** anglais(e) 10; *(language)* l'anglais (m.) 3

**enjoy: Enjoy your meal!** Bon Appétit! 4

**enough (of)** assez (de) 6

to **enter** entrer 8

**environment** l'environnement (m.) 9

**especially** surtout 4

**euro** un euro 3

**Europe** l'Europe (f.) 10

**evening** le soir 2

**everyone** le monde 1

**everywhere** partout 9

**exactly** exactement 8

**expensive** cher, chère 3

**expression** une mine 9

**eye** l'œil (m.) 9; *eyes* les yeux (m.) 5

## F

**fabric** un tissu 7

**face** la figure 9

**factory** une usine 9

**family** une famille 5

**fantastic** génial(e) 2

**far (from)** loin (de) 10

**fast** vite 8

**fat** gros, grosse 6

**father** un père 1; *stepfather* un beau-père 5

**favorite** préféré(e) 2

**February** février 5

to **feel: to feel like** avoir envie de 8; *to feel nauseous* avoir mal au cœur 9

**fertilizer** l'engrais (m.) 9

**fever** la fièvre 9

**fifteen** quinze 2

**fifth** cinquième 7

**fifty** cinquante 3

to **fight** combattre 9

**figure** la ligne 8; *your figure* ta ligne 8

**film** un film 4; *film showing* une séance 4

**finally** enfin 4

to **find** trouver 6

**fine** fin(e) 7

to **finish** finir 5

**finger** le doigt 9

**first** premier, première 5; *first of all* d'abord 6; *first name* un prénom 1

**fish: (gold)fish** un poisson (rouge) 8

**five** cinq 2

**fixed menu** un menu fixe 4

**flag** un drapeau 10

**floor** un étage 7; *ground floor* le rez-de-chaussée 7; *second floor* le premier étage 7

**flu** la grippe 9

**fond of food** gourmand(e) 8

**foot** le pied 9; *on foot* à pied 9

**for** comme 1; pour 3; pendant 8

**forest** une forêt 10

to **forget** oublier 8

**fork** une fourchette 7

**forty** quarante 3

**four** quatre 2

**fourteen** quatorze 2

**fourth** quatrième 7

**France** la France 3

**free** disponible 8

**French** français(e) 1; *(language)* le français 3; *French fries* les frites (f.) 2; *French-speaking* francophone 5; *from, of French-speaking Canada* francanadien(ne) 10

**fresh** frais, fraîche 6

**Friday** vendredi 2

**friend** un(e) ami(e) 2; *(boy/girl) friend* un copain, une copine 1

**fritters: cod fritters** les accras de morue (m.) 5

**from** d', de 1; *from (the)* du, des 5

**front: in front of** devant 3

**fruit** un fruit 6; *fruit tart* une tarte aux fruits 6

**funny** drôle 3

**furniture: piece of furniture** un meuble 7

# G

**Gabon** le Gabon 5

**Gabonese** gabonais(e) 5

to **gain weight** grossir 5

**game** un match 4

**garden** un jardin 8

**generous** généreux, généreuse 5

**German** allemand(e) 10; *(language)* l'allemand (m.) 3

**Germany** l'Allemagne (f.) 10

to **get: to get around** circuler 9; *to get in/on* monter 8; *to get off* descendre 8

**giant** géant(e) 9

**gift** un cadeau 5; *gift card* une carte cadeau 5

**girl** une fille 2

to **give** donner 4; offrir 5; *give me* donnez-moi 4

**glass** un verre 7

to **go** aller 1; *Go for it!* Vas-y! 6; *to go down* descendre 8; *to go for a walk* faire une promenade 8; *to go grocery shopping* faire les courses 6; *to go out* sortir 2; *to go running* faire du footing 2; *to go shopping* faire du shopping 2; *to go up* monter 8

**goal** un but 4

**(gold)fish** un poisson (rouge) 8

**good** bon(ne) 1; *Good-bye.* Au revoir., Salut. 1; *Good idea!* Bonne idée! 8; *Have a good trip!* Bon voyage! 10

**gorilla** un gorille 9; *mountain gorilla* un gorille des montagnes 9

**grade** une note 3

**gram (of)** un gramme (de) 6

**grandfather** un grand-père 5

**grandmother** une grand-mère 5

**grandparents** les grands-parents (m.) 5

**grape** un raisin 6

**grapefruit** un pamplemousse 6

**graphic designer** un(e) graphiste 5

**great** génial(e) 2; chouette 8

**green** vert(e) 5; *green beans* des haricots verts (m.) 6

**grey** gris 5

**grocery store** une épicerie 6

**ground floor** le rez-de-chaussée 7

to **grow** grandir 5

**guest** un(e) invité(e) 7

**guidebook** un guide 10

**gym** un fitness 9; *gym class* l'éducation physique et sportive (l'EPS) (f.) 3

**gymnastics** la gym (gymnastique) 2

# H

**hair** les cheveux (m.) 5

**half** demi(e) 3; *half-brother* un demi-frère 5; *half past* et demie 3; *half-sister* une demi-sœur 5

**hallway** un couloir 7

**ham** le jambon 4; *ham sandwich* un sandwich au jambon 4

**hamburger** un hamburger 2

**hand** la main 8; *hand in hand* la main dans la main 8

**handsome** beau, bel, belle 7

**hat** un chapeau 6

to **have** avoir 3; *(food or drink)* prendre 4; *one/we/you have to* il faut 8; *to have a/an… ache* avoir mal (à…) 9; *to have dinner* dîner 7; *to have to* devoir 7; falloir 9

**he** il 1

**head** la tête 9

**health club** un fitness 9

**heart** le cœur 9

**to heat up** réchauffer 9

**hello** bonjour 1; *(on the telephone)* allô 1

**to help** aider 1

**her** son, sa, ses 5

**here** ici 7; *here is/are* voilà 4

**hey** tiens 6

**hi** salut 1

**high school** un lycée 9

**highway** une route 10

**hill** une colline 10

**hip-hop** le hip-hop 2

**his** son, sa, ses 5

**history** l'histoire (f.) 3

**home** une maison 1; *home health worker* un accompagnateur, une accompagnatrice 9

**homework** les devoirs (m.) 1

**horror** l'horreur (f.) 4

**horse** un cheval 8

**hot** chaud(e); *to be hot* avoir chaud 8; *it's hot* il fait chaud 8; *I am hot* j'ai chaud 8

**hotel** un hôtel 8

**hour** l'heure (f.) 3

**house** une maison 1

**how** comment 1; *How are things going?* Ça va? 1; *How are you?* Comment allez-vous? [form.] 1; *how much* combien 3; *How much is it?* Ça fait combien? 6; *How much per kilo?* C'est combien le kilo? 6; *How old are you?* Tu as quel âge? 5; *How's the weather?* Quel temps fait-il? 8

**humanitarian** humanitaire 10

**hundred: (one) hundred** cent 3

**hungry: to be hungry** avoir faim 4

**hurt: to be hurt** avoir mal (à...) 9

**husband** un mari 5

**hybrid** hybride 9

**hydrotherapeutic** thermal(e) 9

## I

**I** je/ j' 1

**ice cream** une glace 4; *chocolate ice cream* une glace au chocolat 4; *vanilla ice cream* une glace à la vanille 4

**ice-skating (figure skating)** le patinage (artistique) 2

**if** si 4

**illness** une maladie 9

**impossible** impossible 7

**in** dans, en 3; à 5; *in circles* en rondelles 7; *in-line skating* le roller 2; *in front of* devant 3; *in my opinion* à mon avis 9; *in the* au, aux 3; *In what color(s)?* De quelle(s) couleur(s)? 6

**inhabitant** un(e) habitant(e) 10

**to install** installer 9

**intelligent** intelligent(e) 3

**interesting** intéressant(e) 3

**international** international(e) 10

**Internet** (l')Internet (m.) 2

**to introduce** présenter 1; *I'd like to introduce you to...* Je te/vous présente... 1

**to invite** inviter 2

**is** (see **to be**) 1; *Isn't that so?* N'est-ce pas? 2

**it** ça, ce 1; elle, il 3; le, la, l' (object pronoun) 4; *it doesn't surprise me* ça ne me surprend pas 4; *It has a totally vintage look!* Total vintage! 3; *it is* c'est 1; *it is necessary* il faut 8; *it's beautiful out* il fait beau 2; *it's cold* il fait froid 8; *it's cool* il fait frais 8; *it's hot* il fait chaud 8; *it's raining* il pleut 8; *it's snowing* il neige 8; *it's sunny* il fait du soleil 8; *It's the (+ date).* C'est le (+ date). Nous sommes le (+ date). 5; *it's windy* il fait du vent 8

**its** son, sa, ses 5

**Italian** italien(ne) 10

**Italy** l'Italie (f.) 10

**Ivory Coast** la Côte-d'Ivoire 5; *from, of the Ivory Coast* ivorien(ne) 5

## J

**jacket** un blouson 4; une veste 6

**jam** la confiture 4

**January** janvier 5

**jar (of)** un pot (de) 6

**jasmine** le jasmin 7

**jeans** un jean 6

**jersey** un maillot 4

**job** un métier 5

**juice** un jus 4; *orange juice* un jus d'orange 4

**July** juillet 5

**June** juin 5

## K

**ketchup** le ketchup 6

**key (on keyboard)** une touche 7

**keyboard** un clavier 7

**kilogram (of)** un kilo (de) 6

**kilometer** un kilomètre 5

**to kiss** embrasser 8

**kitchen** la cuisine 7

**knee** le genou 9

**knife** un couteau 7

**know** être au courant 9; *I know* je connais 5; je sais 4; *you know* tu sais 9

## L

**lab: computer lab** une salle d'informatique 3; *science lab* un labo (laboratoire) 3

**lake** un lac 10

**lamp** une lampe 7

**language** une langue 3

**large** grand(e) 5; gros, grosse 6

**last** dernier, dernière 8

**late** en retard 4

**to laugh** rire 4; rigoler 8

**lawyer** un(e) avocat(e) 5

**lazy** paresseux, paresseuse 5

**to learn** apprendre 4

**to leave** partir 8; laisser, quitter 9

**left: on the left** à gauche 7; *to(on) the left of* à gauche de 7

**leg** la jambe 9

**less** moins 7

**to let** laisser 9; *Let me finish!* Laisse-moi finir! 8

**lettuce** une salade 6

**like** comme 5

to **like** aimer 2

**link** un lien 7

to **listen (to)** écouter 2; *to listen to music* écouter de la musique 2; *to listen to my MP3 player* écouter mon lecteur MP3 2

**liter (of)** un litre (de) 6

**little** petit(e) 5; *(a) little* (un) peu 2; *a little of* un peu de 6

to **live** habiter 7

**living room** un salon, un séjour 7

**located** situé(e) 10; *to be located* être situé(e) 10

**logo: team logo** un blason 4

**long** long, longue 7

to **look for** chercher 6; *to look awful* avoir mauvaise mine 9; *to look healthy* avoir bonne mine 9; *to look like (something from) my country* avoir un petit air du pays 7; *Does this... look good on me?* Tu trouves que... me va bien? 6

to **lose** perdre 4; *to lose weight* maigrir 5

**lost** perdu(e) 10

**lot: a lot** beaucoup 2; *a lot of* beaucoup de 6

to **love** aimer 2

**lunch** le déjeuner 3

**Luxembourg** le Luxembourg 10; *from, of Luxembourg* luxembourgeois(e)

**lyrics** les paroles (f.) 7

# M

**Ma'am** madame (Mme) 1

**made: made of aluminum** en aluminium 9; *made of plastic* en plastique 9

to **make** faire 1; *to make a call* téléphoner 2; *to make (something) work* faire marcher 9

**Mali** le Mali 5

**Malian** malien(ne) 5

**mall** un centre commercial 1

**man** un homme 5

**mandatory** obligatoire 8

**map** une carte 3; *city map* un plan 10

**March** mars 5

**market: flea market** un marché aux puces 6; *outdoor market* un marché 6

**Martinique** la Martinique 5

**math** les maths (f.) 1

**May** mai 5

**may: May I help you?** Je peux vous aider? 6

**maybe** peut-être 4

**mayo** la mayonnaise 6

**me** m', moi 1; me 4

**meal** un repas 7

**mean** méchant(e) 5

**media center** une médiathèque 3

**medium** moyen(ne) 5

to **meet** faire la connaissance (de) 10; se retrouver 4; *we'll meet* on se retrouve 3

**meeting** un rendez-vous 4

**melon** un melon 6

**memory** un souvenir 8

**menu** une carte 4

**merchant** un(e) marchand(e) 6

**microwave** un micro-onde 7

**midnight** minuit 3

**milk** le lait 6

**million** un million 5

**mineral water** une eau minérale 4

**minute** une minute 7

**Miss** mademoiselle (Mlle) 1

**model** un mannequin 6

**moment** un instant 9; *for the moment* pour l'instant 9

**Monday** lundi 2

**money** l'argent (m.) 8

**monitor** un écran 7; un moniteur 7

**month** un mois 5

**monument** un monument 8

**more** plus 7

**morning** le matin 3

**mosque** une mosquée 7

**most: the most (+ adjective)** le/la/les plus (+ adjectif) 10

**mother** une mère 1; *stepmother* une belle-mère 5

**motto** une devise 10

**mountain** une montagne 9

**mouse** une souris 7

**mouth** la bouche 9

to **move** bouger 9

**movies** le cinéma 2; *action movie* un film d'action 4; *adventure movie* un film d'aventure 4; *detective movie* un film policier 4; *horror movie* un film d'horreur 4; *movie theatre* un ciné (cinéma) 1; *science fiction movie* un film de science-fiction 4

**MP3 player** un lecteur de MP3 3

**Mr.** monsieur (M.) 1

**Mrs.** madame (Mme) 1

**Ms.** madame (Mme), mademoiselle (Mlle) 1

**much: very much** beaucoup 2; *How much is it?* Ça fait combien? 6

**museum** un musée 8

**mushroom** un champignon 6

**music** la musique 2; *alternative music* la musique alternative 2

**musical** un film musical 4

**must (see to have to)** 1; *one/we/you must* il faut 8

**mustard** la moutarde 6

**my** mon, ma, mes 1

# N

**name: first name** un prénom 1; *my name is* je m'appelle 1; *your name is* tu t'appelles 1

**napkin** une serviette 7

**nauseous: to feel nauseous** avoir mal au cœur 9

**near** près de 7

**nearly** presque 9

**neck** le cou 9

to **need** avoir besoin de 3

**never** ne (n')... jamais 10

**new** nouvelle 2; nouveau, nouvel 8

**New Brunswick** le Nouveau-Brunswick 10

**news report** un reportage 9

**newstand** un kiosque à journaux 4

**next** prochain(e) 4; ensuite 6; *next to* à côté (de) 7

**nice** sympa 5

**night** la nuit 3

**nine** neuf 2

**nineteen** dix-neuf 2

**ninety** quatre-vingt-dix 3

**ninth** neuvième 7

**no** non 1; *no longer* ne (n')… plus 10; *no one* ne (n')… personne 10

**nobody** ne (n')… personne 10

**noon** midi 3

**north** le nord 10

**nose** le nez 9

**not** ne (n')… pas, pas 1; *not anymore* ne (n')… plus 10; *not anyone* ne (n')… personne 10; *not at all* pas du tout 10; *not bad* pas mal 1; *not well* pas très bien 1

**notebook** un cahier 3

**nothing** ne (n')… rien 3

**November** novembre 5

**now** maintenant 3

**nuclear** nucléaire 9

**number** un nombre, un numéro 2; *phone number* un numéro de téléphone 2

# O

**ocean** un océan 9

**o'clock** l'heure (f.) 3

**October** octobre 5

**of** de/d' 1; en (pronoun), sur 8; *of (the)* des 5; du 4; *of average height* de taille moyenne 5; *of course* pardi (regional) 7

**often** souvent 10

to **offer** offrir 5

**office** un bureau 3; *principal's office* le bureau du proviseur 3

**oh** ah, oh 1; *oh dear* oh là là 9; *oh no* oh là là 9

**oil slick** une marée noire 9

**OK** d'accord 1

**old** vieil, vielle, vieux 8

**olive** une olive 6

**Olympic Games** les Jeux Olympiques (m.) 2

**omelette** une omelette 4

**on** sur 2; à, en 4; *on board* à bord 7; *on foot* à pied 9; *on sale* en solde 4; *on the* au, du 8; *on the corner* du coin 8; *on the left* à gauche 7; *on the right* à droite 7; *on time* à l'heure 4

**one** on 1; un 2; une 3; *one's* son, sa, ses 5

**onion** un oignon 6

**online** en ligne 6

**open: she opens** elle ouvre 7

**opinion** un avis 9; *in my opinion* à mon avis 9

**or** ou 2

**orange** une orange 4; orange 6; *orange juice* un jus d'orange 4

**organic** biologique 9

**other** autre 7

**otherwise** autrement 6

**ouch** ouille 9

**our** notre, nos 5

**outfit** un ensemble 6

**oven** un four 7

**over there** là-bas 6

# P

**packet (of)** un paquet (de) 6

**painting** un tableau 8

**panda** un panda 9; *giant panda* un panda géant 9

**panel** un panneau 9

**pants** un pantalon 6

**paper** le papier 3; *sheet of paper* une feuille de papier 3

**pardon: pardon me** pardon 8

**parents** les parents (m.) 5

**park** un jardin 8; un parc 7

**party** une fête, une teuf 1

to **pass (a test)** réussir (à) 5

**passion** une passion 10

**passionate (about)** passionné(e) (de) 5

**pasta** les pâtes (f.) 2

**past: half past** et demie 3

**pastime** un passe-temps 2

**pastry: cream puff pastry** une religieuse 8; *layered custard pastry* un millefeuille 8; *pastry shop* une patisserie 6

**pâté** le pâté 6

**path** un chemin 10; une voie 9

to **pay** payer 9; *someone who pays* un payeur, une payeuse 9

**peach** une pêche 6

**pear** une poire 10

**peas** les petits-pois (m.) 6

**pen** un stylo 3

**pencil** un crayon 3; *pencil case* une trousse 3; *pencil sharpener* un taille-crayon 3

**people** les gens (m.) 9

**pepper** le poivre 7; *bell pepper* un poivron 6

**person** une personne 1

**persuaded** persuadé(e) 9

to **phone (someone)** téléphoner 2

**photo** une photo 7; *another photo* re-photo 8

**physics** la physique 3

**pie** une tarte 6; *apple pie* une tarte aux pommes 6

**piece (of)** un morceau (de) 6; *piece of furniture* un meuble 7

**pillow** un coussin 7

**pineapple** un ananas 6

**pink** rose 6

**pizza** une pizza 2

**place** un endroit 3; *place yourself in front of the TV* mets-toi devant l'écran 9

**planet** une planète 9

**plastic** le plastique 9; *made of plastic* en plastique 9

**plate** une assiette 7

**platform** un quai 10

to **play** jouer 2; *to play a role* jouer un rôle 4; *to play basketball* jouer au basket (basketball) 2; *to play ice hockey* jouer au hockey sur glace 2; *to play soccer* jouer au foot (football) 2; *to play sports* faire du sport 2; *to play video games* jouer aux jeux vidéo 2

**please** s'il vous plaît 4

**pleasure** un plaisir 10

**police officer** un agent de police 5

to **pollute** polluer 9

**polluter** un pollueur, une pollueuse 9

**polluting** polluant 9

**pollution** la pollution 9

**pond** un étang 10

**pork** le porc 6

**potato** une pomme de terre 6

**pound** une livre 6

**possible** possible 1

**post office** une poste 8

**poster** une affiche 3

to **prefer** préférer 2

to **prepare** préparer 5

**preposition** une préposition 10

**pretty** joli(e) 6

**principal** un proviseur 3

to **print** imprimer 7

**printer** une imprimante 7

**problem** un problème 7

**profession** la profession 5; *What is your profession?* Quelle est votre profession? 5

**profile** un profil 10

**program: television program** une émission 9

**project** un projet 5

to **protect** protéger, sauvegarder 9

**Provence: from, of Provence** provençal(e) 7

**province** une province 10

**purchase** un achat 6

**purple** violet, violette 6

to **put (on)** mettre 7

# Q

**quarter** un quart 3; *quarter past* et quart 3; *quarter to* moins le quart 3

**Quebec** le Québec 10; *from, of Quebec* québécois(e) 10

**question** une question 7

**quiche** une quiche 4

**quickly** vite 8

# R

**radiation** la radiation 9

to **rain** pleuvoir 8; *it's raining* il pleut 8

**ratatouille** la ratatouille 10

to **read** lire 2

**ready** prêt(e) 6

to **realize** réaliser 10

**really** bien 2; vraiment 5

**recipe** une recette 7

to **recycle** recycler 9

**red** rouge 6; *red (hair)* roux, rousse 5

**refrigirator** un frigo 7

to **reimburse** rembourser 4

**relaxed** décontracté(e) 9

to **remain** rester 8

to **remember: I remember** je me souviens 10

to **rent** louer 10

to **replace** remplacer 9

**report: news report** un reportage 9

to **resemble** ressembler (à) 5

**resident** un(e) habitant(e) 10

**resolution** une résolution 9

**respiratory** respiratoire 9

**restaurant** un restaurant 8

to **return** rentrer, retourner, revenir 8

**riad** une riad 7

**right: That's right.** C'est ça. 1; *to the right* à droite 7; *to (on) the right of* à droite de 7

**ripe** mûr(e) 6

**river** un fleuve 8; une rivière 10

**R&B: R&B concert** un concert R'n'B 2

**road** une route 10

**rock (music)** le rock 2

**role** un rôle 5

**roof** un toit 9

**room** une salle 3; une pièce 7; *bathroom* une salle de bains 7; *classroom* une salle de classe 3; *dining room* une salle à manger 7; *living room* un salon 7

**route** une route 10

**rug** un tapis 7

**running** le footing 2

**Rwanda** le Rwanda 9

# S

**salad** une salade 2; *tuna salad* une salade niçoise 6

**salami** le saucisson 6

**sale: on sale** en solde 4

**salesperson** un vendeur, une vendeuse 6

**salt** le sel 7

**same** même 6

**sandwich** un sandwich 4; *cheese sandwich* un sandwich au fromage 4; *ham sandwich* un sandwich au jambon 4; *grilled ham and cheese sandwich* un croque-monsieur 4

**Saturday** samedi 2

to **save** sauvegarder 7

**say** dis 1; *let's say* disons 4

**scarf** une écharpe 4; un foulard 6

**school** une école 3; *school cafeteria* une cantine 3

**science** les sciences (f.) 3; *science fiction* la science-fiction 4; *science lab* un labo (laboratoire) 3

to **score** marquer 4

**screen** un écran 7

**seat** un siège 10

**second** deuxième 7

to **see** voir 3; *to see each other/ one another* se voir 8; *See you soon.* À bientôt. 1; *See you tomorrow.* À demain. 1

**selfish** égoïste 5

to **sell** vendre 6

to **send** envoyer 2; *to send text messages* envoyer des textos 2

**Senegal** le Sénégal 5

**Senegalese** sénégalais(e) 5

**September** septembre 5

**series** une série 4

**serious** grave 8

**server** un serveur, une serveuse 4

to **set** mettre 7; *to set the table* mettre le couvert 7

**seven** sept 2

**seventeen** dix-sept 2

**seventh** septième 7

**seventy** soixante-dix 3

**she** elle 1

**sheet of paper** une feuille de papier 3

**shirt** une chemise 6

**shoe** une chaussure 4; **tennis shoe** tennis 6

**shop** une boutique 6; *butcher shop* une boucherie 6

**shopping** le shopping 2; commerçant(e) 6; *shopping center* un centre commercial 1

**short** petit(e) 5

**shorts** un short 4

**shoulder** l'épaule (f.) 9

to **show** montrer 8

**shower** une douche 7

**shy** timide 5

**sick** malade 9; *sick person* un(e) malade 9

**simple** simple 10

to **sing** chanter 5

**singer** un chanteur, une chanteuse 5

**sink** un évier 7

**sir** monsieur (M.) 1

**sister** une sœur 5; *half-sister* une demi-sœur 5; *stepsister* une belle-sœur 5

**six** six 2

**sixteen** seize 2

**sixth** sixième 7

**sixty** soixante 3

**size** une taille 5

to **skate: to (figure) skate** faire du patinage (artistique) 2; *to in-line skate* faire du roller 2

**skating: (figure) skating** le patinage (artistique) 2

to **ski: to (downhill) ski** faire du ski (alpin) 2

**skiing (downhill)** le ski (alpin) 2

**skirt** une jupe 6

to **sleep** dormir 2

**slice (of)** une tranche (de) 6

**small** petit(e) 5

to **smell** sentir 7; *What does it smell like?* Ça sent quoi? 7

**snack** le goûter 7

**sneakers** des tennis (f.) 6

**snow: it's snowing** il neige 8

**so** alors 3; donc 4; *so-so* comme ci, comme ça 1

**soccer** le foot 2; *soccer ball* un ballon de foot 4; *soccer player* un footballeur, une footballeuse 4

**sock** une chaussette 4

**soda: lemon-lime soda** une limonade 4

**sofa** un canapé 7

**software** un logiciel 7

**solar** solaire 9; *solar energy* l'énergie (f.) solaire 9

**some** d', de, des, du 2

**somebody** quelqu'un 10

**someday** un jour 5

**someone** quelqu'un 10

**something** quelque chose 10

**son** un fils 5

**song** une chanson 7

**songwriter** un compositeur 5

**soon** bientôt 1

**sorry** désolé(e) 8

**soup** la soupe 6

**south** le sud 10

**spa treatment** une cure 9

**Spain** l'Espagne (f.) 10

**Spanish** espagnol(e) 10; *(language)* l'espagnol (m.) 3

to **speak** parler 3

**species: endangered species** les animaux (m.) en voie de disparition 9

to **spend (time)** passer 7

**spoon** une cuiller 7

**sport** un sport 2

**spring** le printemps 8

**square** un carré 7; une place 8; *in squares* en carrés 7

**stadium** un stade 4

to **start** démarrer 7

**statue** une statue 8

to **stay** rester 8

**steak: steak with fries** un steak-frites 4

**step: step aerobics** le step 9; *stepbrother* un beau-frère 5; *stepfather* un beau-père 5; *stepmother* une belle-mère 5; *stepsister* une belle-sœur 5

**stereo** une stéréo 3

**still** toujours 4

**stomach** l'estomac (m.), le ventre 9

to **stop** s'arrêter 8; arrêter 9

**store** un magasin 3; *dairy store* une crémerie 6; *grocery store* une épicerie 6

**story** un étage 7

**stove** une cuisinière 7

**straight ahead** tout droit 10

**strawberry** une fraise 10

**street** une rue 6

**strict** strict(e) 1

**strong** fort(e) 7

**student** un(e) élève 3

to **study** étudier 2

**subway** le métro 4; *subway entrance* une bouche du métro 4

to **succeed** réussir (à) 5

**sugar** le sucre 7

**suitcase** une valise 10

**summer** l'été (m.) 2

**Sunday** dimanche 2

**sunny: it's sunny** il fait du soleil 8

**supermarket** un supermarché 6

to **support** soutenir; *I support* je soutiens 2

**sure** sûr(e) 7

to **surf** surfer 2; *to surf the Web* surfer sur Internet 2

**survey** une enquête 2

to **survive** survivre 9

**sweater** un pull 6

to **swim** nager 2

**swimming pool** une piscine 3

**Swiss** suisse 10

**Switzerland** la Suisse 10

to **synchronize** synchroniser 7

# T

**table** une table 3; *table setting* le couvert 7

**tablecloth** une nappe 7

**Tahitian** tahitien(ne) 3

to **take** prendre 4; *I'll take* je prends 3; *to take advantage of* profiter 8

to **talk** parler 3; *to talk to each other/one another* se parler 8

**talkative** bavard(e) 5

**tall** grand(e) 5

**tart: fruit tart** une tarte aux fruits 6

**teacher** un(e) prof 1

**team** une équipe 4; *team logo* un blason 4

**television** une télé (télévision) 2; *television program* une émission 9

**temperature** la température 8

**ten** dix 2

**tenth** dixième 7

**terrace** une terrasse 8

**terrific** génial(e) 2

**test** un contrôle 1

**text message** un texto 2

**thank you** merci 4

**than** que 7

**that** ça 2; qui 3; que 5; ce, cet, cette, ces 6; *that is* c'est 1; *That's awesome!* C'est le top! 1; *That's right.* C'est ça. 1

**the** le, la, l' 1; les 2; *the most (+ adjectif)* le/la/les plus (+ adjective) 10

**their** leur, leurs 5

**then** alors, puis 3

**there** là 1; *there is/are* il y a 3; *Are we going (there)?* On y va? 3; *over there* là-bas 6

**therefore** donc 4

**these** ce, cet, cette, ces 6

**they** *they (f.)* elles 2; *they (m.)* on 1; ils 2

to **think** penser 7; *to think over* réfléchir (à) 5

**third** troisième 7

**thirsty: to be thirsty** avoir soif 4

**thirteen** treize 2

**thirty** trente 3

**this** ce, cet, cette, ces 6; *this is* c'est 1

**those** ce, cet, cette, ces 6

**thousand** mille 4

**three** trois 2

**thriller** un thriller 4

**throat** la gorge 9

**Thursday** jeudi 2

**ticket** un billet 10; un ticket 4; *ticket booth* un guichet 4; *ticket collector* un contrôleur, une contrôleuse 10; *ticket-stamping machine* un composteur 10

**tide** une marée 9

**tiger** un tigre; *Sumatran tiger* un tigre de Sumatra 9

**time** l'heure (f.) 3; *on time* à l'heure 4; *What time is it?* Quelle heure est-il? 3

**tired** fatigué(e) 8

**to** à 1; chez 3; *to my house* chez moi 3; *to the* au 1; aux 3; *to him* lui 5; *to her* lui 5; *to me* moi 4; *to you* te 1; vous 5

**today** aujourd'hui 4

**toe** le doigt de pied 9

**together** ensemble 3

**Togo** le Togo 5

**Togolese** togolais(e) 5

**toilet** les toilettes (f.), les W.C. (m.) 7

**tomato** une tomate 6

**tomorrow** demain 1; *See you tomorrow.* À demain. 1

**too** trop 1; aussi 2; *too bad* tant pis 6; *too much of* trop de 6

**tooth** une dent 9

**top** le haut 8

**topic** un thème 9

**tour** un tour 8

**tourist guide** un guide touristique 8

**towards** vers 10

**train** un train 10; *train station* une gare 8; *train track* une voie 10

to **travel** voyager 5

**traveller** un voyageur, une voyageuse 10

**trip** un voyage 8

**true** vrai(e) 10

to **try (on)** essayer 6

**T-shirt** un tee-shirt 6

**Tuesday** mardi 2

**tuna** le thon 6; *tuna salad* une salade niçoise 6

to **turn** tourner 10

**TV** une télé (télévision) 2

**twelve** douze 2

**twenty** vingt 2

**two** deux 2

**type** un genre 4

# U

**ugly** moche 6

**um** euh 3

**uncle** un oncle 5

**under** sous 3

to **understand** comprendre 10

**unintelligent** bête 5

**United States** les États-Unis (m.) 5

**unpleasant** désagréable 8

**until** jusqu'à 10

**us** nous 5

**USB key** une clé USB 7

# V

**vacation** les vacances (f.) 10

to **validate (a ticket)** composter 10

**valley** une vallée 10

**vegetable** un légume 6

**versus** contre 4

**very** très 1; *Very well, and you?* Très bien, et toi/vous? 1

**video: video games** les jeux vidéo (m.) 2; *video game tester* un testeur de jeux vidéo 5

**view** une vue 7; *What a beautiful view!* Quelle belle vue! 7

**visit** une visite 10

to **visit** visiter 8

**visual arts** les arts plastiques (m.) 3

# W

to **wait (for)** attendre 4

**walk** une promenade 8

to **walk** marcher 9

to **want** désirer 4; avoir envie de 8; vouloir 6

**wardrobe** une armoire 7

to **watch** regarder 2; *Watch out!* Attention! 7

water l'eau (f.) 4

waterfall une cascade 10

watermelon une pastèque 6

way un chemin 10

we on 1; nous 2; *We'll call each other.* On s'appelle. 1

to wear porter 4

weather le temps 8; *the weather's bad* il fait mauvais 2

website un site web 7

Wednesday mercredi 2

week une semaine 2

weekend le weekend 2

welcome bienvenue 4

well bien, eh bien 1; ben 7; *Are things going well?* Tu vas bien? 2

west l'ouest (m.) 10

what comment 1; qu'est-ce que, quel, quelle 2; quoi 3; ce que 9; *What a beautiful view!* Quelle belle vue! 7; *What are you doing?* Qu'est-ce que tu fais? 2; *What do you like to do?* Qu'est-ce que tu aimes faire? 2; *What does it smell like?* Ça sent quoi? 7; *What is... like?*

Comment est...? 5; *What is your profession?* Quelle est votre profession? 5; *What size are you?* Quelle taille faites-vous? 6; *What's the weather like?* Quel temps fait-il? 8; *What's wrong with her?* Qu'est-ce qu'elle a? 9; *What's your name?* Tu t'appelles comment? 1

when où 8; quand 2

where où 3

which quel, quelle 2

white blanc, blanche 6

who qui 3

why pourquoi 2

wife une femme 5

wild sauvage 9

to win gagner 4

wind turbine une éolienne 9

window une fenêtre 3

windy: it's windy il fait du vent 8

winter l'hiver (m.) 8

with avec 1; par 7

work un taf 7

to work travailler 5

world le monde 1

world music la world 2

would: I would like je voudrais 5; *you would like* tu voudrais 1; *Would you like...?* Vous voulez...? 4

wow oh là là 9

to write écrire 3

writer un écrivain 5

## Y

year un an, une année 5

yellow jaune 6

yes oui 1; *yes (on the contrary)* si 2

yesterday hier 8

yoga le yoga 9

yogurt le yaourt 6

you te/t', toi, tu, vous 1

your ton, ta 1; tes, votre, vos 5; *your name is* tu t'appelles 1

## Z

zero zéro 2

zucchini une courgette 6

# Grammar Index

This index contains material from Textbook 1A (pages 1–272) and Textbook 1B (pages 273–568). The number included with each entry is the page location in both books.

# Credits

Abbreviations: top (t), bottom (b), right (r), center (c), left (l)

Each listing in the photo, reading, art, and realia credits contains a page number corresponding to the location in Textbook 1A (pages 1–272), and Textbook 1B (Bridge Parts pages B01–B58 and pages 273–568).

## Bridge Photo Credits

AliJa/iStockphoto: B17

Aimstock/iStockphoto: B28 (#5)

Alle12/iStockphoto: B14 (ice cream)

Amelia, John R./Fotolia.com: B12 (soccer)

Anderson, Leslie: B08; B42 (poster, cell phone)

Arattansi/iStockphoto: B42 (iPod)

Bobbieo/iStockphoto: B05

Bowdenimages/iStockphoto: B12 (biking)

Brown, Ken/iStockphoto: B50 (c)

Capude1957/Fotolia.com: B02 (street)

Carlosgaw/iStockphoto: B56 (#8)

Debljames/iStockphoto: B28 (#6)

Digital Skillet/iStockphoto: B04 (t)

Eléonore H/Fotolia.com: B36

EMC Publishing, LLC: B12 (running); B14 (fries, movies, party hats, cheeseburger); B39 (#4, #6); B56 (#2, #4, #7 coke)

"Essentia" studio/iStockphoto: B10 (graffiti)

Ewg3D/iStockphoto: B14 (pool)

Floortje/iStockphoto: B56 (#1)

Fox, Hillary/iStockphoto: B13

Fstop123/iStockphoto: B24

Funwithfood/iStockphoto: B57 (tl)

Greg M. Cooper Photography/iStockphoto: B39 (#2)

Hart Creations/iStockphoto: B04 (b)

iSebastian/iStockphoto: B42 (dictionary)

Jankowska, Magdalena/iStockphoto: B06

Kali Nine Photography/iStockphoto: B12 (swimming)

Kaspi - Kilikpela's Aperture Studio Photography Inc./iStockphoto: B12 (gym); B28 (#4)

Kranendonk, Jan/iStockphoto: B51 (r)

Kupicoo/iStockphoto: B23

Laflor Photography/iStockphoto: B02 (kids); B46

Lattapictures/iStockphoto: B10 (boy)

Lee/iStockphoto: B56 (#6)

LoopAll/iStockphoto: B52

Margouillatphotos/iStockphoto: B56 (#5)

Medicine Hat Photography/iStockphoto: B12 (basketball)

Microsoft.com: B14 (flag); B28 (Modèle); B39 (#1, #3, #5)

Mocker_bat/iStockphoto: B50 (t)

Monkey Business Images/iStockphoto: B51 (l); B57 (tr)

Nailzchap/iStockphoto: B39 (#7)

Nikada, Alex/iStockphoto: B49

Olsen, Morten/iStockphoto: B42 (iPod)

Phdpsx/iStockphoto: B28 (#1)

Prince32/iStockphoto: B35 (l)

Rhoberazzi/iStockphoto: B12 (diving)

Richter, Dirk/iStockphoto: B42 (omelet); B56 (#7 croque-monsieur)

Robynmac/iStockphoto: B08 (tr)

Santa Maria Studio/iStockphoto: B14 (ball)

Sinenko, Vladimir/iStockphoto: B42 (poster)

SoleilC Photography/iStockphoto: B56 (#3)

Steve Debenport Imagery/iStockphoto: B28 (#3); B30; B35 (r)

Topchii, Max/Fotolia.com: B28 (#2)

Vasiliki/iStockphoto: B42 (tart)

Vinogradova, Lilyana/iStockphoto: B39 (Modèle)

Walik/iStockphoto: B14 (hockey)

Wooster, Ignatus/Fotolia.com: B14 (downtown)

Zoom-zoom/iStockphoto: B39 (#8)

## Photo Credits

3alexd/iStockphoto: 487 (#3)

4x6/iStockphoto: 220 (l'oncle)

A & M Photography/iStockphoto: 486 (tiger), 487 (#5)

Acilo Photography/iStockphoto: 111 (l)

AGMIT/iStockphoto: 89

Aguilarphoto/iStockphoto: 536 (t)

Ahturner/iStockphoto: 276 (tr)

Alberto Pomares Photography/iStockphoto: 76

AlcelVision/Fotolia.com: 360 (tl)

Aldomurillo/iStockphoto: 6 (3. #5), 69 (dormir)

Alex/iStockphoto: 276 (une veste), 277 (tc)

Alex Nikada | Photography/iStockphoto: 52 (sortir avec mes amis), 413 (A)

Alfieri, Michele/iStockphoto: x (bl)

Almeida, Helder/Istock: 240

Alvarez, Luis/Fotolia.com: 4 (algérien)

Alxpin/iStockphoto: 371 (b: software)

Amoceptum/iStockphoto: 310 (les petits-pois)

Amysuem/iStockphoto: 169 (t)

Andersen, ULF/SIPA Press: 41

Anderson, Leslie: 16 (t), 78 (le hip-hop, le rock, la musique alternative, la world), 86 (#1), 118 (#2, #5, #6), 164 (un ticket), 197 (Amélie poster), 292 (mayonnaise, soupe), 294 (spaghetti, soup), 300 (Orangina), 324 (metro ticket), 351 (Mississippi Market), 487 (#7), 541 (r)

Andykazie/iStockphoto: 310 (les pêches)

AngiePhotos/iStockphoto: 123 (intelligent(e))

Anmarie98121/iStockphoto: 27 (tr)

Apomares/iStockphoto: 99 (t)

Arcurs, Yuri/Fotolia.com: 31 (#3)

Arianespace/SIPA Press: 35

Arnau Design/iStockphoto: 348 (#3)

Arpad, Benedek/iStockphoto: 426 (#4), 516 (Ontario)

Wey, Peter/Fotolia.com: x (br)
Wierink, Ivonne/Fotolia.com: 480 (t)
Wisbauer, Camilla/iStockphoto: 245 (#6)
Wooster, Ignatius/Fotolia.com: 349
Wragg, Mark/iStockphoto: 245 (#1)
XtravaganT/Fotolia.com: 416
Xxmmxx/iStockphoto: 86 (Modèle), 499 (#6, b)
Yakovlev, Alexander/iStockphoto: 460 (t)
YangYin/iStockphoto: 342 (#4)
Yefimov, Artyom/Fotolia.com: 185 (t)
Yolanda, Linda/iStockphoto: 220 (la belle-sœur)
Zaihan/Fotolia.com: 325 (l)
Zilli/iStockphoto: 245 (#5)
Zoomstudio/iStockphoto: 276 (un tee-shirt)
ZTS/iStockphoto: 499 (#1, L)

# Reading Credits

Apollinaire, Guillaume, "Le chat," *Le Bestiaire*, Deplanche, 1911 (poem): 386

Aragon, Louis, "Je me souviens," Album Montand 7, (paroles), 1967 (poem/song): 558

Ben Jelloun, Tahar, *L'Homme rompu*, Seuil, Paris 1994, pp. 74–75 (novel): 504

Chédid, Andrée, *L'Enfant multiple*, J'ai Lu, Flammarion, 1989 (novel): 266

Cohen, Albert, *Belle du Seigneur*, Folio Gallimard, 1998 (novel): 41

Goscinny, René, *Le Petit Nicolas*. Gallimard, Folio n° 423 (story): 153

Perec, Georges, *Penser/Classer*, Hachette, 1985 (essay): 95

Pons, Maurice, "Le fils du Boulanger," *Douce-amère*, Denoël, 1985 (short story): 328

Prévert, Jacques, "Chanson de la Seine (III)" ("Aubervilliers"), *Spectacle*, © Éditions GALLIMARD, Paris (poem): 446

# Art Credits

The Bridgeman Art Library International: *The Private Conversation*, 1904 (oil on canvas), Beraud, Jean (1849–1935)/J. Kugel Collection, Paris, France/© DACS/Giraudon: 42; *Saint Germain-Des-Pres* (oil on canvas), Boissegur, Beatrice (Contemporary Artist)/Private Collection): 95; *Nafea Faaipoipo* (When are you Getting Married?), 1892 (oil on canvas), Gauguin, Paul (1848–1903)/Rudolph Staechelin Family Foundation, Basel, Switzerland: 106, 129; *Ball at the Moulin de la Galette*, 1876 (oil on canvas), Renoir, Pierre Auguste(1841–1919)/Private Collection, *Self Portrait*, 1889 (oil on canvas): 223; Gogh, Vincent van (1853–90)/Private Collection, Zurich, Switzerland, *Ginger Jar*, c.1895 (oil on canvas): 223; Cezanne, Paul (1839–1906)/©The Barnes Foundation, Merion, Pennsylvania, USA: 223; *The Lily Pond* (oil on canvas), Monet, Claude (1840–1926)/Private Collection/Photo © Christie's Images: 223; *Ms 65/1284 f.7v July: harvesting and sheep shearing* by the Limbourg brothers, from the 'Tres Riches Heures du Duc de Berry' (vellum)(for facsimile copy see 65830) by Pol deLimbourg (d.c.1416) Musee Conde, Chantilly, France/Giraudon: 269, 359 (b); *Landscape near Arles*, 1888 (oil on canvas), Gauguin, Paul (1848–1903)/Indianapolis Museum of Art, USA/Gift in memory of William Ray Adams/The Bridgeman Art Library International: 260; *The Starry Night*, June 1889 (oil on canvas), Gogh, Vincent van (1853–90)/Museum of Modern Art, New York, USA: 359; *In the Oise Valley* (oil on canvas), Cezanne, Paul (1839–1906)/Private Collection/Photo © Christie's Images/The Bridgeman Art Library International: 386; *The Pont de l'Europe*, Gare Saint-Lazare, 1877 (oil on canvas), Monet, Claude (1840–1926)/Musee Marmottan, Paris, France/Giraudon: 449; *The Seated Man*, or *The Architect* (oil on canvas), La Fresnaye, Roger de (1885–1925)/Musee National d'Art Moderne, Centre Pompidou, Paris, France/Giraudon: 506

Christie's Images/CORBIS: *The Pont Neuf* (*Notre Dame in Paris, View of the Pont Neuf*) by Paul Signac©: 447

Doisneau, Robert/Gamma-Rapho: 153 (Information scolaire, 1956)

Varin, Achille/*Le cerf-volant*, 1925. Château-musée municipal de Nemours, France: 558

# Realia Credits

Anderson, Leslie: 230
ASPTT de Paris: 466
Association Québec-France: 13
Atraveo GmbH: 353
Beach Volley/Défi des îles: 226
Carrefour/Groupe Carrefour: 112, 240 (logo), 301, 326, 363
Comité Départemental du Tourisme, Loir-et-Cher: 537
Commémoration du Génocide du Rwanda: 478
Crêperie "Chez Suzette" Inc. Montréal, Québec: 187
Dots United GmbH: 324 (PSG logo)
Eurosport: 171
Famille Chabert-4 restaurants, Lyon, France: 73
Fédération Nationale des Cinémas Français, la Fête du cinéma: 206
Festival Waga Hip Hop/Ali DIALLO: 262
Fête de la musique/Strasbourg.eu: 83
Fête des Lumières, Lyon, France: 74
Fête du cinéma: 206
Francofolies de Montréal: 523
Francoscopie: 379
Genève Tourisme & Congrès: 551
Goldenpass.ch: 24
Musée Grévin: 418
Pariscope, France: 201
Pathé Production, ©2008—PATHE Production—Bethsabée Mucho—TF1 Films Production—M6 Films: 207, 373, 374 (poster of movie LOL)
Plan de Paris: © parisholidays.fr (Find an apartment in Paris.): 403
Pureshopping: 324 (gift card)
RATP: 436
Redoute, la: 283
Résidence des Bateliers: 349
Top-Office.com: 22, 25, 112, 114 (school supplies), 499 (Modèle)
Vélib' Paris: © 2011 Vélib'/Marie de Paris: 494

We have attempted to locate owners of copyright materials used in this book. If an error or omission has occurred, EMC Publishing, LLC will acknowledge the contribution in subsequent printings.

# Appendix

## Phonetic Alphabet

### L'alphabet phonétique pour le français

In its *Prononciation* sections, *T'es branché?* uses the standard phonetic symbols of the International Phonetic Alphabet (IPA). This system was created by the International Phonetic Association as a way to represent the different sounds of spoken languages. The comprehensive list below contains the symbols most commonly used for the French language.

### Voyelles

- [a]  ami, mamy
- [ɑ]  pâtes, bas
- [e]  été, nager
- [ɛ]  étais, belle
- [ə]  le, demain
- [œ]  œuf, sœur
- [ø]  peu, bleu, œufs
- [i]  dix, gris
- [o]  dos, chaud
- [ɔ]  bol, bottes
- [u]  nous, douze
- [y]  pur, sucre, bûcher

### Voyelles nasales

- [ɑ̃]  banque, chambre, enchanté
- [ɛ̃]  cinq, impatient
- [ɔ̃]  bonbons, long
- [œ̃]  un, lundi, parfum

### Consonnes

- [b]  bien, bonbon
- [k]  café, ski, quinze
- [ʃ]  chaud, chien, short
- [d]  douze, dents
- [f]  neuf, pharmacie
- [g]  gris, gant
- [ʒ]  jaune, géant, aubergine
- [ɲ]  agneau, mignon, peigner
- [l]  lampe, mille

- [m]  mille, mère
- [n]  nage, noir
- [ŋ]  le smoking
- [p]  père, pêche
- [R]  rare, père
- [s]  cela, français, poisson, attention, soixante
- [t]  tarte, théâtre
- [v]  violet, avion, wagon
- [z]  visage, zèbre

### Semi-consonnes

- [j]  adieu, œil, fille, yaourt
- [ɥ]  nuit, fruit, huit
- [w]  oui, boire, ouest

---

## Functions in Level 1 Textbook

### Unité 1

#### Leçon A:
- Je m'appelle... *(Sophie)*.
- Je suis... *(Bruno)*.
- Bonjour!/ Salut!
- Enchanté(e).
- Je te/vous présente... *(Jean-Luc)*.
- C'est... *(mon camarade de classe)*.
- Tu t'appelles comment?

#### Leçon B:
- Ça va?
- Comment allez-vous?
- Très bien, et toi/vous?

#### Leçon C:
- On va... *(au café)*?
- Tu voudrais aller...?
- D'accord.
- Oui, je veux bien.
- Pas possible. Je dois... *(faire mes devoirs)*.
- Je ne peux pas. J'aide... *(ma mère)*.

### Unité 2

#### Leçon A:
- Qu'est-ce que tu aimes/vous aimez faire?
- Tu aimes manger... *(des hamburgers)*?
- J'aime... *(sortir)*.
- Je n'aime pas... *(faire du ski)*.

#### Leçon B:
- Tu aimes beaucoup... *(lire)*?
- J'aime un peu... *(lire)*.
- J'aime bien... *(envoyer des textos)*.
- J'aime beaucoup... *(faire du sport)*.

#### Leçon C:
- Moi, je préfère... *(lire les blogues)*.
- Tu préfères... *(la world ou le hip-hop)*?
- Moi aussi.
- Pas moi. Je n'aime pas....
- Quel est le numéro de téléphone de... *(Yasmine)*?

### Unité 3

#### Leçon A:
- J'ai besoin d'... *(une trousse)*.
- Tu as besoin d'... *(un cahier)*?

- *(La trousse)*..., elle coûte combien?
- *(Le cahier)*..., il coûte combien?
- Il coûte... *(2,59 euros)*.

**Leçon B:**
- Mon cours de... *(maths)* est difficile.
- Elle est comment... *(ta prof d'informatique)*?
- Elle est... *(intéressante)*.

**Leçon C:**
- Où est-ce que tu vas après... *(le déjeuner)*?
- Quand est-ce qu'... *(on y va)*?
- Pourquoi est-ce que tu ne peux pas?
- On se retrouve... *(à la piscine)* à *(4h00)*.

## Unité 4

**Leçon A:**
- *(Je vais soutenir Marseille)*... parce qu'ils sont les meilleurs.
- Rendez-vous à... *(3h00)* devant... *(la bouche de métro)*.
- Disons... *(3h15)*.

**Leçon B:**
- Vous désirez?
- Et comme... *(boisson)*?
- Donnez-moi... *(la spécialité du jour)*.
- Je vais prendre... *(le menu fixe)*.
- L'addition, s'il vous plaît.

**Leçon C:**
- Tu vas aimer ça.
- Tu vas rire.
- Tu vas pleurer.
- Peut-être.
- On va voir.

## Unité 5

**Leçon A:**
- Comment est... *(ma tante)*?
- Tu ressembles à... *(ton grand-père)*.

**Leçon B:**
- Tu as quel âge?
- J'ai... ans.
- J'offre... *(un CD à Alice)*.
- Tu peux apporter... *(les boissons)*?

**Leçon C:**
- Quelle est votre profession?
- Je suis... *(actrice)*.
- Vous venez/Tu viens d'où?
- Je viens des... *(États-Unis)*.
- Je viens du... *(Canada)*.
- Je viens de... *(France)*.

## Unité 6

**Leçon A:**
- Je cherche... *(une jupe)*.
- Vous avez... *(le pantalon)* en... *(gris/38)*?
- Je peux vous aider?
- De quelle couleur?
- Quelle taille faites-vous?

**Leçon B:**
- *(Je vais)*... d'abord... *(à la crémerie acheter du beurre et du fromage)*.
- Ensuite,... *(je vais à la charcuterie)*.
- Enfin,... *(je vais à l'épicerie)*.

**Leçon C:**
- *(Les pêches)*... sont mûres?
- C'est combien le kilo?
- Je prends... *(500 grammes)*.
- Et avec ça?
- C'est tout?

## Unité 7

**Leçon A:**
- Là, c'est... *(le séjour où nous regardons des DVDs)*.
- À côté, c'est... *(la salle à manger où nous dînons ce soir)*.
- Au fond du couloir, c'est... *(ma chambre)*.
- Où est-ce que tu habites?
- Je pense que *(oui)*.
- Je pense que *(non)*.

**Leçon B:**
- Tu peux couper... *(les courgettes)* en rondelles.
- Ensuite, tu mets le couvert.

**Leçon C:**
- Je ne comprends pas... *(ce problème de maths)*.
- *(La chanson de Natasha St-Pier?)* Je la télécharge.
- Tu imprimes... *(les paroles)*?

## Unité 8

**Leçon A:**
- Tu as envie de... *(faire une promenade avec moi)*?
- Bonne idée! Je suis disponible.
- Désolé(e). Je suis occupé(e).

**Leçon B:**
- Oh, pardon....
- Nous avons fini... *(sur la terrasse de l'arc de triomphe)*.
- Le premier jour,... *(nous avons visité la tour Eiffel)*.

**Leçon C:**
- On est allé... *(aux Tuileries)*.
- Nous sommes vite descendus... *(prendre le métro)*.
- Nous sommes arrivés... *(chez moi)*.
- *(On a passé un super jour)*... samedi dernier!

## Unité 9

**Leçon A:**
- Il faut....
- Il ne faut pas....

**Leçon B:**
- Qu'est-ce que tu me conseilles?
- À mon avis,... *(il faut prendre le thème des accompagnateurs)*.

**Leçon C:**
- Je pense qu'on doit... *(faire tout ce qu'on peut pour sauvegarder la planète)*.
- Je suis prêt(e)... *(à recycler)*.
- Je ne suis pas prêt(e)... *(à m'engager)*.

## Unité 10

**Leçon A:**
- *(Québec)*... est situé(e)... *(au nord-est de Montréal).*

**Leçon B:**
- N'oublie pas de... *(composter ton billet).*
- Bon voyage!

**Leçon C:**
- Pardon, où se trouve... *(le Musée international de la Croix-Rouge)?*
- Va/ Allez vers... *(l'est).*
- Continue/Continuez tout droit.
- Tourne/Tournez à... *(droite).*
- Prends/Prenez... *(la plus grande avenue).*

---

# Additional Sources of Information

Below you will find search words to help you and your students find Internet sites for a multitude of activities to enrich your classroom instruction.

Cinema:
- académie des arts et techniques du cinéma
- allocine
- festival de cannes

Francophone News:
- l'actualité
- allafrica
- le devoir
- le figaro
- france amérique
- l'humanité
- jeune afrique
- libération
- le monde.fr
- tv5

Francophonie:
- franc parler
- francofil.net
- organization internationale de la francophonie

French Cheeses:
- petit lexique du chabichou et des fromages de chèvre
- ermitage fromage

Governmental Sites:
- ambassade de france
- campus france
- campus france resource center
- french embassy washington d.c.
- ministere de l'education nationale

Grammar:
- conjuguemos french
- french.about.com

Miscellaneous:
- météo france
- phosphore france
- ABU france

Online Activities:
- fsl activities with m. Renaud
- corporate classroom connect

Paris:
- arc de triomphe
- louvre
- musée d'orsay
- notre dame de paris
- paris office du tourisme
- sacré-cœur
- la sorbonne

- tour Eiffel

Pedagogical Sites and Testing:
- ap central french
- carla mn
- center for applied linguistics language testing
- le cndp
- linguafolio
- planète enseignante

Radio Stations:
- europe1
- radio canada
- radio france international
- rci martinique
- tf1 en direct

Sports:
- france football
- le foot français
- quebec hockey sur glace
- pari roller
- tour de france

Teacher Associations:
- aatf
- actfl
- alliance française
- alliance française usa
- center for applied linguistics

Tourist Offices:
- genève tourisme
- guyane française tourisme
- montréal tourisme
- nouveau brunswick tourisme
- office du tourisme antilles françaises
- office du tourisme lyon
- office du tourisme maroc
- office du tourisme marseille
- office du tourisme québec
- office national de tourisme algérien
- office national de tourisme tunisien
- rwanda tourism
- sénégal tourisme
- tahiti office du tourisme
- tourisme guadeloupe
- tourisme loire
- tourisme martinique
- tourist office new orleans la
- tours tourisme

# Culture Index

# French Survey Respondents

In 2009, we conducted a survey of French teachers to find out what they wanted in a new French textbook series. We would like to thank the following teachers for their participation, which helped us design *T'es branché?*

**Alabama:** Judy Byram, Melissa Copeland, Chris Eubanks, Shelley Fordice, Julie Norvelle Fantoni, Cheryl Hall, Cindy Lepore, Stephanie McGee, Maxanna Nichols-Lefebvre, Sara C. Runner, Susanne Rives, Candance Thomason; **Alaska:** Virginia G. Boyd, Claudia Markham, Kathleen Walgren; **Arizona:** Catherine Burke, Linda Dunbar, Ruth Eiseman, Sarah Fowler, Jarred Gainey, Margaret Hanna, Ann-Marie Hyland, Hope Loveland, Randall Nissly, Jennifer Patrick, Leigh Thomas, Diane Waters; **Arkansas:** Chris Becnel, Nola Harrison, Carey Lagarrigue, Gray Langston, Jan Nixon, Kim Scarbrough; **California:** Maria Adame, Sally K. Adams, Joan Adometto Taylor, Judy Avila, Silvia Battigalli, Anne Bazile, Nathalie Belitti, Mary Anne Berry, Justin Brooks, Arlene Boruzki, Leah Boselli, Kathy Calvin, Corinne Carlson, Samantha Carr, Karina Chin, Rachel Cornec, Sandy Dana-Kildow, Sebastian P. DeClerck, James DeKay, Susan Delateur, Michael Delbar, Karen Donner, Mary Dowden, Yvonne Duong, Lynda Fine, Lorraine Fong, Joan Fox, Shelley Friedman, Natalie Freitas, Edwige Gamache, Andrea Gannon, Patricia Grogan, Rhonda Habersham, Janet Hedeline, Lynn Heyman-Hogue, Sharon Hendrickson, Mira Jamadi, Eva Johnson, Shana Kamper, Karen Kessinger, Michelle Klein, Patti Kussman, Brigitte Kyle, Jessica Lawrence, Denise LeBlavant, Valerie Lent, Cecile Lunetta, Azita Mahmoudi, Michelle Marriott, Sheila McCumber, Sadie Medina, Lise Mélin, Deborah Mogel, Micheline Moreau, Starlight Murray, Mariela Neira, Sara Niles, Todd Oesterman, Yvonne Oliver, Brenda Parrish, Carolyn Quinby, Karen Ransom, Dee Robbins, Jetta Rodal, Linda Rosenberg, Rachel Safier, Melisa Salvato, Allison Sass, Robert Schaffer, Claudine Senac-Urtecho, Bertha Sevilla, Francine W. Shivers, Michelle Shockey, Audrey Smith, Patty Stephenson, Judy Stout, Isabelle Teraoka, Tatjana Trout, Beth Tudor, Judith Uriarte, Mary Van de Bovenkamp, Geraldine Van Roie Stoddard, Christine Veilleux, Verna Verspieren, Barbara Vinolus, Elizabeth Vitanza, Agnieszka Waclawek, Catherine Welter, Judy Werner, Jacki Williams-Jones, Francois Wolman; **Colorado:** Jane Backer, Laura Battisti, Leslie Casanova, Debbie Cody, Anne Damanti, Lisa Davis, Ellen Grimsdale, Paul Kirschling, Elaine Kurbegov, Marlene Ladouceur, Patty Ross-Baldwin, Florence Schranz, Ann Snow, Austin Wallace, Linda Zimmerman; **Connecticut:** Magdalena Alvarado, Garry Apgar, Ann Barton, Lisa Ahlstrom-Nasy, Martine Berjet, Maria Cahill, Constance Carrington, Nathalie Casey, Carol Coderre-Marx, Rossana Crudele, Aline Dennison, Justin Ehrenberg, Abdoulaye Fall, Mark Foster, Myriam Franquesa, Paula Greenfield, Diane Holskin, Susan Hudson, Ruth Jones, Nancy Katsaros, Angela Kelleher, Thomas Kelly, Corinne Khawaja, Bruno Koffi, Barbara H. Lathrop, Kathy Martin-Orain, Susan Mason, Gail McKenna, Nancy Moran, Mary E. Periot, Nicandra Perusi, Barbara E. Polley, Dorothy Raviele, Claudine Rose, Jane See, Ed Smith, Jennifer Sturges, Renee M. Sylvestre, Ann Tinkaus, Magloula Tsilibocos, Patricia Viliella, Heather Way, Emily Wentworth, Marianna Wikarska, Sandra P. Wilson, Linda Zabor; **Delaware:** Megan Cover, Roch Luberti, Mary Ann Ryan, Pamela Scholla, Joyce Stojny; **Florida:** Shirley R. Bayard, Sandra Bierkan, Christelle Carter, Sansan Dah, Valerie Eastman, Valerie Gentilini, Gianna Ireland, Susan Laffitte, Herve le Guilloux, Laura Hollands, H. Leonard, Sheila Mansier, Barbara M. Murray, Mary B. Nobun, Susan Olevia-Wagner, Sherry Parker, Erin Pendergast, Doriane Rencker, Simone Schoeni, Sorela Schultz, Teresa Suarez, Mary C. Sweet, Brenda Velez, Kathryn Anne Vensel, Barbara Woolley, Paula Yaniglos; **Georgia:** Patricia Bailey, Valerie Bathurst, Denise Bedell, Christy Belbey, Claire Bell, Kirsten Bittiff, David Bobkowski, Nan Brightwell, Sally Brock, Agnes Browning, Angela Burgess, Brita Buhrman, Cecilia Burns, Karen Canady, Fejokwuc Comfort, Liana Cox, Caryn Craft, Michele Diament, Michael Dockery, Gabrielle Durden-Coffee, Gail Ehrhart, Catherine Francisse, Reesa Frezier, Judy Fritz, Tracey Glass Fuchs, Rhonda Habersham, Shanda D. Hester, Nessa Hoppe, Valerie Hughey, Elizabeth John, Jeanne S. Jones, Mary Lane Jukes, Edna-May King, Susan Logan, Phyllis Loiacono, Patricia A. B. Macmillan, Rachel G. Martellus, Irene Marxsen, Alanna McEachin, Lesya McGee, Katy McManus, Eugenia McMillan, Jennifer Miller, Annie Muir, Nancy Nichols, Laure-Anne Pennell, Kathleen A. Porto, Christohe Powers, Benjamin Riekhof, Tracy Rucker, Sharon Shirah, Marianne Simeneta, Katie Sisterhen, Travis Spell, Carol Stevens, Kenneth Swanson, Cynthia Toups, Lauren Watson, Kristin Webb, Jeanette Webster-Whyte, MaryIou Wiesendanger, Debra Welch, Valerie White, Elizabeth Williams, Jennifer Willis, Thelma Wise; **Hawaii:** Erin C. Cleveland, Kathie Dinges, Dayna Fukunaga, Catherine Pettit, Norma Young; **Idaho:** Gabrielle Applequist, Sharon Bartlow, Jerre Coleman, Claudia Creek, Sally Husted, Aliene Shearer, Dana L. Stockman; **Illinois:** Jason Anderson, Martha Behlow, Caryn Boltz, Jo Anne A. Bratkovich, Liette Brisebois, Tracy Cowper, Angelique Dorchies, Cynthia Driesner, Sharon Eichenehr, Carolyn Fitzgerald, Julie Frost, Michelle Garesche, Barb Goldberg, Sandra Grandolfo, Francis Greaux, Sue Harsa, Ann K. Hartman, Melanie Hillegass, Andrea K. Isabelli, Kathleen Iverson, Jura Jancys, Eric Laird, Lynette Lang, Toni Lowery, Melissa Lo, Joyce Marcorcini, Suzanne McKeigue, Michelle Morelli, Maryann Pliss, Sara Kahle Ruiz, Janet Rzeszutko, Michele Sakauskas, Heather Song, Laura Sperling, Roz Sunquist, William Swiderski, Jeanne Trengove, Judy Weiss; **Indiana:** Michele Balma, Elizabeth Breidinger, Alisha Burcham, Heather Carey, Gwen Craig, Susie Deneen, Philip D. Didier, Kirsty Donley, Rebecca Elkins, Melanie Enkoff, Pamela Forth, Diane Furtwangler, Jessica Geisinger, Cheryl Herman, Jill Hildegmeier, Kathy Jaroszewski, Ellen Landers, Martha Layton, Lisa Liberge, Bryan Macke, Vicki Mannweiler, Paula Morton, Debora Olejniczek, Andrea S. Pieh, Regina Portman, Adrienne Qualls, Carol Shumate, Beth Strodel, Kimberly Summers, Susan Van Fleit, Safia Virgil, Janice Vote, Lisa Walborn, Jill Wiley, Kay A. Wood; **Iowa:** Michele Marie Arman, Laura Catron, Jae Dwyer, Vicki Gallagher, Christine K. Gilbertson, Janet Johnson, Deb Paulsen, Melanie Sartori, Erin Schafer, Christina Snyder-Scott; **Kansas:** Melanie Adams, Christina Beard, Rebecca Bock, Sandra Chastan, Linda S. Clark, Jan Denning, Lisa DeVore, Clara A. George, April S. Gomez, Nora Kelting, Susan Lehr, Karen Pearson, Leslie Ransdall, Alyssa Rydant, Christa L. Ruhlen, Vicki Swetz; **Kentucky:** Elizabeth W. Cooke, Jocelyne Cross, Scottye Eakin, Jennifer Kirby, Elizabeth B. Rambo, Susan Robbins; **Louisiana:** Marilyn J. Ashton, Theresa Barr, Yannick Brignac, Mini Brooks, Pam Broussard, Valerie Burton, Isabelle Callens-Shirazi, Marie Cipolla, Vicki K. Clem, Charles Darby, Marguerite Dietrich, Brother Derek W. Foster, William Gautreaux, Cosima Hasenstein, Mary C. Herget, Linda Lafont, Norma Michaud, Marie-France Price, Martine Smith, Rebecah Smith, Stephanie Viator; **Maine:** Kirsten Andrews, Andrea Askerdunn, Seth Briggs, Linda Butt, Lisa Chartier, Leslie Hatlun, Irene Marchenay, Margaret Nulle, Anne E. Smith; **Maryland:** Amanda Arnoult, Larissa Arist, Monique Brend-Walker, Denise W. Diegel, Elizabeth Foyle, Elizabeth Gray, Nancy Claire Gritzinger, Kenneth Haines, Kathleen Kirk-Leason, Marie-Pierre Manrique, Phyllis McCauley, Paul Newhouse, Keila Otopeza, Angela Porcella, Lexi Sargent, Emilie Shipman, Robert A. Silkworth, Debora Speier, Jeanne Touzeau, Richard Tuckerman, Laurie Whitley, Teresa Wilson, Yimei Wu; **Massachusetts:** Marie Dunell, Justin Evans, Rina Farber-Mazor, Christine Geueke, Christopher Johnson, Janice Joyce, Norma Kozaka, Deborah Leavitt, Michelle Lewison, Susanne Markus, Robert F. Peolquin, Yiota Simoglou; **Michigan:** Dick Ahlers, Faye M. Amo, Amy Begenrie, Michelle Burley, Nancy Busard, Crystal Cannon, Amy Clement, Susan Clugston, Laura Davis, Kelley DeGraaf, Veronica Dewey, Mary Drouillard, Sheryl Foster, Kim Frisinger, Eileen Gifford, Christine Haack, Cindy Hern, Valerie Jablonski, Jennifer M. Kay, Michelle Kuehnlein, Marti Larson, Jeanine LeMieux, Sheryl Moll, Diana Morgenstern, Theresa Nilsen, Victoria Potter, Kathy Refice, Pam Romanelli, Kim Rouvelin, Melissa Saeed, Sister Rose Sam, Melissa Samluk, Barbara St. Louis, Patrick Teahan, Dana Tiputita, Raghida West; **Minnesota:** Susan Brown, Jen Bouchard, Michele Campbell, Kari Christensen, Joyce Cogdell-Travis, Coleen Cotton, K. Droske, Jessica Gillespie, Camilla J. Glattly, Laurie Hennen, Phyllis Hicks, Sara Holcombe, Margaret Laboe, Amy Lemme, Elizabeth Manning, Elizabeth Marin, Mary Lynn Montgomery, Susan Palmer, Kris Ryland, Sue Sephati, Twyla Sha, Kathleen Stoddart, Christina Sturm, Kyle Sweeney, Scott Swedin,; **Mississippi:** Bridget Carmody, Susan Callon, Debbie Gorney, Brigitte Herbert, Jessica Powell, Janis Risley, Jacquelyn Sergi, Jacqueline Wilson; **Missouri:** Vicki Barmann, Julie Beguaud, Fran Burnet, April

Burton, Lauren Coleman, Teresa Connolly, Linda Crane, Judith Crenshaw, Lynne Evans, Karen Gibson, Kathryn L. Hedrick, Annie Hulmes, Nita Jackson, Andrea Junkans, Richard Keefe, Jenifer Kidwell, Nicole King, Chad Lower, Catherine Marquart, Sandy Mason, Kimberlee Moyer, Myriam Palmer, Sarah Rausch, Sarah Scoggins, Laura Snead, Amy Stemke, Mike Summers, Jennifer Tadsen, Lori Turnage, Della Thompson, Julie West, Krista White; **Nebraska:** Jeanne Cronin, Kathy Haidenbergh, Pamela Kooiker; **Nevada:** Richard Bangert, Jonathan Reynolds, Leslie Righetti, Ginnae Stamanis; **New Hampshire:** Leslie Anton, Evelyn Christoph, Elaine Jubinville, David Page, Jayne Wing; **New Jersey:** Gerard Amsellem, Lauren Arcusi, Debbie Barca, Angela Barone, Bonnie Baumert, Karen Beetham, Helene Blanton, Joan Bonnell, G. Cahayla, Eileen Campanella, Geraldine G. Castaldo, Alda Cornec, Claire D'Angelo, Kerrie Decker, Claudy Delne, Phyllis Dimick, Meredith Donato, Maria Kostis Economals, Laurence Farhat, Brigitte Fischer, Diana Flynn, Cynthia Foxworth, Martine Gabler, Kinga Galica, Linda Geldmacher, Sylvia Guensch, Marie-Marthelle Guervil, Jenn Haff, Suzanne Hennessey, Carol Hill, Maryanne Kain, Rebecca Kazimir, Raana Khan, Maria Kostis, Karen Kozlowski, Barbara A. Lehman, Karen Lester, Joan Lipkowitz, Jeanine Losito, Marianne Ly, Sonia Magalhaes, Carol McKay, Carol Mitich, Daniel Moraske, Valerie Morris, Nancy Mousavi, Cristin O'Connor, Ellen O'Meara, Ellen Reiss, Jane Roxbury, Kimberlee J. Safranek, Fritzner Salomon, Paula Schaffer, Susan Shourds, Diana Shults, Lise Simard, Debra Soriano, Joelle Stark, Laura Thomas, Margaret Tisa, Stephanie Walczak, Marguerite Wall, Tammy Wubbenhorst, Marlene Yoskowitz, Susan Roque Zeitz; **New Mexico:** John Coleman, Louise Gentile, Suzanne Holman; **New York:** Elsie Augustave, Jeff Brown, Nancy Burns, Susan Chatoun, Tom Davian, Paula DeFilippo, Ousmane Diouf, Mary Ellen Donovan, Elizabeth A. Emenwein, Alba Gallegos, Andrea Grady, Marie Guagliardo-Day, Lisa Judd, Laurine Haefner, Rose Marie Hawver, Lizette Liebold, Louise J. Lindemann, Patricia Long, Matthew Nani, Monique Navalet, Denise Nichols, Debbie Pelletiere, Giovanni Ruggiero, Ellen Scheiderer, Catherine Scher, Kathryn Siegel, Alla Shustorovich, Jo Ann Thomasson, Jerry Treadwell, Laura Veraili, Lindsay Wahler, Wendy Winters, Lauren Wood-Radcliffe; **North Carolina:** Debra Ashe, Abeer Awad, Erin Bockoras, Maria G. Bonito, Stephanie Castevens, Elizabeth Corinne, Carolyn L. Cooper, Mary Turner Dalton, Ann Herminjard Davis, Richard Dubois, Teresa Engebretsen, Erin Feltman, Shannon Ferguson, Evelyn Marie Freeman, Jill Friesen, Angela Hagler, Angela Harris, Stephanie Helfert, Ana Hummel, James T. Hunter, Dawn Jones, Alicia Lewis, Kim Lemons, Sylvie Little, Kathryn C. Marker, Deborah P. Marks, Victoria Matisko, Sue Mead, Roland Menestres, Laraleigh Moffitt, Symphorien Momet, Wanda Moore, Wendy Mumy, Kirsten Noland, Annie P.G. Norris, Hannah Pao, Alix Pavlic Phillips, Leslie Pyler, Kathleen Rhodes, Cynthia Richards, Julia Royall, Diane Smith, James Sonier, Ashlee Bree Stillings, Dyana Walker Talford, Alain Tourret, Sarah Walden, Ines Weikel, Sharon Williams, Kim Young; **North Dakota:** Patricia Jessen, Melissa R. Klajda, Valerie King, Lynee Meier; **Ohio:** Brandon Arnold, Maria Baker, Madith Barton, Shelbrey Blanc, Patricia Boon, Marguerite Bourgeois, Audra Buckley, Rebekah Clark, Nancy Compton, Parthena Draggett, Lisa Devlin, Carol J. Drescher, Kim Easley, Susan M. Eyron, Rachel Fawcett, Erin Gavula, Marianne Gooding, Suzanne Gyurgyik, Vinka Hartman, Suzanne Heacock, Jeanette Marie Hecker, Tina Hodge, Etchri Kekessi, Kelli Izzo, Patricia Jawn, Madeline LaJeunesse, Tracy Loar, Cynthia Mathias, Judith Mielbrecht, Linda Morell, JoAnn O'Connor, Gretchen Petrie, Juliana Porter, Davara Potel, Ann Marie Radefeld, Ann Ryan, Robert J. Roesbery, Jeff Royer, D. Saunders, Ellen Schaf, Patricia Schorr, Lynne Sebring, Lynette V. Seith, Cheryl Shank, Jacqueline Shrake, Kathryn M. Siegel, Adrienne Six, Bonnie Thompson, Mary Russell Townsend, Milton Alan Turner, Susan Vrooman, Stephanie Waugh, Melinda White, Barbara Yedidsion, Kimberly Young, Nicole Zistler; **Oklahoma:** Patricia Box, Joan King, Janet Gorton, Carol Little, Melinda Minshall, Julie Nesser, Jennifer Taylor, Micki Taylor, Wendy Toscani; **Oregon:** Penny Bazanele, Angela Barley, Eloise S. Bates, Terry Benge, David Burke, Rhonda Case, Mike Curtis, Brenda Eichten, Annette Hallaux, Gina Johnson, Marc McAvoy, Laurelin Muir, Sandra Rands, Jean Redrejo, Anick Southwood, Lexie Tombleson, Kathleen Williams, Erica Zimmerman; **Pennsylvania:** Denis N. Asselin, Colette Ballew, Pamela Barentine, Brenda Barndt, Betty Benton, Linda Bistline, Linda Blum, Colleen Bognet, Mary Bollinger, Kathleen H. Brown, Carolyn Busque, Gloria Carfagno, Gregory W. Coleman, Cindy Comstock, Bruce A. Cope, Virginia Cosgrove, Elaine Danford, Linda Donahue, Sandra Dubansky, Michelle Emery, Jill Fersch, Karen Fickes, Lydia Fichtman, Linda E. Fosselman, Paula Foster, Linda Girard, Jessica Grey, Andrew D. Grim, Dorothea Hackett, Scott Holland, Maureen Klingaman, Andrea Kupprion, Tricia Larson, Annette Lee, Susan Lobb, Cecile McKernan, Nancy McKnight, Ann Menichelli, Linda Mercier, Amy Montgomery, Laura Nagle, Laurie Nelson, Courtney Nelson, Jill Nickerson, Claudine Nicolay, Hallie Olson, Conni Petrie, Andrew Reaman, Joanne Robb, Regina Rooney, Anita Sapadidis, Jennifer Sharp, Susan E. Shuman, Kathy Simonovich, R. Sklar, Jan Hostler Stewart, Kyrston Strauch, Deborah A. Swann, Kathleen Tatala, Jill Trate, Amy Varacallu, Maureen L. Verwey, Nicole Wagner, Vanessa Weinlein, Ellen R. Wiberley, Katie Wilhelm, Diane Yanez, Barbara Zaun; **Rhode Island:** Sarah Brady, Kathleen DePasquale, Coleen Griffith, Sandra Tessier; **South Carolina:** Cathy Boudrie, Susannah Elliot, Jill Hnat, Kristina Holst, Sara Johnson, Justin T. Jones, Marisa Keenan, Lilly Mikol, Michele Mouyeos, Jennifer Teague; **South Dakota:** Jane Perman; **Tennessee:** Marsha Barrom, Marcia Bowen, Elizabeth Buchignani, Edith Jane Cain, Melanie L. Calhoun, Dustin Denzin, Marina Fernandez, Janet Kaller Geerlings, Larry Justis, Ashley Lawrence, Laura Leonard, Alexis Mattingly, Katie Paduch-Ledford, Jacob Truax, Robin Lynn Woo; **Texas:** Ann Abercrombie, Andrea Adams, Veronica Angel, Cheryl Babb, Joanna Gipson Bacon, Rose E. Balboa, Dawn M. Barett, Maria Barraza, Penny Beauchamp, Allison Bennett, Claire Breaux, Kathleen Carsey, Jose H. Castro, Richard J. Catania, Ann Clogan, Jacqueline Costanza, Randi Costenbader, Leslie Cushman, Lan Doan, Florence Dossett, Susan Dworaczyk, Francisca Florent, Allison Foster, Karlyn Fuquay, Erin Gallagher, M. Carla Geiger, Cathy Gelzleichter, Everett Gillette, Stacey Griffin, Rita A. Guidry, Julie Hanson, Phill Hemmings, Esther Hendrick, Jenifer Herndon, Melissa Hezlep, Bruce Hoang, Kitty Hutchcroft, Diana Jacob, Jeanne Johnson, Anne Jones, Penny Korenek, Aaron Levine, Cecilee C. Lindsey, Leigh Marshall, Joel Mayer, Cindy McBrayer, Denise McCage, Rita Mendoza, Diane Meyrat, Patricia Mills, Adam Morton, Deborah Murphy, Mark Myers, Cathy Nacol, Mary Nichols, Rhonda Palmer, Terry Pierce, Elizabeth Porter, Micaela Pitre, Natalya Belova Ramirez, Beverly Randall, Celeste Renza-Guren, Heather Richardson, Jill A. Rock, Serge Schragin, Rachel Schulz, Tara Smith, Maribel Squibb, Karen Stephens, Dore Sulistyo, Gail Sutcliffe, Roger Thomas, J. M. Turner, Kristen Villarreal, Alicia Villavazo, R. D. Wade, Elizabeth Walker, Brandon Walters, Sharon Wendzel, Mary Westlake, Kristin Wright, Pamela Young, Amina Ztot; **Utah:** Christina Brown, Art Burnah, Alisan Mills, Dave Miller, Lorraine Peterson; **Vermont:** Diane Ingham, Norman W. McLure, Kendra Paupst; **Virginia:** Amanda Amos, Kandie Bradshaw, Susan Broaddus, Kay Choi, Anna Collins, Susan Courtney, Cynthia Dahl, Genevieve DeFosse, Kathy Flynn, LaVerne E. Flowers, Monica Johnston, Rinata Lewis, Sue McCloud, Michelle M. Morningstar, Elizabeth Schollaert, Craig F. Seal, Ghislaine Tulou, Cynthia van de Kamp, Dawn Whitehurst; **Washington:** Catherine Blair, Olivia Caulfuex, Roslyn Cooper, Svetlana Cuello, Daniel Dole, Ann Elliot, Jeanne Federovitch, Greg Isham, Jenny Hallenbeck, Tina Irish, Gregg Kasner, Josette Martin, Merissa McGregor, Molly McKinnon, Sarah McMenamin, Kara Miller, Heidi Monrad, Meghan Morahan, JoAnne Peterson, Kathleen Pointec, Esther Reignam, Robert Slabodnik, Kaisa Swenddal-White, Deana Watt; **West Virginia:** Rita Denton; **Wisconsin:** Ramona Armour, Margaret Bussone, Linda Christen, Guy Dayen, Natalia Delaat, Maura Devarie, Jana Gasiorkiewicz, Kathy A. Hawkins, Susanne Krasovich, Mary A. Martin, Jennifer Muchka, Julie Nji, Angela Olson, Jamie Pittmann, Vicky Thompson; Deborah Walther, Michelle Webster, Sally Weems, Brian Wopat.

EMC

# T'es branché?

**1B**

## Annotated Teacher's Edition

### Authors

Colleen C. Josephson
Terry L. Meyers
Emily Wentworth

**Contributing Writer**

Patricia Teefy

EMC
Publishing

ST. PAUL

**Editorial Director:** Alejandro Vargas

**Developmental Editor:** Diana I. Moen

**Associate Editors:** Nathalie Gaillot, Patricia Teefy

**Assistant Editor:** Kristina Merrick

**Copy Editor:** Kristin Hoffman

**Production Editor:** Bob Dreas

**Cover Designer:** Leslie Anderson

**Text Designer:** Leslie Anderson

**Production Specialist:** Julie Johnston

ISBN 978-0-82196-672-3

© 2014 by EMC Publishing, LLC

875 Montreal Way

St. Paul, MN 55102

Email: educate@emcp.com

Website: www.emcschool.com

Printed in the United States of America

22 21 20 19 18 17 16 15 14 13     1 2 3 4 5 6 7 8 9 10

# Meet the Textbook Authors

**Toni Theisen**, the 2009 ACTFL Teacher of the Year and ACTFL President in 2013, is a National Board Certified Teacher of French at Loveland High School in Loveland, Colorado and the Thompson School District World Language Curriculum Representative. She holds an M.A. in Foreign Language Teaching and an M. A. in Education of Diverse Learners. She is also a Google Certified teacher.

A passionate and active world language advocate, Theisen has presented numerous workshops, keynotes, and webinars for national, regional, and state conferences and institutes. Also an author, she has written several middle and high school French language series and many articles on Multiple Intelligences, Differentiated Instruction, and Technology for the 21st-century learner. Theisen presented "Activating Communication" as part of the first ACTFL Webinar series and also presented at the 2011 LARC (National Language Acquisition Resource Center) STARTALK Institute at San Diego State University.

Theisen led the effort in 2009 to revise the Colorado World Languages Academic Standards and co-chaired the revision committee of the National Board for Professional Teacher Standards for WLOE (World Languages Other than English) in 2009. Most recently she chaired the ACTFL 21st Century Skills Map committee in collaboration with the Partnership for 21st Century Learning.

Theisen's many additional honors include the ACTFL Nelson Brooks Award for the Teaching of Culture, the Colorado Governor's Award for Excellence in Teaching, the SWCOLT Excellence in Teaching Award, and the Genevieve Overman Memorial Service Award from the Colorado Congress of Foreign Language Teachers.

**Jacques Pécheur** is the Chief Editor of the French review *Le français dans le monde*. He has worked as Director of the Cultural Center of Palermo and Sicily, and as Cultural Ambassador to the French Embassy in Switzerland. As head of the Mission to the General Delegation for the Languages of France (DGLF), Pécheur has conducted numerous missions to promote multilingualism, the French language, and la Francophonie in the world. He also worked for the French Ministry of Foreign Affairs, the European Council, the European Union, and the Intergovernmental Agency of la Francophonie (AIF). As such he was entrusted with conducting and managing conferences and training workshops in more than 50 countries.

Pécheur's numerous involvements in political, cultural, and language-related occupations have led him to gain expertise in language policies and the language marketplace. As someone who has developed many strategies to promote the learning of French, Pécheur has been a spokesman in numerous conferences related to language learning, and has published many articles. His 20 years of experience in *Le francais dans le monde*, as well as his many publications on French civilization, cinema, and contemporary literature, have shaped his proactive approach to the editorial world.

Honorary member of the AATF, Pécheur is recognized in the United States by the Cultural Services of the French Consulate in the United States (SCAC), the Alliance Française, and many American universities.

# Table of Contents

# Scope and Sequences

## T'es branché? Level 1

| Vocabulaire | Fonctions | Culture | Structure | Stratégies |
|---|---|---|---|---|
| **Unité 1    Bonjour, tout le monde!** | | | | |
| *Essential question: In what ways is learning another language beneficial?* | | | | |
| • Greetings<br>• Nationalities (in **Vocabulaire actif**) | • Introduce oneself<br>• Introduce someone else<br>• Respond to an introduction<br>• Ask someone's name (in **Pour la conversation**) | • Greetings<br>• Popular first names<br>• **La Francophonie:** Francophones in France and North America (in **Points de départ**) | | |
| • Respond to **Ça va?**<br>• Say good-bye | • Ask how someone is<br>• Say how I am doing | • Back to school<br>• Ways to say good-bye<br>• **La Francophonie:** Europe and North Africa | | **Communication:** Register in speaking and writing (in **Stratégies communicatives**) |
| • Locations<br>• Parents | • Extend an invitation<br>• Accept an invitation<br>• Refuse an invitation | • French teens<br>• **La Francophonie:** Sub-Saharan Africa, Caribbean, and South America<br><br>**Produits:**<br>**La Négritude** | | **Culture:** Assess comfort level with Francophone cultures (in **La culture sur place**)<br><br>**Fine art:** Impressionistic techniques (Jean Béraud) (in **Le monde visuel**)<br><br>**Reading:** Answer the five "W" questions and decipher words (in **Lecture thématique**) |
| **Unité 2    Les passe-temps** | | | | |
| *Essential question: What do activities and pastimes reveal about a culture?* | | | | |
| • Pastimes<br>• Olympic sports<br>• Weather<br>• Food | • Ask what someone likes to do<br>• Say what I like to do<br>• Say what I don't like to do | • **Pari Roller**<br>• Olympics<br>• Paris<br><br>**La Francophonie (Sports):**<br>• **Tour de France**<br>• Hockey in Canada<br><br>**Produits:**<br>Cubism in Paris | • Subject pronouns<br>• **tu** vs. **vous**<br>• Present tense of regular **-er** verbs | |
| • More pastimes<br>• Adverbs | • Ask how much someone likes to do something<br>• Say how much I enjoy doing things | • Lyon<br><br>**La Francophonie (Les passe-temps):**<br>• Mancala in Africa<br><br>**Produits:**<br>Guignol | • Position of adverbs | **Communication:** Cognates |

| Vocabulaire | Fonctions | Culture | Structure | Stratégies |
|---|---|---|---|---|
| • Nouns:<br>Sports<br>Music<br>Pastimes<br>• Numbers 0–20 | • State my preferences<br>• Ask what someone prefers<br>• Agree and disagree | • Count on fingers<br>• Rachid Taha and World music<br>• Singer Corneille<br>• **Fête de la musique**<br><br>**La Francophonie (Instruments):**<br>• Kora in Africa | • Gender of nouns and definite articles<br>• The verb **préférer**<br>• Negation with **ne... pas** | **Culture:**<br>Sports viewing habits<br><br>**Fine art:**<br>Coloration (Béatrice Boisségur)<br><br>**Reading:**<br>Paraphrasing and finding meaning in repetition |

## Bilan cumulatif: Unités 1 – 2

## Unité 3   À l'école

*Essential question: How does education shape individuals and societies?*

| | | | | |
|---|---|---|---|---|
| • Classroom objects<br>• Numbers 20–100 | • Say what I need<br>• Ask what someone else needs<br>• Ask what something costs<br>• State what something costs | • Carrefour<br>• School supplies<br>• The euro and the Eurozone<br>• Online instruction | • Indefinite articles<br>• Plurals of articles and nouns<br>• Present tense of the irregular verb **avoir**<br>• **Avoir besoin de** | |
| • Classroom subjects<br>• Adjectives<br>• Time expressions | • Describe a class<br>• Ask for a description of someone<br>• Describe someone | • 24-hour clock<br>• Wednesday afternoon<br>• Classes and exams<br>• The **lycée** and the **bac**<br>• Naming schools<br><br>**La Francophonie:**<br>• French Polynesia<br><br>**Produits:**<br>**Le paréo** in French Polynesia | • Telling time<br>• Present tense of the irregular verb **être**<br>• Agreement and position of regular adjectives | **Communication:**<br>Combine sentences |
| • Places in school<br>• Places in the city | • Ask where someone is going<br>• Ask when someone is going somewhere<br>• Ask why someone cannot do something<br>• Establish a place and time to meet | • **La cantine** and school meals<br>• **Lycées hôteliers**<br>• **Fête de la musique**<br>• English words of French origin<br><br>**La Francophonie (Éducation):**<br>• Education in Mali | • Present tense of the irregular verb **aller**<br>• **À** + definite articles<br>• Forming questions with **est-ce que** | **Culture:**<br>Reflect on learning about French schools and compare them to schools in the United States<br><br>**Fine art:**<br>Focal point (Robert Doisneau)<br><br>**Reading:**<br>Point of view and Context clues |

| Vocabulaire | Fonctions | Culture | Structure | Stratégies |
|---|---|---|---|---|
| **Unité 4    Le weekend ensemble** | | | | |
| *Essential question: What activities do friends in other countries do together?* | | | | |
| • Soccer<br>• Soccer clothes<br>• The **métro** | • Give a reason<br>• Set a time and place to meet<br>• Suggest a different time | • Soccer in France<br>• Soccer clubs<br>• Famous soccer players<br><br>**Produits:**<br>The media and soccer in France | • **Aller** + infinitive<br>• Forming questions | |
| • Food and drink<br>• Numbers 100–1.000 | • Understand what the server will ask<br>• Order food<br>• Ask for the bill | • Cafés and **bistrots**<br>• Paris cafés and famous writers<br>• Fast food chains in France<br><br>**Produits:**<br>Le croissant | • Present tense of the irregular verb **prendre**<br>• Avoir expressions: **avoir faim/soif** | **Communication:**<br>Use adjectives and adverbs |
| • Movie genres<br>• Early, on time, and late | • Make a prediction<br>• Respond to a prediction | • French cinema<br>• French comedies<br>• *Bienvenue chez les Ch'tis*, French comedy<br><br>**Produits:**<br>French film starring Johnny Depp | • The interrogative adjective **quel**<br>• Present tense of the irregular verb **voir** | **Culture:**<br>Remakes of French films<br><br>**Fine art:**<br>Poster art<br><br>**Reading:**<br>Identify the conflict in a story and recognize false cognates |
| **Bilan cumulatif: Unités 3 – 4** | | | | |
| **Unité 5    Les gens que je connais** | | | | |
| *Essential question: What is the nature of relationships in other cultures?* | | | | |
| • Family members<br>• Physical descriptions<br>• Numbers 1.000–1.000.000 | • Ask for a description<br>• Point out resemblances | • The metric system<br><br>**La Francophonie:**<br>• Martinique<br><br>**Produits:**<br>Zouk music | • Possessive adjectives<br>• Indefinite articles in negative sentences | |
| • Months of the year<br>• Birthdays<br>• Descriptions of character | • Ask someone's age<br>• Tell my age<br>• Tell what gift I am giving<br>• Plan a party with others | • Birthdays and saints' days<br>• **La FNAC**<br><br>**La Francophonie (Fêtes d'anniversaire):**<br>• Birthday celebrations in Guadeloupe, North Africa, and Sub-saharan Africa | • Present tense of regular verbs ending in **-ir**<br>• Dates<br>• Expressions with **avoir: J'ai… ans**<br>• Present tense of the irregular verb **offrir** | **Communication:**<br>Ask questions to extend a conversation |
| • French-speaking African countries and nationalities<br>• Professions | • Find out someone's profession<br>• Ask where someone comes from<br>• Tell where I come from | • Singers Amadou and Mariam<br><br>**La Francophonie:**<br>Sub-saharan Francophone Africa<br><br>**Produits:**<br>African masks | • **C'est** vs. **il/elle est**<br>• Present tense of the irregular verb **venir**<br>• **De** + definite articles | **Culture:**<br>Collect anecdotal evidence about a Francophone family<br><br>**Fine art:**<br>Composition (Alfred Wolf)<br><br>**Reading:**<br>Theme and Monitoring comprehension |

| Vocabulaire | Fonctions | Culture | Structure | Stratégies |
|---|---|---|---|---|

## Unité 6    La rue commerçante

*Essential question: How is shopping different in other countries?*

| Vocabulaire | Fonctions | Culture | Structure | Stratégies |
|---|---|---|---|---|
| • Articles of clothing<br>• Colors | • What to ask the salesperson<br>• What the salesperson says | • Shopping online<br>• French flea markets<br>• High fashion houses in Paris<br><br>**La Francophonie (Vêtements):** Clothing in West Africa | • Present tense of the verb **acheter**<br>• Present tense of the irregular verb **vouloir**<br>• Demonstrative adjectives | |
| • Stores and grocery items<br>• Quantities | • Sequence my activities | • Superstores vs. small shops<br>• French cheeses<br>• Metric measurements<br><br>**Produits:**<br>**Le pâté** | • Present tense of regular verbs ending in **-re**<br>• Expressions of quantity | **Communication:** Tell a story through pictures |
| • Fruits and vegetables | • Make a purchase at the market<br>• Respond to questions from the vendor | • Outdoor markets<br>• Slow food movement<br><br>**La francophonie (Le marché):**<br>**Les souks** in North Africa<br><br>**Produits:**<br>North African arts and crafts | • The partitive article<br>• The partitive in negative sentences | **Culture:** Go shopping online<br><br>**Fine art:** Black and white photography **d'après-guerre** (Sabine Weiss)<br><br>**Reading:** Setting and Word families |

## Bilan cumulatif: Unités 5 – 6

## Unité 7    À la maison

*Essential question: What makes a house a "home"?*

| Vocabulaire | Fonctions | Culture | Structure | Stratégies |
|---|---|---|---|---|
| • Stories in a building<br>• Rooms in a house<br>• Furniture in the kitchen and living room | • Give a tour of a house or an apartment<br>• Ask where someone lives<br>• Agree and disagree | • Housing in France<br>• Bathrooms in France<br><br>**La Francophonie (Habitations):** North African dwellings, focus on Algeria<br><br>**Produits:**<br>**Le raï** | • Ordinal numbers | |
| • Meals<br>• Table setting | • Give directions in the kitchen | • Marseille<br>• Provence<br>• Regional culinary specialties<br><br>**Produits:**<br>*The Starry Night* by Van Gogh And **"La Marseillaise"** | • Comparative of adjectives<br>• Present tense of the irregular verb **devoir**<br>• Present tense of the irregular verb **mettre** | **Communication:** Write descriptions |

| Vocabulaire | Fonctions | Culture | Structure | Stratégies |
|---|---|---|---|---|
| • The bedroom and bathroom<br>• Computer and other technology | • Say that I don't understand<br>• Talk about computers | • Technology and French youth<br>**La Francophonie:**<br>• New Brunswick<br>• The **Grand Dérangement** of the Acadians<br>• Singer Natasha St-Pier<br>**Produits:**<br>Zydeco music | • Present tense of the irregular verb **pouvoir** | **Culture:**<br>Evaluate whether student's home is like or unlike Francophone homes<br>**Fine art:**<br>Impressionism and Cubism (Paul Cézanne)<br>**Reading:**<br>Rhyme Scheme and Deciphering new grammatical structures |

## Unité 8    À Paris

*Essential question: How do major world cities tell their stories?*

| Vocabulaire | Fonctions | Culture | Structure | Stratégies |
|---|---|---|---|---|
| • Weather<br>• Seasons<br>• Pets | • Extend an invitation<br>• Accept or refuse an invitation | • Paris<br>• Parisian pastries<br>**La Francophonie (Une autre capitale):**<br>Port-au-Prince<br>**Produits:**<br>**La galette des rois** | • Present tense of the irregular verb **faire**<br>• Expressions with **avoir: avoir froid, avoir chaud, avoir envie de** | |
| • Places in the city<br>• Monuments in Paris | • Excuse oneself<br>• Describe actions that took place in the past<br>• Sequence past events | • **Notre-Dame**<br>• **L'arc de triomphe**<br>• **La tour Eiffel** | • **Passé composé** with **avoir**<br>• Irregular past participles<br>• Position of irregular adjectives | **Communication:**<br>Personal narrative |
| • Time expressions | • Express actions that took place in the past<br>• Sequence past events | • **Le jardin des Tuileries**<br>• **Le métro** | • **Passé composé** with **être**<br>• Position of adverbs in the **passé composé** | **Culture:**<br>Identify customs and React to French culture<br>**Fine art:**<br>Pointillism (Paul Signac)<br>**Reading:**<br>Personification and Making inferences |

## Bilan cumulatif: Unités 7 – 8

## Unité 9    En forme

*Essential question: How do people stay healthy and maintain a healthy environment?*

| Vocabulaire | Fonctions | Culture | Structure | Stratégies |
|---|---|---|---|---|
| • Parts of the body<br>• Parts of the face | • Say it is necessary to do, or not do, something | • **La sécu** in France<br>• "**Manger-bouger**" ad campaign<br>• **Le thermalisme**<br>**Produits:**<br>Homeopathic medications | • Present tense of the irregular verb **falloir** | |

| Vocabulaire | Fonctions | Culture | Structure | Stratégies |
|---|---|---|---|---|
| • Illnesses and other health expressions | • Ask for advice<br>• Give advice | **La Francophonie:**<br>Rwanda<br>• Fighting AIDS in Rwanda<br>• Home health care workers in Rwanda<br><br>**Produits:**<br>Languages and language education in Rwanda | • The imperative | **Communication:**<br>"How-to" writing |
| • Environmental problems<br>• Environmental solutions<br>• Endangered species | • Persuade someone<br>• Respond to persuasion | • **Les Verts** in France<br>• **Vélib' Paris**<br>**Produits:**<br>*La souris verte*, online magazine for young people | • Verbs + infinitives<br>• **De** + plural adjectives | **Culture:**<br>Hunting for diabetes education aids in Francophone countries<br><br>**Fine art:**<br>Cubism (Roger de La Fresnaye)<br><br>**Reading:**<br>Characterization, Text organization, and Making a prediction |

## Unité 10　Les grandes vacances

*Essential question: How do travel experiences shape our worldview?*

| Vocabulaire | Fonctions | Culture | Structure | Stratégies |
|---|---|---|---|---|
| • Places in North America<br>• Quebec essentials<br>• Compass directions | • Tell someone where a place is located | **La Francophonie:**<br>• Quebec<br>• Montreal<br>• **FrancoFolies** festival in Montreal<br><br>**Produits:**<br>Maple syrup | • Prepositions before cities, countries, and continents | |
| • At the train station<br>• Features of the countryside | • Remind someone to do something<br>• Wish someone a good trip | • Departments and regions of France<br>• Loire castles<br>• Tours | • Other negative expressions | **Communication:**<br>Writing a postcard |
| • European countries<br>• European nationalities<br>• Expressions for giving directions | • Ask for directions<br>• Give directions | **La Francophonie:**<br>• Switzerland<br>• Geneva<br>• International museum of the **Croix-Rouge**<br><br>**Produits:**<br>Swiss watches | • Superlative of adjectives | **Culture:**<br>Interviewing a traveler who has visited a Francophone location<br><br>**Fine art:**<br>Perspective (Achille Varin)<br><br>**Reading:**<br>Imagery and the Progression of stanzas |

## Bilan cumulatif: Unités 9 – 10

# T'es branché? Level 2

| Vocabulaire | Fonctions | Culture | Structure | Stratégies |
|---|---|---|---|---|
| **Unité 1    Comment je passe l'été** | | | | |
| *Essential question: What do young people do in the summer in other cultures?* | | | | |
| • Holidays in France, Quebec, and the United States | • Ask someone if they celebrate a particular holiday<br>• Ask when something takes place and respond | • Quebec City<br>• 400th anniversary of the founding of Québec<br>**La Francophonie (Les fêtes):**<br>• Celebrations in Quebec and France<br>• Native Singer Samian<br>**Produits:**<br>**Le cirque du soleil** | • Present tense of regular verbs ending in **-er**, **-ir**, and **-re**<br>• Negation<br>• Possessive adjectives<br>• Forming questions<br>• Dates | |
| • Television programs<br>• Television professions | • Ask for an opinion<br>• Give an opinion<br>• Find out what someone is thinking<br>• Agree or disagree | **La Francophonie:**<br>• Luxemburg<br>• French and Luxemburg TV channels<br>• Reality shows in France<br>**Produits:**<br>• Canal +<br>• "La Nouvelle Star" | • Present tense of the irregular verbs **avoir** and **être**<br>• Indefinite articles in negative sentences<br>• Demonstrative adjectives<br>• Agreement and position of adjectives<br>• Comparative of adjectives | **Communication:**<br>Create a TV commercial |
| • Rides and attractions at amusement parks | • Inquire about future plans<br>• Respond | • French fair **la Fête des Loges**<br>• Amusement parks and other attractions in France<br>**La Francophonie (Parcs d'attractions):**<br>**La Ronde**<br>**Produits:**<br>**Le Parc d'Astérix** | • Present tense of the irregular verbs **aller** and **faire**<br>• **De** and **à** + definite articles<br>• The irregular verb **venir** and **venir de** + infinitive<br>• Telling time | **Culture:**<br>Investigate bilinguism in Canada<br>**Fine art:**<br>Realism (Jean-Louis Ernest Meissonier)<br>**Reading:**<br>Paraphrasing and Learning from the title |
| **Unité 2    Dans la capitale** | | | | |
| *Essential question: What stories does Paris tell about art and architecture?* | | | | |
| • Art terms<br>• Types of paintings | • Describe a painting | • The **Louvre**<br>• The **musée d'Orsay**<br>• The **Centre Pompidou**<br>**Produits:**<br>La *Joconde* | • Present tense of the irregular verb **suivre**<br>• **Passé composé** with **avoir**<br>• Present tense of the irregular verbs **mettre**, **prendre**, and **voir** | |
| • Places in the neighborhood | • Say I'm lost<br>• Tell someone not to worry<br>• Ask for directions<br>• Give directions | • Paris **arrondissements**<br>• **Le Quartier latin**<br>• **Saint-Germain des Prés**<br>**Produits:**<br>**La Sainte-Chapelle** | • Present tense of the irregular verbs **vouloir**, **pouvoir**, **devoir**, and **falloir**<br>• Irregular past participles<br>• Imperative | **Communication:**<br>Describe art |

| Vocabulaire | Fonctions | Culture | Structure | Stratégies |
|---|---|---|---|---|
| • Modes of transportation<br>• Versailles | • Ask about transportation<br>• Respond | • Tourist offices<br>• The R.E.R.<br>• **Versailles** | • Present tense of the irregular verbs **partir** and **sortir**<br>• **Passé composé** with **être**<br>• Superlative of adjectives | **Culture:**<br>Explore **le musée d'Orsay**<br><br>**Fine art:**<br>Modern Art (Marc Laberge)<br><br>**Reading:**<br>Drama basics and Finding evidence in the text |

## Bilan cumulatif: Unités 1 – 2

## Unité 3    La vie quotidienne

*Essential question: How do the routines of people in other cultures differ from mine?*

| Vocabulaire | Fonctions | Culture | Structure | Stratégies |
|---|---|---|---|---|
| • Toiletries<br>• Daily routine | • Complain<br>• Respond to a complaint<br>• Express frustration<br>• Respond | **La Francophonie:**<br>• Cameroon<br>• Goals of the community of **la Francophonie**<br><br>**Produits:**<br>**Le Ngondo** | • Present tense of reflexive verbs<br>• Irregular plural forms of nouns and adjectives | |
| • Household items<br>• Household chores | • Make comparisons<br>• Respond to comparisons<br>• Express injustice | **La Francophonie:**<br>• Ivory Coast<br>• Artists from the Ivory Coast<br>• Africa today<br>• African immigrants in France today<br><br>**Produits:**<br>**Zouglou** music | • Present tense of the irregular verb **s'asseoir**<br>• The imperative of reflexive verbs | **Communication:**<br>Tell a story through pictures |
| • More reflexive verbs | • Find out if someone remembers something<br>• Recount past events | **La Francophonie:**<br>• Senegal<br>• Senagalese artists<br>• **Griots**<br>• Singer Youssou N'Dour<br><br>**Produits:**<br>**L'hymne national sénégalais** | • **Passé composé** of reflexive verbs | **Culture:**<br>Examine the controversy of Halal meat in fast-food restaurants<br><br>**Fine art:**<br>Batik (Anonyme)<br><br>**Reading:**<br>Sensory details and Making inferences |

## Unité 4    Autrefois

*Essential question: How does the past shape us?*

| Vocabulaire | Fonctions | Culture | Structure | Stratégies |
|---|---|---|---|---|
| • Farm<br>• Farm animals | • Reminisce<br>• Describe past events | • Agriculture in France<br>• World ranking of France's agricultural products<br>• French rural life today<br><br>**Produits:**<br>**Emmental** | • Imperfect tense<br>• Present tense of the irregular verb **croire** | |

| Vocabulaire | Fonctions | Culture | Structure | Stratégies |
|---|---|---|---|---|
| • Professions of the past | • Describe past events | • Montmartre<br>• Toulouse-Lautrec<br><br>**Produits:**<br>Poster art | • **Il y a** + time<br>• Imperfect and **passé composé** | **Communication:**<br>Write an oral history |
| • University life | • Make a suggestion | • Demonstrations<br>• May 1968<br>• University of Vincennes vs. Sorbonne | **Si on** + imperfect | **Culture:**<br>Discover the reasons why people demonstrate<br><br>**Fine art:**<br>Impressionism's use of light (Camille Pissarro)<br><br>**Reading:**<br>Text organization and Fact vs. opinion |

## Bilan cumulatif: Unités 3 – 4

## Unité 5    Bon voyage et bonne route!

*Essential question: What do you need to know to travel successfully?*

| Vocabulaire | Fonctions | Culture | Structure | Stratégies |
|---|---|---|---|---|
| • At the airport | • Describe a health problem<br>• Give instructions | • **Air France**<br>• Airports in Paris<br>• Bordeaux<br><br>**Produits:**<br>**Les Nubians**, hip-hop group from Bordeaux | • Direct object pronouns: **me, te, nous, vous** | |
| • Types of cars<br>• Exterior of cars<br>• Interior of cars | • Express that I'm looking forward to something | • **Peugeot-Citroën** and **Renault** car companies<br>• Learning to drive in France<br><br>**Produits:**<br>**Renault** and General Motors | • Direct object pronouns: **le, la, l', les**<br>• Direct object pronouns in the **passé composé**<br>• Present tense of the irregular verb **conduire** | **Communication:**<br>Write a dialogue |
| • Hotel room<br>• French breakfast<br>• North American breakfast | • Ask for a hotel room<br>• Ask if something's included in the price<br>• Understand what the receptionist asks | • Hotels, inns, and bed & breakfasts in France<br>• Luxury hotels and the movies<br><br>**Produits:**<br>Sofitel, hotel chain | • Indirect object pronouns: **lui, leur**<br>• Indirect object pronouns: **me, te, nous, vous**<br>• Present tense of the irregular verb **boire**<br>• The adjective **tout** | **Culture:**<br>Find a hotel that meets your needs<br><br>**Fine art:**<br>Pop art (François Le Diascorn)<br><br>**Reading:**<br>Motif and Cause and effect |

## Unité 6    Les arts maghrébins

*Essential question: How do other cultures enrich our lives?*

| Vocabulaire | Fonctions | Culture | Structure | Stratégies |
|---|---|---|---|---|
| • Things we read<br>• Things we write | • Say what a book is about<br>• Introduce an author or a novel<br>• Borrow something | **La Francophonie:**<br>• Morocco<br>• French language comic books<br>**Produits:**<br>• Henna decoration in North Africa<br>• *Le racisme expliqué à ma fille* by Tahar Ben Jelloun | • Present tense of the irregular verb **lire**<br>• Present tense of the irregular verb **écrire** | |

| Vocabulaire | Fonctions | Culture | Structure | Stratégies |
|---|---|---|---|---|
| • Music genres<br>• Musical instruments | • Ask if someone plays a particular instrument<br>• Say what instrument I play | **La Francophonie:**<br>• Algeria<br>• **Raï** music<br>• Singer Faudel<br>• North African music instruments<br><br>**Produits:**<br>*Indigènes*, French film about North African soldiers | • Present tense of the irregular verb **savoir**<br>• Present tense of the irregular verb **connaître** | **Communication:**<br>Write a character sketch |
| • Accessories and fabrics<br>• Jewelry | • Begin and end a letter<br>• Thank someone formally | **La Francophonie:**<br>• Tunisia<br>• **Souks**<br><br>• How to write a formal letter<br><br>**Produits:**<br>Carthage | • Present tense of the irregular verb **recevoir**<br>• Present tense of the irregular verb **ouvrir** | **Culture:**<br>Reflect on negotiating a price in North African souks and in North America<br><br>**Fine art:**<br>Perspective in modern photography (Peet Simard)<br><br>**Reading:**<br>Images and Refrain |

**Bilan cumulatif: Unités 5 – 6**

**Unité 7    En province**

*Essential question: How do smaller communities enrich a country's culture?*

| Vocabulaire | Fonctions | Culture | Structure | Stratégies |
|---|---|---|---|---|
| • Foods and courses | • Compliment the host or hostess<br>• Politely refuse more food<br>• Offer help | • Alsace<br>• Strasbourg<br><br>**La Francophonie (Une autre province):**<br>**Kabylie** in Algeria<br><br>**Produits:**<br>**La choucroute garnie** | • The relative pronouns **qui** and **que**<br>• The partitive<br>• The pronoun **en** | |
| • French regions and their adjectives | • Ask a friend what's new<br>• Find out someone's associations with a place<br>• Say I like a suggestion | • Normandy<br>• Rouen<br><br>**Produits:**<br>• French influence on the English language<br>• Bayeux tapestry<br>• Cider<br>• Claude Monet museum in Giverny | • Interrogative pronouns | **Communication:**<br>Combine sentences |
| • Things to eat and drink in a **crêperie**<br>• Youth hostels | • Understand what the server asks<br>• Order food | • Brittany<br>• Saint-Malo<br>• Youth hostels<br><br>**Produits:**<br>Food specialties of Brittany | • Stress pronouns | **Culture:**<br>Explore regional identity<br><br>**Fine art:**<br>Still lifes (Paul Cézanne)<br><br>**Reading:**<br>Refrain and tone, and Anticipating vocabulary |

| Vocabulaire | Fonctions | Culture | Structure | Stratégies |
|---|---|---|---|---|
| **Unité 8 Les Antilles** | | | | |
| **Essential question: What are the benefits of encountering other cultures?** | | | | |
| • Flora in Guadeloupe<br>• Fauna in Guadeloupe | • Ask what someone prefers<br>• State ambivalence | **La Francophonie:**<br>• Guadeloupe<br>• **Parc national de la Guadeloupe**<br>• Green tourism<br><br>**Produits:**<br>**"Prière d'un Petit enfant nègre"**<br>by Guy Tirolien | • Present tense of the irregular verb **vivre**<br>• Pronoun **y** | |
| • Carnival in Martinique<br>• Weddings | • Make an observation | **La Francophonie:**<br>• Martinique<br>• Carnival in Martinique<br><br>**Produits:**<br>*La Rue Cases-Nègres* | • Double object pronouns | **Communication:**<br>Circumlocution |
| • Water management<br>• Seafood | • Say what I'm in charge of<br>• Express appreciation | **La Francophonie:**<br>• Haiti<br>• Toussaint Louverture<br>• Haitian cuisine<br><br>**Produits:**<br>Haitian music | • **Depuis** + present tense | **Culture:**<br>Find a good humanitarian organization<br><br>**Fine art:**<br>Seascapes (Claude Salez)<br><br>**Reading:**<br>Theme and Citing others' works |
| **Bilan cumulatif: Unités 7 – 8** | | | | |
| **Unité 9 La vie contemporaine** | | | | |
| **Essential question: What influences and changes contemporary society?** | | | | |
| • Features of smartphones<br>• Steps for taking a digital photo | • Ask someone to lend me something<br>• Say that I know or do not know how to use something<br>• Express what someone was happy about | • French transportation technologies: aviation, space program, rail<br><br>**Produits:**<br>Rubber from Indochina and Michelin | • Conditional tense | |
| • Problems in contemporary society<br>• Possible solutions | • Hypothesize<br>• Propose solutions | • Nuclear energy<br>• Objectives and problems in French education<br>• Unemployed young people<br><br>**Produits:**<br>French **Grandes Écoles** | • Conditional tense in sentences with **si** | **Communication:**<br>Write a proposal |

| Vocabulaire | Fonctions | Culture | Structure | Stratégies |
|---|---|---|---|---|
| • Job sectors<br>• Today's professions | • Express my future goals<br>• Give a reason | **La Francophonie:**<br>• Belgium<br>• Famous Belgians<br>• Brussels<br>• European Union<br><br>**Produits:**<br>Flemish/French song by Jacques Brel | • Future tense | **Culture:**<br>Investigate what new words in *Le Petit Larousse* reveal about contemporary French culture<br><br>**Fine art:**<br>Textures of acrylic paints (Daniel Cacouault)<br><br>**Reading:**<br>Dystopias in fiction and Social commentary |

## Unité 10  En vacances

*Essential question: What opportunities does travel afford us?*

| Vocabulaire | Fonctions | Culture | Structure | Stratégies |
|---|---|---|---|---|
| • At the beach | • Say I've been wanting to do something for a long time | • French Riviera<br>• Nice<br>• Chagall museum<br>• Matisse museum<br><br>**Produits:**<br>The **promenade des Anglais** in Nice | • Adverbs<br>• Verbs + infinitives | |
| • Camping | • Say I need something<br>• Ask someone to return something as soon as possible | • Alps<br>• Grenoble<br>• Camping in France<br><br>**Produits:**<br>**Téléphérique** in Grenoble | • Present tense of the irregular verb **dormir**<br>• Comparative of adverbs | **Communication:**<br>Travel writing |
| • Continents and bodies of water<br>• Adventure tourism | • Ask what to bring | **La Francophonie:**<br>• French Guiana<br>• Kourou<br>• Prisons<br><br>**La Francophonie (Tourisme d'aventure):**<br>Adventure tourism in France and French Guiana<br><br>**Produits:**<br>• Poems of Léon Gontran-Damas<br>• *Papillon* | • Superlative of adverbs | **Culture:**<br>Compare French and American vacation destinations<br><br>**Fine art:**<br>Point of view (Delphine D. Garcia)<br><br>**Reading:**<br>Point of view and Characterization |

## Bilan cumulatif: Unités 9 – 10

# T'es branché? Level 3

| Vocabulaire | Fonctions | Culture | Structure | Stratégies |
|---|---|---|---|---|
| **Unité 1   Les moments de la vie** | | | | |
| *Essential question: Comment les objectifs et les intérêts des Francophones évoluent-ils avec le temps?* | | | | |
| • Human emotions<br>• Teen destinations | • Say where I met someone<br>• Advise someone<br>• Tell someone not to worry<br>• Describe how someone seems | • Teen socialization<br>• **Maisons des Jeunes et de la Culture (MJC)**<br>**Produits:**<br>French blogs | • Present tense of regular -**er**,-**ir**, and -**re** verbs<br>• Present tense of irregular verbs<br>• **Depuis** + present tense | |
| • Different types of families<br>• Childhood games and activities | • Explain how something happened<br>• Say what I discovered<br>• Ask for a suggestion | • Different types of families in France<br>**La Francophonie (Les familles):**<br>• Families and family values in Africa<br>• **Provence-Alpes-Côte d'Azur**<br>**Produits:**<br>Perfumes and Grasse | • The irregular verb **courir**<br>• **Passé composé** with **avoir**<br>• **Passé composé** with **être**<br>• Imperfect tense<br>• Imperfect and **passé composé** | **Communication:**<br>Write a personal narrative |
| • Weddings<br>• Workplaces | • Say I don't care<br>• Say where I'd like to work | • Preparatory and Ivy league schools<br>• Civil and religious marriage ceremonies<br>**La Francophonie (Le mariage):**<br>• Marriage ceremony in Maghreb<br>**Produits:**<br>French wedding cake | • Conditional tense<br>• Conditional tense with **si**<br>• Future tense | **Culture:** Describing adolescent cultures<br>**Fine art:**<br>Line drawing (Édouard Albert)<br>**Reading:**<br>Setting and Using context clues (***Les petits enfants du siècle***, Christiane Rochefort) |
| **Unité 2   Les rapports personnels** | | | | |
| *Essential question: Qu'y a-t-il d'universel dans les rapports entre les gens?* | | | | |
| • Christmas eve dinner | • Talk on the phone<br>• Invite someone<br>• Respond affirmatively to an invitation<br>• Say that a proposal works for me | • Christmas Eve holiday<br>**Produits: Bûche de Noël**<br>**La Francophonie (Les fêtes):**<br>• Ramadan<br>• **Aïd-el-Fitre** | • Interrogative pronouns<br>• Direct object pronouns | |
| • Descriptions: shapes, sizes, material, and usage<br>• Kitchen utensils | • Ask for help<br>• Respond to a request for help | • Classic French cooking<br>• **La nouvelle cuisine**<br>**Produits:**<br>Le Cordon Bleu | • Indirect object pronouns<br>• **C'est** vs. **il/elle est** | **Communication:**<br>Using circumlocution |

| Vocabulaire | Fonctions | Culture | Structure | Stratégies |
|---|---|---|---|---|
| • Dinner table topics of conversation | • Express that I can't stop myself<br>• Say someone is right<br>• Ask about dinner table topics | • Traditional meal for Christmas Eve<br>• Rules of table etiquette<br><br>**Produits:** French wine | • Relative pronouns **qui, que**<br>• Relative pronouns **ce qui, ce que** | **Culture:** Identify food preferences<br><br>**Fine art:** Landscapes behind portraits (Jules Ernest Renoux)<br><br>**Reading:** Dialogue and Conflict (*Deux couverts*, Sacha Guitry) |

**Bilan cumulatif: Unités 1 – 2**

**Unité 3    La Francophonie**

*Essential question: Comment les Francophones restent-ils fidèles à leurs traditions?*

| Vocabulaire | Fonctions | Culture | Structure | Stratégies |
|---|---|---|---|---|
| • Extended family members<br>• States in the United States | • Say where my ancestors came from<br>• Say where my ancestors settled | • **Alliance Française** and its outreach programs<br>• French immigration to Quebec and **île d'Orléans**<br>• French-Canadian immigration to New England | • Pronouns **y, en**<br>• Double object pronouns | |
| • Types of stories<br>• Words from a North African children's story | • Start a fairy-tale | **La Francophonie:**<br>• Tunisia<br>• Immigration of **Maghrébins** in France<br><br>**La Francophonie (Les contes):**<br>• Overview of **contes maghrébins**<br><br>**Produits:** North African cuisine | • Reflexive verbs | **Communication:** Describe in detail |
| • Types of housing<br>• Home repair terms | • Respond to an introduction<br>• Say where I grew up<br>• Give a compliment | • HLMs and **allocations familiales**<br><br>**La Francophonie:**<br>• Senegal **(Logement):**<br>• African housing<br><br>**Produits:** Oral tradition in Africa | • Comparative of adverbs<br>• Superlative of adverbs | **Culture:** Needs of new immigrants<br><br>**Fine art:** Primitive Art (Cécile Delorme)<br><br>**Reading:** Make cultural inferences, Gender criticism (*Une si longue lettre*, Mariama Bâ) |

| Vocabulaire | Fonctions | Culture | Structure | Stratégies |
|---|---|---|---|---|

**Unité 4    Préparatifs de départ**

*Essential question: Qu'est-ce qu'on doit connaître de sa destination pour réussir son voyage?*

| Vocabulaire | Fonctions | Culture | Structure | Stratégies |
|---|---|---|---|---|
| • Sports and activities to do on vacation | • Ask someone's opinion<br>• React positively to someone's opinion<br>• React negatively to someone's opinion | **La Francophonie:**<br>**La Réunion**<br>• Chamonix and other **stations de ski** in France<br><br>**La Francophonie (Stations de ski):**<br>• Switzerland<br><br>**Produits:**<br>Training Saint Bernard dogs | • Present participle<br>• Negation<br>• Other negative expressions | |
| • At the ski resort<br>• Ski clothing and equipment | • Say what I must do<br>• Tell someone they'll have an opportunity<br>• Say I was expecting something | • Haute Savoie traditions and specialties<br>• **Classes de neige**<br><br>**Produits:**<br>**La raclette savoyarde**<br><br>**La Francophonie (La récréation):**<br>Aquatic or "bleu" activities in Saint-Martin | • **Savoir** vs. **connaître**<br>• Subjunctive of regular verbs after **il faut que**<br>• Subjunctive of irregular verbs | **Communication:**<br>Write a "how-to" piece using subjunctive |
| • Other winter sports<br>• Travel planning expressions | • Say I'm doing something different<br>• Tell someone to not hurt himself or herself | • Volunteer travel experiences in Francophone countries<br><br>**Produits:**<br>Sports in the Winter Olympics | • Subjunctive after impersonal expressions | **Culture:** Volunteer travel experiences<br><br>**Fine art:** Classicism (Sébastien Bourdon)<br><br>**Reading:**<br>Structure and Meaning, Allusions ("**Heureux qui, comme Ulysse, a fait un beau voyage**," Joachim du Bellay) |

**Bilan cumulatif: Unités 3 – 4**

**Unité 5    Comment se renseigner en voyage**

*Essential question: De quelles compétences ai-je besoin pour réussir un séjour?*

| Vocabulaire | Fonctions | Culture | Structure | Stratégies |
|---|---|---|---|---|
| • At the hotel<br>• Hotel amenities | • Ask for information | **La Francophonie:**<br>• Monaco<br>• Monte Carlo<br>• Rainier family<br><br>**Produits:**<br>**Le Bal de la Rose** | • Subjunctive after expressions of wish, will, desire | |
| • Food in Bourgogne: meats, dishes, sauces | • Ask about restaurant specialties<br>• Ask what a dish is served with | • Dijon and its region<br>• Food specialties in Bourgogne<br><br>**Produits:** Dijon museum and mustard<br><br>**La Francophonie (La cuisine):**<br>• North African dishes | • Subjunctive after expressions of emotion<br>• Subjunctive after expressions of doubt or uncertainty | **Communication:**<br>Write a movie review |

| Vocabulaire | Fonctions | Culture | Structure | Stratégies |
|---|---|---|---|---|
| • Movie expressions | • Say what I'm not in the mood for<br>• Report a review of a film<br>• Ask someone's reaction (to a piece of art)<br>• Express disagreement | • **Le septième art**<br>• **Les Césars**<br><br>**Produits:** Lumière brothers and birth of cinematography | • Interrogative adjective **quel**<br>• Interrogative pronoun **lequel** (**duquel, auquel**) | **Culture:** Planning a trip online<br><br>**Fine art:** Cartoons (Christian Cailleaux)<br><br>**Reading:** Comedy Sketch, Straight Man ("**Les croissants,**" Fernand Reynaud) |

## Unité 6    On se débrouille en France.

*Essential question: Comment s'intégrer à une autre culture?*

| Vocabulaire | Fonctions | Culture | Structure | Stratégies |
|---|---|---|---|---|
| • Banking terms<br>• University departments | • Open a bank account<br>• Get a credit card<br>• Make a promise | • French banks<br>• French universities and free education<br><br>**Produits:**<br>**La Carte bleue** | • Future tense in sentences with **si**<br>• Future tense after **quand** | |
| • Things to read | • Ask what a book is about<br>• Say I can't decide | • French reading habits<br>• Le Clézio<br><br>**Produits:**<br>French TV shows about books<br><br>**La Francophonie (Les écrivains):**<br>Maryse Condé | • Verbs + **de** + nouns<br>• Relative pronoun **dont** | **Communication:** Persuade someone to read a book or see a movie |
| • At the post office | • Say what I need<br>• Specify items | • French post office and its services<br><br>**Produits:**<br>Films that feature mail carriers | • Demonstrative adjectives<br>• Demonstrative pronouns | **Culture:** Problem solving **sur place**<br><br>**Fine art:** Cartoon art (Marjane Satrapi)<br><br>**Reading:** Narrator and Narration, Direct and Indirect Reporting (*Petropolis*, Marjane Satrapi) |

## Bilan cumulatif: Unités 5 – 6

## Unité 7    Les Arts

*Essential question: Comment l'art est-il un reflet de la culture?*

| Vocabulaire | Fonctions | Culture | Structure | Stratégies |
|---|---|---|---|---|
| • Art descriptions<br>• Art movements | • Say when a painting was painted<br>• Describe an artist's approach<br>• Describe colors in a painting | • **Académie, salons**<br>• **Atelier** vs. **en plein air**<br>• **Salon des refusés**<br><br>**Produits:**<br>Monet painting that gave name to Impressionnists, *Sunday in the Park with George* | • Agreement and position of adjectives<br>• Comparative of adjectives<br>• Superlative of adjectives | |

| Vocabulaire | Fonctions | Culture | Structure | Stratégies |
|---|---|---|---|---|
| • Music | • Describe an artist's development<br>• Say that an artist was successful<br>• Describe an artist's ability to connect with his or her audience | • The modern French song and its themes<br><br>**Produits:**<br>"La vie en rose"<br><br>**La Francophonie (Les chansons):**<br>Quebec group<br><br>**Produits:** "Mon pays," Gilles Vigneault | • The irregular verb **plaire** | **Communication:**<br>Compare and Contrast |
| • Poetry | • Describe how an artist raises themes<br>• Describe how a work of art takes a position<br>• Describe what an artist worked on<br>• Attribute new inventions<br>• Describe how an artist fits into a culture | • French poets<br><br>**Produits:**<br>Apollinaire's **calligrammes** | • **Pour** + infinitive<br>• Subjunctive after **pour que** | **Culture:**<br>Compare French and American music<br><br>**Fine art:**<br>Multiple exposure (Walter Limot)<br><br>**Reading:** Free Verse and Oxymorons ("**Familiale**," Jacques Prévert) |

## Unité 8    La France hier et aujourd'hui

*Essential question: Comment le passé influence-t-il le présent?*

| Vocabulaire | Fonctions | Culture | Structure | Stratégies |
|---|---|---|---|---|
| • French Revolution | • Express what someone was obligated to do<br>• Find that someone is forced to do something | • Louis XVI and Marie-Antoinette<br>• **Les États généraux**<br>• La *Déclaration des Droits de l'homme et du citoyen*<br><br>**Produits:**<br>La **Conciergerie**, guillotine, La *Déclaration des Droits de la femme et de la citoyenne*<br><br>**La Francophonie (La révolution):**<br>Arab Spring in Tunisia | • Expressions with **faire**<br>• **Faire** + infinitive | |
| • Applying and interviewing for a job | • Indicate quantity<br>• Say I did something in vain | • European Union Institutions<br><br>**Produits:**<br>Flag of E.U. | • Expressions with **avoir**<br>• Past infinitive | **Communication:**<br>Write a CV |
| • Health care terms<br>• Debate terms | • Express that someone has a right<br>• Express that someone can afford something<br>• Say I want to discuss something more later | • Rights of the French citizen under **la sécu:** unemployment, health care, family, disabled protection, retirement<br><br>**Produits:**<br>La crèche | • Expressions with **être**<br>• Pluperfect tense | **Culture:**<br>Rights issues and challenges the press faces abroad<br><br>**Fine art:**<br>Theatrical photography (Joseph Nicéphore Niépce)<br><br>**Reading:**<br>Word families and setting (*Le bourgeois gentilhomme*, Molière) |

**Bilan cumulatif: Unités 7 – 8**

| Vocabulaire | Fonctions | Culture | Structure | Stratégies |
|---|---|---|---|---|

## Unité 9    Récits de la vie contemporaine

*Essential question: Quels sont les défis de la vie contemporaire?*

| Vocabulaire | Fonctions | Culture | Structure | Stratégies |
|---|---|---|---|---|
| • Emotions | • Express how someone looked | • Recent changes to French school system<br>• **Le bac** and student stress<br><br>**Produits: Les annales du bac** | • Past conditional tense<br>• Past conditional tense with **si** | |
| • Physical description: hair, age, ethnicity, clothing | • Say I realized something | • Different types of French police<br>• Crime in France<br><br>**Produits: Une déclaration de vol<br>Le château d'If** | • Possessive adjectives<br>• Possessive pronouns | **Communication:**<br>Tell a story through pictures |
| • Reactions | • Say I did not expect something | • Internet resources for teens<br><br>**Produits: Loisirs ados** | • Indefinite adjectives<br>• Indefinite pronouns | **Culture:**<br>Interview a French speaker about challenges of life today<br><br>**Fine art:**<br>Book illustrations (Anonymous)<br><br>**Reading:**<br>Characterization and **Le passé simple**<br>(**Les Misérables,** Victor Hugo) |

## Unité 10    La culture des affaires

*Essential question: Qu'est-ce qu'on apprend de la culture d'un pays en étudiant son économie?*

| Vocabulaire | Fonctions | Culture | Structure | Stratégies |
|---|---|---|---|---|
| • Export products | • Say where an item was made | • French attitude toward globalization<br>• **Luxury products** and LVMH<br><br>**Produits:** Louis Vuitton brand | | |
| • Types of companies<br>• French and U.S. trade | • Ask if someone's been here a long time<br>• Say I wanted to get away | • France's position in world trade<br>• Multinational companies<br>• French business etiquette and taboos<br><br>**Produits:** Ariane rockets | | **Communication:**<br>Make a storyboard to sell a North American product in France |
| • Professional qualifications<br>• Job positions within a company | • Describe adaptability<br>• Say what I'm interested in | • Evolution of French marketing strategies<br><br>**Produits:**<br>Advertisements for **La vache qui rit** | | **Culture:**<br>How globalization affects our lives<br><br>**Fine art:**<br>Advertising photography<br><br>**Reading:**<br>(**14.99 €,** Frédéric Beigbeder) |

**Bilan cumulatif: Unités 9 – 10**

# Introduction

*T'es branché?* was designed to give French teachers a program that focuses on the three modes of communication—interpersonal, presentational, and interpretive—while ensuring their students become proficient in the five skill areas. Based on detailed surveys involving hundreds of experienced French educators, the textbook program responds to teachers' expressed interests and priorities. The filmed dialogues in the *Rencontres culturelles* section were written in France by native speakers, so that students learn idiomatic and natural expression. Grammar exercises are designed to build proficiency. Students develop reading skills with comprehensible input paragraphs in the vocabulary practice section. They also learn to appreciate literary writing in *Lecture thématique*. Activities move from mechanical exercises to more creative and open-ended projects. An essential question molds all the learning in any given unit.

Because paired, small group, and cooperative group activities are at the heart of today's student-centered classroom, *T'es branché?* offers many opportunities for students to work with their classmates on activities and projects that have clear guidelines and expectations. Students assume a more active role in their learning as they focus on how to learn as well as how to communicate in French. Opportunities for critical thinking can be found throughout the program, for example, in comparing francophone cultures to American culture and French grammar to English grammar.

Finally, the *T'es branché?* program was written to incorporate the National Standards. Let's look at how the textbook covers 2.1 and 2.2 from the standards below, for example. Students read culture notes about practices in the francophone world, as well as the content in *Produits* boxes that describe products from these locations. *Perspectives* are presented that may be in the form of a poem or song or quote from a French-speaker about their beliefs, experience, or observations. A new approach to teaching culture is presented in *La culture sur place*, allowing students to engage with francophone culture as they investigate topics of interest to teens and reflect on their "experience." Whatever element you are teaching, *T'es branché?* provides the tools you need to address standards in the following areas:

## Communication

### Communicate in Languages Other Than English

**Standard 1.1:** Students engage in conversations, provide and obtain information, express feelings and emotions, and exchange opinions.

**Standard 1.2:** Students understand and interpret written and spoken language on a variety of topics.

**Standard 1.3:** Students present information, concepts, and ideas to an audience of listeners or readers on a variety of topics.

## Cultures

### Gain Knowledge and Understanding of Other Cultures

**Standard 2.1:** Students demonstrate an understanding of the relationship between the practices and perspectives of the culture studied.

**Standard 2.2:** Students demonstrate an understanding of the relationship between the products and perspectives of the culture studied.

## Connections

### Connect with Other Disciplines and Acquire Information

**Standard 3.1:** Students reinforce and further their knowledge of other disciplines through the foreign language.

**Standard 3.2:** Students acquire information and recognize the distinctive viewpoints that are only available through the foreign language and its cultures.

## Comparisons

**Develop Insight into the Nature of Language and Culture**

**Standard 4.1:** Students demonstrate understanding of the nature of language through comparisons of the language studied and their own.

**Standard 4.2:** Students demonstrate understanding of the concept of culture through comparisons of the cultures studied and their own.

## Communities

**Participate in Multilingual Communities at Home & Around the World**

**Standard 5.1:** Students use the language both within and beyond the school setting.

**Standard 5.2:** Students show evidence of becoming life-long learners by using the language for personal enjoyment and enrichment.

Since a modern challenge in world language instruction is reaching all students—those with varying abilities, backgrounds, interests, and learning styles—the *T'es branché?* program has many opportunities beyond the textbook to help meet those needs. The Annotated Teacher's Edition provides suggested activities for different types of learners, from those with special needs to those who would benefit from enrichment. The Workbook contains Basic and Advanced activities so that students can make progress from where they begin and at their own pace. The online Drill and Practice games provide immediate feedback, allowing students to find out what they need more practice on well in advance of the test. Online Pre-tests also have immediate feedback, so that students can find out what they need to study more before their assessment experiences. Tailor-made products such as these ensure that each student makes progress and meets their potential as they embrace the French language and francophone culture.

## Common Core State Standards

The Common Core State Standards (CCSS) initiative seeks to raise academic standards for students and provide articulation of academic standards between states. The CCSS is designed for courses in English Language Arts, History/Social Studies, Science, and Technical Subjects, each containing four strands: Reading, Writing, Speaking and Listening, and Language. Having CCSS drive curricula will result in new assessment benchmarks for students.

*T'es branché?* was designed with the CCSS in mind. It emphasizes the purpose behind the communication by labeling activities that provide interpersonal (speaking-listening or writing-reading), interpretive (reading, listening, viewing), and presentational (writing, speaking, representing visually) communication. The goal of the textbooks is to move students from novice, to intermediate, to advanced proficiency levels by the time they complete the *T'es branché?* four-level program. Connections activities in *T'es branché?* that are specific to history and science allow students to learn about francophone history and scientific contributions made by Francophones. Technology skills are developed, as in the readings of *Points de départ*, where students research online using search words provided, and the *Projets finaux*, which allows for individual, pair, and group work using technology such as the Internet, video, smartphone, and online programs. *T'es branché?* uses the CCSS to make sure all students are ready for post-secondary learning, working, and becoming global citizens. A correlation of *T'es branché?* to the CCSS is at the end of the Annotated Teacher's Edition front pages.

Welcome to *T'es branché?*!

# Key Features: Student Textbook

**Students are excited to speak targeted communic...**

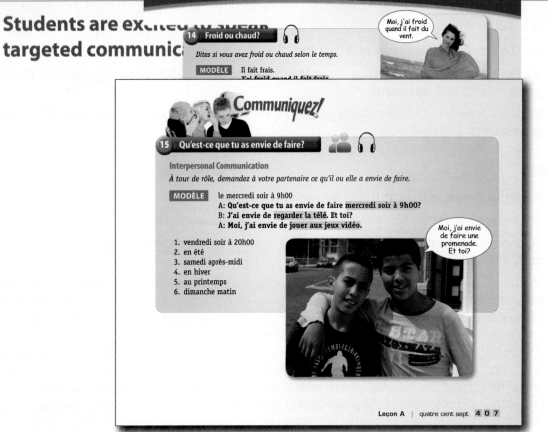

## and opportunities for creative self-expression.

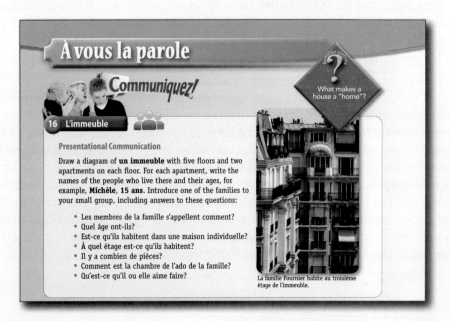

# Unit content is centered on an essential question to anchor learning:

**Unit 3** How does education shape individuals and societies?

**Unit 5** What is the nature of relationships in other cultures?

**Unit 7** What makes a house a "home"?

**Unit 9** How do people stay healthy and maintain a healthy environment?

# Students analyze the essential question in the *Projets finaux* section.

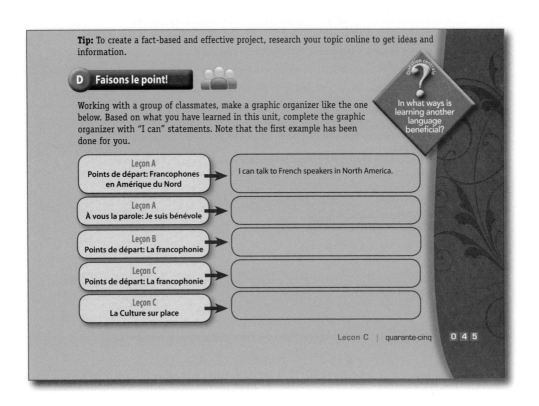

**Tip:** To create a fact-based and effective project, research your topic online to get ideas and information.

**D** Faisons le point!

Working with a group of classmates, make a graphic organizer like the one below. Based on what you have learned in this unit, complete the graphic organizer with "I can" statements. Note that the first example has been done for you.

In what ways is learning another language beneficial?

| Leçon A Points de départ: Francophones en Amérique du Nord | → | I can talk to French speakers in North America. |
| Leçon A À vous la parole: Je suis bénévole | → | |
| Leçon B Points de départ: La francophonie | → | |
| Leçon C Points de départ: La francophonie | → | |
| Leçon C La Culture sur place | → | |

Leçon C | quarante-cinq  0 4 5

# Students investigate francophone cultures "on location."

## La culture sur place

? Question centrale — What activities do friends in other countries do together?

### Les remakes de films français

#### Introduction

One place to find modern versions of a culture's collected stories is in movies. In this section, you and your classmates will use the Internet to learn about French movies that have been "remade" in the United States.

#### Investigation

Moviemakers in the United States often borrow ideas and themes of movies from other cultures. You and your classmates will use the suggestions below to identify American movies based on French films.

---

**10  Un remake d'un film français**

First, use one or more of the following techniques to find a list of American remakes of French films:

- enter the phrase "remakes américains de films français" in an online search engine. Click on a site that comes up and see if it includes a list of remakes.
- search for "remake of French films" on the Internet Movie Database site (www.imdb.com).
- look up the box office results for "Remake-French" on the Box Office Mojo site (www.boxofficemojo.com/genres.com).

Second, select a movie that you are familiar with or that interests you.

Third, look for information that will help you answer the following questions.

1. Compare the French title with the American title. Do they have the same meaning? Or, has the title completely changed?
2. In what ways are the plots similar?
3. In what ways is the American remake different from the French original version? For example, are the main characters the same? Did the setting change? Are elements of the plot different?
4. How popular were the French and American versions in each country? (You may want to include information about box office earnings, film critiques, fan pages, etc.)

---

**11  Un film français et américain**

Share your research with your small group.

# The francophone world is seen through its

- ## Practices

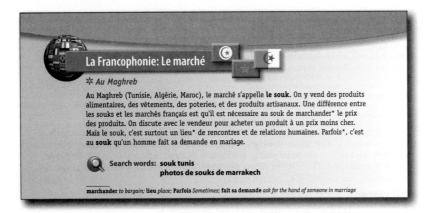

- ## Products

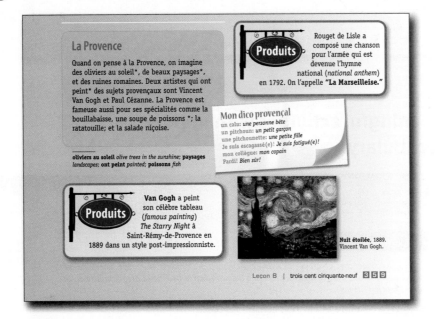

- ## and Perspectives.

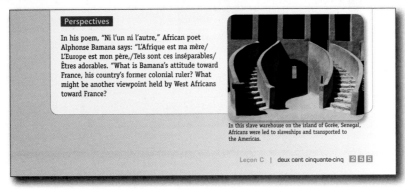

# Students master core vocabulary by reading comprehensible-input texts…

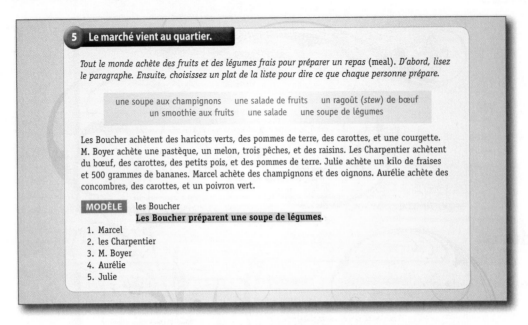

**5  Le marché vient au quartier.**

*Tout le monde achète des fruits et des légumes frais pour préparer un repas (meal). D'abord, lisez le paragraphe. Ensuite, choisissez un plat de la liste pour dire ce que chaque personne prépare.*

| une soupe aux champignons   une salade de fruits   un ragoût (*stew*) de bœuf |
| un smoothie aux fruits   une salade   une soupe de légumes |

Les Boucher achètent des haricots verts, des pommes de terre, des carottes, et une courgette. M. Boyer achète une pastèque, un melon, trois pêches, et des raisins. Les Charpentier achètent du bœuf, des carottes, des petits pois, et des pommes de terre. Julie achète un kilo de fraises et 500 grammes de bananes. Marcel achète des champignons et des oignons. Aurélie achète des concombres, des carottes, et un poivron vert.

**MODÈLE**  les Boucher
**Les Boucher préparent une soupe de légumes.**

1. Marcel
2. les Charpentier
3. M. Boyer
4. Aurélie
5. Julie

# and doing meaningful activities with high frequency vocabulary.

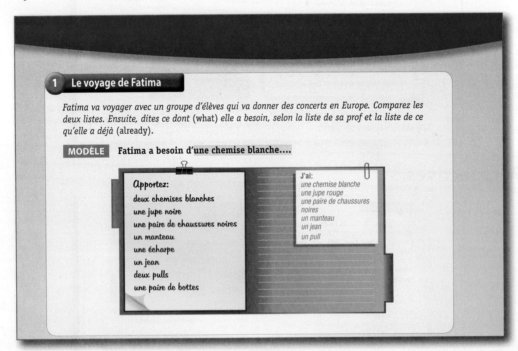

**1  Le voyage de Fatima**

*Fatima va voyager avec un groupe d'élèves qui va donner des concerts en Europe. Comparez les deux listes. Ensuite, dites ce dont (what) elle a besoin, selon la liste de sa prof et la liste de ce qu'elle a déjà (already).*

**MODÈLE**  **Fatima a besoin d'une chemise blanche….**

Apportez:
deux chemises blanches
une jupe noire
une paire de chaussures noires
un manteau
une écharpe
un jean
deux pulls
une paire de bottes

J'ai:
une chemise blanche
une jupe rouge
une paire de chaussures noires
un manteau
un jean
un pull

# Students connect to each structure topic...

- ## visually

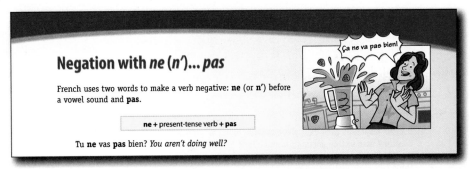

- ## contextually

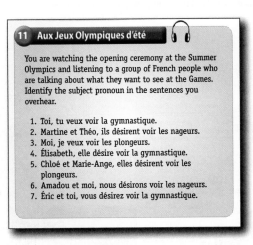

- ## meaningfully

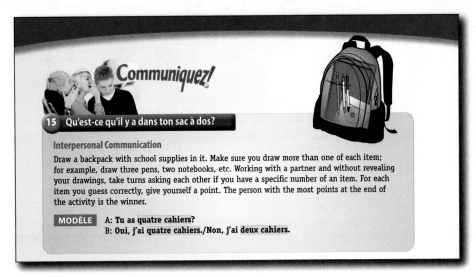

### Le Petit Nicolas

**22** Activités d'expansion

1. Use the responses from your chart to write a paragraph describing the point of view Goscinny uses in this selection from *Le Petit Nicolas*.
2. Rewrite the classroom scene above from the teacher's or George's point of view, using the third-person or first-person point of view.
3. Write a scene for a play based on the selection. Include parts for a narrator, the teacher, Georges, Maixent, and Joachim. Perform your scene for the class.

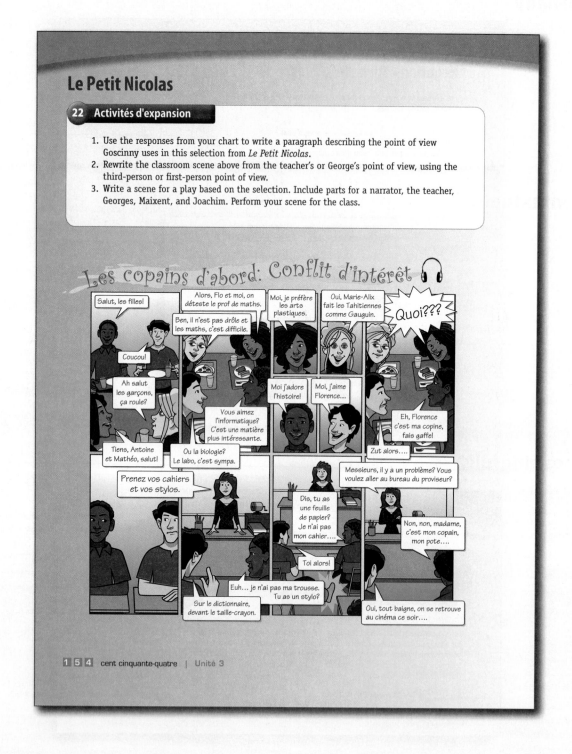

# *T'es branché?* provides two opportunities for reviewing:

## Évaluation

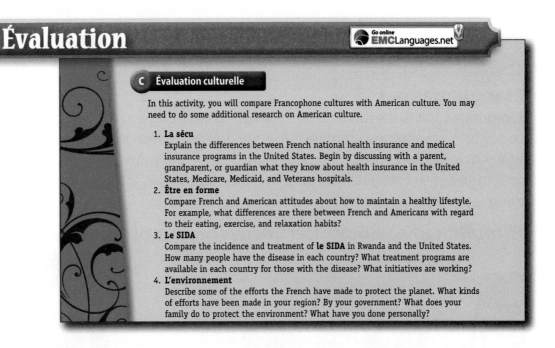

### C Évaluation culturelle

In this activity, you will compare Francophone cultures with American culture. You may need to do some additional research on American culture.

1. **La sécu**
   Explain the differences between French national health insurance and medical insurance programs in the United States. Begin by discussing with a parent, grandparent, or guardian what they know about health insurance in the United States, Medicare, Medicaid, and Veterans hospitals.

2. **Être en forme**
   Compare French and American attitudes about how to maintain a healthy lifestyle. For example, what differences are there between French and Americans with regard to their eating, exercise, and relaxation habits?

3. **Le SIDA**
   Compare the incidence and treatment of **le SIDA** in Rwanda and the United States. How many people have the disease in each country? What treatment programs are available in each country for those with the disease? What initiatives are working?

4. **L'environnement**
   Describe some of the efforts the French have made to protect the planet. What kinds of efforts have been made in your region? By your government? What does your family do to protect the environment? What have you done personally?

## Unité 8 Bilan cumulatif

### Speaking

VII. Tell the four stories suggested by the images.

A. Bruno et Caro    B. Antoine et ses copains    C. Malika    D. tu

1. Give the date, identify the season in each illustration, and describe the weather.
2. Describe what the people are doing in each illustration.
3. Then describe two to three activities that you like to do during each season.

# Key Features: Technology for Students

**Students have the technological tools they need to excel and learn at their own pace:**

- **EMCLanguages.net**
  **EMCLanguages.net** is the ideal blended-learning environment for world language students, and the ultimate, time-saving companion for teachers. This innovative online Learning Management System integrates proven methodologies with EMC's rich content to deliver authentic, interactive, and engaging learning experiences.

- **EPUB multimedia eBook offers delivery on multiple devices.**

- **Electronic flash cards help students master core vocabulary.**

une chemise

- **e-visuals allow for motivating vocabulary practice.**

| prêt-à-porter | chaussures | accessoires | mon panier |
|---|---|---|---|

**Faites votre shopping en ligne!**

lamodeados.fr

*Toute la mode du printemps!*

**La mode des filles**

Pantalon Fantaisie
Couleur: fushia
25,99 €

Jupe bicolore
Couleur: pas de variation
12,99 €

Pull-tunique
Couleur: vert, beige, blanc
21,99 €

**Pour les garçons**

Short Cargo KAPORAL
Couleur: disponible en beige, gris ou noir
15,99 €

T-shirt manches longues
Couleur: orange, bleu ou vert
27,99 €

Tenue Élégance
Couleur: pas de variation
67,99 €

- **Online Pre-tests offer immediate feedback.**

### Unité 1

### Leçon B

Complete the mini-dialogues by filling in the blanks.

1. -Salut, Nasser!
   -Salut, Aurélie! [ ]?
   -Oui. Top!

2. -Bonjour Professeur Novak. [ ]?
   -Très bien merci, Marcus.

3. -Ça va Mélanie?
   - Non, pas [ ].

4. -Au [ ]!
   -Ciao!

5. -Salut!
   -À [ ]!

6. -Moi, ça va. Et toi?
   -Comme [ ].

- **New continuous storyline DVD series, filmed on location in Nice, excites students.**

- **QR codes provide access to videos.**

Weihrauch, Michael/Tellus Vision Production AB, Lund Sweden

Online, print, and electronic resources for the page in question are listed here.

The Reference Desk offers additional background information, linguistic and pronunciation notes, and other relevant information about items on the page.

The Communication box includes Interpersonal, Presentational, and Interpretive activities for additional practice.

Additional information about cultural Practices, Products, or Perspectives is offered here, or additional culture activities.

Here you can find the essential parts of the day's lesson; these tips will help teachers organize the lesson and suggest a logical order of approach.

## RESOURCES

 **e-visuals 28-29**

 **Workbook 1–6**

 **Flash Cards**

 **Listening Activity**

## Reference Desk

The basic formula for determining temperature conversions is as follows ($T_f$ = Temperature in Fahrenheit; $T_c$ = temperature in Celsius):

$(T_f - 32) \times 5/9 = T_c$
$T_c \times 9/5 - 32 = T_f$

## Communication

**Interpersonal: Paired Practice**
Have students research the weather online for about 20 international cities. In groups, students will take turns saying what the weather is in a city according to their findings.

**Interpersonal: Cooperative Groups**

To practice weather expressions, have students sit in small groups. One student starts a round by saying a weather word, such as **beau**. The next student must use the word in a complete sentence about, as in **Il fait beau**. The next student must say that phrase in the negative. The activity continues until all have had a turn.

## Culture

**Practices: Information**
Consider showing the i-Culture video entitled **"L'équitation"** (2010-2011) to provide your students with a culturally authentic perspective related to the theme of this **Leçon**.

**3 9 6**

---

**Leçon A**

## Vocabulaire actif

 **Go online EMCLanguages.net**

### Quel temps fait-il? 🎧

**En été...**
il fait beau.
il fait du soleil.
il fait chaud.

**Au printemps...**
il pleut.

**En automne...**
il fait frais.
il fait du vent.

La température est de 20 degrés./Il fait 20 degrés. (Celsius).

**En hiver...**
il fait froid.
il neige.
il fait mauvais.

Chloé a chaud.  Pierre a froid.

**3 9 6**  trois cent quatre-vingt-seize  |  **Unité 8**

### Essential Instruction

1. Write the seasons on the board with the prepositions **en/au** and the articles **l'/le**. Have students practice saying and spelling them. Point out the silent "m" in **automne**.
2. Ask students, **"Quel temps fait-il aujourd'hui?"** Project images of the weather expressions, act them out, or draw them on the board. Have students repeat as a class, then practice in pairs.
3. Explain the difference between **il fait froid/ chaud** and **il a froid/chaud**.
4. Review and practice the Fahrenheit to Celsius conversion and vice versa.
5. Make the animal sounds in **Les animaux domestiques** and have students identify the animal. Demonstrate a few extra ones, such as **cocorico** (le coq/rooster), **meuh** (une vâche/cow), **hihan** (un âne/donkey), **coin coin** (un canard/duck).
6. Play the audio of **Pour la conversation** and have students repeat the sentences.
7. Present the vocabulary in **Et si je voulais dire...?**, explaining the difference between **il pleut** and **la pluie**, **il neige** and **la neige**.

## Les animaux domestiques

un chat

un oiseau

un chien

un poisson rouge

un cheval

## Pour la conversation 🎧

**H**ow do I extend an invitation?

> **Tu as envie de** faire une promenade avec moi?
> *Do you want to take a walk with me?*

**H**ow do I accept an invitation?

> **Bonne idée! Je suis disponible.**
> *Good idea! I'm free.*

**H**ow do I refuse an invitation?

> **Désolé(e). Je suis occupé(e).**
> *Sorry. I'm busy.*

### Et si je voulais dire...? 🎧

| | |
|---|---|
| **bruiner** | *to drizzle* |
| **Il fait du brouillard.** | *It's foggy.* |
| **Il y a des éclairs.** | *It's lightning.* |
| **la grêle** | *hail* |
| **la neige** | *snow* |
| **la pluie** | *rain* |
| **la météo** | *weather report* |

---

### RESOURCES

📖 Workbook 7–8

### Communication

**Presentational: Cooperative Groups**

Have students write a description about a pet that belongs to their family, a friend, or a celebrity, including the pet's name and what the pet likes to do in certain weather. Ask them to accompany the paragraph with a photo or drawing. Students will make a gallery of pet portraits for the wall and present them to the class. Consider having a contest to vote for the most handsome, funniest, oddest, etc.

### Game

**Des animaux domestiques**

Have students use gestures and actions to "describe" their pets as the rest of the class shouts out French phrases such as **Il est grand! Il dit Miaou!**, etc. to match the actor's movements. Students should continue until they guess the pet.

### Connections

Teach students that the metric system is used in most of the world, including Europe. Give them a set of temperatures in Celsius and ask them to convert them to Fahrenheit temperatures.

### Critical Thinking

Ask students to come up with a rule for describing many weather conditions after looking at those on the page. Then ask them to come up with a rule for saying "I'm hot" or "I'm cold." (Many weather expressions use the third-person-singular form of **faire**, while people's body temperatures are described with **avoir**.)

**3 9 7**

---

**Games may practice vocabulary, grammar, or culture knowledge.**

**Connections provides additional cross-curricular activities.**

**Critical Thinking activities ask students to apply, choose, interpret, solve, categorize, compare, contrast, criticize, distinguish, compose, construct, create, propose, etc.**

---

**Differentiated Learning**
**Expand**
Have students respond **vrai** or **faux** in response to statements you make about the weather in various places and seasons. Ask students to describe the weather in favorite locations. Demonstrate a weather expression and have students say what it is. Switch roles.

**Special Needs Students**
**Linguistically Challenged**
1. To help organize the vocabulary for students, have them complete a chart according to headings such as seasons, weather expressions, verbs, etc. You could also organize weather expressions by adjectives (**beau/chaud/frais**, etc.), nouns (**du vent, du brouillard,** and **du soleil**), and verbs (**il pleut, il neige**).
2. Go over the use of **il y a + du/de la/des + nom**, using the **Et si je voulais dire...?** vocabulary.

---

**Differentiated Learning tips help the teacher make sure advanced and slower-paced students have successful learning experiences.**

**Here teachers find tips for how to reach students with different learning styles, including multiple intelligences, or special needs.**

# Components

*T'es branché?* is a comprehensive four-level French language program written to meet the needs of French students of all abilities in the twenty-first century. The first-level program includes the following components:

- Student Textbook
- Annotated Teacher's Edition
- Workbook
- Workbook Teacher's Edition
- At-Standard Assessment Manual
- Communicative Activities
- Listening Activities
- Audio Program
- DVD Manual
- TPR Storytelling Manual
- EMCLanguages.net

## Student Textbook

*T'es branché?* contains ten units. Each unit is composed of three lessons, labeled A, B, and C. All the units are designed similarly so that both teachers and students will know what to expect. Each lesson gives students the vocabulary, functions, structures, and cultural information necessary to communicate in authentic French about a variety of everyday situations designed to appeal to teenagers. Vocabulary and structures are recycled in the first-level textbook and subsequent textbooks so that students can attain mastery of the concepts that are introduced by the time they complete the program. The headphones icon ⌒ indicates activities that are recorded in the audio program.

***Unit Opener*** – The unit begins with a photo spread, quotation (**Citation**) by a Francophone person of note, and fact (**À savoir**) that connect to the unit theme. The **Question centrale** is an essential question that frames the unit's contents, and that reappears throughout the unit. There is also a culture question accompanied by a photo for which students will find the answer somewhere in the culture readings of the unit. The electronic device pictured in the Unit Opener contains an image from the DVD program that accompanies the textbook; a question is asked to get students excited about seeing the episode that is aligned with the unit in question.

***Vocabulaire actif*** – Each lesson begins with colorful photos or illustrations that introduce coherent vocabulary groupings in a meaningful context. Students need to know that they are expected to learn these words and expressions. Also in this section are one or more functions under the *Pour la conversation* heading, and more advanced vocabulary for the students who want to move at a faster pace (*Et si je voulais dire...?*) and assimilate even more vocabulary in order to express themselves. Vocabulary practice activities follow the presentation, culminating in questions that are designed to elicit responses from students about their lives (*Questions personnelles*). One of the vocabulary practice options includes a listening activity. Another is a paragraph or other text that puts comprehensible input into practice, allowing students to "read" and understand the vocabulary words before using them.

***Rencontres culturelles*** – Next comes a short dialogue that dramatizes a situation typical of everyday life in Francophone regions. Written in France, these dialogues use authentic French speech and current expressions. Speakers may include one or more of the four main characters, their friends, parents, other relatives, or teachers. These teens all live in Paris.

**Yasmine** is an Algerian girl who is dating Maxim. She likes to shop with Camille and finds biology difficult. She is good friends with the other teens below.

**Maxime** is Yasmine's boyfriend. In Unit 8, Maxime and Yasmine have a romantic rendez-vous at the Tuileries. Maxime has a dog, and he has introduced Yasmine to his mother.

**Camille** likes to go inline skating at Pari Roller on Friday nights. In Unit 6 she goes clothes shopping with Yasmine.

**Julien** is an athletic boy who is good friends with Maxim. In Unit 10 he goes to Geneva with his parents.

These dialogues include the functions from the *Pour la conversation* box in the vocabulary spread. Also in the dialogue you will find an example of each structure topic that models for students how it can be used. All words in the dialogue are active vocabulary, though not all of them appear in the vocabulary presentation that precedes it. All dialogues were filmed in France, and the accompanying photo is a still shot from the film. A comprehension activity follows the dialogue to make sure students understand what transpired.

*Extension* – This is another dialogue but of a more advanced nature that requires students to read in context and perhaps even look up some words in their French-English dictionary. A critical thinking question follows each of these dialogues. The vocabulary in this dialogue will not be tested.

*Points de départ* – Directly after the dialogues, information about the francophone world is presented, in English through Unit 5, then in French beginning with Unit 6. These notes reflect the themes introduced in the first dialogue in the *Rencontres culturelles* section. Accompanying photos open a window on cultural practices, perspectives, and products. Certain products are defined and described in the *Produits* boxes, such as African masks, **pâté**, and Coco Chanel's little black dress. In this section, students are also asked to draw comparisons between Francophone cultures and their own (see *Comparaisons* graphic). After answering the *Questions culturelles*, students engage with culture further by participating in a discussion (*À discuter*) or reading a *Perspectives* note and answering a critical thinking question.

*Du côté des medias* – In this section, students read or skim or scan francophone realia and answer questions or complete an activity based on it. The realia ties into one of the notes in the *Points de départ*. Students might see a grocery store advertisement, a restaurant menu, or film ratings.

*La culture sur place* – In Lesson C, this section follows the culture notes and gets students to investigate and engage in an aspect of French culture. For example, students might be asked to examine American remakes of French movies, interview a traveler who has been to a francophone location, or shop online at French stores. The philosophy behind this section is explained in the Philosophy and Approach section of the Annotated Teacher's Edition front pages.

*Structure de la langue* – One or more grammar topics is presented and practiced in this section. You can find all the grammar topics covered in *T'es branché?* in the Scope and Sequence at the beginning of this Annotated Teacher's Edition. The contextualized practice activities that follow move from more mechanical activities to those that are more creative and open-ended. The activities allow for oral and written practice of the language structures, and students may be asked to work with a partner or group. Practice for one of the grammar topics includes a listening activity. (Unit 1 contains no grammar.) Where there is a model, the model sentence is highlighted so students know which parts of the sentence to replace.

*À vous la parole* – A series of proficiency-based activities follows the grammar section. Students have an opportunity to practice interpersonal, presentational, and interpretive communication here as well as in the vocabulary and grammar sections. In this section, the vocabulary, structures, and culture all come together and are integrated into activities that may be cooperative, task-based, oral, or written. For example, students may be asked to conduct a survey, engage in a dialogue at a store or restaurant, develop a book of recipes, perform metric conversations, organize a fashion show, or plan a trip to do humanitarian work.

*Prononciation* – This section is presented at the end of Lesson A in each unit. Written by a pronunciation expert in France who works with English speakers, it centers on pronunciation problems English speakers have with French sounds and pronunciation patterns.

*Stratégie communicative* – This section is presented at the end of Lesson B in each unit. Students learn various strategies for successful function-based oral and written communication activities. For example, students learn how to decode cognates, combine sentences to make longer sentences, write a postcard, practice descriptive writing or the art of communication, and tell a story through pictures.

**Lecture thématique** – This section is presented at the end of Lesson C in each unit. Authentic texts in French are studied with scaffolding that allows students to learn about literature, Francophone authors, and francophone art. First, students read a paragraph about the author, which concludes with a question designed to get students to focus on one of the main ideas of the text. Next, students learn a strategy with which to approach the text, always accompanied by a graphic organizer. A secondary tool for understanding another aspect of the text is highlighted with the *Outil de lecture*. With the pre-reading question, students connect to the theme of the text by comparing it to their own experience or observations. During reading questions, alongside the text, check to make sure students comprehend what is happening in the text. A post-reading question asks students to draw a main conclusion about the text. A painting or other art form accompanies the text. Students learn to appreciate art and art periods and techniques in *Le monde visuel*, which is designed to promote literacy in the visual arts. In the *Activités d'expansion*, students use the information from their graphic organizer to write about the meaning of the text in the first activity. Then, other, more creative activities connect students to the text. Further reading is provided in the *Les copains d'abord* cartoon; here students have the opportunity to learn some idioms and slang expressions in French. The *Lecture thématique* section provides students opportunities to improve their reading skills and helps to prepare them for the AP language exam.

**Projets finaux** – This section was designed for teachers who prefer performance-based assessment to traditional testing, or who like unit work to culminate in a meaningful project. The first activity, *Connexions par Internet*, provides a cross-curricular project that may be connected to art, architecture, math, science, or any number of academic disciplines. The focus of *Communautés en ligne* is to have students build online communities in the French-speaking world in projects that relate to the unit's theme. *Passez à l'action!* provides an engaging activity for students to work with their classmates to complete a project. Finally, *Faisons le point!* asks students to pull together all their learning from the unit and analyze it; one format occurs in odd-numbered units, another in even-numbered units.

**Évaluation** – There are six opportunities for reviewing unit content in this section: (A) listening comprehension; (B) oral communication; (C) culture comparisons; (D) written expression; (E) oral or written response to a visual; and (F) telling a story that uses unit content.

**Vocabulaire** – All words and expressions introduced as active vocabulary in *T'es branché?* appear in the end-of-unit vocabulary list.

**Bilan cumulatif** – Based on the AP exam, this section appears after every even-numbered unit and provides an assessment of listening, reading, writing, and speaking skills.

## Annotated Teacher's Edition

This Annotated Teacher's Edition contains a front section and an annotated version of the student textbook.

Front Section:

- Scope and Sequence charts for Levels 1 – 3
- Introduction
- Key program features
- Description of all the components in the program
- Author biographies
- Philosophy and approach
- Transcript of Textbook Listening Activities
- Correlation to Common Core State Standards

Annotated Version of the Student Textbook:

- Correlations of ancillary materials to the textbook (*Resources*)
- Answers to both oral and written activities
- Informational notes for teachers in the *Reference Desk*
- Culture notes or activities about products, practices, or perspectives (*Culture*)
- Interpersonal, presentational, or interpretive communicative activities (*Communication*)

- Total Physical Response (TPR) activities
- Activities that use critical thinking skills (*Critical Thinking*)
- Additional cross-curricular activities (*Connections*)
- Games
- Additional activities or adaptations of textbook activities (*Expansion*)

The annotated version of the expanded student textbook contains icons in the Resource boxes at the top of the wraparound pages. These icons are:

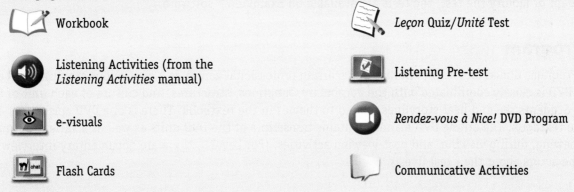

| | | | |
|---|---|---|---|
| Workbook | | Leçon Quiz/*Unité* Test | |
| Listening Activities (from the *Listening Activities* manual) | | Listening Pre-test | |
| e-visuals | | *Rendez-vous à Nice!* DVD Program | |
| Flash Cards | | Communicative Activities | |

## Workbook

The workbook reviews and expands on the material covered in the textbook with additional written exercises that reinforce students' language skills and cultural awareness. To make sure the workbook provides for differentiated instruction, there are basic activities marked with an "A" and more advanced activities marked with a "B," for example "1A" and "6B."

## Workbook Teacher's Edition

This is the student workbook, but with answers in bold.

## Communicative Activities

Since effective communicative activities are integral to the success of a proficiency-oriented French-language program, this online manual provides additional oral and written communicative practice for students. Information gap activities and situation cards allow for interpersonal communication and student-to-student interaction. Also in this manual are conversation grids, activities based on an illustration, and surveys; an e-mail writing activity; and a writing activity based on the conversation grids, activities based on an illustration, or surveys.

## Listening Activities

This online manual provides seven additional listening comprehension activities for each unit, two for each lesson and a cumulative dialogue that synthesizes the vocabulary and grammar from the whole unit. Students are provided with an answer sheet they fill in while they listen. These activities help prepare students for the listening comprehension sections of the Unit Tests in the Assessment Program. An answer key is provided at the end of the manual that also includes complete scripts.

## Textbook Audio Program

The online audio program contains language-production activities, and all the listening comprehension activities in the textbook: one vocabulary and grammar activity for every lesson, the listening activity in the *Évaluation* section, and the first activity of the *Bilan cumulatif*. The *Vocabulaire actif*, dialogues, *Points de départ*, and reading selection have also been recorded.

## Assessment Manual

The *T'es branché? Assessment Manual* is a print version of the At-Standard test that is also found as a prescribed test on the *Teacher Resources DVD* (see Multimedia Technology and Teacher Resources DVD). It contains Lesson Quizzes, Unit Tests, and Proficiency Tests. Each quiz tests student achievement in vocabulary, culture, structure, and speaking. There are three quizzes for each unit, or one per lesson. The Unit Tests contain these sections: vocabulary, structure, proficiency writing, speaking, listening comprehension, reading, and culture. Teachers are encouraged to test their students in the areas that have been practiced in class during the unit. For teachers who want to adapt or modify the test, the tests are available on ExamView® software.

## DVD Program

The DVD Program, filmed on location in Nice and starring professional actors, is a continuous storyline for Levels 1-2. Each DVD is closely coordinated with the vocabulary, functions, structures, and culture of each unit of the textbook. Students see and hear storylines related to themes in the textbook. There is one DVD episode for each unit in the textbook. The online DVD manual contains transcripts of the DVD units as well as a variety of innovative pre-viewing, during viewing, and post-viewing activities. (For Level 3, there are documentary interviews with some of the actors about their real lives.)

## TPR Storytelling Manual

Each unit of this manual contains three mini-stories, one for each lesson, and a comprehensive unit story that are correlated to the content of *T'es branché?* Teachers can present each mini-story and unit story as a class reading, a homework reading, or a reading comprehension assessment. In the beginning of the manual, the TPR Storytelling philosophy is explained, and there is an introductory story that uses high-frequency vocabulary so teachers can see if they like the TPR storytelling approach and decide if they would like to incorporate the stories for the units into their instruction. Each story is accompanied by a series of illustrations.

## Lectures thématiques

Additional readings, including some realia pieces, are available in this manual. The format is similar to the *Lecture thématique* section of the student book.

## Activities for Mastery

The activities presented here offer ideas for instruction from an experienced French teacher who has taught all the levels of high school French. Whether teachers have a few minutes at the end of the class, or need to introduce or reinforce a concept, *Activities for Mastery* is there to help teachers plan their instruction with activities that are fun, educational, and innovative.

## Copy Masters

To save time in the class, there is a manual with blackline masters for all the graphs, charts, maps and other graphics that are in the student edition.

# Multimedia Technology

## EMCLanguages.net

EMCLanguages.net is EMC Publishing's online resource center for many of the *T'es branché?* ancillary materials. Online delivery of classroom materials allows students to access them in an electronic, interactive format and connect to the classroom in new ways using blended instruction. Visit EMCLanguages.net to see all that is available for your students.

- **Lesson Planner**

  Each day's lesson plan, whether for a traditional class or block scheduling, presents the core materials from the textbook and key ancillaries to include in instruction. Teachers can access the ancillary manuals within the lesson planner.

- **e-visuals**

  These digital "transparencies" reinforce the vocabulary presented in the textbook. Some of them are interactive.

- **Electronic Flash Cards**

  These flash cards are an essential component of the differentiated-learning classroom because students can practice over and over again until they master the vocabulary. Each vocabulary word is illustrated and the vocabulary word or expression is also visible spelled out.

- **Drill and Practice Games**

  Students master the vocabulary and structures in *T'es branché?* with activities that provide immediate feedback, telling students if their answer is right or wrong.

- **WebQuests**

  A WebQuest is an inquiry-oriented activity for which students use online resources. There is a WebQuest for each lesson of *T'es branché?*

- **Pre-AP Listening**

  Students hear a short listening segment and answer multiple-choice questions as on the AP test. If they get any of the questions wrong, they can then see and hear the video in order to have a more successful listening experience.

- **Pre-tests**

  There is a pre-test for each lesson of *T'es branché?* Students receive immediate feedback by completing sentences about vocabulary, grammar, culture, and listening so that they know what they need to review before they take each Lesson Quiz or Unit Test.

- **ExamView® Assessment Program**

  Teachers choose between a prescribed test for At-Standard, Slower-Paced, or Advanced students, or they can make their own test that responds to the needs of their students. There is a quiz for every lesson. Each quiz consists of vocabulary, culture, structure, and speaking. Each prescribed Unit Test covers vocabulary, structure, proficiency writing, speaking prep, speaking, listening comprehension, reading, and culture.

## Teacher Resources DVD

The Teacher Resources DVD is a one-stop resource where teachers can find all the resources for the program:

- Annotated Teacher's Edition
- Textbook Audio Program
- Lesson Plans
- Workbook
- Drill and Practice Games
- e-visuals
- Textbook Dialogue Videos
- DVD Program
- Listening Activities
- Activities for Mastery
- Communicative Activities
- Copy Masters
- Lectures thématiques Manual
- TPR Storytelling
- Pre-AP Listening
- Electronic Flash Cards
- Assessment (ExamView® and Print)

# Philosophy and Approach

## World Language Learning in the 21st Century

**By Toni Theisen**

Our world is an ever increasingly diverse, globalized, and complex, media-saturated society. Our 21st-century learners need a multi-sensory and multi-layered learning environment that is designed to inspire creativity, synthesis, and collaboration, as well as provide opportunities to analyze, reflect, and evaluate. So what are the critical skills and multiple literacies that our students will need in order to successfully participate in the global community of today's world? How do we engage them in meaningful contexts that are relevant and challenging? How do we provide project-based learning opportunities that help students reach higher levels of proficiency? How do we help students set personal learning goals and become self-directed learners? How do we personalize learning?

Quite often 21st-century skills are equated with technology. True, technology is a part of the skills learners will need to master, but this concept is much broader. In 2010 ACTFL, in collaboration with the Partnership for 21st Century Skills organization, created the ACTFL World Languages 21st Century Skills Map for Pre-K-16. The Partnership for 21st Century Skills P21 is a national organization that advocates for 21st-century readiness for every student framed within 12 skill areas and four interdisciplinary themes.

**Here are the twelve skills statements from the ACTFL World Languages 21st Century Skills Map and their topics:**

1. **Communication**
   Students as effective communicators use languages to engage in meaningful conversation; to understand and interpret spoken language and written text; and to present information, concepts, and ideas.

2. **Collaboration**
   Students as collaborators use their native and acquired languages to learn from and work cooperatively across cultures with global team members, sharing responsibility and making necessary compromises while working toward a common goal.

3. **Critical Thinking and Problem Solving**
   Students as inquirers frame, analyze, and synthesize information as well as negotiate meaning across language and culture in order to explore problems and issues from their own and different perspectives.

4. **Creativity and Innovation**
   Students as creators and innovators respond to new and diverse perspectives as they use language in imaginative and original ways to make useful contributions.

5. **Information Literacy**
   Students as informed global citizens access, manage, and effectively use culturally authentic sources in ethical and legal ways.

6. **Media Literacy**
   Students as active global citizens evaluate authentic sources to understand how media reflect and influence language and culture.

7. **Technology Literacy**
   Students as productive global citizens use appropriate technologies when interpreting messages; interacting with others; and producing written, oral, and visual messages.

8. **Flexibility and Adaptability**
   Students as flexible and adaptable language learners are open-minded, willing to take risks, and accept the ambiguity of language while balancing diverse global perspectives.

9. **Initiative and Self-Direction**
   Students as life-long learners are motivated to set their own goals and reflect on their progress as they grow and improve their linguistic and cultural competence.

10. **Social and Cross-Cultural Skills**

    Students as adept language learners understand diverse cultural perspectives and use appropriate socio-linguistic skills in order to function in diverse cultural and linguistic contexts.

11. **Productivity and Accountability**

    Students as productive and accountable learners take responsibility for their own learning by actively working to increase their language proficiency and cultural knowledge.

12. **Leadership and Responsibility**

    Students as responsible leaders leverage their linguistic and cross-cultural skills to inspire others to be fair, accepting, open, and understanding within and beyond the local community.

## Interdisciplinary Themes

### Global Awareness

Language education and cultural understanding are at the heart of developing global awareness for students. In order to understand and address global issues, it is important to understand the perspectives on the world that speakers of other languages bring to the table. By learning other languages, students develop respect and openness to those whose culture, religion, and views on the world may be different. Language students are able to interact with students from the target language in order to discuss and reach solutions regarding global issues.

### Financial, Economic, Business, and Entrepreneurial Literacy

Students in language classes learn about the financial and economic issues from the target language culture and are able to compare and contrast with those of the U.S. According to the Committee for Economic Development (CED), "...cultural competence and foreign language skills can prove invaluable when working on global business teams or negotiating with overseas clients." Those who are able to communicate with others in their native language will naturally feel more empowered to negotiate with those around the world as they engage in entrepreneurial activities.

### Civic Literacy

Language learners become aware of the judicial, legislative, and government functions of the target language country/countries and are able to compare and contrast those with the civil liberties and responsibilities in the U.S. Because they can communicate in the target language, they are able to engage in discussions with other students to participate in activities in which they discuss civic life in their respective countries.

### Health Literacy

Language learners are engaged in a value-added activity as they can address global health and environmental issues in the target language and understand materials that were written for native speakers of that language. They have access to information because they can understand the language and can thus engage in global discussions on health, environmental, and public safety issues as they prepare for careers in these fields.

So by focusing on these essential skills, the interdisciplinary themes and the integration of technology in a meaningful, relevant standards-based curriculum, teachers can empower students to actively participate in the global community.

Sources:

ACTFL World Languages 21st Century Skills Map

Partnership for 21st Century Skills

# Oral Proficiency in the 21st Century

### By Toni Theisen

"I want to learn how to speak the language" is the most common goal of most world language learners. But what is oral proficiency and how do learners demonstrate their progress toward this goal?

At the center of the national standards are the three modes of communication. The interpersonal and the presentational modes are focused on both oral and written communication. In the interpersonal mode learners engage in conversation, provide and obtain information, express feeling and emotion, and exchange opinions. This mode occurs in two-way, spontaneous exchanges that involve negotiation of meaning and is unrehearsed. Activities and strategies include debates, discussions, phone calls, Skyping, asking for and giving directions, and conversations with friends about making plans.

In the presentational mode, learners present information, concepts and ideas to an audience of listeners or readers on a variety of topics. It is one-way, planned and can be rehearsed. There is no feedback from another person. Some activities and strategies include creating videos, telling a story, delivering a speech, creating a public service announcement or other podcasts, or presenting a skit or play.

Teachers can assess language performance in terms of ability to use the language effectively and appropriately in real-life situations using a rubric that can measure proficiency. Students need to demonstrate what they "can do." The Linguafolio is an excellent source for "can do" statements at different proficiency levels. The "can do" statements are a perfect resource to use to create learner targets for each thematic unit, help students set personal goals and provide a clearer explanation to parents about what their children are learning in their language classes.

Open-ended performance assessments are the best ways to determine growth in oral proficiency. Rubrics and feedback should be put in kid-friendly terms, so students know what they can do to improve. Each assessment needs to be designed to show what a student is able to do with the language in order to elicit meaningful feedback.

With *T'es branché?*, students gain practice in the three modes of communication in vocabulary and structure activities, as well as the *À vous la parole* and *Projets finaux* sections. Rubrics for spoken and written communication can be found at emclanguages.net. A student contract on the Unit Opener page makes it clear to students what material they will be responsible for learning and helps them take ownership of this content from the beginning. Students reflect on what they can do and what they can learn to do better in *Faisons le point!* at the end of each unit. The final projects are designed to showcase student learning and make students feel successful, engaged, and purpose-driven in their French language learning experiences with *T'es branché?*

# A New Emphasis in Teaching Culture: Explore and Investigate *sur place*

### By Pamela M. Wesely

Foreign language teachers have examined and debated the issue of teaching culture in the foreign language classroom for many years. One of the ways that *T'es branché?* attempts to respond to this debate is through the presentation of *La culture sur place* sections in every unit. They are designed to engage students differently with francophone culture(s) by promoting a spirit of inquiry and treating the students as social actors, not as passive recipients of culture. The idea of developing intercultural competence in the language classroom rather than relying solely on teaching *about* the target culture(s) is not a new one, but it is one that has rarely been incorporated into a textbook.

The format of these sections varies throughout the text, but generally one of six different styles of activity is used for each one.

- **Submersion:** Students are encouraged to feel that they are "on location" in a francophone culture observing, asking questions, finding answers, drawing conclusions, and finding different perspectives and viewpoints. They report on their findings to the class.

- **Poll:** Students conduct a survey of their fellow students that parallels a survey of French or Francophone people. The students can then draw conclusions from a comparison of the results, focusing on current characteristics and realities in francophone cultures, as well as the diversity of their own lives.

- **Advocacy:** Students write a plan for taking action, getting their voices heard, and/or advocating for a specific population in the face of human rights abuses, current events issues, or other potential areas for discussion.

- **Reaction**: Via self-assessment, students examine potential areas of discomfort with French or Francophone cultures, and perhaps identify what they might need to do to gain more comfort in or become more habituated to the practices of these cultures.
- **Comparison**: Students take two explicitly different but related phenomena (encompassing products, practices, and perspectives) in their own culture and the target culture(s) and examine why those two phenomena might be different.
- **Contact**: Students investigate the reality of one individual from a French-speaking culture through an interview conducted in written form or face-to-face.

  "Culture" in *La culture sur place* is thus not intended to be something to be learned, but rather something to be explored, questioned, and examined. Students will be able to use their 21st-century skills in applying themselves to get through the steps of these activities that are meaningful, structured, and that allow for student self-expression.
- **Note**: Some of the activities in *La Culture sur place* might take some preparation several weeks before the actual activity takes place. One notable example of this is the *Unité 5* activity involving identifying individuals from French-speaking countries for the students to interview.

## Teaching Grammar to Enhance Communication

"I took French for three years and I can't say anything." Perhaps you know someone with such an experience with language instruction. The drill-and-practice instruction of yesteryear relied on mechanical, repetitive exercises that were not linked to meaningful expression. Today's teachers still want their students to learn grammatical concepts incrementally so that their language production doesn't fossilize. They also want their students' oral and written expression to be comprehensible to native speakers, acceptable in different social contexts, and accurate. To reach these goals, today's teachers often provide activities that allow for structured input (learning the grammar rules and examining models), structured output (practicing the grammar point in communicative exercises), and communicative output (doing a communicative task that uses the grammar point).

### Structured Input

In *T'es branché?*, grammar points are presented concisely with the use of charts and examples. Students can use these pages as reference when they want to try to expand on their expression; they don't have to learn everything at once. For example, they may learn quickly how to use the **passé composé** in declarative sentences, but can refer back to the grammar presentation later in order to see how to form a question using inversion in the **passé composé** for an interview or survey. Many of the examples used in the grammar presentation come from the first *Rencontres culturelles* dialogue that students can hear and see as many times as they'd like on their mobile devices.

### Structured Output

*T'es branché?* begins with more mechanical activities, then builds to activities that are more creative, meaningful, and open-ended. A mechanical activity might ask students to insert the right preposition before the names of cities, countries, and continents they learned about in the culture readings. A creative activity might have them use the adverbs **bien**, **un peu**, **beaucoup** with the verb **aimer** to report on critics' reviews of new French films. A meaningful and more open-ended activity might include interviewing their partner about their lifestyle habits for the week and then writing sentences using **toujours**, **souvent**, or **ne (n')... pas souvent** or **ne (n')... jamais** to describe those weekly activities. For example: **Zach ne mange jamais de légumes frais.**

### Communicative Output

In the *À vous la parole* section, students put their knowledge of grammar to use in interpretive, presentational, and interpersonal communication activities. For example, they might use **il faut** in a conversation at the doctor's office, describe a photo of their family using possessive adjectives, or use a French TV guide to tell what programs they choose (**choisir**, regular **-ir** verb).

## Communicative Competence

Students build communicative competence by using *T'es branché?* in part because they learn grammar from a logical grammatical syllabus that builds on and recycles grammar points. Some teachers like to provide an immersion experience, having their students build structural knowledge naturally. For these teachers we have the TPR Storytelling manual, which is correlated to the textbook. Students will pick up on the grammar topics in the original story and soon be able to tell their own variation, using accurate and comprehensible grammar.

# Meeting the Needs of the 21st-Century Reader

**"Qui que vous soyez qui voulez cultiver, vivifier, edifier, attendrir, apaiser, mettez des livres partout."**

—Victor Hugo

*Whoever wishes to cultivate, enliven, edify, soften, pacify, put books everywhere.*

Reading research shows that successful readers read extensively, integrate information in the text with pre-existing knowledge, have a reading style that adapts to the text, are motivated, read for a purpose, and rely on different skills to comprehend a text. The readings in *T'es branché?* were designed to provide contextual reading activities that hone all of these skills and guide the reader to greater comprehension. These readings are always accompanied with supports to make every French student a successful reader.

## Successful Readers Read Extensively

In *T'es branché?* students read the dialogues (the second one in *Rencontres culturelles* is for students who want to go farther and faster), which incorporate the vocabulary, functions, structure, and culture of the lesson. In each lesson there is a comprehensible-input paragraph so that students can build understanding of the new vocabulary before using it. A piece of realia, such as a transportation schedule, calendar, movie schedule, map, or tourism website, appears in the section *Du côté des médias*. Beginning in Unit 6 of Level 1, students read the culture readings in French also. Their unit learning culminates in a literary selection, linked to the theme of the unit; pre-reading questions, strategies, guided reading questions, and post-reading questions help students feel that they can tackle literary selections with ideas and themes.

## Successful Readers Integrate Information in the Text With Pre-Existing Knowledge and Adapt to the Text

In the culture section, students are asked to connect to what they know about culture in the United States and Canada with *Comparaisons* questions, which become their starting point for comparisons with francophone cultures. The *Perspectives* questions ask students to consider a certain point of view of a French speaker in excerpts from songs, poems, blogs, etc. In the literary selection, students are asked a pre-reading question to connect the theme of the selection to their own experience. The repeated supports in these sections help students to adapt to the text, whether it is experiential (*Rencontres culturelles*), factual (*Points de départ*), opinion (*Perspectives*), informational (*Du côté des médias*), or literary (*Lecture thématique*).

## Successful Readers Are Motivated and Read for a Purpose

For whatever reason students are learning French (a love of languages, to test out of college French, to travel to French-speaking countries, to have an interesting career, etc.), the texts in *T'es branché?* underline their reasons for study, thus motivating them toward their goal. Students also read with a purpose: for enjoyment (the serial cartoon *Les copains d'abord*), for information (the culture section), to confirm prior knowledge (dialogues and the culture section), or to evaluate ideas (the literary selections), and to grapple with other points of view (*Perspectives*). Students who want to learn more about a certain culture topic will benefit from the "Search words" underneath each culture paragraph that connect them to texts online.

### Successful Students Rely on Different Skills to Comprehend a Text

Although woven throughout the various reading activities of each unit, specific strategies that can help students read more quickly and effectively receive greater focus in *Lecture thématique* and the manual with the same name, and include previewing, predicting, skimming and scanning, monitoring their comprehension, using text organization, tacking difficult vocabulary, visualizing, writing things down (with the help of graphic organizers), guessing from context, and paraphrasing.

Since research has shown that reading is the skill that endures the longest, French students who study with *T'es branché?* will be on their way to becoming life-long readers of French: successfully reading literary selections; reading nonfiction; and reading Internet, reference, and visual materials.

## Immersion Lessons in the Non-immersion Classroom

### Connecting to Literature and Art

"The subject matter class is a language class if it is made comprehensible to the language student."

—Krashen

Research has shown that immersion experiences provide the best experience for language acquisition outside of interaction with a native community. Beginning with Unit 6, the sections of *T'es branché?* that easily lend themselves to immersion experiences are the *Lecture thématique* and *Le monde visuel*, both in Lesson C. Students can build a literary and artistic vocabulary, which will result in an appreciation and understanding of literature and art.

### La littérature

Begin the reading lesson by asking students to read the **Rencontre avec l'auteur**. Identify the time period of the writer by making a timeline on the wall and placing the names of the authors, as you encounter them, where they belong, along with a flag identifying their nationality. Have students identify the question at the end of the paragraph that they should be able to answer after having read the selection; you may want them to write it in their notebook and jot down ideas as they come to them when they read. Have students share responses to the **Pré-lecture** question as a class, unless you consider the question personal and want students to write a response in their notebook. Although the strategy is presented in English, you can give directions on how to complete it in French. Since interaction is the key to a good immersion experience, have students compare their graphic organizers in pairs or small groups. Put useful expressions on the board to help students share information, such as, **J'ai mis….**, **Pourquoi n'as-tu pas considéré…?**, **J'ai une autre idée**, etc.

You may want to begin the selection by playing the audio recording. Point out that there will be words students won't know, but these words are glossed below the selection. Wherever possible, a French synonym is given. Ask students to answer the **Pendant la lecture** questions after listening to the recording, or pause the recording where there is a question in order to monitor their comprehension. Then have students share their responses to the **Post-lecture** question in pairs or small groups, and ask for volunteers to share once you reassemble as a class. Finally, students do the **Activités d'expansion**. Encourage students to publish their writings on the Internet and put some in their portfolio so they can see how they improve at analyzing literature over time.

### L'art

To familiarize your students with keys to understanding art as presented in **Le monde visuel**, you may want to have students keep a notebook in which they define the art terms they encounter with each new painting. Provide them with some words and expressions to answer the question(s) at the end of each paragraph. Have students work in pairs to answer the question(s).

In Level 2, you might begin with an overview of the basic art movements, since not all the art movements are covered in *T'es branché?*, so that students understand the basic characteristics of each movement. The chart that follows provides simple phrases you can use to distinguish these movements. Bring in art books and pass around paintings by the artists mentioned so students understand which artists are associated with each movement and the evolution of French art. Students should learn these types of paintings: **la nature morte, le portrait, l'auto-portrait, le paysage, la scène**. Post some examples in class and do a station activity in which they identify the type of painting and the movement.

## Overview of Art Movements

| Mouvement | Dates approximatives | Charactéristiques | Peintres |
|---|---|---|---|
| Renaissance | 1492 – 1600 | Inspirée par la Renaissance italienne<br><br>Conception nouvelle du portait<br><br>Débuts du paysage, par exemple, dans la *joconde* | Léonard de Vinci<br><br>Fouquet<br><br>Clouet<br><br>Dubreuil<br><br>(Ambroise) Dubois |
| Classicisme | 1575 – 1700 | Sujets nobles de l'antiquité, de la mythologie, de la Bible<br><br>La symétrie dans la composition | Poussin<br><br>Charles Le Brun |
| Baroque | 1625 – 1700 | Histoires viennent des légendes, de la mythologie, de la Bible<br><br>Couleurs chaudes et vives<br><br>Sentiments visibles sur les visages<br><br>L'asymétrie dans la composition<br><br>Impression du mouvement | Chardin<br><br>Fragonard<br><br>Lebrun<br><br>Lorrain<br><br>Poussin |
| Rococo | 1730 – 1789 | Compositions frivoles et légères<br><br>Scènes pastorales et aristocrates | Boucher<br><br>Watteau |
| Néo-classicisme | 1760 – 1830 | Inspiré par Rome antique<br><br>Style plus simple que rococo<br><br>Allégories, mythologie comme sujets | David<br><br>Gérard<br><br>Gros |
| Romantisme | 1775 – 1850 | Rejet du classicisme (trop rigide)<br><br>Désir de montrer l'idéal, les sentiments, l'exotique, les fantaisies du peintre | Delacroix<br><br>Gros<br><br>Géricault |
| Réalisme | 1830 – 1890 | Sujets les scènes de la vie courante<br><br>Observation<br><br>Stylisation<br><br>Coloration sombre | Corot<br><br>Courbet<br><br>Daumier<br><br>Millet<br><br>Fantin-Latour |
| Impressionnisme | 1850 – 1900 | Rejet de l'art académique<br><br>Note les impressions fugitives avec une touche rapide<br><br>Taches de couleurs juxtaposées se recomposent à une distance | Monet<br><br>Renoir<br><br>Pissarro<br><br>Sisley<br><br>Morisot<br><br>Bazille<br><br>Manet |
| Cubisme | 1907 – 1914 | Sujets décomposés<br><br>Formes géométriques | Picasso, Gris<br><br>Braque |

# Differentiated Instruction and *T'es branché?*

Differentiated instruction occurs when teachers design learning to meet individual student needs. It differentiates between **content** (the materials the student needs to learn); **process** (practice that allows the student to learn the material; **products** (projects that get the student to rehearse, apply, and extend his or her learning); and, according to Carol Ann Tomlinson, fosters a positive **learning environment** (the way the classroom functions and feels).

Tailoring activities to different ability levels in your classroom can be time-consuming, so having a program like *T'es branché?* that is designed to meet differing ability levels and learning styles means you won't have to develop many materials on your own. Below are a few examples from *T'es branché?* for each aspect of differentiated instruction.

## Content

1. **Use reading materials for different ability levels.**

   *T'es branché?* has a basic dialogue and a more advanced dialogue in each lesson; the advanced dialogue is called *Extension*. If a literary selection in *Lecture thématique* is too easy or hard for a student, pick an alternative for him or her in the *Lectures thématiques* manual. Ideas for differentiated learning appear in the Annotated Teacher's Edition wraparound notes.

2. **Present materials visually and auditorily.**

   For the visual learner, *T'es branché?* includes many activities based on a visual illustration, piece of realia, or graphic. Take advantage of the e-visuals and electronic flash cards for learning vocabulary, for example. Students are encouraged to fill out graphic organizers throughout *T'es branché?* to help them conceptualize and form ideas. *T'es branché?* has seven listening activities in every odd-numbered unit, eight for even-numbered units; also, the first dialogue in the *Rencontres culturelles* section is available as a video and an audio mp3 file; these listening activities will help students who learn best aurally.

3. **Use materials that result in analysis and evaluation.**

   While some students may find their comfort area in knowledge, comprehension, and application, *T'es branché?* allows for analysis and evaluation as students progress and move forward to reach their potential.

## Process

1. **Provide opportunities for students to work in pairs and groups.**

   Students learning with *T'es branché?* receive many opportunities to work cooperatively in pairs and groups.

2. **Adapt instruction to meet Multiple Intelligences and other learning styles.**

   Different learning styles are built into the activities of *T'es branché?*; suggestions for implementation appear in the Annotated Teacher's Edition wraparound notes.

3. **Provide differentiated testing.**

   With *T'es branché?*, students can be tested with a slower-paced test, an at-standard test, or an advanced test.

## Products

1. **Provide opportunities for communication.**

   With the *T'es branché?* program, students learn to enact dialogues (interpersonal communication); write memos, e-mails, postcards, etc. (presentational communication); and make presentations based on online research (interpretive/presentational communication).

2. **Provide challenging and engaging tasks.**

   The activities in *T'es branché?* move from those that are more mechanical to those that are meaningful, open-ended, and creative. Students practice recalling, check their comprehension, apply what they have learned, analyze, synthesize, and evaluate using *T'es branché?*

3. **Provide a variety of final projects based on learning styles.**

   Students have the opportunity to develop three types of final projects in *T'es branché?*: *Connexions par Internet, Communautés en ligne,* and *Passez à l'action!* In the first students do cross-disciplinary research in

French using presentational communication. In the second they reach out to or learn about a francophone community online that results in interpersonal or presentational communication. The third activity may have them designing the house of the future, researching French links to the Olympics, or donating books to Africa, often as a group activity.

## Learning Environment

People passing by your classroom will see a lot of activity when you teach with *T'es branché?*, but it is a good idea to have days for working quietly without distraction too to keep all your students comfortable. Qualitative assignments in *T'es branché?* mean that students dig deeper and go beyond comprehension questions; learning revolves around an essential question that ties each unit together and that allows for reflection on learning in *Faisons le point!* The technology that accompanies *T'es branché?* means that your students can be engaged every day with video, audio, interactive e-visuals, electronic flash cards—using a variety of electronic devices—having fun while they learn at their own pace because you have planned and organized instruction that accommodates their learning styles.

# Blended Learning in the Second Language Environment

## A Blended Learning Success Story

The overwhelming success of the Khan Academy, which provides free lessons on the Internet, is a wake-up call for teachers who are not using much online instruction in the classroom. Khan Academy currently has 3.5 million users per month, and its free lessons have been viewed more than 82 million times. The increased success rate of students using this free tool is a testament to the potential of blended learning.

## What Is Blended Learning?

Blended learning occurs when teachers combine face-to-face learning with online learning. With self-paced e-learning, students experience differentiated learning. In a blended learning environment activities that may have previously taken place during classroom time are moved online. In one model, student might meet in the traditional classroom only a couple times per week and do the rest of their learning online.

## What Kind of Blended Learning Experience Can I Create for My Students with *T'es branché?*

Today's students are digitally literate, interactive, experiential, social, and possess strong visual-spatial skills. They look for fast response times and are adept at multi-tasking. *T'es branché?* is motivated by the belief that to be successful teachers need to communicate in the language and style of today's students. To achieve this goal, we have created materials that coordinate with a blended learning approach that allows for three types of learning:

| Face-to-Face Learning | Self-Paced Learning | Online Collaborative Learning |
| --- | --- | --- |

## Face-to-Face Learning

Classroom learning with *T'es branché?* centers on the three modes of communication: interpersonal, presentational, and interpretive, or a combination of these. Activities move from mechanical to meaningful to more creative and open-ended as students progress with concepts and information. Assessment is geared to the level of the student with three possibilities for testing: tests for the advanced learner, tests for the at-standard learner, and tests for the slower-paced learner.

## Self-Paced Learning

In today's student-centered classroom, students need to be able to learn at their own pace. To learn vocabulary, *T'es branché?* allows for students to learn words and expressions at their own pace with electronic flash cards and e-visuals, some of which are interactive. In the culture section, called *Points de départ*, students can find out more online about any covered topic by using Search words that are provided under each informational (cultural practices) paragraph. Students can learn each unit's content at their own pace with the interactive textbook; for example, they can listen to and watch the dialogues as many times as they need to. Students can see if they have learned the vocabulary and structure content by playing the *Drill and Practice Games*, which allow for immediate feedback. Immediate feedback is also provided in the online *Pre-tests* so that students can see what they need to go back and review before the Unit Tests. These are a few of the features of *T'es branché?* available on EMC's platform for online learning, emclanguages.net.

## Online Collaborative Learning

Students work collaboratively using *T'es branché?* in the *À vous la parole*, *La culture sur place*, and *Projets finaux* sections. Fun and worthwhile activities that they can participate in online include interviewing or surveying francophone teens, communicating with francophone communities, exchanging videos with other French or francophone classes, participating in a service project with other French speakers, posting and commenting on movie reviews, sharing and describing personal photos, and planning a class trip to a French-speaking location.

The blended learning approach of *T'es branché?* provides a technology-rich learning environment that responds to the needs and expectations of students and teachers of the 21st century and extends the second-language environment beyond the classroom. *T'es branché?* in conjunction with emclanguages.net speak the multi-media language of students today. *On est branché!*

# Pre-AP French Language and Culture

The new AP French Language and Culture exam is centered around themes, incorporates overarching essential questions, and focuses on the three modes of communication (interpersonal, presentational, interpretive). It also relies on authentic print, audio, and video materials, and requires students to comprehend cultural perspectives and make comparisons among cultures. These are some ways in which *T'es branché?* prepares students for the eventual AP French language exam:

- Units are organized thematically, for example, *La rue commerçante*, *Les gens que je connais*, and *Le weekend ensemble*.
- All units have an overarching question, a *Question centrale*, or essential question around which students frame their learning, for example: In what ways is learning another language beneficial? How is shopping different in other cultures? What makes a house a "home"?
- The culture readings (*Points de départ*) take students to French-speaking locations. The *Produits* boxes introduce key cultural products in French-speaking countries. The *Perspectives* questions get students to read excerpts from songs, poems, blogs, etc. and think about cultural perspectives in **la Francophonie**. Students also make comparisons to the cultures they know in this culture section. In *La culture sur place*, students experience French culture by investigating it and reflecting on it.
- Filmed dialogues (*Rencontres culturelles*) and a soap opera DVD program filmed in France allow for student engagement with authentic listening experiences. There are also seven listening opportunities in each unit, eight in the even units.
- *The Stratégies communicatives* provide clear and effective strategies to help students use the three modes of communication in activities that are meaningful, creative, and use criticial thinking skills.
- The *Lectures thématiques* present authentic texts from the French-speaking world (novels, poetry, dialogues, blogs, etc.) that students engage with using critical thinking skills. There are also readings in French in the culture section (beginning with Unit 6) and authentic texts in *Du côté des médias*.
- The *Projets finaux* allow students to build communities (*Communautés en ligne*), make connections (*Connexions par Internet*), and communicate in French to complete a French-based project (*Passez à l'action!*).

- Finally, the *Bilan cumulatif*, at the end of every other unit, provides a practice test experience in listening, reading, writing, composition, and speaking.
- The online resource Pre-AP Listening allows students to listen to audio that is followed by multiple-choice questions as on the AP French exam. However, since this is Pre-AP, students who can't answer the questions with audio alone are prompted to "watch" the video to help them understand before trying the questions again.

Students who use *T'es branché?* will learn to use French in real-life settings (Communities), demonstrate an understanding of francophone cultures (Culture), incorporate interdisciplinary learning (Connections), make comparisons between their cultures and languages and French-speaking cultures and French language (Comparisons), all the while communicating in French (Communication).

## *T'es branché?* and the International Baccalaureat

The International Baccalaureat (IB) program is recognized in many schools in 141 countries, with more than 1,300 schools participating in the United States. It seeks to develop global citizens with a strong sense of cultural awareness who recognize and develop universal human values. The program stimulates curiosity and inquiry as students learn and acquire knowledge across different disciplines in a quest toward lifelong learning.

With *T'es branché?*, students are exposed to **la Francophonie** in culture readings, activities, projects, and literature selections, so they move towards becoming global citizens who can embrace the big "C" and small "c" of places where French is spoken. They interact with Francophone students in *À vous la parole* and *Projets finaux* activities and projects. The section *La culture sur place* asks students to interact directly with Francophone culture as participants. Students see universal human values at work in the *Lecture thématique* selections and *Points de départ* sections, and build relationships working collaboratively with others in pair and group work. Pushing the boundaries of their knowledge in cross-disciplinary activities, they connect to math, literature, meteorology, art, science, technology, and many other subject areas.

Each unit of *T'es branché?* is organized around a *question centrale*, in a sense an umbrella under which all the content of the unit falls. At the end of the unit, students are asked to recapture and reflect on what they have learned and self-assess in the *Faisons le point!* section.

As students learn with *T'es branché?*, they begin to acquire important IB characteristics, becoming....

- **knowledgeable** about French language and culture
- **inquiring** about many subject areas
- **reflective** about human values, social issues, and their own learning process
- **open-minded** about other cultures, their values, and points of view
- **caring** about their classmates and Francophone students with whom they collaborate
- **communicative** as they interact orally and write memos, web pages, formal and informal letters, journal articles, reports on surveys they have taken, brochures, and critiques of books and films

With *T'es branché?* as a tool, IB students become great communicators who practice interpersonal, presentational, and interpretive language skills in activities and projects that are engaging, challenging, penetrating, and open-ended.

# Transcript of Textbook Listening Activities

The following is the transcript of the listening comprehension activities included in the *T'es branché?* These activities are recorded in the Audio Program. The following section contains a transcript of these recorded activities for teachers who prefer to read the activities aloud instead of using the recorded version. There is one vocabulary, one structure listening activity in each lesson, plus one in the *Évaluation* section; in every even unit there is also one for the *Bilan cumulatif*. (Unit 1 has fewer listening activities as it has no grammar.)

## Unité 1

### Leçon A

#### Vocabulaire

#### 1  Les présentations

Listen to the following short introductions and decide if the person who is being introduced is male or female. Write **M** for male or **F** for female.

1. Raoul:            Bonjour, Myriam! Je te présente ma copine, Catherine.
   Myriam:          Salut, Catherine!

2. Raoul:            Salut, Jean! Je te présente mon copain, Ahmed. Il est algérien.
   Jean:             Salut, Ahmed!

3. Raoul:            Bonjour, Madame Duteil! Je vous présente Monsieur Pradier.
   Mme Duteil:     Enchantée, Monsieur Pradier!

4. Raoul:            Salut, Nathalie! C'est Thomas, mon camarade de classe.
   Nathalie:        Salut, Thomas!

5. Raoul:            Bonjour, tout le monde! Je vous présente Mademoiselle Gentille.
   Tout le monde:  Bonjour, Mademoiselle!

6. Raoul:            Salut, Hugo! C'est ma copine, Leïla. Elle est française.
   Hugo:             Salut, Leïla! Enchanté.

### Leçon B

#### Vocabulaire

#### 1  Bonjour ou au revoir

Imagine you are on the streets of Paris listening to greetings and good-byes. Write **H** if the speaker says hello or **G** if the speaker says good-bye.

1. -Bonjour, Monsieur Sorette!
   -Bonjour, Madame Picard! Comment allez-vous?
2. -Salut, Hervé!
   -Salut, Gabrielle! À demain!
3. -Au revoir, Sophie!
   -Au revoir, Ahmed!
4. -À demain, Lilou!
   -À demain, Antoine!
5. -Salut, Christophe. Ça va?
   -Bonjour, Sabrina. Ça va très bien.
6. -À bientôt, Camille!
   -À bientôt, Jérémy!

## Leçon C

### Vocabulaire

### 1 On accepte, oui ou non?

You will hear a series of short conversations. Write **oui** if the second speaker accepts the invitation or **non** if he or she declines.

1. -On va au café?
   -Pas possible. J'aide ma mère.
2. -Tu voudrais aller à la teuf de Sandrine avec moi et ma copine Armelle?
   -Non, je ne peux pas.
3. -On va au centre commercial?
   -D'accord.
4. -Salut, Henri! Tu voudrais aller au centre commercial avec moi?
   -Je ne peux pas. Je dois faire mes devoirs.
5. -Salut, Ahmed! Je te présente mon copain, Xavier. On va au cinéma. Et toi?
   -Oui. Je veux bien.
6. -On va à la maison?
   -Eh bien, oui!
7. -Tu voudrais aller au café demain?
   -Non, je dois aider mon père.

### Évaluation

### A Évaluation de compréhension auditive

Listen to the dialogue, then read the statements below. Write **V** if the statement is **vrai** (*true*) and **F** if it is **faux** (*false*).

| | |
|---|---|
| Aïcha: | Bonjour, Maude. |
| Maude: | Bonjour, Aïcha. Comment ça va? |
| Aïcha: | Ça va bien, et toi? |
| Maude: | Pas mal. |
| Aïcha: | Je te présente mon cousin, Ahmed. Ahmed est algérien. |
| Maude: | Enchantée, Ahmed. |
| Ahmed: | Salut, Maude. On va au café. Et toi? |
| Maude: | Pas possible. Je dois faire mes devoirs. |
| Aïcha: | Bon alors, à demain. |
| Maude: | Oui, à demain. |

## Unité 2

### Leçon A

### Vocabulaire

### 1 Les projets de la semaine

Some students are talking about their week. In English write the day of the week each activity will take place.

1. Tu fais du vélo dimanche.
2. Mardi, je peux aller au cinéma.
3. Lundi, je fais du roller avec mes copains.
4. Jeudi, on va au café manger des hamburgers.
5. Vendredi soir, je fais du shopping après les cours.
6. Samedi, on va au centre commercial.
7. Mercredi, je peux sortir avec mes amis.

**Grammaire**

## 10 Identifiez le sujet!

Write the letter of the French subject pronoun that could replace each name or set of names.

1. Élodie
2. Marcel et Joël
3. Marie et Bruno
4. Jeanne et Anne
5. Amadou
6. Leïla

## Leçon B

**Vocabulaire**

### 1 C'est quelle activité?

Clément is asking his classmates about activities they enjoy. Choose the image that matches the activity you hear.

1. Clément: Salut, Fatima! Qu'est-ce que tu aimes faire?
   Fatima: J'aime beaucoup écouter de la musique.
2. Clément: Bonjour, Lucas! Qu'est-ce que tu aimes bien faire?
   Lucas: J'aime bien envoyer des textos.
3. Clément: Jean-Marc et Yasmine, qu'est-ce que vous aimez faire?
   Jean-Marc & Yasmine: Nous aimons lire.
4. Clément: Et vous, Maude et Mégane?
   Maude & Mégane: Nous aimons jouer aux jeux vidéo.
5. Clément: Cédric, tu aimes surfer sur Internet?
   Cédric: Oui, j'adore surfer sur Internet. C'est génial!
6. Clément: Et Coralie? Elle aime étudier?
   Cédric: Ah! Oui. Elle aime étudier.
7. Clément: Et Éric et Anaïs, ils aiment cuisiner?
   Cédric: Oui, ils aiment beaucoup cuisiner.

**Grammaire**

### 8 On aime un peu, bien, ou beaucoup?

Fill out a chart like the one below. Listen to each sentence twice. Then write the activity each teenager likes to do under the heading that indicates the degree to which they like doing that activity. Listen first to the model.

**Modèle: Fatima aime beaucoup téléphoner.**

1. Lucas aime beaucoup écouter de la musique.
2. Coralie aime un peu lire.
3. Lucas aime un peu cuisiner.
4. Lucas aime bien surfer sur Internet.
5. Coralie aime beaucoup faire du sport.
6. Lucas aime bien étudier.
7. Coralie aime bien envoyer des textos.
8. Lucas aime un peu regarder la télé.
9. Coralie aime beaucoup jouer aux jeux vidéo.

## Leçon C

### Vocabulaire

### 1 Les numéros de téléphone

Florence wants to invite her classmates to a party. She asks Thomas for their phone numbers. Write each phone number you hear.

1. Florence: Quel est le numéro de téléphone de Jasmine?
   Thomas: C'est le 01.19.02.12.03.
2. Florence: Quel est le numéro de Bertrand?
   Thomas: C'est le 01.13.13.18.07.
3. Florence: Et le numéro de Paul?
   Thomas: C'est le 01.05.09.17.11.
4. Florence: Quel est le numéro de Nasser?
   Thomas: C'est le 01.06.08.10.13.
5. Florence: Quel est le numéro de Moussa?
   Thomas: C'est le 01.15.15.03.04.
6. Florence: Et le numéro de Romane?
   Thomas: C'est le 01.14.20.11.04.
7. Florence: Quel est le numéro de Juliette?
   Thomas: C'est le 01.05.07.18.16.

### Grammaire

### 13 Un e-mail de France

French teenagers have written an e-mail to your class. Listen to each sentence twice. If you hear a masculine noun, write **M**. If you hear a feminine noun, write **F**.

1. Nous aimons bien le sport.
2. Nous aimons beaucoup le football.
3. Nous aimons la télé.
4. Nous préférons le cinéma américain.
5. Nous aimons la musique alternative.
6. Nous préférons le hip-hop américain et français.
7. Nous aimons bien la pizza.
8. Nous aimons bien le roller.
9. Nous aimons un peu le basket.

### Évaluation

### A Évaluation de compréhension auditive

Listen to the phone conversation and decide if the statements you hear are **vrai (V)** or **faux (F)**.

Nayah: Allô, Koffi?
Koffi: Salut, Nayah. Tu vas bien?
Nayah: Pas mal. Qu'est-ce que tu fais?
Koffi: Je surfe sur Internet et j'écoute de la musique.
Nayah: Qu'est-ce que tu écoutes?
Koffi: J'écoute Rachid Taha. C'est génial!
Nayah: Moi, je préfère le hip-hop.
Koffi: Tu voudrais aller au concert mercredi?
Nayah: Oui, je peux. J'invite Alexandre?
Koffi: Ah, non. Il préfère la musique alternative!
Nayah: Coralie? Elle aime bien le R'n'B et le hip-hop.
Koffi: D'accord. Quel est le numéro de téléphone de Coralie?
Naya: C'est le 05.03.13.20.19. À bientôt!
Koffi: Salut!

Recorded statements:

1. Koffi surfe sur Internet.
2. Nayah écoute la musique.
3. Koffi écoute Rachid Taha.
4. Nayah préfère la musique alternative.
5. Le concert, c'est vendredi.
6. Koffi invite Alexandre au concert.
7. Coralie adore le R'n'B et le hip-hop.
8. Le numéro de Coralie est le 01.02.12.20.17.

## Bilan cumulatif

### Listening

**I.**

You will hear a short conversation. Select the reply that would come next. You will hear the conversation twice.

| | |
|---|---|
| Marie: | Salut, Djamel! |
| Djamel: | Salut, Marie! Tu vas bien? |
| Marie: | Oui, super! Mon weekend est génial! |
| Djamel: | Qu'est-ce que tu fais ce weekend, mon amie? |
| Marie: | Mon père et moi, on regarde un film pendant qu'il fait mauvais. Et toi, tu joues aux jeux vidéo? |
| Djamel: | Non, je ne joue pas aux jeux vidéo ce weekend. |
| Marie: | Eh bien, qu'est-ce que tu fais? |

**II.**

Listen to the conversation. Select the best completion to each statement that follows.

| | |
|---|---|
| Alexis: | Natasha! On va fait du roller? Il fait beau! |
| Natasha: | Alexis, moi je préfère surfer sur Internet quand il fait beau. |
| Alexis: | Ah bon! Je déteste ça l'Internet, les blogues, les textos, et la télé! Et bien moi, je préfère faire du sport! |
| Natasha: | Ah oui!? Tu aimes jouer au basket? |
| Alexis: | Oui j'aime bien le basket et le foot, et je préfère faire du roller quand il fait soleil. C'est mon passe-temps préféré en été! Et toi? |
| Natasha: | Moi, je n'aime pas faire du roller. Je regarde beaucoup les Jeux Olympiques à la télé: le patinage artistique et le hockey sur glace. Et toi? |
| Alexis: | Regarder les Jeux Olympiques avec mon père et ma mère, c'est mon passe-temps préféré le weekend! C'est génial! |
| Natasha: | Tu voudrais bien regarder la télé? |
| Alexis: | D'accord! On regarde le hockey sur glace, le patinage artistique, et le ski alpin! |

# Unité 3
## Leçon A

### Vocabulaire

#### 2 Les prix

Some students are buying school supplies and items for their bedroom at the store. Number your paper from 1-8. Then match the correct price to the picture of each item you hear.

A. 79,89€     B. 2,30€     C. 5,75€     D. 4,49€     E. 1,29€     F. 56,30€
G. 30,50€     H. 3, 99€

1. - Bonjour, madame. J'ai besoin d'une trousse. Elle coûte combien, s'il vous plait?
   - Elle coûte cinq euros soixante-quinze.
2. - Lilou, tu as besoin d'un dictionnaire?
   - Oui, d'un dictionnaire français-anglais. C'est combien?
   - Trente euros cinquante.

3. - Combien coûtent les cahiers?
   - Ils coûtent deux euros trente.
4. - Léa a besoin d'un crayon.
   - Ce n'est pas cher! Un euro vingt-neuf.
5. - Et le taille-crayon, il coûte combien?
   - Il coûte trois euros quatre-vingt-dix-neuf.
6. - Pardon, monsieur. Il coûte combien l'ordinateur portable HP?
   - Il coûte soixante-dix-neuf euros quatre-vingt-neuf.
7. - Maman, j'ai besoin d'un cédérom français-espagnol.
   - Cinquante-six euros trente. D'accord!
8. - Mathis, ils coûtent combien les cinq stylos?
   - Ils coûtent quatre euros quarante-neuf.

## Grammaire

### 13 Qu'est-ce qu'on a?

Select the correct answer for each question you hear.

1. Tu as un livre de maths?
2. Marielle a une feuille de papier?
3. Vous avez un taille-crayon?
4. J'ai mon cahier d'histoire?
5. Sébastien et Rose ont un cédérom?

## Leçon B

### Vocabulaire

### 2 Les emplois du temps

Listen to Rosalie and Mathis talk about their schedules. Write in French each class or activity in the order it is mentioned.

Mathis: Salut, Rosalie!
Rosalie: Salut Mathis! On a quels cours ce matin?
Mathis: On a biologie à neuf heures. Puis, on a deux heures de maths avec Monsieur Lahalle.
Rosalie: Vraiment? Après les maths, on a quoi?
Mathis: On a anglais et après on mange à la cantine.
Rosalie: Et cet après-midi? On a informatique, espagnol, et EPS, n'est-ce pas?
Mathis: Oui, c'est ça!

## Grammaire

### 7 L'heure

Listen to each statement. Write **oui** if the time you hear matches the clock. Write **non** if it does not match.

1. Je vais à la maison à cinq heures et demie, le lundi.
2. Léa a cours de maths à dix heures et quart du matin.
3. Il est minuit vingt.
4. Kemajou et Jean-Luc jouent au foot à trois heures quarante-cinq le mercredi après-midi.
5. Tu as histoire-géo à neuf heures?
6. Le film sur Gauguin est à huit heures moins le quart du soir.
7. Le matin, Alexandre a cours à huit heures moins vingt-cinq.
8. On rencontre Thomas à quatre heures et demie, mercredi après-midi.
9. On va au centre commercial à trois heures moins le quart?
10. Sandrine mange le déjeuner à midi vingt-cinq.

## Leçon C

### Vocabulaire

### 2 Mercredi après-midi

Number your paper 1-6. Listen to Maxime interview his classmates about their activities on Wednesday afternoon. Identify each location.

1. Maxime: Omar, tu fais quoi le mercredi après-midi?
   Omar: J'étudie à la médiathèque.
2. Maxime: Et toi, Coralie?
   Coralie: Moi, je nage à la piscine.
3. Maxime: Salut Sabine, tu fais quoi mercredi après-midi?
   Sabine: Salut, Maxime! Je vais au café.
4. Maxime: Tu vas où, Sarah?
   Sarah: Je vais à la salle d'informatique pour mon projet d'histoire.
5. Maxime: Bonjour, Noémie! Tu fais du sport?
   Noémie: Non, moi, je fais mes devoirs à la maison.
6. Maxime: Et toi, Justin?
   Justin: Moi, je vais en ville au magasin de sports.

### Grammaire

### 16 Répondez aux questions!

A group of Tahitian teenagers is answering their friends' questions. Select the correct response to each question.

1. Est-ce que tu aimes ta prof de français?
2. Quand est-ce que vous avez chimie?
3. Combien coûte le taille-crayon?
4. Où est-ce que tu veux étudier samedi?
5. Avec qui est qu'ils vont au labo?
6. Tu as besoin de quoi pour le cours d'anglais?
7. Pourquoi est-ce que tu ne vas pas à la piscine avec nous?

### Évaluation

### A Evaluation de compréhension auditive

Listen to the conversation between Félix and his mother. Choose the appropriate answer to the questions.

Félix: Maman, j'ai besoin d'aller à Carrefour.
Maman: Bien sûr. Tu veux y aller à quelle heure?
Félix: À 5h30, après les cours.
Maman: D'accord. Tu as besoin de quoi?
Félix: J'ai besoin de crayons, de stylos, d'un cahier pour le cours de maths, de feuilles de papiers, et d'un cédérom français-anglais pour l'anglais bien-sûr.
Maman: Pourquoi tu as besoin d'un cédérom? Tu as un livre d'anglais, n'est-ce pas?
Félix: Oui, mais le prof veut aussi le cédérom.
Maman: Il coûte combien?
Félix: Il coûte 69 euros.
Maman: Oh là là, c'est cher. Je téléphone au proviseur pour lui demander pourquoi tu dois acheter un cédérom avec ton livre d'anglais.
Félix: Oh, non! Maman!!!

# Unité 4
## Leçon A

### Vocabulaire

### 3 Mélanie fait du shopping.

Mélanie is shopping at a sporting goods store. Write the name of the person she is shopping for and what she is buying in English.

1. J'achète un ballon de foot pour Pierre.
2. Sandrine va avoir le maillot de l'équipe de Marseille.
3. Pour Koffi, les chaussettes de mon équipe.
4. Je vais acheter un blouson pour Samia.
5. J'achète un blason pour le blouson de Thierry.
6. Pour Norbert, une casquette.
7. Je donne une écharpe à mon copain Loïc.
8. Marie-Hélène... pour elle des chaussures de foot!

### Grammaire

### 10 C'est le weekend!

*C'est le weekend! Choisissez la lettre de l'image qui correspond à chaque activité que vous et vos amis allez faire.*

1. Ce weekend, Vincent va aider sa mère.
2. Timéo va regarder le film avec moi.
3. Parce qu'il fait beau, nous allons nager.
4. Elles vont acheter des maillots de notre équipe de foot.
5. Je vais prendre un sandwich.
6. Rahina et Myriam, vous allez jouer aux jeux vidéo.

## Leçon B

### Vocabulaire

### 2 Une fête chez Jérémy

*Écrivez **A** si la personne à la fête de Jérémy a soif ou **B** si elle a faim.*

1. -Tu voudrais quoi, Coralie?
   -Un jus d'orange.
2. -Et toi, Laurent, tu vas prendre un coca?
   -Non, je vais prendre une limonade.
3. -Koffi?
   -Pour moi, une pizza.
4. -Emma, qu'est-ce que tu voudrais?
   -Une quiche.
5. -Héloïse, tu prends quoi?
   -Je prends un café.
6. -Et toi, Salim?
   -J'aime les sandwichs. Je prends un sandwich au jambon.
7. -Et toi, Florence?
   -Pour moi, un coca!
8. -Noah, tu veux une crêpe à la confiture?
   -Oui, d'accord.
9. -Evenye, tu veux quoi?
   -Une eau minérale.
10. -Nicole, tu prends une glace?
    -Non, pour moi, un jus d'orange.

## Grammaire

### 12 Qu'est-ce qu'on va prendre?

*Tout le monde prend quelque chose à manger ou à boire. Écrivez 1 si on parle d'une personne ou 2 si on parle de deux ou plusieurs personnes.* (Everyone is having something to eat or drink. Write **1** if what you hear refers to one person or **2** if it refers to two people or more.)

1. Je prends une limonade et un croque-monsieur.
2. Marcel prend un steak-frites.
3. Mon père et ma mère prennent des hamburgers.
4. Nous ne prenons pas une salade, nous prenons une quiche.
5. Tu prends une glace à la vanille et une eau minérale.

## Leçon C

### Vocabulaire

### 2 Nous allons être à l'heure, n'est-ce pas?

*Regardez l'horaire des films et pour chaque phrase que vous entendez, décidez si les personnes vont être....*

A. en avance    B. à l'heure    C. en retard

1. Lois est devant le cinéma pour voir *Shrek* à 15h00.
2. Amir va au cinéma à 20h10 pour voir *Prince of Persia*.
3. Moi, je retrouve Cédric à 13h45 pour voir *Fatal*.
4. Alexandre va voir *Tournée* au ciné à 20h15.
5. Frédéric et Sandrine se retrouvent à 19h55 pour voir *Tournée*.
6. Kémajou achète un billet pour *Millenium 2*, à 21h00.
7. Saniyya et Amir se retrouvent devant le cinéma à 16h05 pour voir *Shrek 4*
8. Julie va voir *Prince of Persia* à 20h15.
9. On va voir *Fatal* à 13h55.
10. Nous achetons le billet pour *Millenium 2* à 21h30.

### Grammaire

### 14 Qui voit quoi?

*Tout le monde* (Everyone) *voit un film ce weekend. Écrivez la lettre qui correspond à la forme du verbe voir que vous entendez dans chaque phrase.*

A. vois    B. voit    C. voyons    D. voyez    E. voient

1. Alain voit *Avatar* à 17h00.
2. Aline et moi voyons *Saw* au cinéma.
3. Martine et Françoise voient *Star-Trek*.
4. Je vois *Bienvenue chez les Ch'tis* pour rire!
5. Vous voyez *Harry Potter* ce weekend?
6. Nous voyons *Batman*.
7. Mohamed voit *New Moon* sur internet.
8. On voit Iron Man ensemble?

### Évaluation

### A Évaluation de compréhension auditive

Listen as Marine and Khaled talk about their plans for Wednesday afternoon. For each statement you hear, write **V** if it is true (**vrai**) or **F** if it is false (**faux**).

| | |
|---|---|
| Khaled: | Salut, Marine. Tu voudrais aller au cinéma mercredi après-midi? |
| Marine: | Oui, j'aime beaucoup le cinéma. On va voir un film d'horreur ou une comédie? |
| Khaled: | Je préfère voir une comédie ou un film policier. |
| Marine: | On peut voir *Shrek 4* ou *Millenium 2*. |
| Khaled: | Oui, j'aime bien *Shrek 4*. À quelle heure? |
| Marine: | À 13h50 ou 16h30. |

| Khaled: | On va manger au café après les cours et on va à la séance de 16h30? |
|---|---|
| Marine: | Oui, d'accord. Nous nous retrouvons devant le Café des Artistes à midi. |
| Khaled: | On invite Sylvain et Rahina? |
| Marine: | Ils vont voir le match du PSG au Parc des Princes cet après-midi. |
| Khaled: | Bon, alors rendez-vous à midi. |
| Marine: | Oui, à bientôt. |

**Recorded statements:**

1. Khaled veut voir le match de foot du PSG au Parc des Princes.
2. Marine va voir le match du PSG avec Sylvain et Rahina.
3. Marine adore le cinéma.
4. Khaled veut voir un film de science-fiction.
5. Marine préfère une comédie ou un film policier.
6. Khaled et Marine décident de voir *Shrek 4*.
7. Khaled et Marine vont à la séance de 13h50.
8. Khaled et Marine décident de manger au Café des Artistes.
9. Khaled et Marine se rencontrent à midi et demie devant le Café des Artistes.
10. Khaled et Marine vont au cinéma avec Sylvain et Rahina.

## Bilan cumulatif

### Listening

**I.**

You will hear a short conversation. Select the reply that would come next. You will hear the conversation twice.

| Stéphane: | Dis, Virginie, qu'est-ce que tu voudrais faire après le cours d'espagnol? |
|---|---|
| Virginie: | Je voudrais aller au cinéma! |
| Stéphane: | Ah, le cinéma, j'adore! On y va à midi? |
| Virginie: | Non, je ne peux pas! J'ai besoin de manger un croque-monsieur et une glace! |
| Stéphane: | Très bien, mais on se retrouve quand? |

**II.**

Listen to the conversation. Select the best completion to each statement that follows.

| Alexis: | Allô, Séverine, c'est Alexis, ton camarade de classe! |
|---|---|
| Séverine: | Ah, salut Alexis! |
| Alexis: | Ça va? |
| Séverine: | Oui très bien, merci! Et toi? |
| Alexis: | Bien, merci! On va au match de foot dimanche. Dis, tu aimes le foot? |
| Séverine: | Oui, j'adore! J'aime aller au stade et regarder les matchs! |
| Alexis: | Moi aussi! Tu voudrais sortir dimanche avec moi et mes copains? |
| Séverine: | Oui, je veux bien! |
| Alexis: | Et bien, rendez-vous dimanche devant le stade! |
| Séverine: | On se retrouve après le déjeuner? |
| Alexis: | Oui, à 2h00! |

# Unité 5
## Leçon A

### Vocabulaire

#### 5 Ma famille

*Simone décrit* (is describing) *sa famille. Regardez l'arbre généalogique* (family tree) *et dites si chaque phrase est* **vraie (V)** *ou* **fausse (F)**.

1. Je ressemble à mon père.
2. Ma sœur est Romane.

3.  Mon oncle et ma tante ont deux enfants.
4.  Raoul est mon oncle.
5.  Anaïs est ma tante.
6.  Ma cousine est Philippe.
7.  Françoise est ma grand-mère.

## Grammaire

### 10  Comparons nos familles!

*Juliette compare sa famille à la famille de Xavier. Écrivez **J** si elle parle de sa famille, **X** si elle parle de la famille de Xavier, ou **J** et **X** si elle parle des deux familles.*

1.  Sa cousine est très bête.
2.  Mes frères sont sympa et intéressants.
3.  J'adore ma famille. Elle est super!
4.  Ses oncles sont un peu paresseux!
5.  Je ressemble à ma grand-mère Thérèse.
6.  J'aime beaucoup son père. Il est très généreux.
7.  Son demi-frère a les cheveux roux.
8.  Nos grands-pères sont aussi de très bons copains.

## Leçon B

### Vocabulaire

### 3  Les jumeaux

*Les jumeaux souvent se ressemblent. Écoutez chaque description et écrivez l'adjectif qui décrit le jumeau de cette personne. (Twins often look and act alike. Listen to each description and write the adjective that describes that person's twin.)*

> **Modèle:**   Vous entendez:    Christian est méchant. Comment est sa sœur Delphine?
> Vous écrivez:    **méchante**

1.  Madeleine est sympa. Comment est son frère Alain?
2.  Kemajou est timide. Comment est sa sœur Rahina?
3.  Saniyya est égoïste. Comment est son frère Nasser?
4.  Noah est bavard. Comment est sa sœur Noémie?
5.  Claire est paresseuse. Comment est son frère Sébastien?
6.  Salim est diligent. Comment est sa sœur Leïla?
7.  Émile est généreux. Comment est sa sœur Émilie?

## Grammaire

### 16  Les dates

*Catherine et sa sœur parlent des dates importantes. Écoutez leur conversation et écrivez les dates que vous entendez à la française: le jour/le mois. Par exemple, la date de Noël (Christmas) s'écrit (is written) 25/12.*

> **Modèle:**   Vous entendez:    L'anniversaire de Richard est le 12 mai.
> Vous écrivez:    **12/5**

1.  L'anniversaire de mon père est le 31 juin.
2.  Karim va avoir 13 ans le 8 janvier.
3.  On va à la fête de Marie le 15 août.
4.  C'est le 25 novembre. C'est l'anniversaire de ma sœur.
5.  Nous n'allons pas à l'école le 1$^{er}$ mai en France.
6.  Laura et Laurent vont voyager à Tahiti le 13 mars.
7.  J'invite nos amis le 15 octobre pour l'anniversaire de Jean.
8.  Nous offrons un CD à Valentin pour sa fête. C'est le 14 février.
9.  En France, on ne va pas à l'école le 11 novembre.
10.  Maxime, qu'est-ce que tu fais le 17 avril?

## Leçon C

### Vocabulaire

### 3 Les professions

*Choisissez l'image qui correspond à la phrase que vous entendez.*

> **Modèle:** Vous entendez: M. Diouf? C'est un dentiste congolais.
> Vous écrivez: **E**

1. Mlle Chérie est blonde et diligente. C'est une prof.
2. J'adore ce metteur en scène. Elle fait des films intéressants.
3. Mon père adore manger et c'est un bon cuisinier.
4. Il est français; il a les yeux bleus et les cheveux blonds. Il est chanteur.
5. Elle est intelligente. C'est une femme d'affaires.
6. Il gagne beaucoup de matchs. C'est un bon athlète et un footballeur.
7. Elle est diligente. Elle a les cheveux bruns et les yeux marron. C'est une actrice.
8. Elle aime écrire et lire des romans. Elle désire être écrivain.
9. Il est drôle et intelligent. C'est un testeur de jeux vidéo.

### Grammaire

### 16 Les pays d'origine

*Écrivez en anglais le nom du pays* (country) *d'où viennent ces personnes.*

> **Modèle:** Vous entendez: Koffi vient du Togo.
> Vous écrivez: Togo

1. Nous venons des États-Unis.
2. Tu viens du Canada.
3. Rahina vient du Cameroun.
4. Amidou vient de Côte-d'Ivoire.
5. Abdoulaye et Awa viennent du Gabon.
6. Marc et toi, vous venez de France.

### Évaluation

### A Évaluation de comprehension auditive

Listen to the conversation between Rahina and Mathéo. Afterward, you will hear some statements. Write **oui** if the statement is correct. Write **non** if the statement is incorrect.

> Mathéo: Salut, Rahina. Tu vas à l'anniversaire d'Antoine vendredi soir?
> Rahina: Oui, j'y vais. Quel âge a-t-il?
> Mathéo: Il va avoir 18 ans le 23 juin. Il prépare une super teuf! Son oncle, le metteur en scène, offre à Antoine de voyager en Martinique.
> Rahina: Quelle chance! Il vient de Martinique, n'est-ce pas?
> Mathéo: Oui, sa famille vient de Fort-de-France. Sa mère va préparer des accras de morue et des crêpes. Ça va être délicieux!
> Rahina: Quelle est la profession de son père?
> Mathéo: Son père est dentiste.
> Rahina: Et sa mère, elle est comment?
> Mathéo: Elle est gentille. Et, c'est une super cuisinière.
> Rahina: Tu offres quoi à Antoine?
> Mathéo: J'offre un CD de Corneille. À vendredi alors?
> Rahina: Oui, c'est ça. Salut!

Recorded statements:

1. C'est l'anniversaire de Rahina.
2. Mathéo ne va pas à l'anniversaire d'Antoine.

3. Antoine va avoir 18 ans.
4. La famille d'Antoine vient de Martinique.
5. La mère d'Antoine va acheter des accras de morue.
6. Le père d'Antoine est metteur en scène.
7. La mère d'Antoine est une bonne cuisinière.
8. Mathéo va offrir un CD de Corneille.

# Unité 6
## Leçon A

### Vocabulaire

### 3  Qu'est-ce qu'on porte?

*Choisissez l'illustration qui correspond à chaque description que vous entendez.*

1. Justine porte une jupe rouge et des bottes noires. Elle est chic.
2. Amir porte un jean rose. C'est pas mal!
3. Nayah porte un jean, un tee-shirt jaune, et des baskets orange. C'est très sympa.
4. Moussa porte un jean et une veste blanche. Il est sympa!
5. Malika porte un beau manteau vert. C'est pas mal!
6. Anh porte une robe blanche et un chapeau bleu. Elle est très chic!
7. Théo porte un jean et une chemise noire. C'est pas mal!
8. Rahina porte un ensemble marron et des bottes beiges. Elle est chic!

### Grammaire

### 12  Faisons du shopping!

*Choisissez le rayon (department) du magasin où M. et Mme Chambon et leurs enfants, Gabrielle (5 ans) et Julien (10 ans), trouvent les vêtements.*

A. rayon *(department)* garçons     B. rayon filles     C. rayon hommes     D. rayon femmes

1. Mme Chambon veut acheter un ensemble pour le travail. Elle choisit une jupe noire et un pull rose.
2. Gabrielle va bientôt avoir six ans. Ses parents veulent acheter une robe rose pour sa fête d'anniversaire samedi.
3. M. Chambon veut acheter un pantalon bleu et une chemise bleue pour le travail.
4. Julien et Gabrielle veulent acheter un ensemble pour faire du sport. Ils choisissent des shorts verts, des tee-shirts blancs, et des baskets.
5. Mme Chambon veut acheter un vêtement pour l'hiver. Elle choisit un anorak rouge.

## Leçon B

### Vocabulaire

### 6  La chronologie

*Indiquez le magasin où François achète les choses que vous entendez.*

A. la boulangerie     B. la crémerie     C. la boucherie     D. le supermarché     E. la pâtisserie
F. la charcuterie

1. François prend du ketchup, de la mayonnaise, et de la moutarde.
2. Il achète aussi un kilo de bœuf.
3. Il choisit quatre tranches de jambon et un saucisson.
4. Il prend une tarte aux pommes pour samedi.
5. Je n'ai pas de lait ou de beurre; prends un camembert aussi.
6. Tu achètes une baguette et des croissants pour demain matin.

**Grammaire**

## 19 Au supermarché

*Choisissez l'expression de quantité qui correspond à l'aliment (food) que Nicole achète.*

A. une boite    B. une bouteille    C. un kilo    D. un litre    E. un morceau
F. des tranches    G. un paquet    H. un pot

1. J'ai besoin de pommes.
2. J'achète du jambon.
3. J'ai besoin de lait.
4. J'achète aussi du fromage.
5. Je prends du café.
6. J'achète de l'eau minérale.
7. Je prends des pâtes.
8. J'ai besoin de moutarde.

## Leçon C

**Vocabulaire**

## 3 À l'épicerie

*Choisissez l'illustration qui correspond à ce que les clients achètent au marché.*

1. Bonjour, madame. Je voudrais cinq bananes, s'il vous plaît.
2. Bonjour, monsieur. Je fais une ratatouille. J'ai besoin d'une aubergine, de tomates, d'olives, et de courgettes.
3. Madame, donnez-moi un kilo de pommes de terre.
4. Vos poires sont bien mûres? Je prends 500 grammes de poires, s'il vous plaît.
5. Je vais faire une tarte pour le déjeuner. J'achète 200 grammes de fraises, s'il vous plaît.
6. J'ai besoin de poivrons pour ma salade. Donnez-moi deux poivrons rouges, Monsieur.
7. Pour ma salade de fruits, je prends des raisins, des cerises, des pommes, et des oranges, s'il vous plaît, madame.
8. Monsieur, je prends deux kilos de champignons, s'il vous plaît.
9. Je prépare une salade niçoise. J'achète des haricots verts, des tomates, un concombre, un poivron rouge, des olives, et un orange pour le dessert. Merci, mademoiselle.
10. Donnez-moi deux grosses pastèques, s'il vous plaît, mademoiselle.

**Grammaire**

## 16 Le marché

*Choisissez l'image qui correspond à la quantité de l'aliment qu'on décrit (describes).*

**Modèle**    You hear:    M. Martin prend du pain.
              You select:    **A**

1. J'achète un poulet.
2. Mme Mercier prend du jambon.
3. M. Laurent mange de la salade.
4. Justine désire une glace.
5. Claude prend de l'eau.
6. Mlle Michel mange de la tarte aux fraises.
7. Théo achète un saucisson.

**Évaluation**

## A Evaluation de compréhension auditive

Jean-Luc and Christian are going to a market in a village while on vacation. Make a list in English of what they buy.

Jean-Luc:    Qu'est-ce qu'on prend pour le déjeuner et le dîner?
Christian:    Achetons des tomates, elles sont bien mûres, et des courgettes. Tout est frais!

| Jean-Luc: | Je n'aime pas les courgettes. Je préfère prendre des concombres et petits pois. Ils sont très bons et bon marché. |
|---|---|
| Christian: | D'accord. Nous avons besoin d'un kilo de champignons aussi. C'est délicieux! |
| Jean-Luc: | Bonjour, madame. Je voudrais un kilo de tomates bien mûres, deux kilos de courgettes, deux concombres, et 500 grammes de petits pois. C'est combien le kilo de champignons? |
| Vendeuse: | C'est cinq euros. |
| Jean-Luc: | C'est beaucoup trop! |
| Vendeuse: | Je vous fais un prix, quatre euros le kilo. |
| Jean-Luc: | D'accord, 500 grammes alors. Ça fait combien? |
| Vendeuse: | Onze euros, s'il vous plait. |

## Bilan cumulatif

### Listening

**I.**

You will hear a short conversation. Select the reply that would come next. You will hear the conversation twice.

| Vendeuse: | Vous désirez, Mademoiselle? |
|---|---|
| Demoiselle: | Je cherche des pêches. |
| Vendeuse: | Des pêches jaunes ou blanches? |
| Demoiselle: | Des pêches blanches. C'est combien le kilo, s'il vous plaît? |

**II.**

Listen to the conversation. Select the best completion to each statement that follows.

| Marion: | Céline, dis, tu veux bien aller faire du shopping avec moi? |
|---|---|
| Céline: | Oui, je veux bien! Quand ça, Marion? |
| Marion: | Après les cours? |
| Céline: | Génial! Qu'est-ce que tu veux acheter? |
| Marion: | J'ai besoin d'une robe pour la fête, samedi! |
| Céline: | Ah oui! Tu veux une robe de quelle couleur? |
| Marion: | Je voudrais une robe noire. J'aime les robes noires et rouges. |
| Céline: | Pas moi, je préfère les vêtements blancs et roses. Tu as trop de noir, Marion! |
| Marion: | Oui, mais moi, c'est ma couleur, le noir! |
| Céline: | On se retrouve devant la salle de classe de Mademoiselle Lecourt? |
| Marion: | Non, Je préfère devant la médiathèque à 17h00. |
| Céline: | Bon, à 17h00 devant la médiathèque, d'accord? |
| Marion: | D'accord! |
| Céline: | Je vais à la pâtisserie prendre deux tartes aux pommes d'abord: une pour toi et une pour moi, et après, c'est le shopping! |
| Marion: | J'adore faire du shopping avec toi, Céline! |

## Unité 7
### Leçon A

#### Vocabulaire
#### 6  Chez moi!

*Écrivez **L** si la description de la maison est **logique** ou **I** si la description est **illogique**.*

1. Dans la chambre, il y a un évier.
2. Dans la salle à manger, il y a une table.
3. Dans le salon, il y a un tapis et une lampe.
4. Dans la salle de bain, il y a un frigo.
5. Dans la cuisine, il y a des placards.
6. Dans les toilettes, il y a une micro-onde.
7. Dans le couloir, il y a un fauteuil.

## Grammaire

### 15 La maison de Coralie

*Coralie parle de sa maison à Julie. Écrivez **0** si la pièce que Coralie décrit (describes) est au rez-de-chausséeet **1** si c'est au premier étage.*

1. Mes parents et moi, on habite une maison charmante. Au rez-de-chaussée, il y a un grand couloir avec un tapis berbère et une table pour le téléphone.
2. À droite, il y a la cuisine et à gauche du couloir, il y a le salon et la salle de séjour.
3. Il y a aussi des W.C. avec un lavabo au fond du couloir.
4. La chambre de ma sœur Myriam est au premier étage à droite de ma chambre.
5. A côté de ma chambre, il y a aussi une salle de bains.
6. Au fond du couloir, il y a la chambre de mon frère Sébastien et le bureau de mon père. J'adore notre maison. Elle est fantastique!

## Leçon B

### Vocabulaire

### 2 À table!

*La mère de Maxime explique comment mettre le couvert. Faites un dessin selon ses explications.*

1. Tu vas mettre la nappe sur la table.
2. Tu vas mettre quatre assiettes sur la table.
3. Tu vas mettre un couteau à droite de chaque assiette.
4. Tu vas mettre une fourchette à gauche de chaque assiette.
5. Tu vas mettre une cuiller au-dessus de chaque assiette.
6. Tu vas mettre un verre au-dessus et à droite de chaque cuiller.
7. Tu vas mettre une serviette sur chaque assiette.
8. Tu vas mettre le sel et le poivre sur la table.

### Grammaire

### 16 La recette de grand-mère

*Écrivez les numéros 1-7 sur votre papier. Écoutez la grand-mère de Romane donner une recette d'une ratatouille. Choisissez l'illustration qui correspond à chaque phrase.*

1. D'abord, je mets de l'huile dans la poêle.
2. Tu mets un peu d'ail.
3. Puis, on met des oignons.
4. Ensuite, je mets des aubergines coupées en carrés.
5. Ensuite, tu mets les courgettes coupées en rondelles fines.
6. Beaucoup de cuisiniers mettent les tomates après les autres légumes.
7. Et ensuite, vous mettez du sel et du poivre. Voilà, c'est tout.

## Leçon C

### Vocabulaire

### 3 La chambre de Julien

*Écrivez les lettres des illustrations qui représentent les meubles et les accessoires que Julien a dans sa chambre.*

Dans ma chambre, il y mon bureau rouge avec une chaise sous la fenêtre. Sur le bureau, il y a mon nouvel ordinateur. Il y a le clavier et la souris devant l'écran. J'ai une imprimante à droite du bureau à coté de mon armoire. Sur les murs, j'ai aussi une affiche de mon film préféré. Et toi, comment est ta chambre?

### Grammaire

### 15 La technologie: on peut...?

*Écrivez les numéros 1-6 sur un papier. Écrivez **oui** si on peut faire les choses mentionnées ou **non**, si on ne peut pas les faire.*

1. Tu peux taper avec le mp3.
2. Mme Mercier peut télécharger un document avec son imprimante.
3. M. Laurent peut surfer sur Internet.
4. Vous pouvez cliquer avec la souris.
5. Ils peuvent démarrer l'ordinateur avec leur mp3.
6. Mlle Michel peut voir le site web sur l'écran.

## Évaluation

### A Évaluation de compréhension auditive

M. and Mme Petit are looking for an apartment. They have two children. Listen to their conversation with the real estate agent and read the sentences. Write **V** if the statement is **vrai** (true) or **F** if it is **faux** (false).

| | |
|---|---|
| L'agent immobilier: | Est-ce que vous préférez un appartement au rez-de chaussée ou au premier étage? |
| M. Petit: | Nous désirons un appartement au quatrième ou cinquième étage près d'une rue commerçante et d'une bouche de métro. |
| L'agent immobilier: | De combien de chambres avez-vous besoin? |
| Mme Petit: | Nous devons avoir trois chambres, quatre c'est mieux. |
| L'agent immobilier: | Et combien de salle de bains désirez-vous? |
| M. Petit: | Nous voulons deux salles de bains et deux W.C. Une avec baignoire et une douche pour nous, et une avec une douche pour les enfants. |
| L'agent immobilier: | Je pense avoir exactement ce que vous désirez. C'est un appartement avec quatre chambres, deux salles de bain, une cuisine moderne, et une salle à manger, un salon important, et un bureau. Il est au quatrième et dernier étage. Mais il n'y a pas de terrasse et seulement un W.C. séparé. Le marché est à côté le mercredi et le samedi, et vous pouvez être au métro dans cinq minutes. |
| M. et Mme Petit: | Pas de problème pour les toilettes. Ça a l'air super. Quand pouvons-nous le visiter? |
| L'agent immobilier: | Vous pouvez le voir mardi à 17h00? |
| M. et Mme Petit: | Oui, c'est parfait. À mardi alors. |

## Unité 8
### Leçon A

#### Vocabulaire

#### 4 Quel temps fait-il?

*Écrivez les numéros 1–6 sur votre papier. Écoutez la météo (weather forecast) des villes différentes. Ensuite, choisissez la lettre de l'illustration qui correspond à chaque description.*

1. Aujourd'hui, dimanche 20 mars, il pleut et il fait frais.
2. En ce beau jour de printemps, il fait frais et du soleil. La température est de 16 degrés.
3. Il fait mauvais et il fait du vent.
4. Sortez votre manteau! Il neige et il fait froid.
5. C'est l'été! Il fait beau et très chaud. Pourquoi pas nager?
6. Il ne fait pas froid mais il ne fait pas beau.

#### Grammaire

#### 13 Qu'est-ce que Malika fait?

*Écrivez les numéros 1–5 sur un papier. Écoutez et choisissez l'image qui correspond à chaque activité que Malika fait.*

1. Elle fait du shopping.
2. Elle fait une salade.
3. Elle fait ses devoirs.
4. Elle fait du vélo.
5. Elle fait une promenade avec une copine.

## Leçon B

### Vocabulaire

### 4  C'est où?

*Écrivez les numéros 1–7 sur un papier. Écoutez chaque description et écrivez la lettre de l'endroit (location) correspondant.*

1. Les touristes arrivent à l'aéroport Charles de Gaulle.
2. Ils choisissent un hôtel sur la rive gauche.
3. Ils prennent une photo du monument.
4. Ils font une promenade sur la grande avenue.
5. Ils vont au musée d'art.
6. Ils dînent à un restaurant algérien.
7. Ils vont à la gare pour aller à Lyon.

### Grammaire

### 13  Paris ou non?

*Si Brad parle de ses vacances de l'été dernier à Paris, écrivez **P**. S'il parle de sa vie à Boston maintenant, écrivez **B**.*

1. J'ai visité le monument à la place de la Concorde.
2. Nous faisons une promenade à Fort Point le dimanche.
3. On aime bien manger au restaurant Union Oyster.
4. Ma grand-mère n'a pas aimé le bateau-mouche.
5. Ma copine va acheter un manteau au centre commercial Roslindale.
6. On a fini notre visite au quartier Latin.
7. Le soir, nous avons attendu le bus devant l'arc de triomphe.
8. J'ai choisi de visiter La tour Eiffel notre dernier jour.

### Grammaire

### 19  Le weekend de Juliette

*Écrivez les numéros 1–8 sur votre papier. Écoutez la description de Juliette qui a passé le samedi dernier à Paris avec sa grand-mère. Ensuite, indiquez si chaque (each) phrase que vous entendez (hear) est **vraie** (true) ou **fausse** (false).*

Samedi, j'ai attendu ma grand-mère à la gare. Nous avons fait une promenade, puis nous avons mangé dans un restaurant italien. L'après-midi nous avons fait du shopping. Ma grand-mère m'a offert une belle robe bleue et un chapeau. Le soir, nous avons fait une promenade dans l'avenue des Champs-Élysées, la plus grande avenue de Paris. Là, on a pris une glace au café et on a discuté. Dimanche nous avons pris le petit déjeuner à l'hôtel.

1. Juliette a attendu sa grand-mère à l'aéroport.
2. Juliette et sa grand-mère ont nagé dans la Seine.
3. Elles ont mangé de la cuisine italienne.
4. Juliette a acheté une robe et un chapeau.
5. Elles ont fait une promenade sur les Champs-Élysées.
6. Le soir, elles ont vu un film.
7. Juliette a pris un dessert au café.
8. Dimanche elles ont pris des croissants à la pâtisserie.

## Leçon C

### Vocabulaire

### 4  Ça s'est passé quand?

*Écrivez les numéros 1–8 sur votre papier. Aujourd'hui, c'est samedi 17 mars. Écoutez les phrases et indiquez la date (en français) qui correspond à chaque description.*

1. Samedi dernier, j'ai visité le musée d'Orsay. J'ai adoré!

2. Hier soir, Alain et moi sommes allés à la cathédrale Notre-Dame.
3. Janine a passé une mauvaise journée mercredi dernier.
4. Nous sommes allés au cinéma hier après-midi.
5. Ils sont allés au jardin de Luxembourg dimanche dernier.
6. Je suis arrivée à la gare hier matin à 9h00.
7. Le weekend dernier, M. et Mme Gérard sont sortis au restaurant.
8. Je suis restée à l'hôtel lundi de la semaine dernière.

## Grammaire

### 15 Le passé ou le présent?

*Écrivez les numéros 1–8 sur votre papier. Écoutez les phrases et indiquez si chaque phrase est au passé composé* (**PC**) *ou au présent* (**PRÉS**).

1. Michelle est allée au Louvre avec son école la semaine dernière.
2. Jean est sorti avec des amis samedi soir.
3. Ils restent à l'hôtel.
4. Nathalie et Jasmine sont descendues du bus.
5. Je monte dans le métro.
6. Thibaut et moi, on est arrivé à la teuf à 21h00 heures.
7. Je rentre à deux heures du matin.
8. Nora et moi sommes revenu(e)s de Paris hier soir.

## Évaluation

### A Évaluation de compréhension auditive

Amélie went to Paris for Christmas vacation. Listen to her conversation with Pierre. Then, indicate if each sentence about her trip is **vrai** or **faux**.

| | |
|---|---|
| Pierre: | Alors, tes vacances à Paris? |
| Amélie: | C'était génial! J'ai adoré! Je suis allée avec mes parents et mon frère. Il a fait du soleil, mais il a aussi fait froid. |
| Pierre: | Ah bon. Quel âge a ton frère? |
| Amélie: | Il a 19 ans. Il a commencé ses études à l'université à Paris l'année dernière. |
| Pierre: | Alors, qu'est-ce que vous avez fait? |
| Amélie: | Oh, beaucoup. D'abord, nous avons visité trois grands musées. Nous sommes allés au Louvre, au Centre Pompidou, et au musée Grévin. |
| Pierre: | Tu as vu la *Joconde* de Léonard da Vinci? Elle est comment? |
| Amélie: | Bien sûr! Elle est très belle, mais très petite. Et tu ne peux pas prendre de photos. Moi, j'ai préféré le Centre Pompidou. |
| Pierre: | Où est le Louvre? |
| Amélie: | Le Louvre est près de la Seine. |
| Pierre: | Tu as pris le métro? |
| Amélie: | Oui, tous les jours. Quelle vue magnifique de Paris de la tour Eiffel! On a voulu aller manger au restaurant de la tour, mais c'est trop cher. |
| Pierre: | Tu as mangé des spécialités? |
| Amélie: | Pas vraiment, mais j'ai mangé beaucoup de pâtisseries. Les religieuses, c'est bon! |
| Pierre: | Vous avez fait une promenade aux Champs-Élysées? |
| Amélie: | Oui. Nous avons visité la place de la Concorde, l'arc de triomphe, et bien sûr, nous avons fait du shopping pour des souvenirs. |

Recorded statements:

1. Amélie a visité le Louvre, le Centre Pompidou, et le musée Grévin.
2. Elle a vu la *Joconde*.
3. Elle a préféré le Louvre comme musée d'art.
4. Amélie a pris le métro avec ses parents et son frère.
5. Amélie et sa famille ont mangé au restaurant de la tour Eiffel.

6. Elle a fait une promenade aux Champs-Élysées.
7. Amélie n'a pas acheté de souvenirs.
8. Amélie a passé de bonnes vacances.

## Bilan cumulatif

### Listening

**I.**

You will hear a short conversation. Select the reply that would come next. You will hear the conversation twice.

- Ah maman, hier Pascal et moi, nous avons....
- Oui, nous avons regardé....
- Dis, Pascal, laisse-moi finir!

**II.**

Listen to the conversation between a tourist and a French man. Select the best completion to each statement that follows.

Touriste:   S'il vous plaît, monsieur!
Français:   Oui, mademoiselle?
Touriste:   Pardon, excusez-moi, où est la bouche du métro le plus près d'ici?
Français:   Où désirez-vous aller, mademoiselle?
Touriste:   Je voudrais aller à la cathédrale de Notre-Dame.
Français:   Ah Paris et sa cathédrale! Et bien, le métro pour Notre-Dame est derrière vous.
Touriste:   Merci bien, monsieur!
Français:   Vous êtes touriste, mademoiselle?
Touriste:   Oui, c'est ma première fois dans la capitale.
Français:   Vous êtes anglaise? Américaine?
Touriste:   Non, je suis canadienne. Je suis de Montréal!
Français:   Ah, j'adore Montréal et les bateaux sur le fleuve Saint-Laurent.
Touriste:   Moi aussi, j'aime beaucoup Montréal, mais je préfère Paris—ses petits cafés, ses beaux monuments, ses musées, et ses cathédrales! Merci beaucoup, monsieur. Au revoir.

## Unité 9
### Leçon A

### Vocabulaire

### 3  Qu'est-ce que Jacques dit?

*Écrivez les numéros 1–10 sur votre papier. Écoutez Jacques et écrivez la lettre qui correspond à la partie du corps mentionné.*

1. Jacques dit: "Touchez le nez."
2. Jacques dit: "Touchez le cou."
3. Jacques dit: "Touchez la main."
4. Jacques dit: "Touchez la jambe."
5. Jacques dit: "Touchez les yeux."
6. Jacques dit: "Touchez le dos."
7. Jacques dit: "Touchez le pied."
8. Jacques dit: "Touchez l'estomac."
9. Jacques dit: "Touchez la bouche."
10. Jacques dit: "Touchez les doigts."

**Grammaire**

**11  Qu'est-ce qu'il faut faire pour être en forme?**

*Écrivez les numéros 1–10 sur votre papier. Écoutez chaque suggestion et écrivez **L** si elle est **logique** ou **I** si elle est **illogique**.*

1. Il faut faire du sport tous les jours.
2. Il ne faut pas manger de fruits et de légumes.
3. Il ne faut pas regarder la télévision six heures par jour.
4. Il faut manger beaucoup de chocolat pour maigrir.
5. Il faut jouer au basket au fitness.
6. Il faut faire une cure thermale pour se décontracter.
7. Il faut aller au supermarché quand on veut faire du sport.
8. Il ne faut pas prendre de l'eau.
9. Il ne faut pas porter des chaussures de sport pour faire du footing.
10. Il faut manger-bouger pour être en bonne santé.

## Leçon B

**Vocabulaire**

**5  On est malade!**

*Écrivez les numéros 1–9 sur votre papier. Écoutez chaque description et écrivez la lettre de l'image correspondante.*

1. Il a mal au dos.
2. Elle a mal aux oreilles.
3. Elle a mal à la gorge.
4. Il a mal à la tête.
5. Elle a un rhume.
6. Il a mal à la jambe.
7. Il a mal au bras.
8. Elle a mal au pied.
9. Elle a mal au ventre.

**Grammaire**

**12  Les bons conseils!**

*Écrivez les numéros 1–10 sur un papier. Écoutez chaque phrase et indiquez l'image qui correspond à la forme de l'impératif utilisée.*

1. Va chez le médecin quand tu as mal partout!
2. Faites de l'aérobic pour rester en bonne forme!
3. Mange des fruits et des légumes tous les jours!
4. Prenons le thème des accompagnateurs pour le devoir sur l'Afrique!
5. Allez au fitness pour faire un cours de yoga!
6. Regardons l'émission à la télé sur le Rwanda!
7. Allez voir le médecin si vous avez de la fièvre.
8. Finissons le cours de step et allons faire une cure thermale!
9. Quelle mauvaise mine! Demande des conseils à ta mère!
10. Dors bien!

## Leçon C

**Vocabulaire**

**6  Sauvons la planète!**

*Faites correspondre l'image avec la description pour indiquer ce que les Morin font pour sauvegarder l'environnement.*

1. La famille Morin habite dans une belle maison. Pour conserver l'énergie, ils ont installé des panneaux solaires sur le toit.

2. Monsieur Morin donne de l'argent pour aider les animaux en danger.
3. Marion recycle les papiers, les boîtes, et les bouteilles à la maison.
4. Christophe ne prend pas le bus pour aller à l'école. Il y va à pied.
5. La famille prend toujours leur voiture hybride quand ils font de longs voyages.
6. Pour aider à éliminer le dioxyde de carbone, Madame Morin circule à vélo.

**Grammaire**

### 14 Engagé(e) ou non?

*Écoutez les phrases suivantes et écrivez **E** si la personne est engagée et **NE** si la personne n'est pas engagée pour sauvegarder la planète.*

> **Modèle:**     -Tu veux recycler?
>                      -Non, je ne veux pas recycler.
> You write:   **NE** (pas engagé)

1. -Pourquoi Marc ne veut-il pas acheter de canettes de coca?
   -Il n'aime pas recycler les boîtes d'aluminium.
2. -Qu'est-ce qu'on peut faire pour protéger les animaux des marées noires?
   -On ne peut rien faire.
3. -La ville de Lyon va-t-elle construire des éoliennes pour lutter contre la pollution?
   -Non, mais elle va construire des panneaux solaires sur le toit des usines.
4. -Ton père préfère acheter de l'engrais biologique ou de l'engrais chimique?
   -Il préfère acheter de l'engrais chimique parce que c'est moins cher.
5. -Est-ce que tu détestes circuler en voiture?
   -Non, mais j'aime mieux circuler en voiture hybride.
6. -Pourquoi est-ce qu'il faut aller à la conférence des Verts?
   -On désire s'engager à protéger les espaces verts dans les villes.

**Évaluation**

### A Évaluation de compréhension auditive

Number from 1–12 on your paper. Then listen to the conversation between Anissa and Michel. Finally, indicate if each statement you hear is **vrai** (**V**) or **faux** (**F**).

| | |
|---|---|
| Anissa: | Salut, Michel. Ça n'a pas l'air d'aller! Qu'est-ce que tu as? |
| Michel: | Oh, là là! Je ne sais pas. J'ai mal partout! |
| Anissa: | Tu as fait de l'exercice? |
| Michel: | Non, pas du tout. Je déteste faire de l'exercice. Je préfère regarder la télé ou surfer sur Internet. |
| Anissa: | À quelle heure est-ce que tu te couches? |
| Michel: | Normalement, vers 23h00. |
| Anissa: | Il faut dormir plus et, à mon avis, tu dois faire de l'exercice pour être en forme. Il faut faire du sport au moins trois ou quatre fois par semaine, bien manger, et boire beaucoup d'eau. |
| Michel: | Je déteste l'eau. Je préfère prendre du coca et j'aime trop manger des frites. |
| Anissa: | Voilà pourquoi tu as mauvaise mine. En plus, les boîtes de coca, c'est mauvais pour l'environnement. |
| Michel: | Mais je recycle. Ma famille s'engage à protéger l'environnement. On fait partie des Verts. On a même installé des panneaux solaires sur les toits de la maison. |
| Anissa: | Alors, mangez des produits bios! |
| Michel: | Mes parents et ma sœur préfèrent manger bio mais pas moi. Je n'aime pas les légumes. Aie! J'ai mal au ventre et à la tête! J'ai des frissons aussi. |
| Anissa: | Et tu as de la fièvre. Peut-être que tu as la grippe. Je te conseille d'aller chez le médecin! |
| Michel: | Bonne idée! Je vais téléphoner maintenant. |

Recorded statements:

1. Michel est malade.
2. Michel a trop fait d'exercice.

3. Michel adore regarder la télé.
4. Anissa conseille à Michel de faire du sport.
5. Anissa pense que Michel va beaucoup dormir.
6. Anissa pense que Michel pollue avec les boîtes de coca.
7. Anissa pense que Michel a mauvaise mine.
8. Michel aime faire du sport et boire de l'eau.
9. La famille de Michel recycle.
10. Michel mange des produits bios.
11. Michel a très mal au dos.
12. Michel ne veut pas aller chez le médecin.

## Unité 10
### Leçon A

#### Vocabulaire

#### 3 Ils viennent d'où au Québec?

*Écrivez les numéros 1–6 sur votre papier. Ensuite, écoutez les descriptions et choisissez la lettre de la ville qui correspond à chaque description.*

1. Cette ville, qui est située au sud-ouest de Rimouski, est la capitale du Québec.
2. Cette ville est située au sud de la ville de Québec et à l'est de Montréal.
3. C'est au nord de Québec sur le fleuve Saint-Laurent.
4. Cette ville est située entre Québec et Laval.
5. C'est entre Montréal et Trois-Rivières.
6. Cette grande ville est à l'ouest de Sherbrooke au bord du fleuve Saint-Laurent.

#### Grammaire

#### 13 Quel pays habites-tu?

*Écrivez les numéros 1–8 sur votre papier. Ces personnes parlent du pays où elles habitent. Écoutez et écrivez la lettre qui correspond au continent où le pays ou la province est situé.*

1. Salut! Je m'appelle Koffi et j'habite à Abidjan en Côte-d'Ivoire.
2. Bonjour. Je suis Madame Abdou. J'habite à Bruxelles en Belgique.
3. Moi, c'est Rashid et j'habite à Alger en Algérie.
4. Je m'appelle Christine et j'habite à Los Angeles en Californie.
5. Je m'appelle Brian. J'habite à New York aux États-Unis.
6. Bonjour, je m'appelle Juliette et j'habite à Marseille en France.
7. Je suis Félix et j'habite à Montréal, au Canada.
8. Moi, c'est Demba. J'habite à Bamako au Mali.

### Leçon B

#### Vocabulaire

#### 3 Les vacances à Québec!

*Annie parle de son voyage en train de Vancouver à Québec. Faites correspondre la phrase avec l'illustration.*

1. Pour aller chez ma cousine Armelle à Québec, je dois acheter un billet de train. C'est facile, je peux aussi l'acheter à la gare.
2. Heureusement, j'ai un siège confortable.
3. La voyageuse à côté de moi est très sympa.
4. À la gare, je regarde le tableau des arrivées et des départs.
5. Attention! Il faut composter mon billet!
6. Je vais prendre le déjeuner dans le wagon-restaurant du train.

## Grammaire

### 10  Le voyage de Julien!

*Écrivez les numéros 1–8 sur votre papier. Ensuite, écoutez l'histoire de Julien et indiquez si les phrases sont **vraies** (**V**) ou **fausses** (**F**).*

À la gare, Julien a composté son billet et ensuite est allé directement au wagon-restaurant. Il n'a rien trouvé, alors il a pris sa place. Normalement, Julien prend la voiture parce que c'est plus rapide. Il aime bien la voiture, mais en ville, il préfère faire du vélo! C'est sympa et moins pollueur! Il fait du vélo tous les jours! Dans le train, Julien a regardé le paysage de la campagne. Les collines, les étangs, et les rivières sont très beaux! De la gare de Chenonceau, il est allé jusqu'au château à pied. Le château est très joli! C'est la première fois qu'il a visité un château de la Loire. Dans le train du retour, il a vu sa copine Aurélie. Ça alors, quelle coïncidence! Ils ont pris un café et ont parlé de leur visite du château.

Recorded statements:

1. Julien n'a jamais pris le train.
2. Il prend souvent sa voiture.
3. Il n'a rien mangé dans le train.
4. Il ne fait plus de vélo.
5. Il n'a rien vu par la fenêtre.
6. Il ne marche pas jusqu'à Chenonceau.
7. Il n'a jamais visité de châteaux avant sa visite à Chenonceau.
8. Il n'a vu personne pendant son voyage.

## Leçon C

### Vocabulaire

### 3  En vacances où?

*Écrivez les numéros 1–6 sur votre papier. Écoutez chaque description de vacances et choisissez la lettre du pays correspondant.*

A. l'Espagne    B. la France    C. la Suisse    D. la Belgique    E. l'Angleterre

1. -Salut, Eric. Tu as passé de bonnes vacances de printemps?
   -Salut, Marie. Super! Je suis allé dans les Alpes. J'ai fait du ski alpin et j'ai marché. Le paysage est magnifique! J'ai vu des cascades, et bien sûr de beaux lacs!
2. -Et toi, Cécile? Tu es allée où?
   -Je suis restée à la maison. Mais, j'ai fait beaucoup de choses. J'ai visité le musée du Louvre. J'ai traversé tout Paris à pied. Je suis allée à l'Opéra et j'ai fait des courses aux grands magasins avec une copine.
3. -Rahina, qu'est-ce que tu as fait pendant les vacances?
   -Je suis allée à Madrid pour voir ma famille. Je suis allée à la plage tous les jours. J'ai mangé de la paëlla, bien sûr!
4. -Salut, Johann, qu'est-ce que tu as fait pendant les vacances?
   -Moi? J'ai aidé mes grands-parents belges qui habitent à la campagne. Ils ont beaucoup d'animaux.
5. -Et toi, Karim? Qu'est-ce que tu as fait?
   -Je suis allé voir mes cousins anglais. Nous sommes restés dans un hôtel super au bord de la mer! Ensuite, on a traversé le pays en voiture.
6. -Et Gabrielle. Tu as aimé Genève? Qu'est-ce que tu y as fait?
   -Génial et super intéressant! J'ai visité la vieille ville et le musée de la Croix-Rouge. J'ai aussi fait du bateau sur le Lac Léman.

**Grammaire**

**14  Qui est l'élève le plus…?**

*Écoutez chaque description des personnes suivantes au superlatif et écrivez la lettre qui correspond à l'image la plus logique.*

1. Qui est l'élève la plus chic?
2. Qui est la plus petite élève?
3. Quel élève est le meilleur footballeur?
4. Qui est le plus grand élève?
5. Qui est l'élève le plus intelligent?
6. Qui est l'élève le plus bavard?

**Évaluation**

**A  Évaluation de compréhension auditive**

*Écoutez Sandrine et Lucas décrire leur journée aux châteaux de la Loire. Choisissez la réponse appropriée.*

| | |
|---|---|
| Sandrine: | OK, il est 8h00. Nous avons le temps de visiter deux ou trois châteaux de la Loire aujourd'hui. |
| Lucas: | Ca dépend. On prend la voiture ou le bus? |
| Sandrine: | Pourquoi on ne fait pas de vélo? On peut faire de l'exercice et admirer la campagne. En plus, on peut s'arrêter quand on veut et peut-être faire un pique-nique au bord de la rivière! |
| Lucas: | D'accord, quel château on visite d'abord? |
| Sandrine: | Le plus grand des châteaux de la Loire, Chambord! |
| Lucas: | Tu as un plan pour y aller? |
| Sandrine: | Oui, regarde! C'est facile. Sur la route d'Orléans, on va tout droit. Le château est sur la droite. À gauche, il y a le village. |
| Lucas: | Oh! Regarde, il y a un bureau de poste et des cafés. En plus, on peut aller à Cheverny facilement après. |
| Sandrine: | Oui, c'est simple, on entre dans le village et on tourne à gauche et c'est tout droit. Tu es d'accord? |
| Lucas: | Oui, on peut faire Chambord et Cheverny et prendre le train pour retourner à la maison. |
| Sandrine: | Bonne idée, allons-y! |

**Bilan cumulatif**

**Listening**

**I.**

You will hear a short conversation. Select the reply that would come next. You will hear the conversation twice.

-Dis, Anne-Sophie! Tu as mauvaise mine!
-Oui, j'ai froid et j'ai très mal à la tête.
-Qu'est-ce que tu me conseilles, maman?

**II.**

Listen to the conversation. Select the best completion to each statement that follows.

| | |
|---|---|
| Mme Sanchez: | Bonjour, Monsieur Duris! |
| M. Duris: | Bonjour, Madame Sanchez! Comment allez-vous aujourd'hui? |
| Mme Sanchez: | Ah, pas très bien! Je suis très fatiguée, j'ai mal à la tête, à la gorge, et j'ai chaud! |
| M. Duris | Ah, madame, à mon avis vous êtes malade; il fait très froid aujourd'hui. Et puis, vous êtes très pâle ce matin. |
| Mme Sanchez: | Oh non, il ne faut pas rester comme ça! Bon, je dois aller chez le médecin. |
| M. Duris: | Bonne idée, Madame Sanchez! Et ne circulez pas à pied; le dioxyde de carbone, ce n'est pas bon pour vous! |
| Mme Sanchez: | Vous avez raison, Monsieur Duris! Je dois me protéger! Je vais prendre le train pour aller en ville! |

# Correlation of Common Core State Standards

| Common Core State Standards—ELA | Standards for Learning Languages | *T'es branché?* Level 1 |
|---|---|---|
| **Key Ideas and Details** | | |
| **Reading 1–3** | **Interpretive (Reading, Listening, Viewing)** | **Page Number** |
| 1. Read closely to determine what the text says explicitly and to make logical inferences from it; cite specific textual evidence when writing or speaking to support conclusions drawn from the text<br>2. Determine central ideas or themes of a text and analyze their development; summarize key supporting details and ideas<br>3. Analyze how and why individuals, events, or ideas develop and interact over the course of a text | Interpretive Communication (Standard 1.2) | 4, 5, 8, 13, 16, 19, 22, 23, 28, 36, 37, 41, 42, 43, 46, 52, 53, 56, 60, 72, 77, 81, 94, 96, 103, 111, 114, 119, 120, 126, 135, 138, 140, 143, 145, 153, 171, 182, 197, 198, 199, 207, 214, 215, 224, 235, 236, 253, 256, 263, 264, 265, 266, 280, 295, 299, 308, 313, 314, 317, 335, 342, 349, 356, 358, 361, 373, 376, 398, 401, 412, 415, 429, 431, 433, 437, 447, 454, 463, 475, 478, 488, 491, 503, 504, 505, 520, 531, 534, 547, 549, 559, 567 |
| | Cultures: Practices and Products (Standard 2.1 and 2.2) | 4, 5, 16, 22, 23, 24, 29, 31, 32, 35, 36, 37, 41, 42, 46, 55, 60, 72, 77, 81, 126, 128, 140, 143, 152, 153, 171, 182, 197, 198, 199, 208, 215, 224, 236, 253, 263, 264, 265, 266, 280, 295, 299, 313, 314, 317, 328, 335, 342, 349, 356, 358, 361, 376, 386, 398, 401, 412, 415, 429, 432, 433, 437, 446, 447, 451, 454, 463, 475, 478, 488, 491, 503, 504, 505, 520, 531, 534, 547, 549, 559, 567 |
| | Connections: Acquiring New Information (Standard 3.2) | 44, 106, 208, 266, 376, 433, 447, 464, 465, 475, 476, 478, 488, 549 |
| **Craft and Structure** | | |
| **Reading 4–6** | **Interpretive (Reading, Listening, Viewing)** | **Page Number** |
| 4. Interpret words and phrases as they are used in a text, including determining technical, connotative, and figurative meanings, and analyze how specific word choices shape meaning or tone<br>5. Analyze the structure of texts, including how specific sentences, paragraphs, and larger portions of the text relate to each other and the whole<br>6. Assess how point of view or purpose shapes the content and style of a text | Interpretive Communication (Standard 1.2) | 6, 7, 15, 57, 61, 65, 68, 69, 75, 86, 87, 89, 94, 102, 103, 108, 109, 110, 114, 115, 132, 133, 134, 136, 137, 139, 144, 147, 149, 152, 160, 164, 165, 172, 174, 178, 179, 180, 188, 190, 191, 194, 195, 203, 204, 207, 212, 220, 221, 227, 229, 231, 232, 233, 239, 241, 243, 244, 248, 249, 250, 258, 260, 261, 272, 276, 277, 284, 285, 287, 290, 291, 292, 293, 304, 305, 310, 311, 320, 323, 340-341, 350, 354, 355-356, 361, 364, 367, 371-372, 381, 392, 396-397, 404, 406, 409, 410, 411, 419-420, 423, 425, 430-431, 438-439, 443, 453, 460, 461, 467, 470, 471, 472, 479, 485, 486, 489, 496, 499, 510, 512, 516-517, 525, 529, 530, 531, 538, 544-545, 546, 554, 558, 566 |
| | Cultures: Practices and Products (Standards 2.1 and 2.2) | 6, 7, 12, 19, 26, 27, 54, 60, 69, 70, 71, 75, 86, 89, 110, 111, 112, 113, 122, 123, 124, 132, 134, 146, 147, 148, 149, 166, 172, 173, 176, 181, 182, 189, 191, 193, 196, 203, 204, 205, 222, 223, 228, 234, 235, 240, 245, 247, 251, 252, 259, 260, 261, 262, 270, 278, 279, 284, 286, 294, 296, 297, 302, 303, 305, 306, 311, 312, 313, 320, 321, 322, 323, 324, 327, 332, 334, 336, 341, 342, 343, 344, 349, 350, 351, 357, 360, 361, 362, 363, 364, 373, 374, 375, 376, 382, 383, 385, 390, 398, 399, 405, 406, 407, 420, 421, 422, 423, 424, 426, 427, 431, 432, 440, 441, 443, 444, 461, 462, 466, 467, 468, 472, 473, 480, 481, 487, 499, 500, 501, 525, 526, 532, 533, 539, 540, 543, 546, 556, 568 |

| Common Core State Standards—ELA | Standards for Learning Languages | *T'es branché?* Level 1 |
|---|---|---|
| | Connections: Reinforce Other Disciplines (Standard 3.1) | 136, 462, 466, 472, 473, 558 |
| | Comparisons: Language (Standard 4.1) | 2, 9, 10, 19, 38, 46, 65, 115, 117, 128, 132, 133, 142, 149, 152, 153, 172, 175, 185, 188, 190, 203, 204, 226, 227, 239, 243, 258, 260, 284, 302, 304, 327, 347, 350, 359, 362, 365, 381, 404, 406, 439, 443, 467, 479, 496, 522, 539, 543, 551, 554 |
| | Comparisons: Cultures (Standard 4.2) | 9, 10, 38, 46, 82, 112, 113, 208, 350, 458, 468 |

## Integration of Knowledge and Ideas

| Reading 7–9 | Interpretive (Reading, Listening, Viewing) | Page Number |
|---|---|---|
| 7. Integrate and evaluate content presented in diverse formats and media, including visually and quantitatively, as well as in words<br>8. Delineate and evaluate the argument and specific claims in a text, including the validity of the reasoning as well as the relevance and sufficiency of the evidence<br>9. Analyze how two or more texts address similar themes or topics in order to build knowledge or to compare the approaches the authors take<br>10. Read and comprehend complex literary and informational texts independently and proficiently | Interpretive Communication (Standard 1.2) | 6, 7, 8, 14, 18, 25, 40, 52, 53, 82, 83, 127, 128, 129, 130, 141, 142, 152, 162, 168, 169, 170, 185, 186, 187, 200, 202, 206, 225, 226, 237, 254, 255, 265, 281, 282, 289, 299, 300, 315, 316, 318, 327, 346, 347, 348, 353, 359, 360, 377, 378, 379, 385, 387, 401, 402, 416, 434, 445, 446, 449, 454, 464, 465, 476, 477, 492, 493, 503, 518, 521, 522, 523, 528, 535, 541, 542, 550, 551, 552, 557, 558, 560 |
| | Cultures: Practices and Products (Standards 2.1 and 2.2) | 6, 7, 21, 47, 55, 58, 59, 60, 74, 78, 127, 128, 129, 141, 153, 168, 170, 186, 187, 201, 226, 237, 254, 255, 283, 301, 315, 316, 327, 346, 347, 348, 358, 359, 378, 379, 390, 401, 402, 416, 434, 435, 445, 446, 449, 454, 465, 477, 491, 492, 493, 502, 518, 541, 542, 551, 552 |
| | Connections: Reinforce Other Disciplines (Standard 3.1) | 21, 95, 185, 200, 237, 254, 255, 281, 282, 299, 300, 377, 387, 390, 413, 434, 445, 446, 449, 476, 491, 492, 493, 518, 522, 542, 550, 551, 552, 557, 559 |
| | Comparisons: Cultures (Standard 4.2) | 9, 20, 21, 33, 34, 39, 51, 57, 58, 59, 73, 74, 82, 83, 127, 128, 129, 141, 142, 153, 159, 169, 185, 186, 200, 208, 237, 254, 274, 281, 282, 300, 301, 316, 346, 347, 358, 359, 377, 387, 390, 394, 401, 402, 416, 417, 434, 464, 477, 492, 493, 522 |
| | Communities: Beyond the School Setting (Standard 5.1) | 237, 254, 255, 281, 299, 300, 307, 315, 346, 347, 359, 377, 464, 465, 476, 477, 492, 493, 502, 535, 542, 550, 551 |

## Range of Reading and Level of Text Complexity

| Reading 10 | Interpretive (Reading, Listening, Viewing) | Page Number |
|---|---|---|
| 10. Read and comprehend complex literary and informational texts independently and proficiently | Interpretive Communication (Standard 1.2) | 154, 197, 215, 226, 256, 263, 264, 267, 315, 316, 328, 329, 335, 345, 349, 387, 448, 454, 473, 494, 505, 536, 540, 559 |
| | Comparisons: Cultures (Standard 4.2) | 315, 328, 448, 538 |
| | Communities: Beyond the School Setting (Standard 5.1) | 494, 536, 559 |

| Common Core State Standards—ELA | Standards for Learning Languages | *T'es branché?* Level 1 |
|---|---|---|

## Text Types and Purposes

| Writing 1–3 | Presentational (Writing, Speaking, Visually Representing) | Page Number |
|---|---|---|
| 1. Write arguments to support claims in an analysis of substantive topics or texts using valid reasoning and relevant and sufficient evidence<br>2. Write informative/explanatory texts to examine and convey complex ideas and information clearly and accurately through the effective selection, organization, and analysis of content<br>3. Write narratives to develop real or imagined experiences or events using effective technique, well-chosen details, and well-structured event sequences | **Presentational Communication (Standard 1.3)**<br>Present information, concepts, and ideas to an audience of listeners or readers on a variety of topics.<br>• Produce a variety of creative oral and written presentations (e.g. original story, personal narrative, script).<br>• Retell or summarize information in narrative form, demonstrating a consideration of audience.<br>• Create and give persuasive speeches and write persuasive essays.<br>• Produce expository writing. | 27, 42, 67, 75, 96, 97,101, 152, 154, 159, 192, 193, 201, 209, 213, 271, 287, 289, 308, 309, 332, 336, 384, 391, 429, 445, 450, 452, 473, 478, 480, 507, 543, 560, 568 |
| | **Comparisons: Language (Standard 4.1)**<br>Demonstrate understanding of the nature of language through comparisons of the language studied and one's own. | 86, 89, 289, 309, 473, 480, 507, 543 |

## Production and Distribution of Writing

| Writing 4–6 | Presentational (Writing, Speaking, Visually Representing) | Page Number |
|---|---|---|
| 4. Produce clear and coherent writing in which the development, organization, and style are appropriate to task, purpose, and audience<br>5. Develop and strengthen writing as needed by planning, revising, editing, rewriting, or trying a new approach<br>6. Use technology, including the Internet, to produce and publish writing and to interact and collaborate with others | **Presentational Communication (Standard 1.3)**<br>Present information, concepts, and ideas to an audience of listeners or readers on a variety of topics, knowing how, when, and why to say what to whom.<br>• Retell or summarize information in narrative form, demonstrating a consideration of audience.<br>• Self-edit written work for content, organization, and grammar. | 84, 94, 101, 159, 210, 211, 213, 216, 307, 319, 329, 387, 413, 445, 488, 495, 508, 557 |
| | **Cultures: Practices and Perspectives (Standard 2.1):**<br>Demonstrate an understanding of the relationship between the practices and perspectives of the cultures studied. | 11, 12, 17, 32, 35, 40, 47, 54, 62, 131, 136, 210, 211, 216, 257, 264, 261, 319, 326, 333, 417, 425, 445, 450, 484, 508, 510, 557 |
| | **Cultures: Products and Perspectives (Standard 2.2)**<br>Demonstrate an understanding of the relationship between the products and perspectives of the cultures studied. | 11, 25, 40, 211, 216, 261, 299, 307,319,326, 333, 445, 450 |
| | **Comparisons: Language (Standard 4.1)**<br>Demonstrate understanding of the nature of language through comparisons of the language studied and one's own. | 211, 329, 329, 558 |

| Common Core State Standards—ELA | Standards for Learning Languages | *T'es branché?* Level 1 |
|---|---|---|
| | **Communities: Beyond the School Setting (Standard 5.1)** Use the language both within and beyond the school setting. | 44, 98, 257, 271, 388, 488, 510, 550 |

## Research to Build and Present Knowledge

| Writing 7–9 | Presentational (Writing, Speaking, Visually Representing) | Page Number |
|---|---|---|
| 7. Conduct short as well as more sustained research projects based on focused questions, demonstrating understanding of the subject under investigation<br>8. Gather relevant information from multiple print and digital sources, assess the credibility and accuracy of each source, and integrate the information while avoiding plagiarism<br>9. Draw evidence from literary or informational texts to support analysis, reflection, and research | **Presentational Communication (Standard 1.3)** Present information, concepts, and ideas to an audience of listeners or readers on a variety of topics.<br>• Expound on familiar topics and those requiring research.<br>• Produce expository writing including researched reports.<br>• Use reference tools, acknowledge sources and cite them appropriately.<br>• Demonstrate an understanding of features of target culture communities (e.g. geographic, historical, artistic, social and/or political).<br>• Demonstrate knowledge and understanding of content across disciplines. | 14, 25, 42, 45, 60, 67, 73, 74, 80, 84, 85, 89, 93, 95, 98, 99, 125, 126, 142, 151, 157, 159, 202, 210, 211, 212, 225, 268, 269, 283, 307, 330, 332, 352, 387, 391, 408, 449, 493, 495, 498, 502, 510, 523, 524, 527, 528, 537, 541, 542, 552, 557, 561, 562 |
| | **Interpretive Communication (Standard 1.2)** Understand and interpret written and spoken language on a variety of topics. | 13, 30, 47, 90, 92, 97, 114, 115, 116, 125, 128, 202, 230, 268, 330, 380, 449, 495, 523, 524, 535, 537, 541, 542, 550, 553, 555, 561, 562, 563 |
| | **Cultures: Practices and Perspectives (Standard 2.1)** Demonstrate an understanding of the relationship between the practices and perspectives of cultures studied. | 13, 30, 42, 43, 45, 47, 56, 97, 98, 125, 128, 142, 144, 202, 225, 230, 269, 281, 282, 327, 332, 380, 385, 389, 418, 435, 449, 451, 464, 465, 466, 469, 474, 492, 493, 506, 522, 523, 524, 535, 536, 541, 542, 550, 552, 553, 562, 564 |
| | **Cultures: Products and Perspectives (Standard 2.2)** Demonstrate an understanding of the relationship between the products and perspectives of cultures studied. | 25, 47, 202, 269, 283, 332, 356, 389, 435, 449, 451, 469, 484, 527, 528, 541, 561, 562, 564 |
| | **Connections: Reinforce Other Disciplines (Standard 3.1)** Reinforce and further knowledge of other disciplines through the target language. | 225, 271, 330, 332, 387, 435, 449, 451, 493, 506, 509, 510, 523, 527, 528, 541, 561 |
| | **Connections: Acquiring New Information (Standard 3.2)** Acquire information and recognize the distinctive viewpoints that are only available through the target language and its cultures. | 225, 271, 283, 330, 332, 387, 449, 451, 493, 495, 506, 509, 510, 523, 542, 550, 561, 562 |
| | **Comparisons: Culture (Standard 4.2)** Demonstrate understanding | 100, 144, 151, 157, 202, 212, 225, 230, 269, 271, 330, 332, 382, 451, 493, 495, 509, 510, 523, 527 |

| Common Core State Standards—ELA | Standards for Learning Languages | *T'es branché?* Level 1 |
|---|---|---|

## Range of Writing

| **Writing 10** | **Presentational (Writing, Speaking, Visually Representing)** | **Page Number** |
|---|---|---|
| 10. Write routinely over extended time frames (time for research, reflection, and revision) and shorter time frames (a single sitting or a day or two) for a range of tasks, purposes, and audiences | **Presentational Communication (Standard 1.3)** Present information, concepts, and ideas to an audience of listeners or readers on a variety of topics. <br> • Self-monitor and adjust language production. <br> • Self-edit written work for content, organization, and grammar. | 76, 80, 82, 83, 92, 93, 98, 101, 104, 138, 155, 157, 169, 170, 177, 181, 200, 206, 223, 228, 230, 271, 333, 368, 391, 443, 448, 450, 456, 503, 506, 511, 518, 560, 564, 565 |
| | **Cultures: Practices and Perspectives (Standard 2.1)** Demonstrate an understanding of the relationship between practices and perspectives of the cultures studied. | 60, 64, 79, 104, 135, 144, 155, 157, 158, 181, 183, 216, 226, 241, 242, 243, 244, 246, 262, 263, 286, 331, 344, 345, 370, 385, 391, 398, 441, 448, 450, 455, 506, 511, 518, 526 |
| | **Cultures: Products and Perspectives (Standard 2.2)** Demonstrate an understanding of the relationship between the products and perspectives of the cultures studied. | 60, 155, 166, 183, 331, 391, 448, 511 |

## Comprehension and Collaboration

| **Speaking and Listening 1–3** | **Interpersonal (Speaking & Listening; Reading & Writing)** | **Page Number** |
|---|---|---|
| 1. Prepare for and participate effectively in a range of conversations and collaborations with diverse partners, building on others' ideas and expressing their own clearly and persuasively <br><br> 2. Integrate and evaluate information presented in diverse media and formats, including visually, quantitatively, and orally <br><br> 3. Evaluate a speaker's point of view, reasoning, and use of evidence and rhetoric | **Interpersonal Communication (Standard 1.1)** Engage in conversations, provide and obtain information, express feelings and emotions, and exchange opinions. <br> • Engage in the oral exchange of ideas in formal and informal situations. <br> • Elicit information and clarify meaning by using a variety of strategies. <br> • State and support opinions in oral interactions. <br> • Self-monitor and adjust language production. <br> • Converse in ways that reflect knowledge of target culture communities (e.g., geographic, historical, artistic, social and/or political. | 4, 5, 6, 7, 8, 14, 18, 19, 21, 26, 27, 31, 36, 43, 46, 52, 53, 54, 59, 60, 63, 64, 65, 66, 67,69, 70, 71, 72, 74, 75,79, 80, 82, 83, 84, 86, 87, 88, 91, 92, 96, 98, 100, 103, 104, 114, 121, 131, 135, 139, 150, 152, 153, 157, 158, 159, 167, 173, 177, 183, 187, 190, 192, 196, 197, 198, 202, 206, 211, 226, 229, 230, 240, 242, 245, 246, 247, 257, 264, 278, 279, 285, 286, 287, 288, 295, 296, 297, 303, 305, 306, 307, 313, 319, 324, 325, 330, 331, 332, 336, 343, 344, 352, 357, 363, 367, 368, 369, 375, 378, 380, 383, 384, 388, 389, 390, 391, 399, 407, 417, 421, 424, 427, 428, 435, 437, 442, 450, 451, 456, 462, 469, 474, 482, 483, 489, 497, 508, 509, 510, 511, 519, 527, 528, 533, 536, 540, 541, 542, 548, 553, 555, 563, 564, 568 |
| | **Cultures: Practices and Perspectives (Standard 2.1)** Use appropriate verbal and non-verbal behavior in interpersonal communication. | 4, 5, 6, 7, 9, 10, 16, 17, 26, 29, 30, 38, 47, 56, 62, 66, 82, 136, 139, 142, 144, 150, 167, 174, 181, 182, 188, 196, 229, 257, 270, 279, 332, 352, 384, 414, 432, 442, 451, 482, 489, 497, 508, 511, 519, 527, 548, 564 |
| | **Cultures: Products and Perspectives (Standard 2.2)** Compare and contrast artifacts, themes, ideas, and perspectives across cultures. | 21, 23, 25, 32, 33, 34, 45, 51, 58, 59, 85, 114, 202, 212, 289, 296, 301, 316, 368, 389, 509, 564 |

| Common Core State Standards—ELA | Standards for Learning Languages | *T'es branché?* Level 1 |
|---|---|---|
| | **Connections: Acquiring New Information (Standard 3.2)** Use age-appropriate authentic sources to prepare for discussions. | 22, 44, 316, 529, 564 |
| | **Comparisons: Language (Standard 4.1)** Demonstrate an awareness of formal and informal language expressions in other languages and one's own. | 5, 9, 10, 16, 17,20, 26, 27, 46, 47, 63, 119, 257, 278, 527, 528, 553 |
| | **Communities: Lifelong Learning (Standard 5.2)** Establish and/or maintain interpersonal relations with speakers of the target language. | 257 |

## Presentation of Knowledge and Ideas

| Speaking and Listening 4–6 | Interpersonal (Speaking & Listening; Reading & Writing) | Page Number |
|---|---|---|
| 4. Present information, findings, and supporting evidence such that listeners can follow the line of reasoning and the organization, development, and style are appropriate to task, purpose, and audience<br>5. Make strategic use of digital media and visual displays of data to express information and enhance understanding of presentations<br>6. Adapt speech to a variety of contexts and communicative tasks, demonstrating command of formal English when indicated or appropriate | **Presentational Communication: (Standard 1.3)** Present information, concepts, and ideas to an audience of listeners or readers on a variety of topics.<br>• Produce a variety of creative oral presentations (e.g. original story, personal narrative, speech, performance).<br>• Retell or summarize information in narrative form, demonstrating a consideration of audience.<br>• Create and give persuasive speeches.<br>• Expound on familiar topics and those requiring research.<br>• Self-monitor and adjust language production.<br>• Use information about features of target culture communities (e.g. geographic, historical, artistic, social and/or political) in presentations.<br>• Incorporate content across disciplines in presentations. | 19, 21, 40, 76, 91, 92, 93, 115-119, 120, 121, 151, 156, 159, 167, 206, 207, 212, 216, 246, 257, 331, 353, 368, 380, 389, 450, 456, 469, 508, 509, 528, 536, 542, 553 |
| | **Connections: Acquiring information (Standard 3.2)** Use age-appropriate authentic sources to prepare for discussions. | 331 |

EMC

# T'es branché?

**1B**

## Author

**Toni Theisen**

With the collaboration of
**Jacques Pécheur**

## Contributing Writers

**Caroline Busse**
Pasadena, CA

**Nathalie E. Gaillot**
Lyon, France

**Lynne I. Lipkind**
West Hartford, CT

**Todd Losié**
Detroit, MI

**Diana I. Moen**
St. Paul, MN

**Annie-Claude Motron**
Paris, France

**Virginie Pied**
Salt Lake City, UT

**Ann Trinkaus**
Middletown, CT

**Pamela M. Wesely**
Iowa City, IA

**EMC Publishing**

ST. PAUL

**Editorial Director:** Alejandro Vargas

**Developmental Editor:** Diana I. Moen

**Associate Editors:** Nathalie Gaillot, Patricia Teefy, Scott Homler

**Assistant Editor:** Kristina Merrick

**Director of Production:** Deanna Quinn

**Cover Designer:** Leslie Anderson

**Text Designers:** Diane Beasley Design, Leslie Anderson

**Illustrators:** Marty Harris; Patti Isaacs, Parrot Graphics; Katherine Knutson

**Production Specialists:** Leslie Anderson (lead), Jaana Bykonich, Ryan Hamner, Julie Johnston, Valerie King, Timothy W. Larson, Jack Ross, Sara Schmidt Boldon

**Copy Editor:** Mayanne Wright

**Proofreader:** Jamie Gleich Bryant

**Reviewers:** Sébastien De Clerck, Ojai, CA; Nicole Fandel, Acton, MA; Linda Mercier, Elizabethtown, PA; Gretchen Petrie, Medina, OH; Anne Marie Plante, Minneapolis, MN; Celeste Renza-Guren, Dallas, TX

Care has been taken to verify the accuracy of information presented in this book. However, the authors, editors, and publisher cannot accept responsibility for Web, e-mail, newsgroup, or chat room subject matter or content, or for consequences from application of the information in this book, and make no warranty, expressed or implied, with respect to its content.

**Trademarks:** Some of the product names and company names included in this book have been used for identification purposes only and may be trademarks or registered trade names of their respective manufacturers and sellers. The authors, editors, and publisher disclaim any affiliation, association, or connection with, or sponsorship or endorsement by, such owners.

**Credits:** Bridge Photo Credits, Photo Credits, Reading Credits, Art Credits, and Realia Credits follow the Index.

We have made every effort to trace the ownership of all copyrighted material and to secure permission from copyright holders. In the event of any question arising as to the use of any material, we will be pleased to make the necessary corrections in future printings. Thanks are due to the aforementioned authors, publishers, and agents for permission to use the materials indicated.

ISBN 978-0-82196-667-9
© 2014 by EMC Publishing, LLC
875 Montreal Way
St. Paul, MN 55102
Email: educate@emcp.com
Website: www.emcschool.com

Printed in the United States of America

22  21  20  19  18  17  16  15  14  13      1  2  3  4  5  6  7  8  9  10

# To the Student

**Bienvenue au monde de *T'es branché?*** Welcome to the world of *T'es branché?* As you learn French with this exciting and innovative series, you will enjoy many opportunities to explore contemporary life in the Francophone world through your textbook and supplemental materials, online research, and on-location videos filmed in France.

You are on a voyage of discovery. You will meet people from many French-speaking countries and find out what it is like to live there. You will gain knowledge of diverse cultures, traditions, history, and language that will make you travel-ready and multicultural.

From the first day of your apprenticeship at becoming a citizen of the world, you will communicate in French with your classmates, teachers, and other French-speaking teens around the world. You will become skilled at working with a partner, in a group, and at making presentations. You will realize that learning another language expands your horizons, develops your intellect, and prepares you to experience the rich and engaging world in which we live.

Why is it important to learn French? Did you know that...?

1. there are over 200 million people in the world in more than 50 countries on five continents who speak French
2. there are over 20 million French speakers nearby—win Canada, the Caribbean, South America, and even closer to home, in Louisiana, and New England
3. French is, either directly or indirectly, the means of communication of over a quarter of a billion people in Africa where it is the official language of 18 countries
4. French opens doors in Canada, the top trading partner of the United States
5. French is the Romance language most similar to English; about 30% of all English words can be traced to French, so learning French will improve your English-language skills
6. French is among the official languages of the United Nations, UNESCO, the International Monetary Fund, the International Labor Organization, the International Olympic Committee, the 31-member Council of Europe, the European Community, the International Red Cross, postal services around the world, the organization for African Unity, and the International Council of Sport Science and Physical Education (to name a few of the organizations)
7. a second language is often a college requirement and, through its connections to English, can boost your success at your studies
8. French gives you access to discoveries and prominent persons in the world of art, government, food, literature, architecture, science, medicine, technology, music, diplomacy, fashion, and cinema
9. French connects you to the history of the United States and the thousands of places whose names are derived from French

Whatever your personal reasons for learning French, have a good journey as you discover French language and culture!

**Bonne chance!** (*Good luck!*)

# Table of Contents

# Map of Paris

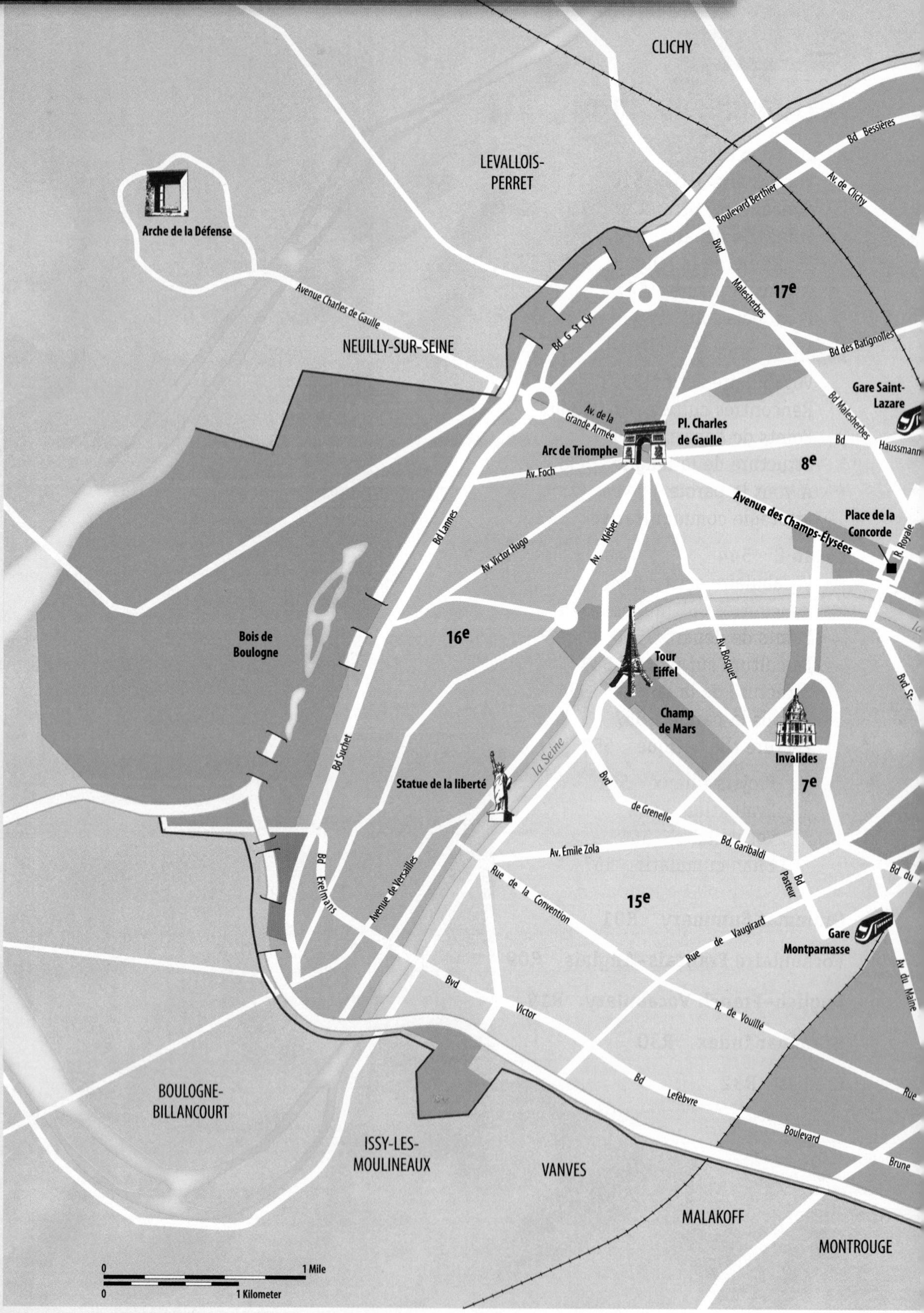

CLICHY

LEVALLOIS-
PERRET

Bd. Bessières

Av. de Clichy

Boulevard Berthier

Arche de la Défense

Bd Malesherbes

17e

Bd des Batignolles

Avenue Charles de Gaulle

NEUILLY-SUR-SEINE

Bd. G. St. Cyr

Gare Saint-
Lazare

Bd Malesherbes

Av. de la
Grande Armée

Pl. Charles
de Gaulle

Bd

Haussmann

Arc de Triomphe

8e

Av. Foch

Bd Lannes

Av. Kléber

Avenue des Champs-Elysées

Place de la
Concorde

R. Royale

Av. Victor Hugo

Bois de
Boulogne

16e

Tour
Eiffel

Av. Bosquet

Champ
de Mars

Bd St-

Bd Suchet

Invalides

la Seine

Statue de la liberté

7e

Bd

de Grenelle

Bd. Garibaldi

Bd. du

Av. Émile Zola

Bd Exelmans

Avenue de Versailles

Rue de la Convention

15e

Bd
Pasteur

Rue de Vaugirard

Gare
Montparnasse

Av. du Maine

R. de Vouillé

Bvd

Victor

Bd

Lefêbvre

Rue

BOULOGNE-
BILLANCOURT

Boulevard

Brune

ISSY-LES-
MOULINEAUX

VANVES

MALAKOFF

MONTROUGE

0       1 Mile

0       1 Kilometer

# Administrative Map of France

# Map of France

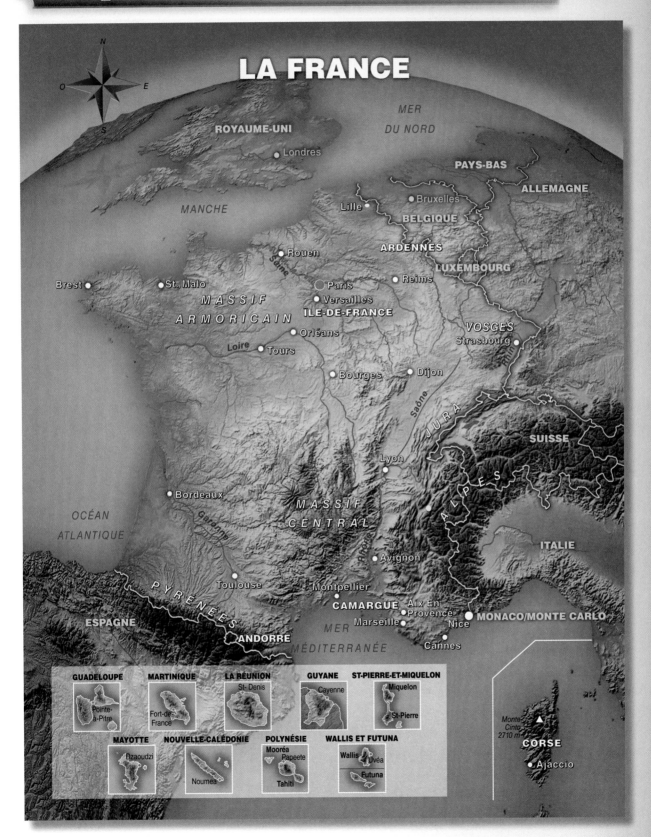

LA FRANCE

ROYAUME-UNI

MER DU NORD

Londres

PAYS-BAS

ALLEMAGNE

MANCHE

Lille

Bruxelles

BELGIQUE

ARDENNES

LUXEMBOURG

Rouen

Reims

Seine

Brest

St. Malo

MASSIF ARMORICAIN

Paris

Versailles

ÎLE-DE-FRANCE

VOSGES

Orléans

Strasbourg

Loire

Tours

Bourges

Dijon

Saône

JURA

SUISSE

Lyon

Bordeaux

OCÉAN ATLANTIQUE

Garonne

MASSIF CENTRAL

ALPES

ITALIE

Avignon

Toulouse

Montpellier

PYRÉNÉES

CAMARGUE

Aix En Provence

MONACO/MONTE CARLO

ESPAGNE

Marseille

Nice

ANDORRE

MER MÉDITERRANÉE

Cannes

**GUADELOUPE**

Pointe-à-Pitre

**MARTINIQUE**

Fort-de-France

**LA RÉUNION**

St- Denis

**GUYANE**

Cayenne

**ST-PIERRE-ET-MIQUELON**

Miquelon

St-Pierre

Monte Cinto 2710 m

**CORSE**

Ajaccio

**MAYOTTE**

Dzaoudzi

**NOUVELLE-CALÉDONIE**

Noumea

**POLYNÉSIE**

Mooréa

Papeete

Tahiti

**WALLIS ET FUTUNA**

Wallis

Uvéa

Futuna

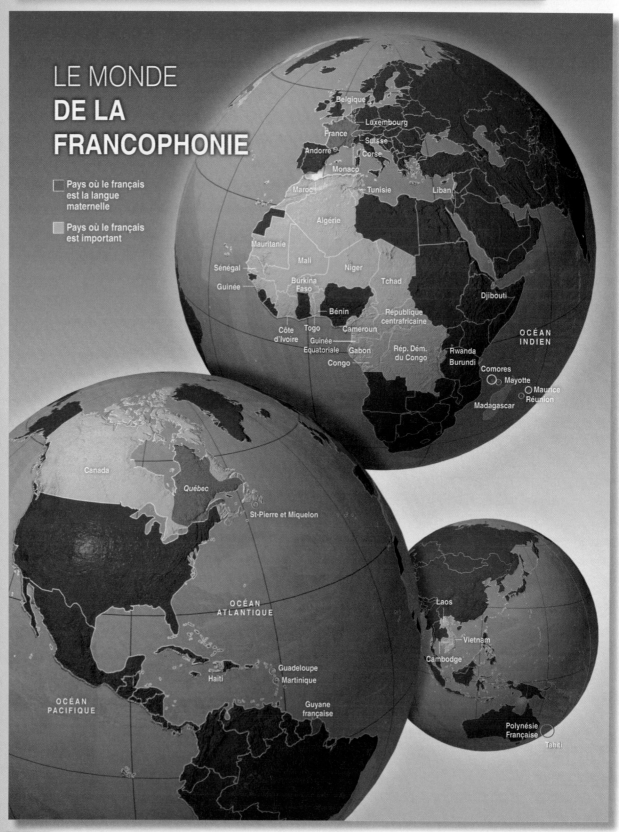

LE MONDE
**DE LA
FRANCOPHONIE**

Pays où le français
est la langue
maternelle

Pays où le français
est important

Belgique
Luxembourg
France
Suisse
Andorre
Corse
Monaco
Maroc
Tunisie
Liban
Algérie
Mauritanie
Mali
Niger
Sénégal
Burkina
Faso
Tchad
Guinée
Djibouti
Bénin
République
centrafricaine
Côte
d'Ivoire
Togo
Cameroun
OCÉAN
INDIEN
Guinée
Equatoriale
Gabon
Rép. Dém.
du Congo
Rwanda
Burundi
Congo
Comores
Mayotte
Maurice
Réunion
Madagascar

Canada
Québec
St-Pierre et Miquelon
OCÉAN
ATLANTIQUE
Laos
Vietnam
Cambodge
Guadeloupe
Martinique
Haïti
OCÉAN
PACIFIQUE
Guyane
française
Polynésie
Française
Tahiti

# Level 1B

# Bridge

## Parties

### Première partie
**I will be able to:**

» introduce someone, tell my name, ask and tell how things are going, and take leave of someone.

### Deuxième partie
**I will be able to:**

» say what I like and don't like to do, and to what degree.

### Troisième partie
**I will be able to:**

» say what I have, need, prefer; tell my age; and ask specific questions.

### Quatrième partie
**I will be able to:**

» say where I am going and what I see there.

### Cinquième partie
**I will be able to:**

» describe my friends and family and order in a café.

Bridge parties   **B 0 1**

## Reference Desk

1. The *T'es branché? Level 1B* Bridge section is divided into five **parties** that review the vocabulary and grammar presented in **Unités** 1–5 of *T'es branché? Level 1A*. Each of the language objectives presented here connects to material from Units 1–5. However, the materials are not always reviewed in the same order as they were presented in Level 1A. Since the Bridge aims to provide an inclusive review of the Level 1A text in a limited amount of space, the presentation of materials has been reorganized into a logical and concise sequence of review points and activities.

2. Review activities consist of controlled vocabulary and grammar practice, as well as a variety of communicative activities. Students have the opportunity to apply previously-learned material within the context of interpersonal and presentational communicative opportunities.

## Essential Instruction
Have a student read the objective aloud for the **Première partie**. Then have pairs identify words and phrases that they remember to accomplish the objective. Have them share their words and phrases with the class. Repeat for the other objectives.

## Learning Styles
### Visual Learners
Direct visual learners to the photos on the page. Have them talk about which photos correspond with each objective. Encourage students think about another photo that could go in the blank square. Have them describe what would be in the photo and how it represents one or more of the objectives presented.

### Critical Thinking

#### Comparisons

Have students think about the words and gestures that they use when they greet their best friend, as well as the school principal. Have students identify the proper way to greet each person in French, being sure to talk about language and gestures in their responses.

### Communication

#### Interpersonal: Paired Practice

Host a meet-and-greet party. Turn the lights off and play soft background music. During this time, students get out of their seats and mingle. Have students "go to the party" with a partner. Students must introduce themselves and their partner to others. Students should also make small talk, asking how one another is doing and saying their nationality. Students should say good-bye before moving on to the next pair. Participate in the party with your students. After several moments, turn the music off and put the lights back on to signal that the party is over and that students should return to their seats.

B02

### Essential Instruction

1. Direct students to the title **Bonjour, tout le monde!** Remind them that the phrase **tout le monde** was chosen because students are introduced to people from all parts of the French-speaking world in this book. Have students work with a partner to brainstorm as many francophone countries as they can remember.

2. Before students begin **Activité 1**, read each bulleted point aloud. Pause after each one and have students identify words and phrases that can be used to achieve each task. Remind them to use a variety of greetings, and not to limit themselves to what is in the model.

3. Have students copy the dialogue for **Activité 2** in the correct order. Remind students of the abbreviations **M.**, **Mme**, and **Mlle**, and to use them as appropriate when they copy the dialogue.

# Vocabulaire

## 1 Présentations

### Interpersonal Communication

Working with two classmates, take turns making introductions.

- Greet the first person.
- Introduce the second person to him/her.
- Indicate whether the second person is your friend or your classmate.
- State his/her nationality.

**MODÈLE**  Isabelle/Sarah/camarade de classe/États-Unis
**Salut, Isabelle. Je te présente Sarah. C'est ma camarade de classe. Elle est américaine.**

1. Mathieu/Fatima/camarade de classe/Algérie (*Algeria*)
2. Madame Binot/Nicolas/camarade de classe/Canada
3. Nathalie/Gabriel/copain/France
4. Monsieur Sang/Florence/copine/États-Unis

## 2 Une nouvelle élève

### Interpersonal Communication

First, reorder the dialogue so that it flows in a logical order. Then, role-play the dialogue by taking on the identities of a different student and teacher.

"Enchantée, Élodie. Tu es canadienne?"
"Bonjour, Madame."
"Je m'appelle Élodie. Mon nom (*name*) de famille est Duchamp."
"Bonjour, Mademoiselle. Tu t'appelles comment?"
"Non, je suis française."

Première partie 1B  **B 0 3**

## Differentiated Instruction
### Accelerate
As students role-play the dialogue for **Activité 2**, have them extend the conversation to include other topics that they are able to discuss, such as favorite pastimes or classes. Remind students to conclude their conversation with an appropriate good-bye.

## Learning Styles
### Kinesthetic Learners
You may want to copy each sentence for **Activité 2** onto separate strips of paper, and place them in an envelope. Give an envelope to each of your kinesthetic learners, and have them align the conversation by placing the strips in the logical order on their desk.

## Answers

**①**

*Possible answers:*
1. Bonjour Mathieu, je te présente Fatima. C'est ma camarade de classe. Elle est algérienne.
2. Bonjour Madame Binot. Je vous présente Nicolas. C'est mon camarade de classe. Il est canadien.
3. Salut Nathalie! C'est Gabriel, mon copain français.
4. Bonjour Monsieur Sang. Je vous présente Florence, ma copine. Elle est américaine.

**②**

*Dialog order:* l.2, l.4, l.3, l.1, l.5;
*Answers will vary.*

## Reference Desk

Students learned names that are popular in France and Canada, as well as those that are popular in French-speaking Africa. Point out the name Fatima, used in **Activité 1**, and explain to students that it is of Arabic origin. Remind students that most of the population of Algeria, Tunisia, and Morocco is Muslim, and that both Arabic and French are spoken in these countries. Have students identify other names of Arabic origin that they may be familiar with, such as Ahmed, Aïcha, Khaled, and Hamza. Offer extra credit to students who are willing to find the meaning of these names on the Internet.

## Culture

### Practices: Information

Students may remember that in France, people often shake hands or do a quick kiss on both cheeks (**faire la bise**) when they greet friends and family. Explain that greeting practices vary in the French-speaking world. In Morocco, for example, people shake hands when they meet. They might also then touch their own heart to express warmth at seeing the other person. In Algeria, any greeting that does not include a handshake is considered to be impolite.

**Answers** _____

 **3**

Greeting: Bonsoir
Farewell: À demain, À bientôt,
Au revoir
Neither: Vas-y, Très bien, Pas mal,
Ça va mal, Et toi?
Both: Salut

**4**

1. Ça va?/Ça va (très) bien.
2. Comment allez-vous?/Ça va mal.
3. Ça va?/Ça va mal.
4. Ça va?/Ça va (très) bien.
5. Ça va?/Ça va. (*or*) Pas mal.
6. Ça va?/Ça va très bien.

## Reference Desk

1. Refer to pp. 016–017 of *T'es branché? Level 1A* for words and phrases that will help students do the activities on this page. Use the e-visual to review words and phrases that talk about how people are doing and good-byes.
2. Point out that the phrase **Vas-y!** in **Activité 3** translates as "Go on!" or "Go for it!"
3. See p. 063 of *T'es branché? Level 1A* to review the difference between **tu** and **vous**.

## Expansion

Say how you are feeling and have students make a gesture based on what they hear. They should give a thumbs-up sign if you are feeling well, a thumbs-down sign if you are not, or shrug their shoulders if you are just okay. Use words and expressions on this page, as well as the **Et si je voulais dire…?** words found on p. 016 of *T'es branché? Level 1A*. Use the activity as an opportunity to review the meaning of these additional phrases. Encourage students to incorporate them into their speech when appropriate.

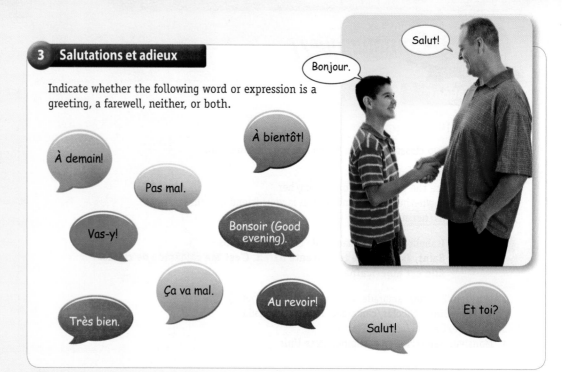

**3** **Salutations et adieux**

Indicate whether the following word or expression is a greeting, a farewell, neither, or both.

À demain!

À bientôt!

Pas mal.

Vas-y!

Bonsoir (Good evening).

Ça va mal.

Au revoir!

Très bien.

Salut!

Et toi?

Bonjour.

Salut!

## Communiquez!

**4** **Ça va?**

**Interpersonal Communication**

With a partner, play the roles of a student and the people below. Ask **Ça va?** or **Comment allez-vous?** as appropriate. Respond with an appropriate expression that fits the situation.

1. Simon: His family just got a new puppy.
2. Mlle Beaufort: She just got a parking ticket.
3. Rose: She has to clean the garage after school.
4. Alima: She discovered a cupcake in her lunch bag.
5. M. Zakaria: His day has been totally ordinary.
6. Mme Rachedi: Her husband gave her an iPad for her birthday today.

Je te présente BlackJack!

## Essential Instruction

1. Ask students how they are feeling. Then have them ask you the same. Review the difference between **tu** and **vous**. Direct students' attention to the photo. Remind them that the boy is using a more formal greeting than the man. Ask students to identify phrases they might use in greeting and leave-taking that are not appropriate in formal situations.
2. Before students begin **Activité 4**, remind them that when they tell how they are, they might follow their response with the question "and you?" Review the tag questions **et toi?** and **et vous?** with students, and have them use the questions to extend their dialogues.
3. Have students close their books. Remind them what a subject pronoun is, using examples in English (I, you, etc.). Ask students to list the subject pronouns in French based on memory. Have them open their books to p. B05 and check their lists against what is found on the page.

# Structure de la langue

**Passons en revue!**

## Subject Pronouns

Subject pronouns are used to talk **to** or **about** someone. They are singular or plural.

| Singular | | Plural | |
|---|---|---|---|
| je | I | nous | we |
| tu | you (*singular informal*) | vous | you (*singular formal and/or plural*) |
| il | he | ils | they |
| elle | she | elles | they (*females only*) |
| on | one/they/we | | |

**5  Quel sujet?**

Which subject pronoun would you use in the following situations?

You are talking...
1. *to* your best friend
2. *about* Julien and Cédric
3. *about* yourself
4. *to* your Graphic Design teacher
5. *about* you and your Mom
6. *to* your cat, Misha
7. *about* M. Leblanc
8. *about* Awa
9. *to* two of your classmates
10. *about* two girls in your P.E. class
11. *to* the lunchroom supervisor
12. *about* Sophie and her boyfriend

C'est Sophie et Charles.

## Present Tense of the Irregular Verb *être*

The verb **être** (*to be*) does not follow a predictable pattern. It is an ***irregular*** verb.

| | | | |
|---|---|---|---|
| je | **suis** | nous | **sommes** |
| tu | **es** | vous | **êtes** |
| ils/elles | **est** | il/elle/on | **sont** |

Première partie 1B   **B05**

---

**Answers**

**5**
1. tu
2. ils
3. je
4. vous
5. nous
6. tu
7. il
8. elle
9. vous
10. elles
11. vous
12. ils

### Reference Desk

1. Refer to p. 061 of *T'es branché? Level 1A* to review subject pronouns with students.
2. Students have also learned the subject pronoun **on** which is often used interchangeably with **nous** in everyday French. Students may remember the suggestion **On va au cinéma?** to mean *Are we going to the movies? /Shall we go to the movies?* The subject pronoun **on** is also used as the impersonal *one* or *you,* as in **On doit étudier** meaning *You / One should study.*
3. Refer to p.132 of *T'es branché? Level 1A* to review the forms of the verb **être** with students.

### Game

**Retrouvez les sujets**

Working in pairs, students create a matching game by cutting a sheet of paper into six even strips. Then have students cut the strips in half, creating 12 total cards. Students divide the cards into two groups. They will write a form of the verb **être** on each of the cards in the first group. Students will write a subject pronoun or subject (i.e. **nous** or **Jean et moi**) for each of the cards in the second group. Students will shuffle all cards and place them face-down. They take turns looking for a subject-verb match by turning two cards over at a time. Students keep matches when they find them.

---

### Differentiated Learning

**Decelerate**

Have students list subject pronouns that would be used in English for each of the situations in **Activité 5.** Then have them use the list at the top of the page to find the French equivalent.

**Special Needs Students**

**Dyslexia**

Students with dyslexia may struggle with the disconnect between the sounds of the forms of the verb **être** and the way they are written. Work with students on French phonology, offering examples of the verb forms used in context and alone, to highlight how **liason** can change pronunciation. Help them to master the pronunciation and spelling by having them create index cards with the French word on one side and a simple phonological spelling on the other. For example, students might write **suis / swee** (as in sweet), **es/ay** (as in day). Allow students to use these cards as a reference when they are participating in activities or reading aloud.

**1.** so**mm**es
**2.** **so**n**t**
**3.** **e**s
**4.** **sui**s
**5.** **êt**es

**7**

**1.** je
**2.** elle
**3.** ils
**4.** nous
**5.** tu
**6.** il
**7.** vous
**8.** elles

## Reference Desk

At this point, students are beginning to see direction lines written in French, as in **Activité 6**. Read these direction lines aloud. Have students apply reading strategies such as using context cues and cognates for comprehension. If students are still unclear about the directions, have them scan the activity itself to better understand what it is asking them to do. Confirm students' understanding of the French direction lines with each activity, until you feel that students are at an appropriate language level to work through them independently.

## Communication

**Interpersonal: Cooperative Groups**

Divide students into groups of four to practice using the verb **être** to play a guessing game. Have students give sentences about a teacher, without naming him or her. For example students might say, **Il est mon prof de maths. Il est dans la salle 302. Il est américain.** Encourage students to say as many sentences with **être** as they can in their descriptions. Group members must guess which teacher is being described. Have students continue until each member of the group has described a teacher.

**B 0 6**

The verb **être** is used...

* to identify people.

  *M. Durocher est mon prof.*

* with nationalities and other adjectives.

  *Thomas est algérien.*
  *Es-tu bavard(e)?*

* to say where someone is or where someone is from.

  *Ma mère est à la maison.*
  *Je suis de Lyon.*

* to say what day it is and to give the date.

  *Nous sommes mercredi.*
  *Nous sommes le 20 octobre.*
  *C'est le 20 octobre.*

**6** **Où sont les lettres?**

*Copiez 1–5 sur votre papier. Écrivez les formes du verbe* **être** *avec les lettres qui manquent* (are missing)*. À côté de* (Next to) *chaque* (each) *forme, écrivez le pronom* (pronoun) *qui correspond* (matches)*.*

**MODÈLE**   il/elle/on   __e__ st

1. nous          __ om __ es
2. les Tremblay  __ on __
3. tu            __ s
4. je            __ ui __
5. vous          __ __es

Ils sont en ville.

**7** **Quel sujet correspond?**

Look at the following phrases and sentences. Which subject pronoun corresponds to the underlined word(s)?

| je | tu | il | elle | on | nous | vous | ils | elles |
|----|----|----|----|----|----|----|----|----|

1. <u>Moi</u> aussi.
2. <u>Yasmine</u> est algérienne.
3. <u>Georges et Salim</u> aiment faire du roller.
4. <u>Daniel et moi</u> aimons manger de la salade.
5. Et <u>toi</u>?
6. <u>Khaled</u> est mon copain.
7. <u>Vincent et toi</u> aimez faire de la gym.
8. Voici (*Here is/are*) <u>Véronique et Isabelle</u>.

**B 0 6**

### Essential Instruction

1. Read each bulleted point aloud for the uses of the verb **être**. After each one, pause and ask students personal questions to practice that use. For example, ask **Qui est votre prof d'anglais?** Students can reply, for example, **Mlle Smith est ma prof d'anglais.** Continue until you have reviewed all of the uses.

2. For **Activité 7** explain that **moi** and **toi** are also pronouns. They are called stress pronouns, and their English equivalents are *me* and *you*. Have students identify the subject pronouns that correspond with *me* and *you* in English to help them find the words in French.

3. For **Activité 9**, divide the class into two groups, and have them survey only the people in their group. Then have students choose a partner from the other group. Students report to their partner what they learned, using the third person. For example, they might say **Katie et Tim sont de St. Louis.**

## 8 Quelle forme?

*Donnez la forme convenable (appropriate) du verbe **être**.*

1. Jeanne... ma camarade de classe.
2. Nous... vendredi. Youpi!
3. Ousmane et Bruno... au cinéma avec Karine et Delphine.
4. Tu... de Marseille. Tu... français.
5. Simon et toi, vous... intelligents!
6. Je... canadien. Je... de Montréal.
7. C'... le 25 novembre.... la fête de l'Action de grâce (*Thanksgiving*).
8. Jacqueline et moi, nous ne... pas énergiques.

## 9 Tu es d'où?

**Interpersonal/Presentational Communication**

*Demandez à dix camarades de classe d'où ils sont (where they're from originally). Présent l'information.*

> **MODÈLE**   A: **Tu es d'où**?
> B: **Je suis de Chicago**.
>
> **Trois élèves sont de Chicago....**

## 10 Une présentation

**Presentational Communication**

*Formez un groupe de 4–6 camarades. Prenez des tours en présentant (introducing) vos camarades de classe.*

- Say where two students in your class are from.
- State that two other classmates are from a different city.
- State that you and Aurélie are from a city in France.

Première partie 1B   **B 0 7**

**8**
1. est
2. sommes
3. sont
4. es, es
5. êtes
6. suis, suis
7. est, C'est
8. sommes

**9** *Answers will vary.*

**10** *Presentations will vary.*

### Reference Desk

1. The phrase **être de** is being used to talk about being from a city. If students want to say that they are from a state or a country, they must also use the definite article (**le**, **la**, **les**) with the phrase. For example, **Je suis des États-Unis** or **Je suis de la Californie**. Teach students how to say the name of your state in French. Most states carry masculine gender. The states that carry feminine gender are **Californie, Caroline du Nord, Caroline du Sud, Floride, Géorgie, Louisiane, Pennsylvanie, Virginie**, and **Virginie-Occidentale**.

2. Display a U.S. map on your bulletin board. Have students locate the city and state where they were born and to mark that space using a push pin. Use the map to review saying where people are from, and to help teach students the state names in French. Have students use the map as a visual when they give their presentations for **Activité 10**.

## Differentiated Learning

### Accelerate
Have students use other questions with **être**, such as **Comment es-tu?**, to find out more about their classmates as they do **Activité 9**.

### Decelerate
Do **Activité 8** as a class. Read each item aloud and say two forms of the verb **être** – one correct and one incorrect. Have students choose the correct form from the pair and write their answer.

## Learning Styles

### Auditory Learners
After all students present the information for **Activité 10**, play a quiz game. Ask students questions such as **Qui est de New York?** or **D'où sont Aurélie et Rachel?** Have students respond orally based on what they heard in their classmates' presentations.

**Answers**

**11** *Dialogues will vary.*

**12** *Possible dialogue:*

–Allô, oui?
–Bonjour, c'est (prénom). Ça va?
–Ça va bien, et toi?
–Très bien, merci. On va à la teuf?
–Je ne peux pas. Je dois aider ma
mère.
–OK, à bientôt.
–Au revoir.

**13**

1. Martine est française?
2. Tu t'appelles comment?
3. On va au centre commercial?
4. Comment allez-vous?
5. Et David?

### Reference Desk

1. Refer to ***T'es Branché?*** *Level 1A* pp. 028–029 to review vocabulary for inviting, accepting, and declining invitations. Show e-visual 5 to students to review place names, and the words and expressions used to discuss invitations.
2. Remember that the word **teuf**, which means party, is **verlan**, a spoken form of French in which the syllables of words are inverted. **Verlan** is roughly the equivalent of Pig Latin in English. Ask students to provide an example of words in Pig Latin. Give additional examples of **verlan** words such as **zonmai** (**maison**) and **meuf** (**femme**).
3. Remind students that the word **âllo** is used as a greeting when answering the telephone.

## Communiquez!

**11** **Tu voudrais aller...?**

### Interpersonal Communication

With a partner, play the roles of an American student and his or her host brother in Québec. The American suggests activities to do, beginning with "**On va...?**"

1. see the movie *Amélie*
2. eat **une tourtière** (*Canadian meat pie*)
3. meet some teenagers and dance
4. buy some gifts to take home to his family
5. watch a hockey game on TV

## Communiquez!

**12** **Dring! Dring! Un coup de téléphone**

### Interpersonal Communication

With a partner, role-play the following conversation.

| **Toi** | **Ton copain/Ta copine** |
|---|---|
| Answer the phone. | Identify yourself. Ask how things are going. |
| Respond and add, "And you?" | Respond; invite your friend to go to a party. |
| Say that you can't. Give an excuse. | Say OK and that you'll see your friend soon. |
| Respond, "See you later!" | |

**13** **Quelle est la question?**

Here are answers to common questions. Choose a question from the box that goes with each answer. Then role-play the short dialogues with a classmate.

> On va au centre commercial?
> Et David?
> Tu t'appelles comment?
> Comment allez-vous?
> Martine est française?

1. _____
   Non, elle est canadienne.
2. _____
   Je m'appelle Amidou, a-emme-i-dé-o-u.
3. _____
   D'accord, je veux bien.

4. _____
   Comme ci, comme ça.
5. _____
   C'est mon camarade de classe.

### Essential Instruction

1. Before students begin **Activité 11**, review words for activities mentioned. Remind students that the movie ***Amélie*** is a comedy about the adventures of a Parisian café waitress. Have students answer according to whether they would actually want to do each activity, based on their own knowledge and preferences. When students finish, have them switch roles and repeat the activity.
2. Have two students act out **Activité 12** using cell phones (real or pretend) as props. Students should stand on opposite sides of the room to carry out their conversation. After the conversation ends, have the student who declined the invitation give the phone back to the first student. She will "call" a different classmate to invite him to the party by handing the phone to a student of her choice. The students will role-play the conversation again, and this time the student who received the phone call will accept the invitation.

# Communiquez!

**14  Présentations - C'est à vous!**

## Interpersonal and Presentational Communication

Write a brief dialogue for the first two situations. Then role-play with a partner the third and fourth situations.

1. Walking downtown, you meet your French friend, Lucie, who is with her classmate, Léo. Greet her. Lucie will introduce you to Léo and state that he is a classmate. Say that you are pleased to meet him.

**En ville**

Toi: _____

Lucie: _____

Toi: _____

2. You are talking to your friend, Coralie, at an International Club meeting. Coralie points out Myriam across the room. You ask if Myriam is Canadian. Coralie tells you no, that she is Algerian.

**Au club**

Coralie: _____

Toi: _____

Coralie: _____

3. You see your French teacher, M. Lebeau, at the movie theater. Greet him and ask him how he is. He tells you that he is so-so. He asks you how you are doing and you tell him how you are.

**Au cinéma**

A: Greet your French teacher, M. Lebeau. Ask how he is.

B: Say you are so-so. Ask your student how things are going.

A: Say how things are going.

4. You are talking to your friend, Olivier, on your cell phone. You invite him to go to the café. He tells you that it's not possible. He has to help his mother. He asks you if you would like to go to the party tomorrow. Tell him that you would like that and add that you will see him tomorrow.

**Au téléphone**

A: Invite your friend, Olivier, to go to the café.

B: Say that it's not possible. You have to help your mother. Ask your friend if he or she would like to go to the party tomorrow.

A: Tell him that you would like that. Say that you will see him tomorrow.

## Multiple Intelligences
### Verbal-Linguistic

Although the instructions for **Activité 14** say that students should write the first two dialogues and role play the others, verbal-linguistic learners will benefit from the opportunity to write and say each one. Encourage these students to write scripts for all four items, and then review them aloud in pairs. After they have had time to practice, have students present their dialogues without their scripts.

## Special Needs Students
### Behavioral Problems

To keep students on task during cooperative activities, assign each group member a role: one group member can be the recorder, who takes notes on the group's discussion. Another might be the reporter, who gives the group's response to the class. A third might work as a leader, who guides the group members through the activities. A fourth student might act as a liaison between the group and the teacher.

# Les passe-temps

B10

### Essential Instruction

1. Have students close their books, and ask them to list as many pastimes as they can remember in French. Remind them to include indoor and outdoor activities. After several moments, call on students to share their responses. Create a class list and leave it displayed during the lesson for students' reference.
2. Direct students' attention to the photo on p. B10. Have students identify in French what they boy is doing. Then ask **Est-ce qu'il aime écouter de la musique?** Have a student respond, and then ask several others whether they like to listen to music.
3. Before beginning **Activité 1** on p. B11, review the pronunciation of each pastime listed in the blue box. Add any new pastimes from the box to your class list.
4. Read the directions to **Activité 2** aloud, and check for comprehension of the instructions before students begin the activity.

# Vocabulaire

## 1 Qu'est-ce que tu aimes faire?

Say what you like to do ("**J'aime**") and don't like to do ("**Je n'aime pas**") on different days of the week or in different weather conditions. Choose from the activities in the box.

| | | |
|---|---|---|
| sortir avec mes amis | travailler | faire du shopping |
| faire du footing | aller à une teuf | jouer au foot |
| manger de la pizza | danser (*dance*) | faire du vélo |
| jouer au basket | faire du roller | aller au cinéma |

**MODÈLE**   Le lundi
**Le lundi**, j'aime **jouer au foot**, mais je n'aime pas **faire du roller**.

1. Le lundi, _____ .
2. Le mardi, _____ .
3. Le mercredi,_____ .
4. Le jeudi,_____ .
5. Le vendredi,_____ .
6. Le samedi, _____ .
7. Le dimanche,_____ .
8. Quand il fait beau, _____ .
9. Quand il fait mauvais,_____ .

## 2 Les Jeux Olympiques

*Voici les champions/championnes des Jeux Olympiques d'été à Beijing et des Jeux Olympiques d'hiver à Vancouver. Dites ce que (what) chaque athlète aime faire.*

**MODÈLE**  Kristin Armstrong
**Elle aime faire du vélo**.

1. Michael Phelps

2. Didier Défago

3. Patrice Bergeron

4. Émilie Heymans

5. Evan Lysacek

6. Thomas Bouhail

Deuxième partie 1B   **B 1 1**

## Differentiated Learning
### Accelerate
Challenge students to provide a more detailed description of each athlete mentioned in **Activité 2**. Students can include nationality, physical characteristics, and personality traits. Have students present their descriptions to the class. Students may also say what other activities the athlete might do, in addition to those mentioned in **Activité 2**.

## Special Needs Students
### Visually Impaired
Visually challenged students may benefit from an explanation of the illustrations in **Activité 2**. Describe each illustration in English and have students supply the French word or phrase orally before they do the activity.

---

**Answers** _____

**1** *Answers will vary.*

**2**

1. Michael Phelps aime nager.
2. Didier Défago aime faire du ski (alpin).
3. Patrice Bergeron aime jouer au hockey.
4. Émilie Heymans aime plonger.
5. Evan Lysacek aime faire du patinage (artistique).
6. Thomas Bouhail aime faire de la gym.

### Reference Desk

1. Highlight the expression **ne... pas**. Remind students that it is used for negation, and that it goes around the conjugated verb. In these activities, the conjugated verb is **aimer**, so students should avoid putting the **ne... pas** around the infinitive.

2. The 2008 Summer Olympics were held in Beijing, China and some Francophones participated. That year, American swimmer Michael Phelps won eight gold medals, breaking the record for the most gold medals ever won in a single Olympics. Diver Émilie Heymans, who won a silver medal, was born in Belgium and raised outside of Montreal. She participated on the Canadian team. The Algerian-born French gymnast Thomas Bouhail won the silver medal for the vault.

3. The 2010 Winter Olympics were held in Vancouver, British Columbia. Patrice Bergeron, a native of Quebec who plays for the Boston Bruins, was a part of the gold medal-winning Canadian ice hockey team. Swiss skier Didier Défago won the gold medal for downhill skiing that winter, and American Evan Lysacek won the gold medal for men's figure skating.

**3** Une semaine occupée

*Regardez l'agenda de Solange, puis et répondez aux phrases suivantes (following) avec "C'est vrai" ou "C'est faux."*

| lundi | mardi | mercredi | jeudi | vendredi | samedi | dimanche |
|---|---|---|---|---|---|---|
| faire | match | étudier | contrôle | sortir | aller au | faire du |
| du | de | pour le | de maths | avec Luc | café | vélo avec |
| footing | basket | contrôle | | et Lilou | | Amélie |
| | ESPN | de maths | | | | |

1. Solange is going out on Saturday.
2. She is going to focus on fitness on Monday.
3. She is probably looking forward to Thursday.
4. She is going to watch TV on Tuesday.
5. She hopes that the weather will be good on Sunday.
6. She is free to go shopping on Wednesday evening.

## Communiquez!

**4** Colonie de vacances

**Interpersonal Communication**

You and your classmate are going to the same camp during vacation. You just received the brochure with pictures of the activities offered. Take turns asking each other if you like each of the activities. Answer with "**Oui**, **j'aime**…" or "**Non**, **je n'aime pas**…" Which one of you will probably be happier at this camp?

### 5 Une lettre

Claire is spending spring break with her relatives in **la Louisiane**. In the first letter that she writes home, she tells her family about the activities that her aunt, uncle and cousins like to do. Read her letter, and replace the pictures with the missing infinitives or verbal expressions.

*Bonjour!*

*Comment allez-vous? Moi, ça va fort! J'aime passer la semaine ici à la Nouvelle Orléans.*

*Oncle Paul aime bien*  *. Tante Héloïse aime*  *. Cousine Virginie aime un peu*

 *, mais elle n'aime pas beaucoup*  *. Cousin Jean aime bien*  *et*

 *. Mon petit cousin Samuel aime un peu*  *et il adore*  *. Moi, j'aime*

*beaucoup*  *avec mon nouveau lecteur MP3. À bientôt!*

*Bisous,*

*Claire*

Quartier français, La Nouvelle Orléans.

B 1 3

---

**Answers**

**5**

faire la cuisine, lire les magazines, surfer sur Internet, dormir, envoyer des textos, téléphoner, jouer aux jeux vidéo, regarder la télé, écouter de la musique

### Reference Desk

The photo at the bottom of this page shows the French Quarter in New Orleans, also known as the **Vieux Carré**. The French Quarter is the oldest neighborhood in the city, and a very popular tourist attraction. Millions of people visit the French Quarter each year. They may go to hear jazz or zydeco music at a local club, or eat some jambalaya or **beignets** at one of the Quarter's many well-known restaurants. Visitors to the French Quarter will note the mix of European and Cajun influences in the music, architecture, and culture.

### TPR

Say activities that you do and don't do. Have students draw the activities under the correct column. For example, if you say **J'aime bien plonger**, students might draw hands together as if the person is preparing to dive.

---

**Differentiated Instruction**

**Decelerate**

Before students begin **Activité 5**, review the words and phrases that each drawing represents.

**Expand**

Using the letter in **Activité 5** as a model, have students imagine that they are staying at the home of an extended family member. Ask them to write a letter to their own parents or caregivers, talking about the likes and dislikes of their host.

**Multiple Intelligences**

**Naturalist**

Have students research summer camp programs offered in France. Ask them to find one that they would be interested in participating in. Have them prepare a presentation in which they say where and when the camp is, what outdoor activities they can do there, and who can attend. If applicable, have students compare the French program with summer camp programs that they have attended in the United States.

## Reference Desk

1. Refer to p. 065 **of T'es branché?** *Level 1A* and e-visual 6 to review the present tense of regular verbs ending in –**er**.
2. Remind students that the verb is divided into two parts: the stem (**la racine**) and the ending (**la terminaison**).
3. Review pronunciation of the –**er** verb forms with students, stressing that four of the forms sound the same (**je**, **tu**, **il/elle/on**, **ils/elles**). Point out to students that the verb forms in the darker parts of the chart have the same pronunciation.
4. Point out how the letter **e** is added in the first-person plural (**nous**) form of verbs whose stem ends in **g**, such as **nager** and **plonger**. Explain that the letter **g** followed by an **o** (as in the –**ons** ending) makes a hard **g** sound in French, as well as in English. Give the borrowed word **gourmet** as an example. Explain that the spelling change keeps the soft **g** sound that is heard in the infinitive and other forms.

# Structure de la langue

**Passons en revue!**

## Present Tense of Regular Verbs ending in –*er*

To form the present tense of regular –**er** verbs, drop the –**er** from the infinitive to find the stem. Add the ending that corresponds to each of the subject pronouns. Regular –**er** verbs follow a predictable pattern. Remember that for verbs whose stem ends in –**g** you must put an **e** before the –**ons** of the nous form (*nous nag**e**ons*). Here is the present tense of the verb **jouer**.

| subject pronoun | stem | ending | subject pronoun | stem | ending |
|---|---|---|---|---|---|
| je | jou | **e** | nous | jou | **ons** |
| tu | jou | **es** | vous | jou | **ez** |
| il/elle/on | jou | **e** | ils/elles | jou | **ent** |

**6** **Choisissez le sujet!**

Look at the following list of verbs with their endings. Write the letter of the subject that corresponds to the verb ending. **Attention!** Some verbs may have *two* possible subjects.

1. joues
2. nagent
3. plongeons
4. dansez
5. aime
6. travailles
7. joue
8. mangez
9. aiment
10. dansons

A. il/elle/on
B. nous
C. ils/elles
D. tu
E. vous
F. je/j'

**7** **Phrases logiques.!**

Choose a subject from column A, a verb from column B, and an expression from column C to create logical sentences. Remember to use the correct verb ending to correspond with the subject you choose. How many sentences can you create?

**MODÈLE**   *Ils plongent dans l'Océan Atlantique.*

| A | B | C |
|---|---|---|
| elle | aimer | à la maison |
| elles | danser | au basket |
| il | inviter | au café |
| ils | jouer | au cinéma |
| je | manger | dans l'océan Atlantique |
| nous | nager | de la glace au chocolat |
| on | plonger | le copain de Barbara |
| tu | travailler | le tango |
| vous | | quand il fait beau |
| | | sortir avec mon copain |

## Essential Instruction

1. Use e-visual 6 to review the present tense of regular verbs ending in –**er**. Give students additional infinitives, including those whose stem ends in **g**, to practice conjugating. Given the similarities in pronunciation, it is important to have students both say and write the verb forms, to ensure that they are producing the correct form.
2. For **Activité 7**, challenge students by timing them. Determine a time frame that is appropriate for your students and your schedule (perhaps between 2–5 minutes), and set a timer. Have students write as many sentences as they can in the allotted time. Award an extra point to the student who writes the most correct sentences. If students write fewer than 10 sentences in the allotted time, have them write the remaining sentences for homework.
3. Students will work in pairs to do **Activité 8**. To ensure that both partners are getting practice, have students take turns playing the role of Salim.

# Communiquez!

## 8 Qu'est-ce qu'on fait?

**Interpersonal Communication**

Salim has just transferred to your school. He is curious about his new classmates. Answer his questions based on the visual cues.

**MODÈLE**  Mamadou parle français?
**Oui, il parle français.**

 Chloé voyage?
**Non, elle nage.**

1. Clément et Pierre jouent au basket?

2. Karima achète une limonade au café?

3. Tu manges des frites?

4. Malika et Valérie travaillent au café?

5. Assane et toi, vous organisez une teuf?

6. Patrick joue au hockey sur glace?

7. Jamila et Thierry préparent une crêpe?

8. Tu aimes aller en ville?

Answers

**8**

1. Non, ils jouent au foot.
2. Non, elle achète une glace.
3. Oui, je mange des frites.
4. Non, elles travaillent au cinéma.
5. Oui, nous organisons une teuf.
6. Oui, il joue au hockey sur glace.
7. Non, ils préparent un hamburger.
8. Oui, j'aime aller en ville. (or) Non, je n'aime pas aller en ville.

## Game

### Jeu de l'âne

Have students play a variation of "Pin the tail on the donkey." Draw a large circle on the board, and five concentric circles inside. The drawing should look like a dart board with a bull's eye and five rings. In the middle, write **je**. Write the other subject pronouns in the other rings. Divide the class into two teams. Give each student an index card with a different **–er** verb written in its infinitive form, and a piece of tape. Call students to the front of the room one at a time, then blindfold them. Have each student walk toward the board and tape his card within the circle. Then have him remove his blindfold and conjugate his verb according to where he placed his card. Have him say and write the word. For example, if he taped the verb **travailler** in the ring with **il**, he should say and write **travaille**. Award a point for correct answers, and award a second point if the student uses the subject/verb combination in a sentence. Have teams take turns. The team which has the most points after everyone has had a turn is the winner.

## Multiple Intelligences
### Intrapersonal

Some students may prefer to work alone. In an activity such as **Activité 8**, where the questions are already provided, allow students to write their responses independently if they choose to do so. To encourage oral practice for students who prefer to work alone, have them read or say their responses to you. Alternatively, you may ask that students record the responses and submit to you electronically.

## Special Needs Students
### Auditory Impairment

Hearing impaired students may have trouble understanding if they do not hear the entire sentence, especially when verb forms sound alike. To ensure that students hear each part of a sentence, move closer to the student and repeat the sentence, being sure to clearly enunciate the subject or subject pronoun. Students can better distinguish what is being said to them when background noise is at a minimum and the speaker is fewer than three feet away.

**9** **Complétez!**

Choose a verb from the word bank that fits logically into the sentence. Then write the correct form of the verb. Each verb will be used only once.

| regarder | porter | marquer | manger | écouter | surfer | aimer | étudier |
|---|---|---|---|---|---|---|---|

1. Je _____ de la quiche au café.
2. Robert et Manu _____ pour le contrôle de sciences.
3. Nous _____ les comédies au cinéma.
4. Marc _____ un but.
5. Tu _____ un peu la radio?
6. Nadia et Claudette _____ des casquettes.
7. On _____ beaucoup sur Internet.
8. Vous _____ lire, Mme Bouchard?

## Communiquez!

**10** **Tout le monde aime une fête!**

### Interpersonal Communication

*Madame Courbin et sa classe de français organisent (organize) une fête. Madame a besoin d'aide. Qui fait quoi (what) pour la fête? Jouez les rôles de Mme Courbin et son assistant(e).*

**MODÈLE** inviter tout le monde/Martine et Claire
A: **Qui invite tout le monde**?
B: **Martine et Claire invitent tout le monde**.

1. apporter les boissons/Luc et moi
2. préparer la quiche/Stéphanie
3. acheter les desserts/moi
4. organiser les jeux/Serge et Abdou
5. inviter le proviseur/vous
6. parler français/nous

### Essential Instruction

1. Assign **Activité 9** as homework.
2. Place students in pairs for **Activité 10**. Before they begin, review forming questions with **qui**. Remind them that **qui** takes the third-person singular form of the verb. As students provide responses, encourage them to add their own details. For example, they might say: **Luc et moi, nous apportons les boissons comme le coca et le jus d'orange.**
3. Set the stage for a review of adverbs of degree by asking **Aimez-vous jouer aux jeux-vidéo?** Get several responses, and ask the question again to the same students, this time adding the word **beaucoup**. After students respond, ask them if they can name the other two adverbs they learned for degree. Review the information and examples in the yellow box on p. B17.
4. For **Activité 11**, have students correct false statements using information in the paragraph.

# Adverbs of Degree

In French, adverbs are usually placed right after the verb. The common adverbs, **un peu**, **bien**, and **beaucoup** tell how much a person likes to do an activity. Adverbs also tell how, when, where, and why.

| | |
|---|---|
| Jacques aime **un peu** voyager. | *Jacques likes to travel a little.* |
| J'aime **bien** parler français. | *I really like to speak French.* |
| Nous aimons **beaucoup** nager. | *We like to swim a lot.* |

**11  Un peu, bien, ou beaucoup?**

Students in Mlle Senghor's class have been asked to write a descriptive paragraph about a classmate. Read the following description of Delphine and say whether the statements that follow are **vrai** or **faux**.

*Ma copine, Delphine, est très active et intéressante. Elle joue au basket, au tennis, et au foot. Elle adore les films, surtout les films français. Elle n'aime pas étudier, mais elle aime bien lire et écouter de la musique. Elle adore manger des spaghetti, mais elle n'aime pas faire la cuisine.*

1. Delphine joue à beaucoup aux sports.
2. Elle aime un peu aller au cinéma.
3. Elle aime bien étudier.

4. Elle aime un peu écouter de la musique.
5. Elle aime beaucoup manger des pâtes.

Deuxième partie 1B    B17

## Reference Desk

1. Refer to p. 075 of **_T'es branché?_** *Level 1A* to review position of adverbs.
2. Direct students' attention to the photo. Explain that the Eiffel Tower, or **La Tour Eiffel**, was constructed to be part of the 1889 World's Fair. At that time, it was the tallest structure on Earth.

## Connections

### History

Explain that although it's a very popular tourist attraction today, at the time of its construction, many of the French were displeased with the Eiffel Tower. Have students work in pairs to research the structure's history and learn about famous people's reaction to it. Have them imagine that it's 1889, and that they are newspaper reporters. Students will work together to publish a short article in English detailing the public's reaction to the "new" structure. After they finish, allow time for students to read the news articles.

## Differentiated Learning

### Expand

Give students additional practice with adverbs of degree. Have them rewrite the sentences in **Activité 9** using the verb **aimer** followed by an adverb of degree and the infinitive form of the verb.

### Special Needs Students

### Linguistically Challenged

Students may have trouble with the different word order that is used with adverbs. Point out that the adverb of degree is placed directly after the conjugated verb. Highlight how the three examples in the grammar box have both the verb **aimer** and another infinitive. Explain that **aimer** is the conjugated verb, and therefore the adverbs follow the form of this verb, since they are describing how much something is liked. When students are faced with a structure that follows a different pattern than English, advise them to focus on memorizing a couple examples.

**Answers**

**⑫**

1. Tu aimes manger de la glace?
   *Answers will vary.*
2. Tu aimes envoyer des textos?
   *Answers will vary.*
3. Tu aimes lire? *Answers will vary.*
4. Tu aimes gagner? *Answers will vary.*
5. Tu aimes sortir avec des amis?
   *Answers will vary.*
6. Tu aimes dormir? *Answers will vary.*
7. Tu aimes écouter de la musique?
   *Answers will vary.*
8. Tu aimes voyager? *Answers will vary.*
9. Tu aimes parler français? *Answers will vary.*

**⑬**

1. soixante-quinze pour cent
2. trente pour cent
3. cinquante-quatre pour cent
4. quatre-vingt-treize pour cent
5. vingt et un pour cent
6. quarante-six pour cent
7. soixante-deux pour cent
8. quatre-vingt-trois pour cent

## Reference Desk

1. You may want to review the Dialogue Video that accompanies the **Rencontres culturelles** for **Unité 2**, **Leçon A** of *T'es branché? Level 1A*. Students can use this dialogue as a model when doing **Activité 12**.
2. The English word *interview* has several French translations. **Une entrevue** and **un entretien** can both refer to job interviews. **Une interview** can also be used to talk about an interview conducted for a newspaper or magazine article.
3. You may want to refer to the information on p.033 of *T'es branché? Level 1A* to compare cell phone use between French and American teens. Point out that 80% of French teens have their own cell phones, as opposed to 75% of American teens.

 **Communiquez!**

### 12 Une entrevue

**Interpersonal/Presentational Communication**

You and your classmates are interviewing each other for the school newspaper. Work with a partner and find out **how much** he/she likes to do the following activities. Your partner will, in turn, ask you the questions. Take notes! When you have interviewed each other, join another pair of students and tell them what you learned in the interview about your partner. Remember to use **un peu**, **bien**, or **beaucoup** in your responses.

> **MODÈLE** regarder la télé
> A: **Tu aimes regarder la télé**?
> B: **J'aime bien regarder la télé**.

1. manger de la glace
2. envoyer des textos
3. lire
4. gagner
5. sortir avec des amis
6. dormir
7. écouter de la musique
8. voyager
9. parler français

| **Les nombres** |
|---|
| zéro  un  deux  trois  quatre  cinq  six  sept  huit  neuf  dix  onze  douze  treize |
| quatorze  quinze  seize  dix-sept  dix-huit  dix-neuf  vingt  trente  quarante |
| cinquante  soixante  soixante-dix  quatre-vingts  quatre-vingt-dix  cent |

### 13 Les jeunes et les portables

State the percentage (for example, **vingt pourcent**) of 12- to 17-year-old American teens who....

| | |
|---|---|
| 1. own a cell phone | 75% |
| 2. talk on a land-line phone daily | 30% |
| 3. send text messages every day | 54% |
| 4. feel safer because they have a cell phone | 93% |
| 5. use e-mail on their phones | 21% |
| 6. play games on their phones | 46% |
| 7. can have their phones in school but not in class | 62% |
| 8. take pictures with their phones | 83% |

**B 1 8**

## Essential Instruction

1. After students have discussed their responses to **Activité 12** in small groups, review them as a class. Use students' input to determine which two activities on the list are most and least popular in the class.
2. Direct students' attention to the numbers in the box. Use your hands to count as you say numbers **zéro** to **dix**. Refer to p. 082 of *T'es branché? Level 1A* to review how the French count on their fingers. Say several digits aloud, and have students show you the corresponding gestures used by the French.

3. Before students begin **Activité 15**, review the pronunciation of the names of the restaurants and the meanings of their names.
4. Begin a review of the date by saying today's date in French. Then say the date of your birthday. Write it on the board, emphasizing how you say and write the number before the month. Call on several students to say their birthdays.

## 14 Les séries

*Quels sont les nombres qui manquent?* (What numbers are missing?)

1. un, trois, _____, _____, _____, _____, treize
2. deux, quatre, _____, _____, _____, douze, _____, _____
3. dix, vingt, _____, _____, _____
4. cent, quatre-vingt-dix, _____, _____, _____

## 15 Quel est le numéro de téléphone?

**Interpersonal Communication**

Take turns with a partner asking and answering the question about phone numbers of restaurants in Avignon, France.

**MODÈLE** La Vieille Ferme: 04.20.15.37.52
A: **Quel est le numéro de téléphone de La Vieille Ferme**?
B: **C'est le zéro quatre, vingt, quinze, trente-sept, cinquante-deux**.

1. La Cour du Palais      04.11.15.07.43
2. La Cuillère      04.10.19.81.12
3. L'Île Sauvage      04.64.17.12.90
4. La Bonne Mère      04.36.18.50.16
5. L'Étoile      04.16.14.99.25
6. La Vache Brune      04.13.08.61.74

## Les dates

To give a date in French, follow this pattern:

To express the first of the month use: **le premier**. Remember that the day comes before the month in an abbreviation: **11.5**

**le + number + month**
C'est le seize mars.
C'est le premier avril.

C'est le onze mai.

janvier   février   mars   avril   mai   juin   juillet   août   septembre   octobre   novembre   décembre

1. cinq, sept, neuf, onze
2. six, huit, dix, quatorze, seize
3. trente, quarante, cinquante
4. quatre-vingts, soixante-dix, soixante

1. –Quel est le numéro de téléphone de La Cour du Palais?
   –C'est le zéro quatre, onze, quinze, zéro sept, quarante-trois.
2. –Quel est le numéro de téléphone de La Cuillère?
   –C'est le zéro quatre, dix, dix-neuf, quatre-vingt-un, douze.
3. –Quel est le numéro de téléphone de L'Île Sauvage?
   –C'est le zéro quatre, soixante-quatre, dix-sept, douze, quatre-vingt-dix.
4. –Quel est le numéro de téléphone de La Bonne Mère?
   –C'est le zéro quatre, trente-six, dix-huit, cinquante, seize.
5. –Quel est le numéro de téléphone de Quel est le numéro de téléphone de L'Étoile?
   –C'est le zéro quatre, seize, quatorze, quatre-vingt-dix-neuf, vingt-cinq.
6. –Quel est le numéro de téléphone de La Vache Brune?
   –C'est le zéro quatre, treize, zéro huit, soixante et un, soixante-quatorze.

### Reference Desk

Refer to p. 241 of *T'es branché?* *Level 1A* for information on expressing dates in French.

### Communication

**Interpersonal: Cooperative Groups**

Find ads for businesses on the Internet and give an ad to each student. Divide students into small groups. Each student should first say the name of their business. Then students will take turns asking for the phone number of the businesses, using **Activité 15** as a guide. Students will write each phone number as their classmate says it. After they finish, students should compare their work to see if they have the same phone numbers.

---

**Multiple Intelligences**
**Mathematical-Logical**
Encourage students to create additional number games and sequencing activities that will help their classmates practice numbers. Have students write their games on the board and lead the class through them.

**Special Needs Students**
**At-Risk Students**
Some at-risk teens are prone to changing schools at unconventional times. If you have a new student who seems to be having trouble adjusting to group work or grasping the content, offer extra support. To integrate the student socially, assign **un (e) ami(e)** who will help familiarize him or her with the other students, the classroom routine, and the process of turning in work. To provide academic support, you may wish to loan the student a copy of **T'es branché?** *Level 1A* if it is available, so that she may have more access to previously taught material. Offer to schedule one-on-one time to provide academic assistance as well as transitional support.

**16**

1. C'est le dix-huit septembre.
2. C'est le vingt-deux décembre.
3. C'est le premier octobre.
4. C'est le dix-sept novembre.
5. C'est le vingt-trois juillet.
6. C'est le quatre février.
7. C'est le neuf août.
8. C'est le vingt-six janvier.
9. C'est le vingt-trois juin.

1. masculine
2. feminine
3. masculine
4. plural
5. feminine
6. feminine
7. feminine
8. plural
9. masculine
10. masculine
11. masculine
12. plural

### Reference Desk

Refer to p. 086 of *T'es branché?*
*Level 1A* for information on the gender of nouns and definite articles.

### Culture

**Practices: Information**

In France, people may sing **Joyeux anniversaire** to the tune of *Happy Birthday to You*. However, the French commonly sing the song below instead. You may want to teach the lyrics of the song. Display the lyrics in the room and review their meaning.
*Bon anniversaire,*
*mes vœux les plus sincères*
*Que ces quelques fleurs*
*vous apportent le bonheur*
*Que l'année entière vous*
*soit douce et légère*
*Et que l'an fini,*
*nous soyons tous réunis*
*Pour chanter en chœur:*
*"Bon Anniversaire!"*

---

**16   C'est quand, l'anniversaire de...?**

*Donnez la date en français de l'anniversaire de chaque personne célèbre.* (Two suggested model responses are provided.)

> **MODÈLE**   Johnny Depp   9.6
> **C'est le neuf juin.**
> **Son anniversaire est le neuf juin.**

| | | | | | |
|---|---|---|---|---|---|
| 1. Rachid Taha | 18.9 | 4. Sophie Marceau | 17.11 | 7. Audrey Tautou | 9.8 |
| 2. Vanessa Paradis | 22.12 | 5. Daniel Radcliffe | 23.7 | 8. Michel Sardou | 26.1 |
| 3. Youssou N'Dour | 1.10 | 6. Leslie Bourgoin | 4.2 | 9. Zinédine Zidane | 23.6 |

## Gender of Nouns and Definite Articles

All nouns in French are either masculine or feminine. To refer to a specific noun or a noun in a general sense, use a definite article. The singular definite articles are **le**, **la** and **l'**. The plural definite article is **les**. They all mean *"the"* in English.

- **Le** precedes masculine singular nouns.
- **La** precedes feminine singular nouns.
- **L'** precedes a masculine or feminine singular noun that begins with a vowel.
- **Les** precedes plural nouns (which usually end in *"s"* and occasionally *"x"*.)

**17   Allons au cinéma!**

All of the following movie titles contain a definite article. Indicate whether the nouns following the movie list are masculine or feminine or plural.

| | | | |
|---|---|---|---|
| La planète des singes | Le discours d'un roi | Les sept Samourais | Le sixième sens |
| C'est l'apocalypse | Le voleur de bicyclette | Il faut sauver le soldat Ryan | L'homme éléphant |
| Le roi lion | Les indestructibles | Le pont de la rivière Kwai | Les temps modernes |
| Les sentiers de la gloire | La guerre des étoiles | La mélodie du Bonheur | La couleur pourpre |

**Masculin ou féminin ou pluriel?**

1. voleur
2. guerre
3. roi
4. indestructibles
5. mélodie
6. couleur
7. planète
8. sentiers
9. discours
10. pont
11. soldat
12. Samourais

**Essential Instruction**

1. Extend **Activité 16** by having students say the birthdays of three classmates, using the activity as a model.
2. Review the information on the gender of nouns and the definite article. List familiar nouns on the board for students, such as **livre**, **copine**, and **amies**, and have students provide their definite articles.
3. Before students begin **Activité 17**, challenge them to identify as many of the movies as they can. Remind them to look for cognates or familiar words in the movie titles. They can use context cues to help them figure out the meaning of unknown words. Review the movies as a class.
4. Review the phrases **Moi aussi**, **Pas moi**, and **Moi non plus**. After students complete the activity with a partner, have them present their information using the first-person plural.
5. Review the information on negation. Remind students that the **ne... pas** always goes around the conjugated verb in sentences with more than one verb.

# Communiquez!

## 18 Moi aussi!

**Interpersonal/Presentational Communication**

Find out which likes and dislikes you and a classmate have in common. Follow the model. In answering the question, **"Et toi?"** use these expressions: **Moi aussi** (*Me too*), **Pas moi** (*Not me*), **Moi non plus** (*Me neither*). Report to the class the things that you and your partner both like, and begin with: **Nous aimons...**

> **MODÈLE** les films policiers
> A: **Tu aimes les films policiers?**
> B: **Oui, j'aime les films policiers. Et toi?**
> A: **Pas moi, je n'aime pas les films policiers.**

1. l'eau minérale
2. la glace
3. les crêpes
4. le hip-hop
5. les films d'aventure
6. le croque-monsieur
7. les films de science-fiction
8. la world
9. la glace à la vanille
10. les casquettes de sport

## Negation with *ne... pas*

To make a sentence negative, place **ne** (or **n'** before a vowel sound) before the present tense verb and **pas** after the verb.

Nous **ne** jouons **pas** au foot.    *We don't play soccer.*
Nous **n'**aimons **pas** le tennis.    *We don't like tennis.*

## 19 Oui et non!

State that the following people do the first activity, but not the second. Follow the model.

> **MODÈLE** Moussa/jouer au basket/plonger
> **Moussa joue au basket, mais il ne plonge pas.**

1. Je/nager en été/étudier
2. Raphaël et Mathis/jouer au foot/marquer un but
3. Monique/danser bien/jouer au hockey
4. Vous/parler français/parler espagnol
5. Tu/travailler à la maison/aider ta mère
6. On/surfer sur Internet/jouer aux jeux vidéo
7. Nous/organiser une teuf/préparer les desserts

Deuxième partie 1B    **B 2 1**

## RESOURCES

 **e-visual 7**

**Answers**

**18**

1. Tu aimes l'eau minérale? *Answers will vary.*
2. Tu aimes la glace? *Answers will vary.*
3. Tu aimes les crêpes? *Answers will vary.*
4. Tu aimes le hip-hop? *Answers will vary.*
5. Tu aimes les films d'aventure? *Answers will vary.*
6. Tu aimes le croque-monsieur? *Answers will vary.*
7. Tu aimes les films de science-fiction? *Answers will vary.*
8. Tu aimes la world? *Answers will vary.*
9. Tu aimes la glace à la vanille? *Answers will vary.*
10. Tu aimes les casquettes de sport? *Answers will vary.*

**19**

1. Je nage en été, mais je n'étudie pas.
2. Raphaël et Mathis jouent au foot, mais ils ne marquent pas un but.
3. Monique danse bien, mais elle ne joue pas au hockey.
4. Vous parlez français, mais vous ne parlez pas espagnol.
5. Tu travailles à la maison, mais tu n'aides pas ta mère.
6. On surfe sur Internet, mais on ne joue pas aux jeux vidéo.
7. Nous organisons une teuf, mais nous ne préparons pas les desserts.

### Reference Desk

Refer to p.089 of *T'es branché? Level 1A* for information on negation with **ne (n') ... pas**. Use e-visual 7 to review the structure.

## Multiple Intelligences
### Visual-Spatial

Help visual learners to pick up the gender of nouns by adding a visual cue. Have students create a vocabulary list in their notebooks. Assign students a color for each gender, such as blue for masculine and red for feminine. Students can write each word in a different color, based on its gender, or use the different colored pens to underline each word. Students might also wish to create two columns in their notebook—one for masculine nouns, and one for feminine nouns—and write the column head in the corresponding color. Students can then organize the vocabulary under the correct column head.

**20**

1. –Tu manges à la maison?
   –Non, je ne mange pas à la maison.
2. –Anaïs et Méline dansent bien?
   –Non, elles ne dansent pas bien.
3. –Ta mère écoute de la musique alternative?
   –Non, elle n'écoute pas de musique alternative.
4. –Xavier et toi, vous jouez beaucoup aux jeux vidéo?
   –Non, nous ne jouons pas beaucoup aux jeux vidéo.
5. –Tu nages samedi?
   –Non, je ne nage pas samedi.
6. –Augustin et moi, nous jouons au foot mercredi?
   –Non, vous ne jouez pas au foot mercredi.
7. –Noah plonge un peu?
   –Non, il ne plonge pas (un peu).
8. –Je joue au hockey en hiver?
   –Non, tu ne joues pas au hockey en hiver.
9. –René téléphone à Sabrina?
   –Non, il ne téléphone pas à Sabrina.
10. –Étienne et Lucas achètent une pizza?
    –Non, ils n'achètent pas de pizza.

**21** *Possible dialogue:*

–Salut, Max! Ça va?
–Oui, bien. Et toi?
–Pas mal. Quel est ton numéro de téléphone?
–C'est le zéro deux, treize, cinquante et un, quinze, trente-huit. Pourquoi?
–Je t'invite à la teuf samedi.
–Bonne idée! On joue au basket jeudi?
–Je ne joue pas au basket, mais j'aime faire du vélo.
–D'accord.
–À bientôt!
–Au revoir.

## Culture

### Products: Activity

Have students name their favorite types of music, and then do an Internet search to find the name of French artists who play that type of music. Have students give the name and a brief description of the group. Then have them share a song title or audio file so that classmates can hear a sample of the artist's music.

# Communiquez!

**20  Très négatif!**

### Interpersonal Communication

*Create questions using the cues given. With a partner, take turns asking and answering the questions, and respond only in the negative.*

**MODÈLE**   ton père/**regarder** beaucoup la télé
A: **Ton père regarde beaucoup la télé**?
B: **Non, il ne regarde pas beaucoup la télé**.

1. tu/**manger** à la maison
2. Anaïs et Méline/**danser** bien
3. ta mère /**écouter** de la musique alternative
4. Xavier et toi/**jouer** beaucoup aux jeux vidéo
5. tu/**nager** samedi
6. Augustin et moi/**jouer** au foot mercredi
7. Noah/**plonger** un peu
8. je/**jouer** au hockey en hiver
9. René/**téléphoner** à Sabrina
10. Étienne et Lucas/**acheter** une pizza

# Communiquez!

**21  Conversation dirigée**

### Interpersonal/Presentational Communication

*Prepare the following conversation with a partner, and present it to a group of classmates.*

| A | B |
|---|---|
| Greet your partner, and ask how things are going. | Respond. Ask, "And you?" |
| Respond. Ask for a classmate's telephone number. | Say that it's "02.13.51.15.38." Ask why. |
| Say that you would like to invite (classmate's name) to a party on Saturday. | Say, "Good idea!" Ask your partner if he/she wants to play basketball on Thursday. |
| Say that you don't play basketball and that you like to go bicycling. | Say, "OK." |
| Respond, "See you soon!" | Say, "Good-bye." |

## Essential Instruction

1. Have students work in pairs to complete **Activité 20**. Remind them that their responses must be in the negative. Have students extend the activity by asking an additional, personal question to their partner, who should answer in the negative.

2. Assign partners for **Activité 21**, and have students do the activity. As an alternative follow-up activity, have students switch partners and do the activity with someone else, performing the opposite role.

3. For **Activité 22**, remind students to extend their grid to poll 10 classmates. Point out that students can vary the column heads, adding more if necessary. Allow time for students to write their summaries. For a more concise summary, have students summarize their survey results by writing separate paragraphs about pastimes, not individual students. Direct them to follow the model.

# Communiquez!

## 22 Les passe-temps favoris

**Interpersonal Communication**

Create a grid like the one below. Poll ten classmates to find out each one's favorite pastime. Put an X in the corresponding column. Then write a description of the poll to turn into your teacher.

**MODÈLE**
A: Qu'est-ce que tu aimes faire?
B: J'aime beaucoup **écouter de la musique**.

**Deux élèves aiment écouter de la musique et aller au cinéma....**

| Nom | Sport | Musique | Technologie | Film | Autre activité |
|---|---|---|---|---|---|
| Christine | | X | | | |
| Bruno | X | | | | |
| Sébastien | | | | X | |
| Michelle | | X | | | |
| Océane | | | | X | |

Tu aimes faire du sport?

Oui, de la danse.

Deuxième partie 1B  B 2 3

**Answers** _____
22 *Answers will vary.*

### Reference Desk

Remind students that *a survey* is **une enquête** or **un sondage d'opinion**.

### Connections

**Math**

Have students summarize their survey results for **Activité 22** using a double bar graph. They can write the activities along the x-axis of the graph, and numbers one through 10 along the y-axis. Students will create two bars for each activity. They should use one color to represent likes, and one to represent dislikes. Students will count how many classmates liked or disliked each activity, and then graph the results. Remind students to include a graph title, to label each axis, and to provide a legend to explain their color coding.

**Differentiated Learning**
**Accelerate**
As students respond to **Activité 20**, have them add additional information about what each person might do or like to do. For example, a student may say: **Mon père ne regarde pas beaucoup la télé, mais il aime bien lire.**

**Special Needs Students**
**AD(H)D**
Provide students with more structure for **Activité 22** by creating the extended chart for them, and completing it with the names of 10 classmates and five pastimes. Assign a responsible student to help them through the remainder of the exercise, and help them summarize their data.

# À l'école

B 2 4

## Essential Instruction

1. Write the phrase **À l'école** on the board. With their books closed, have students identify all of the words that they can remember for school and school supplies. Compile a class list on the board. Then display e-visual 8 to review vocabulary for school supplies, adding any words that students missed.

2. Review prepositions using a small stuffed toy. For example, bring in a teddy bear (**M. Nounours**) and place him on a table in the front of the room. Ask questions such as **Est-ce que M. Nounours est sur la table ou sous la table?** Change his position and continue asking questions to review all prepositions.

3. Have students create a chart for **Activité 1**. They should label one column **dans ma trousse** and the other **dans mon sac à dos**. Have students copy the items in the appropriate column, and compare charts with a partner to check their answers.

# Vocabulaire

## 1 Dans mon casier

*Dites ce qu'on met dans* **la trousse** *et ce qu'on met dans* **le sac à dos.** (Write what you put into the pencil case and what you put into the backpack.)

| MODÈLE | le livre de français | le crayon |
|---|---|---|
| | **dans mon sac à dos** | **dans ma trousse** |

1. le stylo
2. le cahier
3. l'ordinateur portable
4. le dictionnaire
5. la trousse
6. le feuille de papier
7. le taille-crayon
8. le CD

## 2 Tu aimes dessiner?

*Dessinez (Draw) les choses suivantes.*

1. une feuille de papier **sur** un bureau
2. une affiche **sous** une pendule
3. un sac à dos **devant** une porte
4. un stylo **dans** une trousse
5. une élève **avec** une prof

Troisième partie 1B  **B 2 5**

---

## Answers

**1**
1. dans ma trousse
2. dans mon sac à dos
3. dans mon sac à dos
4. dans mon sac à dos
5. dans mon sac à dos
6. dans mon sac à dos
7. dans ma trousse
8. dans mon sac à dos

**2** *Students should draw:*
1. sheet of paper on teacher desk
2. poster under a clock
3. backpack in front of door
4. pen in a pencil case
5. female student with teacher

### Reference Desk

Refer to pp. 108–109 of *T'es branché? Level 1A* to review the vocabulary for school supplies and prepositions.

### TPR

Have students stand up next to their desks and remove one of their shoes. Review prepositional vocabulary, as well as the words **un bureau** and **une chaise**. Give students directives such as **Mettez vos chaussures sous le bureau** or **Mettez vos chaussures derrière la chaise**. After students have responded, repeat the instruction while performing the action yourself so they can assess if they interpreted your command correctly.

---

## Differentiated Learning

### Decelerate

Make a drawing representing each of the phrases in **Activité 2**, or ask an art student to draw it for you. Photocopy the drawing and give each student a copy. Read the sentences aloud, and have students write the sentence number next to the corresponding drawing.

## Learning Styles

### Kinesthetic Learners

Students may better internalize the vocabulary practiced in **Activité 1** by actually placing each item in the appropriate place. Have students identify the items on the list and place them on their desk. Have students draw a picture to represent any items that they don't have readily available. Ask them to place their opened book bags and pencil cases on their chairs. As they go down the list, students should read the word aloud, find the item on their desk, and say where they are putting it, as they place it in the book bag or pencil case. Walk around the room and have students tell you about what they are putting in each bag.

**3**

Il y a des cédéroms, des affiches, des livres, un dictionnaire, un blouson, une casquette, des chaussettes, un ordinateur portable, une pendule, et une fenêtre.

## Reference Desk

1. Refer to p. 115 of *T'es branché?* Level 1A to review indefinite articles.
2. Point out the phrase **il y a** to students. Remind them that its English equivalent depends on what follows it. If the phrase **il y a** is followed by a singular noun (**il y a une chaise**), it means "There is…" If it is followed by a plural noun (**Il y a des chaises**), it means "There are…"

## Expansion

Have students draw a picture of a room in their house, being sure to include at least five objects that represent vocabulary words. Students exchange drawings with a partner, who will write five sentences based on what he or she sees in the drawing, using the phrase **il y a…**. Review the activity by asking questions such as **Est-ce qu'il y a une affiche dans la maison de Natalie?**

# Structure de la langue

**Passons en revue!**

## Indefinite Articles

Indefinite articles indicate whether a noun is masculine or feminine. They mean "a," "an," "one."

- **un** precedes a masculine singular noun
- **une** precedes a feminine singular noun
- **des** precedes a plural noun and is often translated as "some"

**Je prends un Orangina, une salade, et des frites.**

*I'm having an Orangina, a salad and some fries.*

**3** **Dans ma chambre**

*Dites ce qu'il y a dans la chambre.* (Say what is in the bedroom.)

| MODÈLE | **Il y a des cédéroms….** |

**Essential Instruction**

1. Remind students that they reviewed gender of nouns and definite articles in **Partie 2**. Have students identify the definite articles; write them on the board. Next to each one, write the corresponding indefinite article, emphasizing the gender and number. Review pronunciation of the indefinite articles by saying them aloud and having students repeat.
2. Preview **Activité 3** by gesturing around your classroom and saying what is there using the phrase **Il y a…**.
3. Review the forms of the verb **avoir** and the phrase **avoir besoin de**. To make sure each student is speaking throughout **Activité 4**, provide the following question on the board: **De quoi as-tu besoin pour le cours de _____?** Have students take turns asking the question and answering using the model in the book.
4. Before students begin **Activité 5**, ask them to identify each of the items pictured. Use e-visual 12 as necessary.

## Communiquez!

### 4 Soyez préparé(e) préparé(e)!

**Interpersonal Communication**

*À tour de rôle, dites à votre partenaire ce dont vous avez besoin pour les cours suivants.* (Working with a partner, take turns telling each other what you need for the following classes.)

**MODÈLE**   les arts plastiques   →   **J'ai besoin d'un crayon et d'une feuille de papier.**

1. les maths
2. le français
3. l'anglais
4. les sciences
5. l'informatique
6. l'histoire

## Communiquez!

### 5 Au magasin de sport

**Interpersonal Communication**

*Des jeunes footballeurs vont au magasin de sport avec leurs mères. Jouez les rôles du footballeur et sa mère avec un partenaire.*

 9€

 43€

 19€

 35€

 38€

 152€

 70€

**MODÈLE**   A: **Voici 35€.**
            B: **J'achète une écharpe.**

1. Voici 19€.
2. Voici 38€.
3. Voici 152€.
4. Voici 9€.
5. Voici 70€.
6. Voici 43€.

**RESOURCES**

 e-visual 12

**Answers**

**4** *Possible answers:*

1. J'ai besoin d'un livre de maths, d'un cahier (d'une feuille de papier), et d'un crayon.
2. J'ai besoin d'un livre de français.
3. J'ai besoin d'un dictionnaire françaisanglais, d'un cahier, et d'un stylo.
4. J'ai besoin d'un livre de biologie, (de chimie) d'un cahier, et d'un crayon.
5. J'ai besoin d'un ordinateur et de cédéroms.
6. J'ai besoin d'un livre d'histoire.

**5**

1. –Voici dix-neuf euros.
   –J'achète une casquette.
2. –Voici trente-huit euros.
   –J'achète un short.
3. –Voici cent cinquante-deux euros.
   –J'achète des chaussures (de sport).
4. –Voici neuf euros.
   –J'achète des chaussettes.
5. –Voici soixante-dix euros.
   –J'achète un blouson.
6. –Voici quarante-trois euros.
   –J'achète un maillot.

### Reference Desk

1. Refer to pp. 119–120 of *T'es branché? Level 1A* to review the forms of the verb **avoir** and the expression **avoir besoin de**.
2. Refer to p. 109 of *T'es branché? Level 1A* to review numbers from 20 to 100. Refer to p. 180 of *T'es branché? Level 1A* to review numbers from 101 to 1,000.
3. Refer to p. 165 of *T'es branché? Level 1A* to review vocabulary related to clothing.

### Differentiated Learning

**Accelerate**

Have students use prepositions of place to describe the drawing found in **Activité 3** in more detail.

**Decelerate**

Review numbers with students. Then have them write the word for each number before doing **Activité 5** orally.

### Special Needs Students
**Visually Impaired**

Students may have difficulty seeing the details in the drawing for **Activité 3**. As an alternative to using the illustration, have students write about what is in your classroom using **Il y a…**.

**Answers**

**6**

1. Théo nage à six heures et demie (à six heures trente).
2. Claudine et Raoul dansent à dix heures dix.
3. Nous étudions à neuf heures et quart (à neuf heures quinze).
4. Je joue au foot à trois heures moins le quart (à deux heures quarante-cinq).
5. Vous regardez la télé à midi.
6. Tu écoutes de la musique à neuf heures moins cinq (à huit heures cinquante-cinq).

## Reference Desk

1. Refer to p. 124 and pp.130–131 of *T'es branché?* *Level 1A* and e-visual 9 to review telling time.
2. Review the 24-hour time system, and remind students that most events (classes, movie times, etc.) are listed using this system in France.
3. Remind students that when a time is written in French, the letter h (for **heures**) is used in place of the colon that is used in English. For example, seven o'clock is written 7h00, not 7:00.
4. Point out the similarities between the French word **quart** and the English word "quarter." Remind students to add the definite article **le** when saying it is "a quarter to the hour."
5. Explain that the word **demi** takes the masculine form after **midi** and **minuit**, as both are masculine nouns. Otherwise, it takes the feminine form (**demie**) in reference to the feminine noun **heure**.
6. Verbs like **préférer** whose accent marks change depending on the subject are sometimes called stem-changing verbs.

## Telling Time

| | |
|---|---|
| Quelle heure est-il? | *What time is it?* |
| Il est une heure. | *It is 1:00.* |
| Il est deux heure**s** cinq. | *It is 2:05.* |
| Il est trois heures et quart (trois heures quinze). | *It is 3:15.* |
| Il est quatre heures et demie (quatre heures trente). | *It is 4:30.* |
| Il est six heures moins dix (cinq heures cinquante). | *It is 5:50.* |
| Il est sept heures moins le quart (six heures quarante-cinq). | *It is 6:45.* |
| Il est midi. | *It is noon.* |
| Il est minuit. | *It is midnight.* |
| Il est dix-neuf heures vingt. (19h20) *official time* | *It is 7:20 p.m.* |
| On va au café à quelle heure? | *At what time are we going to the café?* |

### 6 À quelle heure?

State that each of the following people is doing the activity at the indicated time.

**MODÈLE**  Mme Thibault/à 7h25
**Mme Thibault téléphone à sept heures vingt-cinq.**

1. Théo/à 6h30

2. Claudine et Raoul/à 10h10

3. nous/à 9h15

4. je/à 2h45

5. vous/à 12h00

6. tu/à 8h55

### Essential Instruction

1. Use e-visual 9 to review telling time. Give students additional practice by writing different times (i.e., 8h30) on index cards, and placing them in a bag. Walk around the room to have students draw a card out of the bag, and say the time they see. Challenge students to say the time using the 24-hour system, when appropriate.
2. Before students do **Activité 6**, review the use of the preposition **à** to say at what time something is done. Have students say what time they do the following activities: **étudier**, **diner**, **regarder la télé**.
3. Before reteaching the forms of the verb **préférer**, review the sounds and uses of the **e accent aigu** and the **e accent grave**, referring to *T'es branché? Level 1A* p. 015, if necessary. Remind students that **préférer** takes regular –er verb endings, and is only considered irregular because of the variation in accent marks.

## Communiquez!

### 7 Votre emploi du temps

**Interpersonal Communication**

*Imaginez que votre emploi du temps ressemble à celui de dessous. À tour de rôle, demandez à votre partenaire quand et à quelle heure il/elle a chaque cours.* (With a partner, take turns asking each other when and at what time you have the following classes.)

| heures | lundi | mardi | mercredi | jeudi | vendredi |
|---|---|---|---|---|---|
| 8h30-9h20 | sciences | sciences | sciences | sciences | informatique |
| 9h25-10h15 | anglais | informatique | anglais | anglais | anglais |
| 10h20-11h10 | informatique | histoire | histoire | histoire | histoire |
| 11h15-12h05 | maths | maths | musique | maths | maths |
| 12h10-12h40 | déjeuner | → | → | → | → |
| 12h45-13h35 | littérature | littérature | littérature | musique | littérature |
| 13h40-14h30 | EPS | EPS | musique | EPS | EPS |
| 14h35-15h25 | français | français | français | français | français |

**MODÈLE**
A: **Quand as-tu ton cours de maths?**
B: **J'ai mon cours de maths le lundi, le mardi, le jeudi, et le vendredi.**
A: **À quelle heure?**
B: **À onze heures et quart.**

---

## Present Tense of *préférer*

The endings for the verb **préférer** follow the same pattern as regular **–er** verbs; however take note of the pattern of its accent marks:

| | |
|---|---|
| je préf**è**re | nous préf**é**rons |
| tu préf**è**res | vous préf**é**rez |
| il/elle/on préf**è**re | ils/elles préf**è**rent |

The verb **préférer** can be followed by a definite article + noun (*Je préfère le rock*) or by an infinitive (*Je préfère écouter le rock.*)

---

Answers (right column):

**7**

–cours de science: le lundi, lemardi, le mercredi, et le jeudi; à huit heures et demie.

–cours d'informatique: le lundi à dix heures vingt, le mardi à neuf heures vingt-cinq, et le vendredi à huit heures et demie.

–cours d'anglais: le lundi, le mercredi, le jeudi, et le vendredi; à neuf heures vingt-cinq.

–cours d'histoire: le mardi, le mercredi, le jeudi et le vendredi; à dix heures vingt.

–cours de littérature: le lundi, le mardi, et le mercredi; à une heure moins le quart (à douze heures quarante-cinq).

–cours d'EPS: le lundi, le mardi, le jeudi, et le vendredi; à deux heures moins vingt (à une heure quarante).

–cours de musique: le mercredi; à deux heures moins vingt (à une heure quarante).

–cours de français: le lundi, le mardi, le mercredi, le jeudi, et le vendredi; à trois heures moins vingt-cinq (à deux heures trente-cinq).

### Reference Desk

Refer to p. 087 of *T'es branché? Level 1A* to review the verb **préférer**.

### Communication

**Interpersonal: Paired Practice**
Have students prepare four questions to interview a classmate about their preferences for leisure activities, schedules, and classes. Provide a model question such as, **Qu'est-ce que tu préfères faire à quatre heures de l'après-midi?** Have students take turns interviewing their partner and taking notes on the responses. Then, have pairs report back to the class, using the verb **préférer** in the third person: **Sonia préfère....**

---

### Multiple Intelligences
**Interpersonal**
Encourage students to take activities that are designed to be done independently, such as **Activité 6**, and turn them into pair work by asking questions or providing follow-up comments in addition to what is being requested in the activity. For example, students might form the question **À quelle heure est-ce que Mme Thibaut téléphone?** to ask before their partner provides an answer. Or they can follow up the sentence with **Et toi? À quelle heure est-ce que tu téléphones à tes amis?**

### Learning Styles
**Visual Learners**
The review of telling time on p. B28 is entirely text-based. To better assist visual-spatial students with this material, draw analog clocks and then write and say each time in French. Encourage students to include these drawings in the notes that they take on your presentation. Have them refer to the drawings and their notes as they complete the review activities. (Another option is to make clocks using paper plates.)

**Answers**

**8**

1. Pauline préfère la chimie.
2. Je préfère l'histoire.
3. Nous préférons les sacs à dos vintage.
4. Bruno et Charles préfèrent le français.
5. Tu préfères les DVD canadiens.
6. On préfère le cours de maths.
7. Vous préférez les plastiques.
8. Malika et Justine préfèrent l'informatique.

**9** *Answers will vary.*

## 8 Préférences

*Écrivez des phrases complètes. Utilisez (Use) la forme correcte du verbe **préférer** et l'**article défini** qui manque.*

> **MODÈLE**    Samuel/préférer/cours de l'EPS
> **Samuel préfère le cours de l'EPS.**

1. Pauline/chimie
2. Je/histoire
3. Nous/sacs à dos vintage
4. Bruno et Charles/français
5. Tu/DVD canadiens
6. On/cours de maths
7. Vous/arts plastiques
8. Malika et Justine/informatique

## 9 Une enquête

**Interpersonal/Presentational Communication**

*Demandez à dix camarades de classe quel cours ils préfèrent. Dites à votre groupe le résultat de votre enquête.* (Poll ten classmates to find out their favorite class, and then report to your group which class is the most popular.)

> **MODÈLE**    A: **Tu préfères quel cours?**
> B: **Je préfère le cours de sciences.**

La majorité préfère...

# Present Tense of the Irregular Verb *avoir*

The forms of the verb **avoir** (*to have*) do not follow a predictable pattern. It is an irregular verb.

| j'**ai** | nous **avons** |
|---|---|
| tu **as** | vous **avez** |
| il/elle/on **a** | ils/elles **ont** |

Several expressions use the verb **avoir**:

- avoir besoin de    *to need*
- avoir faim    *to be hungry*
- avoir soif    *to be thirsty*
- avoir... ans    *to be... years old*
- Tu as quel âge?    *How old are you?*
- J'ai treize ans.    *I'm thirteen years old.*

## 10 Qu'est-ce qu'on a?

Read where people are and say what they have.

> un crayon　　un dictionnaire　　un ordinateur portable　　un maillot　　un stylo
>
> des CD　　un short　　une feuille de papier　　un livre　　un cahier

**MODÈLE**　　Jean-François est en cours de géométrie.
**Il a un crayon, un cahier, et un livre.**

1. Omar est en cours de maths.
2. Nous sommes en cours de physique.
3. Les élèves sont en cours de musique.
4. Je suis en cours d'histoire.
5. Joëlle et Rahina sont en cours d'arts plastiques.
6. Tu es en cours de français.
7. Étienne et toi, vous êtes en cours d'informatique.
8. Je suis en cours d'EPS.

## 11 On a quel âge?

*Donnez l'âge de chaque personne selon leur date de naissance (*birthdate*).*

**MODÈLE**　　moi (1999)
**J'ai treize ans.**

1. ma mère (1973)
2. mon père (1970)
3. nous (1998)
4. Karim et Olivier (1996)
5. toi (2001)
6. ma prof de français (1981)
7. Yasmine et toi (1990)
8. mon prof de maths (1950)

## 12 Questions personnelles

**Interpersonal Communication**

*À tour de rôle, posez les questions et répondez.*

1. Tu as quel âge?
2. Tu as faim à midi?
3. Tu as besoin d'un ordinateur portable?
4. Tu as beaucoup de DVD?
5. Tu as une piscine chez toi?
6. Tu as besoin d'aller au bureau du proviseur?
7. Toi et ton copain, vous avez des sacs à dos?
8. Ton prof de français a une carte de France?
9. Ta copine a une stéréo?
10. Ton école a une salle d'informatique?

### Reference Desk

Remind students that **l'EPS** stands for **l'éducation physique et sportive**. In France, **l'EPS** goes beyond simply doing exercise. The goals of **l'EPS** include developing physical and emotional health, improving motor skills, and learning about sport and physical education as part of the greater culture of France. Students are expected to meet benchmarks for physical performance, including artistic performance, such as dance or acrobatics. Students are also expected to develop life skills such as adaptation to different circumstances, collaboration to achieve a goal, and respect for self and others.

### Connections

#### History

Give students a list of historical figures. Have them work in pairs to find out the birth years of each person. Ask them to give the age of each person if he/she were still alive today, using **Activité 11** as a model. Place two pairs together in a group of four, and have students check their work.

### Differentiated Learning

#### Accelerate

Have students cover the word bank in **Activité 10** with a sheet of paper and complete the activity without using it.

#### Decelerate

Before students do **Activité 11**, identify each person's age in English as a class. Then have students use the information to write their sentences.

### Multiple Intelligences

#### Verbal-Linguistic

Students will benefit from extra instruction on linguistic aspects that will make their conversations more engaging and authentic. Review proper intonation with students and have them apply French intonation in the question and answer activities on this page. Remind students to be mindful of using punctuation to guide their speaking when reading sentences aloud. Teach non-verbal communication that students can use appropriately to supplement their dialogue when they work in pairs or groups.

## Reference Desk

1. Refer to pp.174–175 of *T'es branché? Level 1A* to review forming questions in French.
2. Remind students that the tag question **n'est-ce pas?** is added to the end of a sentence to confirm what is being said. It is used less in France now than in former years. Tag questions in English include *isn't that so?*, *isn't he/she/it?*, and *right?*
3. Refer to p. 203 of *T'es branché? Level 1A* to review the interrogative word **quel** and its forms.
4. Explain that when inversion is used to form questions, a **t** is added with the subject pronouns **il, elle**, and **on**. Point out that this **t** prevents the *hiatus*, or the occurrence of two consecutive vowel sounds that would break the melodic sound of the language.

## Critical Thinking

### Comparisons

Have students think about the ways they have learned how to form questions in French (**n'est-ce pas**, **est-ce que**, inversion, interrogative words and phrases, etc.). Then have them compare methods for asking questions in English. Have students give examples of how the two methods are used in each language. For example, students might write **Avez-vous faim?** and *Are you hungry?* as examples of inversion.

# Forming Questions

To ask a yes/no question in French:

1. Raise your voice at the end of a sentence.
   **Cléo est à la cantine**? (Cléo → est → à → la cantine?)
2. Add the expression **n'est-ce pas** to the end of a sentence.
   **Thierry Henry est un bon footballeur, n'est-ce pas**? (*isn't he?*)
3. Use the expression **est-ce que** (est-ce qu' + vowel sound) before a statement.
   **Est-ce que tu as un ticket pour le match?**     (*do you...?*)
   **Est-ce qu'elle a un maillot de foot?**     (*does she...?*)

To ask an information question, follow this pattern:

> interrogative expression + **est-ce que** + a subject + a verb

| | |
|---|---|
| *(where)* | **Où est-ce que** l'équipe joue au foot? |
| *(how)* | **Comment est-ce que** tu prépares une salade? |
| *(why)* | **Pourquoi est-ce qu'**on va au stade? |
| *(when)* | **Quand est-ce que** Dominique a son cours de sciences? |
| *(at what time)* | **À quelle heure est-ce que** nous avons rendez-vous? |
| *(who)* | **Qui est-ce que** vous invitez à la teuf? |
| *(what)* | **Qu'est-ce que** Martine achète? |

When **qui** is used as a subject, it is followed directly by the verb.

**Qui est ton prof d'histoire?**     *Who is your history teacher?*
**Qui marque un but?**     *Who is scoring a goal?*

To ask "which" or "what," use the interrogative adjective **quel**. It may be followed by a noun or by the verb **être**. It has four forms and agrees in gender (m. or f.) and number (sing. or pl.).

| singular | | plural | |
|---|---|---|---|
| Masculine | Feminine | Masculine | Feminine |
| quel | quelle | quels | quelles |

**Quelle équipe gagne?**     *What team is winning?*
**Quels copains nagent?**     *Which friends swim?*
**Quel est le devoir de maths?**     *What is the math homework?*

Use inversion as another way to ask a yes/no or an information question. The order of the subject pronoun and the verb is reversed or inverted and connected by a hyphen.

**As-tu un ballon de foot?**     *Do you have a soccer ball?*
**Pourquoi aimez-vous le français?**     *Why do you like French?*

When using inversion with the pronouns **il**, **elle**, **on** and a verb form that ends with a vowel, add a **-t-** between the verb and the pronoun.

**Aime-t-elle faire du shopping en ville?**     *Does she like shopping downtown?*
**Pourquoi a-t-il besoin d'une chaise?**     *Why does he need a chair?*

B 3 2

## Essential Instruction

1. As you review how to ask questions, be sure to include personalized examples of each type of question. Ask individuals these personalized questions, and have students repeat them to other classmates for additional practice. Emphasize proper intonation and pronunciation throughout the review.
2. When reviewing the interrogative word **quel**, point out that students have seen it appear at the beginning of a question or in the middle. Give examples, such as **Quels cours aimes-tu?** or **Il voit quel film?**
3. Have students scan **Activité 12** and ask them if there are any words or phrases that need to be reviewed. Then assign **Activité 12** for homework.
4. Remind students that in **Activité 13**, they should use both inversion and **est-ce que** to ask their questions. After they finish writing questions, have them take turns reading their questions to a partner, who should invent a logical response.
5. If you feel comfortable, you might tell students you will answer any of their questions, as long as they are in French.

## 13 Beaucoup de questions!

*C'est la fin du semestre et Élodie a beaucoup de contrôles. Sa mère lui pose beaucoup de questions. Quelles sont les réponses (responses/answers) d'Élodie?*

1. Quand est ton contrôle d'histoire?
2. Où est-ce que tu désires étudier à 3h30?
3. Qui est ta prof de français?
4. Comment est ton prof d'informatique?
5. Avec qui est-ce que tu dois parler?
6. À quelle heure vas-tu arriver à l'école?
7. Pourquoi est-ce que tu vas apporter ton ordinateur portable à l'école?
8. Quel contrôle va être difficile?
9. Mme Masson est sénégalaise, n'est-ce pas?
10. Est-ce que ton sac à dos est sur ton bureau?

A. Mme Masson
B. à sept heures et demie
C. le contrôle de sciences
D. parce que j'ai besoin de préparer un projet pour mon cours d'informatique
E. vendredi
F. non, ivoirienne
G. à la médiathèque
H. non, sous mon bureau
I. strict
J. avec le proviseur

## 14 Quelle est la question?

*Préparez des questions selon les indices (cues).*

**MODÈLE**  où/ta mère/
**Où est-ce que ta mère achète des chaussures?**

1. à quelle heure/vous/

2. comment/ton camarade de classe/

3. où/Juliette/

4. quand/nous/

5. que/tu/

6. où/Henri/

7. pourquoi/Paul et Julien

8. qui/tu/

Troisième partie 1B   B 3 3

### Game

**Méli-Mélo!**

Have students play a game to practice asking questions. Begin by writing familiar topics on index cards. Use topics that were introduced in **Unités 1–5** of *T'es branché?* Level 1A. Topics can be general (family, jobs, movies) or more specific (**Pari Roller**, French Polynesia, etc.), depending on the level of your students. Divide the class into five teams. Have a member of one team select a card, and say the topic aloud. Then set a timer for two minutes. Have all students work together with their team to write as many questions as they can about that topic. For example, if the topic is movies, students might write **Quel film aimes-tu?** or **Qui joue le rôle d'Amélie Poulain?** (Students don't need to know the answers.) After each topic, have a member from each group read their questions aloud. Give a point for each correct question. (Option: If the team is unable to formulate their question correctly, give a point to the team who can say it correctly.) Once each group has read its questions, distribute a new index card to each team and repeat the game. Continue until all of the cards have been used, or as time allows.

### Differentiated Learning

**Expand**

Assign each student a celebrity, either French or American. Call on each student to come to the front of the class and describe the celebrity she was assigned in French (e.g., **Je suis brune et très jolie. Brad Pitt est mon mari**). Ask the "celebrity" to reveal his or her identity, and have the class write one interview question. Allow each student to take one or two questions from the class before moving on to the next student.

### Special Needs Students

**Speech Impairment**

If students have difficulty producing proper intonation patterns in French, encourage them to include the phrases **est-ce que** and **n'est-ce pas** as lexical clues to make it clear that they are asking questions.

1. Sonia porte quelle casquette?
2. Quels sacs à dos coûtent vingt euros?
3. Nous apportons quels CD à la teuf?
4. Quels desserts sont chers?
5. Tu achètes quelle écharpe?
6. Quelle fille a soif?
7. On aime quels sandwichs à la cantine?
8. Vous préférez quelle musique?
9. Frédéric invite quelles filles au café?

## Reference Desk

Direct students' attention to the plural form **les sacs à dos**, found in **Activité 16**. Explain that the noun (**sac**) is pluralized, but the modifier (**à dos**) is not. Point to the phrase **les sandwichs** in the same activity. Explain that although in English the **–es** is added to pluralize words ending in **–ch**, in French this rule does not apply.

## Culture

### Practices: Information

Shopping malls are increasingly popular in France. However, many people still shop **en ville**—downtown—where both chain stores and independent boutiques can be found in a central area. Popular French teen clothing retailers that might be found in a mall or in town include **Pimkie**, **Naf Naf**, **Promod**, and **Kookaï**, all of which sell to women and girls. The international chains **Zara** and **H&M** are also popular among both teen boys and girls in France.

---

### 15 Une réponse logique

**Interpersonal Communication**

*À tour de rôle, posez les questions de l'Activité 14 à votre partenaire. Donnez une réponse logique.*

> **MODÈLE**
> A: **Où est-ce que ta mère achète des chaussures?**
> B: **Elle achète des chaussures au centre commercial.**

### 16 Plus spécifique, s'il vous plaît!

**Interpersonal Communication**

*Lisez la phrase. Votre partenaire va poser (ask) une question en employant (using) une forme de **quel**.*

> **MODÈLE**
> Le contrôle va être facile.
> **Quel contrôle va être facile?**

1. Sonia porte une casquette.
2. Les sacs à dos coûtent (*cost*) vingt euros.
3. Nous apportons les CD à la teuf.
4. Les desserts sont chers.
5. J'achète une écharpe.
6. La fille a soif.
7. On aime les sandwichs à la cantine.
8. Nous préférons la musique alternative.
9. Frédéric invite les filles au café.

## Essential Instruction

1. Remind students that for **Activité 15**, their response must be logical. Point out that they should invent logical answers for items 3, 6, and 7. Students can use personal information to respond to the remaining items.
2. Review the forms of **quel** with students before doing **Activité 16**. Remind students to take turns reading the sentences and asking the questions.
3. Tell students not to repeat question words for **Activité 17**. Students may want to exchange questions with a partner for peer editing before they discuss them in **Activité 18**.
4. If the technology at your school permits, have students use audio or video conferencing to complete **Activité 18**.

## 17 Skypons!

*Vous avez l'occasion to skyper avec votre nouveau/nouvelle correspondant(e) (pen pal) français(e). Écrivez six questions que vous voulez lui poser. Employez (Use): **où, quand, à quelle heure, comment, pourquoi, qui, avec qui, quel, qu'est-ce que**. Employez l'inversion deux fois (times).*

> **MODÈLE**  **Quand as-tu ton cours d'anglais?**

## 18 Répondez, s'il vous plaît!

**Interpersonal Communication**

*Posez les questions de l'Activité 17 à votre camarade de classe. Il/elle va répondre (respond) en jouant (by playing) le rôle de votre correspondant(e).*

> **MODÈLE**  A: **Quand as-tu ton cours d'anglais?**
> B: **J'ai mon cours d'anglais le lundi, mardi, et vendredi.**

Pourquoi ne vas-tu pas en cours de chimie?

Pour que Sébastien m'aide.

Et toi, à quelle heure est-ce tu vas au cours de français?

Troisième partie 1B  **B 3 5**

### Reference Desk

1. If students are not familiar with *Skype*™, explain that it is an online videoconferencing program that lets people communicate with others around the world through their computer, provided that it is equipped with a webcam and a microphone. The French have adopted the verb **skyper**, though they might also simply use the company's name as in the following examples: **Qui veut skype avec moi?/Je vais parler sur skype.**

2. There are numerous online organizations that work to connect classrooms in different countries, including *Skype*™, which has an educational program to help link teachers from around the world. Use the search term "connect classrooms France to America" to find resources on how to connect classrooms and engage students in authentic conversations. You might feel that students are not yet prepared to engage in authentic conversations with native speakers, but many experts feel this type of activity can be beneficial even at the earliest levels. They can apply what they have learned for short, simple conversations. They can also communicate in English to learn more about francophone culture from those peers.

**Differentiated Learning**
**Decelerate**
Provide students with the questions on the board for **Activité 16**. Leave a blank at the beginning of the question, and have them supply the correct form of **quel**.

**Multiple Intelligences**
**Interpersonal**
Most of the activities on pp. B34–B35 require students to work with one another, and interpersonal learners will benefit from these types of activities. Remind students to go above and beyond the question and answer sets in the activities. Encourage them to compare notes, correct one another's errors, and work together to practice proper pronunciation and intonation.

## Reference Desk

1. Highlight the title of **Partie 4, Ados en action!** Remind students that the term **ados** is an abbreviation for the term **adolescent**.
2. Have students identify where the girl in the photo is (a chain coffee shop). Point out that in 2012 there were over 60 Starbucks coffee shops throughout France, but that in general, the French prefer the traditional café experience. Unlike Americans, the French rarely take coffee to go in a paper cup.

## Communication

**Interpersonal: Paired Practice**

Have students write three questions about the photo on p. B36. Students might ask **Qu'est-ce qu'elle mange?** or **Quelle heure est-il?** Then place students in pairs. Have partners take turns asking one another their questions. Have students discuss possible responses based on the details of the photo.

# Quatrième partie   Ados en action!

B 3 6

## Essential Instruction

1. Have students think about their own daily activities. Direct them to close their books, and then ask them to brainstorm as many places and activities as they can remember in French. Make a class list of their responses.
2. Use model phrases and questions to review places in the school. Give sentences such as **Je vais à la cantine à une heure. Est-ce que vous allez à la cantine après le cours de français?** or **Pourquoi allez-vous en ville? Moi, je vais en ville pour faire du shopping**. Continue until you have reviewed each of the places in the blue box on p. B37.
3. Have students read the sentences in **Activité 1** independently. Ask them to identify any unfamiliar words, and review them as a class. Then, have students complete the activity.
4. Remind students to alternate roles in **Activité 2**, so that each partner has the opportunity to make a suggestion.

# Vocabulaire

## 1 Où est-ce qu'on est?

*Dites où chaque personne est selon ce qu'il/elle fait.* (Say where each person is based on what he/she is doing.)

> à la cantine     au stade     en ville     chez moi     à la piscine
> au labo     à la médiathèque     au cinéma     à la salle d'informatique

**MODÈLE**     Vous surfez sur Internet. Vous préparez un projet pour le cours d'histoire.
**Vous êtes à la salle d'informatique.**

1. Kemajou prépare une expérience *(experiment)* de chimie. Il parle à son partenaire.
2. Catherine et son copain nagent, mais ils ne plongent pas.
3. J'aide mon père à faire la cuisine, et je joue avec mon chien.
4. Tu achètes un cadeau pour l'anniversaire de ta copine, et tu vas au café après.
5. Romain porte un maillot de foot. Il marque un but.
6. Nous mangeons un croque-monsieur, et nous parlons à nos camarades de classe.
7. Vous regardez un film de science-fiction. Vous ne parlez pas.
8. Les deux élèves étudient pour un contrôle d'anglais, et ils regardent des cédéroms.

## 2 Disons quinze minutes plus tard!

*Dites où vous allez vous retrouver et à quelle heure. Votre partenaire va suggérer* (suggest) *quinze minutes plus tard* (later). *Alternez les rôles.*

**MODÈLE**     Je voudrais acheter /      15h15
A: **Je voudrais acheter une casquette.**
B: **On se retrouve au magasin à trois heures et quart?**
A: **Disons trois heures et demie.**

1. J'ai très  / 13h00

2. J'ai besoin de faire  / 14h30

3. Nous avons un match de  / 16h05

4. Il y a un bon  / 19h15

5. J'ai très  / 12h

6. Nous avons besoin d'étudier  / 10h10

---

## Differentiated Learning

### Decelerate
Students might struggle with the symbols used in **Activité 2**. Point out that students won't need to use the French words for what is actually pictured, but rather should consider what that picture represents. For example, in number 1, they will not provide **l'eau minérale**, but rather the word **soif**. To avoid confusion, it may be necessary to discuss what each image represents with students before they begin the activity.

### Accelerate
Although most activities have models, you may want to challenge more proficient students to be more creative with their language use. For example, in **Activité 2**, students might instead say, "**Tu voudrais aller au magasin? On se retrouve à trois heures et quart.**" Not only will students produce more spontaneous and creative speech, but they will also get additional practice reviewing words and phrases.

---

**1**
1. ll est au labo.
2. Ils sont à la piscine.
3. Je suis chez moi.
4. Tu es en ville.
5. Il est au stade.
6. Nous sommes à la cantine.
7. Vous êtes au cinéma.
8. Ils sont à la médiathèque.

**2** *Possible answers:*
1. –J'ai très soif.
   –On se retrouve à la cantine à une heure?
   –Disons une heure et quart.
2. –J'ai besoin de faire mes devoirs.
   –On se retrouve à la médiathèque à deux heures et demie?
   –Disons trois heures moins le quart.
3. –Nous avons un match de foot.
   –On se retrouve au stade à quatres heures cinq?
   –Disons quatre heures vingt.
4. –Il y a un bon film d'horreur.
   –On se retrouve au cinéma à sept heures et quart?
   –Disons sept heures et demie.
5. –J'ai très faim.
   –On se retrouve à la cantine à midi?
   –Disons midi et quart.
6. –Nous avons besoin d'étudier la physique.
   –On se retrouve au labo à dix heures dix?
   –Disons dix heures vingt-cinq.

### Reference Desk

1. Refer to p. 137 of *T'es branché? Level 1A* to review vocabulary for place names.
2. Refer to p. 138 and p. 165 of *T'es branché? Level 1A* to review words and phrases for making plans to meet.
3. Students may struggle with **les faux amis** — false cognates. Point to the word **une éxperience** in **Activité 1** and explain the discrepancy.

### Culture

**Practices: Information**

Point out that in France, a typical breakfast for young people consists of a **tartine** (bread with jam) or a croissant. To drink, they might have fruit juice, hot chocolate, coffee, or tea.

**3**

1. Je vais faire du roller.
2. Nadia et moi, nous allons aller au cinéma.
3. Michèle et Richard vont aller à la teuf.
4. Normand va dormir.
5. Tu vas étudier.
6. Vous allez faire la cuisine.

## Reference Desk

1. Refer to p. 145 of *T'es branché? Level 1A* to review the verb **aller**.
2. Refer to p. 172 of *T'es branché? Level 1A* to review how the verb **aller** + infinitive is used to express what is going to happen in the near future.

## Expansion

Have students conduct a survey about their classmates' plans for the week. Ask students to write questions to ask about five different times this week (**après le cours de français**, **samedi soir**, **lundi après-midi**, etc.). Remind them to include the expression **aller** + infinitive in their questions. Give them a model, such as **Qu'est-ce que tu vas faire après le cours?** Then give students five minutes to interview as many classmates as they can. Have student write their results in a paragraph, using the phrase **aller** + infinitive to talk about their classmates' plans.

# Structure de la langue

**Passons en revue!**

## Present Tense of the Irregular Verb *aller*

### *Aller* + near future

Although the verb **aller** (*to go*) is an **–er** verb, it does not follow the regular pattern. It is an irregular verb.

| je | **vais** | nous | **allons** |
|---|---|---|---|
| tu | **vas** | vous | **allez** |
| il/elle/on | **va** | ils/elles | **vont** |

The verb **aller** is used...

1. to say where someone is going.
   **Les élèves vont au labo.**  *The students are going to the lab.*
2. to talk about how someone is feeling.
   **Ça va très mal aujourd'hui.**  *Things are going very badly today.*
3. to say what someone is going to do in the near future.
   **Suzanne va envoyer un texto à Serge.**  *Suzanne is going to send a text message to Serge.*
   **Nous n'allons pas parler anglais.**  *We're not going to speak English.*

**3**  **Qu'est-ce qu'on va faire samedi?**

*Dites ce que les gens suivants* (following people) *vont faire samedi.*

 **MODÈLE**  Édouard
**Édouard va envoyer des textos.**

1. je

2. Nadia et moi

3. Michèle et Richard

4. Normand

5. tu

6. vous

B38

## Essential Instruction

1. Ask several students: **Comment allez-vous?** Then, ask them to identify what verb they hear in the question (**aller**). Explain to students that the verb **aller** has several uses. Review the uses of the verb found in the yellow box on p. B38.
2. Have a student volunteer give the correct form of **aller** orally after these cues: **tu**, **Karim**, **nous**, **les Duval**, **Mlle Forestier**, **je**, **Éric et toi**, **Élodie**.
3. **Activités 3** and **4** can be assigned for homework. Point out that in **Activité 3**, students will be saying what they are going to do, and in **Activité 4**, they will say where they are going.

## 4 On va à Paris ou à New York?

*Dites si les gens vont à Paris ou à New York selon* (according to) *leur préférence.*

| MODÈLE | Antoine préfère manger un  .
**Antoine préfère manger un croque-monsieur. Il va à Paris.**

1. Je préfère visiter la  .

2. Timéo et Vincent préfèrent regarder les  .

3. Nous préférons parler  .

4. Tu préfères manger un  .

5. Vous préférez parler  .

6. M. et Mme Toulon préfèrent visiter la grande  .

7. Lucienne et moi, nous préférons regarder le  .

8. Je préfère acheter un  .

Quatrème partie 1B  **B 3 9**

**4**

1. Je préfère visiter la tour Eiffel. Je vais à Paris.
2. Timéo et Vincent préfèrent regarder un match de basket. Ils vont à New York. (à Paris)
3. Nous préférons parler anglais. Nous allons à New York.
4. Tu préfères manger un hamburger. Tu vas à New York.
5. Vous préférez parler français. Vous allez à Paris.
6. M. et Mme Toulon préfèrent visiter la grande statue de la Liberté. Ils vont à New York.
7. Lucienne et moi, nous préférons regarder le Tour de France. Nous allons à Paris.
8. Je préfère acheter un magazine français. Je vais à Paris.

### Reference Desk

Although basketball is more popular in the United States, it has been played in France for nearly a century. In 1932, the **Fédération Française de Basket-Ball** was formed to promote the sport throughout the country. The organization works to develop players and encourage their participation in basketball competitions in France and internationally. Many cities in France have professional teams, and some French players play in the National Basketball Association. For example, NBA star Tony Parker, who was born in Belgium and raised in France, played in the French national league before beginning his career in the United States.

### Connections

#### History

Explain that the Statue of Liberty was a gift to the United States from the people of France. Have students use the Internet to learn more about when the statue was built, how it was transported from France, who created it, and what it symbolizes. Have students share what they learned in small groups or with the class.

### Differentiated Learning
#### Accelerate

Have students extend **Activité 4** by writing three additional examples and using additional images that represent Paris and New York. Students may draw images or find them in magazines or online.

### Multiple Intelligences
#### Musical-Rhythmic

Challenge students to write a song that reviews the forms and uses of the verb **aller**. Have them choose a familiar tune, such as "Twinkle Twinkle Little Star" or "**Frère Jacques**" and write lyrics that include examples of the verb in each of its conjugations, with different subject pronouns. Encourage students to teach their songs to their classmates and sing them together as a group.

**5**

1. Nous n'allons pas parler anglais.
2. Il va porter un maillot.
3. Je vais aider ma mère.
4. Elles ne vont pas jouer au volley.
5. Vous allez nager.
6. Tu ne vas pas sortir avec des copains.
7. Il va marquer un but.
8. Il va acheter un cadeau.

**6** *All answers to questions will vary.*

1. Est-ce que tu vas téléphoner à un copain?
2. Est-ce que tu vas acheter une écharpe?
3. Est-ce que tu vas manger une glace?
4. Est-ce que tu vas faire le devoir?
5. Est-ce que tu vas aller au cinéma?
6. Est-ce que tu vas étudier pour une interro?
7. Est-ce que tu vas parler français?
8. Est-ce que tu vas préparer un sandwich?
9. Est-ce que tu vas jouer aux jeux vidéo?
10. Est-ce que tu vas faire du shopping?

## Reference Desk

1. Refer to p. 147 of *T'es branché? Level 1A* to review **à** + definite articles.
2. Refer to p. 261 of *T'es branché? Level 1A* to review **de** + definite articles.

## Communication

**Interpersonal: Cooperative Groups**

Tell students to imagine that a French exchange student is coming to spend the week with them. Have students work in small groups to prepare an itinerary for the student. Students should include information about where they are going to go. They will also discuss what they are going to do, and what they are not going to do, with the student. Have each group present its itinerary to the class, who will vote on the best one.

---

**5 Oui ou non?**

*Selon (According to) la première phrase, est-ce qu'on va faire l'activité entre parenthèses?*

**MODÈLE** Béatrice est au stade. (regarder le film policier)
**Elle ne va pas regarder le film policier.**

1. Nous sommes en France. (parler anglais)
2. Éric a un match de basket. (porter un maillot)
3. Je travaille chez moi. (aider ma mère)
4. Yasmine et Sara préfèrent le tennis. (jouer au volley)
5. Il fait beau. (vous/nager)
6. Tu as un contrôle de maths demain. (sortir avec des copains)
7. Salim est un excellent footballeur. (marquer un but)
8. Demain c'est l'anniversaire de la copine de Gilbert. (acheter un cadeau)

## Communiquez!

**6 Enfin le weekend!**

**Interpersonal Communication**

*À tour de rôle, demandez à votre partenaire s'il ou elle va faire les activités suivantes ce weekend. Écoutez bien ses réponses.*

**MODÈLE** organiser une teuf
A: **Est-ce que tu vas organiser une teuf ce weekend?**
B: **Non, je ne vais pas organiser de teuf. Et toi?**
A: **Oui, je vais organiser une teuf.**

1. téléphoner à un copain
2. acheter une écharpe
3. manger une glace
4. faire le devoir
5. aller au cinéma
6. étudier pour une interro
7. parler français
8. préparer un sandwich
9. jouer aux jeux vidéo
10. faire du shopping

## À and *de* plus Definite Articles

The preposition **à** means "to," "at," "in." It forms a contraction when it is followed by **le** and **les**, but not when it is followed by **la** and **l'**.

**B 4 0**

---

**Essential Instruction**

1. Review negation with students before they begin **Activité 5**. Point out that the expression **ne... pas** goes around only the conjugated verb (**aller**).
2. Have students take notes on their partner's response for **Activité 6**. When they finish, discuss their responses as a class. Have students talk about their partners in the third person. For example, students may say **George ne va pas acheter une écharpe ce week-end.**

3. Be sure to provide personalized examples in the review of **à** and **de** + definite articles. For example, ask questions such as **Qu'est-ce que vous allez acheter au magasin?** or **Qui est des États-Unis?** Have students use the target structures in their responses, and then use the examples in your review.
4. **Activités 7** and **8** can be assigned for homework.

| | |
|---|---|
| à + le = **au** | à + la = **à la** |
| à + les = **aux** | à + l' = **à l** |

**Corinne va <u>au</u> café.**
**Jean voyage <u>aux</u> États-Unis.**

**Philippe est <u>à la</u> maison.**
**Delphine étudie <u>à l'</u>école.**

The preposition **de** means "of," "from." It forms a contraction when it is followed by **le** and **les**, but not when it is followed by **la** or **l'**. When **de** means "of," it indicates possession.

| | |
|---|---|
| de + le = **du** | de + la = **de la** |
| de + les = **des** | de + l' = **de l'** |

**J'aime le maillot <u>du</u> footballeur.**
**C'est le secret <u>des</u> copains.**

**C'est l'anniversaire <u>de la</u> cuisinière.**
**Nous aimons le blason <u>de l'</u>équipe.**

---

**7  Choisissez!**

*Complétez les phrases avec la forme correcte de la préposition à + l'article défini.*

| au | aux | à la | à l' |
|---|---|---|---|

**MODÈLE**   **Nous aimons voyager <u>au</u> Canada.**

1. Nous sommes... magasin.
2. Malick et Clément vont... cantine.
3. Jérôme téléphone... fille canadienne.
4. M. Lévesque parle... élèves.

5. Tu n'aimes pas faire les devoirs... école.
6. Vous arrivez... match de basket à l'heure.
7. J'ai besoin de parler... proviseur.
8. Je voudrais voyager... États-Unis.

---

**8  Beaucoup de questions!**

*Répondez aux questions suivantes avec une réponse de la boîte.*

| la copine | le camarade de classe | l'actrice | le prof de maths |
|---|---|---|---|
| les élèves | la prof de français | la dentiste | les copains |

**MODÈL**   **À qui est-ce que tu ressembles?**
**Je ressemble à l'actrice.**

1. À qui est-ce que tu parles français?
2. À qui est-ce que tu téléphones beaucoup?
3. À qui est-ce que tu ne téléphones pas?
4. À qui est-ce que le prof de musique parle?

5. À qui est-ce que le cuisinier donne un gâteau?
6. À qui est-ce que tu apportes un cadeau?
7. À qui est-ce que l'agent de police donne une contravention (*ticket*)?

---

**Answers**

1. au
2. à la
3. à la
4. aux
5. à l'
6. au
7. au
8. aux

1. Je parle français à la prof de français.
2. Je téléphone beaucoup aux copains.
3. Je ne téléphone pas au prof de maths.
4. Le prof de musique parle aux élèves.
5. Le cuisinier donne un gâteau au camarade de classe.
6. J'apporte un cadeau à la copine.
7. L'agent de police donne une contravention à la dentiste.

---

**Reference Desk**

Point out that some verbs in French are followed by prepositions that wouldn't be used in English. Two examples of this are the verbs **téléphoner à** and **ressembler à**. As you review sentences with these verbs in the activities on this page, discuss their English equivalents, emphasizing the absence of the preposition in English after the verbs *call* and *look like*.

---

**Critical Thinking**

**Comparisons**

Point out to students that the words **au** and **du** are contractions. Have students give examples of contractions in English (*won't, don't, can't*). Ask students to think about the difference in use of contractions in both languages (optional in English, mandatory in French).

---

**Learning Styles**
**Auditory Learners**
Encourage auditory learners to do **Activités 7** and **8** aloud in pairs before they write their responses. This will give students additional practice hearing the prepositions **à** and **de** in the various contexts and forms. After they have said each item aloud once, have students start over, writing each item down as they say it again.

**Special Needs Students**
**Behavior Problems**
Students may get bored and off task while practicing structures such as those practiced on pp. B40–B41, which may seem more abstract or irrelevant to them than a vocabulary lesson would. Be sure to keep these types of lessons relevant by giving personal, contextualized examples as you review, and asking students questions about themselves to encourage them to use the structure. By making the lesson relevant and connecting students to the material, you will keep them engaged and on task.

## Answers

 *Possible questions:*

1. Est-ce que tu aimes jouer au foot au stade?
2. Est-ce que tu aimes danser aux teufs?
3. Est-ce que tu aimes porter un maillot de sport au cours d'EPS?
4. Est-ce que tu aimes faire le devoir de sciences au labo?
5. Est-ce que tu aimes regarder un documentaire à la maison?
6. Est-ce que tu aimes parler aux copains à la cantine?
7. Est-ce que tu aimes manger un sandwich au café?
8. Est-ce que tu aimes acheter des frites à la cantine?

**10**

1. Ce sont les magazines de la dentiste.
2. C'est le portable du copain de Camille.
3. C'est le dictionnaire des élèves.
4. C'est le lecteur de MP3 de la copine d'André.
5. C'est l'omelette de l'homme d'affaires.
6. C'est la tarte aux fraises des chefs.
7. *No answer needed.*
8. C'est le ballon de foot de l'athlète.

### Reference Desk

1. The activities on this page use vocabulary for food and beverages. Have students create a t-chart with the left column labeled **la cuisine** and the right column labeled **les boissons**. Ask students to list as many food and beverage words that they can remember in the appropriate columns. Review their lists with them. Compile a class list and have individuals fill in any words that they did not originally include on their charts.
2. Refer to pp. 179–180 of *T'es branché?* Level 1A to review vocabulary for food and beverages.

---

## Communiquez!

**9  À quel endroit?**

### Interpersonal Communication

*À tour de rôle, devinez (guess) où votre partenaire aime aller pour faire les activités suivantes.*

**MODÈLE**  étudier
A: **Est-ce que tu aimes étudier à la maison?**
B: **Non, je préfère étudier à la médiathèque.**

1. jouer au foot
2. danser
3. porter un maillot de sport
4. faire le devoir de sciences
5. regarder un documentaire
6. parler aux copains
7. manger un sandwich
8. acheter des frites

**10  À qui est-ce?**

*Lisez ce que les gens aiment faire. À qui est chaque objet?* (To whom does each object belong?)

**MODÈLE**  Le médecin aime aller au cinéma.
**C'est l'affiche du médecin.**

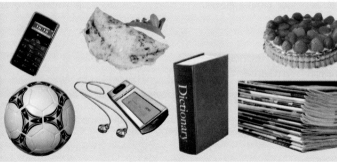

1. La dentiste aime lire.
2. Le copain de Camille aime envoyer des textos.
3. Les élèves aiment étudier l'anglais.
4. La copine d'André aime écouter de la musique.
5. L'homme d'affaires aime beaucoup manger.
6. Les chefs aiment préparer les desserts.
7. Le prof de français aime voyager.
8. L'athlète aime jouer au foot.

### Essential Instruction

1. Before students begin **Activité 9**, have them review the activities on the list. Encourage students to think about two or three possible places where they could do each activity.
2. Assign **Activité 10** for homework.
3. Before reviewing the verb **venir** with students, ask them to explain what an irregular verb is. Have them provide examples of other regular verbs that you have reviewed so far in the Bridge Unit (**être**, **avoir**, and **aller**).
4. Have students complete **Activité 11** individually, then place them in small groups to check each other's work.
5. Remind students to take turns asking and answering questions for **Activité 12**. Have them extend the activity by saying where they just came from, and asking their partner for the same information.

# Present Tense of the Irregular Verb *Venir*

The verb **venir** (*to come*) does not follow a regular pattern. It is irregular.

| je **viens** | nous **venons** |
|---|---|
| tu **viens** | vous **venez** |
| il/elle/on **vient** | ils/elles **viennent** |

Two verbs that are conjugated like **venir** are **devenir** (*to become*) and **revenir** (*to come back*).

To ask where someone is coming from, use the interrogative expression **d'où?**

## 11 Qui vient à la fête?

*Les jeunes* (young) *qui apportent de la nourriture* (food) *ou des boissons viennent à la fête. Dites qui vient et qui ne vient pas.*

> **MODÈLE**  Adèle apporte un gâteau.
> **Elle vient.**
>
> Damien apporte un ballon de basket.
> **Il ne vient pas.**

1. Tu apportes une quiche.
2. François et Françoise apportent des sandwichs au jambon.
3. Mon camarade de classe apporte un DVD.
4. Nous apportons de l'eau minérale.
5. J'apporte mon ordinateur portable.
6. Vous apportez des crêpes.
7. Les copains apportent des cédéroms.
8. On apporte une petite table.

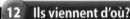

## 12 Ils viennent d'où?

### Interpersonal Communication

*À tour de rôle, demandez à votre partenaire d'où viennent les gens suivants.*

> **MODÈLE**  Mlle Dupuis/le bureau du proviseur
> A: **Mlle Dupuis vient d'où?**
> B: **Elle vient du bureau du proviseur.**

1. tu/le labo
2. Ahmed et Benjamin/la cantine
3. Magali et moi/les magasins
4. M. Dubourg/la salle d'informatique
5. les élèves/l'école
6. Hervé et toi/le stade

Quatrème partie 1B    **B 4 3**

### Reference Desk

1. Refer to p. 260 of ***T'es branché?*** *Level 1A* to review the present tense of the irregular verb **venir**.
2. Remind students that the singular forms of the verb **venir** are all pronounced the same.
3. Point out that the verb **venir** is often, but not always, followed by the preposition **de** to say where someone comes from.
4. You may want to take the opportunity to teach the phrase **venir de** + verb to mean that one "has just done something." Explain the construction and ask students simple questions such as **Vous venez de manger?** Have them respond in complete sentences.

## Differentiated Learning
### Decelerate
Provide students with a list of places to choose from to help them complete **Activité 9**.

### Expand
For **Activité 11**, have students give an additional sentence to say where the person is going if he/she is not coming to the party. Students should base their sentences on what that person is bringing with him/her.

## Multiple Intelligences
### Linguistic
Students may want to know what makes verbs like **venir** irregular. Encourage them to analyze the verb and think about what makes it different. For example, it is an –**ir** verb, but does not take –**ir** verb forms. Its stem changes in some forms, and the third-person plural form takes a double **n** before the ending. Have students discuss their ideas in pairs and then share them with you. Encourage these students to check the etymology of words to see the link; many French words come from Latin.

**13**

*Possible conversation:*

–Salut. Ça va?

–Bien, et toi?

–Pas mal. Tu viens d'où?

–Je viens de la médiathèque.

–Pourquoi?

–J'ai un contrôle de maths demain. Où vas-tu?

–Je vais au magasin.

–Pourquoi?

–J'ai besoin d'acheter des chaussures.

–Tu vas regarder le match de foot à six heures?

–Oui.

–Moi aussi!

–On se retrouve au stade à six heures moins le quart?

–D'accord.

–À bientôt!

–À six heures moins le quart!

**14** *Possible answers:*

1. –Qu'est-ce que tu vois à la médiathèque?
   –Je vois des ordinateurs et des DVD.
2. –Qu'est-ce que nous voyons à la salle d'informatique?
   –Vous voyez des ordinateurs et des cédéroms.
3. –Qu'est-ce que Julien et Jérémy voient à la cantine?
   –Ils voient des élèves qui mangent.
4. –Qu'est-ce que vous voyez au centre commercial?
   –Nous voyons des magasins.
5. –Qu'est-ce que Zohra voit en classe?
   –Elle voit un bureau, une fenêtre, une porte, des livres, des cahiers .
6. –Qu'est-ce que les copains voient en ville?
   –Ils voient des magasins et des cafés.

---

### Reference Desk

Refer to p. 204 of *T'es branché? Level 1A* to review the present tense forms of the irregular verb **voir**.

---

---

## Communiquez!

**13 Conversation dirigée**

**Interpersonal/Presentational Communication**

*Préparez la conversation suivante avec un partenaire, et puis (then) présentez la conversation à un groupe d'élèves.*

| **A** | **B** |
|---|---|
| Greet your partner, and ask how things are going. | Respond. Ask, "And you?" |
| Respond. Ask, "Where are you coming from?" | Say that you are coming from the media center. |
| Ask why. | Say because you have a history test tomorrow. Ask, "Where are you going?" |
| Say that you are going to the store. | Ask why. |
| Explain that you have to buy some shoes. | Ask, "Are you going to watch the soccer game at 6:00?" |
| Say, "Yes." | Say, "Me too!" |
| Suggest meeting at the stadium at 5:45. | Reply, "OK." |
| Say, "See you soon." | Reply. |

---

## Present Tense of the Irregular Verb *Voir*

The verb **voir** (*to see*) is irregular. There is an "i" to "y" change in the **nous** and **vous** forms.

| je **vois** | nous **voyons** |
|---|---|
| tu **vois** | vous **voyez** |
| il/elle/on **voit** | ils/elles **voient** |

## Communiquez!

**14 Qu'est-ce qu'on voit?**

**Interpersonal Communication**

*À tour de rôle, demandez à votre partenaire ce qu'on voit à chaque endroit. Soyez logique! (Be logical!)*

**MODÈLE** Chloé/au magasin
A: **Qu'est-ce que Chloé voit au magasin?**
B: **Elle voit des blousons.**

1. tu/à la médiathèque
2. nous/à la salle d'informatique
3. Julien et Jérémy/à la cantine
4. vous/au centre commercial
5. Zohra/classe
6. les copains/en ville

---

**Essential Instruction**

1. Have students prepare the dialogue in **Activité 13** with a partner. Once students have prepared and practiced their conversations, divide the class into two large groups. Have pairs act out their dialogues in front of the whole group. Encourage group members to offer feedback after each dialogue.

2. As you review the verb **voir**, remind students that the three singular forms and the third-person plural form are all pronounced in the same way.

3. Read the directions aloud for **Activité 15**. Pause after the word **gauche** and point to the left. Pause again after the word **droite** and point to the right. Then, assign the activity for homework. Remind students to look up the movies that they are not familiar with.

4. Read the text messages aloud for students before they begin **Activité 17**. Refer to p. 035 of *T'es branché? Level 1A* to review some phrases used in text messaging.

## 15 Tu aimes le cinéma?

*Faites correspondre (match) le titre des films à gauche avec le genre de film à droite. Vous pouvez faire des recherches en ligne.*

1. *Les Pirates des Caraïbes*
2. *Bienvenue chez les Ch'tis*
3. *Les 3 ninjas contre-attaquent*
4. *La Rafle*
5. *E.T. l'extra-terrestre*
6. *Halloween: Résurrection*
7. *Être et avoir*
8. *Amélie*

A. un film d'horreur
B. un documentaire
C. un film de science-fiction
D. une comédie romantique
E. une comédie
F. un drame
G. un film d'action
H. un film d'aventures

## 16 On va tous au cinéma!

*Indiquez le genre de film qu'on voit.*

> **MODÈLE**  Victor aime rigoler.
> **Il voit une comédie.**

1. Henri et moi, nous aimons voir les monstres, comme Frankenstein.
2. Solange et Hélène aiment pleurer.
3. La copine d'Henri aime les films où les acteurs et les actrices chantent (*sing*).
4. Sylvie adore Johnny Depp et tous les films "pirates."
5. Tu aimes l'histoire et les films biographiques.
6. Moi, j'aime les films où il y a des crimes et du mystère.
7. Georges et toi, vous préférez voir les extra-terrestres.

## 17 Lisons des textos!

### Presentational Communication

*Avec un partenaire, lisez les textos suivants. Récrivez-les en français standard.*

| Phone 1 | Phone 2 |
|---|---|
| 1. Slt. sava? | bi1. mr6. |
| 2. T ché 3?" | Chui o kfé. Pkoi? |
| 3. Je vé o 6né. Tu vi1? | 1posibl. p-ê 2m1? |
| 4. dak. Rdv 2m1 à 7h o 6né. | dak. ab1to! |

---

**Differentiated Instruction**
**Accelerate**
More proficient students should be encouraged to personalize structured dialogue activities, such as **Activité 13**. As long as students are practicing the targeted structures, they should try to include as many creative and personal details in the conversations as possible.

**Special Needs Students**
**Dyslexia**
Dyslexic students will have difficulty completing **Activité 17** unassisted. Write the contents of the text messages out of order and in French. Provide the student with the text. Pair him with a partner who will read the text messages aloud from the book. The dyslexic student should look on the list of sentences that you provided and match what he hears with your sentence. Then the students' partner can work with him to show how the text symbols correspond with the written sentences.

---

**15**
1. H
2. E
3. G
4. F
5. C
6. A
7. B
8. D

**16**
1. Nous voyons un film d'horreur.
2. Elles voient un drame.
3. Elle voit une comédie musicale.
4. Il voit un film d'aventures.
5. Tu vois un documentaire.
6. Je vois un drame.
7. Vous voyez un film de science-fiction.

**17**
1. –Salut. Ça va?
   –Bien, merci.
2. –T'es chez toi?
   –Je suis au café. Pourquoi?
3. –Je vais au ciné. Tu viens?
   –Impossible, peut-être demain.
4. –D'accord. Rendez-vous demain à sept heures au ciné.
   –D'accord. À bientôt!

### Reference Desk

1. Refer to pp. 194–195 of *T'es branché? Level 1A* to review vocabulary related to movies.
2. Remind students that the French film *Bienvenue chez les Ch'tis* is one of the most popular French movies of all time, with over 20 million tickets sold. You may want to introduce *Intouchables*, a more recent French hit.

### Culture

**Practices: Activity**
If your school allows phones, challenge students to text a classmate in French. Encourage students to send text messages to greet one another, find out where the other is, and make arrangements to meet. Have students show you their text message log, and award extra credit points to students who successfully message in French.

1. Refer to p. 220 **of *T'es branché?** Level 1A* to review vocabulary for family members.
2. Remember to be sensitive when talking about family members. Some students may not want to talk about their families. Give students the option to talk about families that they know from television shows, books, or movies, if they prefer not to talk about their own family.
3. Remind students that when talking about grandparents, the word **grand** stays in the masculine for both **grand-mère** and **grand-père**. It takes the plural form in the word **grands-parents**.
4. You may also want to review the following words for family members: **le neveu**, **la nièce**, **le petit-fils**, **la petite-fille**, **l'époux**, **l'épouse**, **les beaux-parents**, **l'enfant unique**, **les jumeaux/les jumelles**.

### Culture

**Perspectives: Information**

In France, the government is very supportive of families. When a baby is born, both parents get paid leave from their jobs. Childcare is subsidized by the government, and parents of multiple children even get a stipend from the government to help with the costs of raising them. Furthermore, parents can take time off from their jobs—up to three years—to be with their children, without worrying about whether the job will still be there when they are ready to return.

Cinquième partie

# Les gens

**B46**

**Essential Instruction**

1. Direct students to the photo on p. B46. Hold up your book and point to the people in the photo. As you point to each person, ask students to identify who that person is in the family.
2. Use e-visual 16 to review words for family members.
3. Review the information in the yellow box on p. B47. Direct students to describe each of the people pictured on p. B46 based on their physical characteristics. Encourage them to invent details about each person's personality as well.

4. Assign **Activité 1** for homework.

# Vocabulaire

### 1  Ma famille

*Qui sont les membres de votre famille?*

| | | | | |
|---|---|---|---|---|
| mon père | ma mère | mon frère | ma sœur | mon grand-père |
| ma tante | mon oncle | ma cousine | mon cousin | ma grand-mère | moi |

**MODÈLE**  **La femme** de **mon grand-père**, c'est **ma grand-mère**.

1. Le père de ma mère, c'est....
2. La fille de mon oncle, c'est....
3. La sœur de mon père, c'est....
4. Le fils de ma mère, c'est....
5. Le frère de ma cousine, c'est....
6. Le père de mon cousin, c'est....
7. La femme de mon père, c'est....
8. La fille de mon père, c'est....

**Answers**

**1**
1. mon grand-père
2. ma cousine
3. ma tante
4. mon frère/mon demi-frère
5. mon cousin
6. mon oncle
7. ma mère/ma belle-mère
8. ma sœur/ma demi-sœur

## Structure de la langue

**Passons en revue!**

### Agreement and Position of Regular Adjectives

Adjectives agree in gender (masculine or feminine) and in number (singular or plural) with the nouns or pronouns that they describe.

Most adjectives are made feminine by adding an **e** to the masculine singular form.

**Alain est un garçon bavard.**   **Anne est une fille bavard<u>e</u>.**

Some masculine adjectives end in **e**; consequently, there is no change to the feminine form.

**Le cours de maths est facil<u>e</u>.**   **La chimie est facil<u>e</u> aussi.**

Some adjectives are irregular and do not follow the patterns above.

**Maxime est canadien.**   **Isabelle est canadie<u>nne</u>.**
**Bastien est généreux.**   **Sandrine est généreu<u>se</u>.**

Most adjectives are made plural by adding an **s** to the singular form.

**Corinne est une élève drôle.**   **Sara et Marie sont des élèves drôle<u>s</u>.**

Some adjectives end in **s** in the singular, and therefore, there is no change for the plural form.

**J'ai un livre français.**   **Vous avez des livres français.**

In French, adjectives are usually placed after the noun that they describe.

**Mon copain a une copine paresseuse.**

Cinquième partie 1B  **B 4 7**

## Reference Desk

1. Refer to p. 123 and p. 221 of *T'es branché? Level 1A* to review vocabulary for descriptive adjectives.
2. Refer to p. 133 of *T'es branché? Level 1A* to review agreement and position of regular adjectives.

## Communication

**Presentational: Cooperative Groups**

Have students form groups of three. Distribute old magazines and catalogues to each group, and have students cut out pictures of people to create a family. Ask students to paste their pictures on poster board to form a family tree. Have them name each family member and label them with the appropriate word in French. Then have students present their family to the class. In addition to introducing each person, students should describe what each person looks like and his/her personality and likes. Encourage students to include at least six family members, so that each group member can describe at least two people to the class.

## Differentiated Learning
### Accelerate

Have students write a description of a family from a popular television show. Ask them to include each person's role in the family, as well as a description of his/her appearance and personality. Encourage students to use detailed descriptions, including phrases such as **les yeux marron**, etc. and **les cheveux raides**, etc. Have students read their descriptions aloud to the class, who will guess the family being described.

## Learning Styles
### Visual Learners

Encourage students to use visuals in their notes to help them review the vocabulary terms. For example, students might copy a family tree diagram into their notebooks instead of listing vocabulary. Students can use colored pencils or crayons to draw people in their notebooks to show hair and eye color. They could draw stick figures to show differences in height.

**2**

1. Le meilleur copain d'Abdou est bavard.
2. La meilleure copine de Pauline est égoïste.
3. La meilleure copine de Sylvie est sympa.
4. Le meilleur ami de Georges est paresseux.
5. La meilleure copine de Janine est grande.
6. Le meilleur copain de Victor est intelligent.

**3**

1. Il est diligent.
2. Elle est généreuse.
3. Il est généreux.
4. Elles sont bavardes.
5. Ils sont diligents.
6. Il est timide.
7. Elles sont paresseuses.

**4** *Dialogues will vary.*

## Reference Desk

1. The numbers used in the model for **Activité 3** are from the French grading system, which is on a scale of one to 20. In this system, students are rarely awarded grades of 16–20, which are considered to be very high honors. Grades of 14–16 are equivalent to an A in the American system, and 12–13 are equivalent to a B. Students can pass with a grade of 10 out of 20, even though in the American system this is considered to be a failing grade (50%).
2. You may want to review possession with **de** before students begin **Activité 2.** Remind students that the preposition **de** is used instead of **'s** to show possession in French. Give additional examples by walking around the room, holding up student objects, and saying sentences such as **C'est le stylo de Jonas. C'est la trousse d'Addison.**

---

### 2 Les meilleurs copains

*Les contraires s'attirent.* (Opposites attract.) *Décrivez* (Describe) *le meilleur copain ou la meilleure copine des élèves suivants. Utilisez les adjectifs contraires.*

> **MODÈLE** Aurélie est paresseuse.
> **La meilleure copine d'Aurélie est diligente.**

1. Abdou est timide.
2. Pauline est généreuse.
3. Sylvie est méchante.
4. Georges est diligent.
5. Janine est petite.
6. Victor est bête.

### 3 Comment sont-ils?

*Décrivez les gens suivants selon leurs activités. Faites attention à l'accord.* (Pay attention to agreement.)

> **MODÈLE** Rosalie a un 17 en sciences, un 18 en maths, et un 16,5 en histoire.
> **Elle est intelligente.**

1. Abdoulaye étudie beaucoup.
2. Evenye donne cinq euros à Méline.
3. Gabriel aide son grand-père le samedi.
4. Clara et Alima parlent beaucoup.
5. Amir et Alain jouent au basket, nagent, et travaillent au magasin.
6. Nicolas n'aime pas parler en public.
7. Sabine et sa sœur aiment dormir et regarder la télé tout le weekend.

## Communiquez!

### 4 Décrivez, s'il vous plait!

**Interpersonal Communication**

*À tour de rôle, demandez à votre partenaire de décrire* (describe) *les gens suivants. Décrivez les cheveux, la taille* (size)*, la personnalité au minimum. Puis, essayez de deviner* (guess) *l'identité de la personne.*

> **MODÈLE** ta chanteuse préférée
> A: **Comment est ta chanteuse préférée?**
> B: **Elle a les cheveux blonds. Elle est grande. Elle est drôle. Elle est anglaise.**
> A: **C'est Adèle?**
> B: **Oui, c'est elle.**

1. un footballeur
2. une actrice
3. un acteur
4. un chanteur
5. un prof
6. une camarade de classe

---

**Essential Instruction**

1. Review opposites before students begin **Activité 2.** Say adjectives such as **timide**, **drôle**, and **diligent**, and have students say the opposite aloud. Then have students complete the activity individually.
2. Encourage students to use more than one adjective whenever possible for **Activité 3.**
3. For **Activité 4**, allow students to write about **un(e) athlète** in general for Question 1, if they are not able to think of a description for a soccer player.
4. Summarize the information in the yellow box on p. B49 in a t-chart on the board. Label one column **C'est** and the other **Il/Elle est.** Then make a bulleted list underneath each heading to show when to use each phrase. Review these forms in both the plural (**ce sont, ils/elles sont**) and the negative.

# C'est versus il/elle est

C'est and il/elle est are used to describe a person or a thing, and they both mean "he is" or "she is" as well as "it is."

Use c'est:
- with an article/possessive adjective + noun
  **C'est ma prof d'histoire.**          *She's my history teacher.*
- with an article + noun + adjective
  **C'est un avocat bavard.**            *He's a talkative lawyer.*
- with a name
  **C'est Justine.**                     *She's Justine.*

C'est becomes **ce n'est pas** in a negative sentence. The plural form of **c'est** is **ce sont**.

**C'est M. Tran. C'est mon médecin. Ce n'est pas mon oncle.**
**Voici M. et Mme Vigier. Ce sont des graphistes français.**

Use il/elle est:
- with an adjective by itself
  **Il est égoïste.**                    *He is selfish.*
- with a profession
  **Elle est cuisinière.**               *She's a cook.*

The plural form of **il/elle est** is **ils/elles sont**.

**Voici M. Odier et Mme Renaud. Ils sont agents de police.**

Note the use of **c'est** and **il/elle est** with nationalities.

**C'est un Français.**                   *He's a Frenchman.*
**Il est français.**                     *He is French.*

M. Aknouch? C'est un Algérien.

## Reference Desk

Refer to p. 258 of *T'es branché? Level 1A* to review **C'est** vs. **il/elle est**.

## Connections

### Language Arts/Art
Have students work in groups to write a children's book about a family. Encourage students to write about at least four family members, and to include names, ages, descriptions of appearance and personality, and details about what each person likes to do. Have students use **C'est** and **Il/Elle est** as appropriate in their books. Students should illustrate each page of their book, and include a title and a cover. Bind students' books for them, and display them in the classroom. Encourage students to read one another's books whenever time permits in class. For example, offer students a book if they finish a test, quiz, or in-class assignment early.

## Multiple Intelligences
### Intrapersonal
If students are uncomfortable working with a partner, allow them to write their descriptions for **Activité 4** on a sheet of paper. Have students exchange papers with a partner who will write their guess. Collect students' work after they finish. Arrange a time to meet with students individually. During this time, have students read their descriptions aloud, and offer feedback on their language use and pronunciation.

## Special Needs Students
### Auditory Impairment
Students with hearing impairments may have trouble distinguishing gender of adjectives based on sound alone. While you discuss the activities, be sure to write the adjective and the noun that it modifies on the board as you say it. This will give hearing impaired students a visual cue to help them to connect the sounds with the words.

**5  Ma dentiste!**

*Complétez le paragraphe avec **c'est, ce sont, elle est, ils sont**.*

Je vous présente Madame Diouf. _____ ma dentiste. _____ sénégalaise. _____ une femme très intéressante. Ses fils s'appellent Moussa et Kemajou. _____ mes camarades de classe. _____ drôles et sympa. _____ des élèves diligents aussi. Ils ont une sœur. _____ petite, et elle ressemble à ses frères. _____ une fille timide, mais énergique.

Mme Diouf

## Communiquez!

**6  Les gens célèbres**

### Interpersonal Communication

*Demandez à votre partenaire avec qui il ou elle veut (wants) faire les activités suivantes. Choisissez la personne célèbre (famous) de la colonne A (column A) et la profession de la colonne B. Suivez le modèle.*

**MODÈLE**  faire la cuisine
A: **Avec qui est-ce que tu veux faire la cuisine?**
B: **Avec Emeril Lagasse.**
A: **Pourquoi?**
B: **Parce que c'est un cuisinier drôle.**

| A | B |
|---|---|
| Emeril Lagasse | une actrice sympa |
| Einstein | une femme généreuse |
| Steve Jobs | un chanteur populaire |
| Zinédine Zidane | un cuisinier drôle |
| Le Président des États-Unis | un prof intelligent |
| J. K. Rowling | un homme d'affaires riche |
| Vanessa Paradis | un écrivain intéressant |
| Youssou N'Dour | un homme diligent |
| Oprah Winfrey | un athlète énergique |

1. faire la cuisine
2. jouer au foot
3. chanter
4. lire
5. étudier pour le contrôle de physique
6. parler
7. voir un film
8. travailler
9. aller en ville

## Essential Instruction

1. Have students complete **Activité 5** alone, and then check their work in small groups. Walk around the room to monitor students' discussions, and provide clarification as necessary.
2. Have students look at the list of people for **Activité 6**, and check to see that they are familiar with each one. Encourage students to provide one or two adjectives to describe each person before they begin the activity. Then allow time for students to do the activities in pairs.
3. Review possessive adjectives with students. Read the information in the yellow box on p. B51 aloud. Model using possessive adjectives by holding up things in the room, and using the appropriate adjectives to describe them. For example, hold up a copy of the textbook and say **C'est notre livre de français**. Hold up your own copy and say **C'est mon livre**. Repeat for several students in order to use a variety of possessive adjectives.

# Possessive Adjectives

Possessive adjectives are used to show ownership or relationship. In French, they agree in gender and number with the noun that follows them.

|  | Singular | | Plural |
|---|---|---|---|
|  | **Masculine** | **Feminine** |  |
| my | **mon** | **ma** | **mes** |
| your | **ton** | **ta** | **tes** |
| his, her, its, one's | **son** | **sa** | **ses** |
| our | **notre** | **notre** | **nos** |
| your | **votre** | **votre** | **vos** |
| their | **leur** | **leur** | **leurs** |

### Reference Desk

1. Refer to p. 227 of *T'es branché? Level 1A* for a review of possessive adjectives.
2. Remind students that even though they are masculine, the adjectives **mon**, **ton**, and **son** are used before feminine nouns that start with a vowel. Point out that this prevents the occurrence of two consecutive vowel sounds, and maintains the melodic sound of the language. Give students examples such as **mon amie**, **ton épouse**, etc.

Possessive adjectives agree with what is possessed and not with the owner.

Marie, tu aimes **tes** cousins, n'est-ce pas?

**Son, sa** and **ses** may mean "his," "her," "its," "one's." They agree in gender and number with the noun that follows and not with the owner.

Claire apporte **son** sac à dos à l'école.
Pierre a rendez-vous avec **ses** copains.

Directly before a feminine singular noun beginning with a vowel sound, use **mon, ton, son** rather than **ma, ta, sa**.

Je dois étudier pour **mon** interro d'anglais.

Les enfants aiment visiter leurs grands-parents.

Minouche regarde sa carte.

Cinquième partie 1B  **B 5 1**

## Differentiated Learning
### Expand
After students finish **Activité 6**, have them switch partners and do the activity again. This time, have students say with whom they would prefer to do each activity. Students might choose another celebrity to answer each question, or they may simply name a friend or family member. Remind students to provide reasons for their choices. Have pairs share their dialogues with the class.

## Special Needs Students
### Linguistically Challenged
Students may struggle with possessive adjectives in French. Provide additional support for students. Write the following sentence on the board: **Julie travaille avec son père.** Circle the phrase **son père**, and ask students what the possessive adjective is (**son**). Explain that it is modifying **père** – a masculine noun. Erase the circled text and write "_____ **mère**." Have students supply the missing possessive adjective (**sa**).

**7**

1. C'est mon gâteau.
2. C'est son cadeau.
3. C'est notre maison.
4. Ce sont vos dictionnaires.
5. C'est ton café.
6. C'est son stylo.
7. C'est ma trousse.
8. C'est leur ordinateur.
9. Ce sont leurs CD.
10. C'est notre photo.

**8**

1. son
2. leurs
3. ses
4. sa
5. leurs
6. leur
7. sa
8. leur

## Reference Desk

Some activities on this page include vocabulary for birthdays and birthday gifts. Refer to p. 232 of **T'es branché?** Level 1A to review this vocabulary.

## Culture

### Practices: Information

It is common for the French to put sparklers on birthday cakes instead of candles.

---

**7  À qui est-ce?**

*Dites à qui chaque objet appartient (belongs) en utilisant (by using) les adjectifs possessifs. Suivez le modèle.*

MODÈLE **C'est ta carte cadeau.**
toi

**Ce sont ses chaussettes.**
Léa

1. moi   2. Virginie   3. nous   4. vous   5. toi

6. Maude   7. moi   8. Romain et Raoul   9. Naya et Emma   10. Dominique et moi

---

**8  On est très généreux!**

*Dans la grande famille de Rose, tout le monde offre des cadeaux pour la fête de la St-Valentin. Complétez les phrases avec **son, sa, ses, leur** ou **leurs**.*

1. Mme Colbert offre un blouson à... mari.
2. Les jumelles (*twins*), Juliette et Justine, donnent une carte cadeau à... grands-parents.
3. M. Colbert achète un ballon de foot pour... fils, Xavier et Louis.
4. Cédric offre une écharpe à... mère.
5. Xavier et Louis préparent un gâteau pour... parents.
6. Juliette et Cédric achètent une casquette pou... oncle.
7. M. Colbert donne un nouveau portable à... femme.
8. M. et Mme Colbert achète des roses pour... fille, Rose.

---

### Essential Instruction

1. Remind students to change the verb to the plural for Questions 4 and 9 of **Activité 7**. Refer them to the model.
2. **Activités 7** and **8** can be done as homework.
3. Before they begin **Activité 9**, students can review the list of items and determine how they will respond to each question. Encourage students to add their own details to each answer. For example, for Question 1, students might reply: **Ma maison n'est pas grande, mais elle est belle**.

4. Assign students to groups of three to complete **Activité 10**. Remind them that one student will ask the other two questions. A student from that pair will answer on behalf of both students. Walk around the room to monitor students and make sure that they are alternating roles.

## Communiquez!

### 9 Tu es trop curieux!

**Interpersonal Communication**

*À tour de rôle, jouez le rôle du camarade de classe trop curieux (curious). Suivez le modèle. Utilisez les adjectifs possessifs.*

**MODÈLE** cours de maths/facile
A: **Est-ce que ton cours de maths est facile?**
B: **Oui, mon cours de maths est facile. (Non, mon cours de maths est difficile.)**

1. maison/grand
2. copains/drôle
3. prof de français/sympa
4. cours de sciences/intéressant
5. cousins/timide
6. sac à dos/petit
7. grand-mère/généreux
8. camarade de classe/bavard

## Communiquez!

### 10 Une petite enquête

**Interpersonal Communication**

*À tour de rôle et en groupes de trois, posez les questions suivantes et répondez. Utilisez **votre, vos, notre** et **nos.***

**MODÈLE** école/grand/petit
A: **Est-ce que votre école est grande ou petite?** (une personne)
B: **Notre école est grande.** (deux personnes)

1. cours d'EPS/facile/difficile
2. ordinateurs/être à la maison/à l'école
3. où/copains/à midi
4. prof de français/parler/anglais
5. médiathèque/avoir/beaucoup de tables
6. école/avoir/une piscine

Cinquième partie 1B **B 5 3**

---

**11** *Answers from A will vary.*
1. Est-ce que tu grossis?
2. Quel cadeau est-ce que tu choisis?
3. À quelle heure sont tes cours?
4. Est-ce qu'elle rougit?
5. Est-ce que tu réussis?
6. Qu'est-ce que vous choisissez?
7. Est-ce qu'elle maigrit?
8. À quelle heure est-ce que vous finissez?

## Reference Desk

1. Refer to p. 239 of *T'es branché? Level 1A* to review the present tense of regular verbs ending in **–ir**.
2. Remind students that they already reviewed verb conjugations for regular verbs ending in **–er** in the **Deuxième partie**. Ask a student to explain the process of conjugating a regular verb. Remind them of the terms **la racine** and **la terminaison**. Have students identify the stems for each of the **–ir** verbs.
3. Point out that the pronunciation of the three singular forms is identical. Model the **z** sound that the letters **–issent** make in the third-person plural form.

## Critical Thinking

### Analysis

Have students identify French words related to the following verbs: **grossir, maigrir, rougir, finir, choisir,** and **grandir**. Have students make connections among the words in the word families in order to explain the meanings of the verbs. If necessary, students may use their glossary, a bilingual dictionary, or the Internet to help them.

# Regular –*ir* verbs

To form the present tense of regular **–ir** verbs, drop the **–ir** from the infinitive to find the stem. Add the ending that corresponds to each of the subject pronouns. Regular **–ir** verbs follow a predictable pattern. Here is the present tense of the verb **choisir** (*to choose*).

| je | chois**is** | nous | chois**issons** |
|----|------------|------|-----------------|
| tu | chois**is** | vous | chois**issez** |
| il/elle/on | chois**it** | ils/elles | chois**issent** |

Other **–ir** verbs include **finir** (*to finish*), **grandir** (*to grow*), **grossir** (*to put on weight*), **maigrir** (*to lose weight*), **réfléchir (à)** (*to think over*), **réussir (à)** (*to succeed, to pass a test*), and **rougir** (*to blush*).

## Communiquez!

**11  Parlons!**

### Interpersonal Communication

*À tour de rôle, utilisez l'information suivante pour former des questions qui emploient (use) les verbes **–ir**. Parlez avec votre partenaire.*

| choisir | réussir | maigrir | grossir | finir | rougir |

**MODÈLE**  A: J'aime bien mon cours de musique. (À quelle heure)
B: **À quelle heure est-ce que ton cours de musique finit?**
A: **Il finit à 2h30.**

1. Je mange beaucoup de desserts en été. (Est-ce que)
2. L'anniversaire de ma cousine est dimanche. (Quel cadeau)
3. J'ai six cours le vendredi. (À quelle heure)
4. Gabrielle est très timide, et elle doit parler devant la classe. (Est-ce que)
5. J'étudie un peu pour mon contrôle d'histoire. (Est-ce que)
6. Nous allons déjeuner au café. (Qu'est-ce que)
7. Ma sœur fait beaucoup de sports. (Est-ce qu'elle)
8. Nous allons voir un bon film ce soir. (À quelle heure)

## Essential Instruction

1. Review with students the forms of regular verbs that end in **–ir**. Read the information in the yellow box on p. B54. Then call on volunteers to conjugate other verbs on the board.
2. Guide students through **Activité 11**. Have them read each sentence aloud, and discuss each one as a class to determine which verb should be used in the question.
3. Assign **Activité 12** for homework.

4. Review words for food and drinks before students begin **Activité 13**. Have students copy and complete the menu on a separate sheet of paper. Encourage them to add other items that they may know for each category. Have students compare their menu with that of a partner after they finish.

## 12 Oui ou non?

*Lisez la phrase. Est-ce que l'activité entre parenthèses arrivera (will happen)?*

**MODÈLE**  Éléonore adore les desserts. (choisir la glace?)
**Elle choisit la glace.**

Étienne est très actif (*active*). (grossir?)
**Il ne grossit pas.**

1. Gabriel mange des hamburgers et des frites. (maigrir?)
2. Nous étudions beaucoup. (réussir?)
3. Vous allez au magasin de sport. (choisir un short?)
4. Anaïs et Lilou vont à la médiathèque. (finir le devoir?)
5. Tu es très timide. (rougir?)
6. Je joue au foot, et je nage. (grossir?)
7. Mon frère regarde la télé de 18h00 à 22h00 lundi soir. (réussir au contrôle mardi?)
8. Tu veux acheter un cadeau pour ta mère. (réfléchir à ses besoins?)

## 13 Au Café Bon Ami

*Votre oncle va ouvrir (open) un nouveau café français en ville. Aidez-le à créer la carte. (Help him create the menu.) Mettez les mots (words) dans une des trois catégories sur une carte comme celle (the one) de dessous: plats (main dishes), boissons, ou desserts.*

pizza    limonade    quiche

glace à la vanille    café

crêpe à la confiture

steak-frites    coca    gâteau

omelette    croque-monsieur

eau minérale    glace au chocolat

sandwich au fromage

jus d'orange

sandwich au jambon    salade

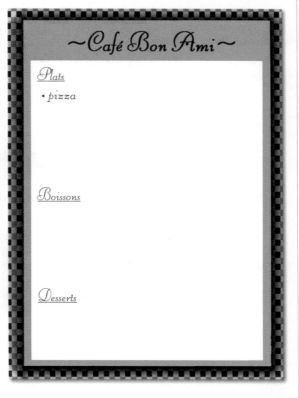

~Café Bon Ami~

*Plats*
• *pizza*

*Boissons*

*Desserts*

1. Il ne maigrit pas.
2. Nous réussissons.
3. Vous choisissez un short.
4. Elles finissent le devoir.
5. Tu rougis.
6. Je ne grossis pas.
7. Il ne réussit pas au contrôle mardi.
8. Tu réfléchis à ses besoins.

**Plats:** pizza, quiche, steak-frites, omelette, croque-monsieur, sandwich au fromage, sandwich au jambon, salade
**Boissons:** limonade, café, coca, eau minérale, jus d'orange
**Desserts:** glace à la vanilla, crêpe à la confiture, gâteau, glace au chocolat

### Reference Desk

1. Refer to pp. 179–180 of *T'es branché?* Level 1A to review words and phrases for ordering food and beverages in a café.
2. Remind students that cafés and restaurants in France typically serve a **prix-fixe** (*fixed price*) meal that includes two or three courses. A two-course **menu** (*meal*) might include **une entrée** (*appetizer*) and **un plat principal** (*main course*). A three-course **menu** includes **une entrée**, **un plat principal**, and **un dessert**. When ordering a **menu**, customers typically pay one price and have the choice among two or three dishes for each course. **Menus** are generally advertised by price.

### Expansion

Have students use the menu that they create for **Activité 13** as a prop in a role-play between a server and a customer. Ask students to write a short dialogue. Encourage them to use verbs ending in **–ir**, such as **choisir** and **finir**. Have students choose menu items to order. They should also ask for the check, and say thank you and good-bye. Have students perform their dialogues in front of the class.

## Differentiated Learning
### Decelerate
If students have trouble making the necessary inferences to form questions for **Activité 11**, write the appropriate question for each item on the board, leaving a blank where the verb goes. Have students complete each question with the correct form of the verb ending in **–ir**.

## Special Needs Students
### Speech Impairment
Students may have trouble pronouncing the distinct verb forms. To show what they know, have students write each verb ending on a separate index card. As students do the activities, have them reinforce their answer by saying the sentence and holding up the appropriate verb ending at the same time.

**14**

1. Koffi prend un sandwich au fromage.
2. Mes parents prennent un café.
3. Moi, je prends un steak-frites.
4. Ma sœur prend une eau minérale.
5. Toi, tu prends une crêpe.
6. Mégane et moi, nous prenons une pizza.
7. Noah et Inès prennent un coca et un croque-monsieur.
8. Simon et toi, vous prenez une glace à la vanille.

## Reference Desk

1. Refer to p. 188 of *T'es branché?* Level 1A to review the present tense of the irregular verb **prendre**.
2. Remind students that the verb **prendre** is frequently used in reference to ordering and consuming both food and drink. Give examples such as: **Je vais prendre une salade. Ma mère prend du café.**

## Culture

### Products: Information

1. In France, sandwiches are often served on long, crusty bread called a **baguette**. Cheese, ham, turkey, tuna, and vegetables (**crudités**) are popular sandwiches.
2. A **café américain** is a filtered coffee, similar to what people drink in the United States. If one orders just **un café** in France, she will receive a strong coffee, similar to an espresso.
3. **La quiche** is a popular lunchtime dish in France and is available in many **cafés** and **boulangeries. Quiche Lorraine**, which has **lardons** (*bacon*) and **gruyère** cheese, is very common. However, **quiche** is also available with ham, cheese, and vegetables such as broccoli or spinach.
4. In France, ice cream is often served with a long, tube-shaped cookie in it. This type of cookie is referred to as **une cigarette russe**.

# *Prendre* in the Present Tense

The irregular verb **prendre** means "to take" or "to have" when referring to food or beverage. Its forms are:

| je | **prends** | nous | **prenons** |
|---|---|---|---|
| tu | **prends** | vous | **prenez** |
| il/elle/on | **prend** | ils/elles | **prennent** |

Saniyya <u>prend</u> son ordinateur à l'école.
Mathis <u>prend</u> un sandwich au café.

*Saniyya is taking her computer to school.*
*Mathis is having a sandwich at the café.*

Other verbs that follow the same pattern as **prendre** are **apprendre** (*to learn*) and **comprendre** (*to understand*).

## 14  Qu'est-ce qu'on prend?

*Regardez la carte du Café Bon Ami que vous avez faite, et dites ce que tout lemonde prend pour le déjeuner.*

1. Koffi  2. mes parents  3. moi, je  4. ma sœur

 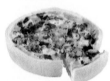  

5. toi, tu  6. Mégane et moi, nous  7. Noah et Inès  8. Simon et toi, vous

### Essential Instruction

1. Review the forms of the verb **prendre** with students. Have volunteers use the verbs **comprendre** and **apprendre** in original sentences.
2. Have students scan the photos before they begin **Activité 14**. Review the words as necessary.
3. Say the name of each café in **Activité 15** aloud, and have students guess its meaning. For each café, discuss possible foods and beverages that one might have there. Allow time for students to complete the activity in pairs. After they finish, listen to several dialogues for each item.
4. Assign students to groups of three to prepare and rehearse the dialogues in **Activité 16**. Create a café in your classroom by bringing in a table cloth, a vase of silk flowers, and items such as cups and plates for students to use as props.

# Unité

# 6 La rue commerçante

*Rendez-vous à Nice!*

**Épisode 6:**
*Au travail!*

Go online
**EMC**Languages.net

deux cent soixante-treize 273

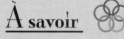

# Citation

"La beauté échappe aux modes passagères."

Beauty escapes passing styles.

—Robert Doisneau, photographe français

## À savoir 4.2

The tradition of the French open-air market dates back to the Middle Ages, and continues today. Meat, candy, flowers, fruit and vegetables, and clothing are some of the most popular items.

# Unité 6
# La rue commerçante

**Answers** _____

The answer to the video question is B.

## Question centrale

### How is shopping different in other countries?

Go online
EMCLanguages.net

**Why is Jean-Charles upset?**
A. Charlotte is ill.
B. He caught Patrick at Charlotte's house.
C. He caught Patrick kissing Charlotte.

In what parts of the francophone world can you find open-air markets like this?

## Contrat de l'élève

### Leçon A  I will be able to:

» shop for clothes.

» talk about shopping online in France, French flea markets, designers, and clothing in West Africa.

» use the verbs **acheter** and **vouloir** and demonstrative adjectives.

### Leçon B  I will be able to:

» sequence activities.

» talk about French stores, cheeses, and metric measurements.

» use regular –**re** verbs and expressions of quantity.

### Leçon C  I will be able to:

» make purchases at the market.

» talk about French and North African markets and the slow food movement in France.

» use the partitive in affirmative and negative sentences.

deux cent soixante-quinze **275**

## Reference Desk

In the Arab world, a **souk** is a market which may be located in a designated commercial section of the city, or in an open-air location. **Souks** are an important part of life in North Africa, and merchants sell everything from rugs to vegetables. By tradition, shoppers at a **souk** must negotiate with shopkeepers to reach a price. For large items, customers are expected to sit down with the shopkeeper who will offer them tea and snacks while the price is discussed.

## Critical Thinking

### Comparisons
If your students are keeping a Culture Journal, you might have them brainstorm possible answers to the **Question centrale** and the photo question. Or, offer students the alternative to write about a unique (funny, challenging, etc.) shopping experience they've had.

**Learning Styles**
**Kinesthetic/Visual Learners**
Have students create a photo collage, either online or using poster board, of different places to shop and things they like to buy, including favorite foods. As they move through the unit, they can add French labels to the items on their collage.

## Reference Desk

1. Consider teaching your students the expression **faire du lèche-vitrine** (to go window shopping).

2. **Un pull** is the shortened form of **un pull-over**. In French-speaking Canada, **un chandail** is often used for **un pull**.

3. **Un manteau** is a coat, and **une veste** is a jacket for a male or female.

4. Nowadays, with unisex clothing, a woman's shirt that resembles the form of a man's shirt (with collar, sleeves, and cuffs) may be called **une chemise**. Take note also that **une blouse** is a work shirt or lab coat worn over regular clothes and a **blouson** is a blousy, bulky jacket.

5. Students learned **une écharpe** in **Leçon A, Unité 5**. Explain that **écharpe** is the term for scarves of rectangular-shaped material (hence, the Paris Saint-Germain **écharpe**), but **foulard** is for square-shaped material.

6. Other related terms: **un survêtement** (*warm-up suit*), **une ceinture** (*belt*), **un imper**, **un imperméable** (*raincoat*), **des gants (m.)** (*gloves*), **un collant** (*tights*), **des lunettes (f.)** (*glasses*), **des lunettes de soleil (f.)** (*sunglasses*), **des verres de contact (m.)** (*contact lenses*).

7. Note that the word **tennis** is masculine, although people may use the feminine form for short in place of the complete expression **les chaussures de tennis**.

 **Leçon A**

# Vocabulaire actif

 Go online EMCLanguages.net

## À la boutique   1.2

**Les vêtements (m.)**

un manteau
un chapeau
une chemise
un pull
un pantalon
un ensemble
une jupe

| un maillot de bain | une veste | | |
| un tee-shirt | un foulard | une robe | un jean |

**Les chaussures (f.)**

| des tennis (m.) | des bottes (f.) |

## Essential Instruction

1. Show pictures of the clothing presented in the **Vocabulaire actif** and poll your students in French to find out what they're wearing today. Ask questions using cognates, such as, **Qui porte un jean aujourd'hui? Un tee-shirt?** Write the vocabulary on the board as you proceed.

2. Have students listen to and repeat the vocabulary in **À la boutique**, then tell a partner what they are or are not wearing.

3. Review the masculine and feminine forms of the adjectives of color. Brainstorm cognates or French terms used in English, such as "blank," "to blanch," and "bleach" for **blanc/blanche**, "jaundice" for **jaune**, a **film noir** for a dark film, and "Vermont" for **vert/verte**.

4. Point out the cognate for **chercher** (*search*) in **Pour la conversation**.

**2 7 6**

1.2

## Les couleurs (f.)

| | |
|---|---|
| noir/noire | blanc/blanche |
| violet/violette | marron |
| bleu/bleue | beige |
| vert/verte | gris/grise |
| rouge | rose |
| jaune | orange |

Le pull **violet** est **joli.**

La chemise **violette** est **moche.**

## Pour la conversation

**W**hat do I say to find the clothes I want?

> **Je cherche** une jupe.
> *I'm looking for a skirt.*

> **Vous avez** le pantalon **en** gris/**en** 38?
> *Do you have the pants in gray/in a size 38?*

**W**hat does the salesperson say?

> **Je peux vous aider?**
> *May I help you?*

> **De quelle couleur?**
> *What color?*

> **Quelle taille faites-vous?**
> *What's your size?*

### Et si je voulais dire...?

| | |
|---|---|
| **à la mode** | *in style* |
| **un anorak** | *ski jacket* |
| **des bas** | *(panty) hose* |
| **un costume** | *man's suit* |
| **court(e)** | *short* |
| **une cravate** | *tie* |
| **long(ue)** | *long* |
| **un sweat** | *sweatshirt* |
| **un tailleur** | *woman's suit* |

## TPR

If you have flash cards or pictures of the clothing items, you might give students commands, such as **Montrez-moi la robe**, while holding up the picture of the dress and another item of clothing. Students respond by pointing to the card that shows the dress. Continue this activity by commanding students to pair up two items, using **Mets le foulard avec la veste**.

Students can demonstrate comprehension by manipulating the flash cards/pictures as directed.

## Communication

**Interpersonal: Cooperative Groups**

Gather enough pictures of the clothing items in this lesson for each student to have one. Create a separate set of 3×5 cards with the vocabulary words in French, again enough for each student to have one. Distribute two different pictures to half the students in class and hand out two different vocabulary cards to the rest of the class. Instruct students to circulate and find a match to their cards by saying what they are looking for, "**Je cherche....**" After a designated amount of time, stop the activity and ask students to hold up the picture and matching card and say what it is.

## Differentiated Learning
### Expand

1. Ask students to research and report the origin of the expression **pie à la mode**. The term first appears in American English at the end of the 19th century.
2. Discuss the Eskimo word **anorak,** which refers to a ski jacket or parka in English.

### Learning Styles
### Visual Learners

1. You may wish to have students create their own picture flash cards for the vocabulary.

2. When teaching the colors, distribute colored paper to each student. Ask, "**Qui a le papier bleu? orange?**" etc. Students hold up the corresponding colored paper to show their comprehension. Expand this activity and ask, "**De quelle couleur est...?**" using the vocabulary from the lesson and classroom objects students know.

## 1 Le voyage de Fatima

2.1, 2.2

*Fatima va voyager avec un groupe d'élèves qui va donner des concerts en Europe. Comparez les deux listes. Ensuite, dites ce dont (what) elle a besoin, selon la liste de sa prof et la liste de ce qu'elle a déjà (already).*

**MODÈLE** **Fatima a besoin d'une chemise blanche....**

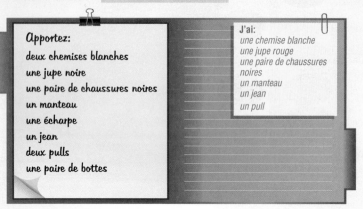

Apportez:
deux chemises blanches
une jupe noire
une paire de chaussures noires
un manteau
une écharpe
un jean
deux pulls
une paire de bottes

J'ai:
*une chemise blanche
une jupe rouge
une paire de chaussures noires
un manteau
un jean
un pull*

## Communiquez!

1.1, 4.1

## 2 On fait du shopping!

**Interpersonal Communication**

*Vous cherchez les vêtements suivants dans un magasin. Avec un partenaire, jouez les rôles du vendeur et son client.*

**MODÈLE**
A: **Je peux vous aider?**
B: **Oui, je cherche un pull.**
A: **De quelle couleur?**
B: **Un pull vert, s'il vous plaît.**
A: **Voilà un pull vert.**
B: **Combien coûte le pull?**
A: **Trente-six euros.**

1. 176€
2. 85€
3. 129€
4. 84€
5. 62€
6. 13€
36€

### 3 Qu'est-ce qu'on porte?  2.1, 2.2

*Choisissez l'illustration qui correspond à chaque description que vous entendez.*

A.

B.

C.

D.

E.

F.

G.

H.

### 4 Qu'est-ce qu'ils portent aujourd'hui?

*Choisissez un ado. Dites ce qu'il ou elle porte aujourd'hui. Votre partenaire va identifier la personne basée sur votre description.*

1.1

### 5 Questions personnelles

2.1

*Répondez aux questions.*

> J'aime acheter les chapeaux!

1. Est-ce que tu aimes faire du shopping?
2. Préfères-tu faire du shopping au centre commercial, au magasin, ou à une boutique?
3. Quels vêtements est-ce que tu cherches d'habitude au magasin?
4. Aimes-tu porter des chapeaux? Des chaussures? Des maillots de bain?
5. As-tu un manteau et des bottes pour le mois de janvier?
6. As-tu besoin d'un nouveau pull? D'un nouveau jean?
7. Qu'est-ce que tes amis et toi, vous portez quand vous allez à l'école?
8. Qu'est-ce que tes amis et toi, vous portez quand vous allez au restaurant avec vos parents?
9. Qu'est-ce que tu apportes quand tu voyages?

Leçon A | deux cent soixante-dix-neuf **2 7 9**

## Answers

**3** Script can be found in the front pages of the Annotated Teacher's Edition.

1. E
2. A
3. G
4. F
5. H
6. C
7. D
8. B

**4**

1. Elle porte une jupe grise, un pull rose, des bottes noires, et une écharpe grise.
2. Il porte une chemise violette, un pantalon noir, des baskets rouges, une casquette rouge, et une veste jaune.
3. Elle porte une robe orange, des chaussures marron, un manteau vert, et un chapeau vert.

**5** *Answers will vary.*

### Expansion

Find a simple children's coloring book with line drawings of people wearing different outfits. Photocopy the pages and pass out a different page to each student. Tell students to color every clothing item with a different color. Students may then write out descriptions of what each model is wearing, including color. Ask each student to choose one outfit to describe orally to the class.

### Game

**C'est quelle couleur?**
Distribute small flags if available, or pictures of flags, and have students ask each other what the color of the flag is. Example:
A: **Quelle est la couleur du drapeau de la France?** B: **bleu, blanc, rouge**

### Differentiated Learning
#### Accelerate
Assign students to find two photos (magazine, online source) of people and write a detailed description of the clothing they are wearing, including colors, and other adjectives students know. Have them use **foncé** (dark) and **clair** (light) in their descriptions. In class the next day, have small accelerated groups shuffle all the photos, and then match each one to the description as students read them aloud.

### Special Needs Students
#### Linguistically Challenged
In **Activité 5**, you may want to provide the beginning of each answer for students. For example, write on the board:, #7. **Mes amis et moi, nous portons....**

**Answers** _____

**Extension**

*Answers will vary.*

## Reference Desk

1. Ask students if they have heard of fashion designer Jean-Paul Gaultier (b. 1952 –). Gaultier never formally studied design, but he started sending his sketches to high-fashion designers from a very early age. Hired as an assistant by Pierre Cardin at the age of 18, Gaultier developed his irreverent style and skill to become the highly successful **enfant terrible** of the fashion world. He is popular with musicians and film directors who often commission his designs.
2. The color **framboise** is a light reddish pink color, whereas **mauve** is darker and closer to purple.
3. **S'affoler**, mentioned in the **Extension** dialogue, is a slang term that means "to go crazy." Find and show pictures of different outfits and ask students which ones "make them go crazy." Ask what other topics students go crazy for, such as a type of music, a specific film, school subject, or a sports activity.

## Communication

### Presentational

Have students make a presentation in which they describe what clothes they own, which items are their favorites, and which ones they don't like. Which clothes are they most likely to wear or not wear, and where?

---

# Rencontres culturelles

## Camille cherche un ensemble.    1.2

Yasmine et Camille font du shopping dans une boutique.

Yasmine: Mais, qu'est-ce que tu cherches?
Camille: Je cherche une jupe et un pull pour la teuf vendredi soir.
Vendeuse: Je peux vous aider?
Yasmine: Ma copine cherche une jupe et un pull, taille *small*.
Vendeuse: De quelles couleurs?
Camille: Je veux une jupe noire et un pull rose.
Vendeuse: Alors, c'est là-bas. Allez voir.
Camille: Je veux essayer cette jupe et ce pull.
Yasmine: Vas-y!

*(Camille sort de la cabine d'essayage.)*

Camille: Tu trouves que cet ensemble me va bien?
Yasmine: Tu es très chic, comme un mannequin de Gaultier!
Camille: Donc, j'achète. Ensuite, le marché aux puces pour trouver un foulard bon marché.
Yasmine: Autrement, tu peux trouver un foulard en ligne.

**6** **Camille cherche un ensemble.**   **2.1, 2.2**

*Complétez chaque phrase.*

1. Yasmine et Camille sont dans....
2. Camille cherche un ensemble pour....
3. ... aide Camille.
4. Camille désire essayer....
5. Yasmine compare Camille à....
6. Comme accessoire, Camille désire trouver....

**Extension** **Lucas est chic?**   1.2

Lucas fait du shopping dans une boutique avec son copain Théo.

Lucas: Pardon, Monsieur, je cherche un pantalon en coton.
Vendeur: Tu aimes ce jean framboise?
Lucas: Oui, ce jean framboise et ce polo mauve....
Théo: Comme ça, les filles, elles vont s'affoler....
Lucas: Tu penses, vraiment?

**Extension** How would you describe Lucas' style?

---

**Essential Instruction**

1. Show the filmed dialogue. Ask students to discuss what they understood, then to read the dialogue aloud with a partner. Assign **Activité 6** in pairs. Have groups role-play the dialogue for their classmates.

2. Revisit the **Question centrale** before you have students read the topics in **Points de départ**. You may wish to assign research of the topics in **Points de départ** using the search words. Ask students to share with the class two or three specific facts they found. Ask students about their experiences with online shopping and if they have been to a flea market.

# Points de départ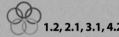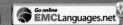

## e-commerce: acheter en ligne  1.2, 2.1, 3.1, 4.2

Cinquante-huit pourcent des personnes qui utilisent l'Internet en France font du shopping en ligne. Ils achètent des produits de tourisme (56%); des billets* de concerts, de théâtre, etc.; des CD, des DVD, et des livres (45%); des vêtements (48%); et des produits techniques (type téléviseur, 50%). Il y a aussi des personnes qui achètent des choses à manger au supermarché en ligne. Le e-commerce représente 30.000.000.000 d'euros par an* en France.

🔍 **Search words: la redoute, 3 suisses, tati**

――――――
**billet** *ticket*; **par an** *yearly*

**Question centrale**

**How is shopping different in other countries?**

**COMPARAISONS** 2.1, 5.1

What percentage of your clothing do you and your friends buy online? What else do you buy online?

## Les marchés aux puces* 1.2, 2.1, 4.2

Un marché aux puces est un marché en plein air* où on vend des articles d'occasion* et des antiquités. Il y a environ 10.000 marchés aux puces en France, mais le plus important est le marché de Saint-Ouen, à côté de Paris. C'est le plus grand marché d'antiquités au monde avec 2.000 stands dispersés dans un ensemble de 17 marchés différents. "Aller aux puces" est une promenade* que des millions de Parisiens et de touristes aiment faire chaque année.

Le marché aux Puces de Saint-Ouen est ouvert du lundi au samedi, de 9h00 à 18h00.

🔍 **Search words: paris puces, marché aux puces de saint-ouen**

――――――
**plein air** *open-air*; **d'occasion** *used*; **promenade** *outing*; **marchésaux puces** *Flea Markets*

---

**Answers** _____

**Question Centrale**
*Answers will vary.*

**Comparaisons**
*Answers will vary.*

### Reference Desk

1. **Un créateur de mode** is French for fashion designer.
2. Ask students to scan **Points de départ** for English cognates (**supermarchés, antiquités, stands, dispersés, tailleurs,** etc.). For words they don't recognize (**environ, monde,** etc.), make connections with English when possible.

### Culture

**Products: Activity**
**3 Suisses** has a great web site that students might enjoy navigating. Consider creating an online shopping activity based on the site.

### Critical Thinking

**Analysis**
Ask students to research why people use the word **puces** to talk about these age-old markets. Discuss the idea of buying used objects vs. new products, negotiating prices, sanitation, social mores, recycling, etc. Point out another meaning of **puce** that has arisen with new technologies. (Electronic chip embedded in debit and phone cards.)

### Expansion

Encourage students to create a "French quarter" stand with a banner **Marché aux puces** at a school, team, or community fundraising event.

---

**Differentiated Learning**
**Accelerate**
After students watch the **Rencontres culturelles,** have them write three yes/no questions and three information questions using **est-ce que** and then ask each other about the dialogue in groups. Expand this exercise by asking them to rewrite their questions using inversion and then exchange papers to check each other's accuracy.

**Special Needs Students**
**AD(H)D**
To help these students focus on the **Rencontres culturelles** reading, provide a completion activity to guide students to specific information you want them to find. For example, for **Les marchés aux puces,** write: "At a flea market in France, they sell...;" "There are... flea markets in France;" etc.

**Gabrielle Bonheur "Coco" Chanel** (1883 – 1971): innovative French fashion designer whose contemporary designs and menswear-inspired fashions earned her a place on *Time* magazine's list of 100 most influential people of the 20th century.

**Christian Dior** (1905 – 1957): famous French fashion designer who founded one of the world's top fashion houses.

**Jeanne-Marie Lanvin** (1867 – 1946): French fashion designer of the 1920s and '30s whose trademarks were skillful embroideries and beaded decorations.

**Pierre Cardin** (b.1922 –): Known for his avant-garde style and his Space Age designs, Cardin favors geometric shapes and motifs, often ignoring the female form.

**Yves Saint Laurent** (1936 – 2008): Grew up in Algeria, then a French colony. He left for Paris at the age of 17 and was hired as Christian Dior's assistant. YSL introduced the tuxedo suit for women and was the first designer to use ethnic models in his runway shows and reference other non-European cultures in his work.

**Cristóbal Balenciaga** (1895 – 1972): Spanish Basque designer whom Dior referred to as "the master of us all." The French multinational company PPR now owns the house of Balenciaga.

**Jean-Paul Gaultier:** see notes on p. 280.

**Christian Marie Marc Lacroix** (b. 1951 –): studied Art History and aspired to become a museum curator. He launched his own **haute couture** house after working at Hermès.

---

## La haute couture*  1.2, 2.1, 3.1, 4.2

Chanel, Dior, Givenchy, Lanvin, Cardin, Saint-Laurent, Balenciaga, Jean-Paul Gaultier, et Christian Lacroix sont les grands noms de la haute couture française. Ils présentent leurs collections de vêtements (été et hiver) deux fois* par an. Chaque robe, tailleur (*suit*), ou ensemble est unique et peut coûter 100.000 euros. Les stars du show business servent souvent d'inspiration pour les collections de certains couturiers*: Madonna et Jean-Paul Gaultier; Catherine Deneuve et Saint-Laurent; Vanessa Paradis, Nicole Kidman, et Audrey Tautou pour Chanel.

 **Search words: chanel paris, jean paul gaultier**

_____
**haute couture** *high fashion;* **fois** *times;* **couturiers** *designers*

Le mannequin porte un manteau rose et bleu Chanel.

---

 **Produits**

C'est Coco Chanel qui a créé (*created*) "**la petite robe noire**" dans les années 20. Beaucoup de femmes considèrent cette robe courte et simple un vêtement essentiel. On la porte le soir pour sortir et son dessin classique assure qu'elle va être toujours à la mode (*in fashion*).  **1.2, 4.2**

---

 **La Francophonie** 1.2, 4.2

### ✳ En Afrique: Les vêtements

En Afrique de l'Ouest, les vêtements sont souvent en **pagne**, un tissu* très coloré. Les femmes portent des tailleurs, de grandes robes, et des foulards de tête* en **pagne**. Les hommes portent des **boubous** (une sorte de robe pour homme) et des chemises en **pagne**. Pour les jours de fête, on porte des vêtements en **bazin**, un tissu en coton coloré qui a un aspect de papier glacé*.

_____
**tissu** *fabric;* **foulards de tête** *headscarves;* **glacé** *glazed*

Beaucoup de femmes africaines portent des foulards de tête.

---

## 7 Questions culturelles   2.1, 2.2

*Répondez aux questions.*

1. Au sujet du e-commerce, à quoi correspondent ces chiffres?
   - 56%
   - 45%
   - 48%
2. Qu'est-ce qu'on achète au marché aux puces?
3. Comment s'appelle le plus grand marché aux puces en France?
4. Quels sont les noms de trois grands couturiers en France?
5. Quels couturiers sont associés avec ces stars?
   - Audrey Tautou et Nicole Kidman
   - Madonna
   - Catherine Deneuve
6. Quels sont les vêtements traditionnels pour les femmes et les hommes africains?

La petite fille sénégalaise porte une robe en pagne.

### Perspectives

Some French people say they can pick out Americans traveling in France even before they speak. What styles and clothing do you think they consider as "American"?

## Du côté des médias

## 8 Shopping en ligne  1.3, 2.1, 2.2, 3.2

*Regardez cette page de catalogue. Ensuite, répondez aux questions ou complétez le projet.*

1. Ces vêtements sont pour les filles de quel âge?
2. Pour compléter ces ensembles, vous choisissez quelles catégories (à gauche)?
3. Comparez les prix (*prices*) des trois produits avec les prix d'un catalogue américain.
4. Faites votre propre (*own*) page de catalogue Internet. Sélectionnez des images de vêtements, décrivez-les (*describe them*) en français, et dites combien chaque article coûte.

Leçon A | deux cent quatre-vingt-trois **283**

**Answers**

**7**

1. 56% des personnes qui utilisent l'Internet achètent des produits de tourisme.
   45% des personnes qui utilisent l'Internet achètent des CD, des DVD, et des livres.
   48% des personnes qui utilisent l'Internet achètent des vêtements.
2. On achète des articles d'occasion et des antiquités.
3. Le plus grand marché aux puces en France s'appelle le marché de Saint-Ouen.
4. Chanel, Dior, Givenchy, Lanvin, Cardin, Saint-Laurent, Balenciaga, Jean-Paul Gaultier, et Christian Lacroix
5. Nicole Kidman et Audrey Tautou sont associées à Chanel.
   Madonna est associée à Jean-Paul Gaultier
   Catherine Deneuve est associée à Saint Laurent
6. Les vêtements en Afrique de l'Ouest sont souvent en pagne, un tissu très coloré. Les femmes portent des tailleurs, de grandes robes, et des foulards de tête en pagne. Les hommes portent des boubous et des chemises en pagne.

**Perspectives**
*Answers will vary.*

**8**

1. de 8 à 18 ans.
2. Blouse, tunique; Pull, gilet, sweat; Jean; Pantalon, pantalon court; Bermuda, short; Robe, jupe; Manteau, blouson, parka; Maillot de bain; Sport; Pyjama, robe de chambre; Sous-vêtements; Chaussettes, collants; Chaussures; Accessoires
3. *Answers will vary.*
4. *Answers will vary.*

**Culture**

**Products: Activity**
Put students in groups and see which groups can recognize the most logos and products that correspond to famous **couturiers**. You could use French designers mentioned in **Points de départ**, designers from other francophone countries, or designers from the United States, Canada, or Japan who also participate in Paris fashion week.

**Answers**

**9**

1. Amidou et sa sœur préfèrent le steak-frites, mais ils achètent le croque-monsieur.
2. Ma tante préfère la glace à la vanille, mais elle achète une orange.
3. Noémie et moi, nous préférons la limonade, mais nous achetons de l'eau minérale.
4. Rahina et toi, vous préférez la glace au chocolat, mais vous achetez le sandwich au fromage
5. Moi, je préfère..., mais j'achète...

## TPR

Project sentences that contain a different form of the verbs listed in the practice above, but without any accents on the final **e** of the verb stem. Cover all the sentences so that you can reveal them one at a time. As you uncover each sentence, point to the **e** in the verb's stem. If there should be an accent on that **e**, students raise their hands slanting them in the direction the accent should go. If no accent is needed, students do not raise their hands.

## Communication

**Interpretive: Cooperative Groups**

To practice writing the silent 3rd person plural ending of the verb **acheter**, have students complete **dictée** sentences that start with **Les Français achètent...., Les Américains achètent....**, etc. Practice similar cognate verbs involving the spelling change with the **accent grave**, such as: **répéter, considérer, suggérer**, etc.

# Structure de la langue

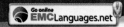

## Present Tense of the Verb *acheter*

The endings of the verb **acheter** (*to buy*) are regular, but there is an **accent grave** over the final **e** (**è**) in the stem of the **je, tu, il/elle/on**, and **ils/elles** forms like in the verb **préférer**.

|  | acheter |  |  |
|---|---|---|---|
| j' | **achète** | nous | **achetons** |
| tu | **achètes** | vous | **achetez** |
| il/elle/on | **achète** | ils/elles | **achètent** |

**1.2**

*Mme Diouf achète une robe pour sa fille ou pour elle-même? Les deux achètent des vêtements?*

### Pronunciation Tip

The shaded section shows you which forms have a spelling change in the verb stem. All these forms are pronounced the same way.

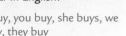

## COMPARAISONS

Is the verb *to buy* regular or irregular in English?

I buy, you buy, she buys, we buy, they buy

**4.1**

Tu **achètes** le maillot de bain orange? — *Are you buying the orange bathing suit?*

Je n'**achète** pas ça! — *I'm not buying that!*

### 9  À Flunch

 **2.1, 2.2**

*Dites ce qu'on préfère et ce qu'on achète à la cafétéria Flunch.*

**MODÈLE**  **Sabrina préfère la glace au chocolat, mais elle achète la salade.**

Sabrina

1. Amidou et sa sœur        2. ma tante

3. Noémie et moi, nous    4. Rahina et toi, vous    5. moi, je

**COMPARAISONS:** In English the verb "to buy" is regular.

**Essential Instruction**

1. Review the conjugation of the verb **préférer**, then present **acheter**, which follows the same pattern. As the class conjugates the verb, ask students to raise their hands (making the **accent grave**) every time it appears in the verb form.
2. Divide the class into two groups and do **Activité 9** chorally, with half the class saying the first part of the answer using **préférer** and the other half completing the second part of the sentence with **acheter.** Then have them switch roles.
3. Assign **Activité 10** as pair work. Ask them to think of three additional situations and say what clothing they would buy for those.
4. For the verb **vouloir**, point out that few verbs in French share the conjugation singular forms ending in -**x**/-**x**/-**t**. Contrast these endings with those of the -**er** verbs, **e, es, e**.
5. Review the **Comparaisons** question and confirm that students understand the different verb tenses.

# Communiquez!

**10  Qu'est-ce que tu achètes?**

> Qu'est-ce que tu achètes pour la teuf?

> J'achète un pantalon et des tennis.

**Interpersonal Communication**

*À tour de rôle, discutez avec un partenaire de ce que vous achetez pour chaque (each) situation.*

**MODÈLE**  A: **Qu'est-ce que tu achètes pour la rentrée?**
B: **J'achète un jean, des tee-shirts, et des pulls.**

1. la rentrée
2. la teuf d'un(e) ami(e)
3. un voyage en décembre
4. un voyage en juillet
5. pour jouer au foot
6. pour faire du footing

1.1

## Present Tense of the Irregular Verb *vouloir*

1.2

The verb **vouloir** (*to want*) is irregular.

| vouloir | | | |
|---|---|---|---|
| je | **veux** | nous | **voulons** |
| tu | **veux** | vous | **voulez** |
| il/elle/on | **veut** | ils/elles | **veulent** |

### Pronunciation Tip

The singular forms of **vouloir (veux, veux, veut)** are all pronounced the same way.

### Usage Tip

The verb **vouloir** can be followed by a verb or a noun.

Quand **voulez**-vous faire du shopping?  *When do you want to go shopping?*
Je **veux** un nouveau pantalon maintenant!  *I want a new pair of pants now!*

**COMPARAISONS**

4.1

You already know one form of the verb vouloir that you use when you ask for something politely: Je voudrais essayer le pantalon gris. What would the English equivalent of this sentence be? In both French and English, the conjugated verb is in what tense?

COMPARAISONS: **Je voudrais** and "I would like," both translations, are in the conditional tense. In this instance, the conditional is used to make a polite request.

Leçon A | deux cent quatre-vingt-cinq  **285**

**11** Je veux; on veut; Lucas veut; nous voulons; Lucas et Juliette veulent; vous voulez

**12** Script can be found in the front pages of the Annotated Teacher's Edition.

1. D
2. B
3. C
4. A & B
5. D

**13** *Answers will vary.*

1. A: Quand tu as faim, qu'est-ce que tu veux manger d'habitude?
2. A: Quand tu vas à une teuf, qu'est-ce que tu veux porter d'habitude?
3. A: Quand c'est l'anniversaire de ton ami(e), qu'est-ce que tu veux offrir d'habitude?
4. A: Quand tu vas au centre commercial, qu'est-ce que tu veux acheter d'habitude?
5. A: Quand tu vas au cinéma, qu'est-ce que tu veux voir d'habitude?
6. A: Quand tu as soif, qu'est-ce que tu veux prendre d'habitude?

## Communication

**Interpretive**

Find online and copy the words to the popular song *Je veux* by French artist Zaz (Isabelle Geoffroy, b. 1980 –) who is known for her mix of jazz, pop, and acoustic music. Ask students to identify cognates. Explain the theme of wanting love, joy, and happiness over riches, then play the original video of Zaz singing her hit several times. Ask students to sing the refrain, which offers practice of **je veux**.

## Expansion

1. Have students find and display images of people going to different events and venues. Ask students to describe several scenes using **vouloir**, **prendre**, and **préférer**.
2. To vary this activity, use francophone destinations and have students describe what they would wear on a trip there.

---

**11** On veut faire du shopping.  2.1

*Alexis, son frère, et sa sœur veulent faire du shopping au marché aux puces. Complétez la note d'Alexis à ses parents avec la forme appropriée du verbe **vouloir**.*

*Salut! Je ▨ aller au marché aux puces avec Lucas et Juliette ce weekend. On ▨ chercher des soldes. Lucas ▨ 10 euros pour une chemise. Juliette et moi, nous ▨ 10 euros pour des livres. Lucas et Juliette ▨ 5 euros pour des tee-shirts. Est-ce que vous ▨ aider vos enfants?*

*Bisous,*
*Alexis*

**12** Faisons du shopping!  2.1, 2.2

*Choisissez le rayon (department) du magasin où M. et Mme Chambon et leurs enfants, Gabrielle (5 ans) et Julien (10 ans), trouvent les vêtements.*

A. rayon (*department*) garçons
B. rayon filles
C. rayon hommes
D. rayon femmes

M. et Mme Chambon trouvent une robe pour leur fille au rayon filles.

### Communiquez!

**13** Qu'est-ce que tu veux d'habitude (*usually*)? 1.1

**Interpersonal Communication**

*Interviewez votre partenaire pour trouver ce qu'il ou elle veut dans les situations suivantes.*

| MODÈLE | tu as soif/prendre |
|---|---|

A: **Quand tu as soif, qu'est-ce que tu veux prendre d'habitude?**
B: **Je veux prendre une eau minérale. Et toi, qu'est-ce que tu veux prendre d'habitude?**
A: **Je veux prendre un jus d'orange.**

1. tu as faim/manger
2. tu vas à une teuf/porter
3. c'est l'anniversaire de ton ami(e)/offrir
4. tu vas au centre commercial/acheter
5. tu vas au cinéma/voir
6. tu as soif/prendre

Je veux porter une chemise et une jupe. Et toi?

Quand tu vas à une teuf, qu'est-ce que tu veux porter d'habitude?

---

**Essential Instruction**

1. Model the pronunciation of the note in **Activité 11**, then have students read it aloud with a partner.
2. After listening to **Activité 12**, ask students in which department (**rayon**), they usually find certain clothing items.
3. Review the instructions in **Activité 13**, and then ask volunteer pairs to present the mini-dialogues.
4. Draw a chart on the board that you complete with the demonstrative adjectives as you present them in context. Using the demonstrative adjectives, pictures of clothing, and colors, ask students to choose between singular and plural and masculine and feminine items, for example, **Tu veux ce pantalon bleu ou cette chemise blanche?**
5. Have students write one demonstrative adjective on each side of two index cards that you provide. Provide verbal cues using vocabulary that students know, such as, **la (une) casquette.** Students must hold up the correct demonstrative adjective, and say, **Cette casquette.**
6. Ask students to present and display their **album de photos** from **Activité 14**.

# Demonstrative Adjectives  1.2

Demonstrative adjectives are used to point out specific people or things. The demonstrative adjectives in French are **ce**, **cet**, and **cette**, which mean "this" or "that," and **ces**, which means "these" or "those." These adjectives agree with the nouns that follow them.

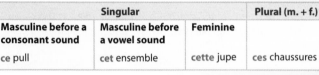

> Tu veux cette glace, ce yaourt, ou ces bonbons comme dessert?

|  | Singular |  | Plural (m. + f.) |
|---|---|---|---|
| **Masculine before a consonant sound** | **Masculine before a vowel sound** | **Feminine** | |
| ce pull | cet ensemble | cette jupe | ces chaussures |

## 14 Mon album de photos  1.3

*Faites un album de photos. Écrivez une légende* (caption) *pour chaque photo de votre famille réelle ou imaginaire.*

**MODÈLE** Cet homme est mon oncle, Bill.

# Communiquez!

## 15 C'est combien?    1.1

**Interpersonal Communication**

*Avec un partenaire, jouez les rôles d'un(e) client(e) et un vendeur ou vendeuse dans une boutique.*

**MODÈLE**
A: C'est combien, cette robe jaune?
B: Cette robe jaune coûte 80 euros.

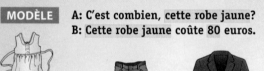

80 €

1. 37 €     2. 120 €     3. 38 €     4. 69 €

5. 72 €     6. 25 €     7. 97 €     8. 77 €     9. 152 €

**RESOURCES**

 **Workbook 13–15**

Answers _____

**14** *Photo albums will vary.*

**15**

1. A: C'est combien, ce pantalon bleu?
   B: Ce pantalon bleu coûte 37 euros.
2. A: C'est combien, cette veste marron?
   B: Cette veste marron coûte 120 euros.
3. A: C'est combien, ce chapeau bleu?
   B: Ce chapeau bleu coûte 38 euros.
4. A: C'est combien, cette jupe rose?
   B: Cette jupe rose coûte 69 euros.
5. A: C'est combien, cette chemise verte?
   B: Cette chemise verte coûte 72 euros.
6. A: C'est combien, cette écharpe orange et jaune?
   B: Cette écharpe rouge coûte 25 euros.
7. A: C'est combien, ces bottes noires?
   B: Ces bottes noires coûtent 97 euros.
8. A: C'est combien, cet ensemble?
   B: Cet ensemble coûte 77 euros.
9. A: C'est combien, ces tennis blanches?
   B: Ces tennis blancs coûtent 152 euros.

## Game

**Je veux....**
Create four large demonstrative adjective cards and project or display them. Have students form two teams. As you call out a vocabulary word from this lesson or previous units, a designated student from each team runs to the board and taps or grabs the correct card. In order to earn the point, however, the teammate next in line must quickly complete the sentence, **Je veux...**, adding the demonstrative article and the noun.

**Differentiated Learning**
**Expand**
For **Activité 14**, give the students the option to include family photos or to profile an imaginary family by using magazine or online photos. Have students include six people and pets, such as, **chat/chatte**, **chien/chienne**, and **oiseau**.

**Decelerate**
Find and project a photo of a family. Write sentences about the different members in which the demonstrative adjective is missing. Have students read the sentences aloud, inserting the missing adjective.

**Multiple Intelligences**
**Verbal-Linguistic/Interpersonal**
Have students write out the questions for **Activité 13**. Then have them circulate and interview at least six people in the class and respond to each other's questions. Finally, have students share what they learned about their classmates.

## Communiquez!

**16**    **Comment est-ce que tu trouves...?**      1.1

### Interpersonal Communication

*Trouvez huit photos d'athlètes, chanteurs, metteurs-en-scène, et acteurs. À tour de rôle, demandez à votre partenaire son opinion de ces personnes célèbres. Utilisez une profession de la liste dans chacune (each) de vos réponses.*

| |
|---|
| un chanteur    une chanteuse    un acteur    une actrice |
| un metteur en scène    un(e) athlète |

**MODÈLE**    Shaun White
A: **Comment est-ce que tu trouves Shaun White?**
B: **J'aime bien cet athlète. Il est énergique.**
    ou
    **Je n'aime pas cet athlète. Il est égoïste.**

Comment est-ce que tu trouves Audrey Tautou?

J'aime un peu cette actrice. Elle est sympa.

# À vous la parole

## Communiquez!

### 17 Le prêt-à-porter

**1.1, 2.2**

**Interpersonal Communication**

With a partner, role-play a scene between a salesperson and customer shopping in **un grand magasin,** or department store. In the conversation, the salesperson finds out what the customer is looking for, what color he or she would like, and the customer's size. The salesperson then finds the item and they discuss its price.

## Communiquez!

### 18 Un défilé de mode

**1.2, 1.3, 4.1**

**Interpretive/Presentational Communication**

Follow the steps below to create a plan for a fashion show for your classmates.

- Visit the online catalogues of French stores **La Redoute** or **3Suisses** or **Tati**.
- Select six to eight outfits for different occasions.
- Print photos or create drawings for your selections.
- Prepare a detailed description of each outfit. Present your outfits to a group of classmates.

 **Search words:  la redoute, 3suisses, tati**

---

**Answers**

**17** *Answers will vary.*

**18** *Presentations will vary.*

## Reference Desk

The first department store, **Le Bon Marché**, opened in Paris in 1852. Created by Aristide Boucicaut, the new type of store presented a revolutionary new way to shop, which allowed customers to browse the merchandise and get reimbursed if not satisfied. **Le Printemps** opened 13 years later. **La Samaritaine**, on the right bank of the Seine near the **Pont Neuf**, opened in 1869 and closed in 2005 due to financial difficulties. There are plans to convert the 19th century building, with its beautiful view of Paris, into a luxury **hôtel**, apartments, and shops.

### Blended Instruction

Consider using blended instruction, a combination of in-class learning and computer-mediated instruction or learning opportunities. Ask students to complete activities on the computer or using their cell phone, smartphone, or other emerging electronic technology. This will allow students to hone their tech skills and become more independent learners. Schedule routine Internet and e-book learning in class and in the lab.

---

## Differentiated Learning

### Accelerate
Encourage students to write several additional lines when creating the scene for **Activité 17**.

### Expansion
For **Activité 18**, students could bring in an image, draw a picture, or create a very short slideshow presentation to show in class.

### Decelerate
To help students who may have difficulty forming the corresponding question in French from the cue, "what the customer is looking for," provide them with the first few words of each question.

## Learning Styles

### Kinesthetic Learners
For **Activité 18**, offer the option of organizing the presentation as a fashion show. Tell students to provide commentary in French. Other students may prefer to draw the items or create paper clothing and model the fashions.

### Reference Desk

1. Have students practice other words that end in **-eau**, such as **château**, **gâteau**, **bateau**, **cadeau**. Note that the sound **/o/** as in **beau** is also written as **au**, as in **haut(e)**, **chaud**, and **o** as in **dos** and **rose**.

2. Have students practice other words with French nasal vowel **/õ/** such as: **mon**, **ton**, **son**, **sont**, **font**, **blond**, and 1st person plural verb endings **-ons**. Note that the spelling can be **-om**, as in **nom**, **comprendre**.

### Game

**Les comptines**
To further contrast the vowel sounds **/o/** and **/õ/**, have students repeat the following nursery rhymes (**comptines**) that French children learn for this purpose.

**Le mot**
*Tourne, tourne autour du pot*
*Quelqu'un se cache dans ton dos*
*Il te dépose un anneau*
*A toi de trouver un mot*
*En "o"*
*Robot*
*Pot*
*Piano*
*Vélo ...*

**Menu du jour**
*Du poisson?*
*Non.*
*Du jambon?*
*Non.*
*Des champignons?*
*Non.*
*Du melon?*
*Non.*
*Alors quoi donc?*
*Des cornichons.*
*Ah bon!*

# Prononciation  1.2

## No Liaison

- As a general rule, words in a sentence are connected. However, liaison does not occur between the **tu** form of **aller** and a verb beginning with a vowel. For example, there is no liaison in **Tu vas° aller° au cinéma?**

 **A** **Les endroits**

*Listen to the question, then replace the location.*

> **MODÈLE**
> You see: **à la salle d'informatique**
> You say: **Tu vas° à la salle d'informatique?**

1. au stade
2. au labo
3. à la piscine
4. à la médiathèque

- Liaison does not occur before or after the word **et**.

 **B** **Au café**

*Repeat the statement, replacing the food items and/or drinks.*

S'il vous plaît, **un thé° et° un coca!**
1. un café° et° un coca!
2. un croissant° et° une limonade!
3. un chocolat° et° un café!

## Pronunciation of /o/ and /õ/

- The vowel /o/ in **beau** is different from the nasal vowel /õ/ in **bon**.

 **C** **Les sons /o/ et /õ/**

*Repeat the sentences, paying careful attention to the sounds /o/ and /õ/.*

1. C'est un beau blouson. C'est un beau pantalon.
2. C'est un bon gâteau. C'est un bon cadeau.

 **D** **Eh bien, dis donc...!**

*Pronounced /ebjēdidō/, **Eh bien, dis donc** expresses surprise. Repeat each of these sentences to practice the sound /õ/.*

Eh bien, dis donc, ce jambon est... spécial!
Eh bien, dis donc, ce melon est... génial!
Eh bien, dis donc, ce saucisson est... original!

**E** **Choisissez le son correct.**

*Write **V** if you hear the vowel /o/ or **N** if you hear the nasal vowel /õ/.*

**Essential Instruction**

1. Contrast the **liaison** in **les hôtels** to **les hamburgers** in which there is no **liaison**. Play the first part of the audio **Prononciation**.

2. Have students practice the nasal /õ/ by plugging their nose to feel the slight vibration when they make the sound correctly; contrast this to /o/.

3. Present the **Vocabulaire actif** and explain that shopping in different specialty stores is still common practice in Europe and other francophone countries. Add that some products are sold differently, such as milk in cartons that doesn't need refrigeration until opened, blocks of butter sold by weight, and "young" or "ripe" cheese. Clarify the difference between **une boulangerie** and **une pâtisserie** and **une boucherie** and **une charcuterie**.

# Vocabulaire actif

1.2

## On fait les courses.

la boulangerie

la baguette

le croissant · le pain

la crémerie

le lait

le beurre · les œufs (m.)

le fromage

le yaourt · le camembert

la pâtisserie

la tarte aux pommes · le gâteau

la boucherie

le porc · le bœuf · le poulet

Leçon B | deux cent quatre-vingt-onze 291

## RESOURCES

 e-visual 21

 Workbook 16–17

 Flash Cards

 Listening Activities

## Reference Desk

1. **Une boucherie** is a butcher shop that sells all meats, but few or no pork products, whereas a **charcuterie** specializes in pork products. Unless they have dietary or religious reasons, most French eat pork products quite frequently. The French equivalent of the classic American sandwich might be considered **un sandwich au jambon-beurre**.
2. While a **pâtisserie** may have baguettes, croissants, and other items found in a **boulangerie**, it mainly offers pastries.
3. Teach students the expression **l'épicerie du coin** (literally, the corner store). Ask them if there is such a store in their neighborhood.

## TPR

To identify if foods or stores are masculine or feminine, say the vocabulary item and have students raise their left hand if they hear a masculine noun and their right hand if they hear a feminine noun.

## Culture

**Products: Activity**
Have students draw shops on large sheets of white paper. Tape the "shops" on the wall to form **une rue commerçante**.

## Differentiated Learning

**Expand**
Reinforce the vocabulary by asking students their preferences, **Tu aimes/préfères le bœuf, le porc?**, etc.

## Multiple Intelligences

**Bodily-Kinesthetic/Naturalistic**
If possible, organize a cheese tasting day. Have volunteers bring in different French cheeses (**Camembert**, **Gruyère**, **Boursin**, **La vache qui rit**, **Brie**, etc.). Have students taste one cheese at a time and record their reactions according to a list of adjectives you provide (**délicieux**, **crémeux**, etc.).

The same **Activité** can be done with mineral waters and even salt (**le sel industriel**, **sel de mer**, **fleur de sel**).

## Special Needs Students

**Auditory Impairment**
Encourage students to repeat the **Activités de prononciation** outside of class where they can individually control the volume, pause the recording, repeat each answer as needed, and listen to their responses. Consider having students turn in a recording of their work.

l' épicerie (f.)

la charcuterie

la mayonnaise    la moutarde

le jambon    le pâté    le saucisson

le ketchup    la confiture    la soupe

## Quelle quantité de mayonnaise a-t-on? 🎧

M. Durand a trop de mayonnaise.

Mme Durand a assez de mayonnaise.

Marie-Alix a beaucoup de mayonnaise.

Guillaume a un peu de mayonnaise.

**Essential Instruction**

1. Using adverbs of quantity, ask students how much they have of certain items. For example, ask if they have **trop de** or **un peu de devoirs**.

2. Ask students to identify cognates and other French vocabulary used in English (**croissant**, **baguette**) in the **Vocabulaire actif**. Use various types of food packaging as you present the **Liste d'achats** vocabulary. Contrast **pâtes** and **pâté**. Note that a vowel with an accent circumflex indicates an older spelling that included an "s," as in **pastes** (pasta). Knowing this can help to decode meaning.

3. Listen to and practice **Pour la conversation**. Explain the sequencing value of adverbs: **d'abord**, **ensuite**, and **enfin**.

Mme Roussin fait les courses au supermarché.

**Liste d'achats**
6 tranches (f.) de jambon
un kilo de beurre
un paquet de café
un pot de moutarde
un paquet de pâtes
un morceau de fromage
un litre de lait
une bouteille d'eau minérale
une boîte de soupe

**RESOURCES**

 **Workbook 18–20**

**Reference Desk**

Note that expressions of quantity, such as slices of…, a packet of…, a piece of…, a bottle of…, a kilo of…, etc. all have the same structure with the word **de** or **d'**, and not **de la**, **du** or **des**. Reinforce **beaucoup de** as a model to help students follow the pattern. (See p. 304.)

## Pour la conversation

How do I sequence my activities?

> Je vais **d'abord** à la crémerie acheter du beurre et du fromage.
> *First I'll go to the dairy store to buy some butter and cheese.*

> **Ensuite**, je vais à la charcuterie.
> *Then I'll go to the delicatessen.*

> **Enfin**, je vais à l'épicerie.
> *Finally, I'll go to the grocery store.*

### Et si je voulais dire…?

| | |
|---|---|
| **une barre céréalière** | *nutrition bar* |
| **des biscuits (m.)** | *cookies* |
| **une brioche** | *sweet bread* |
| **la boucherie chevaline** | *horse meat shop* |
| **des chips (m.)** | *potato chips* |
| **un flan** | *custard pie* |
| **une livre de** | *a pound of* |
| **un pain au chocolat** | *chocolate croissant* |
| **le poisson** | *fish* |
| **la poissonerie** | *fish shop* |

**Differentiated Learning**
**Expand**
Prepare students for learning the metric system later in this unit by asking if anyone knows how many pounds are in **un kilo** (a kilogram). Answer: 2.2 pounds = 1 kilo.

**Accelerate**
Review **Et si je voulais dire…?** Students may be surprised about the existence of **la boucherie chevaline**. Ask them to research the benefits of eating horsemeat, find photos of this type of store, and share their findings and reactions.

**Multiple Intelligences**
**Intrapersonal/Logical-Mathematical**
To practice the sequencing words presented in **Pour la conversation**, have pairs use them to plan a shopping excursion, naming where they would go first, next, and last.

**1** Je fais les courses.  2.1, 2.2

*Choisissez la description qui correspond à chaque illustration.*

1.  2.  3.

4.  5.

6.  7.  8.

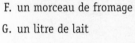

A. six tranches de jambon

B. un kilo de beurre

C. une boîte de soupe

D. un pot de moutarde

E. un paquet de pâtes

F. un morceau de fromage

G. un litre de lait

H. une bouteille d'eau minérale

**2** Une tartine pour le petit déjeuner 2.1, 2.2

*On prépare le petit déjeuner (breakfast). Dites quelle quantité de confiture chaque personne a.*

1. Mélanie    2. Paul

3. M. Leroy    4. Mme Leroy

### Essential Instruction

1. Say the quantities in **Activité 1** and have students call out the number. Then say the number, and ask the class to identify the quantity and the item.
2. Have students complete **Activités 2 – 4** with a partner. Encourage them to add additional vocabulary to **Activité 4**.

3 Mme Deschanel va à la crémerie, à la boucherie, à la pâtisserie, à la boulangerie, et à la charcuterie.

4 *Answers to the questions will vary.*
1. A: Tu préfères le café ou la limonade?
2. A: Tu préfères le bœuf ou le poulet?
3. A: Tu préfères la mayonnaise ou le ketchup?
4. A: Tu préfères le gâteau au chocolat ou la tarte aux pommes?
5. A: Tu préfères la glace au chocolat ou la glace à la vanille?

## 3 Mme Deschanel fait les courses.  1.2, 2.1, 2.2

*Lisez le paragraphe. Ensuite, répondez à la question.*

Madame Deschanel a besoin de faire les courses parce qu'elle invite ses parents pour le dîner. Elle préfère acheter ses provisions chez les petits commerçants. D'abord, elle achète cinq cent grammes de fromage et une douzaine d'œufs. Ensuite, elle achète un poulet, une tarte aux pommes, et deux baguettes. Enfin, elle va acheter une tranche de pâté et deux saucissons.

Madame Deschanel va faire les courses à quels magasins?

Mme Deschanel va acheter une tarte aux pommes à la pâtisserie.

# Communiquez!

## 4 Le dîner  1.1

**Interpersonal Communication**

*À tour de rôle, demandez à votre partenaire quels aliments* (foods) *il ou elle préfère.*

**MODÈLE**   A: **Tu préfères le pâté ou le saucisson?**
B: **Je préfère le saucisson.**

1.                    2.

3.                    4.                    5.

### Reference Desk

Explain that an **épicerie** is a small grocery store, but in Paris, for example, it is usually a small shop "down the street" or "on the corner" that sells a little of everything, from an assortment of fruits and vegetables to canned goods and bath tissue (**produits alimentaires et non-alimentaires**). Can your students find a clue to its meaning or origins within the word **épicerie**? **Épice** means spice. Spices are sold in bags or other containers in open-air or specialty markets around the world, but especially in Africa and Asia. Dating from the Middle Ages **épiceries** traditionally sold just spices, but eventually came to offer other food items. Now food and a few household goods make up the majority of their products. What is **pain d'épices**? Gingerbread-tasting (spice) bread!

## Differentiated Learning
### Decelerate
1. Read aloud the quantity descriptions in **Activité 1** and have students draw an imaginary line connecting the description to the item.
2. Write the four expressions of quantity on the board or on a card so students have a visual cue when doing **Activité 2**.

## Special Needs Students
### AD(H)D/Visually Challenged
Enlarge the paragraph in **Activité 3** or retype it, separating it into five sentences and removing the photo. Having less visual stimulation may help some students better focus their attention on the task of reading. Choosing a different font, type size, text color, or underlining the quantities may help as well.

# Communiquez!

**5** **Les petits commerçants**    1.1, 2.2

### Interpersonal Communication

*À tour de rôle, demandez à votre partenaire s'il ou elle a besoin d'acheter l'objet. Votre partenaire va dire "oui" et où il ou elle va pour l'acheter.*

**MODÈLE** A: **Tu as besoin de fromage?**
B. **Oui, je vais à la crémerie.**

1.     2.     3.

4.     5.     6.     7.     8.

**6** **La chronologie**

*Indiquez le magasin où François achète les choses que vous entendez.*

A. la boulangerie
B. la crémerie
C. la boucherie
D. le supermarché    **1.2, 2.1, 2.2**
E. la pâtisserie
F. la charcuterie

**7** **En ville**     2.1, 2.2

*Dites où vous allez, ensuite ce que vous y (there) faites.*

**MODÈLE**    Je regarde un match.
**D'abord, je vais au stade.**
**Ensuite, je regarde un match.**

1. J'étudie.
2. Je prends un croque-monsieur et un coca.
3. Je nage.
4. J'achète un ensemble bleu.
5. Je surfe sur Internet.
6. Je fais du shopping.
7. Je fais les courses.
8. Je vois un drame français.
9. J'achète un pot de confiture.

### Essential Instruction

1. Check that students understand the title of **Activité 5**, **Les petits commerçants**. Review the expression **avoir besoin de**, and then have partners complete the exercise.
2. Check answers to the listening **Activité 6**.
3. Have students do **Activité 7** in small groups. Survey the class to see how many different places they referenced for each activity.
4. For **Activité 8**, ask students to respond chorally.
5. Have students expand on the **Questions personnelles** by adding other foods for questions 1-2.

## Answers

**8**

1. Enfin, Mme Vaillancourt trouve le poulet.
2. Enfin, Mlle Fleury trouve le lait.
3. Enfin, M. Moreau trouve le camembert.
4. Enfin, Jules trouve les œufs.
5. Enfin, Mlle Martin trouve la moutarde.
6. Enfin, Anne-Marie trouve le saucisson.

**9** *Answers will vary.*

### Reference Desk

In **Activités 8** and **9**, the definite article is used, not the partitive (some). Remind students that to express likes/dislikes and preferences for a general category such as food, one uses the definite article in French, but the article is generally absent in English. For example, one would say in French, **Je préfère le café.** or **J'adore le fromage.** In English, however, we say "I prefer coffee." or "I love cheese." The partitive article is explained in **Leçon C**.

---

**8** **Au nouveau supermarché**  2.1, 2.2

*On fait les courses au nouveau supermarché, mais c'est difficile de trouver certains produits. Dites que, enfin, les gens trouvent ce qu'ils cherchent.*

**MODÈLE** M. Roussel
**Enfin, M. Roussel trouve le bœuf.**

1. Mme Vaillancourt   2. Mlle Fleury   3. M. Moreau

4. Jules   5. Mlle Martin   6. Anne-Marie

**9** **Questions personnelles**

*Répondez aux questions.*

1. Est-ce que tu préfères le porc, le bœuf, ou le poulet?
2. Manges-tu un peu ou beaucoup de fromage? De yaourt?
3. Dans ta famille, qui aime faire les courses?
4. Est-ce que tu aimes faire les courses?
5. Qu'est-ce que ta famille va acheter au supermarché ce weekend?

 1.1, 2.1, 2.2

Mon grand frère aime faire les courses.

---

## Differentiated Learning
### Accelerate
1. To challenge more advanced students, do **Activité 6** with additional cognates (**des broccolis, des tartelettes**, etc.).
2. Ask students to use sequencing words to tell about three things they do during the week or on the weekend.

## Learning Styles
### Kinesthetic Learners
Have students imagine that they are journalists as they circulate to survey classmates using the **Questions personnelles**.

## Special Needs Students
### Dyslexia
A multi-sensory approach offers further support of dyslexic students. Have students read aloud directions and answer choices before completing the **Activités**. Project or post numbered photos of the stores referenced in **Activité 6**. Ask students to respond to the listening activity questions by selecting the correct photo rather than reading the answer.

## Answers

**⑩**

1. Les parents de Julien ne sont pas à la maison ce soir.
2. Ils vont manger du couscous.
3. Julien va prendre 500 grammes de légumes.
4. Oui, ils ont soif.
5. Momo offre du pain comme cadeau.
6. Ils vont à la pâtisserie et à la crémerie.

### Extension

Ham and melon, a lime sherbet with strawberries and raspberries.

### Reference Desk

You might show a short, carefully selected clip from the film **Monsieur Ibrahim** showing scenes of the **épicerie**, managed at the beginning of the film by Monsieur Ibrahim (played by Omar Sharif) and at the end by his adopted son Momo. The film is based on the novel **Monsieur Ibrahim et les fleurs du Coran** by the prolific Alsatian dramatist, novelist, and fiction writer Éric-Emmanuel Schmitt. His plays have been staged in over fifty countries all over the world.

# Rencontres culturelles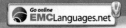

## Chez Momo     1.2

Julien et Maxime font les courses dans l'épicerie de Momo.

Julien: Bon, mes parents ne sont pas à la maison ce soir. Je t'invite à manger. Qu'est-ce que tu veux?

Maxime: Du couscous. On achète combien de paquets? Deux?

Julien: D'accord.

Momo: Tiens, j'ai des légumes tous prêts pour préparer le couscous.

Maxime: Ils sont frais?

Momo: Tout frais d'aujourd'hui, mon ami.

Julien: Alors, 500 grammes. On prend aussi un litre de coca, s'il vous plaît. Ça coûte combien?

Momo: 9,50 euros. Et prends ce pain pour manger avec, c'est un cadeau.

Julien: Merci, Momo. À bientôt!

Maxime: Dis, Julien, où est-ce qu'on vend des tartes aux fruits?

Julien: À la pâtisserie Giscard.

Maxime: C'est moi qui les offre. Enfin, on cherche une crémerie pour acheter un peu de camembert.

### 10 Chez Momo   1.2, 2.1

*Répondez aux questions.*

1. Qui n'est pas à la maison de Julien ce soir?
2. Qu'est-ce que Julien et Maxime vont manger?
3. Combien de légumes frais Julien va-t-il prendre?
4. Julien et Maxime ont-ils soif?
5. Qu'est-ce que Momo offre comme cadeau?
6. Julien et Maxime vont aller à quels magasins maintenant?

### Extension  Au rayon charcutier du supermarché

Apolline et François font les courses.

Apolline: Alors, on prend quoi comme hors-d'œuvre?

François: Coppa et jambon corse, c'est bien, non?

Apolline: Avec le melon, parfait!

François: Ça veut dire pas de melon au dessert….

Apolline: Non, on prend du sorbet avec des fraises et des framboises.

François: Alors, sorbet citron vert et deux bouteilles de Badoit!

### Extension   Qu'est-ce qu'Apolline et François vont prendre comme hors-d'œuvre et dessert?  1.2

## Essential Learning

1. Have students observe the photo and guess what the dialogue is about.
2. Instruct students to scan the dialogue for cognates. Ask them to comment on the difference between **les courses** and **le couscous**.
3. Show the video. Assign groups to read the dialogue aloud and do **Activité 10**. Finally, replay the filmed dialogue. Instruct students to review the dialogue again outside of class as needed.
4. Review the **Question centrale**. Have students read **Les hypermarchés et les petits commerçants** silently. Ask them to discern what **hyper** means and connect to the English "hyperactive." Show the progression from **grand→super→hyper**.
5. Have students identify cognates in the **Produits** section. Survey students to see who has eaten **pâté**. If possible bring in some **pâté** for willing students to sample.

# Points de départ

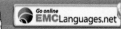

## Les hypermarchés et les petits commerces

**1.2, 3.1, 5.1**

De plus en plus de Français font les courses aux hypermarchés, des grands magasins qui vendent des produits alimentaires* et non alimentaires. Depuis le début des années 60, les hypermarchés ont influencé comment les Français font leurs courses et ce qu'ils* achètent. Les plus importants sont Carrefour, Auchan, Leclerc, et Intermarché. Aujourd'hui les petits commerces représentent seulement* 15% du total du commerce dans l'alimentation (boucherie, crémerie, épicerie....)

 **Search words: supermarchés en ligne**

Avec Carrefour en ligne vous n'avez pas besoin d'aller au magasin.

___

**alimentaires** *food*; **ce qu'ils** *what they*; **seulement** *only*

**Produits**

**Le pâté** est une préparation à base de viande hachée (*minced meat*) souvent mélangée (*mixed*) avec du gras (*fat*), des épices (*spices*), des herbes, des légumes, ou du vin (*wine*). On achète du pâté à la charcuterie ou au supermarché. Cherchez des photos et des recettes en ligne.

**1.2, 2.2**

## Communication

**Presentational: Paired Practice**
Draw or reproduce on a piece of paper a spacious but simple large grocery cart. Make copies for your class. Divide the class into four groups called **Carrefour, Auchan, Leclerc,** and **Intermarché.** Within each group, have students work in pairs as they shop online at their assigned **hypermarché.** Instruct them to consult at least four different **rayons,** and select 10–15 items to put in their **chariot** (*cart*). They must sketch the items in the cart and list them in French on the back of their sheet, using expressions with the partitive. Have each pair present the contents of their shopping cart and turn in a written shopping list, for example, **Au rayon charcuterie nous prenons du jambon.**

## Critical Thinking

**Comparisons**
Ask students to discuss and compare different opportunities for shopping (from small specialized shops to **hypermarchés** to online experiences) in the United States and France.

## Expansion

Tell groups that they have a weekly allowance of **100€** to spend online on groceries for a family of four. Have students use the search words in **Points de départ** to find a **hypermarché** or **des petits commerces** where they can buy certain items. For a challenge, tell students that one member of the family is allergic to a certain item, lactose intolerant, or requires a gluten-free diet. Have them share their virtual purchases with the class.

## Differentiated Learning
### Accelerate
1. Have students re-write the dialogue in paragraph format using the sequencing words.
2. Once students learn what **un citron** (*lemon*) is, ask them to deduce the meaning of **un citron vert** (*lime*).
3. Define or show pictures of **coppa** (*an aged, cured pork shoulder, usually thinly sliced*). Then have pairs read the **Extension** dialogue.

## Multiple Intelligences
### Bodily-Kinesthetic
Bring in some couscous and pass it around so students can touch it. Explain that a common misconception is that it is a form of rice. In fact, couscous is hard wheat semolina rolled into tiny balls.

### Reference Desk

1. Although **emmental** cheese originated as a Swiss cheese from the Emme valley near Berne, it is also made in other European countries. In France, **emmental** cheese is made in the Savoie region. **Emmental** has holes in it, and should not be confused with **gruyère**, another cheese from Switzerland, also made in France, but without holes.
2. Charles De Gaulle was Minister of Defense prior to World War II, Leader of the Free French Forces based in Great Britain during WWII, then President of France post-WWII.

### Expansion

1. Instruct students to make a grocery list of items they would need for certain situations, such as holiday or seasonal meals.
2. Have students research and make a French cheese region map to display in the classroom.
3. Organize a monthly tasting of a French cheese from a different region if possible.

## Les fromages  1.2, 3.1

"Comment voulez-vous gouverner un pays où il existe 258 variétés de fromage?"

—Charles De Gaulle, président de la France (1959–1969)

Chaque région en France a ses spécialités. La Normandie a le camembert; l'Auvergne, le bleu; le Jura, le comté; la Savoie, la tomme; l'Alsace, le munster…. Mais l'emmental, de Savoie, et le camembert sont les fromages les plus populaires en France.

Le fromage est si important en France qu'il entre dans de nombreuses expressions, comme par exemple: "en faire tout un fromage" qui signifie exagérer et "entre la poire* et le fromage" qui indique le bon moment pour discuter d'une affaire.

🔍 **Search words: fromage français**

> **Producteurs de fromage:** 1. USA 2. Allemagne 3. France
>
> **Exportateurs de fromage:** 1. France 2. Allemagne 3. Pays-Bas
>
> **Consommateurs de fromage (par habitant):** 1. Grèce 2. France 3. Italie

_____

**si** *so*; **poire** *pear*

## COMPARAISONS

What cheeses are popular where you live?

4.2

## L'expression des mesures 1.2, 3.1, 4.2

En France, on utilise le système métrique. Pour le poids* (fruits, légumes, viande), on utilise le kilo (1.000 grammes), la livre (500 grammes), ou la demi-livre (250 grammes). Pour les quantités de moins d'une demi-livre on utilise les grammes. Certaines expressions sous-entendent* des quantités.

| Quantité | Mesure métrique |
|---|---|
| le paquet de café | 250 grammes |
| la plaquette de beurre | 125 grammes |
| la barquette de fruits | Entre 100 et 250 grammes |
| une maxi bouteille de coca | 1,5 litres |
| une bouteille | 1 litre |
| une demi-bouteille | 0,50 litres |
| une canette / boîte | 33 centilitres |
| un pack ou une boîte de lait | 1 litre |

🔍 **Search words: tableau système métrique**

_____

**poids** *weight*; **sous-entendent** *imply*

## COMPARAISONS

If you were to buy a maxi bouteille of your favorite soft drink in France, would it be more or less than a gallon?

4.2, 5.1

Au supermarché, on vend des litres d'Orangina au rayon des boissons.

### Essential Instruction

1. Ask students to silently read **Les fromages** for comprehension. Provide pushpins or colored flag pins to volunteers and ask them to indicate on a map of France the regions mentioned in the paragraph. Discuss the idiomatic expressions.
2. If the resources are available, you may wish to purchase some of the cheeses mentioned in **Les fromages**. Have willing students taste, then rate each one according to smell and flavor.
3. Ask students where and when they might use the metric system. Have students who know the metric system clarify the weights on a chart, showing equivalencies in pounds and ounces.
4. Divide the class into nine groups and assign one **Question culturelle** to each group. Have a volunteer from each group report back to the class.

## 11 Questions culturelles 🎧  2.1, 2.2, 4.2

*Répondez aux questions.*

1. Comment s'appellent les quatre grands hypermarchés français?
2. Le petit commerce représente quel pourcentage du commerce dans l'alimentation?
3. Quel est l'ingrédient principal du pâté?
4. Quelles sont les spécialités de fromage dans ces régions?
   * Normandie
   * Auvergne
   * Alsace
5. Quels sont les deux fromages les plus populaires en France?
6. L'expression "entre la poire et le fromage" suggère quelle activité?
7. Quel pays est le premier exportateur de fromage?
8. Quelles sont les mesures principales pour le poids en France?
9. En quoi est-ce qu'on achète de l'eau ou du coca?

La vache qui rit est un fromage français qu'on trouve aux États-Unis.

### À discuter

What can the small shop owner offer that the **hypermarchés** cannot? What does the increasing popularity of **hypermarchés** suggest about a shift in priorities in France? Which type of store would you prefer if you lived in France? Why?

## Du côté des médias

## 12 Au supermarché  2.2

*Faites les activités suivantes.*

1. Dites pour quel repas on prend ces produits.
2. Dites quelle sorte de produits on achète de la marque:
   * Quaker ou Kellogg's
   * Illy ou Maison du café
   * Grany LU
3. Vous avez 8 euros. Qu'est-ce que vous achetez pour le petit déjeuner?

Leçon B | trois cent un **301**

### ⑪

1. Carrefour, Auchan, Leclerc, et Intermarché
2. 15%
3. la viande hachée
4. en Normandie: le camembert; en Auvergne: le bleu; en Alsace: le munster
5. l'emmental et le camembert
6. un bon moment pour discuter d'une affaire
7. la France
8. le kilo (1.000 grammes), la livre (500 grammes), et la demi-livre (250 grammes)
9. On achète de l'eau en maxi bouteille (1,5 litres), en bouteille (1 litre), et en demi-bouteille (0,50 litres). On achète du coca en canette ou en petite bouteille (25 ou 33 centilitres).

### À discuter
*Answers will vary.*

### ⑫

1. On prend ces produits pour le petit déjeuner.
2. On achète les céréales de la marque Quaker ou Kellogg's, le café de la marque Illy ou Maison du café, les barres céréalières de la marque Grany LU.
3. *Answers will vary.*

### Reference Desk

**Une livre** (a pound/500 gr.) is feminine and **un livre** (*book*) is masculine.

### Communication

**Interpretive: Cooperative Groups**
Make a collage for the classroom wall of packaging labels from French items sold in American supermarkets. Challenge teams to find or photograph the most items. Consider having a fund-raiser to buy the items and celebrate with a **fête** to taste everything.

---

## Differentiated Learning
### Accelerate
Have students analyze and draw conclusions about the statistics in **Les fromages**. Are the highest cheese-consuming nations also the highest producers, etc.?

## Multiple Intelligences
### Bodily-Kinesthetic
Borrow some small scales from the science department and weigh some items from the list in **L'expression des mesures**. Have students give equivalent weights in ounces and pounds.

## Mathematical-Logical
After studying the metric system, ask students to go online and research current gas prices in the United States, converting liters into gallons. Then have them find out how much a gallon of gas costs in France or other francophone countries. Have them share this information with the class. Point out how European gas prices have always been much higher than prices in the United States. Speculate as to why that might be. Tell students they will learn more about energy sources in **Unité 9**.

## Communication

**Presentational: Cooperative Groups**

To practice the verb **vendre,** put students in small groups. Use pictures or cards of food items. Mix them up and place them face down on a large table. All students select two pictures at random and return to their group to tell what each is selling. For example, (**fromage/yaourt**) **Je vends du fromage et des yaourts.** A second student must say what that person is selling, using **tu**, **il**, or **elle** as the subject.

Encourage students to be as creative as possible and to use all subject pronouns and forms of **vendre**.

## Communication

**Interpersonal: Paired Practice**

Have students write and present a skit about shopping in a **supermarché**.

# Structure de la langue

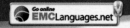

## Present Tense of Regular Verbs Ending in –*re*  1.2

The infinitives of many French verbs end in **-re**. Most of these verbs, such as **vendre** (*to sell*) and **attendre** (*to wait for*), are regular. To form the present tense of a regular **-re** verb, drop the **-re** ending from the infinitive to find the stem, and add the appropriate ending. Note that no ending is added for the **il/elle/on** form.

| Qu'est-ce que | Qui attend |
| Samantha attend? | Samantha au musée? |

| vendre | | |
|---|---|---|
| je | **vends** | nous | **vendons** |
| tu | **vends** | vous | **vendez** |
| il/elle/on | **vend** | ils/elles | **vendent** |

Qu'est-ce que vous **vendez**?     *What do you sell?*
Nous **vendons** du pain.          *We sell bread.*

### Pronunciation Tip

The singular forms of **-re** verbs are all pronounced the same way.

### Usage Tip

You don't need to add an ending after **il/elle/on.**

### COMPARAISONS

How does the English version of the verbs in these two sentences differ?

On attend!
On attend le médecin.

What word is omitted in French, but necessary in English in the second sentence?

**4.1**

Damien attend Rachida au café.

COMPARAISONS: In the second sentence "for" needs to be added after the verb in English.

## Essential Instruction

1. Ask a volunteer to conjugate at the board an **-er** verb as you simultaneously write out the conjugated forms of the verb **vendre,** highlighting the endings in a different color. Have the students note the similarities and differences. Then model the pronunciation of the new verb and point out that only the endings **-ons** and **-ez** are pronounced. The letter **d** is silent in the singular forms and pronounced [d] in the plural forms. The **d** is pronounced [t] in the inverted forms of **il/elle/on: Où vend-on du pain?** Have students practice the verb in the affirmative, negative, and interrogative forms on white boards.

2. Instruct the students to do **Activités 13** and **14** orally with a partner. Ask volunteers to present the dialogues in **Activité 14**.

## 13 Les commerçants   2.1, 2.2

*Dites ce que ces personnes vendent dans leurs magasins.*

**MODÈLE** Monsieur Dufort
**Monsieur Dufort vend du poulet.**

1. Madame Salomé et son fils
2. Sarah et moi, nous
3. toi, tu

4. Hamza et toi, vous
5. on
6. moi, je
7. mon amie Élodie

## Communiquez!  1.1

### 14 Qu'est-ce que tu attends?

Est-ce que tu attends les jeux Olympiques d'été?

Non, j'attends le match des Lakers.

**Interpersonal Communication**

*Demandez à votre partenaire s'il ou elle attend la chose suivante. Ensuite, changez de rôles.*

**MODÈLE** le nouveau livre de Stephanie Meyer
A: **Est-ce que tu attends le nouveau livre de Stephanie Meyer?**
B: **Oui, j'attends le nouveau livre de Stephanie Meyer.**
ou
**Non, je n'attends pas le nouveau livre de Stephanie Meyer. J'attends le nouveau livre de Stephen King.**

1. le nouveau CD de Snow Patrol
2. le nouveau film de Robert Pattinson
3. le match des Red Sox
4. la fête de ton ami(e)
5. les Jeux Olympiques d'été
6. le nouveau film de Kristen Stewart
7. le match des Lakers

---

**Answers**

**13**
1. Madame Salomé et son fils vendent des tartes.
2. Sarah et moi, nous vendons du bœuf.
3. Toi, tu vends de la moutarde.
4. Hamza et toi, vous vendez du pâté.
5. On vend du pain.
6. Moi, je vends du beurre.
7. Mon amie Élodie vend du camembert.

**14** *All questions will follow the model. Answers will vary.*

1. B: Oui, j'attends…. ou Non, je n'attends pas….
2. B: Oui, j'attends…. ou Non, je n'attends pas….
3. B: Oui, j'attends…. ou Non, je n'attends pas….
4. B: Oui, j'attends…. ou Non, je n'attends pas….
5. B: Oui, j'attends…. ou Non, je n'attends pas….
6. B: Oui, j'attends…. ou Non, je n'attends pas….
7. B: Oui, j'attends…. ou Non, je n'attends pas….

### Reference Desk

Tell students **attendre** is **un faux ami**. It means "to wait for," not "to attend." **Assister** is also a false friend. The verb **assister à** means "to attend or be present" (at an event) and not "to assist" (**aider**)!

### Expansion

Assign each of six groups the name of a French food store. As you call out a food, the group where it is sold stands up and uses it in a sentence, for example, **On vend du beurre à la crémerie.**

---

## Differentiated Learning

### Expand/Accelerate

1. To practice the verb **vendre**, the demonstrative adjectives, and the stores, show pictures of different foods and ask, **Où vend-on ces pommes? ces tartes,** etc.?
2. Point out other regular -**re** verbs: **attendre**, **répondre**, **descendre**, **entendre**.
3. You may wish to explain to students that there are many "subcategories" of -**re** verbs (**rire**, **mettre**, **conduire**) that they will learn later.

## Learning Styles

### Auditory Learners

For additional practice, ask questions using **vendre** and vocabulary from previous units, for example, **On vend des dictionnaires à la FNAC? On vend des ordinateurs à l'école?** etc. Ask students to create additional questions, and you can use them as a warm-up drill for the next day's class.

### Multiple Intelligences

**Visual-Spatial**

Have students create colorful illustrated sentences with -**re** verbs.

*Vous voulez un morceau de fromage, monsieur? Un peu de pain?*

# Expressions of Quantity

To ask "how many" or "how much," use the expression **combien de (d')** before a noun.

| | |
|---|---|
| **Combien de** tartes est-ce que tu veux? | *How many pies do you want?* |
| Il y a **combien d'**œufs dans cette omelette? | *How many eggs are there in this omelette?* |

To tell "how many" or "how much," use one of these general expressions of quantity before a noun:

| | |
|---|---|
| **(un) peu de** | *(a) little, few* |
| **assez de** | *enough* |
| **beaucoup de** | *a lot of, many* |
| **trop de** | *too much, too many* |

| | |
|---|---|
| Je voudrais **un peu de** fromage. | *I would like a little cheese.* |
| Non, merci, j'ai **assez d'**eau. | *No thanks, I have enough water.* |

Certain nouns express a specific quantity. They are followed by **de (d')** and a noun.

| | |
|---|---|
| **une boîte de** | *a can of* |
| **une bouteille de** | *a bottle of* |
| **un gramme de** | *a gram of* |
| **un kilo de** | *a kilogram of* |
| **un litre de** | *a liter of* |
| **un morceau de** | *a piece of* |
| **un paquet de** | *a package of* |
| **un pot de** | *a jar of* |
| **une tranche de** | *a slice of* |

*Est-ce que Jean a acheté une bouteille d'eau?*

| | |
|---|---|
| Donnez-moi **une tranche de** jambon. | *Give me a slice of ham.* |
| Je vais acheter **un litre d'**eau minérale. | *I am going to buy a liter of mineral water.* |

### COMPARAISONS

What do these sentences mean in English?

J'aime beaucoup le fromage.
J'aime beaucoup de fromages.

What part of speech is each boldfaced word or expression?

4.1

COMPARAISONS: The sentences mean "I like cheese a lot" and "I like a lot of cheeses." In the first sentence, **beaucoup** is an adverb; in the second, **beaucoup de** expresses a quantity.

## Essential Instruction

1. Model the pronunciation of the expressions of quantity followed by different foods and beverages. You can expand the practice of the expressions of quantity to include vocabulary from previous units, for example, **beaucoup de devoirs**, **assez de stylos**, etc.
2. For a quick drill, say an expression of quantity, and then ask students to provide a different noun to use with an expression of quantity.
4. Ask students to complete **Activités 15** and **16** with a partner.
5. Review the **Comparaisons** and ask students to brainstorm a list of French adverbs that they know, such as **bien**, **trop de**, **aussi**, **mais**, **d'abord**, **ensuite**, etc. Students may be surprised at the number of adverbs that they know.

## 15 Maman fait les courses.

 2.1, 2.2

Dites si votre mère achète **trop de**, **assez de**, ou **pas assez de** provisions pour les membres de votre famille.

**MODÈLE** **Maman achète trop de jambon.**

 1.
 2.
 3.
 4.
 5.

 6.
 7.
 8.
 9.
 10.

# Communiquez!

## 16 Le pique-nique

 1.1

**Interpersonal Communication**

*Vous faites un pique-nique avec quatre amis. À tour de rôle, demandez à votre partenaire combien il y a de chaque aliment.*

**MODÈLE**
A: **Il y a combien de tartes?**
B: **Il y a beaucoup de tartes.**

A: **Il y a combien de cocas?**
B: **Il y a assez de cocas.**

Leçon B | trois cent cinq **305**

---

## Answers

**15** *Answers will vary according to the family size:*

Trop/assez/pas assez:
1. de poulet
2. de confiture
3. d'oeufs
4. de fromage
5. de mayonnaise
6. de croissants
7. de beurre
8. de café
9. de lait
10. d'eau

**16**

A: Il y a combien de yaourts?
B: ... un peu de yaourts.
A: Il y a combien de fromage?
B: ...un peu de fromage.
A: Il y a combien de saucissons?
B: ...assez de saucissons.
A: Il y a combien de moutarde?
B: ... trop de moutarde.
A: Il y a combien de pain?
B: ... peu de pain.
A: Il y a combien de poulets?
B: ... beaucoup de poulets.
A: Il y a combien d'eau minérale?
B: ... peu d'eau minérale.
A: Il y a combien de tartes?
B: ... beaucoup de tartes.
A: Il y a combien de coca?
B: ... assez de coca.

### Game

**On fait les courses.**
Display empty cartons, packages, food wrappings, bottles, and images of quantities and food items. Divide students into two to four teams and give each an imaginary **panier** (*shopping basket*) and a dinner **entrée** to shop for, such as spaghetti with a salad. At the signal, one student at a time from each team goes to the table to "shop" for one ingredient. The "shopping" continues until time is called. The team that has procured the most items needed for their specific **entrée** and that can identify what they have in their **panier** wins the game.

---

**Differentiated Learning**
**Expand**
Ask students to focus on the cartoon at the top of p. 304. What expression of quantity might the mouse use to answer the question?

**Learning Styles**
**Auditory/Visual Learners**
Show pictures of food and ask students to call out all the quantities that logically correspond to food items that you show.

**Kinesthetic Learners**
Have students create their own cartoon, using one or more expressions of quantity.

## Answers

**17**
1. un paquet de mayonnaise
2. un morceau de fromage
3. 250 grammes de beurre
4. un pot de moutarde
5. une boîte de café
6. un litre de lait
7. une bouteille d'eau minérale
8. six tranches de jambon
9. une boîte de soupe

**18** *Answers will vary.*

**19** Script can be found in the front pages of the Annotated Teacher's Edition.
1. C
2. F
3. B, D
4. C, E
5. G
6. B, D
7. A, G
8. H

---

**17 Quelle quantité?**  2.1, 2.2

*Choisissez la quantité appropriée.*

| un litre de | une bouteille de | six tranches de | une boîte de |
| un morceau de | 250 grammes de | un pot de | un kilo de | un paquet de |

**MODÈLE** pommes
**un kilo de pommes**

1. mayonnaise
2. fromage
3. beurre
4. moutarde
5. café
6. lait
7. eau minérale
8. jambon
9. soupe

> J'ai un kilo de pommes et 500 grammes de poivrons dans mon panier.

**18 Dans mon panier**  1.1

**Interpersonal Communication**

*Dessinez un panier (basket) avec six aliments différents.*
*À tour de rôle, demandez ce que votre partenaire a dans son panier.*

| un kilo de | un paquet de | un pot de | un morceau de |
| une bouteille de | un litre de | une tranche de | une boîte de |

**MODÈLE** A: **Tu as un litre de lait?**
B: **Oui, j'ai un litre de lait. Tu as un pot de confiture?**
ou
**Non. Tu as un pot de confiture?**

**19 Au supermarché** 2.1, 2.2

*Choisissez l'expression de quantité qui correspond à l'aliment (food) que Nicole achète.*

A. une boîte
B. une bouteille
C. un kilo
D. un litre
E. un morceau
F. des tranches
G. un paquet
H. un pot

# À vous la parole  1.1, 1.3

*Question centrale*
**?**
How is shopping different in other countries?

## Communiquez!

### 20 Les mesures métriques

**Presentational Communication**

In this lesson, you have learned to express some units of measurements in the metric system. Bring in an item or a photo of an item that is given in a metric measurement, for example, the odometer in your car or a product from the grocery store. (Since Canada uses metric measurements, you might easily find a Canadian product.) Present your product or photo to your group, giving the measurements of your product in the metric system and our system. Finally, discuss how you would feel if the United States adopted the metric system and for what careers knowing the metric system would be useful.

 **Search words: convertisseur métrique**

## Communiquez!

### 21 Je fais les courses en ligne.
1.1, 1.3, 5.1

**Interpretive/Interpersonal Communication**

Make a grocery store flyer with this week's specials. Draw, cut out, or download pictures of at least ten different items, then visit an online grocery store to find out how much each item costs in euros. Write the quantity and cost of each item on the flyer. Then with a partner, role-play placing a telephone order for groceries. Your partner will use your flyer to tell you how much money each item costs and how much you owe for your order.

 **Search words: carrefour shopping en ligne, mon supercasino, auchan en direct**

## Communiquez!

### 22 La recette
1.1, 1.3, 2.2

**Interpretive/Interpersonal Communication**

Find a recipe of a French dish online, then role play a conversation with a partner in which you discuss the ingredients you need to buy to make the dish. Be sure to talk about the amount of each ingredient you need and which stores you will go to in order to purchase the items.

 **Search words: recettes**

On a besoin de cerises pour faire un clafoutis.

## RESOURCES

📝 **Communicative Activities**

**Answers** _____

20 *Presentations will vary.*

21 *Role plays will vary.*

22 *Role plays will vary.*

## Reference Desk

Suggest that students look at home or in a store to find five different categories of items, such as health and beauty products, produce, home and office supplies, and auto-motive supplies with both metric and English measures. Discuss how widespread use of the metric system is in the United States.

**Blended Instruction**
Consider using blended instruction, a combination of in-class learning and computer-mediated instruction or learning opportunities. Ask students to complete activities on the computer or using their cell phone, smartphone, or other emerging electronic technology. This will allow students to hone their tech skills and become more independent learners. Schedule routine Internet and e-book learning in class and in the lab.

**Differentiated Instruction**
**Decelerate**
Ask students in English how the food items in **Activité 17** would be packaged.

**Learning Styles**
**Kinesthetic/Visual/Auditory Learners**
Place the food packages you brought in for earlier **Activités** on a desk or table. Divide students into teams. As you call out one of the items in **Activité 17**, one student from each team must try to be the first to come and select the appropriate package

for that particular item and say it in a sentence, for example, **J'achète une bouteille d'eau minérale.** Award a point for the correct quantity and a point for a correct sentence.

**Special Needs Students**
**Social Anxiety/Autism**
To ease anxiety, suggest that students complete the **Activité** of their choice from **À vous la parole** in a written format. Another option is to ask students to video record themselves as they present.

# Stratégie communicative

## Telling a Story through Pictures  1.2, 1.3

One way to develop your speaking skills is to practice telling a story. Use the following strategies to describe the sequence of pictures that follows.

1. Study the pictures. Think about the people in the picture, where they are, and what they are doing.
2. Review the vocabulary and structures you have learned in this and previous units. This will help you to describe what you see.
3. Use as many of the words and expressions that you know to tell the story. You may be surprised by just how much you can say!

### Vocabulaire utile

**parler de** *to talk about;* **une photo** *photo;* **du fast-food** *some fast-food*

---

When you told the story, did you include everything you saw in the pictures? Did you use your imagination to make up details about the story? Did you use vocabulary from Unit 6 and from previous units? Read the following paragraphs to see how one student told the story.

Marianne et son amie Françoise sont à la maison de Marianne. Marianne parle de sa famille à son amie. Son père a 50 ans. Il a les yeux noirs et les cheveux bruns. Il est homme d'affaires. Sa mère est médecin. Elle a aussi 50 ans. Elle a les cheveux blonds et les yeux bleus. Ses grand-parents viennent du Sénégal. Ils sont généreux et sympa. Son frère ressemble à leur père. Il a 20 ans et il est testeur de jeux vidéo. Il est timide, mais très intelligent. Il travaille beaucoup. Il n'est pas paresseux!

Françoise étudie les maths parce qu'elle va être prof de maths. Elle est très diligente. Marianne achète des vêtements à Tati en ligne. Les filles mangent une pizza, des hamburgers, et des frites. Elle prennent aussi des cocas.

---

### Essential Instruction

1. Explain that telling a story through pictures is a skill that requires practice and that the goal is to incorporate as much vocabulary and grammar from all previous units as possible. You may decide that students will not be graded on this type of exercise until they have learned some basic strategies.

2. Review the example illustrations and story, and then have students brainstorm vocabulary that they might use to describe the illustrations in **Activité 23**. You can organize them into categories if you wish, such as nouns, verbs, adjectives. Add adverbs (quantity, sequencing, etc.) and linking words (**et, mais, alors**) to the list.

3. Encourage partners to have fun with this activity and to include as much humor as they can. This is the place for them to be creative!

**23** Je raconte une histoire!  1.3, 4.1

**Les rues commerçantes** are often filled with shoppers on the weekends. Carefully study the following storyboard featuring two girls doing their weekend shopping. Then with a partner, tell a story based on the pictures. In the first frame, name the characters; describe their relationship, physical appearance, clothing, and character; tell how old they are, and what they like to do. Then move on to describing the events. Remember to use the strategies you just learned.

Answers _____

 **23** *Stories will vary.*

1.

2.

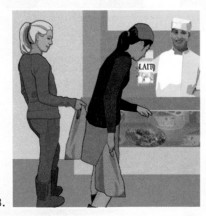

3.

4.

**Vocabulaire utile**

**dit** *says;* **la liste** *list*

### Expansion

Students may wish to make their own comic strips or illustrated stories. Use digital storytelling software that allows students to upload images and record narration. These presentations can be part of the evaluation process or saved to student portfolios. With some coordination between international partners, you can have your students make storybooks and share them with French e-pals by snail mail, e-mail, or on a blog. You might choose a theme such as "An afternoon shopping trip with friends." This can lead to interesting discussions and comparisons. Another option might be to have students select several family members or friends to use as the main characters in the story.

### Differentiated Learning
#### Accelerate
This is an opportunity for students to model high quality language production. You may consider asking these students to help struggling learners with their presentations.

#### Learning Styles
#### Visual Learners
Have students check off the items they need to include in their description of the illustrations as a way to review before presenting their story.

### Special Needs Students
#### Social Anxiety
To ease anxiety, tell students that they will not be required to make presentations in front of the class. If it is appropriate for your particular students, tell them that they can present to you alone. Alternatively, they can make a recording of their description and give it to you. You can also offer them the added security of being able to have note cards.

## Reference Desk

Explain that **raisins secs** are raisins in English. Explain that they are, in fact, dried grapes, which makes the French term logical.

## Culture

### Products: Activity
Have students look at the photos of items pictured in the **Vocabulaire actif**. What American and French dishes would they make with these ingredients? Can your students suggest recipes? Discuss how some of these items would be served in American or French restaurants or settings. Look up recipes for some of the ingredients in American and French cookbooks to compare usage.

### Practices: Information
Consider showing the i-Culture video entitled **"Le marché"** (2009-2010) to provide your students with a culturally authentic perspective related to the theme of this **Leçon**.

## Game

### Au marché
Have students form one or two large circles. One student starts by saying what fruit or vegetable he or she is buying at the **marché**. The next student must repeat what the other is buying and add a fruit or vegetable, for example, **Il/Elle achète des bananes. Moi, j'achète une tomate.** Each student must repeat the entire shopping list before adding another item. To challenge students further, ask them to add quantities.

**310**

 **Leçon C**

# Vocabulaire actif

## Au marché   1.2

**Les légumes (m.)**

les salades (f.)
les champignons (m.)
les pommes de terre (f.)
les tomates (f.)
les carottes (f.)
les courgettes (f.)
les haricots verts (m.)

 les petits pois (m.)   les oignons (m.)   les aubergines (f.)   les poivrons (m.)   les concombres (m.)

**Les fruits (m.)**

les pommes (f.)
les poires (f.)
les oranges (f.)
les cerises (f.)
les fraises (f.)
les bananes (f.)
les melons (m.)

 les ananas (m.)   les pêches (f.)   les raisins (m.)   les pamplemousses (m.)

## Essential Instruction

1. Recycle questions about who at home does the shopping for food and how often. Announce to students that they are going to a **marché** to buy fresh fruits and vegetables like the French do several times a week.
2. Play the audio for **Au marché** while students look at the pictures. Ask them to point out cognates.
3. Present and model the vocabulary in **Pour la conversation** using real or plastic fruits and vegetables if possible. Distribute the props, or pictures of the food items, and have students role-play with a partner.
4. Have students ask questions using the fruits and vegetables, such as, **Qui aime les courgettes? De quelle couleur sont les melons?**
5. Have partners indicate in French whether or not they like each of the foods pictured. Have them share with the class what they learned about their partner's preferences.
6. Assign **Activité 1** as partner work.

# Pour la conversation

How do I make a purchase at the market?

> Les pêches **sont mûres?**
>
> *Are the peaches ripe?*

> **C'est combien le kilo?**
>
> *How much is it per kilo?*

> **Je prends 500 grammes.**
>
> *I'll take 500 grams.*

What will the vendor say?

> **Et avec ça?**
>
> *And with that?*

> **C'est tout?**
>
> *Is that all?*

## Et si je voulais dire...?

| | |
|---|---|
| **l'ail (m.)** | *garlic* |
| **les framboises (f.)** | *raspberries* |
| **les mangues (f.)** | *mangoes* |
| **les myrtilles (f.)** | *blueberries* |
| **les patates (f.) [slang]** | *potatoes* |
| **les poireaux (m.)** | *leeks* |

---

**1** **Les marchands de légumes**  **2.1, 2.2**

*Dites quels légumes chaque marchand vend.*

**MODÈLE** **Mlle Rousseau** vend **des aubergines, des tomates, et des haricots verts.**

1. M. Gaumont     2. Mme Bernier

3. Mlle LeForestier     4. M. Sofralot

---

## Answers

 **1**

1. M. Gaumont vend des haricots verts, des carottes, et des tomates.
2. Mme Bernier vend des pommes de terre, des petits pois, et des oignons.
3. Mlle LeForestier vend des poivrons verts, des poivrons rouges, et des champignons.
4. M. et Mme Sofralot vendent des concombres, des courgettes, et des aubergines.

### Reference Desk

1. **Patates** is not a slang word in Quebec, but rather the commonly used noun to refer to potatoes. Have students look up the recipe for the Quebec dish **la poutine** (*potato fries, gravy, cheese curds*). Explain that **myrtilles** (*blueberries*) are called **bleuets** in Quebec, because of the color **bleu**. Note that **bleuets** means cornflowers in France. And cranberries? **Les airelles** in France and **les canneberges** in French-speaking Canada.

2. Present the two types of silent **h**: the **h muet**, which allows for a contraction and liaison, as in **l'homme/les hommes** (**lay-zuhm**), as if the **h** were invisible. Words with an **h muet** are often of Latin origin (**habile, habiller, habiter**, etc.).

   The **h aspire** is never contracted, nor pronounced with the liaison, since the **h** is treated like a consonant. Most French words borrowed from other languages have an **h aspiré**. The **h** of **haricots** is an **h aspiré**, so there is no liaison between the final **-s** of **les** or **des** and **haricots** (**lay-ah-ree-koh**). (Consider also pointing out **le hockey, la halle, le hamburger, le héros**, etc.)

---

## Differentiated Learning

### Expand
To practice spelling, have groups of three or four choose a student who will say a word while the others in the group write it (books open), write and draw it (books closed), or take turns drawing the item(s) as the others identify it.

### Accelerate
Challenge students to ask a partner about the fruits and vegetables that family members like or dislike, then share with the class what they learned.

## Learning Styles

### Visual/Kinesthetic Learners
Play the role of **le/la marchand(e)** and have students role-play a customer. Use plastic fruits and vegetables (or flash cards or pictures), and ask each student to say what item he or she would like to buy. Once all students or pairs have an item, call out a color in French. Whoever has an item of that color shows it and calls out the name of the item. Then have students ask each other for, and exchange, items.

**2**

1. Les bananes coûtent 1,90 euros le kilo.
2. Les tomates coûtent 5,30 euros le kilo.
3. Les poires coûtent 4,90 euros le kilo.
4. Les raisins coûtent 4,11 euros le kilo.
5. Les fraises coûtent 13,80 euros le kilo.
6. Les cerises coûtent 3,14 euros le kilo.
7. Les pêches coûtent 4,55 euros le kilo.

**3** Script can be found in the front pages of the Annotated Teacher's Edition.

1. E
2. G
3. B
4. D
5. H
6. A
7. C
8. H
9. J
10. I

## Connections

### Math

Bring a scale into class that can be used to weigh fruits and vegetables, along with a sampling of food items. Weigh different items such as bananas, apples, potatoes, tomatoes, grapes, etc. so that students gain a sense of how much items weigh. Make a comparative wall chart with amounts in pounds versus grams/kilos. Would students go into a market and order kilos of raspberries? How many would that be? Would you ask for potatoes in grams or kilos? For what produce items would you use the term **une livre**? Which food items can you ask for as counted items (such as **trois bananes**)? Does one order bananas differently from grapes?

---

**2** C'est combien le kilo?  2.1, 2.2

*Pour chaque aliment, répondez à la question.*

**MODÈLE** Les **oranges** coûtent **4,55 euros le kilo.**

 1.
 2.
 3.

 4.
 5.
 6.
 7.

**3** À l'épicerie   2.1, 2.2

*Choisissez l'illustration qui correspond à ce que les clients achètent au marché.*

A.

B.

C.

D.

E.

F.

G.

H.

I.

J.

---

**Essential Instruction**

1. Have students do **Activités 2** and **4** in pairs. Point out how **4,55 euros le kilo** is expressed in English with a decimal point and the words per kilo. Ask them the current dollar value of the euro.
2. After abundant practice of the new vocabulary, have students do the listening activity.
3. Read aloud the paragraph in **Activité 5**, and then ask students to read it aloud in pairs.

Give examples similar to **une salade de fruits** and explain the constructions noun + **de** + noun (food) to indicate something composed of a particular ingredient, and **à** + definite article (**aux/ à la/ à l'/au**) + food, such as in **une glace à la vanille** to indicate a flavor or something added, like a sauce. Have students answer chorally as you give the cues.

4. Assign **Activité 6** with a new partner.

Answers _____

**4**
1. C
2. E
3. B
4. D
5. A

**5**
1. Marcel prépare une soupe aux champignons.
2. Les Charpentiers préparent un ragoût de bœuf.
3. M. Boyer prépare une salade de fruits.
4. Aurélie prépare une salade.
5. Julie prépare une smoothie aux fruits.

**6** *Answers will vary.*

**4** **De petites conversations au marché**  **2.1, 2.2**

*Choisissez la lettre qui correspond à la bonne* (correct) *réponse.*

1. Nous n'avons pas de pêches aujourd'hui.
2. Bonjour, Monsieur. Vous désirez?
3. C'est combien le kilo?
4. Vos poires sont fraîches?
5. On achète combien de haricots verts, maman?

A. Cinq cent grammes.
B. C'est trois euros quatre-vingt-dix.
C. Donc, je prends 500 grammes de cerises.
D. Toutes fraîches d'aujourd'hui.
E. Un kilo d'oignons, s'il vous plaît.

**5** **Le marché vient au quartier.**  **1.2, 2.1, 2.2**

*Tout le monde achète des fruits et des légumes frais pour préparer un repas* (meal)*. D'abord, lisez le paragraphe. Ensuite, choisissez un plat de la liste pour dire ce que chaque personne prépare.*

> une soupe aux champignons   une salade de fruits   un ragoût (*stew*) de bœuf
> un smoothie aux fruits   une salade   une soupe de légumes

Les Boucher achètent des haricots verts, des pommes de terre, des carottes, et une courgette. M. Boyer achète une pastèque, un melon, trois pêches, et des raisins. Les Charpentier achètent du bœuf, des carottes, des petits pois, et des pommes de terre. Julie achète un kilo de fraises et 500 grammes de bananes. Marcel achète des champignons et des oignons. Aurélie achète des concombres, des carottes, et un poivron vert.

**MODÈLE**  les Boucher
**Les Boucher préparent une soupe de légumes.**

1. Marcel
2. les Charpentier
3. M. Boyer
4. Aurélie
5. Julie

**6** **Questions personnelles**

*Répondez aux questions.*

1. Préfères-tu les melons ou les poires?
2. Quels légumes est-ce que tu n'aimes pas?     **1.2, 2.1, 2.2**
3. Est-ce que tu manges assez de fruits et de légumes?
4. Qu'est-ce que tu achètes pour faire une bonne salade?
5. Quels légumes est-ce que tu préfères dans une soupe?
6. Est-ce que ta famille va au marché pour acheter des fruits et des légumes frais?

> Je n'aime pas les carottes!

**Communication**

**Presentational: Cooperative Groups**

To practice numbers, counting, euro currency, and the unit vocabulary, make a **marché de fruits et légumes** display for your classroom wall. Students can draw or print images of fruits and vegetables to make a market showcase. Prices should be appropriate. Use this wall as a backdrop for a market skit with students acting as vendors and customers. Put students in teams. Assign an amount (in euros) for each team to spend, and items needed for a meal. The teams then report back on what quantities and items they have purchased and how they have used their money.

Leçon C | trois cent treize **313**

**Differentiated Learning**
**Decelerate**
Ask students to check off which words from the **Vocabulaire actif** they already know.

**Learning Styles**
**Kinesthetic Learners**
1. Time students as they circulate to ask the **Questions personnelles**. Stop the clock and call on volunteers to share something about their classmates. Repeat several times.
2. Play **Tapette à mouches** (*Flyswatter*) to practice the vocabulary. Organize two teams. Provide a flyswatter to the first player from each team, or have them use their hands. Project or post unlabeled images of the vocabulary. As you say an item, players try to be first person to swat it (**taper**), thus earning a point for the team.

**Multiple Intelligences**
**Visual-Spatial**
Distribute large pieces of paper. Tell students to create and label **un repas dégoûtant**, using **Unité 6** vocabulary. Provide examples, such as **une soupe de légumes et du chocolat**, or **un sandwich aux bananes et au poisson**.

## Camille et sa mère au marché     1.2

Camille et sa mère font les courses pour le déjeuner.

| | |
|---|---|
| Marchand: | Bonjour, Madame! Vous désirez? |
| Mère: | Vos tomates sont mûres? |
| Marchand: | Oui, oui. |
| Mère: | C'est combien le kilo? |
| Marchand: | C'est 3,89 euros. |
| Mère: | Alors, un kilo de tomates, s'il vous plaît. Des concombres, une livre; deux poivrons, un vert et un orange. |
| Camille: | Des olives noires, Maman! Et, du thon. |
| Marchand: | Ah! Y'a de la salade niçoise dans l'air. |
| Mère: | On achète du thon et des olives à l'épicerie. |
| Camille: | Et, pour la salade de fruits, Maman? |
| Mère: | Oh! Alors, je prends un kilo de pêches, une livre de fraises, et un melon. |
| Marchand: | Nous n'avons pas de pêches aujourd'hui. |
| Mère: | Tant pis. Ça fait combien? |
| Marchand: | 22 euros, Madame. |

*(La mère de Camille donne un billet de 50 euros.)*

| | |
|---|---|
| Marchand: | Ah! Vous êtes toutes les mêmes avec vos gros billets, hein? |

**Answers**

**7**

1. Faux, elle achète un kilo de tomates.
2. Faux, elle achète un poivron vert et un poivron orange.
3. Faux, elles vont préparer une salade niçoise.
4. Vrai
5. Faux, elle prend une livre de concombres.
6. Faux, elles vont manger une salade de fruits.
7. Vrai

**Extension**

He says he will give her a deal and suggests recipes to use the fruit.

**Communication**

**Interpretive: Cooperative Groups**
Use the market display that shows fruit and vegetables with prices created for the activity mentioned in the notes on p. 313. Put students into teams of four. Read off a selection of four items and various amounts purchased, such as those depicted in the conversation with Camille (**un kilo de pêches, une livre de fraises**, etc.). All students should calculate the total cost for each item in euros and compare with other group members.

**7 Camille et sa mère au marché**

*Dites si la phrase est vraie ou fausse. Corrigez (correct) les phrases qui sont fausses.*

1. La mère de Camille achète 500 grammes de tomates.
2. Elle achète deux poivrons verts.
3. Camille et sa mère vont préparer une quiche.
4. Elles vont acheter du thon à l'épicerie.
5. La mère de Camille prend une livre d'olives vertes.
6. Comme dessert, Camille et sa mère vont manger une glace à la vanille.
7. Le marchand n'est pas content (*happy*).

2.1, 2.2

**Extension Au marché**   1.2, 2.1, 2.2

Sarah s'arrête devant le marchand de fruits.

| | |
|---|---|
| Marchand: | Je vous fais un prix sur les cerises… profitez-en! |
| Sarah: | Combien? |
| Marchand: | Quatre euros 50 le kilo, sept euros les deux kilos. |
| Sarah: | C'est beaucoup trop! Qu'est-ce que je vais en faire? |
| Marchand: | Des clafoutis! Des tartes! Des yaourts! Tout le monde aime les cerises…. |
| Sarah: | Ah! Oui, c'est une idée. Je prends un kilo de cerises. |
| Marchand: | Trois euros 75 et c'est bien, parce que je suis gentil! |

**Extension** Que fait le vendeur pour vendre son produit à Sarah?

**Essential Instruction**

1. Ask students if they would like to "visit" a French open-air market. Then show the filmed dialogue with books closed. Have students share what they noticed about the market and what they understood.
2. Have students read aloud the dialogue in small groups, noting any words that they do not know.
3. Discuss and define vocabulary before showing the filmed dialogue a second time.
4. Have the students do **Activité 7** in pairs and ask them to think of one additional true-false statement to share with the class.
5. Assign students to read about the topics in **Points de départ**, including **La Francophonie: Au marché**. Have students revisit the **Question centrale** and discuss the **Comparaisons** questions with a partner, then share with the class.
6. To further explore the topics, you could ask students to do online research using the search words and then report three things they learned.

# Points de départ

**RESOURCES**

👁 **e-visual 22**

📓 **Workbook 31–32**

## Au marché 🌸 1.2, 2.1, 2.2

En général, il y a des marchés une ou deux fois* par semaine dans les villes et villages de la France. On trouve sur les marchés des produits alimentaires*, surtout* des fruits et des légumes. Mais on peut aussi acheter des spécialités locales ou régionales, des produits bio*, des spécialités étrangères (italiennes, africaines) ou exotiques, de la viande et de la charcuterie, des fromages et des produits laitiers*, des fleurs*, et du pain ou des gâteaux. Les prix sont souvent moins chers que dans les épiceries, mais plus chers que dans les supermarchés ou hypermarchés.

 **Search words: marchés de paris, marchés provence**

> **Question centrale**
> How is shopping different in other countries?

> ### COMPARAISONS
> How many farmers' markets are there where you live? How is it different from shopping at a supermarket? How is it similar to French markets?
>
> **4.2, 5.1**

Au marché, le marchand de fruits et légumes vend beaucoup de pêches.

_____
**fois** *times*; **alimentaires** *food*; **surtout** *especially*; **bio** *organic*; **laitiers** *milk*; **fleurs** *flowers*

## Le mouvement slow food en France 🌸 1.2, 2.1, 2.2

D'origine italienne, le mouvement *slow food* existe en France depuis* 2003. C'est une réaction à la restauration rapide ou le *fast-food*. Le mouvement encourage la consommation* de produits régionaux, une alimentation* diversifiée, et des traditions gastronomiques. Des associations *slow food* sont surtout présentes dans le sud de la France.

 **Search words: slow food france**

_____
**depuis** *since*; **consommation** *consumption (eating)*; **alimentation** *diet*

Leçon C | trois cent quinze **315**

---

**Answers** _____

**Comparaisons**
*Answers will vary.* You might want to ask students first to make a list of the differences between farmer's markets and supermarkets. Help students think in categories: location, size, type of produce, price, crowd, etc. Then check the similarities between the local farmer's markets and French **marchés**.

### Reference Desk

The Slow Food movement is an international movement founded by Carlo Petrini in 1986, to react against the invasion of fast-food. It was the first movement of its kind that sought to preserve a natural relationship between people and food, and maintain a balance in the ecosystem. Adherents of the slow food movements encourage traditional and regional cuisine, the use of local plants, seeds, and livestock. A manifesto was signed in Paris in 1989 and many European and international countries have adopted this movement.

### Critical Thinking

**Evaluation**
Have some class discussions about the Slow Food movement and what your students know about it. Have they become aware of changes in their own or their family's attitudes toward food, food shopping, freshness of produce, local markets, organic farming, restaurant choices, etc.? What are the advantages of the Slow Food movement?

---

**Differentiated Learning**
**Accelerate**
Have accelerated students read aloud and discuss the **Extension** dialogue in class. You may want to write a short glossary on the board before they read the dialogue, such as, **s'arrête**, **profitez-en**, **c'est une idée**….

**Multiple Intelligences**
**Bodily-Kinesthetic**
Find a photo and a recipe online of **clafoutis** to show students. Encourage them to make the recipe at home, take a picture of their dish, and report back to the class on the taste. You may wish to offer extra credit to students who complete this activity.

## La Francophonie: le marché

1.2, 2.1, 2.2, 3.2

### ✳ Au Maghreb

Au Maghreb (Tunisie, Algérie, Maroc), le marché s'appelle **le souk**. On y vend des produits alimentaires, des vêtements, des poteries, et des produits artisanaux. Une différence entre les souks et les marchés français est qu'il est nécessaire au souk de marchander* le prix des produits. On discute avec le vendeur pour acheter un produit à un prix moins cher. Mais le souk, c'est surtout un lieu* de rencontres et de relations humaines. Parfois*, c'est au **souk** qu'un homme fait sa demande en mariage.

🔍 **Search words:** souk tunis photos de souks de marrakech

_____

**marchander** *to bargain;* **lieu** *place;* **Parfois** *Sometimes;* **fait sa demande** *ask for the hand of someone in marriage*

1.2, 4.2
2.2

**Produits**

Les Algériens, les Marocains, et les Tunisiens sont populaires pour leurs poteries, tapis (*carpets*), bijoux (*jewelry*), sacs, et autres **produits artisanaux** faits selon (*according to*) des techniques traditionnelles et avec des dessins géométriques.

Il y a des marchés, ou souks, comme ça en Tunisie, en Algérie, et au Maroc.

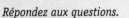  

**❽ Questions culturelles**

2.1, 2.2, 4.2

*Répondez aux questions.*

1. En général, combien de fois par semaine est-ce qu'il y a des marchés en France?
2. Quels sont les produits spécifiques que vous pouvez trouver sur un marché?
3. Est-ce que les prix sont moins chers au marché ou au supermarché?
4. Comment s'appelle le mouvement qui encourage les traditions gastronomiques et la consommation des produits régionaux?
5. Qu'est-ce que c'est un **souk**?
6. Qu'est-ce qu'on fait pour marchander dans un souk?

Au Maroc, le **souk** est aussi un lieu de rencontres.

**Perspectives**

"J'aime le marché parce que je peux voir, sentir, et toucher la nourriture et il y a une ambiance sociale." Pourquoi est-ce que cette Française ne va pas au supermarché pour ses fruits, légumes, et certains autres produits alimentaires?

## Du côté des médias  1.2

*Lisez les informations sur le Marché de Chambéry.*

# Marché, Commerces et entreprises

## Marché de Chambéry

Le marché de Chambéry situé à l'ouest de Lyon, place du marché, propose une diversité de produits de consommation : fruits et légumes, viande et fromages frais, fleurs et plantes, produits d'habillement et artisanaux.

- le mercredi et le dimanche matin

Tous les mercredis matins, un car desservant les quartiers de Givros, Chambéry et Villeurbanne, est gratuit pour les personnes âgées désirant se rendre au marché.

- départ à 8h30, rue Camailleux, arrivée au centre-ville à 9h 15
- retour à 11h30

---

**9  Marché de Chambéry**  **2.1, 2.2**

*Répondez aux questions.*

1. Où est-ce qu'on trouve Chambéry?
2. Le marché de Chambéry ressemble à quoi?
3. Qu'est-ce qu'on trouve sur ce marché?
4. Quels jours ont lieu (*takes place*) le marché de Chambéry?
5. Quelles facilités sont offertes aux habitants pour venir au marché?

Leçon C | trois cent dix-sept **317**

**9**
1. C'est une petite banlieue parisienne dans le département de l'Île-de-France.
2. Il ressemble à un petit supermarché en plein air.
3. On y trouve une variété de produits: des aliments et des vêtements.
4. Le marché a lieu le jeudi et le dimanche.
5. On offre un car (un autobus) pour les personnes âgées.

## Culture

### Practices: Activity
Ask students to discuss how the elderly shop in the local community. What provisions are made for transportation to supermarkets and shopping centers? How convenient is access to markets in French towns and cities compared to those in the United States?

---

## Differentiated Learning
### Decelerate
For **Activité 8**, have students discuss the more complex questions, such as #4 and #6, in English.

## Learning Styles
### Visual Learners
Have students create a visual representation of the answers in **Questions culturelles** and a cartoon illustrating the **Perspectives**.

### Auditory Learners
Read aloud the **Perspectives** and have students list reasons the speaker gives for not shopping at a supermarket.

**RESOURCES**

e-visual 24

**Expansion**

Have students research current **looks** in France, Quebec, and Senegal, and compare them with the local **looks** of teens in their community. What **looks** are promoted in American versus French fashion magazines? Which overseas **looks** have caught on here in the United States? Is a **look** imported from Europe or exported from the United States first? Students with e-pals may wish to discuss their findings with their francophone partners.

# La culture sur place

## Je fais du shopping en ligne.

### Introduction

Faire du shopping en ligne est un passe-temps qui est populaire dans tout le monde (*world*), surtout dans les pays (*especially in countries*) où les individus ont accès à l'Internet. Mais quels "looks" est-ce qu'on peut acheter?

**LES LOOKS FRANÇAIS** 1.2

Il y a beaucoup de "looks"en France, mais voilà trois exemples:
- **Le look BCBG**, qui ressemble à notre look "*preppy.*"
- **Le look fashion**, qui représente tout ce qui est à la mode (*in style*) en ce moment.
- **Le look bobo**, qu'on peut décrire (*describe*) comme "bohème bourgeois" (*hippy chic*).

Isabelle a un look BCBG.

Emma aime le style bobo.

Marc a un look fashion.

**Essential Instruction**

1. Read the **Introduction** together before students do online research in class. You may want to show them additional examples of the three styles or **looks**.
2. For students who are not interested in fashion, offer the choice to research specific sports clothing. Be sure to establish what appropriate clothing to include.
3. Distribute the **Copy Masters** grid for **Activité 10**.

4. As an alternative to having students print each article of clothing, have them create a slide show to use for the visual presentation of their research in **Activité 11**. Another possibility is to have students circulate and view the selections on others' computer screens.
5. Have groups of four do the discussion in **Activité 12**.

## Enquête

### 10 Acheter en ligne

1.3, 2.1, 2.2

*Suivez ces étapes pour trouver des vêtements en ligne:*

1. Cherchez des exemples des trois looks en ligne.

**Search words: le look BCBG, le look fashion, le look bobo**

2. Trouvez deux exemples de chaque look en ligne dans ces compagnies.

**Search words: www.laredoute.fr**
**www.les3suisses.fr**
**www.tati.fr**

3. Complétez une grille comme celle-ci avec des détails pour chaque vêtement.

| Numéro et compagnie | Le look | Description | Prix | Couleur | Taille | Autre (accessoires....) |
|---|---|---|---|---|---|---|
| | | | | | | |
| | | | | | | |
| | | | | | | |

4. Imprimez (*Print*) une copie de chaque vêtement que vous choisissez.

### 11 Ma présentation

1.3

*Présentez les vêtements que vous avez choisis* (that you chose) *à vos camarades de classe en montrant* (showing them) *les images.*

## Faisons l'inventaire!

### 12 Une discussion

1.1

*Répondez individuellement en anglais aux questions suivantes. Ensuite, discutez vos idées avec vos camarades de classe.*

1. Were you always aware that you were looking at a website in French, or did you sometimes forget? Was there something specific that reminded you that you were looking at a website in French? If so, what?
2. In what ways is French fashion the same as in North America? In what ways is it different?
3. Did you learn anything about the cultures of French-speaking countries during your online shopping experience? If so, what?



**Answers**

10 *Projects will vary.*

11 *Presentations will vary.*

12 *Answers will vary.*

**Communication**

**Presentational**

Students may enjoy preparing, designing, and presenting a comparative fashion show, a wall display, or catalogue flyer of the latest **looks** from Paris and New York.

**Differentiated Learning**

**Decelerate, Adapt, Accelerate**

If you do not have computer access for the entire class at this time, have students do the research for **Activité 10** at home or in the library, and upload the selected photos to a photo-sharing site that you can access in class. You could also ask them to print the pictures, preferably in color. Ask students to practice their presentations with partners before presenting.

**Special Needs Students**

**AD(H)D**

To help these students focus while doing the research for **Activité 10**, have them find clothes for one or more special occasions, such as a traditional family holiday, a rock concert, or religious event.

## Answers

1. de la; les
2. de la; des, les
3. des
4. le; la
5. des; des; des
6. de la

## Reference Desk

1. The partitive article (**du**, **de la**, or **de l'**) is required in French, but often omitted in English.
2. Point out that there is a liaison between **des** and a plural noun beginning with a vowel sound.
3. Point out that partitive articles are not used after **vouloir**, **acheter**, **manger**, **donner**, **désirer**, **avoir**, **voici**, **voilà** and **il y a** when referring to whole items. For example, **Christine mange la tarte** and **Je voudrais une salade.**

# Structure de la langue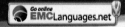

## The Partitive Article  1.2

For nouns that can't be counted, like bread, ice-cream, and water, use **du**, **de la**, or **de l'** to express the idea of "some" or "any." These are called partitive articles.

| | |
|---|---|
| On va acheter **du** pain. | *We're going to buy (some) bread.* |
| Vous avez **de la** glace? | *Do you have (any) ice cream?* |
| Je voudrais **de l'**eau. | *I would like (some) water.* |

Maintenant prenez du chocolat....
Ensuite, du sucre et de la crème.

For nouns that can be counted, such as potatoes and carrots, use **des** to express the idea of "some" or "any." Remember, **des** is the plural of the indefinite article **un(e)**.

Je veux **des** pommes de terre.      *I want (some) potatoes.*

Partitive articles are often used after the verbs and expressions **acheter**, **avoir**, **désirer**, **donner**, **manger**, **prendre**, **vouloir**, **voilà**, and **il y a** to indicate a quantity. Partitive articles are not used after the verbs **aimer** and **préférer**. The definite articles **le**, **le**, **l'**, and **les** are used.

| | |
|---|---|
| Il y a **de la salade**? | *Is there (any) salad?* |
| Catherine aime bien **les** carottes. | *Catherine really likes carrots.* |

| some, any | in general, for ex., after *aimer* |
|---|---|
| **du** pain (before a masculine noun) | **le** pain |
| **de la** mayonnaise (before a feminine noun) | **la** mayonnaise |
| **de l'**eau minérale (before a noun beginning with a vowel) | **l'**eau minérale |
| **des** pommes de terre (before a plural noun) | **les** pommes de terre |

## 13 Les mini-dialogues  2.1, 2.2

*Complétez chaque phrase avec l'article approprié.*

| du | de la | des | le | la | les |
|---|---|---|---|---|---|

1. Mme Thomas:   Vous voulez… tarte?
   Mlle Robert:   Non, merci. Je n'aime pas… pommes.
2. Mme Lefevre:   Et pour le dessert, il y a… glace à la vanille.
   Annick:   Je voudrais… fruits frais. J'aime bien… pommes.
3. Serveuse:   Vous désirez, Monsieur?
   M. Guerin:   Un steak avec… pommes de terre, s'il vous plaît.
4. Mme Roussel:   Qu'est-ce qu'on prépare? Tu aimes bien… couscous?
   M. Roussel:   Non, je préfère… quiche.
5. Karine:   Voilà… légumes!
   Léon:   On achète… aubergines et… tomates?
6. Émilie:   J'ai un sandwich au poulet pour toi.
   Chantal:   Merci. Tu as… mayonnaise?

## Essential Instruction

1. Explain the partitive article, and then have students read the explanation.
2. On the board, list the verbs that are often used with the partitive (beginning with **acheter**).
3. In small groups, have students use plastic foods, if available, and take turns creating sentences with the verbs on the board, the food vocabulary from **Unité 6**, and the partitive, such as, **Je veux du pain et de la tarte.**
4. Have pairs do **Activité 13**, and then role-play the mini-dialogues for the class.
5. Clarify remaining questions about the use of the partitive as students do **Activité 14**. Explain or show with pictures the difference between **un gâteau/du gâteau**, **un yaourt/du yaourt**, etc.
6. For **Activité 15**, tell groups that they can also choose foods not listed.

 **14  À la cantine**  **2.1, 2.2**

*Dites ce qu'on va manger cette semaine à la cantine.*

**MODÈLE**  Lundi, on va manger des carottes….

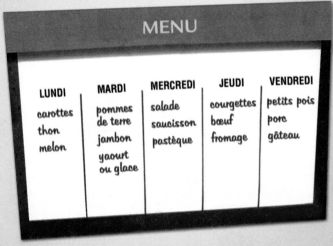

## MENU

| LUNDI | MARDI | MERCREDI | JEUDI | VENDREDI |
|-------|-------|----------|-------|----------|
| carottes | pommes de terre | salade | courgettes | petits pois |
| thon | jambon | saucisson | bœuf | porc |
| melon | yaourt ou glace | pastèque | fromage | gâteau |

 **15  Les trois repas** **2.1, 2.2**

*Dites ce que vous prenez du placard (cupboard) ou du frigo (refrigerator) pour faire chaque repas indiqué. Vous n'allez pas utiliser tous les mots.*

| la mayonnaise | les fraises | le beurre | le jambon | la confiture de fraises |
|---|---|---|---|---|
| le poulet | la confiture de pêches | le pain | la salade | le bœuf | le chocolat |

1.     2.     3.

**MODÈLE**  Je prends du pain avec du beurre et….

---

1. Lundi, on va manger des carottes, du thon, et du melon.
2. Mardi, on va manger des pommes de terre, du jambon, et un yaourt ou une glace.
3. Mercredi, on va manger une salade, du saucisson et de la pastèque.
4. Jeudi, on va manger des courgettes, du bœuf, et du fromage.
5. Vendredi, on va manger des petits pois, du porc, et du gâteau.

1. Pour faire le petit-déjeuner, je prends le pain du placard, et la confiture de fraises/de pêches et le beurre du frigo.
2. Pour faire le déjeuner, je prends le pain du placard, et la mayonnaise (ou le beurre), le jambon, et la salade du frigo.
3. Pour faire le dîner, je prends le pain et le chocolat du placard.

## Communication

**Presentational**

Ask students to keep a food diary in French for a week, noting each day's meals. In class have all the students present what they ate for their favorite meal of the week, paying attention to use of the partitive and definite articles.

---

**Differentiated Learning**
**Decelerate**
The partitive is a difficult concept in English because it is often omitted, for example, "I'd like to eat French fries." (**Je voudrais manger des frites.**) Reinforce that in French the verb can help to determine if the **partitif** is needed.

**Learning Styles**
**Visual/Kinesthetic Learners**
Provide several plastic foods to pairs of students. Have students ask each other for one or more foods

and create a sentence with the appropriate **partitif**, for example, **Je voudrais du steak**. The partner can respond **Voilà du steak**. You can also use photos of food.

**Multiple Intelligences**
**Verbal-Linguistic**
Have students write a list of ten or more foods in the refrigerator at home, then compare lists with a partner and create sentences containing the items they both have. Ask pairs to share their respective lists.

**321**

**16** Script can be found in the front pages of the Annotated Teacher's Edition.

1. A
2. B
3. B
4. A
5. B
6. B
7. A

## Communication

### Presentational: Cooperative Groups

Put students in groups to design and make a menu for an imaginary restaurant. Have different groups work on breakfast, lunch, or dinner menus. Have each group present their menus by performing a group skit in which they play the roles of the server and the customers ordering their meal.

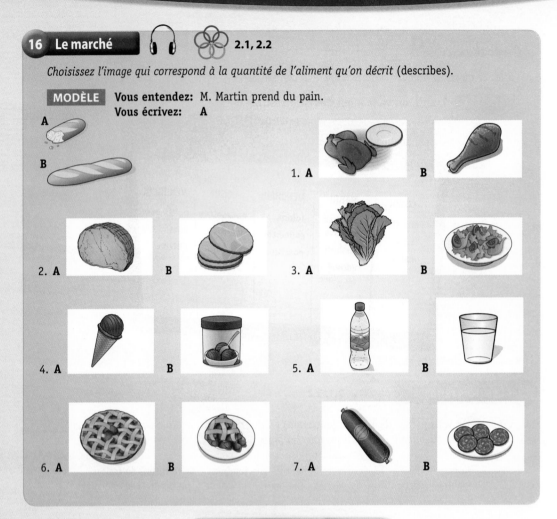

**16  Le marché**        2.1, 2.2

*Choisissez l'image qui correspond à la quantité de l'aliment qu'on décrit (describes).*

**MODÈLE**   **Vous entendez:** M. Martin prend du pain.
             **Vous écrivez:**   **A**

Tu veux prendre de la tarte aux pommes?

**Essential Learning**

1. Review the listening **Activité 16** as a class. Ask students to provide the partitive or article for the other illustration.

2. As you model the partitive in negative sentences, write the forms on the board. Then have students read aloud the examples on p. 323.

3. Review what items students have in their refrigerators at home; have them include the partitive, and then have them write six items that are not in their refrigerator. Finally, ask them to compare with a partner's list.

4. Assign students to do **Activité 17** in pairs.

# The Partitive in Negative Sentences

 1.2

You've already learned that in negative sentences (except with **être**), **des** becomes **de** or **d'**.

The partitive article becomes **de** or **d'** after negated verbs.

Tu achètes **du** fromage?
*Are you buying some cheese?*

Non, je n'achète pas **de** fromage.
*No, I'm not buying any cheese.*

Vous avez **de la** glace?
*Do you have (any) ice cream?*

Nous n'avons pas **de** glace.
*We don't have any ice cream.*

Tu veux **de l'**eau?
*Do you want some water?*

Je ne veux pas **d'**eau.
*I don't want any water.*

Est-ce qu'il y a **des** pommes de terre?
*Are there any potatoes?*

Il n'y a pas **de** pommes de terre.
*There aren't any potatoes.*

**17** | L'intolérance au lactose   2.1, 2.2

*Brigitte ne peut pas manger de produits laitiers* (milk products). *Dites si elle mange ou non les aliments suivants.*

**MODÈLES**  melons
**Elle mange des melons.**

yaourt
**Elle ne mange pas de yaourt.**

1. poulet
2. glace
3. fraises
4. camembert
5. champignons
6. petits pois
7. saucisson
8. fromage
9. aubergines
10. beurre

Leçon C | trois cent vingt-trois **3 2 3**

**RESOURCES**

**Workbook 37–38**

Answers _____

**17**
1. Elle mange du poulet.
2. Elle ne mange pas de glace.
3. Elle mange des fraises.
4. Elle ne mange pas de camembert.
5. Elle mange des champignons.
6. Elle mange des petits pois.
7. Elle mange du saucisson.
8. Elle ne mange pas de fromage.
9. Elle mange des aubergines.
10. Elle ne mange pas de beurre.

## Communication

**Presentational**
Use food flash cards made for previous activities. Show three or four cards of a specific category (**fruits**, **légumes**, **patisseries**, etc.) to the class. Students must use **il y a...** to tell you in succession what food items are presented and suggest additional food items from the same category that are not shown. For example, you might show three cards displaying peaches, strawberries, and grapes, but not apples or melon. Choose four or more students to use **il n'y a pas de...** to say what is missing.

## Differentiated Learning
**Expand**
For additional oral practice of **il y a un/une/des** and **il n'y a pas de (d')**, ask questions using the classroom vocabulary, for example, **Est-ce qu'il y a des livres dans la salle de classe?**

## Learning Styles
**Kinesthetic Learners**
Pass out plastic food items or large pictures of food to half the class, who will play the role of the **marchand(e)s** at the **marché**. The other half of the class will play the role of the **client(e)s** shopping for food. As they circulate, they should ask the **marchand(e)** what products he or she has, adding the appropriate **partitif**.

**3 2 3**

**18** **Des plats populaires**  **2.1, 2.2**

*Dites quels aliments principaux manquent (are missing) pour faire ces plats. Soyez logique! (Be logical!)*

**MODÈLE** les spaghetti bolognaise
**Il n'y a pas de bœuf ou de pâtes.**

| concombres | bœuf | chocolat | carottes | jambon |
|---|---|---|---|---|
| fromage | pâtes | pommes de terre | œufs | thon |

1. une omelette au fromage  2. un steak-frites  3. une salade niçoise

4. un croque-monsieur  5. une crêpe au chocolat  6. une soupe aux légumes

## Communiquez!  1.1

**19** **Activité sur la culture française**

### Interpersonal Communication

*Dessinez huit objets ou aliments français sur une feuille de papier. Ensuite, posez des questions à votre partenaire pour voir s'il ou elle a les mêmes objets ou aliments.*

**MODÈLE** A: **Est-ce que tu as une trousse?**
B: **Oui, j'ai une trousse.**
ou
**Non, je n'ai pas de trousse.**

### Essential Instruction

1. Do **Activité 18** together as a class to ensure accuracy, then ask the students to repeat it with a partner.
2. To start reviewing, ask students to begin to draw or write specific **Unité 6** vocabulary.
3. Because **Activité 20** is more open-ended than other **Activités**, you may want to review question formation and instruct students to use either **est-ce que** or inversion when forming questions. Remind students to use the formal when addressing an adult they don't know. Encourage them to extend the conversation if they wish. Make sure that students understand that the blue arrows require two-way communication and that the yellow-green arrows indicate the speaker.

# À vous la parole

## Communiquez!

How is shopping different in other countries?

**20 Au marché**   1.1

**Interpersonal Communication**

Role play a conversation between a customer and a vegetable or fruit vendor at the market. In the conversation:

Greet each other.

Ask each other how things are going.

Ask a question about the produce.

Respond.

Ask the price of three items.

Give prices.

Say what quantity you need.

Say how much the customer owes.

Thank the merchant.

Say good-bye.

**Special Needs Students**
**Linguistically Challenged**
You can facilitate **Activité 20** for students by playing the role of one of the characters, thus assuring that they have an appropriate stimulus for their rejoinder.

## Reference Desk

Remind students to use the **vous** for the conversation in **Activité 20** since it is not a personal relationship.

**Blended Instruction**
Consider using blended instruction, a combination of in-class learning and computer-mediated instruction or learning opportunities. Ask students to complete activities on the computer, or using their cell phone, smartphone, or other emerging electronic technology. This will allow students to hone their tech skills and become more independent learners. Schedule routine Internet and e-book learning in class and in the lab.

## Expansion

Place groups in different parts of the room and assign each the responsibility of a store with a display of items for sale and prices, such as **une pâtisserie, une boulangerie, une charcuterie, une crémerie, une épicerie** and **marchand de fruits et légumes**. During different rounds of the activity, one student from each group "shops" for one item from each store, noting the purchases on a piece of paper. Students must converse imitating the dialogue pattern of **Activité 20**. After all the rounds, students within each group tell each other what they have purchased and note a few items they did not purchase.

## Expansion

Students may return to their research of French supermarket websites (p. 299) such as **Carrefour**, **Auchan**, **Leclerc**, and **Intermarché**. Find out what food items may be ordered online and if there is home delivery service. Have them compare results with each other and compare with online supermarket shopping and delivery services in their communities.

### Communiquez!

**21** **Un sondage**  1.1, 2.1, 2.2

#### Interpersonal/Presentational Communication

Create a chart like the one below, listing three fruits and three vegetables that you like or dislike. Then ask ten students if they like each fruit or vegetable a lot (**beaucoup, +**), a little (**un peu, =**), or not at all (**ne... pas, -**). Note your classmates' responses in the chart, as indicated by the symbols in parentheses.

**MODÈLE**  A: **Est-ce que tu aimes les pommes?**
B: **Oui, j'aime beaucoup/un peu les pommes.**
ou
**Non, je n'aime pas les pommes.**

| Fruit/Légume | 1 | 2 | 3 | 4 | 5 | 6 | 7 | 8 | 9 | 10 |
|---|---|---|---|---|---|---|---|---|---|---|
| Pommes | + | + | - | = | + | - | = | - | = | + |
| Oranges | | | | | | | | | | |
| Fraises | | | | | | | | | | |

Write a summary of your five most interesting results and share it with your classmates.

**MODÈLE**  **Trois élèves aiment un peu les pommes. Quatre élèves aiment beaucoup les pommes. Trois élèves n'aiment pas les pommes.**

### Communiquez!

**22** **Au supermarché en ligne**  1.1

#### Interpretive Communication

Answer the following questions about the supermarket advertisement.

1. Quels sont deux fruits dans cette publicité que tu aimes beaucoup?
2. Quel est un fruit que tu n'aimes pas?
3. Ça coûte combien deux kilos de bananes?

### Essential Instruction

1. Tailor **Activité 21** to the number of students in your class (20 students = two groups with ten slots, 24 students = three groups with eight slots, 32 students = four groups with eight slots, etc.).
2. Use **Activité 22** to review the verbs **adorer**, **détester**, and **préférer**, numbers, and the metric system. Ask students to calculate the cost of a half kilo (**500gm, une livre, un demi-kilo**) of the fruits in the advertisement.
3. Before asking students to read **Rencontre avec l'auteur**, write the word **nouvelle** on the board

and ask them what it means. Explain that in this context the word is a noun. Have students silently read the biography, then answer the **pré-lecture** question.
4. Distribute the **Copy Master** of the grid on p. 327.
5. Ask students what they think the expression **Outils de lecture** means and point out the similarity in pronunciation with the English word "tools." Before students read and listen to the passage, have them brainstorm a list of word families.

# Lecture thématique

## Le fils du boulanger

### Rencontre avec l'auteur  1.2

**Maurice Pons** (1925– ) est un écrivain français dont l'œuvre a servi d'inspiration pour beaucoup de metteurs en scène et de chorégraphes. *Le fils du boulanger* est la première des onze nouvelles (*short stories*) qui composent le recueil (*collection*) *Douce Amère* (1985). Qu'est-ce que vous comptez (*plan*) lire dans une nouvelle qui s'appelle "Le fils du boulanger?"

## Pré-lecture  2.1, 2.2

Décrivez une visite réelle ou imaginaire à une boulangerie-pâtisserie. Qu'est-ce que vous voyez? Qu'est-ce que vous sentez (*smell*)?

## Stratégie de lecture  2.1

### Setting

The setting of a story is the time, place, and circumstances in which the action takes place. In this selection, the setting is revealed through descriptive details. Create a chart like the one below. Then, as you read, note what each adjective or noun tells you about the bakery where the story take place.

| Descriptions | Explication |
|---|---|
| 1. prospère | |
| 2. bien placée | |
| 3. régulière | |
| 4. cette initiative | |
| 5. un succès | |

## Outils de lecture  2.1, 2.2, 4.1

### Word Families

Sometimes a noun, a verb, an adjective, or another part of speech may share the same root. For example, the adjective **aimable** (*amicable*) and the nouns **amitié** (*friendship*) and **ami(e)** all share the root **ami-** from Latin. You know what **une boulangerie** is. What do you think **un boulanger** does for a living?

Leçon C | trois cent vingt-sept **327**

**Answers** _____

Pré-lecture
*Answers will vary.*

Stratégie de lecture
1. prospère/ It was *prosperous*, the business was working and making money.
2. bien placée/ It was a good location, well positioned at the center of the village to attract customers.
3. régulière/ It was *regular*, a habitual action, probably every day.
4. cette initiative/ This enterprise (from *initiate*), the start of producing meat pastries.
5. un succès/ This is a succesful enterprise.

### Reference Desk

Have students research and read Marcel Pagnol's 1938 play *La Femme du Boulanger*. You may be able to play excerpts from a film of this online. Compare with Maurice Pons' story *Le fils du Boulanger*.

---

**Differentiated Learning**
**Accelerate**
For **Activité 21**, assign more advanced students the role of group leader and ask them to summarize the results and share with the class.

**Learning Styles**
**Visual Learners**
To review the vocabulary in **Leçons B** and **C**, prepare a slide show with images of food items you find online.

## Culture

**Products: Activity**
Students will most certainly enjoy researching and learning about the famous Parisian bakery called **Poilâne**, its history and, of course, its world-renowned 4 lb. sourdough bread loaf. The original location is on the **rue du Cherche-Midi** in the Paris **6e arrondissement**. You may have a local importer of European foods that distributes this bread, or consider ordering a **boule** online for your class! Perhaps join with the school's cooking class or kitchen to bake some French bread.

 1.2, 2.1, 2.2, 4.2

Mon père était* boulanger et fils de boulanger. J'étais* gamin* quand il reprit à son compte* l'unique boulangerie de Saint-Gratien, dans la Creuse*. Je me souviens* de façon très précise de notre installation dans ce nouveau pays*, dans cette nouvelle maison, cette nouvelle boutique. (…)

La boulangerie de Saint-Gratien était une affaire* prospère. Elle était bien placée au centre du village et attirait* une clientèle régulière. Le dimanche, ma mère et sa vendeuse écoulaient* un nombre considérable de tartes et de pâtisseries.

Mon père avait vite remarqué que les jeunes ouvrières* de la fabrique,* pendant la pause de midi, plutôt que d'aller déjeuner à la cantine, se rendaient* en bande à la boulangerie pour acheter des pains au chocolat et des croissants. (…) Il décida d'engager un commis* et se mit à* faire des friands à la viande,* des croque-monsieurs au jambon et au fromage, et même des pizzas. Cette initiative, rarement entreprise à l'époque*, connu un succès considérable dans tout Saint-Gratien.

**Pendant la lecture**
1. Quelle est la profession du père du narrateur?

**Pendant la lecture**
2. Que vendent sa mère et son assistante le dimanche?

**Pendant la lecture**
3. Pour quelle raison le père du narrateur est-il un entrepreneur?

**était/étais** *was;* **gamin** *enfant;* **reprit à son compte** *bought back his business;* **la Creuse** *department in central France?;* **Je me souviens** *I remember;* **pays** *région;* **une affaire** *un business;* **attirait** *attracted;* **écoulaient** *moved;* **ouvrières** *personnes qui travaillent;* **la fabrique** *factory;* **se rendaient** *went;* **d'engager un commis** *to hire a helper;* **se mit à** *began;* **friands à la viande** *meat pies;* **à l'époque** *at that time*

## Post-lecture  2.1, 2.2

Est-ce que le narrateur aime vivre dans ce village et travailler dans cette boulangerie? Justifiez votre réponse.

## Le monde visuel  1.2, 4.2

Sabine Weiss (1924– ) est connue (*known*) pour ses photos en noir et blanc de la France après la deuxième Guerre Mondiale (*WWII*), une période difficile pour le pays économiquement, psychologiquement, et moralement. Elle fait partie des photographes humanistes qui aident la reconstruction de l'identité française. Ces photographes célèbrent et documentent les institutions et les événements ordinaires et habituels. Quel aspect de la vie de tous les jours et quelle institution française sont représentés sur cette photo?

*Enfant à la sortie de la boulangerie,* 1960. Sabine Weiss.

**3 2 8** trois cent vingt-huit | Unité 6

## Essential Learning

1. Before listening to the reading, review the glossed vocabulary. Then have students skim the passage for cognates as you write them on the board. Make sure the students understand the meaning of the English translation, for example **un entrepreneur**.

2. Review the guided reading questions together, listen to the passage, and discuss the answers.

3. Before reading the cartoon, explain the slang vocabulary **les mecs**, **les fringues**, **T'es radon**, and **c'est ingrat**. After the students read the cartoon silently, ask them to read the story aloud and discuss their opinions of the characters in small groups.

**23** **Activités d'expansion** **1.3, 4.1**

1. Écrivez une description du milieu (*setting*) de cette lecture, incorporant l'information de votre grille. La boulangérie représente une réussite (*success*)? Expliquez.
2. Commencez des phrases avec ces expressions pour faire un poème sur un endroit:
   - A. Je vois....
   - B. Je sens (*smell*)....
   - C. J'entends (*hear*)....
   - D. Je goûte (*taste*)....
   - E. Je pense (*think*)....

   Pensez à un titre. Ensuite, lisez votre poème à votre groupe.

3. Dessinez l'image d'une boulangerie-pâtisserie. Ou bien, imprimez des photos que vous trouvez en ligne et mettez des légendes (*captions*).

    **Search words: boulangerie patisserie bonneau paris**

## Les copains d'abord: Au marché de Saint-Ouen

**1.2**

Leçon C | trois cent vingt-neuf **329**

## Differentiated Learning
### Expand
After discussing the **Lecture thématique**, ask students to read the story aloud in small groups to practice pronunciation. Have them share any personal connections to the story (parents who work together, etc.). Suggest **Activité 23** for extra credit. Provide the students with a chart with the five senses (**le toucher, l'ouïe, l'odorat, la vue,** and **le goûter**) and have them find examples in the text that correlate to each sense.

## Multiple Intelligences
### Visual-Spatial
Students interested in photography might want to research the work of Sabine Weiss as well as other famous French photojournalists such as Robert Doisneau, Henri Cartier-Bresson, and Frank Capa, and others who worked for **Photo Magnum**.

## RESOURCES

 **Pre-test**

*Leçon* **Quiz**

**Answers** _____

**23**

*Answers will vary.* La boulangerie est placée au centre du village, elle attire des clients régulièrement. C'est un commerce prospère. C'est une réussite parce que le boulanger a pris une initiative, celle de faire des friands à la viande.

## Reference Desk

Have students research flea markets in Paris. Discuss any student experiences at a flea market and explore how to shop at a flea market.

## Les copains d'abord

Here is the translation for **Les copains d'abord**:
A = Antoine
F = Florence
MA = Marie-Alix
M = Mathéo
V = le vendeur (salesman)

M: OK girls, us guys are going to look for clothes. MA: All right, and we are going to buy food for the picnic. F: So, we already have bread, so, fruit and vegetables? MA: Yes, a head of lettuce, 500 grams of tomatoes, one melon. F: Let's go to the deli to get a bit of pâté. MA: And the dairy store to get some good cheese. M: I'm going to buy a pair of jeans for Florence. A: Oh, a present, nice! M: Good morning, sir, I am looking for a pair of Kaporal jeans. V: OK, that will be 60 euros. M: No, that's too much, 30 euros. V: All right, 40 euros. A: 39 euros for the jeans, last offer! M: You are stingy! A: You know, girls are so ungrateful, keep your money Mathéo. MA: Ah, we did well! F: Indeed, we have everything the boys like! MA: Our friends are so nice.

List of slang and idiomatic expressions:
**les mecs (m.):** *the guys;* **les fringues:** *clothes;* **radin:** *stingy;* **ingrat(e):** *ungrateful*

**329**

*T'es branché?*

# Projets finaux

**A** **Connexions par internet: Les finances personnelles**

 **1.1, 1.3, 2.1, 3.2**

Imagine you have saved 100 euros to throw a party. Follow these steps to plan your party.

- With a partner, make a list in French of beverages, snacks, and other items that you will need for the party.
- Research and compare prices for the items on your list at three French supermarket sites online to get the best deals.
- Create a document to show the results of your research.
- What did you purchase? Were you able to stay within your budget? Share your results with your partner.

 **Search words: carrefour shopping en ligne, mon supercasino, auchandirect**

**B** **Communautés en ligne**  **1.3, 3.2, 4.2**

**Un appartement à Paris**

Imagine your family has rented an apartment for a month in Paris. Your parents belong to one of the food movements below. Look for a blog and/or articles online to find out which stores sell foods that will meet your needs, which restaurants and cafés serve those foods, and which outdoor markets have them available.

**Search words: bio-organique** (organic), **végétalien** (vegan), **manger slow**, **le fooding**

Nous allons acheter la nourriture bio-organique à Vitalibio.

**Essential Learning**

1. Invite your students to choose **Activité A** or **B** in the **Projets finaux** section to accommodate their learning preferences, and then have them share with their groups.
2. Ask students if they remember how to say "taking stock" of something from previous units. Tell them that reflecting about their thinking (meta-cognition) is an important step in the learning process. Then have all students fill out the

chart in **Activité D** as a self-evaluation of their progress after this unit. Distribute copies of this graphic organizer which is located in the **Copy Masters** supplement.

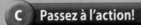 **C** **Passez à l'action!**   **1.1, 1.3, 3.2**

*Question centrale*
**?**
How is shopping different in other countries?

### Les marchés en France

In groups of three, research the following topics to find out more about markets in France. Each person in your group should research two topics.

- regional and seasonal specialties, such as different cheeses, herbs from the south of France, camembert from Normandy
- the history of French markets
- compare and contrast an American farmers' market with a **marché**
- compare and contrast a French supermarket with a **marché**
- what Rungis is and what you can buy there
- **les Halles** in Paris, yesterday and today

Share what you learn with the members of your group and create a presentation to share with the class. You might create a website, podcast, slide presentation, booklet, or use some other media for your presentation.

**D** **Faisons le point!**  **2.1, 2.2**

Your teacher will give you a chart like the one below. Fill it in with what you've learned about how shopping is different in other cultures.

| Je comprends | Je ne comprends pas encore | Mes connexions |
|---|---|---|
|  |  |  |

| | |
|---|---|
| What did I do well to learn and use the content of this unit? | What should I do in the next unit to better learn and use the content? |
| How can I effectively communicate to others what I have learned? | What was the most important information I learned in this unit? |

**Answers** _____

**A** Script can be found in the front pages of the Annotated Teacher's Edition.

one kilo of tomatoes, two kilos of zucchini, two cucumbers, 500 grams of peas, 500 grams of mushrooms

**B** *Dialogues will vary.*

**C** *Research and findings will vary.*

## Expansion

Locate the **rues commerçantes** of Paris (**rue Cler, rue Mouffetard, rue Montorgueil,** etc.). In which areas are they located? Show pictures. Discuss their attractions. Have students research and learn about the old market at **Les Halles** and what kind of shopping place it has become.

---

# Évaluation

### A   Évaluation de compréhension auditive   2.1, 2.2

Jean-Luc and Christian are going to the market in a village while on vacation. Make a list in English of what they buy.

### B   Évaluation orale

*Tu as besoin de chaussures?*

*Oui, allons au magasin de chaussures.*

You and a friend are talking about what you plan to buy on **la rue commerçante** today. You will each make three stops. In your conversation, state what you need and where you are going to buy it. For clothing include colors and for grocery items include quantities.

1.1, 2.2

### C   Évaluation culturelle   1.3, 2.1, 2.2, 3.1, 3.2, 4.2

In this activity, you will compare francophone cultures with American culture. You may need to complete additional research about American culture.

1. **On fait du shopping.**
   Where do you and your friends typically buy clothes? Where else can you buy clothes in France and the United States other than at the stores themselves?
2. **Les essentiels**
   How does France's "little black dress" compare with American jeans? In what ways are they used similarly? In what ways are they used differently?
3. **Les vêtements en Afrique**
   What does West Africa's traditional style of dress reveal about Western influences on the culture regarding clothing? In what ways would you expect West African clothing to be different from what people wear in France and the United States?
4. **L'exportation de l'alimentation**
   The French export many food products, such as cheese. What packaged foods does the United States export?
5. **On fait les courses.**
   Where do people in France and North Africa traditionally prefer to buy fresh food? Where do you and your family grocery shop? Are there any outdoor markets in your area? If so, what are some local specialties you would find there?
6. **Le mouvement** *slow food*
   What kinds of food should people buy, according to the slow food movement? Does the United States have a slow food movement? Are both France and the United States trying to maintain food traditions, or start new ones?

## Essential Learning

1. Discuss any errors students make in doing listening **Activité A**.
2. Have students do **Activité B** with a partner of their choice and present the conversation to the class. Consider awarding extra points to students who memorize the dialogue.
3. Ask students to choose a topic from **Activité C** to research. To prepare the presentation, divide students into groups so that all topics are represented. Ask students to share their research with the group.
4. Have students prepare **Activité D** and **E** at home, then share with the entire class.
5. Consider having students use the storyboard in **Activité F** as a means of assessment for the **unité**.

In France, people prefer to shop in small boutiques along **la rue commerçante**.

7. **Les mesures métriques**
Explain the differences between how most francophone nations measure weight and volume, and compare it to the system used in the United States. Make a list of products you buy on a weekly basis with the metric weight or volume you would need in francophone countries.

8. **Les marchés francophones**
Look at photos of French markets and North African *souks* online. How do they compare? How different are these markets from your shopping experience? In which places would you need to learn to negotiate the price? Would that be a new experience for you? How comfortable or uncomfortable would you be bargaining?

**D** **Évaluation écrite**  **1.3**

Write your family's grocery list (**liste d'achats**) for the week in French. Be sure to include appropriate quantities.

**E** **Évaluation visuelle**  **2.1, 2.2**

Use your answers to the questions below to write a paragraph about the fashion show (**le défilé de mode**) in the illustration.

1. On est où?
2. C'est le défilé de mode de qui?
3. Que porte la première femme?
4. Que porte la deuxième femme?
5. Que porte la troisième femme?

**F** **Évaluation compréhensive**  **1.3**

Create a storyboard with six frames. Write captions for each frame, telling about your shopping day on **la rue commerçante**. Share your story with a group of classmates.

**E**
1. *Answers will vary.*
2. *Answers will vary.*
3. Elle porte une longue jupe rouge et une chemise grise.
4. Elle porte un ensemble jaune: un pantalon jaune et une veste jaune, et une chemise blanche.
5. Elle porte une robe violette.

**F** *Stories will vary.*

### Expansion

Have students research French fashion shows and select **couturiers** whose presentations they wish to describe. When and where are these fashion shows held? Which **couturiers** do your students favor?

## Differentiated Learning
### Accelerate
Suggest that students do **Activité F** and present their work to the class. Then post the storyboards in class.

### Special Needs Students
**AD(H)D**
Provide students with more structure and step-by-step guidelines to use when doing the **Évaluation**. Time permitting, work individually with students or write additional instructions for them to follow.

## Game

### Pictionary
Write each word from the list of vocabulary on a separate piece of paper and put them in an envelope. Divide the class into two teams. Teams take turns having one student select a word and create a drawing on the board while the other team members try to guess the word. Explain the rules of not using letters, numbers, or oral cues. Alternate teams. Vary the activity by having a student from each team come to the board. Award one point for a correct guess.

# Vocabulaire de l'Unité 6  1.2

un **achat** purchase *B*
l' **air (m.)** air *C*
**aller: Tu trouves que… me va bien?** Does this… look good on me? *A*; **Vas-y!** Go for it! *A*
**assez (de)** enough (of) *B*
**autrement** otherwise *A*
une **baguette** long thin loaf of bread *B*
**beaucoup de** a lot of *B*
le **beurre** butter *B*
un **billet** bill (money) *C*
le **bœuf** beef *B*
une **boîte de** a can of *B*
**bon marché** cheap *A*
la **boucherie** butcher shop *B*
la **boulangerie** bakery *B*
une **bouteille (de)** bottle (of) *B*
une **boutique** shop *A*
la **cabine: cabine d'essayage** dressing room *A*
le **camembert** camembert cheese *B*
**ce, cet, cette; ces** this, that, these, those *A*
la **charcuterie** delicatessen *B*
**chercher** to look for *A*
**chic** chic *A*
**combien: C'est combien le kilo?** How much per kilo? *C*
**commerçant(e)** shopping, business *A*
une **couleur** color *A*; **De quelle(s) couleur(s)?** In what color(s)? *A*
le **couscous** couscous *B*
une **crémerie** dairy store *B*
un **croissant** croissant *B*
**d'abord** first of all *B*
**en: en ligne** online *A*
un **ensemble** outfit *A*
**ensuite** next *A*
une **épicerie** grocery store *B*
**essayer** to try (on) *A*
**faire: faire les courses** to go grocery shopping *B*
**fait: Ça fait combien?** How much is it? *C*
**faites: Quelle taille faites-vous?** What size do you wear? *A*
**frais, fraîche** fresh *B*
un **fruit** fruit *C*
un **gramme (de)** gram (of) *B*
**gros, grosse** big, fat, large *C*
**joli(e)** pretty *A*
le **ketchup** ketchup *B*
un **kilo (de)** a kilogram (of) *B*
le **lait** milk *B*
un **légume** vegetable *B*

**ligne: en ligne** online *A*
un **litre (de)** a liter (of) *B*
une **livre** pound *C*
un **mannequin** model *A*
un(e) **marchand(e)** merchant *C*
le **marché** outdoor market *C*; **marché aux puces** flea market *A*
la **mayonnaise** mayo *B*
**même** same *C*
**moche** ugly *A*
un **morceau (de)** a piece (of) *B*
la **moutarde** mustard *B*
**mûr(e)** ripe *C*
**niçoise: la salade niçoise** tuna salad *C*
un **œuf** egg *B*
une **olive** olive *C*
le **pain** bread *B*
un **paquet (de)** a packet (of) *B*
le **pâté** pâté *B*
la **pâtisserie** bakery/pastry shop *B*
**peu: un peu (de)** a little (of) *B*
**peux: Je peux vous aider?** May I help you? *A*
le **porc** pork *B*
un **pot (de)** a jar (of) *B*
le **poulet** chicken *B*
**prêt(e)** ready *B*
la **rue** street *A*
le **saucisson** salami *B*
**sort: sortir** to come out *A*
la **soupe** soup *B*
le **supermarché** supermarket *B*
la **taille: Quelle taille faites-vous?** What size are you? *A*
**tant pis** too bad *C*
une **tarte**: pie *B*; **tarte aux fruits** fruit pie *B*; **tarte aux pommes** apple pie *B*
le **thon** tuna *C*
**Tiens!** Hey! *B*
**tous** all *B*; **toutes** all *C*
une **tranche (de)** a slice (of) *B*
**trop (de)** too much (of) *B*
**trouver** to find *A*
un **vendeur, une vendeuse** salesperson *A*
**vendre** to sell *B*
des **vêtements (m.)** clothes *A*
**vouloir** to want *A*
le **yaourt** yogurt *B*

Clothing… see p. 276
Colors… see p. 277
Fruits and vegetables… see p. 310

## Listening   1.2, 2.1, 2.2

I. You will hear a short conversation. Select the reply that would come next. You will hear the conversation twice.

1. A. C'est quatre euros le kilo.
   B. J'ai besoin de quatre tranches.
   C. C'est mon supermarché là, devant le cinéma.
   D. Je voudrais une jupe blanche en 38.

II. Listen to the conversation. Select the best completion to each statement that follows.

1. Marion cherche....
   A. Céline
   B. une pâtisserie
   C. un centre commercial
   D. un vêtement noir pour samedi

2. Céline n'aime pas....
   A. le noir
   B. le blanc et le rose
   C. Mademoiselle Lecourt
   D. les robes

3. Céline veut d'abord....
   A. acheter une robe noire
   B. aller à la pâtisserie
   C. manger
   D. faire les devoirs

## Reading 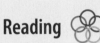 1.2, 2.1, 2.2

III. Read the letter that Alexis, a Canadian studying at a French university, writes to her parents describing what she likes about life in France. Then select the best completion to each statement.

Chers papa et maman,

Voilà, je suis à Lyon! J'adore la France! J'aime l'université de Lyon et j'aime beaucoup parler français. Les weekends en France sont super. Le vendredi, je cherche souvent des CD à la médiathèque. La musique française et la musique algérienne sont géniales. Le samedi, je vais à la boulangerie chercher des croissants et du pain. Ils sont fantastiques à huit heures du matin. Ensuite, je vais au café avec ma baguette et mes deux crois-sants. Je prends un jus d'orange et je mange mes croissants. Au café, j'adore lire mon magazine, regarder et aussi écouter les Français parler. À dix heures, je vais au marché. Je n'aime pas faire mes courses au supermarché. Je préfère le marché parce que les fruits et les légumes sont frais. À midi, mes copains et moi, on se retrouve au restaurant. Enfin, à deux heures, on va au cinéma regarder un film américain ou un film français. Après le film, j'achète souvent de petits gâteaux à la pâtisserie derrière le cinéma, et je mange mon dessert à la maison devant la télé. J'adore la France!

Et vous, ça va à Montréal?

Bises,
Alexis

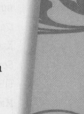

Answers _____

 Script can be found in the front pages of the Annotated Teacher's Edition.

1. A

II
1. D
2. A
3. B

III
1. B
2. A
3. D

**IV**

1. shopping
2. de
3. vais/dois
4. légumes
5. à
6. vous
7. kilo
8. Ensuite/puis
9. Les
10. mûres
11. combien
12. cher
13. va
14. cherchons
15. est
16. veut
17. regardent
18. sont
19. a
20. est
21. voulons

**V** *Compositions will vary*

**VI** *Dialogues will vary.*

---

### Reference Desk

1. Remind students to use adjectives and adverbs to add details to their composition. Also, ask them to vary the subjects of their sentences so they can practice conjugating verbs.
2. Remind students to use the **vous** form in a formal setting.

---

1. Alexis est....
   A. avec ses parents
   B. à Lyon
   C. dans une université américaine
   D. à Los Angeles

2. Le samedi matin Alexis mange....
   A. à la boulangerie
   B. au café
   C. au restaurant

3. Alexis aime....
   A. la musique française
   B. le pain et les gâteaux français
   C. les films français
   D. A, B, et C

## Writing  2.1, 2.2

IV. Complete this conversation at Carrefour with appropriate words or expressions.

Maxime:       On va faire du __1__ , maman? J'ai besoin __2__ vêtements pour l'école.
Maman:        Et moi, je __3__ acheter des fruits et des __4__ d'abord. Ensuite on va __5__ Carrefour.
Le vendeur: Je peux __6__ aider, Madame?
Maman:        Je prends un __7__ de tomates. __8__ , je prends des bananes.
Le vendeur: Madame, c'est l'été! __9__ pêches sont très __10__ et délicieuses!
Maman:        C'est __11__ la livre?
Le vendeur: Un euro cinquante. Ce n'est pas __12__ !

Complete the paragraph with the correct form of the verbs.

Quand on __13__ au marché aux puces,          13. (aller)

nous __14__ des vêtements.                          14. (chercher)

C'est amusant quand on __15__ ensemble.       15. (être)

Xavier __16__ des tennis noires.                     16. (vouloir)

Sophie et Sarah __17__ les robes.                   17. (regarder)

Elles __18__ top!                                         18. (être)

Maxime __19__ besoin de jeans.                     19. (avoir)

Le vendeur __20__ sympa.                              20. (être)

Nous __21__ essayer les vêtements et les chaussures!   21. (vouloir)

## Composition  1.3

V. It's your birthday, and you are at a restaurant with family and friends celebrating. Write a paragraph describing the celebration. In your paragraph:

- tell which family members are there.
- state the names and ages of your friends.
- describe the clothes you are wearing.
- tell what you are having to eat.
- tell what people are giving you.

## Speaking   1.1

VI. Étienne and Salim are buying a shirt to give to their friend Abdoulaye for his birthday. In groups of three, play the roles of Étienne, Salim, and the saleswoman.

# Unité 7

## À la maison

*Rendez-vous à Nice!*

**Épisode 7:**

*Changement de cœur*

Go online
**EMC**Languages.net

1. As students study the photo, discuss their observations. Compare the houses and setting of this modern subdivision with dwellings in students' neighborhoods or near the school. What differences are there in style and design, architectural elements, size, building materials, spacing, etc.? Would this image be on the cover of an American architectural or **décor** magazine? Show magazine cover samples to the class and discuss.

2. What does it mean to be king in one's house? How does (do) the occupant(s) of a house express individuality, even when at first glance a house looks similar to the neighboring ones?

3. How important is a garden or a yard or other personal outdoor space to people in different cultures? Have students find images of houses in Belgium, Switzerland, French Canada, Monaco, and North Africa. Post the images on the board and discuss.

# Citation

"Chacun est roi en sa maison."

Everyone is a king in his own house.

—Proverbe français

## À savoir

Three out of four Fren people have a garden terrace.

## Essential Instruction

1. Read the **Citation** to the class and ask students if they agree with the quote. Is this value uniquely French or do Americans share it? Ask students to find a similar saying in English, or another idiom related to the home, such as "A man's home is his castle" or "There's no place like home."

2. Explore what the students will learn in **Unité 7** by going through the **Contrat de l'élève**.

3. Show the relevant video clip from *Rendez-vous à Nice!*, Episode 7, and discuss the related question as a class.

4. Briefly discuss the **Question centrale** and the difference between the connotation (the associated meaning) and the denotation (the explicit or direct meaning) of words.

# À la maison

**Answers**

The answer to the video question is B.

## Question centrale

### What makes a house a "home"?

Go online
**EMCLanguages.net**

**What is Patrick showing Charlotte?**
A. a secret that Jean-Charles has been hiding
B. a poster
C. an award from a contest in English

In what city is this port located?

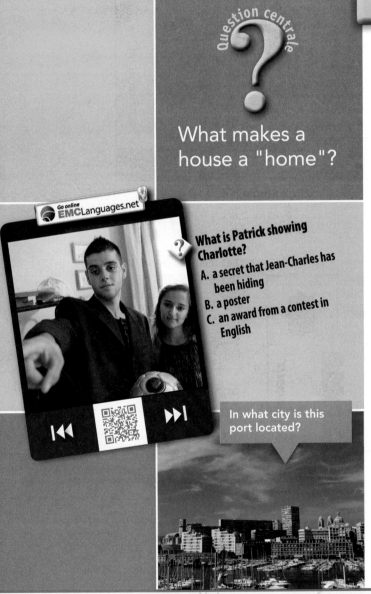

## Contrat de l'élève

### Leçon A  I will be able to:

>> give a tour of my home and ask where someone lives.

>> talk about housing in France and **le Maghreb** and share facts about Algeria.

>> use ordinal numbers.

### Leçon B  I will be able to:

>> give directions in the kitchen.

>> talk about Marseille and Provence.

>> use the verbs **devoir** and **mettre** in the present tense and make comparisons with adjectives.

### Leçon C  I will be able to:

>> talk about the computer and say I don't understand something.

>> talk about technology that young French people use, the province of New Brunswick in Canada, and the singer Natasha St-Pier.

>> use the verb **pouvoir** in the present tense.

trois cent trente-neuf **3 3 9**

## Reference Desk

1. **Leçon A:** Explain that the numbers one, two, three, etc. are called cardinal numbers. Cardinal comes from the Latin **cardinalis**, or principal, chief, essential. The ordinal (L. **ordinalis**, showing order) numbers depend on the cardinal numbers, hence the name. In French, cardinal and ordinal numbers are called **les nombres cardinaux et ordinaux**.
2. **Leçon B:** Explain that students will learn how to say "have to" (**devoir**) do something and how to compare things.
3. **Leçon C:** Explain to students that they will learn the irregular verb **pouvoir** and be able to express that someone can or is able to do something.

## Connections

**Geography**
The students will learn about the port in the photo in the **Points de départ** of **Leçon A.** You may wish to make a photo display of different ports in France, North Africa, and New Brunswick, the three locations featured in the unit. France has numerous ports, for example Calais, Saint-Malo, Brest, Bordeaux, Marseille, and Sète. The Maghreb countries of Morocco, Algeria, and Tunisia have dozens of commercial and fishing ports of all sizes. New Brunswick is home to the major commercial port of Saint Jean. Compare ports in these locations with other European ports such as Monte Carlo (Monaco), Rotterdam (Holland), and some in North America, for example, Montreal, New York, New Orleans, and Houston.

## Reference Desk

1. The first or ground floor is the **rez-de-chaussée** in French, whereas a French first floor (**premier étage**) is the equivalent of the American second floor.
2. Discuss the layout of the rooms in the illustration. Note that the bath and toilet are separate rooms. (See **Points de départ** on p. 346.)
3. The word **salle** (**la salle de classe**) is reserved for rooms with a public function, but **chambre** means bedroom.
4. Other useful vocabulary: **un appartement de grand standing** (penthouse); **un ascenseur** (elevator); **une maison individuelle** (single-family home); **une tour** (high rise).
5. **Jardin** is French for garden and yard.

## Communication

**Interpersonal: Cooperative Groups**

Have groups ask each other true/false questions about the **Vocabulaire actif**, for example, **Cet immeuble a cinq étages.** (**Faux. Il a huit étages.**) **Le rez-de-chaussée est au premier étage.** (**Faux. Il est au R-de-C.**)

## Game

**C'est quelle pièce?**
Have students identify rooms from your cues. For example, **C'est la pièce où vous allez dormir.** (**la chambre**)

Leçon A

# Vocabulaire actif

## La maison   1.2

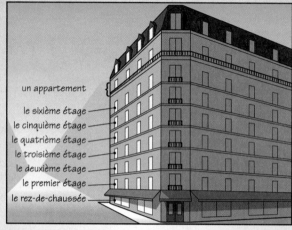

un appartement
le sixième étage
le cinquième étage
le quatrième étage
le troisième étage
le deuxième étage
le premier étage
le rez-de-chaussée

un immeuble

**Les pièces (f.):**

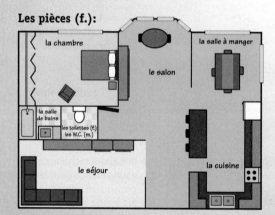

la chambre
la salle à manger
le salon
la salle de bains
les toilettes (f.)
les W.C. (m.)
le séjour
la cuisine

**Les meubles (m.):**

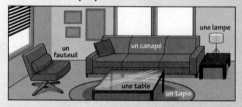

une lampe
un fauteuil
un canapé
une table
un tapis

un micro-onde
un placard
un frigo
une cuisinière
un évier
un four

## Essential Instruction

1. Explain the root meaning of the word **immeuble** (something that cannot be moved) vs. **meuble** (something that can be moved) to anchor the concept of buildings and furniture.
2. Compare the way floors in a building are counted in francophone countries and the United States. Ask if students see a relationship between **rez-de-chaussée** and the words **chaussettes** and **chaussures**. Suggest that this will help them remember the expression for the ground floor.
3. Do **Pour la conversation** with the audio.

# Pour la conversation

How can I give a tour of my house or apartment?

> **Là, c'est** le séjour où nous regardons des DVD.
>
> *That's the family room where we watch DVDs.*

> **À côté, c'est** la salle à manger où nous dînons ce soir.
>
> *Next to it is the dining room where we'll dine tonight.*

> **Au fond du couloir, c'est** ma chambre.
>
> *At the end of the hallway is my bedroom.*

How do I ask where someone lives?

> **Où est-ce que tu habites?**
>
> *Where do you live?*

How do I agree and disagree?

> **Je pense que** oui.
>
> *I think so.*

> **Je pense que** non.
>
> *I don't think so.*

### Et si je voulais dire...?

| | |
|---|---|
| **la banlieue** | *suburb* |
| **une cafetière** | *coffee maker* |
| **un congélateur** | *freezer* |
| **une cuisine aménagée** | *equipped kitchen* |
| **un grille-pain** | *toaster* |
| **un jardin** | *garden* |
| **une maison de campagne** | *country house* |
| **un mixeur** | *blender* |

---

### 1 · Les maisons des Roux  2.1, 2.2

*Les Roux ont déménagé (moved) avec chaque promotion de M. Roux. Choisissez la légende (caption) qui correspond à chaque photo.*

1.

2.

3.

A. leur deuxième maison
B. leur première maison
C. leur troisième maison

**Answers** _____

**1** *Answers will vary.*

1. A
2. C
3. B

## Communication

**Presentational: Paired Practice**

Ask students to bring in a picture of a house to describe. Students take turns describing their home while the partner draws it. Once they've finished, they verify the accuracy of their partner's illustration compared to the photos.

## Expansion

1. Brainstorm different types of housing such as an apartment, a houseboat, a small cottage in the country, a Parisian apartment, the White House, a château, a ranch, etc. Have students imagine what three of their future homes will be like. Assign research of different types of residences, and ask students to bring in three photos or draw pictures that they label with **ma première maison**, **ma deuxième maison**, etc. Students can present their dream homes in groups.

2. Use students' pictures of dream rooms or houses, or images gathered from house and **décor** magazines. Show one picture at a time to the class and say a statement about the picture such as, **Il y a un canapé jaune dans le salon.** Or **Le garage est à droite de/derrière le jardin,** etc. Students must decide if the statement is **vrai** or **faux**.

---

## Differentiated Learning

### Decelerate

Ask students to find cognates. Remind them that there is approximately a thirty percent lexical overlap between French and English.

### Accelerate

Using the vocabulary in **Et si je voulais dire...?** have students write original sentences or prepare original dialogues using some of the expressions.

## Multiple Intelligences

### Visual-Spatial

Ask students to draw a floor plan of their own home or find a floor plan in a magazine or on the Internet and label it with the vocabulary. Have students share their pictures in small groups and present what items are found in which rooms.

# Answers

## ❷

1. Le frigo va dans la cuisine.
2. La télé va dans le séjour.
3. La table va dans la salle à manger.
4. La chaise va dans la salle à manger ou dans la cuisine.
5. Le four va dans la cuisine.
6. Le bureau va dans la bureau.
7. L'ordinateur va dans la bureau ou dans la salle de séjour.
8. Le fauteuil va dans le séjour.
9. Le micro-onde va dans la cuisine.
10. Le canapé va dans le séjour.
11. Le tapis va dans le séjour.

## Reference Desk

1. The **nous** form of **déménager** (-**eons**) is similar to the verbs **manger, changer, nager**.
2. Students can expand their vocabulary by learning words related to **déménager**, such as **un ménage, emménager**, and **une femme de ménage**. As for **déménager**, have them think of **ménage** as a household. Add the prefix **dé-** and you are literally un-doing or dismantling (moving) the household.

## TPR

Have students cut out images of home furnishings and furniture from magazines. Prepare large and varied house floor plans and make copies. Additionally, have each student draw a house floor plan on a large sheet of paper. First, students will "furnish" their houses using the magazine pictures. Then distribute a new floor plan and have students "move" houses and arrange the furnishings in the new home. Students can compare their homes and furnishings with each other.

---

## 2 Nous déménageons! 🎧 ✿ 2.1, 2.2

*Dites dans quelle pièce va le meuble* (piece of furniture) *ou l'appareil électroménager* (appliance).

**MODÈLE** la lampe
**La lampe va dans la chambre.**

la chambre   la cuisine   la salle à manger   le séjour   le bureau

1.
2.
3.
4.
5.
6.
7.
8.
9.
10.
11.

---

## Essential Instruction

1. Ask students to work on **Activité 2** in pairs.
2. Once pairs complete **Activité 3**, have them share with the class what they learned about each other.
3. Before students do **Activité 4**, clarify that **frigo** is an abbreviation for **réfrigérateur**. Ask students if they know what **canapé** means (a type of appetizer or **hors d'œuvre**). Explain that it is a **faux ami**. In English, a **canapé** is a type of appetizer or **hors d'œuvre**, but in French **un canapé** is a sofa. Provide additional vocabulary such as **un canapé-lit** or **un canapé clic clac** (sofa bed).
4. For more writing practice, ask students to write out the answers for **Activité 4**.

# Communiquez!

## 3 Dans quelle pièce?

**Interpersonal Communication**

*À tour de rôle, demandez à votre partenaire dans quelle pièce il ou elle aime faire les activités suivantes.*

**MODÈLE**   écouter de la musique
> **A: Dans quelle pièce est-ce que tu aimes écouter de la musique?**
> **B: J'aime écouter de la musique dans ma chambre.**

> Dans quelle pièce est-ce que tu aimes lire?
>
> Dans le salon.

1. dormir
2. manger
3. étudier
4. regarder la télé
5. téléphoner
6. voir un film
7. surfer sur Internet
8. lire
9. envoyer des textos
10. jouer aux jeux vidéo

## 4 Complétez!    2.1, 2.2

*Choisissez le mot logique qui complète chaque phrase.*

> lampe   pièces   cuisine   canapé   séjour
> immeuble   frigo   tapis

1. L'appartement des Moreau est dans un… à Marseille.
2. Il y a six… dans l'appartement.
3. Dans le salon, il y a un… et deux fauteuils.
4. Sur la table il y a une lampe rouge; sous la table, il y a un… Algérien qui est rouge aussi.
5. Dans la…, un micro-ondes est sous le placard.
6. On regarde la télé dans le….
7. Pour faire ses devoirs, Maxime a un bureau et une… sur le bureau.
8. M. Moreau est en retard et va manger; sa salade est dans le….

**Answers** _____

**3** *Dialogues will vary.*

**4**
1. immeuble
2. pièces
3. canapé
4. tapis
5. cuisine
6. séjour (la salle de séjour)
7. lampe
8. frigo

### TPR

Make copies of a blank **Loto** (*Bingo*) template for all students and ask them to draw items from the **Vocabulaire actif** randomly in the squares. Call out vocabulary until someone has completed a row. To win, a student must show you his or her game board.

### Expansion

Have students search interior design or home decor magazines or websites, perhaps from a francophone country (Switzerland, Canada, Tahiti, or Morocco, for example) or particular regions in France. Have students select an image of a room they like and write a description of all the items pictured in the room. Students should then show and describe their picture to the class without looking at their written descriptions. Post the images and descriptions on the wall and have students vote on their favorites.

## Differentiated Learning
### Accelerate
Create some sentences incorporating vocabulary from previous units with these new expressions (**un micro-onde**, for example) from **Unité 3, Les endroits: On trouve dans la cantine du lycée, des fauteuils à la piscine municipale**, etc. Have students identify them as **logique** or **illogique**.

## Learning Styles
### Visual Learners
Have students create a picture that illustrates the family apartment described in **Activité 4**.

## Special Needs Students
### Linguistically Challenged
For **Activité 2**, have students draw an imaginary line from the item to the room in which it is usually found. Then have them say and spell (in French) the vocabulary words in this activity.

**Answers** _____

**5**

Sabrina a besoin d'acheter deux lampes, un canapé, un micro-ondes, et trois chaises.

**6**

Script can be found in the front pages of the Annotated Teacher's Edition.

1. I
2. L
3. L
4. I
5. L
6. I
7. I

**7** *Answers will vary.*

**8** *Answers will vary.*

## Game

**Ça rime**
Play a rhyming game with students. Say a vocabulary word from this unit and ask students to call out words that rhyme. For example, if you say **salle de bains**, students might say **faim, demain, copain**, etc.

---

**5** **L'appartement de Sabrina**  **1.2, 2.1, 2.2**

*Sabrina a besoin de meubles pour son nouvel appartement et demande de l'aide à sa grand-mère. Lisez sa liste et la réponse à son e-mail. Ensuite, répondez à la question.*

3 lampes
1 canapé
1 micro-ondes
4 chaises
1 tapis
1 table de nuit

À: Sabrina
Cc:
Sujet: Je peux t'aider.

Ma chère Sabrina,

Je regarde ta liste. Je peux te donner la table de nuit de ta mère quand elle était (*was*) petite, un tapis rouge algérien, une chaise bleue, et une jolie lampe jaune pour ton salon. Je sais que ça coûte cher d'acheter des meubles pour un appartement. C'est pourquoi je t'envoie ce chèque pour 100 euros. Envoie-moi une photo de ton premier appartement!

Je t'embrasse,
Mémé

*Enfin, qu'est-ce que Sabrina a besoin d'acheter?*

---

**6** **Chez moi!**  **2.1, 2.2**

*Écrivez **L** si la description de la maison est **logique** ou **I** si la description est **illogique**.*

**7** **La maison de mes rêves**  **2.1**

*Votre famille achète la maison de vos rêves. De quoi est-ce que vous avez besoin pour chaque pièce? Faites un dessin de la maison et écrivez le nom des pièces, des meubles, et des appareils électroménagers.*

---

**8** **Questions personnelles**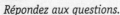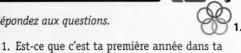

*Répondez aux questions.* **1.1**

Il n'y a pas de télé dans ma chambre.

1. Est-ce que c'est ta première année dans ta maison ou ton appartement?
2. Est-ce qu'il y a une télé dans ta chambre?
3. Dans quelle pièce est-ce que tu aimes faire tes devoirs?
4. Où est-ce que tu manges?
5. De quelle couleur est ton frigo?
6. Où est-ce que ta famille regarde la télé?

**3 4 4** trois cent quarante-quatre | Unité 7

---

## Essential Instruction

1. Set the stage for **Activité 5** by asking students if they have ever asked their grandparents or other relatives to help them with a personal project. Have pairs or small groups answer the question **Enfin, qu'est-ce que Sabrina a besoin d'acheter?**

2. For **Activité 7**, consider having students use an online drawing tool to create their dream homes. Ask students to vote on the best design.

3. Show the filmed dialogue and discuss the questions in **Activité 9** together. Ask students, **"Comment dit-on…?"** followed by questions in English such as, "It kind of feels like home/ the old country," "What does it smell like?", etc. to guide them to discover the meanings of the French sentences. Finally, show the filmed dialogue a second time.

# Rencontres culturelles

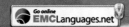

## Une invitée

 1.2

Camille arrive chez Yasmine, où elle va passer la nuit, et elles parlent dans le salon.

Camille: Oh, tu habites près du parc? Quelle belle vue!

Yasmine: Oui, nous sommes au septième étage. On voit tout—le parc, les magasins, la mosquée.

Camille: C'est beau cette pièce! C'est le séjour?

Yasmine: Oui. Ça a un petit air du pays, n'est-ce pas?

Camille: Je pense que oui. J'aime les tapis!

Yasmine: Ce sont des tapis berbères… ils viennent de Kabylie, le pays de mes grands-parents. Regarde, c'est une photo de leur riad.

Camille: Charmant! Les meubles, les lampes, les coussins, ils viennent aussi de là?

Yasmine: Il y a des meubles de mes grands-parents, une lampe aussi. Les autres lampes, les tissus, on peut tout trouver ici….

Camille: Et ça sent quoi?

Yasmine: Ah ça, c'est du jasmin. À droite, c'est la salle à manger où nous dînons avec ma famille ce soir. Là, au fond du couloir, c'est ma chambre.

Camille: Où sont les toilettes?

Yasmine: À gauche de ma chambre.

Camille: J'arrive dans cinq minutes!

### 9 Une invitée

2.1

*Complétez la phrase.*

1. … invite son amie à passer la nuit.
2. Yasmine et sa famille ont une vue du….
3. On va dîner avec….
4. Les tapis de la maison viennent de….
5. En Kabylie, c'est possible d'habiter dans un… comme les grands-parents de Yasmine.
6. Ça sent le….
7. Camille a besoin de….

### Extension   Les futurs colocataires 1.2, 2.1

Deux étudiants, qui veulent louer un appartement, parlent à l'agent immobilier. (*Two college students who want to rent an apartment speak to a real estate agent.*)

L'agent: Entrez. Alors vous voyez, c'est un deux pièces classique; il est refait à neuf. C'est ce que vous cherchez?

Alexandre: Euh oui… un grand séjour à tout faire et une chambre.

L'agent: À tout faire?

Julie: Oui, on va mettre deux bureaux face à face devant la fenêtre et ici une table pour déjeuner.

Alexandre: Il y a une prise internet?

L'agent: L'immeuble est câblé: vous n'avez qu'à choisir l'opérateur.

Julie: Contre ce mur la bibliothèque et au milieu, le canapé.

Alexandre: On peut accrocher la télé au mur?

L'agent: Commençons par votre dossier. Il est complet?

### Extension   Alexandre et Julie sont-ils sûrs d'avoir cet appartement? Justifiez votre réponse.

## RESOURCES

 **Dialogue Video**

Answers _____

**9**
1. Yasmine
2. septième étage
3. la famille de Yasmine
4. Kabylie
5. riad
6. le jasmin
7. toilettes

### Extension

*Answers will vary.*

## Reference Desk

Students might enjoy knowing the word **un appart** as a short version for **appartement**. Teach students how to say their address in French: **J'habite** (house number) **rue** (street number) **à** (city).

## Communication

**Interpersonal: Paired Practice**

Have pairs compare their **maisons de rêve** using the drawings they made for **Activité 7**. Remind students to use expressions such as, **Moi, je préfère…, Ah, non, j'aime mieux…, J'adore, Il y a…,** etc. Have students ask classmates where the rooms are in relation to each other and how they are furnished.

## Differentiated Learning
### Adapt/Decelerate
Assign **Activité 7** as homework. It is a suitable writing activity for students to prepare as homework. Alternatively, you could limit the scope of this assignment to just one room of their choice.

### Accelerate
Use the **Extension** dialogue as supplemental work for the more advanced students. Ask them to answer the **Extension** question that requires higher level critical thinking skills.

## Learning Styles
### Visual Learners
Find and project a map of Algeria and of the Maghreb, and pictures of the Kabyle people (a branch of Berber people living in northeast Algeria and Tunisia), Berber rugs, a mosque, and jasmine. Use the pictures to help students visualize the context of the dialogue. Alternatively, ask students to find these images and post them to the class website for review.

### Reference Desk

1. Instruct pairs to peruse the readings in **Points de départ** for unfamiliar words and to try to figure out their meaning in context.
2. Underscore the importance in meaning between the singular form vs. the plural of **la toilette** (as in **faire sa toilette**) and **les toilettes**. In French, **on va aux toilettes** is plural, whereas in Belgium and Quebec, one often hears **On va à la toilette**. Ask students the meaning and origin of **W.C.** (*water closet*). Note that it, too, is a plural noun in French!

### Game

**Dans ma maison**
Have each student draw a picture of a household furnishing item (toilet, sink, night table, etc.) on one side of a piece of paper and write the name of the item on the other. One student begins the game by holding up his or her picture for the rest of the circle to see and says **"Dans ma maison, il y a …,"** finishing the sentence with the item in the drawing. The next student holds up his or her picture and repeats the sentence the first student said and adds his or her own item to the list. Students continue showing their drawings and adding to the list as they go around the circle.

# Points de départ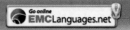

Question centrale
What makes a house a "home"?

## Les logements  1.2, 2.1, 2.2, 5.1

Individualistes, 57% des familles françaises choisissent d'habiter dans une maison individuelle et 43% seulement dans un immeuble. Il existe aussi des logements sociaux (des HLM—habitations à loyer modéré*). Ils sont occupés surtout par de jeunes couples, des gens qui ont de faibles revenus*, et des retraités*. Beaucoup de jeunes continuent aujourd'hui à habiter chez leurs parents après l'âge de 20 ans, mais ils sont indépendants financièrement et émotionnellement. D'autres jeunes choisissent la colocation*, qui permet* d'avoir plus d'espace et de payer aussi un loyer* moins cher.

🔍 **Search words: immobilier paris, immobilier lyon, immobilier marseille**

Un HLM en banlieue a en moyenne (*average*) douze étages; le plus grand a 29 étages.

**habitations à loyer modéré** *low-rent housing;* **faibles revenus** *low incomes;* **des retraités** *retired people;* **la colocation** *sharing of an apartment;* **permet** *allows;* **un loyer** *rent*

### COMPARAISONS

How does the rate of home ownership in the United States compare to that in France?
4.2

## La salle de bains et les toilettes 1.2

D'habitude, la salle de bains (la douche* ou la baignoire*) est séparée des toilettes (ou W.C.) en France. C'est un espace pour faire sa toilette*, s'habiller*, etc. Des fois, les baignoires sont même* remplacées par des douches avec jet. Les constructions les plus modernes ont tendance aussi à inclure les toilettes dans la salle de bains.

**douche** *shower:* **baignoire** *bathtub;* **faire sa toilette** *wash up;* **s'habiller** *get dressed;* **même** *even*

Dans cette salle de bains, il y a des W.C., un évier pour la toilette générale, et un bidet pour la toilette privée.

**Essential Instruction**

1. As they read the **Points de départ**, ask students to search for specific information, for example who lives in an HLM.
2. Reflect on the meaning of **eau de toilette**.
3. Show students that French bathrooms often have a bidet, now also found in a number of newer American bathrooms. Bidets are considered extremely hygienic and have existed since the Middle Ages because bathing facilities used to be scarcer than they are today.
4. Have students identify cognates before reading and discussing the paragraphs. Explain that the word **le Maghreb** is Arabic and means "place of the sunset" or "the west."
5. Point out that some of the vocabulary in **Mon dico maghrébin** is slang (**un bled, un toubib**).
6. Ask students to identify the flags of **Le Maghreb**.

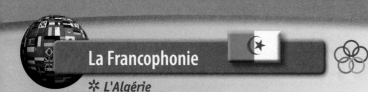

## La Francophonie

 1.2, 5.1

### ✳ L'Algérie

L'Algérie fait partie* du Maghreb. (Les autres pays de cette région sont la Tunisie et le Maroc.) Colonie française pendant 130 ans, l'Algérie est devenue* indépendante en 1962. La guerre de libération a duré huit ans, de 1954 à 1962. L'économie algérienne est basée essentiellement sur les ressources pétrolières*, mais un chômage très élevé* force beaucoup de gens à émigrer. La langue officielle est l'arabe, mais souvent l'expression au cinéma, dans la littérature et la musique (le raï) est en français.

 **Search words:** tourisme algérie
state department travel advisory
algérie

---

**fait partie** *belongs to*; **est devenue** *became*; **pétrolières** *oil*; **un chômage très élevé** *high unemployment*

**Produits**

**Le raï** est une musique qui vient de l'Algérie. Aujourd'hui, il est populaire partout au Maghreb. On peut trouver cette musique en France aussi. Parfois ces chansons sont en arabe et français. Vous pouvez trouver des chansons et vidéos de raï sur Internet; cherchez les noms "Cheb Bilal" et "Cheb Khaled," par exemple.

**4.2**

### Mon dico maghrébin

4.1

un **bédouin**: un homme (du désert)
un **bled**: un petit village
**cheb**: titre (*title*) pour un chanteur de raï
le **couscous**: un plat à base de semoule de blé (*wheat grain*), servi avec viande et légumes
un **souk**: un marché
un **toubib**: un médecin

## La Francophonie: Habitations au Maghreb

1.2, 2.1, 2.2, 5.1

Les trois types d'habitation traditionnelle sont les *riads*, les *khaimas* (tentes), et les *kasbahs*. Les riads sont des maisons construites autour* d'un patio en forme de jardin. Les khaimas sont de grandes tentes. L'espace intérieur est divisé* en deux, l'un, caché*, réservé aux femmes; l'autre, ouvert*, réservé aux hommes et aux visiteurs. Il y a souvent des tapis et des coussins au sol*. Les kasbahs sont de superbes mais fragiles bâtisses en terre* avec un rez-de-chaussée pour les activités agricoles*, un premier étage pour la cuisine et les femmes, et un deuxième étage qui sert de salon de réception.

**Perspectives**

How are the values and traditions of **le Maghreb** reflected in its traditional housing?

---

**construites autour** *constructed around*; **divisé** *divided*; **caché** *hidden*; **ouvert** *open*; **sol** *ground*; **bâtisses en terre** *clay buildings*; **agricoles** *agricultural*

Leçon A | trois cent quarante-sept **3 4 7**

**Answers** _____

### Perspectives

In general, Algerian cultural and religious values shape the traditions concerning the roles of men and women. In their homes, women and men are generally separated in common spaces. Also, in **kasbahs** (ancient, traditional fortresses often restored for modern living), women spend time on the second floor (**premier étage**) where the kitchen is also located, while farm-related activities take place on the ground floor (**r-de-c**); the third floor (**deuxième étage**) is reserved for receiving guests.

### Expansion

Ask students to restate the following sentences, translating the Arabic expression into French.

1. Qui est ce bédouin?
2. Nous habitons un petit bled pas loin de la capitale.
3. Je vais au souk pour acheter des provisions.
4. Son père est toubib.

### Game

**Où et quoi?**
Have students think of an activity that they do in a particular room of a house. Ask a volunteer to call out the activity, saying for example, **Je fais mes devoirs....** Another student must respond by saying where he or she does that activity, for example, **Je fais mes devoirs dans ma chambre**. That student then calls out a different room (e.g., **la cuisine**) for which the next student responds with an activity to complete the phrase. (**Je fais un gâteau au chocolat dans la cuisine.**) Continue until all have had the chance to play.

---

**Differentiated Learning**

**Accelerate**
Discuss historical and political reasons for the immigration of Algerians to France, and compare to an immigration story that exists in the United States (Vietnam War, Central America, East Africa, etc.).

**Learning Styles**

**Auditory/Visual Learners**
1. Find out which students are familiar with **raï** singers and share that Cheb Mami recorded the hit "Desert Rose" with Sting. Ask them to find and share in class another song and lyrics in French by Cheb Mami or Khaled. Do a cloze listening exercise using the song **"Mon Pays"** by Faudel. Have students create two columns labeled **France** (Paris) and **mon pays**, then list descriptions for each (weather, smells, landscape). Finally, ask groups to name similar things that characterize the city or region where they live.

2. Find images from the Internet of the three types of housing in **La Francophonie: Habitations au Maghreb**, label, and post in the classroom.

## Answers

**10**

1. La plupart habitent chez leurs parents.
2. Les salles de bain sont souvent séparées des toilettes.
3. fiche d'identité de l'Algérie:
   Langue officielle: l'arabe
   Ressource principale: le pétrole
   Date de l'indépendance: 1962
   Langue de l'expression du cinéma, dans la littérature et la musique: le français
   Genre de musique populaire: le raï
4. habitations algériennes :
   une maison construite autour d'un patio: un riad
   une tente: un khaima
   une bâtisse en terre: un kasbah
5. Le raï est un genre de musique dont des musiciens célèbres sont Cheb Mami ou Cheb Khaled

**10** Questions culturelles

*Répondez aux questions.*

1. Où habitent les jeunes en France?
2. Comment sont les salles de bains en France?
3. Remplissez (*Fill out*) la fiche d'identité de l'Algérie.
   * Langue officielle
   * Ressource principale
   * Date de l'indépendance
   * Langue de l'expression du cinéma, dans la littérature et la musique
   * Genre de musique populaire
4. Comment appelle-t-on les habitations suivantes au Maghreb?
   * une maison construite autour d'un patio
   * une tente
   * une bâtisse en terre
5. Qu'est-ce que c'est que le raï? Faites une recherche sur Internet sur l'origine, les caractéristiques, les chanteurs, ou les tendances du raï. Chaque membre du groupe choisit un sujet et fait une présentation au groupe.

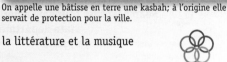
On appelle une bâtisse en terre une kasbah; à l'origine elle servait de protection pour la ville.

**2.1, 2.2, 4.2**

## Du côté des médias  **1.2**

*Voici des petites annonces* (want ads) *pour des appartements à Paris. Remarquez toutes les abréviations!*

1. Paris, 14ème
   Bel imm, appt de 90 m2. Entrée, double séj. proche de la cuis. 2 ch., 1 SdB avec wc. Parquet, cheminée. **750.00 €**

3. Magnif. Appt 4 pces avec espaces verts. Séj., 2 chs, SdB, wc, parc. **225.000 €**

2. Paris, 8ème
   Bel imm. PdT: 2 pces, 50 m2, 5ème ét., dche. **180.000 €**

4. Paris, 9ème
   Appt avec entrée, cuis, séjour, 3 chs, balcon. RdC. Park. Proche de toutes commodités! **280.000 €**

**Essential Instruction**

1. Assign the **Questions culturelles** as homework or in small groups in class. Review with the entire class.
2. For **Du côté des médias**, assign small groups the task of deciphering the abbreviations of one of the advertisements. Tell them to look at **Activité 11** for help. Then have each group read its ad aloud with the reconstituted words.
3. Pull this learning together with **Activité 12**. Ask volunteers to read the item aloud for pronunciation practice, and have the class decide on the right apartment.
4. Look at the realia together. Ask the class what they think **un immeuble de standing** and **un cadre verdoyant** mean.

## 11 Les petites annonces

 2.1, 2.2

*Pour chaque expression suivante, écrivez une abréviation.*

1. appartement
2. cuisine
3. rez-de-chaussée
4. salle de bains
5. parking
6. pièces
7. séjour
8. immeuble
9. étage

## 12 On cherche un appartement à Paris!

 1.2, 2.1, 2.2

*Aidez les personnes suivantes à trouver un appartement à Paris. Dites le numéro de l'annonce qui les intéresserait (would interest them).*

1. Éric a besoin d'un bureau parce qu'il travaille à la maison. Il a besoin d'espaces verts pour promener son chien (*dog*).
2. Les Clément ont deux filles de 14 et 8 ans; donc, on a besoin de deux chambres pour elles. Ils veulent avoir un garage pour leur voiture (*car*). Ils voudraient être proches (*near*) de la rue commerçante.
3. Anne-Marie a 23 ans et elle est célibataire (*single*). Elle a besoin d'un petit appartement bon marché. Elle n'a pas besoin d'un ascenseur (*elevator*).
4. Les Bonnet ont un petit garçon, Mathieu. Ils ont besoin d'un grand séjour parce que Mathieu aime jouer à l'intérieur. Ils désirent un appartement de 100 m² approximativement.

 1.2

EN TERRAIN DE CONFIANCE

À DUNKERQUE

Portes ouvertes tous les dimanches et sur RDV en semaine.

LA RÉSIDENCE DES TOURNESOLS

Venez découvrir cette nouvelle résidence de standing, comprenant 11 logements de 2 à 4 pièces, avec de très belles prestations: chauffage individuel, au gaz par condensation, normes THPE, terrasses, jardins privatifs, parkings, garages et caves, dans un cadre verdoyant exceptionnel.

AVANTAGES FISCAUX SUR CES PROPRIÉTÉS

Leçon A | trois cent quarante-neuf **349**

**Differentiated Learning**
**Adapt**
Ask students to look for housing ads on the Internet or in magazines and present them in French.

**Multiple Intelligences**
**Logical-Mathematical**
Ask students to measure the square footage of your classroom or their living room or bedroom at home and convert the measurement into square meters. Then ask them to convert the square meters in the housing ads into square feet. Finally, ask them to change the euros into dollars. What observations can they make about apartment size and price in Paris?

Answers _____

**13**

1. Ils habitent au quatrième étage.
2. Elle habite au premier étage.
3. Ils habitent au troisième étage.
4. Elle habite au sixième étage.
5. Ils habitent au cinquième étage.

### Reference Desk

1. Remind students that ordinal means "of or pertaining to order."
2. While **premier/première** is the ordinal number for one, numbers such as twenty-first (**vingt-et-unième**), thirty-first (**trente-et-unième**), etc. follow the normal formation for ordinals.
3. Explain the spelling changes for **cinquième** and **neuvième**, and the pronunciation change (**neuf** to **neuvième**).
4. Show that ordinals are used for fractions: 1/5, 1/6, 1/7, 1/8, etc. Ask students to find the expressions for 1/2 (**une moitié**), 1/3 (**un tiers**), 2/3 (**deux tiers**), 1/4 (**un quart**), and 3/4 (**trois quarts**).
5. Note the abbreviations for ordinals: 1$^{er}$ and 1$^{ère}$, 2$^{e}$ or 2$^{ième}$ (using the last letter **e** or letters **ième** of the word **deuxième**), etc.
6. The use of ordinals (often expressed with Roman numerals) for Parisian city districts or **arrondissements** is common (ex. **J'habite dans le 18$^{e}$**). For example the 18$^{th}$ **arrondissement** may be written as **le XVIII$^{e}$**.

### Communication

**Presentational**

Ask students to think of two things that could be referenced with ordinal numbers, such as the first day of school, third day of the week, fourth class of the day, etc. Call on all students to say their ordinal statement.

---

# Structure de la langue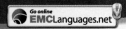

## Ordinal Numbers  1.2

Numbers like "first," "second," and "third" are called ordinal numbers. They show the order in which things are placed.

All ordinal numbers in French, except **premier** and **première** ("first"), end in **-ième**. To form most ordinal numbers, add **-ième** to the cardinal number. If a cardinal number ends in **-e**, drop the **e** before adding **-ième**. Note that "first," "fifth," and "ninth" are irregular.

Nicole est deuxième dans le marathon.

| | | |
|---|---|---|
| un, une | → | **premier** (m.), **première** (f.) |
| deux | → | **deuxième** |
| trois | → | **troisième** |
| quatre | → | **quatrième** |
| cinq | → | **cinquième** |
| six | → | **sixième** |
| sept | → | **septième** |
| huit | → | **huitième** |
| neuf | → | **neuvième** |
| dix | → | **dixième** |

**COMPARAISONS**

How would you express this sentence in English? 4.1
Mon appartement est au cinquième étage.

Mon **premier** jour en Algérie, je vais manger du couscous.

*On my first day in Algeria, I'm going to eat couscous.*

Le **deuxième** jour, nous allons à un concert de raï.

*On the second day, we are going to a rai concert.*

**Culture Note**  4.2

In French-speaking countries, **le rez-de-chaussée** is the equivalent of the ground or first floor in English-speaking countries. **Le premier étage** refers to the second floor.

**13 C'est quel étage?**  2.1, 2.2

*Dites à quel étage ces personnes habitent.*

**MODÈLE** Cédric
**Cédric habite au deuxième étage.**

1. Noémie et Jean-Luc
2. Charlotte
3. Karim et Claude
4. Sabrina
5. Sarah et Lucas

Charlotte
Cédric
Karim et Claude
Noémie et Jean-Luc
Sarah et Lucas
Sabrina
le rez-de-chaussée

**350** trois cent cinquante | Unité 7

COMPARAISONS: "My apartment is on the sixth floor."

---

**Essential Instruction**

1. Provide practice by saying aloud a cardinal number and having the class respond together with the ordinal equivalent. Briefly review the way floors are numbered in francophone countries. Ask students on which floor(s) their classroom, the school library, their bedroom, etc. are located.

2. Complete **Activité 14** in pairs and listen as a class to **Activité 15**.

3. Name a day of the week and ask for the corresponding ordinal number in the French week, reminding students that **lundi** is the first day of the week.

## 14 Mme Fournier fait les courses au supermarché.

 2.1, 2.2

*À Monoprix, il y a une caméra à l'extérieur et à l'intérieur, mais les photos de Mme Fournier sont dans le désordre (in disorder). Retrouvez l'ordre des photos d'après (according to) les phrases ci-dessous.*

**MODÈLE**    **Photo A: C'est la première photo.**

A.

B.

C.

D.

E.

F.

1. Elle arrive au supermarché Monoprix.
2. Elle prend un chariot (*cart*).
3. Elle regarde les annonces (*adds*) de Monoprix.
4. Elle met du poulet dans le chariot (*cart*).
5. Elle achète la nourriture.
6. Elle met un sac dans sa voiture.

## 15 La maison de Coralie

  2.1, 2.2

*Coralie parle de sa maison à Julie. Écrivez **0** si la pièce que Coralie décrit (describes) est au rez-de-chaussée et **1** si c'est au premier étage.*

---

---

**Answers**

**16** *Presentations will vary.*

**17** *Dialogues will vary.*

# À vous la parole

**16  L'immeuble**    1.1, 1.3

### Presentational Communication

Draw a diagram of **un immeuble** with five floors and two apartments on each floor. For each apartment, write the names of the people who live there and their ages, for example, **Michèle, 15 ans**. Introduce one of the families to your small group, including answers to these questions:

- Les membres de la famille s'appellent comment?
- Quel âge ont-ils?
- Est-ce qu'ils habitent dans une maison individuelle?
- À quel étage est-ce qu'ils habitent?
- Il y a combien de pièces?
- Comment est la chambre de l'ado de la famille?
- Qu'est-ce qu'il ou elle aime faire?

La famille Fournier habite au troisième étage de l'immeuble.

**17  La visite**  1.1, 2.1

Tu veux un coca ou une limonade?

### Interpersonal Communication

With a partner, roleplay the following conversation between an American host student (**A**) and an exchange student from Algeria (**B**). Then switch roles.

Je voudrais une limonade, merci.

A: Welcome your guest and asks if he or she would like a sandwich or a salad, a cola or a mineral water.
B: Say which food and beverage you would like.
A: Give a tour of your house or apartment, ending in the exchange student's bedroom. Ask if he or she needs anything.
B: Respond and thank the host.
A: Say good night (**Bonne nuit!**) and see you tomorrow.
B: Say good night (**Bonne nuit!**) and see you tomorrow.

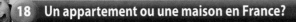

# Communiquez!

**18** **Un appartement ou une maison en France?**   **1.2, 1.3**

### Interpretive/Presentational Communication

You and your family plan to spend a month in France this summer. Since your parents don't speak French, they have asked you to help them find a furnished apartment or house to rent. Follow these steps to complete this task.

- Choose a city or region of France you would like to visit.
- Then find vacation rental agency sites in French on the Internet and select three possible rentals.
- Complete the chart, ranking your choices in order of preference.

| | Ville ou région? | Appartement ou maison? | Nombre de pièces? | Nombre de chambres? | Piscine? Jardin ou terrasse? | Attractions de la région? | Prix? |
|---|---|---|---|---|---|---|---|
| 1. | | | | | | | |
| 2. | | | | | | | |
| 3. | | | | | | | |

Now, explain your choices in French to a partner, using your diagram to organize your presentation.

 **Search words: location de maisons de vacances en France**

Lancer la recherche ▶

**Locations de vacances France**

Page 1 2 3 ... 999 ▶ ▶|          Classement  Importance  ▼

Faites une recherche ciblée en inscrivant les dates du séjour! Ainsi, seuls les logements disponibles avec les prix respectifs seront affichés.

**Maison de vacances France pour 8 personnes env. 140 m², Saint-Pée-sur-Nivelle, Aquitaine (Pyrénées-Atlantiques)**
4 chambres à coucher, 2 salles de bains, TV par satellite, lave-vaisselle, lac 350 m, plage 500 m, point d'eau 350 m, lave-linge, chien admis

de € 359 à € 1.016
pour 1 semaine

Détails ▶

courte descriptiontypemaison de vacancessuperficie6 pièces, 2 étages ou niveaux, 140 m² de surface ... ▼ Plus d'infos

Location N° 274532

**Appartement France pour 4 personnes env. 30 m², Le Barcarès, Languedoc-Roussillon (Pyrénées-Orientales)**
1 chambre à coucher, 1 salle de bains, TV, lave-vaisselle, lave-linge

de € 279 à € 699
pour 1 semaine

Détails ▶

Les logements proposés sont confortables, bien équipés et régulièrement entretenus. Certains à ... ▼ Plus d'infos

Location N° 772109

☐ Nouvelle offre

---

### Expansion

Have students research online the answers to the following questions about film, or create your own set of questions about a particular theme.
Famous French film magazine (*Première*)
Cinema is sometimes known as the...? (**le septième art**)
Which film by French director François Truffaut, starring Catherine Deneuve and Gérard Dépardieu, had the word "last" in the title (opposite of "first")? (*Le Dernier Métro*)

### Critical Thinking

**Evaluate**
Ask students to come up with a list of criteria in order to judge which would be the best dwelling for their family.

---

**Differentiated Learning**
**Decelerate**
For **Activité 18**, pre-select a city or area and a corresponding website that students will review. Ask them to select one vacation rental.

# Prononciation  1.2

## Unpronounced Internal /ə/

- Sometimes the sound /ə/, as in **je** and **de**, is unpronounced in the middle of words.

**A** Le /ə/ interne non prononcé

*Repeat each sentence. Do not pronounce the sound /ə/ except when it is in bold.*

1. Au revoir!
2. À samedi!
3. Au revoir! On revient demain matin.
4. Au revoir! On revient le samedi quinze.
5. La boulangerie est près d**e** la crémerie.
6. La boucherie est près d**e** la charcuterie.

**B** Je la fais tout de suite!

*Answer the question according to the example.* ***Tout de suite*** *means "right away."*

| MODÈLE | Vous entendez: | **Tu prépares la salade?** |
| | Vous dites: | **Je la prépare tout de suite!** |

1. Tu fais la sauce?     Je la fais tout de suite!
2. Tu coupes les pommes?     Je les coupe tout de suite!
3. Tu mets les serviettes?     Je les mets tout de suite!

**C** Style standard, familier, ou relâché?

*Listen to the same sentences pronounced in different styles, and repeat.*

Excusez-moi, j**e** suis en retard!    (standard)
Excusez-moi, j**e** suis en retard!    (familiar)
Excuse-moi, je suis en retard!    (relaxed)
Excuse-moi, je suis en retard!    (relaxed)

## The Sound /R/

- The French **r** is made by closing the back of the throat almost completely as if gargling or preventing liquid from passing, then pushing air through. Exceptions to the /R/ sound include **monsieur** and the infinitive form of **-er** verbs.

**D** Pratiquons le son /R/!

*Repeat the following words and phrases.*

1. mon père, ma mère, mon frère, ma sœur
2. Bonjour. Bonsoir. D'accord. Bien sûr.
3. le sport
4. un tournoi de rugby
5. le Tour de France
6. Roland Garros

**E** Tu vas...?

*Answer according to the example.*

| MODÈLE | Vous entendez: | **Tu vas lire?** |
| | Vous dites: | **Ça oui! Je voudrais lire!** |

1. Tu vas dormir?   Ça oui! Je voudrais dormir!
2. Tu vas partir?   Ça oui! Je voudrais partir *(to leave)*!
3. Tu vas sortir?   Ça oui! Je voudrais sortir!

**F** Il y a un "r"?

*Write **R** if you hear /R/ or **0** if you do not hear /R/.*

| MODÈLES | Vous entendez: | **C'est un four.** |
| | Vous écrivez: | **R** |
| | Vous entendez: | **C'est une affiche.** |
| | Vous écrivez: | **0** |

### Essential Instruction

1. For **Activité A**, brainstorm examples of silent letters in spoken English, then play the audio and model the pronunciation.
2. Review that the French **r** sound is similar to the "ch" in Loch Ness or "kh" in Khaled. Instruct students to close the back of the throat as if they're going to gargle and say "k" several times, then "ra-ra-ra." Ask pairs to create some funny sentences with the letter "r" like **Le grand gros rat mangera trop de fromage de Gruyère et grossira et mourra**. This will also prepare them for learning the future tense later on.
3. Write on the board **Les repas** and list the four meals in French from **Vocabulaire actif** in **Leçon B**. Model the pronunciation, then ask students to tell a partner what time they eat each meal.
4. Review the vocabulary and prepositions by asking students where certain items of the table setting are located. Have students draw a table setting on small white boards. Then say **"Montrez-moi..."** and students respond by pointing to them.

# Leçon B

## Vocabulaire actif

*Go online* EMCLanguages.net

### Les repas  1.2

- un bol
- le sel
- le poivre
- une cuiller
- une serviette
- une fourchette
- le sucre
- une tasse
- un verre
- une assiette
- un couteau
- une nappe

La fourchette est à gauche de l'assiette.

Le couteau est à droite de l'assiette.

La cuiller est au-dessus de l'assiette.

le petit déjeuner

le goûter

le déjeuner

le dîner

Leçon B | trois cent cinquante-cinq 355

## RESOURCES

 Workbook 14–17

 Flash Cards

 Listening Activity

## Reference Desk

French lunch and dinner are usually several course meals and include **une entrée** (an appetizer), **un plat principal** (a main course), cheese and/or dessert. **Entrées** are typically salads, soups, **pâté**, or a delicacy from the deli. Main courses are composed of a meat or fish dish, rice, potatoes, or pasta with vegetables, or a more traditional **plat** (dish) (**choucroute**, **bouillabaisse**, etc.). Not everyone eats cheese or dessert at every meal, but often the French choose cheese, fruit, or yogurt to end their meal.

## TPR

Energize students with a relay outside or in the gym. Have teams line up behind a starting line. Provide a set of plastic cutlery and paper plates and cups. At the signal, one student from each team races to the "table" to deposit the item you identify in the correct position for a table setting. Then, they race back to tag the next wave. The first team to "set the table" wins.

## Expansion

Have students note the differences between how tables are set at home and at restaurants in America and what they see in the photos.

## Culture

**Practices: Information**
Consider showing the i-Culture video entitled **"La cuisine française"** (2010-2011) to provide your students with a culturally authentic perspective related to the theme of this **Leçon**.

### Learning Styles

**Kinesthetic/Visual/Auditory Learners**
Have students do any or all of these activities with a partner, using the card stock vocabulary or white boards: show or draw each item as you give its name in French; remove or erase items from a table setting as you say them; set the table based on cues such as, **Mettez** (introduced in **Leçon B**) **le couteau à droite de l'assiette.**

**Visual Learners**
Draw pictures or find images online of the table setting vocabulary. Make enough copies on card stock for a classroom set and place them in a plastic bag. Then, have volunteers identify items that they pull out of the bag.

355

## Pour la conversation

How do I give directions in the kitchen?

> **Tu peux couper** les courgettes **en rondelles.**
> _You can cut the zucchini in rounds._

> **Ensuite, tu mets le couvert.**
> _Next, you set the table._

**Et si je voulais dire...?**

| | |
|---|---|
| **une assiette à soupe** | _soup plate_ |
| **le couvert** | _silverware_ |
| **une cuiller à soupe** | _tablespoon_ |
| **une cuiller à café** | _teaspoon_ |
| **une poêle** | _frying pan_ |
| **grignoter** | _to snack_ |
| **un hors-d'œuvre** | _appetizer_ |
| **des chips (m.)** | _chips_ |
| **les snacks (m.)** | _snacks_ |

**1  Nicole met le couvert.**  1.2, 2.1, 2.2

_Lisez comment Nicole met le couvert, puis répondez à la question._

Je mets la nappe et une assiette. Le couteau est à droite de l'assiette. La fourchette est à gauche de l'assiette avec la serviette. Le verre est au-dessus du couteau. La tasse est à droite du couteau. La petite cuiller et la cuiller à soupe sont au-dessus de l'assiette.

Nicole est-elle américaine ou française?

**2  À table!**   2.2

_La mère de Maxime explique comment mettre le couvert. Faites un dessin selon ses explications._

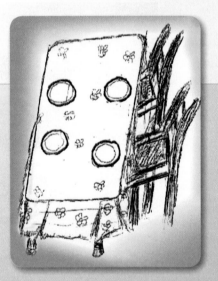

**Essential Instruction**

1. Ask students, **"Qui met la table à la maison? Qui aime faire la cuisine?"**, then present **Pour la conversation** with the audio.

2. If possible, bring in items listed in **Et si je voulais dire...?** Model the pronunciation, then challenge pairs to create one sentence using all of the vocabulary.

3. As you read each sentence in **Activité 1**, have students render it on a white board or paper.

4. Have students share their drawings from listening **Activité 2** and check for understanding.

5. Review the expression **avoir besoin de**, then assign **Activités 3** and **4** in pairs.

6. Ask students to answer the questions in **Activité 5** in pairs.

## 3 Je prépare le dîner!  2.1, 2.2

*Dites quels ustensiles de la liste vous prenez pour préparer ces plats.*

| un couteau | une fourchette | une cuiller | un bol |
|---|---|---|---|

**MODÈLE** **Je prends un bol, une fourchette, et un couteau.**

1.

2.

3.

4.

## 4 Mets le couvert! 2.1, 2.2

*Selon le repas, dites ce dont vous avez besoin pour mettre le couvert. N'oubliez pas la nappe, la serviette, le sel, le poivre, et le sucre!*

**MODÈLE** une soupe aux légumes, une crêpe au poulet et au fromage, une salade, et un café
**J'ai besoin d'un bol, d'une cuiller, d'une assiette, d'une fourchette, d'une tasse, d'une nappe, d'une serviette, du sel, du poivre, et du sucre.**

1. une omelette au jambon, des petits pois, de l'eau minérale, et un yaourt
2. du bœuf avec des pommes de terre, des haricots verts, un gâteau, et un café
3. une soupe aux carottes, du porc, des courgettes, du café au lait, et une glace au chocolat
4. une soupe aux champignons, un sandwich au fromage, une pomme, une limonade, et une crêpe

## 5 Questions personnelles  1.1

*Répondez aux questions.*

Je prends le déjeuner à l'école.

1. Qu'est-ce que tu prends au petit déjeuner?
2. À quelle heure est-ce que tu prends le déjeuner?
3. Où est-ce que tu prends le déjeuner?
4. Qu'est-ce que tu prends comme dessert?
5. Qu'est-ce que tu prends comme goûter après l'école?
6. Est-ce que ta famille prend un grand dîner?
7. Est-ce que tu aides ta famille à préparer le dîner?
8. Quel est ton dîner préféré?

Answers _____

**3**
1. ... une assiette et un couteau, une fourchette, une assiette.
2. ... un bol, un couteau et une fourchette.
3. ... une assiette et un couteau.
4. ... un bol, un couteau, une cuillère et une fourchette.

**4**
1. .... assiette, fourchette, couteau, cuillère, petite cuillère, nappe, serviette, verre, sel, poivre, sucre.
2. ... assiette, fourchette, couteau, cuillère, tasse, petite cuillère, petite fourchette, petite assiette, nappe, serviette, sel, poivre, sucre.
3. ...bol, cuillères, assiette, fourchette, couteau, tasse, petite cuillère, petit bol, nappe, serviette, sel, poivre, sucre
4. ... bol, cuillère, assiette, couteau, verre, petite fourchette, nappe, serviette, sel, poivre, sucre.

**5** *Answers will vary.*

### Game

Have students form a circle. Toss a lightweight ball to one student and call out the name of a utensil (**fourchette**). The student who catches the ball must name a food dish appropriate to the utensil (**une omelette**).

### Expansion

1. Have kitchen tools (bowl, plates, plastic knives, forks, etc.) on hand for demonstrations of simple imaginary or real recipes.
2. Have teams compete to be first to set the table properly as you call out a meal (**déjeuner**, etc.).
3. Bring in food items and, as you hold one up, have students write down how they would cut it up, using **couper** and **en rondelles**, **en carrés**, **en tranches**, **en morceaux**.

### Differentiated Learning
#### Accelerate
After doing **Activité 1**, ask pairs to draw a crazy table setting using all the vocabulary from **Vocabulaire actif**. Then have them take turns instructing their partner how to draw the table setting according to their own illustration.

### Multiple Intelligences
#### Interpersonal/Visual-Spatial
Have students on one side of the room set the table the French way. Then tell the students on the other side of the room to remove one item at a time from the table setting while the other students close their eyes, then say what is missing. Reverse roles.

**Answers**

**6**

1. une ratatouille
2. des aubergines, des courgettes, des poivrons, des tomates
3. Il coupe les courgettes et les aubergines.
4. en rondelles
5. en carrés
6. Maxime
7. dans la salle à manger
8. On va utiliser les assiettes de sa tante de Marseille parce qu'elles sont plus jolies.

### Extension

Lauren puts the fork on the right, the knife on the left, the spoon on the outer left, and the small spoon between the glasses and plate in the middle. Mateo puts the glass above the plate and the napkin on the left.

### Reference Desk

The word **ben** is a familiar expression, derived from the word **bien**. However, **Ben ...,** at the beginning of a sentence marks hesitation. It does not replace the word **bien** as in **Je vais bien**.

# Rencontres culturelles

## Un repas provençal     1.2

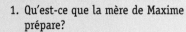

**6 Un repas provençal** 2.1, 2.2

*Repondez aux questions.*

1. Qu'est-ce que la mère de Maxime prépare?
2. Quels sont les légumes que Maxime et sa mère préparent?
3. Que fait Maxime pour aider sa mère dans la cuisine?
4. Comment doit-il couper les courgettes?
5. Comment doit-il couper les aubergines?
6. Qui va mettre le couvert?
7. Dans quelle pièce est-ce qu'on va prendre le déjeuner?
8. On va utiliser quelles assiettes? Pourquoi?

Dans la cuisine, Maxime attend la ratatouille que sa mère prépare pour le déjeuner.

| | |
|---|---|
| Maxime: | Je veux prendre le déjeuner maintenant. C'est trop long à préparer ta recette de grand-mère. |
| Mère: | Ah, c'est sûr! On n'est pas chez McDo! |
| Maxime: | Bon alors, qu'est-ce que je fais pour t'aider? |
| Mère: | Eh bien, tu coupes les aubergines et les courgettes. Je vais couper des poivrons et des tomates. |
| Maxime: | Comment? |
| Mère: | Comment quoi? |
| Maxime: | Ben, les courgettes et les aubergines, je les coupe comment? |
| Mère: | Tu peux couper les courgettes en rondelles. Attention! Tu fais des rondelles fines, les aubergines en carrés. |
| Maxime: | Et les carrés comment? |
| Mère: | Les carrés comme des carrés, pardi! Ensuite tu mets le couvert dans la salle à manger. Prends les assiettes de ta tante de Marseille. Elles sont plus jolies que nos assiettes jaunes. |
| Maxime: | Je dois tout faire dans cette maison! |

### Extension   Bon appétit! 1.2, 2.1, 2.2

Des participants de la télé-réalité show "Bon appétit" essaient de mettre la table.

| | |
|---|---|
| Maître d'hôtel: | Non, Lauren, on recommence.... |
| Lauren: | La fourchette à droite, c'est sûr. Donc... le couteau à gauche. Ah oui, la cuiller à gauche à l'extérieur, et la petite cuiller entre les verres et l'assiette, bien au centre. |
| Maître d'hôtel: | Très bien, Lauren, vous voyez, vous y arrivez quand vous faites attention.... Bon, Matéo, le verre et la serviette maintenant. |
| Matéo: | Je mets le verre d'eau au-dessus du couteau? |
| Maître d'hôtel: | C'est ça. Et la serviette? |
| Matéo: | À gauche de la fourchette. |
| Maître d'hôtel: | Bravo, tous les deux! |

### Extension Quand Lauren et Matéo mettent le couvert, qui fait quoi?

## Essential Instruction

1. Read aloud **La Provence** in **Points de départ**, then view the dialogue **Un repas provençal**. Ask if any students have seen the movie *Ratatouille*, or eaten this dish. Have pairs read aloud the dialogue, discuss any questions, and do **Activité 6**. Show the filmed dialogue a second time. Ask how much more they understood the second time and what they noticed.
2. Show online slide shows provided by the tourist offices of Marseille and the region of **Provence**.
3. Explain that the regional language **provençal** is still spoken by some **en Provence** as you dicuss the examples in **Mon dico provençal**. Discuss the differences among regional languages and dialects in France. Compare to regional differences in the United States.
4. Find and play an online version of **"La Marseillaise,"** then read **Produits**. Ask students to share their opinions of this **hymne national** and that of the United States.
5. If possible, play an online slide show of Van Gogh paintings as the class reads about him.

# Points de départ

**Go online**
**EMCLanguages.net**

**Question centrale**

**?**

What makes a house a "home"?

## Marseille  1.2, 2.1, 2.2, 5.1

Marseille est la deuxième ville de France. C'est le plus grand port de la Méditerranée et le quatrième port européen. Elle est un centre économique pour le transport maritime et les hélicoptères, pour les explorations sous-marines*, et pour la restauration*. L'agglomération* marseillaise a 1,4 millions d'habitants. Ils viennent de pays différents, surtout d'Italie, d'Arménie, d'Espagne, de Turquie, et des pays nord-africains.

🔍 **Search words: visiter marseille tourisme marseille**

Avec son port qui facilite les migrations on appelle Marseille "le carrefour des mondes" (*world crossroads*).

**sous-marines** *underwater*; **la restauration** *restaurant business*; **L'agglomération** *urban area*

## La Provence  1.2, 5.1

Quand on pense à la Provence, on imagine des oliviers au soleil*, de beaux paysages*, et des ruines romaines. Deux artistes qui ont peint* des sujets provençaux sont Vincent Van Gogh et Paul Cézanne. La Provence est fameuse aussi pour ses spécialités comme la bouillabaisse, une soupe de poissons *; la ratatouille; et la salade niçoise.

**oliviers au soleil** *olive trees in the sunshine*; **paysages** *landscapes*; **ont peint** *painted*; **poissons** *fish*

**Produits**  Rouget de Lisle a composé une chanson pour l'armée qui est devenue l'hymne national (*national anthem*) en 1792. On l'appelle *La Marseilleise*. **4.2**

### Mon dico provençal  4.1
un calu: *une personne bête*
un pitchoun: *un petit garçon*
une pitchounette: *une petite fille*
Je suis escagassé(e)! *Je suis fatigué(e)!*
mon collègue: *mon copain*
Pardi! *Bien sûr!*

**Produits**  **Van Gogh** a peint son célèbre tableau (*famous painting*) *The Starry Night* à Saint-Rémy-de-Provence en 1889 dans un style post-impressionniste. **4.2**

**Nuit étoilée**, 1889. Vincent Van Gogh.

Leçon B | trois cent cinquante-neuf **3 5 9**

---

**3 5 9**

## Gastronomie: spécialités régionales  1.2

Chaque région de France a ses spécialités qui illustrent la diversité des climats et des terroirs (*lands*). Voici des exemples:

Les crêpes (Bretagne).

La bouillabaisse (Marseille).

### 7 Questions culturelles  2.1, 2.2

**COMPARAISONS**

For what special foods and beverages is your city or region famous? 4.2

*Faites les petits projets suivants.*

1. Retrouvez les informations suivantes sur Marseille pour faire un profil.
   - Importance en France et en Europe
   - Activités économiques
   - Population
   - Principaux pays d'origine des immigrants
2. Quels sont les ingrédients pour une bouillabaisse marseillaise? Faites des recherches en ligne et écrivez une liste.
3. Écrivez le nom de la région associée avec ces plats:
   - les crêpes
   - le camembert
   - la ratatouille
   - la choucroute garnie
   - les escargots
   - le cassoulet
   - la fondue savoyarde
   - la quiche lorraine
   - le roquefort
4. Écrivez un petit dialogue en français avec des mots en provençal.

**À discuter**

What is the most important room in your house?

La ratatouille.

### Essential Instruction

1. Discuss student experiences with French foods, such as **crêpes** or **bouillabaisse**, and compare those foods to regional food specialties in your area.
2. Ask students to research and prepare a visual presentation of one of the topics in **Activité 7**. Provide a note-taking template with all topics listed and have students write three interesting or important things they learn from each presentation.
3. Have students present their **provençal** dialogues.
4. Dictate the ingredients and directions for the **Salade niçoise**, then have students compare what they wrote to the recipe in the book.
5. Do **Activité 8** in groups to check comprehension.

## Du côté des médias  1.2

*Lisez la recette.*

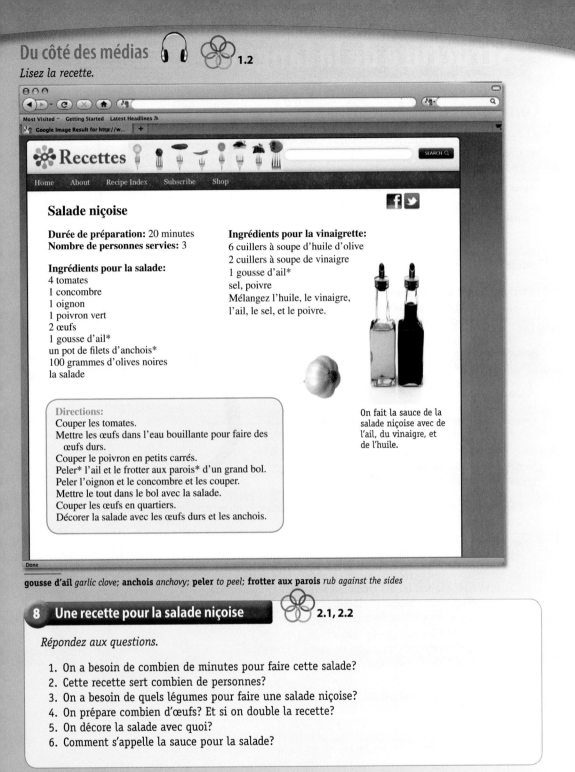

### Recettes

Home | About | Recipe Index | Subscribe | Shop

#### Salade niçoise

**Durée de préparation:** 20 minutes
**Nombre de personnes servies:** 3

**Ingrédients pour la salade:**
4 tomates
1 concombre
1 oignon
1 poivron vert
2 œufs
1 gousse d'ail*
un pot de filets d'anchois*
100 grammes d'olives noires
la salade

**Ingrédients pour la vinaigrette:**
6 cuillers à soupe d'huile d'olive
2 cuillers à soupe de vinaigre
1 gousse d'ail*
sel, poivre
Mélangez l'huile, le vinaigre, l'ail, le sel, et le poivre.

On fait la sauce de la salade niçoise avec de l'ail, du vinaigre, et de l'huile.

**Directions:**
Couper les tomates.
Mettre les œufs dans l'eau bouillante pour faire des œufs durs.
Couper le poivron en petits carrés.
Peler* l'ail et le frotter aux parois* d'un grand bol.
Peler l'oignon et le concombre et les couper.
Mettre le tout dans le bol avec la salade.
Couper les œufs en quartiers.
Décorer la salade avec les œufs durs et les anchois.

Done

**gousse d'ail** *garlic clove*; **anchois** *anchovy*; **peler** *to peel*; **frotter aux parois** *rub against the sides*

### 8 Une recette pour la salade niçoise — 2.1, 2.2

*Répondez aux questions.*

1. On a besoin de combien de minutes pour faire cette salade?
2. Cette recette sert combien de personnes?
3. On a besoin de quels légumes pour faire une salade niçoise?
4. On prépare combien d'œufs? Et si on double la recette?
5. On décore la salade avec quoi?
6. Comment s'appelle la sauce pour la salade?

---

**Answers** _____

**9** *Answers will vary.*

## Communication

### Presentational: Cooperative Groups

Students may enjoy having a cooking contest to see which team can prepare the tastiest **salade niçoise** or other French dish. Ask teams to prepare the dishes at home, take pictures throughout the process, and bring the pictures and the dishes to class. Invite other language teachers to be food judges. Once the judging is complete, students can eat the dishes.

## Expansion

1. Watch the animated movie *Ratatouille* in French and ask groups to note culinary vocabulary from the dialogues.
2. Display a list of regular **-er**, **-ir**, and **-re** cooking-related verbs (**ajouter**, **couper**, **griller**, **cuisiner**, **séparer**, **verser**, **trancher**, **tourner**, **incorporer**, **bouillir**, **rôtir**, **noircir**, **fonder**) and practice verb conjugations. Later, write each verb on a separate index card and place the cards in a hat. Divide students into teams. Show a verb card to one student from each team. At your signal, students conjugate the verb on the board. Award one point for finishing first, one point for the correct conjugation, and one point for correct pronunciation of the conjugation.

---

# Structure de la langue

**Go online EMCLanguages.net**

## Comparative of Adjectives  1.2

To compare people and things in French, use the following constructions.

| | | | | |
|---|---|---|---|---|
| **plus** (*more*) | + | adjective | + | **que** (*than*) |
| **moins** (*less*) | + | adjective | + | **que** (*than*) |
| **aussi** (*as*) | + | adjective | + | **que** (*as*) |

In the following examples, note how the adjective agrees with the first noun in the comparison.

La ratatouille **est plus délicieuse que** la salade niçoise.
Les assiettes **sont moins jolies que** les verres.
Fatima est **aussi charmante qu'**Aïcha.

*Ratatouille is more delicious than nicoise salad.*
*The plates are less pretty than the glasses.*
*Fatima is as charming as Aïcha.*

### Spelling Tip

Remember that **que** becomes **qu'** before a vowel or vowel sound.

**Le petit déjeuner est moins cher que le déjeuner. Le dîner est plus cher que le déjeuner.**

### COMPARAISONS

How are two things or people compared in English?
4.1
Nathalie is taller than David.
A lemon is more sour than an orange.

**9** **Comparons les gens!** 🌸 2.1, 2.2

*Comparez la première personne à la deuxième. Utilisez la forme correcte d'un adjectif de la liste suivante.*

**MODÈLE** Anne/Delphine (− grand)
**Anne est moins grande que Delphine.**

| | |
|---|---|
| **+** | plus |
| **−** | moins |
| **=** | aussi |

1. mon meilleur ami ou ma meilleure amie/moi (+ généreux)
2. mon cousin/ma cousine (− intelligent)
3. les acteurs/les artistes (= passionné)
4. ma mère/ma grand-mère (− bavard)
5. mon prof de français/mon prof de gym (= énergique)
6. moi/mon frère ou ma sœur (+ sympa)

*COMPARAISONS: To make comparisons in English, add -er to the adjective or place "more" before the adjective. This compares to French comparisons made with plus.*

---

## Essential Instruction

1. Use classroom nouns and people in the school community to present the comparative. Emphasize adjective agreement and the use of **qu'** before a vowel or an **h**. Then have students read aloud the examples in the textbook.
2. Assign **Activités 9** and **10** in pairs. Review again the adjective agreement on the board.
3. For **Activité 11**, remind students that the verb needs to agree with the subject. Ask students to create some additional original comparisons and share with the class what they learn about their partner.

## 10 À Carrefour  2.1, 2.2

*Utilisez* **plus cher que, moins cher que,** *ou* **aussi cher que** *pour comparer les prix à Carrefour.*

**MODÈLE** Le yaourt est **moins cher que** le fromage.
Le fromage est **plus cher que** le yaourt.

 1€11  2€96

1.  5€10  3€12

2.  2€96  2€96

3.  1€48  2€12

4.  1€60  1€60

5.  2€49  2€97

# Communiquez!

## 11 À mon avis  1.1

> Tu penses que la world est plus culturelle que le hip-hop?

### Interpersonal Communication

*À tour de rôle, demandez l'opinion de votre partenaire.*

**MODÈLE** Jon Stewart/drôle/Stephen Colbert
A: **Tu penses que Jon Stewart est plus drôle que Stephen Colbert?**
B: **Non, je pense que Jon Stewart est moins drôle que Stephen Colbert.**

1. ton prof d'anglais/strict/ton prof d'histoire
2. les élèves d'espagnol/diligent/les élèves de français
3. l'équipe de foot/passionné/l'équipe de basket
4. les pommes/délicieux/les bananes
5. Ben Stiller/drôle/Tina Fey
6. la world/culturel/le hip-hop
7. U2/généreux/Bill Gates
8. les sciences/intéressant/les langues

Leçon B | trois cent soixante-trois **363**

---

**Answers**

**10**
1. La pizza est plus chère que le yaourt.
2. Le fromage est aussi cher que le thon.
3. Le pain est moins cher que la confiture.
4. La moutarde est aussi chère que la mayonnaise.
5. Le jus d'orange de gauche est moins cher que l'eau minérale.

**11** *Answers will vary.*
1. A: … ton prof d'anglais est plus strict que ton prof d'histoire?
2. A: … les élèves d'espagnol sont plus diligents que les élèves de français?
3. A: … l'équipe de foot est plus passionnée que l'équipe de basket?
4. A: … les pommes sont plus délicieuses que les bananes?
5. A: … Ben Stiller est plus drôle que Tina Fey?
6. A: … la world est plus culturelle que le hip-hop?
7. A: … U2 sont plus généreux que Bill Gates?
8. A: … les sciences sont plus intéressantes que les langues?

### Communication

**Interpersonal: Cooperative Groups**

Solicit and display adjectives in French: e.g., **drôle, difficile, facile, intéressant, joli, sympa, délicieux, cher,** etc. Ask pairs to compose a list of 10 comparisons of books, movies, food dishes, restaurants, subjects of study, actors/actresses, cities, etc. such as: **Le quatrième livre de Harry Potter est plus intéressant que le deuxième.** Pairs will share their preferences and get reactions from their peers. Comparisons concerning people should be appropriate.

---

### Differentiated Learning
**Decelerate**
For **Activité 11,** ask students to write the answers, then share with a partner to help reinforce this more complex sentence structure.

**Accelerate**
For **Activité 11,** provide additional categories, such as sports, cities, states, cars, movies, and TV shows, and have students create and share original comparisons.

### Multiple Intelligences
**Intrapersonal/Interpersonal**
For **Activité 11,** have small groups subsitute nouns, then adjectives, to create more comparisons about their own lives, for example **ton prof de français/ton prof de maths,** etc.

**Answers**

**12**

1. Tu dois étudier pour les contrôles.
2. Vous ne devez pas envoyer des textos en classe.
3. Il doit finir ses devoirs.
4. Nous ne devons pas parler en classe.
5. Je ne dois pas regarder par la fenêtre.
6. Ils doivent participer aux discussions.

**13** *Answers will vary.*

### Reference Desk

Point out that for the verb **devoir**, the final **t** of the forms **doit** and **doivent** of the verb **devoir** is only pronounced in the inverted form, for example **Doit-il venir?**

### Communication

**Interpersonal: Paired Practice**

Have students work in pairs to ask and answer questions about what they have to do on certain days of the week. For example, **Qu'est-ce que tu dois faire le samedi? Je dois travailler le samedi.**

### Expansion

1. In groups, have students make a list of **ce qu'on doit faire en classe** and **ce qu'on ne doit pas faire en classe**.
2. Ask students to make an illustration of an activity one must not do in life to be safe and healthy, such as smoking, playing with fire, not looking both ways in traffic, eating too much, exercising in extreme heat or cold, etc. Students will show their drawings to the class, saying, for example, **On ne doit pas fumer. On doit faire de l'exercice.**

# Present Tense of the Irregular Verb *devoir*  1.2

The verb **devoir** (*to have to*) is irregular. It is usually followed by an infinitive to express obligation.

| devoir | | | |
|---|---|---|---|
| je | **dois** | nous | **devons** |
| tu | **dois** | vous | **devez** |
| il/elle/on | **doit** | ils/elles | **doivent** |

Qu'est-ce que vous **devez** faire?    *What do you have to do?*
Je **dois** préparer une ratatouille.    *I have to make ratatouille.*

Annie doit faire les courses.

## 12 Les bulletins de notes  2.1, 2.2

*Tous les élèves ont leurs bulletins de notes. Pour le cours d'histoire, dites ce que chacun doit ou ne doit pas faire pour améliorer (improve) sa note.*

**MODÈLE** Stéphanie
**Elle ne doit pas arriver en retard.**

| Élève(s) | Commentaires de M. Mathieu: |
|---|---|
| **Modèle** Stéphanie | Arrive en retard. |
| 1. tu | N'étudie pas pour les contrôles. |
| 2. Nayah et toi, vous | Envoient des textos en classe. |
| 3. Olivier | Ne finit pas ses devoirs. |
| 4. Timéo et moi, nous | Parlent en classe. |
| 5. je | Regarde par la fenêtre. |
| 6. Maude et Clément | Ne participent pas aux discussions. |

## 13 Des conseils   2.1, 2.2

*Donnez deux ou trois conseils aux personnes suivantes. Utilisez le pronom **tu**.*

**MODÈLE** Ton cousin veut être un bon athlète.
**Tu dois manger beaucoup de fruits et de légumes.**
**Tu dois jouer aux sports tous les jours.**

> Tu veux être une bonne amie? Tu dois me parler.

1. Ton cousin veut devenir chanteur et compositeur de la musique world.
2. Ton voisin (*neighbor*) veut ouvrir (*open*) un restaurant français.
3. Ta petite sœur veut être une bonne amie.
4. Ton grand frère veut être un bon prof un jour.
5. Ta copine veut être une bonne élève.

## Essential Instruction

1. Present the verb **devoir**, pointing out that the **nous** and **vous** forms have the same stem as the infinitive, like many irregular verbs.
2. Emphasize the construction **devoir** + infinitive. Then ask questions about household tasks, such as, **Qui doit mettre la table chaque soir? Qui doit promener le chien?**
3. After students practice the conjugation, do **Activité 12** as a class.
4. For **Activité 13**, have groups of three write three pieces of advice they would give each person in the group. Then have them share what they wrote.
5. Have students practice the oral and written conjugation of **mettre** before writing the missing verb forms in **Activité 14**. Allow partners to read the conversation aloud, helping each other with comprehension.

# Present Tense of the Irregular Verb *mettre*

The verb **mettre** (*to put, to put on, to set*) is irregular.

| mettre | | | |
|---|---|---|---|
| je | **mets** | nous | **mettons** |
| tu | **mets** | vous | **mettez** |
| il/elle/on | **met** | ils/elles | **mettent** |

Où **mets**-tu les cuillers? — *Where are you putting the spoons?*
Je **mets** les cuillers au-dessus des assiettes. — *I'm putting the spoons above the plates.*

*Amidou met le couvert dans la salle à manger.*

### Pronunciation Tip

The singular verb forms all sound the same.

### COMPARAISONS

4.1

What is the English equivalent of this sentence?

En hiver, je mets un manteau.

## 14 Un dîner important
 2.1, 2.2

*Mathieu choisit des vêtements, et son grand frère Guillaume offre des conseils. Complétez la conversation avec la forme appropriée du verbe* **mettre**.

Mathieu: Je vais dîner chez les parents de Romane. Est ce que je __1__ un tee-shirt ou une chemise, et un jean ou un pantalon?

Guillaume: Tu __2__ une chemise et un pantalon, c'est sûr.

Mathieu: Vraiment? Mais on ne va pas au restaurant. On __3__ des vêtements de tous les jours à la maison, n'est-ce pas?

Guillaume: Quand les parents invitent les copains à dîner, les copains __4__ un pantalon et une chemise. C'est simple!

Mathieu: Mais Romane et moi, nous __5__ toujours un jean. Pourquoi est-ce différent?

Guillaume: Parce que les parents t'invitent. Je suis sûr que ce soir Romane __6__ un pantalon ou une jupe.

Mathieu: Et toi et Virginie, qu'est-ce que vous __7__ quand vous dînez chez ses parents?

Guillaume: Nous __8__ un jean, mais c'est différent. On n'a pas besoin de faire bonne impression!

COMPARAISONS: This sentence says "In winter, I put on a coat." Note that no preposition is needed in French, while the preposition "on" is needed in English.

---

## RESOURCES

**Workbook 26–27**

**Answers**

**14**

1. mets
2. mets
3. met
4. mettent
5. mettons
6. met
7. mettez
8. mettons

### Reference Desk

1. Point out that the **-t** is silent in the singular forms of the **présent** of **mettre**, but pronounced in the plural and the inverted forms, as in, **Met-il son manteau?**
2. Emphasize the different meanings of the verb **mettre** and that the preposition is built in as part of the verb when expressing "to put on" clothes.

### TPR

Have groups practice setting plastic tableware appropriately for a dinner of several courses as you tell them in French where each piece goes. For example, **On met la fourchette à gauche de l'assiette.** Then ask a student volunteer to do the same in front of the class. Or have a volunteer put all the utensils in the wrong places as students call out how the settings should be corrected.

---

## Differentiated Learning
### Expand/Accelerate

1. Explain that **devoir quelquechose à quelqu'un** means "to owe something to someone." Have students create sentences about what or how much they owe to whom, using all subject pronouns.
2. Present some of the prefixes added to the verb **mettre** to form new verbs (**permettre, promettre, remettre, admettre, commettre, soumettre**), and ask them what these verbs mean.

You might consider adding the corresponding nouns, **la permission, l'admission, la commission, la soumission**, but **la promesse**.

## Multiple Intelligences
### Verbal-Linguistic/Interpersonal

Have small groups stage a talk show where several "guests" present and ask advice about personal problems and the hosts respond using the verb **devoir**.

**3 6 5**

**15**

1. Tu mets la nappe.
2. Mohammed met les fourchettes.
3. Paul et toi, vous mettez les bols.
4. Martinet met les couteaux.
5. Karim et moi, nous mettons les cuillères.
6. Angèle et Héloïse mettent les serviettes.
7. Je mets les verres.
8. Noémie et Nayah mettent le sel et le poivre.
9. Hervé met le sucre.

**16** Script can be found in the front pages of the Annotated Teacher's Edition.

1. B
2. D
3. E
4. G
5. A
6. C
7. F

### Reference Desk

Ask students to share a family recipe, perhaps from grandparents or another family member, that has been passed down through the generations or has special meaning and is served for very special occasions.

### Game

**Dans la cuisine**
Display about 15 unlabeled images of kitchen utensils and place setting items on an interactive or manual whiteboard. Have each student make a list of 10 meal-related vocabulary items, such **le petit déjeuner**, **le déjeuner**, **une omelette au fromage**, **une ratatouille**, **une glace**, etc. Taking turns, one student at a time will say a statement about the meal or dish along with an item from the board, such as: **Je mets des couteaux et des fourchettes pour manger une glace. (faux)** The rest of the class answers **vrai** or **faux**. Students should correct any false statements and try to be creative in making both probable and improbable matches.

---

**15** **Au lac du bois**   **2.1, 2.2**

*En colonie de vacances, tous les ados doivent mettre le couvert. Vous êtes le chef ce soir. Dites ce que chacun met.*

**MODÈLE**  Raphaël
**Raphaël met les assiettes.**

1. tu            2. Mohammed      3. Paul et toi,    4. Martine
                                     vous

5. Karim et moi,   6. Angèle et    7. je    8. Noémie et    9. Hervé
   nous              Héloïse                    Nayah

**16** **La recette de grand-mère**   **2.1, 2.2**

**Vocabulaire utile**

**l'huile** *oil*; **une poêle** *frying pan*;
**des herbes** *herbs/seasonings*

*Écrivez les numéros 1–7 sur votre papier. Écoutez la grand-mère de Romane donner une recette d'une ratatouille. Choisissez l'illustration qui correspond à chaque phrase.*

A.                B.                C.

 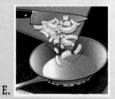  
D.                E.                F.                G.

### Essential Instruction

1. Review the forms of the verb **mettre** and then have students do **Activité 15** chorally.
2. Tell the class they are going to learn how to make **ratatouille** by listening to Grandma's instructions in **Activité 16**.
3. Have pairs do **Activités 17** and **18** orally.

 **17 Dans le frigo**  **2.1, 2.2**

*Dites ce qu'on met dans le frigo.*

**MODÈLE** Marc
**Marc met les oranges dans le frigo.**

1. Julie et moi, nous

2. tu

3. Julien

4. mes parents

5. je

6. Éric et toi, vous

 **Communiquez!** 🎧 **1.1**

**18 Qu'est-ce que tu mets?**

**Interpersonal Communication**

*À tour de rôle, demandez à votre partenaire ce qu'il ou elle met pour faire chaque activité.*

**MODÈLE** dîner au restaurant avec tes parents
A: **Qu'est-ce que tu mets quand tu dînes au restaurant avec tes parents?**
B: **Je mets un pantalon, une chemise, et des chaussures noires.**

1. aller à la piscine
2. faire la cuisine
3. jouer au foot
4. faire du footing
5. aller au cinéma
6. faire du camping
7. aller à l'école
8. faire les courses

*Qu'est-ce que tu mets quand tu fais la cuisine?*

*Je mets un jean et un tee-shirt.*

Leçon B | trois cent soixante-sept **3 6 7**

**Answers**

**17**

1. Julie et moi, nous mettons des tomates dans le frigo.
2. Tu mets de la salade dans le frigo.
3. Julien met le lait dans le frigo.
4. Mes parents mettent des cannettes dans le frigo.
5. Je mets du fromage dans le frigo.
6. Éric et toi, vous mettez des fraises dans le frigo.

**18** *Answers for partner B will vary.*

1. A: Qu'est-ce que tu mets quand tu vas à la piscine?
2. A: ...tu fais la cuisine?
3. A: ...tu joues au foot?
4. A: ...tu fais du footing?
5. A: ...tu vas au cinéma?
6. A: ...tu fais du camping?
7. A: ...tu vas à l'école?
8. A: ...tu fais les courses?

**Communication**

**Interpersonal: Paired Practice**
Switch up **Activité 18** by having one partner share what different people wear, followed by the other partner who completes the sentence stating where one wears that clothing. Students should vary subjects and scenarios as much as possible.

**Game**

**Qu'est-ce qu'on met?**
Students sit in a circle. One student starts by providing a scenario similar to those in **Activité 18** and adds clothing one might wear in that situation, for example, **Quand je vais au match de foot je mets mon écharpe PSG**. The following student must repeat the previous sentence and add another appropriate article of clothing. Students continue until they exhaust the scenario. The game continues with a new scenario.

**Differentiated Learning**
**Decelerate**
Assign **Activité 18** first as a writing assignment in order to practice the spelling of the verb forms, clothing vocabulary, and adjective agreement. Then ask pairs to peer-correct their work. Finally, have different pairs role-play the dialogues.

**Learning Styles**
**Kinesthetic/Auditory Learners**
Play listening **Activité 16** a second time, asking students to demonstrate the instructions they hear using gestures and imaginary cooking utensils.

📘 **Communicative Activities**

## Answers

19. *Recipes will vary.*
20. *Presentations will vary.*
21. *Presentations will vary.*

### Culture

**Products: Activity**
Ask students to prepare a French dish for their family who will write feedback.

### Communication

**Interpretive, Presentational: Cooperative Groups**

Teams choose a classic French dish, such as **une tarte aux pommes, un sandwich au jambon**, etc., for which they prepare a display of the recipe with a picture and a table setting. However, they must leave out one ingredient from the recipe and one item from the table setting. Teams inspect each other's presentations to determine what is missing from the display, which they note on a card and leave face down at each station.

### Expansion

Distribute recipes in French. Have students convert amounts for three ingredients to American measures and show the results.

### Reference Desk

**Blended Instruction**
Consider using blended instruction, a combination of in-class learning and computer-mediated instruction or learning opportunities. Ask students to complete activities on the computer or using their cell phone, smartphone, or other emerging technology. This will allow students to hone their tech skills and become more independent learners. Schedule routine Internet and e-book learning in class and in the lab.

# À vous la parole

## Communiquez!

**Question centrale: What makes a house a "home"?**

### 19 Un livre de recettes  1.1, 1.3

**Interpretive/Presentational Communication**

In small groups, decide on an American recipe to create for a Francophone teen. Write each step of the recipe on a separate note card, including the necessary quantities of the ingredients. Then turn in your cards to your teacher, who will mix up all the cards from the class and give a couple to each student, along with the name of a dish. Ask your classmates if they have a card for your recipe. You will need to anticipate the steps of the recipe in order to do this. Finally, put the cards for your recipe in order and type up the ingredients and instructions to make a recipe page for the cookbook for a French-speaking teen.

> **MODÈLE**  Recipe: banana split
> **Est-ce que tu as la carte "Couper les bananes"?**

**Vocabulaire utile**

| | |
|---|---|
| **mélanger** | to mix |
| **ajouter** | to add |
| **peler** | to peel |
| **faire cuire** | to cook |
| **laver** | to wash |

## Communiquez!

### 20 À table aux USA!  1.3, 2.2

**Presentational Communication**

Prepare a demonstration in French for Francophone exchange students about the way your family sets the table. Remember to use props such as silverware, plates, bowls, and glasses. Present your demonstration to the class live or via video or podcast.

## Communiquez!

### 21 Bon Appétit!  1.1, 1.3, 2.2

**Interpersonal/Presentational Communication**

Working with a partner, choose an easy recipe and demonstrate how to prepare it for a French cooking show. As you demonstrate, be sure to state the quantities of the ingredients you are using. The class will be your audience. Dishes you might prepare include: a banana split, tacos, a smoothie, burgers or veggie burgers, a casserole, or a taco salad.

## Essential Instruction

1. For **Activité 19**, have each student type up the recipes before class. Explain that infinitives are often used for recipes, but that using the **vous** imperative (command) form is also acceptable.
2. Have students choose either **Activité 20** or **21**. For **Activité 20**, use card stock table settings or white boards so students can show each other how their family sets the table for guests. If there are any exchange students in school, consider inviting them to demonstrate how they set a table at home.
3. As volunteers read aloud the **Stratégie communicative**, review the prepositions, **c'est** vs. **il/elle est**, and brainstorm a list of adjectives. Then, assign **Activité 22** as pair work.

# Stratégie communicative

## Descriptive Writing

Effective descriptive writing depends on the writer's ability to paint pictures with words, and then organize those pictures into an effective pattern. To describe where things are in relationship to each other, use prepositions such as: **dans**, **derrière**, **devant**, **sous**, **sur**, **à droite de**, **à gauche de**, **à côté de**, **au fond de**.

Once you establish relationships among items, you can add adjectives describing colors, sizes, and nationalities to make your description more vivid. Here is a review of how adjectives are formed in French.

Remember, nouns are either masculine or feminine and singular or plural in French. Adjectives agree in gender and number with the nouns they modify. There are some exceptions, however, such as the adjective **marron**, which is invariable.

| Masc. singular | Fem. Singular | Masc. plural | Fem. plural |
|---|---|---|---|
| intelligent | intelligente | intelligents | intelligentes |
| algérien | algérienne | algériens | algériennes |
| généreux | généreuse | généreux | généreuses |
| marron | marron | marron | marron |

In addition, French adjectives are usually placed after the noun they modify: **une lampe algérienne**.

## Communiquez!

**22  Je décris ma vie.**  1.1

### Interpersonal Communication

Ask your partner to describe people and things in his or her life.

**MODÈLE**   ton ami(e)
A: **Comment est ton amie, Élisabeth?**
B: **C'est une amie sympa et intelligente.**

1. ta maison ou ton appartement
2. ton film préféré
3. ta mère
4. ton cours d'anglais
5. ton prof préféré
6. ton frère ou ta sœur
7. ton acteur ou ton actrice préféré(e)

Comment est ton acteur préféré?

Il est drôle comme toi.

## Differentiated Learning
### Adapt
Brainstorm easy recipes and assign one per group for **Activité 19**. After groups peer-correct their recipes, set a timer and have them do the recipe re-assemble, returning to the original group to verify if the recipe makes sense.

## Special Needs Students
### Linguistically Challenged
1. Balance groups according to ability for **Activité 19**. Before writing the recipe instructions, have students list the key verbs and vocabulary for each step.
2. You may wish to provide vocabulary for a simple recipe or limit the steps to help students do **Activité 21**. Ask students to bring in props to make their demonstration more fun to watch and easier to understand for the rest of the class.

**Answers** _____

**23** *Drawings will vary.*

**24** *Drawings will vary.*

## Communication

### Presentational

Hand out an image of a room to pairs of students. Each pair will show their image to another pair for 10 — 15 seconds. Students must study the image but are not allowed to write anything down. After the time limit, pairs write a list of every item they can remember from the picture they studied. When their lists are complete, the pairs exchange pictures and check how closely their list corresponds to the pictured items. Students can then present their descriptions to the rest of the class.

## Expansion

For **Activité 24,** have students prepare their drawing before class. To vary this activity, post magazine pictures and have partners describe them in writing in several brief paragraphs.

**23 Je dessine!**   2.1

Your partner will describe a living room orally. Draw the room that he or she describes. Then switch roles.

**24 Ma chambre**  2.1

Draw a picture of your real or imaginary bedroom that includes furniture and other items that make your bedroom special. Write a description of your actual or dream bedroom using the prepositions and adjectives you already know. For additional adjectives and prepositions, use a bilingual dictionary. Be creative!

### Essential Instruction

1. Have students bring in a photo or drawing of a living room to use for **Activité 23.**
2. For **Activité 24**, have students list furnishings and adjectives, then write their descriptions using the words on their list. Discuss the use of online dictionaries and establish a policy regarding online translators, many of which do not provide a context and thus lead to misinterpretation.
3. Listen to the **Leçon C** vocabulary and have students repeat.
4. If possible, have students quiz each other about their laptops' features in class using the vocabulary, for example, **Qu'est-ce que c'est?** or **C'est le clavier.**

# Vocabulaire actif

## La chambre 🎧 ❀ 1.2

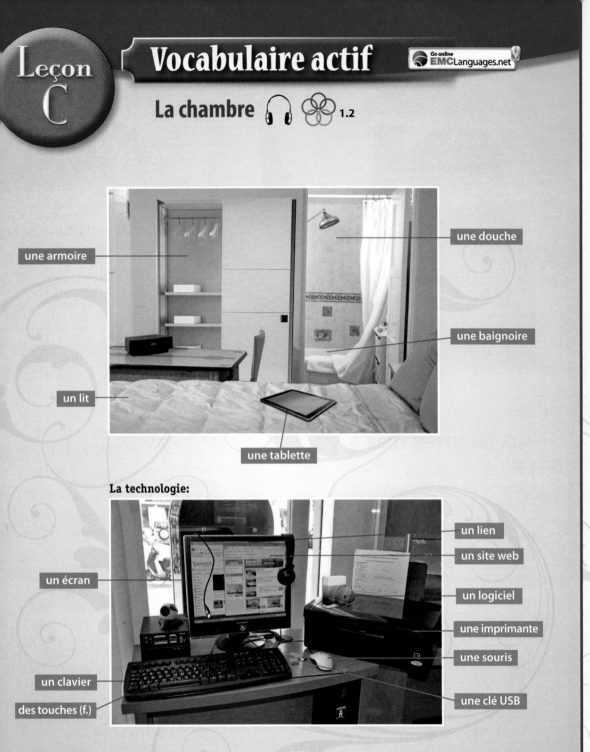

une armoire

une douche

une baignoire

un lit

une tablette

**La technologie:**

un écran

un clavier

des touches (f.)

un lien

un site web

un logiciel

une imprimante

une souris

une clé USB

## Reference Desk

1. Have students study the images and the corresponding vocabulary. Challenge them to find what other items are pictured but not labeled. Have students research new vocabulary as needed. For example, from **la chambre: les ceintres, les oreillers, le duvet, la radio-réveil, les étagère**; from **la technologie: les fils** *(wires)*, **les câbles, le disque dur externe** *(external disk drive)*, **la webcam, le lecteur de disques, le matériel** *(hardware)*.

2. Point out that **placard** can refer to closets or kitchen cabinets (both used to store things) and that many French bedrooms contain **armoires** rather than closets. Explain that **un clavier** is a keyboard on a computer, a piano, an accordion (fingerboard), and a phone (keypad). **Une souris** is not only a computer mouse, but also the word for the animal itself.

## Critical Thinking

**Evaluate**
Ask students how their rooms and computer work areas compare to those in the **Vocabulaire actif**. Are the images in the textbook necessarily French or European? Why or why not?

## Differentiated Learning

**Decelerate**
To facilitate the task in **Activité 23**, give students a diagram of a room that you have already drawn so that they have something concrete to work from. For **Activité 24**, give students sentence starters such as, **Dans ma chambre idéale, il y a....** When they look at their illustration or photo, remind them to focus on vocabulary they know and keep sentences simple.

**Expand, Accelerate**
Students can also describe a kitchen, dining room, or home office for **Activité 23**. Students have already seen the word **tapis**, so ask them to guess the meaning of **un tapis de souris** *(mouse pad)*.

## Learning Styles

**Kinesthetic/Auditory Learners**
Students can use dollhouse furniture or pictures of furniture from magazines or coloring books to arrange according to their partner's description in **Activité 23**, using their desk as the floor plan.

**Qu'est-ce que Sophie fait pour télécharger une chanson?**

1. Elle démarre l'ordinateur.
2. Elle clique avec la souris.
3. Elle ouvre le logiciel.
4. Elle navigue sur le site.
5. Elle paie.
6. Elle télécharge sa chanson préférée.
7. Elle synchronise son lecteur MP3.
8. Elle ferme le logiciel.

## Pour la conversation

**H**ow do I say that I don't understand?

> **Je ne comprends pas** ce problème de maths.
> *I don't understand this math problem.*

**H**ow do I talk about the computer?

> La chanson de Natasha St-Pier? **Je la télécharge.**
> *Natasha Saint-Pier's song? I'm downloading it.*

> **Tu imprimes** les paroles?
> *Are you printing the lyrics?*

### Et si je voulais dire…?

| | |
|---|---|
| **une armoire à pharmacie** | *medicine cabinet* |
| **un bidet** | *bidet* |
| **une commode** | *dresser* |
| **un lavabo** | *bathroom sink* |
| **un réveil-matin** | *alarm clock* |
| **une table de nuit** | *night stand* |

### Essential Instruction

1. Ask students to scan the process for downloading to see if they can find cognates, and have them decide if they would add or modify any steps in the process.
2. Listen to **Pour la conversation** and have students share what songs they download or lyrics they print out.
3. For **Activité 1**, to review numbers, call out a number out of order and have students respond with the vocabulary.
4. Have students sketch the bedroom in **Activité 2** as they read the description.

**1**
1. Il a un bureau.
2. Il a une chaise.
3. Il a une lampe de bureau.
4. Il a un ordinateur portable.
5. Il a une imprimante.
6. Il a une clé USB.
7. Il a un lit.

**2** *Drawings will vary.*

**1** **La chambre de Karim**  **2.1, 2.2**

*Dites ce que Karim a dans sa chambre.*

**MODÈLE** **Il a une affiche de film.**

1.

2.

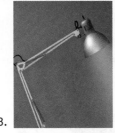
3.

4.

5.

6.

7.

**2** **La chambre de Rahina** **1.2**

*Lisez la description de la chambre de Rahina, puis faites un dessin avec tous les détails.*

La chambre de Rahina est jaune. Dans sa chambre, elle a un grand lit. Son lecteur MP3 et des photos de ses copains sont sur le lit. Elle a un bureau où elle fait ses devoirs. Devant le bureau, il y a une chaise confortable. Sur le bureau, il y a un ordinateur, des cahiers, des livres, et une trousse. Sur la table de nuit, il y a une lampe orange. Le tapis dans sa chambre est orange et marron. Elle collectionne des affiches de films. Elle met ses vêtements dans un placard.

**Differentiated Learning**
**Adapt/Accelerate**
Students can have fun by rewriting the paragraph in **Activité 2** by changing the location of items, for example, **Ses livres et cahiers sont sous le lit. La lampe est dans le placard, etc.**

**Multiple Intelligences**
**Bodily-Kinesthetic/Visual-Spatial**
Have one member of each pair of students draw part of the bedroom in **Activité 2** at the board or using individual white boards while his or her partner reads half of the description. Have students switch roles to complete the task.

Script can be found in the front pages of the Annotated Teacher's Edition.

A, B, C, E, G

**④**

1. Je démarre mon ordinateur.
2. Je navigue le site.
3. Je trouve ma chanson préférée.
4. Je télécharge la chanson.
5. Je synchronise mon lecteur MP3.
6. Je ferme le logiciel.

**⑤**

1. démarre
2. clique
3. navigue
4. paie
5. télécharge
6. synchronise
7. ferme

## Reference Desk

French actress, director, screen-writer, and author Sophie Marceau (b. 1966-) has appeared in more than 38 films. Marceau earned fame as a teen when she appeared in *La boum* (1980) and *La boum II* (1982) for which she received the **César** (French film industry award) for Most Promising Actress. In *LOL*, Marceau plays the mother of 16-year old Lola, nicknamed Lol, whose life is split among her high school studies, her secret diary, her friends, boyfriends, and her divorced parents.

## Communication

**Presentational**

Challenge students to design and display an original film poster for a favorite film. Students could describe the poster, withholding the film title or actors' names, as the class tries to guess the title.

## Culture

**Perspectives: Activity**

Have students research posters of French and American films. Are the images changed for a different audience? What kinds of pictures illustrate a French vs. an American comedy? Would students know the poster was for a French film if they didn't see the title?

---

**3** **La chambre de Julien**   **2.1, 2.2**

*Écrivez les lettres des illustrations qui représentent les meubles et les accessoires que Julien a dans sa chambre.*

A.

B.

C.

D.

E.

F.

G.

**4** **En ordre, s'il vous plaît!** **2.1, 2.2**

*Mettez les phrases suivantes dans l'ordre logique.*

1. Je télécharge la chanson.
2. Je trouve ma chanson préférée.
3. Je navigue sur le site.
4. Je démarre mon ordinateur.
5. Je synchronise mon lecteur MP3.
6. Je ferme le logiciel.

**5** **Moussa télécharge une chanson.** **2.1, 2.2**

*Complétez chaque phrase avec un verbe de la liste.*

| synchronise | ferme | clique |
| télécharge | démarre | paie | navigue |

1. D'abord, Moussa... son ordinateur.
2. Ensuite, il... avec la souris pour ouvrir le logiciel.
3. Il... sur le site pour trouver sa chanson préférée.
4. Il... pour la chanson.
5. Il... la chanson.
6. Il... son lecteur MP3.
7. Enfin, il... le logiciel.

**Essential Instruction**

1. Do listening **Activité 3** as a class and assign **Activités 4** and **5** in pairs.
2. For a change of pace, write each of the **Questions personnelles** in **Activité 7** on a card or a slip of paper. Then have students pick from **un beret** one of the questions to answer.

## 6 J'achète des billets de cinéma en ligne.  2.1, 2.2

*Mettez les phrases suivantes dans l'ordre pour expliquer ce que vous faites pour acheter des billets de cinéma en ligne.*

1. Je paie avec ma carte de crédit.
2. Je démarre mon ordinateur.
3. Je choisis "AlloCiné."
4. Mais je clique sur le lien "Billetterie et sorties de cinéma," et "Réservez."
5. J'imprime la page web.
6. Je ne télécharge pas le film sur mon ordinateur.
7. Je navigue sur le web pour trouver un bon site.

## 7 Questions personnelles    1.1

*Répondez aux questions.*

1. De quelle couleur est ta chambre?
2. Est-ce que tu as un grand lit ou un petit lit?
3. Où est-ce que tu mets tes vêtements?
4. Est-ce que tu as des affiches? De quoi sont-elles?
5. Qu'est-ce qu'il y a sur ton bureau?
6. Qu'est-ce que tu fais pour trouver une chanson que tu aimes en ligne?

> J'ai un ordinateur sur mon bureau.

Answers _____

**6**

1. Je démarre mon ordinateur.
2. Je navigue le web pour trouver un bon site.
3. Je choisis «AlloCiné.»
4. Je ne télécharge pas le film sur mon ordinateur,
5. mais je clique sur le lien «Billetterie et sorties de cinéma,» et «Réservez».
6. Je paie avec ma carte de crédit.
7. J'imprime la page web.

**7** *Answers will vary.*

## Communication

**Interpersonal, Presentational: Paired Practice**

Tell pairs that they have a certain allowance to spend at an online tech store to buy items for French class. Students should check out the products online, decide on what to buy and how much items cost, and share their "purchases" with the class, explaining their choices.

## Game

Have teams randomly list on the board the subject-verb of each sentence in **Activité 4** (**Je navigue, Je démarre**, etc). Assign a different list to each team. As you call out the corresponding object (**la chanson**, **mon ordinateur**), teams rush to complete the sentences. Award points to the team that correctly completes and reorders the sentences.

## Differentiated Learning
### Adapt
Create a list of different online purchases that students might make (CDs, songs, books, apps, etc.) and have them write out the process of online buying similar to **Activité 6**. Ask students to write and share in small groups a description of a room (parent bedroom, kitchen, etc.) in their home, while others guess which room it is.

## Accelerate
Ask students to add sequencing words introduced in **Unité 6** (**d'abord, ensuite, enfin**) for **Activité 6**. Encourage them to take their writing to a new level by embellishing the description of their room.

## RESOURCES

**Dialogue Video**

**Answers**

1. Thomas
2. Julien
3. Maxime
4. Maxime et Julien
5. Maxime

### Extension

She backed it up on her USB key or thumb drive because her computer is slow. She says, "**il rame,**" which means literally, "it rows" (her computer is slow).

### Communication

**Presentational: Paired Practice**

Students may work in pairs to create a comic strip with 4–6 panels illustrating **un problème électronique**. Encourage students to take inspiration from the **Rencontres culturelles** dialogues for the **bulles** (word bubbles), but to write about and illustrate unique situations. Display the comic strips and invite another French class to judge. Students may also enjoy role-playing their "stories" to another class.

### Expansion

Have groups make a French dictionary of tech terms. They should include illustrated cardboard covers, a title page, illustrated pages, etc. To make it more fun, the dictionary could be in an oversized format so it can be displayed in class. On a visit to elementary schools in your district, students can teach some tech terms to younger students using their dictionaries. By teaching the younger ones, they will reinforce their vocabulary.

# Rencontres culturelles

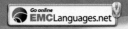

## Une chanson téléchargée     1.2

### 8 Une chanson téléchargée

*Identifiez ces personnes.*

1. Cette personne va venir aider Julien et Maxime avec leurs devoirs de maths.
2. Cette personne envoie un SMS.
3. Cette personne télécharge une chanson.
4. Cette personne aime la chanson de Natasha St-Pier.
5. Cette personne va chanter une chanson à son amie. **2.1, 2.2, 3.2**

Julien et Maxime sont en train d'étudier dans la chambre de Maxime.

**Julien:** Je ne comprends pas ce problème de maths. À qui est-ce qu'on peut demander?

**Maxime:** À Thomas, il est fort en maths. Tu as ton portable?

**Julien:** Et qu'est-ce que je...?

**Maxime:** Ben, un texto!

**Julien:** Alors... "Taf impossible en maths. Viens!"

*(Julien regarde son portable.)*

Il arrive.

**Maxime:** Super!

**Julien:** Qu'est-ce que tu fais?

**Maxime:** Je vais sur un site de musique. Nous allons écouter une chanson de Natasha St-Pier.

**Julien:** Qui?

**Maxime:** Une chanteuse du Nouveau-Brunswick. Tu vas voir. La chanson est géniale.

*(Ils écoutent la chanson.)*

**Julien:** Je suis d'accord avec toi. Elle est géniale. Tu peux m'envoyer le lien?

**Maxime:** Non, donne-moi ton portable. Il est là-bas, sur le lit. Je télécharge la chanson.

**Julien:** Merci. Tu imprimes les paroles? Tu vas chanter la chanson à qui?

**Maxime:** À... ça commence par un "Y," ça finit par un "E"!

### Extension Un problème électronique   1.2, 2.1, 2.2

Marie et Alyssa sont dans la salle d'informatique.

**Alyssa:** Planté!

**Marie:** Eh bien, ferme tout et redémarre.

**Alyssa:** Qu'est-ce que j'ai fait encore?

**Marie:** Pas de panique... tu cliques ici, tu tapes là, et le tour est joué!

**Alyssa:** Heureusement, j'ai fait une sauvegarde sur ma clé USB juste avant.

**Marie:** Tu as trop de programmes inutiles. Ton ordinateur, il rame et il plante. C'est aussi simple....

**Alyssa:** Alors, éliminons! Avant, je peux vérifier si je n'ai rien perdu....

**Marie:** Bien sûr que non! Tu as fait une sauvegarde! Ah! L'informatique avec toi, ce n'est pas simple!

### Extension Que fait Alyssa pour sauvegarder son travail?

### Essential Instruction

1. Set the stage for the video by surveying how many students text or call friends when they need help with homework. As students watch the video, ask them to complete Julien's line: **Qu'est ce que je...** and to guess from context what **taf** means (**travail à faire**).
2. Do **Activité 8** to verify comprehension and then replay the dialogue.
3. Be sure that students can locate New Brunswick on a map.
4. Discuss the **Comparaisons** question (forced relocation and movement of Native American nations from southeastern parts of the United States following the Indian Removal Act of 1830) as a class. Play some Zydeco music in class to introduce them to the **Produits** topic.

# Points de départ

What makes a house a "home"?

## RESOURCES

👁 **e-visual 27**

📖 **Workbook 33–34**

## Les jeunes et les technologies

Les jeunes Français habitent un univers des technologies de l'information et de la communication: textos, blogues, téléchargements *peer to peer*, web 2.0, flux vidéo et audio. C'est une culture du "tout, tout de suite." Les différents types d'écrans (télévision, ordinateur, console de jeux, téléphone portable) occupent une place très importante dans les loisirs* des jeunes Français. Dans la maison, il y a en moyenne* dix écrans par famille.

Il y a combien d'écrans dans cette pièce?

**1.2, 3.1, 4.2**

———
**loisirs** *leisure activities;* **en moyenne** *an average of*

## La Francophonie: Le Nouveau-Brunswick

**1.2**

Le Nouveau-Brunswick est une province canadienne dans l'est du pays. C'est la seule* province d'être officiellement bilingue (anglais et français). (Le Québec est officiellement francophone.) Plus de 30% des habitants parlent français. Le Nouveau-Brunswick est l'ancien pays des Acadiens, les ancêtres des Cajuns de Louisiane. Aujourd'hui, sa population est assez multiculturelle avec des personnes d'origine acadienne et indigène* parmi* d'autres.

———
**seule** *only;* **indigène** *native;* **parmi** *among*

### COMPARAISONS

What people in America were forced to abandon their lands? What was the Trail of Tears?

**4.2**

## Le Grand Dérangement

**1.2, 5.1**

Les Cajuns, habitants de la Louisiane, et les Acadiens, habitants du Nouveau-Brunswick et de la Nouvelle Écosse*, sont très marqués par ce qu'ils appellent **le Grand Dérangement**. En 1755, 13.000 Acadiens Francophones sont chassés* par les Anglophones de ces provinces canadiennes. Entre 7.000 et 8.000 meurent* et beaucoup de familles sont séparées. Dispersés sur les territoires britanniques, ils sont nombreux à se réfugier* aux États-Unis où ils forment la communauté des Cajuns qui est aujourd'hui située principalement au sud* des États-Unis en Louisiane.

———
**Nouvelle Écosse** *Nova Scotia;* **chassés** *chased out;* **meurent** *die;* **ils sont nombreux à se réfugier** *many take refuge;* **sud** *south*

### Produits

**Zydeco**, ou **Zarico** en français, est un exemple de la musique folklorique de Louisiane et d'autres états du Sud. Cette musique est liée (*tied*) à la musique de l'Acadie. Deux instruments de musique qu'on emploie (*uses*) en faisant cette musique sont l'accordéon et le frottoir (*washboard*).

**1.2**

## Reference Desk

1. Bring your class discussion of the history of **Acadie** and the tragedy of **Le Grand Dérangement** to life with the music of the Acadian folk band **Grand Dérangement**, from southwestern Nova Scotia. The band's evocative songs and instrumentals have helped spread the music and history of **Acadie** around the world. While the band's name echoes Acadian history, and their song **"Y a jamais de Grand Dérangement"** tells the sad tale, the name of the band also suggests a desire to stir up the listening audience.
2. Ask students to find out what the flag of **Acadie** has in common with the French tricolor.
3. Discuss and debate with students whether the forced expulsion of the French during **Le Grand Dérangement** constitutes ethnic cleansing during the 18th century.
4. Show the movie *Bellizaire the Cajun* to your class.

## Expansion

Divide the class into regional groups: Cajun, Acadian, Breton, West African, etc. Each group will choose and practice singing one or more songs representative of their group's regional music. Students will present the songs in a karaoke performance to the class. You may wish to invite other language classes to the performance and other language teachers for judging.

## Differentiated Learning
### Accelerate
For the **Extension** dialogue, first explain that **ramer** literally means to row a boat (moving slowly) and that **planté** means planted (not moving at all). Then ask the students to guess what these words mean in the context of computer language (slowing down and then crashing). You can also teach them the difference between **sauver** and **sauvegarder**.

## Learning Styles
### Auditory Learners
Find an online radio station from Louisiana that features Zydeco or Cajun music and listen to a few songs in class.

### Multiple Intelligences
**Musical-Rhythmic/Bodily-Kinesthetic**
Play samples of Zydeco music from the Internet.

1. L'Univers des technologies de l'information et de la communication
2. On y parle l'anglais et le français.
3. Ils viennent du Nouveau-Brunswick et de la Nouvelle-Écosse.
4. Date: 1755
   Nombre d'Acadiens chassés du Canada: 13.000
   Nombre de morts: entre 7.000 et 8.000
5. *Answers will vary.*

**À discuter**
*Discussions will vary.*

### Reference Desk

1. The creole word "Cajun" is a phonetic distortion of the word **Acadien**.
2. With some research on the expulsion of the French from the Canadian Maritimes, students can create a class map showing the routes of dispersement and the diaspora of **Acadiens,** including those forced by ship along the Atlantic coast of America, only to be lost at sea, or those landed at points along the coast of New England, Virginia, Louisiana, etc., or others who traveled overland into Maine and the rest of New England. Some students may have descended from Acadian exiles.

### Culture

**Perspectives: Activity**
Students may be able to interview local people with Acadian heritage. Students may also research Acadian cultural groups in New England and Louisiana that work to keep their heritage alive, and find out what activities they do to promote the Acadian culture. Have students research online and share common French expressions in Cajun and Louisiana Creole.

## Natasha St-Pier  1.2

Natasha St-Pier est une chanteuse de chansons sentimentales et romantiques. Elle vient du Nouveau-Brunswick et débute sa carrière internationale en 1999 à l'âge de 18 ans. Aujourd'hui, elle continue à être adorée au Canada et en France.

*Natasha St-Pier*

**Tracklist**
01 - Embrasse-moi
02 - L'Esprit De Famille
03 - 1, 2, 3
04 - L'Orient-Express
05 - John
06 - Pardonnez-moi
07 - L'instinct de Survie
08 - J'irai te chercher

Natasha St-Pier chante pour la radio Chérie FM.

**9 Questions culturelles**  1.1, 1.2, 2.1, 2.2

*Répondez aux questions.*

1. Comment est-ce qu'on décrit (*describe*) l'univers des jeunes Français?
2. Quelles langues est-ce qu'on parle au Nouveau-Brunswick?
3. D'où viennent les Cajuns et les Acadiens?
4. Qu'est-ce que vous savez du Grand Dérangement? Faites un profil:
   - Date
   - Nombre d'Acadiens chassés du Canada
   - Nombre de morts
5. Quelles sont les meilleures (*best*) chansons de Natasha St-Pier? Écoutez ses chansons en ligne. Ensuite, faites une liste de vos cinq chansons préférées.

**À discuter**

How important is technology in your household?

Nathaniel Williams du groupe Nathan and the Zydeco Cha Chas joue de l'accordéon à la Nouvelle-Orléans.

### Essential Instruction

1. Play **Natasha St-Pier's** music in the background while students work with a partner to answer the questions in **Activité 9**.
2. Use the **À discuter** question to prepare students for **Du coté des médias**. Assign small groups to analyze the survey results. Ask each group to prepare three comparative sentences about Internet usage in France and between France and the United States.

## Du côté des médias

*Lisez ce sondage (poll) sur l'usage d'Internet en France.*

| en % | Télécharger des logiciels | Télécharger des films | Télécharger de la musique | Effectuer* un achat en ligne | Téléphoner grâce à* un logiciel (Skype, etc.) | Rechercher des offres d'emploi* | Utiliser Internet pour la formation* ou les études | Utiliser Internet pour un travail ou les études | Effectuer une démarche administrative ou fiscale* |
|---|---|---|---|---|---|---|---|---|---|
| **Hommes** | 34 | 20 | 27 | 41 | 11 | 19 | 18 | 25 | 39 |
| **Femmes** | 18 | 11 | 20 | 34 | 6 | 20 | 16 | 20 | 34 |
| **12-17 ans** | 49 | 32 | 56 | 28 | ns | ns | 35 | 14 | ns |
| **18-24 ans** | 56 | 47 | 59 | 56 | 14 | 54 | 33 | 43 | 55 |
| **25-39 ans** | 17 | 7 | 13 | 38 | 7 | 15 | 13 | 16 | 40 |
| **60-69 ans** | ns | ns | ns | 17 | ns | ns | ns | ns | 20 |

**effectuer** *carry out;* **grâce à** *thanks to;* **offres d'emploi** *want ads;* **formation** *training;* **démarche administrative ou fiscale** *adminstrative or tax-related task*

**10** **L'Internet et les Français**  **1.2, 2.1, 2.2**

*Répondez aux questions.*

1. Est-ce que plus de femmes ou d'hommes téléchargent de la musique? Des logiciels? Des films?
2. Quel groupe achète le plus en ligne?
3. Quel est le pourcentage de personnes âgées de 18–24 ans qui téléphonent grâce à un logiciel? C'est la majorité?
4. Quel groupe utilise l'Internet le plus pour un travail ou des études?
5. Pour quel groupe est-ce que l'Internet est le plus important?
6. Quels sont les résultats pour les ados américains? Faites un sondage *(survey)* basé sur le sondage français.

Ce sont les gens âgés de 25 à 39 ans qui achètent le plus en ligne, pardi!

**Answers** _____

**10**
1. plus d'hommes
2. les 25 à 39 ans
3. 6%; non
4. les 18 à 24 ans
5. pour le groupe des 18 à 24 ans
6. *Answers will vary.*

### Communication

**Interpersonal, Presentational**
Have students devise questions to poll other class members about their Internet use, using the chart in **Du côté des médias** for inspiration. Make a chart showing the results from one or more classes or age groups. After discussing the results in class, ask students to summarize their findings in writing. Students with e-pals can also inquire about their international peers' Internet usage. Provide search terms for students to use as they look online for recent polls on teen use of the Internet and tech devices in the French news.

### Differentiated Learning

**Decelerate**
Assign groups of mixed abilities to complete the **Questions culturelles** in order to ensure balance and encourage peer-helping.

**Accelerate**
Ask students to express if they think Internet usage would be the same in the United States as in France if the same cross-section of the population were polled. Why or why not?

### Multiple Intelligences
**Visual-Spatial**
Ask students to create a graph or other visual to present the results in a different way. Were they surprised by their findings?

# La culture sur place

## Nos maisons
### Introduction

Quand on entre dans la maison d'une autre personne, on peut voir comment est sa vie (*life*) de tous les jours. C'est une occasion de voir la culture sur place.

### 11 Dans ma maison  1.2, 1.3

*Lisez les descriptions suivantes des six maisons qu'on trouve dans des pays francophones. Est-ce que votre maison est comme ces maisons? Écrivez chaque description dans la bonne colonne d'une grille comme celle-ci pour faire des comparaisons.*

| Ma maison est comme ça. | Ma maison est un peu comme ça. | Ma maison n'est pas comme ça. |
|---|---|---|
| = | + | − |

1. Il y a beaucoup de photos de famille.
2. Les enfants aident les parents dans la cuisine.
3. Les enfants mettent la table.
4. On prépare des spécialités du pays d'origine.
5. L'espace intérieur est divisé en deux, avec un espace pour les femmes et un espace pour les hommes.
6. Il y a des tapis et des meubles qui viennent du Maghreb.
7. La baignoire est séparée des toilettes.
8. Il y a dix écrans dans la maison.
9. On télécharge la musique d'autres pays.
10. Les enfants invitent leurs camarades de classe à la maison.

### Faisons l'inventaire!

### 12 Présentation et discussion   1.1, 1.3

1. *Donnez votre réaction aux dix phrases de l'Activité 11.*
2. *Parlez à une personne qui parle français et demandez-lui sa réaction aux dix phrases.*
3. *En groupes de trois ou quatre personnes, discutez vos réponses à l'activité avec l'organigramme en utilisant les questions suivantes.*

A. Are your answers different from those of your classmates? Discuss possible reasons for this.
B. Are most homes in your community similar to or different from each other? Why do you think this is so?
C. Have you ever visited someone's home that is very different from your own? In what ways was it different? What do you think of these differences?

**Essential Instruction**

1. Ask students how one says "on site" in French (**sur place**).
2. Have students complete **Activité 11** individually, then compare and contrast their results with other students in **Activité 12**. Tally the results.
3. Present and practice the forms of the verb **pouvoir**. Connect the singular verb endings to the verb **vouloir**. Write the proverb **Vouloir, c'est pouvoir** on the board and ask students to guess the corresponding English proverb. ("Where there's a will, there's a way.")

4. Poll your students, asking a variety of questions about what they can do, such as, **"Qui peut skier? parler chinois? jouer du piano?"** Use cognates and gestures to help with comprehension.
5. Have partners share three things they can do and three things they can't do in various places or situations (**dans le cours de français, au stade, dans la chambre, avec ses profs**, etc.). Ask each pair to share with the class something they learned about each other.

# Structure de la langue

## Present Tense of the Irregular Verb *pouvoir*  1.2

### RESOURCES

📖 **Workbook 35–38**

🔊 **Listening Activity**

Annie peut acheter l'ordinateur.

The verb **pouvoir**, which means "can" or "to be able (to)," is irregular. In the following examples, note the different ways to express **pouvoir** in English.

| pouvoir | | | |
|---|---|---|---|
| je | **peux** | nous | **pouvons** |
| tu | **peux** | vous | **pouvez** |
| il/elle/on | **peut** | ils/elles | **peuvent** |

**Pouvez**-vous cliquer sur le lien?     *Are you able to click on the link?*

Non, je ne **peux** pas.     *No, I can't.*

### Pronunciation Tip

The colored verb forms all have the same vowel sound that is different from that in the infinitive and the **nous** and **vous** forms.

### COMPARAISONS

In English, is "can" also usually followed by an infinitive?

I can speak French.

 4.1

Nous pouvons télécharger la chanson "Embrasse-moi!"

> COMPARAISONS: You might just respond "I can" if someone asks, "Can you come to the game?" But most times the verb "can" is followed by an infinitive in English also; "I can swim."

### Reference Desk

1. Remind students of the similar conjugation of the present tense of **pouvoir** and **vouloir**.
2. Both **pouvoir** and **vouloir** are often followed by infinitives.
3. Reinforce that the final -t in **peut** and **peuvent** is only pronounced in the inverted question form, as in **Peuvent-ils venir?**

### Communication

**Interpersonal: Paired Practice**

Pair up each student with a classmate to present a dialogue. Students find out if their partner can do a certain activity, then invite him or her to do it, settling on a time and place to meet.

**Special Needs Students**
**At-Risk Teens**
Be mindful that every family's circumstance is unique and that talking about one's home and family situation might be uncomfortable for some students For these students, allow them to discuss imaginary or media families.

**Possible answers:**

1. J'ai cinquante euros. Donc, je peux acheter le lecteur MP3, mais je ne peux pas acheter l'imprimante.
2. M. et Mme Lambert ont 500 euros. Donc, ils peuvent acheter l'ordinateur portable.
3. Tu as 35 euros. Donc, tu peux acheter la clé USB, mais tu ne peux pas acheter la clé USB et la souris.
4. On a 85 euros. Donc, on peut acheter l'imprimante, mais on ne peut pas acheter le téléphone portable.
5. Mon frère et moi, nous avons 75 euros. Donc, nous pouvons acheter la clé USB et le lecteur MP3, mais nous ne pouvons pas acheter l'ordinateur portable.
6. Toi et tes amis, vous avez 20 euros. Donc, vous pouvez acheter le clavier, mais vous ne pouvez pas acheter le lecteur MP3.

1. Simon et moi, nous pouvons voir le film d'aventures.
2. Angèle et Marie-Alix peuvent voir la comédie romantique.
3. Jérôme et toi, vous ne pouvez pas voir le film d'action.
4. Toi, tu peux voir le film de science-fiction.
5. Martine ne peut pas voir le thriller.
6. Abdoulaye et Karim ne peuvent pas voir le film policier.
7. Karine peut voir le film musical
8. *Answers will vary.*

## Communication

**Interpersonal: Paired Practice**

Have students make a list of questions with **pouvoir** such as, **Est-ce que tu peux faire des recherches en ligne dans la salle de classe? Est-ce que tu peux utiliser ton portable en classe?** If possible, have students exchange questions with e-pals and post the answers.

## Culture

**Products: Activity**

Challenge students to list films that fall into the different categories listed in **Activité 14.**

---

### 13 Le rayon d'appareils électroniques  2.1, 2.2

*Utilisez la forme appropriée du verbe **pouvoir** pour dire quels appareils électroniques et accessoires ces personnes peuvent ou ne peuvent pas acheter avec l'argent qu'elles ont.*

**clé USB**    32 €    **imprimante**    61 €    **ordinateur portable**    495 €    **lecteur MP3**    35 €

**portable**    89 €    **clavier**    18 €    **souris**    15 €    **tablette**    489 €

**MODÈLE**   Alexis a quinze euros.

**Alexis a quinze euros. Donc, il peut acheter la souris, mais il ne peut pas acheter le clavier.**

1. J'ai 50 euros.
2. M. et Mme Lambert ont 500 euros.
3. Tu as 35 euros.
4. On a 85 euros.
5. Mon frère et moi, nous avons 75 euros.
6. Toi et tes amis, vous avez 20 euros.

### 14 Au cinéma  2.1, 2.2

*Les parents au Québec insistent que leurs enfants qui ont 15 ans voient seulement (only) des films "Visa général" (PG) ou "13 ans +" (13 and older). Dites qui peut et qui ne peut pas voir les films au cinéma Mega-Plex Marché Central à Montréal cette semaine.*

| Genre de film | Classification |
|---|---|
| le drame | 16 ans + |
| le film d'aventures | Visa général |
| la comédie | 13 ans + |
| le film policier | 18 ans + |
| le film de science-fiction | Visa général |
| la comédie romantique | 13 ans + |
| le film d'action | 18 ans + |
| le thriller | 16 ans + |
| le film musical | Visa général |

1. Simon et moi, nous voulons voir le film d'aventures.
2. Angèle et Marie-Alix veulent voir la comédie romantique.
3. Jérôme et toi, vous voulez voir le film d'action.
4. Toi, tu veux voir le film de science-fiction.
5. Martine veut voir le thriller.
6. Abdoulaye et Karim veulent voir le film policier.
7. Karine veut voir le film musical.
8. Et toi? Qu'est-ce que tu veux voir? Est-ce que tu peux?

**Essential Instruction**

1. Review counting to 500, then assign groups to complete **Activité 13.**
2. Ask students to list the American movie ratings in English before they do **Activité 14.**
3. Check listening comprehension in **Activité 15.** Once they have finished listening, ask students to add original things that they can do with technology.
4. Once partners practice the dialogues in **Activité 16,** have volunteers present to the class. Encourage students to modify responses as they wish.

**Answers** _____

**15** Script can be found in the front pages of the Annotated Teacher's Edition.

1. non
2. non
3. oui
4. oui
5. non
6. oui

**16** *Answers follow model.*

## 15  La technologie: on peut...?   **2.1, 2.2**

*Écrivez les numéros 1–6 sur un papier. Écrivez **oui** si on peut faire les choses mentionnées ou **non**, si on ne peut pas les faire.*

*Communiquez!*

## 16  Tu peux...?  **1.1**

*À tour de rôle, demandez si votre partenaire a la permission de ses parents de faire les activités suivantes. Ensuite, écrivez un paragraphe qui décrit ce que votre partenaire peut et ne peut pas faire.*

**MODÈLE**   A: **Tu peux aller au café à 23h00?**
B: **Oui, je peux aller au café à 23h00. Et toi?**
ou
**Non, je ne peux pas aller au café à 23h00.**

1. envoyer des textos pendant le dîner
2. faire du footing ou du roller après 20h00
3. essayer les vêtements de ton frère ou de ta sœur
4. aller au centre commercial à 20h00 mercredi soir
5. choisir un film à regarder pour la famille
6. regarder la télé à 23h00 le mardi soir
7. manger devant la télévision
8. apporter ton ordinateur portable à l'école

*Tu peux faire du roller après 20h00?*

*Oui, je peux.*

*Tu peux apporter ton portable à l'école?*

*Non, je ne peux pas.*

## Communication

**Interpersonal: Cooperative Groups**

1. Ask two teams to make a list of "dos" and "don'ts" for the classroom in French, using forms of **pouvoir** followed by an infinitive. Compare which topics they listed in common and which ones they had not included but that the other team had.

2. Brainstorm a list of films currently showing for each genre listed in **Activité 14**. Ask students to survey each other about whether or not they can and want to see several of them. Finally, students can share one or two things that they learned about their classmates.

## Game

**Je veux et Je peux**
Introduce a sentence using **vouloir** or **pouvoir** (ex: **Je peux parler français**). Then point to a student introducing a new subject (ex: **tu**). The student must come up with the correct form (ex: **Tu peux parler français**). If the student responds correctly, he or she then points to another student and states a different subject (ex. **nous**). The game continues until all subjects have been used.

---

**Multiple Intelligences**
**Verbal-Linguistic/Intrapersonal**
Ask students to share on a class social network what they can or cannot do in two of the following areas: technology, sports, music, at home, at school, and in friendships.

**Special Needs Students**
**Social Anxiety**
Have students write out their responses to **Activité 16**.

## Reference Desk

Review the **Question centrale**. How have students' responses evolved since the beginning of the **Unité**?

**Blended Instruction**
Consider using blended instruction, a combination of in-class learning and computer-mediated instruction or learning opportunities. Ask students to complete activities on the computer or using their cell phone, smartphone, or other emerging electronic technology. This will allow students to hone their tech skills and become more independent learners. Schedule routine Internet and e-book learning in class and in the lab.

## Communication

**Interpersonal: Cooperative Groups**

Challenge students in groups to create skits about computer difficulties and act these out for the class. They may wish to have their skits show an online discussion, a conversation on the phone or in a computer store, or other situations.

**Presentational: Cooperative Groups**

Have students ask their parents what they were allowed to do as teens and compare findings in class.

---

## À vous la parole

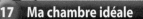

**What makes a house a "home"?**

**17 Ma chambre idéale**  1.3

**Presentational Communication**

You decide to enter a bedroom makeover contest sponsored by a French Canadian teen magazine. To win, you must submit a 100-word paragraph that describes your ideal bedroom and explains why you should win. Be specific in your description. Tell the color, size, and location of furniture, technology components, and other items in the bedroom.

> **MODÈLE** Ma chambre idéale a **un grand bureau sous la fenêtre....**

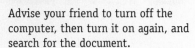

**18 Signal de détresse!** 1.1, 2.1

| Vocabulaire utile | |
|---|---|
| un document | *document* |
| envoie-moi | *send me* |
| utiliser | *to use* |

**Interpersonal Communication**

With a partner, role-play the following conversation between a tech whiz (A) and a friend (B) who calls in a panic because his or her computer has crashed while working on a French assignment. In your conversation:

Calm your friend down and ask what the problem is.  → Say you cannot find a document.

Advise your friend to turn off the computer, then turn it on again, and search for the document.  → Say you have the document.

Advise your friend to use an external flash drive to save the document. Then tell your friend that if he or she has a problem again, he or she can send you a text message.  → Thank your friend.

**Essential Instruction**

1. Students can use the description of an ideal bedroom they wrote for **Leçon B Activité 24**, or create a new one as a basis for **Activité 17**. Instruct them to add tech components and more details (color, size, and location of furniture).

2. For **Activité 18**, review vocabulary and expressions students will need, then assign pairs to prepare and practice the dialogue. Finally, have volunteers role-play the conversation.

3. Ask students to scan the **Rencontre avec l'auteur** for cognates and then read the paragraph for the following information: **nom, nationalité, profession, ami, philosophie, inspiration**.

4. Find and provide a simple poem and demonstrate how to assign letters to the end rhymes.

# Lecture thématique

## Le chat

### Rencontre avec l'auteur  1.2

**Guillaume Apollinaire** (1880–1918), un poète français, est le nom de plume (*pen name*) de Wilhelm Albert Wlodzimierz Apolinary de Waz-Kostrowicki. Il était (*was*) écrivain de l'avant-garde et membre d'un groupe artistique qui comprenait (*included*) Picasso. Selon (*according to*) Apollinaire, l'imagination doit gouverner l'écriture (*writing*), pas la théorie. Il a trouvé son inspiration dans la nature et la vie. Qu'est-ce qu'il y a dans sa maison idéale?

## Pré-lecture  2.1

Vous avez besoin de quelles personnes et de quels objets dans votre maison?

## Stratégie de lecture  2.1

### Rhyme Scheme

A rhyme scheme is the pattern of end rhymes, or rhymed words at the end of the lines of a poem. Rhyme schemes are labeled with letters, each letter indicating a particular sound. For example, the rhyme scheme of the first four lines of "Twinkle, Twinkle, Little Star" is A-A-B-B. Sometimes rhyming lines are also linked in meaning. Complete the chart below, noting the rhyme scheme and explaining how ideas are linked. Consider these questions as you read: Who does the narrator want in his house besides his wife and the cat? What does **lesquels** (*which*) link to besides his friends? In other words, what else can he not live without? Part of the chart has been filled out for you.

| End words | Rhyme scheme letters | Linked ideas |
|-----------|---------------------|--------------|
| Maison | A | |
| Raison | A | **la rime maison/raison:** the attitude of the narrator's wife contributes to his happiness at home |
| Livres | | |
| Saison | | |
| Vivre | | |

## Outils de lecture  2.1, 2.2

### Present Participles

When you read a selection and come across a grammatical construction you haven't learned yet, look up its meaning to see if you can figure out what it is. For example, you will see that **ayant** from line 2 is defined under the poem. It is the present participle of **avoir** (the *–ing* form of a verb in English). When used with **raison**, it literally means "having reason." What is another example of a present participle in this poem? Hint: it comes from the verb "to pass."

### Reference Desk

Enhance your students' appreciation of Apollinaire's work, much of which is accessible to the beginning student of French, by introducing them to more of his poetry.

### Communication

#### Presentational
Print out a selection of some of Apollinaire's pictoral **calligrammes** (the typography and layout make a picture related to the theme of the each poem) for groups to figure out. After gaining some familiarity with Apollinaire's style, have students make and share their own **calligrammes** with pictoral typographic structure.

### Differentiated Learning

#### Decelerate
1. Provide sentence starters and key words for the conversation in **Activité 18**.
2. Suggest answers to those challenged by the critical thinking skills needed to complete the **Stratégie de lecture** chart.

#### Accelerate
Suggest that interested students research rhyme patterns in French poetry and bring in examples. Provide search words such as **une rime riche, une rime plate, une rime féminine/masculine, des rimes croisées/embrassees.**

### Learning Styles

#### Auditory Learners
Find recordings online of poets reading poems with the AABB rhyme scheme. Have students listen and try to identify the rhyming sounds.

### Multiple Intelligences

#### Verbal-Linguistic/Musical-Rythmic
1. Assign research of traditional French poetry: **un sonnet, une ode,** and **une ballade**.
2. Play French music with an identifiable rhyme scheme.

## Answers

*Possible examples*: his house, his wife, his cat, his books, his friends.

**Activités d'expansion**
*Poems will vary.*

**Le monde visuel**
Il y a des rectangles dans le reflet de l'eau, dans le champ, et les maisons à l'arrière-plan. Il y a quatre plans horizontaux: le lac, le champ, les maisons, et le ciel. La peinture est impressionniste à cause des lumières et des touches floues (*blurry strokes*) comme dans les arbres et le champ. Elle est cubiste à cause des formes géométriques.

**Activités d'expansion**
*Activities will vary.*

---

### Critical Thinking

**Analysis**
Ask students why the poem is called **"Le chat."** What elements of the poem make this animal stand out among others? Ask students to reflect on the poet's purpose in choosing what seems to be the least important item as a title for the poem. What does this contrast suggest? Remind students to look at rhythm, rhyme, images, and semantic associations.

---

### Connections

**Art**
Have students research and display pictures of the Provence-inspired paintings of Cézanne and Van Gogh (presented in **Leçon B**, **Points de départ**). Locate on a map Arles, St. Rémy (Van Gogh), Mont Ste-Victoire, and Aix-en-Provence (Cézanne). Discuss what attracted Cézanne, Monet, Renoir, Pissarro, Seurat, Picasso, Matisse, and other artists to the region of Provence. Select one of these painters and compare a painting of a landscape he did of Provence and one he painted of another area of France. Discuss the differences in light and the kinds of activities depicted when these painters painted in the south vs. the north of France.

**386**

---

 **2.1, 2.2**

Je souhaite* dans ma maison:

Une femme ayant raison*,

Un chat passant* parmi* les livres,

Des amis en toute saison,

Sans lesquels* je ne peux pas vivre.*

---
**souhaite** *voudrais*; **ayant raison** *who's reasonable*; **passant** *passing*; **parmi** *among*; **sans lesquels** *without which*; **vivre** *to live*

## Post-lecture  2.1, 2.2

Le narrateur a besoin de quoi pour vivre?

## Le monde visuel  1.2, 3.1, 4.2

L'artiste Paul Cézanne (1839–1906) habitait en Provence et ses peintures (*paintings*) reflètent les paysages (*landscapes*) de sa région. Il a été (*was*) influencé par l'impressionnisme, un mouvement d'artistes qui voulaient peindre (*wanted to print*) une impression d'une chose, pas prendre une "photo" avec tous les détails. Mais, on considère Cézanne le père de la peinture moderne et du Cubisme par ses formes géométriques et son expression personnelle. Il est connu aussi pour sa perspective linéaire. Quelles formes géométriques est-ce que vous trouvez dans cette peinture? Combien de plans (*planes*) horizontaux est-ce que vous observez? Comment la peinture est-elle impressionniste et cubiste?

*Dans la vallée de l'Oise*, 1873. Paul Cézanne. Collection privée.

---

### 19  Activités d'expansion

1. Écrivez un paragraphe sur la maison que le narrateur désire. Utilisez les notes dans votre grille pour vous aider: **Le narrateur désire une maison avec....**
2. Écrivez un paragraphe sur la maison de vos rêves (*dreams*).
3. Écrivez un poème qui commence avec: **Je souhaite dans ma vie....** (*I wish in my life*). Continuez ensuite avec une liste de personnes et/ou de choses.
4. Écrivez un poème sur un thème qui vous intéresse avec l'agencement des rimes (*rhyme scheme*) A-A-B-A-B.

**386** trois cent quatre-vingt-six | Unité 7

---

### Essential Instruction

1. Explain that the glossed vocabulary expressions are defined in French whenever possible. Discuss the meaning of **une femme ayant raison** and **des amis en toute saison**. Then, complete the chart on the previous page, and answer the **Post-lecture** question. To practice pronunciation, consider asking students to memorize the poem.

2. What linguistic clues do students find in the words Impressionism and Cubism that may help to understand the style of painting (**impression**, **cube**)? Ask students to share what they might already know about these movements.

3. Have students view the Cézanne painting, and then jot down their one-word impressions in French. Next, ask them to scan **Le monde visuel** for cognates. List and discuss characteristics of the painting.

4. Answer questions about new vocabulary in **Les copains d'abord**. Students can read, and then role-play in their groups.

## Les copains d'abord: Il est beau, mon HLM

**RESOURCES**

✓ **Pre-test**

📝 *Leçon* **Quiz**

### Les copains d'abord

Here is the translation for **Les copains d'abord:**

A = Antoine
F = Florence
MA = Marie-Alix
M = Mathéo
Maman = la maman de Mathéo

Maman: Are you staying for dinner, Florence? I'm making a ratatouille. M: But, Mom, you know we're going to the restaurant with our friends. They're on their way. F: Still, I can help you set the table. Maman: Thank you. The plates are in the cupboard, behind the bowls. F: I like your new refrigerator! But where is the microwave? Maman: My husband likes it better in our room. A: All right, where does Mathéo live? In this building? MA: No, he is in that housing complex, on the seventh floor… or the fourth? MA: Hold on, I'll send him a text. A: Put that away! Someone will take it! MA: You're a jerk! It's not because people live in subsidized housing that they steal. A: Still, it's horrible here… MA: People aren't desperate; it just means that they have a modest income. A: You know, that's true, Mathéo has an iPhone and a computer! MA: … and a TV in his room, a Moroccan rug in his living room… A: Well, in any case, I hope he has a bathroom!

List of slang and idiomatic expressions:
**le resto:** short for **restaurant**; **piquer:** *steal*; **nul:** *jerk*; **ça craint:** *that's horrible*; **tsais:** Quebécois short for **tu sais**; **en tout cas:** *either way*; **la piaule:** *bedroom*

**Differentiated Learning**
**Accelerate**
Assign students to choose and write about one of the **Activités d'expansion**, and then share in small groups. Have them peer-edit each other's work. Collect the draft, edited, and final corrected versions to better gauge student progress.

**Multiple Intelligences**
**Visual-Spatial**
Have some students look online for Paul Cézanne paintings and other Impressionist or Cubist paintings to show to the class.

**Bodily-Kinesthetic**
As students read the poem out loud several times, have them tap their desks or clap their hands to show the meter.

*T'es branché?*

## Projets finaux

**A** **Connexions par Internet**  **1.3, 3.1, 3.2, 4.2**

### L'histoire, la littérature, le cinéma, la musique

Working in small groups, choose one of the topics below to research on the Internet and create a PowerPoint™ or some other form of presentation. Divide up project tasks among group members by assigning a role to each person. For example, roles might be note taker, researcher, summarizer, creator of visual images, and data-entry person. Make your presentation to the rest of the class.

- The connection between the Acadians and Cajuns
- The colonization of New Brunswick and the Canadian Maritimes
- The islands of Saint-Pierre and Miquelon, featured in the film *La veuve de St. Pierre*
- The story of *Evangeline* by Henry Wadsworth Longfellow
- The movie *Belizaire the Cajun*
- Cajun and Acadian music

**B** **Communautés en ligne** **1.1, 1.3, 5.1**

### La semaine du goût

The yearly celebration of **la semaine du goût** (*National "Taste" Week*) in France reflects the country's attitudes and cultural values about food and cuisine. Research **la semaine du goût** on the Internet to find out more about this event, and complete a chart like the one below with your findings. Then, discuss as a class the different communities that participate in **la semaine du goût** and the values reflected in this event.

| Le site officiel de la semaine du goût | |
|---|---|
| Deux ou trois valeurs (*values*) de la semaine du goût | |
| Deux adresses gourmandes | |
| C'est quoi un atelier du goût? | |
| Description des événements (*events*) dans une école pendant la semaine du goût | |

 **Search words: la semaine du goût**

### Essential Instruction

1. Design a rubric for **Activité A** that includes the number of slides, type and quantity of information for students to include, and the opportunity to evaluate each group's final product.
2. Assign research for **Activité B** as homework. Have students share and compare in groups. Finally, ask each group to share two observations or conclusions.
3. Provide a rubric to explain expectations clearly for **Activité C**. You might have each student in the group design a different room. Students

should first decide what format they will use for their presentation (slide show presentation, poster, diorama, or brochure). Allow for in-class and at-home work on this project.

4. Have groups revisit the **Question centrale** and complete **Activité D** using the graphic organizer provided in the **Copy Masters** supplement. Do students feel their cultural understanding has increased compared to when they began the unit? How would they define a "home" now?

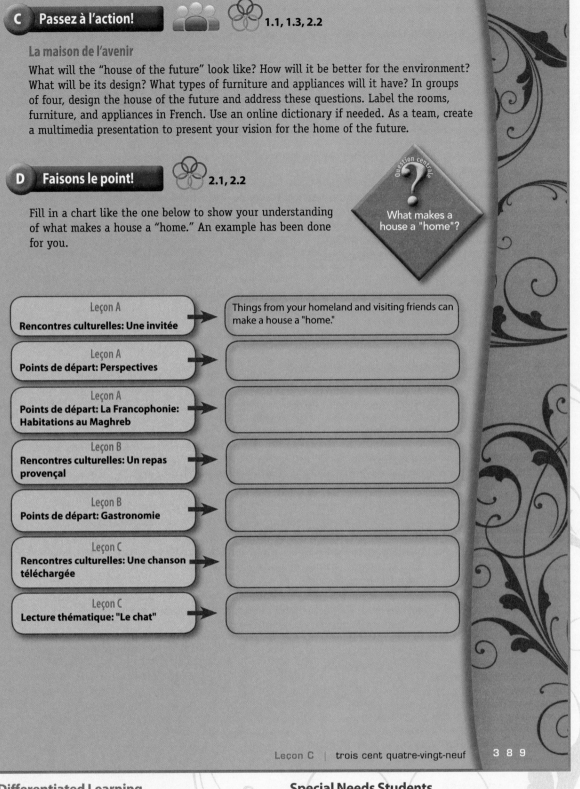

## C · Passez à l'action! 1.1, 1.3, 2.2

### La maison de l'avenir

What will the "house of the future" look like? How will it be better for the environment? What will be its design? What types of furniture and appliances will it have? In groups of four, design the house of the future and address these questions. Label the rooms, furniture, and appliances in French. Use an online dictionary if needed. As a team, create a multimedia presentation to present your vision for the home of the future.

## D · Faisons le point! 2.1, 2.2

Fill in a chart like the one below to show your understanding of what makes a house a "home." An example has been done for you.

**Question centrale**
What makes a house a "home"?

| | |
|---|---|
| **Leçon A**<br>Rencontres culturelles: Une invitée | Things from your homeland and visiting friends can make a house a "home." |
| **Leçon A**<br>Points de départ: Perspectives | |
| **Leçon A**<br>Points de départ: La Francophonie: Habitations au Maghreb | |
| **Leçon B**<br>Rencontres culturelles: Un repas provençal | |
| **Leçon B**<br>Points de départ: Gastronomie | |
| **Leçon C**<br>Rencontres culturelles: Une chanson téléchargée | |
| **Leçon C**<br>Lecture thématique: "Le chat" | |

---

## Differentiated Learning

### Decelerate
Give students the choice of doing **Activité A** or **B**. Provide specific parameters and step-by-step directions to make this project more manageable.

### Accelerate
For **Faisons le point!** ask students to share their answers in French with the class.

## Special Needs Students
### AD(H)D
For **Activité A**, provide a checklist of defined tasks for each role. Allow special needs students to choose their role in the group.

---

**C** *Presentations will vary.*

**D**

**Leçon A:** The houses in Maghreb are in harmony with the natural elements.
**Leçon A:** Dwellings in Maghreb divide space according to the positions of men and women.
**Leçon B:** Cooking a meal together with your family makes it special.
**Leçon B:** Every region has its own gastronomic specialty.
**Leçon C:** Songs can be personalized and remind you of your family or friends.
**Leçon C:** People, animals, and objects of sentimental value make your house a home.

### Reference Desk

1. To evaluate the **Projets finaux**, teachers might assess oral communication (language control), vocabulary use, accuracy, comprehensibility, how well students demonstrate cultural understanding, and overall organization of the projects.
2. Teachers may want to offer some of the **Projets finaux** as individual projects to assess each student's progress.

### Critical Thinking

**Evaluation**
Once they've completed **Activité B**, ask students to discuss the value of having **une semaine de goût**.

## Answers

**A** Script can be found in the front pages of the Annotated Teacher's Edition.

1. F
2. V
3. F
4. F
5. F

**B** *Dialogues will vary.*

**C** *Comparisons will vary.*

---

## Reference Desk

1. Students can research traditional French homes from the Maritime Provinces of Canada to compare with those of the Maghreb and Provence.
2. Display photos of classic regional dishes and food from Brittany, Normandy, Provence, etc. for students to identify the dish and region in quiz format or for review. For variety, have students say, **À Québec (Paris/La Nouvelle Orléans)/ En Provence (Normandie, Bretagne, Louisiane)/Au Maroc (Canada, Sénégal...) etc.), je peux manger....** as they name the dish in the image.

---

# Évaluation

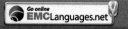  

### A  Évaluation de compréhension auditive      2.1, 2.2

M. and Mme Petit are looking for an apartment. They have two children. Listen to their conversation with the real estate agent and read the sentences. Write **V** if the statement is **vrai** (*true*) or **F** if it is **faux** (*false*).

1. M. et Mme Petit désirent un appartement au rez-de-chaussée.
2. M. et Mme Petit veulent être près des magasins.
3. M. et Mme Petit ont besoin de deux chambres.
4. M. et Mme Petit veulent trois salles de bains.
5. M. et Mme Petit préfèrent les salles de bains et les toilettes ensemble.

### B  Évaluation orale     1.1, 2.1, 2.2, 3.1, 3.2

Draw a design of a home, perhaps your ideal home, and describe it to your partner, for example, **Dans ma maison, il y a un salon**.... Then describe your bedroom and its furnishings to your partner, who should draw a picture of it based on your clear description.

### C  Évaluation culturelle    1.1

In this activity, you will compare francophone cultures with American culture. You may need to do some additional research on American culture.

1. **La salle de bains et les toilettes**
   Compare bathrooms in France to those in your home and in your friends' homes.
2. **La maison**
   Compare traditional homes in **le Maghreb** with traditional homes in the United States, for example, log cabins, farm houses, pueblos. You may want to look at some American homes in areas of the United States other than where you live.
3. **L'Algérie et la France comparées au Puerto Rico et les États-Unis**
   What similarities and differences can you identify between Algeria and its relationship to France and that of Puerto Rico and its relationship to the United States? Consider history, language, and immigration.
4. **Marseille et la diversité**
   How far do you have to travel from your home to find a city with as diverse a population as that of Marseille? Compare the cultural diversity in your local or regional community to that in Marseille.
5. **Les caractéristiques de Provence et de ma région**
   What makes Provence famous? Are any of these characteristics the same as those in your region? What is your region famous for?

---

## Essential Instruction

1. Play listening **Activité A** twice, then check understanding.
2. Consider having students record **Activité B** in the lab or outside of class. If time to evaluate is short, provide a rubric and assign students to peer-review their classmate's work. Or, assign this as practice for oral assessment later.
3. Allow students to choose the **Évaluation** topic(s) that interest(s) them, ensuring that no more than four or five people have the same topics. Prepare a note-taking template for students to

complete on all topics. Discuss what they found the most interesting or enlightening.
4. If you assign **Activité D**, give students a rubric indicating the word count, how much new vocabulary to include, and how you will assess the accuracy of their writing.
5. For **Activité E**, have groups list download instructions and then compare them with another group's instructions. Are they the same? Play in class the Natasha St-Pier songs mentioned.

6. **Les jeunes et la technologie**
   What kinds of technology do you use regularly? How does this compare with the technology used by teens in France? Would you mind being called the "**tout, tout de suite**" generation? Why, or why not?
7. **Le Grand Dérangement**
   Compare the **Grand Dérangement** in Acadia to "The Trail of Tears" in the United States. How are these two events similar? How are they different?

 **D Évaluation écrite** 🌸 1.3, 2.1, 2.2

You are planning to exchange homes with a family in New Brunswick over spring break. Write a detailed description of your home for the Canadian family. Also tell them how close your home is to shopping areas, parks, and other attractions in your area.

**Vocabulaire utile**

| | |
|---|---|
| **à un kilomètre** | *a kilometer away* |
| **pas loin** | *not far* |

 **E Évaluation visuelle** 🌸 1.3

Julie is listening to the song "**L'Orient-Express**" by Natasha St-Pier. Describe the steps she uses on the computer to download this and other songs in French.

"L'Orient-Express"
"M'attend sur le quai"
"D'un mot d'un geste"
"Tu vois je m'en vais"

 **F Évaluation compréhensive** 🌸 1.3

Create a six-frame storyboard with illustrations and captions that describe the house you will live in someday. Begin by saying in what city you will live.

**Answers** _____
**D** *Descriptions will vary.*
**E** *Descriptions will vary.*
**F** *Stories will vary.*

**Reference Desk**

Students may also review by acting out the steps for **Activité E**.

**Differentiated Learning**
**Accelerate**
Leave instructions more open-ended and encourage students to expand or change the parameters given for the activities in **Évaluation**. Then grade students based on the parameters they set for themselves.

**Multiple Intelligences**
**Visual-Spatial/Verbal-Linguistic**
Have partners collaborate on **Activité F** and present their work to the class.

## RESOURCES

 Flash Cards

 *Rendez-vous à Nice!*
Episode 7

 Listening Pre-test D

 *Unité* Test

# Vocabulaire de l'Unité 7  1.2

**à: à côté (de)** beside, next to *A*
**air: un petit air du pays** looks like (something from) my country *A*
un **appartement** apartment *A*
une **armoire** wardrobe *A*
**Attention!** Watch out! Be careful! *B*
**aussi** as *B*
**autre** other *A*
une **baignoire** bathtub *C*
**beau, bel, belle** handsome, beautiful *A*
**ben** well *B*
**berbère** Berber *A*
un **carré** square *B*; **en carrés** in squares *B*
la **chambre** bedroom *A*
une **chanson** song *C*
**charmant(e)** charming *A*
**cliquer** to click *C*
**commencer** to begin *C*
le **couloir** hallway *A*
**couper** to cut *B*
un **coussin** pillow *A*
le **couvert:** table setting *B*; **mettre le couvert** to set the table *B*
la **cuisine** kitchen *A*
**demander** to ask (for) *C*
**démarrer** to start *C*
**dessus: au dessus de** above *B*
**devoir** to have to *B*
**dîner** to have dinner *A*
une **douche** shower *C*
**droite: à droite (de)** to (on) the right of *B*
un **étage** floor, story *A*; **le premier étage** second floor *A*
**être: être d'accord** to agree *C*; **être en train de (+ infinitive)** to be (busy) doing something *C*
**fermer** to close *C*
**fin(e)** fine *B*
**fond: au fond de** at the end of *A*
**fort(e)** strong, good at *C*
**gauche: à gauche (de)** to (on) the left of *A*
**habiter** to live *A*
**ici** here *A*
un **immeuble** apartment building *A*
**impossible** impossible *C*
**imprimer** to print *C*
un(e) **invité(e)** guest *A*
le **jasmin** jasmine *A*
la **la** it (object pronoun) *C*
un **lit** bed *C*
**long, longue** long *B*
**mettre** to put (on), to set *B*

une **minute** minute *A*
**moins** less *B*
la **mosquée** mosque *A*
**naviguer** to browse *C*
le **Nouveau-Brunswick** New Brunswick *C*
**ouvre: elle ouvre** she opens *C*
**paie: elle paie** she pays *C*
**par** with *C*
un **parc** park *A*
**pardi (régional)** of course *B*
les **paroles (f.)** lyrics *C*
**passer** to spend (time) *A*
le **pays** country *A*
**penser** to think *A*
une **photo** photo *A*
une **pièce** room *A*
**plus** more *B*
un **portable** cell phone, laptop *C*
**pouvoir** can, to be able (to) *C*
**près (de)** near *A*
un **problème** problem *C*
**provençal(e)** from, of Provence *B*
**que** as, than *B*
la **ratatouille** ratatouille *B*
une **recette** recipe *B*
un **repas** meal *B*
le **rez-de-chaussée** ground floor *A*
une **riad** riad *A*
une **rondelle:** circle *B* **en rondelles** in circles *B*
le **salon** living room *A*
la **salle à manger** dining room *A*
la **salle de bains** bathroom *A*
**sauvegarder** to save *C*
le **séjour** living room *A*
**sentir** to smell *A*; **Ça sent quoi?** What does it smell like? *A*
**sûr(e)** sure *B*
**synchroniser** to synchronize *C*
une **tablette** tablet *C*
un **taf** work *C*
**télécharger** to download *C*
le **tissu** fabric *A*
les **toilettes (f.)** bathroom *A*
une **vue** view *A*; **Quelle belle vue!** What a beautiful view! *A*
les **W.C. (m.)** toilet *A*

Computer… see p. 371
Household furnishings and appliances… see p. 340
Meals… see p. 355
Ordinal numbers… see p. 340
Place setting… see p. 355

# Unité
# 8 À Paris

*Rendez-vous à Nice!*
**Épisode 8:**
*Meilleurs résultats!*

Go online
**EMC**Languages.net

trois cent quatre-vingt-treize **3 9 3**

**3 9 3**

1. Have students look at the photo on p. 394 and talk about what they see in the picture: the Eiffel Tower, the gardens of the **Trocadero** (across the river from the Eiffel Tower), the **Champs de Mars**, the **École Militaire**, etc.
2. Paris Motto: Have students research an image for the emblem or coat of arms of Paris. This depicts a ship being tossed about on the waves. Ask students why water is a key element in this motto and emblem. The reference is to the river Seine, boatmen, and the importance of trade and commerce for the city since Roman times. Remind them that boats and cities are usually referred to as feminine, despite the word **bâteau** being masculine.
3. Look at the geographic location of Paris on your classroom map of France and have students trace the route of the Seine. It originates near Dijon and flows out into the English Channel at Le Havre. Remind them that its direction then determines what is called the **rive droite** and **rive gauche**.

**Expansion**

Give each student an 8.5 x 17 sheet of paper. As you draw the Seine and monuments to the north and south of it, students draw and label their own version.

# Citation

"La province crée le talent: Paris la renommée."

The provinces create talent: Paris, fame.

**Augusta Amiel–Lapeyre, écrivain français**

## À savoir   4.2

The motto of Paris is "It floats but doesn't sink." (*Fluctuat nec mergitur* in Latin, *Il flotte mais il ne sombre pas* in French).

**Essential Instruction**

1. To set the stage for **Unité 8**, ask students to share any travel experiences they may have had, either in Paris or another big city.
2. Explore the idea that cities have their own personality and ask for real-life and fictional examples (literature, song, film). Then discuss the **Question centrale**.
3. Have students read the **Citation** and **À savoir**. Discuss what they tell us about Paris.
4. Call on students to read aloud the **Contrat de l'élève**. Elaborate and expand on some of the topics such as the past tense.
5. Show the relevant video clip from *Rendez-vous à Nice!*, Episode 8, and discuss the related question as a class.

# Unité 8
# À Paris

Question centrale

**?**

## How do major world cities tell their stories?

**What is Patrick about to do?**
A. say the right answer
B. admit his love for Charlotte
C. tell the teacher Jean-Charles cheated on the test

What is the name of this Parisian monument?

Go online
**EMC**Languages.net

## Contrat de l'élève

### Leçon A  I will be able to:

>> extend an invitation and accept or refuse an invitation.

>> discuss Paris sites; famous pastries; and Port-au-Prince, the capital of Haiti.

>> use the verb **faire** when describing the weather, sports and other activities; and learn how to say "I'm hot" and "I'm cold."

### Leçon B  I will be able to:

>> excuse myself and talk about past events.

>> discuss three famous Paris monuments.

>> describe events completed in the past, including those that take irregular past participles; and use irregular adjectives.

### Leçon C  I will be able to:

>> sequence events in the past.

>> discuss **le jardin des Tuileries** and the **métro**.

>> describe past events and specify with adverbs.

trois cent quatre-vingt-quinze **3 9 5**

## RESOURCES

 *Rendez-vous à Nice!* **Episode 8**

Answers _____

The answer to the video question is A.

### Reference Desk

1. Students will learn about Haiti in **Leçon A** and Parisian monuments in **Leçon B**. There is a link between many Parisian monuments and Napoleon (**l'arc de triomphe, l'arc du carrousel, l'École Militaire, rue de Rivoli**, etc.). Ask students to consider what link exists between Napoleon and Haiti. (Napoleon played a role in the Haitian Revolution by trying to reestablish French rule and reinstate slavery in French overseas colonies.)

2. **Question centrale:** Discuss what constitutes a city being designated as "major."

3. Does the photo of the **arc de triomphe** reveal a notion about the **place de l'Étoile** and the 12 avenues radiating from the monument? Can students guess whose triumphs it celebrates? (Napoleon) Although a controversial political and military figure, ultimately exiled for his mistakes (1812 invasion of Russia, tyrannical rule, 17 years of war), Napoleon is also celebrated. Why? (Establishing order after the French Revolution, legal reforms, Napoleonic Code, extension of French sphere of influence) Who defeated Napoleon? (Wellington at the Battle of Waterloo in Belgium 1815)

### Culture

**Perspectives: Information**
Reserve a section of your board for students to display what they learn about Napoleon (**l'arc de triomphe, rue de Rivoli**, etc.) vs. the monarchy in Paris (**le Louvre, les Tuileries, la place de la Concorde**) as it relates to urban development of Paris.

## Differentiated Learning
**Expand**
You may want to have students share postcards, travel brochures, and/or photos from Paris and other major world cities they have visited.

## Learning Styles
**Visual Learners**
Find online, create, or ask students to create a slide show of monuments and landmarks of Paris featured in this unit. Play the images in the background as you present various monuments and landmarks.

## Reference Desk

The basic formula for determining temperature conversions is as follows ($T_f$ = temperature in Fahrenheit; $T_c$ = temperature in Celsius):

$$(T_f - 32) \times {}^5/_9 = T_c$$
$$T_c \times {}^9/_5 - 32 = T_f$$

## Communication

### Presentational

Have students research the weather online for about 20 international cities and present their findings to the class.

### Interpersonal: Cooperative Groups

To practice weather expressions, have students sit in small groups. One student starts a round by saying a weather word, such as **beau**. The next student must use the word in a complete sentence as in **Il fait beau**. The next student must say that phrase in the negative. The activity continues until all have had a turn.

## Culture

### Practices: Information

Consider showing the i-Culture video entitled **"L'équitation"** (2010-2011) to provide your students with a culturally authentic perspective related to the theme of this **Leçon**.

---

# Vocabulaire actif

## Quel temps fait-il?   1.2

**En été...**

il fait beau.
il fait du soleil.
il fait chaud.

**En automne...**

il fait frais.
il fait du vent.

**En hiver...**

il fait froid.
il neige.
il fait mauvais.

**Au printemps...**

il pleut.

La température est de 20 degrés./Il fait 20 degrés (Celsius).

Chloé a chaud.       Pierre a froid.

**3 9 6**   trois cent quatre-vingt-seize | Unité 8

## Essential Instruction

1. Write the seasons on the board with the prepositions **en/au** and the articles **l'/le**. Have students practice saying and spelling them. Point out the silent "m" in **automne**.
2. Ask students, **"Quel temps fait-il aujourd'hui?"** Project images of the weather expressions, act them out, or draw them on the board. Have students repeat as a class, then practice in pairs.
3. Explain the difference between **il fait froid/ chaud** and **il a froid/chaud**.
4. Review and practice the Fahrenheit to Celsius conversion and vice versa.
5. Make the animal sounds in **Les animaux domestiques** and have students identify the animal. Demonstrate a few extra ones, such as **cocorico** (**le coq**/rooster), **meuh** (**une vâche**/cow), **hihan** (**un âne**/donkey), **coin coin** (**un canard**/duck).
6. Play the audio of **Pour la conversation** and have students repeat the sentences.

# Les animaux domestiques

*Miaou!* — un chat

*Cui cui!* — un oiseau

*Hî-hî-hî!* — un cheval

*Ouaf ouaf!* — un chien

*Glou glou!* — un poisson rouge

un cheval

## Pour la conversation

**H**ow do I extend an invitation?

> **Tu as envie de** faire une promenade avec moi?
>
> *Do you want to take a walk with me?*

**H**ow do I accept an invitation?

> **Bonne idée! Je suis disponible.**
>
> *Good idea! I'm free.*

**H**ow do I refuse an invitation?

> **Désolé(e). Je suis occupé(e).**
>
> *Sorry. I'm busy.*

### Et si je voulais dire...?

| | |
|---|---|
| **bruiner** | *to drizzle* |
| **Il fait du brouillard.** | *It's foggy.* |
| **Il y a des éclairs.** | *It's lightning.* |
| **la grêle** | *hail* |
| **la neige** | *snow* |
| **la pluie** | *rain* |
| **la météo** | *weather report* |

## Communication

**Presentational**

Have students write a description about a pet that belongs to their family, a friend, or a celebrity, including the pet's name and what the pet likes to do in certain weather. Ask them to accompany the paragraph with a photo or drawing. Students will make a gallery of pet portraits for the wall and present them to the class. Consider having a contest to vote for the most handsome, funniest, oddest, etc.

## Game

**Des animaux domestiques**

Have students use gestures and actions to "describe" their pets as the rest of the class shouts out French phrases such as **Il est grand! Il dit "Miaou!"**, etc. to match the actor's movements. Students should continue until they guess the pet.

## Differentiated Learning

**Expand**

Have students say **vrai** or **faux** in response to statements you make about the weather in various places and seasons. Ask students to describe the weather in their favorite locations.

**Accelerate**

Present the vocabulary in **Et si je voulais dire...?**, then ask students to use these words in original sentences.

## Special Needs Students

**Linguistically Challenged**

To help organize the vocabulary for students, have them complete a chart according to headings such as seasons, weather expressions, verbs, etc. You could also organize weather expressions by adjectives (**beau, chaud, frais**, etc.), nouns (**du vent, du brouillard**, and **du soleil**), and verbs (**il pleut, il neige**).

## Connections

### Math
Find online a map of France that shows the weather, and project it. Have students locate cities and describe the weather. Practice converting Celsius to Fahrenheit and Fahrenheit to Celsius. Give the weather and temperature in Celsius for a city. Students should mark a corresponding symbol (sun, rain, etc.) and the correct temperature on the map. Have students compare their results afterwards.

## Expansion

Show landscape photos of francophone countries. Write sentences starting with the name of the country and a season, for example, **Au Canada, en été,** .... or **En Algérie, en hiver**.... Students must finish each sentence with a weather expression.

## Game

### C'est quel mois?
Say a month and ask students to say the month that comes before and after.

---

### 1 Bruno et les sports  1.2, 2.1, 2.2

*Lisez et répondez à la question.*

Bruno aime les sports. Il fait du sport presque toute l'année. Au printemps il aime faire du vélo et du footing quand il fait beau et un peu frais. En été il aime nager et aller plonger quand il fait chaud et du soleil. En automne il aime jouer au foot et au basket avec des copains. En hiver il n'aime pas faire du ski, et il n'aime pas jouer au hockey. Il préfère regarder le basket à la télé.

En quelle saison est-ce que Bruno ne fait pas de sport?

### 2 Que porter? 2.1, 2.2

*Dites quel vêtement vous portez dans les situations suivantes.*

**MODÈLE** Quand il fait chaud, ....
(un pantalon, un short)
**Quand il fait chaud, je porte un short.**

1. Quand il fait frais, .... (un tee-shirt, un pull)
2. Quand il neige, .... (des bottes, des chaussures)
3. Quand il fait du soleil, .... (un manteau, un chapeau)
4. Quand il fait froid, .... (une chemise, un manteau)
5. Quand il fait chaud, .... (un maillot de bain, une veste)

### 3 En quelle saison?   2.1, 2.2

*Dites en quelle saison les ados suivants font chaque activité.*

1. Damien aime faire du roller quand il fait frais; il aime faire du roller....
2. Martine aime nager quand il fait du soleil; elle aime nager....
3. Joëlle aime jouer aux jeux vidéo quand il pleut; elle aime jouer aux jeux vidéo....
4. Luc aime plonger quand il fait chaud; il aime plonger....
5. Julie aime faire du vélo quand il fait beau; elle aime faire du vélo....
6. Sébastien aime faire du ski quand il neige; il aime faire du ski....

### 4 Quel temps fait-il?   2.1

*Écrivez les numéros 1–6 sur votre papier. Écoutez la météo (weather forecast) des villes différentes. Ensuite, choisissez la lettre de l'illustration qui correspond à chaque description.*

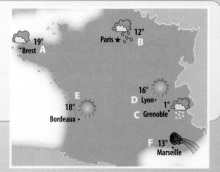

3 9 8 | trois cent quatre-vingt-dix-huit | Unité 8

---

## Essential Instruction

1. Instruct pairs to read aloud the paragraph in **Activité 1** and provide answers in a complete sentence for **Activités 2, 3,** and listening **Activité 4.**
2. Have students do **Activité 5** chorally. Research online and discuss popular pet names in France, such as **Minou, Filou,** etc.
3. Give students a few minutes to write in French eight different activities they're planning to do during the weekday evenings or on the weekend. Write several examples on the board, such as **faire mes devoirs, aller au ciné,** and **jouer au foot.** Then review the directions for **Activité 6** and assign it in pairs, using the activities they wrote.
4. Have students write the answers to **Activité 7** and check for accuracy. Then assign small groups to do the **Activité** orally without looking at their written answers.

## 5 Comment s'appellent les animaux?

*Dites comment s'appellent les animaux suivants.*

**MODÈLE**    Flou-Flou

**Le chat s'appelle Flou-Flou.**

 1. Toto

 2. Tweety

 3. Samuel

 4. Bellino

 5. Prince

## Communiquez!

### 6 Des invitations

 1.1

As-tu envie de jouer au basket?

Quel jour?

**Interpersonal Communication**

*Faites un agenda pour le soir et le weekend de cette semaine pour voir quand vous êtes disponible. Ensuite, invitez un(e) camarade de classe différent(e) à faire une activité.*

**MODÈLE**    jouer aux jeux vidéo chez moi/mardi/15h40

A: **As-tu envie de jouer aux jeux vidéo chez moi?**
B: **Quel jour?**
A: **Mardi.**
B: **À quelle heure?**
A: **À quatre heures moins vingt.**
B: **Bonne idée! Je suis disponible.** ou **Désolé(e), je suis occupé(e).**

### 7 Questions personnelles

   1.2, 2.1, 2.2

*Répondez aux questions.*

1. Quel temps fait-il aujourd'hui?
2. Est-ce que tu préfères les sports d'hiver ou les sports d'été?
3. Qu'est-ce que tu aimes faire en hiver? en été?
4. Qu'est-ce que tu portes quand il fait froid?
5. Es-tu occupé(e) samedi soir?
6. Qu'est-ce que tu as envie de faire dimanche?

---

**5**
1. Le chien s'appelle Toto.
2. L'oiseau s'appelle Tweety.
3. Le poisson s'appelle Samuel.
4. Le cheval s'appelle Bellino.
5. Le chat s'appelle Prince.

**6**   *Dialogues will vary.*

**7**   *Answers will vary.*

### Expansion

Gather pictures of various pets featured in the **Vocabulaire actif**. Have students gather around the "pet portrait gallery" and make statements describing each pet.

### Communication

**Interpersonal: Paired Practice**
Have partners use old telephones or their cell phones as props while they act out calling one or more partners to invite them to an evening or weekend activity.

---

## Differentiated Learning

**Decelerate**
Have students write out their answers to the **Activités**. Circulate to answer questions and check for understanding, then have small groups do the activities orally.

**Accelerate**
For additional practice of the vocabulary, students could write and present a paragraph similar to the one in **Activité 1**.

## Multiple Intelligences

**Verbal-Linguistic**
Have students create additional sentences for **Activité 3** and ask their partner to complete each sentence.

**Answers** _____

**8**

4. Maxime fait une promenade avec son chien.
5. Maxime voit Yasmine.
2. On s'arrête devant une pâtisserie.
1. On achète une religieuse.
3. On va aux Tuileries.

### Extension

_Answers may vary_, but most likely yes, since the agent makes it sound romantic and exciting.

### Communication

**Interpersonal: Paired Practice**

Using the video dialogue as a model, have students create and present a scenario that takes place around their city or town.

**Presentational**

To show comprehension, have students draw illustrations of the sentences in **Activité 8** before they put them in order.

---

# Rencontres culturelles

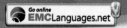

## Une promenade à Paris     1.2

Yasmine et Maxime se voient dans la rue.

Maxime: Tu as envie de faire une promenade avec Snoopy et moi?

Yasmine: Oui, bonne idée! Si on s'arrête à la pâtisserie du coin? J'ai envie d'un gâteau....

Maxime: Trop gourmande! Attention! Ta ligne....

Yasmine: Ce n'est pas grave! Qu'est-ce que je vais prendre? Une tarte? Non. Un millefeuille? Peut-être. Un éclair au chocolat.... Oh! Oui... non, mieux! Une religieuse. Comme ça, tu manges le haut et je mange le bas.

_(Maxime et Yasmine entrent dans la pâtisserie avec le chien.)_

Maxime: _(à Yasmine)_ Et maintenant, qu'est-ce qu'on fait?

Yasmine: En cette belle journée de printemps, pourquoi pas une chouette promenade aux Tuileries?

Maxime: Il ne va pas pleuvoir?

Yasmine: Mais non!

**8** **Une promenade à Paris**

**2.1, 2.2**

_Mettez les événements_ (events) _suivants dans l'ordre chronologique._

1. On achète une religieuse.
2. On s'arrête devant une pâtisserie.
3. On va aux Tuileries.
4. Maxime fait une promenade avec son chien.
5. Maxime voit Yasmine.

### Extension    À l'agence de voyage  1.2, 2.1, 2.2

Emma et Loïk parlent au tour-opérateur à l'agence de voyage.

Opérateur: J'ai ce très beau produit... quatre jours à Paris.

Loïk: Ah! Oui, pourquoi pas. On va au bout du monde et on ne va jamais à Paris.

Emma: Et qu'est-ce qu'on fait pendant quatre jours?

Opérateur: Pour voir la Seine et les monuments, une superbe promenade en bateau-mouche; pour dîner en couple, une soirée à la tour Eiffel; côté culture, le Louvre pour vous tous seuls....

### Extension    Est-ce que vous imaginez que Loïk et Emma vont accepter ce que le tour opérateur propose? Justifiez votre réponse.

**Essential Instruction**

1. Before viewing the dialogue, have students scan the text for cognates and any new vocabulary. Survey students about what French pastries they've tried and/or know. Ask them to guess what **un millefeuille** (literally a thousand sheets) might be. Show the dialogue and instruct small groups to identify the season, weather, and what **pâtisserie** the two friends decide to order.

2. Have partners role-play the dialogue, then ask volunteers to present the conversation. Finally, have them complete **Activité 8**.

3. Before students read **Paris, capitale de la France**, briefly revisit the **Question centrale** and brainstorm local sites listed in the **Comparaisons**. Show a map of Paris and identify the landmarks listed in the **Activité** if students did not make the maps as described on p. 394. Divide the listed Paris landmarks in **Points de départ** for pairs to research. Ask them to include several images, maps, or diagrams in their presentation.

# Points de départ

How do major world cities tell their stories?

## RESOURCES

Workbook 9

## Paris, capitale de la France   1.2, 2.1, 2.2

La Seine divise Paris en deux parties: la rive* droite (au nord de la Seine) et la rive gauche (au sud de la Seine). L'île* de la Cité, où la cathédrale Notre-Dame de Paris est située, est une île sur la Seine. Le nom romain de Paris était* Lutèce, mais c'est son nom celte, le nom de ses premiers habitants, les *Parisii*, qu'on utilise. Son destin est lié aux rois*, aux empereurs, aux présidents de la République, et aux hommes d'Église* qui ont construit* ses monuments.

| Période | Construction | Responsables |
|---|---|---|
| XIIème siècle* | Notre-Dame | Maurice de Sully |
| XIIème siècle | le Louvre | Philippe Auguste |
| XVIIème siècle | places Dauphine, Vosges, les Champs-Élysées, les Invalides | Henri IV, Marie de Médicis, Louis XIV |
| XVIIIème siècle | le Champ de Mars, le Palais-Royal | Louis XV |
| 1852–1875 | les grands boulevards et parcs, l'Opéra | Napoléon III, le Baron Haussman, Charles Garnier |
| 1887–1900 | la tour Eiffel, le Petit et le Grand Palais | Gustave Eiffel, Charles Girault, etc. |
| 1970–1989 | le Centre Pompidou, la Pyramide du Louvre, l'arche de la Défense | Georges Pompidou, François Mitterrand |

 **Search words:** **pages de paris**
**paris info**
**louvre site officiel**

---

**rive** *bank*; **l'île** *island*; **était** *was*; **lié aux rois** *linked to kings*;
**Église** *Church*; **ont construit** *built*; **siècle** *century*

L'arche de la Défense.

 **COMPARAISONS** 4.2

What monuments, churches, museums, and statues are there in your state's capital city?

## Game

If possible, obtain a Paris city version of Monopoly or have students make a French version of the board game. Playing the game is a fun way to reinforce the names of famous Parisian landmarks and locations.

## Connections

### History
Have students do research on who these historical figures were, then make a horizontal time line in the classroom that features images of the locations.

---

**Differentiated Learning**
### Adapt
Ask students to summarize the video segment using sequencing adverbs (**d'abord, ensuite,** etc.).

### Accelerate
Have pairs read the **Extension** dialogue and answer the question.

**Multiple Intelligences**
### Visual-Spatial
Distribute Paris maps, and have students identify the sites in relation to each other. To obtain a classroom set of detailed Paris maps, contact the French consulate in your region or the Paris tourist office.

## Les pâtisseries parisiennes  1.2, 2.1, 2.2

Il n'est pas nécessaire d'aller loin à Paris pour trouver une pâtisserie ou une boulangerie-pâtisserie. Des gâteaux traditionnels qu'on y achète sont les flans, les éclairs, les religieuses, et les millefeuilles. Avant les fêtes, on peut y acheter une bûche de Noël* ou une galette des Rois* pour fêter l'Épiphanie. À Paris il y a aussi des salons de thé comme Angelina ou Ladurée qui servent des gâteaux de toutes sortes.

 Search words: **angelina paris**
**ladurée**
**maison pierre hermé**

———
**bûche de Noël** *Yule log;* **galette des Rois** *Kings' Cake*

Les enfants aiment porter la couronne (*crown*) que les pâtisseries distribuent avec la galette des Rois.

 **Produits**

La **galette des Rois** est un gâteau qu'on sert pour l'Épiphanie. On met une fève (*bean*) dedans, et la personne qui la trouve devient le roi (*king*) ou la reine (*queen*) de la journée. On peut aussi trouver cette tradition en Belgique et en Louisiane, où on le sert pendant la fête de Mardi Gras.

1.2, 4.2

## La Francophonie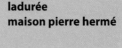

1.2, 2.1, 2.2

✻ *Une autre capitale*

Port-au-Prince est la capitale d'Haïti, la partie ouest de l'île Hispaniola dans la mer des Caraïbes*. (À l'est est la République Dominicaine.) Comme partout* en Haïti, les résidents de la capitale parlent français et créole. Port-au-Prince est un port et la plus grande ville de la République. Il y a une université nationale dans la ville. L'art est partout, même sur les autobus, qu'on appelle des "tap-tap." En général, les artistes haïtiens aiment les couleurs vives* et la décoration. Le 12 janvier 2010 Port-au-Prince a été* dévastée par un tremblement de terre*. Le coût de la reconstruction de la ville est estimé entre 8 et 14 milliards* de dollars.

 Search words: **haïti tourisme**

Tu voudrais circuler dans un autobus tap-tap à Port-au-Prince, Haïti?

———
**mer des Caraïbes** *Caribbean Sea;* **partout** *everywhere;* **vives** *bright;* **a été** *was;* **tremblement de terre** *earthquake;*
**milliards** *billions*

**Essential Instruction**

1. Have students read the **Points de départ** and **Produits** paragraphs silently. Ask students to use the search words to research online French pastry shops and Port-au-Prince, then share several additional facts that they learned.

2. Ask students to prepare the research in **Perspectives** as homework and briefly discuss their findings in class the next day when they do **Activité 9.**

3. Have pairs compare the charts they created for **Activité 10.**

## 9 Questions culturelles

2.1, 2.2, 3.1, 4.2

*Répondez aux questions et faites les activités suivantes.*

1. À qui doit-on les transformations de Paris?
   - la place des Vosges
   - les Champs-Élysées
   - l'Opéra Garnier
2. Qui étaient (*were*) les responsables des transformations de Paris moderne? Faites des recherches en ligne.
3. Regardez des photos en ligne des pâtisseries mentionnées. Laquelle voudriez-vous goûter?
4. Où est située la République d'Haïti?
5. Qu'est-ce qui y (*there*) est arrivé le 12 janvier 2010?

La cathédrale de Notre-Dame est située sur l'île de la Cité.

### Perspectives

More than 20 million tourists visit Paris each year, including many Americans. But where do the French travel? Do online research to find out where they like to travel the most.

**Search words: destination des séjours personnels**

## Du côté des médias

## 10 Le plan de Paris

2.1, 2.2

*Regardez le plan de Paris et complétez une grille comme celle-ci en mettant chaque endroit dans la colonne appropriée.*

| rive droite | rive gauche |
|---|---|
| **Modèle** | la tour Eiffel |
| 1. | |
| 2. | |

1. l'arc de triomphe
2. l'Opéra
3. le Louvre
4. les Invalides
5. le Sacré-Cœur
6. les Champs-Élysées
7. le Panthéon
8. le Cimetière du Père-Lachaise

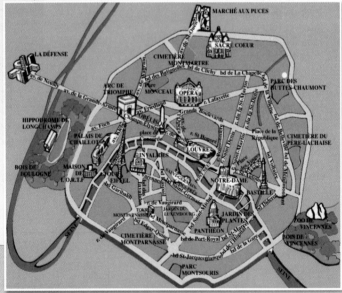

Leçon A | quatre cent trois **403**

## Structure de la langue

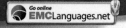

### Present Tense of the Irregular Verb *faire* 1.2

The irregular verb **faire** means "to do" or "to make."

| faire | | | |
|---|---|---|---|
| je | **fais** | nous | **faisons** |
| tu | **fais** | vous | **faites** |
| il/elle/on | **fait** | ils/elles | **font** |

Juliette fait une promenade dans le jardin des Tuileries.

Qu'est-ce que vous **faites**?   *What are you doing?*
Nous **faisons** une salade niçoise.   *We're making a niçoise salad.*

Like the irregular verbs **aller**, **être**, and **avoir**, **faire** is used in many expressions in which a verb other than *to do* or *to make* is used in English, such as in sports and weather expressions.

Tu **fais** du sport?   *Do you play sports?*
Oui, je **fais** de la gym.   *Yes, I do gymnastics.*
Il **fait** chaud.   *It's (The weather's) hot/warm.*

Do you remember these **faire** expressions?

* faire ses devoirs
* faire la cuisine
* faire les courses
* faire du footing
* faire du patinage artistique
* faire du roller
* faire du shopping
* faire du ski alpin
* faire du vélo

**COMPARAISONS** 4.1

When someone asks you, "What are you doing?", do you use the verb "to do" in your answer?

What are you doing?
I'm taking a walk.

Gisèle et Marc font du patinage artistique.

COMPARAISONS: When someone asks you, "What are you doing?" you can answer with a variety of verbs, just as in French: **Qu'est-ce que tu fais? J'écoute de la musique.**

## 11 Dans la cuisine

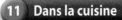 

2.1, 2.2

*Dites ce que tout le monde fait dans la cuisine.*

1. tu

2. Éric et moi, nous

3. Danielle et Awa

4. Rahina

5. je

6. vous

## 12 Mercredi après-midi

2.1, 2.2

*Dites où tout le monde est, puis ce qu'ils y font.*

**MODÈLE** Charlotte
**Charlotte est dans le jardin. Elle fait du sport.**

1. Nicole

2. je

3. Vincent et toi, vous

4. Simone et Clara

5. tu

6. Alima et moi, nous

---

### Reference Desk

It might help students to compare **faire** to other irregular verbs, such as **avoir** and **aller**. To aid pronunciation and aural discrimination of irregular verb forms, read pairs such as: **il/elle est/a; ils/elles sont/ont; ils/elles font/vont**, etc. and ask students to identify the appropriate infinitives. For a more challenging task, add reading comprehension and cloze listening. Prepare and remove the subject and irregular verb of sentences. Distribute to students. As you read one of the subject-verb pairings, students must correctly complete the sentence. For example, students might see on their paper **à la plage en France** as you say **vous êtes/vous faites**.

### Expansion

Ask students to role-play a dialogue in which they talk to their friend on the phone about what they are doing.

---

### Differentiated Learning
#### Accelerate
1. Introduce other expressions with **faire**, such as **faire un voyage**, **faire de la musique**, **faire une faute/une erreur/une gaffe**.
2. Have students review inversion question formation using **faire**.

### Learning Styles
#### Kinesthetic Learners
Play **Tapette à mouches** to practice **faire**. Post on the board pictures of people doing different **faire** activities. Divide the class into teams and, if possible, provide a flyswatter to each team. As you call out an activity, a student from each team tries to be first to tap the correct picture. Award a point for identifying the picture and another for a correct complete sentence.

### Multiple Intelligences
#### Visual-Spatial
Create a set of large flash cards with pictures/photos of **faire** activities on one side and the **faire** expression on the back. Use for conjugation drills, questions, vocabulary, and spelling practice.

**Answers** _____

 Script can be found in the front pages of the Annotated Teacher's Edition.

1. B
2. A
3. E
4. D
5. C

## Game

Divide students into two teams. For the first round, assign **avoir chaud** to Team A and **avoir froid** to Team B. At a given signal, ask the teams to compile a list of as many expressions as possible, using infinitives, that complete the sentence: **Quand j'ai chaud** (Team A)/**froid** (Team B), **j'ai envie de** + infinitive phrase. After the designated time is up, teams will swap expressions and do the same for round two, making up a list of phrases to complete the sentences. Then, teams take turns having one member at a time share their team answers with the rest of the class. Any answers that do not make sense must be replaced with another, until the sentence is correct. The team that can provide the most logical answers wins.

**13  Qu'est-ce que Malika fait?**   2.1, 2.2

*Écrivez les numéros 1–5 sur un papier. Écoutez et choisissez l'image qui correspond à chaque activité que Malika fait.*

A.

B.

C.

D.

E.

## Expressions with *avoir*: *avoir froid, avoir chaud, avoir envie de*

1.2

You have already seen that the verb **avoir** is used in several French expressions where English uses another verb: **avoir besoin de**, **avoir faim**, **avoir soif**, **avoir... ans**. Three more **avoir** expressions are **avoir froid** (*to be cold*), **avoir chaud** (*to be hot*), and **avoir envie de** (*to want to*).

**Est-ce qu'Amidou a chaud ou froid?**

### COMPARAISONS
4.1

What is the best way to put this sentence into English? A good, idiomatic translation doesn't always rely on translating word-by-word, but by considering the sense of the whole sentence.

*J'ai froid, mais tu as chaud.*

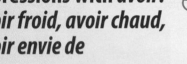
COMPARAISONS: **J'ai froid, mais tu as chaud** is best expressed as "I'm cold, but you are hot."

## Essential Instruction

1. Before doing listening **Activité 13**, ask students to create a sentence with **faire** to describe each illustration.

2. Review the conjugation of **avoir** by asking questions with the **avoir** expressions in affirmative and negative sentences that students already know. Use gestures as you add new **avoir** expressions to your questions.

3. To practice the expressions, point to an expression, or make a gesture, and provide a subject pronoun; have the class respond chorally. Drill negative sentences as well.

4. Before students do **Activités 14** and **15**, discuss the **Comparaisons** question and the problem with a word-for-word translation.

**14**

1. J'ai froid quand il pleut.
2. J'ai chaud quand il fait du soleil.
3. J'ai froid quand il neige.
4. J'ai chaud quand il fait beau.
5. J'ai froid quand il fait du vent.

**15** *All dialogues will vary.*

**14** **Froid ou chaud?**   2.1, 2.2

*Dites si vous avez froid ou chaud selon le temps.*

> **MODÈLE**  Il fait frais.
> **J'ai froid quand il fait frais.**

1. Il pleut.
2. Il fait du soleil.
3. Il neige.
4. Il fait beau.
5. Il fait du vent.

> Moi, j'ai froid quand il fait du vent.

# Communiquez!

**15** **Qu'est-ce que tu as envie de faire?** 1.1

**Interpersonal Communication**

*À tour de rôle, demandez à votre partenaire ce qu'il ou elle a envie de faire.*

> **MODÈLE**  le mercredi soir à 9h00
> A: **Qu'est-ce que tu as envie de faire mercredi soir à 9h00?**
> B: **J'ai envie de regarder la télé. Et toi?**
> A: **Moi, j'ai envie de jouer aux jeux vidéo.**

1. vendredi soir à 20h00
2. en été
3. samedi après-midi
4. en hiver
5. au printemps
6. dimanche matin

> Moi, j'ai envie de faire une promenade. Et toi?

**Reference Desk**

Although an Anglicism and a grammatical error to say **je suis chaud(e)**, in **québecois** young people say "**C'est hot!**" without pronouncing the <h> to express something is great.

**Expansion**

1. Re-purpose sentences students have made up for the game on p. 406 for a **logique/pas logique** listening quiz or practice. Create illogical sentences by mixing and matching some of the sentence portions. For example, change **Quand il fait chaud, j'ai envie de nager dans l'océan** to the illogical sentence **Quand il neige, j'ai envie de nager dans l'océan.** As you read statements, students check **Logique** or **Pas logique**. For fun, challenge students to make up humorous, illogical statements to share with the rest of the class.
2. Have pairs of students present a dialogue in which two **avoir** expressions are used, including those they learned earlier.

**Differentiated Learning**
**Accelerate**
Give students additional **avoir** expressions such as **avoir de la chance**, **avoir peur**, **avoir sommeil**, **avoir raison**, and **avoir tort**. Ask them to write a short paragraph using a couple of these expressions.

**Decelerate**
Have students be responsible for one dialogue with their partner in **Activité 15** before role-playing them.

**Special Needs Students**
**Auditory Impairment**
When vocabulary overlaps, as in the phrases **il a froid**, **il fait froid**, and **il fait frais**, some students may have difficulty distinguishing between **faire** vs. **avoir** or between **froid** and **frais**. You may consider pairing sentences with a visual to further aid in deciphering sound and meaning.

**Answers** _____

**16** *Presentations will vary.*

**17** *Albums will vary.*

## Reference Desk

**Blended Instruction**
Consider using blended instruction, a combination of in-class learning and computer-mediated instruction or learning opportunities. Ask students to complete activities on the computer, using their cell or smartphone, or other emerging electronic technology. This will allow students to hone their tech skills and become more independent learners. Schedule routine Internet and e-book learning in class and in the lab.

## Communication

TV5Monde and other French-language TV stations present short world-wide weather bulletins. Using those reports as models, challenge small groups (one student per continent in each group) to create and present skits of television weather reports. Each student will stand in front of a map (ideally projected on a screen behind the student) and give the general weather for key cities in a particular region. Record the skits and have students evaluate them according to a rubric you provide.

## Expansion

To expand the Parisian photo album project, assign a specific number of photos and sentences per photo that you expect students to include in their album.

**4 0 8**

# À vous la parole

 **Communiquez!**

**How do major world cities tell their stories?**

**16  La météo**  **1.3**

**Presentational Communication**
Select a francophone city and look it up on a map. (If it is located south of the equator, remember that seasons are reversed from those in the Northern Hemisphere). Next, research what the weather is like there in the winter, spring, summer, and fall. Also find out the average temperatures in each season and note them in Celsius. Finally, create a weather report or a weather map for your city for a particular date in each season. Share your weather report with the class.

> **MODÈLE**  C'est le **23 décembre**. Vous avez besoin de mettre votre manteau. Ici à **Paris** il **pleut** et il **fait du vent**. La température ce matin: **8 degrés**. La température cet après-midi va être de **4 degrés**. Demain il va **neiger**.

 **Search words:  météo (+ name of location)**

**Communiquez!**

**17  Album de photos des monuments parisiens**  **1.3**

**Presentational Communication**
Make a photo album of five sites from the culture reading "Paris, capitale de la France." For each image, write a caption in French identifying the location and stating what you can see or do there. To find this out, it may be necessary to do some online research. Next, create a timeline showing when each site was built. Put your album online or print it out. Present it to a partner.

> **MODÈLE**  C'est le **Centre Pompidou**. Il est sur la **rive droite** à Paris. On va **au Centre Pompidou pour visiter les musées, manger dans les restaurants, et regarder les musiciens et mimes devant le musée.**

 **Search words:  tour eiffel, notre-dame de paris, louvre, opéra garnier, grand palais, centre pompidou**

**Essential Instruction**

1. For **Activité 16**, first review and practice Celsius/Fahrenheit temperature conversions. Brainstorm a list of francophone countries and cities. Assign or have students select a different city to research. Before students present their weather report, ask them to practice with a partner. Then have students present their weather report in small groups. Finally, poll the class in French about what cities have warm, cool, and cold weather in different seasons.

2. Give students the opportunity to reflect on the **Question centrale** in their Culture Journal.

3. Ask students to compare standard to casual English, for example, "do not" and "don't." Then listen to the **Prononciation** section on page 409 and do the activities.

# Prononciation   1.2

## Ellipses

- There is a difference between standard spoken French that you use in class and casual spoken French that you might use with friends. In the casual style, speakers sometimes drop some sounds that can modify the number of syllables and the rhythm of the sentence.

**A** Style standard et style relâché, le son /l/

*Repeat the sentences, paying attention to the sound /l/.*

| Standard French | Casual French |
| --- | --- |
| 1. Il faut. Il ne faut pas. | Il faut. Il ne faut pas. |
| 2. S'il te plaît. | S'il te plaît. |
| 3. Ils ont fini? | Ils ont fini? |

**B** Style standard et style relâché, les sons /l/ et /R/

*Repeat the sentences, paying attention to the sounds /l/ and /R/.*

| Standard French | Casual French |
| --- | --- |
| 1. Ferme la fenêtre! | Ferme la fenêtre! |
| 2. Tu as quatre sœurs? | Tu as quatre sœurs? |
| 3. Il n'a plus faim. | Il n'a plus faim. |

**C** Style standard ou style relâché?

*Write **S** if you hear standard French or **C** if you hear casual French.*

## Closed and Open Vowels

- *Closed vowels are usually at the end of a syllable, whereas open vowels are usually followed by a pronounced consonant.*

**D** La voyelle fermée /e/ et la voyelle ouverte /ɛ/

*Repeat the words, paying attention to the sounds /e/ and /ɛ/.*

| Chloé. | Inès. |
| --- | --- |
| Hervé. | Djamel. |

**E** Le son /e/ ou le son /ɛ/?

*Write /e/ if you hear the closed vowel /e/ as in Chloé or /ɛ/ if you hear the open vowel /ɛ/ as in Inès.*

**RESOURCES**

 **Pre-test**

 *Leçon* **Quiz**

**Answers** _____

**C**
1. S
2. S
3. C
4. C

**E**
1. /ɛ/
2. /e/
3. /ɛ/
4. /e/
5. /ɛ/
6. /e/
7. /e/
8. /ɛ/

### Expansion

The sound /e/ can be written as **é**. Challenge groups to list as many words from memory with **é**. How many did they find? Then, distribute a paragraph students are familiar with and one that is new (both with several words with **é**) and ask students to identify words that contain **é**. Circulate and ask students to pronounce a word from the list. If they know how to pronounce **é**, they should be able to pronounce all new words. Next give them a text (or a page with a mosaic of words) that contains words with the /e/ sound rendered by -**er** (**chevalier**, **rester**, **donner**, etc.), -**ez** (**jouez**, **allez**, **nez**, etc.), -**ef** (**clef**), and -**ed** (**pied**), -**es** (**les**, **des**, **mes**), etc. For greater challenge, include words that do *not* have the /e/ or the /ɛ/ sound. Ask students to circle words with /e/. Write on the board: **forêt, neige, maison, fais, es, est, professeur**. Ask what sound is in these words. Answer? /ɛ/! Practice pronunciation and compare words with /ɛ/ and /e/.

---

**Differentiated Learning**

**Adapt**
Assign **Activité 17** in groups, dividing the research tasks and presentation.

**Decelerate**
Provide clear guidelines about the information to research for **Activité 17**.

**Learning Styles**

**Visual Learners**
Have students find or create a Farenheit/Celsius conversion chart.

**Special Needs Students**
**AD(H)D**
Have students choose either **Activité 16** or **17**. Write step-by-step instructions for them. Add a checklist for these students to assess their work.

## Reference Desk

1. The Statue of Liberty in New York was a gift from the French. Built in 1876 by French sculptor Frédéric Auguste Bartholdi, it commemorated the friendship between France and America, their mutual quest for independence, and their reciprocal help to achieve it during their successive revolutions. Students might be interested to know that the two nations even shared the cost of the statue.
2. Ask students to find out where in Paris there is a Statue of Liberty. (Near the Grenelle bridge on the man-made **l'île aux Cygnes**)
3. Looking at the map, ask students how many of these monuments they recognize.
4. Give one important fact about each numbered place in Paris.
5. Capitalization of the names of monuments and sites is taken from *le Petit Robert, Dictionnaire universel des noms propres*.

# Leçon B

# Vocabulaire actif

 Go online EMCLanguages.net

## Les endroits en ville  1.2

**Départ**

la statue de la **Liberté**

① une statue

la **Seine**

② un fleuve

l'avenue des **Champs-Élysées**

③ une avenue

la place de **la Concorde**

④ une place

le monum de la place **Vendôme**

⑤ un monument

Paris

**Arrivée**

13 un aéroport

l'aéroport Roissy—Charles de Gaulle

Bienvenue en gare de Paris-Nord

12 une gare

la gare du Nord

4 1 0 quatre cent dix | Unité 8

**Essential Instruction**

1. To present the vocabulary and model the pronunciation, present **rive droite** and **rive gauche**, then ask where each place is located. Discuss the **faux ami** (false cognate) **une place** (a square) and make the distinction between **un endroit** and **une place**.

2. Remind students that **h** is always silent in French, as in **cathédrale**, **hôtel**, etc. Give other examples, such as **un thé**, **Thierry**, etc.

le musée
du Louvre

le Pont-Neuf

**6** un musée

**7** un pont

la Coupole

un restaurant

la rue de Rivoli

un restaurant

**8** une rue

l'hôtel du Quartier latin

un hôtel

l'hôtel de ville
(du 2ème
arrondissement)

**9** un hôtel de ville

la poste du quartier

une poste

la cathédrale
Notre-Dame
de Paris

l'argent

la Banque de France

une banque

**11** un bateau

**10** une cathédrale

le bateau-mouche

---

---

**1**

Les touristes voient la Tour Eiffel, Notre-Dame, le Louvre, la Seine, la Statue de la Liberté, la Place de la Concorde, des restaurants français et des magasins.

**2** Questions personnelles

*Answers will vary.*

---

### Reference Desk

1. Ask students to research why the vocabulary word **cimetière** has been included in **Et si je voulais dire...?** Can they locate the **Cimetière de Père-Lachaise** or **Cimetière Montparnasse** on a map? Why are these cemeteries important? (Thousands of tourists visit these cemeteries each year, as many famous people from around the world are buried in each.)
2. Have students add the following to their maps: the word **quai**, **Quartier Latin**, and the sites of **fontaines** in the **Jardin des Tuileries**, the **Luxembourg Gardens**, and **Versailles**.

---

### Culture

**Activity: Products**
Distribute a large, unlined index card to each student. Have them draw and color one side with an image of Paris. On the reverse, divide the card into a message section and an address section, similar to a real postcard. Have students address their cards to a real or imaginary pen pal in France (with street names in French, real city names, and postcodes). Have students write a message about a (real or imaginary) visit to Paris. Students can research the price of postage and print French stamps images.

---

# Pour la conversation   1.2

**H**ow do I excuse myself?

> ❭ **Oh, pardon....**
>
> *Oh, pardon me....*

**H**ow do I describe actions that took place in the past?

> ❭ **Nous avons fini** sur la terrasse de l'arc de triomphe.
>
> *We finished on the terrace of the Arch of Triumph.*

**H**ow do I sequence past events?

> ❭ **Le premier jour,** nous avons visité la tour Eiffel.
>
> *The first day, we visited the Eiffel Tower.*

### Et si je voulais dire...?

| | |
|---|---|
| **un cimetière** | *cemetery* |
| **le distributeur de billets** | *ATM machine* |
| **une fontaine** | *fountain* |
| **un quai** | *train platform, river quay* |
| **un quartier** | *neighborhood* |
| **un tableau** | *painting* |

---

### 1  Les touristes américains à Paris

*Lisez le paragraphe. Ensuite, répondez à la question.*

Les touristes américains arrivent à l'aéroport Roissy–Charles de Gaulle. Ils prennent un taxi pour aller à leur hôtel. Ils achètent des tickets de métro et commencent un tour de Paris. Ils prennent des photos à la tour Eiffel, un monument célèbre. Il visitent Notre-Dame, une vieille cathédrale. Au Louvre, un vieux musée d'art, ils voient la *Joconde* (*Mona Lisa*) de Léonard de Vinci. Sur la Seine, le fleuve de Paris, ils voient du bateau que la statue de la Liberté est plus petite que la même statue à New York. Ils voient que la place de la Concorde est très grande. Ils vont aux restaurants français pour dîner et aux magasins pour acheter des souvenirs.

Quels sites à Paris est-ce que les touristes américains sont sûrs de voir?

1.1, 2.1, 2.2

### 2  Questions personnelles

*Répondez aux questions.*

1. Aimes-tu visiter les musées?
2. Quand est-ce que tu vas à la poste?
3. Quand est-ce que tu vas à la banque?
4. Quel est ton restaurant préféré?
5. Il y a une statue dans ta ville? Si oui, de qui?
6. Il y a un fleuve dans ta région? Si oui, comment s'appelle le fleuve?
7. Quels monuments voudrais-tu voir à Paris?

Non, ma ville n'est pas près d'un fleuve.

2.1, 2.2

---

**Essential Instruction**

1. To practice pronunciation, have students listen to **Pour la conversation** and ask them to repeat the sentences. Have students say **Pardon** with the titles **madame**, **monsieur**, and **mademoiselle**.
2. After students read the paragraph in **Activité 1**, check for comprehension.
3. Assign **Activités 2** and **3** as pair work.
4. Ask the class to orally give the missing vocabulary word in **Activité 3** as you randomly call the numbers. Then have them spell the words aloud.
5. Have students identify the places in the photos in **Activité 4** as a class, then do the listening.

Answers _____

**3**
1. aéroport
2. pont
3. musée
4. place
5. gare
6. statue
7. avenue

**4** Script can be found in the front pages of the Annotated Teacher's Edition.

1. D
2. A
3. G
4. E
5. B
6. F
7. C

**3 Une visite à New York**  1.3

*Faites des recherches sur New York pour compléter chaque phrase.*

1. LaGuardia est un grand... à New York.
2. On peut aussi entrer dans la ville sur le... Georges Washington.
3. Le Métropolitain est un... d'art intéressant.
4. "Washington" est aussi le nom d'une... importante.
5. On peut prendre le train à la.... Grand Central.
6. La... de la Liberté est sur Staten Island.
7. "Fifth" est une... avec de beaux immeubles et de belles boutiques.

**4 C'est où?**   1.3, 3.1

*Écrivez les numéros 1–7 sur un papier. Écoutez chaque description et écrivez la lettre de l'endroit (location) correspondant.*

A.

B.

C.

D.

E.

F.

G.

**Leçon B** | quatre cent treize **413**

# Communiquez!

## 5 Où vas-tu? 2.1

### Interpersonal Communication

*Vous rencontrez des amis qui vont à des destinations différentes. À tour de rôle, dites ce que vous faites et où vous allez.*

**MODÈLE** faire du shopping
A: **Je vais faire du shopping.**
B: **Alors, tu vas à la rue commerçante?**
A: **Oui, c'est ça.**

> la gare    le restaurant    le musée    la poste    l'aéroport
> l'hôtel    la rue commerçante

1. envoyer un cadeau
2. voyager à Marseille
3. voir l'exposition (*exhibit*) de Cézanne
4. visiter Hong Kong
5. travailler comme serveur ou serveuse
6. faire les courses
7. travailler comme réceptionniste
8. envoyer une lettre

*Je vais voyager à Marseille.*

*Alors, tu vas à la gare?*

## 6 Un voyage à Paris 2.1

*Les Nelson organisent un voyage à Paris. Terminez les phrases en choisissant le bon mot de vocabulaire de la liste ci-dessous. Ensuite, mettez les phrases en ordre.*

> la Seine    l'arc de triomphe    Paris    la statue    la cathédrale
> la place    l'avenue    le Louvre

1. Le troisième jour, nous allons visiter _____ Notre-Dame de Paris.
2. Le premier jour, nous allons voir _____ sur _____ des Champs-Élysées.
3. Le cinquième jour, nous allons prendre des photos de _____ de la Concorde.
4. Le quatrième jour, nous allons en bateau sur _____ pour voir _____ de la Liberté.
5. Le deuxième jour, nous allons visiter _____ et voir la *Joconde*.
6. Le sixième jour, nous allons acheter des souvenirs de _____.

### Essential Instruction

1. Have students prepare and present the dialogues of **Activité 5**. Have them do **Activité 6** with a partner.
2. As they watch and listen to the **Rencontres culturelles** dialogue, ask students to determine which two people are cousins and to jot down answers to the questions in **Activité 7**.

# Rencontres culturelles

 Go online EMCLanguages.net

## Un tour de Paris     1.2

Yasmine attend Camille devant son immeuble.

Yasmine: Enfin!

Camille: Quoi, enfin? J'arrive de la gare de Lyon! Mon petit cousin… tu as oublié?

Yasmine: Oh, pardon! Alors, tu as fait le guide touristique pendant deux jours. Et qu'est-ce que vous avez fait?

Camille: Le premier jour, nous avons visité la tour Eiffel et le musée Grévin. On a vu Céline Dion et Michael Jackson!

Yasmine: Et aujourd'hui, le deuxième jour?

Camille: TOUT! Lucas est parti fatigué. D'abord, on a visité Notre-Dame de Paris. Puis il a vu le tableau la *Joconde* au Louvre. Ensuite, la jolie rue de Rivoli, la grande place de la Concorde, ici photo obligatoire de sa jolie cousine avec son cousin….

Yasmine: Très charmant… quand est-ce que tu me montres la photo?

Camille: Laisse-moi finir! Donc, place de la Concorde, puis les Champs-Elysées, et nous avons fini sur la terrasse de l'arc de triomphe. Quelle belle vue sur Paris!

Yasmine: Et re-photo!

Camille: Exactement!

 2.1, 2.2

### 7 Un tour de Paris

*Répondez aux questions.*

1. Pourquoi est-ce que Camille arrive de la gare?
2. Qui est fatigué?
3. On a visité quels monuments parisiens?
4. Où est-ce qu'on a une belle vue sur Paris?
5. Camille a combien de photos d'elle avec son cousin?

### Extension   Les grands magasins de Paris

1.2, 2.1, 2.2

*Laura et Maya se parlent à une terrasse de café.*

Laura: Alors, c'était bien ce weekend?

Maya: Trop court. Quand tu es à Paris, tu as envie de rester là une semaine… rien que pour le shopping. C'est de la folie!

Laura: Je vois… tu as beaucoup acheté au Printemps, aux Galeries Lafayette, et au Bon Marché?

Maya: J'ai acheté cette paire de ballerines, ce sac, et une petite marinière.

Laura: Rien que ça!!!

### Extension   Quels sont trois magasins à Paris?

---

## Differentiated Learning

**Accelerate**

After students complete **Activité 6**, ask them to reorder the sentences according to their own personal preferences. What places in Paris would they visit first, second, etc.?

Assign pairs to role-play the **Extension** dialogue and identify three department stores in Paris.

## Multiple Intelligences

**Visual-Spatial**

1. Ask three students to sketch on the board the items that Maya bought in the **Extension** dialogue, and then ask the class to identify them in French.

---

## RESOURCES

 **Dialogue Video**

**Answers** _____

**7**

1. Elle a fait le guide touristique à son petit cousin à Paris pendant deux jours.
2. Lucas, le petit cousin de Camille.
3. On a visité Notre-Dame de Paris, le Louvre, la rue de Rivoli, la place de la Concorde, les Champs-Élysées et l'arc de Triomphe.
4. Depuis la terrasse de l'arc de triomphe.
5. deux photos

### Extension

Printemps, Galeries Lafayettes, Bon Marché

### Reference Desk

1. Tell students that **il a vu** literally means "he has seen." Ask them what period of time this reflects (past). Ask them to find more examples of the past tense.
2. Show students pictures you find online of the three **grands magasins** mentioned in the **Extension** dialogue and then tell them a little bit about their beginnings in the 19th century.

### TPR

Assign groups to write and act out a dialogue between travelers and knowledgeable Parisians who help them visit the city more efficiently. Create a rubric of elements that students must use.

### Communication

**Interpersonal: Cooperative Groups**

Students can take turns describing a Paris monument in a few phrases, including hints about its location, and have the rest of the class guess which one they are talking about. Alternatively, students can play a version of Pictionary on the board and draw famous places in Paris as their peers guess.

## Reference Desk

Challenge your students to research the history, art, and style of **Notre-Dame** and to discover other gothic cathedrals of France. Make a map showing their locations around the country with photos from the Internet. Compare sizes and main features (spires, length of nave, stained glass art). Discuss which ones they may have heard about previously, which ones were damaged in World War II, and which ones they would incorporate into their visits to France.

## Connections

### Art History

Students working individually or in pairs may enjoy making rose window decorations for the class windows. Cut out a circle of black construction paper with symmetrical cut-out patterns from the edge to the center for stone framework designs like a rose window. Spray glue onto a sheet of tracing paper and sprinkle with miniature bits of colored paper. Apply another sheet of tracing paper and place this sandwich of sheets behind the cut-out tracery of the black paper and hang in class windows to simulate the **rosaces**. Research windows from various cathedrals and trace their designs.

# Points de départ

Les fenêtres multicolores de la cathédrale s'appellent des "vitraux."

**Question centrale**
How do major world cities tell their stories?

## Notre-Dame de Paris  1.2, 2.1, 2.2

La cathédrale **Notre-Dame de Paris** est un symbole important de la ville et marque le point zéro de toutes les distances calculées à partir de Paris. Sa construction a duré* deux siècles (1163–1363). C'est un exemple de l'architecture gothique. Approximativement 13,5 millions de visiteurs par an viennent visiter la cathédrale.

Search words: **cathédrale notre dame de paris**

———
**a duré** *lasted*

**Produits**

L'écrivain célèbre **Victor Hugo** a sauvé la cathédrale en 1831 avec le succès de son roman *Notre-Dame de Paris*, avec le bossu (*hunchback*) Quasimodo.

 4.2

## L'arc de triomphe  1.2, 2.1, 2.2

Napoléon est responsable pour la construction de **l'arc de triomphe** qui devient le centre de la place de l'Étoile (aujourd'hui la place Charles de Gaulle). C'est ici où 12 avenues différentes débouchent sur un rond-point*. **L'arc de triomphe** est associé avec plusieurs moments historiques comme les funérailles de Victor Hugo en 1885 et le défilé* de victoire après la Première guerre mondiale de 1914–1918. Depuis 1921, on trouve la tombe du Soldat inconnu* et la flamme du Souvenir sous l'arc.

Search words: **arc de triomphe centre de monuments nationaux**

———
**débouchent sur un rond-point** *flow into a traffic circle*; **défilé** *parade*; **Soldat inconnu** *Unknown Soldier*

## Essential Instruction

1. Briefly revisit the **Question centrale**. Tell students a story about the history of a monument in your city.
2. Ask students to brainstorm what they may know about Victor Hugo and Napoleon. Focus on how both personalities are associated with the two monuments before reading about **Notre-Dame** and the **arc de triomphe**.
3. Show a map of **La place de l'Étoile** and discuss why this is an appropriate name. Explain that its official **métro** name is **Étoile-Charles de Gaulle**. What does this tell them about the importance of the late president?
4. Discuss the **Questions culturelles** or assign them as group projects.

## La tour Eiffel  1.2, 2.1, 2.2

On a construit* la tour Eiffel pour l'Exposition universelle de 1889. La construction de la tour par l'ingénieur Gustave Eiffel a duré deux ans. On a mis 7.000 tonnes d'acier* et deux millions de rivets pour la construire. La tour a trois étages et elle est haute de 300 mètres. Elle est repeinte* tous les sept ans avec 50 tonnes de peinture. Attraction universelle, elle est le symbole de Paris et est célébrée par les plus grands artistes, peintres, poètes, photographes, et metteurs en scène.

**Search words: tour eiffel site officiel**

_____
**a construit** *built*; **acier** *steel*; **repeinte** *repainted*

---

## 8 Questions culturelles  1.1, 2.1, 2.2, 4.2

*Répondez aux questions.*

1. Faites des recherches sur les parties d'une cathédrale gothique comme Notre-Dame. Ensuite, trouvez des photos de la cathédrale Notre-Dame de Paris en ligne qui montrent ces parties.
2. Recherchez l'intrigue (plot) du roman de Victor Hugo, *Notre-Dame de Paris*. C'est un roman intéressant pour vous? Pourquoi, ou pourquoi pas?
3. Trouvez autre chose, à part l'arc de triomphe, que Napoléon a fait construire.
4. Avec un convertisseur en ligne, donnez l'équivalent de 300 mètres (la taille de la tour Eiffel) en "feet."

**Search words: cartes postales virtuelles de paris**

### À discuter

Why do societies build monuments?

L'arc de triomphe forme une étoile au centre de douze avenues de Paris, comme l'avenue des Champs-Élysées.

**Leçon B** | quatre cent dix-sept **417**

---

### Reference Desk

1. Point out that Victor Hugo's novel *Notre-Dame de Paris* is one of the reasons the cathedral is still standing today and was never destroyed during WWII. The name of its main character, **Quasimodo**, is Latin for "almost (*quasi*) human." Consider showing a clip from one of the many French or English film versions of this classic of French literature. Show the 2000 musical version by Quebec composer and lyricist Luc Plamondon. Print out the lyrics for some of the songs and have students sing along.
2. Point out to students that there is another monument in Paris with the same shape as the **arc de triomphe**. It's the **L'arc du carrousel**, near the Louvre.

### Communication

**Interpersonal: Cooperative Groups**

On individual maps of Paris or on a large classroom display or mural, students should draw a straight alignment of monuments from the **Pyramide du Louvre**, **l'arc du carrousel**, **le jardin des Tuileries**, **l'Obelisque** at **place de la Concorde** along **avenue des Champs-Élysées** to **l'arc de triomphe** and to **la Grande Arche** at **La Défense**. Explain that **La Défense** is a suburb outside Paris. Find and show students an aerial photo from **la Grande Arche** to the **Louvre** and the reverse view from the **Louvre** Pyramid to **la Grande Arche**.

---

## Differentiated Learning
### Expand, Accelerate

1. To learn more about the **tour Eiffel**, create a timeline on the board. Solicit the answer to when the monument was built and add to the timeline. Then ask students to guess what anniversary the construction of the Eiffel Tower commemorated (**Fête nationale française**), and present the word **centenaire**. Finally ask them to give you the year of the **bicentenaire** of this monument.
2. Ask if students know which ancient culture celebrated victories with triumphal arches (the Romans). Then ask them if they can guess why Napoleon built this monument.
3. Explain the difference between **une tour** (a tower) and **un tour** (**faire un tour**: a visit or a ride, e.g., **le Tour de France**).

### Special Needs Students
### AD(H)D/Visually Challenged

Enlarge the paragraphs or retype them, separating each paragraph into sentences so that students can focus their attention.

**417**

**9**

1. *Answers will vary.*
2. Métro Grands Boulevards
3. five
4. *Answers will vary.*

---

### Reference Desk

1. Ask students which celebrities and notables should get a statue in the **Musée Grévin**. Some students may enjoy the challenge of making a figurine out of wax or clay to propose as an addition to the museum.

2. Introduce students to some less well-known museums in Paris: **le musée Marmottan, le musée Jacquemart-André, le musée Rodin, le musée d'Orsay, le Petit Palais, le Grand Palais, le musée d'Art Moderne, le musée Carnavalet, le musée des Arts décoratifs, le musée de la Mode, la maison de Victor Hugo, la maison de Balzac, le musée Zadkine, le musée Cernuschi, le musée Bordelle,** etc. There's also a museum of magic in the **Marais**.

3. Challenge students to find the most unique museum in Paris and the one that would be the most interesting for them to visit.

---

### Communication

**Interpersonal: Paired Practice**

Draw up a list of Paris museums and their locations. Have students sit in pairs facing each other. Taking turns, one student will describe a museum and what it offers. The partner will try to guess which museum it is and give its location.

---

## Du côté des médias

*Lisez la brochure sur le musée Grévin.*

**9** Le musée Grévin  2.1

*Répondez aux questions.*

1. Allez au site officiel du musée Grévin. Combien coûte un billet pour un adulte pour un jour férié?
2. Le musée est près de quelle bouche de métro?
3. Combien de personnages sont représentés sur la brochure?
4. Qui est-ce que vous reconnaissez (*recognize*) sur les photos? Que savez-vous de ces personnes?

### Essential Instruction

1. Consider projecting the website in **Du côté des médias** as your students read about the museum and complete **Activité 9**.

2. Explain that students are going to learn a new tense to describe past events, then present **Structure de la langue**. Divide students into three groups and distribute a large piece of paper with the categories **infinitif, participe passé, sens** (meaning). Have groups list -**er**, -**ir**, or -**re** infinitives they know, then present their poster to the class. If wall space is available, post their work around the room.

3. Explain that, while French past participles are like the past tense "-ed" in English, the helping verb and the past participle together form one thought unit. Model the **passé composé** for each verb group, and ask students to call out past participles as you provide infinitives.

4. Ask students to complete their posters by adding **participes passés** and **sens**.

5. Students will learn **adverbes de temps** to use with **passé composé** (such as **hier, avant-hier**, etc.) in **Leçon C**.

# Structure de la langue

 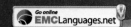

## Passé composé with avoir  1.2

The **passé composé** is a verb tense used to discuss completed events in the past. This tense is composed of two words: a helping verb and a past participle. To form the **passé composé** of most verbs, use the appropriate present tense form of the helping verb **avoir** and the past participle of the main verb.

To form the past participle of –er verbs, drop the –er of the infinitive and add **é**: regarder → regard**é**.

*Qu'est-ce que Samuel a oublié dans la médiathèque?*

J'**ai regardé** des monuments.　　　　*I looked at (some) monuments.*

| regarder | | | | | |
|---|---|---|---|---|---|
| j' | **ai** | regard**é** | nous | **avons** | regard**é** |
| tu | **as** | regard**é** | vous | **avez** | regard**é** |
| il/elle/on | **a** | regard**é** | ils/elles | **ont** | regard**é** |

**Est-ce que tu as regardé** la télé?　　*Did you watch TV?*
Non, j'**ai écouté** de la musique.　　　*No, I listened to music.*

To form the past participle of most –**ir** verbs, drop the –**ir** and add **i**: fin**ir** → fin**i**.

| finir | | | | | |
|---|---|---|---|---|---|
| j' | **ai** | fin**i** | nous | **avons** | fin**i** |
| tu | **as** | fin**i** | vous | **avez** | fin**i** |
| il/elle/on | **a** | fin**i** | ils/elles | **ont** | fin**i** |

Most infinitives that end in –**re** form their past participles by dropping the –**re** and adding **u**: vend**re** → vend**u**.

| vendre | | | | | |
|---|---|---|---|---|---|
| j' | **ai** | vend**u** | nous | **avons** | vend**u** |
| tu | **as** | vend**u** | vous | **avez** | vend**u** |
| il/elle/on | **a** | vend**u** | ils/elles | **ont** | vend**u** |

To make a negative sentence in the **passé composé**, put **n'** before the form of **avoir** and **pas** after it.

Les élèves **n'**ont **pas** visité le musée.　　*The students didn't visit the museum.*

To ask a question in the **passé composé** using inversion, put the subject pronoun after the form of **avoir**.

**RESOURCES**

Workbook 26–29

## Reference Desk

To help students grasp the important structure and concept of the placement of **ne** and **pas** in a negative past tense sentence, use the imagery of a sandwich: the two "bread slices" are **ne** and **pas**. In between the "bread" is the "jam" or the auxiliary conjugated verb from of **être** or **avoir**. Teach them that this will be the standard pattern for negative formation in the past for all other compound past tenses, which they will learn eventually (**plus-que-parfait**, past conditional, future perfect, past subjunctive).

## Expansion

Have all students make up a list of 12 sentences about visiting Paris, using different verbs: four -**er**, -**ir** verbs, and -**re** verbs. In pairs, each student takes turns reading a sentence in the affirmative, while the partner responds by saying the sentence in the negative.

## Communication

**Interpersonal: Paired Practice**
Put students in pairs to discuss what they did last weekend.

**Differentiated Learning**
**Decelerate**
Focus on practice of **tu** and **je** forms in the **passé composé** to get these students started.

**Learning Styles**
**Visual Learners**
To practice the **passé composé**, play **Loto**. Create or have students design bingo cards with pictures that correspond to regular verbs they know. Randomly distribute a card to each student and provide playing pieces. Call out phrases in the **passé composé**.

Have the first student to call **Loto** repeat the past participle to be declared **gagnant(e)**.

**Kinesthetic Learners**
Create sets of 3 × 5 cards with subject pronouns, all forms of **avoir**, and -**er**, -**ir**, and -**re** past participles. Distribute one set to each pair of students. As you call out a past tense phrase in English (I ate, she spoke, etc.), students try to be first to combine three elements to show the French equivalent.

**As**-tu **parlé** français à Paris?     *Did you speak French in Paris?*

The **passé composé** has more than one meaning in English.

Elle **a mangé** trois religieuses.     { *She **ate** three cream puffs.*
                                     *She **has eaten** three cream puffs.*

**A**-t-elle **mangé** trois religieuses?     *Did she eat three cream puffs?*

**COMPARAISONS**  4.1

What are three ways to express this sentence in English?

Ils ont parlé français à Paris.

---

**10**   **On a fait le tour de Paris!**   2.1, 2.2

*Dites quels sites tout le monde a visité.*

**MODÈLE**   moi, je
**Moi, j'ai visité le jardin des Tuileries.**

1. tu

2. M. Dupont

3. Maman et moi     4. Les élèves

5. Éric et toi

---

COMPARAISONS: The sentence **Ils ont parlé français à Paris** can be expressed three ways in English:
1. They spoke French in Paris.
2. They have spoken French in Paris.
3. They did speak French in Paris.

An auxiliary verb is always needed in French to express the past tense, but not always needed in English.

### Essential Instruction

1. Review **Comparaisons** and discuss how students will discern which English translation corresponds to the French **passé composé** (context).
2. Have students do **Activité 10** orally in pairs or listen to the audio.
3. Assign students to write, then peer-correct, the stories in **Activité 12**.
4. Present and practice the negative **passé composé** and inversion. Reinforce the "sandwich" analogy to help students remember how to formulate the negative of a past tense verb. Write the example sentence on the board, circle the helping verb (calling it the sandwich filling), and draw squares around **ne** and **pas** (the bread).

## 11 Salut de Paris!

 2.1, 2.2

*Complétez l'e-mail avec les verbes appropriés au passé composé.*

> manger    perdre    attendre    finir    visiter    acheter    regarder

À   Saniyya
Cc:
Sujet: Salut de Paris!

Salut, Saniyya!

Paris est super! Le métro est facile à naviguer, et Sylvie et moi, nous __1__ le Louvre aujourd'hui!
Hugo préfère le sport, alors il __2__ un match au Stade de France. On l' __3__ au restaurant algérien.
Est-ce que tu __4__ le couscous à Paris? J' __5__ ma casquette; donc, j' __6__ une autre casquette avec le
blason du PSG. Bien sûr, j'ai aussi un cadeau pour toi! Bon, j' __7__ mon mail!

À très bientôt,
Timéo

## 12 Le weekend prolongé

 2.1, 2.2

*Dites ce qu'on a fait chaque jour. Choisissez un verbe de la liste pour décrire chaque illustration.*

> regarder    vendre    finir    synchroniser    dormir    manger    jouer    attendre

**MODÈLE**  **Le premier jour Ambre a synchronisé son lecteur mp3.**

1. Ambre

2. Mes copines et moi, nous

3. Julian et Clark

Leçon B | quatre cent vingt et un **4 2 1**

Answers _____

**11**
1. avons visité
2. a regardé
3. a attendu
4. as mangé
5. ai perdu
6. ai acheté
7. ai fini

**12**
1. Le deuxième jour, Amber a dormi. Le troisième jour, elle a attendu son amie au cinéma.
2. Le premier jour, mes copains et moi, nous avons joué au foot. Le deuxième jour, nous avons mangé des pâtes dans un restaurant italien. Le troisième jour, nous avons regardé la télé.
3. Le premier jour, Julian et Clark ont acheté des jeux vidéo. Le deuxième jour, ils ont joué aux jeux vidéo. Le troisième jour, ils ont fini leurs devoirs!

### Game

Have pairs place their set of flash cards from the paired practice activity on p. 420 face down on a desk. Taking turns, they lift two cards. If the cards match according to category, the student removes them and earns a point. If they don't match, the student returns the cards to their face-down position. Ask students to express what they "did" at each place.

### Expansion

Challenge your students to compose an account of what they did during vacation or on a three-day weekend. Have students peer-edit the stories and then read them aloud.

## Differentiated Learning
### Decelerate
For **Activité 11,** provide the past-tense English verb needed for the blanks and then have students complete the e-mail with the French **passé composé.**

Before assigning **Activité 12,** identify the infinitive needed to describe each picture.

## Special Needs Students
### Linguistically Challenged
To provide additional practice, prepare and hand out a list of core infinitives that students know. Ask them to provide the **passé composé** of each verb.

**4 2 1**

**4 2 2**

---

**13** **Paris ou non?** 2.1, 2.2

*Si Brad parle de ses vacances de l'été dernier à Paris, écrivez **P**. S'il parle de sa vie à Boston maintenant, écrivez **B**.*

**14** **Oui et non!** 2.1, 2.2

*Dites que les personnes suivantes ont fait la première chose, mais pas la deuxième.*

**MODÈLE** moi, je (acheter des pommes/préparer la tarte)
**Moi, j'ai acheté des pommes, mais je n'ai pas préparé la tarte.**

1. Abdoul et toi, vous (jouer au foot/perdre le match)
2. Maude et moi, nous (trouver des cartes postales au musée/trouver le guide touristique)
3. Sarah (finir le dîner/aider sa mère dans la cuisine)
4. toi, tu (surfer sur Internet/synchroniser ton lecteur MP3)
5. Moussa (téléphoner à Émilie/inviter Émilie à la teuf)
6. Thomas et Julien (choisir un CD au magasin/donner le CD à Vincent pour son anniversaire)

Abdoul et toi, vous avez joué au foot, mais vous n'avez pas perdu le match.

**Communiquez!**

As-tu visité la tour Eiffel?

Oui, j'ai visité la tour Eiffel.

**15** **Un voyage imaginaire à Paris**

**Interpersonal communication**

*Imaginez que vous et votre partenaire avez voyagé à Paris. À tour de rôle, demandez ce que votre partenaire a fait.*

**MODÈLE** passer une heure au jardin des Tuileries
A: **As-tu passé une heure au jardin des Tuileries?**
B: **Oui, j'ai passé une heure au jardin des Tuileries.**
   ou
**Non, je n'ai pas passé une heure au jardin des Tuileries.**

1. choisir un hôtel sur la rive droite ou la rive gauche
2. visiter la tour Eiffel
3. manger des pâtisseries
4. manger un croque-monsieur
5. téléphoner à tes parents
6. acheter des souvenirs
7. attendre le guide au Louvre
8. parler français

 1.1

**4 2 2** quatre cent vingt-deux | Unité 8

---

**Essential Instruction**

1. Before doing **Activité 13**, have students provide the infinitives of the past-tense verbs.
2. Ask students to write the answers for **Activité 14**, then peer-correct.
3. Review yes/no question formation of **passé composé** sentences, then use inversion in the **passé composé** and assign **Activité 15** as pair work.
4. Model pronunciation of /u/ before introducing the irregular forms. Point out that the past participle **dû** is written with a circumflex to distinguish it from the word **du** (*of/from the, some*).
5. Have students call out the past participles (include regular verbs) when you give infinitives. Ask students to identify if it is regular or irregular.
6. Discuss the **Comparaison** question and point out that there are many irregularities in English as well.
7. Ask partners to present their storyboards after completing **Activité 16**.

# Irregular Past Participles  1.2

Some verbs that use **avoir** in the **passé composé** have irregular past participles.

| Verb | Past Participle | Meaning |
|---|---|---|
| avoir | j'ai **eu** | I had |
| devoir | j'ai **dû** | I had to |
| pleuvoir | il a **plu** | It rained. |
| pouvoir | j'ai **pu** | I was able to |
| voir | j'ai **vu** | I saw |
| vouloir | j'ai **voulu** | I wanted (to) |
| mettre | j'ai **mis** | I put (on) |
| prendre | j'ai **pris** | I took |
| être | j'ai **été** | I was |
| faire | j'ai **fait** | I did, made |
| offrir | j'ai **offert** | I offered |

Heather a pris le métro à Paris.

Qu'est-ce que tu **as vu**? — *What did you see?*
J'**ai vu** l'arc de triomphe. — *I saw the Arch of Triumph.*

 **COMPARAISONS** 4.1

Which of these verbs with irregular past participles in French have regular past participles ending in "-ed" in English?

## 16 Un cadeau d'anniversaire  2.1, 2.2

*Complétez chaque phrase avec le passé composé des verbes entre parenthèses. Puis, faites un storyboard avec un partenaire pour montrer votre compréhension de l'histoire.*

1. Marc... en ville. (être)
2. Il... l'idée d'acheter un cadeau pour sa mère pour son anniversaire. (avoir)
3. Il... trouver un cadeau bon marché. (devoir)
4. Il... une promenade dans la rue commerçante. (faire)
5. Il... des écharpes. (voir)
6. Il... une écharpe violette. (choisir)
7. Il... le métro à la maison. (prendre)
8. Il... l'écharpe à sa mère. (offrir)
9. Il... donner le cadeau à sa mère. (pouvoir)
10. Sa mère... l'écharpe et a dit (*said*), "C'est splendide!" (mettre)

Marc a fait une promenade dans la rue commerçante.

COMPARAISONS: **Offrir** ("offered"), **pleuvoir** ("rained") and **vouloir** ("wanted") are the only three verbs on this list that have regular past participles in English.

**Answers** _____

**16**
1. a été
2. a eu
3. a dû
4. a fait
5. a vu
6. a choisi
7. a pris
8. a offert
9. a pu
10. a mis

## Game

Divide the class into two groups, one designated as the infinitive group and the other the past participle group. A student in the infinitive group calls out an irregular verb. The other group must then respond in unison with the matching past participle. Repeat until you have exhausted the infinitive/past participle pairings that your students know. Now have a student from the past participle group call out a past participle to which the other group must respond in unison with the correct infinitive. For variety, see how fast students can call out and respond with all correct pairings.

## Differentiated Learning
**Expand, Decelerate**
Have students play **le jeu des dés** (Dice Game) to practice irregular past participles. Provide three dice to each group of four: one for the subject pronoun and two for the verb form. Number and write on the board the subject pronouns and the irregular past participles. Each student rolls one die to determine the subject pronoun and then two more to determine the verb. He or she then says and writes the correct form of the **passé composé** on a white board. The other group members verify it and keep individual scores. If possible, award a prize to the winner of each group.

## Multiple Intelligences
**Bodily-Kinesthetic**
Prepare a matching card game with **passé composé** and **infinitifs**. You can also use the cards to play Concentration or Memory, where students turn over cards to match infinitives with their irregular past participles.

**17** Samedi

*Dites où tout le monde a été. Ensuite, dites ce qu'ils n'ont pas fait et ont fait.*

MODÈLE

**Chloé et moi, nous avons été à la teuf. Nous n'avons pas offert le CD. Nous avons offert le cadeau.**

 2.1, 2.2

1. Alima et Leïla/surfer sur Internet
2. Sébastien/acheter des vêtements
3. toi, tu/regarder la la télé

4. je/voir la comédie
5. Monique/mettre un short et un tee-shirt
6. Laurence et toi, vous/ prendre le steak-frites

## Communiquez!

 As-tu pris le métro à Paris?

 Oui, j'ai pris le métro.

**18** Un voyage à Paris

### Interpersonal Communication

*À tour de rôle, demandez si votre partenaire a fait les choses suivantes pendant ses vacances à Paris.*

MODÈLE prendre des photos de la place de la Concorde
A: **As-tu pris des photos de la place de la Concorde?**
B: **Oui, j'ai pris des photos de la place de la Concorde.**
   ou
**Non, je n'ai pas pris de photos de la place de la Concorde.**

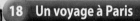 1.1

1. voir un match du PSG
2. mettre une écharpe française
3. faire une promenade aux Champs-Élysées
4. prendre le métro
5. voir la cathédrale de Notre-Dame de Paris
6. être au jardin des Tuileries
7. prendre du couscous dans un restaurant **algérien**

**19** Le weekend de Juliette 🎧  2.1

*Écrivez les numéros 1–8 sur votre papier. Écoutez la description de Juliette qui a passé le samedi dernier à Paris avec sa grand-mère. Ensuite, indiquez si chaque (each) phrase que vous entendez (hear) est **vraie** (true) ou **fausse** (false).*

# Position of Irregular Adjectives

In French, adjectives usually follow the nouns they describe.

  J'ai trouvé une jupe **noire**.  *I found a black skirt.*

Some frequently used adjectives precede the nouns they describe. These adjectives often express *b*eauty, *a*ge, *g*oodness, and *s*ize. (You can remember these categories easily by associating them with the word "BAGS.") Some of these adjectives are **beau**, **joli**, **nouveau**, **vieux** (*old*), **bon**, **mauvais** (*bad*), **grand**, and **petit**.

Les Petit ont choisi un beau restaurant.

|  |  |
|---|---|
| Ma **petite** sœur va au centre commercial. | *My little sister is going to the mall.* |
| Elle a besoin d'un **nouveau** jean. | *She needs new jeans.* |
| Elle trouve un **beau** pull rose. | *She finds a beautiful pink sweater.* |
| Quel **grand** magasin! | *What a big store!* |

The adjectives **nouveau**, **vieux**, and **beau** have irregular feminine forms as well as irregular forms before a masculine noun beginning with a vowel sound.

1.2

| Masculine singular | Masculine singular | Feminine singular |
|---|---|---|
| before a consonant sound | before a vowel sound | |
| un **beau** chien | un **bel** achat | une **belle** promenade |
| un **nouveau** bateau | un **nouvel** hôtel | une **nouvelle** idée |
| un **vieux** musée | un **vieil** aéroport | une **vieille** cathédrale |

The irregular masculine plural forms of **beau**, **nouveau**, and **vieux** are **beaux**, **nouveaux**, and **vieux**.

**Pronunciation Tip**

When **bon** comes before a masculine word that begins with a vowel, it sounds more like the feminine form **bonne: Bon appétit!**

## Answers

**20**

1. C'est un vieux monument.
2. C'est une vieille cathédrale.
3. C'est un vieux fleuve.
4. C'est un nouveau musée.
5. C'est une nouvelle statue.
6. C'est un nouvel aéroport.
7. C'est un vieil hôtel.

### Critical Thinking

**Comparisons**
Give each student a sheet of paper folded twice to create four quadrants. In one square, have students draw an image of some place or thing that is considered "old" in their region. In another, have them draw some place or thing that is considered "modern" in their region. In the two remaining squares, students should draw an image of something "old" and something "modern" in Paris. Students will present their illustratins to the class. Have students reflect on the concept of what is "old" and "modern" in both French and American cultures.

---

**20 Paris—une ville moderne ou une vieille ville?**

*Dites si les endroits à Paris sont vieux ou nouveaux.*

**MODÈLE** gare
**C'est une vieille gare.**

2.1, 2.2

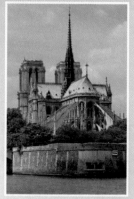

1. monument          2. cathédrale

3. fleuve

4. musée          5. statue

6. aéroport          7. hôtel

**4 2 6** quatre cent vingt-six | **Unité 8**

---

**Essential Instruction**

1. Ask for student volunteers to form sentences for **Activité 20**. As you confirm or correct the pronunciation of each answer, ask the entire class to repeat the answer several times. Explain that part of language learning involves "training the ear."

2. **Activité 21** can be done with the audio or as an entire class.

3. Before having students do **Activité 22**, brainstorm a list of adjectives, including the BAGS (or BANGS) adjectives, and write them on the board. Then ask students to present one of their partner dialogues.

**㉑**
1. Mehdi a acheté une veste moche.
2. Madeleine et sa sœur ont acheté une jolie jupe.
3. Justine a acheté un petit maillot de bain.
4. Nayah a acheté une chemise rose.
5. Alexis a acheté un beau pantalon.

**㉒**  *Answers will vary.*

**㉑ Aux Galeries Lafayette**  2.1, 2.2

*Tout le monde a fait du shopping aux Galeries Lafayette à Paris. Dites ce qu'ils ont acheté et décrivez leurs nouveaux vêtements.*

**MODÈLE**  Stéphanie/joli
**Stéphanie a acheté un joli ensemble.**

1. Mehdi/moche

2. Madeleine et sa sœur/joli

3. Justine/petit

4. Nayah/rose

5. Alexis/beau

**㉒ Bon ou mauvais?** 1.1

**Interpersonal Communication**

*À tour de rôle, demandez à votre partenaire son opinion de huit personnes ou choses suivantes: des films, des acteurs, des livres, des sports, des athlètes, des écrivains, des chanteurs, etc.*

**MODÈLE**  Usher/chanteur
A: **Usher est un bon ou un mauvais chanteur?**
B: **C'est un bon chanteur.**
      ou
    **C'est un mauvais chanteur.**

**Differentiated Learning**
**Decelerate**
For **Activité 22**, students will benefit from a list of written cues such as specific films, books, sports etc., to work from. Having a list of cues will reduce the pressure of thinking of an item and instead focus efforts on the grammar and communication practice.

# À vous la parole

**How do major world cities tell their stories?**

**23  Un voyage à la capitale**  1.1

**Interpersonal Communication**

With a partner, play the roles of a student who just spent three wonderful days in Paris and a friend from Quebec who wants to know all about the visit. The Quebecker asks what the friend saw and did in Paris. When the traveler mentions a place, the Quebecker always asks a follow-up question.

1.1

**24  Guide touristique sur un bateau-mouche**

**Vocabulaire utile**

a été construit(e)   *was built*
au XIX^ème siècle   *in the 19th century*

**Presentational Communication**

To prepare for a job interview as a tour guide on one of the Paris tour boats (**bateaux-mouches**), you need to be able to identify three famous monuments, museums, or bridges along the Seine. Select three locations visible from the boats (go to the website below and select **promenade**, then **plan du parcours**). Then find out if each place is **sur la rive droite ou gauche**, in which century it was built (use ordinal numbers), and what tourists can see or do there. Write out the information about your three locations. You will be asked to present one of them orally before turning your project in.

**MODÈLE**   La tour Eiffel est sur la rive gauche. Elle a été construite au XIX^ème siècle pour une exposition universelle. Les touristes peuvent manger dans un restaurant de la tour Eiffel et regarder les vues de Paris. On peut prendre des photos de la Seine et du Palais de Chaillot.

   **Search words:  compagnie des bateaux mouches site officiel**

# Stratégie communicative

## Personal Narrative

A personal narrative tells about a life experience, observation, or idea. You are going to write a personal narrative about your own past experiences. In order to do this, it may be helpful for you to review the **passé composé** with **avoir** on pages 419 and 423 in this lesson.

**25** Le voyage à Paris de Jameson  **1.2, 2.1, 2.2**

Read Jameson's narrative in the **passé composé** about his first day in Paris. Finally, put sentences 1-5 in chronological order.

Le 18 juin, à 10h15, j'ai vu d'abord la tour Eiffel où j'ai acheté des cartes postales pour mes copains. Au café à midi, j'ai pris une omelette, des frites, et une limonade. J'ai envoyé mes cartes postales à la poste à 14h00. Ensuite, j'ai visité le jardin des Tuileries où j'ai fait une promenade. Enfin, le soir, j'ai vu les monuments de Paris d'un bateau sur la Seine.

1. Jameson a pris le déjeuner.
2. Jameson a vu les monuments de Paris d'un bateau.
3. Jameson a envoyé ses cartes postales.
4. Jameson a vu la tour Eiffel où il a acheté des cartes postales.
5. Jameson a fait une promenade au jardin des Tuileries.

**26** Mon weekend  **1.3**

Create a timeline of your activities last weekend. Using the information on your timeline, write a personal narrative about your weekend. Add adjectives and adverbs to make your writing more descriptive. Be specific about the time of day each action occurred, using times or expressions such as **samedi soir**.

**MODÈLE**  Vendredi soir, j'ai regardé un match de basket.
Samedi matin, j'ai aidé ma mère à la maison.
Samedi après-midi....
Samedi soir....

Answers _____

 **25**
4. Jameson a vu la tour Eiffel où il a acheté des cartes postales.
1. Jameson a pris le déjeuner.
3. Jameson a envoyé ses cartes postales.
5. Jameson a fait une promenade au jardin des Tuileries.
2. Jameson a vu les monuments de Paris d'un bateau.

 **26**
*Narratives will vary.*

### Reference Desk

Students' writing benefits from editing. Create peer-editing checklists that students must complete and return to the author of the narrative. Students should consult the peer checklists they received while they make final corrections to their work before handing in the assignment. Have students submit their work with its peer-editing list attached.

### Communication

**Interpersonal: Paired Practice**
Have students read a sentence to a partner from their Paris composition (**Activité 23**). The partner can say whether he or she did or did not do that activity during a Paris trip.

### Expansion

Have students imagine they are taking a trip to Paris and ask them what they would do first when they arrived and what they would do last before heading home. Challenge students to make a written narrative recounting a morning, an afternoon, an evening, or a day in Paris. Select a few students to read excerpts from their accounts.

**4 2 9**

### Reference Desk

French calendars usually include the national holidays and school vacations, many of which are based on Christian celebrations. Though France's population includes groups from many diverse ethnic backgrounds and religious traditions, the calendar does not usually reflect these celebrations.

### Communication

**Interpersonal: Cooperative Groups**

Have students design a personalized calendar for last month that includes their activities and uses appropriate time expressions in relation to **aujourd'hui**. Then, in groups, have students share with each other what they did throughout the month.

### Critical Thinking

**Comparisons**

Ask students to research and compare the ethnic and religious background of the French population to that of the United States. Next, have them research and compare calendars from both countries. What holidays and traditions are represented on each? What does each calendar say about the values of these two countries, both democratic and secular?

### Expansion

For additional practice with the vocabulary, suggest that students temporarily change their smartphone calendars and other features to French.

**4 3 0**

---

# Leçon C — Vocabulaire actif

## Expressions de temps   1.2

### DÉCEMBRE 2011

| lu | ma | me | je | ve | sa | di |
|---|---|---|---|---|---|---|
| | | | 1 | 2 | 3 | 4 |
| 5 | 6 | 7 | 8 | 9 | 10 | 11 |
| 12 | 13 | 14 | 15 | 16 | 17 | 18 |
| 19 | 20 | 21 | 22 | 23 | 24 | 25 |
| 26 | 27 | 28 | 29 | 30 | 31 | |

le mois dernier
l'année (f.) dernière
en 2011

### JANVIER 2012

| lundi | mardi | mercredi | jeudi | vendredi | samedi | dimanche |
|---|---|---|---|---|---|---|
| | | | | | | 1 |
| 2 | 3 | 4 mercredi dernier | 5 | 6 | 7 | 8 le weekend dernier |

## la semaine dernière

| | | | | | | |
|---|---|---|---|---|---|---|
| 9 | 10 hier matin 9h00 / hier après-midi 14h00 / hier soir 20h00 | 11 X aujourd'hui | 12 | 13 | 14 | 15 |
| 16 | 17 | 18 | 19 | 20 | 21 | 22 |

**4 3 0** quatre cent trente | **Unité 8**

**Essential Instruction**

1. Have pairs of students dictate the months as a review. Students can check their spelling against the vocabulary list in **Unité 5**.
2. As students look at the calendar months, discuss and model the pronunciation of the new time expressions, pointing out the noun-adjective agreement.
3. Have students read silently the paragraph in **Activité 1**. Read the paragraph aloud and clarify any comprehension questions students may have. After they write their answer to the question, they can compare responses with a classmate.
4. Have students do **Activité 2** in pairs.

# Pour la conversation  1.2

**H**ow do I express actions that took place in the past?

> **On est allé** aux Tuileries.

  *We went to the Tuileries.*

> **Nous sommes vite descendus** prendre le métro.

  *We quickly went down to take the metro.*

> **Nous sommes arrivés** chez moi.

  *We arrived at my house.*

**H**ow do I sequence past events?

> On a passé un super jour **samedi dernier**!

  *We spent a super day last Saturday.*

## Et si je voulais dire...?

| | |
|---|---|
| **avant-hier** | *day before yesterday* |
| **l'été passé** | *last summer* |
| **il y a 15 jours** | *two weeks ago* |

## 1 Les voyages de Mlle Teefy  1.2, 2.1, 2.2

*Lisez le paragraphe. Ensuite, répondez à la question.*

Mlle Teefy voyage beaucoup. Elle est femme d'affaires. L'année dernière elle a visité Hong Kong. Le mois dernier elle a voyagé en Haïti. Elle a parlé français aussi la semaine dernière quand elle a voyagé à Paris. Samedi soir elle a mangé dans un restaurant français avec une amie parisienne. Dimanche après-midi elle a visité le Louvre. Lundi elle a pris des photos de la tour Eiffel. Et hier soir? Elle a très bien dormi dans son lit!

Où est-ce que Mlle Teefy a voyagé l'année dernière?

## 2 Qu'est-ce qui s'est passé?  2.1, 2.2

*Choisissez l'expression la plus logique pour compléter chaque phrase.*

1. J'ai fait mes devoirs (jeudi matin, hier soir, maintenant).
2. Abdoulaye a vu un film au cinéma (samedi soir, mardi matin, en 2001).
3. Nous avons fait du shopping (le weekend dernier, l'année dernière, hier à 23h00).
4. Chris et Justin ont pris une photo de la tour Eiffel (cet après-midi, l'année dernière, aujourd'hui).
5. Vous avez voyagé à la Martinique (le mois dernier, aujourd'hui, hier soir).

Nous avons fait du shopping le weekend dernier.

# Communiquez!

1.1

**3 Mes activités passées**

**Interpersonal Communication**

*À tour de rôle, dites quand vous avez fait les activités suivantes.*

> **MODÈLE** A: **Quand as-tu voyagé?**
> B: **J'ai voyagé l'été dernier.**

1. faire une promenade
2. télécharger une chanson
3. visiter un monument
4. préparer un gâteau
5. finir tes devoirs
6. rigoler
7. choisir un DVD
8. consommer du fromage

> Quand as-tu téléchargé la chanson de Salif Keita?
>
> Ce matin!

**4 Ça s'est passé quand?**

2.1, 2.2

*Écrivez les numéros 1–8 sur votre papier. Aujourd'hui, c'est samedi 17 mars. Écoutez les phrases et indiquez la date (en français) qui correspond à chaque description.*

**mars**

| lundi | mardi | mercredi | jeudi | vendredi | samedi | dimanche |
|---|---|---|---|---|---|---|
| | | | 1 | 2 | 3 | 4 |
| 5 | 6 | 7 | 8 | 9 | 10 | 11 |
| 12 | 13 | 14 | 15 | 16 | 17 | 18 |
| 19 | 20 | 21 | 22 | 23 | 24 | 25 |
| 26 | 27 | 28 | 29 | 30 | 31 | |

**5 Questions personnelles**

2.1

*Répondez aux questions.*

1. Qu'est-ce que tu as fait ce matin?
2. Est-ce que tu as fait tes devoirs hier soir?
3. As-tu fait du sport le weekend dernier?
4. As-tu voyagé l'été dernier?
5. Tu as vu combien de films le mois dernier?

> Oui, j'ai voyagé en France l'été dernier.

# Rencontres culturelles

## Un beau souvenir

    1.2, 3.2

Maxime et Yasmine se parlent au téléphone du jour où ils sont allés aux Tuileries.

**Maxime:** On a passé une super journée samedi dernier!

**Yasmine:** Le jour où on est allé aux Tuileries? J'ai a-do-ré. On a commencé à la pâtisserie....

**Maxime:** On a mangé la religieuse sur un banc aux Tuileries. Mais aux Tuileries il a commencé à pleuvoir. Nous sommes vite descendus prendre le métro.

**Yasmine:** Oui, et tu as fait comme au cinéma; tu en as profité pour m'embrasser!

**Maxime:** Tu n'as pas trouvé ça désagréable?

**Yasmine:** Bien sûr que non! Nous sommes arrivés chez moi....

**Maxime:** Et ta petite sœur a rigolé de nous voir la main dans la main.

**6 Un beau souvenir**   2.1, 2.2

*Répondez aux questions.*

1. Avec qui Maxime a-t-il passé un bon après-midi?
2. Où est-ce que tout a commencé?
3. Est-ce qu'il a fait beau ce jour?
4. Qu'est-ce que les deux jeunes ont fait après les Tuileries?
5. Pourquoi la petite sœur a-t-elle rigolé?

**Extension** **La Ville lumière**  1.2, 2.1, 2.2, 3.2

Le professeur de français de Jack, Emma, Lily, et Nick commente à ses élèves leur visite à Paris en bateau-mouche.

**Le prof:** Bon, alors, vous reconnaissez les monuments de Paris? Nous avons étudié ces monuments en classe.

**Jack:** Oui, la tour Eiffel devant à gauche et le jardin des Tuileries, à droite.

**Nick:** Ah, ils sont beaux, les monuments de Paris!

**Emma:** Regardez, la place de la Concorde est vachement bien éclairée!

**Le prof:** Oui, on appelle Paris la "Ville lumière." Vous savez pourquoi?

**Lily:** Parce qu'elle est très éclairée? La tour Eiffel, par exemple....

**Le prof:** Oui, mais il y a une autre explication aussi. C'est au XIX^ème siècle que les Anglais ont appelé Paris "Ville lumière," à cause de ses passages commerçants illuminés.

**Extension** Qu'est-ce que les élèves peuvent voir du bateau-mouche?

Leçon C | quatre cent trente-trois **433**

## RESOURCES

**Dialogue Video**

**Answers**

**6** *Answers will vary.*

1. avec Yasmine
2. à la pâtisserie
3. Non, il a plu.
4. Ils ont pris le métro pour aller chez Maxime.
5. Elle a rigolé parce que Maxime et Yasmine ont marché la main dans la main.

**Extension**

Ils peuvent voir les monuments de Paris.

## Reference Desk

Paris is called the "City of Light" because so many of its monuments are illuminated at night.

## Critical Thinking

### Comparisons
Have students make a list of 15 things they did over the weekend—in French! How do your students think their peers in Paris may have spent the weekend? If your class has e-pals, have students ask them what they *actually* did over the weekend and discuss why there are similarities or differences.

## Culture

### Perspectives
Hemingway said, "If you are lucky enough to have lived in Paris as a young man, then wherever you go for the rest of your life, it stays with you, for Paris is a moveable feast." Discuss with your students what Hemingway meant. (Hemingway lived in Paris from 1921-29.)

## Differentiated Learning

### Decelerate
For additional practice, have students find, list, and write the meanings of the past tense phrases in the dialogue **Un beau souvenir.**

### Accelerate
For **Activité 5,** have students ask for more information when interviewing a partner, then share with rest of the class.

## Multiple Intelligences

### Verbal-Linguistic/Bodily-Kinesthetic
To help students distinguish between the **passé composé** and the **présent** with **avoir,** say a variety of sentences using both tenses, in the affirmative and negative. Have students raise their hands when they hear the helping verb **avoir.** Do the activity again, this time raising their right hand if they hear an infinitive and their left hand if they hear a past participle.

# Points de départ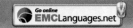

 **Question centrale**
How do major world cities tell their stories?

## Le jardin des Tuileries  1.2, 2.1, 2.2

Le jardin des Tuileries est entre la place de la Concorde et le Louvre à Paris. C'est un jardin pour les gens de tous les âges. Les adultes peuvent faire une promenade et admirer les statues et les fleurs*. Les enfants peuvent faire du vélo, jouer au ballon, ou assister à un spectacle* du théâtre de Guignol. Il y a de vrais poneys et des faux au manège de chevaux de bois*. Les petits peuvent même faire naviguer de petits bateaux sur le grand bassin.

 **Search words: parcs et jardins de paris**

Le jardin des Tuileries est le plus vaste jardin public de Paris.

fleurs *flowers*; **assister à un spectacle** *attend a show*; **manège de chevaux de bois** *merry-go-round with wooden horses*

## Le métro  1.2, 2.1, 2.2

Il y a 16 lignes de métro à Paris. Elles offrent aux voyageurs un système de transport très rapide et bon marché. Avec 297 stations de métro à l'intérieur de Paris, on n'est jamais loin d'une "bouche de métro." Vous prenez le train qui va en direction d'où vous voulez aller. Pour savoir quelle direction prendre, vous regardez le nom de la station à la fin de la ligne. Des fois, il est nécessaire de changer de ligne. En ce cas, vous cherchez le panneau "correspondances" pour changer à la ligne qui va à votre destination. À beaucoup de stations de métro, il y a deux ou trois lignes qui se rejoignent*. Le métro, c'est facile à utiliser!

 **Search words: ratp paris**

qui se rejoignent *intersect*

**COMPARAISONS**

What activities for children are there in the parks in your region?  4.2

Les bouches du métro style "Art Nouveau" ont des structures linéaires métalliques.

 **Produits** 4.2

Quand on voulait décorer les stations de métro en 1902, on a mis des panneaux (*signs*) dans le style **Art Nouveau**. On peut toujours trouver 86 de ces panneaux, classés maintenant comme monuments historiques.

### Essential Instruction

1. As an introduction to the **Points de départ**, you may want to find online and show a video of people in the **Tuileries** and/or the **métro**.
2. Ask students to scan the paragraphs for cognates and new vocabulary. Have them read the paragraphs silently.
3. Assign small groups additional research. Have them present several interesting facts that they learned.
4. Have students do **Activité 7** in groups of three and respond to the **À discuter** question. Ask them to share a summary of their conversation.
5. Using either the **métro** map on p. 436 or one you find online, show students how to use the Paris **métro** before having them do **Activité 8** in small groups.

*Répondez aux questions.*

1. Où est situé le jardin des Tuileries à Paris?
2. Qu'est-ce que les adultes et les enfants peuvent faire au jardin des Tuileries?
3. Il y a combien de lignes et stations de métro?
4. Comment est-ce qu'on utilise le métro?
5. Quel panneau (*sign*) devez-vous chercher pour changer de métro?

Il faut aller à droite pour prendre la correspondance pour la Défense.

**À discuter**

What, if any, commitments are being made in your region to have public transportation that is fast and cheap?

## Du côté des médias

8 **Plan du métro**  2.1, 2.2, 3.1

*Complétez une grille comme celle-ci pour indiquer votre chemin dans le métro aux destinations ci-dessous. Utilisez le plan du métro à la page 436 pour trouver le chemin le plus direct.*

| Point de départ et destination finale | Direction (numéro et nom de la ligne) | Correspondances (nom de la station) | Direction (numéro et nom de la nouvelle ligne) | Destination finale: monument à visiter |
|---|---|---|---|---|
| **MODÈLE** Invalides—République | 13. St. Denis—Université | Miromesnil | 9. Mairie de Montreuil | monument à la République—statue de Marianne |
| 1. Champs-Élysées—Anvers | | | | Sacré Cœur, funiculaire à Montmartre |
| 2. Cité—Bir Hakeim | | | | la tour Eiffel |
| 3. Opéra—Assemblée Nationale | | | | l'Assemblée nationale |
| 4. Arts et Métiers—Concorde | | | | Place de la Concorde |
| 5. Place d'Italie—Cluny-La Sorbonne | | | | le Musée de Cluny/National du Moyen Âge, la Sorbonne, le Collège de France |
| 6. destination que vous choisissez | | | | |
| 7. destination que vous choisissez | | | | |

http://www.ratp.fr

## Differentiated Learning
### Adapt
Give the students plenty of time to practice learning to use the **métro**. Point out that the most important things to remember are the line number (color) and the name of its two end points.

## Multiple Intelligences
### Visual-Spatial/Logical-Mathematical
Tell students they are staying in Paris at a hotel near a certain **métro** stop that you give them. Have pairs choose three monuments or landmarks they want to visit. Then have them plan and write how they will get from the hotel to the three places and back to the hotel at the end of the day.

---

**Answers** _____

7

1. Il est situé entre la place de la Concorde et le Louvre.
2. Les adultes peuvent faire une promenade et admirer les statues et les fleurs. Les enfants peuvent faire du vélo, jouer au ballon, ou assister à un spectacle du théâtre de Guignol.
3. Il y a 16 lignes et 297 stations de métro.
4. On cherche une bouche de métro, on regarde le nom de la station à la fin de la ligne.
5. On doit chercher le "**panneau correspondances.**"

**À discuter**
*Discussions will vary.*

8

1. Champs-Élysées—Answers: 13. St Denis-»Université; Place de Clichy; 2. Nation
2. Cité—Bir-Hakeim: 4. Porte d'Orléans; Gare Montparnasse; 6. Charles de Gaulle Étoile
3. Opéra—Assemblée Nationale: 8. Balard; Madeleine; 12. Mairie d'Issy
4. Arts-et-Métiers—Concorde: 11.Châtelet; Hôtel de Ville; 1. La Défense
5. Place d'Italie—Cluny-La Sorbonne: 5. Bobigny Pablo Picasso; Gare d'Austerlitz; 10. Boulogne Pont de St-Cloud
6. *Answers will vary.*
7. *Answers will vary.*

### Communication

**Interpersonal: Paired Practice**
Bring in a **métro** ticket, or have students look online to find an image of one to use as a model to make a **carnet** (book of 10 tickets). Create a **guichet** (subway ticket window) in your classroom. Groups of three or more will then create skits about buying tickets and asking for directions at the subway ticket booth for getting to various destinations in Paris.

### Products: Activity

Have students access the interactive **RATP** maps of Paris (reprint and distribute, or use ones from a previous trip) to practice how to determine the direction they are going by looking for the terminus station of each line. Practice finding the most efficient routes from one Parisian landmark to another. If one lived in the south of Paris at the **Cité Universitaire**, what would be the most efficient way to get there from CDG-Roissy airport? What is the fastest way to get from the Louvre to **la Grande Arche at La Défense**? What is the nearest station to the Eiffel Tower? To **Sacre-Cœur** in Montmartre? Students may enjoy some timed competitions to find the most efficient routes between locations. After practicing giving directions and following routes on the **métro**, use familiar phrases for **dictées** for listening compréhension and writing practice.

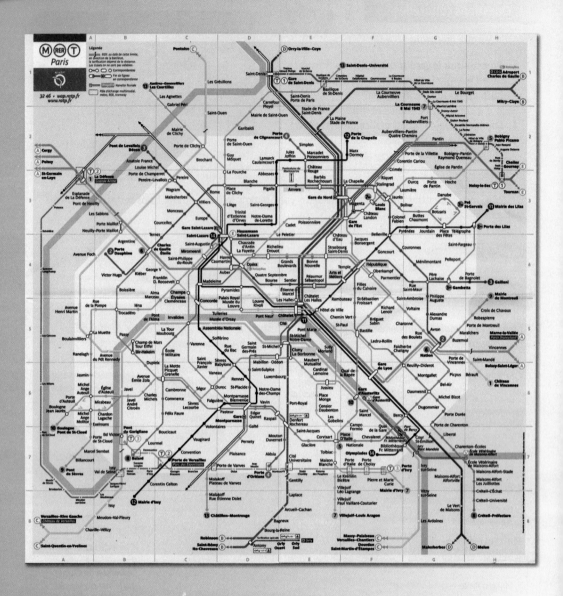

### Essential Instruction

1. Read aloud and explain the introduction to **La culture sur place**. Ask students about their experiences and the importance of observing a different culture (a different group at school, in a city, in a location within the city, etc.) to better understand it.

2. For **Activité 9**, ask for volunteers to read aloud each observation and give the rule or custom. Ask students to write their reactions in their Culture Journal.

3. Have students discuss **Activité 10** in groups.

# La culture sur place

## L'étiquette

### Introduction

Afin de (*In order to*) mieux apprécier la culture sur place et comprendre comment montrer son respect dans une autre culture, on doit chercher à comprendre les coutumes (*customs*) de la société. Pour ça, on a besoin d'être bon observateur.

*Lisez les observations suivantes qui ont lieu (take place) en France. Ensuite, donnez votre réponse ou réaction à la question.*

| Observation | Règles (*Rules*)/Coutumes | Votre réaction en France |
|---|---|---|
| **MODÈLE** Un jeune couple à table dans un café appelle le serveur: "S'il vous plaît, monsieur!" | *One should call a waiter by saying "S'il vous-plaît!," and not "Garçon!"* | Qu'est-ce que vous dites au café à la serveuse quand vous avez soif? *I say* "S'il vous plaît, mademoiselle, je voudrais une limonade." |
| 1. Un jeune étudiant français entre dans le métro. Il enlève (*removes*) son sac à dos et le porte à la main. | | Qu'est-ce que vous faites avec votre sac à dos quand vous entrez dans un train de métro? |
| 2. Un jeune homme traverse (*walks through*) une foule (*crowd*) dans la station du métro, murmurant "Pardon" à chaque personne devant qui il passe. | | Qu'est-ce que vous dites quand vous avez besoin de passer quelqu'un quand vous entrez dans un ascenseur (*elevator*)? |
| 3. Quatre jeunes femmes sont à la terrasse d'un café, et elles parlent doucement (*quietly*) et calmement. | | Vous êtes très content d'être à la tour Eiffel. Comment est-ce que vous parlez à vos camarades de classe? |
| 4. À la boulangerie, une femme dit "Bonjour, Monsieur" quand elle entre et "Merci, au revoir" quand elle sort. | | Vous entrez dans un magasin de souvenirs. Qu'est-ce que vous dites à la commerçante? Et quand vous partez? |
| 5. Au marché de fruits et de légumes, le marchand dit "Je peux vous aider?" à un client. Ensuite, le client choisit des fruits. | | Vous voulez prendre une pomme au marché. Qu'est-ce que vous faites? |

 **Faisons l'inventaire**  1.2

*Discutez les questions en anglais.*

1. Was it easy to identify the rules of etiquette in the situations described above? Why, or why not?
2. What are the advantages to observing people in different social situations? Are there any disadvantages? Would you feel uncomfortable people watching? Why, or why not?
3. Now that you are more aware of what the French say or do in certain situations, would you dress or behave differently if you traveled to France? Why, or why not?

---

## Answers

**9**

1. One should make sure the objects one carries on the bus or the métro are not obstructing the way for others.
2. You should excuse yourself as you walk in front of people.
3. When in a public place, it is polite not to be too noisy as you could prevent others from hearing their own conversations.
4. It is a rule of thumb to say hello and good-bye when you enter a place where you will interact with people.
5. Generally, merchants are attentive and helpful to the customers and ask them if they need help as soon as they arrive.

*Reactions will vary.*

**10** *Discussions will vary.*

### Critical Thinking

**Comparisons**

Have students discuss how they think the French should react in different situations in the United States. Then ask them to enumerate rules of etiquette in the United States that may not be familiar to the French. What reactions to cultural differences have they experienced on trips overseas, and if any, to France or other European destinations? Perhaps you can invite some foreign exchange students from a local university to visit your classroom and discuss etiquette in the home, the classroom, the workplace, and in public places like parks, the subway, museums, restaurants, etc.

---

## Differentiated Learning

**Decelerate**

For **Activité 9**, group the students so that there is someone available to help the challenged students with understanding the observations/questions and with forming answers in French.

## Special Needs Students

**Visually Challenged**

For **Activité 8**, if possible, print a larger **métro** map for these students, or project one that you find online.

## Reference Desk

1. You may want to add the verbs **tomber**, **passer**, **naître**, **mourir** to complete the list of 17 verbs that use the auxiliary **être** in the past. Draw a pictorial expression or find one online, such as **La maison d'être** (where you go in/out of, arrive/leave, are born and can die, etc.), to encourage your students to remember all "house" verbs.

2. Introduce the name **DR. MRS. VANDERTRAMPP** as a mnemonic device to recall all the verbs on the list.

3. For more challenge, you may wish to introduce the concept that the verbs **rentrer**, **sortir**, **monter**, **descendre**, **passer** from the list can take **avoir** or **être** depending on whether or not they are followed by a direct object, which changes the meaning. For example, **Je suis passé devant la maison hier** (I passed by....), but **J'ai passé une heure au musée** (I spent one hour....).

## Critical Thinking

### Application

Before introducing the verbs that take **être** as an auxiliary in the past, have a discussion about verbs. List sentences (with direct objects) in the **passé composé** that take **avoir**. Next, list **passé composé** sentences that take **être** (without direct objects) and discuss that group's commonality, then compare them with the **avoir** group. Be sure that students understand the notion and meaning of transitive versus intransitive verbs which will help them grasp and recognize **être** verbs.

---

## Structure de la langue

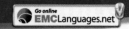 *Go online* **EMC**Languages.net

### *Passé composé* with *être* 🍀 1.2

**Madame Solange a dû attendre le train.
Il est arrivé en avance ou en retard?**

To form the **passé composé** of certain verbs, you use a present tense form of the helping verb **être** and the past participle of the main verb.

> Monsieur, vous **êtes allé** à l'hôtel de ville?   *Sir, you went to the city hall?*
>
>        (helping verb) (past participle of **aller**)

To form the past participle of verbs that use **être** in the **passé composé**, follow the same rules that you learned in **Leçon B**: drop the infinitive ending and add **–é** for **–er** verbs, **–i** for **–ir** verbs, and **–u** for **–re** verbs. For example, for the verb **aller**, which is regular in the **passé composé**, drop the **–er** of the infinitive and add an **é**: aller → allé.

The difference with verbs that take **être** is that the past participle of the verb agrees in gender (masculine or feminine) and in number (singular or plural) with the subject:

- for a masculine singular subject, add nothing.
- for a masculine plural subject, add an **s**.
- for a feminine singular subject, add –**e**.
- for a feminine plural subject, add -**es**.

|  | **aller** |
|---|---|
| je suis allé(e) | nous sommes allés<br>nous sommes allé(e)s |
| tu es allé(e) | vous êtes allé<br>vous êtes allé(e)(s) |
| il est allé<br>elle est allée<br>on est allé | ils sont allés<br>elles sont allées |

> Virginie, tu **es allée** au restaurant?   *Virginie, did you go to the restaurant?*
> Non, je **suis allée** au musée.   *No, I went to the museum.*

Most of the verbs that use **être** in the **passé composé** *express motion* or *movement*, but not all verbs of movement are conjugated with **être** in the **passé composé**, so it's important to learn those that are.

**4 3 8** quatre cent trente-huit | Unité 8

---

### Essential Instruction

1. Write the **passé composé** conjugation of the verb **aller** on the board with color-coded endings. Ask students why they think there are endings added to the past participles. Discuss the explanation in **Structure de la langue** as you read it together as a class.

2. After students look at the list of verbs conjugated with **être**, point out that most of the verbs have regular endings. Ask them what the verb meanings have in common. (They do not take a direct object.)

3. Discuss **Comparaisons** together as a class and compare to the answers students discussed with **passé composé** with **avoir**.

| Infinitive | Past Participle | Meaning |
|---|---|---|
| aller (*to go*) | all**é** | *went* |
| arriv**er** (*to arrive*) | arriv**é** | *arrived* |
| entr**er** (*to enter*) | entr**é** | *entered* |
| mont**er** (*to go up, to get in/on*) | mont**é** | *went up, got in/on* |
| rentr**er** (*to come home, to return, to come back*) | rentr**é** | *came home, returned, came back* |
| rest**er** (*to stay, remain*) | rest**é** | *stayed, remained* |
| retourn**er** (*to return*) | retourn**é** | *returned* |
| part**ir** (*to leave*) | part**i** | *left* |
| sort**ir** (*to go out*) | sort**i** | *went out* |
| descend**re** (*to go down, to get off*) | descend**u** | *went down, got off* |
| **But:** | | |
| ven**ir** (*to come*) | ven**u** | *came* |
| reven**ir** (*to come back, to return*) | reven**u** | *came back, returned* |
| deven**ir** (*to become*) | deven**u** | *became* |

To make a negative sentence in the **passé composé**, put **ne** (**n'**) before the form of **être** and **pas** after it.

Annie **n'**est **pas** allée au musée Grévin.

*Annie didn't go to the Grevin museum.*

To ask a question in the **passé composé** using inversion, put the subject pronoun after the form of **être**.

Awa **est**-elle **partie** ce matin?

*Did Awa leave this morning?*

Pierre est resté avec son petit frère.

**COMPARAISONS**  4.1

Does English ever use a helping verb to express an action that took place in the past?

We have gone to the convenience store.
Justin has bought a snack.
We did get back on time.

COMPARAISONS: In English, a form of the verb "to have" is sometimes used to express actions in the past. A form of "to do" may also be used. However, it is most common to use no helping verb at all: "We went to the convenience store." rather than "We have gone..." or "We did go....

**Expansion**

Ask students to create their own **Maison d'être** based on the different stages in life (childhood, adulthood, the top floor for old age) and including illustrations of all 17 verbs. They could choose a real or imaginary person, or even an animal that lives in the house.

**Communication**

**Interpersonal: Cooperative Groups**

Have groups share the **Maison d'être** that they created for the previous activity and create sentences about the main character in their respective drawings.

**Interpersonal: Paired Practice**

Have students prepare a dialogue in pairs. One has just returned from Paris and the other asks questions about what he or she saw and did, using verbs that take **être** and **avoir**.

**Differentiated Learning**

**Adapt**

To provide practice in forming the affirmative and negative **passé composé** with **être**, have students use white boards to write the past participles as you call out infinitives. Then have them write the entire conjugation of two or three verbs you choose. Next, say an infinitive and a subject, such as **descendre** (**elles**). Students write **elles sont descendues**. Do sentences in the negative as well.

**Decelerate**

After students practice writing the **passé composé** with **être**, have them work in groups of three to create sentences. The first student creates a sentence about something he or she did last week, for example, **Je suis rentré(e) à minuit samedi soir.** The next student restates the sentence using **tu** and the third student restates it using **il/elle**. A different student starts the next sentence, this time with **nous**, and the others in the group restate the sentence with the remaining subjects.

**11**

1. Tiffany et moi, nous sommes allé(e)s à la boucherie pour acheter du jambon.
2. Hannah et Amber sont allées au marché pour acheter des pommes et des oranges.
3. Je suis allé(e) à l'épicerie pour acheter de la moutarde.
4. Noah et Jennifer sont allés à la crémerie pour acheter du fromage.
5. Amanda et toi, vous êtes allé(e)s à la pâtisserie pour acheter des éclairs au chocolat.
6. Tu es allé(e) à l'épicerie pour acheter de la mayonnaise.

**12**

1. Olivier est parti ce matin à dix heures et quart.
2. Rosalie est partie lundi matin à neuf heures.
3. Florence et toi, vous êtes parti(e)s mercredi après-midi à deux heures et demie.
4. René et Alexandre sont partis hier après-midi à une heure et demie.
5. Michèle, Alima, et Élodie sont parties hier soir à sept heures.
6. Lamine est parti mercredi soir à huit heures.
7. Gaby est parti(e) mardi après-midi à trois heures moins le quart.
8. Moi, je suis parti(e) lundi soir à dix heures moins le quart.

## Reference Desk

Remind students of the "sandwich" placement of **ne** and **pas** around the auxiliary form of **être** or **avoir** in compound past tense sentences.

## Game

**Loto maison**

In order to hone students' awareness of the "house" verbs that take **être** as an auxiliary in the past, create Loto cards with randomly placed verbs that take both **être** and **avoir**. As you call a verb, have students complete their Loto card with a sentence in the **passé composé**. The first person to call Loto must read the sentences from his or her card. If all sentences are correct, the student wins the game.

**4 4 0**

---

**11 Un pique-nique au jardin des Tuileries**   2.1, 2.2

*Votre classe a organisé un pique-nique. Dites où tout le monde est allé pour acheter les provisions.*

**MODÈLE** Mme Olsen
**Mme Olsen est allée à la boulangerie pour acheter les baguettes.**

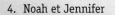

1. Tiffany et moi, nous
2. Hannah et Amber
3. je

4. Noah et Jennifer
5. Amanda et toi, vous
6. tu

**12 On part en vacances.**  2.1, 2.2

*Alain parle à un ami des projets de vacances. Quel jour et à quelle heure est-ce que tout le monde est parti en vacances?*

| Les départs | | | | | |
|---|---|---|---|---|---|
| **lundi** | **mardi** | **mercredi** | **jeudi** | **vendredi HIER** | **samedi AUJOURD'HUI** |
| Rosalie (9h00) | | Florence et toi (14h30) | Sophie (8h00) | Lilou (11h00) | Olivier (10h15) |
| | Gaby (14h45) | | | René et Alexandre (13h30) | X |
| moi (21h45) | | Lamine (20h00) | | Michèle, Alima, et Élodie (19h00) | |

**MODÈLE** Sophie
**Sophie est partie jeudi matin à huit heures.**

1. Olivier
2. Rosalie
3. Florence et toi, vous
4. René et Alexandre

5. Michèle, Alima, et Élodie
6. Lamine
7. Gaby
8. moi, je

**Essential Instruction**

1. Ask partners to do **Activité 11** orally and to write **Activité 12** in pairs. Have them exchange papers with another pair to check each other's work.

2. For **Activités 13** and **14**, have individuals say the missing verb form, and then read the sentences to their partner, checking to see that they wrote the same verb form.

3. As students listen to the sentences in **Activité 15**, ask them to identify additional details such as what location, when, who is mentioned.

**13** Une soirée au cinéma  2.1, 2.2

*Marie-Ange raconte une soirée passée au cinéma. Complétez la phrase avec le passé composé du verbe entre parenthèses.*

1. Je... au Gaumont hier avec des amies. (aller)
2. Ma sœur... avec nous. (venir)
3. Nous... à 19h00. (partir)
4. Ma sœur et moi, nous... à 19h20. Mes copains, cinq minutes après. (arriver)
5. Nous... au cinéma pendant deux heures. (rester)
6. Mes amies... prendre le métro, à l'exception de Sophie. (descendre)
7. Sophie et moi, nous... au Café des Artistes. (aller)
8. Je... en retard! (rentrer)

**14** Aux Césars  2.1, 2.2

*Complétez chaque phrase avec la forme correcte du passé composé du verbe entre parenthèses pour raconter l'histoire d'Awa Soumaré et Kemajou Diouf. Vérifiez que vous avez utilisé le bon verbe auxiliaire, être ou avoir.*

1. Awa... metteur en scène à l'âge de 34 ans. (devenir)
2. Kemajou... acteur l'année dernière. (devenir)
3. Kemajou... son premier rôle dans le film d'Awa, un drame en français qui s'appelle *Loin de chez moi*. (jouer)
4. Ensemble, ils... à Paris pour les Césars. (aller)
5. Pour la cérémonie, Awa... un ensemble traditionnel, et Kemajou un smoking (*tuxedo*). (mettre)
6. Aux Césars ils... deux prix (*awards*) pour leur film. (gagner)
7. Quand ils partaient (*were leaving*), beaucoup de photographes... leur photo. (prendre)
8. Awa et Kemajou... au Sénégal des héros! (retourner)

**15** Le passé ou le présent?  2.1

*Écrivez les numéros 1–8 sur votre papier. Écoutez les phrases et indiquez si chaque phrase est au passé composé (PC) ou au présent (PRÉS).*

**13**
1. suis allée
2. est venue
3. sommes parti(e)s
4. sommes arrivées
5. sommes restées
6. sommes descendues
7. sommes allées
8. suis rentrée

**14**
1. est devenue
2. est devenu
3. a joué
4. sont allés
5. a mis
6. ont gagné
7. ont pris
8. sont retournés

**15** Script can be found in the front pages of the Annotated Teacher's Edition.
1. PC
2. PC
3. PRÉS
4. PC
5. PRÉS
6. PC
7. PRÉS
8. PC

### Critical Thinking

**Analysis**
Ask students to reflect on their learning style and evaluate the best method (visual, auditory, TPR) for them to learn and remember the **être** verbs as a special group.

**Differentiated Learning**
**Adapt**
In **Activité 14**, ask students to research the **Césars** and share who won various awards last year.

**Accelerate**
Have students rewrite **Activité 14** as a paragraph, summarizing the information they learned. Or, ask them to create an original paragraph of a famous couple or themselves at the **Césars** or Oscars.

**Special Needs Students**
**Linguistically Challenged**
Pair more advanced students with others who may need help reading the chart in **Activité 12** and understanding the sentences in **Activité 14**. Remind students to first scan for cognates, try to guess meaning of words in context, and then read the text.

**16**

1. A: As-tu attendu des amis devant l'école?
   B: Oui, j'ai attendu .... / Non, je n'ai pas attendu ....
2. A: As-tu parlé français dans la classe de français?
   B: Oui, j'ai parlé .... / Non, je n'ai pas parlé ....
3. A: Es-tu allé(e) à la cantine à midi?
   B: Oui, je suis allé(e) ... / .Non, je ne suis pas allé(e) ....
4. A: As-tu pris un sandwich au jambon pour le déjeuner?
   B: Oui, j'ai pris... / Non, je n'ai pas pris ....
5. A: Es-tu parti(e) de l'école en avance?
   B: Oui, je suis parti(e) .... / Non, je ne suis pas parti(e) ....
6. A: Es-tu allé(e) à la banque?
   B: Oui, je suis allé(e) ... / Non, je ne suis pas allé(e) ....
7. A: Es-tu sorti(e) avec des amis hier soir?
   B: Oui, je suis sorti(e) .... / Non, je ne suis pas sorti(e) ....
8. A: Es-tu resté(e) à la maison hier soir?
   B: Oui, je suis resté(e) .... / Non, je ne suis pas resté(e) ....

## Critical Thinking

### Application

Project about 15 sentences in **passé composé** with different verbs that take **être** or **avoir**, but do not complete any past participle agreement for those verbs that take **être**. Ask students to consider where changes need to be made as they look over the sentences with you. For a second round, ask students to volunteer to suggest a new subject for each sentence and how the agreement must change accordingly.

# Communiquez!

**16** Hier  🎧 🌸 1.1, 2.1

### Interpersonal Communication

*À tour de rôle, demandez à votre partenaire s'il ou elle a fait les activités suivantes hier. Faites attention au verbe auxiliaire.*

> **MODÈLE**  arriver à l'école en retard
> A: **Es-tu arrivé (e) à l'école en retard hier?**
> B: **Oui, je suis arrivé(e) à l'école en retard hier.**
> ou
> **Non, je ne suis pas arrivé(e) à l'école en retard hier.**
>
> finir tes devoirs dans la médiathèque
> A: **As-tu fini tes devoirs dans la médiathèque?**
> B: **Oui, j'ai fini mes devoirs dans la médiathèque.**
> ou
> **Non, je n'ai pas fini mes devoirs dans la médiathèque.**

1. attendre des amis devant l'école
2. parler français dans la classe de français
3. aller à la cantine à midi
4. prendre un sandwich au jambon pour le déjeuner
5. partir de l'école en avance
6. aller à la banque
7. sortir avec des amis hier soir
8. rester à la maison hier soir

*Tu as parlé français dans la classe de français?*

*Oui.*

### Essential Instruction

1. Before students do **Activité 16** in pairs, review how to form questions using inversion, emphasizing the difference between **Es-tu...?** and **As-tu...?** Say several questions using both **être** and **avoir**. Ask students to call out which helping verb they need. After students complete the activity, ask volunteers to present their dialogues.

2. Ask students to define what an adverb is and provide examples in English. Have students give you the declarative form of the verb in the cartoon caption and write it on the board: **Il est vite parti.** Have students repeat each sentence as you insert a different adverb from the list. Then, do **Activité 17.**

3. Discuss the **Comparaisons** question and contrast adverbs in English and French.

# Position of Adverbs in the *passé composé*  1.1

You may wish to add an adverb when expressing an idea in the **passé composé**. The short adverbs below are generally placed between the auxiliary verb (**avoir** or **être**) and the past participle.

| | |
|---|---|
| **assez** | *enough* |
| **beaucoup** | *a lot* |
| **bien** | *well* |
| **déjà** | *already* |
| **enfin** | *finally* |
| **mal** | *badly* |
| **peu** | *a little* |
| **trop** | *too much* |
| **vite** | *fast, quickly* |

Pourquoi M. Gauthier est-il vite parti?

Tes amis sont-ils **déjà** partis?    *Did your friends leave already?*
Oui, ils sont **enfin** partis!    *Yes, they finally left!*

---

**17**   **Le premier match de foot**   🎧    1.3, 2.1, 2.2

*Mettez l'adverbe entre parenthèses dans la phrase. Quand vous finissez, faites un sommaire de l'histoire en anglais pour votre partenaire.*

1. Thierry a acheté un maillot avec le blason de sa nouvelle équipe. (déjà)
2. Il a mis son maillot, son short, ses chaussettes, et ses chaussures. (déjà)
3. Il est allé au stade en métro. (vite)
4. Il a parlé aux autres footballeurs. (peu)
5. Il a pris le ballon avec ses pieds. (bien)
6. Il a marqué un but pour son équipe. (bien)
7. Son équipe a gagné, 1 à 0. (enfin)

---

**COMPARAISONS**  4.1

Where are adverbs placed in past tense sentences in English?

I ate a lot yesterday.
We really did like the movie.
He has finally arrived.

COMPARAISONS: In past tense sentences in English, adverbs may be placed after the verb, before the verb, or between the helping verb and past participle.

---

**RESOURCES**

📖 **Workbook 44-45**

**Answers** _____

**17**

1. Thierry a déjà acheté un maillot avec le blason de sa nouvelle équipe.
2. Il a déjà mis son maillot, son short, ses chaussettes, et ses chaussures.
3. Il est vite allé au stade en métro.
4. Il a peu parlé aux autres footballeurs.
5. Il a bien pris le ballon avec ses pieds.
6. Il a bien marqué un but pour son équipe.
7. Son équipe a enfin gagné, 1 à 0.

*Summaries will vary.*

**Reference Desk**

Remind students that some longer adverbs (**généralement**, **lentement**, etc.) are generally placed at the beginning or end of a sentence.

**Expansion**

1. Have students practice saying sentences out loud that contain adverbs within **passé composé** verbs to get used to giving tonic stress to emphasize the adverbs.
2. Put a list of adverbs on the board. Distribute a list of 25 sentences in the present tense. Ask students to take turns volunteering to put the sentences in **passé composé** and then choosing an appropriate adverb from the list to complete the sentence.

---

**Differentiated Learning**
**Accelerate**
Brainstorm a list of activities students do on the weekend. Then have them write questions according to the model in **Activité 16**. Have them survey several students and share about what they learned.

**Learning Styles**
**Visual Learners**
Have students create a three-frame storyboard in which two characters ask each other about their activities last weekend.

### Reference Desk

Note that a grade of 20 is extremely rare, especially as a term grade. Although it is possible to get a 20 on a math test or a grammar test (where questions are either right or wrong), it is virtually impossible to do so on essays or short-answer tests (where questions involve subjectivity).

### Critical Thinking

**Comparisons**
Start a discussion on your classroom blog or with e-pals about different grading systems. How do your students like the French system vs. theirs? Perhaps exhange quizzes with a partner teacher to grade in the other's system or grade your students on a quiz according to the French method and discuss students' reactions.

---

**18 Les phrases brouillées**  2.1, 2.2

*Mettez les phrases en ordre.*

1. bien / Marcel / samedi soir / a / dormi
2. l'équipe / joué / de Marseille / mal / a / dimanche
3. as / au restaurant / tu / mangé / trop
4. partis / vous / êtes / de l'école / vite
5. avons / enfin / eu / un contrôle français / 20 / nous / sur
6. mon / déjà / père / a / la cuisine / fait
7. a / Mlle Desjardins / à la crémerie / acheté / assez
8. peu / les / étudié / élèves / ont / pour le contrôle de maths
9. beaucoup / j'ai / le film d'action / aimé

Ils ont trop mangé au restaurant?

**19 Le contrôle d'histoire**   2.1, 2.2

*Dans les écoles françaises, 18 sur 20 est une très bonne note, 16 est très bien. Les élèves qui ont 12 sur 20 sont contents. On a besoin de 10 pour réussir à un examen. Dites si ces élèves ont **bien**, **assez bien**, ou **peu** étudié pour le contrôle d'histoire, selon les résultats.*

| | |
|---|---|
| Héloïse | 18 |
| Marianne | 7 |
| Karim | 20 |
| Étienne | 12 |
| Evenye | 19 |
| Marc-Antoine | 13 |
| Virginie | 8 |
| Nasser | 14 |

**MODÈLE** **Virginie a peu étudié pour le contrôle d'histoire.**

1. Héloïse
2. Marc-Antoine
3. Nasser
4. Marianne
5. Karim
6. Evenye
7. Étienne

### Essential Instruction

1. Do **Activité 18** together as a class to check for understanding, then ask the students to repeat it with a partner.
2. Explain the differences between **contrôle**, **interrogation**, **examen**, **concours**.
3. On the board, show students the spread of grades from 1–20, labeling the cutoffs described in **Activité 19**. Ask for their observations about how the American system differs. (Would they consider getting a 50% to be acceptable?) Do **Activité 19** as a class.
4. Use **Activité 20** as a guided writing assignment. Remind students to use their sequencing words and remind them that they will need both the **passé composé** and the **futur proche**.

# À vous la parole

## Communiquez!

### 20 Une carte postale de Paris! 1.3

**Presentational Communication**

Find a virtual postcard of Paris online and send it to one of your classmates. In your postcard:

- Use the salutation **Cher** or **Chère** followed by the student's name.
- Say when you arrived in Paris.
- Name three sites you saw and when (use expressions of time such as **hier soir**). Then tell what you did at each one.
- Say what you are going to do tonight.
- Say you'll see your friend soon and sign your name.

Print a copy of your postcard or e-mail a copy to your teacher.

 **Search words: carte postale virtuelle de paris**

## Communiquez!

### 21 On prend le métro? 1.2, 1.3, 2.1, 2.2, 3.1

**Interpretive/Presentational Communication**

A. Explore the official Paris metro website to find out the information below.
- cost of a single metro ticket in euros and dollars
- advantage of purchasing a book of 10 tickets (un carnet, ou "t+")
- cost of a **Paris visite** pass in euros and dollars
- hours the metro is open

B. Next, use the interactive map to find the best routes to five different tourist sites, following the directions below.
- Start your trip at the Gare d'Austerlitz.
- Find your first location.
- Print out the itinerary.
- Be sure to print out your other itineraries.

C. Show one of your itineraries to your partner. Tell him or her how you got from one tourist site in Paris to another, using the metro.

 **MODÈLE** **Je suis allé(e) de la Gare d'Austerlitz à la tour Eiffel. J'ai pris le métro en direction de Boulogne—Pont de St. Cloud. J'ai fait une correspondance (*transferred*) à La Motte Picquet en direction de Charles de Gaulle—Étoile. Je suis descendu(e) à la station Bir Hakeim.**

 **Search words: paris ratp**

## RESOURCES

**Communicative Activities**

## Answers

**20** *Postcards will vary.*

**21** *Presentations will vary.*

## Reference Desk

1. If someone starts using a Paris Pass in the late afternoon on Day 1, a two-day pass is only valid for one more full day. In order to use it most efficiently, it should be used starting in the morning of Day 1.
2. Students may be interested in exploring what other offers are available for residents who use the Paris metro (monthly passes, passes that include different regions and the **RER**).

**Blended Instruction**
Consider using blended instruction, a combination of in-class learning and computer-mediated instruction or learning opportunities. Ask students to complete activities on the computer, using their cell or smartphone, or other emerging electronic technology. This will allow students to hone their tech skills and become more independent learners. Schedule routine Internet and e-book learning in class and in the lab.

## Expansion

To practice the distinction between future actions with **aller**, and past actions with **avoir**, give students ten sentences in the present tense about a person and his or her family (it could be a famous person they like). Have pairs of students transform those sentences into the near future with **aller**, while others transform them into the past with **avoir**. Then ask for volunteers to read the **futur proche** sentences first, then the sentences in the past.

---

## Differentiated Instruction

### Decelerate
Provide a clear rubric for **Activité 21**. Limit the search to one tourist site. Pair students who may be challenged with more capable students.

### Multiple Intelligences
#### Bodily-Kinesthetic
 Enlarge and cut up the **phrases brouillées**. Put them in separate envelopes and distribute one envelope to each group. Have them compete to put their sentence together.

### Intrapersonal
To personalize the concept in **Activité 19**, write various scores from 1–20 on a 3 × 5 card, distribute them randomly to the students (or have them draw from a hat), and have them tell if they studied well for the test or not based on their score. Invite them to add another sentence as an explanation, for example, **J'ai eu 17 sur l'examen. J'ai très bien étudié…je n'ai pas regardé la télévision le soir avant l'interro.**

# Lecture thématique

## Chanson de la Seine

### Rencontre avec l'auteur  1.2, 3.1

**Jacques Prévert** (1900–1977) connaît un vrai succès populaire. Il est l'auteur de chansons célèbres, de films importants, et de quatre volumes de poésie: *Paroles* (1945), *La Pluie et le beau temps* (1955), *Histoires* (1963), et *Choses et autres* (1972). Sa poésie ressemble à la langue parlée et ses thèmes touchent directement la vie de tous les jours avec ses misères et ses joies. Quelles misères est-ce qu'il trouve à Paris dans "Chanson de la Seine"?

### Pré-lecture  2.1, 2.2

Avez-vous passé du temps au bord (*along the banks*) d'un fleuve ou d'une rivière? Quelles activités avez-vous faites?

### Stratégie de lecture  2.1, 2.2

#### Personification

Jacques Prévert uses personification in his poem "Chanson de la Seine." Personification is the attribution of human qualities to something that is not human. For example, the phrase "The wind danced in the trees" describes the action of the wind as if it were dancing like a person. As you read the poem, fill in the chart with examples of personification; then explain what human characteristics the poet is giving the river.

| Examples of personification | Explanation |
|---|---|
| 1. La Seine n'a pas de souci. | The river is carefree like a young person. |
| 2. | |
| 3. | |

### Outils de lecture 2.1, 2.2

#### Inference

An inference is a conclusion reached due to evidence provided in a literary text. What inference can you make about Prévert's attitude toward the Seine? For example, does he respect it, is he indifferent towards it, or does he dislike it? What evidence in the text supports your position?

 **1.2, 2.1, 2.2**

¹La Seine a de la chance*
Elle n'a pas de souci*
Elle se la coule douce*
Le jour comme la nuit
⁵Et elle sort de sa source
Tout doucement*, sans bruit* sans sortir de son lit
Et sans se faire de mousse*,
Elle s'en va vers la mer*
En passant par Paris.
¹⁰La Seine a de la chance
Elle n'a pas de souci
Et quand elle se promène*
Tout au long de ses quais
Avec sa belle robe verte
¹⁵Et ses lumières dorées*
Notre-Dame, jalouse*, immobile et sévère
Du haut de* toutes ses pierres*
La regarde de travers*
Mais la Seine s'en balance
²⁰Elle n'a pas de souci
Elle se la coule douce
Le jour comme la nuit
Et s'en va vers le Havre, et s'en va vers la mer
En passant comme un rêve
²⁵Au milieu des* mystères
Des misères de Paris.

_____
**a de la chance** *is lucky*; **un souci** *worry*; **se la coule douce** *is peaceful*;
**doucement** *gently*; **sans bruit** *without noise*; **la mousse** *foam*; **la mer** *sea*; **se
promène** *fait une promenade*; **doré(e)** *golden*; **jalouse** *jealous*; **du haut de** *atop*;
**pierres** *stones*; **de travers** *askance*; **au milieu de** *in the middle of*

> **Pendant la lecture**
> 1. Comment est la Seine?

> **Pendant la lecture**
> 2. Qui est jalouse de la Seine?

> **Pendant la lecture**
> 3. La Seine comprend-elle ce qui se passe à Paris? (*Does the Seine understand what's going on in Paris?*)

## Post-lecture  **2.1, 2.2**

Est-ce que le portrait de la Seine par Prévert est romantique? Expliquez.

## Le monde visuel **1.2, 3.2**

Paul Signac (1863-1935), peintre français, était un co-fondateur du pointillisme, qui consiste à peindre par juxtaposition de petites touches de couleurs primaires (rouge, bleu, et jaune) et de couleurs complémentaires (orange, violet, et vert) pour créer des formes. Connu pour ses couleurs lumineuses, Signac a peint beaucoup de tableaux de la Seine. Dans ce tableau, le fleuve semble être vivant avec sa luminosité et son mouvement. Est-ce que le style de Signac est plus proche de l'art de Monet (recherchez *Impression, soleil levant*) ou de Corot (recherchez *Le Pont de Mantes*)? Pourquoi?

*Le Pont Neuf*, 1927. Paul Signac. Galerie Daniel Malingue, Paris, France.

**Answers**

**Activités d'expansion**
*Paragraphs will vary.*

## Les copains d'abord

Here is the translation for **Les copains d'abord:**

A = Antoine
F = Florence
MA = Marie-Alix

A: Hi Flo! It's not a good day for a walk along the Seine, it's about to rain! A: Uh…what's going on? F: Mathéo doesn't want to be my boyfriend any more, he broke up with me. A: Really? Well, he's stupid, he's a jerk… Come on; let's get out of the rain! Text message: URGENT meet us at the café, Flo is stressed out. MA: Flo, I'm sorry, but you can't fall apart. Here, I brought you a cream puff pastry. F: Mathéo treated me to a cream puff pastry last week! A: Here you go, girls, hot chocolates. And for you, Flo, a layered custard pastry! F: Oh, it's Mathéo's favorite pastry… A: Look, the sun is out, now. Let's go to the Louvre! F: Oh, Mathéo and I went… A: OK, Mathéo, he's a loser, but us, we are your friends! MA:… Yes, listen, the birds are singing. Let's rediscover Paris together! F: Oh, you're so nice. Thank you, my friends.

List of slang and idiomatic expressions:
**rompu** (past participle: **rompre**): *break up;* **nul**: *a jerk;* **s'effondrer**: *fall apart;* **perdant**: *loser*

## Expansion

1. Have students write a contemporary conversation for a comic they illustrate about Paris.
2. Find some comic illustrations of Paris, but leave out the captions for students to fill in.

---

### 22 Activités d'expansion  1.3, 2.1, 2.2

1. Utilisez les informations dans votre grille pour écrire un paragraphe qui explique la personnification dans le poème. La Seine est-elle un homme ou une femme? Quelles sont ses caractéristiques?
2. Comparez ce poème à un autre poème qui décrit (*describes*) un fleuve, par exemple, le Mississippi, le Nil, ou l'Amazone. Comment est-ce que l'attitude de ce poète ressemble à celle (*the one*) de Prévert dans "Chanson de la Seine"?
3. Quand les lignes d'un poème ressemblent à un objet, c'est un "shape poem." Écrivez un "shape poem" au sujet d'un endroit à Paris.
4. Écrivez un poème qui énumère (*lists*) les gens et les endroits de Paris. Commencez avec **Paris est une ville de….** Trouvez un moyen (*way*) d'organiser vos idées.

1.2, 4.2

### Essential Instruction

1. Offer students the choice of **Activités d'expansion.**
2. Explain that the title of the cartoon is also that of a famous poem by Verlaine. Explain the vocabulary **se balader, rompre, nul, s'effrondrer, une religieuse, un millefeuille, le perdant,** and decipher the text message: **rendez-vous au café…**
3. Have students read the cartoon silently. Then have them role-play the story aloud in groups of three. What do the students think of Flo's problem and of her friends?
4. For the **Projets finaux** offer students the choice of **Activité A** or **B.**

# T'es branché?

## Projets finaux

### A Connexions par Internet: L'art

1.2, 1.3, 2.1, 2.2, 3.1, 3.2

**Interpretive/Presentational**

Many art movements, such as Cubism, were founded in Paris. The city also has a lot of street art—statues, fountains, sidewalk drawings in chalk, etc. Research a piece of art featuring Paris. For example, you might look up works by Jean Béraud, Béatrice Boisségur, Georges Dupuis, Toulouse-Lautrec, Albert Marquet, Jules Ernest Renoux, Paul Signac, Edgar Degas, or Maurice Utrillo. Then present your piece of art to a small group of classmates.

**Le pont de l'Europe, Gare Saint-Lazare**, 1877. Claude Monet. Musée l'Harmattant, Paris, France.

**Search words: bridgeman art library**
**musée d'orsay site officiel**
**louvre site officiel**

MODÈLE  Ce tableau montre le Pont de l'Europe et la Gare Saint-Lazare de Paris. L'artiste est Claude Monet. J'aime ce tableau parce que....

### B Communautés en ligne

1.2, 1.3

**Les expatriés américains à Paris**

Find a blog about expats living in Paris. Expats are people who have left their home country and now reside somewhere else, in this case Paris. Write a profile of one person, answering the questions below:

1. Comment s'appelle-t-il? Comment s'appelle-t-elle?
2. Il/Elle est à Paris depuis (*since*) quand?
3. Quels sont ses passe-temps?
4. Quelle est sa profession?
5. Est-ce qu'il ou elle cherche quelque chose (*something*)?

Present your profile to your partner. Finally, tell him or her your answers to these questions: **Voudrais-tu habiter ou étudier à Paris? Pour combien de temps?**

**Search words: expatriés américains à paris**
**expat blog paris**

### Reference Desk

Display current views of Paris alongside the older painted versions of Paris by different artists. Discuss which painter's vision of Paris your students prefer. Students may also research where famous artists lived or had their studios in Paris.

### Game

Find pictures of paintings of Paris by various artists. Adjust the image scale to be about 3 × 5, and print the pictures in duplicate. Attach the images to labels on index cards and play a memory game. (Cards face down, student picks two at a time, trying to get a pair.)

Alternatively, use these images for a quiz on artwork and artists, or to accompany statements that are true or false for a listening and cultural comprehension quiz.

**C** **Passez à l'action!**   1.1, 1.3

### Notre voyage imaginaire à Paris

Plan a class trip to Paris where you will stay for five days. Decide as a group when you'd like to go, in what area of Paris you'd like to stay, and what you'd like to see. To plan your trip, give each person in your group a task, for example:

1. Find a reasonable flight and make a document with the name of the airline, the departure and arrival dates and times, and the name of the airports with their codes.
2. Find a reasonable hotel in a neighborhood you all want to stay in. Make a document with the name of the hotel, the number of stars (if any), the address, the number of the **arrondissement** (district of Paris), the phone number, Website, and nearest metro station(s).
3. Decide what museums, parks, and monuments you'd like to see. Make a document that shows your itinerary, or the date, time, and location.
4. Find photos of the places you plan to see.
5. Write captions for the photos, saying what your group saw and did at each place.
6. Place your documents and photos on the Internet to share with other French classes. Ask them to share an imaginary trip to another francophone destination with you.

**D** **Faisons le point!**  2.1, 2.2

Your teacher will give you a chart like the one below. Fill it in to show what you've learned about the French language and francophone cultures.

Question centrale

How do major world cities tell their stories?

| Je comprends | Je ne comprends pas encore | Mes connexions |
|---|---|---|
|  |  |  |
|  |  |  |
|  |  |  |

| | |
|---|---|
| What did I do well to learn and use the content of this unit? | What should I do in the next unit to better learn and use the content? |
| How can I effectively communicate to others what I have learned? | What was the most important concept I learned in this unit? |

**Essential Instruction**

1. **Activité C** is a cumulative class project.
2. Ask all students to complete **Activité D**, since reflecting on one's learning is an important step in solidifying knowledge. Distribute copies of the graphic organizer located in the **Copy Masters** supplement.
3. Remind students to do the online pre-test.
4. Do **Activité A** with the audio. Provide the opportunity for students to do it a second time as needed.
5. If you choose to do the **Évaluation culturelle**, clarify the terms "compare" (showing similarities) and "contrast" (showing differences).

# Évaluation

Go online
EMCLanguages.net

## A | Évaluation de compréhension auditive

  **2.1**

Amélie went to Paris for Christmas vacation. Listen to her conversation with Pierre. Then, indicate if each sentence about her trip is **vrai** or **faux**.

## B | Évaluation orale

**1.1, 2.1**

Imagine that you traveled to your favorite city last week and your partner wants to know what you saw and did. Answer your partner's questions and say on which days you did each activity. Include monuments, museums, restaurants, and other places you visited. Say if you walked or took the metro. Switch roles.

## C | Évaluation culturelle

In this activity, you will compare francophone cultures with American culture. You may need to do some additional research on American culture.

1. **Deux capitales**
   Create a timeline of the construction of two key monuments, one in Washington D.C., one in Paris. The timeline should cover the period 1800–2010. Explain how each monument reveals something important about the history of the city.

2. **La nature et la ville**
   Explain how a geographical feature of Paris (such as the Seine) affected the city's development. Compare Paris's development to that of your own town or city. Is there a geographical feature, such as a river or hill, around which your city was built? How has your city's geography influenced construction and economic activity?

3. **Deux monuments**
   Compare **la tour Eiffel** in Paris and the Statue of Liberty in New York. What do these monuments symbolize in their respective countries, and to the world?

4. **Les gâteaux**
   What are the traditional desserts that you and your family eat on different holidays and for special occasions? Research the origins and traditions regarding one of these foods and compare it to **la galette des Rois**.

5. **La culture des drapeaux**
   Compare your state flag to the flag of Haiti. How do the objects and colors of the flags represent or symbolize aspects of each culture?

6. **Les transports en commun**
   Research the public transportation system in a large city in your state. Do many people use the system? Have you ever used a public transportation system? Compare this public transportation system to the metro in Paris. How are the

---

**Differentiated Learning**
## Accelerate, Adapt, Decelerate
Give students the option of creating their own project. Be sure to provide clear guidelines and an assessment rubric to ensure their success.

---

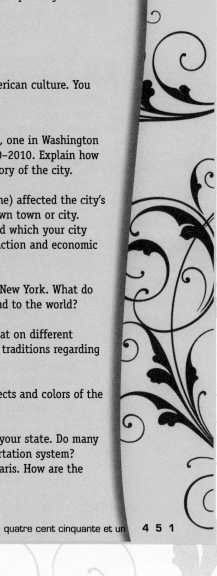

## RESOURCES

🔊 **Listening Activity**
*Synthèse*

### Answers

**A** Script can be found in the front pages of the Annotated Teacher's Edition.

1. V
2. V
3. F
4. V
5. F
6. V
7. F
8. V

**B** *Dialogues will vary.*

**C** Provide information in English or research topics prior to assigning the projects. Here are a few ideas of subjects to mention:

1. Pierre l'Enfant, French-born American architect and engineer who fought in American Revolution, designed New York City Hall, also hired to design Washington D.C. as a capital city.

2. Paris: la Seine divides the south **rive gauche** from the north **rive droite**.

3. Review French pastries learned so far: **une bûche de Noël**, **une galette des Rois**, **un flan**, **un éclair**, **une religieuse**, **un mille-feuille**.

4. Explain the flag of Haiti: the blue represents the freedom of Haitians as first emancipated slaves; the red represents the multi-ethnic population; the coat of arms is a claim for freedom, strength, and independence.

5. *Answers will vary.*

6. The **Jardin des Tuileries** is a formal park in the center of Paris, with the Louvre at one end and the **Jeu de Paume** and the **Orangerie** at the other end. The **Orangerie** was built especially to house a series of Monet's very large water lily paintings. The name **Tuileries** comes from **tuile** or tile. Old tile kilns were located here until Henry II's widow, Catherine de Medici, had a palace built on this site in the 16th century. The palace was destroyed in 1871.

**451**

## Reference Desk

Students may also be inspired to tell stories about Paris through film, making videos with movie-making programs, or even creating films using stills with Ken Burns effects.

## Expansion

Tell your students to imagine they just returned from a three-day trip to Paris and write a Culture Journal entry about their observations.

Crowds of people gather to wait for the **métro** at rush hour.

two systems similar and different? Consider the practicality, affordability, and accessibility of each system, how many people use it, and the area it covers.

7. **Deux parcs**
Compare the **jardin des Tuileries** to a well-known park in your region. Which one is more urban? Which is older? What kinds of activities does each park offer? Do special events take place there?

**D  Évaluation écrite**  **2.1, 2.2, 3.1, 3.2, 4.2**

Write to a friend about where you, your family, or friends went, and what you saw and did over the weekend.

**E  Évaluation visuelle** **1.3**

Imagine that you've spent the last two days sight-seeing in Paris. Write a postcard to a friend telling about your visit based on the image below. Say where you went, what you saw, and what you did there. Be sure to tell on what day you did each activity.

**F  Évaluation compréhensive** **1.3**

Imagine that you were a tour guide for a group of French students visiting your city or town. Create a storyboard with six frames that show the sites you took them to see and what they did there. Include a written caption for each frame.

**Essential Learning**

1. You might have students write the **Évaluation écrite** as a blog entry or e-mail for a francophone audience.
2. Have partners do the **Évaluation visuelle** orally. Encourage students to embellish by looking back to previous chapters for inspiration.

# Vocabulaire de l'Unité 8  1.2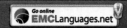

| | | |
|---|---|---|
| un | **aéroport** airport *B* | |
| un | **animal** animal *A* | |
| s' | **arrêter** to stop *A* | |
| | **au** on the *C* | |
| l' | **automne (m.)** autumn *A* | |
| une | **avenue** avenue *B* | |
| | **avoir: avoir chaud** to be hot *A*; **avoir envie de** to want, to feel like *A*; **avoir froid** to be cold *A* | |
| un | **banc** bench *C* | |
| une | **banque** bank *B* | |
| le | **bas** bottom *A* | |
| un | **bateau** boat *B* | |
| une | **cathédrale** cathedral *B* | |
| | **chaud(e): j'ai chaud** I am hot *A* | |
| | **chouette** great *A* | |
| le | **coin** corner *A*; **du coin** on the corner *A* | |
| | **consommer** to consume *A* | |
| un | **degré** degree *A* | |
| | **déjà** already *C* | |
| | **dernier, dernière** last *C* | |
| | **désagréable** unpleasant *C* | |
| | **descendre** to go down, to get off *C* | |
| | **désolé(e)** sorry *A* | |
| | **disponible** free *A* | |
| | **du** on the *A*; about (the) *C* | |
| un | **éclair** eclair *A* | |
| | **embrasser** to kiss *C* | |
| | **en** of *C* | |
| | **entrer** to enter, to come in *A* | |
| | **exactement** exactly *B* | |
| | **faire: faire une promenade** to go for a walk *A* | |
| | **fatigué(e)** tired *B* | |
| un | **fleuve** river *B* | |
| | **froid: cold** *A*; **j'ai froid** I am cold *A* | |
| une | **gare** train station *B* | |
| | **gourmand(e)** fond of food *A* | |
| | **grave** serious *A* | |
| un | **guide touristique** tourist guide *B* | |
| le | **haut** top *A* | |
| | **hier** yesterday *C* | |
| un | **hôtel** hotel *B*; **un hôtel de ville** city hall *B* | |
| une | **idée** idea *A*; **Bonne idée!** Good idea! *A* | |
| un | **jardin** garden, park *B* | |
| une | **journée** day *A* | |
| | **laisser: Laisse-moi finir!** Let me finish! *B* | |
| la | **ligne** figure *A* | |

| | | |
|---|---|---|
| la | **main** hand *C*; **la main dans la main** hand in hand *C* | |
| un | **millefeuille** layered custard pastry *A* | |
| | **monter** to go up, to get in/on *C* | |
| | **montrer** to show *B* | |
| un | **monument** monument *B* | |
| un | **musée** museum *B* | |
| | **nouveau, nouvel, nouvelle** new *B* | |
| | **occupé(e)** busy *A* | |
| | **où** when *B* | |
| | **oublier** to forget *B* | |
| | **pardon** pardon me *B* | |
| se | **parler** to talk to each other/one another *C* | |
| | **partir** to leave *C* | |
| | **pendant** for *B* | |
| une | **photo: re-photo** another photo *B* | |
| une | **place** square *B* | |
| | **pleuvoir** to rain *A*; **il pleut** it's raining *A* | |
| un | **pont** bridge *B* | |
| une | **poste** post office *B* | |
| le | **printemps** spring *A* | |
| | **profiter** to take advantage of *C* | |
| une | **promenade** walk *A* | |
| une | **religieuse** cream puff pastry *A* | |
| | **rentrer** to come home, to return, to come back *C* | |
| un | **restaurant** restaurant *B* | |
| | **rester** to stay, to remain *C* | |
| | **retourner** to return *C* | |
| | **rigoler** to laugh *C* | |
| une | **rue** street *A* | |
| un | **souvenir** memory *C* | |
| une | **statue** statue *B* | |
| | **sur** of *B* | |
| un | **tableau** painting *B* | |
| la | **température** temperature *A* | |
| le | **temps** weather *A*; **Quel temps fait-il ?** What's the weather like? How's the weather? *A* | |
| la | **terrasse** terrace *B* | |
| un | **tour** tour *B* | |
| | **vieux, vieil, vieille** old *B* | |
| | **visiter** to visit *B* | |
| | **vite** fast, quickly *C* | |
| se | **voir** to see one another/each other *A* | |

Animals… see p. 397
Weather… see p. 396

Animals… see p. 397
Weather… see p. 396

## RESOURCES

 **Flash Cards**

 *Rendez-vous à Nice!* **Episode 8**

 **Listening Pre-test D**

 *Unité* **Test**

## Expansion

Have students list antonyms for these vocabulary words: **chaud, dernier, descendre, nouveau, occupé(e), arriver.**

**Answers** _____

Script can be found in the front pages of the Annotated Teacher's Edition.

1. C

2. D
3. A
4. B

**III**
1. A
2. B
3. B

# Unité 8 Bilan cumulatif

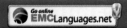

## Listening 🎧  1.2, 2.1, 2.2

I. You will hear a short conversation. Select the reply that would come next. You will hear the conversation twice.

1. A. Désolé, je ne suis pas libre.
   B. À bientôt!
   C. Oh pardon, Mélanie.
   D. J'ai froid.

II. Listen to the conversation between a tourist and a French man. Select the best completion to each statement that follows.

2. La touriste cherche....
   A. la tour Eiffel
   B. un bateau-mouche
   C. le musée du Louvre
   D. le métro, ensuite Notre-Dame

3. Elle est....
   A. canadienne
   B. américaine
   C. anglaise
   D. française

4. Le monsieur aime beaucoup....
   A. Paris et ses cathédrales
   B. Montréal et ses bateaux
   C. Paris et ses monuments
   D. Paris—ses cafés, ses monuments, ses musées et cathédrales

## Reading  1.2, 2.1, 2.2

III. Read Claire's e-mail to her friend Alex about her recent trip to Paris. Then select the best completion to each statement.

Salut Alex!

Ça va? Moi, super. Le weekend dernier, je suis allée à Paris avec ma copine, Céline. Paris est magique! En plus, il a fait très beau. Nous avons visité tous les musées et les monuments de la capitale française! Le premier jour, j'ai visité le musée du Louvre où j'ai vu la *Joconde*! Eh bien, tu sais, je n'ai pas trouvé la *Joconde* géniale. Moi, j'ai préféré le jardin des Tuileries où nous avons fait une promenade samedi après-midi. J'ai pris beaucoup de belles photos. Nous sommes arrivées chez moi dimanche soir. J'ai été très contente, mais aussi très fatiguée après mon weekend très occupé. Et toi, qu'est-ce que tu as fait le weekend dernier? Nous nous retrouvons demain au café sur la place de l'hôtel de ville? Je peux te montrer mes photos, d'accord?

À demain,

Claire

1. Céline et Claire ont vu....
   A. des musées et des monuments
   B. Alex
   C. un petit café français
   D. de petites statues

2. Claire aime....
   A. Alex
   B. le jardin des Tuileries
   C. la *Joconde*
   D. les musées

3. Claire voudrait....
   A. retourner à Paris
   B. prendre un café avec son ami demain
   C. voir Céline
   D. aller à Paris avec Alex

# Writing 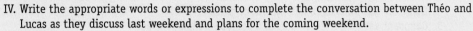 2.1

IV. Write the appropriate words or expressions to complete the conversation between Théo and Lucas as they discuss last weekend and plans for the coming weekend.

Theo: Samedi __1__ après les cours, j'ai fait du vélo avec Marine à Paris. Nous avons passé un super __2__. Il a fait très __3__, très chaud avec du soleil. Et toi, est-ce que tu as fait du sport?

Lucas: Bien __4__ que non! Tu parles. Moi, j'ai étudié pour mon __5__ de maths. Je n'ai pas réussi!

Théo: Ce n'est pas __6__. Tu es __7__ ce weekend? On peut faire du roller près de la tour Eiffel.

Lucas: Non, je suis __8__! Je vais faire une __9__ près de la Seine pour voir la cathédrale Notre-Dame de Paris.

Theo: S'il __10__ mauvais et il __11__, qu'est-ce qu' __12__ fait?

Lucas: On peut voir un film __13__ au Gaumont.

V. Choose the appropriate verb or expression to complete each sentence.

La semaine dernière, Martin __14__ Leïla au restaurant pour son anniversaire.
A. a fini          B. est allé          C. a invité

Ils __15__ à la terrasse d'un café près de Notre-Dame.
A. ont mangé       B. sont partis       C. ont profité

Après, ils ont profité du beau temps pour __16__ au bord de la Seine.
A. faire une promenade   B. consommer    C. partir

Leïla __17__ envie de voir les lumières de la tour Eiffel.
A. a été           B. a eu              C. a fait

Alors, ils ont pris le métro pour __18__ là-bas.
A. aller           B. visiter           C. descendre

Leïla __19__ ça très beau.
A. a trouvé        B. a aimé            C. a eu

Enfin, Martin et Leïla __20__ aux Champs-Élysées pour prendre une boisson.
A. ont rigolé      B. ont fini          C. sont allés

Quel beau souvenir!

Answers _____

1. dernier
2. après-midi
3. beau
4. sûr
5. contrôle
6. grave
7. libre
8. occupé
9. promenade
10. fait
11. pleut
12. on
13. d'aventures

14. a invité (C)
15. ont mangé (A)
16. faire une promenade (A)
17. a eu (B)
18. aller (A)
19. a trouvé (A)
20. sont allés (C)

## Composition  1.3

**VI.** Write a journal entry about your visit to Paris last weekend by responding to the following questions.

1. À quelle heure es-tu arrivé(e) à l'hôtel vendredi soir?
2. Où as-tu mangé?
3. Est-ce qu'il a fait beau?
4. Qu'est-ce que vous avez fait samedi et dimanche?
5. Comment est-ce que tu es allé(e) à l'aéroport dimanche soir?
6. À quelle heure est-ce que tu es arrivé(e) à la maison?
7. Est-ce que tu as aimé ton voyage à Paris?

## Speaking  1.1, 1.3

**VII.** Tell the four stories suggested by the images.

A. Bruno et Caro     B. Antoine et ses copains     C. Malika     D. tu

1. Give the date, identify the season in each illustration, and describe the weather.
2. Describe what the people are doing in each illustration.
3. Then describe two to three activities that you like to do during each season.

# Unité
# 9 En forme

*Rendez-vous à Nice!*

**Épisode 9:**
*Au fitness*

Go online
EMCLanguages.net

quatre cent cinquante-sept 457

457

## Citation

"Le bien-être est un état agréable résultant de la satisfaction des besoins du corps et du calme de l'esprit."

Well-being is an agreeable condition resulting from meeting the needs of the body and the calmness of the mind.

—Le dictionnaire Larousse

## À savoir  4.2

Due in part to dietary changes, cases of Type 1 juvenile diabetes have doubled in France in the last 30 years.

### Essential Instruction

1. Briefly discuss the **Question centrale** to introduce the theme of the **Unité**. Ask students what the state of the environment has to do with personally staying healthy.

2. Read the **Citation** aloud for students. Have them look at the translation and ask them what they think of the mind-body connection. Ask students to reflect on and write their own definition of **bien-être** in their Culture Journal.

3. Explore what students will learn in **Unité 9** by reviewing the **Contrat de l'élève**.

4. Show the relevant video clip from *Rendez-vous à Nice!*, Episode 9, and discuss the related question.

# Unité 9

# En forme

## RESOURCES

*Rendez-vous à Nice!*
**Episode 9**

Answers _____

The answer to the video question is A.

## Question centrale

**?**

How do people stay healthy and maintain a healthy environment?

Go online
EMCLanguages.net

**What is Chadia doing on the phone?**
A. sneaking a phone call to Thomas
B. calling the police
C. making plans to sneak out

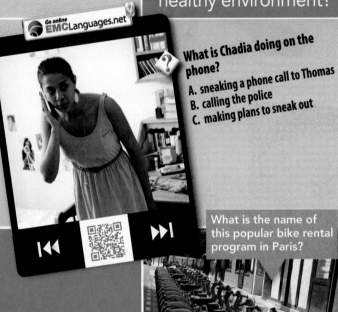

What is the name of this popular bike rental program in Paris?

## Contrat de l'élève

**Leçon A   I will be able to:**

» express need and necessity.

» talk about France's national medical insurance, a government campaign to get people in shape, and thermal spas.

» use the present tense form of the verb **falloir**.

**Leçon B   I will be able to:**

» ask for and give advice.

» talk about Rwanda, its home health care system, and the people who provide it.

» give commands.

**Leçon C   I will be able to:**

» persuade someone and respond to persuasion.

» talk about the Green movement in France and a popular bike rental program in Paris.

» use infinitives after some conjugated verbs and know when to use **des** or **de** with plural nouns modified by adjectives.

quatre cent cinquante-neuf **459**

## Culture

**Practices: Information**
The bike rental program introduced in **Leçon C** started in Paris in 2007 after similar programs were proven successful in Lyon and La Rochelle. A plan to introduce a rental program for small electric cars is under consideration. (See **Leçon C, Points de départs.**)
Discuss whether your students have seen any evidence of these bike rental programs in places they've visited. (Boston, Washington, London, Minneapolis, Barcelona, etc.)
What cities around the world support and encourage cycling? Which countries have suitable terrain and a culture already adapted to cycling? Why is cycling popular in diverse regions like Europe (the Netherlands, Denmark) and Asia (China, among others)?

---

**Differentiated Learning**
**Accelerate**
Ask these students to write their definition of **bien être** in French.

**Learning Styles**
**Visual Learners**
Have students create collages of images associated with well-being. Post their work in the classroom and label the images in French as you move through the unit.

## Reference Desk

1. Vocabulary for the parts of the body offers a good opportunity to review and practice the words **gauche** and **droit(e)** and adjective agreement with respect to **la main**, **le bras**, **le pied**, **la jambe**, **l'épaule**, **le genou**, **l'œil**, **l'oreille**, etc.
2. Students will need to pay special attention to the formation and pronunciation of the plural of **un œil → les yeux** and of **un genou → les genoux**.
3. Note that the definite article is generally used when expressing body vocabulary. (**Il met la main sur la table.**) If the ownership of the body part is unclear, then the possessive may be used. (**On lève une main pour indiquer sa participation.**)
4. Ask if any students study ballet or other forms of dance. Explain that the word ballet comes from the French word for a dance: **un bal**.
5. Other related terms are **le pouce** (thumb, big toe), **le gros orteil** (big toe), **le coude** (elbow), **le cheville** (ankle), **le poignet** (wrist), **le taille** (waist), **la cuisse** (thigh), and **la poitrine** (chest).

## TPR

To help students learn body vocabulary, find an online version of a French song, such as **Alouette, je te plumerai,** or **Savez-vous planter les choux**. Teach it to your students and repeat it often to reinforce the vocabulary. Or, use the song **tête/épaules/ genoux/pieds** and have students sing along as they touch their head, shoulders, knees, and feet.

# Vocabulaire actif

## Le corps et la figure   1.2

Le corps

le doigt de pied
le pied
la jambe
le dos
l'épaule (f.)
le genou
la poitrine
l'estomac (m.)
la tête
le cou
le bras
la main
le doigt

La figure

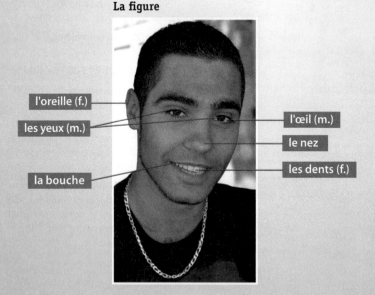

l'oreille (f.)
les yeux (m.)
la bouche
l'œil (m.)
le nez
les dents (f.)

## Essential Instruction

1. Ask students to identify any cognates from the **Vocabulaire actif**. Point out the **faux ami** (*false cognate*) **la figure**.
2. Model the pronunciation of the vocabulary words. Play **Pour la conversation** with the audio and ask students what they must do to be successful in French class.
3. Have students call out the answers in **Activité 1** and have them compare their drawing of the **famille d'extraterrestres** in **Activité 2** with a partner.

# Pour la conversation

Ｈow do I say it is necessary to do, or not do, something?

> **Il faut....**

*It is necessary to...., You must....*

> **Il ne faut pas....**

*You must not....*

**Et si je voulais dire...?**

| | |
|---|---|
| **le front** | *forehead* |
| **les sourcils (m.)** | *eyebrows* |
| **les cils (m.)** | *eyelashes* |
| **les paupières (f.)** | *eyelids* |
| **les joues (f.)** | *cheeks* |
| **la langue** | *tongue, language* |
| **les lèvres (m.)** | *lips* |
| **le menton** | *chin* |
| **les ongles (f.)** | *fingernails* |

## 1 Complétez!  2.1, 2.2

*Choisissez le mot convenable qui complète chaque phrase.*

> oreilles   yeux   bouche   jambes   pieds   dents   mains   doigts   tête

**MODÈLE**   On fait du footing avec les... et les....
**On fait du footing avec les jambes et les pieds.**

1. On mange avec les....
2. On parle avec la....
3. On regarde la télé avec les....
4. On joue au foot avec les... et la....
5. On fait une promenade avec les... et les....
6. On fait la cuisine avec les....
7. On écoute son lecteur MP3 avec les....

On mange avec la bouche.

## 2 Portrait d'une famille d'extraterrestres  1.2, 2.1, 2.2

*Dessinez la famille selon la description.*

L'ado a une petite tête avec un grand œil au centre. Il a de longs cheveux violets et des yeux jaunes. Il a un long cou. Il a un bras avec deux mains. Il a trois jambes et trois pieds avec quatre, cinq, et six doigts de pied. Il porte un tee-shirt bleu et un short rouge. Il écoute de la musique sur son lecteur MP3. Il ressemble à son père mais pas à sa mère. Son père porte un short vert et une chemise rouge. Sa mère a deux têtes avec un œil sur chaque tête. Elle n'a pas de cou. Elle a deux bras, deux mains, et une jambe avec un grand pied. Le pied a huit doigts de pied. Elle porte une jupe orange et un tee-shirt jaune.

---

### RESOURCES

📖 **Workbook 6–8**

**Answers** _____

**1**

1. mains
2. bouche
3. yeux
4. pieds, tête
5. pieds, jambes
6. mains
7. oreilles

**2** *Drawings will vary.*

### TPR

Play **Jacques a dit** to practice the vocabulary. (**Jacques a dit**, "**Touchez la bouche...**"). Each time you mention a body part, students must touch that part of the body. If a student moves when you do not say **Jacques a dit**, he or she is eliminated from the game.

### Expansion

1. Tell students they witnessed a crime and have to describe the criminal to a police sketch artist. Students role-play the witness and the sketch artist using the vocabulary for **le corps et la figure**.
2. Use the description of the alien in **Activité 2** as **dictée** material and ask students to draw what they hear. (You can also describe a figurative but abstract painting by Picasso as the basis for this **dictée**.)

---

## Differentiated Learning
### Expand

1. Provide the vocabulary words **la ligne** and **la silhouette** for a figure of a body and contrast to **la figure**. Teach students the alternate word for face, **le visage**.
2. Ask students to look at the vocabulary words and try to find words in English that are in the same word family, for example, **nez** (*nasal*), **main** (*manual*), **genou** (*genuflect*).

## Learning Styles
### Kinesthetic Learners

Organize teams. As you read a sentence from **Activité 2**, have one student from each team come to the board and add to a collective drawing. After reading the last instruction, compare the teams' drawings.

### Multiple Intelligences
### Verbal-Linguistic

Ask volunteers to prepare and read aloud a description of an extra-terrestrial (or a fictional animal, or action figure) as students draw it.

---

**3** **Qu'est-ce que Jacques dit?**

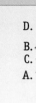 *Écrivez les numéros 1–10 sur votre papier. Écoutez Jacques et écrivez la lettre qui correspond à la partie du corps mentionnée.*

**2.1, 2.2**

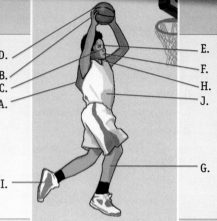

**4** **Qu'est-ce qu'il faut faire?**  **2.1, 2.2, 3.1**

*Choisissez la lettre qui correspond à ce qu'il faut faire selon la situation.*

**MODÈLE**    Mme Delaunay veut faire la cuisine.
   **B**

1. Cédric doit maigrir.
2. Océane a un contrôle d'histoire.
3. Salim veut voir un film.
4. On a faim.
5. Jacqueline veut voir la tour Eiffel.
6. Michel va à une teuf d'anniversaire.
7. Evenye est dans la classe de français.

A. Il faut aller à Paris.
B. Il faut faire les courses.
C. Il faut offrir un cadeau.
D. Il faut faire du sport.
E. Il faut étudier.
F. Il faut faire la cuisine.
G. Il faut parler français.
H. Il faut prendre le métro pour aller au cinéma.

## Communiquez!

**5** **Questions personnelles**   **1.1**

### Interpersonal Communication

*Répondez aux questions.*

1. Est-ce que tu manges de la pizza avec une fourchette ou les doigts?
2. Qu'est-ce que tu mets sur ta tête en hiver?
3. En général, es-tu prêt(e) pour les contrôles?
4. Qu'est-ce qu'il faut faire quand on a faim?
5. Qu'est-ce qu'il faut mettre quand on a froid?
6. Qu'est-ce qu'il ne faut pas faire dans la classe de français?

> Je mets un chapeau sur ma tête en hiver.

---

# Rencontres culturelles

## Au fitness

    1.2

## RESOURCES

 **Dialogue Video**

Yasmine et Camille ont quitté le fitness.

Camille: Tu es prête?
Yasmine: Oh là là, j'ai mal partout!
Camille: Qu'est-ce que tu as fait?
Yasmine: De l'aérobic et du step.
Camille: Ce n'est pas trop difficile?
Yasmine: Si, mais qu'est-ce qu'il faut faire? Je veux maigrir! Toi, qu'est-ce que tu as fait?
Camille: Moi? Du yoga.
Yasmine: Ah! C'est sûr, tu ne dois pas être aussi fatiguée que moi.
Camille: Mes bras, mes jambes, et mon dos sont décontractés.
Yasmine: Ouille! Mes pieds... je ne peux pas marcher!
Camille: Tu profiterais d'une cure thermale! Dis, on mange?
Yasmine: Oui, manger-bouger aujourd'hui!

### 6 Au fitness  2.1, 2.2

*Répondez aux questions.*

1. Qui a mal partout? Pourquoi?
2. Pourquoi est-ce que Yasmine a fait beaucoup d'exercice?
3. Qu'est-ce que Camille a fait comme exercices?
4. Qui a les bras, les jambes, et le dos décontractés?
5. Où vont les filles après le fitness?

### Extension  L'entraînement  1.2, 2.1, 2.2

Timéo parle de sport à son professeur.

Timéo: Qu'est-ce qu'on travaille aujourd'hui?
Professeur: D'abord le dos, puis le cou, les épaules, les bras....
Timéo: Bien... et ensuite....
Professeur: Eh bien, les genoux, les pieds. D'abord, déliez le corps.... Vous avez tout compris! On va travailler tous les points... lentement....
Timéo: On y va!
Professeur: Respirez....

### Extension  Quels sont les conseils du prof pour Timéo?

Leçon A | quatre cent soixante-trois **463**

---

## Answers

**6**

1. Yasmine; elle a fait de l'aérobic et du step
2. Elle veut maigrir.
3. Elle a fait du yoga.
4. Camille
5. Elles vont manger.

### Extension

Il faut travailler progressivement tous les points du corps.

### Reference Desk

At this level, students learn to employ an infinitive after **il faut**. Students will learn the subjunctive after **il faut** in Level 3.

### Game

**Aïe! On a mal!**
Have students line up on one side of the room. One by one (or in pairs), have them pass by the front of the class pretending to have something physically wrong. As they move "off stage," the other students must call out what is wrong using complete sentences: **Il a mal à l'oreille gauche!** or **Elles ont mal au ventre!** For variety, do the pantomimes in teams. Increase difficulty by having the guessing team add a phrase about what must be done to remedy the injury, such as, **Ils ont mal au bras; alors, il faut aller voir le médecin/l'infirmière.**

---

## Differentiated Learning
### Adapt
To review food vocabulary, ask the class what they think the two girls in the dialogue should eat to be **en forme**, using **il faut/il ne faut pas manger....**

### Learning Styles
### Kinesthetic Learners
You can ask volunteers to act out the **Extension** dialogue, indicating each part of the body as it is mentioned. Clarify the meaning of the word **entraînement** (*training*). Ask partners to use French to lead their classmates in a particular exercise, for example jumping jacks or a simple stretch.

### Multiple Intelligences
### Verbal-Linguistic
For vocabulary enrichment, explain that there are two parts to the action of **respirer** (*to breathe*): **aspirer** (*to inhale*) and **expirer** (*to exhale*). In English, when one takes one's last breath, one "expires," while one "aspires" to a goal.

# Points de départ

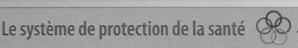

**?** Question centrale

How do people stay healthy and maintain a healthy environment?

## Le système de protection de la santé  1.2, 2.1, 3.2

Les Français sont protégés* par la sécurité sociale (ou "la sécu") quand ils tombent malades*. C'est un système d'assurance* collectif financé par les employés salariés et les compagnies. Chaque Français a un médecin généraliste, mais il peut aussi consulter des spécialistes. Il peut aller dans un hôpital publique ou dans une clinique privée. En conséquence, les Français sont de gros consommateurs de soins*.

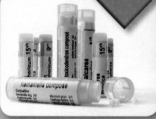

La sécurité sociale couvre la plupart des frais de la médecine homéopathique.

🔍 **Search words:** www.securite-sociale.fr
**sécurité sociale en france**

protégés *protected*; tombent malades *get sick*; assurance *insurance*; soins *care*

 **Produits**

**L'homéopathie** est très populaire en France. On peut trouver ces médicaments, souvent remboursé *(reimbursed)* par la sécu, dans les pharmacies ou en ligne.

 3.2, 4.2

## COMPARAISONS

What national medical programs are there in the United States?

4.2, 5.1

## Garder la forme 1.2, 2.1, 3.2,

"Pour rester en forme*, manger-bouger*." C'est le thème d'un programme national en France pour la nutrition et la santé*. Bien manger signifie manger des légumes et des fruits et éviter les produits gras* et trop sucrés. Toute la France fait un effort. De nouvelles chaînes de restaurants rapides se développent. Elles proposent des menus basses calories, des produits naturels, des salades, des soupes, des jus de fruit frais. Dans les cantines des lycées, on développe aussi une information sur l'équilibre alimentaire*.

À Pat à Pain, vous pouvez prendre du yaourt avec le miel *(honey)*.

🔍 **Search words:** www.mangerbouger.com

rester en forme *to stay fit*; bouger *to move*; santé *health*; gras *fatty*; équilibre alimentaire *balanced diet*

## COMPARAISONS

What opportunities for staying healthy and fit are there in your area?

5.1

## Le thermalisme  1.2, 2.1, 3.2

Le thermalisme est l'utilisation des eaux minérales pour des raisons médicales. Il a commencé à se développer après 1850. On a établi* des stations* thermales dans les Vosges (Vittel), l'Auvergne (Vichy), les Alpes (Évian), et les Pyrénées (Amélie les Bains). Aujourd'hui, 500.000 personnes visitent les 100 villes thermales chaque année. La majorité y va pour soigner* les rhumatismes. Une vraie cure thermale dure* trois semaines. Souvent ces cures sont payées par la sécu.

La ville thermale de Contrexéville a donné son nom à la fameuse eau minérale Contrex.

 **Search words: france thermale, thermalisme**

_____
**a établi** *established*; **stations** *resorts*; **soigner** *to treat*; **dure** *lasts*

---

### 7 Questions culturelles   2.1, 2.2, 5.1

*Répondez aux questions ou faites l'activité.*

1. Qu'est-ce que c'est "la sécu"?
2. Qu'est-ce que vous pouvez faire pour "manger-bouger"?
3. Qu'est-ce qu'on peut trouver maintenant dans certains restaurants rapides?
4. Choisissez un menu à Flunch qui vous aide à rester en forme.

 **Search words: flunch menus**

5. Qu'est-ce que c'est le thermalisme?
6. Choisissez une station thermale et écrivez les maladies qu'elle traite.

 **Search words: stations thermales, france thermale**

#### Perspectives

Do the French consider their health care to be socialized medicine as in Canada and the United Kingdom?

 **Search words: health care lessons from france, french health care**

---

Answers

**7**

1. la "sécurité sociale", un système collectif d'assurance maladie
2. bien manger (manger équilibré) et bouger (faire de l'exercice et du sport)
3. des menus à basses calories, des produits naturels
4. *Answers will vary.*
5. C'est l'utilisation de l'eau minérale pour un but médical.
6. *Answers will vary.*

**Perspectives**
They are very similar.

### Reference Desk

1. Have students locate French thermal stations on their wall map of France and research other well-known thermal spas in Europe (in Germany, Austria, Switzerland, Iceland, England, Hungary, etc.), or in Asia (Japan, Korea). Are there any in the Americas?
2. Compare American and French views on homeopathic remedies and methods, such as the use of herbal drugs and acupuncture.
3. Hold a discussion on western eating habits. How have the French viewed the incursion of American food chains, like McDonald's, into their culture? What French chains exist to rival the American ones? Have these American and French chains modified their offerings now that there is greater focus on healthy eating?

### Critical Thinking

**Comprehension**
Ask students to find the "franglais" words, the incorporation of certain English words in French, in **Points de départ**. Challenge students to keep adding to this list.

---

**Differentiated Learning**
**Adapt/Accelerate**
Ask if students can identify any cities in the United States or Canada that provide services like those in the French **stations thermales**. (Hot Springs, AK; Banff, Canada)

**Multiple Intelligences**
**Logical-Mathematical**
Ask partners to choose one of the search word topics to research online. Provide specific guidelines to help orient their exploration. For example, they should share two or three important points of new information they find about the topics.

**8**

1. l'Association Sportive des Postes Télégrammes et Télécommunication.
2. depuis 1908
3. À l'origine elle a été créée pour les postiers (clubs collectifs, bon marché). Aujourd'hui, tout le monde peut participer à l'association ASPTT.
4. tous les sports
5. partage, évasion, défi, échange, effort
6. *Answers will vary.*
7. *Answers will vary.*

## Reference Desk

While the **ASPTT** (**Association sportive des postes, télégraphes, and et telephones**) was originally the name given to the sporting clubs of French postal workers, it is no longer limited exclusively to them. Now anyone can join this sports club.

## Culture

**Practices: Activity**
Have students research and share about the various extra-curricular clubs in France.

## Critical Thinking

**Comparisons**
Ask groups to discuss the paradox of the French way of life (the consumption of wine, butter, cream, alcohol, and cigarettes) and French people's relative good health as compared to that of Americans. Students could start by making lists of the healthy habits and of the unhealthy habits of the French. How have these habits changed? Do the French set an example or are they following healthy changes initiated in the United States? What is the current French stance on smoking? Have students make posters for the classroom, school health center, and cafeteria illustrating good study, health, and dietary habits with captions in French employing **Il faut** or **Il ne faut pas** (or both).

---

**ASPTT Paris IDF**

Depuis 1908

*Du sport pour tous...*

**Partage**

**Évasion**

**Défi**

PARIS

**Échange**

**Effort**

**GUIDE DU SPORT**
**2011/2012**

**ADULTES** & **JEUNES**

TEL : 01 58 14 21 80

www.paris.asptt.com

## Du côté des médias

*Lisez les informations sur ce centre sportif.*
Vous allez avoir besoin d'aller sur le site web pour répondre à certaines questions.

**8  ASPTT de Paris et Île de France**    **1.2, 2.1, 2.2, 3.1**

*Répondez aux questions.*

1. C'est quoi l'ASPTT?
2. Depuis quand existe cette association?
3. Allez sur le site web de l'ASPTT. À l'origine, cette association a été créée pour quelles personnes? Aujourd'hui, qui peut utiliser l'ASPTT?

  **Search words:  ASPTT, acronym**

4. Selon les images de la brochure, quels genres de sports peut-on pratiquer à l'ASPTT de Paris?
5. Quels sont les bénéfices des activités sportives?
6. Nommez deux sports modernes que vous ne connaissez pas bien, par exemple:
   • **vol à moteur**
   • **capoeira**
   • **krav maga**
   • **qi gong**
7. Finalement, identifiez ces sports.

**Essential Instruction**

1. Ask students to infer the meaning of the words that form the five goals of the **ASPTT** by using English (effort, escape/diversion, sharing, personal exchange/contact, challenge).
2. Emphasize that **il faut** is an impersonal expression and contrast **il faut parler** with the personal subject pronoun in **Il parle**. Provide several more examples on the board before beginning **Activité 9**.

# Structure de la langue

 Go online EMCLanguages.net

## Present Tense of the Irregular Verb *falloir*  1.2

*Il faut faire du sport pour rester en forme.*

 **COMPARAISONS**  4.1

What are two ways to express this sentence in English?

*Il faut manger des fruits et légumes frais.*

The verb **falloir** (*to be necessary, to have to*) has only one present tense form: **il faut**. **Il faut** means "it is necessary," "one has to/must," or "we/you have to/must." **Il faut** is often followed by an infinitive.

**Il faut** travailler les épaules et les bras.  *You have to work your shoulders and your arms.*

**Il** ne **faut** pas trop travailler les genoux.  *You mustn't work your knees too much.*

---

**9** De bons élèves   2.1, 2.2

*Dites s'il faut faire l'activité ou pas pour être un(e) bon(ne) élève.*

**MODÈLES** faire ses devoirs
**Il faut faire ses devoirs.**

téléphoner en classe
**Il ne faut pas téléphoner en classe.**

> Il faut réussir aux contrôles pour être bonne élève.

1. parler aux copains en classe
2. arriver en retard
3. réussir aux contrôles
4. finir les devoirs
5. écouter son lecteur MP3 en classe
6. prendre des notes
7. étudier
8. envoyer des textos en classe

---

COMPARAISONS: "Il faut manger des fruits et légumes frais." can be expressed in two ways: (1) You have to eat fresh fruits and vegetables; and (2) It is necessary to eat fresh fruits and vegetables.

---

**RESOURCES**

📖 **Workbook 12–14**

🔊 **Listening Activity**

**Answers** _____

**9**

1. Il ne faut pas parler ....
2. Il ne faut pas arriver ....
3. Il faut réussir ....
4. Il faut finir ....
5. Il ne faut pas écouter ....
6. Il faut prendre ....
7. Il faut étudier ....
8. Il ne faut pas envoyer ....

---

## Reference Desk

1. Note that in the phrase **Il ne faut pas trop travailler les genoux** the adverb modifies the infinitive and not the verb **falloir**.
2. Remind students that **élève** can refer to a male or female student and that any adjective must agree with the person about whom the reference is made. **Bons élèves** is the masculine plural (used in the exercise title), whereas **bonne élève** is the feminine singular (used in the girl's speech bubble).

---

## Communication

**Presentational: Cooperative Groups**

Put students in groups. Give each group a list of teen problems, for example, "**J'ai des boutons** (*pimples*). **Que faire?**" (Jennifer) Ask students to type up solutions, for example, "**Chère Jennifer, Il faut acheter (produit).**" Students can post the problems and solutions online.

---

## Differentiated Learning

### Decelerate

Ask the class some humorous **vrai-faux** questions (either orally or in writing or both) to check for understanding, for example, **Il faut donner beaucoup de cadeaux au prof à Noël? Il faut manger deux kilos de chocolat quand on a faim? Il faut laver le chien dans la machine à laver? Il faut dormir sous le lit?**

### Accelerate

Introduce the formula **il faut** + noun (+ infinitive), as in **Il faut un ballon pour jouer au foot.** Ask students to choose an activity and say what one needs/has in order to participate in that activity.

**10** On voyage.  **2.1, 2.2, 4.2**

*Donnez des suggestions de ce qu'il faut faire dans chaque ville quand on est touriste.*

> **MODÈLE**  manger de la ratatouille
> **À Marseille il faut manger de la ratatouille.**

| New York | San Francisco | Londres | Paris | Orlando | Alger | Marseille |

1. marcher sur les Champs-Élysées
2. faire un tour en trolley
3. voir la Statue de la Liberté
4. prendre une photo de Big Ben
5. dîner dans un restaurant algérien
6. parler avec Mickey Mouse

**11** Qu'est-ce qu'il faut faire pour être en forme?   **2.1, 2.2**

*Écrivez les numéros 1–10 sur votre papier. Écoutez chaque suggestion et écrivez **L** si elle est **logique** ou **I** si elle est **illogique**.*

**12** Qu'est-ce qu'il faut faire?  **2.1, 2.2**

*Dites à vos amis ce qu'il faut faire dans chaque situation.*

> **MODÈLE**  Il n'y a pas de soupe dans le placard.
> **Il faut faire les courses au supermarché.**

1. Je voudrais voir la nouvelle comédie au Gaumont.
2. J'ai froid.
3. Il fait beau.
4. J'ai soif.
5. Il n'y a pas de fruits dans le frigo.
6. Il neige.
7. Samedi soir il y a une teuf pour l'anniversaire de Gilberte.

**Essential Instruction**

1. Do **Activité 10** as a class since some students might not have the cultural references needed to successfully complete these questions individually.
2. You might have students give a thumbs up for **logique** and thumbs down for **illogique** as they listen to **Activité 11**.
3. Challenge students to come up with as many suggestions as possible in a set amount of time for answers in **Activité 12**. Compare lists and award points for the number of logical suggestions.
4. For **Activité 13**, ask for volunteers to model the guided conversation for the class. Then divide the class into pairs and have them practice. Finally, ask several pairs to present the exchange.

# À vous la parole

How do people stay healthy and maintain a healthy environment?

## Communiquez!

### 13  Au fitness    1.1

**Interpersonal Communication**

You and a friend run into each other at the gym. In your conversation:

Greet your friend. Ask how he or she is.        Greet your friend. Say that you want to stay in shape.

Say that you do too. Ask what activities your friend likes to do.    Respond. Suggest an activity to do together.

Invite your friend to go and eat something when you're done.    Accept or refuse the invitation.

## Communiquez!

### 14  Un centre de fitness parisien    1.1, 1.3, 2.2

**Interpretive/Presentational Communication**

Imagine you live in Paris and would like to get in shape. Find a fitness center in Paris online. Research the classes the center offers, when they are scheduled, and how much each costs. List five classes you would like to take, what areas of the body they work, what time the activities are offered, and how much you will have to spend.

**MODÈLE**  Je vais faire un cours de yoga le lundi à 18h00. Je vais travailler les épaules, les bras, et les jambes. Ça coûte 10 euros.

  **Search words:  centre de sports à paris, fitness à paris**

Leçon A  |  quatre cent soixante-neuf  4 6 9

---

## RESOURCES

**Communicative Activities**

**Answers** _____

**13** *Dialogues will vary.*

**14** *Research will vary.*

### Reference Desk

**Blended Instruction**
Consider using blended instruction, a combination of in-class learning and computer-mediated instruction or learning opportunities. Ask students to complete activities on the computer, using their cell or smartphone, or other emerging electronic technology. This will allow students to hone their tech skills and become more independent learners. Schedule routine Internet and e-book learning in class and in the lab.

### Communication

**Interpersonal, Presentational: Cooperative Groups**
Brainstorm a list of specific healthy habits that students might like to institute (more fruits and vegetables, less fast food, fewer screen hours, etc.). Have students or teams make posters in French promoting healthy eating and lifestyle habits, and record their progress over several months or for an academic term. Students can be encouraged to average the success of their efforts and compare with a rival class.

### Expansion

1. For **Activité 13**, suggest an alternative dialogue activity, such as making New Year's resolutions about eating better or getting more in shape.
2. Challenge students to create a story about, or a description of, the ultimate in-shape person: what would he or she look like and what kind of lifestyle would he or she lead?

---

## Differentiated Learning
### Adapt/Accelerate
**Activité 14** provides students the opportunity to explore authentic resources. Ask students to present their findings to the class by giving a guided tour of the website that they selected.

### Learning Styles
**Visual Learners**
For **Activité 14**, assign students a poster or brochure to illustrate the **centre de fitness** and important details about participating in activities there.

## Special Needs Students
### Linguistically Challenged
For **Activité 13**, provide a template with sentences in French for students to complete. In addition, consider giving students a word bank to use as a reference.
For **Activité 14**, preselect a website and provide a questionnaire to guide students through the activity.

### Auditory Impairment
Provide an opportunity for students to repeat **Activité 11** with the audio or read these sentences aloud for them at a slower pace.

# Prononciation  1.2

## Final Pronounced Consonants

- Often an **–e** is added to a noun or adjective to make it feminine. When this occurs the final consonant preceding the **–e** is pronounced.

**A** Paires masculines et féminines

*Repeat the feminine and masculine pairs you hear and see below.*

1. Elle est allemande. Il est allemand.
2. Elle est première. Il est premier.
3. Elle est mauvaise. Il est mauvais.
4. Elle est intéressante. Il est intéressant.

**B** Langues et nationalités

*Ask what each person's nationality is, based on the language she speaks. Be sure to pronounce the final consonant /z/. Follow the model.*

> **MODÈLE**   You hear:   Notre cousine parle portugais.
> You say:   Elle est portugaise?

1. Ma prof parle français.
2. Cette musicienne chante en anglais.
3. La journaliste aime lire le japonais.

**C** Masculin ou féminin?

*Write **F** if you hear a feminine adjective, or **M** if you hear a masculine adjective.*

> **MODÈLE**   You hear: Tu es intelligente.
> You write: **F**

## End Consonants

- Most final consonants are not pronounced. Many final consonants are only pronounced when **liaison** occurs before a vowel, with the exception of "c," "f," "l," and sometimes "r."

**D** Un match de foot

*Repeat the following sentences, paying attention to the last letter in each number.*

1. Il y a huit matchs et huit ‿ équipes.
2. Il y a six joueurs et six ‿ entraîneurs (*coaches*).
3. Il y a dix joueuses et dix ‿ arbitres (*referees*).

**E** Consonnes finales ou pas?

*Write **C** if you hear a final consonant, or **NC** if you do not.*

# Leçon B

## Vocabulaire actif

### On n'est pas en forme.   1.2

**Où as-tu mal?**

J'ai mal à la tête.

J'ai mal aux oreilles.

J'ai mal au dos.

J'ai mal au cœur.

J'ai mal aux dents.

J'ai mal à la gorge.

J'ai mal au ventre.

**Qu'est-ce qu'elle a?**

Elle a la grippe.

Elle a de la fièvre.

Elle a un rhume.

Elle a des frissons.

Elle a mauvaise mine.

Elle a bonne mine.

Elle est en bonne forme.

Elle est malade.

Elle n'est pas en forme.

Leçon B | quatre cent soixante et onze **471**

## RESOURCES

 e-visual 34

 Workbook 15–19

 Flash Cards

 Listening Activity

### Reference Desk

1. Review the construction **à** + definite article (**le**, **la**, **l'**, **les**).
2. Note descriptions that employ **avoir** and the ones that employ **être**: **Elle a des frissons** but **Elle est malade.**
3. Other related terms: **avoir une angine** (*to have tonsillitis*), **des boutons (m.)** (*pimples*), **une ordonnance** (*a prescription*), **un médicament** (*médicine*), **un mouchoir** (*a handkerchief*), **un/une malade** (*a patient, sick person*).

### TPR

Play **Jacques a mal**, a version of **Jacques a dit** that uses illnesses rather than movements. If the teacher says **Jacques a mal au dos**, students must touch their back. Students who move when you do not precede the body expression with **Jacques a...** are out of the game.

### Communication

**Interpersonal**

Working with a partner, ask students to role-play a sick person who goes to the pharmacist, and the pharmacist, who recommends a product, for example, **Achetez de l'aspirine.**

---

## Differentiated Learning
### Adapt

1. Have students use the **avoir** health expressions, changing the subject pronoun or adding the negative. You may want to review the inversion **as-tu**, **a-t-il**, **a-t-elle**, **avez-vous**, and **ont-ils (elles)**, and then ask students to poll a partner on his or her condition.
2. Have one partner practice spelling aloud the nouns following **avoir** as the other deciphers the answer.
3. For more listening comprehension practice, say silly **vrai-faux** sentences, for example, **Quand je mange trois pizzas, j'ai mal aux oreilles.**

Students respond chorally by saying, **Faux!** Then ask a student to correct the sentence by responding with a more logical sentence, such as **Je n'ai pas mal aux oreilles. J'ai mal au ventre.**

### Multiple Intelligences
### Bodily-Kinesthetic

Use gestures and have students indicate your condition. Remind them to use the formal **vous**. Ask for volunteers to act out the health vocabulary and have the class call out the corresponding expression.

**471**

## Communication

**Interpersonal, Presentational: Paired Practice**

Have students create and present funny skits that take place in a health setting, with perhaps a patient who has multiple symptoms or who imagines his illness(es). Challenge students to use as much unit vocabulary as possible.

## Culture

**Perspectives: Activity**
You may want to show your students a video clip from a French performance of Molière's *Le Malade imaginaire* (especially Act III).

# Pour la conversation   1.2

**H**ow do I ask for advice?

> **Qu'est-ce que tu me conseilles?**
>
> *What do you advise me to do?*

**H**ow do I give advice?

> **À mon avis,** il faut prendre le thème des accompagnateurs.
>
> *In my opinion, you should take the topic of home health care workers.*

| **Et si je voulais dire...?** | |
|---|---|
| **éternuer** | *to sneeze* |
| **être raplapla** | *to be wiped out* |
| **tousser** | *to cough* |
| **J'ai le nez qui coule.** | *I have a runny nose.* |
| **Je me sens bien.** | *I feel good.* |
| **Je suis crevé(e).** | *I'm exhausted.* |

**1  Qu'est-ce qu'on prend?**  2.1, 2.2, 3.1

*Tous les élèves de la classe de français sont malades. Indiquez ce que chaque élève doit prendre ou utiliser pour sa maladie (illness).*

**MODÈLE**  Joseph a des frissons.
    **C**

1. Sandrine a mal à la tête.
2. Bruno a mal au ventre.
3. Charles a mal à la gorge.
4. Delphine a mal au cœur.
5. Patrick a de la fièvre.
6. Assia a un rhume.

A.

B.

C.

D.

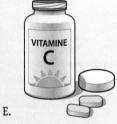

E.

F.

G.

**Essential Instruction**

1. Model the vocabulary in **Pour la conversation**, then add a specific condition and ask for advice, such as, **Je suis très fatigué(e). Qu'est-ce que tu me conseilles?**
2. Review direction lines in **Activités 1** and **3** to ensure comprehension.
3. As they are reading the paragraph in **Activité 2** silently, tell students to think about and discuss which advice they follow, by saying sentences such as, **Je (ne) prends (pas) souvent du (de) jus d'orange.**

Answers _____

**2** *Posters will vary.*

**3**

1. Elle a mal au ventre.
2. Elle a un rhume.
3. Il a mal à la tête.
4. Il est malade.
5. Il est en forme.
6. Elle a mal à la gorge.
7. Elle a mal aux dents.
8. Il a la grippe.

## 2 Pour rester en forme

  1.2, 1.3, 4.1

*Lisez le paragraphe et faites l'activité suivante.*

Pour rester en forme, d'abord, il faut dormir au moins huit heures par nuit. Ensuite, il faut bien manger: des fruits et des légumes frais. Il faut prendre souvent du jus d'orange. Il ne faut pas consommer trop de sel ou prendre trop de desserts. Il ne faut pas manger beaucoup de chocolat. Puis, il faut aussi faire du sport ou faire d'autres formes d'exercice, peut-être du footing ou des promenades dans le parc. Enfin, il faut avoir de bons copains avec qui on peut parler, et il faut choisir des passe-temps intéressants. Et n'oubliez pas: il faut voir le médecin une fois par an!

Faites une affiche qui montre un conseil pour rester en bonne forme et écrivez une légende (*caption*).

## 3 Qu'est-ce qu'ils ont?

 2.1, 2.2, 3.1

*Les personnes suivantes vont mal. Dites ce qu'elles ont.*

**MODÈLE**   Yasmine a une température de 39°.
**Elle a de la fièvre.**

1. Monique a mangé trop de chocolat.
2. Le nez de Lamine est très rouge.
3. Olivier a regardé la télé pendant cinq heures.
4. Gaston n'est pas à l'école; il reste au lit.
5. Yves a fini le Tour de France.
6. Chloé ne peut pas parler.
7. Zohra parle au dentiste.
8. André a très froid.

Yves a mal aux jambes.

## Answers _____

**4** *All questions and answers follow model.*

**5** *Script can be found in the front pages of the Annotated Teacher's Edition.*

1. D
2. I
3. E
4. H
5. C
6. G
7. B
8. F
9. A

**6** *Answers will vary.*

### Reference Desk

To help students remember the meaning of **besoin**, post the French proverb *C'est dans le besoin qu'on reconnaît ses vrais amis.* (*A friend in need is a friend indeed.*)

### Communication

**Interpersonal: Paired Practice**

Ask all students to make a list of five to ten items (nouns and articles) they need for everyday situations and a list of ten things they need to do (infinitives). In pairs, one student expresses what he or she needs from the list, for example, **J'ai besoin de chaussettes** and the partner offers advice on what the partner needs to do by saying **Tu as besoin d'aller au magasin**. Once partners have used all nouns on their lists, they will repeat the activity with the verb lists. This time, the partner will say what the person needs for doing that activity.

### Communiquez!

**4  Qu'est-ce que tu me conseilles?**  1.1

**Interpersonal Communication**

*À tour de rôle, expliquez votre problème et demandez les conseils de votre partenaire.*

**MODÈLE**  J'ai besoin d'un jeu vidéo.
A: **J'ai besoin d'un jeu vidéo. Qu'est-ce que tu me conseilles?**
B: **À mon avis, il faut aller à la FNAC.**

Je voudrais voyager cet été.

À mon avis, il faut visiter la Martinique.

1. J'ai un contrôle de français demain.
2. C'est l'anniversaire de mon copain dimanche.
3. Il y a un match de foot au stade samedi.
4. J'ai besoin de fruits et de légumes frais.
5. J'ai la grippe.
6. Je voudrais prendre une belle photo de Paris.
7. J'ai besoin de jambon et de pâté.
8. Je voudrais voir *la Joconde*.

**5  On est malade!**   2.1

*Écrivez les numéros 1–9 sur votre papier. Écoutez chaque description et écrivez la lettre de l'image correspondante.*

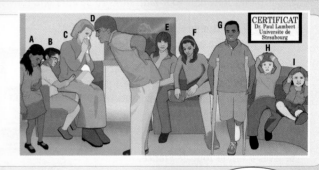

### Communiquez!

**6  Questions personnelles**  1.1

**Interpersonal Communication**

*Répondez aux questions.*

Je prends de l'aspirine quand j'ai mal à la tête.

1. Es-tu fatigué(e) aujourd'hui?
2. Qu'est-ce que tu fais quand tu es malade?
3. Est-ce que tu as beaucoup de rhumes en hiver?
4. Es-tu en bonne forme en été?
5. Quand est-ce que tu prends de l'aspirine?
6. Qu'est-ce que tu fais quand tu as des frissons?
7. Je voudrais faire du sport. Qu'est-ce que tu me conseilles?

### Essential Instruction

1. Review **avoir besoin de** and **il faut + infinitif** before having students do **Activité 4** in pairs. Ask volunteers to role-play their dialogues.
2. Play the audio for **Activité 5**.
3. For **Activité 6**, go over the verb changes students will need to make before having them write the answers. Then ask them to take turns asking and answering.
4. To introduce the topic in the **Rencontres culturelles** dialogue, consider first presenting the background material about Rwanda from **Points de départ** on p. 476.
5. Show the video dialogue, discuss vocabulary and questions, and then have students role-play the dialogue in pairs. Show the filmed dialogue a second time. Finally, do **Activité 7** as a class.

# Rencontres culturelles

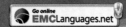

## Les malades au Rwanda

    1.2

Julien parle à son père dans le salon.

Julien: Qu'est-ce que tu regardes?

Père de Julien: Un reportage sur les accompagnateurs. Tu sais, les gens qui aident les personnes malades au Rwanda.

Julien: Et cette femme-là, qui n'est pas en forme et qui a mauvaise mine?

Père de Julien: Elle est presque morte du SIDA. Mais maintenant, un accompagnateur vient chez elle et, avec les antirétroviraux, elle va survivre.

Julien: Bon, alors je te laisse regarder.

Père de Julien: Pourquoi?

Julien: Non, rien, enfin... si—j'ai un devoir à faire sur l'Afrique et je voudrais ton avis.

Père de Julien: Mon avis? Sur quoi?

Julien: Qu'est-ce que tu me conseilles, comme thème?

Père de Julien: Eh bien, le voilà ton thème. À mon avis, il faut prendre le thème des accompagnateurs! Mets-toi devant l'écran et regarde l'émission avec moi.

### 7 Les malades au Rwanda

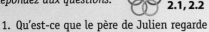

*Répondez aux questions.* 2.1, 2.2

1. Qu'est-ce que le père de Julien regarde à la télé?
2. Qui sont les "accompagnateurs"?
3. Qui n'est pas en forme et a mauvaise mine?
4. Qu'est-ce que Julien doit faire?
5. Qu'est-ce que le père de Julien suggère comme thème pour le devoir?
6. Qu'est-ce que Julien va faire maintenant?

**Extension** Un diagnostic   1.2, 2.1, 2.2

Au cabinet du médecin, un patient parle avec son médecin.

Patient: Non, vraiment, Docteur, ça ne va pas du tout... je ne me sens pas très bien.

Médecin: Oui. On va regarder ça. Vous avez mal où?

Patient: J'ai des frissons, puis j'ai mal à la tête et à la gorge... j'ai très mauvaise mine, n'est-ce pas?

Médecin: Ah bon? Non je ne trouve pas... peut-être un peu de fatigue... du stress, comme tout le monde.... Mais, ce n'est pas grave.

**Extension** Quel est le diagnostic du patient?

Leçon B | quatre cent soixante-quinze **475**

# Points de départ

Go online
EMCLanguages.net

How do people stay healthy and maintain a healthy environment?

## La Francophonie

1.2, 3.1, 3.2

### ✳ Le Rwanda

Le Rwanda est un assez petit pays dans l'Afrique Centrale avec une population d'environ huit millions d'habitants. La capitale est Kigali. Son climat est tempéré, et il y pleut beaucoup. Ce climat favorise l'agriculture, la base de l'économie rwandaise. Ancienne colonie de la Belgique, le Rwanda a gagné son indépendence en 1962. Mais des conflits entre deux groupes ethniques, les Hutus et les Tutsis, ont terminé en guerre* civile en 1994. Entre 500.000 et 1.000.000 de personnes sont mortes.

**guerre** *war*

Je parle kinyarwanda et français.

**Produits**

Une ancienne (*former*) colonie belge, le Rwanda insistait sur le français dans ses écoles. Mais plus récemment (*recently*), le pays a décidé que ses élèves doivent apprendre l'anglais comme deuxième langue. Mais le français reste toujours une option dans les écoles.

5.1

## La lutte* contre le SIDA au Rwanda

1.2, 3.1, 3.2

Le Rwanda est touché par le SIDA depuis* 1983. Trois pour cent des Rwandais sont infectés par le VIH, surtout* les femmes. Il existe un grand programme de protection de soins* pour les femmes et les enfants atteints de* la maladie et pour éviter* la transmission du VIH de la mère à l'enfant. La proportion d'enfants infectés par le VIH par leur mère a diminué*. Aujourd'hui beaucoup plus de personnes ont accès aussi aux médicaments*.

**lutte** *fight;* **depuis** *since;* **surtout** *especially;* **soins** *care;* **atteints de** *affected by;* **éviter** *to avoid;* **a diminué** *has lessened;* **medicaments** *medecine*

**Essential Instruction**

1. Assign each topic in **Points de départ** to at least two groups and have them report in English about what they learned. By having more than one group read each topic, the most important information will be presented more thoroughly.

2. Ask students to share their reaction to life in Rwanda and discuss the **Comparaisons** question, and the **Question centrale**. Can they relate anything about their lives, or those of people they know, to the experiences of the Rwandans they read about?

4. If possible, show examples of **Kinyarwanda** mentioned in **Produits** and reflect on what might be the historical, cultural, and political importance of learning all of these languages in school.

5. Have groups do **Activité 8** and assign each student responsibility for sharing about at least one topic.

6. Find online and share lyrics and a music video of the Youssou N'Dour song mentioned in **Perspectives**.

## Les accompagnateurs  1.2, 5.1

Dans les zones rurales du Rwanda, des malades (infectés du SIDA, de la tuberculose, du paludisme*, etc.) prennent leurs médicaments régulièrement grâce anx accompagnateurs. Ce sont des gens qui vont dans les maisons des malades qui n'ont pas accès à un hôpital ou une clinique. Cette initiative donne un job aux gens pauvres, qui gagnent environ $30 par mois, et préserve des milliers de vies humaines.

Le groupe international Partners in Health a organisé le système d'accompagnateurs au Rwanda, en Haïti, et autres pays en voie de développement.

**paludisme** *malaria;* **grâce à** *thanks to*

### COMPARAISONS

Does anyone you know receive home health care? What are the benefits? Disadvantages?

 4.2

## 8 Questions culturelles 🎧

1.2, 2.1, 2.2, 4.2

*Faites les activités suivantes.*

1. Remplissez la carte d'identité du Rwanda:
   • Population
   • Ethnies
   • Langues
   • Capitale
2. Répondez aux questions suivantes sur la lutte contre le SIDA.
   • Depuis quand existe le SIDA au Rwanda?
   • Quel est l'objectif du grand programme de protection?
   • Il y a plus ou moins de cas d'enfants infectés?
   • Qu'est-ce qui aide aujourd'hui dans la lutte contre le SIDA?
3. Décrivez les avantages du programme qui met un accompagnateur dans les maisons des malades.

### Perspectives

Read the lyrics to the song "La ronde des écoliers du monde" by Senegalese singer Youssou N'Dour online. What is his viewpoint on maintaining healthy relationships within and between nations?

Kigali est la capitale du Rwanda.

Answers

8
1. 8 millions d'habitants; Hutus, Tutsi; anglais, kinyarwanda, et français; Kigali
2. depuis 1983; éviter la transmission du virus de la mère à l'enfant; Il y en a moins; les médicaments
3. Ils peuvent apporter des médicaments aux malades loin des hôpitaux et cliniques.

Perspectives
He thinks that nations should not go to war on the grounds that the children deserve happiness and health.

### Reference Desk

You may want to show a video about home health care workers in Rwanda. One is available at PBS. Search words: **House Calls and Health Care in Africa - Breakthrough health care innovation in Rwanda DVD**.

### Communication

**Interpersonal, Interpretive, Presentational: Cooperative Groups**

Have groups research the effects of AIDS on the populations of different francophone African countries. Provide a rubric to complete with specific information they find (**la population du Rwanda qui a le SIDA en 1983**, etc.). Students may make posters to tell the story of the statistics and the efforts being made to solve this social problem. Consider having students compare their findings with those of non-francophone African countries. What role do European francophone countries (France, Belgium, Luxemburg, Monaco, Andorre) currently play in helping alleviate the AIDS crisis in Africa? What role does Sting play?

**Differentiated Learning**
**Accelerate**
Have students read all three **Points de départ** topics and prepare a written summary in French of the most important and interesting facts for a group discussion.

**Multiple Intelligences**
**Visual-Spatial**
Have students go online to find photos of Rwanda that depict its climate, geography, homes, daily life, schools, clinics, people, and clothing. Ask them to use an online presentation tool to share their findings with the class.

**9**

1. Elles sont françaises.
2. Elle est belge à l'origine.
3. *Collages will vary.*
4. *Messages will vary.*

### Expansion

1. Students may wish to work together to make their own class poster or have a poster contest to commemorate the Rwandan genocide and remember these troubles. Determine a time best suited to have a class-, course-, or school-wide commemoration.

2. If your school allows mural painting, perhaps dedicate a wall (or walls in a corridor) in the school to be **le mur de la paix**. Have student groups submit project ideas for painting suitable and varied peace commemorations. Perhaps join with other language classes in order to have a French wall, a Spanish wall, and others. Or, consider making a paper mural that can be displayed in the hallway.

## Du côté des médias

**9 Commémoration du génocide rwandais**    1.2, 1.3, 2.1, 2.2

*Répondez à la question ou faites l'activité.*

1. Qu'est-ce que les différentes associations qui soutiennent (*support*) cette commémoration ont en commun?
2. Allez sur le site Internet d'Ibuka. Cette association est de quel pays?
3. Faites un collage au sujet de "le mur de la paix (*peace*)" de Paris.
4. Écrivez le message de la paix que vous aimeriez (*would like*) mettre au mur de la paix.

### Essential Instruction

1. Go over the poster in **Du côté des médias** as a class. If time allows, have students pick one of the topics in **Activité 9** to do and share in class.

2. To introduce the imperative, project the charts for the three regular verb groups. Ask students what they notice about the command form **Étudie!** (It is missing the **-s.**)

3. To practice commands, have students form a circle and toss a koosh ball (or other soft object) calling out the pronouns **tu**, **nous**, and **vous** alternately.

4. Ask students to brainstorm suggestions for an imaginary class field trip using the **nous** imperative form.

# Structure de la langue

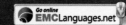 Go online **EMCLanguages.net**

## The Imperative  1.2

Use imperative verb forms to give commands and make suggestions. There are three imperative forms, **tu**, **vous**, and **nous**, yet these pronouns are not used with commands. Compare the following present tense forms of the verb **étudier** with their corresponding commands. Note that the **tu** imperative form of **–er** verbs (including **aller**) does **not** end in **-s**.

Faites une promenade tous les jours!

| Present tense | Imperative –er verbs |
|---|---|
| tu étudies | **Étudie!** *Study!* |
| vous étudiez | **Étudiez!** *Study!* |
| nous étudions | **Étudions!** *Let's study!* |

| Present tense | Imperative –ir verbs |
|---|---|
| tu finis | **Finis!** *Finish!* |
| vous finissez | **Finissez!** *Finish!* |
| nous finissons | **Finissons!** *Let's finish!* |

Ouvrez la bouche!

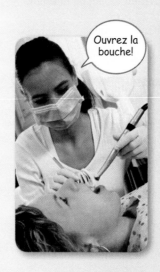

| Present tense | Imperative –re verbs |
|---|---|
| tu vends | **Vends!** *Sell!* |
| vous vendez | **Vendez!** *Sell!* |
| nous vendons | **Vendons!** *Let's sell!* |

The **nous** form of the imperative is used to make a suggestion and means "Let's + *verb*."

What do these imperatives addressed to a friend mean?
**Prends un gâteau! Va à l'école! Fais tes devoirs!
Offre un conseil! Achète un cadeau! Viens au café!**

Form the negative imperative by putting **ne** before the verb and **pas** after the verb.

**Ne** va **pas** au centre commercial! *Don't go to the mall!*

## COMPARAISONS

How would you express this sentence in English?

Visitons **Paris!**  4.1

COMPARAISONS: The French command **Visitons Paris!** can be translated as "Let's visit Paris!"

---

**Differentiated Learning**
**Accelerate**
Have students explore the topics in **Activité 9** in greater detail and write a paragraph or prepare a visual presentation in French to report their findings.

Or, ask volunteers to give a description of one of the member organizations or make a presentation on **le mur de la paix**.

**Multiple Intelligences**
**Bodily-Kinesthetic**
Now that students know the imperative forms and the parts of the body, play **Jacques a dit** using different verbs and having students give the commands using **tu** and **vous** forms. For example, **Jacques a dit chante/tousse/éternue/etc....** If students miss a command, or do the command when you haven't said **Jacques a dit**, they are eliminated. The last student(s) standing win(s).

**10** Une teuf d'anniversaire   1.3, 4.1

*Écrivez des textos à vos amis pour leur dire comment ils peuvent aider avec la teuf d'anniversaire pour Lilou que vous organisez.*

MODÈLE   préparer des pizzas
**Prépare des pizzas!**

1. préparer un gâteau
2. acheter un cadeau
3. inviter ton copain ou ta copine
4. apporter des boissons
5. choisir la musique

Apporte un gâteau pour la teuf!

**11** Une vie équilibrée   2.1, 2.2

*Dites ce que les médecins disent aux ados pour avoir une vie équilibrée.*

MODÈLE   manger des fruits frais
**Mangez des fruits frais!**

1. manger des légumes frais
2. choisir des passe-temps
3. faire du sport
4. prendre du jus d'orange
5. aller à l'école en vélo

Faites du sport!!

**12** Les bons conseils!   2.1, 2.2

*Écrivez les numéros 1–10 sur un papier. Écoutez chaque phrase et indiquez l'image qui correspond à la forme de l'impératif utilisée.*

A. tu

B. vous

C. je

**Essential Instruction**

1. For **Activité 10**, have students write the messages on index cards if your school prohibits cell phones in class.
2. Review with students when and with whom they should use the **vous** form of the verb and the irregular forms for **faire** and **prendre**. Then have pairs take turns role-playing **Activité 11**.
3. You may want to have students call out their responses to listening **Activité 12**.

Answers _____

**13**
1. Ne faites pas la cuisine! Allez au lit!
2. Ne joue pas au foot! Reste à la maison!
3. Ne regarde pas la télé! Fais de l'aérobic!
4. Ne passez pas le week-end à la maison! Voyagez!
5. Ne porte pas la vieille robe! Achète une nouvelle robe!
6. Ne mange pas de pizza! Prépare une ratatouille!

## 13 Des conseils

2.1, 2.2

*Donnez des conseils à ces personnes.*

**MODÈLES**

(à M. Lucas)

manger des desserts, faire une promenade
**Ne mangez pas de desserts! Faites une promenade!**

(à Bruno)

jouer aux jeux vidéo, étudier
**Ne joue pas aux jeux vidéo! Étudie!**

(à Mme Montaigne)
1. faire la cuisine, aller au lit

(à Chloé)
2. jouer au foot, rester à la maison

(à Véro)
3. regarder la télé, faire de l'aérobic

(à M. Duval)
4. passer le weekend à la maison, sortir

(à Julie)
5. porter cette vieille robe, acheter une nouvelle robe

(à Guy)
6. manger de la pizza, préparer une ratatouille

Leçon B | quatre cent quatre-vingt-un **481**

**Communication**

**Interpretive, Presentational: Cooperative Groups**
Challenge students to devise skits in pairs using the Peanuts cartoon character Lucy and her advice booth as a model. After students recreate a 3D version of Lucy's booth with the sign **Chez le docteur**, one partner plays the role of the patient with needs (use forms of **avoir** with **besoin/envie/soif/faim**/etc.), while the other plays **Lucie**, dispensing advice (using the imperative). Film the skits and add to student portfolios or post to the class website. For a second, more challenging round, ask groups of students to run through their skits as quickly and as accurately as possible. How much advice can be dispensed for how many patients (in rotation) during a set amount of time?

**TPR**

**Les ordres**
If you have pictures or flash cards of the items in a home or apartment that were introduced in **Leçon A**, display them for all students to see. Then give commands to indivdual students that use these visuals. For example, **Anne, prends la table!** and **Donne la table à Jérome!** Students demonstrate comprehension by manipulating the visuals as directed.

**Differentiated Learning**
**Decelerate**
Before groups complete **Activité 13** orally, ask students to indicate chorally if the **tu** or **vous** imperative form is appropriate with each person shown.

**Accelerate**
Students may enjoy writing commands telling specific teachers, or the principal, what to do.

## Communiquez!

**14** **Qu'est-ce qu'on fait ce weekend?** 1.1, 2.1

**Interpersonal Communication**

*À tour de rôle, suggérez à votre partenaire une activité à faire ce weekend. Développez votre projet avec une deuxième suggestion.*

> **MODÈLE**
> A: **Je ne veux pas sortir ce weekend.**
> B: **Alors, regardons un DVD!**
> A: **D'accord. Choisissons un film d'action!**

1. Je veux faire du sport.
2. Je voudrais sortir vendredi soir.
3. Je veux faire la cuisine.
4. Je voudrais écouter de la musique.
5. Je veux faire du shopping.
6. Je voudrais aller au fitness.
7. Je veux aller à un concert.

Je voudrais écouter de la musique ce weekend.

Alors, téléchargeons des chansons!

Je voudrais faire du shopping.

D'ac. Achetons ...une jupe et une chemise.

**Essential Instruction**

1. For **Activité 14**, have pairs practice their dialogues aloud. Then instruct them to join with two other pairs to share their dialogues.
2. Model the dialogue in **Activité 15** with an accelerated student. Allow for sufficient practice so that they can present it to another pair without reading it.

# À vous la parole

## Communiquez!

**Question centrale**

How do people stay healthy and maintain a healthy environment?

### 15 Comment vas-tu?

 1.1

**Interpersonal Communication**

With a partner, play the roles of a parent and a child who is not feeling well. In your conversation:

Say that you are sick.

→ Tell your child that he or she doesn't look well and ask what the problem is.

Explain what is wrong, listing several symptoms.

→ Tell your child he or she has a fever.

Ask your parent for advice.

→ Tell your child what to do to feel better and whether or not he or she should go to school.

## Communiquez!

### 16 Qu'est-ce que tu as?

  1.1

**Interpersonal Communication**

Your teacher will assign partners and an illness or body ache to both of you. Ask questions to find out what is wrong with your partner. Once you have guessed the condition correctly, switch roles.

## Differentiated Learning

**Decelerate**

Some students will probably need to write out the three conversations on these pages before they try to present them from memory. Consider allowing them to memorize portions or use index cards with cues when they present.

**Accelerate**

Allow students to choose the illness or body ache for **Activité 16**.

## Special Needs Students

**Social Anxiety**

For some students, activities that include presentations and memorization may cause greater anxiety. To encourage a more comfortable learning environment, offer the opportunity to present only to a chosen partner or to video record outside of class.

## RESOURCES

 **e-visuals 35–36**

 **Pre-test**

 *Leçon* **Quiz**

## Answers

 **17**

1. lavez
2. coupez
3. mélangez
4. ajoutez
5. Mettez
6. Remuez
7. Servez
8. mangez

**18** *Presentations will vary.*

## Communication

**Interpersonal, Presentational: Cooperative Groups**

Challenge students to work in groups to create skits about how to do a task. The winner(s) will have the most detailed, yet clearest, instructions.

## Expansion

Have students make a simple origami figure or do another simple project according to your instructions or those on a list you provide, like solve a math problem or send a photo using their smartphones.

# Stratégie communicative

## "How-to" Writing

When you want to give instructions on how to do something, communicate the steps in completing a process, or make suggestions, you can use the imperative, or command forms of verbs. To review the imperative, see page 479.

Follow these tips to write the steps in a process:

1. Make a list of all the steps in the process and put them in order, using the imperative form for the pronoun **vous**.
2. Be brief and concise.
3. To make the order of the steps clear, use words like **d'abord**, **ensuite**, **après**, and **enfin**.
4. Edit your writing and have someone else proofread it.
5. Use pictures or photos to illustrate each step.

---

**17** **Une recette française: la ratatouille**  **2.1**

Complete the following recipe with the commands from the list.

> mélangez   coupez   remuez   lavez   mangez   mettez   ajoutez   servez

D'abord, __(1)__ les tomates, poivrons rouges et verts, courgettes, et aubergines. Puis, __(2)__ tout en petits cubes et __(3)__ les cubes dans un bol. Ensuite, __(4)__ les oignons et la gousse d'ail coupés en petits morceaux. __(5)__ un peu d'huile d'olive, du sel, et du poivre sur les légumes, les oignons, et l'ail. Après, faites cuire au four 45 minutes dans une cocotte (*pressure cooker*). __(6)__ de temps en temps. __(7)__ et pour finir, __(8)__ bien!  Bon appétit!

---

**18** **Des instructions**  **2.2**

Use the imperative to give directions on how to prepare your favorite family recipe. Or, you might select an original topic like providing steps to install a DVD, send a photo on your phone, or do an aerobic exercise.

**Essential Instruction**

1. Ask students if they follow any of the suggested writing tips in the **Stratégie communicative** and add additional tips to the list.
2. Before students do **Activité 17** with a partner, review the meaning and pronunciation of each command and any additional new vocabulary.
3. Provide guidelines about how many commands you want students to include for **Activité 18**. Stress that they are not to translate a recipe, but to simplify it into easy instructions.
4. Introduce the **Leçon C** theme by asking how many students are concerned about **le bien-être de notre planète**. Discuss the **faux ami** verb **s'engager** (*to commit to*) and the English expression "a wedding engagement," which means to make a commitment to marry.
5. Have students look at the pictures and identify any cognates before playing the audio.

# Vocabulaire actif

## Je m'engage pour sauvegarder la planète!

  1.2

### Quels sont les problèmes de l'environnement?

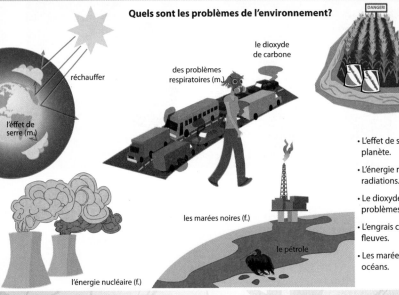

réchauffer

l'éffet de serre (m.)

des problèmes respiratoires (m.)

le dioxyde de carbone

l'engrais chimique (f.)

DANGER!

les marées noires (f.)

le pétrole

l'énergie nucléaire (f.)

- L'effet de serre réchauffe la planète.
- L'énergie nucléaire peut causer des radiations.
- Le dioxyde de carbone cause des problèmes respiratoires.
- L'engrais chimique pollue les fleuves.
- Les marées noires polluent les océans.

### Comment éliminer les problèmes de l'environnement?

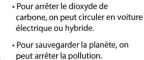

des éoliennes (f.)

une usine

le toit

les panneaux solaires (m.)

les espaces sauvages (m.)

les animaux (m.)

la pollution

L'ENGRAIS BIOLOGIQUE

Légumes Biologiques

une voiture hybride

une voiture électrique

recycler

le papier

les boîtes (f.) en aluminium

les bouteilles (f.) en plastique

- Pour arrêter le dioxyde de carbone, on peut circuler en voiture électrique ou hybride.
- Pour sauvegarder la planète, on peut arrêter la pollution.
- Pour sauvegarder les animaux, on peut protéger les espaces sauvages.
- Pour arrêter la pollution, on peut recycler le papier, les boîtes en aluminium, et les bouteilles en plastique.
- Pour arrêter la pollution, on peut remplacer l'engrais chimique par l'engrais biologique.
- Pour combattre l'effet de serre, on peut installer des panneaux solaires sur les toits.
- Pour combattre l'effet de serre, on peut faire marcher une usine avec des éoliennes.

## RESOURCES

Workbook 28–32

Flash Cards

Listening Activity

## Reference Desk

First, have students discuss what they and their families are doing to help save the planet. Then, broaden the discussion to include their school, their communities, their town, state, and the nation. How do the efforts of American citizens compare with those of francophone nations? What countries in the world are leaders and innovators with bold new ideas? (Germany pledged in 2011 to phase out the use of nuclear reactors.) How have recent natural disasters influenced countries' decisions concerning energy use, agriculture, housing, etc.?

## Culture

**Practices: Information**
Consider showing the i-Culture video entitled **"Planète bio"** (2004–2005) to provide your students with a culturally authentic perspective related to the theme of this **Leçon**.

## Differentiated Learning
**Adapt**
Create a two-column chart with problems in one column and a solution in another column.

**Accelerate**
Tell these students that "how-to" tasks can also be described using infinitives, and ask them to provide an example.

## Multiple Intelligences
**Visual-Spatial**
Ask interested students what major concerns they might have about the environment and what they are doing to resolve ecological problems. Have these students make signs for the French classroom, such as turning off some or all of the lights, recycling paper, etc.

**Les animaux en voie de disparition**

le panda géant

le gorille des montagnes    l'ours polaire (m.)    le tigre de Sumatra

## Pour la conversation

**H**ow do I persuade someone?

> **Je pense qu'on doit** faire tout ce qu'on peut pour sauvegarder la planète.
> *I think one must do everything one can to save the planet.*

**H**ow do I respond to persuasion?

> **Je suis prêt(e)** à recycler.
> *I'm ready to recycle.*

> **Mais, je ne suis pas prêt(e)** à m'engager.
> *But I'm not ready to commit.*

### Et si je voulais dire...?

| | |
|---|---|
| **covoiturer** | *to carpool* |
| **les aérosols (m.)** | *aerosols* |
| **les déchets radioactifs (m.)** | *radioactive waste* |
| **les emballages (m.)** | *packaging* |
| **les transports en commun (m.)** | *public transportation* |
| **gaspiller** | *to waste* |
| **renoncer à** | *to give up* |

## Essential Instruction

1. Model the pronunciation of the endangered species and then, to review vocabulary, poll the class: **Quel est votre animal préfère? Quel animal est blanc? Quel animal est le plus grand? Quel animal a de grosses dents?**, etc.
2. After you listen to **Pour la conversation**, ask students to create a role-play with a partner about being ready or not ready for a party, test, trip, etc.
3. Ask for individual responses to **Activité 1**, and then have all students respond chorally.

## 1 Des choses et des animaux sur la planète

 2.1, 2.2

*Identifiez chaque chose ou animal.*

**MODÈLE**  C'est un **ours polaire.**

 Ce sont des **bouteilles en plastique.**

1.

2.

3.

4.

5.

6.

7.

8.

9.

10.

**2** **Les problèmes de la planète**   **1.2, 2.1, 2.2, 3.2**

*Lisez le paragraphe, et ensuite répondez à la question.*

Il y a de graves problèmes de l'environnement. Beaucoup d'usines polluent l'air. Les marées noires polluent les océans. L'engrais pollue les fleuves. Des gens mettent les boîtes et les bouteilles dans les lacs et les océans. Ils ne recyclent pas leur papier. L'effet de serre réchauffe la planète. Le dioxyde de carbone des voitures et des autobus cause des problèmes respiratoires. L'énergie nucléaire peut causer la radiation. Il y a des animaux qui sont en voie de disparition. Il faut sauvegarder la planète.

Quelles sortes de pollution sont mentionnées?

**3** **Sauvegardons la planète!**  **1.3, 5.1**

*Écrivez une phrase qui explique ce qu'on peut faire pour résoudre (solve) chaque problème.*

> **MODÈLE** L'effet de serre réchauffe la planète.
> **On peut installer des panneaux solaires et des éoliennes.**

1. L'énergie nucléaire peut causer la radiation.
2. Le dioxyde de carbone cause des problèmes respiratoires.
3. Les marées noires polluent les océans.
4. L'engrais pollue les fleuves et les océans.
5. Les tigres de Sumatra sont en voie de disparition.
6. Les usines polluent l'air.

On peut installer des panneaux solaires dans les usines.

## Essential Instruction

1. **Activité 3** requires higher level thinking skills (Application). Divide the class into six groups; assign each group one question for which there are multiple answers. As students share their answers, correct and develop them as you write them on the board.
2. To help students remember the word **prêt/prête** in **Activité 4**, introduce **prêt-à-porter** vs. **haute couture** clothing.
3. For a change of pace, put the individual questions in **Questions personnelles** on index cards, a set for each group. Students randomly pick one to answer. Ask students to pick a question randomly to answer for the class.

**4 Tu es prêt(e)?** 2.1, 2.2

*Dites que chaque personne est prêt(e) à faire les activités suivantes pour être en bonne forme.*

**MODÈLE** **Sophie est prête à dormir huit heures.**

prendre du jus d'orange    dormir huit heures    voir son médecin
faire du sport    acheter des fruits et des légumes frais
faire une promenade au parc    parler avec un camarade de classe

Sophie

1. Bernard

2. Brigitte

3. Khaled

4. Rahina

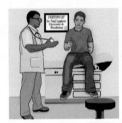
5. Hervé

6. Charlotte

# Communiquez!

**5 Questions personnelles**

**Interpersonal Communication**    1.1, 2.1

*Répondez aux questions.*

À mon avis, on doit faire marcher les usines à l'énergie solaire.

1. Qu'est-ce que tu recycles?
2. Comment est-ce que tu viens à l'école?
3. Est-ce que ta famille et toi, vous circulez en voiture électrique ou hybride?
4. À ton avis, pourquoi est-ce qu'il faut protéger les espaces sauvages?
5. À ton avis, comment est-ce qu'on doit faire marcher les usines?
6. Es-tu prêt(e) à t'engager pour sauvegarder l'environnement?

---

**Answers** _____

**4**
1. Bernard est prêt à acheter des fruits et des légumes frais.
2. Brigitte est prête à faire du sport.
3. Khaled est prêt à prendre du jus d'orange.
4. Rahina est prête à faire une promenade au parc.
5. Hervé est prêt à voir son médecin.
6. Charlotte est prête à parler avec un camarade de classe.

**5** *Answers will vary.*

## Reference Desk

Some students might ask you for the word "litter" (**des ordures, des déchets**) and the word "litterbug" (**un malpropre qui jette ses ordures**).

## TPR

Act out a different activity or action in front of the class and have students write what you are ready to do, for example, **Vous êtes prêt(e) à voyager.**

---

**Differentiated Learning**
**Expand**
You may want students to write the answers to **Activités 4** and/or **5** for extra practice with spelling, sentence construction, and using new vocabulary correctly.

**Special Needs Students**
**Dyslexia/AD(H)D**
Copy, enlarge, and cut up the sentences in **Activité 2** to enable students to focus on less visual stimuli at one time. Ask students to list sentences according to specific environments such as air, water, or land.

**6** Script can be found in the front pages of the Annotated Teacher's Edition.

1. D
2. F
3. A
4. C
5. B
6. E

**6** **Sauvons la planète!**   **2.1, 2.2, 3.1**

*Faites correspondre l'image avec la description pour indiquer ce que les Morin font pour sauvegarder l'environnement.*

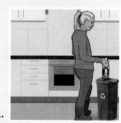 A.

 B.

 C.

 D.

 E.

 F.

La poubelle bleue est pour le recyclage du papier.

**Essential Instruction**

1. As students listen to **Activité 6**, have them call out the answers.
2. After students watch the video, check for general comprehension. Read the dialogue and discuss the expression **au courant** (*to be in the know*) and the meaning of **jaune** in this context (*to be fearful or cowardly*). Ask how many students have their parents drive them to school.
3. Do **Activité 7** together and listen to the dialogue a second time.

# Rencontres culturelles

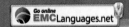

## Maxime n'est pas persuadé.

    1.2

Camille et Maxime sont devant le lycée après les cours.

**Camille:** Tu es paresseux.

**Maxime:** Qui? Moi, paresseux? Pourquoi?

**Camille:** Tous les jours… en voiture… avec ma-man!

**Maxime:** Je ne veux pas venir à pied.

**Camille:** Non, mais tu pourrais venir à vélo!

**Maxime:** Pourquoi?

**Camille:** C'est moins polluant! La planète… tu n'es peut-être pas au courant?

**Maxime:** Si, si, l'effet de serre… l'ours polaire….

**Camille:** Je pense qu'on doit faire tout ce qu'on peut pour sauvegarder la planète. Moi, j'ai de nouvelles résolutions; je vais recycler les papiers, les boîtes, les bouteilles en plastique. Cette semaine je suis venue à l'école à vélo, et je vais continuer!

**Maxime:** Mais je ne suis pas prêt à m'engager. Je suis plutôt jaune, pas "vert."

**Camille:** Tiens, offre-moi un coca au café!

**Maxime:** C'est ça: pollueur, payeur! Pour l'instant, je préfère payer.

### 7 — Maxime n'est pas persuadé.

*Complétez les phrases.* 2.1, 2.2

1. À l'avis de Camille, … est paresseux.
2. Maxime vient à l'école….
3. Camille dit qu'il est moins polluant de venir à l'école….
4. Camille fait tout ce qu'elle peut pour….
5. Camille va recycler….
6. Maxime n'est pas….

### Extension — En direct: Des gestes pour sauvegarder la planète

2.1, 2.2, 3.2

Un journaliste fait une enquête sur les gestes pour sauvegarder la planète.

**Journaliste:** Sauvegarder l'environnement, mieux utiliser l'énergie solaire, protéger les espaces vierges….

**Jeune homme:** Je suis breton, et en Bretagne, il y a beaucoup de vent. Dans mon village, on a décidé d'installer des éoliennes.

**Adolescent:** Nous, à la cantine au lycée, on fait très attention au tri des déchets et notre professeur de SVT est très vigilant!

### Extension

Quels gestes pour sauvegarder la planète sont mentionnés?

---

## RESOURCES

 **Dialogue Video**

### Answers

**7**

1. Maxime
2. en voiture
3. à vélo
4. sauvegarder la planète
5. les papiers, les boîtes, les bouteilles en plastique
6. vert

### Extension

Utliser l'énergie solaire, protéger les espaces vierges, installer des éoliennes, faire le tri des déchets

### Reference Desk

These dialogues present two opposite views on pollution and the environment so students can learn to debate or support either position.

### Critical Thinking

**Application**
Using the white board or a large presentation pad, write down environmental problems and solutions such as pollution, protecting endangered species and their habitats, saving the planet, etc. Then ask the students to vote on them and put them in order of priority. Display the ordered class list and compare with that of other classes that complete this activity.

---

## Differentiated Learning
### Adapt/Accelerate

1. If you include the **Extension** dialogue, explain the terms **gestes** (*acts or actions*, not *gestures* in this context), **vierge** (*untouched*), **faire le tri** (*to separate*; ask the students if they know what medical triage is), and **SVT: Sciences de la vie et de la terre** (*Earth Science*).

2. Project a map of Brittany for students to see that the province juts out into the Atlantic, thus exposing it to strong winds, which makes it an ideal place for wind power plants. For fun, give students the name of the department **Finistère** and ask them to use their reading strategies to justify this name: **la fin de la terre**.

## Connections

### Environment

What green movements exist in the United States? And in francophone countries? Are the major issues and activities comparable? What is the position on the environment of the major political parties in the United States? Who are the major leaders or organizations of the American environmental movement? Have students explore this topic with e-pals.

# Points de départ

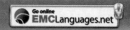 Go online EMCLanguages.net

**Question centrale?** How do people stay healthy and maintain a healthy environment?

## Les Verts en France

Le mouvement écologiste des Verts est né* au début des années 1970. Aujourd'hui ils représentent une population jeune, urbaine, et intellectuelle. Cette population est soucieuse du* cadre de vie*, du respect écologique, de la transparence démocratique. Elle est aussi progressiste sur les questions de société. Les Verts sont une vraie force politique. Ils présentent des candidats à chaque élection présidentielle et

Daniel Cohn Bendit parle aux assises nationales (conférences nationales) du rassemblement des Verts à Lyon.

participent dans les gouvernements régionaux et municipaux. Mais les Verts ne sont pas les seuls* à donner de l'importance aux thèmes écologistes de protection: sauvegarde de la nature (animaux en voie de disparition), lutte contre la pollution urbaine (dioxyde de carbone), lutte contre la pollution agricole (engrais), lutte contre la pollution des côtes (marées noires). Tous les partis politiques le font. Les Verts se distinguent* par des propositions radicales sur les transports (développement des transports en commun, de la voiture électrique) ou sur les choix énergétiques (contre le nucléaire, pour les énergies renouvelables*).

 **Search words: les verts france**

 **1.2, 2.1, 2.2, 3.1, 5.1**

---

**est né** *was born*; **soucieuse du** *concerned about*; **cadre de vie** *living environment*; **les seuls** *the only ones*; **se distinguent** *distinguish themselves*; **renouvelables** *renewable*

---

 **Produits**

*La souris verte* est un magazine en ligne écrit par *les Jeunes Verts* en France. C'est un groupe qui voudrait préserver l'environnement. Trouvez leur slogan en ligne.

 **Search words: les jeunes verts la souris verte**

 **2.1, 4.2**

## Essential Instruction

1. Provide a graphic organizer for the reading **Les Verts**. On a Venn diagram show **Les Verts** and **d'autres partis politiques** and ask the class to determine what environmental interests they share and what distinguishes them. You may wish to discuss the concepts of progressive (progressing forward for change) vs. conservative (conserving traditional values) and radical (favoring extreme change), and regional vs. municipal.

2. Briefly discuss the **Produits** reading and ask students to propose an appropriate slogan for the French youth green party before looking for it online.

3. Have students work in small groups to explore one of the **Questions culturelles** to research online and report on.

## Vélib' Paris  1.2, 2.1, 5.1

Vélib' est un mot qui combine les mots "vélo" et "liberté."
Ce système de location* de bicyclettes existe à Paris depuis
juillet 2007. On loue un vélo dans une station et on laisse le
vélo dans une autre. Aujourd'hui on compte 20.000 vélos de
location dans 1.200 stations. C'est un moyen de transport*
public utilisé par beaucoup de Parisiens et de touristes.

 **Search words: velib paris**

_____
**location** *rental;* **moyen de transport** *means of transportation*

Les stations Vélib' Paris sont bien situées.

### COMPARAISONS

Does your area offer a bike
rental program? On what forms of
transportation do you depend? What
form of public transportation would
you like to see in your region?

**2.1, 2.2, 4.2**

### 8 Questions culturelles  1.3, 2.1, 3.1, 3.2, 4.2

*Faites les activités suivantes.*

1. Faites des recherches sur les Verts en ligne et nommez
   un de leurs buts (*goals*) récents.
2. Faites un profil de Vélib' Paris:
   • Ce que c'est
   • Comment on l'utilise
   • Nombre de vélos
   • Nombre de stations
3. Faites des recherches en ligne pour trouver une autre
   ville française où un programme Vélib' existe.

### À discuter

What actions can you and your classmates take to create a
healthier planet?

Il y a environ 17 millions d'utilisateurs du
Vélib' à Paris.

## Differentiated Learning
### Expand/Accelerate
For the **À discuter** question, ask students to brainstorm something that the school does already to
create a healthier planet. Have students reflect on
personal actions they could take by re-asking the
question, **Quels gestes pouvez-vous faire pour
aider la planète?**

**Comparaisons**
*Discussions will vary.*

**8**
1. *Answers will vary.*
2. un système de vélos en libre-
   service; on achète un ticket, on
   prend un vélo dans une station
   et on le laisse dans une autre station; *answers will vary; answers
   will vary.*
3. *Answers will vary*

**À discuter**
*Discussions will vary.*

### Reference Desk

1. Discuss the pros and cons
   of the bike rental service
   (economical, ecological, need
   for maintenance, a high percentage of vandalism, safety).
   You might wish to have students study a topographical
   map of Paris in addition to
   one showing cultural sites and
   attractions in order to consider
   the practicality of cycling in
   various (hilly or flat) parts of
   the city.
2. Have students find out where
   and when other bike share programs have been started (nearly
   300 around the world, including London, Boston, Miami,
   Minneapolis, Washington,
   Mumbai, Barcelona, Mexico City,
   and Montreal), and compare
   their scale and success with that
   of the Parisian program.

### Expansion

Have partners make a collage
showing the different bike logos
and designs from bike share programs around the world. Then ask
them to design a logo for a bike-
share program in their community.

**9**

1. des vélos
2. vélo, liberté.
3. Elle indique qu'on peut sortir de la pollution et on peut aller (presque) où on veut.
4. la météo: oui; des chansons: non; des vidéos: oui; des livres: non; les stations de vélib: oui; des informations: oui

### Reference Desk

Using e-pals, or another social network, have students interview peers about their opinions of the success and problems associated with the **Vélib'** program. Consider asking students to interview several local town officials to find out about whether such a service could be established in their area. In what city would your students most like to try the bike share program? What city lacks this service, but should have it, according to your students?

## Du côté des médias

*Lisez cette page qui décrit une application pour Vélib'.*

**9 Vélib' Paris**  **1.3, 5.1**

*Répondez à la question ou faites l'activité.*

1. Que voit-on sur les petits ballons verts et sur le fond d'écran (*background*)?
2. "Vélib'" combine deux mots: ... et ....
3. Qu'est-ce qui indique l'idée de la liberté?
4. Avec l'application Vélib', dites si on peut trouver ces choses (**oui**) ou pas (**non**).
   * la météo
   * des chansons
   * des vidéos
   * des livres
   * les stations de Vélib'
   * les informations

### Essential Instruction

1. Use the questions in **Activité 9** to guide the exploration of the poster in **Du côté des médias** as a class. Ask **Combien d'applications avez-vous téléchargées sur votre portable?**
2. To introduce **La culture sur place**, ask students to reflect on why diabetes is a growing problem in western countries.
3. For **Activité 10**, project the two sites and have the class complete the **Activité** together.

# La culture sur place

## Le diabète chez les jeunes en Occident
### Introduction

Le diabète chez les jeunes est un problème sérieux dans l'Ouest, par exemple, les Etats-Unis, le Canada, la Belgique, le Luxembourg, la Suisse, et la France. Dans cette **Culture sur place**, vous allez faire des recherches et réfléchir (*to think about*) à ce problème global qui a besoin de l'engagement de jeunes de votre âge.

**10 Première étape: Les sites web**  1.2, 1.3

 *Trouvez les sites français ci-dessous. Cherchez les renseignements (information) suivants sur le diabète. Marquez à quel site vous trouvez les renseignements.*

**Search words:** Site #1 – **journée mondiale du diabète**
Site #2 – **fédération internationale du diabète**

| | Site #1 | Site #2 |
|---|---|---|
| Les posters multilingues avec les signes précurseurs de diabètes | | |
| Les pourcentages des décès attribuables au diabète | | |
| Une liste de facteurs de risque pour le diabète | | |
| Les posters pour la Journée Mondiale du Diabète | | |
| Une définition du diabète | | |
| Les estimations du nombre de cas de diabète chez les jeunes | | |

**11 Une affiche du diabète**  1.3

*Faites une affiche sur laquelle vous mettez les informations les plus importantes sur le diabète que vous avez apprises en lisant les sites web.*

**12 Deuxième étape: Faites une comparaison**  3.2, 4.2

*Choisissez un autre pays francophone en Occident (le Canada, la Belgique, le Luxembourg, la Suisse) et trouvez un site sur le diabète dans ce pays. Faites une recherche pour voir si les mêmes informations de l'organigramme sont disponibles (available) dans ce pays.*

 **Search words:** **le diabète en suisse** (exemple)

---

**Answers** _____

**10** *Answers will vary.*

**11** *Presentations will vary.*

**12** *Comparisons will vary.*

### Connections

**Medicine**
Have students do research in English to find out the risk factors for diabetes so they will be able to understand the information they locate in **Activité 10** on websites that are in French.

### Expansion

**Taking inventory**
Have students discuss the following questions to see what they have learned about diabetes and juvenile diabetes in the francophone world:
1. What are some ideas for increasing awareness of diabetes in your community? And global awareness?
2. What resources do you need to create awareness of an issue outside your community? How do these resources differ from those you would need to create awareness locally?
3. How might a multilingual website help promote global awareness of and advocacy for a particular issue?
4. Was there any information listed in the chart that you did not find for the particular country you researched? Was there any important information you found that was not included in the chart? How might you make this information available to people?

### Reference Desk

Many Fench verbs may be fol-lowed by an infinitive, including this group of nine common verbs: **adorer, aimer, aller, désirer, falloir, pouvoir, préférer, venir, and vouloir.** Have pairs create a clever or silly acronym using the first letter of these verbs to help them remember the list.

### Communication

**Interpersonal: Cooperative Groups**

Ask each student to choose an endangered animal, especially those found in francophone coun-tries. (Include Antarctica, where one may choose the penguin or a species that may be the topic of the French polar research post.) Have students research, illus-trate, and write a report on their selected animal and its habitat, challenges to its survival, and ways researchers are trying to protect it. Make a large mural with the title **Parc Zoölogique** and post it in the classroom. Have students place their animal illustration in the **zoo**. Then brainstorm a list of pertinent questions one needs to ask in order to learn about a new animal. Once the questionnaire is finalized, make copies and distrib-ute. Then, have students circulate around the class and interview their classmates about their ani-mals. Students can consult the **zoo** during the activity so they are sure to interview all their classmates.

# Structure de la langue

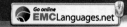

## Verbs + Infinitives  1.2

Many French verbs may be directly followed by an infinitive.

| | |
|---|---|
| **aimer** | **Aimez**-vous **voyager**? |
| **aller** | Je **vais faire** du yoga. |
| **désirer** | Est-ce que vous **désirez prendre** un dessert? |
| **devoir** | Nous **devons mettre** le couvert. |
| **falloir** | Il ne **faut** pas **étudier** ce soir. |
| **pouvoir** | Est-ce que vous **pouvez venir** demain? |
| **préférer** | Je **préfère faire** du ski. |
| **venir** | Mes grands-parents **viennent dîner**. |
| **vouloir** | Qu'est-ce que tu **veux faire** maintenant? |

### COMPARAISONS

Some verbs in English are also followed by an infinitive, but the form the infinitive takes may vary. How would you express these sentences in English?

Nous devons être en forme pour le match.
J'aime faire des promenades en ville.

**4.1**

COMPARAISONS: In the first sentence, the infinitive does not include the word "to": We must be in shape for the game. In the second sentence, the infinitive uses the word "to": I like to take walks in town.

### Essential Instruction

1. To anchor this grammar concept, remind your students that they already know the **futur proche** (aller + infinitif): **Je vais recycler, tu vas sauvegarder la planète**, etc.
2. Remind them that the **falloir** is used only with the impersonal subject pronoun **il**.
3. Model the negative of the **verbe + infinitif**, reminding students to make the **ne... pas** "sand-wich" with the conjugated verb. Have students take note of the English translation differences in **Comparaisons**.
4. Ask students to complete **Activité 13** in pairs; randomly select students to share what they learned about their partner.
5. Have students call out **engagé(e)** and **pas engagé(e)** as they listen to **Activité 14**.

# Communiquez!

**Answers** _____

13  *Answers to questions will follow the model*

1. A: … tu aimes faire du sport?
2. A: … tu désires bien faire du patinage?
3. A: … que tu vas faire du shopping cette semaine?
4. A: … tu préfères écouter la world ou le hip-hop ?
5. A: … tu veux voyager en France un jour?
6. A: … tu préfères jouer au basket ou jouer au foot?
7. A: … tu aimes voir les comédies ou les films de science-fiction?

14  Script can be found in the front pages of the Annotated Teacher's Edition.

1. NE
2. NE
3. E
4. NE
5. E
6. E

**13  Une interview**   1.1

### Interpersonal Communication

*Choisissez un partenaire que vous ne connaissez pas (don't know) bien. À tour de rôle, posez des questions à votre partenaire. Après l'interview, écrivez un paragraphe sur ce que vous savez maintenant de votre partenaire.*

**MODÈLE**   aimer/lire "Les copains d'abord"
**A: Est-ce que tu aimes lire "Les copains d'abord?"**
**B: Oui, j'aime lire "Les copains d'abord."**
      ou
**Non, je n'aime pas lire "Les copains d'abord."**

1. aimer/faire du sport
2. désirer/faire du patinage
3. aller/faire du shopping cette semaine
4. préférer/écouter la world ou le hip-hop
5. vouloir/voyager en France un jour
6. préférer/jouer au basket ou jouer au foot
7. aimer/voir les comédies ou les films de science-fiction

**14  Engagé(e) ou pas engagé(e)?**

*Écoutez les phrases suivantes et écrivez* **E** *si la personne est engagée et* **NE** *si la personne n'est pas engagée pour sauvegarder la planète.*

2.1

### Expansion

Have small groups make two sets of notecards, one set with each of the nine verbs followed directly by an infinitive and the other set with an infinitive that might logically follow one of the nine verbs. Each student in the group randomly selects one card from each set and makes a complete sentence using a verb followed by an infinitive. For example, **pouvoir/skier → Nous pouvons skier quand il neige.** After cycling through the cards, groups exchange their second set of note cards with each other and the game begins again. Vary this activity by asking students to form a question from two cards they select. Another student in the group responds.

**Multiple Intelligences**
**Interpersonal**
Put students in pairs to create a dialogue about what they are going to do this summer.

**Answers**

**15** *Answers will vary.*

 **Communiquez!**

**15  Une enquête**      **1.1, 1.3**

### Interpersonal Communication

*Faites une grille comme celle de dessous. Dans la grille, écrivez quatre activités que vous pensez que vos amis aiment faire pendant le weekend. Ensuite, demandez à dix camarades quelle activité ils préfèrent faire et notez leurs réponses dans la grille. Ensuite, faites un rapport à votre groupe. Dites-leur combien de personnes préfèrent faire chaque activité.*

| Qu'est-ce que tu préfères faire le weekend? | 1 | 2 | 3 | 4 | 5 | 6 | 7 | 8 | 9 | 10 |
|---|---|---|---|---|---|---|---|---|---|---|
| aller à un concert | | | | | | | | | | |
| voir un film | | | | | | | | | | |
| faire du shopping | | | | | | | | | | |
| aller à une teuf | | | | | | | | | | |

**MODÈLE**

Vous: **Qu'est-ce que tu préfères faire le weekend—aller à un concert, faire du shopping, voir un film, ou aller à une teuf?**

Élève 1: **Je préfère voir un film.**

**Cinq personnes préfèrent aller à une teuf, trois personnes préfèrent voir un film, et deux personnes préfèrent aller à un concert.**

## De + Plural Adjectives      **1.2**

*Il y a de grands gorilles au zoo.*

### Essential Instruction

1. Distribute a copy of the grid in **Activité 15** to each student, review the instructions together, and ask volunteers to present the model dialogue. The grid can be found in the **Copy Masters** supplement. Give students a set amount of time to survey each other. Poll students to find out the results.

2. Review adjective placement and the BAGS adjectives that come before a noun. Ask students questions using **de** + plural adjective + plural noun, writing the combination on the board as you proceed. Ask them what they notice, then point out the use of **de** instead of **des**. In general, students do not find this grammar point difficult to understand.

3. Have students do **Activité 16** in pairs.

You already know to use **des** before a plural noun when the adjective follows the noun.

Il vend **des** voitures électriques.    *He sells electric cars.*

When the adjective precedes a plural noun, however, **des** often becomes **de** or **d'**. Remember, adjectives that usually come before the noun include **beau**, **joli**, **nouveau**, **vieux**, **bon**, **mauvais**, **grand**, and **petit.**

Tu portes **de** nouvelles chaussures?    *Are you wearing new shoes?*

However, when an adjective preceding a noun is a part of that noun, **des** does not become **de** or **d'**.

Je voudrais **des** petits pois.    *I would like (some) peas.*

---

### 16 La rentrée  2.1, 2.2

*Dites que les élèves de Mme Gaillot achètent de nouvelles choses pour l'année scolaire.*

**MODÈLE**    Les élèves achètent de **nouveaux stylos.**

**Answers** _____

**16**

1. Les élèves achètent de nouvelles imprimantes.
2. Les élèves achètent de nouveaux livres.
3. Les élèves achètent de nouveaux dictionnaires.
4. Les élèves achètent de nouvelles trousses.
5. Les élèves achètent de nouveaux cahiers.
6. Les élèves achètent de nouvelles clés USB.
7. Les élèves achètent de nouveaux ordinateurs.
8. Les élèves achètent de nouveaux taille-crayons.

**Reference Desk**

Review the formation of the irregular adjectives **nouveau** and **vieux** before doing **Activités 16, 17,** and **18.**

**Communication**

**Interpersonal: Paired Practice**

Have students create a dialogue about an imaginary house that one is giving a tour of to the other, using four examples of **de** + plural adjective, for example, **Nous avons de vieux tapis!**

---

**Differentiated Learning**
**Adapt/Accelerate**
Brainstorm a list of adjectives that students know. In another column, solicit about 20 different plural nouns. Have students form sentences using **de** and placing the adjectives in the proper position relative to the noun.

**Multiple Intelligences**
**Verbal-Linguistic**
Ask students to write a paragraph using **de** + plural adjective + plural noun. Tell them they have a shop and must describe what they sell in their shop, using each of the BAGS adjectives that they know. Ask them to be creative and/or funny in choosing what they sell, for example, **Dans mon magasin, je vends de jeunes girafes.** Then have them share their paragraphs in groups of four and select the most original sentences to read to the class.

**17**

1. Ce sont de vieux ponts à Paris.
2. Ce sont de nouvelles statues à Paris.
3. Ce sont de vieux hôtels à Paris.
4. Ce sont de nouveaux monuments à Paris.
5. Ce sont de vieilles gares à Paris.
6. Ce sont de nouveaux musées à Paris.

## Expansion

Using the images in **Activité 17** as a model, challenge students to find similar pairings of places in their area that are new or young/old, handsome/pretty, good/bad, or big/small (using **nouveau**, **jeune**, **vieux**, **beau**, **joli**, **bon**, **mauvais**, **grand**, and **petit**) and then make an online display or post in class. Point to different pairings and ask students to describe them with the formula **ce sont de** + plural adjective + noun. Use some phrases in **dictées** for writing practice and listening comprehension.

**17** À Paris   2.1, 2.2

*Dites si les édifices à Paris sont nouveaux ou vieux.*

**MODÈLE** Ce sont de <u>nouveaux restaurants</u> à Paris.

1.

2.    3.    4.

5.

6.

**Essential Instruction**

1. Before doing **Activité 17**, review with students the various structures shown in the pictures. See if they remember their names, such as **le Pont Alexandre III**, **la Grande Arche de la Défense**, and so forth.
2. Play a location game like "Where's Waldo?" asking students to point to the items in the illustration they will need to locate in order to do **Activité 18**.

**18** *Possible answers:*
1. Il y a de vieilles usines dans la ville.
2. Il y a de grands pandas dans le zoo.
3. Il y a des petites voitures électriques dans la ville.
4. Il y a de grands gorilles dans le zoo.
5. Il y a de nouveaux espaces sauvages dans la ville.
6. Il y a de nouveaux immeubles dans la ville.

**18 Une ville verte**  **2.1, 2.2**

*Utilisez les adjectifs **grand**, **petit**, **nouveau**, et **vieux** pour décrire les animaux et les choses dans cette ville verte.*

| MODÈLE | les écoles |
|--------|-----------|
| | **Il y a de grands panneaux solaires sur les écoles.** |

vieux

nouveau

grand

petit

1. les usines
2. les pandas
3. les voitures électriques
4. les gorilles
5. les espaces sauvages
6. les immeubles

### Expansion

Project images from previous exercises that students are familiar with and ask them to describe the pairings with plural adjectives. Then insert some new images that one could also describe with the BAGS adjectives. Randomly select students to describe them.

---

**Differentiated Learning**
**Decelerate**
These students would benefit by writing **Activités 17** and **18** before doing them orally.

**Learning Styles**
**Visual Learners**
Have students draw or find a picture of a store or town that has a number of familiar items or places in it for which they could create their own version of **Activité 18**.

**Multiple Intelligences**
**Bodily-Kinesthetic**
Print out and cut up the pictures in **Activité 17**. Have students arrange them on a poster board with their sentences, or use them as flash cards with a partner who will create sentences using a BAGS adjective.

**Answers** _____

**19** *Answers will vary.*

**20** *Posters will vary.*

### Reference Desk

Students may wish to learn about the explorer, inventor, scientist, and ecologist Jacques-Yves Cousteau (1910–1997) and his efforts to save the seas.

#### Blended Instruction
Consider using blended instruction, a combination of in-class learning and computer-mediated instruction or learning opportunities. Ask students to complete activities on the computer, using their cell or smartphone, or other emerging electronic technology. This will allow students to hone their tech skills and become more independent learners. Schedule routine Internet and e-book learning in class and in the lab.

### Critical Thinking

#### Synthesis
Have groups make a giant paw shape on a large piece of paper. On one finger/claw section of the paw, mark the current month or date. Have students write some statistics about their carbon footprint in this area of the illustration. In a month's time, ask the students if they have made any changes to their carbon footprint. Mark the new date on another section of the paw and have students note the changes they have reported. Check in later to see if students' carbon footprints have changed.

# À vous la parole

## Communiquez!

**Question centrale**
How do people stay healthy and maintain a healthy environment?

### 19 Calculez votre empreinte écologique (*carbon footprint*).

**1.3, 2.1, 2.2, 5.1**

**Interpretive Communication**

Complete the quiz below about your family's carbon footprint. Then assess your family's rating.

| | oui | non |
|---|---|---|
| 1. Nous recyclons les boîtes, les bouteilles, et le papier. | | |
| 2. Nous circulons dans une voiture hybride ou électrique. | | |
| 3. Nous utilisons les transports en commun. | | |
| 4. Nous travaillons pour sauver les animaux en voie de disparition. | | |
| 5. Nous travaillons pour sauvegarder les espaces sauvages. | | |
| 6. Nous utilisons des ampoules (*light bulbs*) CFL. | | |
| 7. Nous ne voyageons pas en avion ou nous prenons l'avion une fois par an. | | |
| 8. Nous avons des panneaux solaires sur le toit. | | |
| 9. Nous mangeons beaucoup de fruits et de légumes. | | |
| 10. Nous ne mangeons pas beaucoup de bœuf. | | |

**Les résultats:**

Des réponses oui de 7/10 à 10/10: **Bravo! Vous êtes une famille écolo!**

Des réponses oui de 4/10 à 6/10: **Bien! Vous êtes sur le chemin écolo!**

Des réponses oui de 0/10 à 3/10: **Attention! Vous avez du progrès à faire pour devenir une famille écolo!**

## Communiquez!

### 20 Des affiches écologiques

**1.3**

**Presentational Communication**

Working in small groups, make a poster for other French classes, telling them what they can do to preserve the environment and be better stewards of the Earth. Your poster could be part of an Earth Day celebration with songs, dances, poems, etc.

### Essential Instruction

1. Discuss the survey items in **Activité 19** before students ask their family about their carbon footprint. Make sharing about activity results optional.

2. For **Activité 20**, consider posting the **affiches** throughout the school or having students present them at an Earth Day celebration.

3. Create a rubric for **Activité 21** detailing your expectations for content, vocabulary, length, and structures to include. Brainstorm a list of potential topics and additional French search words.

4. After students read aloud the paragraph about tigers in **Activité 22** with a partner, review the three questions as a class.

 Communiquez!

## 21 Une brochure écolo

 1.3

**Presentational Communication**

Design a three-fold brochure about any aspect of environmental protection that interests you. You might state some facts about your topic to raise people's awareness or write a list of steps to become more **écolo**. If you choose the latter, you might also find it useful to review the **Stratégie communicative** in **Leçon B** before you begin writing.

 **Search words: paris vélib'**

 Communiquez!

## 22 Protégez les tigres!

 1.2, 2.1, 2.2

**Interpretive Communication**

Read the information about tigers and answer these questions.

1. What does the number 6.000 refer to in this passage?
   A. There are currently 6,000 tigers left in the world.
   B. Ten years ago there were 6,000 tigers.
   C. 95% of 6,000 tigers still exist.
2. How many tigers currently exist, according to this article?
   A. 25
   B. 3,200
   C. 95
3. How many species of tiger are extinct?
   A. 4–5
   B. 2–3
   C. 3–4

Le nombre de tigres a diminué de 95% depuis cinquante-cinq ans. Aujourd'hui, il ne reste que 3.200 tigres sauvages sur 6.000 il y a dix ans. C'est une population très faible qui tient en compte la disparition de trois à quatre espèces de tigres.

### Expansion

Discuss how **écolo** students consider themselves. How about their school or community? Have things changed in the last few years as students have grown up and become more aware of the environment? What steps do your students feel they could and should take in the future to reduce their carbon footprint or that of their family, school, or community? Students may wish to research environmental organizations that they admire or would like to support. Check out the French or francophone sites of various environmental organizations. (World Wildlife Fund, National Geographic, Jane Goodall's Roots and Shoots) Which ones are experiencing success? What image (animal, plant, or other) would the class adopt as their **écolo** symbol? Compare with the choice of other classes.

### Differentiated Learning
**Decelerate**

Consider assigning **Activité 20** or **21** as an extra-credit project. Provide a list of sentences and vocabulary for students to include in these projects. Provide the beginning of sentences for students to complete for a brief overview of their poster or brochure.

### Multiple Intelligences
**Logical-Mathematical**

Have students calculate and present the potential energy and financial savings for their family if they use **ampoules CFL** (compact fluorescent) or **une voiture hybride**.

### Naturalistic

Some students may enjoy researching online one or more of the items mentioned in **Activité 19**. Have them focus on the local or national scene, or a francophone country. Students could make a poster or display in French and English to promote ecological practices in your school.

# Lecture thématique

## L'homme rompu

### Rencontre avec l'auteur  1.2, 2.1, 2.2

Écrivain et poète franco-marocain, **Tahar Ben Jelloun** (1944– ) est né à Fez, au Maroc. Il a étudié la philosophie et la psychologie. En 1985, il a publié *L'enfant de sable* et en 1987, *La nuit sacrée*—deux grands succès. Dans ses livres, il parle de la dignité humaine et du racisme. Vous allez lire un extrait de *L'homme rompu (The Broken Man)*. Dans cet extrait, Mourad, un fonctionnaire (*civil servant*) honnête fait de nouvelles résolutions. Quelle sorte d'homme est-ce qu'il veut devenir?

### Pré-lecture  2.1, 2.2

Si vous pouviez changer une chose dans votre vie, qu'est-ce que vous changeriez? (*If you could change one thing in your life, what would it be?*)

### Stratégie de lecture  2.1, 2.2

**Characterization and Inference**

**Characterization** is the act of creating or describing a character. **Inference** is reading between the lines to draw conclusions based on evidence. As you go through the text, draw conclusions about the narrator's character based on what you read. In the left-hand column, write what you infer about how he is now. In the right-hand column, note how he would like to be. An example has been done for you.

| How the narrator is now | How the narrator would like to be |
|---|---|
| 1. He walks with his head down, hunched over, and his hands don't move. | He wants to be more confident and energetic, which indicates that he does not currently see himself as a powerful man of action. |
| 2. | |
| 3. | |
| 4. | |
| 5. | |
| 6. | |
| 7. | |

## Outils de lecture  2.1, 2.2

### Using Text Organization and Making a Prediction

Writers may organize events or information in their text chronologically, using words like **d'abord, ensuite,** and **enfin**; writers may also put events in random order, or, they may use detail to show the importance of an event. How does Ben Jelloun organize this selection? Notice the structure of the text. Where is there more detail? Where is there less? How does the organization help you read the selection? How successful do you think the narrator will be in changing his life? Do you think he will change everything on his list?

  1.2, 2.1, 2.2

Je prends un bloc-notes* tout neuf et inscris* sur la première page quelques décisions:

À partir de ce jour, je décide de changer. Je m'arrête* et me pose la question: "Comment un homme de quarante ans peut-il encore changer? Tu sais bien que c'est impossible. On change quand on est jeune, quand on se cherche*, on ne change pas à cet âge-là." (...) Mais changer quoi? Avant toute chose ma manière de marcher. Il faut absolument que je marche la tête haute, le dos droit et les mains en mouvement. (...)

Je décide aussi de cesser de fumer*. J'attends le Ramadan* pour cesser de m'empoisonner les poumons*.

Je ne regarderai plus la télévision. À la place je lirai*, j'écouterai de la musique. (...)

Je ne passerai plus le week-end à la maison. J'emmènerai* ma famille à la mer* ou à la montagne. Il faut vivre*. (...)

Manger lentement*. (Ne plus* manger entre les repas.)

Faire du sport (de la gymnastique ou du vélo).

Tenir* un journal.

**Pendant la lecture**
1. Le narrateur veut marcher comment?

**Pendant la lecture**
2. Pourquoi veut-il cesser de fumer pendant Ramadan?

**Pendant la lecture**
3. Il veut changer aussi les vies de quelles autres personnes?

---

**un bloc-notes** *cahier;* **inscris** *write;* **m'arrête** *stop;* **se cherche** *is finding oneself;* **cesser de fumer** *to stop smoking;* **le Ramadan** *ninth month of the Islamic calendar when faithful Muslims fast;* **poumons** *lungs;* **lirai** *will read;* **emmènerai** *will take;* **la mer** *sea;* **vivre** *to live;* **lentement** *slowly;* **Ne plus** *No longer;* **tenir** *to keep*

## Answers

### Outils de lecture
The author lists facts from health to emotional and intellectual well-being. There is more detail given to the initial question. *Other answers will vary.*

### Pendant la lecture
1. Il veut marcher la tête haute.
2. Il ne veut pas s'empoisonner les poumons.
3. Il veut changer la vie de sa famille.

### Culture

**Practices: Activity**
Have a discussion with students about smoking in France and the perceptions of French and Americans concerning certain habits.

### Critical Thinking

**Synthesis**
Do Ben Jelloun's **bloc-notes** inspire your students? Discuss with them what inspires them to change, to better their character or their lives. Would they be willing to write a list of things to improve? Have students draw up individual lists of five to ten things they want to change in their personal life. Have students use infinitives (as Ben Jelloun did at the end of his list).

## Differentiated Learning
### Accelerate
Ask students to list the verbs in the reading and identify the tenses that they know. Although students will formally learn the **futur simple** in Level 2, explain the concept and point out the verbs in the reading.

## Multiple Intelligences
### Visual-Spatial
Use an online graphic organizer to help students structure the reading or ask them to draw and label two pictures of the character **Mourad**—one of him **à 40 ans** and another of him **dans l'avenir**.

### Special Needs Students
### Linguistically Challenged
Ask partners to make a list of all cognates.

## Post-lecture  2.1

Quel changement le narrateur a-t-il déjà commencé?

*L'homme assis* ou *L'architecte*, 1914. Roger de La Fresnaye.
Musée National d'Art Moderne, Centre Pompidou, Paris, France.

## Le monde visuel  3.1, 3.2

Roger de La Fresnaye (1885–1925) peint (*paints*) dans le style cubiste. Le Cubisme est un mouvement artistique où les personnes et les objets deviennent fragmentés. Fresnaye utilise les formes géométriques pour former l'homme et l'arrière-plan (*background*) dans ce tableau. Quelles formes géométriques est-ce que vous observez? L'artiste utilise-t-il les couleurs sombres (*dark*) ou brillantes? Qu'est-ce qu'on sait de cet homme assis (*seated*)?

### 23 Activités d'expansion  1.3, 2.1

1. Écrivez un paragraphe qui décrit le narrateur aujourd'hui et comment il voudrait changer dans l'avenir (*future*). Servez-vous (*use*) des informations dans votre grille.
2. Faites une grille avec deux colonnes, une pour les bonnes activités et l'autre pour les mauvaises. Écrivez les expressions ci-dessous dans la colonne appropriée.

> marcher droit / tenir un journal / fumer / lire / manger entre les repas
>
> manger lentement / faire du sport / quitter la ville le weekend

3. Dites si chaque phrase est un fait (*fact*) ou une opinion.
   A. On change quand on est jeune.
   B. Il vaut mieux lire que regarder la télévision.
   C. Faire du sport est bon pour la santé.
   D. Il vaut mieux aller à la mer que rester à la maison.
   E. Fumer empoisonne les poumons.
4. Faites une résolution pour votre vie (*life*). Nommez une chose que vous pouvez faire aujourd'hui, une chose que vous pouvez faire ce mois, et plusieurs choses que vous pouvez faire cette année.

**Essential Instruction**

1. Review the answer to the **Post-lecture** question.
2. If possible, find online some examples of Roger de La Fresnaye's paintings. Ask students for their reaction and opinion of his work. Then read **Le monde visuel**. Discuss new vocabulary and briefly explain the Cubist art movement.
3. Have groups of four work together to decode the meaning of the cartoon, jotting down vocabulary questions they have. Discuss any questions. Have them role-play the cartoon. Ask their opinions of each of the characters. What predictions can they make about what will happen in subsequent episodes? Ask for a volunteer group to present the episode to the class.

## Les copains d'abord

Here is the translation for **Les copains d'abord**:

A = Antoine
F = Florence
MA = Marie-Alix
M = Mathéo

A: Oh I love the feel of the wind blowing…. MA: Me too, but you need to recycle your plastic bottle, don't be lazy! A: All right, I'll pick up my bottle and recycle it… MA: Wait, Flo stopped. Are you coming? Are you hurt? F: I've had enough, my back hurts. I'm out of breath! A: OK let's take a break, but not for long, please. MA: Hey, we could go check out the sporting goods…. F: So, no one is waiting for me? Nice, I hurt everywhere, I have the chills, I might have a fever! M: Florence! Are you OK? You don't look so good…. F: I'm just fine, thanks. And you? M: Do you need help? F: Yes, I hate sports. M: You need to push with your left leg. F: Ouch, my leg hurts! M: Sorry, here, give me your hand…. F: My arms hurt! M: I'd better carry you…. F: OK. M: You know, doing sports is good for you… F: I just don't like biking, that's all. M: Maybe I can help you; you're very beautiful…. F: You're very strong…. M: I love you. F: I love you too. A: Ah, look at these two lovebirds! MA: OK. Drop the **Vélib'** (bike share). Want to go roller-blading?

List of slang and idiomatic expressions:
**flemmard:** *lazy;* **en avoir marre:** *to be fed up;* **être à bout de souffle:** *to be out of breath;* **les oiseaux qui se bécotent:** *lovebirds;* **aïe:** *ouch*

## Differentiated Learning
### Accelerate
Assign the first two activities of the **Activités d'expansion** as homework, then ask students to share in small groups.

## Special Needs Students
### Dyslexia
Some students may find the layout of the dialogue in the cartoon challenging to follow. You may want to rewrite it in a more linear dialogue form, so they can better determine the order of the conversation. Consider also using a larger font.

# T'es branché?

## Projets finaux

### Ⓐ Connexions par internet  1.3, 2.1

**Sciences de la vie et de la terre**

Research and find images of the USDA's new "My Plate" graphic that replaces the food pyramid. Make a graphic similar to the one on the USDA's web site, but with the labels in French. Write five sentences in French stating what one must eat for each food group. For example: **Il faut manger du poulet, du porc, ou du bœuf….**

🔍 **Search words: usda my plate**

### Ⓑ Communautés en ligne  1.1, 1.3, 2.1

**Les habitudes alimentaires**

Working in groups, design a survey with five questions in French to find out about the eating habits of ten Francophone teens. (A few examples follow for you.) Give your survey to students at a school in a Francophone country that your teacher will help you find. After the survey is returned to you, report the results to your class. Be sure to state what the students can do to keep in better shape.

Sample questions:
1. Vous prenez combien de repas par jour?
2. Est-ce que vous mangez rapidement?
3. Est-ce que vous mangez entre les repas?
4. Combien de fois par jour est-ce que vous prenez un coca ou une limonade?
5. Combien de fruits est-ce que vous mangez par jour?
6. Combien de portions de légumes est-ce que vous prenez?
7. Est-ce que vous faites des promenades?
8. Est-ce que vous faites du sport?

Possible report:
**Six élèves canadiens sur dix prennent deux repas par jour, quatre sur dix prennent un repas. Ces élèves peuvent être en forme s'ils prennent trois repas par jour….**

**Essential Instruction**

1. Have students work with a partner to research the "MyPlate" graphic in **Activité A**.
2. Divide students into groups to complete **Activité C** or **Activité D**. Distribute copies of the graphic organizer, which can be found in the **Copy Masters** supplement, to complete **Activité D**.

**C** Passez à l'action!  1.1, 1.3, 2.2

**Un plan pour la classe**

Join one of two groups in class: one that wants to brainstorm ways to keep physically healthy, and one that wants to brainstorm things you can do to preserve the environment. Develop a statement about your group's beliefs and/or actions you want to take and put them on a poster, in a PowerPoint™ presentation, or on a web page.

**D** Faisons le point! 3.1, 3.2, 4.2

Make a diagram like the one that follows and fill it in to demonstrate your understanding of how other cultures maintain a healthy lifestyle and environment. An example has been done for you.

Question centrale
**?**
How do people stay healthy and maintain a healthy environment?

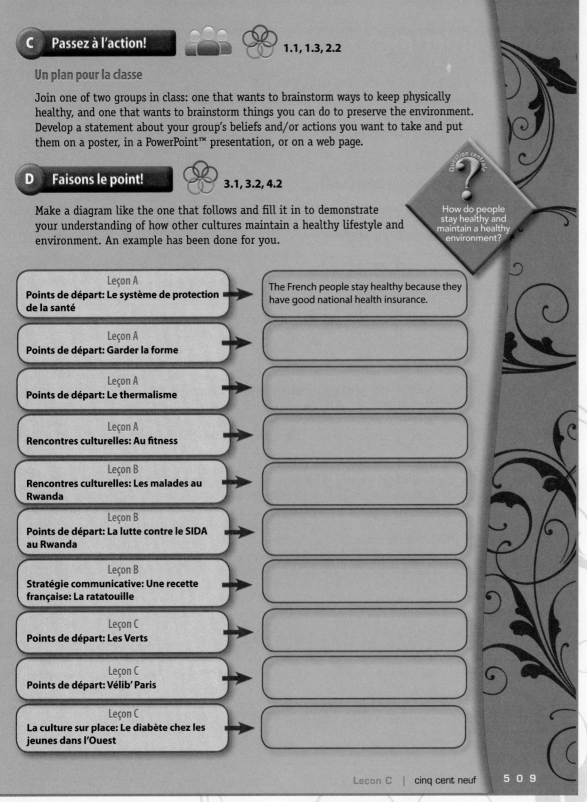

| Leçon A **Points de départ: Le système de protection de la santé** | → | The French people stay healthy because they have good national health insurance. |

Leçon A
**Points de départ: Garder la forme** →

Leçon A
**Points de départ: Le thermalisme** →

Leçon A
**Rencontres culturelles: Au fitness** →

Leçon B
**Rencontres culturelles: Les malades au Rwanda** →

Leçon B
**Points de départ: La lutte contre le SIDA au Rwanda** →

Leçon B
**Stratégie communicative: Une recette française: La ratatouille** →

Leçon C
**Points de départ: Les Verts** →

Leçon C
**Points de départ: Vélib' Paris** →

Leçon C
**La culture sur place: Le diabète chez les jeunes dans l'Ouest** →

Leçon C | cinq cent neuf | **5 0 9**

---

**Answers**

**C** *Presentations will vary.*

**D**

**Leçon A:** French people stay healthy because they have good national health insurance.

**Leçon A:** The **manger-bouger** program provides tips on how to stay healthy.

**Leçon A:.** Thermal cures help with illnesses like arthritis.

**Leçon A:** French people stay healthy by going to their health clubs and participating in exercise programs.

**Leçon B:** Rwandans who are ill benefit from the visits of home health workers.

**Leçon B:.** Rwandans stay healthy due to programs that fight AIDS.

**Leçon B:** The French stay healthy by eating healthy dishes like ratatouille, which is made with fresh vegetables.

**Leçon C:** The French maintain a healthy environment due to the influence of the Green Party which pushes for environmentally-friendly changes in social and political policies.

**Leçon C:** The French maintain a healthy environment and personal health by using bike rental programs.

**Leçon C:** Countries like France, Belgium, Switzerland, and Luxemburg promote the health of young people by providing important information about diseases such as diabetes.

**Reference Desk**

Review student answers to **La Question centrale:** How do people stay healthy and maintain a healthy environment? What have students learned about themselves, their school and community, and the world at large from this **Unité**?

---

**Differentiated Learning**

**Adapt**
Have students research the French **pyramide alimentaire** and compare to the American food pyramid called "MyPlate."

**Accelerate**
Ask students to create the survey in **Activité B**, modifying the sample questions and adding a few of their own as they wish. If they have access to students from francophone countries during the year, they could post the survey online.

**Multiple Intelligences**

**Bodily-Kinesthetic/Musical-Rhythmic**
Have students create and present a commercial with music and/or dance that illustrates the French food pyramid or the American "MyPlate."

**Intrapersonal**
For **Activité B**, instead of posing the sample survey questions to students from francophone countries, have students write personal answers to the questions and share them in groups afterwards.

## Answers

**A** Script can be found in the front pages of the Annotated Teacher's Edition.

1. V
2. F
3. V
4. V
5. F
6. V
7. V
8. F
9. V
10. F
11. F
12. F

**B** *Conversations will vary.*

**C** *Comparisons will vary.*

# Évaluation

**A** **Évaluation de compréhension auditive**   **1.2**

Number from 1–12 on your paper. Then listen to the conversation between Anissa and Michel. Finally, indicate if each statement you hear is **vrai** (**V**) or **faux** (**F**).

**B** **Évaluation orale**   **1.1**

With a partner, play the roles of a teen with a problem and his or her friend. The teen with a problem describes what's wrong. Then the friend offers a solution to the problem, saying what it is necessary to do.

**C** **Évaluation culturelle**  **1.3, 3.1, 3.2, 4.2**

In this activity, you will compare Francophone cultures with American culture. You may need to do some additional research on American culture.

1. **La sécu**
   Explain the differences between French national health insurance and medical insurance programs in the United States. Begin by discussing with a parent, grandparent, or guardian what they know about health insurance in the United States, Medicare, Medicaid, and Veterans hospitals.

2. **Être en forme**
   Compare French and American attitudes about how to maintain a healthy lifestyle. For example, what differences are there between French and Americans with regard to their eating, exercise, and relaxation habits?

3. **Le SIDA**
   Compare the incidence and treatment of **le SIDA** in Rwanda and the United States. How many people have the disease in each country? What treatment programs are available in each country for those with the disease? What initiatives are working?

4. **L'environnement**
   Describe some of the efforts the French have made to protect the planet. What kinds of efforts have been made in your region? By your government? What does your family do to protect the environment? What have you done personally?

5. **Les Verts**
   Research the history of the American green party and what it stands for. Compare these to the French party **Les Verts**. Share five facts that you learn.

6. **La souris verte**
   What kind of background do you have in environmental studies? Do you have a way to make your opinions known like French teens do with the online magazine **La souris verte**? How can young people in the United States get involved in environmental causes? What is a forum for French teens who are interested in preserving the environment?

## Essential Instruction

1. Have students call out the answers as they listen to **Activité A**.
2. Consider assigning **Activité B** or **E** and have students record their dialogue. Use this as the oral assessment for the **Unité**.
3. Time permitting, have partners choose one topic in **Activité C** to research. They can write a report for you and share their findings with another pair during class.
4. Use **Activité D** to gauge how well students have learned the material from this **Unité**. Provide a clear rubric and expectations about vocabulary, structures, etc. that they should integrate into their writing.

**D Évaluation écrite** 2.1, 5.1

Write a letter to your cousin Ryan, who is studying in Montreal. Respond to his letter below, giving him advice on how to live a healthier lifestyle.

Bonjour de Montréal!

Je ne vais pas bien. Je suis toujours fatigué. Je ne prends pas le petit déjeuner parce que mon premier cours est à 9h00. Le weekend je vais à beaucoup de fêtes. J'étudie de minuit à 4h00. Je peux dormir cinq heures par nuit. Je prends toujours le métro. Je ne vais pas au fitness. Je ne fais pas de sport. Maintenant je suis fatigué, j'ai mal à la gorge, et j'ai de la fièvre. Qu'est-ce que tu me conseilles? Et toi, tu vas bien?

Ton cousin,
Ryan

  **E Évaluation visuelle** 1.1, 2.1

With a partner, role-play a conversation between the teens in the illustrations. Talk about how you are feeling and your symptoms. Give advice to your partner about what he or she should or should not do to feel better.

Élève 1

Élève 2

 **F Évaluation compréhensive** 1.3, 2.1, 2.2

You work for a health care organization. Create a storyboard with six frames. Write captions for each frame that present advice on how to stay healthy. Include what to do in the case of certain symptoms and the environmental problems that can contribute to health issues. Share your storyboard with a group of classmates.

Answers _____

**D** *Letters will vary.*

**E** *Conversations will vary.*

**F** *Conversations will vary.*

**Expansion**

Consider having students film a role-play for the **Évaluation orale**. Provide a rubric that includes guidelines about the number of structures, functions, and vocabulary to use from the **Unité**. Encourage students to use props and memorize the dialogue.

**Differentiated Learning**
**Accelerate**
Have these students do items 1-6 in **Activité C** with a partner.

**Special Needs Students**
**Linguistically Challenged**
Consider creating shorter alternative oral and written evaluations. Design an oral evaluation with clear guidelines, for example requiring students to come up with and say six sentences about their general health and dietary habits using a set number of vocabulary expressions. As a written assessment, offer the option of writing a short dialogue (ten complete sentences) between a patient and a doctor. Provide a rubric with specific expectations and the opportunity for self-evaluation.

# Vocabulaire de l'Unité 9  1.2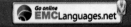

**à: à mon avis** in my opinion *B*; **à pied** on foot *C*; **à vélo** by bike *C*

un **accompagnateur, une accompagnatrice** home health worker *B*

l' **aérobic (m.)** aerobics *A*

les **antirétroviraux (m.)** antiretroviral drugs *B*

**arrêter** to stop *C*

**avoir: avoir bonne mine** to look healthy *B*; **avoir mauvaise mine** to look sick *B*

**biologique** organic *C*

**bouger** to move *A*

**causer** to cause *C*

**ce: ce que** what *C*

**chimique** chemical *C*

**circuler** to drive, to get around *C*

**combattre** to fight *C*

**conseiller** to advise *B*

**continuer** to continue *C*

le **corps** body *A*

une **cure** spa treatment *A*

**décontracté(e)** relaxed *A*

un **devoir** assignment *B*

le **dioxyde de carbone** carbon dioxide *C*

l' **effet (m.)** effect *C*; **l'effet de serre** greenhouse effect *C*

**électrique** electric *C*

**éliminer** to eliminate *C*

l' **émission (f.)** television program *B*

en **en aluminium, plastique** made of aluminium, plastic *C*

l' **énergie (f.)** energy *C*; **l'énergie nucléaire** nuclear energy *C*; **l'énergie solaire** solar energy *C*

s' **engager** to commit to *C*

l' **engrais (m.)** fertilizer *C*

l' **environnement (m.)** environment *C*

une **éolienne** wind turbine *C*

un **espace** area *C*

**être: être au courant** to be informed, to know *C*; **être en (bonne, mauvaise) forme** to be in (good, bad) shape *B*; **être vert** to be environmentally friendly *C*

**faire: faire marcher** to make (something) work *C*

**falloir** to be necessary, to have to *A*

la **figure** face *A*

le **fitness** health club, gym *A*

**géant(e)** giant *C*

**installer** to install *C*

l' **instant (m.)** moment *C*; **pour l'instant** for the moment *C*

**laisser** to leave, to let *B*

un(e) **malade** sick person *B*

une **maladie** illness *B*

**marcher** to walk *A*

la **marée** tide *C*; **marée noire** oil slick *C*

se **mettre: mets-toi** set yourself down *B*

la **montagne** mountain *C*

**mort(e)** dead *B*

**nucléaire** nuclear *C*

un **océan** ocean *C*

**oh là là** oh dear, oh no, wow *A*

**ouille** ouch *A*

un **panneau: panneau solaire** solar panel *C*

**partout** everywhere *A*

**payer** to pay *C*

un **payeur, une payeuse** someone who pays *C*

une **personne** person *B*

**persuadé(e)** persuaded *C*

le **pétrole** petroleum *C*

la **planète** planet *C*

**polluant(e)** polluting *C*

**polluer** to pollute *C*

un **pollueur, une pollueuse** polluter *C*

la **pollution** pollution *C*

**pourrais: tu pourrais** you could *C*

**presque** nearly *B*

**profiter de** to benefit from *A*; **tu profiterais de** you would benefit from *A*

**protéger** to protect *C*

**quitter** to leave *A*

la **radiation** radiation *C*

**réchauffer** to heat up *C*

**recycler** to recycle *C*

**remplacer** to replace *C*

un **reportage** news report *B*

une **résolution** resolution *C*

**respiratoire** respiratory *C*

le **Rwanda** Rwanda *B*

**sais: tu sais** you know *B*

**sauvage** wild *C*

**sauvegarder** to protect *C*

le **SIDA** AIDS *B*

le **step** step aerobics *A*

**survivre** to survive *B*

le **thème** topic *C*

**thermal(e)** hydrotherapeutic *A*

le **toit** roof *C*

une **usine** factory *C*

une **voie** path *C*; **les animaux (m.) en voie de disparition** endangered species *C*

une **voiture** car *C*; **voiture électrique** electric car *C*; **voiture hybride** hybrid car *C*

le **yoga** yoga *A*

Avoir mal + (body part) see p. 471
Endangered species… see p. 486
Illnesses… see p. 471
Parts of the body… see p. 460
Parts of the face… see p. 460

# Unité
# 10 Les grandes vacances

*Rendez-vous à Nice!*
**Épisode 10:**
*La grande fête*

Go online
**EMC**Languages.net

513

## Reference Desk

1. Ask students how often they travel. How do vacations differ depending on the season, goals, means, etc.? Does it matter if vacations are long or short?
2. Discuss Lamartine's words. What is a "complete man"? How does travel "complete" a person? Is it a contradiction in terms to say "complete" and "transform twenty times"?
3. Ask if students can identify the city and season pictured on this page. What cities or regions have your students visited in Canada? Why might Quebec have been chosen as the city to be illustrated here? What other large North American French-speaking city do your students know of?
4. Tell students to use an article when referring to the province **le Québec**. Ask what the difference is between these phrases: **Je vais au Québec.** and **Je vais à Québec.** (The first is the province; the second is the city.)

## Expansion

Have students find Quebec on the classroom wall map. Point out the location of Quebec city and the territorial extent of Quebec province.

## Citation

"Il n'y a d'homme plus complet que celui qui a beaucoup voyagé, qui a changé vingt fois la forme de sa pensée et de sa vie."

**There is no man more complete than the one who has traveled a lot, who has changed his thinking and his lifestyle twenty times.**

—Alphonse de Lamartine, poète romantique français

## À savoir

The people of France and visitors to the country take 80 million train trips a year.

### Essential Instruction

1. Read the **Question centrale** as students look at the page spread. Ask if anyone has been to Quebec or Switzerland. Ask where they have traveled, including experiences closer to home, such as summer (day) camp or exploring a different town.

2. Have small groups discuss whether or not they agree with the **Citation** based on their own travel experiences. Can they cite specific examples of how their thoughts, impressions, and assumptions about a place or people change after a travel experience?

3. Review the **Contrat de l'élève**.

4. Show the relevant video clip from *Rendez-vous à Nice!*, Episode 10, and discuss the related question as a class.

# Unité 10
# Les grandes vacances

**RESOURCES**

*Rendez-vous à Nice!*
**Episode 10**

Answers _____

The answer to the video question is C.

### Question centrale

**?**

How do travel experiences shape our worldview?

Go online
**EMC**Languages.net

**Why are Thomas and Chadia sad?**
A. They must stop seeing each other.
B. Thomas is moving to Paris.
C. Chadia is leaving for the summer.

What is the name of this square in Montreal?

## Contrat de l'élève

**Leçon A  I will be able to:**

>> say where places are located.

>> talk about Quebec and Montreal.

>> use prepositions before cities, countries, and continents.

**Leçon B  I will be able to:**

>> remind people and wish them a good trip.

>> talk about French departments and regions, and French castles.

>> use more negative expressions.

**Leçon C  I will be able to:**

>> give directions.

>> talk about Switzerland, Geneva, and the Red Cross.

>> say that people and things are the best, prettiest, oldest, etc.

### Reference Desk

1. Ask students to discuss the title **Les grandes vacances**. Why might vacation be called "big" or "great" in French? Point out that **vacances** is a plural (fem.) noun.

2. Students will be able to answer the culture question after reading **Points de départ** in **Leçon A**. This square is the historic city center. It is surrounded by the **Séminaire de Saint-Sulpice** (earliest construction dates back to 1684), Notre-Dame Basilica (completed in the 1820s; replaced the 17th-century church), the Bank of Montreal head office, two early 20th-century skyscrapers, and a modernist office tower built in the 1960s. In the center of the square is a monument to Montreal's founder, Paul de Chomedey de Maisonneuve. The work of sculptor Louis-Philippe Hébert, it portrays Maisonneuve surrounded by Charles Lemoyne, Lambert Closse, Jeanne Mance, and an Iroquois brave.

### Game

**Où vas-tu?**
Have students stand or sit in a circle. Toss a koosh ball to one student and ask, **"Où est-ce tu vas en vacances?"** The student answers with the present of **aller à** with a city. Challenge students to use the names of places they have learned. That student then tosses the ball to a classmate and asks the same question. For variety, have students answer with **prendre les vacances**. Note that while most cities retain their own name, some have a French version such as **Londres**, **La Nouvelle-Orléans**, etc.

## Differentiated Learning
### Adapt
Many cities, regions, and countries have extensive websites that include video and photos featuring key natural and man-made tourist attractions. Challenge students to find an online presentation of the cities of Quebec, Montreal, and Geneva to stimulate interest in learning about these places.

### Decelerate
Help students anticipate what they will learn as you review the **Contrat de l'élève** with them. Define terms such as prepositions and negative expressions. Ask pairs to provide two examples of each grammar topic in English.

## Learning Styles
### Visual Learners
Have small groups discuss the advantages and disadvantages of travel and create a visual that illustrates the results of their reflection.

## Connections

### Geography

Ask students to point out places they have visited in Canada. Where are the two Quebecs? How would they compare the size of Canadian territory to American? Ask students where they would like to go in Canada. Why is the province of Quebec singled out in orange on this map? (It is the predominantly French portion of Canada, whereas the rest of Canada became predominantly English-speaking.) Discuss what American states are in closest proximity to French Canada. How many U.S. states border Canada? What influence might the proximity of the two cultures have had on one another?

# Leçon A

# Vocabulaire actif

## Le Québec 🎧 ◉ 1.2

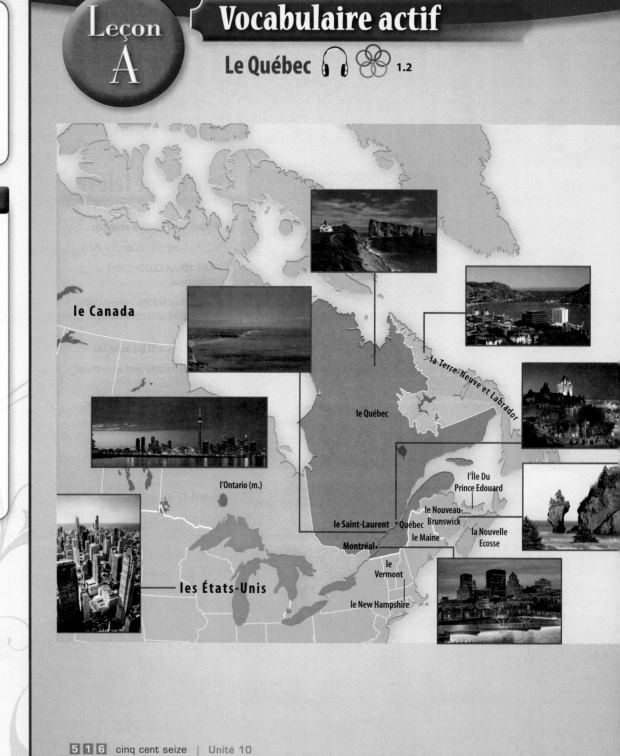

le Canada

la Terre-Neuve et Labrador

le Québec

l'Ontario (m.)

le Saint-Laurent — Québec

Montréal

le Nouveau-Brunswick

l'Île Du Prince Edouard

le Maine

la Nouvelle Ecosse

le Vermont

les États-Unis

le New Hampshire

## Essential Instruction

1. Ask students to scan the vocabulary and identify any cognates. Play the audio for the **Vocabulaire actif** and **Pour la conversation** and have students repeat several times.

2. Provide the English translation of the **devise** (*motto*) of provincial Quebec that figures on the license plate (*I remember*). Offer bonus points to students who research and share the significance of the motto. (Although there are many stories about the origin, most agree that it is a declaration of the French Canadians remembering the glories, misfortunes, and lessons of its past.)

le nord
le nord-ouest — le nord-est
l'ouest — l'est
le sud-ouest — le sud-est
le sud

La capitale: la ville de Québec.

Le drapeau du Québec.

Je me souviens

La devise du Québec: Je me souviens.

Les habitants: les Québécois, les Francanadiens.

## Pour la conversation

How do I tell someone where a place is located?

> **Québec est situé** au nord-est de Montréal.
> *Quebec is located northeast of Montreal.*

| Et si je voulais dire...? | |
|---|---|
| **à l'étranger** | *abroad* |
| **un circuit** | *organized tour* |
| **la frontière** | *border* |
| **un séjour linguistique** | *language study program* |
| **un(e) touriste** | *tourist* |
| **un(e) vacancier(ière)** | *vacationer* |

### Reference Desk

1. Ask students what decorative symbol is present in the Quebec flag and the license plate. (**fleur de lys**) Tell students a **fleur de lys** actually is a stylized version of a lily or iris plant. It has been associated with European royalty and heraldry for centuries, particularly French monarchy. The symbol is also associated with areas first settled by the French.

2. The **devise** of Quebec refers to what the French Canadians always remember/never forget: their homeland and being defeated in Quebec City on the Plains of Abraham by the English.

### Expansion

You may wish to have a **fleur de lys** treasure hunt for the duration of the lesson. Ask students to find **fleur de lys** symbols around town and in their everyday life such as on buildings, statuary, food packaging, clothing, etc., and bring in examples to add to your classroom display.

### Differentiated Learning
**Adapt**
To practice the compass directions, project a map of Canada and write pairs of cities on the board (**Montréal/Québec**). Ask students to form sentences, for example, **Montréal est situé au sud-ouest de Québec.**

### Multiple Intelligences
**Visual-Spatial**
Copy and distribute a map without place names. Have students complete the map with the vocabulary and personalize it by adding their own illustrations or images.

### Special Needs Students
**Visually Challenged**
Provide an enlarged copy of the map on p. 516 for visually challenged students, or consider giving them a map without the pictures.

## Answers

**❶**

1. Québec
2. Terre-Neuve-et-Labrador
3. Nouveau Brunswick
4. Maine
5. New Hampshire
6. Vermont
7. Ontario
8. Québec

**❷**

1. province
2. capitale
3. Francanadiens
4. drapeau
5. devise
6. ouest
7. nord
8. Nouveau-Brunswick
9. sud

**❸** Script can be found in the front pages of the Annotated Teacher's Edition.

1. D
2. E
3. A
4. F
5. C
6. B

### Reference Desk

The map mentioned in **Activité 1** is a blackline master that can be found in the **Copy Masters** ancillary.

### Communication

**Interpersonal: Paired Practice**

Have students use the formula **Je viens de + ville** to answer the question posed by a partner: **D'où viens-tu?** Using a map, students take turns pointing to a city (start with francophone cities around the world) and asking the question to a partner, who replies. Avoid city or country names that contain articles (such as **La Nouvelle-Orléans**).

---

**1** La plus grande province du Canada  **1.2, 1.3, 3.1**

*Lisez les paragraphes. Ensuite écrivez des légendes (captions) pour la carte que votre prof va vous donner.*

Quelle est la plus grande province du Canada? C'est le Québec. Au nord du Québec est la Terre-Neuve-et-Labrador. À l'est est le Nouveau-Brunswick. Au sud-est sont des états américains: le Maine, le New Hampshire, et le Vermont. À l'ouest est la province d'Ontario.

Dû à sa situation géographique, il fait très froid au Québec en hiver. On aime jouer au hockey sur glace, faire du patinage, et faire du ski.

La capitale de cette belle province s'appelle aussi Québec. On appelle ses habitants des Québécois ou des Francanadiens. Sa devise est "Je me souviens" (*I remember*).

**2** Le Québec  **2.1, 2.2**

*Complétez chaque phrase avec un mot de la liste.*

| | | | | |
|---|---|---|---|---|
| sud | drapeau | ouest | province | Nouveau-Brunswick |
| | Francanadiens | devise | capitale | nord |

1. Le Québec est une… canadienne.
2. Sa… est la ville de Québec.
3. Les personnes qui habitent au Québec s'appellent des….
4. Le… québécois est bleu et blanc.
5. "Je me souviens" est la… du Québec.
6. La province d'Ontario est à l'… du Québec.
7. La Terre-Neuve-et-Labrador est au… du Québec.
8. Le… est à l'est du Québec.
9. Les États-Unis sont le pays au… du Québec.

**3** Ils viennent d'où au Québec?

*Écrivez les numéros 1–6 sur votre papier. Ensuite, écoutez les descriptions et choisissez la lettre de la ville qui correspond à chaque description.*

 **2.1**

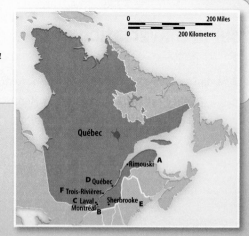

### Essential Instruction

1. Distribute the map for **Activité 1**. Project a completed map afterwards so students can check their answers.
2. Complete **Activité 2** as a class.
3. Have students call out the answers as they listen to **Activité 3**.
4. Assign **Activité 2** in pairs and ask for volunteers to present the dialogues in **Activité 4**.
5. For **Activité 5**, have students ask each other the **questions personnelles**. Present expressions to refer to inhabitants from various places in the United States, for example, **les Californiens, les New Yorkais, les Texans,** or more generally, **les gens du/de la/de l' + endroit** in order to expand on question 5. Explain the construction **tu te souviens de…**.

# Communiquez!

**4** **Dans ma ville**  **1.1, 2.1**

**Interpersonal Communication**

*À tour de rôle, demandez à votre partenaire si les endroits suivants sont près de chez toi.*

**MODÈLE** A: **Est-ce qu'il y a une poste près de chez toi?**
B: **Oui, il y a une poste au nord-est de chez moi.**

1. une école
2. un centre commercial
3. un cinéma
4. l'hôtel de ville
5. un restaurant
6. un hôtel
7. une banque
8. un supermarché

# Communiquez!

**5** **Questions personnelles**   **1.1, 2.1**

**Interpersonal Communication**

*Répondez aux questions.*

1. Est-ce que ton école est au nord, au sud, à l'est, ou à l'ouest de ta maison?
2. Es-tu allé(e) au Canada? au Québec? à Montréal? à Québec?
3. Est-ce qu'il y a des drapeaux dans ta salle de classe? De quel pays?
4. Est-ce que tu te souviens de l'été dernier? De ton anniversaire? Du dernier film que tu as vu?
5. Les habitants de Montréal s'appellent des Montréalais. Comment s'appellent les habitants de ta ville? de ton état?

Les habitants de ma ville s'appellent les New-Yorkais.

**4** *Answers for B will vary.*

1. A: Est-ce qu'il y a une école près de chez toi?
2. A: Est-ce qu'il y a un centre commercial près de chez toi?
3. A: Est-ce qu'il y a un cinéma près de chez toi?
4. A: Est-ce que l'hôtel de ville est près de chez toi?
5. A: Est-ce qu'il y a un restaurant près de chez toi?
6. A: Est-ce qu'il y a un hôtel près de chez toi?
7. A: Est-ce qu'il y a une banque près de chez toi?
8. A: Est-ce qu'il y a un supermarché près de chez toi?

**5** *Answers will vary.*

## Game

To recycle the vocabulary for places in the city, have your students work in teams to give compass directions for places in your area, for example, **Il est au nord-est de la ville** or **Elle est au sud de la mairie.** If the team that hears the clue can guess the location (**l'aéroport**, **la piscine**, etc.), the team that prepared the clue earns a point for their excellent description.

## Differentiated Learning
### Decelerate

1. For **Activité 2**, make sure students understand the meanings of the words in the box.
2. For **Activité 5**, write the beginning of each response on the board to help students get started writing out their answers. Then have them share with the other group members.

## Special Needs Students
### Auditory Impairment

Before listening to **Activité 3**, provide a written copy of the script for students.

**Reference Desk**

Ask students what other pairing of region/country and city mirrors the **au Québec/à Québec** formula. (**au Luxembourg/à Luxembourg**) Are there any others?

**Communication**

**Interpersonal: Group Practice**

To practice compass directions, ask students to name cities north/south/east/west of a particular American city, for example, **Quelle ville est au nord de Memphis? Boston est au nord de Memphis. Quelle ville est au sud de San Francisco? Los Angeles est au sud de San Francisco.** As they get used to the pattern and pronouncing the points of the compass, have students begin taking turns formulating the questions themselves. Practice also with metropolitan French cities.

Ask students to re-write the dialogue (or at least Robert's **québecois** portions) in "French" French. Have students practice the dialogue in groups of three. The group with the best rendition in "French" French or **québecois** French can perform for the class. Consider also having groups or pairs record dialogues for later evaluation.

# Rencontres culturelles

## Une visite à Montréal     1.2

À Montréal, Yasmine fait la connaissance de Robert, un copain québécois de sa cousine, Fatima. Elle réalise que le français au Québec est différent que le français en France.

Fatima: C'est ma cousine, Yasmine, qui vit en France. Elle est en visite chez nous autres cet été.
Robert: Allô, c'est un plaisir!
Yasmine: Moi aussi. Qu'est-ce qu'il y a à faire à Montréal en été?
Robert: Ta visite est bien cédulée. Il reste encore un couple de jours des FrancoFolies. Je peux vous offrir des billets parce que je vas avec ma famille à Québec.
Yasmine: Mais tu es déjà à Québec?
Robert: Chu-t *au* Québec, la province, mais je vas *à* Québec, la ville, qui est située au nord-est de Montréal.
Yasmine: Une question de prépositions!
Robert: C'est correct. Pis, vous voulez les billets?
Fatima: Sais-tu pour quel concert c'est?
Robert: Andrea Lindsay.
Fatima: Wô! Merci gros!

## Essential Instruction

1. Most languages have different dialects, accents, and vocabulary depending on where they're spoken. Compare the differences among British, Australian, and American English and ask students if they can think of some examples of different vocabulary in these languages, for example, apartment vs. flat, elevator vs. lift, trunk vs. boot, or chum/mate vs. friend. Explain that similar to English, there are many differences between the French spoken in Quebec and the French spoken in France. Discuss the vocabulary in **Les expressions** on p. 521.

3. Before showing the **Rencontres culturelles** video, have groups read the dialogue aloud. Answer any questions they have.

4. Show the filmed dialogue, asking students to note differences in accent among the characters.

5. Do **Activité 6** chorally, with or without the audio.

## Les expressions

| Au Québec | En France |
|---|---|
| vit | habite |
| chez nous autres | chez nous |
| allô | bonjour |
| c'est un plaisir | enchanté(e) |
| Ta visite est bien cédulée. | Ta visite tombe bien. |
| un couple de jours | quelques jours |
| je vas | je vais |
| chu | je suis |
| c'est correct | c'est ça |
| wô | ouah |
| merci gros | merci beaucoup |

## 6 Une visite à Montréal  2.1, 2.2

*Identifiez la personne décrite.*

1. ... est la cousine de Yasmine.
2. ... est un copain de Fatima.
3. ... offre des billets pour les FrancoFolies à Montréal.
4. ... va chanter aux FrancoFolies.
5. ... accepte le cadeau.

## Extension Table ronde  1.2, 2.1, 2.2

Les participants d'une table ronde se présentent.

**Animatrice:** Je me présente, Apolline, de Paris. Merci d'être venus. C'est une réunion importante sur la francophonie. Vous voulez bien vous présenter aux spectateurs?

**Abdoulaye:** Je commence.... Bonjour, je m'appelle Abdoulaye. Je viens de Dakar, au Sénégal.

**Claire:** Moi, c'est Claire et j'habite à Genève, en Suisse.

**Emmanuelle:** Je suis Emmanuelle, et j'habite à Monaco.

**Jean:** Bonjour, Jean. J'habite à Luxembourg, au Luxembourg.

**Gilberte:** Je m'appelle Gilberte. J'habite à Montréal, au Québec.

**Rosalie:** C'est moi la dernière? Alors moi, c'est Rosalie et j'habite à Bruxelles, en Belgique.

## Extension De quels continents, pays, et villes est-ce que les participants viennent?

---

## Differentiated Learning
### Accelerate
Have small groups read aloud the **Extension** dialogue, then present to the class. As an introduction to the grammar point of this lesson, ask students to scan the dialogue and deduce what prepositions are used to express in a city or in a country.

## Learning Styles
### Kinesthetic Learners
As students watch the filmed dialogue, ask them to stand or raise their hand when they hear a French-Canadian expression.

### Multiple Intelligences
**Bodily-Kinesthetic**
Have groups create name tags, adopting the role of one of the characters in the dialogue as they read the lines aloud. Remind students that it is common to shake hands when meeting someone for the first time, especially in a formal situation.

---

**6**
1. Fatima
2. Robert
3. Robert
4. Andrea Lindsay
5. Fatima

## Extension

Europe, Paris, France; Afrique, Dakar, Sénégal; Europe, Genève, Suisse; Europe, Monaco; Europe, ville de Luxembourg, Luxembourg; Amérique du Nord, Montréal, Québec; Europe, Bruxelles, Belgique

## Reference Desk

1. Before assigning **Activité 6**, have students first identify the **québécois** expressions from the dialogue on p. 520.
2. In anticipation of learning about prepositions with geographical places, have students choose a country from a list of feminine countries. Ask **Où vas-tu?** and demonstrate how to answer using **en**. For another round, have students choose from a list of masculine countries using **au**. Ask what the difference might be between these two groups. Remind students that, similar to other nouns, country names require an article, but generally cities do not. If a city name has an article (**Le Havre, Le Caire, La Paz, Les Andelys**) it must be included and follow the general rule when using **à** (**à+le = au, à+les = aux**, etc.) and **de** (**de+le = du, de+les = des**, etc.).

## Communication

**Interpersonal: Group Practice**
Have students model a conversation like the one used in the **Extension** dialogue.

### Reference Desk

1. Students should be sensitized to the importance of French in Quebec. In general, the **Québecois** are fiercely invested in their French-speaking heritage. People in Quebec do not consider themselves bilingual, but rather francophone. TV and radio programs, street signs, classes, and political affairs are conducted mostly in French.
2. For what dishes do people generally use maple syrup? Ask students to research and share how Canadians use maple syrup.
3. Note that the language used by young people in Quebec is influenced greatly by American English. Hence a number of English words appear in **qué-becois** daily vocabulary (*cash, flashlight, hot, peanut,* etc.) and retain their original meaning.

### Communication

**Interpersonal: Paired Practice**

With a partner, have students play the role of a resident of Montreal and a visitor who has never been to Montreal before. The resident and visitor are walking, and the resident answers the visitor's questions about what they are seeing, which could be anything from a neighborhood park or café to places mentioned in the culture reading.

---

# Points de départ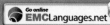

 **La Francophonie**

 **Question centrale** How do travel experiences shape our worldview?

✳ *Le Québec* ✿ **1.2, 2.1**

Le Québec est souvent appelé "La belle province." C'est la plus grande province du Canada (2 millions de km²) et avec le plus de personnes (7,8 millions d'habitants). Elle est traversée* par le fleuve Saint-Laurent. Sa capitale est Québec (500.000 habitants), mais la plus grande ville est Montréal. Le drapeau du Québec est bleu et blanc à quatre fleurs de lys, le symbole des rois* de France, et la devise du Québec est "Je me souviens," qui montre la conviction des Québécois de préserver leur héritage francophone dans cette province où le français est la langue officielle.

🔍 **Search words: bonjour québec**

**traversée** *crossed;* **rois** *kings*

### COMPARAISONS

French is Canada's second language. What do you consider to be the second language of the United States? **4.2**

 **3.1** **Produits** La province de Québec est responsable pour 75% **du sirop d'érable** (*maple syrup*) du monde. Les premiers Européens en Amérique ont appris à le faire des Américains autochtones.

 **Mon dico québécois** **4.1**

un dépanneur: *convenience store*
Étatsunien(ne): *américain(e)*
magasiner: *faire du shopping*
une piasse: *un dollar canadien ou américain*
la poutine: *frites avec cheese curds et sauce*
C'est le fun!: *C'est amusant!*

 ✳ *Montréal*

**1.2, 2.1** Montréal est la deuxième ville du Canada après Toronto et la deuxième ville francophone du monde après Paris. (Elle a 2 millions d'habitants, 4 millions d'habitants pour la métropole.) La ville est dominée par le Mont Royal: cet immense espace vert donne son nom à la ville. La vieille ville est constituée par* le Vieux Port, la place Jacques Cartier, l'Hôtel de ville, la Place d'Armes, et la basilique Notre-Dame. La vie culturelle est particulièrement intense avec de nombreux festivals: le Festival International de Jazz, les FrancoFolies, le Festival Juste pour Rire, et le Festival des Films du Monde.

🔍 **Search words: montréal guide touristique tourisme montréal**

**constituée par** *made up of*

La place d'Armes honore Paul Chomedey de Maisonneuve, qui a fondé Montréal en 1642.

522 cinq cent vingt-deux | Unité 10

---

### Essential Instruction

1. Expand on **québecois** expressions with the vocabulary in **Mon dico québécois**. Then discuss the question in **Comparaisons**. While the United States has no official language, most consider Spanish the unofficial second language. Reflect on the advantages and disadvantages of the United States officially becoming a bilingual nation instead of being an English-only country. Expand to include statistics on languages spoken in the region and nationally. Which language would students select to be the official second language?

2. Assign students to read the **Questions culturelles** on p. 523 before reading the culture paragraphs so that they can focus on the information they are expected to learn.

3. Once students learn about **Les FrancoFolies**, find and play a song by Andrea Lindsay or one of the other featured musicians.

4. Have pairs complete **Activité 7.**

## Les FrancoFolies  1.2, 2.1

Les FrancoFolies sont un festival de musique qui a lieu* tous les étés à Montréal. Il y a plus de 1.000 chanteurs de rock, de hip-hop, de rai, de punk, et d'autres genres de musique, venus du monde entier*. Certains concerts sont gratuits* pour le public. Andrea Lindsay, une canadienne anglophone d'Ontario, a chanté aux FrancoFolies récemment. Elle est tombée amoureuse du français lors* d'un voyage à Paris. Elle a étudié la traduction* et a commencé à chanter des chansons et à faire des tournées* en français.

 **Search words: francofolies montréal andrea lindsay vidéo**

**a lieu** *takes place*; **entier** *whole*; **gratuits** *free*; **lors** *during*; **traduction** *translation*; **faire des tournées** *to go on tour*

**Horaire** des spectacles en salle

LES FRANCOFOLIES DE MONTRÉAL

À venir plus de **150** spectacles extérieurs GRATUITS

17e édition

---

**7  Questions culturelles**   1.3, 3.1, 3.2, 4.2

*Faites les activités suivantes.*

1. Remplissez la carte d'identité du Québec:
   Population:
   Capitale:
   Principale ville:
   Langue officielle:
2. Situez sur un plan du centre historique de Montréal le Mont Royal, le Vieux Port, la place Jacques Cartier, l'Hôtel de ville, la Place d'Armes, et la basilique Notre-Dame.
3. Faites des recherches sur Internet et trouvez le sens de ces mots québécois:
   * mon best • ma blonde • char • chum • déjeuner

### Perspectives

What do you think it would be like to live in a French-speaking province in a country of mostly English speakers? What do you think it is like for people who have just moved to the United States and don't know how to speak English yet?

Leçon A | cinq cent vingt-trois **523**

---

---

**Differentiated Learning**
**Accelerate**
Ask these students to write original **vrai-faux** or completion statements to distribute to the other students.

**Decelerate**
Provide questions about the readings.

**Learning Styles**
**Kinesthetic Learners**
For #2 of **Activité 7**, distribute a map of the historic center of Montreal and words of the places mentioned in **Points de départ**. Students locate each place as you show images.

**Visual Learners**
Have students research the line up for the next **FrancoFolies** or for another music festival. Then have them create a poster in French for one of the concerts.

**Multiple Intelligences**
**Visual-Spatial**
Have students create a word cloud with **québécois** expressions.

**8**

1. F
2. V
3. V
4. F
5. V
6. V

**9**

**Vieux Montréal**

1. Place Jacques Cartier; Hôtel de ville; Champ-de-Mars; Place d'Armes
2. *Presentations will vary.*

## Connections

Divide students into two groups and assign research on the lives of the French explorers Samuel de Champlain and Jacques Cartier, specifically their cities of origin, voyages of discovery in the New World, and respective contributions to the founding of French Canada. To present their work, have students stage a press conference and come in costume as their respective explorer and/or a member of his crew. Have some volunteers play the role of members of the press, asking questions to learn about the other explorer and his crew.

## Expansion

Divide students into groups according to their interest in visiting Quebec or Montreal during the summer or winter. Subdivide these seasonal groups into smaller groups that will research interesting and fun activities tourists can do in each city during that season. Students should create a promotional brochure to present their findings to the class, and then poll the class on its preferences.

## TPR

Read the statements in **Activité 8**, and have students raise one hand for **vrai** and two hands for **faux**.

# Du côté des médias  1.2

*Lisez le paragraphe sur le Vieux-Montréal.*

## La place d'Armes

Située au centre du quartier historique du Vieux-Montréal, la Place d'Armes est une représentation de toutes les périodes de l'histoire de Montréal. Du plus vieil immeuble de la ville à la grande église modernisée avec le temps, du siège social de la première banque du pays au premier gratte-ciel de huit étages du Canada, le New York Life, construit en 1888, la place a gardé son histoire tout en se modernisant!

**8  Vrai ou faux?**  2.1

*Écrivez **V** si les phrases suivantes sont vraies, et **F** si elles sont fausses.*

1. La place d'Armes est un immeuble à Montréal.
2. Le Vieux-Montréal est un quartier historique.
3. Il y a de vieux immeubles sur la place d'Armes.
4. Le New York Life est un monument ancien.
5. Le gratte-ciel (*skyscraper*) moderne a huit étages.
6. La place d'Armes représente l'histoire ancienne et moderne de Montréal.

**9  Vieux Montréal**  1.3, 2.1

*Faites des recherches et répondez aux questions.*

1. Quel est ce monument?
   - Ce lieu public a une statue de l'amiral Nelson.
   - Ce lieu municipal a eu la visite du Général de Gaulle.
   - Ce lieu public a eu beaucoup de batailles (*battles*).
   - Ce lieu public montre toutes les périodes historiques de Montréal.
2. Choisissez un monument, un édifice, ou un lieu dans le Vieux-Montréal. Ensuite, recherchez des informations sur Internet et faites une présentation à la classe.

## Essential Instruction

1. Start by having students read the description in **À côté des médias** silently. Explain that a **gratte-ciel** is a skyscraper. Brainstorm a list of skyscrapers students are familiar with locally or nationally.
2. Before introducing the use of prepositions to mean "to" or "in" before geographical expressions, review the use of **de** (+ definite article + place), meaning "from" or "of."
3. Read aloud and discuss the grammar explanation. Do **Activité 10** together and write the answers on the board.

# Structure de la langue

Go online EMCLanguages.net

## Prepositions before Cities, Countries, and Continents 1.2

You have already learned that countries have gender and are singular or plural. You also know how to use a form of **de** with a place to say where you come from or are arriving from. Now you are going to learn how to say "to" or "in" a country or place. Use **au** if the country's name is masculine and singular and **aux** if it is masculine and plural.

J'habite à Montréal, au Québec.

Tu vas **au** Canada?
Non, je vais **aux** États-Unis.

*Are you going to Canada?*
*No, I'm going to the United States.*

Use **en** before countries or continents with feminine names.

Nous allons **en** Côte-d'Ivoire, **en** Afrique.

*We're going to the Ivory Coast, in Africa.*

Use **à** before the names of cities.

On est allé **à** Dakar, au Sénégal.

*We went to Dakar, in Senegal.*

---

**10  Deux voyages à destinations différentes**  2.1, 2.2

*Sabrina et son ami Théo vont voyager pour les vacances, mais ils ne vont pas voyager ensemble. Dites où ils vont.*

Sabrina voyage....

le Canada

les États-Unis

Théo voyage....

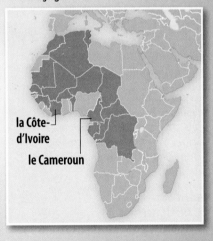

la Côte-d'Ivoire

le Cameroun

Leçon A  |  cinq cent vingt-cinq  **525**

---

**RESOURCES**

Workbook 8–11

Listening Activity

**Answers**

**10**
Sabrina voyage au Canada et aux États-Unis.
Théo voyage en Côte-d'Ivoire et au Cameroun.

**Reference Desk**

1. Show students a list of common masculine country names (**le Pérou, le Danemark, le Brésil,** etc., but note **le Mexique** is masculine!).
2. Use **à** with large islands: **Je vais à Cuba, à Tahiti,** etc.
3. You may want to introduce the French names for francophone countries students haven't learned yet.

---

## Differentiated Learning
### Expand

Distribute a list of the 50 United States in French. Remark on the inconsistencies, for example, some states ending in "a" in English change to a final **e** (**la Floride, la Californie**) in French, yet others do not (**l'Arizona, l'Alaska**).

States ending in "-ia" change to **ie** in French and are usually feminine. Other states are generally masculine. Mention the alternative of using **dans l'état de** + state name.

## Learning Styles
### Audio Learners

Do a rapid drill of prepositions with geographical places. Name a city, country, or continent including the direct article when applicable and have students reply with **Je vais au/à la/à l'** or **en** + location.

### Multiple Intelligences
#### Intrapersonal/Interpersonal

Ask students to share sentences about where they would like to go and why.

### Reference Desk

Students should note that in **Activité 12** the verb **rentrer** means to come back TO a place. However, **rentrer** can also mean to come FROM a place. Depending on the context, **rentrer** may take **de** + article (*from*) or **en** or **à** + article (*to*).

### Communication

**Interpersonal: Paired Practice**

Have students work in pairs to create a role-play in which they say where they are going in a city they do not name. The class listens to the clues in the dialogue and tries to identify the city.

---

**11** Où est-ce qu'ils habitent?

 *Dites dans quelle capitale et dans quel pays chaque personne habite.*

**2.1, 2.2**
1. Abdoulaye habite… Dakar, … Sénégal.
2. Pierre habite… Paris, … France.
3. Mohamed habite… Bamako, … Mali.
4. Awa habite… Yaoundé, … Cameroun.
5. Evenye habite… Yamoussoukro, … Côte-d'Ivoire.
6. Robert habite… Ottawa, … Canada.
7. Julian habite… Washington, … États-Unis.
8. Djamel habite… Libreville, … Gabon.

Abdoulaye habite en Afrique.

---

**12** Le lycée international

 *Éric, un élève à une école internationale en Europe, écrit à sa mère à propos des voyages de ses amis pour les grandes vacances. Complétez son e-mail avec les bonnes prépositions (à, au, aux, en).*

**2.1, 2.2** Salut, Maman!

Tout le monde va voyager bientôt. Ma copine Delphine rentre __1__ Marseille, et mon copain Philippe __2__ Lyon. Lance va __3__ Boise, dans l'Idaho, __4__ États-Unis. Rahina voyage __5__ Burkina Faso, et Amidou __6__ Togo. Naya va __7__ Côte-d'Ivoire. Comme tu le sais bien, j'arrive __8__ France demain!

Bisous,
Éric

---

**13** Quel pays habites-tu?

 *Écrivez les numéros 1–8 sur votre papier. Ces personnes parlent du pays où elles habitent. Écoutez et écrivez la lettre qui correspond au continent où le pays ou la province est situé.*

**2.1**

A. Europe
B. North America
C. Africa

---

**14** Mes voyages

*Nommez cinq villes et pays où vous voudriez voyager.*

**MODÈLE**

**Je voudrais voyager à Paris, en France.**

**2.1**

*Je voudrais voyager à la Nouvelle-Orléans, en Louisiane, aux États-Unis.*

---

**Essential Instruction**

1. Assign **Activités 11**, **12**, and **14** to small groups, then have students correct their answers.
2. Have students call out the answers as they listen to **Activité 13**.
3. Ask volunteers to present their dialogues from **Activité 15**.
4. Ask partners to collaborate on **Activité 16**, reminding them to ensure that each student speaks an equal amount during the presentation.

# À vous la parole

How do travel experiences shape our worldview?

## Communiquez!

### 15 Visitons Montréal! 1.1, 2.1, 4.1

**Interpersonal Communication**

With a partner, play the role of a tourist and an employee at the Montreal tourist office. In your conversation:

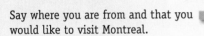

Greet the tourist office employee. → Greet the tourist and ask where he or she is from.

Say where you are from and that you would like to visit Montreal. → Say that Quebec is called the "beautiful province" and he or she will like Montreal. Suggest a few places in the old part of the city for the tourist to visit.

Ask what else you can do in the city. → Give the name of a festival the tourist can go to.

Say thank you. → Say good-bye.

## Communiquez!

### 16 Les musiciens aux FrancoFolies 1.3, 2.2, 3.1, 4.2

**Presentational Communication**

Research and create a profile of a Francophone musician or group who will play or who has played at the Montreal music festival **les FrancoFolies**. Tell your classmates where the musicians are from, the type of music they play, and the names of some of their songs. Include an audio sample in your profile if possible.

 **Search words: francofolies, vidéo francofolies montréal**

---

## Differentiated Learning
### Decelerate
Allow students to write out the conversation in **Activité 15** before presenting it. Or, provide a template for the conversation with the first few words suggested for each line.

### Learning Styles
**Visual Learners**
Have these students draw and color a backdrop for the dialogue in **Activité 15**.

## Multiple Intelligences
### Musical-Rhythmic
Ask students to select an audio sample to accompany their presentation for **Activité 16**. Consider having students create a playlist of the featured musicians at the **FrancoFolies** and upload it to the class website. Ask students to listen to several selections and post a critique.

### Special Needs Students
**Social Anxiety**
Offer students the option of filming the dialogue or presentation in **Activités 15 and 16**.

---

**RESOURCES**

 **Communicative Activities**

**Answers**

**15** *Dialogues will vary.*

**16** *Discussions will vary.*

## Communication

**Presentational: Cooperative Groups**

If some of your students have musical talents, have them put on a variety performance for your class or other classes. Students could imagine they are playing at the **FrancoFolies** event. Beside those who will play instruments or sing, some students can play the roles of announcer and emcee, while others may enjoy creating a short skit or comic sketch to present during an **entr'acte** (*intermission*). Have students design the programs and make announcements in the school newspaper, etc.

## Reference Desk

**Blended Instruction**

Consider using blended instruction, a combination of in-class learning and computer-mediated instruction or learning opportunities. Ask students to complete activities on the computer, using their cell or smartphone, or other emerging electronic technology. This will allow students to hone their tech skills and become more independent learners. Schedule routine Internet and e-book learning in class and in the lab.

**17** *Presentations will vary.*

**18** *Presentations will vary.*

**19** *Dialogues will vary.*

**17** **Une leçon de géographie** **1.3, 3.1**

**Presentational Communication**

Pick a Francophone location and give a geography lesson to a small group of your classmates. Begin by making or finding a map that is large enough for everyone to see. In your presentation:

- point out the names of the countries or provinces that surround the location (**La France est située à l'ouest de….**)
- show where the capital city is (**Voilà la capitale, Paris.**)
- point out four other important cities and where they are located in relationship to the capital (**au nord-est**, etc.)

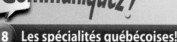  

**18** **Les spécialités québécoises!** **1.2, 1.3, 2.2**

**Interpretive/Presentational Communication**

Research online the history and ingredients of a traditional or popular dish from Quebec. Then prepare a presentation with visual aids about the dish and how to make it. (There are a lot of dishes that are made with maple syrup.) Use the imperative.

**Search words: plats québécois**
**recette sirop d'érable**

La poutine est composée de frites, avec cheese curds et sauce.

**19** **Chu-t au Québec!** **1.1, 1.3, 3.2, 4.1**

**Interpersonal Communication**

With a partner, create a dictionary of ten vocabulary words and expressions from Québec. Then, write a dialogue with a partner using some of the expressions you found and some of the ones presented in this lesson. Present the dialogue to the class. Ask your classmates to guess the meaning of the expressions given their context in the dialogue.

 **Search words: expressions québécoises**

**Essential Instruction**

1. Have partners choose one of the communication **Activités** to present. Ensure that there are no duplicate recipes or locations. Allow for in-class research, peer editing, and practice. Help students with pronunciation. Create a rubric detailing expectations, and use the presentations as an assessment for this lesson.

2. As you work through the **Prononciation** section with the audio, ask students to add more examples, such as additional questions for **Activité A** and similar vocabulary (**puis, suis, depuis**). In **Activité E** point out that words containing -**ill** are sometimes pronounced **/il/**, as in the words **Lille, mille, ville**, and **village** and that they are sometimes pronounced **/ij/**, as in the words **fille, bille** (*marble*), and **papillon** (*butterfly*). There is no hard and fast rule to explain this inconsistency.

# Prononciation   1.2

## Descending Intonation in Questions

- In general, intonation rises for questions that can be answered with "yes" or "no," and falls in questions that ask for information.

 **A** **L'intonation interrogative descendante**

*Listen to questions 1-2, paying attention to the type of intonation at the end of the sentence. Then repeat questions 3-4 after the speaker.*

1. Tu as beaucoup voyagé?
2. Où es-tu allé(e)?
3. Tu as visité beaucoup de pays?
4. Tu as visité quels pays?

**B** **Une interview**

*Write **up** if the intonation you hear at the end of the question rises, or **down** if the intonation falls.*

| MODÈLE | Tu as quel âge? |
|---|---|
| | **down** |

**C** **Prononcez les questions!**

*Read the questions that follow out loud, then listen to the speaker to see if your intonation was correct.*

1. Tu aimes le basket?
2. Tes parents vont au Sénégal en été?
3. Quelle est ta nationalité?
4. Où voudrais-tu passer les vacances?
5. Comment s'appelle ton top chum?

## The Semi-consonants /ɥ/ and /j/

- The sounds /ɥ/ and /j/ are semi-consonants.

 **D** **Le son /ɥ/**

*Listen to the following words that contain the sound /ɥ/. Then, the speaker will say them a second time, when you can repeat them.*

1. huit
2. la nuit
3. ensuite

**E** **Le son /j/**

*Listen to the following words that contain the sound /j/. Then, the speaker will say them a second time, when you can repeat them.*

1. le billet
2. le maillot
3. la famille

**F** **J'entends une semi-consonne?**

*Write **S** if you hear a sentence with a semi-consonant, or **0** if the sentence does not contain a semi-consonant.*

Leçon A | cinq cent vingt-neuf **529**

### Reference Desk

Ask if students can identify the high-speed train featured in the **Vocabulaire actif** illustration. Explain that track was laid for the **TGV** (**Train à grande vitesse**) in France in 1976, and the inaugural voyage from Paris to Lyon was made in 1981 and took only 2:40 (previously four hours).

### Culture

**Products: Information**
Have students research and report on the various high-speed trains in Europe. How do they compare to trains and train travel in the United States?

Bring in French timetables and ask students in French when certain trains are leaving and arriving.

**Practices: Information**
Consider showing the i-Culture video entitled **"Le tramway"** (2009-2010) to provide your students with a culturally authentic perspective related to the theme of this **leçon**.

 **Leçon B**

# Vocabulaire actif

 Go online EMCLanguages.net

## Un voyage en train à la campagne   1.2

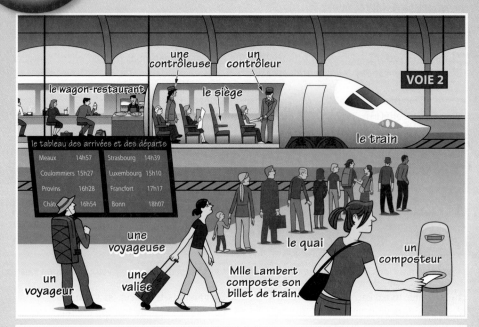

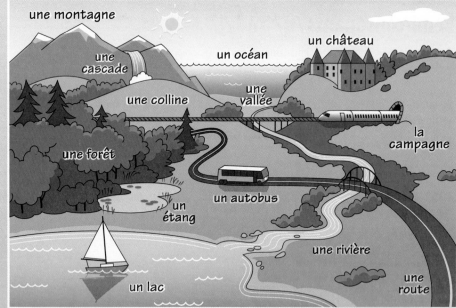

### Essential Instruction

1. Ask students to look at the picture of the train station and identify where it is (continent or region) based on the cities listed on the arrival and departure table.
2. Explain the necessity of validating one's train ticket in **le composteur** (the station ticket machine) before boarding the train. Unlike in the United States, a traveler can be fined for not doing this.
3. Have students point to the vocabulary on the page as they listen to the audio.
4. After students listen to the first function in **Pour la conversation**, ask them to identify the verb tense (**l'impératif**). Ask what the command would be if they were addressing more than one person or **un docteur** (**N'oubliez pas de....**) or to include oneself in the subject (**N'oublions pas de ...**). Model the pronunciation of the vocabulary. Have students repeat the words.
5. Review answers with students for **Activités 1** and 2.

# Pour la conversation

Ⓗow do I remind someone to do something?

> **N'oublie pas de** composter ton billet.

*Don't forget to validate your ticket.*

Ⓗow do I wish someone a good trip?

> **Bon voyage!**

*Have a good trip!*

**Et si je voulais dire...?**

| | |
|---|---|
| **un appareil-photo** | *camera* |
| **les champs (m.)** | *fields* |
| **un guide Michelin** | *Michelin tourist guidebook* |
| **piqueniquer** | *to picnic* |

## ❶ Un voyage en train 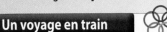    1.2, 2.1, 2.2

*Djamel fait un voyage en train. Lisez le paragraphe. Ensuite, mettez les phrases en ordre chronologique.*

Djamel a acheté son billet en ligne. Le 20 juin, il est allé à la gare en avance. Il a regardé le tableau des arrivées et des départs. Il a vu que son train était à l'heure. Il a composté son billet dans le composteur orange. Puis, il a trouvé la voie numéro 5. Il est monté dans le train et a trouvé son siège à côté de la fenêtre. À midi, il est parti trouver le wagon-restaurant où il a pris un sandwich au jambon et une limonade. Il a parlé à une voyageuse canadienne. Pendant son voyage, il a vu une rivière, une vallée, et un château. Il a pris des photos par la fenêtre. Quand il est arrivé à Tours, il a trouvé son hôtel près de l'hôtel de ville. Demain, il va visiter les châteaux de la Loire en vélo.

1. Djamel a composté son billet.
2. Djamel a mangé dans le wagon-restaurant.
3. Djamel a regardé le tableau des arrivées et des départs.
4. Djamel a trouvé son hôtel.
5. Djamel est monté dans le train.
6. Djamel a visité les châteaux de la Loire.
7. Djamel a acheté un billet de train.

## ❷ Caro voyage.     2.1, 2.2

*Mettez les phrases en ordre chronologique. Utilisez les mots **d'abord** et **ensuite**.*

**MODÈLE**   Caro a cherché son hôtel.
Elle est descendue du train.
**D'abord, Caro est descendue du train.**
**Ensuite, elle a cherché son hôtel.**

*D'abord, Caro a regardé la campagne par la fenêtre.*

1. Caro est entrée dans la gare.
   Elle a regardé le tableau des arrivées et des départs.
2. Caro est allée sur la voie numéro 2.
   Elle a acheté son billet au guichet.
3. Caro a composté son billet. Elle est montée dans le train.
4. Caro est allée au wagon-restaurant.
   Elle a trouvé son siège.
5. Caro a regardé la campagne par la fenêtre.
   Elle est arrivée à Tours.

**❷**

1. D'abord, Caro est entrée dans la gare.
   Ensuite, elle a regardé le tableau des arrivées et des départs.
2. D'abord, Caro a acheté son billet au guichet.
   Ensuite, elle est allée sur la voie numéro 2.
3. D'abord, Caro a composté son billet.
   Ensuite, elle est montée dans le train.
4. D'abord, Caro a trouvé son siège.
   Ensuite, elle est allée au wagon-restaurant.
5. D'abord, Caro a regardé la campagne par la fenêtre.
   Ensuite, elle est arrivée à Tours.

### Communication

**Presentational**
Have students describe a train trip that includes:
1. finding out when the train leaves
2. where they are going
3. what they ate on the train
4. what they saw from the train window

You might allow students to choose to present orally or in writing, depending on their comfort level.

### Expansion

Show samples of **Guides Michelin** and explain that the tire company created the guides to promote car travel (and their tires). Point out that the green Michelin guide details tourist sites whereas the red guide rates hotels and restaurants. Have pairs of students plan an itinerary to a French location using the guidebooks.

---

**Differentiated Learning**

**Adapt/Accelerate**

1. Give a definition of the word you want to elicit, for example, **l'eau qui tombe d'une montagne** (**une cascade**), **beaucoup d'arbres** (**une forêt**), etc.
2. Ask students to reword the imperative in **Pour la conversation** by using the impersonal **il faut** expression they learned in **Unité 9**.

3. Write **Bon voyage** on the board and make a list of similar expressions with **bon/bonne** (**bon anniversaire**, **bon appétit**, **bonne année**, etc.).

4. Have students write a Michelin-style ranking and review of their favorite restaurant.

**3** **Les vacances à Québec!**   **2.1, 2.2**

*Annie parle de son voyage en train de Vancouver à Québec. Faites correspondre la phrase avec l'illustration.*

A.

B.

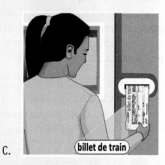

C.

D.

| départs | arrivées |
| --- | --- |
| 16:33 | 18:47 |
| 17:20 | 20:33 |
| 17:40 | 19:50 |
| 16:33 | 22:14 |
| 17:47 | 22:00 |

billet de train

E.

F.

### Essential Instruction

1. Have students call out the answers as they listen to **Activité 3**.
2. Assign partners for **Activités 4** and **5**. Then have them share what they learned about their partner by doing **Activité 5**.
3. Allow students to ask you some **questions personnelles**. Remind them to use the formal **vous**.

**4** **Bonne route!** 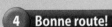 **2.1, 2.2**

*Dites ce que ces familles francanadiennes ont vu en route à leurs destinations.*

les Tremblay

MODÈLE **Les Tremblay ont vu un lac et une cascade.**

1. les Charbonneau

2. les Mercier

3. les Vaillancourt

4. les Bouchard

5. les Michaud

**Communiquez!**

**5** **Questions personnelles**

**Interpersonal Communication**  **1.1**

*Répondez aux questions.*

1. Préfères-tu faire des promenades à la campagne ou en ville?
2. Est-ce que tu préfères nager dans un lac ou dans l'océan?
3. As-tu voyagé en train? Si oui, où es-tu allé(e)?
4. As-tu jamais visité un château? Si oui, comment s'appelle le château que tu as visité?
5. As-tu jamais oublié tes devoirs de français?

J'ai voyagé en train à Marseille.

Leçon B | cinq cent trente-trois 533

**Dialogue Video**

**Answers** _____

**6**

1. Julien
2. Julien
3. louer
4. un wagon-restaurant
5. composter
6. monte

**Extension**

Ils ne veulent rien faire et ils ne veulent voir personne.

**Reference Desk**

Explain that most legal holidays in France are based on Christian traditions. The Ascension (40 days after Easter) commemorates Jesus' ascent into heaven following his resurrection. Since this feast day falls on a Thursday, most workers and schools have Friday off; this is known as **ils font le pont** (four-day weekend).

# Rencontres culturelles

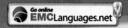

## Un voyage en train à la vallée de la Loire

 **1.2**

Maxime et Julien parlent du voyage de Julien en train.

Julien: Tu es sûr... tu ne veux pas m'accompagner?

Maxime: C'est que... Yasmine et moi, on a des projets pour la semaine. Tu as ton billet?

Julien: Dans mon sac à dos. Départ: Paris. Destination: Tours, dans le département d'Indre-et-Loire....

Maxime: Tu voudrais voir quels châteaux de la Loire cette semaine?

Julien: Chambord, Chenonceau.... Je vais louer un vélo.

Maxime: Où peux-tu louer un vélo?

Julien: Pas loin de l'hôtel.

Maxime: Tu as apporté quelque chose à manger dans le train?

Julien: Non, je n'ai rien apporté, mais il y a un wagon-restaurant.

Maxime: Tu es sûr d'avoir tout—ton argent, ton guide, ta carte, ton portable?

Julien: Bien sûr. Donc, je vais monter dans le train.

Maxime: N'oublie pas de composter ton billet! Bon voyage!

**6** Un voyage en train à la vallée de la Loire   **2.1, 2.2**

*Complétez les phrases.*

1. Maxime parle à....
2. ... voyage à Tours.
3. Julien va... un vélo pour voir les châteaux de la Loire.
4. Il va manger dans... du train.
5. D'abord, il faut... son billet.
6. Ensuite, il... dans le train.

**Extension** Décision: un weekend, mais où? **1.2, 2.1, 2.2**

Léa et Christophe font des projets pour un long weekend.

Léa: Bon, on va où pour le pont de l'Ascension? Quatre jours.... On reste à Paris?

Christophe: Mais c'est dans quatre mois!

Léa: Eh bien, justement, c'est le moment de décider. Alors, la vallée ou la montagne? Lac ou océan?

Christophe: Le plan c'est de ne voir personne et de ne rien faire? Toi, tu as des idées derrière la tête.

Léa: Toutes petites....

Christophe: Bréhat, en Bretagne?

Léa: Oui, j'achète des billets?

Christophe: D'accord!

**Extension** Quelle sorte de vacances désirent Léa et Christophe?

**Essential Instruction**

1. Locate **Le Val de Loire** on a map and introduce the features of this region. View the video for general understanding. After completing **Activité 6,** view the video again. Finally, have students role-play the dialogue.

2. Show a map of French **départements** and **régions** to introduce the **Points de départ** reading. Ask students to read the passage silently and list the responsibilities and powers that each has. Ask what students know about the **Révolution française** and why the administrative divisions were important (decentralization of power).

3. After reading about the **châteaux,** explore the answer to the **Comparaisons** question.

## Points de départ

Go online EMCLanguages.net

**Question centrale ?**
How do travel experiences shape our worldview?

### Les départements et les régions  1.2, 2.1

La France est composée de 101 départements. Un département est une division administrative du territoire français créé* sous la Révolution française. Les départements sont responsables de l'entretien* des routes départementales, des écoles primaires, et des affaires culturelles. La France est aussi composée de 22 régions. Les régions ont commencé à avoir de vrais pouvoirs en 1982. La conséquence? Un véritable développement régional. Certaines villes ou régions sont maintenant identifiées avec leur spécialités, par exemple, Toulouse avec l'Airbus et l'aérospatiale et Strasbourg avec la génétique.

🔍 **Search words: carte des départements de France**

créé *created*; l'entretien *maintenance*

**COMPARAISONS**

What is the oldest historical building in your city or region?

4.2, 5.1

### Les châteaux de la Loire  1.2, 2.1

Les châteaux de la Loire ont été construits* pendant la Renaissance, et particulièrement sous le règne* de François Ier (1497–1550). Chambord est le plus grand château avec 440 pièces. Chenonceau a une galerie qui traverse* une rivière qui s'appelle le Cher. Il est connu comme "le château des six femmes" parce que des femmes en ont été les propriétaires*. D'autres châteaux qui sont populaires à visiter sont Amboise, Blois, Cheverny, et Azay-le-Rideau. Quarante-deux châteaux peuvent être aujourd'hui appelés châteaux de la Loire.

🔍 **Search words: carte châteaux de la loire domaine national de chambord château de chenonceau**

construits *built*; le règne *the reign*; traverse *crosses*; en ont été propriétaires *were owners of it*

le château de Chambord

le château de Chenonceau

### RESOURCES

 **e-visual 38**

 **Workbook 17–18**

### Reference Desk

1. Show an image of a French **plaque d'immatriculation**. Explain that the last two digits in the border on the right represent the department number where the car is registered. French children often play a license plate department identification game on road trips.
2. Some **chateaux** served as large country estates. François I had Chambord built on the original site of a small hunting lodge within a vast, thick forest. Containing 440 rooms, it is the largest of the Loire castles and the symbol of the French Renaissance at its height. Chambord has a very harmonious shape with its four central towers connected to the outer ones by two floors of galleries.
3. Chenonceau spans the river Cher, combining fine proportions with a delightful setting. François I took the castle as payment for a debt when it was not much more than a block of towers close to the shore. His son, Henri II, gave it to his mistress, Diane de Poitiers, who had a bridge built to the opposite side of the river.

---

**Differentiated Learning**
**Expand/Accelerate**
Play the role of **Julien** in **Rencontres culturelles** and have students use the imperative to recommend other "essential" items to you.

**Decelerate**
Have students evaluate suggested items as **essentiel**, **pratique**, or **peu pratique**.

**Multiple Intelligences**
**Logical-Mathematical**
Review numbers by explaining that departments are assigned a number (01 – 101, including the six overseas departments) based on their alphabetical order. Project a map of France that includes cities and department numbers. Name a city and have students provide the corresponding department.

**7**

1. 101, 22
2. *Possible answers:* Toulouse: l'aérospatiale; Strasbourg: la génétique
3. *Teacher might want to refer students to a website.*
4. *Answers will vary.*

**À discuter**
*Discussions will vary.*

---

### Reference Desk

Some French experts say that studying/living in Tours will help students develop the best French accent.

---

### Expansion

The **châteaux** of the **Loire** are popular tourist destinations and familiar symbols of France. Help students learn the names and locations of a few iconic **châteaux** by having them create a pair of cards. Students can make either an identical pair of cards (for example, two cards with pictures of Chambord) or a related pair (for example, one card with the picture of Chambord and a related card with a map of the Loire valley and the location of Chambord marked with a dot). Decide how you want the pairs to be before assigning students to make them. Have students bring their cards to class. Shuffle the decks and use them to play Memory.

---

## Tours  1.2, 2.1

Tours est une ville de 300.000 habitants. Elle est située au centre de la vallée de la Loire. Beaucoup de touristes restent à Tours quand ils visitent les châteaux de la région. Fameuse pour son architecture et histoire, Tours est classée Ville d'Art et d'Histoire. Elle est aussi inscrite au Patrimoine mondiale de l'Humanité de l'UNESCO. Les écrivains Rabelais et Balzac sont originaires de Tours, aussi le compositeur Francis Poulenc, le réalisateur Patrice Leconte, et les acteurs Jean Carmet, Jean-Hugues Anglade, et Jacques Villeret.

**Search words: site de la ville de tours**
**tours office de tourisme**
**au pays des châteaux de la loire**

---

**7** **Questions culturelles**

*Faites les activités suivantes.* 1.1, 1.3, 4.2, 5.1

1. Retrouvez ces informations.
   * le nombre de départements en France
   * le nombre de régions
2. Associez une spécialité à chaque ville.
   * Toulouse
   * Strasbourg
3. Situez sur une carte ces châteaux: Chambord, Chenonceau, Amboise, Blois, Cheverny, Azay-le-Rideau.
4. Choisissez une personnalité originaire de Tours et faites son portrait.

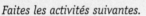

Les Airbus viennent de Toulouse, en France.

### À discuter

Do you primarily think of France as having old or new buildings and monuments? Which ones would you most want to see on a trip there? Explain your response.

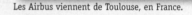

**Essential Instruction**

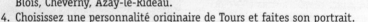

1. Before reading the passage on Tours, mention that UNESCO (United Nations Education, Scientific and Cultural Organization) encourages international peace and universal respect by promoting collaboration among nations. One of its roles is to name **le Patrimoine** (world heritage sites).

2. You may choose to discuss the **Questions culturelles** or assign them to students as research projects or extra credit work.

3. Ask students if they recognize the **château** in the **Du côté des medias** brochure picture (Chambord) and complete the questions in **Activité 8** as a class.

## Du côté des médias

*Lisez les informations dans la brochure.*

COMITÉ DÉPARTEMENTAL
DU TOURISME DE LOIR-ET-CHER
5 rue de la Voûte du Château
BP 149 – 41005 BLOIS Cedex

Tél. 02 54 57 00 41
Fax 02 54 57 00 47

www.coeur-val-de-loire.com
www.sejour-en-val-de-loire.com
www.randonnee-en-val-de-loire.com
infos@cdt41.com

*Cœur Val de Loire*
LOIR-ET-CHER ◆ LOIRE VALLEY

LOIR-ET-CHER
COMITÉ
DÉPARTEMENTAL
DU TOURISME

**8** | **Dans la vallée de la Loire**  **1.2, 1.3, 2.1**

*Répondez aux questions 1 et 2 et faites les activités qui suivent.*

1. Les touristes arrivent dans quelle ville?
2. Dans quel département se situe cette ville?
3. Faites une recherche et cherchez quel château on peut voir dans cette ville.
4. Faites des recherches sur un château de la Loire que vous aimeriez visiter et dites pourquoi.
5. Allez sur le site Internet mentionné dans la brochure et faites une liste des visites suggérées.

Leçon B | cinq cent trente-sept **537**

### Connections

**History**

The **châteaux** of the **Loire** have fascinating royal connections and histories. Students may enjoy preparing historical presentations with some class members dressing up and playing the roles of the most famous royal figures and aristocratic patrons associated with the **châteaux,** such as **Louis XI, Louis XII, François 1er, Henri II, Henri III, Henri IV, Diane de Poitiers, Catherine de Medici, Louis XIV.** Challenge students to find out what royal connections **Leonardo da Vinci** and **Molière** had to the **châteaux.** Royal patronage of artists and musicians helped shape the life and culture at these **châteaux** and other royal dwellings.

### Expansion

1. Challenge students to find French words that incorporate the word **tour** (before you reveal any) and to make a funny and clever sentence using these words, for example, **Eh, touriste! C'est ton tour! Regardez la tour qui entoure ce château!**
2. Have students each research a different **château** of the Loire and make a folded brochure describing the **château**, its location, when it was built, who built it, its outstanding features, hours, tours, etc. They can also make a large wall map of the Loire region and surround it with strategically placed pictures of their **châteaux.** Attach strings from the pictures to the locations marked on the map.

**Learning Styles**
**Visual Learners**
Assign small groups to research another French site that is part of the **Patrimoine mondiale de l'Humanité de l'UNESCO.** Ask them to select illustrations of the main features of the site and to prepare two to three sentences for an oral presentation about each illustration.

**Multiple Intelligences**
**Visual-Spatial**
Show a slide-show of Chambord. Emphasize the enormity of the chateau by sharing that King François I used to ride his horse up and down the marble stairways.

# Structure de la langue

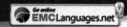
Go online
EMCLanguages.net

## Negative Expressions  1.2

Mme Roseau aime toujours la Suisse,
mais elle ne voyage plus.

There are other negative expressions that follow the same pattern as **ne (n')... pas** to make a verb negative. Compare the following expressions.

| Affirmative | Negative |
|---|---|
| **souvent** *often* <br> **toujours** *always* | **ne (n')... jamais** *never* |
| **toujours** *still* | **ne (n')... plus** *no longer, not anymore* |
| **quelqu'un** *someone, somebody* | **ne (n')... personne** *no one, nobody, not anyone* |
| **quelque chose** *something* | **ne (n')... rien** *nothing, not anything* |

| | |
|---|---|
| Tu voyages **souvent** en train? | *Do you often travel by train?* |
| Non, je **ne** voyage **jamais** en train. | *No, I never travel by train.* |
| | |
| Vous avez **toujours** des vélos à louer? | *Do you still have bicycles to rent?* |
| Non, nous n'avons **plus** de vélos à louer. | *No, we don't have any more bicycles to rent.* |
| | |
| Il y a **quelqu'un** à la porte? | *Is there someone at the door?* |
| Non, il **n'**y a **personne** à la porte. | *No, there's no one at the door.* |
| | |
| Tu prends **quelque chose**? | *Are you having something (to eat)?* |
| Non, je **ne** prends **rien**. | *No, I'm not having anything (to eat).* |

Note that in each of these negative expressions, **ne (n')** comes before the verb and **jamais**, **plus**, **personne**, or **rien** follows the verb. Remember that indefinite articles (**un**, **une**, **des**) and partitive articles (**du**, **de la**, **de l'**) become **de** or **d'** in a negative sentence.

| | |
|---|---|
| Tu veux **des** cerises? | *Do you want some cherries?* |
| Non, je **ne** veux **plus de** cerises. | *No, I don't want any more cherries.* |

**Personne** may also be used after a preposition.

> Je **ne** parle **à personne**.        *I'm not talking to anyone.*

In the **passé composé**, **ne (n')** precedes the helping verb and **pas**, **plus**, **jamais**, or **rien** follows it. **Personne**, however, follows the past participle.

> Je **n'**ai **rien** apporté.        *I brought nothing. /I didn't bring anyhthing.*
> Il **n'**a vu **personne**.        *He saw no one. /He didn't see anybody.*

### COMPARAISONS  4.1

Where are negative expressions in English placed?
I never travel to the mountains.
I no longer ski.
I spend nothing on vacation at home.
There is no one to travel with.

---

**9  Les phrases négatives**     2.1, 2.2

*Mettez les phrases au négatif. Utilisez **ne (n')... pas**, **ne (n')... jamais**, **ne (n')... plus**, **ne (n')... personne**, ou **ne (n')... rien**.*

> MODÈLE   Jean-Luc a quelque chose à lire.
> **Jean-Luc n'a rien à lire.**

1. Heather parle à quelqu'un en français.
2. Jean va souvent au stade du PSG.
3. Caro a un dictionnaire français-allemand.
4. J'ai toujours un chat blanc.
5. Tu apportes quelque chose à la fête.
6. Martin a un portable américain.
7. Nous faisons toujours du sport.
8. Jacqueline fait toujours ses devoirs.

Mlle Mercier n'aime plus les chiens?

**COMPARAISONS:** In English, negative expressions come before or after the verb.

---

**9**
1. Heather ne parle à personne en français.
2. Jean ne va jamais au stade du PSG.
3. Caro n'a pas de dictionnaire français-allemand.
4. Je n'ai plus de chat blanc.
5. Tu n'apportes rien à la fête.
6. Martin n'a pas de portable américain.
7. Nous ne faisons jamais de sport.
8. Jacqueline ne fait jamais ses devoirs

### Reference Desk

1. For **Activité 9**, teachers need to make students aware that when the word **toujours** means "always," its negative correspondent is **jamais**, but when it means "still," its negative correspondent is **plus**.

2. Students will need practice matching the appropriate affirmative and negative expressions and completing sentences to readily assimilate the pairings. To practice the notions of **personne/quelqu'un** and **rien/quelque chose**, make four cards to illustrate their meaning: one showing someone opening a door with no one outside, one finding a person outside, one with a person opening a box with nothing inside, and one finding a package on the doorstep. Show these to the class one at a time to elicit the responses: **Il n'y a personne; il y a quelqu'un; il n'y a rien; il y a quelque chose.** For further practice, have students take turns asking and answering the questions.

---

**Differentiated Learning**
**Decelerate**
Have students write out **Activité 9**, or pair students who find this concept challenging with more confident students.

**Multiple Intelligences**
**Bodily-Kinesthetic**
Post the words **souvent**, **toujours**, **quelqu'un**, **quelque chose**. Then ask students to tape cards with the negative expressions next to their antonyms.

<br>

## Answers

**10** Script can be found in the front pages of the Annotated Teacher's Edition.

1. F
2. V
3. V
4. F
5. F
6. F
7. V
8. F

**11**

1. Alain prend toujours ....
2. Alain mange souvent ....
3. Alain ne fait pas souvent ....
4. Alain mange souvent ....
5. Alain ne mange jamais ....
6. Alain ne fait pas souvent ....
7. Alain ne dort jamais ....

*Answers to the title question will vary.*

**12**

*Answers to the questions will vary.*

1. A: Tu écoutes de la musique alternative?
2. A: Tu manges du pâté?
3. A: Tu étudies pour les contrôles d'histoire?
4. A: Tu fais du ski alpin?
5. A: Tu voyages au Québec?
6. A: Tu visites un château?
7. A: Tu attends tes amis à la cantine?
8. A: Tu fais du vélo?
9. A: Tu prends un hamburger après les cours?
10. A: Tu marches à l'école?

### Expansion

Ask students to fold a piece of paper in half. Have them list ten things they always do and ten things they never do under the appropriate heading **toujours** or **jamais**. In pairs, students will take turns reading each sentence to a partner, but omit the key words **toujours** and **jamais**. The partner must repeat the sentence and supply the correct missing word.

---

**10  Le voyage de Julien**   1.2

*Écrivez les numéros 1–8 sur votre papier. Ensuite, écoutez l'histoire de Julien et indiquez si les phrases sont vraies (**V**) ou fausses (**F**).*

1. Julien n'a jamais pris le train.
2. Il prend souvent sa voiture.
3. Il n'a rien mangé dans le train.
4. Il ne fait plus de vélo.
5. Il n'a rien vu par la fenêtre.
6. Il ne marche pas à Chenonceau.
7. Il n'a jamais visité de châteaux avant sa visite à Chenonceau.
8. Il n'a vu personne pendant son voyage.

**11  Alain est en forme ou pas?**  2.1, 2.2

*Le graphique suivant montre quand Alain a fait certaines choses cette semaine. Pour chaque activité, écrivez une phrase qui utilise **toujours, souvent, ne (n')... pas souvent**, ou **ne (n')... jamais**. Enfin, répondez à la question dans le titre de cette activité.*

- prendre un jus d'orange le matin (100%)
- manger du fast-food (85%)
- faire du sport (10%)
- manger des fruits frais (75%)
- manger des légumes frais (0%)
- faire des promenades (10%)
- dormir huit heures par nuit (0%)

## Communiquez!

**12  Nos activités**   1.1

**Interpersonal Communication**

*À tour de rôle, demandez si votre partenaire fait les activités suivantes. Répondez avec **ne (n')... jamais, ne (n')... plus**, ou **toujours**.*

**MODÈLE**  A: **Tu joues au foot?**
B: **Je joue toujours au foot.**
ou
**Je ne joue jamais au foot.**
ou
**Je ne joue plus au foot.**

1. écouter de la musique alternative
2. manger du pâté
3. étudier pour les contrôles d'histoire
4. faire du ski alpin
5. voyager au Québec
6. visiter un château
7. attendre tes amis à la cantine
8. faire du vélo
9. prendre un hamburger après les cours
10. marcher pour aller à l'école

### Essential Instruction

1. Have students call out the answers as they listen to **Activité 10**.
2. Ask volunteers to write answers on the board for **Activité 11**. Then ask students to vote on the question **Alain est en forme ou pas?**
3. Select pairs to present the dialogues in **Activité 12**.
4. For **Activités 13** and **14**, consider filming the dialogues and posting to the class website.

Encourage students to bring in props and to practice. If possible, film a rough cut and allow time for students to watch and evaluate their own performance. Have them practice again and film the final version.

5. In discussing the **Question centrale**, ask students to reflect on how travel or their experience of a place changed any pre-conceived notions they may have had about it.

# À vous la parole

How do travel experiences shape our worldview?

**Communiquez!**

### 13 À la gare  1.1

**Interpersonal Communication**

With a partner, play the roles of a traveler and the ticket agent at the train station. In your conversation:

| Traveler | Ticket agent |
|---|---|
| Greet the ticket agent and say that you would like to buy a train ticket from Paris to another destination in France. | Ask the traveler if he or she would like to leave in the morning, afternoon, or evening. |
| Select a departure time and ask the price of the ticket. | Provide the price of the ticket and departure and arrival times. |
| Purchase the ticket and ask where you can find the train. | Tell the traveler which train track to go to. |
| Ask if the train is on time. | Remind the traveler to look at the arrivals and departures board. |
| Thank the ticket agent. | Wish him or her a good trip. |

**Communiquez!**

### 14 Voyage en TGV!  1.2, 1.3, 2.1, 2.2, 3.1

**Interpretive/Presentational Communication**

With a partner, explore the website for the national French railway (**SNCF: Société nationale des chemins de fer français**) and plan a trip on the high speed French train, the TGV (**train à grande vitesse**) from Paris to another city in France. Then, tell your classmates where you are going, the departure and arrival times of your train, the cost of the ticket, what you can eat on the train, and what geographical features you might see from the train window on the trip. (Note: ticket prices will vary based on the age of the traveler and the class in which you wish to travel.)

 **Search words: sncf, tgv, idtgv, idzen, idzap, idnight**

---

## RESOURCES

**Communicative Activities**

**Answers** _____

**13** *Dialogues will vary.*

**14** *Presentations will vary.*

---

## Reference Desk

**Blended Instruction**

Consider using blended instruction, a combination of in-class learning and computer-mediated instruction or learning opportunities. Ask students to complete activities on the computer, using their cell or smartphone, or other emerging electronic technology. This will allow students to hone their tech skills and become more independent learners. Schedule routine Internet and e-book learning in class and in the lab.

---

**Differentiated Learning**
**Adapt**

For those who voted **non** in **Activité 11**, ask **Qu'est qu'Alain doit faire pour être en forme?** Tell students to answer using **Il faut…/Il ne faut pas…** to recycle vocabulary from previous units.

**Special Needs Students**
**Social Anxiety**

Offer an alternate way of presenting **Activités 13** and **14** that would not require having attention focused on students in front of the class. Perhaps they could perform for a smaller group of students, just you, or film themselves at home.

**541**

## Reference Desk

Show students examples of French postcards that you have, or find some on the Internet. Students may be interested in seeing samples of French handwriting. Penmanship is still an important skill in France and distinctly different from American handwriting. Find some examples online and share with students.

## Culture

### Products: Activity

Have students research the different regional **TGV** train lines of France and those to Brussels and London, and further into Europe, and study relevant maps of the rail system. What are these lines called? (**TGV Elipsos** to Spain; **TGV Lyria** to Switzerland; **TGV Artesia** to Italy) If one takes the **Eurostar** or the **Thalys**, where is one traveling? (**Paris-Londres**; **Paris-Bruxelles/Amsterdam/Cologne**, etc.)

 **Communiquez!**

 **15** Itinéraire au "jardin de la France"   1.2, 1.3, 2.1, 2.2, 3.1, .3.2, 5.1

### Interpretive/Presentational Communication

Research the Loire Valley region of France and prepare a travel poster or PowerPoint™ presentation to share what you learn. Include the following:

- three castles to visit
- the location of each castle in relation to Tours (**à l'est de Tours**, etc.)
- the entrance fee, opening hours, and dates when the castle is closed
- one special feature of each castle
- where you can stay while visiting **les châteaux de la Loire**
- three additional activities you can do in the region

 **Search words: châteaux de la loire, vallée de la loire, tours**

**Communiquez!**

**16** Une enquête   1.1, 1.3

### Interpersonal Communication

Poll ten of your classmates to find out if they have traveled to three Francophone cities or countries of your choosing. Record their answers in a grid like the one below by checking the box next to each place the person has traveled. After polling your classmates, report the percentage of people who have traveled to each place.

**As-tu jamais voyagé à/au/aux/en...?**

|                    | 1 | 2 | 3 | 4 | 5 | 6 | 7 | 8 | 9 | 10 |
|--------------------|---|---|---|---|---|---|---|---|---|----|
| **Montréal**       |   |   | ✔ |   | ✔ |   |   |   | ✔ |    |
| **Paris**          |   | ✔ |   |   | ✔ |   |   |   |   |    |
| **Québec (ville)** |   |   |   |   |   |   |   |   |   |    |

**MODÈLE**   A: As-tu jamais voyagé à Montréal?
             B: **Oui, j'ai voyagé à Montréal.**
                ou
                **Non, je n'ai jamais voyagé à Montréal.**

**Report: Vingt pourcent des élèves ont voyagé à Paris; trente pourcent ont voyagé à Montréal, mais il n'y a personne qui a voyagé à Québec.**

### Essential Instruction

1. Have the class do **Activité 15** as described or assign groups to present one castle.
2. For **Activité 16**, ask students to personalize their survey with local, regional, or national locations for those who have not traveled much.
3. Show students examples of French postcards that you have, or find some on the Internet. Students may be interested in seeing samples of French handwriting. Penmanship is still an important skill in France and distinctly different from American handwriting. Find some examples online and share with students.
4. Assign **Activité 17** as pair work.
5. For **Activité 18**, have the students make a printed copy of their postcard and post them on a bulletin board.

# Stratégie communicative

## Writing a Postcard  4.1

1. When writing someone a postcard, always begin with the date, for example, **le 18 mai**. Remember that in French the day comes before the month.
2. Next, use a French salutation, or greeting, such as:
   - **Salut, Coralie!**
   - **Cher Patrick** (*Dear Patrick*)
   - **Chère Catherine** (*Dear Catherine*)
   - **Mes chers grands-parents** (*My dear grandparents*)
   - **Mes chères cousines** (*My dear cousins*)

When addressing someone you don't know well, use **Monsieur**, **Madame**, or **Mademoiselle**, followed by the person's last name.

3. After writing the content of your postcard, always finish with an appropriate closing. The following are some possibilities when writing to your family or friends or adults you don't know very well.

| Informal | Formal |
|----------|--------|
| **Gros bisous** (*Big kisses*) | **Cordialement** (*Cordially*) |
| **Je pense à toi.** (*Thinking about you.*) | **Amitiés** (*Best regards*) |
| **Je t'embrasse très fort.** (*Big kisses.*) | **Bien à vous** (*Sincerely*) |

### 17 Une Américaine à Paris  2.1, 2.2

What did Jennifer write about her first day in Paris to her pen pal in Morocco? Put the expressions and sentences in logical order on the postcard that your teacher will give you.

1. Je suis arrivée à l'aéroport Roissy—Charles de Gaulle.
2. Ma chère Yasmine,
3. Enfin, j'ai mangé une crêpe au chocolat sur les bords de la Seine.
4. D'abord, je suis allée au Louvre pour admirer la Joconde.
5. Je t'embrasse très fort, Jennifer
6. Puis, je suis montée dans un bâteau-mouche sur la rive gauche.
7. Comment vas-tu?
8. J'ai pris le métro direction la tour Eiffel.
9. Ensuite, je suis montée tout en haut de la tour Eiffel où j'ai pris des photos de tout Paris.
10. le 25 juillet

### 18 Mon voyage en train  1.3, 4.1

Send a virtual postcard to a friend, relative, or another adult in your life from Montreal or the Loire Valley. Describe your stay, using the **passé composé**, time expressions (**hier matin, mercredi soir, etc.**), and linking words (**d'abord, ensuite, après, enfin**).

 **Search words:** carte virtuelle montréal, carte virtuelle châteaux de la loire

## Answers

**17**

10, 2, 7, 1, 4, 8, 9, 6, 3, 5

**18** *Postcards will vary.*

## Communication

**Presentational: Cooperative Groups**

Have students sit in a circle. Each student is going to contribute a phrase to an oral postcard. The first student will give the date. The next student will repeat that and give the salutation. The next student repeats what the previous two have said and starts the body of the message. Students continue around until the postcard is finished. Students should help each other out as they try to remember previous comments. To help them, ask students just to repeat two previous students' comments before adding their own so that the content does not get too cumbersome to remember.

## Differentiated Learning
### Accelerate

You may want to teach indefinite negative subject pronouns **personne ne...** and **rien ne...** Ask students questions that elicit the response "no one" or "nothing" in French, for example, **Qui aime les devoirs?** or **Qu'est-ce qu'il y sur la tête du prof?**

For the **Stratégie communicative,** offer variations of French salutations and closings, such as, **Mon cher amour, Mon petit chou, Mon âme, Grosses bises, Affectueusement**, etc.

## Learning Styles
### Kinesthetic Learners

Copy and cut up the sentences in **Activité 17**. Distribute a line (or more, as needed depending on class size) to each student, and have them get up and arrange themselves in logical order. Once they think they have the order correct, have them read their line aloud.

# Leçon C

# Vocabulaire actif

## L'Europe et les directions   1.2

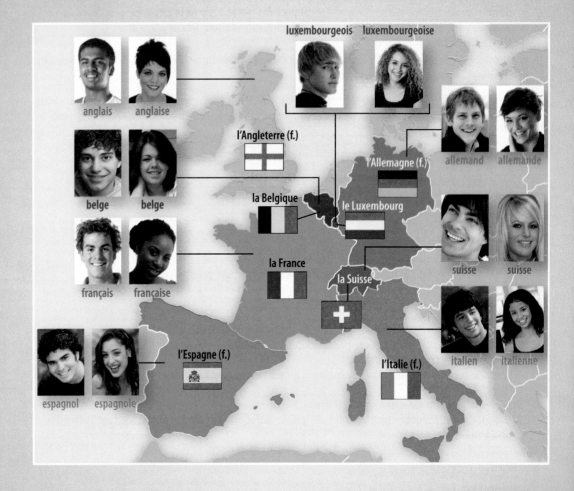

## Essential Instruction

1. Model the pronunciation as you point to a country and indicate the country and nationality of the youth pictured here. Then name a country and have students provide the correct preposition and the country, for example **en Belgique**.

2. Create a chart using the **Vocabulaire actif**. Group together nationalities with similar endings and leave some blanks in each category for students to complete.

3. Brainstorm prepositions students have learned thus far, including **près (de)** and **loin (de)**. Then practice the vocabulary for giving directions. Select some locations in and near the school and provide directions (write on board, provide a list) from the classroom to these locations. Underline the prepositions you use and write the imperatives on the board.

4. Offer extra credit to students who bring in color maps of all the countries listed on these two pages.

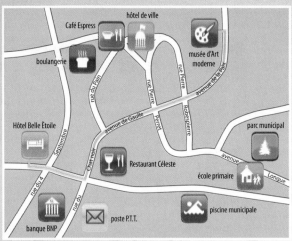

Traversez la rue du 4 septembre.
Tournez à gauche quand vous arrivez au restaurant.
Prenez l'avenue de Gaulle jusqu'à l'avenue de la Paix.
Allez tout droit.
Le musée est sur votre gauche.

La banque est **en face de** la poste.
Le café est **à côté de** l'hôtel de ville.
L'école est **entre** le parc et la piscine.

Traversez la rue du 4 septembre.

## Pour la conversation

**H**ow do I ask for directions?

> **Pardon, où se trouve** le Musée international de la Croix-Rouge?

*Excuse me, where is the International Red Cross Museum located?*

**H**ow do I give directions?

> **Va/Allez vers** l'est.

*Go towards the east.*

> **Continue/Continuez tout droit.**

*Continue straight ahead.*

> **Tourne/Tournez à** droite.

*Turn right.*

> **Prends/Prenez** la plus grande avenue.

*Take the biggest avenue.*

### Et si je voulais dire...?

| | |
|---|---|
| **l'Autriche (f.)** | *Austria* |
| **autrichien(ne)** | *Austrian* |
| **la Chine** | *China* |
| **chinois(e)** | *Chinese* |
| **le Japon** | *Japan* |
| **japonais(e)** | *Japanese* |
| **le Madagascar** | *Madagascar* |
| **malgache** | *from Madagascar* |
| **le Maroc** | *Morocco* |
| **marocain(e)** | *Moroccan* |
| **le Mexique** | *Mexico* |
| **mexicain(e)** | *Mexican* |
| **le Portugal** | *Portugal* |
| **portugais(e)** | *Portuguese* |
| **la Tunisie** | *Tunisia* |
| **tunisien(ne)** | *Tunisian* |

Leçon C | cinq cent quarante-cinq **545**

### Expansion

Taking turns, a student can give directions for an unnamed location within your school. The other students must guess the location and provide feedback on how efficient or correct the directions are. Alternatively, students can tell what route they take to get from their home to school or to a well-known local destination.

---

**Differentiated Learning**
**Adapt**

To practice directions, pass out enlarged copies of the map in **Le vocabulaire actif** or a map you create or find online. Choose a starting point on which students place a token. Give directions in French, telling them to move their token with each instruction. See where they are after several instructions. Challenge students by saying **la première/deuxième rue**, rather than the street names.

**Multiple Intelligences**
**Bodily-Kinesthetic/Visual-Spatial**

Use the rows of desks as the streets of a village. Ask students to create street and shop signs, such as **la banque, le restaurant,** etc. and post in different locations. Have volunteers follow your directions in the classroom.

Give students time to write and give directions based on the map. Create a treasure hunt within the school building, giving directions to certain clues that students pick up.

**1** Les drapeaux européens  **1.2**

*Identifiez le drapeau.*

**MODÈLE** C'est le drapeau français.
Il est bleu, blanc, et rouge.

 1.   2.   3.

 4.   5.   6.   7.

**2** Ils sont européens.  **2.1, 2.2**

*Les personnes suivantes font des activités dans leurs pays ce weekend. Complétez la phrase avec un adjectif qui réflète leur pays d'origine.*

**MODÈLE** Angèle est luxembourgeoise.
Elle regarde un match....
**luxembourgeois**

1. Marie-Alix est française. Elle dîne dans un restaurant....
2. Gunther est allemand. Il circule dans une voiture....
3. Carlos est espagnol. Il invite une amie....
4. Gemma est anglaise. Elle regarde un match....
5. Jean-Luc est suisse. Il achète une imprimante....
6. Louis-Jacques est belge. Il va à une gare....
7. Luigi est italien. Il fait les courses dans une boutique....

Marie-Alix dîne sur la terrace d'un café français.

**3** En vacances où?   **2.1**

*Écrivez les numéros 1–5 sur votre papier. Écoutez chaque description de vacances et choisissez la lettre du pays correspondant.*

A. l'Espagne    B. la France    C. la Suisse    D. la Belgique    E. l'Angleterre

Answers _____

4
1. la piscine
2. le café
3. l'hôtel de ville
4. la statue
5. la banque
6. la poste

## 4 Où est-ce qu'ils vont?

 1.2, 2.1, 2.2

*Lisez les indications que chaque personne reçoit de l'Office de Tourisme. Lisez les phrases pour trouver la destination sur le plan (on the map).*

**MODÈLE**  M. Simon
Prenez l'avenue du 14 juillet au nord et tournez à droite sur la rue Frédéric Chopin. C'est en face de la cathédrale.
**le musée**

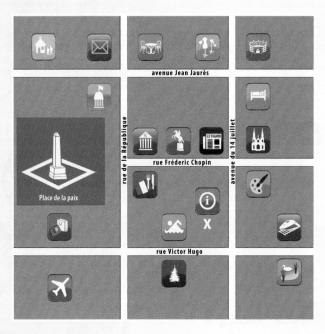

1. Mme Collins
Tournez à droite sur l'avenue du 14 juillet. Prenez la rue Victor Hugo vers l'ouest. C'est sur votre droite en face du parc.

2. M. Martinelli
Prenez l'avenue du 14 juillet vers le nord et traversez la rue Frédéric Chopin. Tournez à gauche sur l'avenue Jean Jaurès. C'est à côté d'une boutique.

3. Mlle Clément
Prenez l'avenue du 14 juillet à gauche et allez tout droit à la rue Frédéric Chopin. Tournez à gauche et allez jusqu'à la rue de la République. Tournez à droite et allez tout droit à l'avenue Jean Jaurès. Tournez à gauche. C'est sur votre gauche.

4. Mme Kraft
Prenez l'avenue du 14 juillet à gauche. Tournez à gauche sur la rue Frédéric Chopin. C'est entre le kiosque à journaux et la banque.

5. M. Redgrave
Tournez à gauche sur l'avenue du 14 juillet. Allez jusqu'à la rue Frédéric Chopin. Tournez à gauche. C'est en face du restaurant italien.

6. Mlle Olsen
Prenez l'avenue du 14 juillet à droite. Allez jusqu'à la rue Victor Hugo. Tournez à droite. Prenez la rue de la République. Allez tout droit. À l'avenue Jean Jaurès tournez à gauche. C'est sur votre droite à côté de l'école.

**Differentiated Learning**
**Accelerate**
Have students continue **Activité 4** by writing original directions and reading them to their group who will then determine the destination.

**Decelerate**
For students who find understanding directions difficult, break them down into shorter parts. Have students say where they are after each instruction.

**Special Needs Students**
**Visually Challenged**
For **Activité 4**, have students number each step of the instructions to make it easier to follow them.

**Auditory Impairment**
You may want to give students additional listening practice to distinguish among masculine and feminine nationalities as well as countries. Say sentences where students can't determine gender just from the name of the person, but must listen for the adjective ending, such as **Dominique est allemande**.

**5**
1. A: Pardon, où se trouve la piscine?
2. A: Pardon, où se trouve le centre commercial?
3. A: Pardon, où se trouve l'hôtel de ville?
4. A: Pardon, où se trouve la banque?
5. A: Pardon, où se trouve le restaurant italien?
6. A: Pardon, où se trouve le supermarché?

*Answers to B will vary.*

**6** *Answers will vary.*

## Expansion

After students practice finding locations and giving directions, distribute a sample map of Paris to every student. Read out a list of directions. Students must trace the directions on the map and then write down the destination they discover. Repeat the exercise for about five locations. Have students discuss and review their findings to see how well they did or what they misunderstood. (Remind students of the difference between the expressions **allez tout droit** and **tournez à droite**.)

# Communiquez!

**5** **Dans ma ville** 1.1, 2.1

**Interpersonal Communication**

*À tour de rôle, jouez les rôles d'un élève francophone qui visite votre école et d'un élève qui l'aide avec des directions.*

**MODÈLE**

A: **Pardon, où se trouve la poste?**

B: **Prenez High Street jusqu'à Oak Road. Tournez à droite. C'est à côté de la banque.**

1. la piscine
2. le centre commercial
3. l'hôtel de ville
4. la banque
5. le restaurant italien
6. le supermarché

# Communiquez!

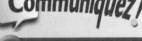 

**6** **Questions personnelles**     1.1

**Interpersonal Communication**

*Répondez aux questions.*

1. Dans ta ville, est-ce qu'il y a un centre commercial au nord de ton école?
2. Où se trouve la poste dans ta ville?
3. Comment est-ce que tu vas au cinéma?
4. As-tu voyagé en Europe? Si oui, où es-tu allé(e)?
5. Veux-tu faire du ski alpin dans les montagnes suisses?
6. Ta famille a-t-elle une voiture allemande?

## Essential Instruction

1. For **Activité 5**, have small groups work together to give directions starting from the school. Tell them to add additional locations in their town, such as a certain park, museum, teen hangout, transit station, etc.

2. Before students do **Activité 6** orally, review the use of **se trouve** in #2 and the use of the **passé composé** in #4.

3. Have students scan the **Rencontres culturelles** dialogue for cognates and any new vocabulary. Then show the filmed dialogue. Have students read aloud and discuss the meaning of the dialogue in small groups. Answer any questions they may have before showing the filmed dialogue a second time. Finally, ask volunteers to role-play the dialogue.

4. Review the answers for **Activité 7** as a class.

# Rencontres culturelles

## Julien et ses parents à Genève     1.2

Julien et ses parents cherchent le Musée international de la Croix-Rouge, à Genève, en Suisse.

**Julien:** Qu'est-ce qu'on fait cet après-midi? Pas un autre musée!

**Mère de Julien:** On est à Genève, on visite le Musée international de la Croix-Rouge! C'est le musée le plus intéressant pour moi!

**Père de Julien:** Ta passion pour les causes humanitaires, c'est fini?

**Julien:** Non, pas du tout!

*(Le père de Julien regarde son plan de Genève.)*

**Père de Julien:** Bon alors… je suis perdu.

**Mère de Julien:** Julien, demande le chemin à ce monsieur.

**Julien:** Pardon, monsieur. Où se trouve le Musée international de la Croix-Rouge?

**Monsieur:** C'est simple. Continuez tout droit. Au bout de la rue, tournez à droite. Puis allez tout droit, ensuite le pont, le lac. Prenez la plus grande avenue et vous y êtes.

**Julien:** Merci, monsieur.

### 7 Julien et ses parents à Genève

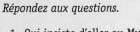

*Répondez aux questions.* 2.1, 2.2

1. Qui insiste d'aller au Musée international de la Croix-Rouge?
2. Julien aime-t-il cette idée?
3. Qui regarde le plan de Genève?
4. Les parents de Julien ont trouvé le musée?
5. Qui demande le chemin?
6. Qu'est-ce qu'il faut faire pour arriver au musée?

### Extension  Tourisme à deux   1.2, 3.2

Léo et Ludivine passent un weekend à Paris. Ils sont à pied.

**Léo:** On aurait pu prendre le métro.

**Ludivine:** Pour ne rien voir… merci. Je préfère la lumière, la couleur de la pierre, les gens qui bougent. Regarde les gens, c'est ça la vie!

**Léo:** Alors, on est venu à Paris pour voir la lumière et les gens? Moi, j'aurais préféré voir les monuments.

### Extension  Comment les idées de tourisme de Léo et Ludivine sont-elles différentes?

## RESOURCES

 **Dialogue Video**

**Answers** _____

**7**

1. la mère de Julien
2. non
3. le père de Julien
4. non
5. Julien
6. Il faut continuer tout droit et tourner à droite au bout de la rue.

**Extension**

Leo is a tourist, Ludivine, a traveler.

## Reference Desk

Point out where Switzerland and Geneva are on a map. Ask students what they know about the Red Cross.

## Culture

**Perspectives**
Discuss with your students the notion of a "traveler" and a "tourist," the ideas brought up in the conversation between Léo and Ludivine. Which category do your students feel they belong to? Would this change if they spent more time in a country rather than making a quick visit? Discuss how they believe Americans to be perceived abroad. How can one avoid seeming like the stereotypical American tourist? Remind students of the **Question centrale** of the unit!

## Differentiated Learning
**Accelerate**
Read aloud the **Extension** dialogue, pointing out new expressions such as **On aurait pu prendre** and **j'aurais préféré**. Then have pairs read it aloud and answer the question orally.

## Multiple Intelligences
**Interpersonal/Verbal-Linguistic**
For homework, have students write directions from school to their place of residence (real or imaginary). The next day, as they read their directions to each other in groups, the other members of the group can draw a map corresponding to the directions given. Then tell them to compare their maps with each other.

# Points de départ

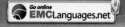

## La Francophonie

**How do travel experiences shape our worldview?**

### ✷ La Suisse

**1.2, 2.1**

La Suisse est un pays formé de 26 cantons. Un canton est une division administrative du territoire. Sa capitale est Berne. Il y a quatre langues nationales: le français, l'allemand, l'italien, et le romanche. La Suisse a une longue tradition de neutralité politique et militaire. Elle est connue aussi pour la fabrication de montres*, ses chocolats délicieux, ses banques, et ses stations de ski.

🔍 **Search words: myswitzerland.com**

La capitale de Berne est dans le canton de Berne.

---

**fabrication de montres** *manufacturing of watches*

**3.1, 3.2**

**Produits**

En Suisse on fabrique (*make*) beaucoup de **montres**. Une marque de luxe est Rolex, connu au monde entier (*entire*) pour sa beauté et précision. Rolex produit environ 2.000 montres, avec 20 modèles, chaque année. Une autre marque de montre suisse est Swatch, qui est bon marché.

### COMPARAISONS

For what products is your state or region known?

**5.1**

### ✷ Genève

**1.2, 2.1**

Genève est située sur les bords du Lac Léman et du Rhône*. C'est la deuxième ville de Suisse après Zurich et la première ville francophone en Suisse. Elle est le centre d'une agglomération de 1,2 millions d'habitants. Genève est une capitale financière et le siège* de 250 institutions internationales dont* l'Office de Nations Unies à Genève (ONUG) et le Comité international de la Croix-Rouge (CICR). Avec son jet d'eau*, haut de 140 mètres, et d'autres attraits* comme sa Vieille Ville, Genève est aussi une ville très touristique.

🔍 **Search words: genève tourisme**

Il y a près de 200.000 habitants à Genève.

---

**Rhône** *Rhone River*; **siège** *headquarters*; **dont** *including*; **jet d'eau** *fountain*; **attraits** *attractions*

## Musée international de la Croix-Rouge* et du Croissant-Rouge

 1.2, 2.1, 2.2, 3.1

Genève, berceau* de la Croix-Rouge*, a inauguré en 1988 un musée consacré à l'œuvre* d'Henry Dunant, fondateur de la Croix-Rouge en 1863. Le musée évoque l'aventure d'hommes et de femmes dans leur mission au service de l'humanité depuis presque 150 ans. Son objectif est de faire connaître* les principes*, l'histoire, et les interventions de la Croix-Rouge et du Croissant-Rouge. Le rôle de la Croix-Rouge est d'assurer une assistance aux blessés*, aux prisonniers, et aux civiles victimes des conflits. Aujourd'hui la Croix-Rouge c'est 12.000 personnes à travers* le monde et des interventions dans 80 pays.

**Search words: musée international de la croix-rouge**

berceau *cradle*; Croix-Rouge *Red Cross*; consacré à l'œuvre *dedicated to the work*; faire connaître *to make known*; principes *principles*; blessés *wounded*; à travers *throughout*

### À discuter

How could a visit to Geneva lead to an interest in humanitarian work? What kind of studies do you think you would need to undertake to pursue these types of jobs?

### Mon dico suisse

souper: *dîner*
donner un bec: *faire la bise*
Il fait bon chaud.: *Il fait très chaud.*
septante: *soixante-dix*
octante: *quatre-vingts*
nonante: *quatre-vingt-dix*

4.1

### COMPARAISONS

What has the Red Cross done for residents of your city or region last year or this year?

5.1

---

## Musées
### *Museums*

MUSEE INTERNATIONAL DE LA CROIX-ROUGE ET DU CROISSANT-ROUGE

AVENUE DE LA PAIX 17 • 1202 GENEVE

☎ 022 748 95 25        FX 022 748 95 28

www.micr.org

🕐: Me au lu: 10h-17h – Fermé: Ma

📠: Accès: CHF 10.– /
Gratuit pour les moins de 12 ans /

👫: Sur rendez-vous / *by appointment*
tél. 022 748 95 06

🚌: n° 8, 28, F, V, Z

P: Nations

♿: Accessible

📚, Médiathèque: sur rendez-vous

🎦: Restaurant

🎁: Cadeaux, souvenirs

---

**Answers**

**À discuter**
*Answers will vary.*

**Comparaisons**
*Answers will vary.*

### Reference Desk

Remind students about their previous study of **Médecins sans frontières,** and discuss how important it is for multiple humanitarian agencies to be ready to help in times of crisis. Where has the Red Cross been involved recently around the world? Do students feel a connection with people and countries in need of aid worldwide when they make a donation or give blood for the Red Cross? Reiterate that the Red Cross is an international organization, not solely an American one.

---

### Differentiated Learning
#### Accelerate/Expand

Have students use the search words to learn more online about Switzerland. Break down the research into more specific topics that students can choose such as Swiss chocolates, ski resorts, watches, Romanche, and so forth. Form groups to share information in class, with different topics being discussed within a group.

### Special Needs Students
#### Linguistically Challenged

You may want to provide a handout with bullet points in English of the important information to aid students who have difficulty with reading comprehension so they can glean the main facts.

## Communication

### Presentational: Cooperative Groups

Students will work in two groups, one for Geneva and one for Berne, to put together a proposal for a class trip to Switzerland. The finished project will be illustrated with informative posters and brochures about international, business, and cultural attractions and a five-day program for visiting each city. Students should note places to see on city maps of Geneva and propose a couple of walking tours with directions from their hotels (use the material presented on pp. 545–47 for reference), as well as excursions on Lake Geneva or into the Alps. Students will present their work orally. Encourage the use of the **futur proche** (**aller** + infinitives). Use a carefully devised rubric to evaluate for participation, content, and accuracy.

**8** **Questions culturelles**  1.3, 2.1

*Faites les activités suivantes.*

1. Faites un profil de la Suisse:
   - Langues officielles
   - Capitale
   - Produits
2. Retrouvez les informations suivantes sur Genève:
   - Situation
   - Nombre d'habitants
   - Nombre d'institutions internationales
3. Situez sur un plan de Genève:
   - Le jet d'eau
   - Le Palais des Nations
   - La Vieille Ville
4. Citez des évènements où la Croix-Rouge est intervenue:
   - Conflit militaire
   - Catastrophe naturelle
   - Catastrophe sanitaire

Le jet d'eau de Genève est haut de 140 m. (*459 feet*).

## Du côté des médias

*Lisez la carte suisse.*

### Restaurant La Raclette

**ENTRÉES**
Raclette nature ou au poivre
Salade composée, asperges et parmesan, vinaigrette à l'érable
Carpaccio de bœuf, tapenade d'olives, et persil
Antipasto misto
(esturgeon fumé, œufs de cailles, rosette de Lyon, olives, câpres, anchois)

**PLATS PRINCIPAUX**
Raclette traditionnelle garnie de jambon, et de bœuf des Grisons
Émincé de veau à la zurichoise
Pavé de truite, salsa de concombre, aneth, yogourt, et saumon fumé
Escalope de saumon à la moutarde de Meaux
Fondue au fromage suisse
Fondue au fromage suisse aux cèpes et au thym
Poulet grillé aux olives, raisins, et citron
Foie de veau, sauce à l'ail rôti et pleurotes grillés
Bavette de bœuf marinée, vinaigrette aux herbes fraîches

**DESSERTS**
Poire Belle-Hélène
Vermicelles de marrons glacés
Clafoutis aux cerises noires
Torte au chocolat
Nougat glacé aux fruits séchés et aux noix

**À LA CARTE**
Portion de rösti
Viandes des Grisons
100G Fromage Raclette

**9** **Restaurant La Raclette**

*Faites les activités suivantes.*

1. Retrouvez sur la carte l'origine de ces produits:
   - rosette de….
   - moutarde….
   - veau à la….
   - bœuf des….

   1.2, 2.1, 2.2, 3.1

2. Trouvez sur la carte trois plats typiquement suisses:
   - un plat de fromage:
   - un plat de viande:
   - un plat de légumes:
3. Citez dans la carte deux plats qui viennent de la gastronomie…
   - italienne:
   - française:
4. Choisissez votre menu (une entrée, un plat, un dessert).

## Essential Instruction

1. For **Activité 8**, pass out maps of Geneva. Have groups of four collaborate to locate the places in #3.
2. After reviewing the main categories on the menu, complete **Activité 9** as a class.
3. For the interview in **La culture sur place**, give students the choice of interviewing a real or imaginary person. If students prepare an interview of an imaginary person, have them work with a partner and exchange questions, then do **Activités 10** and **11**.
4. After students present their interviews, discuss the questions in **Activité 12** as a class or in small groups.

# La culture sur place

## Interview avec un voyageur/une voyageuse

### Introduction

Est-ce que vous connaissez (*know*) quelqu'un qui a voyagé à une destination où l'on parle français? Ça peut être un ami, un membre de votre famille, un camarade de classe, ou une connaissance sur votre réseau social (*social network*). Pour ce projet vous allez interviewer cette personne.

### 10 Investigation: Les questions  1.2, 2.1, 4.1

*Faites des recherches en ligne sur la destination de la personne que vous interviewez. Préparez une liste de questions. Si la personne parle français, posez les questions en français. Sinon, posez les questions en anglais. Commencez avec des questions comme les suivantes.*

1. Où est-ce que vous êtes allé(e)?
2. Qu'est-ce que vous avez vu?
3. Qu'est-ce que vous avez fait?
4. Qu'est-ce que vous avez aimé?
5. Qu'est-ce que vous n'avez pas aimé?

*Posez encore trois ou quatre questions plus précises sur le voyage, basées sur votre recherche. Évitez (Avoid) les questions avec les réponses "oui" et "non."*

### 11 Présentation et discussion  1.3

*Préparez un résumé (summary) de votre interview. Vous devez parler du pays ou de la région francophone où la personne est allée, de ses expériences, et de ses souvenirs. Ensuite, présentez votre résumé à un groupe de trois ou quatre camarades de classe.*

> **MODÈLE** **Mon sujet est allé à/au/en.... Il/Elle a vu.... Il/Elle a fait, a visité, a pris, etc.  Il/Elle a aimé.... Il/Elle n'a pas aimé....**

### 12 Faisons l'inventaire!  1.1

*Discutez ces questions avec vos camarades de classe.*

1. What patterns or trends do you see in the experiences of the people who were interviewed by those in your group? Was it an obstacle for them to not speak French?
2. Do you feel like you can make any general statements about what it might be like to travel to a country or a region where French is the primary language spoken?

### Reference Desk

1. For conducting an interview, remind students that they know many ways to ask questions and get information: **est-ce que**, intonation, and inversion. They can now use inversion for making questions in the **passé composé**. They should use a variety of interrogative adverbs (**combien**, **comment**, **où**, **quand**, and **pourquoi**); pronouns **qui** and **que**; and interrogative adjectives, such as **quelle(s)** and **quel(s)**.
2. Post the presentations online and ask students which trip they would like to take someday.

### Differentiated Learning
**Decelerate**

For the interview, create a worksheet containing the questions in **Activité 10** with a line for each answer and a second line for students to change it to the third person (**Activité 11**).

### Learning Styles
**Visual Learners**

Before you look at the Swiss menu, offer extra credit for students who volunteer to bring in images of three food items from the menu (printed, copied, or drawn). Assign each student different items.

# Structure de la langue

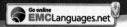

## Superlative of Adjectives  1.2

*Quelle fille est la plus chic? Quelle est la plus grande fille?*

To say that a person or thing has the most of a certain quality compared to all others, use the superlative construction.

> **le/la/les + plus + adjectif**

| | |
|---|---|
| Solange est l'athlète **la plus fatiguée**. | *Solange is the most tired athlete.* |
| La tour Eiffel est **le plus beau** monument. | *The Eiffel Tower is the most beautiful monument.* |

If an adjective usually precedes a noun, its superlative form also precedes a noun. If an adjective usually follows a noun, so does its superlative form. Both the definite article and the adjective agree in gender and in number with the noun they describe.

Sometimes the superlative is followed by a form of **de**.

Québec est la ville la plus charmante **du** Québec.   *Quebec is the most charming city in Quebec.*

The superlative of **bon(s)** is **le/la/les meilleur(s)**.

Ce sont **les meilleurs** footballeurs.   *They are the best soccer players.*

### COMPARAISONS  4.1

How do you form the superlative in English?
New York is the biggest American city.
Daniel is one of its most elegant restaurants.
What is the superlative of "good" in English?

COMPARAISONS: In English superlatives are made by adding –est to the adjective or most before the adjective. The superlative of "good" is "best," and, like in French, is irregular.

# Communiquez!

⑬ Answers to questions will vary.
1. A: Quelle est l'équipe de basket la plus paresseuse?
2. A: Quelle est l'école la plus stricte?
3. A: Quel est le musée le plus intéressant?
4. A: Quel est le restaurant le plus chic?
5. A: Quelle est la boutique la plus chère?
6. A: Quel est l'homme ou la femme d'affaires le plus généreux?

⑭ Script can be found in the front pages of the Annotated Teacher's Edition.
1. D
2. E
3. F
4. A
5. B
6. C

## 13 Ma ville  1.1

**Interpersonal Communication**

*À tour de rôle, demandez l'opinion de votre partenaire des endroits et personnes dans votre ville ou région.*

**MODÈLE**  le parc/splendide
A: **Quel est le parc le plus splendide?**
B: **Regions est le parc le plus splendide.**

1. l'équipe de basket/paresseux
2. l'école/strict
3. le musée/intéressant
4. le restaurant/chic
5. la boutique/cher
6. l'homme ou la femme d'affaires/généreux

Quel est le musée le plus intéressant?

Le musée d'art.

## 14 Qui est l'élève le plus...?  1.2

*Écoutez chaque description des personnes suivantes au superlatif et écrivez la lettre qui correspond à l'image la plus logique.*

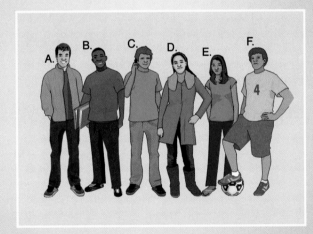

### Game

**Le meilleur jeu!**
As students get used to forming the superlative of adjectives, you can increase the difficulty of the game on p. 554 with a paperless version: have students sit in a circle. One by one, a student will call out a noun, such as car, movie, book, restaurant, store, etc. As soon as students think of an appropriate superlative adjective and can use it in a sentence, they raise their hands. Call on several students to try out their answers. Alternatively, make it a Pictionary-type game. One student thinks of an item and a pertinent adjective and goes to the board to illustrate this notion. The other students, either as a team or the class as a whole, must guess what the sentence would be using a superlative adjective. Teams can compete for the best or most creative sentences.

**Differentiated Learning**
**Decelerate**
1. To help students with the order of the superlative, have pairs write a sample sentence for each BAGS adjective, and then share their sentences with another pair, checking for accuracy.
2. Have pairs write sentences on the board for four adjective/noun combinations (masculine, feminine, singular, and plural) that you provide. Have students work with a partner peer-editing his or her work.

**Multiple Intelligences**
**Verbal-Linguistic**
Brainstorm a list of categories in which students could incorporate the superlative, such as school subjects, teachers, sports teams, cities, countries, singers, cars, food, etc. Then ask them to create a sentence using the superlative for several categories in order to express their opinions.

1. Ce sont les élèves les plus diligents.
2. Ce sont les profs les plus intelligents.
3. C'est la plus jolie cantine.
4. C'est le cours le plus intéressant.
5. C'est la plus nouvelle piscine.
6. C'est la médiathèque la plus moderne.
7. C'est le meilleur labo.
8. C'est la meilleure équipe de foot.
9. C'est la plus grande salle de classe.
10. C'est la meilleure école.

1. Mon ami le plus bavard/mon amie la plus bavarde, c'est ....
2. Mon plus grand ami/ma plus grande amie, c'est....
3. Mon ami le plus généreux/mon amie la plus généreuse, c'est....
4. Mon ami le plus égoïste/mon amie la plus égoïste, c'est....
5. Mon ami le plus chic/mon amie la plus chic, c'est....
6. Mon plus joli ami/ma plus jolie amie, c'est....
7. Mon plus bel ami/ma plus belle amie, c'est....

## Game

Challenge teams to come up with the longest list of adjectives they can think of, with a matching list of nouns relevant to each adjective. Have students from each team read statements using the material from their lists and forming superlative adjectives. Compare lists. If a team does not have an adjective that another team has on the list, the first team must create a superlative statement using the missing adjective.

---

**15 Notre école**   **2.1, 2.2**

*Vous êtes le guide pour des visiteurs à votre école. Utilisez le superlatif pour décrire ces choses et personnes.*

**MODÈLES**  nouveau/l'école
**C'est la plus nouvelle école.**

profs/énergique
**Ce sont les profs les plus énergiques.**

1. élèves/diligent
2. profs/intelligent
3. joli/cantine
4. cours/intéressant
5. nouveau/piscine
6. médiathèque/moderne
7. bon/labo
8. bon/équipe de foot
9. grand/salle de classe
10. bon/école

Ce sont les élèves les plus diligents.

**16 Mes amis**  **2.1, 2.2**

*Utilisez le superlatif d'un adjectif de la liste pour écrire des phrases qui décrivent vos amis.*

**MODÈLES**  énergique
**Mon ami le plus énergique, c'est Serge.**
petit
**Ma plus petite amie, c'est Anne.**

1. bavard
2. grand
3. généreux
4. égoïste
5. chic
6. joli
7. beau

**Essential Instruction**

1. Instruct students to write out **Activité 15**, underlining the superlative structure. Then have them review the **Activité** orally with a partner.
2. As a class, quickly identify the adjectives in **Activité 16** that precede the noun vs. those that follow it. Then have the students work with a partner.
3. Give students the choice of doing **Activités 17**, **18**, or **19**.

# À vous la parole

## Communiquez!

**Question centrale**

?

How do travel experiences shape our worldview?

**17   La Suisse**   1.3, 2.1

**Interpretive/Presentational Communication**

Plan a vacation in Switzerland that centers around its natural landscape. Tell your classmates what you will visit and what you will do and see there.

**MODÈLE**   Je vais visiter…. Je vais voir…. Je vais (faire)….

Search words: **myswitzerland.com: une histoire d'eau**
**swissworld: saisons**
**swissworld: paysages**

## Communiquez!

**18   De l'humanitaire avec La Croix-Rouge**   1.3, 3.1

**Interpretive/Presentational Communication**

You and a friend are organizing volunteers for the Red Cross in various Francophone countries. Do online research about current projects and volunteer activities and create a survey listing five of them. Distribute the survey to your classmates and ask them to rank the projects and activities in order of their preferences. Tally the results and present the top volunteer opportunity to the class.

Search words:  **croix rouge suisse: jeunesse**

## Communiquez!

**19   Venez chez moi!**   1.3

**Presentational Communication**

You are throwing a birthday party for a friend. Give your friends detailed directions from school to your house. Include buildings and landmarks they will see on their way.

---

## Answers

**17** *Presentations will vary.*

**18** *Research will vary.*

**19** *Directions will vary.*

### Critical Thinking

**Analysis**
Ask students to reflect on how learning about Quebec and Montreal, the Loire Valley, Switzerland, train travel, and giving directions has enriched their thinking about travel. Do they feel better informed? Ask if any of your students has visited these regions or traveled by **TGV**. If so, what further information could they provide to complement what was presented in the unit? Has this unit given them the curiosity to learn more about these places or to visit them?

### Reference Desk

**Blended Instruction**
Consider using blended instruction, a combination of in-class learning and computer-mediated instruction or learning opportunities. Ask students to complete activities on the computer, using their cell or smartphone, or other emerging electronic technology. This will allow students to hone their tech skills and become more independent learners. Schedule routine Internet and e-book learning in class and in the lab.

---

## Differentiated Learning
### Expand
Invite students to expand on **Activités 15** and **16** with positive sentences of their own creation that use the superlative.

## Learning Styles
### Visual Learners
Ask students to brainstorm adjectives they have already learned and write them on the board in random order. Then, using pictures from magazines or the Internet, have students create some superlative sentences, for example, "the tallest mountain," "the most ferocious dog," "the most delicious dessert," etc. Students love to talk about the funny animal pictures that abound on the Internet.

# Lecture thématique

## Je me souviens

### Rencontre avec l'auteur   1.2

**Louis Aragon** (1897–1982) était écrivain et poète français. Très jeune, il faisait partie du mouvement surréaliste. Pendant la Seconde Guerre mondiale (*WWII*), il est devenu l'un des poètes de la Résistance contre les nazis. Son roman (*novel*) le plus célèbre est **Aurélien** (1945), un roman d'amour autobiographique. Poète majeur de la deuxième partie du XX^{ème} siècle, beaucoup de ses textes ont été popularisés par des compositeurs et chanteurs. Vous allez lire le poème "Je me souviens." Yves Montand a chanté ce poème dans lequel un homme regarde des cartes postales de ses amis dans un album. De quoi se souvient-il quand il regarde ces photos?

### Stratégie de lecture  4.1

**Imagery** is descriptive language used to create word pictures, or **images**. As you read, fill in a graphic organizer like the one below with images from the song lyrics.

Image 1 · Image 2 · Image 3 · Image 4 · Images de "Je me souviens"

### Outils de lecture  1.2, 3.1

#### Stanzas

A stanza, or **strophe**, is a grouping of lines in a poem or song. This song poem has quintains, or five-line stanzas. In French, such a poem is called **un cinquain**. Note that the rhyme scheme in **"Je me souviens"** is A-A-B-B-A in each stanza. These stanzas progress in meaning. In the first stanza, the speaker feels nostalgia (a longing) for trips he and his friends have taken. In the second stanza, he is looking at a postcard album and rereading how his friends signed their postcards. The third stanza is about whose memories?

*Le cerf-volant*, 1925. Achille Varin. Château-musée municipal de Nemours, France.

**Essential Instruction**

1. To introduce the reading, ask if students have ever collected postcards.
2. Provide an overview of the German occupation of France, the Resistance, and surrealism, and then read **Rencontres avec l'auteur**.
3. Ask students to scan the poem and list the final words from each line, and then discuss the rhyme scheme, AABBA.
4. Read the **Stratégies de lecture** and ask if there is anything that students are nostalgic for.

5. Have students listen to the poem with eyes closed. Then have small groups read the poem aloud and answer the **Pendant la lecture** questions. Are they aware that the second stanza contains a series of disconnected excerpts from postcards from different places? Whose memories are described in the third stanza? Are they of trips like those in the second stanza, or of simple everyday pleasures, such as **un verre d'eau fraiche**? Do students have any similar memories of a simple pleasure?

# Pre-lecture  5.1

De quel voyage est-ce que tu te souviens? La nostalgie évoque quelles images de ce voyage?

  1.2, 2.1, 2.2

Ô la nostalgie à retrouver de vieilles cartes postales
Où le ciel* est toujours bleu, l'arbre* toujours vert, la mer étale*
Sans doute on ne les met dans l'album que pour les photographies
Je suis seul à savoir* ce que l'écriture* au dos signifie
Les diminutifs*, les phrases banales

Au-dessus de ce monde mort on voit traîner des cerfs-volants*
Poignées de main* de Castelnaudary, bons baisers* du Mont-Blanc,
Un bonjour de Saint-Jean-de-Luz, salutations de la Baule,
Je suis depuis* trois jours ici, c'est plein de* Parisiens très drôles,
Nous avons fait un voyage excellent

Je me souviens de nuits qui n'ont été rien d'autre que des nuits
Je me souviens de jours où rien d'important ne s'était produit
Un café dans le bois* près de la gare Saint Nom La Bretèche
Le bonheur* extraordinaire en été d'un verre d'eau fraîche
Les Champs-Élysées un soir sous la pluie*

> **Pendant la lecture**
> 1. Les cartes postales sont-elles réalistes ou idéalistes?
> 2. Qui a la clé de la signification des "diminutifs" et "phrases banales"?

> **Pendant la lecture**
> 3. Quels endroits les amis du narrateur ont-ils visités?

> **Pendant la lecture**
> 4. Le narrateur se souvient-il de moments simples ou compliqués?

le ciel *sky*; l'arbre *tree*; étale *spreads out*; ne... que *only*; avoir *to know*; l'écriture *writing*; diminutifs *nicknames*; traîner des cerfs-volants *kites floating*; poignées de main *handshakes*; baisers *kisses*; depuis *since*; plein de *full of*; le bois *woods*; le bonheur *happiness*; la pluie *rain*

# Post-lecture  2.1, 2.2

De quelles façons cette chanson est-elle nostalgique?

# Le monde visuel  3.1

*Le cerf-volant* (The Kite) d'Achille Varin (1863–1942) montre l'utilisation artistique de la perspective. La perspective est une technique utilisée pour montrer la relation spaciale entre objets, donnant une illusion de distance et de profondeur (*depth*). La ligne qui divise la terre et l'herbe (*grass*), la ligne verticale des arbres, et la ligne horizontale de l'horizon attirent l'œil dans la dimension de cette scène en plein air. Comment la perspective utilisée avec le cerf-volant donne-t-elle une vue plongeante (*diving*) dans la peinture?

**20** *Activities will vary.*

## Les copains d'abord

Here is the translation for **Les copains d'abord:**
A = Antoine
F = Florence
MA = Marie-Alix
M = Mathéo

A: Come on, hurry up! M: Yeah, you're gonna miss your train! M: We're coming, we're coming... F: Well, Marie-Alix took us to the wrong train station! MA: Yeah? Well, Florence left our tickets in the taxi cab! We were lucky! F: She looked at the wrong departure screen. MA: Flo forgot to stamp her ticket. M: Well, the summer vacation is off to a good start.... A: All right, girls, let's say 'bye and have a good vacation in Toulouse. MA: That's right, we won't see you for a while. F: Have a good trip to Quebec! M: 'Bye baby, have a good time at your grandma's. I'll miss you. F: Me too, love. Have fun in Quebec! MA: Don't worry, we're only leaving for two weeks! A: Yeah, well, I'll be gone two months! M: OK, now we gotta move. To the airport! A: You're right, the plane takes off in two hours! M: It's so nice of your parents to invite me to Quebec for two weeks. What's your city called again? A: Mont-Saint-Hilaire. It's 40 kilometers from Montréal. A: I promise we'll go hiking and biking in the mountains. M: Cool! And, can we swim in the river... A: ... the Richelieu? Yes, it's a natural spring, a pure water source that hasn't been polluted by industrialization. And further north we can go kayaking because of the rapids! M: Oh, awesome! And, will we be able to go out in Montreal in the evening? A: Well, my parents'll take us out to eat and to Quebec City too. M: And I'll be there during the FrancoFolies festival, right? A: You'll see, you'll have so much fun, the girls will be jealous!

List of slang and idiomatic expressions: **louper:** *to miss;* **avoir du pot:** *to be lucky;* **T'en fais pas:** *don't worry;* **se grouiller:** *to hurry;* **filer:** *to run;* **la classe:** *awesome*

**20** Activités d'expansion  1.3

*Faites les activités suivantes.*

1. Écrivez un paragraphe dans lequel (*in which*) vous expliquez l'organisation de la chanson et la sélection d'images. Servez-vous de votre organigramme.
2. Écrivez une carte postale à un copain qui décrit un voyage réel ou imaginaire. Commencez votre carte postale avec **Cher** (pour un copain) ou **Chère** (pour une copine) et terminez avec une expression de la deuxième strophe du poème. Dessinez ou imprimez une image pour votre carte postale.
3. Écrivez un cinquain avec des images d'un voyage réel ou imaginaire.

 1.2, 2.1

### Essential Instruction

1. Offer the **Activités d'expansion** for extra credit.
2. Before reading the dialogue, ask students to identify where each of the four friends is going. Then guide them through the dialogue.
3. Invite students to choose one of the **Projets finaux**. After they complete the research, have them share their findings in small groups.

## T'es branché?

# Projets finaux

### A Connexions par Internet: L'architecture

**1.2, 1.3, 3.2**

Research online the characteristics of the following architectural styles of French castles: **féodal ou médiéval**, **gothique**, **gothique flamboyant**, **renaissance**, **classique**. Find a French castle that you like that illustrates one of these styles and present it to the class. Include its name, location, style, and the time period of that style. Also include one other interesting piece of information that would make your classmates want to visit the castle.

**MODÈLE**

**C'est le château de Cheverny. Il se trouve à l'est de Tours et entre Chenonceau au sud et Chambord au nord. C'est dans le style classique. Le classicisme est un style du XVIIᵉᵐᵉ siècle. Cheverny est le château de la Loire le plus meublé.**

### B Communautés en ligne

**1.2, 1.3, 2.2, 3.1**

**Les 22 régions de France**

Learn about one of France's 22 regions by writing to the French tourist office or consulate in your area. Begin by finding a map of the regions. Then, select one that looks interesting to you based on preliminary research. Create a list of questions and, using what you learned about writing correspondence in this unit's **Stratégie communicative** section, write an e-mail asking the French consulate or tourist office to send you information and/or web links for each of the following categories: history; regional traditions, festivals, and celebrations; art and architecture; tourist sites; and, food specialties. Create a PowerPoint™ or other visual presentation about your region for the class.

 **Search words: régions de france, office de tourisme de** *(name of region)*

### Reference Desk

Slides of many French historical buildings are available at **La documentation française.**

### Communication

**Presentational**

Ask students to bring in a picture from a travel magazine that contains one or more people and a train or airplane or some other travel situation. Have them write a caption or cartoon dialogue bubble for their picture. Keeping their caption or bubble to one side, students then swap images with a partner and write something appropriate for their classmate's picture. Have partners compare what they have written for each picture.

**Multiple Intelligences**
**Verbal-Linguistic**
Have students role-play the dialogue in the cartoon.

## Expansion

As the class or groups in the class complete **Activité C**, have each student be responsible for presenting one of the locations to the class using the present and the **futur proche** (**aller** + infinitive). Make a gallery on the class wall and have students summarize orally to the class.

**C** **Passez à l'action!**   1.2, 1.3, 2.1, 2.2, 3.2

### Le programme de notre voyage

Plan a class trip to several French-speaking cities in Europe or Africa. Create an itinerary and draw a map to show where you will go. Include information about the cities (population, history, important sites). Also find places where you will stay and eat (hotels and restaurants) and how you will travel (**en train, en bus, en avion, en voiture**—or a combination of these).

 **Search words:** *(place name)* **tourisme**
**voyager à/au/aux/en** *(place name)*

How do travel experiences shape our worldview?

**D** **Faisons le point!**  2.1, 2.2

Your teacher will give you a chart like the one below. Fill it in with what you've learned about how travel in other countries shapes one's worldview.

| Je comprends | Je ne comprends pas encore | Mes connexions |
|---|---|---|
|  |  |  |

| What did I do well to learn and use the content of this unit? | What should I do to better learn and use the content of this unit? |
|---|---|
| How can I effectively communicate to others what I have learned? | What was the most important information I learned in this unit? |

### Essential Instruction

1. For **Activité D**, distribute copies of the graphic organizer located in the **Copy Masters** supplement. After students complete the chart, survey the class about common areas that they need to review. Consider grouping together students who responded similarly and match them with students who can help them.

2. Review answers and discuss any questions after students listen to **Activité A**.

3. Assign **Activité B** to do with a partner. Or, play the role of the traveler and have the class play the role of the friend.

# Évaluation

## A. Évaluation de compréhension auditive

  1.2

*Écoutez Sandrine et Lucas décrire leur journée aux châteaux de la Loire. Choisissez la réponse appropriée.*

1. Quelle heure est-il?
   - A. Il est huit heures.
   - B. Il est neuf heures.
   - C. Il est dix heures.
2. Sandrine et Lucas vont visiter combien de châteaux?
   - A. Ils vont visiter cinq châteaux.
   - B. Ils vont visiter un ou deux châteaux.
   - C. Ils vont visiter deux ou trois châteaux.
3. Comment est-ce qu'ils vont y aller?
   - A. Ils vont y aller en bus.
   - B. Ils vont y aller à vélo.
   - C. Ils vont y aller en voiture.
4. Quel château vont-ils visiter d'abord?
   - A. D'abord ils vont visiter Chambord.
   - B. D'abord ils vont visiter Cheverny.
   - C. D'abord ils vont visiter Chenonceau.
5. Comment peut-on trouver le château?
   - A. Le château est à droite sur la route d'Orléans.
   - B. Le château est à gauche sur la route d'Orléans.
   - C. Le château est à droite sur la route de Cheverny.
6. Qu'est-ce qu'il y a dans le village?
   - A. Il y a un centre commercial près du château.
   - B. Il y a des cafés et un bureau de poste au village.
   - C. Il n'y a rien dans le village.
7. Comment Sandrine et Lucas vont-ils revenir?
   - A. Lucas et Sandrine vont revenir à pied.
   - B. Lucas et Sandrine vont revenir à vélo.
   - C. Lucas et Sandrine vont revenir en train.

## B. Évaluation orale

 1.1

With a partner, role-play a conversation between a traveler who's going somewhere in Quebec, France, or Switzerland by train and a friend who's come to the station to say good-bye. The friend asks if the traveler has bought a ticket, looked at the departures board to see if the train is on time, and brought something to eat. The traveler responds, and then tells the friend what he or she is going to see while on the train. The friend asks what the traveler is going to see and do at his or her destination. After the traveler responds, the friend wishes the traveler a good trip.

Leçon C | cinq cent soixante-trois **563**

**Multiple Intelligences**
**Verbal-Linguistic**
Have students write out the dialogue for **Évaluation Activité B** for homework. In class, pair up students and have them combine their dialogues into one. After they practice, have volunteers present to the class.

## Connections

### Economics

Ask students to make a trip to the supermarket or other local stores. What products can they find that are from Switzerland or Canada? (Swiss chocolate, cheeses, water, candies; beauty products, watches, clothing; Canadian maple products, clothing, etc.) They can list them, take photos, or bring in some (food) samples. As students compare their findings, ask them if they knew about these products beforehand. Are they more aware of these now?

---

**C** **Évaluation culturelle**  **1.1, 2.1, 2.2, 3.2**

In this activity, you will compare Francophone cultures with American culture. You may need to do some additional research on American culture.

1. **La province de Québec**
   Compare the province of Quebec to your state. Compare their languages, flags, populations, largest cities, capitals, and popular sports.

2. **Les destinations touristiques**
   Compare tourist attractions in Montreal or Geneva with those in the area where you live.

3. **Les spectacles**
   Compare les FrancoFolies with a music festival you've heard about, followed online, or attended.

4. **La géographie et l'histoire politique**
   Compare geopolitical political subdivisions (regions, provinces, states, counties, etc.) in France, Switzerland, and Canada with those in the United States.

5. **Les monuments historiques**
   Compare the castles of the Loire Valley with old buildings or homes that people visit in your region or other parts of the United States (i.e., the plantations of the South or the mansions of Newport, R.I.).

6. **Les personnes célèbres**
   Compare one of the famous people of Tours with a famous person from your area. Why are/were these people famous? In what field do/did they work? Do you think they will be remembered 100 years from now? Why, or why not?

7. **Les produits**
   For what products is Switzerland known, and how do these products compare with those produced in your state or region?

8. **Une institution internationale**
   Name the international institution with offices in Geneva and in New York City. What is the goal of this organization?

9. **La Croix-Rouge**
   What is the role of the Red Cross, and what has it done for residents in your city, state, or region?

---

**D** **Évaluation écrite**  **1.3**

A French family friend has arrived at your local or regional airport or other transportation station, and has rented a car. She has texted you that she needs directions to your house. Tell her the most efficient way to get there.

### Essential Instruction

1. Ask students to read through and choose one of the topics in **Activité C** that interests them the most. In class, group together students according to their preferences. Have these groups research and present about their selected topic.

2. Provide a detailed rubric to guide students as they do writing for **Activité D**.

3. Consider having students record their commentary for **Activité E** and randomly assign another student to listen and provide feedback on the recording, using a simple rubric with answers and a rating scale based on how much the listener can understand.

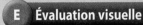 

## E  Évaluation visuelle  1.3

Compare the illustrations of a train station at two different times of the day. Then, answer the questions below to describe each illustration. The questions below will help you organize your paragraph.

**MODÈLE**  Il y a une voyageuse au composteur?
**À 14h00 il y a une voyageuse qui composte son billet.**
**À 23h00, il n'y a personne qui composte son billet.**

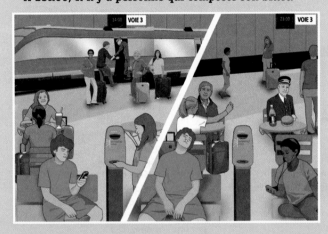

1. Il y a un train sur la voie numéro 3?
2. Il y a des voyageurs qui montent dans le train?
3. Il y a un adolescent qui écoute de la musique?
4. Le conducteur travaille?
5. Les voyageurs prennent quelque chose?

## F  Évaluation compréhensive  1.3

Create a storyboard with six frames. Write captions for each frame, telling about what happened (**passé composé**) on a train trip to Quebec, France, or Switzerland. Begin at the train station, continue with what you saw from the train window and did on the train, and conclude with what happened after you arrived at your destination. Share your storyboard with a group of classmates.

**Answers** _____

**E**

1. À 14h00 il y a un train sur la voie numéro 3. À 23h00, il n'y a plus de train sur la voie numéro 3.
2. À 14h00 il y a des voyageurs qui montent dans le train. À 23h00, il n'y a personne qui monte dans le train.
3. À 14h00 il y a un adolescent qui écoute de la musique. À 23h00, il n'y a pas d'adolescent qui écoute de la musique.
4. À 14h00 le conducteur travaille. À 23h00, le conducteur ne travaille plus.
5. À 14h00 les voyageurs prennent quelque chose à manger et à boire. À 23h00, ils ne prennent rien.

**F**  *Answers will vary.*

### Reference Desk

You may wish to use the illustration on this page to discuss the pros and cons of traveling. When is travel fun and easy? When is it tiresome and arduous? Ask students to relate their experiences.

**Learning Styles**
**Visual Learners**
**Activité F** provides a creative outlet to students who like to draw. Be sure to provide a rubric with clear expectations regarding the required vocabulary and structures.

# Vocabulaire de l'Unité 10  1.2 · Go online EMCLanguages.net

| | | |
|---|---|---|
| | **accompagner** to accompany *B* | |
| l' | **Allemagne (f.)** Germany *C* | |
| l' | **Angleterre (f.)** England *C* | |
| l' | **arrivée (f.)** arrival *B* | |
| un | **autobus** bus *B* | |
| | **belge** Belgian *C* | |
| la | **Belgique** Belgium *C* | |
| un | **billet** ticket *A* | |
| | **bon: Bon voyage!** Have a good trip! *B* | |
| le | **bout** end *C*; **au bout de** at the end of *C* | |
| la | **campagne** country(side) *B* | |
| la | **capitale** capital *A* | |
| une | **cascade** waterfall *B* | |
| une | **cause** cause *C* | |
| un | **château** castle *B* | |
| le | **chemin** way, path *C*; **demander le chemin** ask for directions *C* | |
| une | **colline** hill *B* | |
| | **composter** to validate a ticket *B* | |
| un | **composteur** ticket-stamping machine *B* | |
| un | **contrôleur, une contrôleuse** ticket collector *B* | |
| le | **départ** departure *B* | |
| un | **département** department *B* | |
| une | **destination** destination *B* | |
| une | **devise** motto *A* | |
| une | **direction** direction *C* | |
| un | **drapeau** flag *A* | |
| | **droit: tout droit** straight ahead *C* | |
| | **en: en face (de)** across (from) *C* | |
| | **entre** between *C* | |
| l' | **Espagne (f.)** Spain *C* | |
| l' | **est (m.)** east *A* | |
| un | **étang** pond *B* | |
| l' | **Europe (f.)** Europe *C* | |
| | **faire: faire la connaissance (de)** to meet *A* | |
| une | **forêt** forest *B* | |
| un(e) | **Francanadien(ne)** from French-speaking Canada *A* | |
| un | **guide** guidebook *B* | |
| un(e) | **habitant(e)** inhabitant, resident *A* | |
| | **humanitaire** humanitarian *C* | |
| | **international(e)** international *C* | |
| l' | **Italie (f.)** Italy *C* | |
| | **italien(ne)** Italian *C* | |
| | **jusqu'à** until *C* | |
| un | **lac** lake *B* | |
| | **loin (de)** far (from) *B* | |
| | **louer** to rent *B* | |
| le | **Luxembourg** Luxembourg *C* | |

| | |
|---|---|
| | **luxembourgeois(e)** from, of Luxembourg *C* |
| | **ne (n')… jamais** never *B* |
| | **ne (n')… personne** no one, nobody, not anyone *B* |
| | **ne (n')… plus** no longer, not anymore *B* |
| | **ne (n')… rien** nothing, not anything *B* |
| le | **nord** north *A* |
| l' | **ouest (m.)** west *A* |
| | **pas: pas du tout** not at all *C* |
| la | **passion** passion *C* |
| | **perdu(e)** lost *C* |
| un | **plaisir** pleasure *A* |
| un | **plan** city map *C* |
| | **plus: le/la/les plus (+ adjective)** the most (+ adjective) *C* |
| une | **préposition** preposition *A* |
| le | **profil** profile *A* |
| la | **province** province *A* |
| le | **quai** platform *B* |
| le | **Québec** Quebec *A* |
| | **québécois(e)** from, of Quebec *A* |
| | **quelqu'un** someone, somebody *B* |
| | **quelque chose** something *B* |
| | **réaliser** to realize *A* |
| une | **rivière** river *B* |
| une | **route** road, highway, route *B* |
| un | **siège** seat *B* |
| | **simple** simple *C* |
| | **situé(e)** located *A* |
| | **souvent** often *B* |
| | **souviens: je me souviens** I remember *A* |
| le | **sud** south *A* |
| | **suisse** Swiss *C* |
| la | **Suisse** Switzerland *C* |
| le | **tableau des arrivées et départs** arrival and departure timetable *B* |
| | **toujours** always *B* |
| | **tourner** to turn *C* |
| le | **train** train *B* |
| | **traverser** to cross *C* |
| se | **trouver** to be located *C* |
| les | **vacances (f.)** vacation *A* |
| une | **valise** suitcase *B* |
| une | **vallée** valley *B* |
| | **vers** towards *C* |
| une | **visite** visit *A* |
| une | **voie** train platform *B* |
| un | **voyageur, une voyageuse** traveler *B* |
| | **vrai(e)** true *A* |
| un | **wagon-restaurant** dining car *B* |

**Essential Instruction**
Review and discuss the answers after students complete the listening **Activité**.

**Answers**

Script can be found in the front pages of the Annotated Teacher's Edition.

## Listening   1.2

I. You will hear a short conversation. Select the reply that would come next. You will hear the conversation twice.

1. A. Il ne faut jamais sortir.
   B. Faisons une fête entre amis!
   C. Bon voyage!
   D. Je pense que tu dois rester à la maison ce soir et ne rien faire!

II. Listen to the conversation. Select the best completion to each statement that follows.

2. Comment va Madame Sanchez?
   Mme Sanchez....
   A. a froid
   B. va bien; elle est avec son ami, Monsieur Duris
   C. a mal à la tête et à la gorge
   D. va à la maison

3. Madame Sanchez veut....
   A. demander le chemin
   B. aller chez le médecin
   C. rester à la campagne
   D. rencontrer un médecin

## Reading  1.2, 2.1, 2.2

III. Read Elisa Guttierez' journal of her family vacation in Quebec, Canada. Then select the best completion to each statement.

Nous sommes partis en vacances de Los Angeles dans notre nouvelle voiture hybride mercredi soir. Pour arriver le plus vite, nous avons pris la route qui va tout droit au nord jusqu'au Canada et ensuite, nous sommes allés à l'est en direction de Montréal. Après cinq jours de route, nous sommes enfin arrivés à notre destination. D'abord, nous avons visité Montréal, la ville la plus internationale du Canada. Ensuite, nous sommes allés à la ville de Québec où nous sommes restés trois jours. C'est aussi une très jolie ville qui se trouve au bord du fleuve St. Laurent. Les Québécois sont très sympas! En plus, protéger l'environnement est très important au Canada où l'on fait tout pour arrêter la pollution. J'adore le Canada!

4. Elisa et sa famille sont arrivées au Canada....
   A. à une école internationale
   B. après cinq jours
   C. lundi
   D. pour apprendre le français et l'anglais

5. Les Guttierez ont....
   A. voyagé en train
   B. pris l'avion
   C. circulé en voiture
   D. pris un bateau

6. Elisa pense que....
   A. la ville de Montréal est la capitale du Québec
   B. protéger l'environnement est important pour les Canadiens
   C. Montréal est la plus belle ville du Canada
   D. les Québécois sont généreux

**Answers**

**I**
1. D

**II**
2. C
3. B

**III**
4. B
5. C
6. B

**Differentiated Learning**
**Accelerate/Adapt/Decelerate**
Depending on the level of the students, ask them to create original sentences or a brief story about a vacation, using a number of words from the end-of-unit vocabulary list.

**IV**

1. cet; 2. mois; 3. en; 4. hybride; 5. l'environnement; 6. arrêter; 7. projets; 8. n'; 9. pas; 10. ma; 11. train; 12. voyage; 13. wagon-restaurant; 14. France or Suisse; 15. campagnes; 16. sont allées; 17. ont acheté; 18. ont appris; 19. fait; 20. ont vu; 21. retourner; 22. visiter

**V** *Postcards will vary.*

**VI** *Dialogues will vary.*

# Writing  2.1, 2.2

IV. Complete the dialogue between Julien and Sophie with appropriate words or expressions.

Julien: Qu'est-ce que tu vas faire __1__ été?

Sophie: Pendant le __2__ de juillet, je vais accompagner ma famille __3__ Espagne. On y va avec notre nouvelle voiture __4__ . En août, je vais travailler avec des amis pour protéger __5__ à Paris. Il faut __6__ la pollution. Et toi? Est-ce que tu as des __7__ pour les vacances?

Julien: Je __8__ ai __9__ encore fait des projets avec des copains, mais avec __10__ mère, mon père, et ma sœur, on part pour la Suisse bientôt. On prend le __11__ . Un __12__ en train coûte seulement 15 euros. J'adore manger dans le __13__ du train aussi. En plus, on peut beaucoup voir pendant le voyage. La __14__ , avec ses belles __15__ et montagnes, est vraiment géniale.

V. Complete the paragraph with the correct form of the verbs. Note: there will be verbs in the **passé composé** and others that require the infinitive.

Janvier dernier, Sarah et sa sœur Marie __16__ au Canada pour le Carnaval de Québec. Avant d'y aller, elles __17__ un guide et elles __18__ l'histoire de cette région et ville splendides et francophones. En général, en hiver il __19__ très froid au Québec, mais les deux sœurs ont porté les vêtements nécessaires. Elles __20__ tout au Carnaval. Après cette visite, elles veulent maintenant y __21__ en été. Elles veulent __22__ Montréal pour aller au festival des FrancoFolies. Le Québec, c'est le fun!

16. (aller)
17. (acheter)
18. (apprendre)
19. (faire)
20. (voir)
21. (retourner)
22. (visiter)

# Composition  1.3

VI. Write a postcard about an imaginary trip to Quebec in which you:
- write the date.
- write a salutation and say hello from Montreal in Quebec.
- tell your friends that you went to **les FrancoFolies** and the music genre you liked the best.
- describe the weather.
- name a tourist attraction that you visited and what you saw or did there.
- sign your postcard at the bottom, using an appropriate closing.

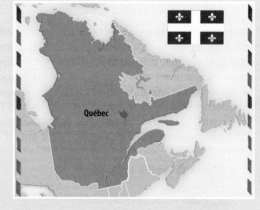

Québec

# Speaking 1.1

VII. Play the roles of an American tourist who speaks French and a **Francanadienne** who meet at the FrancoFolies festival in Montreal. The **Francanadienne** asks the American tourist's name and age, where he or she is from, the classes he or she has, what he or she likes to do, what he or she did last summer, and what he or she plans to do after the concert. The American tourist responds.

**Essential Instruction**

As an alternative to the **Activités** in the **Évaluation** section, consider using the Composition and Speaking from the **Bilan cumulatif** as a way to assess the students' cumulative knowledge.

# Grammar Summary

The material in this section contains information presented in Textbook 1A and Textbook 1B. The Grammar Summary is listed in alphabetical order.

## Adjectives

### Agreement of Regular Adjectives

| Masculine | Masculine Plural | Feminine | Feminine Plural |
|---|---|---|---|
| | **+ s** | **masculine adjective + e** | **masculine adjective + es** |
| grand | grands | grande | grandes |

### Exceptions

| Masculine | Masculine Plural | Feminine | Feminine Plural |
|---|---|---|---|
| Adjectives ending in **e** bête | **+ s** bêtes | no change bête | **+ s** bêtes |
| Adjectives ending in **n, l** bon intellectuel | **+ s** bons intellectuels | **double consonant + e** bonne intellectuelle | **double consonant + es** bonnes intellectuelles |
| Adjectives ending in **s** gros | no change gros | **double consonant + e** grosse | **double consonant + es** grosses |
| Adjectives ending in **eux** généreux | no change généreux | **-euse** généreuse | **-euses** généreuses |

### Irregular Adjectives

| Masculine | Masculine Before a Vowel | Masculine Plural | Feminine | Feminine Plural |
|---|---|---|---|---|
| beau | bel | beaux | belle | **+ s** |
| nouveau | nouvel | nouveaux | nouvelle | |
| vieux | vieil | vieux | vieille | |
| frais | | | fraîche | |
| cher | | } + s | chère | |
| blanc | | | blanche | |
| long | | | longue | |

### Position of Adjectives

| Article + Noun | + Adjective |
|---|---|
| des stylos **bleus** | |

## Exceptions

beau, joli, nouveau, vieux, bon, mauvais, grand, petit, gros *(BAGS: beauty, age, goodness, size)*

| Article + Adjective | + Noun |
|---|---|
| une **belle** voiture ||

## Comparative of Adjectives

| plus | *(more)* | **+ adj** | **+ que** | *(than)* |
|---|---|---|---|---|
| **moins** | *(less)* | **+ adj** | **+ que** | *(than)* |
| **aussi** | *(as)* | **+ adj** | **+ que** | *(as)* |

## Superlative of Adjectives

### For regular adjectives, placed after the noun

**le/la/les** + noun + **le/la/les** + **plus** + adjective

### For adjectives placed before the noun

**le/la/les** + **plus** + adjective + noun

**Exception:** bon = le/la/les **meilleur**(e)(s)

## Interrogative Adjective *quel*

| Masculine | Masculine Plural | Feminine | Feminine Plural |
|---|---|---|---|
| quel | quels | quelle | quelles |

## Possessive Adjectives

| Masculine | Feminine | Plural |
|---|---|---|
| mon | ma | mes |
| ton | ta | tes |
| son | sa | ses |
| notre | notre | nos |
| votre | votre | vos |
| leur | leur | leurs |

# Adverbs

| | |
|---|---|
| assez | mal |
| beaucoup | peu |
| bien | un peu |
| déjà | trop |
| enfin | vite |

## Expressions of Quantity

| | | |
|---|---|---|
| assez de | une boîte de | une bouteille de |
| beaucoup de | un paquet de | un pot de |
| peu de | un morceau de | une tranche de |
| un peu de | un gramme de | un kilo de |
| trop de | un litre de | |

# Articles

## Indefinite Articles

| Singular | | Plural |
|---|---|---|
| Masculine | Feminine | des |
| un | une | |

## Definite Articles

| Singular | | | Plural |
|---|---|---|---|
| Before a Consonant Sound | | Before a Vowel Sound | les |
| Masculine | Feminine | | |
| le | la | l' | |

## *À* + Definite Articles

| Singular | | | Plural |
|---|---|---|---|
| Before a Consonant Sound | | Before a Vowel Sound | aux |
| Masculine | Feminine | | |
| au | à la | à l' | |

## *De* + Definite Articles

| Singular | | | Plural |
|---|---|---|---|
| Before a Consonant Sound | | Before a Vowel Sound | des |
| Masculine | Feminine | | |
| du | de la | de l' | |

## Partitive Articles

| Before a Consonant Sound | | Before a Vowel Sound | In the Negative |
|---|---|---|---|
| Masculine | Feminine | de l' | **pas de** coca<br>**pas de** viande<br>**pas d'**eau minérale |
| du | de la | | |

# C'est vs. il/elle est

| c'est | vs. | ce n'est pas |
|---|---|---|
| C'est un ballon de foot. | | Ce n'est pas un gâteau. |
| **c'est** | **vs.** | **il/elle est** |
| C'est un garçon. C'est une fille. | | Il s'appelle Karim. Elle s'appelle Amélie. |
| **ce sont** | **vs.** | **ils/elles sont** |
| Ce sont des étudiants. Ce sont des étudiantes. | | Ils sont sportifs. Elles sont sympa. |

# Negation

| | |
|---|---|
| ne (n')… pas | Il **ne** joue **pas**.<br>Il **n'**a **pas** joué. |
| ne (n')… plus | Elle **n'**aime **plus** les frites. |
| ne (n')… jamais | Nous **ne** dansons **jamais**. |
| ne (n')… personne | Vous **n'**invitez **personne**? |
| ne (n')… rien | Ma grand-mère **ne** comprend **rien**. |

# Numbers

| Cardinal Numbers | Ordinal Numbers |
|---|---|
| un | premier, première |
| deux | deuxième |
| trois | troisième |
| quatre | quatrième |
| cinq | cinquième |
| six | sixième |
| sept | septième |
| huit | huitième |
| neuf | neuvième |
| dix, etc. | dixième, etc. |

# Prepositions

## Prepositions before Cities, Countries, Continents

| City<br>(no article) | Masculine<br>(le Japon) | Feminine<br>(la France) | Plural<br>(les États-Unis) |
|---|---|---|---|
| à | au | en | aux |

# Pronouns

## Subject Pronouns

| Singular | Plural |
|---|---|
| je | nous |
| tu | vous |
| il/elle/on | ils/elles |

# Questions

## Forming Questions

| | |
|---|---|
| using **n'est-ce-pas** | Il fait chaud, **n'est-ce pas**?<br>Ils regardent un DVD, **n'est-ce pas**? |
| using **est-ce que** | **Est-ce qu'**il fait chaud?<br>**Est-ce qu'**ils regardent un DVD? |
| using **inversion:** Verb-Subject | **Fait-il** chaud?<br>**Regardent-ils** un DVD? |

# Telling Time

**Il est** une **heure**    …et quart.    …et demie.    …moins le quart.
Il est midi.
Il est minuit.

# Verbs

## Regular Verbs—Present Tense

| -er aimer | | | |
|---|---|---|---|
| j' | aim**e** | nous | aim**ons** |
| tu | aim**es** | vous | aim**ez** |
| il/elle/on | aim**e** | ils/elles | aim**ent** |

| -ir finir | | | |
|---|---|---|---|
| je | fin**is** | nous | fin**issons** |
| tu | fin**is** | vous | fin**issez** |
| il/elle/on | fin**it** | ils/elles | fin**issent** |

| -re vendre |
|---|

| je | vend**s** | nous | vend**ons** |
|---|---|---|---|
| tu | vend**s** | vous | vend**ez** |
| il/elle/on | vend | ils/elles | vend**ent** |

## Irregular Verbs—Present Tense

| acheter | | | |
|---|---|---|---|
| j' | ach**è**te | nous | achetons |
| tu | ach**è**tes | vous | achetez |
| il/elle/on | ach**è**te | ils/elles | ach**è**tent |

| aller | | | |
|---|---|---|---|
| je | vais | nous | allons |
| tu | vas | vous | allez |
| il/elle/on | va | ils/elles | vont |

| avoir | | | |
|---|---|---|---|
| (avoir besoin de/avoir chaud/avoir faim/avoir froid/avoir soif) | | | |
| j' | ai | nous | avons |
| tu | as | vous | avez |
| il/elle/on | a | ils/elles | ont |

| devoir | | | |
|---|---|---|---|
| je | dois | nous | devons |
| tu | dois | vous | devez |
| il/elle/on | doit | ils/elles | doivent |

| être | | | |
|---|---|---|---|
| je | suis | nous | sommes |
| tu | es | vous | êtes |
| il/elle/on | est | ils/elles | sont |

| faire | | | |
|---|---|---|---|
| je | fais | nous | faisons |
| tu | fais | vous | faites |
| il/elle/on | fait | ils/elles | font |

| falloir | | | |
|---|---|---|---|
| il faut | | | |

| mettre | | | |
|---|---|---|---|
| je | mets | nous | mettons |
| tu | mets | vous | mettez |
| il/elle/on | met | ils/elles | mettent |

| offrir | | | |
|---|---|---|---|
| j' | offre | nous | offrons |
| tu | offres | vous | offrez |
| il/elle/on | offre | ils/elles | offrent |

| pouvoir | | | |
|---|---|---|---|
| je | peux | nous | pouvons |
| tu | peux | vous | pouvez |
| il/elle/on | peut | ils/elles | peuvent |

| préférer | | | |
|---|---|---|---|
| je | préf**è**re | nous | préférons |
| tu | préf**è**res | vous | préférez |
| il/elle/on | préf**è**re | ils/elles | préf**è**rent |

| prendre | | | |
|---|---|---|---|
| je | prends | nous | prenons |
| tu | prends | vous | prenez |
| il/elle/on | prend | ils/elles | prennent |

## Irregular Verbs—Present Tense *continued*

| venir | | | |
|---|---|---|---|
| je | viens | nous | venons |
| tu | viens | vous | venez |
| il/elle/on | vient | ils/elles | viennent |

| voir | | | |
|---|---|---|---|
| je | vois | nous | voyons |
| tu | vois | vous | voyez |
| il/elle/on | voit | ils/elles | voient |

| vouloir | | | |
|---|---|---|---|
| je | veux | nous | voulons |
| tu | veux | vous | voulez |
| il/elle/on | veut | ils/elles | veulent |

## Regular Imperatives

| -er<br>chanter | -ir<br>choisir | -re<br>pendre |
|---|---|---|
| Chante! | Choisis! | Prends! |
| Chantons! | Choisissons! | Prenons! |
| Chantez! | Choisissez! | Prenez! |

## Expressing the Near Future

| aller + Infinitive |
|---|
| Nous allons dîner. |

## *Passé composé* with *avoir*

| avoir + past participle |
|---|

| -er verbs → é | -ir verbs → i | -re verbs → u |
|---|---|---|
| Nous avons gagné. | Tu as fini. | On a attendu. |

| Irregular Past Participles | | | | | |
|---|---|---|---|---|---|
| avoir | → **eu** | devoir | → **dû** | être | → **été** |
| faire | → **fait** | mettre | → **mis** | offrir | → **offert** |
| pouvoir | → **pu** | prendre | → **pris** | vendre | → **vendu** |
| venir | → **venu** | voir | → **vu** | vouloir | → **voulu** |

## *Passé composé* with *être*

| être + past participle (+ agreement in gender and number) | | | | | |
|---|---|---|---|---|---|
| je | suis | arrivé(e) | nous | sommes | arrivé(e)s |
| tu | es | arrivé(e) | vous | êtes | arrivé(e)s |
| il | est | arrivé | ils | sont | arrivés |
| elle | est | arrivée | elles | sont | arrivées |

Some of the verbs that use *être* as the helping verb in the **passé composé** are:

| Infinitive | Past Participle |
|---|---|
| aller | **allé** |
| arriver | **arrivé** |
| entrer | **entré** |
| monter | **monté** |
| rentrer | **rentré** |
| rester | **resté** |
| retourner | **retourné** |
| partir | **parti** |
| sortir | **sorti** |
| descendre | **descendu** |
| vendre | **vendu** |
| venir | **venu** |

## Verbs + Infinitives

| aimer | aller | désirer |
|---|---|---|
| devoir | falloir | pouvoir |
| préférer | venir | vouloir |

| Nous préférons faire du ski. |
|---|

# Vocabulaire

## Français–Anglais

This vocabulary list combines words from Textbook 1A (Units 1 to 5) and Textbook 1B (Units 6 to 10). The number at the end of each definition is the Unit in which the word is first presented.

**A**    à to 1; at 2; on 4; in 5; by 9; À *bientôt.* See you soon. 1; à *bord* on board 7; à *côté (de)* beside, next to 7; À *demain.* See you tomorrow. 1; à droite on the right 7; à gauche on the left 7; à *l'heure* on time 4; à mon avis in my opinion 9; à pied on foot 9; à vélo by bike 9

un   **accompagnateur, une accompagnatrice** home health worker 9

   **accompagner** to accompany 10

les   **accras de morue (m.)** cod fritters 5

un   **achat** purchase 6

   **acheter** to buy 3

un   **acteur, une actrice** actor 4

l'   **action (f.)** action 4

une   **activité** activity 2

l'   **addition (f.)** bill 4

l'   **aérobic (m.)** aerobics 9

un   **aéroport** airport 8

une   **affiche** poster 3

l'   **Afrique (f.)** Africa 5

l'   **âge (m.)** age 5; *Tu as quel âge?* How old are you? 5

un   **agent de police** police officer 5

l'   **agriculture (f.)** agriculture 9

   **ah** oh 1

   **aider** to help 1

   **aimer** to like, love 2

l'   **air (m.)** air 6

   **algérien(ne)** Algerian 1

l'   **Allemagne (f.)** Germany 10

l'   **allemand (m.)** German (language) 3

   **allemand(e)** German 10

   **aller** to go 1; *Tu trouves que... me va bien?* Does this... look good on me? 6; *Vas-y!* Go for it! 6

   **allô** hello (on telephone) 1

   **alors** so, then 3

l'   **aluminium (m.)** aluminum 9; *en aluminium* made of aluminum 9

   **américain(e)** American 1

un(e)   **ami(e)** friend 2

un   **an** year 5

un   **ananas** pineapple 6

l'   **anglais (m.)** English (language) 3

   **anglais(e)** English 10

l'   **Angleterre (f.)** England 10

un   **animal** animal 8; *animaux en voie de disparition* endangered species 9

une   **année** year 5

un   **anniversaire** birthday 5

les   **antirétroviraux (m.)** antiretroviral drugs 9

   **août** August 5

un   **appartement** apartment 7

s'   **appeler: je m'appelle** my name is 1; *On s'appelle.* We'll call each other. 1; *tu t'appelles* your name is 1

   **apporter** to bring 5

   **apprendre** to learn 4

   **après** after 2

l'   **après-midi (m.)** afternoon 3

l'   **argent (m.)** money 8

une   **armoire** wardrobe 7

   **arrêter** to stop 9

s'   **arrêter** to stop 8

une   **arrivée** arrival 10

   **arriver** to arrive 4

les   **arts plastiques (m.)** visual arts 3

   **assez (de)** enough (of) 6

une   **assiette** plate 7

un(e)   **athlète** athlete 5

   **attendre** to wait (for) 4

   **Attention!** Watch out!, Be careful! 7

   **au** to (the) 1; in (the), on (the) 8; *au bout (de)* at the end (of) 10; *au-dessus de* above 7; *au fond (de)* at the end (of) 7; *Au revoir.* Good-bye. 1

une   **aubergine** eggplant 6

   **aujourd'hui** today 4

   **aussi** also, too 2; as 7

un   **autobus** bus 10

l'   **automne (m.)** autumn 8

   **autre** other 7

   **autrement** otherwise 6

   **aux** at (the), in (the), to (the) 3

   **avance: en avance** early 4

   **avec** with 1

une   **aventure** adventure 4

une   **avenue** avenue 8

un   **avion** airplane 8

un   **avis** opinion 9; *à mon avis* in my opinion 9

un(e)   **avocat(e)** lawyer 5

   **avoir** to have 3; *avoir... an(s)* to be... year(s) old 5; *avoir besoin de* to need 3; *avoir bonne mine* to look healthy 9; *avoir chaud* to be hot 8; *avoir envie de* to want, to feel like 8; *avoir faim* to be hungry 4; *avoir froid* to be cold 8; *avoir mal (à...)* to be hurt, to have a/an... ache 9; *avoir mal au cœur* to feel nauseous 9; *avoir mauvaise mine* to look awful 9; *avoir quel âge* to be how old 5; *avoir soif* to be thirsty 4; *avoir un petit air du pays* to look like (something from) my country 7

   **avril** April 5

**B**

une   **baguette** long thin loaf of bread 6

une   **baignoire** bathtub 7

un   **ballon (de foot)** (soccer) ball 4

   **banal(e)** banal 8

une   **banane** banana 6

un **banc** bench 7

une **banque** bank 8

le **bas** bottom 8

le **basket (basketball)** basketball 2

un **bateau** boat 8

**bavard(e)** talkative 5

**beau, bel, belle** beautiful, handsome 7

**beaucoup** a lot, very much 2; *beaucoup de* a lot of 6

un **beau-frère** stepbrother 5

un **beau-père** stepfather 5

**beige** beige 6

**belge** Belgian 10

la **Belgique** Belgium 10

une **belle-mère** stepmother 5

une **belle-sœur** stepsister 5

**ben** well 7

le **Bénin** Benin 5

**béninois(e)** Beninese 5

**berbère** Berber 7

**bête** unintelligent 5

le **beurre** butter 6

**bien** well 1; really 2

**bientôt** soon 1; *à bientôt* see you soon 1

**bienvenue** welcome 4

un **billet** bill (money) 6; ticket 10

la **biologie** biology 3

**biologique** organic 9

**blanc, blanche** white 6

un **blason** team logo 4

**bleu(e)** blue 5; *la bleue* the blue one 3

un **blogue** blog 2

**blond(e)** blond 5

un **blouson** jacket 4

le **bœuf** beef 6

une **boisson** drink 4

une **boîte (de)** can (of) 6

un **bol** bowl 7

**bon(ne)** good 1; *Bon Appétit!* Enjoy your meal! 4; *bon marché* cheap 6; *Bon voyage!* Have a good trip! 10

**bonjour** hello 1

les **bottes (f.)** boots 6

la **bouche** mouth 9; *bouche du métro* subway entrance 4

une **boucherie** butcher shop 6

**bouger** to move 9

une **boulangerie** bakery 6

le **bout** end 10; *au bout (de)* at the end (of) 10

une **bouteille (de)** bottle (of) 6

une **boutique** shop 6

le **bras** arm 9

**brun(e)** brown, dark (hair) 5

un **bureau** desk, office 3; *bureau du proviseur* principal's office 3

le **Burkina Faso** Burkina Faso 5

**burkinabè** from, of Burkina Faso 5

un **but** goal 4

# C

**c'est** this is, that is, it is 1; *C'est ça.* That's right. 1; *C'est le (+ date)* It's the (+ date) 5; *C'est le top!* That's awesome! 1

**ça** it, this 1; that 2; *Ça fait combien?* How much is it? 6; *Ça va?* How are things going? 1

une **cabine: cabine d'essayage** dressing room 6

un **cadeau** gift 5

un **café** café 1; coffee 4

un **cahier** notebook 3

un **calendrier** calendar 2

un(e) **camarade de classe** classmate 1

le **camembert** camembert cheese 6

le **Cameroun** Cameroon 5

**camerounais(e)** Cameroonian 5

la **campagne** country(side) 10

le **Canada** Canada 5

**canadien(ne)** Canadian 1

un **canapé** sofa 7

une **cantine** school cafeteria 3

une **capitale** capital 10

une **carotte** carrot 6

un **carré** square 7; *en carrés* in squares 7

une **carte** map 3; menu 4; map 5; *carte cadeau* gift card 5

une **cascade** waterfall 10

une **casquette** cap 4

une **cathédrale** cathedral 8

une **cause** cause 10

**causer** to cause 9

un **CD** CD 2

**ce** it 1; this 3; *ce, cet, cette,*

*ces* this, that, these, those 6; *ce que* what 9

un **cédérom** CD 3

**cent** (one) hundred 3

un **centre** center 1; *centre commercial* mall, shopping center 1

une **cerise** cherry 6

une **chaise** chair 3

une **chambre** bedroom 7

un **champignon** mushroom 6

une **chanson** song 7

**chanter** to sing 5

un **chanteur, une chanteuse** singer 5

un **chapeau** hat 6

une **charcuterie** delicatessen 6

**charmant(e)** charming 7

un **chat** cat 8

un **château** castle 10

**chaud(e)** hot 8; *avoir chaud* to be hot 8; *il fait chaud* it's hot 8; *j'ai chaud* I am hot 8

une **chaussette** sock 4

une **chaussure** shoe 4

un **chemin** way, path 10

une **chemise** shirt 6

**cher, chère** expensive 3

**chercher** to look for 6

un **cheval** horse 8

les **cheveux (m.)** hair 5

**chez** to, at the house (home) of 3; *chez moi* at/to my house 3

**chic** chic 6

un **chien** dog 8

la **chimie** chemistry 3

**chimique** chemical 9

le **chocolat** chocolate 4

**choisir** to choose 5

**chouette** great 8

un **ciné (cinéma)** movie theatre 1; *le cinéma* movies 2

**cinq** five 2

**cinquante** fifty 3

**cinquième** fifth 7

**circuler** to drive, to get around 9

une **classe** class 1

un **clavier** keyboard 7

une **clé USB** USB key 7

**cliquer** to click 7

un **coca** cola 4

le **cœur** heart 9; *avoir mal au cœur* to feel nauseous 9

le **coin** corner 8; *du coin* on the corner 8

une **colline** hill 10

**combattre** to fight 9

**combien** how much 3; *Ça fait combien?* How much is it? 6; *C'est combien le kilo?* How much per kilo? 6; *Il coûte combien?* How much does it cost? 3

une **comédie** comedy 4; *comédie romantique* romantic comedy 4

**comme** for 4; like 5; *comme ci, comme ça* so-so 1

**commencer** to begin 7

**comment** how, what 1; *Comment allez-vous? [form.]* How are you? 1; *Comment est...?* What is... like? 5

**commerçant(e)** shopping, business 6

un **compositeur, une compositrice** composer, songwriter 5

**composter** to validate (a ticket) 10

un **composteur** ticket-stamping machine 10

**comprendre** to understand 4

un **concert** concert 2; *concert R'n'B* R&B concert 2

un **concombre** cucumber 6

la **confiture** jam 4

**connais: je connais** I know 5

**conseiller** to advise 9

**consommer** to consume 8

**continuer** to continue 9

**contre** versus, against 4

un **contrôle** test 1

un **contrôleur, une contrôleuse** ticket collector 10

un **copain, une copine** (boy/girl) friend 1

le **corps** body 9

**côté: à côté (de)** beside, next to 7

la **Côte-d'Ivoire** Ivory Coast 5

le **cou** neck 9

une **couleur** color 6; *De quelle(s) couleur(s)?* In what color(s)? 6

un **couloir** hallway 7

**couper** to cut 7

une **courgette** zucchini 6

un **cours** course, class 2

le **couscous** couscous 6

un(e) **cousin(e)** cousin 5

un **coussin** pillow 7

un **couteau** knife 7

**coûter** to cost 3

le **couvert** table setting 7; *mettre le couvert* to set the table 7

un **crayon** pencil 3

une **crémerie** dairy store 6

une **crêpe** crêpe 4

un **croissant** croissant 6

un **croque-monsieur** grilled ham and cheese sandwich 4

une **cuiller** spoon 7

la **cuisine** cooking 2; kitchen 7

un **cuisinier, une cuisinière** cook, chef 5

une **cuisinière** stove 7

**culturel, culturelle** cultural 5

une **cure** spa treatment 9

# D

**d'abord** first of all 6

**d'accord** OK 1

**dans** in 3

**de/d'** of, from 1; some, any 2; *De quelle(s) couleur(s)?* In what color(s)? 6

**décembre** December 5

**décontracté(e)** relaxed 9

un **degré** degree 8

**déjà** already 8

le **déjeuner** lunch 3

**délicieux, délicieuse** delicious 3

**demain** tomorrow 1; *À demain.* See you tomorrow. 1

**demander** to ask (for) 7; *demander le chemin* to ask for directions 10

**démarrer** to start 7

**demi(e)** half 3; *et demie* half past 3

un **demi-frère** half-brother 5

une **demi-sœur** half-sister 5

une **dent** tooth 9

un(e) **dentiste** dentist 5

un **départ** departure 10

un **département** department 10

**dernier, dernière** last 8

**derrière** behind 3

**des** some 2; from (the), of (the) 5

**désagréable** unpleasant 8

**descendre** to go down, to get off 8

**désirer** to want 4

**désolé(e)** sorry 8

un **dessert** dessert 4

**dessus: au-dessus de** above 7

une **destination** destination 10

**deux** two 2

**deuxième** second 7

**devant** in front of 3

**devenir** to become 5

une **devise** motto 10

**devoir** to have to 7

un **devoir** assignment 9; *les devoirs (m.)* homework 1

un **dictionnaire** dictionary 3

**difficile** difficult 3

**diligent(e)** diligent 5

**dimanche** Sunday 2

**dîner** to have dinner 7

le **dîner** dinner 7

le **dioxyde de carbone** carbon dioxide 9

une **direction** direction 10

**dis** say 1; *disons* let's say 4

une **discussion** discussion 5

**disponible** free 8

**divorcé(e)(s)** divorced 5

**dix** ten 2

**dix-huit** eighteen 2

**dix-neuf** nineteen 2

**dix-sept** seventeen 2

**dixième** tenth 7

un **documentaire** documentary 4

le **doigt** finger 9; *doigt de pied* toe 9

**dois** (see **devoir**) 1

**donc** so, therefore 4

**donner** to give 4; *donnez-moi* give me 4

**dormir** to sleep 2

le **dos** back 9

**une** **douche** shower 7

**douze** twelve 2

**un** **drame** drama 4

**un** **drapeau** flag 10

**droite: à droite** to the right 7; *à droite de* to (on) the right of 7; *tout droit* straight ahead 10

**drôle** funny 3

**du** some 2; of (the) 4; from (the) 5; about (the) 8; *du coin* on the corner 8

**un** **DVD** DVD 3

# E

**l'** **eau (f.)** water; *eau minérale* mineral water 4

**une** **écharpe** scarf 4

**un** **éclair** eclair 8

**une** **école** school 3

**écouter** to listen (to) 2; *écouter de la musique* to listen to music 2; *écouter mon lecteur MP3* to listen to my MP3 player 3

**un** **écran** monitor, screen 7

**écrire** to write 3

**un** **écrivain** writer 5

**l'** **éducation physique et sportive (EPS) (f.)** gym class 3

**un** **effet** effect 9; *l'effet de serre* greenhouse effect 9

**égoïste** selfish 5

**eh: eh bien** well 1

**électrique** electric 9

**un(e)** **élève** student 3

**éliminer** to eliminate 9

**elle** she 1; it 3

**elles** they 2

**embrasser** to kiss 8

**une** **émission** television program 9

**en** in 3; on 4; of (pronoun) 8; by 9; *en aluminium, plastique* made of alumnum, plastic 9; *en avance* early 4; *en face de* across from 10; *en ligne* online 6; *en retard* late 4; *en solde* on sale 4; *en ville* downtown 3; *en voiture électrique* by electric car 9; *en voiture hydride* by hybrid car 9

**enchanté(e)** delighted 1

**un** **endroit** place 3

**l'** **énergie (f.)** energy; *énergie nucléaire* nuclear energy 9; *énergie solaire* solar energy 9

**énergique** energetic 3

**un** **enfant** child 5

**enfin** finally 4

**s'** **engager** to commit to, to be committed to 9

**l'** **engrais (m.)** fertilizer 9

**une** **enquête** survey 2

**ensemble** together 4

**un** **ensemble** outfit 6

**ensuite** next 6

**entre** between 10

**entrer** to enter, to come in 8

**l'** **environnement (m.)** environment 9

**envoyer** to send 2; *envoyer des textos* to send text messages 2

**une** **éolienne** wind turbine 9

**l'** **épaule (f.)** shoulder 9

**une** **épicerie** grocery store 6

**l'** **EPS (f.)** gym class 3

**une** **équipe** team 4

**un** **espace** area 9

**l'** **Espagne (f.)** Spain 10

**l'** **espagnol (m.)** Spanish (language) 3

**espagnol(e)** Spanish 10

**essayer** to try (on) 6

**est** (see **être**) 1

**l'** **est (m.)** east 10

**est-ce que** (phrase introducing a question) 3

**l'** **estomac (m.)** stomach 9

**et** and 1; *et demie* half past 3; *et quart* quarter past 3

**un** **étage** floor, story 7; *le premier étage* the second floor 7

**un** **étang** pond 10

**les** **États-Unis (m.)** United States 5

**l'** **été (m.)** summer 2

**être** to be 3; *être au courant* to know, to be informed 9; *être d'accord* to agree 7; *être libre* to be free 8; *être en (bonne, mauvaise) forme* to be in (good, bad) shape 9; *être*

*en train de (+ infinitive)* to be (busy) doing something 7; *être occupé(e)* to be busy 8; *être situé(e)* to be located 10; *être vert* to be environmentally friendly 9; *Nous sommes le (+ date).* It's the (+ date). 5

**étudier** to study 2

**euh** um 3

**un** **euro** euro 3

**l'** **Europe (f.)** Europe 10

**un** **évier** sink 7

**exactement** exactly 8

# F

**face: en face de** across from 10

**facile** easy 3

**faim: avoir faim** to be hungry 4

**faire** to do, to make 1; *faire de la gym (gymnastique)* to do gymnastics 2; *faire du footing* to go running 2; *faire du patinage (artistique)* to (figure) skate 2; *faire du roller* to in-line skate 2; *faire du shopping* to go shopping 2; *faire du ski (alpin)* to (downhill) ski 2; *faire du sport* to play sports 2; *faire du vélo* to bike 2; *faire la connaissance (de)* to meet 10; *faire la cuisine* to cook 2; *faire les courses* to go grocery shopping 6; *faire marcher* to run, make (something) work 9; *faire mes devoirs* to do my homework 1; *faire une promenade* to go for a walk 8

**fais: je fais** (see **faire**) 2

**fait:** *Ça fait combien?* How much is it? 6; *il fait beau* it's beautiful out 2; *il fait chaud* it's hot 8; *il fait du soleil* it's sunny 8; *il fait du vent* it's windy 8; *il fait frais* it's cool 8; *il fait froid* it's cold 8; *il fait mauvais* the weather's bad 2; *Quel temps fait-il?* What's the weather like? 8

**falloir** to be necessary, to have to 9; *il faut* it is necessary, one has to/must, we/you have to/must 9

une **famille** family 5

**fatigué(e)** tired 8

**faut** (see **falloir**) 9

un **fauteuil** armchair 7

une **femme** wife 5; *femme d'affaires* businesswoman 5

une **fenêtre** window 3

**fermer** to close 7

une **fête** party 1

une **feuille de papier** sheet of paper 3

**février** February 5

la **fièvre** fever 9

la **figure** face 9

une **fille** girl 1; daughter 5

un **film** film 4; *film d'action* action movie 4; *film d'aventures* adventure movie 4; *film d'horreur* horror movie 4; *film de science-fiction* science fiction movie 4; *film musical* musical 4; *film policier* detective movie 4

un **fils** son 5

**fin(e)** fine 7

**finir** to finish 5

un **fitness** health club, gym 9

un **fleuve** river 8

**fond: au fond (de)** at the end (of) 7

le **foot** soccer 2

un **footballeur, une footballeuse** soccer player 4

le **footing** running 2

une **forêt** forest 10

**forme: être en (bonne, mauvaise) forme** to be in (good, bad) shape 9

**fort(e)** strong 7

un **foulard** scarf 6

un **four** oven 7

une **fourchette** fork 7

**frais, fraîche** fresh 6; cool 8; *il fait frais* it's cool 8

une **fraise** strawberry 6

le **français** French (language) 3

**français(e)** French 1

**francanadien(ne)** from, of French-speaking Canada 10

la **France** France 3

**francophone** French-speaking 5

un **frère** brother 5; *beau-frère* stepbrother 5; *demi-frère* half-brother 5

un **frigo** refrigerator 7

les **frissons (m.)** chills 9

les **frites (f.)** French fries 2

**froid(e)** cold 8; *avoir froid* to be cold 8; *il fait froid* it's cold 8; *j'ai froid* I am cold 8

le **fromage** cheese 4

un **fruit** fruit 6; *une tarte aux fruits* fruit tart 6

# G

le **Gabon** Gabon 5

**gabonais(e)** Gabonese 5

**gagner** to win 4

un **garçon** boy 1

une **gare** train station 8

un **gâteau** cake 5

**gauche: à gauche** on the left 7; *à gauche de* to (on) the left of 7

**géant(e)** giant 9

**généreux, généreuse** generous 5

**génial(e)** fantastic, great, terrific 2

le **genou** knee 9

un **genre** type 4

les **gens (m.)** people 5

une **glace** ice cream 4; *glace à la vanille* vanilla ice cream 4; *glace au chocolat* chocolate ice cream 4

la **gorge** throat 9

un **gorille** gorilla 9; *gorille des montagnes* mountain gorilla 9

**gourmand(e)** fond of food 8

le **goûter** snack 7

un **gramme (de)** gram (of) 6

**grand(e)** big, large, tall 5

une **grand-mère** grandmother 5

les **grands-parents (m.)** grandparents 5

un **grand-père** grandfather 5

**grandir** to grow 5

un(e) **graphiste** graphic designer 5

**grave** serious 8

la **grippe** flu 9

**gris** grey 5

**gros, grosse** big, fat, large 6

**grossir** to gain weight 5

un **guichet** ticket booth 4

un **guide** guidebook 10; *guide touristique* tourist guide 8

la **gym (gymnastique)** gymnastics 2; *faire de la gym (gymnastique)* to do gymnastics 2

# H

un(e) **habitant(e)** inhabitant, resident 10

**habiter** to live 7

un **hamburger** hamburger 2

les **haricots verts (m.)** green beans 6

le **haut** top 8

l' **heure (f.)** hour, o'clock, time 3; *à l'heure* on time 4; *Quelle heure est-il?* What time is it? 3

**hier** yesterday 8

le **hip-hop** hip-hop 2

l' **histoire (f.)** history 3

l' **hiver (m.)** winter 2

un **homme** man 5; *homme d'affaires* businessman 5

l' **horreur (f.)** horror 4

un **hôtel** hotel 8; *hôtel de ville* city hall 8

**huit** eight 2

**huitième** eighth 7

**humanitaire** humanitarian 10

**hybride** hybrid 9

# I

**ici** here 7

une **idée: Bonne idée!** Good idea! 8

**il** he 1; it 3

**il y a** there is/are 3

**ils** they 2

un **immeuble** apartment building 7

**impossible** impossible 7

une **imprimante** printer 7

**imprimer** to print 7

l' **informatique (f.)** computer science 3

un **ingénieur** engineer 5

**installer** to install 9

un **instant** moment 9; *pour l'instant* for the moment 9

**intelligent(e)** intelligent 3

**intéressant(e)** interesting 3

**international(e)** international 10

(l') **Internet (m.)** Internet 2

un(e) **invité(e)** guest 7

**inviter** to invite 2

l' **Italie (f.)** Italy 10

**italien(ne)** Italian 10

**ivoirien(ne)** from, of the Ivory Coast 5

## J

la **jambe** leg 9

le **jambon** ham 4

**janvier** January 5

un **jardin** garden, park 8

le **jasmin** jasmine 7

**jaune** yellow 6

**je (j')** I 1

un **jean** jeans 6

**jeudi** Thursday 2

les **Jeux Olympiques (m.)** Olympic Games 2

des **jeux vidéo (m.)** video games 2

**joli(e)** pretty 6

**jouer** to play 2; *jouer au basket (basketball)* to play basketball 2; *jouer au foot (football)* to play soccer 2; *jouer au hockey sur glace* to play ice hockey 2; *jouer aux jeux vidéo* to play video games 2; *jouer un rôle* to play a role 4

un **jour** day 2; one day, someday 5

une **journée** day 8

**juillet** July 5

**juin** June 5

une **jupe** skirt 6

un **jus** juice 4; *jus d'orange* orange juice 4

**jusqu'à** until 10

## K

le **ketchup** ketchup 6

un **kilo (de)** kilogram (of) 6

un **kilomètre** kilometer 5

un **kiosque à journaux** newstand 4

## L

**là** there 1

**là-bas** over there 5

un **labo (laboratoire)** science lab 3

un **lac** lake 10

**laisser** to leave, to let 9; *Laisse-moi finir!* Let me finish! 8

le **lait** milk 6

une **lampe** lamp 7

une **langue** language 3

**le, la, l'** the 1; it (object pronoun) 4

un **lecteur de DVD** DVD player 3; *lecteur de MP3* MP3 player 3

un **légume** vegetable 6

**les** the 2

**leur, leurs** their 5

un **lien** link 7

la **ligne** figure 8; *en ligne* online 6

une **limonade** lemon-lime soda 4

**lire** to read 2

un **lit** bed 7

un **litre (de)** liter (of) 6

un **livre** book 3

une **livre** pound 6

un **logiciel** software 7

**loin (de)** far (from) 10

**long, longue** long 7

**louer** to rent 10

**lui** to him/her 5

**lundi** Monday 2

le **Luxembourg** Luxembourg 10

**luxembourgeois(e)** from, of Luxembourg 10

un **lycée** high school 9

## M

**m'appelle: je m'appelle** my name is 1

**madame (Mme)** Ma'am, Mrs., Ms. 1

**mademoiselle (Mlle)** Miss, Ms. 1

un **magasin** store 3

**mai** May 5

**maigrir** to lose weight 5

un **maillot** jersey 4; *maillot de bain* bathing suit 6

la **main** hand 8; *la main dans la main* hand in hand 8

**maintenant** now 3

**mais** but 3

une **maison** house, home 1

**mal** badly 1; *Ça va mal.* Things are going badly. 1; *avoir mal (à…)* to be hurt, to have a/ an… ache 9

**malade** sick 9

un(e) **malade** sick person 9

une **maladie** illness 9

le **Mali** Mali 5

**malien(ne)** Malian 5

**manger** to eat 2

un **mannequin** model 6

un **manteau** coat 6

un(e) **marchand(e)** merchant 6

un **marché** outdoor market 6; *marché aux puces* flea market 6

**marcher** to walk 9; *faire marcher* to make (something) work 9

**mardi** Tuesday 2

une **marée** tide 9; *marée noire* oil slick 9

un **mari** husband 5

**marquer** to score 4

**marron** brown 5

**mars** March 5

la **Martinique** Martinique 5

un **match** game 4

les **maths (f.)** math 1

la **matière** class subject 3

le **matin** morning 3

**mauvais** bad 8; *il fait mauvais* the weather is bad 2

la **mayonnaise** mayo 6

**me (m')** me 4

**méchant(e)** mean 5

un **médecin** doctor 5

une **médiathèque** media center 3

les **meilleurs (m.)** the best 4

un **melon** melon 6

**même** same 6

un **menu fixe** fixed menu 4

**merci** thank you 4

**mercredi** Wednesday 2

une **mère** mother 1; *belle-mère* stepmother 5

**mesdemoiselles (f.)** plural of *mademoiselle* 4

un **métier** job 5

le **métro** subway 4

un **metteur en scène** director 4

**mettre** to put (on), to set 7; *mettre le couvert* to set the table 7

se **mettre: mets-toi devant l'écran** place yourself in front of the TV 9

un **meuble** piece of furniture 7

un **micro-onde** microwave 7

**midi** noon 3

**mieux** better 1

**mille** thousand 4

un **millefeuille** layered custard pastry 8

un **million** million 5

une **mine** appearance, expression 9

une **minute** minute 7

**minuit** midnight 3

**moche** ugly 6

**moi** me 1

**moins** less 7; *moins le quart* quarter to 3

un **mois** month 5

**mon, ma, mes** my 1

le **monde** everyone, world 1

un **moniteur** monitor 7

**monsieur (M.)** Mr., sir 1

une **montagne** mountain 9

**monter** to go up, to get in/on 8

**montrer** to show 8

un **monument** monument 8

un **morceau (de)** piece (of) 6

**mort(e)** dead 9

**morue: accras de morue (m.)** cod fritters 5

une **mosquée** mosque 7

la **moutarde** mustard 6

**moyen(ne)** medium 5

**mûr(e)** ripe 6

un **musée** museum 8

la **musique** music 2; *musique alternative* alternative music 2

# N

**n'est-ce pas?** isn't that so? 2

**nager** to swim 2

une **nappe** tablecloth 7

**naviguer** to browse 7

**ne (n')... jamais** never 10

**ne (n')... pas** not 1

**ne (n')... personne** no one, nobody, not anyone 10

**ne (n')... plus** no longer, not anymore 10

**ne (n')... rien** nothing 3

**neige: il neige** it's snowing 8

**neuf** nine 2

**neuvième** ninth 7

le **nez** nose 9

**niçoise: une salade niçoise** tuna salad 6

**noir(e)** black 5

un **nombre** number 2

**non** no 1

le **nord** north 10

une **note** grade 3

**notre, nos** our 5

**nous** we 2; us 5

**nouveau** new 2; *nouvel, nouvelle* new 8

le **Nouveau-Brunswick** New Brunswick 7

**novembre** November 5

**nucléaire** nuclear 9

la **nuit** night 3

un **numéro** number 2; *numéro de téléphone* phone number 2

# O

**obligatoire** mandatory 8

**occupé(e)** busy 8; *être occupé(e)* to be busy 8

un **océan** ocean 9

**octobre** October 2

l' **œil (m.)** eye 9

un **œuf** egg 6

**offrir** to offer, to give 5

**oh** oh 1

**oh là là** oh dear, oh no, wow 9

un **oignon** onion 6

un **oiseau** bird 8

une **olive** olive 6

une **omelette** omelette 4

**on** they, we, one 1; *On s'appelle.* We'll call each other. 1

un **oncle** uncle 5

**onze** eleven 2

**orange** orange 6

une **orange** orange 4

un **ordinateur** computer 3;

*ordinateur portable* laptop computer 3

l' **oreille (f.)** ear 9

**ou** or 2

**où** where 3; when 8

**oublier** to forget 8

l' **ouest (m.)** west 10

**oui** yes 1

**ouille** ouch 9

un **ours** bear 9; *ours polaire* polar bear 9

**ouvre: elle ouvre** she opens 7

# P

**paie** (see **payer**) 7

le **pain** bread 6

un **pamplemousse** grapefruit 6

un **panda** panda 9; *panda géant* giant panda 9

un **panneau** panel 9

un **pantalon** pants 6

le **papier** paper 3; *une feuille de papier* sheet of paper 3

un **paquet (de)** packet (of) 6

**par** with 7

un **parc** park 7

**parce que** because 3

**pardi (régional)** of course 7

**pardon** pardon me 8

les **parents (m.)** parents 5

**paresseux, paresseuse** lazy 5

**parler** to speak, to talk 5

se **parler** to talk to each other/ one another 8

les **paroles (f.)** lyrics 7

**partir** to leave 8

**partout** everywhere 9

**pas** not 1; *pas du tout* not at all 10; *pas mal* not bad 1; *pas très bien* not very well 1

**passer** to spend (time) 7

un **passe-temps** pastime 2

une **passion** passion 10

**passionné(e) (de)** passionate (about) 5

une **pastèque** watermelon 5

le **pâté** pâté 6

les **pâtes (f.)** pasta 2

le **patinage (artistique)** (figure) skating 2

une **pâtisserie** bakery, pastry shop 6

**payer** to pay 9

un **payeur, une payeuse** someone who pays 9

un **pays** country 7

une **pêche** peach 6

**pendant** during 2; for 8

une **pendule** clock 3

**penser** to think 7

**perdre** to lose 4

**perdu(e)** lost 10

un **père** father 1; *beau-père* stepfather 5

une **personne** person 9; *ne (n')… personne* no one, nobody, not anyone 10

**persuadé(e)** persuaded 9

**petit(e)** little, short, small 5

le **petit déjeuner** breakfast 7

les **petits pois (m.)** peas 6

(un) **peu** (a) little 2; *un peu de* a little of 6

**peut** (see **pouvoir**) 3

**peut-être** maybe 4

**peux** (see **pouvoir**) 1; *Je peux vous aider?* May I help you? 6

une **photo** photo 7; *re-photo* another photo 8

la **physique** physics 3

une **pièce** room 7

le **pied** foot 9; *à pied* on foot 9

une **piscine** swimming pool 3

une **pizza** pizza 2

un **placard** closet 7

une **place** square 8

un **plaisir** pleasure 10

un **plan** city map 10

une **planète** planet 9

le **plastique** plastic 9; *en plastique* made of plastic 9

**pleurer** to cry 4

**pleuvoir** to rain 8; *il pleut* it's raining 8

**plonger** to dive 2

**plus** more 7; *le/la/les plus (+adjectif)* the most (+ adjective) 10

une **poire** pear 6

un **poisson (rouge)** (gold)fish 8

la **poitrine** chest 9

le **poivre** pepper 7

un **poivron** bell pepper 6

**polluant** polluting 9

**polluer** to pollute 9

un **pollueur, une pollueuse** polluter 9

la **pollution** pollution 9

une **pomme** apple 6; *une tarte aux pommes* apple pie 6

une **pomme de terre** potato 6

un **pont** bridge 8

le **porc** pork 6

un **portable** cell phone 7

une **porte** door 3

**porter** to wear 4

**possible** possible 1

une **poste** post office 8

un **pot (de)** jar (of) 6

le **poulet** chicken 6

**pour** for 3

**pourquoi** why 2

**pourrais: tu pourrais** you could 9

**pouvoir** can, to be able (to) 7

**préféré(e)** favorite 2

**préférer** to prefer 2

**premier, première** first 5

**prendre** to take, to have (food or drink) 4; *je prends* I'll take 3

un **prénom** first name 1

**préparer** to prepare 5

une **préposition** preposition 10

**près de** near 7

**présenter** to introduce 1; *Je te/vous présente…* I'd like to introduce you to… 1

**presque** nearly 9

**prêt(e)** ready 6

le **printemps** spring 8

un **problème** problem 7

un(e) **prof** teacher 1

une **profession** profession 5; *Quelle est votre profession?* What is your profession? 5

un **profil** profile 10

**profiter** to take advantage of 8; *profiter de* to benefit from 9; *tu profiterais de* you would benefit from 9

un **projet** project 5

une **promenade** walk 8

**protéger** to protect 9

**provençal(e)** from, of Provence 7

une **province** province 10

un **proviseur** principal 3

**puis** then 3

un **pull** sweater 6

## Q

**qu'est-ce que** what 2; *Qu'est-ce qu'elle a?* What's wrong with her? 9; *Qu'est-ce que tu aimes faire?* What do you like to do? 2; *Qu'est-ce que tu fais?* What are you doing? 2

un **quai** platform 10

**quand** when 2

**quarante** forty 3

un **quart** quarter 3; *et quart* quarter past 3; *moins le quart* a quarter to 3

**quatorze** fourteen 2

**quatre** four 2

**quatre-vingt-dix** ninety 3

**quatre-vingts** eighty 3

**quatrième** fourth 7

**que** that 5; than, as 7

le **Québec** Quebec 10

**québécois(e)** from, of Quebec 10

**quel, quelle** what, which 2

**quelqu'un** somebody, someone 10

**quelque chose** something 10

une **question** question 2

**qui** that, who 3

une **quiche** quiche 4

**quinze** fifteen 2

**quitter** to leave 9

**quoi** what 3

## R

la **radiation** radiation 9

un **raisin** grape 6

la **ratatouille** ratatouille 7

**réaliser** to realize 10

une **recette** recipe 7

**réchauffer** to heat up 9

**recycler** to recycle 9

**réfléchir (à)** to think over, consider 5

**regarder** to watch 2

une **religieuse** cream puff pastry 8

**rembourser** to reimburse 4
**remplacer** to replace 9
un **rendez-vous** meeting 4
**rentrer** to come back, to come home, to return 8
un **repas** meal 7
**re-photo** another photo 8
un **reportage** news report 9
une **résolution** resolution 9
**respiratoire** respiratory 9
**ressembler (à)** to resemble 5
un **restaurant** restaurant 8
**rester** to remain, to stay 8
**retourner** to return 8
se **retrouver** to meet 4; *on se retrouve....* we'll meet.... 3
**réussir (à)** to pass (a test), to succeed 5
**revenir** to come back 5; to return 8
le **rez-de-chaussée** the ground floor 7
un **rhume** cold 9
une **riad** riad 7
**rien: ne (n')... rien** nothing 3
**rigoler** to laugh 8
**rire** to laugh 4
une **rivière** river 10
une **robe** dress 6
le **rock** rock (music) 2
un **rôle** role 5
le **roller** in-line skating 2
une **rondelle** circular piece of food 7; *en rondelles* in circles 7
**rose** pink 6
**rouge** red 6
**rougir** to blush 5
une **route** highway, road, route 10
**roux, rousse** red (hair) 5
une **rue** street 6
le **Rwanda** Rwanda 9

## S

**s'appeler: On s'appelle.** We'll call each other. 1
**s'il vous plaît** please 4
un **sac à dos** backpack 3
**sais: je sais** I know 4; *tu sais* you know 9

une **salade** salad 2; lettuce 6; *salade niçoise* tuna salad 6
une **salle** room 3; *salle à manger* dining room 7; *salle de bains* bathroom 7; *salle de classe* classroom 3; *salle d'informatique* computer lab 3
un **salon** living room 7
**salut** hi, good-bye 1
**samedi** Saturday 2
un **sandwich** sandwich 4; *sandwich au fromage* cheese sandwich 4; *sandwich au jambon* ham sandwich 4
le **saucisson** salami 6
**sauvage** wild 9
**sauvegarder** to protect 9; to save 7
la **science-fiction** science fiction 4
les **sciences (f.)** science 3
une **séance** film showing 4
**seize** sixteen 2
un **séjour** living room 7
le **sel** salt 7
une **semaine** week 2
le **Sénégal** Senegal 5
**sénégalais(e)** Senegalese 5
**sentir** to smell 7; *Ça sent quoi?* What does it smell like? 7
**sept** seven 2
**septembre** September 5
**septième** seventh 7
une **série** series 4
un **serveur, une serveuse** server 4
une **serviette** napkin 7
le **shopping** shopping 2
un **short** shorts 4
**si** yes (on the contrary) 2; if 4
le **SIDA** AIDS 9
un **siège** seat 10
**simple** simple 10
un **site web** website 7
**situé(e)** located 10
**six** six 2
**sixième** sixth 7
le **ski (alpin)** (downhill) skiing 2
une **sœur** sister 5; *belle-sœur* stepsister 5; *demi-sœur* half-sister 5
**soif: avoir soif** to be thirsty 4
le **soir** evening 2

**soixante** sixty 3
**soixante-dix** seventy 3
**solaire** solar 9; *l'énergie (f.) solaire* solar energy 9
**solde: en solde** on sale 4
**soleil: il fait du soleil** it's sunny 8
**son, sa, ses** his, her, one's, its 5
**sortir** to go out 2; to come out 6
la **soupe** soup 6
une **souris** mouse 7
**sous** under 3
**soutenir** to support 4; *je soutiens* I support 4
un **souvenir** memory 8
**souvent** often 10
**souviens: je me souviens** I remember 10
une **spécialité: spécialité du jour** daily special 4
un **sport** sport 2
un **stade** stadium 4
une **statue** statue 8
un **steak-frites** steak with fries 4
le **step** step aerobics 9
une **stéréo** stereo 3
**strict(e)** strict 1
un **stylo** pen 3
le **sucre** sugar 7
le **sud** south 10
**suis** (see **être**) 1
**suisse** Swiss 10
la **Suisse** Switzerland 10
**super** awesome 5
un **supermarché** supermarket 6
**sur** on 2; of 8
**sûr(e)** sure 7
**surfer** to surf 2; *surfer sur Internet* to surf the Web 2
**surprend: ça ne me surprend pas** it doesn't surprise me 4
**surtout** especially 4
**survivre** to survive 9
**sympa** nice 5
**synchroniser** to synchronize 7

## T

**t'appelles: tu t'appelles** your name is 1; *Tu t'appelles comment?* What's your name? 1
une **table** table 3

un **tableau** chalkboard 3; painting 8; *tableau des arrivées et des départs* arrival and departure timetable 10

une **tablette** tablet 7

un **taf** work 7

**tahitien(ne)** Tahitian 3

une **taille** size 5; *de taille moyenne* of average height 5; *Quelle taille faites-vous?* What size are you? 6

un **taille-crayon** pencil sharpener 3

**tant pis** too bad 6

une **tante** aunt 5

un **tapis** rug 7

une **tarte** pie 6; *tarte aux fruits* fruit tart 6; *tarte aux pommes* apple pie 6

une **tasse** cup 7

**te (t')** you, to you 1

un **tee-shirt** T-shirt 6

une **télé (télévision)** TV, television 2

**télécharger** to download 7

**téléphoner** to phone (someone), to make a call 2

la **température** temperature 8

le **temps** weather 8; *Quel temps fait-il?* What's the weather like? How's the weather? 8

des **tennis (m.)** sneakers 6

une **terrasse** terrace 8

un **testeur de jeux vidéo** video game tester 5

la **tête** head 9

une **teuf** party 1

un **texto** text message 2

un **thème** topic 9

**thermal(e)** hydrotherapeutic 9

le **thon** tuna 6

un **thriller** thriller 4

un **ticket** ticket 4

**tiens** hey 6

un **tigre** tiger 9; *tigre de Sumatra* Sumatran tiger 9

**timide** shy 5

un **tissu** fabric 7

le **Togo** Togo 5

**togolais(e)** Togolese 5

**toi** you 1

les **toilettes (f.)** toilet 7

un **toit** roof 9

une **tomate** tomato 6

**ton, ta** your 1; *tes* your 5

**top** awesome 1; *C'est le top!* That's awesome! 1

**total(e): Total vintage!** It has a totally vintage look! 3

une **touche** key (on keyboard) 7

**toujours** always 10; still 4

un **tour** tour 8

**tourner** to turn 10

**tout(e), tous, toutes** all 1; *Tout ça!* All that! 4

un **train** train 10

une **tranche (de)** slice (of) 6

**travailler** to work 5

**traverser** to cross 10

**treize** thirteen 2

**trente** thirty 3

**très** very 1; *Très bien, et toi/vous?* Very well, and you? 1

**trois** three 2

**troisième** third 7

**trop** too 1; *trop de* too much of 6

une **trousse** pencil case 3

**trouver** to find 6

se **trouver** to be located 10

**tu** you 1

# U

**un** a, an 1; one 2

**une** a, an, one 3

une **usine** factory 9

# V

**va** (see **aller**) 1

les **vacances (f.)** vacation 10

une **valise** suitcase 10

une **vallée** valley 10

**vas** (see **aller**) 1; *Tu vas bien?* Are things going well? 2

un **vélo** bike 2; *à vélo* by bike 9

un **vendeur, une vendeuse** salesperson 6

**vendre** to sell 6

**vendredi** Friday 2

**venir** to come 1

**vent: il fait du vent** it's windy 8

le **ventre** stomach 9

un **verre** glass 7

**vers** towards 10

**vert(e)** green 5

une **veste** jacket 6

des **vêtements (m.)** clothes 4

**veux: je veux bien** I'd like that 1

**vieux, vieil, vieille** old 8

une **ville** city 3; *en ville* downtown 3

**vingt** twenty 2

**violet, violette** purple 6

une **visite** visit 10

**visiter** to visit 8

**vite** fast, quickly 8

une **voie** path 9; train track 10; *animaux en voie de disparition* endangered species 9

**voilà** here is/are 4

**voir** to see 3

se **voir** to see each other/one another 8

une **voiture** car 9; *voiture électrique* electric car 9; *voiture hybride* hybrid car 9

**votre, vos** your 5

**voudrais: je voudrais** I would like 5; *tu voudrais* you would like 1

**vouloir** to want 6

**vous** you 1, to you 5; *Vous voulez...?* Would you like...? 4

un **voyage** trip 8

**voyager** to travel 5

un **voyageur, une voyageuse** traveller 10

**vrai(e)** true 10

**vraiment** really 5

une **vue** view 7; *Quelle belle vue!* What a beautiful view! 7

# W

les **W.C. (m.)** toilet 7

un **wagon-restaurant** dining car 10

le **weekend** weekend 2

la **world** world music 2

# Y

**y: On y va?** Are we going (there)? 3

un **yaourt** yogurt 6

les **yeux (m.)** eyes 5

le **yoga** yoga 9

# Z

**zéro** zero 2

# Vocabulary

## English–French

This vocabulary list combines words from Textbook 1A (Units 1 to 5) and Textbook 1B (Units 6 to 10). The number at the end of each definition is the Unit in which the word is first presented.

**A**    **a, an** un 1; une 3; *(a) little* (un) peu 2; *a little of* un peu de 6; *a lot* beaucoup 2; *a lot of* beaucoup de 6

to be   **able (to)** pouvoir 7
**about (the)** du 8
**above** au-dessus de 7
to   **accompany** accompagner 10
**ache: to have a/an... ache** avoir mal (à)... 9
**across from** en face de 10
**action** l'action (f.) 4
**activity** une activité 2
**actor** un acteur, une actrice 4
**adventure** une aventure 4
to   **advise** conseiller 9
**aerobics** l'aérobic (m.) 9; *step aerobics* le step 9
**Africa** l'Afrique (f.) 5
**after** après 2
**afternoon** l'après-midi (m.) 3
**against** contre 4
**age** l'âge (m.) 5
to   **agree** être d'accord 7
**agriculture** l'agriculture (f.) 9
**AIDS** le SIDA 9
**air** l'air (m.) 6
**airplane** un avion 8
**airport** un aéroport 8
**Algerian** algérien(ne) 1
**all** tout(e), toutes, tous 1; *All that!* Tout ça! 4
**already** déjà 8
**also** aussi 2
**aluminum** l'aluminium (m.) 9; *made of aluminum* en aluminium 9
**always** toujours 10
**American** américain(e) 1
**and** et 1
**animal** un animal 8
**another: another photo** re-photo 8
**antiretroviral drugs** les antirétroviraux (m.) 9
**any** d', de 2

**apartment** un appartement 7; *apartment building* un immeuble 7
**appearance** une mine 9
**apple** une pomme 6; *apple pie* une tarte aux pommes 6
**April** avril 5
**area** un espace 9
**arm** le bras 9
**armchair** un fauteuil 7
**arrival** une arrivée 10; *arrival and departure timetable* un tableau des arrivées et des départs 10
to   **arrive** arriver 4
**as** aussi, que 7
to   **ask (for)** demander 7; *to ask for directions* demander le chemin 10
**assignment** un devoir 9
**at** à 2; *at (the)* au, aux 3; *at my house* chez moi 3; *at the end (of)* au fond (de) 7; au bout (de) 10; *at the house (home) of* chez 3
**athlete** un(e) athlète 5
**August** août 5
**aunt** une tante 5
**autumn** l'automne (m.) 8
**avenue** une avenue 8
**awesome** top 1; super 8; *That's awesome!* C'est le top! 1

**B**

**back** le dos 9
**backpack** un sac à dos 3
**bad** mal 1; mauvais 8; *the weather is bad* il fait mauvais 2
**badly** mal 1; *Things are going badly.* Ça va mal. 1
**bakery** une boulangerie, une pâtisserie 6
**banal** banal(e) 8

**banana** une banane 6
**bank** une banque 8
**basketball** le basket (basketball) 2
**bathing suit** un maillot de bain 6
**bathroom** une salle de bains 7
**bathtub** une baignoire 7
to   **be** être 3; *to be able (to)* pouvoir 7; *to be busy* être occupé 8; *to be (busy) doing something* être en train de (+ infinitive) 7; *to be cold* avoir froid 8; *to be committed to* s'engager 9; *to be environmentally friendly* être vert 9; *to be free* être libre 8; *to be hot* avoir chaud 8; *to be how old* avoir quel âge 5; *to be hungry* avoir faim 4; *to be hurt* avoir mal (à...) 9; *to be informed* être au courant 9; *to be in (good, bad) shape* être en (bonne, mauvaise) forme 9; *to be located* être situé(e), se trouver 10; *to be necessary* falloir 8; *to be thirsty* avoir soif 4; *to be... year(s) old* avoir... an(s) 5
**bear** un ours 9; *polar bear* un ours polaire 9
**beautiful** beau, bel, belle 7; *It's beautiful out.* Il fait beau. 2
**because** parce que 3
to   **become** devenir 5
**bed** un lit 7
**bedroom** une chambre 7
**beef** le bœuf 6
to   **begin** commencer 7
**behind** derrière 3
**beige** beige 6
**Belgian** belge 10
**Belgium** la Belgique 10
**bench** un banc 7

**to benefit from** profiter de 9;
*you would benefit from* tu
profiterais de 9

**Benin** le Bénin 5

**Beninese** béninois(e) 5

**Berber** berbère 7

**beside** à côté de 7

**best: the best** les meilleurs (m.) 4

**better** mieux 1

**between** entre 10

**big** grand(e) 5; gros, grosse 6

**bike** un vélo 2

**to bike** faire du vélo 2; *by bike* à
vélo 9

**bill** l'addition (f.) 4; *bill
(money)* un billet 6

**biology** la biologie 3

**bird** un oiseau 8

**birthday** un anniversaire 5

**black** noir(e) 5

**blog** un blogue 2

**blond** blond(e) 5

**blue** bleu(e) 5; *the blue one* la
bleue 3

**to blush** rougir 5

**boat** un bateau 8

**body** le corps 9

**book** un livre 3

**boots** les bottes (f.) 6

**bottle (of)** une bouteille (de) 6

**bottom** le bas 8

**bowl** un bol 7

**boy** un garçon 5

**bread** le pain 6; *long thin
loaf of bread* une baguette 6

**breakfast** le petit déjeuner 7

**bridge** un pont 8

**to bring** apporter 5

**brother** un frère 5; *half-
brother* un demi-frère 5;
*stepbrother* un beau-frère 5

**brown** marron 6; *brown (hair)*
brun(e) 5

**to browse** naviguer 7

**building: apartment building**
un immeuble 7

**Burkina Faso** le Burkina Faso
5; *from, of Burkina Faso*
burkinabè 5

**bus** un autobus 10

**business** commerçant(e) 6

**businessman** un homme
d'affaires 5

**businesswoman** une femme
d'affaires 5

**busy** occupé(e) 8

**to be busy** être occupé(e) 8; *to be
(busy) doing something* être
en train de (+ infinitive) 7

**but** mais 3

**butcher shop** une boucherie 6

**butter** le beurre 6

**to buy** acheter 3

**by** à 9; en 9; *by bike* à vélo 9;
*by electric car* en voiture
électrique 9; *by hybrid car*
en voiture hybride 9

# C

**café** un café 1

**cafeteria: school cafeteria**
une cantine 3

**cake** un gâteau 5

**camembert cheese** le
camembert 6

**Cameroon** le Cameroun 5

**Cameroonian** camerounais(e) 5

**can (of)** une boîte (de) 6

**Canada** le Canada 5

**Canadian** canadien(ne) 1

**cap** une casquette 4

**capital** une capitale 8

**car** une voiture 9; *dining car*
un wagon-restaurant 10;
*electric car* une voiture
électrique 9; *hybrid car* une
voiture hybride 9

**carbon dioxyde** le dioxyde de
carbone 9

**card** une carte 5

**careful: Be careful!** Attention! 7

**carrot** une carotte 6

**castle** un château 10

**cat** un chat 8

**cathedral** une cathédrale 8

**cause** une cause 10

**to cause** causer 9

**CD** un CD 2; un cédérom 3

**cell phone** un portable 7

**center** un centre 1; *shopping
center* un centre commercial 1

**chair** une chaise 3

**chalkboard** un tableau 3

**charming** charmant(e) 7

**cheap** bon marché 6

**cheese** le fromage 4;
*camembert cheese* le
camembert 6; *cheese sandwich*
un sandwich au fromage 4

**chef** un cuisinier, une
cuisinière 5

**chemical** chimique 9

**chemistry** la chimie 3

**cherry** une cerise 6

**chest** la poitrine 9

**chic** chic 6

**chicken** le poulet 6

**child** un enfant 5

**chills** les frissons (m.) 9

**chocolate** le chocolat 4

**to choose** choisir 5

**circular: circular object or
piece of food** une rondelle 7

**city** ville 3

**city hall** un hôtel de ville 8

**class** une classe 1; un cours 2;
*class subject* la matière
3; *gym class* l'éducation
physique et sportive (EPS)
(f.) 3

**classmate** un(e) camarade de
classe 1

**classroom** la salle de classe 3

**to click** cliquer 7

**clock** une pendule 3

**to close** fermer 7

**closet** un placard 7

**clothes** des vêtements (m.) 4

**coat** un manteau 6

**cod fritters** les accras de
morue (m.) 5

**coffee** un café 4

**cola** un coca 4

**cold** froid 8; *I am cold* j'ai froid
8; *it's cold* il fait froid 8; *to
be cold* avoir froid 8

**cold** un rhume 9

**color** une couleur 6; *In what
color(s)?* De quelle(s)
couleur(s) 7

**to come** venir 1; *to come back*
revenir 5; rentrer 8; *to come
home* rentrer 8; *to come in*
entrer 8; *to come out* sortir 6

comedy une comédie 4; *romantic comedy* une comédie romantique 4

to **commit to** s'engager 9

**composer** un compositeur 5

**computer** un ordinateur 3; *computer lab* une salle d'informatique 3; *computer science* l'informatique (f.) 3; *laptop computer* un ordinateur portable 3

**concert** un concert 2

to **consider** réfléchir (à) 5

to **consume** consommer 8

to **continue** continuer 9

**cool** frais, fraîche 8; *it's cool* il fait frais 8

**cook** un cuisinier, une cuisinière 5

to **cook** faire la cuisine 2

**cooking** la cuisine 2

**corner** le coin 8; *on the corner* du coin 8

to **cost** coûter 3

**could: you could** tu pourrais 9

**country** un pays 7

**country(side)** la campagne 10

**course** un cours 2

**couscous** le couscous 6

**cousin** un(e) cousin(e) 5

**cream puff pastry** une religieuse 8

**crêpe** une crêpe 4

**croissant** un croissant 6

to **cross** traverser 10

to **cry** pleurer 4

**cucumber** un concombre 6

**cultural** culturel, culturelle 5

**cup** une tasse 7

**to cut** couper 7

# D

**daily special** une spécialité du jour 4

**dairy store** une crémerie 6

**dark (hair)** brun(e) 5

**daughter** une fille 5

**day** un jour 2; une journée 8; *one day, some day* un jour 5

**dead** mort(e) 9

**December** décembre 5

**degree** un degré 8

**delicatessen** une charcuterie 6

**delicious** délicieux, délicieuse 3

**delighted** enchanté(e) 1

**dentist** un(e) dentiste 5

**department** un département 10

**departure** un départ 10

**desk** un bureau 3

**dessert** un dessert 4

**destination** une destination 10

to **dictionary** un dictionnaire 3

**difficult** difficile 3

**diligent** diligent(e) 5

**dining: dining car** un wagon-restaurant 10; *dining room* la salle à manger 7

**dinner** le dîner 7

to have **dinner** dîner 7

**direction** une direction 10

**director** un metteur en scène 5

**discussion** une discussion 5

to **dive** plonger 2

to **divorced** divorcé(e)(s) 5

to **do** faire 1; *to do gymnastics* faire de la gym (gymnastique) 2; *to do my homework* faire mes devoirs 1

**doctor** un médecin 5

**documentary** un documentaire 4

**dog** un chien 8

**door** une porte 3

to **download** télécharger 7

**downtown** en ville 3

**drama** un drame 4

**dress** une robe 6

**dressing room** une cabine d'essayage 6

**drink** une boisson 4

to **drive** circuler 9

**during** pendant 2

**DVD** un DVD 3; *DVD player* un lecteur de DVD 3

# E

**ear** l'oreille (f.) 9

**early** en avance 4

**east** l'est (m.) 10

**easy** facile 3

to **eat** manger 2

**eclair** un éclair 8

**effect** un effet 9; *greenhouse effect* l'effet de serre 9

**egg** un œuf 6

**eggplant** une aubergine 6

**eight** huit 2

**eighteen** dix-huit 2

**eighth** huitième 7

**eighty** quatre-vingts 3

**electric** électrique 9

**eleven** onze 2

to **eliminate** éliminer 9

**end** le bout 10; *at the end (of)* au fond (de) 7; au bout (de) 10

**endangered species** les animaux en voie de disparition 9

**energetic** énergique 3

**energy** l'énergie (f.) 9; *nuclear energy* l'énergie nucléaire 9; *solar energy* l'énergie solaire 9

**engineer** un ingénieur 5

**England** l'Angleterre (f.) 10

**English** anglais(e) 10; *(language)* l'anglais (m.) 3

**enjoy: Enjoy your meal!** Bon Appétit! 4

**enough (of)** assez (de) 6

to **enter** entrer 8

**environment** l'environnement (m.) 9

**especially** surtout 4

**euro** un euro 3

**Europe** l'Europe (f.) 10

**evening** le soir 2

**everyone** le monde 1

**everywhere** partout 9

**exactly** exactement 8

**expensive** cher, chère 3

**expression** une mine 9

**eye** l'œil (m.) 9; *eyes* les yeux (m.) 5

# F

**fabric** un tissu 7

**face** la figure 9

**factory** une usine 9

**family** une famille 5

**fantastic** génial(e) 2

**far (from)** loin (de) 10

**fast** vite 8

**fat** gros, grosse 6

**father** un père 1; *stepfather* un beau-père 5

**favorite** préféré(e) 2

**February** février 5

to **feel: to feel like** avoir envie de 8; *to feel nauseous* avoir mal au cœur 9

**fertilizer** l'engrais (m.) 9

**fever** la fièvre 9

**fifteen** quinze 2

**fifth** cinquième 7

**fifty** cinquante 3

to **fight** combattre 9

**figure** la ligne 8; *your figure* ta ligne 8

**film** un film 4; *film showing* une séance 4

**finally** enfin 4

to **find** trouver 6

**fine** fin(e) 7

to **finish** finir 5

**finger** le doigt 9

**first** premier, première 5; *first of all* d'abord 6; *first name* un prénom 1

**fish: (gold)fish** un poisson (rouge) 8

**five** cinq 2

**fixed menu** un menu fixe 4

**flag** un drapeau 10

**floor** un étage 7; *ground floor* le rez-de-chaussée 7; *second floor* le premier étage 7

**flu** la grippe 9

**fond of food** gourmand(e) 8

**foot** le pied 9; *on foot* à pied 9

**for** comme 1; pour 3; pendant 8

**forest** une forêt 10

to **forget** oublier 8

**fork** une fourchette 7

**forty** quarante 3

**four** quatre 2

**fourteen** quatorze 2

**fourth** quatrième 7

**France** la France 3

**free** disponible 8

**French** français(e) 1; *(language)* le français 3; *French fries* les frites (f.) 2; *French-speaking* francophone 5; *from, of French-speaking Canada* francanadien(ne) 10

**fresh** frais, fraîche 6

**Friday** vendredi 2

**friend** un(e) ami(e) 2; *(boy/girl) friend* un copain, une copine 1

**fritters: cod fritters** les accras de morue (m.) 5

**from** d', de 1; *from (the)* du, des 5

**front: in front of** devant 3

**fruit** un fruit 6; *fruit tart* une tarte aux fruits 6

**funny** drôle 3

**furniture: piece of furniture** un meuble 7

# G

**Gabon** le Gabon 5

**Gabonese** gabonais(e) 5

to **gain weight** grossir 5

**game** un match 4

**garden** un jardin 8

**generous** généreux, généreuse 5

**German** allemand(e) 10; *(language)* l'allemand (m.) 3

**Germany** l'Allemagne (f.) 10

to **get: to get around** circuler 9; *to get in/on* monter 8; *to get off* descendre 8

**giant** géant(e) 9

**gift** un cadeau 5; *gift card* une carte cadeau 5

**girl** une fille 2

to **give** donner 4; offrir 5; *give me* donnez-moi 4

**glass** un verre 7

to **go** aller 1; *Go for it!* Vas-y! 6; *to go down* descendre 8; *to go for a walk* faire une promenade 8; *to go grocery shopping* faire les courses 6; *to go out* sortir 2; *to go running* faire du footing 2; *to go shopping* faire du shopping 2; *to go up* monter 8

**goal** un but 4

**(gold)fish** un poisson (rouge) 8

**good** bon(ne) 1; *Good-bye.* Au revoir., Salut. 1; *Good idea!* Bonne idée! 8; *Have a good trip!* Bon voyage! 10

**gorilla** un gorille 9; *mountain gorilla* un gorille des montagnes 9

**grade** une note 3

**gram (of)** un gramme (de) 6

**grandfather** un grand-père 5

**grandmother** une grand-mère 5

**grandparents** les grands-parents (m.) 5

**grape** un raisin 6

**grapefruit** un pamplemousse 6

**graphic designer** un(e) graphiste 5

**great** génial(e) 2; chouette 8

**green** vert(e) 5; *green beans* des haricots verts (m.) 6

**grey** gris 5

**grocery store** une épicerie 6

**ground floor** le rez-de-chaussée 7

to **grow** grandir 5

**guest** un(e) invité(e) 7

**guidebook** un guide 10

**gym** un fitness 9; *gym class* l'éducation physique et sportive (l'EPS) (f.) 3

**gymnastics** la gym (gymnastique) 2

# H

**hair** les cheveux (m.) 5

**half** demi(e) 3; *half-brother* un demi-frère 5; *half past* et demie 3; *half-sister* une demi-sœur 5

**hallway** un couloir 7

**ham** le jambon 4; *ham sandwich* un sandwich au jambon 4

**hamburger** un hamburger 2

**hand** la main 8; *hand in hand* la main dans la main 8

**handsome** beau, bel, belle 7

**hat** un chapeau 6

to **have** avoir 3; *(food or drink)* prendre 4; *one/we/you have to* il faut 8; *to have a/an... ache* avoir mal (à...) 9; *to have dinner* dîner 7; *to have to* devoir 7; falloir 9

**he** il 1

**head** la tête 9

**health club** un fitness 9

**heart** le cœur 9

to **heat up** réchauffer 9

**hello** bonjour 1; *(on the telephone)* allô 1

to **help** aider 1

**her** son, sa, ses 5

**here** ici 7; *here is/are* voilà 4

**hey** tiens 6

**hi** salut 1

**high school** un lycée 9

**highway** une route 10

**hill** une colline 10

**hip-hop** le hip-hop 2

**his** son, sa, ses 5

**history** l'histoire (f.) 3

**home** une maison 1; *home health worker* un accompagnateur, une accompagnatrice 9

**homework** les devoirs (m.) 1

**horror** l'horreur (f.) 4

**horse** un cheval 8

**hot** chaud(e); *to be hot* avoir chaud 8; *it's hot* il fait chaud 8; *I am hot* j'ai chaud 8

**hotel** un hôtel 8

**hour** l'heure (f.) 3

**house** une maison 1

**how** comment 1; *How are things going?* Ça va? 1; *How are you?* Comment allez-vous? *[form.]* 1; *how much* combien 3; *How much is it?* Ça fait combien? 6; *How much per kilo?* C'est combien le kilo? 6; *How old are you?* Tu as quel âge? 5; *How's the weather?* Quel temps fait-il? 8

**humanitarian** humanitaire 10

**hundred: (one) hundred** cent 3

**hungry: to be hungry** avoir faim 4

**hurt: to be hurt** avoir mal (à...) 9

**husband** un mari 5

**hybrid** hybride 9

**hydrotherapeutic** thermal(e) 9

# I

**I** je/ j' 1

**ice cream** une glace 4; *chocolate ice cream* une glace au chocolat 4; *vanilla ice cream* une glace à la vanille 4

**ice-skating (figure skating)** le patinage (artistique) 2

**if** si 4

**illness** une maladie 9

**impossible** impossible 7

**in** dans, en 3; à 5; *in circles* en rondelles 7; *in-line skating* le roller 2; *in front of* devant 3; *in my opinion* à mon avis 9; *in the* au, aux 3; *In what color(s)?* De quelle(s) couleur(s)? 6

**inhabitant** un(e) habitant(e) 10

to **install** installer 9

**intelligent** intelligent(e) 3

**interesting** intéressant(e) 3

**international** international(e) 10

**Internet** (l')Internet (m.) 2

to **introduce** présenter 1; *I'd like to introduce you to...* Je te/vous présente... 1

to **invite** inviter 2

**is** (see **to be**) 1; *Isn't that so?* N'est-ce pas? 2

**it** ça, ce 1; elle, il 3; le, la, l' (object pronoun) 4; *it doesn't surprise me* ça ne me surprend pas 4; *It has a totally vintage look!* Total vintage! 3; *it is* c'est 1; *it is necessary* il faut 8; *it's beautiful out* il fait beau 2; *it's cold* il fait froid 8; *it's cool* il fait frais 8; *it's hot* il fait chaud 8; *it's raining* il pleut 8; *it's snowing* il neige 8; *it's sunny* il fait du soleil 8; *It's the (+ date).* C'est le (+ date). Nous sommes le (+ date). 5; *it's windy* il fait du vent 8

**its** son, sa, ses 5

**Italian** italien(ne) 10

**Italy** l'Italie (f.) 10

**Ivory Coast** la Côte-d'Ivoire 5; *from, of the Ivory Coast* ivorien(ne) 5

# J

**jacket** un blouson 4; une veste 6

**jam** la confiture 4

**January** janvier 5

**jar (of)** un pot (de) 6

**jasmine** le jasmin 7

**jeans** un jean 6

**jersey** un maillot 4

**job** un métier 5

**juice** un jus 4; *orange juice* un jus d'orange 4

**July** juillet 5

**June** juin 5

# K

**ketchup** le ketchup 6

**key (on keyboard)** une touche 7

**keyboard** un clavier 7

**kilogram (of)** un kilo (de) 6

**kilometer** un kilomètre 5

to **kiss** embrasser 8

**kitchen** la cuisine 7

**knee** le genou 9

**knife** un couteau 7

**know** être au courant 9; *I know* je connais 5; je sais 4; *you know* tu sais 9

# L

**lab: computer lab** une salle d'informatique 3; *science lab* un labo (laboratoire) 3

**lake** un lac 10

**lamp** une lampe 7

**language** une langue 3

**large** grand(e) 5; gros, grosse 6

**last** dernier, dernière 8

**late** en retard 4

to **laugh** rire 4; rigoler 8

**lawyer** un(e) avocat(e) 5

**lazy** paresseux, paresseuse 5

to **learn** apprendre 4

to **leave** partir 8; laisser, quitter 9

**left: on the left** à gauche 7; *to(on) the left of* à gauche de 7

**leg** la jambe 9

**less** moins 7

to **let** laisser 9; *Let me finish!* Laisse-moi finir! 8

lettuce une salade 6

like comme 5

to like aimer 2

link un lien 7

to listen (to) écouter 2; *to listen to music* écouter de la musique 2; *to listen to my MP3 player* écouter mon lecteur MP3 2

liter (of) un litre (de) 6

little petit(e) 5; *(a) little* (un) peu 2; *a little of* un peu de 6

to live habiter 7

living room un salon, un séjour 7

located situé(e) 10; *to be located* être situé(e) 10

logo: team logo un blason 4

long long, longue 7

to look for chercher 6; *to look awful* avoir mauvaise mine 9; *to look healthy* avoir bonne mine 9; *to look like (something from) my country* avoir un petit air du pays 7; *Does this… look good on me?* Tu trouves que… me va bien? 6

to lose perdre 4; *to lose weight* maigrir 5

lost perdu(e) 10

lot: a lot beaucoup 2; *a lot of* beaucoup de 6

to love aimer 2

lunch le déjeuner 3

Luxembourg le Luxembourg 10; *from, of Luxembourg* luxembourgeois(e)

lyrics les paroles (f.) 7

## M

Ma'am madame (Mme) 1

made: made of aluminum en aluminium 9; *made of plastic* en plastique 9

to make faire 1; *to make a call* téléphoner 2; *to make (something) work* faire marcher 9

Mali le Mali 5

Malian malien(ne) 5

mall un centre commercial 1

man un homme 5

mandatory obligatoire 8

map une carte 3; *city map* un plan 10

March mars 5

market: flea market un marché aux puces 6; *outdoor market* un marché 6

Martinique la Martinique 5

math les maths (f.) 1

May mai 5

may: May I help you? Je peux vous aider? 6

maybe peut-être 4

mayo la mayonnaise 6

me m', moi 1; me 4

meal un repas 7

mean méchant(e) 5

media center une médiathèque 3

medium moyen(ne) 5

to meet faire la connaissance (de) 10; se retrouver 4; *we'll meet* on se retrouve 3

meeting un rendez-vous 4

melon un melon 6

memory un souvenir 8

menu une carte 4

merchant un(e) marchand(e) 6

microwave un micro-onde 7

midnight minuit 3

milk le lait 6

million un million 5

mineral water une eau minérale 4

minute une minute 7

Miss mademoiselle (Mlle) 1

model un mannequin 6

moment un instant 9; *for the moment* pour l'instant 9

Monday lundi 2

money l'argent (m.) 8

monitor un écran 7; un moniteur 7

month un mois 5

monument un monument 8

more plus 7

morning le matin 3

mosque une mosquée 7

most: the most (+ adjective) le/la/les plus (+ adjectif) 10

mother une mère 1; *stepmother* une belle-mère 5

motto une devise 10

mountain une montagne 9

mouse une souris 7

mouth la bouche 9

to move bouger 9

movies le cinéma 2; *action movie* un film d'action 4; *adventure movie* un film d'aventure 4; *detective movie* un film policier 4; *horror movie* un film d'horreur 4; *movie theatre* un ciné (cinéma) 1; *science fiction movie* un film de science-fiction 4

MP3 player un lecteur de MP3 3

Mr. monsieur (M.) 1

Mrs. madame (Mme) 1

Ms. madame (Mme), mademoiselle (Mlle) 1

much: very much beaucoup 2; *How much is it?* Ça fait combien? 6

museum un musée 8

mushroom un champignon 6

music la musique 2; *alternative music* la musique alternative 2

musical un film musical 4

must (see to have to) 1; *one/ we/you must* il faut 8

mustard la moutarde 6

my mon, ma, mes 1

## N

name: first name un prénom 1; *my name is* je m'appelle 1; *your name is* tu t'appelles 1

napkin une serviette 7

nauseous: to feel nauseous avoir mal au cœur 9

near près de 7

nearly presque 9

neck le cou 9

to need avoir besoin de 3

never ne (n')… jamais 10

new nouvelle 2; nouveau, nouvel 8

New Brunswick le Nouveau-Brunswick 10

news report un reportage 9

newstand un kiosque à journaux 4

**next** prochain(e) 4; ensuite 6; *next to* à côté (de) 7

**nice** sympa 5

**night** la nuit 3

**nine** neuf 2

**nineteen** dix-neuf 2

**ninety** quatre-vingt-dix 3

**ninth** neuvième 7

**no** non 1; *no longer* ne (n')... plus 10; *no one* ne (n')... personne 10

**nobody** ne (n')... personne 10

**noon** midi 3

**north** le nord 10

**nose** le nez 9

**not** ne (n')... pas, pas 1; *not anymore* ne (n')... plus 10; *not anyone* ne (n')... personne 10; *not at all* pas du tout 10; *not bad* pas mal 1; *not well* pas très bien 1

**notebook** un cahier 3

**nothing** ne (n')... rien 3

**November** novembre 5

**now** maintenant 3

**nuclear** nucléaire 9

**number** un nombre, un numéro 2; *phone number* un numéro de téléphone 2

**O**

**ocean** un océan 9

**o'clock** l'heure (f.) 3

**October** octobre 5

**of** de/d' 1; en (pronoun), sur 8; *of (the)* des 5; du 4; *of average height* de taille moyenne 5; *of course* pardi (regional) 7

**often** souvent 10

to **offer** offrir 5

**office** un bureau 3; *principal's office* le bureau du proviseur 3

**oh** ah, oh 1; *oh dear* oh là là 9; *oh no* oh là là 9

**oil slick** une marée noire 9

**OK** d'accord 1

**old** vieil, vielle, vieux 8

**olive** une olive 6

**Olympic Games** les Jeux Olympiques (m.) 2

**omelette** une omelette 4

**on** sur 2; à, en 4; *on board* à bord 7; *on foot* à pied 9; *on sale* en solde 4; *on the* au, du 8; *on the corner* du coin 8; *on the left* à gauche 7; *on the right* à droite 7; *on time* à l'heure 4

**one** on 1; un 2; une 3; *one's* son, sa, ses 5

**onion** un oignon 6

**online** en ligne 6

**open: she opens** elle ouvre 7

**opinion** un avis 9; *in my opinion* à mon avis 9

**or** ou 2

**orange** une orange 4; orange 6; *orange juice* un jus d'orange 4

**organic** biologique 9

**other** autre 7

**otherwise** autrement 6

**ouch** ouille 9

**our** notre, nos 5

**outfit** un ensemble 6

**oven** un four 7

**over there** là-bas 6

**P**

**packet (of)** un paquet (de) 6

**painting** un tableau 8

**panda** un panda 9; *giant panda* un panda géant 9

**panel** un panneau 9

**pants** un pantalon 6

**paper** le papier 3; *sheet of paper* une feuille de papier 3

**pardon: pardon me** pardon 8

**parents** les parents (m.) 5

**park** un jardin 8; un parc 7

**party** une fête, une teuf 1

to **pass (a test)** réussir (à) 5

**passion** une passion 10

**passionate (about)** passionné(e) (de) 5

**pasta** les pâtes (f.) 2

**past: half past** et demie 3

**pastime** un passe-temps 2

**pastry: cream puff pastry** une religieuse 8; *layered custard pastry* un millefeuille 8; *pastry shop* une patisserie 6

**pâté** le pâté 6

**path** un chemin 10; une voie 9

to **pay** payer 9; *someone who pays* un payeur, une payeuse 9

**peach** une pêche 6

**pear** une poire 10

**peas** les petits-pois (m.) 6

**pen** un stylo 3

**pencil** un crayon 3; *pencil case* une trousse 3; *pencil sharpener* un taille-crayon 3

**people** les gens (m.) 9

**pepper** le poivre 7; *bell pepper* un poivron 6

**person** une personne 1

**persuaded** persuadé(e) 9

to **phone (someone)** téléphoner 2

**photo** une photo 7; *another photo* re-photo 8

**physics** la physique 3

**pie** une tarte 6; *apple pie* une tarte aux pommes 6

**piece (of)** un morceau (de) 6; *piece of furniture* un meuble 7

**pillow** un coussin 7

**pineapple** un ananas 6

**pink** rose 6

**pizza** une pizza 2

**place** un endroit 3; *place yourself in front of the TV* mets-toi devant l'écran 9

**planet** une planète 9

**plastic** le plastique 9; *made of plastic* en plastique 9

**plate** une assiette 7

**platform** un quai 10

to **play** jouer 2; *to play a role* jouer un rôle 4; *to play basketball* jouer au basket (basketball) 2; *to play ice hockey* jouer au hockey sur glace 2; *to play soccer* jouer au foot (football) 2; *to play sports* faire du sport 2; *to play video games* jouer aux jeux vidéo 2

**please** s'il vous plaît 4

**pleasure** un plaisir 10

**police officer** un agent de police 5

to **pollute** polluer 9

**polluter** un pollueur, une pollueuse 9

**polluting** polluant 9

**pollution** la pollution 9

**pond** un étang 10

**pork** le porc 6

**potato** une pomme de terre 6

**pound** une livre 6

**possible** possible 1

**post office** une poste 8

**poster** une affiche 3

to **prefer** préférer 2

to **prepare** préparer 5

**preposition** une préposition 10

**pretty** joli(e) 6

**principal** un proviseur 3

to **print** imprimer 7

**printer** une imprimante 7

**problem** un problème 7

**profession** la profession 5; *What is your profession?* Quelle est votre profession? 5

**profile** un profil 10

**program: television program** une émission 9

**project** un projet 5

to **protect** protéger, sauvegarder 9

**Provence: from, of Provence** provençal(e) 7

**province** une province 10

**purchase** un achat 6

**purple** violet, violette 6

to **put (on)** mettre 7

## Q

**quarter** un quart 3; *quarter past* et quart 3; *quarter to* moins le quart 3

**Quebec** le Québec 10; *from, of Quebec* québécois(e) 10

**question** une question 7

**quiche** une quiche 4

**quickly** vite 8

## R

**radiation** la radiation 9

to **rain** pleuvoir 8; *it's raining* il pleut 8

**ratatouille** la ratatouille 10

to **read** lire 2

**ready** prêt(e) 6

to **realize** réaliser 10

**really** bien 2; vraiment 5

**recipe** une recette 7

to **recycle** recycler 9

**red** rouge 6; *red (hair)* roux, rousse 5

**refrigirator** un frigo 7

to **reimburse** rembourser 4

**relaxed** décontracté(e) 9

to **remain** rester 8

to **remember: I remember** je me souviens 10

to **rent** louer 10

to **replace** remplacer 9

**report: news report** un reportage 9

to **resemble** ressembler (à) 5

**resident** un(e) habitant(e) 10

**resolution** une résolution 9

**respiratory** respiratoire 9

**restaurant** un restaurant 8

to **return** rentrer, retourner, revenir 8

**riad** une riad 7

**right: That's right.** C'est ça. 1; *to the right* à droite 7; *to (on) the right of* à droite de 7

**ripe** mûr(e) 6

**river** un fleuve 8; une rivière 10

**R&B: R&B concert** un concert R'n'B 2

**road** une route 10

**rock (music)** le rock 2

**role** un rôle 5

**roof** un toit 9

**room** une salle 3; une pièce 7; *bathroom* une salle de bains 7; *classroom* une salle de classe 3; *dining room* une salle à manger 7; *living room* un salon 7

**route** une route 10

**rug** un tapis 7

**running** le footing 2

**Rwanda** le Rwanda 9

## S

**salad** une salade 2; *tuna salad* une salade niçoise 6

**salami** le saucisson 6

**sale: on sale** en solde 4

**salesperson** un vendeur, une vendeuse 6

**salt** le sel 7

**same** même 6

**sandwich** un sandwich 4; *cheese sandwich* un sandwich au fromage 4; *ham sandwich* un sandwich au jambon 4; *grilled ham and cheese sandwich* un croque-monsieur 4

**Saturday** samedi 2

to **save** sauvegarder 7

**say** dis 1; *let's say* disons 4

**scarf** une écharpe 4; un foulard 6

**school** une école 3; *school cafeteria* une cantine 3

**science** les sciences (f.) 3; *science fiction* la science-fiction 4; *science lab* un labo (laboratoire) 3

to **score** marquer 4

**screen** un écran 7

**seat** un siège 10

**second** deuxième 7

to **see** voir 3; *to see each other/ one another* se voir 8; *See you soon.* À bientôt. 1; *See you tomorrow.* À demain. 1

**selfish** égoïste 5

to **sell** vendre 6

to **send** envoyer 2; *to send text messages* envoyer des textos 2

**Senegal** le Sénégal 5

**Senegalese** sénégalais(e) 5

**September** septembre 5

**series** une série 4

**serious** grave 8

**server** un serveur, une serveuse 4

to **set** mettre 7; *to set the table* mettre le couvert 7

**seven** sept 2

**seventeen** dix-sept 2

**seventh** septième 7

**seventy** soixante-dix 3

**she** elle 1

**sheet of paper** une feuille de papier 3

**shirt** une chemise 6

**shoe** une chaussure 4; **tennis shoe** tennis 6

**shop** une boutique 6; *butcher shop* une boucherie 6

**shopping** le shopping 2; commerçant(e) 6; *shopping center* un centre commercial 1

**short** petit(e) 5

**shorts** un short 4

**shoulder** l'épaule (f.) 9

to **show** montrer 8

**shower** une douche 7

**shy** timide 5

**sick** malade 9; *sick person* un(e) malade 9

**simple** simple 10

to **sing** chanter 5

**singer** un chanteur, une chanteuse 5

**sink** un évier 7

**sir** monsieur (M.) 1

**sister** une sœur 5; *half-sister* une demi-sœur 5; *stepsister* une belle-sœur 5

**six** six 2

**sixteen** seize 2

**sixth** sixième 7

**sixty** soixante 3

**size** une taille 5

to **skate: to (figure) skate** faire du patinage (artistique) 2; *to in-line skate* faire du roller 2

**skating: (figure) skating** le patinage (artistique) 2

to **ski: to (downhill) ski** faire du ski (alpin) 2

**skiing (downhill)** le ski (alpin) 2

**skirt** une jupe 6

to **sleep** dormir 2

**slice (of)** une tranche (de) 6

**small** petit(e) 5

to **smell** sentir 7; *What does it smell like?* Ça sent quoi? 7

**snack** le goûter 7

**sneakers** des tennis (f.) 6

**snow: it's snowing** il neige 8

**so** alors 3; donc 4; *so-so* comme ci, comme ça 1

**soccer** le foot 2; *soccer ball* un ballon de foot 4; *soccer player* un footballeur, une footballeuse 4

**sock** une chaussette 4

**soda: lemon-lime soda** une limonade 4

**sofa** un canapé 7

**software** un logiciel 7

**solar** solaire 9; *solar energy* l'énergie (f.) solaire 9

**some** d', de, des, du 2

**somebody** quelqu'un 10

**someday** un jour 5

**someone** quelqu'un 10

**something** quelque chose 10

**son** un fils 5

**song** une chanson 7

**songwriter** un compositeur 5

**soon** bientôt 1

**sorry** désolé(e) 8

**soup** la soupe 6

**south** le sud 10

**spa treatment** une cure 9

**Spain** l'Espagne (f.) 10

**Spanish** espagnol(e) 10; *(language)* l'espagnol (m.) 3

to **speak** parler 3

**species: endangered species** les animaux (m.) en voie de disparition 9

to **spend (time)** passer 7

**spoon** une cuiller 7

**sport** un sport 2

**spring** le printemps 8

**square** un carré 7; une place 8; *in squares* en carrés 7

**stadium** un stade 4

to **start** démarrer 7

**statue** une statue 8

to **stay** rester 8

**steak: steak with fries** un steak-frites 4

**step: step aerobics** le step 9; *stepbrother* un beau-frère 5; *stepfather* un beau-père 5; *stepmother* une belle-mère 5; *stepsister* une belle-sœur 5

**stereo** une stéréo 3

**still** toujours 4

**stomach** l'estomac (m.), le ventre 9

to **stop** s'arrêter 8; arrêter 9

**store** un magasin 3; *dairy store* une crémerie 6; *grocery store* une épicerie 6

**story** un étage 7

**stove** une cuisinière 7

**straight ahead** tout droit 10

**strawberry** une fraise 10

**street** une rue 6

**strict** strict(e) 1

**strong** fort(e) 7

**student** un(e) élève 3

to **study** étudier 2

**subway** le métro 4; *subway entrance* une bouche du métro 4

to **succeed** réussir (à) 5

**sugar** le sucre 7

**suitcase** une valise 10

**summer** l'été (m.) 2

**Sunday** dimanche 2

**sunny: it's sunny** il fait du soleil 8

**supermarket** un supermarché 6

to **support** soutenir; *I support* je soutiens 2

**sure** sûr(e) 7

to **surf** surfer 2; *to surf the Web* surfer sur Internet 2

**survey** une enquête 2

to **survive** survivre 9

**sweater** un pull 6

to **swim** nager 2

**swimming pool** une piscine 3

**Swiss** suisse 10

**Switzerland** la Suisse 10

to **synchronize** synchroniser 7

# T

**table** une table 3; *table setting* le couvert 7

**tablecloth** une nappe 7

**Tahitian** tahitien(ne) 3

to **take** prendre 4; *I'll take* je prends 3; *to take advantage of* profiter 8

to **talk** parler 3; *to talk to each other/one another* se parler 8

**talkative** bavard(e) 5

**tall** grand(e) 5

**tart: fruit tart** une tarte aux fruits 6

**teacher** un(e) prof 1

**team** une équipe 4; *team logo* un blason 4

**television** une télé (télévision) 2; *television program* une émission 9

**temperature** la température 8

**ten** dix 2

**tenth** dixième 7

**terrace** une terrasse 8

**terrific** génial(e) 2

**test** un contrôle 1

**text message** un texto 2

**thank you** merci 4

**than** que 7

**that** ça 2; qui 3; que 5; ce, cet, cette, ces 6; *that is* c'est 1; *That's awesome!* C'est le top! 1; *That's right.* C'est ça. 1

**the** le, la, l' 1; les 2; *the most (+ adjectif)* le/la/les plus (+ adjective) 10

**their** leur, leurs 5

**then** alors, puis 3

**there** là 1; *there is/are* il y a 3; *Are we going (there)?* On y va? 3; *over there* là-bas 6

**therefore** donc 4

**these** ce, cet, cette, ces 6

**they** *they (f.)* elles 2; *they (m.)* on 1; ils 2

to **think** penser 7; *to think over* réfléchir (à) 5

**third** troisième 7

**thirsty: to be thirsty** avoir soif 4

**thirteen** treize 2

**thirty** trente 3

**this** ce, cet, cette, ces 6; *this is* c'est 1

**those** ce, cet, cette, ces 6

**thousand** mille 4

**three** trois 2

**thriller** un thriller 4

**throat** la gorge 9

**Thursday** jeudi 2

**ticket** un billet 10; un ticket 4; *ticket booth* un guichet 4; *ticket collector* un contrôleur, une contrôleuse 10; *ticket-stamping machine* un composteur 10

**tide** une marée 9

**tiger** un tigre; *Sumatran tiger* un tigre de Sumatra 9

**time** l'heure (f.) 3; *on time* à l'heure 4; *What time is it?* Quelle heure est-il? 3

**tired** fatigué(e) 8

**to** à 1; chez 3; *to my house* chez moi 3; *to the* au 1; aux 3; *to him* lui 5; *to her* lui 5; *to me* moi 4; *to you* te 1; vous 5

**today** aujourd'hui 4

**toe** le doigt de pied 9

**together** ensemble 3

**Togo** le Togo 5

**Togolese** togolais(e) 5

**toilet** les toilettes (f.), les W.C. (m.) 7

**tomato** une tomate 6

**tomorrow** demain 1; *See you tomorrow.* À demain. 1

**too** trop 1; aussi 2; *too bad* tant pis 6; *too much of* trop de 6

**tooth** une dent 9

**top** le haut 8

**topic** un thème 9

**tour** un tour 8

**tourist guide** un guide touristique 8

**towards** vers 10

**train** un train 10; *train station* une gare 8; *train track* une voie 10

to **travel** voyager 5

**traveller** un voyageur, une voyageuse 10

**trip** un voyage 8

**true** vrai(e) 10

to **try (on)** essayer 6

**T-shirt** un tee-shirt 6

**Tuesday** mardi 2

**tuna** le thon 6; *tuna salad* une salade niçoise 6

to **turn** tourner 10

**TV** une télé (télévision) 2

**twelve** douze 2

**twenty** vingt 2

**two** deux 2

**type** un genre 4

# U

**ugly** moche 6

**um** euh 3

**uncle** un oncle 5

**under** sous 3

to **understand** comprendre 10

**unintelligent** bête 5

**United States** les États-Unis (m.) 5

**unpleasant** désagréable 8

**until** jusqu'à 10

**us** nous 5

**USB key** une clé USB 7

# V

**vacation** les vacances (f.) 10

to **validate (a ticket)** composter 10

**valley** une vallée 10

**vegetable** un légume 6

**versus** contre 4

**very** très 1; *Very well, and you?* Très bien, et toi/vous? 1

**video: video games** les jeux vidéo (m.) 2; *video game tester* un testeur de jeux vidéo 5

**view** une vue 7; *What a beautiful view!* Quelle belle vue! 7

**visit** une visite 10

to **visit** visiter 8

**visual arts** les arts plastiques (m.) 3

# W

to **wait (for)** attendre 4

**walk** une promenade 8

to **walk** marcher 9

to **want** désirer 4; avoir envie de 8; vouloir 6

**wardrobe** une armoire 7

to **watch** regarder 2; *Watch out!* Attention! 7

**water** l'eau (f.) 4

**waterfall** une cascade 10

**watermelon** une pastèque 6

**way** un chemin 10

**we** on 1; nous 2; *We'll call each other.* On s'appelle. 1

to **wear** porter 4

**weather** le temps 8; *the weather's bad* il fait mauvais 2

**website** un site web 7

**Wednesday** mercredi 2

**week** une semaine 2

**weekend** le weekend 2

**welcome** bienvenue 4

**well** bien, eh bien 1; ben 7; *Are things going well?* Tu vas bien? 2

**west** l'ouest (m.) 10

**what** comment 1; qu'est-ce que, quel, quelle 2; quoi 3; ce que 9; *What a beautiful view!* Quelle belle vue! 7; *What are you doing?* Qu'est-ce que tu fais? 2; *What do you like to do?* Qu'est- ce que tu aimes faire? 2; *What does it smell like?* Ça sent quoi? 7; *What is... like?* Comment est...? 5; *What is your profession?* Quelle est votre profession? 5; *What size are you?* Quelle taille faites-vous? 6; *What's the weather like?* Quel temps fait-il? 8; *What's wrong with her?* Qu'est-ce qu'elle a? 9; *What's your name?* Tu t'appelles comment? 1

**when** où 8; quand 2

**where** où 3

**which** quel, quelle 2

**white** blanc, blanche 6

**who** qui 3

**why** pourquoi 2

**wife** une femme 5

**wild** sauvage 9

to **win** gagner 4

**wind turbine** une éolienne 9

**window** une fenêtre 3

**windy: it's windy** il fait du vent 8

**winter** l'hiver (m.) 8

**with** avec 1; par 7

**work** un taf 7

to **work** travailler 5

**world** le monde 1

**world music** la world 2

**would: I would like** je voudrais 5; *you would like* tu voudrais 1; *Would you like...?* Vous voulez...? 4

**wow** oh là là 9

to **write** écrire 3

**writer** un écrivain 5

## Y

**year** un an, une année 5

**yellow** jaune 6

**yes** oui 1; *yes (on the contrary)* si 2

**yesterday** hier 8

**yoga** le yoga 9

**yogurt** le yaourt 6

**you** te/t', toi, tu, vous 1

**your** ton, ta 1; tes, votre, vos 5; *your name is* tu t'appelles 1

## Z

**zero** zéro 2

**zucchini** une courgette 6

# Grammar Index

This index contains material from Textbook 1A (pages 1–272) and Textbook 1B (pages 273–568). The number included with each entry is the page location in both books.

# Credits

Abbreviations: top (t), bottom (b), right (r), center (c), left (l)

Each listing in the photo, reading, art, and realia credits contains a page number corresponding to the location in Textbook 1A (pages 1–272), and Textbook 1B (Bridge Parts pages B01–B58 and pages 273–568).

## Bridge Photo Credits

AliJa/iStockphoto: B17

Aimstock/iStockphoto: B28 (#5)

Alle12/iStockphoto: B14 (ice cream)

Amelia, John R./Fotolia.com: B12 (soccer)

Anderson, Leslie: B08; B42 (poster, cell phone)

Arattansi/iStockphoto: B42 (iPod)

Bobbieo/iStockphoto: B05

Bowdenimages/iStockphoto: B12 (biking)

Brown, Ken/iStockphoto: B50 (c)

Capude1957/Fotolia.com: B02 (street)

Carlosgaw/iStockphoto: B56 (#8)

Debljames/iStockphoto: B28 (#6)

Digital Skillet/iStockphoto: B04 (t)

Eléonore H/Fotolia.com: B36

EMC Publishing, LLC: B12 (running); B14 (fries, movies, party hats, cheeseburger); B39 (#4, #6); B56 (#2, #4, #7 coke)

"Essentia" studio/iStockphoto: B10 (graffiti)

Ewg3D/iStockphoto: B14 (pool)

Floortje/iStockphoto: B56 (#1)

Fox, Hillary/iStockphoto: B13

Fstop123/iStockphoto: B24

Funwithfood/iStockphoto: B57 (tl)

Greg M. Cooper Photography/iStockphoto: B39 (#2)

Hart Creations/iStockphoto: B04 (b)

iSebastian/iStockphoto: B42 (dictionary)

Jankowska, Magdalena/iStockphoto: B06

Kali Nine Photography/iStockphoto: B12 (swimming)

Kaspi - Kilikpela's Aperture Studio Photography Inc./iStockphoto: B12 (gym); B28 (#4)

Kranendonk, Jan/iStockphoto: B51 (r)

Kupicoo/iStockphoto: B23

Laflor Photography/iStockphoto: B02 (kids); B46

Lattapictures/iStockphoto: B10 (boy)

Lee/iStockphoto: B56 (#6)

LoopAll/iStockphoto: B52

Margouillatphotos/iStockphoto: B56 (#5)

Medicine Hat Photography/iStockphoto: B12 (basketball)

Microsoft.com: B14 (flag); B28 (Modèle); B39 (#1, #3, #5)

Mocker_bat/iStockphoto: B50 (t)

Monkey Business Images/iStockphoto: B51 (l); B57 (tr)

Nailzchap/iStockphoto: B39 (#7)

Nikada, Alex/iStockphoto: B49

Olsen, Morten/iStockphoto: B42 (iPod)

Phdpsx/iStockphoto: B28 (#1)

Prince32/iStockphoto: B35 (l)

Rhoberazzi/iStockphoto: B12 (diving)

Richter, Dirk/iStockphoto: B42 (omelet); B56 (#7 croque-monsieur)

Robynmac/iStockphoto: B08 (tr)

Santa Maria Studio/iStockphoto: B14 (ball)

Sinenko, Vladimir/iStockphoto: B42 (poster)

SoleilC Photography/iStockphoto: B56 (#3)

Steve Debenport Imagery/iStockphoto: B28 (#3); B30; B35 (r)

Topchii, Max/Fotolia.com: B28 (#2)

Vasiliki/iStockphoto: B42 (tart)

Vinogradova, Lilyana/iStockphoto: B39 (Modèle)

Walik/iStockphoto: B14 (hockey)

Wooster, Ignatus/Fotolia.com: B14 (downtown)

Zoom-zoom/iStockphoto: B39 (#8)

## Photo Credits

3alexd/iStockphoto: 487 (#3)

4x6/iStockphoto: 220 (l'oncle)

A & M Photography/iStockphoto: 486 (tiger), 487 (#5)

Acilo Photography/iStockphoto: 111 (l)

AGMIT/iStockphoto: 89

Aguilarphoto/iStockphoto: 536 (t)

Ahturner/iStockphoto: 276 (tr)

Alberto Pomares Photography/iStockphoto: 76

AlcelVision/Fotolia.com: 360 (tl)

Aldomurillo/iStockphoto: 6 (3. #5), 69 (dormir)

Alex/iStockphoto: 276 (une veste), 277 (tc)

Alex Nikada | Photography/iStockphoto: 52 (sortir avec mes amis), 413 (A)

Alfieri, Michele/iStockphoto: x (bl)

Almeida, Helder/Istock: 240

Alvarez, Luis/Fotolia.com: 4 (algérien)

Alxpin/iStockphoto: 371 (b: software)

Amoceptum/iStockphoto: 310 (les petits-pois)

Amysuem/iStockphoto: 169 (t)

Andersen, ULF/SIPA Press: 41

Anderson, Leslie: 16 (t), 78 (le hip-hop, le rock, la musique alternative, la world), 86 (#1), 118 (#2, #5, #6), 164 (un ticket), 197 (Amélie poster), 292 (mayonnaise, soupe), 294 (spaghetti, soup), 300 (Orangina), 324 (metro ticket), 351 (Mississippi Market), 487 (#7), 541 (r)

Andykazie/iStockphoto: 310 (les pêches)

AngiePhotos/iStockphoto: 123 (intelligent(e))

Anmarie98121/iStockphoto: 27 (tr)

Apomares/iStockphoto: 99 (t)

Arcurs, Yuri/Fotolia.com: 31 (#3)

Arianespace/SIPA Press: 35

Arnau Design/iStockphoto: 348 (#3)

Arpad, Benedek/iStockphoto: 426 (#4), 516 (Ontario)

Dononeg/iStockphoto: 382 (mouse)

Doucet, Martine/iStockphoto: 517 (people)

DRB Images/iStockphoto: iv (bl)

Driving South/Fotolia.com: 544 (français)

Drxy/iStockphoto: 99 (b)

DSGpro/iStockphoto: 66 (#5)

Dunouau, Franck/Photononstop: 435

Duris, Guillaume/Fotolia.com: 17, 156 (b)

Edward ONeil Photography Inc./iStockphoto: 374 (E)

Egal/iStockphoto: 323

Elasesinodifuso/Fotolia.com: 550 (t)

Elenathewise/iStockphoto: 364, 500 (#3 l)

Elke, Dennis/Fotolia.com: 544 (italienne)

Elnur/iStockphoto: 277 (tl)

Email2ying/iStockphoto: 191

EMC Publishing, LLC: 29, 53 (de la pizza), 54 (Karim/samedi), 66 (#7), 180 (un coca), 181 (C. coke), 182 (#4 coke), 189 (#3), 210, 211

Encrier/iStockphoto: vii (tr)

Erel photography/iStockphoto: 479

Eremm/iStockphoto: 374 (Modèle)

Erikson Photography/iStockphoto: 182 (Modèle)

Erikwkolstad/iStockphoto: 51, 74 (t)

Eurobanks/iStockphoto: 220 (Théo), 544 (belge, boy)

Evrigen/iStockphoto: 110 (2. #1)

Fabien/Fotolia.com: 108 (un ordinateur portable), 110 (2. #7)

Fabien R. C./Fotolia.com: ix (b)

Fabio Boari Fotografo/iStockphoto: 303 (#1), 322, 405 (#5)

Falataya/iStockphoto: 255 (b)

Falcatraz/iStockphoto: 220 (le père)

Fanfan/Fotolia.com: 410 (un monument)

Fayole, Pascal/SIPA Press: 492

Fei, Wong Sze/Fotolia.com: iv (bc)16 (Pas mal.), 233 (tr)

Felinda/iStockphoto: 276 (un foulard), 324 (scarf)

Ffolas/iStockphoto: 78 (le roller)

Flavyx197/Fotolia.com: 535 (t)

Floris70/Fotolia.com: 78 (le cinéma)

FocalHelicopter/iStockphoto: 242 (t)

Foster, Caleb/Fotolia.com: 552

FotoliaXIV/Fotolia.com: 218

Franco Deriu Photographer/iStockphoto: 310 (les oignons)

Franklin, David/iStockphoto: 393 (b)

Freephoto/Fotolia.com: 127 (b)

French Embassy to the US/Press Office: 44

Freyermuth, Sylvain/Théâtre des Zonzons: 74 (c)

Fried, Robert/robertfriedphotography.com: 4 (tc), 10 (b), 20 (t), 21 (t), 34, 60, 128 (t), 142 (b), 219, 220 (le grand-père, la grand-mère), 225, 238, 245 (#8), 249 (un cuisinier), 262 (#7), 291 (la tarte aux pommes, le gâteau), 296 (#2), 310 (t, les raisins), 316 (b), 324 (crêpe), 332, 344, 348 (t), 357, 375 (b), 394, 397 (horse), 399 (#4), 405 (#3), 410 (une statue), 413 (B), 420 (Modèle, #1, #2, #3), 422 (t), 423, 476, 500 (#4)

Frischhut, Thomas/Tellus Vision Production AB, Lund, Sweden: 8, 19, 32 (tlc), 56, 72 (t), 81, 111 (t), 126, 140, 168, 184, 199, 224, 236, 253, 280, 298, 314, 345, 358, 376, 400, 415, 433, 463, 475, 491, 520, 534, 549

Frincu, Edith/Shutterstock: 307 (b)

Fstop123/iStockphoto: 176

Fuzephoto/iStockphoto: 250 (tr), 251 (#5)

Gaillot, Bernard: 39 (b)

Gchutka/iStockphoto: 404

Ghiea, Vlad/Shutterstock.com: xi (Quebec)

Ghispoppins/Fotolia.com: 517 (plate)

Gillow, Mark/iStockphoto: 180 (une quiche), 181 (B.quiche), 182 (#5 quiche), 189 (#4), 291 (les œufs), 297 (#7)

Ginies/SIPA Press: 265

Glade Christine/iStockphoto: 234 (b), 471 (flu)

Godong/Photononstop: 141

Goldberg, Beryl: 17 (c), 108 (un DVD, une pendule), 109 (1. #2, #3), 115 (Modèle, #4), 121 (t), 129, 136, 137 (à la piscine), 139 (C,D), 148 (t, #7), 181, 179 (t), 198, 205 (#1), 212 (t), 222 (br), 248 (sénégalaise), 254 (b), 282 (b), 291 (la boucherie)

Golden Pixels, LLC/iStockphoto: 26

Gordon's Life Photo/iStockphoto: 4 (américain)

Gorilla/Fotolia.com: 407 (t)

Gough, Laurence/Fotolia.com: 108 (une élève)

Gould, Phillip/CORBIS: 10 (t)

Govin-Sorel/Photononstop: 165

Gray, Michael C/Shutterstock: 180 (une glace au chocolat), 182 (#6. ice-cream), 189 (#3)

Green Machine/iStockphoto: 108 (une stéréo), 115 (#5)

Greg/Fotolia.com: 310 (les ananas)

Gretener Ivo/iStockphoto: 229

Guillet, Frédéric/Fotolia.com: 535 (b)

Hadj/Jobard/SIPA Press: 57

Hähnel, Christoph/Fotolia.com: 544 (anglaise, allemande)

Hart Creations/iStockphoto: 6 (2. #3), 303 (b), 424, 432 (b)

HayesPhotos/iStockphoto (New Brunswick)

Hoa-Qui/Wolf Alfred/Fête foraine auxTuileries, Paris 1/Gamma Rapho: 266

Iconogenic/iStockphoto: 221 (tr)

Idambies/iStockphoto: 52 (Il fait beau.), 54 (météo/lundi, météo/mardi, météo/samedi, météo/dimanche), 90 (Modèle 1, #2, #3, #6)

Ika PrikhodkoPhotography/iStockphoto: 78 (le basketball)

Ileximage/iStockphoto: 52 (faire du vélo), 54 (Suzanne/lundi), 374 (F)

Imagery Majestic/Fotolia.com: 467

Images by Barbara/Fotolia.com: 16 (Comme-ci, comme-ça.)

Imagine/Fotolia.com: 151, 499 (#4, r)

Inkcapture/iStockphoto: 352 (c)

Iophoto/iStockphoto: 137(chez moi), 138 (B)

Iserg/iStockphoto: 371 (b: USB key)

Isik, Sinan/iStockphoto: 249 (un testeur de jeux vidéo)

Simson, David/images by "David SimsonB-6940 SEPTON (dasphoto@hotmail.com)": v (t), vi (bl, br), 4 (tl), (française), 5 (Sandrine, Saniyya), 6 (2. #4; 3. #6), 7 (b), 11, 16 (bl), 18, 28 (au café, au cinéma), 31 (Modèle, #4), 32, 37 (t), 52 (sortire ave c mes amis), 53 (des frites (f.)), 54 (Karim/dimanche), 54 (Suzanne/mercredi), 86 (#3), 88, 92, 108 (t), 113 (b), 117, 121 (b), 134, 137 (au bureau du proviseur, au magasin, en ville), 138 (t), 138 (2. D), 139, 142 (t), 146, 148 (#1, #2), 163, 164 (t, cr), 167, 179 (b), 180 (un sandwich au jambon, une omelette, un steak-frites, une crêpe), 181 (A, C (water and clear soda), D,E), 182 (#1, #2 omelet, #3, #4 sandwich, #5; #6 water, #7 steak and fries, water), 183, 185 (b), 186, 189 (#1, #2, #5, #6), 190, 203, 205 (Modèle, #2, #4, #5, #6), 212 (b), 220 (le demi-frère, la cousine, le cousin, la sœur), 225 (t), 233 (tl), 245 (#7, br), 246, 248 (boy burkinabè, ivoirien, camerounais, camerounaise), 249 (un agent de police, un ingénieur, une chanteuse), 252, 257, 261, 262 (Modèle, #3), 270, 275, 279, 281, 283, 284 (Modèle (ice cream), #1, #3, #4), 285, 286, 288, 291 (la boulangerie, la baguette, le croissant, la pâtisserie, la crémerie, le beurre, le lait, le fromage, le yaourt, le camembert, le porc), 292 (l'épicerie, la moutarde, la confiture, la charcuterie, cl, cr, bl, br), 294 (#1, #2, #3, #4, #5), 295, 296 (#1, #3, #4, #5, #6, #7, #8), 297 (#2, #3, #5, b), 299, 300, 301, 303 (#3, #6, #7), 310 (les fruits), 315, 316 (t), 317, 325(r), 333, 342 (#7, #11), 343, 346 (b), 352 (b), 355 (t, le petit déjeuner, le goûter, le dîner), 363, 367, 370 (b), 371 (b), 372, 399 (#1), 403, 405 (#4, #6), 407 (b), 410 (une gare, une avenue, un aéroport, un fleuve), 411 (un musée, un bateau, un restaurant, une poste), 413 (C, D, E, F, G), 414, 420 (#4), 426 (Modèle, #5, #7), 431, 444 (t), 452, 460 (b), 461, 462, 464, 471 (all but flu, fever, healthy, unhealthy, sick), 473, 474, 482 (t), 487 (#4, 9, 10), 489, 493 (b), 499 (#3), 500 (Modèle t, #2, #5, #6 l), 511 (r), 546, 563

Skup, Lukas/Fotolia.com: 360 (tr)

SoopySue/iStockphoto: 516 (Terre-Neuve)

Sorrentino Angela/iStockphoto: 291 (le pain), 303 (#5)

Spiderbox Photography Inc./iStockphoto: 342 (#3), 373 (#3), 374 (C, D)

SSilver/Fotolia.com: 74 (b)

Stanislaff/iStockphoto: 292 (le jambon)

Stefanphoto/iStockphoto: 127 (t)

Steve__/iStockphoto: 486 (gorilla), 487 (#7, #8)

Steve Debenport Imagery/iStockphoto Photos: 2 (2:#2), 91, 251 (#1), 496,

Stitt, Jason/Fotolia.com: 384 (l)

Struthers, Karen/Fotolia.com: 544 (française)

Studio41/iStockphoto: 221 (les cheveux bruns)

StudioDer/Fotolia.com: 302

Super Sport Photography/iStockphoto: 307 (t)

Susaro/iStockphoto: 78 (le cinéma: *image on screen*)

SV/Fotolia.com: 541 (l)

Syagci/iStockphoto: 397 (bird)

T.M.C/iStockphoto: 487 (#5)

Take A pix Media/iStockphoto: 52 (jouer au foot), 66 (#6), 164 (soccer ball in top photo)

Tangney, Denis Jr./iStockphoto: 516 (Montreal)

Targovcom/iStockphoto: 241

Techno/iStockphoto: 53 (faire du ski)

Terex/iStockphoto: 276 (une robe)

Terraxplorer/iStockphoto: 69 (regarder la télé)

Teun van den Dries Fotografie/iStockphoto: 371 (t: wardrobe)

Texas Media Imaging/iStockphoto: 4 (Allô?)

Tilio & Paolo/Fotolia.com: v (br)

Timchen/iStockphoto: 28 (au centre commercial)

TMAX/Fotolia.com: 411 (une banque), 500 (#3 r)

Tom Fullum Photography/iStockphoto: 52 (Il fait mauvais.), 54 (météo/mercredi, météo/jeudi, météo/vendredi), 90 (Modèle b, #1, #4, #5)

TomS/Fotolia.com: 318 (c)

The Desktop Studio/iStockphoto: 251 (t)

The New Dawn Singers Inc./iStockphoto: 249 (un metteur en scène), 318 (r)

Track5/iStockphoto: 156 (t), 242 (b), 555

Tracy WhitesidePhotography/iStockphoto: 383 (r)

Trigger Photo: 4 (américaine), 86 (#9)

Tulcarion/iStockphoto: 342 (#2)

Tupungato/iStockphoto: 310 (les pamplemousses)

Turay, Lisa/iStockphoto: 544 (belge, girl)

Turtle Pond Photography/iStockphoto: 348 (#2)

Unclesam/Fotolia.com: 110 (2.#2,#3), 499 (#5)

Uolir/Fotolia.com: 105 (b), 108 (une salle de classe), 109 (1.#8), 346 (t)

Urman, Lionel/SIPA Press: 282 (t)

U Star Pix/Istockphoto: x (br)

ValentynVolkov/iStockphoto: 310 (les aubergines)

VanHart/Fotolia.com: x (tl)

Varela Filipe B./iStockphoto: 66 (t)

Varley/SIPA Press: 378 (b)

Vasiliki/iStockphoto: 69 (jouer aux jeux vidéo)

Vasko Miokovic Photography/iStockphoto: 405 (#2)

Viisimaa Peeter/Istock: 248 (girl burkinabè), 254 (t), 339, 359 (t)

Villalon, Richard/Fotolia.com: 108 (un taille-crayon), 109 (1. #5, 2. #5), 402 (t)

Villard/SIPA Press: 195, 259

Vivet, Julien/Fotolia.com: 411 (une rue)

Vkovalcik/iStockphoto: 396 (Versailles in summer)

Vladone/iStockphoto: 514

Vorobyev, Kirill/iStockphoto: 397 (cat)

W A Britten/iStockphoto: 6 (2. #6)

Wagner, Martine/Fotolia.com: 405 (#1)

Wan Bin/Chine Nouvelle/SIPA Press: 98 (b)

Wariatka, Matka/iStockphoto: 499 (#4, L)

Weberfoto/iStockphoto: 28 (à la maison)

Webkojak/iStockphoto: 100

Webphotographeer/iStockphoto: 79 (b)

Webphotographer/iStockphoto: 527

Weihrauch, Michael/Tellus Vision Production AB, Lund, Sweden: 1, 3(b), 49 (tl, tr), 51 (c), 105 (tl, tr), 107 (c), 161 (tl, tr), 163 (c), 217, 219 (c), 273 (tr), 275 (c), 337 (b, tr), 339 (c), 393 (tl), 395 (c), 457 (tl, tr), 459 (c), 513 (tl), 515 (c)

Weiss, Sabine/Rapho/Enfant à la sortie de la boulangerie. Paris, 1960: 327 (b)

Westacoot, Elliot/Fotolia.com: 544 (luxembourgeoise)

Wey, Peter/Fotolia.com: x (br)
Wierink, Ivonne/Fotolia.com: 480 (t)
Wisbauer, Camilla/iStockphoto: 245 (#6)
Wooster, Ignatius/Fotolia.com: 349
Wragg, Mark/iStockphoto: 245 (#1)
XtravaganT/Fotolia.com: 416
Xxmmxx/iStockphoto: 86 (Modèle), 499 (#6, b)
Yakovlev, Alexander/iStockphoto: 460 (t)
YangYin/iStockphoto: 342 (#4)
Yefimov, Artyom/Fotolia.com: 185 (t)
Yolanda, Linda/iStockphoto: 220 (la belle-sœur)
Zaihan/Fotolia.com: 325 (l)
Zilli/iStockphoto: 245 (#5)
Zoomstudio/iStockphoto: 276 (un tee-shirt)
ZTS/iStockphoto: 499 (#1, L)

# Reading Credits

Apollinaire, Guillaume, "Le chat," *Le Bestiaire*, Deplanche, 1911 (poem): 386
Aragon, Louis, "Je me souviens," Album Montand 7, (paroles), 1967 (poem/song): 558
Ben Jelloun, Tahar, *L'Homme rompu*, Seuil, Paris 1994, pp. 74–75 (novel): 504
Chédid, Andrée, *L'Enfant multiple*, J'ai Lu, Flammarion, 1989 (novel): 266
Cohen, Albert, *Belle du Seigneur*, Folio Gallimard, 1998 (novel): 41
Goscinny, René, *Le Petit Nicolas*. Gallimard, Folio n° 423 (story): 153
Perec, Georges, *Penser/Classer*, Hachette, 1985 (essay): 95
Pons, Maurice, "Le fils du Boulanger," *Douce-amère*, Denoël, 1985 (short story): 328
Prévert, Jacques, "Chanson de la Seine (III)" ("Aubervilliers"), *Spectacle*, © Éditions GALLIMARD, Paris (poem): 446

# Art Credits

The Bridgeman Art Library International: *The Private Conversation*, 1904 (oil on canvas), Beraud, Jean (1849–1935)/J. Kugel Collection, Paris, France/© DACS/Giraudon: 42; *Saint Germain-Des-Pres* (oil on canvas), Boissegur, Beatrice (Contemporary Artist)/Private Collection): 95; *Nafea Faaipoipo* (When are you Getting Married?), 1892 (oil on canvas), Gauguin, Paul (1848–1903)/Rudolph Staechelin Family Foundation, Basel, Switzerland: 106, 129; *Ball at the Moulin de la Galette*, 1876 (oil on canvas), Renoir, Pierre Auguste(1841–1919)/Private Collection, *Self Portrait*, 1889 (oil on canvas): 223; Gogh, Vincent van (1853–90)/Private Collection, Zurich, Switzerland, *Ginger Jar*, c.1895 (oil on canvas): 223; Cezanne, Paul (1839–1906)/©The Barnes Foundation, Merion, Pennsylvania, USA: 223; *The Lily Pond* (oil on canvas), Monet, Claude (1840–1926)/Private Collection/Photo © Christie's Images: 223; *Ms 65/1284 f.7v July: harvesting and sheep shearing* by the Limbourg brothers, from the 'Tres Riches Heures du Duc de Berry' (vellum)(for facsimile copy see 65830) by Pol deLimbourg (d.c.1416) Musee Conde, Chantilly, France/Giraudon: 269, 359 (b); *Landscape near Arles*, 1888 (oil on canvas), Gauguin, Paul (1848–1903)/Indianapolis Museum of Art, USA/Gift in memory of William Ray Adams/The Bridgeman Art Library International: 260; *The Starry Night*, June 1889 (oil on canvas), Gogh, Vincent van (1853–90)/Museum of Modern Art, New York, USA: 359; *In the Oise Valley* (oil on canvas), Cezanne, Paul (1839–1906)/Private Collection/Photo © Christie's Images/The Bridgeman Art Library International: 386; *The Pont de l'Europe*, Gare Saint-Lazare, 1877 (oil on canvas), Monet, Claude (1840–1926)/Musee Marmottan, Paris, France/Giraudon: 449; *The Seated Man*, or *The Architect* (oil on canvas), La Fresnaye, Roger de (1885–1925)/Musee National d'Art Moderne, Centre Pompidou, Paris, France/Giraudon: 506
Christie's Images/CORBIS: *The Pont Neuf* (*Notre Dame in Paris, View of the Pont Neuf*) by Paul Signac©: 447
Doisneau, Robert/Gamma-Rapho: 153 (Information scolaire, 1956)
Varin, Achille/*Le cerf-volant*, 1925. Château-musée municipal de Nemours, France: 558

# Realia Credits

Anderson, Leslie: 230
ASPTT de Paris: 466
Association Québec-France: 13
Atraveo GmbH: 353
Beach Volley/Défi des îles: 226
Carrefour/Groupe Carrefour: 112, 240 (logo), 301, 326, 363
Comité Départemental du Tourisme, Loir-et-Cher: 537
Commémoration du Génocide du Rwanda: 478
Crêperie "Chez Suzette" Inc. Montréal, Québec: 187
Dots United GmbH: 324 (PSG logo)
Eurosport: 171
Famille Chabert-4 restaurants, Lyon, France: 73
Fédération Nationale des Cinémas Français, la Fête du cinéma: 206
Festival Waga Hip Hop/Ali DIALLO: 262
Fête de la musique/Strasbourg.eu: 83
Fête des Lumières, Lyon, France: 74
Fête du cinéma: 206
Francofolies de Montréal: 523
Francoscopie: 379
Genève Tourisme & Congrès: 551
Goldenpass.ch: 24
Musée Grévin: 418
Pariscope, France: 201
Pathé Production, ©2008—PATHE Production—Bethsabée Mucho—TF1 Films Production—M6 Films: 207, 373, 374 (poster of movie LOL)
Plan de Paris: © parisholidays.fr (Find an apartment in Paris.): 403
Pureshopping: 324 (gift card)
RATP: 436
Redoute, la: 283
Résidence des Bateliers: 349
Top-Office.com: 22, 25, 112, 114 (school supplies), 499 (Modèle)
Vélib' Paris: © 2011 Vélib'/Marie de Paris: 494

We have attempted to locate owners of copyright materials used in this book. If an error or omission has occurred, EMC Publishing, LLC will acknowledge the contribution in subsequent printings.

# Appendix

## Phonetic Alphabet

### L'alphabet phonétique pour le français

In its *Prononciation* sections, *T'es branché?* uses the standard phonetic symbols of the International Phonetic Alphabet (IPA). This system was created by the International Phonetic Association as a way to represent the different sounds of spoken languages. The comprehensive list below contains the symbols most commonly used for the French language.

### Voyelles

- [a]  ami, mamy
- [ɑ]  pâtes, bas
- [e]  été, nager
- [ɛ]  étais, belle
- [ə]  le, demain
- [œ]  œuf, sœur
- [ø]  peu, bleu, œufs
- [i]  dix, gris
- [o]  dos, chaud
- [ɔ]  bol, bottes
- [u]  nous, douze
- [y]  pur, sucre, bûcher

### Voyelles nasales

- [ɑ̃]  banque, chambre, enchanté
- [ɛ̃]  cinq, impatient
- [ɔ̃]  bonbons, long
- [œ̃]  un, lundi, parfum

### Consonnes

- [b]  bien, bonbon
- [k]  café, ski, quinze
- [ʃ]  chaud, chien, short
- [d]  douze, dents
- [f]  neuf, pharmacie
- [g]  gris, gant
- [ʒ]  jaune, géant, aubergine
- [ɲ]  agneau, mignon, peigner
- [l]  lampe, mille

- [m]  mille, mère
- [n]  nage, noir
- [ŋ]  le smoking
- [p]  père, pêche
- [R]  rare, père
- [s]  cela, français, poisson, attention, soixante
- [t]  tarte, théâtre
- [v]  violet, avion, wagon
- [z]  visage, zèbre

### Semi-consonnes

- [j]  adieu, œil, fille, yaourt
- [ɥ]  nuit, fruit, huit
- [w]  oui, boire, ouest

---

## Functions in Level 1 Textbook

### Unité 1

**Leçon A:**
- Je m'appelle… *(Sophie)*.
- Je suis… *(Bruno)*.
- Bonjour!/ Salut!
- Enchanté(e).
- Je te/vous présente… *(Jean-Luc)*.
- C'est… *(mon camarade de classe)*.
- Tu t'appelles comment?

**Leçon B:**
- Ça va?
- Comment allez-vous?
- Très bien, et toi/vous?

**Leçon C:**
- On va… *(au café)*?
- Tu voudrais aller…?
- D'accord.
- Oui, je veux bien.
- Pas possible. Je dois… *(faire mes devoirs)*.
- Je ne peux pas. J'aide… *(ma mère)*.

### Unité 2

**Leçon A:**
- Qu'est-ce que tu aimes/vous aimez faire?
- Tu aimes manger… *(des hamburgers)*?
- J'aime… *(sortir)*.
- Je n'aime pas… *(faire du ski)*.

**Leçon B:**
- Tu aimes beaucoup… *(lire)*?
- J'aime un peu… *(lire)*.
- J'aime bien… *(envoyer des textos)*.
- J'aime beaucoup… *(faire du sport)*.

**Leçon C:**
- Moi, je préfère… *(lire les blogues)*.
- Tu préfères… *(la world ou le hip-hop)*?
- Moi aussi.
- Pas moi. Je n'aime pas….
- Quel est le numéro de téléphone de… *(Yasmine)*?

### Unité 3

**Leçon A:**
- J'ai besoin d'… *(une trousse)*.
- Tu as besoin d'… *(un cahier)*?

- (La trousse)..., elle coûte combien?
- (Le cahier)..., il coûte combien?
- Il coûte... (2,59 euros).

**Leçon B:**
- Mon cours de... (maths) est difficile.
- Elle est comment... (ta prof d'informatique)?
- Elle est... (intéressante).

**Leçon C:**
- Où est-ce que tu vas après... (le déjeuner)?
- Quand est-ce qu'... (on y va)?
- Pourquoi est-ce que tu ne peux pas?
- On se retrouve... (à la piscine) à (4h00).

## Unité 4

**Leçon A:**
- (Je vais soutenir Marseille)... parce qu'ils sont les meilleurs.
- Rendez-vous à... (3h00) devant... (la bouche de métro).
- Disons... (3h15).

**Leçon B:**
- Vous désirez?
- Et comme... (boisson)?
- Donnez-moi... (la spécialité du jour).
- Je vais prendre... (le menu fixe).
- L'addition, s'il vous plaît.

**Leçon C:**
- Tu vas aimer ça.
- Tu vas rire.
- Tu vas pleurer.
- Peut-être.
- On va voir.

## Unité 5

**Leçon A:**
- Comment est... (ma tante)?
- Tu ressembles à... (ton grand-père).

**Leçon B:**
- Tu as quel âge?
- J'ai... ans.
- J'offre... (un CD à Alice).
- Tu peux apporter... (les boissons)?

**Leçon C:**
- Quelle est votre profession?
- Je suis... (actrice).
- Vous venez/Tu viens d'où?
- Je viens des... (États-Unis).
- Je viens du... (Canada).
- Je viens de... (France).

## Unité 6

**Leçon A:**
- Je cherche... (une jupe).
- Vous avez... (le pantalon) en... (gris/38)?
- Je peux vous aider?
- De quelle couleur?
- Quelle taille faites-vous?

**Leçon B:**
- (Je vais)... d'abord... (à la crémerie acheter du beurre et du fromage).
- Ensuite,... (je vais à la charcuterie).
- Enfin,... (je vais à l'épicerie).

**Leçon C:**
- (Les pêches)... sont mûres?
- C'est combien le kilo?
- Je prends... (500 grammes).
- Et avec ça?
- C'est tout?

## Unité 7

**Leçon A:**
- Là, c'est... (le séjour où nous regardons des DVDs).
- À côté, c'est... (la salle à manger où nous dînons ce soir).
- Au fond du couloir, c'est... (ma chambre).
- Où est-ce que tu habites?
- Je pense que (oui).
- Je pense que (non).

**Leçon B:**
- Tu peux couper... (les courgettes) en rondelles.
- Ensuite, tu mets le couvert.

**Leçon C:**
- Je ne comprends pas... (ce problème de maths).
- (La chanson de Natasha St-Pier?) Je la télécharge.
- Tu imprimes... (les paroles)?

## Unité 8

**Leçon A:**
- Tu as envie de... (faire une promenade avec moi)?
- Bonne idée! Je suis disponible.
- Désolé(e). Je suis occupé(e).

**Leçon B:**
- Oh, pardon....
- Nous avons fini... (sur la terrasse de l'arc de triomphe).
- Le premier jour,... (nous avons visité la tour Eiffel).

**Leçon C:**
- On est allé... (aux Tuileries).
- Nous sommes vite descendus... (prendre le métro).
- Nous sommes arrivés... (chez moi).
- (On a passé un super jour)... samedi dernier!

## Unité 9

**Leçon A:**
- Il faut....
- Il ne faut pas....

**Leçon B:**
- Qu'est-ce que tu me conseilles?
- À mon avis,... (il faut prendre le thème des accompagnateurs).

**Leçon C:**
- Je pense qu'on doit... (faire tout ce qu'on peut pour sauvegarder la planète).
- Je suis prêt(e)... (à recycler).
- Je ne suis pas prêt(e)... (à m'engager).

## Unité 10

### Leçon A:
- *(Québec)... est situé(e)... (au nord-est de Montréal).*

### Leçon B:
- N'oublie pas de... *(composter ton billet).*
- Bon voyage!

### Leçon C:
- Pardon, où se trouve... *(le Musée international de la Croix-Rouge)?*
- Va/ Allez vers... *(l'est).*
- Continue/Continuez tout droit.
- Tourne/Tournez à... *(droite).*
- Prends/Prenez... *(la plus grande avenue).*

---

# Additional Sources of Information

Below you will find search words to help you and your students find Internet sites for a multitude of activities to enrich your classroom instruction.

Cinema:
- académie des arts et techniques du cinéma
- allocine
- festival de cannes

Francophone News:
- l'actualité
- allafrica
- le devoir
- le figaro
- france amérique
- l'humanité
- jeune afrique
- libération
- le monde.fr
- tv5

Francophonie:
- franc parler
- francofil.net
- organization internationale de la francophonie

French Cheeses:
- petit lexique du chabichou et des fromages de chèvre
- ermitage fromage

Governmental Sites:
- ambassade de france
- campus france
- campus france resource center
- french embassy washington d.c.
- ministere de l'education nationale

Grammar:
- conjuguemos french
- french.about.com

Miscellaneous:
- météo france
- phosphore france
- ABU france

Online Activities:
- fsl activities with m. Renaud
- corporate classroom connect

Paris:
- arc de triomphe
- louvre
- musée d'orsay
- notre dame de paris
- paris office du tourisme
- sacré-cœur
- la sorbonne

- tour Eiffel

Pedagogical Sites and Testing:
- ap central french
- carla mn
- center for applied linguistics language testing
- le cndp
- linguafolio
- planète enseignante

Radio Stations:
- europe1
- radio canada
- radio france international
- rci martinique
- tf1 en direct

Sports:
- france football
- le foot français
- quebec hockey sur glace
- pari roller
- tour de france

Teacher Associations:
- aatf
- actfl
- alliance française
- alliance française usa
- center for applied linguistics

Tourist Offices:
- genève tourisme
- guyane française tourisme
- montréal tourisme
- nouveau brunswick tourisme
- office du tourisme antilles françaises
- office du tourisme lyon
- office du tourisme maroc
- office du tourisme marseille
- office du tourisme québec
- office national de tourisme algérien
- office national de tourisme tunisien
- rwanda tourism
- sénégal tourisme
- tahiti office du tourisme
- tourisme guadeloupe
- tourisme loire
- tourisme martinique
- tourist office new orleans la
- tours tourisme

# Culture Index

# French Survey Respondents

In 2009, we conducted a survey of French teachers to find out what they wanted in a new French textbook series. We would like to thank the following teachers for their participation, which helped us design *T'es branché?*

**Alabama:** Judy Byram, Melissa Copeland, Chris Eubanks, Shelley Fordice, Julie Norvelle Fantoni, Cheryl Hall, Cindy Lepore, Stephanie McGee, Maxanna Nichols-Lefebvre, Sara C. Runner, Susanne Rives, Candance Thomason; **Alaska:** Virginia G. Boyd, Claudia Markham, Kathleen Walgren; **Arizona:** Catherine Burke, Linda Dunbar, Ruth Eiseman, Sarah Fowler, Jarred Gainey, Margaret Hanna, Ann-Marie Hyland, Hope Loveland, Randall Nissly, Jennifer Patrick, Leigh Thomas, Diane Waters; **Arkansas:** Chris Becnel, Nola Harrison, Carey Lagarrigue, Gray Langston, Jan Nixon, Kim Scarbrough; **California:** Maria Adame, Sally K. Adams, Joan Adometto Taylor, Judy Avila, Silvia Battigalli, Anne Bazile, Nathalie Bellitti, Mary Anne Berry, Justin Brooks, Ariene Borutzki, Leah Boselli, Kathy Calvin,Corinne Carlson, Samantha Carr, Karina Chin, Rachel Cornec, Sandy Dana-Kildow, Sebastian P. DeClerck, James DeKay, Susan DeLateur, Michael Delbar, Karen Donner, Mary Dowden, Yvonne Duong, Lynda Fine, Lorraine Fong, Joan Fox, Shelley Friedman, Natalie Freitas, Edwige Gamache, Andrea Gannon, Patricia Grogan, Rhonda Habsersham, Janet Hedeline, Lynn Heyman-Hogue, Sharon Hendrickson, Mira Jamadi, Eva Johnson, Shana Kamper, Karen Kessinger, Michelle Klein, Patti Kussman, Brigitte Kyle, Jessica Lawrence, Denise LeBiavant, Valerie Lent, Cecile Lunetta, Azita Mahmoudi, Michelle Marriott, Sheila McCumber, Sadie Medina, Lise Melin, Deborah Mogel, Micheline Moreau, Starlight Murray, Mariela Neira, Sara Niles, Todd Oesterman, Yvonne Oliver, Brenda Parrish, Carolyn Quinby, Karen Ransom, Dee Robbins, Jetta Rodal, Linda Rosenberg, Rachel Safier, Melisa Salvato, Allison Sass, Robert Schaffer, Claudine Senac-Urtecho, Bertha Sevilla, Francine W. Shivers, Michelle Shockey, Audrey Smith, Patty Stephenson, Judy Stout, Isabelle Teraoka, Tatjana Trout, Beth Tudor, Judith Uriarte, Mary Van de BovenKamp, Geraldine Van Roie Stoddard, Christine Veilleux, Verna Verspieren, Barbara Vinolus, Elizabeth Vitanza, , Agnieszka Waclawek, Catherine Welter, Judy Werner, Jacki Williams-Jones, Francois Wolman; **Colorado:** Jane Backer, Laura Battisti, Leslie Casanova, Debbie Cody, Anne Damanti, Lisa Davis, Ellen Grimsdale, Paul Kirschling, Elaine Kurbegov, Marlene Ladouceur, Patty Ross-Baldwin, Florence Schranz, Ann Snow, Austin Wallace, Linda Zimmerman; **Connecticut:** Magdalena Alvarado, Garry Apgar, Ann Barton, Lisa Ahlstrom-Nasy, Martine Berliet, Maria Cahill, Constance Carrington, Nathalie Casey, Carol Coderre-Marx, Rossana Crudele, Aline Dennison, Justin Ehrenberg, Abdoulaye Fall, Mark Foster, Myriam Franquesa, Paula Greenfield, Diane Holskin, Susan Hudson, Ruth Jones, Nancy Katsaros, Angela Kelleher, Thomas Kelly, Corrine Khawaja, Bruno Koffi, Barbara H. Lathrop, Kathy Martin-Ocain, Susan Mason, Gail McKenna, Nancy Moran, Mary E. Perlot, Nicandra Perusi, Barbara C. Polley, Dorothy Raviele, Claudine Rose, Jane See, Ed Smith, Jennifer Sturges, Renee M. Sylvestre, Ann Trinkaus, Magioula Tsilibocos, Patricia Villella, Heather Way, Emily Wentworth, Marianna Wikarska, Sandra P. Wilson, Linda Zabor; **Delaware:** Megan Cover, Roch Luberti, Mary Ann Ryan, Pamela Scholla, Joyce Strojny; **Florida:** Shirley R. Bayard, Sandra Bierkan, Christelle Carter, Sansan Dah, Valerie Eastman, Valerie Gentilini, Gianina Ireland, Susan Laffitte, Herve le Guilloux, Laura Hollands, H. Leonard, Sheila Mansier, Barbara M. Murray, Mary B. Noblin, Susan Olevia-Wagner, Sherry Parker, Erin Pendergast, Doriane Rencker, Simone Schoeni, Sorela Schultz, Teresa Suarez, Mary C. Sweet, Brenda Velez, Kathryn Anne Vensel, Barbara Woolley, Paula Yaniglos; **Georgia:** Patricia Bailey, Valerie Bathurst, Denise Bedell, Christy Belbey, Claire Bell, Kristen Bintlift, David Bobkowski, Nan Brightwell, Sally Brock, Agnes Browning, Angela Burgess, Brita Buhrman, Cecilia Burns, Karen Canady, Fejokwuc Comfort, Liana Cox, Caryn Craft, Michele Diament, Michael Dockery, Gabrielle Durden-Coffee, Gail Ehrhart, Catherine Francisse, Reesa Frezier, Judy Fritz, Tracey Glass Fuchs, Rhonda Habersham, Shanda D. Hester, Nessa Hoppe, Valerie Hughey, Elizabeth John, Jeanne S. Jones, Mary Lane Jukes, Edna-May King, Susan Logan, Phyllis Loiacono, Patricia A. B. Macmillan, Rachel G. Martellus, Irene Marxsen, Alanna McEachin, Lesya McGee, Katy McManus, Eugenia McMillan, Jennifer Miller, Amie Muir, Nancy Nichols, Laure-Anne Pennelli, Kathleen A. Porto, Christohe Powers, Benjamin Riekhof, Tracy Rucker, Sharon Shirah, Marianne Simeneta, Katie Sisterhen, Travis Spell, Carol Stevens, Kenneth Swanson, Cynthia Toups, Lauren Watson, Kristin Webb, Jeanette Webster-Whyte, Marylou Wiesendanger, Debra Welch, Valerie White, Elizabeth Williams, Jennifer Willis, Thelma Wise; **Hawaii:** Erin C. Cleveland, Kathie Dinges, Dayna Fukunaga, Catherine Pettit, Norma Young; **Idaho:** Gabrielle Applequist, Sharon Bartlow, Jerre Coleman, Claudia Creek, Sally Husted, Aliene Shearer, Dana L. Stockman; **Illinois:** Jason Anderson, Martha Behlow, Caryn Boltz, Jo Anne A. Bratkovich, Liette Brisebois, Tracy Cowper, Angelique Dorchies, Cynthia Driesner, Sharon Eichensehr, Carolyn Fitzgerald, Julie Frost, Michelle Garesche, Barb Goldberg, Sandra Grandolfo, Francis Greaux, Sue Harsa, Ann K. Hartman, Melanie Hillegass, Andrea K. Isabelli, Kathleen Iverson, Jura Jancys, Eric Laird, Lynette Lang, Toni Lowery, Melissa Lo, Joyce Marconcini, Suzanne McKeigue, Michelle Morelli, Maryann Pliss, Sara Kahle Ruiz, Janet Rzeszutko, Michele Salkauskas, Heather Song, Laura Sperling, Roz Sunquist, William Swiderski, Jeanne Trengove, Judy Weiss; **Indiana:** Michele Balma, Elizabeth Breidinger, Alisha Burcham, Heather Carey, Gwen Craig, Susie Deneen, Philip D. Didier, Kristy Donley, Rebecca Elkins, Melanie Enkoff, Pamela Forth, Diane Furtwangler, Jessica Geisinger, Sara Harrison, Cheryl Herman, Jill Hildgemeier, Kathy Jaroszewski, Ellen Landers, Martha Layton, Lisa Liberge, Bryan Macke, Vicki Mannweiler, Paula Morton, Debora Olejniczek, Andrea S. Pieh, Regina Portman, Adrienne Qualls, Carol Shumate, Beth Strodel, Kimberly Summers, Susan Van Fleit, Safia Virgil, Janice Vote, Lisa Walborn, Jill Wiley, Kay A. Wood; **Iowa:** Michele Marie Arman, Laura Catron, Jae Dwyer, Vicki Gallagher, Christine K. Gilbertson, Janet Johnson, Deb Paulsen, Melanie Sartori, Erin Schafer, Christina Snyder-Scott; **Kansas:** Melanie Adams, Christina Beard, Rebecca Bock, Sandra Chastan, Linda S. Clark, Jan Denning, Lisa DeVore, Clara A. George, April S. Gomez, Nora Kelting, Susan Lehr, Karen Pearson, Leslie Ransdall, Alyssa Rydant, Christa L. Ruhlen, Vicki Swetz; **Kentucky:** Elizabeth W. Cooke, Jocelyne Cross, Scottye Eakin, Jennifer Kirby, Elizabeth B. Rambo, Susan Robbins; **Louisiana:** Marilyn J. Ashton, Theresa Barr, Yannick Brignac, Mimi Brooks, Pam Broussard, Valerie Burton, Isabelle Callens-Shirazi, Marie Cipolla, Vicki K. Clem, Charles Darby, Marguerite Dietrich, Brother Derek W. Foster, William Gautreaux, Cosima Hasenstein, Mary C. Herget, Linda Lafont, Norma Michaud, Marie-France Price, Martine Smith, Rebeccah Smith, Stephanie Viator; **Maine:** Kristen Andrews, Andrea AskenDunn, Seth Briggs, Linda Butt, Lisa Charlier, Leslie Harlin, Irene Marchenay, Margaret Nulle, Anne E. Smith; **Maryland:** Amanda Arnoult, Larissa Arist, Monique Briend-Walker, Denise W. Diegel, Elizabeth Foyle, Elizabeth Gray, Nancy Claire Gritzinger, Kenneth Haines, Kathleen Kirk-Leason, Marie-Pierre Manrique, Phyllis McCauley, Paul Newhouse, Keila Oropeza, Angela Porcella, Lexi Sargent, Emilie Shipman, Robert A. Silkworth, Debora Speier, Jeanne Touzeau, Richard Tuckerman, Laurie Whitley, Teresa Wilson, Yimei Wu; **Massachusetts:** Marie Dunell, Justin Evans, Rina Farber-Mazor, Christine Geueke, Christopher Johnson, Janice Joyce, Norma Kozaka,  Deborah Leavitt, Michelle Lewison, Susanne Markus, Robert F. Peolquin, Yiota Simoglou; **Michigan:** Dick Ahlers, Faye M. Amo, Amy Begnene, Michelle Burley, Nancy Busard, Crystal Cannon, Amy Clement, Susan Clugston, Laura Davis, Kelley DeGraaf, Veronica Dewey, Mary Drouillard, Sheryl Foster, Kim Frisinger, Eileen Gifford, Christine Haack, Cindy Hern, Valerie Jablonski, Jennifer M. Kay, Michelle Kuehnlein, Marti Larson, Jeanine LeMieux, Sheryl Moll, Diana Morgenstern, Theresa Nilsen, Victoria Potter, Kathy Refice, Pam Romanelli, Kim Rouvelin, Melissa Saeed, Sister Rose Sam, Melissa Samluk, Barbara St. Louis, Patrick Teahan, Dana Tipurita, Raghida West; **Minnesota:** Susan Brown, Jen Bouchard, Michele Campbell, Kari Christensen, Joyce Cogdell-Travis, Coleen Colton, K. Droske, Jessica Gillespie, Camilla J. Glattly, Laurie Hennen, Phyllis Hicks, Sara Holcombe, Margaret Laboe, Amy Lemme, Elizabeth Manning, Elizabeth Marin, Mary Lynn Montgomery, Susan Palmer, Kris Rydland, Sue Sebghati, Twyla Sha, Kathleen Stoddart, Christina Sturm, Kyle Sweeney, Scott Swedin,; **Mississippi:** Bridget Carmody, Susan Callon, Debbie Gorney, Brigitte Herbert, Jessica Powell, Janis Risley, Jacquelyn Sergi, Jacqueline Wilson; **Missouri:** Vicki Barmann, Julie Begnaud, Fran Burnet, April

Burton, Lauren Coleman, Teresa Connolly, Anne-Marie Coreggia, Linda Crane, Judith Crenshaw, Lynne Evans, Karen Gibson, Kathryn L. Hedrick, Annie Hilmes, Nita Jackson, Andrea Junkans, Richard Keefe, Jenifer Kidwell, Nicole King, Chad Lower, Catherine Marquart, Sandy Mason, Kimberlee Moyer, Myriam Palmer, Sarah Rausch, Sarah Scoggins, Laura Snead, Amy Sternke, Mike Summers, Jennifer Tadsen, Lori Turnage, Della Thompson, Julie West, Krista White; **Nebraska:** Jeanne Cronin, Kathy Hardenbergh, Pamela Kooiker; **Nevada:** Richard Bangert, Jonathan Reynolds, Leslie Righetti, Ginnae Stamanis; **New Hampshire:** Leslie Anton, Evelyn Christoph, Elaine Jubinville, David Page, Jayne Wing; **New Jersey:** Gerard Amsellem, Lauren Arcusi, Debbie Barca, Angela Barone, Bonnie Baumert, Karen Beetham, Helene Blanton, Joan Bonnell, G. Cahayla, Eileen Campanella, Geraldine G. Castaldo,  Alda Cornec, Claire D'Angelo, Kerrie Decker, Claudy Delne, Phyllis Dimick, Meredith Donato, Maria Kostis Economals, Laurence Farhat, Brigitte Fischer, Diana Flynn, Cynthia Foxworth, Martine Gabler, Kinga Galica, Linda Geldmacher, Sylvia Guensch, Marie-Marthelle Guervil, Jenn Haff, Suzanne Hennessey, Carol Hill, Maryanne Kain, Rebecca Kazimir, Raana Khan, Maria Kostis, Karen Kozlowski, Barbara A. Lehman, Karen Lester, Joan Lipkowitz, Jeanine Losito, Marianne Ly, Sonia Magalhaes, Carol McKay, Carol Milich, Daniel Moraske, Valerie Morris, Nancy Mousavi, Cristin O'Connor, Ellen O'Meara, Ellen Reiss, Jane Roxbury, Kimberlee J. Safranek, Fritzner Salomon, Paula Schaffer, Susan Shourds, Diana Shults, Lise Simard, Debra Soriano, Joelle Stark, Laura Thomas, Margaret Tisa, Stephanie Walczak, Marguerite Wall, Tammy Wubbenhorst, Marlene Yoskowitz, Susan Roque Zeitz; **New Mexico:** John Coleman, Louise Gentile, Suzanne Holman; **New York:** Elsie Augustave, Jeff Brown, Nancy Burns, Susan Chatoui, Tom Davian, Paula DeFlippo, Ousmane Diouf, Mary Ellen Donovan, Elizabeth A. Ernenwein, Alba Gallegos, Andrea Grady, Marie Guagliardo-Day, Lisa Judd, Laurine Haefner, Rose Marie Hawver, Lizette Liebold, Louise J. Lindemann, Patricia Long, Matthew Nani, Monique Navalet, Denise Nichols, Debbie Pelletiere, Giovanni Ruggiero, Ellen Scheiderer, Catherine Scher, Kathryn Siegel, Alla Shustorovich, Jo Ann Thomasson, Jerry Treadwell, Laura Veralli, Lindsay Wahler, Wendy Winters, Lauren Wood-Radcliffe; **North Carolina:** Debra Ashe, Abeer Awad, Erin Bockoras, Maria G. Bonito, Stephanie Casstevens, Elizabeth Conine, Carolyn L. Cooper, Mary Turner Dalton, Ann Herminjard Davis, Richard Dubois, Teresa Engebretsen, Erin Feltman, Shannon Ferguson, Evelyn Marie Freeman, Jill Friesen, Angela Hagler, Angela Harris, Stephanie Hellert, Ana Hummel, James T. Hunter, Dawn Jones, Kim Lemons, Alicia Lewis, Sylvie Little, Kathryn C. Marker, Deborah P. Marks, Victoria Matisko, Sue Mead, Roland Menestres, Laraleigh Moffitt, Symphorien Momet, Wanda Moore, Wendy Mumy, Kristen Noland, Annie P.G. Norris, Hannah Pao, Alix Pavlic Phillips, Leslie Pyler, Kathleen Rhodes, Cynthia Richards, Julia Royall, Diane Smith, James Sonier, Ashlee Bree Stillings, Dyana Walker Talford, Alain Tourrret, Sarah Walden, Ines Weikel, Sharon Williams, Kim Young; **North Dakota:** Patricia Jessen, Melissa R. Klajda, Valerie Kling, Lynee Meier; **Ohio:**  Brandon Arnold, Maria Baker, Madith Barton, Shelbrey Blanc, Patricia Boon, Marguerite Bourgeois, Audra Buckley, Rebekah Clark, Nancy Compton, Parthena Draggett, Lisa Devlin, Carol J. Drescher, Kim Easley, Susan M. Eynon, Rachel Fawcett, Erin Gavula, Marianne Gooding, Suzanne Gyurgyik, Vinka Hartman, Suzanne Heacock, Jeanette Marie Hecker, Tina Hodge, Etchri Kekessi, Kelli Izzo, Patricia Jawyn, Madeline LaJeunesse, Tracy Loar, Cynthia Mathias, Judith Mielbrecht, Linda Morell, JoAnn O'Connor, Gretchen Petrie, Juliana Porter, Davara Potel, Ann Marie Radefeld, Ann Ryan, Robert J. Roesbery, Jeff Royer, D. Saunders, Ellen Schaf, Patricia Schorr, Lynne Sebring, Lynette A. Seith, Cheryl Shank, Jacqueline Shrake, Kathryn M. Siegel, Adrienne Six, Bonnie Thompson, Mary Russell Townsend, Milton Alan Turner, Susan Vrooman, Stephanie Waugh, Melinda White, Barbara Yedidsion, Kimberly Young, Nicole Zistler; **Oklahoma:**  Patricia Box, Joan King, Janet Gorton, Carol Little, Melinda Minshall, Julie Nesser, Jennifer Taylor, Micki Taylor, Wendy Toscani; **Oregon:**  Penny Bazanele, Angela Barley, Eloise S. Bates, Terry Benge, David Burke, Rhonda Case, Mike Curtis, Brenda Eichten, Annette Hallaux, Gina Johnson, Marc McAvoy, Laurelin Muir, Sandra Rands, Jean Redrejo, Anick Southwood, Lexie Tombleson, Kathleen Williams, Erica Zimmerman; **Pennsylvania:** Denis N. Asselin, Colette Ballew, Pamela Barentine, Brenda Barndt, Betty Benton, Linda Bistline, Linda Blum, Colleen Bognet, Mary Bollinger, Kathleen H. Brown, Carolyn Busque, Gloria Carfagno, Gregory W. Coleman, Cindy Comstock, Bruce A. Cope, Virginia Cosgrove, Elaine Danford, Linda Donahue, Sandra Dubnansky, Michelle Emery, Jill Fersch, Karen Fickes, Lydia Fichtman, Linda E. Fosselman, Paula Foster, Linda Girard, Jessica Grey, Andrew D. Grim, Dorothea Hackett, Scott Holland, Maureen Klingaman, Andrea Kupprion, Tricia Larson, Annette Lee, Susan Lobb, Cecile McKernan, Nancy McKnight, Ann Menichelli, Linda Mercier, Amy Montgomery, Laura Nagle, Laurie Neilson, Courtney Nelson, Jill Nickerson, Claudine Nicolay, Hallie Olson, Conni Petrie, Andrew Reaman, Joanne Robb, Regina Rooney, Anita Sapalidis, Jennifer Sharp, Susan Shelley, Susan E. Shuman, Kathy Simonovich, R. Sklar, Jan Hostler Stewart, Kyrston Strauch, Deborah A. Swann, Kathleen Tatala, Alan M. Tomaszewski, Jill Trate, Amy Varacalli, Maureen L. Verwey,  Nicole Wagner, Vanessa Weinlein, Ellen R. Wiberley, Katie Wilhelm, Diane Yanez, Barbara Zaun; **Rhode Island:**  Sarah Brady, Kathleen DePasquale, Coleen Griffith, Sandra Tessier; **South Carolina:**  Cathy Bouabre, Susannah Elliot, Jill Hnat, Kristina Holst, Sara Johnson, Justin T. Jones, Marisa Keenan, Lilly Mikol, Michele Mouyeos,  Jennifer Teague; **South Dakota:**  Jane Perman; **Tennessee:**  Marsha Barrom, Marcia Bowen, Elizabeth Buchignani, Edith Jane Cain, Melanie L. Calhoun, Dustin Denzin, Marina Fernandez, Maureen Garrett, Janet Kaller Geerlings, Larry Justis, Ashley Lawrence, Laura Leonard, Alexis Mattingly, Katie Paduch-Ledford, Jacob Truax, Robin Lynn Woo; **Texas:**  Ann Abercrombie, Andrea Adams, Veronica Angel, Cheryl Babb, Joanna Gipson Bacon, Rose E. Balboa, Dawn M. Baraett, Maria Barraza, Penny Beauchamp, Allison Bennett, Claire Breaux, Kathleen Carsey, Jose H. Castro, Richard J. Catania, Ann Clogan, Jacqueline Costanza, Randi Costenbader, Leslie Cushman, Lan Doan, Florence Dossett, Susan Dworaczyk, Francisca Florent, Allison Foster, Karlyn Fuquay, Erin Gallagher, M. Carla Geiger, Cathy Gelzleichter, Everett Gillette, Stacey Griffin, Rita A. Guidry, Julie Hanson, Phill Hemmings, Esther Hendrick, Jenifer Herndon, Melissa Hezlep, Bruce Hoang, Kitty Hutchcroft, Diana Jacob, Jeanne Johnson, Anne Jones, Penny Korenek, Aaron Levine, Cecilee C. Lindsey, Leigh Marshall, Joel Mayer, Cindy McBrayer, Denise McCage, Rita Mendoza, Diane Meyrat, Patricia Mills, Adam Morton, Deborah Murphy, Mark Myers, Cathy Nacol, Mary Nichols, Rhonda Palmer, Terry Pierce, Elizabeth Porter, Micaela Pitre, Natalya Belova Ramirez, Beverly Randall, Celeste Renza-Guren, Heather Richardson, Jill A. Rock, Serge Schragin, Rachel Schulz, Tara Smith, Maribel Squibb, Karen Stephens, Dore Sulistyo, Gail Sutcliffe, Roger Thomas, J. M. Turner, Kristen Villalvazo, Alicia Villarreal, R. D. Wade, Elizabeth Walker, Brandon Walters, Sharon Wendzel, Mary Westlake, Kristin Wright, Pamela Young, Amina Ztot; **Utah:**  Christina Brown, Art Burnah, Alisan Mills, Dave Miller, Lorraine Peterson; **Vermont:**  Diane Ingham, Norman W. McLure, Kendrda Paupst; **Virginia:**  Amanda Amos, Kandie Bradshaw, Susan Broaddus, Kay Choi, Anna Collins, Susan Courtney, Cynthia Dahl, Genevieve Delfosse,  Kathy Flinn, LaVerne E. Flowers, Monica Johnston, Rinata Lewis, Sue McCloud, Lynn McCrady, Michelle M. Morningstar, Elizabeth Schollaert, Craig F. Seal, Ghislaine Tulou, Cynthia van de Kamp, Dawn Whitehurst; **Washington:**  Catherine Blair, Olivia Caulhez, Roslyn Cooper, Svetlana Cuello, Daniel Dole, Ann Elliot, Jeanne Federovitch, Greg Isham, Jenny Hallenbeck, Tina Irish, Gregg Kasner, Josette Martin, Merissa McGregor, Molly McKinnon, Sarah McMenamin, Kara Miller, Heidi Monrad, Meghan Morahan, JoAnne Peterson, Kathleen Pointec, Esther Reiquam, Robert Slabodnik, Kaisa Swenddal-White, Deana Wiatr; **West Virginia:** Rita Denton; **Wisconsin:** Ramona Armour, Margaret Bussone, Linda Christen, Guy Dayen, Natalia DeLaat, Maura Devanie, Jana Gasiorkiewicz, Kathy A. Hawkins, Susanne Krasovich, Mary A. Martin, Jennifer Muchka, Julie Nji, Angela Olson, Jamie Pittmann, Vicky Thompson, Deborah Waither, Michelle Webster, Sally Weems, Brian Wopat